Let's Get Started.

Thanks for choosing Kaplan for your SAT Preparation. Get ready to experience Kaplan SAT and score higher—guaranteed or your money back.

STEP 1

Check the contents of your SAT Kit.

You should have the following:

✔ SAT Course Book
✔ Big Book of SAT Practice Tests

STEP 2

Take your Diagnostic Test.

Bring your Big Book of Practice Tests with you to your first class. It contains your first practice test—a full-length SAT. This Diagnostic Test establishes a baseline of your performance and fuels your custom study plan in your online resources.

STEP 3

Log into Your Online Center.

Go to kaptest.com/myhome and log into your online center. After you log in, you can:

• View your Diagnostic Test results
• Get started on your assignments for your next class session

Pg 40
p.65
p.435

P 589 — H-W

D1360124

Ready to score higher? Log in to get started.

Didn't receive your log-in information? Visit kaptest.com/myhome, and we'll resend it.

Need help? Call 1-800-KAP-TEST or email us at customer.care@kaplan.com.

KAPLAN
TEST PREP

NEW SAT®
Course Book

CSG H·W
Pg 316 1-8 (930)
Pg 341 1-8 (940)
Pg 795 Red 795-801
810-812
Review Pg 802-809
(1139)

5) Take Test #4
on saturday
AM

2/24/16

2/10/16 H·W
Pg 217 1-8 (889)
Pg 240 1-8 (900)
Pg 494 1-11 (1022)
Pg 639 1-11 (1091)
12-22

2/8/16 H·W
Pg. 270 # 1-7 (909)
Pg. 296 #1-8 (918)
Pg. 474 #1-11 (1011)
Pg. 684 #1-11
(1106)

2/22/16
Pg 177 1-8 (876)
Pg. 533 #1-21 (1043)
Pg 550 # 1-21 (1055)
Pg. 779 Read passage; fill out line,
write essay on
pg 782

NEW SAT®
Course Book

PUBLISHING

New York

Acknowledgments

Special thanks to those who made this book possible including Arthur Ahn, Laura Aitcheson, Becky Berthiaume, Michael Boothroyd, Matthew Callan, Potoula Chresomales, Kate Fisher, Adam Hinz, Kate Hurley, Brandon Jones, Rebecca Knauer, Celina Lasota, James Radkins, Justin Starr, Bob Verini, Devon Wible, Daniel Wittich, and many others who contributed materials and advice.

ISBN-13: 978-1-62523-291-5

Table of Contents

PART ONE: MATH

UNIT ONE: MATH INTRODUCTION

UNIT TWO: HEART OF ALGEBRA

UNIT THREE: PROBLEM SOLVING & DATA ANALYSIS

Introduction to the SAT

The first step to achieving SAT success is to learn about the structure of the test and why it's so important for your future. The SAT, like any standardized test, is predictable. The more comfortable you are with the test structure, the more confidently you will approach each question type, thus maximizing your score.

SAT STRUCTURE

The SAT is 3 hours long, or 3 hours and 50 minutes long if you choose to complete the optional Essay Test. It is made up of mostly multiple-choice questions that test two subject areas: Math and Evidence-Based Reading and Writing. The latter is broken into a Reading Test and a Writing & Language Test.

Test	Allotted Time (min.)	Question Count
Reading	65	52
Writing & Language	35	44
Math	80	58
Essay (optional)	50	1
Total	180 OR 230 (w/essay)	153 OR 154 (w/essay)

SAT SCORING

SAT scoring can be pretty complex. You will receive one score ranging from 200 to 800 for Evidence-Based Reading and Writing and another for Math. Your overall SAT score will range from 400 to 1600 and is calculated by adding these two scores together. You will receive a separate score for the Essay Test, if you choose to take it.

In addition to your overall scores, you will receive subscores that provide a deeper analysis of your SAT performance. The SAT also gives you a percentile ranking, which allows you to compare your scores with those of other high school students who took the test. For example, a student with a percentile of 63 has earned a score better than 63 percent of test takers.

WHERE AND WHEN TO TAKE THE SAT

The SAT is offered every year on multiple Saturday test dates. Typically, exams are offered in October, November, December, January, March, May, and June. You can take the SAT multiple times. Some states offer special administrations of the SAT on different dates. Sunday tests are available by request for students requiring religious or other exemptions. The SAT is administered at high schools around the country that serve as testing centers. Your high school may or may not be a testing center. Check www.collegeboard.org for a list of testing centers near you. Note that you must register for the SAT approximately one month in advance to avoid paying a late fee. Some SAT test dates also offer SAT Subject Tests. You may not take both the SAT and the Subject Tests in a single sitting.

THE SAT MATH TEST

The SAT Math Test is broken down into a calculator section and a no-calculator section. Questions across the sections consist of multiple-choice, student-produced response (Grid-in), and more comprehensive Multi-Part questions.

	Calculator Section	No-Calculator Section	Total
Duration (minutes)	55	25	80
Multiple-choice	30	15	45
Grid-in	8	5	13
Total Questions	38	20	58

The SAT Math Test is divided into four content areas: Heart of Algebra, Problem Solving and Data Analysis, Passport to Advanced Math, and Additional Topics in Math.

SAT Math Test Content Area Distribution	
Heart of Algebra (19 questions)	Analyzing and fluently solving equations and systems of equations; creating expressions, equations, and inequalities to represent relationships between quantities and to solve problems; rearranging and interpreting formulas
Problem Solving and Data Analysis (17 questions)	Creating and analyzing relationships using ratios, proportions, percentages, and units; describing relationships shown graphically; summarizing qualitative and quantitative data

SAT Math Test Content Area Distribution	
Passport to Advanced Math (16 questions)	Rewriting expressions using their structure; creating, analyzing, and fluently solving quadratic and higher-order equations; purposefully manipulating polynomials to solve problems
Additional Topics in Math (6 questions)	Making area and volume calculations in context; investigating lines, angles, triangles, and circles using theorems; and working with trigonometric functions

A few math questions might look like something you'd expect to see on a science or history test. These "crossover" questions are designed to test your ability to use math in real-world scenarios. There are a total of 16 "crossover" questions that will contribute to subscores that span multiple tests. Eight of the questions will contribute to the Analysis in Science subscore, and eight will contribute to the Analysis in History/Social Studies subscore.

THE SAT READING TEST

The SAT Reading Test will focus on your comprehension and reasoning skills when presented with challenging extended prose passages taken from a variety of content areas.

SAT Reading Test Overview	
Timing	65 minutes
Questions	52 passage-based multiple-choice questions
Passages	4 single passages; 1 set of paired passages
Passage Length	500–750 words per passage or passage set

Passages will draw from U.S. and World Literature, History/Social Studies, and Science. One set of History/Social Studies or Science passages will be paired. History/Social Studies and Science passages can also be accompanied by graphical representations of data such as charts, graphs, tables, and so on.

Reading Test Passage Types	
U.S. and World Literature	1 passage with 10 questions
History/Social Studies	2 passages or 1 passage and 1 paired-passage set with 10–11 questions each
Science	2 passages or 1 passage and 1 paired-passage set with 10–11 questions each

The multiple-choice questions for each passage will be arranged in order from the more general to the more specific so that you can actively engage with the entire passage before answering questions about details.

Skills Tested by Reading Test Questions	
Information and Ideas	Close reading, citing textual evidence, determining central ideas and themes
Summarizing	Understanding relationships, interpreting words and phrases in context
Rhetoric	Analyzing word choice, assessing overall text structure, assessing part-whole relationships, analyzing point of view, determining purpose, analyzing arguments
Synthesis	Analyzing multiple texts, analyzing quantitative information

THE SAT WRITING & LANGUAGE TEST

The SAT Writing & Language Test will focus on your ability to revise and edit text from a range of content areas.

SAT Writing & Language Test Overview	
Timing	35 minutes
Questions	44 passage-based multiple-choice questions
Passages	4 single passages with 11 questions each
Passage Length	400–450 words per passage

The SAT Writing & Language Test will contain four single passages, one from each of the following subject areas: Careers, Humanities, History/Social Studies, and Science.

Writing & Language Passage Types	
Careers	Hot topics in "major fields of work" such as information technology and health care
Humanities	Texts about literature, art, history, music, and philosophy pertaining to human culture
History/Social Studies	Discussion of historical or social sciences topics such as anthropology, communication studies, economics, education, human geography, law, linguistics, political science, psychology, and sociology
Science	Exploration of concepts, findings, and discoveries in the natural sciences including Earth science, biology, chemistry, and physics

Passages will also vary in the "type" of text. A passage can be an argument, an informative or explanatory text, or a nonfiction narrative.

Writing & Language Passage Text Type Distribution	
Argument	1–2 passages
Informative/Explanatory Text	1–2 passages
Nonfiction Narrative	1 passage

Some passages and/or questions will refer to one or more informational graphics that represent data. Questions associated with these graphical representations will ask you to revise and edit the passage based on the data presented in the graphic.

The most prevalent question format on the SAT Writing & Language Test will ask you to choose the best of three alternatives to an underlined portion of the passage or to decide that the current version is the best option. You will be asked to improve the development, organization, and diction in the passages to ensure they conform to conventional standards of English grammar, usage, and style.

Skills Tested by Writing & Language Test Questions	
Expression of Ideas (24 questions)	Development, organization, and effective language use
Standard English Conventions (20 questions)	Sentence structure, conventions of usage, and conventions of punctuation

THE SAT ESSAY TEST (OPTIONAL)

The SAT Essay Test will assess your college and career readiness by testing your abilities to read and analyze a high-quality source document and write a coherent analysis of the source supported with critical reasoning and evidence from the given text.

The SAT Essay Test features an argumentative source text of 650–750 words aimed toward a large audience. Passages will examine ideas, debates, and shifts in the arts and sciences as well as civic, cultural, and political life. Rather than having a simple for/against structure, these passages will be nuanced and will relate views on complex subjects. These passages will also be logical in their structure and reasoning.

It is important to note that prior knowledge is not required.

The SAT Essay Test prompt will ask you to explain how the presented passage's author builds an argument to convince an audience. In writing your essay, you may analyze elements such as the author's use of evidence, reasoning, style, and persuasion; you will not be limited to those elements listed, however.

Rather than writing about whether you agree or disagree with the presented argument, you will write an essay in which you analyze *how* the author makes an argument.

The SAT Essay Test will be broken down into three categories for scoring: Reading, Analysis, and Writing. Each of these elements will be scored on a scale of 1 to 4 by two graders, for a total score of 2 to 8 for each category.

TEST-TAKING STRATEGIES

You have already learned about the overall structure of the SAT as well as the structure of the three tests it entails: Reading, Writing & Language, and Math. The strategies outlined in this section can be applied to any of these tests.

The SAT is different from the tests you are used to taking in school. The good news is that you can use the SAT's particular structure to your advantage.

For example, on a test given in school, you probably go through the questions in order. You spend more time on the harder questions than on the easier ones because harder questions are usually worth more points. You probably often show your work because your teacher tells you that how you approach a question is as important as getting the correct answer.

This approach is not optimal for the SAT. On the SAT, you benefit from moving around within a section if you come across tough questions because the harder questions are worth the same number of points as the easier questions. It doesn't matter how you arrive at the correct answer—only that you bubble in the correct answer choice.

STRATEGY #1: TRIAGING THE TEST

You do not need to complete questions on the SAT in order. Every student has different strengths and should attack the test with those strengths in mind. Your main objective on the SAT should be to score as many points as you can. While approaching questions out of order may seem counterintuitive, it is a surefire way to achieve your best score.

Just remember, you can skip around within each section, but you cannot work on a section other than the one you've been instructed to work on.

To triage the test effectively, do the following:

- First, work through all the easy questions that you can do quickly. Skip questions that are hard or time-consuming

- For the Reading and Writing & Language Tests, start with the passage you find most manageable and work toward the one you find most challenging. You do not need to go in order

- Second, work through the questions that are doable but time-consuming

- Third, work through the hard questions

- If you run out of time, pick a Letter of the Day for remaining questions

A Letter of the Day is an answer choice letter (A, B, C, or D) that you choose before Test Day to select for questions you guess on.

STRATEGY #2: ELIMINATION

Even though there is no wrong-answer penalty on the SAT, Elimination is still a crucial strategy. If you can determine that one or more answer choices are definitely incorrect, you can increase your chances of getting the right answer by paring the selection down.

To eliminate answer choices, do the following:

- Read each answer choice

- Cross out the answer choices that are incorrect

- Remember: There is no wrong-answer penalty, so take your best guess

STRATEGY #3: GUESSING

Each multiple-choice question on the SAT has four answer choices and no wrong-answer penalty. That means if you have no idea how to approach a question, you have a 25 percent chance of randomly choosing the correct answer. Even though there's a 75 percent chance of selecting the incorrect answer, you won't lose any points for doing so. The worst that can happen on the SAT is that you'll earn zero points on a question, which means you should *always* at least take a guess, even when you have no idea what to do.

When guessing on a question, do the following:

- Always try to strategically eliminate answer choices before guessing

- If you run out of time, or have no idea what a question is asking, pick a Letter of the Day

COMMON TESTING MYTHS

Since its inception, the SAT has gone through various revisions, but it has always been an integral part of the college admissions process. As a result of its significance and the changes it has undergone, a number of rumors and myths have circulated about the exam. In this section, we'll dispel some of the most common ones. As always, you can find the most up-to-date information about the SAT at the College Board website (https://www.collegeboard.org).

Myth: **There is a wrong-answer penalty on the SAT to discourage guessing.**

Fact: While this statement was true a few years ago, it is no longer true. Older versions of the SAT had a wrong-answer penalty so that students who guessed on questions would not have an advantage over students who left questions blank. This penalty has been removed; make sure you never leave an SAT question blank!

Myth: **Answer choice C is most likely to be the correct answer.**

Fact: This rumor has roots in human psychology. Apparently, when people such as high school teachers, for example, design an exam, they have a slight bias toward answer choice C when assigning correct answers. While humans do write SAT questions, a computer randomizes the distribution of correct choices; statistically, therefore, each answer choice is equally likely to be the correct answer.

Myth: **The SAT is just like another test in school.**

Fact: While the SAT covers some of the same content as your high school math, literature, and English classes, it also presents concepts in ways that are fundamentally different. While you might be able to solve a math problem in a number of different ways on an algebra test, the SAT places a heavy emphasis on working through questions as quickly and efficiently as possible.

Myth: **You have to get all the questions right to get a perfect score.**

Fact: Many students have reported missing several questions on the SAT and being pleasantly surprised to receive perfect scores. Their experience is not atypical: Usually, you can miss a few questions and still get a coveted perfect score. The makers of the SAT use a technique called scaling to ensure that a SAT score conveys the same information from year to year, so you might be able to miss a couple more questions on a slightly harder SAT exam and miss fewer questions on an easier SAT exam and get the same scores. Keep a positive attitude throughout the SAT, and in many cases, your scores will pleasantly surprise you.

Myth: **You can't prepare for the SAT.**

Fact: You've already proven this myth false by buying this book. While the SAT is designed to fairly test students regardless of preparation, you can gain a huge advantage by familiarizing yourself with the structure and content of the exam. By working through the questions and practice tests available to you, you'll ensure that nothing on the SAT catches you by surprise and that you do everything you can to maximize your score. Your Kaplan resources help you structure this practice in the most efficient way possible, and provide you with helpful strategies and tips as well.

COURSE OVERVIEW

WELCOME TO KAPLAN!

Congratulations on taking this important step in your college admission process! By studying with Kaplan, you'll maximize your score on the SAT, a major factor in your overall college application.

Our experience shows that the greatest SAT score increases result from active engagement in the preparation process. Kaplan will give you direction, focus your preparation, and teach you the specific skills and effective test-taking strategies you need to know for the SAT. We will help you achieve your top performance on Test Day, but your effort is crucial. The more you invest in preparing for the SAT, the greater your chances of achieving your target score and getting into your top-choice college.

This Course Overview serves as a guide to Kaplan's SAT program. Read it carefully. You'll get answers to the following important questions:

- How is the course structured?

- What homework will I need to do?

- What materials does Kaplan provide, and how do I use them effectively?

- What are my online resources, and how do I access them?

- How can I achieve my best score on Test Day?

Are you registered for the SAT? Kaplan cannot register you for the official SAT. If you have not already registered for the upcoming SAT, visit the College Board's website at www.collegeboard.org.

The SAT is administered on Saturday mornings in October, November, December, January, March, May and June. To avoid paying a late fee, students should be registered well in advance of the test dates. Your high school guidance counselor may also have more information about registering for the SAT. Students who have religious needs that prevent them from taking a Saturday exam may request alternate accommodations from the College Board.

COURSE STRUCTURE

Your Kaplan SAT course will consist of ten sessions: four full-length practice tests and six interactive lessons. In addition to your tests and lessons, your Kaplan program includes this extensive Course Book and the Big Book of Practice Tests, as well as additional digital resources.

PRACTICE TESTS

Kaplan's practice tests are just like the actual SAT, except your scores don't count toward the college admissions process. In fact, your Kaplan SAT Practice Test scores are not reported to anyone except you (and your Kaplan instructors). By taking an exam administered by a proctor under test-like conditions, you will prepare yourself for the actual Test Day experience. Your practice tests are included in the Big Book of Practice Tests, so bring it with you on Test Days.

LESSONS

In your lessons, your expert Kaplan instructor will review the key concepts tested on the SAT and teach you Kaplan's proven methods and strategies. Each lesson will cover the content and concepts tested on the SAT and will be interactive, so be ready to participate! You will need your SAT Course Book for all of your lessons.

Each lesson will cover four chapters from your Course Book—a mixture of math and verbal chapters. Each chapter has a three-part structure of Prepare, Practice, and Perform. During the Prepare section, your expert Kaplan instructor will walk you through the chapter's concepts and content, demonstrating how to apply specific Kaplan strategies or methods to answer SAT questions correctly. You will then move into the Practice portion of the chapter, in which you will be given a chance to practice what you learned during Prepare with the help of your instructor and the Course Book. During the ultimate phase—Perform—you will independently apply the skills acquired during the chapter to a short series of test-like questions that your instructor will review with you.

Classroom Session	Chapters Covered
Session 1	Chapters 2, 3, 18, 26
Session 2	Chapters 5, 6, 19, 33
Session 3	Chapters 10, 11, 20, 30
Session 4	Chapters 8, 9, 21, 28
Session 5	Chapters 7, 23, 24, 34
Session 6	Chapters 12, 13, 31, 35

You'll notice that not every chapter of this book will be covered in your SAT class. Class focuses on the most important topics that are likely to be tested on the SAT. You can use the rest of the chapters to brush up on less-frequently tested skills and content independently.

HOMEWORK (EXTRA PRACTICE)

You need to reinforce what you learn in class by practicing the Kaplan Methods and strategies on your own. Your instructor will assign homework after every class session, but your homework assignments are also listed at the end of each chapter. Homework assignments will include extra practice questions in the SAT Course Book. At the top of each homework assignment, there is a list of required and recommended questions. The required questions more directly reinforce that chapter's content but the recommended questions will also help prepare you for Test Day. For immediate results and improved online recommendations, please complete the online bubble grid for the required homework sections you complete.

SMARTPOINTS

Each chapter contains a breakdown of SmartPoints. By studying the information released by the College Board, Kaplan has been able to determine how often certain topics are likely to show up on the SAT, and therefore how many points these topics are worth on Test Day. If you master a given topic, you can expect to earn the corresponding number of SmartPoints on Test Day. The breakdown of SmartPoints for Math, Reading, and Writing & Language are summarized in the following tables. You can also see how these topics align to chapters in this Course Book.

Math			
SmartPoint Category	**# of Points**	**Sub-Categories**	**SAT Chapter(s)**
Linear Equations	110	Linear Equations, Graphs, Word Problems	Ch. 2
Systems of Linear Equations	50	Systems of Equations, Word Problems, Intersecting Graphs	Ch. 3
Inequalities	40	Inequalities, 1-D Graphs of Inequalities, 2-D Graphs of Inequalities	Ch. 4
Rates, Ratios, Proportions, and Percentages	80	Rates, Ratios, Proportions, Measurement/Units, and Percents	Ch. 5
Scatterplots	40	Scatterplots, Lines of Best Fit, Modeling Data	Ch. 6
Statistics and Probability	50	Descriptive Statistics, Probability, Two-Way Tables, Graphical Organizers	Ch. 7
Exponents	80	Exponents, Radicals, Rational Expressions/Equations, and Polynomial Operations	Ch. 8, 9
Functions	50	Functions and Graphs of Functions	Ch. 10
Quadratics	30	Quadratic Equations, Modeling Data, Parabolas, Systems of Mixed Equations	Ch. 11
Imaginary Numbers	10	Imaginary Numbers	Ch. 12
Geometry	10	Lines, Angles, Triangles, Similarity, Congruence, Proofs, Circles, 3D Shapes	Ch. 13-16
Trigonometry	50	Trigonometry	Ch. 17
TOTAL	**600**		

Reading			
SmartPoint Category	**# of Points**	**Sub-Categories**	**SAT Chapter(s)**
Command of Evidence	70	—	Ch. 21
Rhetoric	70	Analyzing Word Choice, Analyzing Overall Text Structure, Analyzing Part-Whole Text Structure, Analyzing Point of View, Analyzing Purpose, Analyzing Claims & Counterclaims, Assessing Reasoning, Analyzing Evidence	Ch. 23, Ch. 24
Vocab-in-Context	55	—	Ch. 22
Inference	40	Determining Implicit Meanings, Using Analogical Reasoning, Understanding Relationships	Ch. 20, Ch. 22
Synthesis	50	Analyzing Multiple Texts, Analyzing Quantitative Information	Ch. 25
Global	20	Determining Central Ideas & Themes, Summarizing	Ch. 21
Detail	20	Determining Explicit Meanings	Ch. 20
TOTAL	**325**		

Writing & Language			
SmartPoint Category	# of Points	Sub-Categories	SAT Chapter(s)
Effective Language Use	50	Precision, Concision, Style & Tone, Syntax	Ch. 29
Organization	50	Logical Sequence; Introductions, Conclusions, and Transitions	Ch. 27
Usage	50	Pronouns, Possessive Determiners, Pronoun-Antecedent Agreement, Subject-Verb Agreement, Noun Agreement, Frequently Confused Words, Logical Comparison, Conventional Expression (Idioms)	Ch. 31
Development	40	Proposition, Support, Focus	Ch. 28
Sentence Formation	40	Sentence Boundaries, Subordination & Coordination, Parallel Structure, Modifier Placement	Ch. 30
Punctuation	30	End-of-Sentence Punctuation, Within-Sentence Punctuation, Possessive Nouns & Pronouns, Items in a Series, Nonrestrictive & Parenthetical Elements, Unnecessary Punctuation	Ch. 32
Quantitative	10	—	Ch. 26
Shifts in Construction	5	Verb Tense, Mood, and Voice; Pronoun Person & Number	Ch. 30
TOTAL	275		

SAT COURSE MATERIALS

Your Kaplan SAT Student Kit contains the following items that you'll use in your preparation for Test Day.

COURSE BOOK

This book contains the lessons you'll work on in each session and the homework assignments you'll complete between sessions. In addition to the chapters taught in class, this book contains many more chapters you can study and review by yourself in order to maximize your score on Test Day. **Bring this book, a calculator, and a pencil to every class.**

BIG BOOK OF PRACTICE TESTS

The Big Book of Practice Tests includes all four practice tests that you will take as part of your course. Bring this book, a calculator, and a few pencils to class on test days.

DIGITAL RESOURCES

In addition to the homework assignments in your book, you have a variety of resources available through your online Kaplan account.

How do you access your online resources? Follow these steps:

1. Go to kaptest.com.

2. Click on Sign In at the top of the page.

3. Input your username and password that were emailed to you and/or your parents when you enrolled in your Kaplan course. This email is sent to the email address you provided with your class registration.

Don't have your username and password? Check your junk email folder for the original user-name and password email from Kaplan. If you cannot locate your username and password, visit kaptest.com, and click on the link next to "Forgot your password?" and enter the email address used when registering for your course. Your login credentials will be re-sent to that email address.

4. Once you are logged in, read and accept the terms and conditions.

5. Use your study plan and recommendations, which are personalized based on your perfor-mance throughout the course, to study effectively and efficiently for the SAT.

Math

Math Introduction

BY THE END OF THIS UNIT, YOU WILL BE ABLE TO:

1. Identify the arithmetic and algebra concepts needed to get the most out of this book

2. Determine which calculators are best to use on the SAT

3. Utilize your calculator effectively

CHAPTER 1

Prerequisite Skills & Calculator Usage

CHAPTER OBJECTIVES

By the end of this chapter, you will be able to:

- Identify skills necessary to obtain the full benefits of the math section of this book and to hone skills not fully developed

- Use efficiency tips to boost your Test Day speed

- Distinguish between questions that need a calculator and questions in which manual calculations are more efficient

- Utilize strategies that can help when you don't know how to start a question

- Identify how expert test takers use their calculators in a balanced way

COURSE PREREQUISITES

This course focuses on the skills that are tested on the SAT. It assumes a working knowledge of arithmetic, algebra, and geometry. Before you dive into the subsequent chapters where you'll try test-like problems, there are a number of concepts—ranging from basic arithmetic to geometry—that you should master. The following sections contain a brief review of these concepts.

Algebra and Arithmetic

- Order of operations is one of the most fundamental of all arithmetic rules. A well-known mnemonic device for remembering this order is PEMDAS: Please Excuse My Dear Aunt Sally. This translates to Parentheses, Exponents, Multiplication/Division, Addition/Subtraction. Note: Multiplication and division have the same priority, as do addition and subtraction. Perform multiplication and division from left to right (even if it means division before multiplication) and treat addition and subtraction the same way.

$$(14 - 4 \div 2)^2 - 3 + (2 - 1)$$
$$(14 - 2)^2 - 3 + (1)$$
$$(12)^2 - 3 + (1)$$
$$144 - 3 + 1$$
$$142$$

- Three basic properties of number (and variable) manipulation—commutative, associative, and distributive—will assist you with algebra on Test Day. These properties are outlined next.

  - Commutative: Numbers can swap places and still provide the same mathematical result. This is valid only for addition and multiplication.

    $$a + b = b + a \rightarrow 3 + 4 = 4 + 3; \text{ also, } 3 \times 4 = 4 \times 3$$
    $$\text{BUT: } 3 - 4 \neq 4 - 3; \ 3 \div 4 \neq 4 \div 3$$

  - Associative: Different number groupings will provide the same mathematical result. This is valid only for addition and multiplication.

    $$(a + b) + c = a + (b + c) \rightarrow (4 + 5) + 6 = 4 + (5 + 6); \text{ also, } (4 \times 5) \times 6 = 4 \times (5 \times 6)$$
    $$\text{BUT: } (4 - 5) - 6 \neq 4 - (5 - 6); \ (4 \div 5) \div 6 \neq 4 \div (5 \div 6)$$

  - Distributive: A number to be multiplied by the sum or difference of two other numbers can be rewritten as the first number multiplied by the two others individually. This does *not* work with division.

    Note: When subtracting an expression in parentheses, such as in $4 - (x + 3)$, distribute the negative sign outside the parentheses first: $4 + (-x - 3) \rightarrow 1 - x$. Be particularly careful with these, as negative signs are easily lost in calculations.

    $$a(b + c) = ab + ac; \ a(b - c) = ab - ac \rightarrow 6(x + 3) = 6x + 6 \times 3; \ 3(y - 2) = 3y - 3 \times 2$$
    $$\text{BUT: } 12 \div (6 + 2) \neq 12 \div 6 + 12 \div 2$$

- Ensure you can correctly manipulate negative numbers and that you understand the additive inverse property: Subtracting a positive number is the same as adding its negative. Likewise, subtracting a negative number is the same as adding its positive.

  $$r - s = r + (-s); \ r - (-s) = r + s \rightarrow 22 - 15 = 22 + (-15) = 7; \ 22 - (-15) = 22 + 15 = 37$$

- You should be comfortable manipulating both proper and improper fractions. To add and subtract fractions, first find a common denominator, then add the numerators together. Multiplication is straightforward: Multiply the numerators together, then repeat for the denominators.

Cancel when possible to simplify your answer. Dividing by a fraction is the same as multiplying by its reciprocal. Once you've rewritten your division problem as one of multiplication, follow the rules for fraction multiplication to solve.

addition/subtraction: $\dfrac{2}{3} + \dfrac{5}{4} \rightarrow$

common denominator: $12 \rightarrow \left(\dfrac{2}{3} \times \dfrac{4}{4}\right) + \left(\dfrac{5}{4} \times \dfrac{3}{3}\right) = \dfrac{8}{12} + \dfrac{15}{12} = \dfrac{23}{12}$

multiplication: $\dfrac{5}{8} \times \dfrac{8}{3} = \dfrac{5}{\cancel{8}} \times \dfrac{\cancel{8}^{1}}{3} = \dfrac{5 \times 1}{1 \times 3} = \dfrac{5}{3}$

division: $\dfrac{3}{4} \div \dfrac{3}{2} = \dfrac{\cancel{3}^{1}}{\cancel{4}_{2}} \times \dfrac{\cancel{2}^{1}}{\cancel{3}_{1}} = \dfrac{1 \times 1}{2 \times 1} = \dfrac{1}{2}$

- Know what absolute value is: The distance a number is from 0 on a number line. Because absolute value is a distance, it is always positive or 0. Absolute value can *never* be negative.

$$|-17| = 17, \; |21| = 21, \; |0| = 0$$

- Follow the Cardinal Rule of Equations: What is done to one side of an equation must be done to the other. For instance, if you multiply one side by 3, you must multiply the other side by 3 as well.

- The ability to solve straightforward, one-variable equations is critical on the SAT. See the following example:

$$\dfrac{4x}{5} - 2 = 10$$

$$\dfrac{4x}{5} = 12$$

$$\dfrac{5}{4} \times \dfrac{4x}{5} = 12 \times \dfrac{5}{4}$$

$$x = 15$$

Note: $\dfrac{4x}{5}$ is the same as $\dfrac{4}{5}x$. You could see either form on the SAT.

- You should be able to extract numbers (and infer their relevance) from word problems like this one:

Annabel bought six pairs of shoes during a sale at her favorite boutique. If this purchase tripled the number of pairs of shoes she had before she went shopping, how many pairs of shoes did Annabel own before she visited the sale?

Let s represent the number of shoe pairs Annabel had before the sale. She adds six pairs (+ 6) to this value, which is equal to triple her original shoe pair count (= 3s). Your equation should read $s + 6 = 3s$. Solving for s reveals $s = 3$, so Annabel had three pairs of shoes before she went shopping at the sale.

- You will encounter irrational numbers, such as certain radicals and π, on Test Day. Carry an irrational as you would a variable (e.g., $4 \times \sqrt{2} = 4\sqrt{2}$). Only convert it to a decimal when you have finished any intermediate steps and when the question asks you to provide an *approximate* value.

For Extra Efficiency

You might be a math whiz, but unless you're Isaac Newton (the inventor of calculus), you can likely benefit from knowing a few extra things that will boost your speed on Test Day.

- Don't abuse your calculator by using it to determine something as simple as $15 \div 3$ (we've seen it many times). Besides, what if you're in the middle of the no-calculator section? Save time on Test Day by reviewing multiplication tables. At a bare minimum, work up through the 10s. If you know them through 12 or 15, that's even better!

- You can save a few seconds of number crunching by memorizing perfect squares. Knowing perfect squares through 10 is a good start; go for 15 or even 20 if you can.

- The ability to recognize a few simple fractions masquerading in decimal or percent form will save you time on Test Day, as you won't have to turn to your calculator to convert them. This is especially helpful when you get to chapter 7 and learn about probability. Memorize the content of the following table.

Fraction	Decimal	Percent
$\dfrac{1}{10}$	0.1	10%
$\dfrac{1}{8}$	0.125	12.5%
$\dfrac{1}{5}$	0.2	20%
$\dfrac{1}{4}$	0.25	25%
$\dfrac{1}{3}$	$0.333\overline{3}$	$33.3\overline{3}\%$
$\dfrac{1}{2}$	0.5	50%

Tip: If you need the decimal (or percent) form of a multiple of one of the fractions shown in the table, such as $\dfrac{3}{8}$, just take the fraction with the corresponding denominator ($\dfrac{1}{8}$ in this case), convert to a decimal (0.125), and multiply by the numerator of the desired fraction to get its decimal equivalent: $\dfrac{3}{8} = \dfrac{1}{8} \times 3 = 0.125 \times 3 = 0.375$.

- Many students assume that every math problem encountered can be solved with a proportion. Proportions are not appropriate for every question. Know when to use them and when not to; review chapter 5 for more information. You must be able to recognize the type of question you have *and* use the right math tools to solve it.

Graphing

- Basic two-dimensional graphing is performed on a coordinate plane. There are two axes, *x* and *y*, that meet at a central point called the origin. Each axis has both positive and negative values that extend outward from the origin at evenly spaced intervals. The axes divide the space into four sections called quadrants, which are labeled I, II, III, and IV. Quadrant I is always the upper-right section, and the rest follow counterclockwise.

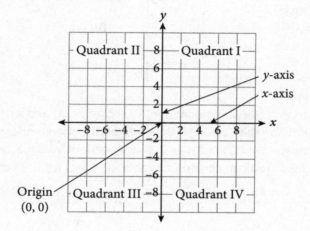

- To plot points on the coordinate plane, you need their coordinates. The *x*-coordinate is where the point falls along the *x*-axis, and the *y*-coordinate is where the point falls along the *y*-axis. The two coordinates together make an ordered pair written as (x, y). When writing ordered pairs, the *x*-coordinate is always listed first. Four points are plotted in the following figure as examples.

- When two points are vertically or horizontally aligned, calculating the distance between them is easy. For a horizontal distance, only the *x*-value changes; for a vertical distance, only the *y*-value changes. Take the positive difference of the *x*-coordinates (or *y*-coordinates) to determine the distance. Two examples are presented here.

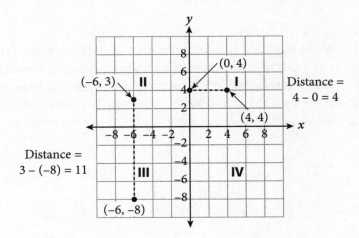

- Two-variable equations have an independent variable (input) and a dependent variable (output). The dependent variable (often *y*), depends on the independent variable (often *x*). For example, in the equation $y = 3x + 4$, *x* is the independent variable; any *y*-value depends on what you plug in for *x*. You can construct a table of values for the equation, which can then be plotted.

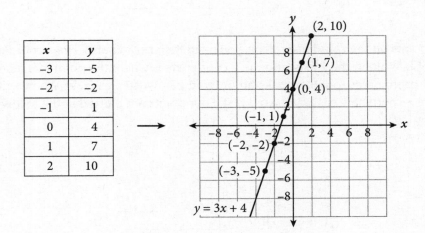

x	y
−3	−5
−2	−2
−1	1
0	4
1	7
2	10

- You can be asked to infer relationships from graphs. In the first of the following graphs, the two variables are time and population. Clearly the year does not depend on how many people live in the town; rather, the population increases over time and thus depends on the year. In the second graph, you can infer that plant height depends on the amount of rain; thus, rainfall is the independent variable. Note that the independent variable for the second graph is the vertical axis; this can happen with certain nonstandard graphs. On the standard coordinate plane, the independent variable is always on the horizontal axis.

- When two straight lines are graphed, one of three possible scenarios will occur:
  - The lines will not intersect at all (no solution).
  - The lines will intersect at one point (one solution).
  - The lines will lie on top of each other (infinitely many solutions).

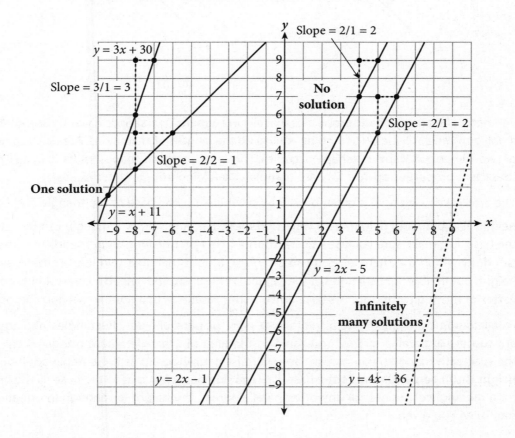

Geometry

- Adjacent angles can be added to find the measure of a larger angle. The following diagram demonstrates this.

- Two distinct lines in a plane will either intersect at one point or extend indefinitely without intersecting. If two lines intersect at a right angle (90°), they are perpendicular and are denoted with ⊥. If the lines never intersect, they are parallel and are denoted with ∥.

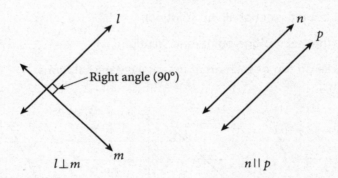

- Perimeter and area are basic properties that all two-dimensional shapes have. The perimeter of a polygon can easily be calculated by adding up the lengths of all its sides. Area is the amount of two-dimensional space a shape occupies. The most common shapes for which you'll need these two properties on Test Day are triangles, parallelograms, and circles.

- The area (A) of a triangle is given by $A = \frac{1}{2}bh$, where b is the base of the triangle and h is its height. The base and height are always perpendicular. Any side of a triangle can be used as the base; just make sure you use its corresponding height (the longest perpendicular line you can draw within the triangle). You can often use a right triangle's two legs as the base and height, but in non-right triangles, if the height is not given, you'll need to draw it in (from the vertex of the angle opposite the base down to the base itself at a right angle) and compute it.

- Parallelograms are quadrilaterals with two pairs of parallel sides. Rectangles and squares are subsets of parallelograms. You can find the area of a parallelogram using $A = bh$. As is the case with triangles, you can use any side of a parallelogram as the base; in addition, the height is still perpendicular to the base. Use the side perpendicular to the base as the height for a rectangle or square; for any other parallelogram, the height (or enough information to find it) will be given.

- A circle's perimeter is known as its circumference (C) and is found using $C = 2\pi r$, where r is the radius (distance from the center of the circle to its edge). Area is given by $A = \pi r^2$. The strange symbol is the lowercase Greek letter pi (π, pronounced "pie"), which is approximately 3.14. As mentioned in the algebra section, you should carry π without rounding unless instructed otherwise.

- A shape is said to have symmetry when it can be split by a line (called an *axis of symmetry*) into two identical parts. Consider folding a shape along a line: If all sides and vertices align once the shape is folded in half, the shape is symmetrical about that line. Some shapes have no axis of symmetry, some have one, some have multiple axes, and still others can have infinite axes of symmetry (e.g., a circle).

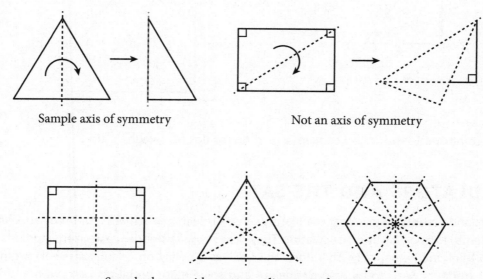

Sample axis of symmetry   Not an axis of symmetry

Sample shapes with corresponding axes of symmetry

- *Congruence* is simply a geometry term that means identical. Angles, lines, and shapes can be congruent. Congruence is indicated by using hash marks: Everything with the same number of hash marks is congruent.

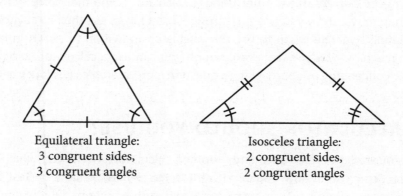

Equilateral triangle:
3 congruent sides,
3 congruent angles

Isosceles triangle:
2 congruent sides,
2 congruent angles

- Similarity between shapes indicates that they have identical angles and proportional sides. Think of taking a shape and stretching or shrinking each side by the same ratio. The resulting shape will have the same angles as the original. While the sides will not be identical, they will be proportional.

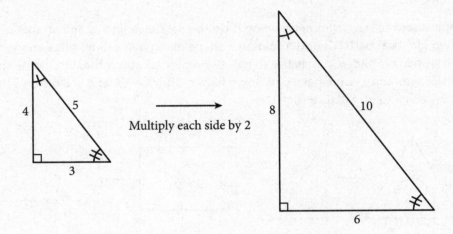

Multiply each side by 2

If you're comfortable with these concepts, read on for tips on calculator use.

CALCULATORS AND THE SAT

Educators and parents believe that calculators serve a role in mathematics, but they are concerned that students rely too heavily on calculators. They believe this dependence weakens students' overall ability to think mathematically. Therefore, the SAT has a policy on calculator use to promote the idea that students need to be able to analyze and solve math problems both with and without a calculator. Some sections will allow you to use a calculator, but others will require you to solve problems without technology. The makers of the SAT walked 12 miles uphill in the snow to school, so why should you have things any easier? Think of this chapter as your personal pair of snow boots that can make that uphill walk a little more comfortable for you.

Many students never stop to ask whether using a calculator is the most efficient way to solve a problem. This chapter will show you how the strongest test takers use their calculators strategically; that is, they carefully evaluate when to use the calculator and when to skip it in favor of a more streamlined approach. As you will see, even though you can use a calculator, sometimes it's more beneficial to save your energy by approaching a question more strategically. Work smarter, not harder.

WHICH CALCULATOR SHOULD YOU USE?

The SAT allows four-function, scientific, and graphing calculators. No matter which calculator you choose, start practicing with it now. You don't want to waste valuable time on Test Day looking for the exponent button or figuring out how to correctly graph equations. Due to the wide range of mathematics topics you'll encounter on Test Day, **we recommend using a graphing calculator**, such as the TI-83/84. If you don't already own one, see if you can borrow one from your school's math department or a local library.

A graphing calculator's capabilities extend well beyond what you'll need for the test, so don't worry about memorizing every function. The next few pages will cover which calculator functions you'll want to know how to use for the SAT. If you're not already familiar with your graphing calculator, you'll want to get the user manual; you can find this on the Internet by searching for your calculator's model number. Identify the calculator functions necessary to answer various SAT math questions, then write down the directions for each to make a handy study sheet.

WHEN SHOULD YOU USE A CALCULATOR?

Some SAT question types are designed based on the idea that students will do some or all of the work using a calculator. As a master test taker, you want to know what to look for so you can identify when calculator use is advantageous. Questions involving linear regression calculations, determining roots of complicated quadratic equations, and other topics are generally designed with calculator use in mind.

Other questions aren't intentionally designed to involve calculator use. Solving some with a calculator can save you time and energy, but you'll waste both if you go for the calculator on others. You will have to decide which method is best when you encounter the following topics:

- Long division and other extensive calculations
- Graphing quadratics
- Simplifying radicals and calculating roots
- Plane and coordinate geometry

Practicing long computations by hand and with the calculator will not only boost your focus and mental math prowess, but it will also help you determine whether it's faster to do the work by hand or reach for the calculator. If you tend to make quick work of long division and multiple-digit multiplication by hand, you can still use the calculator afterward to check your work.

Graphing quadratic equations is a big reason most of you got that fancy calculator in the first place; it makes answering these questions a snap! This is definitely an area where you need to have an in-depth knowledge of your calculator's functions. The key to making these questions easy with the calculator is being meticulous when entering the quadratic. Errors in entry will make it easy to pick a trap answer.

Another stressful area for students is radicals, especially when the answer choices are in decimals. Those two elements are big red flags that trigger a reach for the calculator. Beware: Not all graphing calculators have a built-in radical simplification function, so consider familiarizing yourself with this process.

Geometry can be a gray area for students when it comes to calculator use. Consider working by hand when dealing with angles and lines, specifically when filling in information on complementary, supplementary, and congruent angles. You should be able to work fluidly through those questions sans calculator.

✔ Expert Tip

If you choose to use trigonometric functions to get to the answer on triangle questions, make sure you have your calculator set to degrees or radians as necessitated by the question.

Your calculator will come in handy when you need to work with formulas (volume, distance, arc, etc.) and want to check your work. Because the SAT uses π instead of 3.14…, there is no need to enter the decimal form into your calculator.

TO USE OR NOT TO USE?

A calculator is a double-edged sword on the SAT: Using one can be an asset for verifying work if you struggle when doing math by hand, but turning to it for the simplest computations will cost you time that you could devote to more complex questions. Practice solving questions with and without a calculator to get a sense of your personal style as well as strengths and weaknesses. Think critically about when a calculator saves you time and when mental math is faster. Use the exercises in this book to practice your calculations so that by the time Test Day arrives, you'll be in the habit of using your calculator as effectively as possible!

UNIT TWO

Heart of Algebra

BY THE END OF THIS UNIT, YOU WILL BE ABLE TO:

1. Apply the Kaplan Method for Math to any math question on the SAT

2. Solve linear equations and inequalities

3. Graph linear equations and inequalities

4. Solve systems of equations

5. Translate word problems into math

CHAPTER 2

The Kaplan Method for Math & Linear Equations

CHAPTER OBJECTIVES

By the end of this chapter, you will be able to:

1. Apply the Kaplan Method for Math to Heart of Algebra questions
2. Recognize, simplify, and solve linear equations efficiently
3. Translate complex word problems into equations
4. Interpret the most commonly tested types of linear graphs

SMARTPOINTS

Point Value	SmartPoint Category
Point Builder	Kaplan Method for Math
110 Points	Linear Equations

THE KAPLAN METHOD FOR MATH

Because the SAT is a standardized test, students who approach each question in a consistent way will be rewarded on Test Day. Applying the same basic steps to every math question—whether it asks you about geometry, algebra, or even trigonometry—will help you avoid minor mistakes as well as tempting wrong answer choices.

Use the Kaplan Method for Math for every math question on the SAT. Its steps are applicable to every situation and reflect the best test-taking practices.

The Kaplan Method for Math has three steps:

Step 1: Read the question, identifying and organizing important information as you go

Step 2: Choose the best strategy to answer the question

Step 3: Check that you answered the *right* question

Let's examine each of these steps in more detail.

Step 1: Read the question, identifying and organizing important information as you go

This means:

- **What information am I given?** Take a few seconds to jot down the information you are given and try to group similar items together.

- **Separate the question from the context.** Word problems may include information that is unnecessary to solve the question. Feel free to discard any unnecessary information.

- **How are the answer choices different?** Reading answer choices carefully can help you spot the most efficient way to solve an SAT math question. If the answer choices are decimals, then painstakingly simplifying your final answer as a fraction is a waste of time; you can just use your calculator instead.

- **Should I label or draw a diagram?** If the question describes a shape or figure but doesn't provide one, sketch a diagram so you can see the shape or figure and add notes to it. If a figure is provided, take a few seconds to label it with information from the question.

> **✔ Expert Tip**
>
> Don't assume you understand a question as soon as you see it. Many students see an equation and immediately begin solving. Solving math questions without carefully reading can take you down the wrong path on Test Day.

Step 2: Choose the best strategy to answer the question

- **Look for patterns.** Every SAT math question can be solved in a variety of ways, but not all strategies are created equally. To finish all of the questions, you'll need to solve questions as *efficiently* as possible. If you find yourself about to do time-consuming math, take a moment to look for time-saving shortcuts.

- **Pick numbers or use straightforward math.** While you can always solve an SAT math question with what you've learned in school, doing so won't always be the fastest way. On questions that describe relationships between numbers (such as percentages) but don't actually use numbers, you can often save time on Test Day by using techniques such as Picking Numbers instead of straightforward math.

> ✔ **Expert Tip**
>
> The SAT won't give you any extra points for solving a question the hard way.

Step 3: Check that you answered the *right* question

- When you get the final answer, **resist the urge to immediately bubble in the answer.** Take a moment to:

  - Review the question stem

  - Check units of measurement

  - Double-check your work

- The SAT will often ask you for quantities such as $x + 1$ or the product of x and y. **Be careful on these questions!** They often include tempting answer choices that correspond to the values of x or y individually. There's no partial credit on the SAT, so take a moment at the end of every question to make sure you're answering the right question.

LINEAR EQUATIONS

Linear equations and linear graphs are some of the most common elements on the SAT Math Test. They can be used to model relationships and changes such as those concerning time, temperature, or population.

The graphs of these equations are as important as the equations themselves. The graphs you will see most are either linear or lines of best fit. A sample graph is shown:

When working with a graph like this, you may not know anything about magnetization or cobalt ferrite, but you do see a graph with a straight line on it. That straight line is your clue that you're dealing with a linear equation.

Being able to work with, understand, and interpret linear equations will make up a substantial part of your Math score. In this chapter, we will explore all of those scenarios so you'll be ready to tackle linear equations in whatever form you encounter them on the test.

Many students inadvertently switch on "math autopilot" when solving linear equations, automatically running through the same set of steps on every equation without looking for the best way to solve the question. On the SAT, however, every second counts. You will want to use the *most* efficient strategy for solving questions. Take a look at the following example:

1. $$\frac{4+z-(3+2z)}{6}=\frac{-z-3(5-2)}{7}$$

What is the value of z in the equation above?

A) -61

B) $-\dfrac{61}{27}$

C) $\dfrac{61}{27}$

D) 61

The following table shows Kaplan's strategic thinking on the left, along with suggested math scratchwork on the right. Keeping your notes organized is critical for success on the SAT, so start practicing setting up well-organized scratchwork now.

Strategic Thinking	Math Scratchwork
Step 1: Read the question, identifying and organizing important information as you go This question is straightforward: You're given an equation and need to solve for z.	
Step 2: Choose the best strategy to answer the question Straightforward algebra will work well here. Combine like terms on both sides of the equation first, being mindful of negative signs. Once you've combined, cross-multiply to eliminate the fractions, and then isolate z.	$$\frac{4+z-(3+2z)}{6}=\frac{-z-3(5-2)}{7}$$ $$\frac{1-z}{6}=\frac{-z-9}{7}$$ $$7-7z=-6z-54$$ $$+7z$$ $$-z=-61$$ $$z=61$$
Step 3: Check that you answered the *right* question You've determined that z is equal to 61; therefore, (D) is correct.	$$z=61$$

You could have approached a question like this in many ways, but remember, the goal is to get the correct answer quickly. The faster you solve algebraic equations, the more time you'll be able to devote to challenging questions, setting you up to earn more points on Test Day.

✔ Remember

As you practice, always ask yourself: "Is there a faster way to solve this question?" Use the Answers & Explanations at the back of this book to check!

$$4+z-3-2z \qquad 7-7z$$
$$-2-3(3) \qquad (1-z)7$$
$$(-3z-9)6 = 7-7x$$
$$-18x-54 = 7-7x$$
$$-18v = 61-7x$$

When solving an equation, always keep in mind the fundamental principles of equality: Because both sides of an equation are equal, you need to do the same thing to both sides so that equality is preserved. Try solving another linear equation for extra practice:

2. $3y + 2(y - 2) = -25$

What value of y satisfies the equation above?

A) $-\dfrac{29}{5}$

B) $-\dfrac{21}{5}$

C) $\dfrac{21}{5}$

D) $\dfrac{29}{5}$

Work through the Kaplan Method for Math step-by-step to solve this question. The following table shows Kaplan's strategic thinking on the left, along with suggested math scratchwork on the right.

Strategic Thinking	Math Scratchwork
Step 1: Read the question, identifying and organizing important information as you go This looks similar to the first question: It's asking you to find the value of y.	$3y + 2(y - 2) = -25$
Step 2: Choose the best strategy to answer the question Straightforward algebra is the fastest route to the answer. Start by distributing the 2. Continue by combining like terms until you isolate y.	$3y + 2y - 4 = -25$ $5y - 4 = -25$ $5y = -21$ $y = -\dfrac{21}{5}$
Step 3: Check that you answered the *right* question You found y, so you're done! Choice (B) is correct.	

Notice that none of the answer choices are integers. The SAT may challenge you by designing questions so that the answer is in a form you do not expect. If you arrive at an answer in an unusual form, don't be dissuaded. Fractions and decimals are often correct on the SAT.

Looking carefully at how the SAT uses fractions and decimals can guide your strategy in solving linear equations. The presence of fractions in the answer choices likely means you'll need to rely on techniques for combining and simplifying fractions to get to the right answer. Seeing decimals in the answer choices, on the other hand, likely indicates that you can rely on your calculator and save time on Test Day.

Try to determine the best strategy for solving the next question.

3. $3(y - 8) + 3(6x + 2) = 24 + 3y$

    Which approximate value of x satisfies the equation above?

    A) 0.80

    B) 1.33

    C) 2.33

    D) The value cannot be determined from the given information.

Work through the Kaplan Method for Math step-by-step to solve this question. The following table shows Kaplan's strategic thinking on the left, along with suggested math scratchwork on the right.

Strategic Thinking	Math Scratchwork
Step 1: Read the question, identifying and organizing important information as you go	
The question is asking you to solve for a variable. Note that there are two variables present.	$3(y-8) + 3(6x+2) = 24 + 3y$
Step 2: Choose the best strategy to answer the question	
Before blindly choosing D because there are two variables and only one equation, determine whether the y terms can be eliminated. Divide both sides by 3, and then combine like terms. You'll see that the y terms cancel, leaving one equation with one variable. Isolate x.	$y - 8 + 6x + 2 = 8 + y$ $-8 + 6x + 2 = 8$ $-6 + 6x = 8$
The presence of decimals means your calculator will be a great asset here. Don't worry about reducing the fraction; just punch it into your calculator to find its decimal equivalent.	$6x = 14$ $x = \dfrac{14}{6} = 2.33$
Step 3: Check that you answered the _right_ question	
Double-check the question stem. You've found the value of x, which is 2.33, making (C) correct.	$x = 2.33$

Notice in the previous question that careful use of your calculator can eliminate the need to complete time-consuming tasks by hand. Be conscious of the format of the answer choices—decimal answers are a great clue that you can use your calculator.

> ✔ **Note**
>
> Many graphing calculators have a built-in function that will let you input and solve algebraic equations like the previous one. Consider learning how to use it ahead of Test Day by reading the instruction manual or searching online.

LINEAR WORD PROBLEMS (REAL-WORLD SCENARIOS)

Another way linear equations can be made to look complicated is for them to be disguised in "real-world" word problems, where it's up to you to extract and solve an equation. When you're solving these problems, you may run into trouble translating English into math. The following table shows some of the most common phrases and mathematical equivalents you're likely to see on the SAT.

Word Problems Translation Table	
English	**Math**
equals, is, equivalent to, was, will be, has, costs, adds up to, the same as, as much as	=
times, of, multiplied by, product of, twice, double, by	×
divided by, per, out of, each, ratio	÷
plus, added to, and, sum, combined, total, increased by	+
minus, subtracted from, smaller than, less than, fewer, decreased by, difference between	−
a number, how much, how many, what	x, n, etc.

Linear word problems are made more difficult by complex phrasing and extraneous information. Don't get frustrated—word problems can be broken down in predictable ways. To keep you organized on Test Day, use the **Kaplan Strategy for Translating English into Math:**

- **Define any variables, choosing letters that make sense.**
- **Break sentences into short phrases.**
- **Translate each phrase into a mathematical expression.**
- **Put the expressions together to form an equation.**

Let's apply this to a straightforward example: Colin's age is three less than twice Jim's age.

- **Define any variables, choosing letters that make sense:** We'll choose C for Colin's age and J for Jim's age.

- **Break sentences into short phrases:** The information about Colin and the information about Jim seem like separate phrases.

- **Translate each phrase into a mathematical expression:** Colin's age = C; 3 less than twice Jim's age = $2J - 3$.

- **Put the expressions together to form an equation:** Combine the results to get $C = 2J - 3$.

This strategy fits into the larger framework of the Kaplan Method for Math: When you get to **Step 2: Choose the best strategy to answer the question** and are trying to solve a word problem as efficiently as possible, switch over to this strategy to move forward quickly.

The Kaplan Strategy for Translating English into Math works every time. Apply it here to a test-like example:

4. Malia and Omar want to find the shortest route from their school to a local burger hangout. Route A is 1.5 times longer than Route B and $\frac{3}{4}$ the length of Route C. If Route C is 3 km, how much longer is Route A than Route B?

   A) 0.75 km

   B) 1.5 km

   C) 2 km

   D) 2.25 km

Work through the Kaplan Method for Math step-by-step to solve this question. The following table shows Kaplan's strategic thinking on the left, along with suggested math scratchwork on the right.

Strategic Thinking	Math Scratchwork
Step 1: Read the question, identifying and organizing important information as you go The question is asking you to solve for the difference between the lengths of Routes A and B.	C is 3 km A is $\frac{3}{4}$ of C and 1.5 times B
Step 2: Choose the best strategy to answer the question This looks like a word problem, so go through each step of the Kaplan Strategy for Translating English into Math. Use the route labels for your variables. Note each comparison of the routes in your scratchwork, and then translate them into math. Work carefully through the algebra to find the lengths of routes A and B.	$A = \frac{3}{4} \times C$ $A = \frac{3}{4} \times 3 = \frac{9}{4}$ km $= 2.25$ km $A = 1.5B$ $2.25 = 1.5B$ $1.5 = B$
Step 3: Check that you answered the _right_ question One more step to go. Subtract the length of Route B from the length of Route A to yield (A) as your match.	$A - B = 2.25 - 1.5$ $= 0.75$ km

LINEAR GRAPHS

Working with equations algebraically is only half the battle. The SAT will also expect you to work with graphs of linear equations, which means using lines in slope-intercept form and point-slope form.

One of the most important quantities you'll be working with when graphing a linear equation is the slope. Slope is given by the following equations: $m = \dfrac{(y_2 - y_1)}{(x_2 - x_1)}$, $m = \dfrac{rise}{run}$, and $m = \dfrac{\Delta y}{\Delta x}$, where (x_1, y_1) and (x_2, y_2) are coordinates of points on the line, Δy is the change in the y direction and Δx is the change in the x direction.

One of the most common forms of a linear equation is *slope-intercept form*, which is used to describe the graph of a straight line. The formula is quickly recognizable: $y = mx + b$. The variables y and x represent a point on the graph through which the line passes, while m tells us what the slope of the line is and b represents the point at which the line intersects the y-axis.

Remember: A line with a positive slope runs up and to the right ("uphill"), and a line with a negative slope runs down and to the right ("downhill"). In the following figure, lines n and l have positive and negative slopes, respectively.

Occasionally, you will encounter a line with a slope of 0—meaning it does not rise or fall from left to right. These lines are easy to spot because they are horizontal and are parallel to the x-axis (line k in the figure shown). Lines that are parallel to the y-axis, such as line m in the figure, have slopes that are "undefined." The lines themselves exist, but their slopes cannot be calculated numerically.

The slope of a graph can also tell you valuable information about the rate of change of numbers and variables associated with the line. A positive slope signifies an increase in a variable, while a negative slope indicates a decrease. *Large* numerical values for slope indicate rapid changes, while *small* numerical values point to more gradual changes. Imagine the balance in your checking account is B, and it changes with the number of days that go by, D. Several proposed models are listed here. Think about how each one would impact your life.

$$B = 100\,D + 75$$
$$B = 0.25\,D + 75$$
$$B = -100\,D + 75$$
$$B = -0.25\,D + 75$$

The first equation probably looks pretty good. The second equation isn't as great. An extra quarter a day isn't going to do much for you. The third equation would quickly drive you into bankruptcy, while the fourth equation might be cause for concern after a while.

The *y*-intercept, on the other hand, is much less significant, typically representing the initial condition in a number of models—that is, where the model begins. In the checking account example, the beginning balance was $75 in all four models. Notice, the *y*-intercept didn't change at all.

Look at the following question to see how the SAT might test your ability to match a linear equation with its graph.

5. If a line contains the coordinates $(-\frac{2}{5}, 0)$ and $(0, 1)$, which of the following lines will it never intersect?

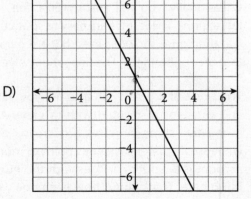

Approach this question by using the Kaplan Method for Math. Try to ask yourself similar questions as you work through questions like this on Test Day.

Strategic Thinking	Math Scratchwork
Step 1: Read the question, identifying and organizing important information as you go This question is asking you to determine which line will never intersect the one that contains the two points provided by the question stem.	
Step 2: Choose the best strategy to answer the question Using your calculator will take too long, so use the slope formula and your critical thinking skills instead. Start by finding the slope of the line in the question stem. Because the slope is positive, you can eliminate C and D, which both contain lines with negative slopes.	$(-\frac{2}{5}, 0), (0, 1)$ $m = \dfrac{y_2 - y_1}{x_2 - x_1}$ $= \dfrac{1-0}{0-(-\frac{2}{5})} = \dfrac{1}{\frac{2}{5}} = \dfrac{5}{2}$
Two lines that never intersect are parallel and therefore have the same slope, so determine which of the remaining answer choices also has a slope of $\frac{5}{2}$. There is no need to calculate the slopes; simply counting units on the graphs will suffice.	$m_A: \dfrac{2}{5}$ $m_B: \dfrac{5}{2}$
Step 3: Check that you answered the *right* question Only (B) contains a line that will not intersect the one described in the question stem. Notice you didn't have to do any additional work, such as finding *y*-intercepts. Only do as much as you need to—this saves time on Test Day.	(B)

Some questions are a little more challenging. They're usually similar in structure to the "checking account" equation described earlier, but they can involve more complicated scenarios. This next question requires you to choose the best model for a given "real-world" situation. See if you can match the graph to an appropriate model. Watch out: It's a science crossover question, so you'll need to be particularly careful to separate the question from the context.

Snowy Tree Cricket Temperature Prediction

6. Snowy tree crickets have long been used to determine the ambient air temperature. The correlation between ambient air temperature and their chirp frequency is highly consistent. The graph shows the correlation between ambient air temperature, t, in degrees Fahrenheit and the number of chirps, c, per minute from a snowy tree cricket. Which of the following represents the line on the graph?

A) $c = 4t - 160$

B) $c = \frac{1}{4}t - 160$

C) $c = \frac{1}{2}t - 40$

D) $c = 4t + 40$

Although you may enjoy learning about science with your math, you don't need to waste time digesting extraneous information. The following table shows the strategic thinking that can help you solve this question.

Strategic Thinking	Math Scratchwork
Step 1: Read the question, identifying and organizing important information as you go Only the last two sentences describe the graph and your task: "The graph above shows the correlation between ambient air temperature, *t*, in degrees Fahrenheit and the number of chirps, *c*, per minute from a snowy tree cricket. Which of the following represents the line on the graph?"	

Strategic Thinking	Math Scratchwork
Step 2: Choose the best strategy to answer the question	
Plotting the equations in the answer choices on your calculator would be time consuming; in addition, the line's *y*-intercept is not visible, thereby introducing another hurdle. Opt for examining the answer choices closely instead.	$(40, 0)$ and $(65, 100)$ $m = \dfrac{100-0}{65-40} = \dfrac{100}{25} = 4$
Pick a couple points on the line of best fit to determine the slope. You'll find it equals 4, so eliminate B and C.	
Looking at the graph, you'll see that 40 cannot be the *y*-intercept because the line does not cross the *y*-axis at that point. Eliminate D.	$b \neq 40$
Step 3: Check that you answered the *right* question	
Choice (A) is the only option remaining. You're done! Note that you didn't have to calculate *b* to find the correct answer, so you saved some time.	

While scatterplots will be described in more detail in subsequent chapters, this next question shows that the principles covered here for graphing linear equations can be equally applied to the line of best fit on a scatterplot. See what you can conclude from the slope and *y*-intercept of the equation of the best-fit line. Note that this question is an example of a very complex word problem—don't be intimidated! If you can tackle this problem, you'll be able to handle the most difficult SAT word problems.

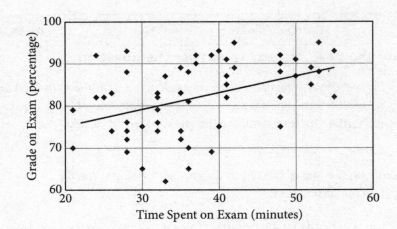

7. A physics professor presented the scatterplot above to his first-year students. What is the significance of the slope of the best-fit line?

A) The slope represents the rate at which time spent on an exam increases based on a student's exam performance.

B) The slope represents the average grade on the exam.

C) The slope represents the rate at which a student's exam grade increases based on time spent on the exam.

D) The slope has no significance.

Use the Kaplan Method for Math to make short work of this question. The following table shows the strategic thinking that can help you solve complex questions like this one.

Strategic Thinking
Step 1: Read the question, identifying and organizing important information as you go
You must determine the significance of the slope of the best-fit line on the scatterplot.
Step 2: Choose the best strategy to answer the question
Look for answer choices you can easily eliminate based on what you know about lines. A line's slope is a rate, so you can eliminate B and D. Examine A and C next. According to the graph, time spent on the exam is the independent variable, and the exam grade is the dependent variable. Pick the answer choice that reflects this.
Step 3: Check that you answered the *right* question
You've determined the significance of the slope of the line of best fit. The correct answer is (C).

Now you'll have a chance to try a few more test-like questions. Use the scaffolding as needed to guide you through the question and get the right answer.

Some guidance is provided, but you'll need to fill in the missing parts of explanations or the step-by-step math to get to the correct answer. Don't worry—after going through the examples at the beginning of this chapter, these questions should be completely doable. If you find yourself struggling, however, review the worked examples in this chapter.

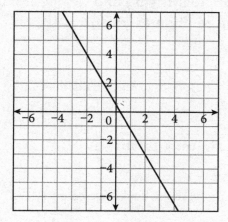

8. The line $y = -\dfrac{7x}{4} + \dfrac{1}{2}$ is shown in the graph. If the line is shifted down 2 units and then reflected over the x-axis, which of the following graphs represents the new line?

A)

B)

C)

D)

The following table can help you structure your thinking as you go about solving this problem. The Kaplan strategic thinking is provided, as are bits of structured scratchwork. If you're not sure how to approach a question like this, start at the top and work your way down.

Strategic Thinking	Math Scratchwork
Step 1: Read the question, identifying and organizing important information as you go *What are you actually solving for here?* You're asked for the graph that corresponds to the described changes made to $y = -\dfrac{7x}{4} + \dfrac{1}{2}$.	
Step 2: Choose the best strategy to answer the question *While you could apply the transformations, could picking a test point be faster?* Pick a test point on the original line. Apply the changes to it. Cross off any choices that don't pass through the new point. You might need to pick more than one point if your initial choice doesn't eliminate all of the answer choices.	
Step 3: Check that you answered the *right* question *Which graph matches the changes described?* Did you get (D)? If so, you're correct! Beware of C; it results from a reflection over the wrong axis.	

Here's another test-like example to try with this method:

9. Three years ago, Madison High School started charging an admission fee for basketball games to raise money for new bleachers. The initial price was \$2 per person; the school raised the price of admission to \$2.50 this year. Assuming this trend continues, which of the following equations can be used to describe the cost of admission, c, y years after the school began charging for admission to games?

A) $c = 6y + 2$

B) $c = \dfrac{y}{6} + 2.5$

C) $c = \dfrac{y}{6} + 2$

D) $c = \dfrac{y}{2} + 2$

The following table can help you structure your thinking as you go about solving this problem. The Kaplan strategic thinking is provided, as are bits of structured scratchwork. If you're not sure how to approach a question like this, start at the top and work your way down.

Strategic Thinking	Math Scratchwork
Step 1: Read the question, identifying and organizing important information as you go *What is this question asking you to find?* You need to identify the equation that correctly relates cost to years after the admission charge implementation.	
Step 2: Choose the best strategy to answer the question *How do you start a question like this?* Look carefully; you're implicitly given two sets of coordinates. You can use these to find a key piece of a linear equation and eliminate two answer choices. *What should you do to determine which remaining choice is correct?* The school started charging admission at a certain point in time; the price at this point is your y-intercept. Use this to pick the correct answer.	$(\underline{}, \underline{})$ $(\underline{}, \underline{})$ $m = \dfrac{\rule{2cm}{0.4pt}}{} = \rule{2cm}{0.4pt}$ *eliminate* $\underline{}$ *and* $\underline{}$ $b = \underline{}$

Strategic Thinking	Math Scratchwork
Step 3: Check that you answered the *right* question *Did you find the correct equation?* Did you come up with (C)? If so, great job! You're correct.	 ———

> **✔ Note**
>
> Because the question says "three years ago," it's tempting to use (–3, 2) and (0, 2.5) as your coordinates. Before you do this, think about what that means: This translates to the first admission charge being $2.50, as it's impossible to have a negative year. B is a trap waiting for students who attempt this route!

Now that you've seen the variety of ways in which the SAT can test you on linear equations, try the following questions to check your understanding. Give yourself 3.5 minutes to tackle the following three questions. Make sure you use the Kaplan Method for Math on every question. Remember, you'll need to emphasize speed and efficiency in addition to simply getting the correct answer.

10. If the line $y = -5x + 8$ is shifted down 3 units and left 2 units, what is the slope of the new line?

(A) –5

B) 0

C) 3

D) 5

11. If $\frac{3}{4}y = 6 - \frac{1}{3}c$, then what is the value of $2c + \frac{9}{2}y$?

12. If m is a constant between 0 and $\frac{1}{2}$ (exclusive), which of the following could be the graph of $x - y = m(2x + y)$?

A)

B)

C)

D)

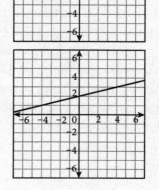

Answers and Explanations for this chapter begin on page 815.

EXTRA PRACTICE

Required	Recommended
Questions 1–8	Questions 9–41

1. Which of the following equations is linear?

   A) $y = \dfrac{3}{x}$

   B) $\sqrt{x} + y = 0$

   C) $\dfrac{1}{2}x - \dfrac{5}{8}y = 11$

   D) $y = x^2 + 2x - 4$

2. Which of the following does not represent a linear relationship?

   A) $y = \dfrac{x}{5}$

   B)

x	y
−4	12
0	2
4	−6
8	2
12	12

   C) $x = \dfrac{9}{7}y + 4$

   D) $y = 4x + 7$

3. The local Farmers' Market usually sells potatoes for $0.90 per pound. On Fridays, they sell potatoes at a 30% discount. The market also sells cantaloupes for $3.50 each. Which of the following represents the total cost, c, if a customer buys 2 cantaloupes and p pounds of potatoes on a Friday?

   A) $c = 0.63p + 7$

   B) $c = 0.9p + 7$

   C) $c = 0.3p + 3.5$

   D) $c = 0.9p + 3.5$

4. If paintbrushes cost $1.50 each and canvases cost 6 times that much, which of the following represents the cost, in dollars, of p paintbrushes and c canvases?

   A) $7.5pc$

   B) $10.5pc$

   C) $9c + 1.5p$

   D) $10.5(p + c)$

5. In states that produce natural gas, the state government typically imposes two types of taxes on producers: a local impact fee, which is a flat tax paid per well drilled, and a severance tax, which is based on the market value of the total volume of gas extracted, v. If a producer's total bill for one well is given by the equation $T = 0.004v + 50{,}000$, then the value 0.004 could represent which of the following?

   A) The local impact fee

   B) The market value of the gas extracted

   C) The total tax bill minus the local impact fee

   D) The amount of the severance tax as a percentage

Expected Property Values 2014-2028

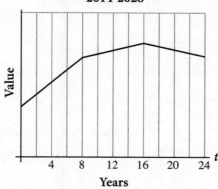

6. A realtor is studying the graph above, which shows the expected value of properties in her area over the next 24 years. If *t* represents the number of years after 2014, in what year should the increase in property values start to slow down?

A) 2008

B) 2018

C) 2022

D) 2030

Number of Songs Purchased

7. The graph above shows the cost of joining and buying music from a music subscription service. What does the *y*-intercept of the line most likely represent?

A) The cost per song

B) The cost to join the service

C) The cost of buying 20 songs

D) The cost of 20 subscriptions to the service

8. A store "breaks even" when its sales equal its expenses. Jon has just opened a new surfboard store at the beach. He buys each surfboard wholesale for $80 and has fixed monthly expenses of $3,600. He sells each surfboard for $120. How many surfboards does Jon need to sell in a month to break even?

A) 18

B) 30

C) 45

D) 90

9. Which value of *x* makes the equation $\frac{8}{5}\left(x+\frac{33}{12}\right)=16$ true?

A) 7.25

B) 8.75

C) 12.75

D) 13.25

Price of One Pound	Projected Number of Pounds Sold
$1.20	15,000
$1.40	12,500
$1.60	10,000
$1.80	7,500
$2.00	5,000
$2.20	2,500

10. Which of the following equations best describes the linear relationship shown in the table, where *g* represents the number of pounds of grain sold and *d* represents the price in dollars of one pound of grain?

A) $g = 1.2d + 12,500$

B) $g = 12,500d + 15,000$

C) $g = -12,500d + 17,500$

D) $g = -12,500d + 30,000$

11. Henry just set up direct deposit from his employer to his checking account. The equation $y = 360x - 126.13$ represents the balance in Henry's account if he deposits his weekly paycheck for x weeks. Based on this equation, which of the following statements is true?

    A) Henry earns $126.13 per week.

    B) Henry made an initial deposit of $126.13.

    C) Before setting up the direct deposit, Henry had overdrawn his account.

    D) When Henry set up the direct deposit, he already had $360 in his account.

12. A printing press running around the clock can print 54,000 black and white pages per day. Based on this information, what could the function $f(x) = 2,250x$ represent?

    A) The number of pages the press can print in x days

    B) The number of pages the press can print in x hours

    C) The number of days it takes the press to print x pages

    D) The number of hours it takes the press to print x pages

13. Nadim is hosting a party and is hiring a catering company to make and serve the food. The caterer charges a flat fee for serving the food plus a per person rate for the meals. If the equation used to calculate the total cost of Nadim's party is $y = 11x + 300$, then which of the following most likely represents the number of people attending the party?

    A) x

    B) y

    C) 11

    D) 300

14. The graph of which of the following linear equations has an undefined slope?

    A) $x = 3$

    B) $y = 0$

    C) $x = -y$

    D) $x - y = 0$

15. The graph shown represents which of the following equations?

    A) $y = -3x + 4$

    B) $y = -\dfrac{1}{3}x + 4$

    C) $y = \dfrac{1}{3}x - 4$

    D) $y = 3x - 4$

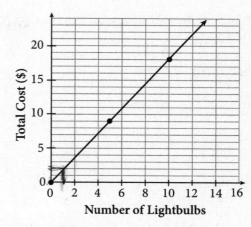

16. If the equation of the line shown in the graph above is written in the form $y = mx + b$, which of the following is true?

A) $m < 0$ and $b < 0$

B) $m < 0$ and $b > 0$

C) $m > 0$ and $b < 0$

D) $m > 0$ and $b > 0$

17. Which of the following scenarios could be supported by the graph shown?

A) As the algae content in a lake increases, the number of fish decreases.

B) As the algae content in a lake decreases, the number of fish decreases.

C) As the algae content in a lake increases, the number of fish increases.

D) As the algae content in a lake increases, the number of fish remains constant.

18. A hardware store sells lightbulbs in different quantities. The graph shows the cost of various quantities. According to the graph, what is the cost of a single lightbulb?

A) $0.56

B) $1.80

C) $2.50

D) $3.60

19. A laser tag arena sells two types of memberships. One package costs $325 for one year of membership with an unlimited number of visits. The second package has a $125 enrollment fee, includes five free visits, and costs an additional $8 per visit after the first five. How many visits would a person need to use for each type of membership to cost the same amount over a one-year period?

A) 20

B) 25

C) 30

D) 40

20. Which of the following equations has no solution?

   A) $\frac{3}{8}(x-2)=\frac{8}{3}(x+2)$

   B) $-\frac{3}{2}(2x-8)=3x-12$

   C) $4\left(\frac{3}{4}x+5\right)=3x+20$

   D) $6\left(\frac{2}{3}x+5\right)=4x+5$

$$2\left(x-\frac{5}{2}\right)=c\left(\frac{4}{5}x-2\right)$$

21. If the equation above has infinitely many solutions and c is a constant, what is the value of c?

   A) -2

   B) $-\frac{4}{5}$

   C) $\frac{5}{4}$

   D) $\frac{5}{2}$

22. If $\frac{1}{4}(10h)-\frac{3}{2}(h+1)=-\frac{2}{3}\left(\frac{9}{2}h\right)+6$, what is the value of h?

   A) $\frac{9}{8}$

   B) $\frac{15}{8}$

   C) There is no value of h for which the equation is true.

   D) There are infinitely many values of h for which the equation is true.

23. Vera is on her school's track and field team. In a practice long-jump competition against her teammates, she gets 5 points for landing over the closer line and 10 points for landing over the farther line. She gets a total of 7 jumps and lands x times over the farther line and the rest of the times over the closer line. Which of the following functions represents Vera's total score?

   A) $f(x) = 10x$

   B) $f(x) = 5x + 35$

   C) $f(x) = 10x + 5$

   D) $f(x) = 70 - 5x$

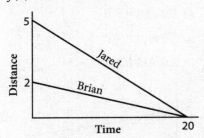

24. Brian and Jared live in the same apartment complex and they both bike to and from work every day. The figure above shows a typical commute home for each of them. Based on the figure, which of the following statements is true?

   A) It takes Brian longer to bike home because his work is farther away.

   B) It takes Jared longer to bike home because his work is farther away.

   C) Jared and Brian arrive home at the same time, so they must bike at about the same rate.

   D) Jared bikes a longer distance than Brian in the same amount of time, so Jared must bike at a faster rate.

25. When graphing a linear equation that is written in the form $y = mx + b$, the variable m represents the slope of the line and b represents the y-intercept. Assuming that $b > 0$, which of the following best describes how reversing the sign of b would affect the graph?

A) The new line will shifted down b units.

B) The new line will be shifted down $b \times 2$ units.

C) The new line will be a perfect reflection across the x-axis.

D) The new line will be a perfect reflection across the y-axis.

Legislation Impact on Population

26. The federal government in the United States has the authority to protect species whose populations have reached dangerously low levels. The graph above represents the expected population of a certain endangered species before and after a proposed law aimed at protecting the animal is passed. Based on the graph, which of the following statements is true?

A) The proposed law is expected to accelerate the decline in population.

B) The proposed law is expected to stop and reverse the decline in population.

C) The proposed law is expected to have no effect on the decline in population.

D) The proposed law is expected to slow, but not stop or reverse, the decline in population.

27. What value of n satisfies the equation $\dfrac{7}{8}(n-6) = \dfrac{21}{2}$?

28. If the equation of line A in the graph above is given by $y = mx + b$ and the equation of line B is given by $y = k(mx + b)$, what is the value of k?

29. If $2x + 5 = 11$, what is the value of $2x - 5$?

    A) −11

    B) −6

    C) 1

    D) 11

30. Which value of x makes the equation

    $\dfrac{3}{2}(x+7)=6$ true?

    A) −5

    B) −3

    C) 9

    D) 11

31. Andrew works at a travel agency. He gets paid $120 for a day's work, plus a bonus of $25 for each cruise he books. Which of the following equations represents the relationship between one day of Andrews's pay d and the number of cruises he books c?

    A) $c = 25d + 120$

    B) $c = 120d + 25$

    C) $d = 25c + 120$

    D) $d = 120c + 25$

32. A company is sponsoring a celebrity charity walk. For each celebrity who participates, the company will donate a flat amount to the charity of the celebrity's choice, plus an additional amount for every mile the celebrity walks. If the amount donated to charity on behalf of one celebrity is represented by $y = 100x + 250$, what does the number 250 best represent?

    A) The flat amount donated

    B) The total amount donated

    C) The amount donated per mile

    D) The number of miles the celebrity walked

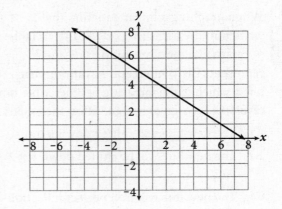

33. What is the slope of the line shown in the graph above?

    A) $-\dfrac{3}{2}$

    B) $-\dfrac{2}{3}$

    C) $\dfrac{2}{3}$

    D) $\dfrac{3}{2}$

x	−9	0	3	9
y	11	8	7	?

34. If the values in the table represent a linear relationship, what is the missing value?

    A) 5

    B) 6

    C) 11

    D) 13

35. A local restaurant is hosting a dance-a-thon 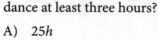 for charity. Each couple must dance a minimum of three hours before earning any money for the charity. After the first three hours, couples earn $50 per half-hour of continuous dancing. Which expression represents the total amount earned by a couple that dances h hours, assuming they dance at least three hours?

A) $25h$

B) $100h$

C) $50(h - 3)$

D) $100h - 300$

Minutes Charging	10	15	30
Percent Charged	34	41.5	64

36. Jose is using his laptop and wants to recharge it before the battery completely runs out. He recorded the battery charge for the first 30 minutes after he plugged it in to get an idea of when it would be completely charged. The table above shows the results. Which linear function represents the percent battery charge on Jose's laptop x minutes after he plugged it in?

A) $f(x) = 1.5x + 19$

B) $f(x) = 2x + 14$

C) $f(x) = 2.5x + 9$

D) $f(x) = 10x + 34$

37. If a is a rational number where $a > 1$, which of the following could be the graph of $y = ay + ax + x + 1$?

A)

B)

C)

D)

38. Some cars are more fuel-efficient than others. Which graph could represent the fuel efficiency of an efficient car, e, and a less efficient car, i?

A)

B)

C)

D)

$$0.55x - 1.04 = 0.35x + 0.16$$

39. In the equation above what is the value of x?

40. For what value of y does the graph of $\frac{3}{2}y - 2x = 18$ cross the y-axis?

Box Airmail

41. A freight airline charges a flat fee to airmail a box, plus an additional charge for each pound the box weighs. The graph above shows the relationship between the weight of the box and the total cost to airmail it. Based on the graph, how much would it cost in dollars to airmail a 40-pound box?

CHAPTER 3

Systems of Equations

CHAPTER OBJECTIVES

By the end of this chapter, you will be able to:

1. Distinguish between independent and dependent equations

2. Solve two-variable systems of equations

3. Determine the most efficient way to solve systems of equations

4. Translate word problems into multiple equations

SMARTPOINTS

Point Value	SmartPoint Category
40 Points	Systems of Linear Equations

SYSTEMS OF EQUATIONS

The linear equations detailed in the previous chapter are well suited for modeling a variety of scenarios and for solving for a single variable in terms of another that is clearly defined (e.g., what is the cost of a data plan if you consume 4 GB of data in a month). However, sometimes you will be given a set of multiple equations with multiple variables that are interdependent. For example, perhaps you know that a $50/month cell phone plan can be consumed by $0.05 text messages and $0.40 voice calls. Further, the plan has a cap of 1,000 combined text messages and voice calls.

This scenario can be represented by the following system of equations:

$$\$0.05t + \$0.40v = \$50$$
$$t + v = 1,000$$

Solving such a system would enable you to determine the maximum number of text messages and voice calls you could make under your plan, optimizing your usage. To solve systems of equations, you'll need to rely on a different set of tools that builds on the algebra you're already familiar with. The following question shows an example of such a system in the context of a test-like question.

1. If $28x - 5y = 36$ and $15x + 5y + 18 = 68$, what is the value of x?

    A) 1

    B) 2

    C) 3

    D) 4

You might be tempted to switch on math autopilot at this point and employ substitution, solving the first equation for y in terms of x:

$$y = \frac{1}{5}(-36 + 28x)$$

You could plug this back into the original question and eventually solve for x, but remember, the SAT tests your ability to solve math problems in the most efficient way. The following table contains some strategic thinking designed to help you find the most efficient way to solve this problem on Test Day, along with some suggested scratchwork.

Strategic Thinking	Math Scratchwork
Step 1: Read the question, identifying and organizing important information as you go	
This question is straightforward: You're being asked to solve for x.	
Step 2: Choose the best strategy to answer the question	
Looking at the coefficients, it's evident that combination will be much faster than substitution. Begin by combining like terms. The y term coefficients are equal in magnitude but opposite in sign, so no equation manipulation is necessary. Once the y terms are eliminated, solve for x.	$28x - 5y = 36$ $15x + 5y + 18 = 68$ $28x - 5y = 36$ $+ \quad 15x + 5y = 50$ ─────────── $43x = 86$ $x = 2$
Step 3: Check that you answered the _right_ question	
You've solved for x, the requested quantity. You can confidently select (B).	$x = 2$

✔ **Note**

We will not explicitly include an explanation for each simplifying step in this chapter. If you get stuck, review the information on simplifying and solving equations in chapter 2.

INDEPENDENT VERSUS DEPENDENT EQUATIONS

Generally, when you are given a situation involving n variables, you will need a system of n independent equations to arrive at fixed values for these variables. Thus, if you have a system of two variables, you'll need two independent equations to solve for each of the variables. Three variables would require three independent equations, and so on and so forth.

Systems of equations are extremely useful in modeling and simulation. Complex mathematical problems such as weather forecasting or crowd control predictions often require 10 or more equations to be simultaneously solved for multiple variables. Fortunately, you won't encounter anything this daunting on Test Day; following is an example of what you might see on the SAT.

$$y - 3x = 14$$
$$x - 5 = 6y$$

Before we outline the process for solving two-variable systems of equations, let's clarify one of the key requirements to solve these problems. We'll need two independent equations to solve for two variables. What exactly is an independent equation? Consider the equation $4x + 2y = 8$. We could use properties of equality to transform this equation in a number of different ways. For example, we could multiply both sides by 2, resulting in the equation $8x + 4y = 16$.

While it seems as though we've just created an additional equation, this is misleading, as our second equation has the same core variables and relationships as our first equation. This is termed a dependent equation, and two dependent equations cannot be used to solve for two variables. Look what happens when we try to use substitution. Let's isolate y in our original equation:

$$y = 4 - 2x$$

If we plug that into our second equation, notice what happens:

$$8x + 4(4 - 2x) = 16$$
$$8x + 16 - 8x = 16$$
$$16 = 16$$

While it's always good to see that $16 = 16$, this doesn't bring us any closer to solving for either of our variables. In fact, if you arrive at a result like this when you are solving a system of equations, it's a strong sign that your two equations are *dependent* on one another. In this case, we'd say that our system has infinitely many solutions because we could choose any number of possible values for x and y.

> ✔ **Note**
>
> When two equations are dependent, one equation could be obtained by algebraically manipulating the other equation. Graphically, dependent equations both describe the same line in the coordinate plane.

At other times, you'll encounter equations that are fundamentally incompatible with each other. For example, if we have the two equations $4x + 2y = 8$ and $4x + 2y = 9$, it should be obvious that there are no values for x and y that will satisfy both equations at the same time. Doing so would violate fundamental laws of math. In this case, we'd have a system of equations with no solution. These two equations define parallel lines, which by definition never intersect.

Knowing how many solutions a set has will tell you how graphing them together should look. Remember, the solution of a system of equations consists of the point or points where their graphs intersect.

If your system has . . .	. . . then it will graph as:	Reasoning
no solution	two parallel lines	Parallel lines never intersect.
one solution	two lines intersecting at a single point	Two straight lines have only one intersection.
infinitely many solutions	a single line (one line directly on top of the other)	One equation is a manipulation of the other—they graph the same line.

Because you could encounter any of these three on Test Day, ensure you are familiar with all of them.

Let's examine a sample problem that investigates the requirements for solving a system of equations:

$$5x - 3y = 10$$
$$6y = kx - 42$$

2. In the system of linear equations above, k represents a constant. If the system of equations has no solution, what is the value of $2k$?

   A) $\dfrac{5}{2}$

   B) 5

   C) 10

   D) 20

Work through the Kaplan Method for Math step-by-step to solve this question. The following table shows Kaplan's strategic thinking on the left, along with suggested math scratchwork on the right.

Strategic Thinking	Math Scratchwork
Step 1: Read the question, identifying and organizing important information as you go You are looking for the value of $2k$. You're given a system of equations with no solution.	
Step 2: Choose the best strategy to answer the question The fact that the system of equations has no solution is key to finding the correct answer. When the two variables have identical coefficients in both equations, they should be equal to different constants. Start by manipulating the second equation into the same format as the first. After manipulating the second equation, divide it by 2 to yield a -3 coefficient for y to match y's coefficient in the first equation. $\dfrac{k}{2}$ must equal 5, the coefficient of x in the first equation. Solve for k.	$5x - 3y = 10$ $6y = kx - 42$ $-kx + 6y = -42$ $kx - 6y = 42$ $\dfrac{k}{2}x - 3y = 21$ $\dfrac{k}{2} = 5$ $k = 10$
Step 3: Check that you answered the *right* question Be careful: You're asked for $2k$, not k. Multiply both sides by 2 to get $2k = 20$, which is (D).	$2k = 20$

SOLVING SYSTEMS OF EQUATIONS: COMBINATION & SUBSTITUTION

Now that you understand the requirements that must be satisfied to solve a system of equations, we can go into more depth about methods for solving these equations effectively. The two main methods of solving a system of linear equations are substitution and combination (sometimes referred to as *linear elimination*).

Substitution is the most straightforward method for solving equations, and it can be applied in every situation. Unfortunately, it is often the longest and most time-consuming route for solving systems of equations as well. To use substitution, solve the simpler of the two equations for one variable, and then substitute that result into the other equation. We could use substitution to answer the question on the next page, but you'll see that there's a quicker way: combination.

Combination involves adding the two equations together to eliminate a variable. Often, one or both of the equations are multiplied by a constant before they are added together. Combination is almost always the best technique to use to solve a system of equations when the question only asks you for the value of one of the variables, but even when a question asks you for both variables, combination is often faster than substitution.

Unfortunately, even though most students prefer substitution, problems on the SAT are often designed to be quickly solved with combination. To really boost your score on Test Day, practice combination as much as you can on Practice Tests and in homework problems so that it becomes second nature.

3. If $\frac{1}{4}x + 2y = \frac{11}{4}$ and $-6y - x = 7$, what is half of y?

Work through the Kaplan Method for Math step-by-step to solve this question. The following table shows Kaplan's strategic thinking on the left, along with suggested math scratchwork on the right.

Strategic Thinking	Math Scratchwork
Step 1: Read the question, identifying and organizing important information as you go Read carefully: You need to find *half* of y.	
Step 2: Choose the best strategy to answer the question Resist the urge to automatically use substitution. The presence of fractions in the question stem tells you that you should use combination. Multiply the first equation by 4 to clear out its fractions, and then add the equations together and solve for y.	$\frac{1}{4}x + 2y = \frac{11}{4}$ $-6y - x = 7$ $4\left(\frac{1}{4}x + 2y = \frac{11}{4}\right) \rightarrow$ $x + 8y = 11$ $\begin{aligned} x + 8y &= 11 \\ +\quad -x - 6y &= 7 \\ \hline 2y &= 18 \\ y &= 9 \end{aligned}$
Step 3: Check that you answered the *right* question Don't stop yet: You need to find half of y. Grid in 9/2 or 4.5, and you're done.	$\frac{y}{2} = \frac{9}{2} = 4.5$

Combination can also be used when the testmakers ask you for a strange quantity, as in the following problem:

4. If $7c - 2b = 15$ and $3b - 6c = 2$, what is the value of $b + c$?

    A) −27

    B) −3

    C) 8

    D) 17

Work through the Kaplan Method for Math step-by-step to solve this question. The following table shows Kaplan's strategic thinking on the left, along with suggested math scratchwork on the right.

Strategic Thinking	Math Scratchwork
Step 1: Read the question, identifying and organizing important information as you go You are being asked to find the value of $b + c$. The question stem provides two equations involving b and c.	$7c - 2b = 15$ $3b - 6c = 2$
Step 2: Choose the best strategy to answer the question The fact that you're solving for $b + c$ suggests that there's a short-cut that will save time on Test Day. Add the equations together to yield $b + c$ equal to a constant.	$-2b + 7c = 15$ $+ \quad 3b - 6c = 2$ ———————— $b + c = 17$
Step 3: Check that you answered the _right_ question Choice (D) correctly reflects the sum of b and c.	$b + c = 17$

That was much easier and faster than substitution. With substitution, you could spend more than two minutes solving a question like this. However, a bit of analysis and combination gets the job done in much less time.

TRANSLATING WORD PROBLEMS INTO MULTIPLE EQUATIONS

While solving systems of equations can be relatively straightforward once you get the hang of it, sometimes, to complicate things, the SAT will give you a complex word problem and make you translate it into a system of equations and then solve. It sounds a lot scarier than it actually is. Remember to use the Kaplan Strategy for Translating English into Math to set up your equations, and then solve using either substitution or combination.

> ✔ **Note**
>
> The Kaplan Strategy for Translating English into Math can be found in chapter 2.

5. At a certain toy store, tiny stuffed pandas cost $3.50 and giant stuffed pandas cost $14. If the store sold 29 panda toys and made $217 in revenue in one week, how many tiny stuffed pandas and giant stuffed pandas were sold?

   A) 18 tiny stuffed pandas, 11 giant stuffed pandas

   B) 11 tiny stuffed pandas, 18 giant stuffed pandas

   C) 12 tiny stuffed pandas, 17 giant stuffed pandas

   D) 18 tiny stuffed pandas, 13 giant stuffed pandas

Work through the Kaplan Method for Math to solve this question step-by-step. The following table shows Kaplan's strategic thinking on the left, along with suggested math scratchwork on the right.

Strategic Thinking	Math Scratchwork
Step 1: Read the question, identifying and organizing important information as you go	
You need to find the number of tiny stuffed pandas and giant stuffed pandas sold.	tiny: $3.50 giant: $14 29 total sold $217.00 in revenue

Strategic Thinking	Math Scratchwork
Step 2: Choose the best strategy to answer the question This is a word problem, so use the Kaplan Strategy for Translating English into Math. Because both toys are pandas, p is likely to be a confusing choice for a variable. Instead, use t for tiny and g for giant. Break off each piece of relevant information into a separate phrase. Translating each phrase into a math expression will get you the components of a system of equations. After piecing together the system of equations, use combination to quickly eliminate g. Multiply the first equation by −14 before combining with the second. Solve for t. Choices B and C have different values for t, so eliminate them. Plug 18 into the first equation for t, and then solve for g.	t = tiny g = giant tiny: \$3.50 → 3.5t giant: \$14 → 14g 29 total sold → = 29 \$217.00 in revenue → = 217 $t + g = 29$ $3.5t + 14g = 217$ $-14t - 14g = -406$ + $3.5t + 14g = 217$ ——————————— $-10.5t = -189$ $t = 18$ $t + g = 29$ $18 + g = 29$ $g = 11$
Step 3: Check that you answered the *right* question The only answer choice that contains both quantities you found is (A).	$t = 18$, $g = 11$

Watch out for B, a trap answer designed to catch students who switched the variables, possibly due to choosing an ambiguous letter such as p. Choosing descriptive variable names might sound silly, but in the high-stakes environment of the SAT, you must do everything you can to avoid careless errors and subsequent lost points.

> ✔ **Note**
>
> Always choose variable names that make sense to you. Countless students struggle on multi-part problems due to disorganized notes. Don't let that happen to you. Move beyond x and y when selecting variable names on the SAT.

Other questions of this type will simply ask you to choose from a series of answer choices that describes the system of equations—they won't actually ask you to calculate a solution! These questions can be great time-savers. Consider the following example:

6. A state college has separate fee rates for resident students and nonresident students. Resident students are charged $421 per semester, and nonresident students are charged $879 per semester. The college's sophomore class of 1,980 students paid a total of $1,170,210 in fees for the most recent semester. Which of the following systems of equations represents the number of resident (r) and nonresident (n) sophomores and the amount of fees the two groups paid?

A) $r + n = 1{,}170{,}210$; $421r + 879n = 1{,}980$

B) $r + n = 1{,}980$; $879r + 421n = 1{,}170{,}210$

C) $r + n = 1{,}980$; $421r + 879n = 1{,}170{,}210$

D) $r + n = 1{,}170{,}210$; $879r + 421n = 1{,}980$

Work through the Kaplan Method for Math to solve this question step-by-step. The following table shows Kaplan's strategic thinking on the left, along with suggested math scratchwork on the right.

Strategic Thinking	Math Scratchwork
Step 1: Read the question, identifying and organizing important information as you go You're asked for the system of equations that represents the given situation.	
Step 2: Choose the best strategy to answer the question This question is wordy, so use the Kaplan Strategy for Translating English into Math. The first step (assigning variables) has been done for you, so you can go right to breaking up the question stem into smaller pieces. Convert these into math, and then assemble your equations.	r = resident n = nonresident r: $421 in fees n: $879 in fees 1,980 students $1,170,210 collected r: $421 → $421r$ n: $879 → $879n$ $= 1{,}980$ $= 1{,}170{,}210$ $r + n = 1{,}980$ $421r + 879n = 1{,}170{,}210$

Strategic Thinking	Math Scratchwork
Step 3: Check that you answered the *right* question Choice (C) is the only answer choice that contains both equations you built.	

Be careful! Choice B is close but switches the fee structure, drastically overcharging the in-state students! Pay close attention to the differences between answer choices to avoid traps on Test Day.

Now you'll have a chance to try a few more test-like questions. Use the scaffolding as needed to guide you through the question and get the right answer.

Some guidance is provided, but you'll need to fill in the missing parts of explanations or the step-by-step math to get to the correct answer. Don't worry—after going through the examples at the beginning of this chapter, these questions should be completely doable. If you find yourself struggling, however, review the worked examples in this chapter and their explanations.

7. A bead shop sells wooden beads for $0.20 each and crystal beads for $0.50 each. If a jewelry artist buys 127 beads total and pays $41 for them, how much more did she spend on crystal beads than wooden beads?

    A) $11

    B) $15

    C) $23

    D) $26

The following table can help you structure your thinking as you go about solving this problem. The Kaplan strategic thinking is provided, as are bits of structured scratchwork. If you're not sure how to approach a question like this, start at the top and work your way down.

Strategic Thinking	Math Scratchwork
Step 1: Read the question, identifying and organizing important information as you go *What are you being asked to do here?* You're asked how much more the jewelry artist spent on crystal beads than on wooden beads.	

Strategic Thinking	Math Scratchwork
Step 2: Choose the best strategy to answer the question *Where should you start?* The Kaplan Strategy for Translating English into Math is a great choice. *What variables should you use?* Variables are easy to pick for this question. Think about what letters the words start with. *How do you break apart the question into smaller phrases? What can you do with them?* Separate each numerical piece into its own phrase, then convert to math.	wooden: _____ crystal: _____ _____ per wooden _____ per crystal _____ total bought _____ spent _____ per wooden → _____ _____ per crystal → _____ _____ total bought → _____ _____ spent → _____
What should you do with the phrases? Assemble a system of equations, then solve. You can use either substitution or combination to solve for the quantity of each bead type. Remember to think critically about which approach would be faster in this situation. *Am I done once I've solved the system?* Almost. Determine how much the jewelry artist spent on each type of bead, then take the difference.	_____ + _____ = _____ _____ + _____ = _____ _____ = _____ _____ = _____ \$ _____ on wooden \$ _____ on crystal _____ − _____ = _____
Step 3: Check that you answered the *right* question *Which answer choice matches the difference you found?* If you came up with (A), you're absolutely correct.	 _____

8. If $y = -x - 15$ and $\dfrac{5y}{2} - 37 = -\dfrac{x}{2}$, what is the value of $2x + 6y$?

Larger numbers don't make this question any different; just be careful with the arithmetic. Again, the following table can help you structure your thinking as you go about solving this problem. The Kaplan strategic thinking is provided, as are bits of structured scratchwork. If you're not sure how to approach a question like this, start at the top and work your way down.

Strategic Thinking	Math Scratchwork
Step 1: Read the question, identifying and organizing important information as you go *What are you being asked to do here?* You're asked to find the value of $2x + 6y$.	
Step 2: Choose the best strategy to answer the question *The equations look complicated. Where should I start?* Start by rearranging the equations so that they're in the same general format. Because you're asked for an expression, look for a shortcut. Don't bother trying to solve for either x or y individually. *Which system of equations tactic would work best here?* A good bet: clearing the fractions from the second equation so you can use combination. Once the fractions are gone, confirm that adding the second equation to the first will yield the expression you need.	$y = -x - 15$ $\dfrac{5y}{2} - 37 = -\dfrac{x}{2}$ _____ + _____ = _____ _____ + _____ = _____ ___(___ + ___ = ___) _____ + _____ = _____ + _____ + _____ = _____ _____ _____ + _____ = _____
Step 3: Check that you answered the *right* question *What's the value of $2x + 6y$?* If your answer is 59, you're correct!	_____

Now that you've seen the variety of ways in which the SAT can test you on systems of linear equations, try the following questions to check your understanding. Give yourself 4.5 minutes to tackle the following three questions.

$$6x + 3y = 18$$
$$qx - \frac{y}{3} = -2$$

9. In the system of linear equations above, q is a constant. If the system has infinitely many solutions, what is the value of q?

    A) −9

    B) $-\dfrac{2}{3}$

    C) $\dfrac{2}{3}$

    D) 9

10. If $12x + 15y = 249$ and $5x + 13y = 124$, then what is $\dfrac{y}{x}$?

11. A pizzeria's top-selling pizzas are The Works and The Hawaiian. The Works sells for $17, and The Hawaiian sells for $13. Ingredient costs for The Works are $450 per week, and ingredient costs for The Hawaiian are $310 per week. Assuming the pizzeria sells an equal number of both pizzas in one week, at what point will profits for one pizza overtake the other?

    A) After 35 pizzas each, Hawaiian profits will overtake Works profits.

    B) After 145 pizzas each, Hawaiian profits will overtake Works profits.

    C) After 35 pizzas each, Works profits will overtake Hawaiian profits.

    D) After 145 pizzas each, Works profits will overtake Hawaiian profits.

Answers and Explanations for this chapter begin on page 830.

EXTRA PRACTICE

Required	Recommended
Questions 1–8	Questions 9–12

1. If $2x - 3y = 14$ and $5x + 3y = 21$, then what is the value of x?

   A) -1

   B) 0

   C) $\dfrac{7}{3}$

   D) 5

$$\begin{cases} 4x + 3y = 14 - y \\ x - 5y = 2 \end{cases}$$

2. If (x, y) is a solution to the system of equations above, what is $x - y$?

   A) $\dfrac{1}{4}$

   B) 1

   C) 3

   D) 18

3. Charlie starts to solve a system of linear equations graphically. He puts both equations into slope-intercept form and notices that the lines have the same slope. Based on this information only, which of the following statements is true?

   A) The system could have no solution, one solution, or infinitely many solutions.

   B) The system has no solution because two equations with the same slope never intersect.

   C) The system has either no solution or infinitely many solutions, depending on the y-intercepts.

   D) The system has infinitely many solutions because two equations with the same slope represent the same line.

$$\begin{cases} hx - 4y = -10 \\ kx + 3y = -15 \end{cases}$$

4. If the graphs of the lines in the system of equations above intersect at $(-3, 1)$, what is the value of $\dfrac{k}{h}$?

   A) $\dfrac{3}{2}$

   B) 2

   C) 3

   D) 6

$$\begin{cases} \dfrac{1}{2}x - \dfrac{2}{3}y = 7 \\ ax - 8y = -1 \end{cases}$$

5. If the system of linear equations above has no solution, and a is a constant, what is the value of a?

   A) -2

   B) $-\dfrac{1}{2}$

   C) 2

   D) 6

6. A party store has 54 packs of plates in stock. The packs are either sets of 8 or sets of 12. If the store has 496 total plates in stock, how many plates would a customer buy if he or she buys all of the packs of 12 that the store has in stock?

   A) 16

   B) 38

   C) 192

   D) 304

$$\begin{cases} 3x - 9y = -6 \\ \dfrac{1}{2}x - \dfrac{3}{2}y = c \end{cases}$$

7. If the system of linear equations above has infinitely many solutions, and c is a constant, what is the value of c?

A) −6

B) −3

C) −2

D) −1

Equation 1		Equation 2	
x	y	x	y
−2	6	−8	−8
0	4	−4	−7
2	2	0	−6
4	0	4	−5

8. The tables above represent data points for two linear equations. If the two equations form a system, what is the x-coordinate of the solution to that system?

9. What is the y-coordinate of the solution to the system shown above?

A) −5

B) 3

C) 5

D) 6

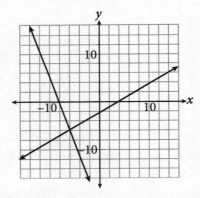

10. If (A, B) is the solution to the system of equations shown above, and A and B are integers, what is the value of $A + B$?

A) −12

B) −6

C) 0

D) 6

11. A sofa costs $50 less than three times the cost of a chair. If the sofa and chair together cost $650, how much more does the sofa cost than the chair?

    A) $175

    B) $225

    C) $300

    D) $475

12. At a certain movie theater, there are 16 rows and each row has either 20 or 24 seats. If the total number of seats in all 16 rows is 348, how many rows have 24 seats?

    A) 7

    B) 9

    C) 11

    D) 13

$$\frac{3}{2}x - \frac{9}{2}y = -3$$

$$\frac{1}{2}x - \frac{3}{2}y = C$$

$$M = \frac{-A}{B} \text{ for the slope of 1 equation}$$

$$\frac{3}{2} \cdot \frac{6}{1}$$

$$\frac{18}{2} = 9$$

CHAPTER 4

Linear Inequalities and Systems of Inequalities

CHAPTER OBJECTIVES

By the end of this section, you will be able to:

1. Identify the key differences between solving inequalities and equations
2. Efficiently solve systems of inequalities

SMARTPOINTS

Point Value	SmartPoint Category
50 Points	Inequalities

RULES FOR SOLVING INEQUALITIES

There's more to algebra than just equations, and inequalities will show up quite frequently on the SAT. Fortunately, many of the same strategies that apply to solving equations also apply to inequalities. There are a few key exceptions to keep in mind, but don't worry—these will be explained later in this section.

First, the language used to describe inequalities tends to be more complex than the language used to describe equations. You "solve" an equation for x, but with an inequality, you might be asked to "describe all possible values of x" or provide an answer that "includes the entire set of solutions for x." This difference in wording exists because an equation describes a specific value of a variable, whereas an inequality describes a range of values. Regardless of the language, your task is the same: Isolate x on one side. The following question tests your basic inequality-solving skills.

1. A bowling alley charges a flat $6.50 fee for shoe and ball rental plus $3.75 per game and 6.325% sales tax. If each person in a group of seven people has $20 to spend on a bowling outing, which inequality represents the maximum number of shoe and ball rentals (r) and games (g) that can be purchased by the group?

   A) $1.06325 (6.5r + 3.75g) \leq 140$

   B) $1.06325 (6.5r + 3.75g) \leq 20$

   C) $1.06325 \left(\dfrac{6.5}{r} + \dfrac{3.75}{g} \right) \leq 140$

   D) $0.06325 (6.5r + 3.75g) \leq 20$

Work through the Kaplan Method for Math step-by-step to solve this question. The following table shows Kaplan's strategic thinking on the left, along with suggested math scratchwork on the right.

Strategic Thinking	Math Scratchwork
Step 1: Read the question, identifying and organizing important information as you go The question asks for an inequality that represents the situation described.	

Strategic Thinking	Math Scratchwork
Step 2: Choose the best strategy to answer the question	
The wordiness of the question should point you toward the Kaplan Strategy for Translating English into Math. The variables are already defined, so you only need to correctly piece them together with the given numbers.	$r \rightarrow$ rentals, $6.5r$ $g \rightarrow$ games, $3.75g$ including tax: 1.06325
The question states that a shoe and ball rental costs \$6.50 and that a game costs \$3.75. Combine these with the correct variables, remembering to incorporate sales tax. Be careful when writing the right side of the inequality; the question asks for an inequality that represents the entire group, not just one person.	total \$: $7 \times 20 = 140$ $1.06325(6.5r + 3.75g)$ ≤ 140
Step 3: Check that you answered the _right_ question	
Choice (A) contains the inequality you derived.	

Notice B is a trap answer. If you write the inequality to reflect the cost for just one person, you'll be led right to it.

> ✔ **Note**
>
> Choice D is a trap waiting for students who improperly incorporate the sales tax component. Using 0.06325 calculates the amount spent on sales tax, not the total amount spent on the bowling outing.

> ✔ **Note**
>
> If the variable ends up on the right-hand side of the symbol when you solve an inequality, be careful when matching it to an answer choice. For instance, $3 > x$ can be rewritten as $x < 3$. Notice that the small end of the symbol stays pointed at x.

Inequalities can also be presented graphically in one or two dimensions. In one dimension, inequalities are graphed on a number line with a shaded region. For example, $x > 1$ could be graphed like this:

Note the open dot at $x = 1$, indicating that 1 is not a solution to the inequality. This is called a **strict** inequality. By contrast, the graph of $x \leq 0$ looks like this:

Notice the closed dot, indicating that 0 should be included in the solution set for the inequality.

 Note

To help remember which way to shade, read the < symbol as "less than," which tells you to shade to the left of the dot. Note the *L*s: *L*ess than means shade *L*eft.

In two dimensions, things get a bit more complicated. While linear equations graph as simple lines, inequalities graph as lines called **boundary lines** with shaded regions known as **half planes**. Solid lines involve inequalities that have $\leq$ or $\geq$ because the line itself is included in the solution set. Dashed lines involve strict inequalities that have $>$ or $<$ because, in these cases, the line itself is not included in the solution set. The shaded region represents all points that make up the solution set for the inequality.

SOLVING SYSTEMS OF INEQUALITIES

Multiple inequalities can be combined to create a system of inequalities. This system can involve multiple variables, or it can be used to provide more detailed bounds for a range of solutions for a single variable. You'll get to try both in questions shortly.

Systems of inequalities can also be presented graphically with multiple boundary lines and multiple shaded regions. Follow the same rules for graphing single inequalities, but keep in mind that the solution set is the region where the shading overlaps. Shading in different directions (e.g., parallel lines slanted up for one inequality and down for the other) makes the overlap easier to see. This is illustrated in an upcoming question.

2. Which of the following graphs represents the solution set for $5x - 10y > 6$?

A)

B)

C)

D)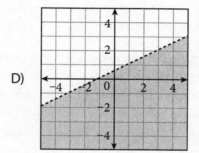

Work through the Kaplan Method for Math step-by-step to solve this question. The following table shows Kaplan's strategic thinking on the left, along with suggested math scratchwork on the right.

Strategic Thinking	Math Scratchwork
Step 1: Read the question, identifying and organizing important information as you go The question is asking for the graph that matches the inequality given.	

Strategic Thinking	Math Scratchwork
Step 2: Choose the best strategy to answer the question	$5x - 10y > 6$
It's risky to eliminate choices now, as the inequality is not in slope-intercept form. Rearrange the inequality so that it's in this form, remembering to flip the inequality symbol in the final step because you're dividing by -10.	$-10y > -5x + 6$ $y < \dfrac{1}{2}x - \dfrac{3}{5}$
The inequality in slope-intercept form indicates a negative y-intercept, so you can eliminate A and D. The "less than" symbol indicates that the shading should be done below the dashed line, meaning (C) must be correct.	
Alternatively, you can plug a point (such as the origin) into the inequality. Notice the origin is not included in the shaded region in choice (C), but it is in choice B. When plugged into the inequality, you'll see that the origin should not be in the solution set because 0 is not greater than $0 + \dfrac{3}{5}$. This means (C) is correct.	
Step 3: Check that you answered the *right* question	
Choice (C) matches the equation given.	

3. If $\dfrac{1}{2}x + \dfrac{2}{3}y \leq 1$ and $\dfrac{1}{2}x + \dfrac{1}{3}y \leq \dfrac{2}{3}$ comprise a system of inequalities, what is one possible value of $x + y$?

Work through the Kaplan Method for Math step-by-step to solve this question. The following table shows Kaplan's strategic thinking on the left, along with suggested math scratchwork on the right.

Strategic Thinking	Math Scratchwork
Step 1: Read the question, identifying and organizing important information as you go The question asks for a possible value of $x + y$.	
Step 2: Choose the best strategy to answer the question Resist the temptation to convert the inequalities to slope-intercept form; the fractions will just make things tougher. Instead, examine the coefficients of the variables carefully. If you write one equation under the other, you'll see that the x term coefficients sum to 1, as do the y term coefficients. You can add the inequalities together as they are and get $x + y$ on one side.	$\frac{1}{2}x + \frac{1}{3}y \le \frac{2}{3}$ $+\frac{1}{2}x + \frac{2}{3}y \le 1$ $\rule{3cm}{0.4pt}$ $x + y \le \frac{5}{3}$
Step 3: Check that you answered the *right* question This is a Grid-in, so pick a number between 0 and $\frac{5}{3}$, inclusive (but no negatives), that satisfies both inequalities.	$0 \le x + y \le \frac{5}{3}$

✔ **Note**

Remember that you can add inequalities only if they have the same symbol.

✔ **Note**

If a question like this is in the calculator section, you can also solve by graphing the two inequalities, selecting a point that lies in the overlap of the shaded regions, and adding the coordinates of the point together.

4. If $12x - 4y > 8$ and $\frac{2}{3}x + 6y \geq 14$ form a system of inequalities, which of the following graphs shows the solution set for the system?

A)

B)

C)

D)

Work through the Kaplan Method for Math step-by-step to solve this question. The following table shows Kaplan's strategic thinking on the left, along with suggested math scratchwork on the right.

Strategic Thinking	Math Scratchwork
Step 1: Read the question, identifying and organizing important information as you go You need to identify the graph that correctly displays the two inequalities given.	

Strategic Thinking	Math Scratchwork
Step 2: Choose the best strategy to answer the question Start by rewriting each one in slope-intercept form. Once finished, determine what the correct graphs will look like. The boundary line for $y < 3x - 2$ should be a dashed line, and the boundary line for $y \geq -\frac{1}{9}x + \frac{7}{3}$ should be a solid line. You can eliminate C based on this. The half-plane below $y < 3x - 2$ should be shaded, and the half-plane above $y \geq -\frac{1}{9}x + \frac{7}{3}$ should be shaded; of the remaining choices, only (B) satisfies this requirement.	$12x - 4y > 8$ $-4y > -12x + 8$ $y < 3x - 2$ $\frac{2}{3}x + 6y \geq 14$ $6y \geq -\frac{2}{3}x + 14$ $y \geq -\frac{1}{9}x + \frac{7}{3}$
Step 3: Check that you answered the *right* question Choice (B) correctly depicts the two inequalities. You can check your answer by plugging a point from (B)'s solution set, such as (10, 10), into both inequalities given in the question and verifying that each is a true statement.	

Now you'll have a chance to try a test-like problem in a scaffolded way. We've provided some guidance, but you'll need to fill in the missing parts of explanations or the step-by-step math to get to the correct answer. Don't worry—after going through the worked examples at the beginning of this section, this problem should be completely doable.

5. A network of hotels across the United States normally charges $180 for an overnight stay at any of its properties. This network also offers a deal for longer trips: a traveler who purchases a hotel discount card for $720 will pay only $120 per night at any of the network's properties for the duration of the traveler's trip. Which of the following inequalities represents the number of nights n a traveler must stay in any combination of the network's hotels during a trip in order to make the discount card a better deal?

    A) $n > 12$

    B) $n < 12$

    C) $n > 9$

    D) $n < 9$

Use the following scaffolding as your map through the question. If you aren't sure where to start, answer the questions in italics and fill in the blanks in the table as you work from top to bottom.

Strategic Thinking	Math Scratchwork
Step 1: Read the question, identifying and organizing important information as you go *What are you being asked to find?* You need to identify the inequality that correctly depicts the situation in the question.	
Step 2: Choose the best strategy to answer the question *What's an efficient way to extract what you need from all the words?* Use the Kaplan Strategy for Translating English into Math. *Are there any variables to define? How much does it cost per night with the discount card? How much is it without the card?* You're told n is the number of overnight stays. The cost of travel with the card is $720 + 120n$. Without the card, a traveler would pay $180n$. Combine these expressions in an inequality and solve for n.	____ < ____ ____ < ____ ____ < ____

Strategic Thinking	Math Scratchwork
Step 3: Check that you answered the *right* question *Which choice matches the situation described?* If you got (A), you're right!	 _____

✔ **Note**

Analyze carefully when translating English into math; it's very easy to misread a question and land yourself in a trap (answer). Kaplan Methods and Strategies will help you avoid the pitfalls.

Now that you've seen the variety of ways in which the SAT can test you on linear inequalities, try the following questions to check your understanding. Give yourself 2 minutes to tackle these two questions.

6. If $-3 < \frac{4}{3}h + \frac{1}{6} < 1$, what is one possible value of $12h - 4$?

7. Sarah and Zena are head sales associates at a dance apparel shop. In addition to their annual raises, the two will be eligible for holiday bonuses if their dance tops and pants sales meet the following criteria in December: between the two of them, the girls must sell an average of 75 items each, and their combined generated revenue must be at least $6,000. Each top costs $35, and each pair of pants costs $60. If Sarah sells t_s tops and p_s pairs of pants and Zena sells t_z tops and p_z pairs of pants, which of the following systems of inequalities correctly depicts the minimum quantities the two must sell to earn a holiday bonus?

    A) $t_s + p_s + t_z + p_z \geq 75$, $35(t_s + t_z) + 60(p_s + p_z) \geq 3,000$

    B) $t_s + p_s + t_z + p_z \geq 150$, $90(t_s + p_s + t_z + p_z) \geq 6,000$

    C) $t_s + p_s + t_z + p_z \geq 150$, $35(t_s + t_z) + 60(p_s + p_z) \geq 6,000$

    D) $t_s + p_s + t_z + p_z \geq 150$, $35(t_s + p_s) + 60(t_z + p_z) \geq 6,000$

    Answers & Explanations are provided on page 838.

EXTRA PRACTICE

Required	Recommended
Questions 1–8	Questions 9–13

$$\frac{1}{5}(7 - 3b) > 2$$

1. Which of the following gives all values of b that satisfy the inequality above?

    A) $b < -1$

    B) $b > -1$

    C) $b < 1$

    D) $b > 1$

2. Which of the following represents the solution to the inequality $2(4x - 1) > 5x + 13$?

    A) ![number line with closed dot at 5, shaded to the right; marks at 0 and 5]

    B) ![number line with closed dot at 5, shaded to the left; marks at 0 and 5]

    C) ![number line with open dot at 5, shaded to the right; marks at 0 and 5]

    D) ![number line with open dot at 5, shaded to the left; marks at 0 and 5]

3. If $n - 3 > 8$ and $n + 1 < 14$, which of the following could be a value for n?

    A) 11

    B) 12

    C) 13

    D) 14

4. Which of the following best describes the graphical solution to the inequality $y < -2x + 3$?

    A) A dashed boundary line that rises from left to right, with shading in the half-plane below the boundary line

    B) A dashed boundary line that falls from left to right, with shading in the half-plane below the boundary line

    C) A dashed boundary line that falls from left to right, with shading in the half-plane above the boundary line

    D) A solid boundary line that falls from left to right, with shading in the half-plane below the boundary line

$$15 - x \;\boxed{}\; 9$$

5. The number line above shows the solution to the inequality. Which of the following symbols would make the statement true?

    A) $<$

    B) $>$

    C) $\leq$

    D) $\geq$

Electric Company	Price (cents per kWh)
Company A	15.2
Company B	17.4
Company C	16.5
Company D	14.8

6. A kilowatt-hour is a unit of measure for consumable energy. A kilowatt-hour, written kWh, is equivalent to using 1,000 watts of power in 1 hour. The table above shows the per-kWh rates charged by several electric companies in New England. According to the United States Energy Information Administration, an average household in New England uses between 530 and 730 kWh of energy per month. Which inequality represents how much less in energy costs a household would pay per month if it uses Company D as its energy supplier, than if it uses Company B?

A) $x \le 0.026$

B) $0.148 \le x \le 0.174$

C) $13.78 \le x \le 18.98$

D) $29.60 \le x \le 34.80$

7. The figure above shows the solution set for the system $\begin{cases} y < \dfrac{3}{5}x - 2 \\ y \le -\dfrac{4}{3}x + 5 \end{cases}$. Which of the following is not a solution to this system?

A) $(-1, -4)$

B) $(1, -1)$

C) $(4, -1)$

D) $(6, -3)$

8. A shipping company employee is in charge of packing cargo containers for shipment. He knows a certain cargo container can hold a maximum of 50 microwaves or a maximum of 15 refrigerators. Each microwave takes up 6 cubic feet of space, and each refrigerator takes up 20 cubic feet. The cargo container can hold a maximum of 300 cubic feet. The employee is trying to figure out how to pack a container containing both microwaves and refrigerators. Which of the following systems of inequalities can the employee use to determine how many of each item (microwaves, m, and refrigerators, r) he can pack into one cargo container?

A) $\begin{cases} m \le 6 \\ r \le 20 \\ 50m + 15r \le 300 \end{cases}$

B) $\begin{cases} m \le 50 \\ r \le 15 \\ m + r \le 300 \end{cases}$

C) $\begin{cases} m \le 50 \\ r \le 15 \\ 6m + 20r \le 300 \end{cases}$

D) $\begin{cases} m \le 50 \\ r \le 15 \\ 50m + 15r \le 300 \end{cases}$

$\begin{cases} y < 2x - 3 \\ y \; \boxed{?} \; mx + 3 \end{cases}$

9. Which value of m and which symbol result in the system of inequalities shown above as having no solution?

A) $m = -2; >$

B) $m = -\dfrac{1}{2}; <$

C) $m = 2; >$

D) $m = 2; <$

10. If $-\dfrac{2}{5} < 3k - 4 < \dfrac{6}{7}$, then which of the following is not a possible value for $-6k + 8$?

A) $-\dfrac{5}{7}$

B) $\dfrac{1}{7}$

C) $\dfrac{1}{3}$

D) $\dfrac{4}{3}$

$\begin{cases} y \le \dfrac{2}{3}x + 1 \\ 2x - 3y \le 12 \end{cases}$

11. Which of the following best describes the solution set for the system of inequalities above?

A) The system has no solution.

B) The solution set consists of a single point.

C) The solution set consists of all real numbers.

D) The solution set consists of all points that lie between the boundary lines.

12. Marco is paid $80 per day plus $15 per hour for overtime. If he works five days per week and wants to make a minimum of $520 this week, what is the fewest number of hours of overtime he must work?

13. The figure above shows the solution for the system of inequalities $\begin{cases} y > -x - 5 \\ y < 2x + 3 \end{cases}$.

Suppose (a, b) is a solution to the system. If $a = 0$, what is the greatest possible integer value of b?

Problem Solving & Data Analysis

BY THE END OF THIS UNIT, YOU WILL BE ABLE TO:

1. Apply the Kaplan Method for Multi-Part Math Questions

2. Use rates, ratios, proportions, and percentages

3. Interpret and extract information from scatterplots and two-way tables

4. Analyze simple and complex data sets using descriptive statistics

CHAPTER 5

Introduction to Problem Solving

CHAPTER OBJECTIVES

By the end of this chapter, you will be able to:

1. Use the Kaplan Method for Multi-Part Math Questions to answer Problem Solving questions effectively

2. Solve multi-part problems involving rates, ratios, and proportions

3. Use appropriate formulas to find percentages and single or multiple percent changes

SMARTPOINTS

Point Value	SmartPoint Category
Point Builder	Kaplan Method for Multi-Part Math Questions
100 Points	Rates, Ratios, Proportions & Percentages

The new SAT contains multiple-choice and Grid-in questions, as well as a new type of question: the Multi-Part Math question. Multi-Part Math questions have multiple parts and require more analysis and planning than multiple-choice questions. To help you answer these questions effectively, use the Kaplan Method for Multi-Part Math Questions.

KAPLAN METHOD FOR MULTI-PART MATH QUESTIONS

Step 1: Read the first part of the question, looking for clues

Step 2: Identify and organize the information you need

Step 3: Based on what you know, plan your steps to navigate the first part

Step 4: Solve, step-by-step, checking units as you go

Step 5: Did I answer the *right* question?

Step 6: Repeat for remaining questions, incorporating results from the previous parts

The next few pages will walk you through each step in more detail.

Step 1: Read the first part of the question, looking for clues

- **Focus all your energy here** instead of diluting it over the whole question; solving a Multi-Part Math question in pieces is far simpler. Further, you may need the results from earlier parts to solve subsequent ones. Don't even consider the later parts of the question until you've solved the first part.

- **Watch for hints** about what you'll need to use or how to solve. Underlining key quantities is often helpful to separate what you need from extraneous prose.

Step 2: Identify and organize the information you need

If you think this sounds like the Kaplan Method for Math, you're absolutely correct. You'll use some of those same skills. The difference: The Multi-Part Math question is just more involved with multiple pieces.

- **What information am I given?** Jot down key notes, and group related quantities to develop your strategy.

- **What am I solving for?** This is your target. As you work your way through subsequent steps, keep your target at the front of your mind. This will help you avoid unnecessary work (and subsequent time loss). You'll sometimes need to tackle these problems from both ends, so always keep your goal in mind.

✔ **Expert Tip**

Many students freeze when they encounter a problem with multiple steps and seemingly massive amounts of information. Don't worry! Take each piece one at a time, and you won't be intimidated.

Step 3: Based on what you know, plan your steps to navigate the first part

- **What pieces am I missing?** Many students become frustrated when faced with a roadblock such as missing information, but it's an easy fix. Sometimes you'll need to do an intermediate calculation to reveal the missing piece or pieces of the puzzle.

Step 4: Solve, step-by-step, checking units as you go

- **Work quickly but carefully**, just as you've done on other SAT math questions.

Step 5: Did I answer the *right* question?

- As is the case with the Kaplan Method for Math, **make sure your final answer is the requested answer**.

- Review the first part of the question.

- Double-check your units and your work.

Step 6: Repeat for remaining questions, incorporating results from the previous parts

- Now take your results from the first part and think critically about how they fit into the subsequent parts. Previous results won't always be applicable, but when they are, they often lead to huge time savings.

When you've finished, congratulate yourself for persevering through such a challenging task. The Multi-Part Math questions are the toughest on the SAT. If you can ace these questions, you'll be poised for a great score on Test Day. Don't worry if the Kaplan Method seems complicated; we'll walk through an example shortly.

> ✔ **Expert Tip**
>
> As these questions take substantially more time, consider saving Multi-Part Math questions for last.

RATES, MEASUREMENT & UNIT CONVERSIONS

By now, you've become adept at using algebra to answer many SAT math questions, which is great, because you'll need those algebraic skills to answer questions involving rates. You're likely already familiar with many different rates—kilometers per hour, meters per second, and even miles per gallon are all considered rates.

A fundamental equation involved with rates is "Distance = Rate × Time" (a.k.a. the DIRT equation—Distance Is Rate × Time). If you have two of the three components of the equation, you can easily find the third. An upcoming Multi-Part Math example demonstrates this nicely.

You'll notice units of measurement are important for rate questions (and others that require a unit conversion) and, therefore, also an opportunity to fall for trap answers if you're not careful. How can you avoid this? Use the factor-label method. The factor-label method is a simple yet powerful way to ensure you're doing your calculations correctly and getting an answer with the requested units.

For example, suppose you're asked how many cups are in two gallons. First, identify your starting quantity's units (gallons) and then identify the end quantity's units (cups). The next step is to piece together a path of relationships that will convert gallons into cups, cancelling out units as you go. Keep in mind that you will often have multiple stepping stones between your starting and ending quantities, so don't panic if you can't get directly from gallons to cups.

The SAT won't expect you to know English measurements by heart. Instead, they'll provide conversion factors when needed. A gallon is the same as 4 quarts, every quart contains 2 pints, and a pint equals 2 cups. And there you have it! Your map from gallons to cups is complete. The last step is to put it together as a giant multiplication problem. Each relationship, called a conversion factor, is written as a fraction. The basic rules of fraction multiplication apply, so you can cancel a unit that appears in both the numerator and denominator.

> ✔ **Note**
>
> The SAT will not require you to memorize conversions for conventional imperial units. If the test asks you to convert miles into inches, for example, you will be provided with enough conversion factors to solve the problem.

Follow along as we convert from gallons to quarts to pints to cups:

$$2\text{ gallons} \times \frac{4\text{ quarts}}{1\text{ gallon}} \times \frac{2\text{ pints}}{1\text{ quart}} \times \frac{2\text{ cups}}{1\text{ pint}} = (2 \times 4 \times 2 \times 2)\text{ cups} = 32\text{ cups}$$

The DIRT equation is actually a variation of this process. Suppose you travel at 60 mph for 5 hours. You would calculate the distance traveled with $d = rt = \frac{60\text{ mi}}{1\text{ h}} \times 5\text{ h} = 300\text{ mi}$. The hour units cancel out, leaving you with miles, which you know is a distance. This built-in check is a great way to ensure your math is correct. If your units are off, check your steps for mistakes along the way. The SAT will never ask you for a quantity such as miles^4 or gallons^3, so if you end up with funky units like that, you've made an error somewhere in your work.

> ✔ **Note**
>
> When using the factor-label method, don't be afraid to flip fractions and rates to make your units cancel out as needed.

1. Quinn wants to rent a self-storage unit for her college dorm room furniture for the summer. She estimates that she will need 700 cubic feet of storage space, but the self-storage provider measures its units in cubic meters. If 1 meter is approximately 3.28 feet, about how many cubic meters of space will Quinn need?

   A) 19.84

   B) 25.93

   C) 65.07

   D) 213.41

Work through the Kaplan Method for Math to solve this question step-by-step. The following table shows Kaplan's strategic thinking on the left, along with suggested math scratchwork on the right.

Strategic Thinking	Math Scratchwork
Step 1: Read the question, identifying and organizing important information as you go You need to determine how many cubic meters of space Quinn needs for her belongings.	700 ft^3 space needed $= ? \text{ m}^3$
Step 2: Choose the best strategy to answer the question The factor-label method will be the quickest path to the correct answer. You're starting in cubic feet and need to convert to cubic meters. You know that 1 m = 3.28 ft, but be careful: 1 m^3 is not the same as 3.28 ft^3! Consider each feet-to-meters conversion separately.	starting qty: 700 ft^3 end qty: $? \text{ m}^3$ $\dfrac{700 \text{ ft}^3}{1} \times \dfrac{1 \text{ m}}{3.28 \text{ ft}} \times \dfrac{1 \text{ m}}{3.28 \text{ ft}} \times \dfrac{1 \text{ m}}{3.28 \text{ ft}}$ $= \dfrac{700}{(3.28)^3} \text{m} \sim 19.84 \text{ m}^3$
Step 3: Check that you answered the *right* question You've correctly converted cubic feet to cubic meters to get the correct answer, which is (A).	19.84 m^3

✔ **Note**

The conversion from feet to meters is not the same as the conversion from cubic feet to cubic meters (or square feet to square meters). Trap answers will often use incorrect conversion factors. Be particularly careful when dealing with conversions that have multiple dimensions.

Next, you'll walk through a test-like Multi-Part Math question that involves rates. Follow along with the Kaplan Method for Multi-Part Math Questions, and think about how knowledge of rates is used to get to the answer.

Remember, even though these questions have multiple parts, you'll rely on the same math skills you'd use in a simple multiple-choice question to solve each part. If you find that there are missing pieces or missing quantities, use techniques such as the factor-label method to bridge the gap.

Think of solving a Multi-Part Math question as building a three-dimensional puzzle. You collect all the relevant pieces and then arrange and assemble them to make the foundation, akin to using information from the first question to map a route to its answer. Just as the top part of a 3D puzzle is built on the foundation, the second part of a Multi-Part Math question builds on what you learned in the introduction and first question. Call on this information to help you solve the second question just as you did with the first.

Use the following information to answer questions 2 and 3:

Dismantling fraud rings, intercepting enemy communications, and protecting national infrastructure are just a few tasks for which Special Agents in the FBI's Cyber Division utilize state-of-the-art computers and other technology. The New Haven field office recently seized 2.43 terabytes (TB) of encrypted information during the raid of an infrastructure-hacking operations base, which agents believe contains information on a planned attack. One TB is equal to 10^6 megabytes (MB).

2. The cyber team's decryption software can decrypt 4.5 MB per second. How many hours will it take to decrypt the entire hard drive?

3. Newly gathered intelligence indicates a high likelihood of an infrastructure attack occurring before the hard drive is fully decrypted; consequently, the New York and Boston field offices have been asked to divert resources to the decryption task. New York's decryption software is 40% faster than New Haven's, but Boston's is 20% slower than New Haven's. By how many hours will the decryption time be reduced with the three cyber teams working in tandem? Round your answer to the nearest hour.

Work through the Kaplan Method for Multi-Part Math Questions step-by-step to solve this question. The following table shows Kaplan's strategic thinking on the left, along with suggested math scratchwork on the right.

Strategic Thinking	Math Scratchwork
Step 1: Read the first part of the question, looking for clues	
You're told the size of the seized hard drive and the speed at which it will be decrypted.	2.43 TB drive 4.5 MB/s decryption

Strategic Thinking	Math Scratchwork
Step 2: Identify and organize the information you need Part 1 asks for the time required to decrypt the hard drive. The given rate will help you determine this amount.	*hours to decrypt: ?*
Step 3: Based on what you know, plan your steps to navigate the first part The hard drive's capacity is in TB, but the rate is in MB/s (and you're asked for time in hours), so the DIRT equation requires a couple of extra calculations before you can use it. The factor-label method will be faster. Map your conversion steps.	*starting qty: 2.43 TB* *desired qty: ? h* $TB \rightarrow MB \rightarrow s \rightarrow min \rightarrow h$
Step 4: Solve, step-by-step, checking units as you go Plug in the appropriate conversion factors. When properly set up, all units except h will cancel, and you'll have the time needed for the decryption.	$2.43 \text{ TB} \times \dfrac{10^6 \text{ MB}}{1 \text{ TB}} \times \dfrac{1 \text{ s}}{4.5 \text{ MB}} \times \dfrac{1 \text{ min}}{60 \text{ s}}$ $\times \dfrac{1 \text{ h}}{60 \text{ min}} = 150 \text{ h}$
Step 5: Did I answer the *right* question? It will take 150 h to fully decrypt the hard drive.	

✔ **Note**

You might be given extra information on questions like these. If you don't need it to get to the answer, then don't worry about it.

Now on to Step 6: Repeat for remaining parts. Kaplan's strategic thinking is on the left, along with suggested math scratchwork on the right.

Strategic Thinking	Math Scratchwork
Step 1: Read the second part of the question, looking for clues	
Part 2 provides a relative description of New York and Boston's decryption software speeds.	NY: 40% faster than NH B: 20% slower than NH
Step 2: Identify and organize the information you need	
You need to determine the reduction in decryption time (in hours) if all three systems work in tandem.	new decryption time: ?
Step 3: Based on what you know, plan your steps to navigate the second part	
You must calculate the decryption speeds of the New York and Boston systems; you can't use the given percents to directly get the final answer. With the speeds in hand, you can find the total rate and the adjusted decryption time.	% → MB/s TB → MB → s → min → h
Step 4: Solve, step-by-step, checking units as you go	
Use the percent three-part formula to determine the speeds of the New York and Boston systems, being mindful when picking which decimal to plug in for what percent.	NY: 1.4 × 4.5 = 6.3 MB/s B: 0.8 × 4.5 = 3.6 MB/s
Apply the factor-label method to calculate the required decryption time with all three systems working, and then find the difference in times.	total rate = 4.5 + 6.3 + 3.6 = 14.4 MB/s $2.43 \text{TB} \times \dfrac{10^6 \text{ MB}}{1 \text{ TB}} \times \dfrac{1 \text{ s}}{14.4 \text{ MB}} \times \dfrac{1 \text{ min}}{60 \text{ s}}$ $\times \dfrac{1 \text{ h}}{60 \text{ min}} = 46.875 \text{ h}$ 150 − 46.875 = 103.125
Step 5: Did I answer the *right* question?	
Round properly per the question stem's instructions, and you're done.	103

As you saw, using the Kaplan Method for Multi-Part Math Questions makes an intimidating question far more straightforward. You'll have a chance to try it yourself later in this chapter.

RATIOS AND PROPORTIONS

Ratios and proportions are ubiquitous in everyday life. Whether it's making a double batch of meatballs or calculating the odds of winning the lottery, you'll find that ratios and proportions are invaluable in myriad situations.

A ratio is a way of comparing one quantity to another. When writing ratios, you can compare part of a group to another part of that group, or you can compare a part to the whole group. Suppose you have a bowl of apples and oranges. You can write ratios that compare apples to oranges (part to part), apples to total fruit (part to whole), and oranges to total fruit (part to whole).

You can also combine ratios. If you have two ratios, *a:b* and *b:c*, you can derive *a:c* by finding a common multiple of the *b* terms. Take a look at the following table to see this in action.

a	:	*b*	:	*c*
3	:	4		
		3	:	5
9	:	12		
		12	:	20
9		:		20

What's a common multiple of the *b* terms? The number 12 is a good choice because it's the least common multiple of 3 and 4 which will reduce the need to simplify later. Where do you go from there? Multiply each ratio by the factor (use 3 for *a:b* and 4 for *b:c*) that will get you to *b* = 12.

The ratio *a:c* equals 9:20. Notice we didn't merely say *a:c* is 3:5; this would be incorrect on Test Day (and likely a wrong-answer trap!).

Proportions are simply two ratios set equal to each other. They are an efficient way to solve certain problems, but you must exercise caution when setting them up. Watching the units of each piece of the proportion will help you with this. Sometimes the SAT will ask you to determine whether certain proportions are equivalent—check this by cross-multiplying. You'll get results that are much easier to compare.

$$\text{If } \frac{a}{b} = \frac{c}{d}, \text{ then: } ad = bc, \frac{a}{c} = \frac{b}{d}, \frac{d}{b} = \frac{c}{a}, \frac{b}{a} = \frac{d}{c}, \text{ BUT } \frac{a}{d} \neq \frac{c}{b}$$

Each derived ratio shown except the last one is simply a manipulation of the first, so all except the last are correct. You can verify this via cross-multiplication (*ad = bc*).

Alternatively, pick numerical values for *a*, *b*, *c*, and *d*; then simplify and confirm the two sides of the equation are equal. For example, take the two equivalent fractions $\frac{2}{3}$ and $\frac{6}{9}$ ($a=2, b=3, c=6, d=9$). Cross-multiplication gives $2 \times 9 = 3 \times 6$, which is a true statement. Dividing *a* and *b* by *c* and *d* gives $\frac{2}{6} = \frac{3}{9}$, also true, and so on. However, attempting to equate $\frac{a}{d}\left(\frac{2}{9}\right)$ and $\frac{b}{c}\left(\frac{3}{6}\right)$ will not work.

Let's take a look at a test-like question that involves ratios:

4. Neil is preparing two cans of paint for a client. The first is 25 parts red paint and 60 parts blue paint; the second is 30 parts yellow paint, 70 parts blue paint, and 15 parts white paint. The client has also asked Neil to prepare a third can containing only white and red paint per the ratios of the first two cans. What ratio of white to red paint should Neil use for the third can?

    A) 35:18

    B) 18:35

    C) 5:3

    D) 3:5

Work through the Kaplan Method for Math step-by-step to solve this question. The following table shows Kaplan's strategic thinking on the left, along with suggested math scratchwork on the right.

Strategic Thinking	Math Scratchwork
Step 1: Read the question, identifying and organizing important information as you go	
You're asked for the ratio of white to red paint in the third can. Two ratios are given.	R:B = 25:60 Y:B:W = 30:70:15

Strategic Thinking	Math Scratchwork
Step 2: Choose the best strategy to answer the question The ratio terms are rather large, so reduce the first ratio with a common factor, and then repeat with the second ratio. To combine two ratios, they must share a common term. Both ratios contain blue paint, but the blue paint terms aren't identical. Find a common multiple of 12 and 14. Once you've found one, merge the two ratios to directly compare white and red paint.	R:B = 25:60 → 5:12 Y:B:W = 30:70:15 → 6:14:3 common multiple of 12 & 14: 84 R:B = (5:12) × 7 = 35:84 Y:B:W = (6:14:3) × 6 = 36:84:18 R:B:Y:W = 35:84:36:18 R:W = 35:18
Step 3: Check that you answered the *right* question The question asks for the ratio of white paint to red paint, so flip your ratio, and you're done. Choice (B) is correct.	W:R = 18:35

✔ Note

Beware of trap answers that contain incorrect ratios, such as A. Always confirm that you've found the ratio requested.

PERCENTAGES

Percentages aren't just for test grades; you'll find them frequently throughout life—discount pricing in stores, income tax brackets, and stock price trackers all use percents in some form. It's critical that you know how to use them correctly, especially on Test Day.

Suppose you have a bag containing 10 blue marbles and 15 pink marbles, and you're asked what percent of the marbles are pink. You can determine this easily by using the formula $\% = \dfrac{\text{Part}}{\text{Whole}} \times 100\%$.

Plug 15 in for the part and 10 + 15 (= 25) for the whole, then compute to get $\dfrac{15}{25} \times 100\% = 60\%$ pink marbles.

Another easy way to solve many percent problems is to use the following statement: (blank) percent of (blank) is (blank). Translating from English into math, you obtain (blank)% × (blank) = (blank). As you saw with the DIRT equation in the rates section, knowledge of any two quantities will unlock the third.

You might also be asked to determine the percent change in a given situation. Fortunately, you can find this easily using a variant of the percent three-part formula:

$$\text{Percent increase or decrease} = \frac{(\text{Amount of increase or decrease})}{(\text{Original amount})} \times 100\%$$

 Note

The percent three-part formula requires the percent component to be in decimal form. Remember to move the decimal point appropriately before using this formula.

Sometimes more than one change will occur. Be especially careful here, as it can be tempting to take a "shortcut" by just adding two percent changes together (which will almost always lead to an incorrect answer). Instead you'll need to find the total amount of increase or decrease and calculate accordingly. We'll demonstrate this in an upcoming problem.

The following is a test-like question involving percentages.

5. Some individuals like to dilute 100% juice drinks with water to lessen the flavor intensity and reduce caloric intake. Kristina, a personal trainer, is preparing several blends of varying juice concentrations to see which ratio her fitness club's clients prefer. She plans to make 240 oz each of 80% juice, 60% juice, 50% juice, 40% juice, and 20% juice blends. If the 100% juice Kristina plans to buy comes in 32 oz bottles and partial bottles cannot be bought, how many bottles will Kristina need to make her blends?

A) 8

B) 18

C) 19

D) 60

Work through the Kaplan Method for Math step-by-step to solve this question. The following table shows Kaplan's strategic thinking on the left, along with suggested math scratchwork on the right.

Strategic Thinking	Math Scratchwork
Step 1: Read the question, identifying and organizing important information as you go You're asked how many bottles of 100% juice Kristina needs to buy to make her five blends. You're given the percent juice content of each.	five blends: 80%, 60%, 50%, 40%, 20% juice
Step 2: Choose the best strategy to answer the question Although this looks like calculator busywork, there's a faster (but less obvious) route to the answer. Notice that each percentage is a multiple of 10. Therefore, all you need to do is find 10% of 240 and multiply by the appropriate number to get the ounces of juice in each blend.	$0.1 \times 240 \ oz = 24 \ oz$ ——— $\times 2: 20\% = 48 \ oz \ juice$ $\times 4: 40\% = 96 \ oz \ juice$ $\times 5: 50\% = 120 \ oz \ juice$ $\times 6: 60\% = 144 \ oz \ juice$ $\times 8: 80\% = 192 \ oz \ juice$ sum: 600 oz. $\dfrac{600}{32} = 18.75 \rightarrow 19$
Step 3: Check that you answered the *right* question You've found the number of juice bottles required; the correct answer is (C).	19

Here's an example of a Multi-Part Math question that tests your percentage expertise.

Use the following information to answer questions 6 and 7.

Projected Undergraduate Costs at the University of California

2014-15	2015-16	2016-17	2017-18	2018-19	2019-20
$12,192	$12,804	$13,446	$14,118	$14,820	$15,564

Source: regents.universityofcalifornia.edu

Over the last decade, colleges have come under fire for significant tuition and fee increases. The University of California recently approved a series of tuition and fee increases over the course of five years. The table above summarizes the total cost per undergraduate per year through the 2019-20 academic year.

6. If fees account for 8.75% of one year's total expenses, what is the average fee increase per academic year? Round your answer to the nearest dollar.

7. Suppose the University of California system wants to extend these increases through the 2022-23 academic year. Assuming the average yearly increase for this extension remains the same as it was from 2014-15 through 2019-20, by what percentage will total tuition and fees have increased at the end of the 2022-23 academic year since their implementation? Round your answer to the nearest whole percent.

Work through the Kaplan Method for Multi-Part Math Questions step-by-step to solve. The following table shows Kaplan's strategic thinking on the left, along with suggested math scratchwork on the right.

Strategic Thinking	Math Scratchwork
Step 1: Read the first part of the question, looking for clues You are given a table with total costs for several academic years. Part 1 states that fees account for 8.75% of one year's expenses.	
Step 2: Identify and organize the information you need Part 1 asks for the portion of the total cost increase that is comprised of fees.	*fees (in $): ?*

Strategic Thinking	Math Scratchwork
Step 3: Based on what you know, plan your steps to navigate the first part You'll need the total cost increase in dollars to start, as well as the average annual increase. From there, you can determine the portion of the increase that fees make up. The percent given in part 1 indicates you should use the three-part formula.	*8.75% is fees* *(blank)% of (blank) is (blank)*
Step 4: Solve, step-by-step, checking units as you go Instead of finding each year-to-year increase, find the total increase from 2014-15 through 2019-20. Once there, determine the average increase for each year. Use the three-part formula to find the fee portion of the average increase.	$15,564 - $12,192 = $3,372 $avg = \dfrac{\$3372}{5}$ = \$674.40 0.0875 x \$674.40 = \$59.01
Step 5: Did I answer the *right* question? You've found the average fee increase per year. Once you round appropriately, part 1 is complete.	59

> **✔ Note**
>
> By finding the total increase instead of each individual increase, you saved yourself a substantial amount of time.

Part 1 is finished! Now on to Step 6: Repeat for the other parts. Kaplan's strategic thinking is on the left, along with suggested math scratchwork on the right.

Strategic Thinking	Math Scratchwork
Step 1: Read the second part of the question, looking for clues There's a proposal to extend the tuition/fee hikes through 2022-23.	
Step 2: Identify and organize the information you need Part 2 asks for the percent increase in total tuition/fee cost between 2014-15 and 2022-23.	% increase: ?
Step 3: Based on what you know, plan your steps to navigate the second part You know the average yearly increase from the first part. Use this to determine what the cost for the 2022-23 year will be, and then calculate the total increase. Use this result to calculate the percent increase.	2014-15 thru 2019-20: $3,372 avg. yearly incr.: $674.40
Step 4: Solve, step-by-step, checking units as you go Extending the increases past 2019-20 means increases for 2020-21, 2021-22, and 2022-23 – 3 years total. Multiply the average yearly increase by 3 to determine the additional increase. Add this to the increase you found in the first part to find the total increase from 2014-15 through 2022-23. To calculate the percent change, divide the total increase by the original cost from 2014-15, and multiply the result by 100.	$674.40 × 3 = $2,023.20 $2,023.20 + $3,372 = $5,395.20 $\dfrac{\$5395.20}{\$12192} \times 100 = 44.252\%$
Step 5: Did I answer the *right* question? Round the percent change per the instructions in the question stem, and you're done.	44

Now you'll have a chance to try a few test-like problems in a scaffolded way. See if you can fill in the missing pieces and solve for the correct answer without a full explanation.

We've provided some guidance, but you'll need to fill in the missing parts of explanations or the step-by-step math to get to the correct answer. Don't worry—after going through the worked examples at the beginning of this section, these problems should be completely doable.

8. Ramp meters are often used in and around metropolitan areas to reduce freeway congestion during AM and PM rush hours. Depending on freeway volume, ramp meters in Milwaukee allow one car onto the freeway every 5-9 seconds. Assuming a constant ramp car queue, between the hours of 3:30 PM and 6:30 PM, how many more cars can move through a ramp meter with a 5-second interval than one with an 8-second interval?

    A) 270

    B) 320

    C) 810

    D) 960

The following table can help you structure your thinking as you go about solving this problem. The Kaplan strategic thinking is provided, as are bits of structured scratchwork. If you're not sure how to approach a question like this, start at the top and work your way down.

Strategic Thinking	Math Scratchwork
Step 1: Read the question, identifying and organizing important information as you go *What are you being asked to find here?* You must determine how many more cars pass through a ramp meter with a 5-second interval.	

Strategic Thinking	Math Scratchwork
Step 2: Choose the best strategy to answer the question	
One car per time interval . . . does this sound familiar?	5-second interval:
It should! One car every 5 (or 8) seconds is a rate, so turn to the DIRT equation. Be careful here; you need to manipulate the given form of the rate before you can use it.	r_5 = 1 car per 5 s = ____ cars/s

8-second interval:

r_8 = 1 car per 8 s = ____ cars/s |
| *Which variable do I need to find?* | 3 h × _____ × _____ = _____ s |
| The 3:30 PM–6:30 PM window translates to 3 h, which is your time. Your rate, however, involves seconds, so you'll need to convert time to seconds. Finding d will give you the number of cars; do this for both intervals. Watch your units! | 5 seconds

d_5 = _____ × _____

d_5 = _____

8 seconds |
| *Are you finished?* | d_8 = _____ × _____

d_8 = _____ |
Almost. Subtract the 8-second car count from the 5-second car count to get the difference.	_____ − _____ = _____
Step 3: Check that you answered the *right* question	
How many more cars are allowed onto the freeway with the shorter interval?	
If your answer is (C), you're correct!	_____

✔ **Expert Tip**

Sometimes your distance or time units won't look like those you're used to (e.g., miles, minutes, etc.). Don't let this deter you. If you have a rate, you can use the DIRT equation.

Here's another test-like example to try using this method:

Murray's Annual Income Tax Liability

Federal (up to $9,225)	Federal ($9,226-$37,450)	Federal ($37,451-$90,750)	State (flat rate)
10%	15%	25%	4.5%

9. Murray has an annual salary of $75,400. He contributes 20% of his pre-tax income to his 401(k), and he pays $150 per month for health insurance (pre-tax, deducted after 401(k)). The table above summarizes Murray's tax liability; all taxes are calculated based on Murray's adjusted gross income (pay remaining after 401(k) and insurance payments). He must pay 10% on the first $9,225 in income, 15% on any income between $9,226 and $37,450, 25% on income between $37,451-$90,750, and a 4.5% state-tax on all of his income. All taxes are deducted simultaneously. What is Murray's biweekly take-home pay after all deductions have been made?

A) $1,537.98

B) $1,586.79

C) $1,699.78

D) $1,748.59

The following table can help you structure your thinking as you go about solving this problem. The Kaplan strategic thinking is provided, as are bits of structured scratchwork. If you're not sure how to approach a question like this, start at the top and work your way down.

Strategic Thinking	Math Scratchwork
Step 1: Read the question, identifying and organizing important information as you go *What is the question asking? What information will help you find the answer?* You need to find Murray's income after deductions. You have information about each deduction, as well as the order in which they're taken.	start ($_____) – _____ 401(k) – _____ insurance – taxes = take-home pay

Strategic Thinking	Math Scratchwork
Step 2: Choose the best strategy to answer the question *There's a lot going on. Where should you start?* The table provides tax information for annual income, so don't convert to biweekly yet. Follow the order you extracted in Step 1 to calculate each deduction first. *How much does Murray deduct before taxes?* Use the three-part percent formula to find his 401(k) contribution, then subtract his health insurance cost. *How should taxes be approached?* The question states that all taxes are deducted simultaneously; that is, don't deduct state tax and then take federal tax on what's left and vice versa. Use the quantity left after the insurance deduction for all tax calculations, and then subtract Murray's total tax liability from the remaining quantity post-insurance. *Am I finished?* The question asks for Murray's biweekly take-home pay. Divide by the number of pay periods in one year to get the final answer.	401(k): _____ × _____ = $ _____ annually insurance: $ _____ × _____ = $ _____ annually $ _____ − $ _____ − $ _____ = $ _____ annual pre-tax taxes: state _____ × _____ = _____ M. owes $ _____ for state fed 10% bracket _____ × _____ = _____ M. owes $ _____ for 10% br. fed 15% bracket _____ × _____ = _____ M. owes $ _____ for 15% br. fed 25% bracket _____ × _____ = _____ M. owes $ _____ for 25% br. total tax: $ _____ take-home: $ _____ − $ _____ = $ _____ annually $\dfrac{\$\ \rule{1cm}{0.4pt}}{wks}$ = $ _____ biweekly
Step 3: Check that you answered the *right* question *How much money does Murray get to take home?* If you chose (D), you're right.	_____

✔ **Note**

Read carefully; it's easy to erroneously take a flat 25% of Murray's check for federal taxes instead of using the tiers (and real-life taxes would be far more painful this way).

Now try your hand at a Multi-Part Math question.

Use the following information to answer questions 10 and 11.

Shuang has a set of square ceramic plates she'd like to glaze. She wants to create evenly spaced concentric squares on the plates with gray and black glaze as shown in the diagram above. The squares' edges are each 0.5 in. apart.

10. What fraction of one plate will Shuang cover with gray glaze?

11. Shuang also plans to glaze smaller square plates with the same type of pattern as the plate in the figure. The smaller plates' squares are the same size and distance apart as those of the larger plates. If a small plate has four concentric squares, By how many times is the fraction of a small plate that Shuang will cover with black glaze greater than that of a large plate?

The following table can help you structure your thinking as you go about solving this problem. The Kaplan strategic thinking is provided, as are bits of structured scratchwork. If you're not sure how to approach a question like this, start at the top and work your way down.

Strategic Thinking	Math Scratchwork
Step 1: Read the first part of the question, looking for clues *What information do part 1 and the intro provide?* You're given a picture of one of Shuang's plates and told that she will use two colors to create the design.	
Step 2: Identify and organize the information you need *What does part 1 ask you to find?* You need to find the fraction of the plate that will be gray.	gray/total: ?
Step 3: Based on what you know, plan your steps to navigate the first part *Anything missing? How do you get around not having the plate's exact dimensions?* You might think this problem is bogus, but it asks for a relative quantity, not an absolute quantity. You'll need to pick a value for the area of one square and calculate the others based on the one you set. Label the squares to help keep your calculations clear.	

Strategic Thinking	Math Scratchwork
Step 4: Solve, step-by-step, checking units as you go *What is the side length of square 1? How do you calculate the others?* Pick a small, manageable number for this value. Remember how far apart the square edges are; this will help you find the side lengths and areas of the other squares. Also keep in mind you'll need to account for the fact that each square outside the first is not actually a full square. *What is the ratio of gray glaze to total glaze?* Divide the gray glaze area by the total glaze area.	sq. 1 = ___ in.^{2} sq. 2 = ___^{2} – ___ = ___ in.^{2} sq. 3 = ___^{2} – ___ = ___ in.^{2} sq. 4 = ___^{2} – ___ = ___ in.^{2} sq. 5 = ___^{2} – ___ = ___ in.^{2} sq. 6 = ___^{2} – ___ = ___ in.^{2} sq. 7 = ___^{2} – ___ = ___ in.^{2} sq. 8 = ___^{2} – ___ = ___ in.^{2} gray: ___ + ___ + ___ + ___ = ___ in.^{2} black: ___ + ___ + ___ + ___ = ___ in.^{2} gray/total = _____
Step 5: Did I answer the *right* question? *What fraction of each plate is gray?* If you got 7/16, great job! You're correct.	_____

Fantastic! Now repeat for the other parts. Once again, Kaplan strategic thinking is provided, as are bits of structured scratchwork. If you're not sure how to approach the second part, start at the top and work your way down.

Strategic Thinking	Math Scratchwork
Step 1: Read the second part of the question, looking for clues *What's new in part 2?* You're told a smaller plate has four concentric squares with edges 0.5 in. apart like in a larger plate.	4 squares in a small plate
Step 2: Identify and organize the information you need *What is needed to solve this part?* You'll need to find the fraction of black glaze on one small plate and one large plate.	sm. black: ? lg. black: ?
Step 3: Based on what you know, plan your steps to navigate the second part *Anything missing? How can the gray fraction from part 1 help?* You'll need to find the black fraction of the two plates. Fortunately, the black fraction for the larger plate is easy to find because you found its gray counterpart for part 1.	lg. black = 1 – ___ = ___
Step 4: Solve, step-by-step, checking units as you go *How do you find the black fraction of the small plate?* Good news: You did most of the work for this calculation in part 1. Just use the same numbers.	sq. 1 (gray) = ___ in.^{2} sq. 2 (black) = ___ in.^{2} sq. 3 (gray) = ___ in.^{2} sq. 4 (black) = ___ in.^{2} sm. gray: ___ + ___ = ___ in.^{2} sm. black: ___ + ___ = ___ in.^{2} sm. bl. vs. lg. bl.: ___ ÷ ___ = ___ × ___ = ___
Step 5: Did I answer the *right* question? *What is part 2 asking?* Did you get 10/9? If so, congrats! You're correct.	

Now that you've seen the variety of ways in which the SAT can test you on ratios, rates, and percentages, try the following questions to check your understanding. Give yourself 5 minutes to tackle the following four questions. Make sure you use the Kaplan Method for Math as often as you can (as well as the Kaplan Method for Multi-Part Math Questions when necessary). Remember, you want to emphasize speed and efficiency in addition to simply getting the correct answer.

12. Grocery stores often differ in how they price fruit; some charge by weight, and others charge per piece. FoodCo sells bananas for $0.60 a pound, Bob's charges $0.29 per banana, Acme charges $1.50 for a two-pound banana bunch, and Stu's offers a special: buying three pounds of bananas at $0.65 per pound gets you a fourth pound free. If one banana weighs $\frac{1}{3}$ lb, which of the following correctly orders the four grocers in order of decreasing cost per banana (assuming all purchases are made in 4 lb increments)?

A) Bob's, Acme, FoodCo, Stu's

B) Bob's, FoodCo, Acme, Stu's

C) Stu's, FoodCo, Acme, Bob's

D) Stu's, Acme, FoodCo, Bob's

13. The owner of an aerial adventure park wants to construct a zipline for kids who aren't tall enough to ride the regular zipline, which starts at a platform in a tree 10 m above the ground and is 26 m in length. The desired platform height for the new zipline is 3 m. If the owner wants the kids' zipline length and platform starting height to be proportional to those of the regular zipline, what will the difference in length of the two ziplines be?

Use the following information to answer questions 14 and 15.

Gas stations in the United States sell gasoline by the gallon, whereas those in Great Britain sell it by the liter. Mark is assembling a budget for a trip to Great Britain. He plans to drive from London to Edinburgh and back with various excursions along the way; he estimates his total mileage to be 960 miles. The Great Britain pound (GBP)-U.S. dollar (USD) exchange rate is currently 1:1.52, and 1 gallon (gal) is approximately 3.785 liters (L).

14. If Mark rents a car that averages 40 mpg throughout the trip and estimates an average gas cost of 1.20 GBP per liter, how much money (in USD) should Mark budget for fuel? Round your answer to the nearest dollar.

15. The rental car firm Mark is using has a special offer: for an extra 30 GBP, Mark can lock in a subsidized fuel cost of 0.75 GBP per liter for the duration of his trip. How much, in USD, would Mark save with this offer? Round your answer to the nearest dollar.

Answers and Explanations for this chapter begin on page 844.

EXTRA PRACTICE

Required	Recommended
Questions 1–8	Questions 9–38

 You may use your calculator for all questions in this section.

1. An expert on car depreciation determines that a certain car that costs $35,000 new will immediately depreciate by $12,000 once it is driven off the lot. After that, for the first 50,000 miles, the car will depreciate approximately $0.15 per mile driven. For every mile after that, it will depreciate by $0.10 per mile driven until the car reaches its scrap value. How much would this car be worth after being driven 92,000 miles?

   A) $11,300
   B) $13,800
   C) $17,000
   D) $27,700

2. While reviewing for exams, a teacher knows that the number of topics he can cover is directly proportional to the length of time he has to review. If he can cover 9 topics in a single 45-minute period, how many topics can he cover in a 1-hour period?

   A) 5
   B) 7
   C) 10
   D) 12

3. Weight is dependent on the gravitational force exerted on an object. In other words, in space, you would weigh nothing because there is no gravity. Likewise, because the moon's gravitational pull is less than Earth's, objects weigh less on the moon. In general, 1 pound on Earth is equal to approximately 0.166 pounds on the moon. If a man weighs 29 pounds on the moon, about how much, in pounds, does he weigh on Earth?

   A) 21
   B) 48
   C) 175
   D) 196

4. At all trials and hearings, a court reporter types every word spoken during the proceedings so that there is a written record of what transpired. Because they must type every word, the average court reporter must be able to type at a minimum rate of 3.75 words per second in order to be certified. Suppose a trial transcript contains 25 pages with an average of 675 words per page. Assuming the court reporter typed the transcript at the minimum rate, how long was she actively typing?

   A) 1 hour, 15 minutes
   B) 1 hour, 45 minutes
   C) 2 hours, 30 minutes
   D) 3 hours

5. In 1912, the original candidates for United States President were Woodrow Wilson and William H. Taft. Because of party disagreements, former President Theodore Roosevelt also decided to run and ended up splitting the vote with his fellow Republican and incumbent, Taft. In a certain state, the ratio of the popular vote of Taft to Roosevelt to Wilson was approximately 35:41:63. If approximately 208,500 votes were cast in that state for the three candidates altogether, how many were cast for Taft?

   A) 15,000

   B) 45,000

   C) 52,500

   D) 69,500

6. When medical tests are conducted, there is always the possibility that the test will return a false positive or a false negative. A false positive means the test shows that a patient has the condition being studied, when the patient actually does not; a false negative indicates that a patient does not have the condition, when the patient actually does. Suppose a certain medical test has a false positive rate of 6 out of 3,500. How many people were tested during a period when 27 false positives came back?

   A) 14,000

   B) 15,750

   C) 17,500

   D) 21,000

$$\frac{6}{3500} = \frac{27}{x}$$

$$6x = 94500$$

7. A tutoring service offers a free one-hour tutoring session. After a client signs up, the next 10 hours of tutoring are billed at a rate of $30 per hour. For all hours after that, the client receives a discounted rate. If a client pays $664 for 25 hours of tutoring, what is the service's discounted hourly rate?

   A) $24.50

   B) $25.54

   C) $26.00

   D) $26.56

   1 – free
   $30 per hour
   300

8. Political canvassers polled voters in two locations on whether they viewed a particular candidate for governor favorably. At the first location, they asked 125 people and of those, 22.4% responded favorably. At the second location, 37.5% of 272 people responded favorably. What percent of all the people surveyed responded favorably?

   A) 25.7%

   B) 30.0%

   C) 31.5%

   D) 32.7%

   $$\frac{125}{22.4} = \frac{272}{375}$$
   60   428   46.875

9. At 350°F, an oven can cook approximately 3 pounds of turkey per hour. At 450°F, it can cook approximately 4.5 pounds per hour. How many more ounces of turkey can the oven cook at 450° than at 350° in 10 minutes? (Note: 1 pound = 16 ounces)

   A) 4

   B) 6

   C) 8

   D) 12

10. In extreme climates, temperatures can vary as much as 20° Celsius in a single day. How much can these climates vary measured in degrees Fahrenheit? $(F = \frac{9}{5} C + 32)$

 A)   20°F

 B)   36°F

 C)   62°F

 D)   68°F

11. A company specializes in converting people's VHS movies and DVDs to digital formats, which, once converted, are approximately 4.5 gigabytes in size. Once converted, the company uploads the videos to a secure cloud drive, where the customers can retrieve their files. The company uploads the videos every day, from closing time at 5:00 PM until 9:00 PM. Their internet service provider has an upload speed of 12 megabytes per second. What is the maximum number of videos the company can upload each evening? (1 gigabyte = 1,024 megabytes)

 A)   2

 B)   37

 C)   242

 D)   682

12. An online movie subscription service charges a dollars for the first month of membership and b dollars per month after that. If a customer has paid $108.60 so far for the service, which of the following expressions represents the number of months he has subscribed to the service?

 A) $\dfrac{108.60}{a+b}$

 B) $\dfrac{108.60-a}{b}$

 C) $\dfrac{108.60-a-b}{b}$

 D) $\dfrac{108.60-a+b}{b}$

13. A certain real estate agent uses what he calls a *step-strategy* to sell houses. He puts a house on the market at a higher-than-expected selling price and if it hasn't sold in two weeks, he drops the price by 5%. If it still hasn't sold in another 2 weeks, he drops the price by another 5%. After that, he continues to drop the price by 3% every two weeks until it reaches a cut-off amount assigned by the homeowner, or the house sells, whichever comes first. If a house is originally listed at $200,000 and the homeowner sets a cut-off amount of $166,000, what is the final selling price given that the house sells after being on the market for 9 weeks?

 A) $162,901.25

 B) $164,737.48

 C) $166,000.00

 D) $169,832.45

14. A museum is building a scale model of Sue, the largest *Tyrannosaurus rex* skeleton ever found. Sue was 13 feet tall and 40 feet long, and her skull had a length of 5 feet. If the length of the museum's scale model skull is 3 feet, 1.5 inches, what is the difference between the scale model's length and its height?

A) 8 feet, 1.5 inches

B) 16 feet, 10.5 inches

C) 25 feet

D) 27 feet, 4 inches

15. A company reimburses employees for a portion of their gas costs for commuting to and from work based on mileage. Based on the following data, what is the rate in dollars per gallon that the company uses to reimburse employees?

- The company has 126 employees who commute.

- The average employee traveled 12,250 miles to and from work over the course of the year.

- The average gas mileage reported by all employees was 22.5 miles per gallon.

- The company paid out a total of $96,040.00 in gas reimbursements.

A) $0.44

B) $0.71

C) $1.40

D) $1.60

16. On average, Betsy reads 1 page of her book every 1.5 minutes. Her book has 116 pages. Raymond starts a 94-page book on Saturday morning at 8:30 AM and reads straight through until he finishes it at 11:38 AM. How many more minutes does it take Raymond to read his book than Betsy to read hers?

17. Katrina is working on a school project and determines that she needs 576 square inches of cardboard, but the craft store only sells cardboard by the square foot. How many square feet of cardboard does she need?

18. A county employee is collecting water samples from all the houses in a subdivision where trace amounts of lead were found in the water. There are 45 houses in the subdivision. If he starts the first house at 9:00 AM and starts the sixth house at 10:00 AM, how many minutes will it take the employee to collect samples from all the houses in the subdivision, assuming it takes the same amount of time at each house?

19. On a map, the scale is the ratio of the distance shown on the map to the actual distance. A geography teacher has a map on her wall with a scale of 1 inch:100 miles. She uses the school's copier to shrink the large wall map down to the size of a piece of paper to hand out to each of her students. To do this, she makes the map $\frac{1}{4}$ of its original size. Suppose on the students' maps, the distance between two cities is 2.5 inches. How many actual miles apart are those cities?

20. A bank offers a long-term savings account with a 1.0% annual interest rate. At the end of each year, the interest is rounded down to the nearest cent and added to the principal. If the initial deposit was $1,500, how much interest has the account earned at the end of 5 years?

21. A power company divides the geographic regions it serves into grids. The company is able to allocate the power it generates based on the usage and needs of a particular grid. Certain grids use more power at certain times of the day, so companies often shift power around to different grids at various times. On any given day, the company makes several changes in the power allocation to Grid 1. First, it increases the power by 20%. Then, it decreases it by 10%. Finally, it increases it by 30%. What is the net percent increase in this grid's power allocation? (Round to the nearest whole percent and ignore the percent sign when entering your answer.)

22. An emergency room doctor prescribes a certain pain medication to be delivered through an IV drip. She prescribes 800 mL of the medication to be delivered over the course of 8 hours. The IV delivers 1 mL of medication over the course of 30 drips. How many drips per minute are needed to deliver the prescribed dosage?

Questions 23 and 24 refer to the following information.
Every Saturday morning, three friends meet for breakfast at 9:00 AM. Andrea walks, Kellan bikes, and Joelle drives.

23. Last Saturday, all three friends were exactly on time. Andrea left her house at 8:30 AM and walked at a rate of 3 miles per hour. Kellan left his house at 8:15 AM and biked at a rate of 14 mph. Joelle left her house at 8:45 AM and drove an average speed of 35 mph. How many miles from the restaurant does the person who travelled the farthest live?

24. Kellan lives 12 miles away from Andrea. On a different Saturday, Kellan biked at a rate of 15 mph to Andrea's house. The two then walked to the restaurant at a rate of 2.5 mph, and they arrived five minutes early. What time did Kellan leave his house? Enter your answer as three digits and ignore the colon. For example, if your answer is 5:30 AM, enter 530.

Questions 25 and 26 refer to the following information.
Mia is planning to work as a hostess at a restaurant. Two restaurants in her area have offered her jobs, both of which utilize "tip share," which means that the hostess gets a portion of all tips left by all customers. Restaurant A has a tip share for hostesses of 7%, while Restaurant B has a tip share of only 4%.

25. Mia does some research and finds that, on average, restaurants in her area bring in approximately $1,100 in tips for the evening shift. Based on this information, how much more in dollars would Mia make in tips at Restaurant A than at Restaurant B if she worked 5 evenings a week for 4 weeks?

26. Upon further research, Mia discovers that Restaurant B is making some improvements to become a more upscale establishment, which will result in an increase in meal prices and, consequently, should also increase tips. Assuming both restaurants originally brought in the average tips given in the previous question, what percent increase would Restaurant B need to experience in tips in order for Mia to make the same amount of money in one evening at both restaurants from the hostess tip share? Assume that Restaurant B doesn't increase its tip share percentage. Enter your answer as a whole number and ignore the percent sign.

Questions 27 and 28 refer to the following information.

Bridget is starting a tutoring business to help adults get their GEDs. She already has five clients and decides they can share a single textbook, which will be kept at her office, and that she also needs one notebook and four pencils for each of them. She records her supply budget, which includes tax, in the table shown.

Supply	Total Number Needed	Cost Each
Textbook	1	$24.99
Notebooks	5	$3.78
Pencils	20	$0.55

27. The textbook makes up what percent of Bridget's total supply budget? Round to the nearest tenth of a percent and ignore the percent sign when entering your answer.

28. Bridget's business does very well, and she needs more supplies. She always orders them according to the table above, for five clients at a time. At the beginning of this year, she orders the supplies for the whole year, which cost $988.02. Halfway through the year, she decides to take inventory of the supplies. She has used $713.57 worth of the supplies. How many pencils should be left, assuming the supplies were used at the rate for which she originally planned?

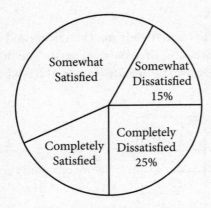

29. A company conducts a customer satisfaction survey. The results are summarized in the pie graph. If 240 customers responded to the survey, how many customers were either completely or somewhat satisfied?

A) 60

B) 96

C) 144

D) 204

30. A general contractor is building an addition onto a home. He budgets 20% for materials, 55% for labor, 10% for equipment rental, and the rest is his fee. If the estimate the contractor gives to the homeowners says he will spend $5,200 on materials, then how much is his fee?

A) $2,600

B) $3,900

C) $5,200

D) $6,500

31. In a week, a light bulb factory produces 12,500 light bulbs. The ratio of light emitting diodes (LED bulbs) to compact fluorescent lamps (CFL bulbs) is 2:3. Of the LED bulbs produced, 3% were defective. How many LED bulbs were not defective?

A) 150

B) 2,425

C) 4,850

D) 7,275

32. In 1950, scientists estimated a certain animal population in a particular geographical area to be 6,400. In 2000, the population had risen to 7,200. If this animal population experiences the same percent increase over the next 50 years, what will the approximate population be?

A) 8,000

B) 8,100

C) 8,400

D) 8,600

33. An architect is designing a new stadium-seating movie theater. The theater company has given the architect the following guidelines for the designing the rows:

- The length of each row must be at least 20 feet long, but no longer than 90 feet.

- Each row should be at least 20% longer than the row in front of it.

- Each row length must be evenly divisible by the width needed for each seat, 2.5 feet.

Which list of row lengths meets the theater company's guidelines and includes as many row lengths as possible?

A) 24, 30, 36, 45, 54, 66, 81

B) 20, 32.5, 45, 57.5, 72.5, 85

C) 20, 30, 40, 50, 60, 70, 80, 90

D) 25, 30, 37.5, 45, 55, 67.5, 82.5

34. Mikal has two saltwater fish tanks in his home. One has eels and lionfish in a ratio of 5 to 2. The second tank has eels and seahorses in a ratio of 2 to 3. Mikal wants to put a tank in his office with seahorses and lionfish, using the same ratio he has at home to make it easier to buy food for them in bulk. What ratio of lionfish to seahorses should he use?

A) 2:3

B) 5:2

C) 7:8

D) 4:15

Questions 35 and 36 refer to the following information.

A restaurant offers a 20% discount to students and to members of the military. The restaurant is also currently participating in a charity drive. If patrons donate a gently used item of clothing, they get an additional 5% off their bill, which is applied before any other discounts, such as student or military discounts.

35. A student brings in an item of clothing and has a total bill, before any discounts, of $13.00. How much does she pay, once all applicable discounts are applied, not including tax?

36. Sharon is a member of the military. She dines with her friend, Damien. Damien brings an item of clothing, but Sharon forgot to bring one. If Sharon's meal before discounts is $16.25 and Damien's is $12.80 before discounts, how much did the discounts save them altogether?

Questions 37 and 38 refer to the following information.

Jordan is beginning a marathon-training program. During his first day of training, he wears a pedometer to get an idea of how far he can currently run. At the end of the run, the pedometer indicates that he took 24,288 steps.

37. Jordan knows from experience that his average stride (step) is 2.5 feet. How many miles did he run on his first day of training?
(Note: 1 mile = 5,280 feet)

38. Jordan was telling his friend Alexa, who is from Europe, about his training and told her how far he ran. Alexa wasn't sure whether that distance was long or short because she is familiar with the metric system, which uses kilometers, instead of miles. Jordan wants to convert the distance for her. If 1 kilometer equals approximately 0.62 miles, what number should he tell Alexa? Round your answer to the nearest tenth of a kilometer.

CHAPTER 6

Scatterplots

CHAPTER OBJECTIVES

By the end of this chapter, you will be able to:

1. Decide whether a linear, quadratic, or exponential model describes the data presented in a scatterplot

2. Use an equation for a line of best fit to describe trends between variables in a scatterplot

SMARTPOINTS

Point Value	SmartPoint Category
30 Points	Scatterplots

SCATTERPLOT BASICS

Some students tend to associate scatterplots with nasty-looking statistical analyses and consequently become nervous when they hear they'll likely encounter a few scatterplots on Test Day. However, these seemingly difficult plots are usually straightforward—if you know what to look for. We'll go over the foundational concepts of scatterplots, growth and decay examples, and modeling with scatterplots over the next several pages.

First, let's look at the anatomy of a scatterplot.

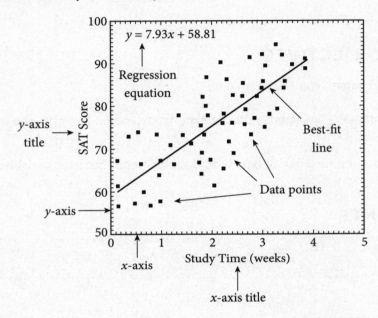

- You're already familiar with the **x- and y-axes**, but something that might be new is their **units**. Most scatterplots that use real data have units on the axes; these are important when trying to draw conclusions and inferences based on data (more on this later).

- The **best-fit line** is drawn through the **data points** to describe the relationship between the two variables as an equation. This line does not need to go through most or all data points, but it should accurately reflect the trend shown by the data with about half the points above the line and half below. As in "plain" equations, x is the independent variable, and y is the dependent variable.

- The **best-fit equation** (also called the **regression equation**) is the equation that describes the best-fit line algebraically. This equation can be linear, quadratic, exponential, or another shape, but the first three are those you'll most likely encounter on Test Day.

> **✔ Note**
>
> A scatterplot outlier is defined as a data point that does not follow the trend exemplified by the other data points. It will appear to have been derived from a different trend.

Below is a test-like question that involves a scatterplot.

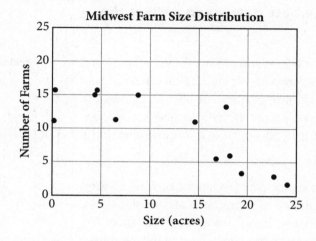

1. In 2012, the United States Department of Agriculture conducted a survey on the frequency of various farm sizes in select areas of the Midwest region of the country. Which of the following best describes the relationship between the size and number of farms?

   A) There is a strong positive correlation between farm size and farm count.

   B) There is a strong negative correlation between farm size and farm count.

   C) There is a weak positive correlation between farm size and farm count.

   D) There is no correlation between farm size and farm count.

Work through the Kaplan Method for Math step-by-step to solve this question. The following table shows Kaplan's strategic thinking on the left, along with suggested math scratchwork on the right.

Strategic Thinking	Math Scratchwork
Step 1: Read the question, identifying and organizing important information as you go You must determine the correlation, if any, between farm count and farm size.	
Step 2: Choose the best strategy to answer the question The answer choices imply that you can model the relationship between the variables with a line or curve. Draw a line of best fit to visualize this relationship. A line of best fit follows the overall trend of the data points. Draw your line accordingly, keeping in mind that it need not pass through the majority of the points. According to the scatterplot and the line of best fit, as farm size increases, the number of farms of that size decreases, which indicates a negative correlation. The majority of the data points are fairly close to the line of best fit, which means the correlation is strong.	**Midwest Farm Size Distribution** Number of Farms (y-axis: 0, 5, 10, 15, 20, 25) Size (acres) (x-axis: 0, 5, 10, 15, 20, 25)
Step 3: Check that you answered the *right* question There is a strong negative correlation between the two variables, making (B) the correct answer.	

✔ **Note**

Remember that the line of best fit does not necessarily pass through the greatest number of points; in fact, it does not have to pass through any.

GROWTH AND DECAY

The real world is full of examples of growth and decay, and you're bound to see some examples on Test Day. To start, let's take a look at the basic structure of linear and exponential equations. Following is the model of the linear equation:

$$y = kx + x_0$$

If this equation looks familiar, it would be for good reason: It's a linear equation in slope-intercept form with different variables standing in for the ones you've seen in the past. You should be able to match each piece to a quantity in the slope-intercept form of an equation. Take a look at the following table for a translation of the new components.

Linear Growth/ Decay Piece	What It Represents	Slope-Intercept Counterpart
x_0	y-intercept or initial quantity in a word problem	b
k	rate of change, slope	m

Recognizing that the previous equation, which might look weird at first glance, is really something you've seen before, will go a long way on Test Day.

> **✔ Note**
>
> You might also see this expressed in function notation. We've included several homework problems in this format for you to try. For an overview of functions and function notation, see chapter 10.

A more complex equation is the exponential equation:

$$y = x_0(1 + r)^x$$

You'll notice most of the terms, such as y, x_0 (pronounced "x-naught"), and x are in both linear and exponential equations which makes exponential equations a bit easier to understand. The lone new variable, r, is the rate of change, akin to k in the linear equation. Also note that x is now an exponent.

What happens if you have a negative exponential rate of change? It's similar to k with linear decay (just like with m in regular linear equations from a few sections back).

Suppose $r = -\frac{3}{4}$ and $x_0 = 100$. This gives $y = 100(1 - \frac{3}{4})^x = 100(\frac{1}{4})^x$. Using our exponent rules to distribute the x, we get $y = 100 \times \frac{1^x}{4^x}$. Because 1^x will always be 1, we can drop it and move

100 to the numerator to give the final equation, $y = \dfrac{100}{4^x}$. This can also be written as $y = 100 \times 0.25^x$, so be ready for both fraction and decimal forms. Here's an easy way to remember whether you have exponential growth or decay: If r is positive, you're looking at growth; if r is negative, decay is occurring. An r of 0 will give you 1^x, which drops out and leaves y equal to a constant (and therefore a horizontal line instead of an exponential curve).

Another key difference to note: The rate of change in linear growth and decay is constant, but it is variable in a case of exponential growth or decay. Graphwise, linear growth/decay is a straight line, whereas exponential growth/decay has a curve. This will often help you identify which is occurring in a given situation.

Now let's look at a question that involves growth. It's up to you to figure out whether it is linear or exponential.

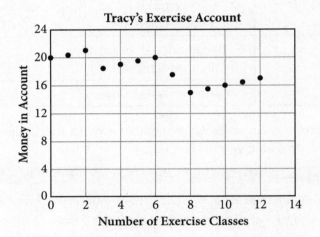

2. Tracy recently joined a workout group in which each member commits to attending three exercise classes per week. To increase accountability, each member sets aside $20 in an account. If a member misses a class, that individual will lose $2.50, which is then equally distributed among the members who attended that class. After missing three classes, Tracy vows to hold herself more accountable and not miss any more. The scatterplot above shows Tracy's account balance over time. Assuming exactly one person is absent from any given class and no one else has joined or left the group since its inception, which of the following equations could represent Tracy's account balance after she resolves not to miss any further classes?

A) $y = 20\,(1.5)^x$

B) $y = x^{1.5} + 11$

C) $y = 0.5x + 11$

D) $y = 0.5x + 20$

Work through the Kaplan Method for Math step-by-step to solve this question. The following table shows Kaplan's strategic thinking on the left, along with suggested math scratchwork on the right.

Strategic Thinking	Math Scratchwork
Step 1: Read the question, identifying and organizing important information as you go You need to determine which equation correctly represents Tracy's account balance after her second missed class, assuming she does not miss any after that. You're given some information about the account's behavior.	$20 @ start present: + x no-show: – $2.50
Step 2: Choose the best strategy to answer the question Find the relevant data points on the scatterplot. The last class Tracy missed corresponds to the third (and final) decrease on the scatterplot. You need the equation that represents Tracy's account balance after that class, so you can disregard her attendance prior to that. Because the no-show count and group size do not change, you can assume Tracy's account balance will increase at a constant rate, indicating a linear equation. You can therefore eliminate A and B. To determine which of the remaining answer choices is correct, draw a line of best fit through the appropriate points. The y-intercept is 11, meaning (C) must be correct.	
Step 3: Check that you answered the _right_ question Only (C) contains a linear equation with the correct y-intercept.	$y = 0.5x + 11$

Nice job! Let's continue our exploration of scatterplots with a section on modeling.

SCATTERPLOT MODELING

As you've seen, the new SAT can ask a variety of questions pertinent to scatterplots. In addition, you might be asked to do some more advanced tasks as mentioned previously, such as drawing conclusions and making predictions. This task sounds daunting, but it's not as challenging as you might think.

Look at the following graphs for a preview of the types of models you might see.

| Linear | Quadratic | Exponential |

A **linear** plot/graph will always increase or decrease at a constant rate, making it easy to spot. By contrast, a **quadratic** plot/graph is U-shaped, indicating a variable rate of change. Quadratics make parabola shapes and have a minimum or maximum known as a vertex (although sometimes it is not shown on the plot). Lastly, an **exponential** plot/graph typically starts with a gradual rate of change, which increases significantly over time. Unlike the quadratic, it does not have a vertex.

There are times when using a graphing calculator on Test Day is prudent; deriving an equation that fits a data set is one of them. These "best-fit" equations are called regression equations and can take several shapes depending on the data's behavior. The correlation coefficient, r, indicates how good a fit the regression line is; the closer to 1 it is for an increasing equation (or −1 for a decreasing equation), the better the fit. The steps for using this function on a TI-83/84 are shown here:

Step 1: Press the [**STAT**] button. Choose [**EDIT**], then enter your data for [L_1] and [L_2].

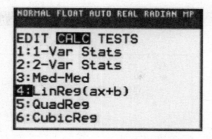

Step 2: Press the [STAT] button again and scroll to [CALC]. Select [4] for a linear regression, [5] for quadratic, or [0] for exponential and press the [ENTER] button. Make sure [L_1] and [L_2] are listed beside [XList] and [YList], respectively.

Step 3: Scroll down to [Calculate], then press the [ENTER] button. The variable values are listed, as is the correlation coefficient. If r is not close to 1/–1, try another regression type.

Note: If r is not displayed, go to the [CATALOG] menu (press [2nd] then [0]), scroll to the Ds, then select [DiagnosticOn].

As mentioned, this is a useful feature, but you must exercise good judgment when deciding whether to use it for a particular question on Test Day.

 Note

If you have a calculator other than the TI-83/84, make sure you read its manual prior to Test Day so you're familiar with how to use this function on it.

Below is a test-like example that asks you to determine a correlation type and extrapolate data.

3. Inhabitants of colder climates are often concerned about frostbite in the winter months and use the wind chill factor to gauge how much time they can safely spend outside. Wind chill reflects the temperature that one feels when outside based on the actual temperature and the wind speed. Wind chill was first introduced in 1939, and the formula was revised in 2001. If the outside temperature is 0°F, what is the approximate wind chill at 40 mph based on the 2001 formula, and what wind speed would produce the same wind chill using the 1939 formula?

    A)   −30°F, 10 mph

    B)   −30°F, 15 mph

    C)   −50°F, 15 mph

    D)   −50°F, 40 mph

Work through the Kaplan Method for Math step-by-step to solve this question. The following table shows Kaplan's strategic thinking on the left, along with suggested math scratchwork on the right.

Strategic Thinking	Math Scratchwork
Step 1: Read the question, identifying and organizing important information as you go You are asked to identify a wind chill value and a wind speed. Although the question stem is lengthy, most of the information is irrelevant. Pay attention to both the title and axes labels on the scatterplot when solving; there are several parameters present, and it's easy to confuse them if you're not careful.	

Strategic Thinking	Math Scratchwork

Step 2: Choose the best strategy to answer the question

Use the trend of the 2001 formula data to draw a line that extends to 40 mph. Next, draw a vertical line from 40 mph on the *x*-axis to intersect the data extension that you drew, and then draw a horizontal line from that intersection to the *y*-axis to estimate the wind chill factor, which is approximately –30°F. You can eliminate C and D based on this finding.

The second part asks for the temperature that would yield the same wind chill (–30°F) using the 1939 formula. The horizontal line that you drew for the first part crosses right through a point on the 1939 curve. Draw another line down to the *x*-axis from that point to find that the wind speed is approximately 15 mph.

Math Scratchwork:

Wind Chill Index at 0˚F

• 1939 Wind Chill Formula
■ 2001 Wind Chill Formula

• 1939 Wind Chill Formula
■ 2001 Wind Chill Formula

Wind Chill Index at 0 ˚F

• 1939 Wind Chill Formula
■ 2001 Wind Chill Formula

Step 3: Check that you answered the *right* question

Choice (B) is the only answer choice that contains both findings.

✔ **Note**

Watch the axis labels. Don't assume each gridline always represents one unit of the given category.

Now you'll have a chance to try a couple test-like problems in a scaffolded way. See if you can fill in the missing pieces and solve for the correct answer without a full explanation.

We've provided some guidance, but you'll need to fill in the missing parts of explanations or the step-by-step math in order to get to the correct answer. Don't worry—after going through the worked examples at the beginning of this section, these problems should be completely doable.

4. Which of the following plots could be modeled by the equation $y = 3^x + 4$?

A)

B)

C)

D)

This question is different from the previous ones, but don't worry. The following table can help you structure your thinking as you go about solving this problem. The Kaplan strategic thinking is provided, as are bits of structured scratchwork. If you're not sure how to approach a question like this, start at the top and work your way down.

Strategic Thinking	Math Scratchwork
Step 1: Read the question, identifying and organizing important information as you go *What are you being asked to do?* You need to match the given equation to the correct plot.	

Strategic Thinking	Math Scratchwork
Step 2: Choose the best strategy to answer the question *What kind of graph does y = 3^x + 4 have?* The *x* in the exponent indicates that you have a certain type of graph; there are two choices you can eliminate based on this. *How do you know which of the remaining choices is correct?* Plug in a manageable value for *x*, and see what *y* is at that point. Determine which graph contains this point.	 *need a(n) _____ graph; eliminate _____* *when x = _____, y = _____* *_____ matches*
Step 3: Check that you answered the *right* question *Did you match the equation to the correct graph?* If you chose (C), you'd be correct!	 _____

✔ **Note**

Remember that 3^x is very different from 3x and x^3.

Here's a chance to try a Multi-Part Math question involving a scatterplot.

The following information applies to questions 5 and 6.

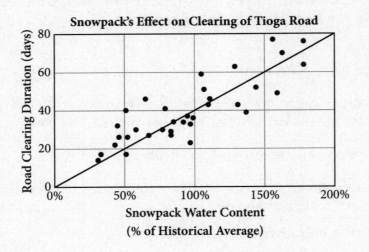

Snowpack's Effect on Clearing of Tioga Road

(data source: www.nps.gov/yose/planyourvisit/tiogaopen.htm)

Tioga (pronounced tie-OH-ga) Road is a mountain pass that crosses the Sierra Nevada through northern Yosemite National Park. Due to its high elevation and the unpredictability of Sierra weather in the winter and early spring, the road is closed from about November through late May. This time period can change depending on the quantity and nature of the season's snowfall, as well as unforeseen obstacles like fallen trees and/or rocks. The scatterplot above compares the snowpack water content on April 1 (for years 1981-2014) as a percent of the historical average to the time it takes the National Park Service to fully clear the road and open it to traffic.

5. For every 5% increase in snowpack water content, how many more days does it take the National Park Service to clear Tioga Road?

6. Assuming no unforeseen obstacles or machinery issues, if the road's snowpack water content on April 1 is 248% of the historical average, how many days will it take to fully clear Tioga Road?

The following table can help you structure your thinking as you go about solving this more involved problem. The Kaplan strategic thinking is provided, as are bits of structured scratchwork. If you're not sure how to approach a question like this, start at the top and work your way down.

Strategic Thinking	Math Scratchwork
Step 1: Read the first part of the question, looking for clues *What useful information are you given?* The infographic shows the relationship between snowpack water content and road clearing duration. A line of best fit is also drawn.	
Step 2: Identify and organize the information you need *What does part 1 ask you to find?* You are asked to find how much the road clearing time increases with each 5% increase in snowpack water content.	
Step 3: Based on what you know, plan your steps to navigate the first part *What missing information will help you find the answer?* You need a rate, which means you need to find the slope of the line of best fit. Pick a pair of points to use (look for places where the line passes through a gridline intersection to minimize error). Read the axes carefully when writing the coordinates!	(____ , ____) (____ , ____)
Step 4: Solve, step-by-step, checking units as you go *How do you find the slope of a line?* Use the slope formula to determine the change in clearing time per 1% increase in snowpack water content.	$m = \dfrac{y_2 - y_1}{x_2 - x_1} = $ _____ = ____ = ____
Step 5: Did I answer the *right* question? *Did you find the clearing duration increase for a 5% increase in snowpack water content?* Be careful; you're not done yet! The slope represents the clearing duration increase for a 1% increase in snowpack water content. Multiply *m* by 5 to get the requested change. If you got 2, you'd be correct!	____ × ____ = ____

Great job! Repeat this for the second part. Kaplan strategic thinking is on the left, and bits of scratchwork guidance are on the right.

Strategic Thinking	Math Scratchwork
Step 1: Read the second part of the question, looking for clues *Any new information presented?* Not a whole lot, just a piece of information on the snowpack water content during a particularly snowy winter.	
Step 2: Identify and organize the information you need *What does part 2 ask you to find? Will anything from part 1 help here?* Part 2 asks for the road clearing duration if snowpack water content is 248% of the historical average. The slope you found in part 1 could be useful here.	$m = $ ___
Step 3: Based on what you know, plan your steps to navigate the second part *How would the slope from part 1 help you?* 248% snowpack water content is not on the graph, and you can easily make an error if you try to extend the line of best fit and estimate 248%. You can use the slope of the line to find the line's equation and extrapolate from there.	$y = mx + b$
Step 4: Solve, step-by-step, checking units as you go *What do you need in order to find the equation of the line of best fit?* Determine where the line of best fit intersects the y-axis to identify the value of b. Once there, plug 248 into the equation for the line of best fit, and then solve for y.	*eqn:* = ___ = ___ + ___ $x = 248$: ___ = ___ × ___ + ___ ___ = ___ + ___ = ___

Strategic Thinking	Math Scratchwork
Step 5: Did I answer the *right* question?	
How many days will it take to clear Tioga Road at 248% snowpack water content?	
Did you get 99.2? If so, you'd be right!	——

Well done! Fortunately, exceedingly heavy snowfall years like the one described in question 6 are relatively rare in the High Sierra of Yosemite.

Now test what you've learned by taking a brief quiz.

Now that you've seen the variety of ways in which the SAT can test you on scatterplots, try the following questions to check your understanding. Give yourself 4 minutes to tackle the following three questions. Make sure you use the Kaplan Method for Math as often as you can. Remember, you want to emphasize speed and efficiency in addition to simply getting the correct answer.

7. The graph above shows the percent of school age children in the United States who received immunizations for various illnesses between 1996 and 2012. What was the average rate of increase in the percent of children immunized over the given time period?

    A) 5%

    B) 10%

    C) 25%

    D) 70%

8. A marketing team is conducting a study on the use of smartphones. In a certain metropolitan area, there were 1.6 million smartphone users at the end of 2014. The marketing team predicts that the number of smartphone users will increase by 35% each year. If y represents the number of smartphone users in this metropolitan area after x years, then which of the following equations best models the number of smartphone users in this area over time?

    A) $y = 1{,}600{,}000(1.35)^x$

    B) $y = 1{,}600{,}000(35)^x$

    C) $y = 35x + 1{,}600{,}000$

    D) $y = 1.35x + 1{,}600{,}000$

9. A microbiologist is comparing the growth rates of two different yeast strains. She indirectly measures the number of yeast cells by recording the optical density (OD600) of each strain every ten hours. The measurements are presented in the graph above. Based on the data, which of the following is NOT a true statement?

    A) Strain 1 had a higher OD600 reading than Strain 2 throughout the monitored period.

    B) The growth rate of Strain 2 was less than the growth rate of Strain 1 until hour 50, at which point Strain 1's growth rate became the lesser one.

    C) Between hours 50 and 70, Strain 2's OD600 reading increased by approximately 0.03 every hour.

    D) The growth rate of Strain 1 was greater than the growth rate of Strain 2 throughout the monitored period.

Answers and Explanations for this chapter begin on page 861.

EXTRA PRACTICE

Required	Recommended
Questions 1–8	Questions 9–24

You may use your calculator for all questions in this section.

1. If a scatterplot shows a strong positive linear correlation, then which of the following best describes the trend of the data points?

    A) Points in a perfectly straight line that rises from left to right

    B) Points in a perfectly straight line that falls from left to right

    C) Points that fit fairly close to a straight line that rises from left to right

    D) Points that fit fairly close to a straight line that falls from left to right

2. Which of the following is the best estimate for the slope of the line that best fits the data shown in the figure above? (Assume that the black bordered area is a square and that the scale of measurement is the same on every side.)

    A) −3

    B) $-\dfrac{1}{3}$

    C) $\dfrac{1}{3}$

    D) 3

3. Which of the following is best modeled using a linear regression equation, $y = ax + b$, where $a < 0$?

A)

B)

C)

D)

4. Adriana used the data from a scatterplot she found on the U.S. Census Bureau's website to determine a regression model showing the relationship between the population in the area where she lived and the number of years, x, after she was born. The result was an exponential growth equation of the form $y = x_0(1 + r)^x$. Which of the following does x_0 most likely represent in the equation?

A) The population in the year that she was born

B) The rate of change of the population over time

C) The maximum population reached during her lifetime

D) The number of years after her birth when the population reached its maximum

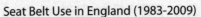

Seat Belt Use in England (1983-2009)

Years After Seat Belt Law Enacted

5. In 1983, the British Parliament enacted a mandatory seat belt law. The scatterplot above shows data collected each year after the law was enacted regarding the percent of drivers and front seat passengers who wore seat belts. Which of the following equations best represents the trend of the data shown in the figure?

A) $y = 0.4x + 25$

B) $y = 1.8x + 15$

C) $y = 2.1x + 35$

D) $y = 2.6x + 25$

**Minor Muscle Strains Sustained
by Athletes**

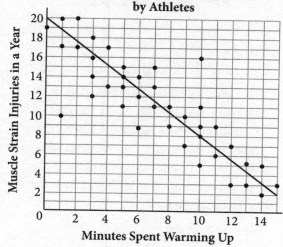

6. The scatterplot above shows the number of minor muscle strain injuries sustained in a year by athletes, plotted against their self-reported amount of time spent stretching and doing other "warm up" activities before engaging in rigorous physical activity. Which of the following best estimates the average rate of change in the number of injuries compared with the number of minutes spent warming up?

A) −1.2

B) −0.8

C) 2

D) 20

7. The Federal Reserve controls certain interest rates in the United States. Investors often try to speculate as to whether the Federal Reserve will raise or lower rates and by how much. Suppose a company conducts extensive interviews with financial analysts, and as a result, predicts that "the Fed" will increase rates by an average of 0.25 percentage points every six months for the foreseeable future. Which type of equation could be used to model the predicted interest rates over the next several years, assuming no other significant changes?

A) A linear equation

B) A quadratic equation

C) A polynomial equation

D) An exponential equation

8. Suppose a scatterplot shows a weak negative linear correlation. Which of the following statements is true?

A) The slope of the line of best fit will be a number less than −1.

B) The slope of the line of best fit will be a number between −1 and 0.

C) The data points will follow, but not closely, the line of best fit, which has a negative slope.

D) The data points will be closely gathered around the line of best fit, which has a negative slope.

Employee Sick Day Usage

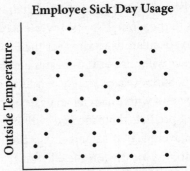

9. The Human Resources department of a company tracks employee sick day usage to see if there are patterns. One of the HR representatives decides to check employee sick day usage against outside temperature. He compiles the information for the employees' sick day usage and temperature in the scatterplot above. Which of the following conclusions can he draw based on this data?

A) There is no relationship between the number of sick days used by employees in general and outside temperature.

B) There is no relationship between the number of sick days used by this company's employees and outside temperature.

C) No conclusions can be drawn about the number of sick days used by this company's employees and outside temperature.

D) There is a relationship between, but not causation by, the number of sick days used by this company's employees and outside temperature.

Regression Line Type	r^2
Linear	0.881
Polynomial	0.983
Exponential	0.623

10. Terence is trying to decide what kind of regression line is appropriate for a set of data. He calculates the r^2 value for three different regression lines, which are summarized in the table above. Given this information, which type of regression line is LEAST appropriate for Terence's data set?

A) Exponential

B) Linear

C) Polynomial

D) It cannot be determined without knowing the data points used.

11. What is the y-value of the data point that has the highest percent error from the mean of the data shown in the scatterplot above?

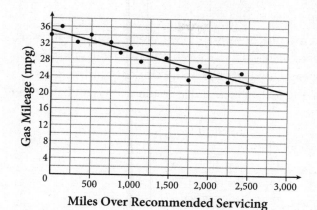

Miles Over Recommended Servicing

12. Research suggests that for any given make and model of car, the more miles the car is driven over the recommended miles between servicing, the worse gas mileage the car gets. Suppose a car dealership compiles data on a specific make and model of car and creates the scatterplot shown above. They then use the equation $y = -\dfrac{1}{200}x + 35$ to model the data.

Based on the information, how many miles per gallon could be expected if this particular car is driven 3,400 miles over the recommended miles between servicing?

Questions 13-15 refer to the following information.

Most chickens reach maturity and begin laying eggs at around 20 weeks of age. From this point forward, however, as the chicken ages, its egg production decreases. A farmer was given a flock of 100 chickens (all of which are the same age) and asked to measure daily egg output for the entire flock at random intervals starting at maturity until the chickens were 70 weeks old. The data is recorded in the scatterplot below and the line of best fit has been drawn.

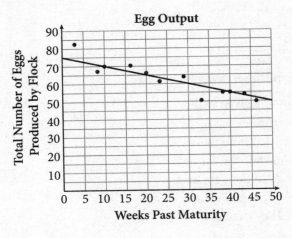

13. How many times did the farmer's data differ by at least 5 eggs from the number of eggs predicted by the line of best fit?

14. Based on the line of best fit, what is the predicted number of eggs that will be produced by the flock when it is 36 weeks past maturity?

15. A different farmer has a flock of 100 chickens that is producing 55 eggs at 20 weeks past maturity. He wants to calculate the percent error of this amount compared to that predicted by the line of best fit. What is the percent error? Round to the nearest whole percent and ignore the percent sign when entering your answer.

16. Which of the lines given by the following equations best fits the data shown above?

    A) $y = 0.5x - 1$

    B) $y = 0.5x + 1$

    C) $y = 1.5x + 1$

    D) $y = 1.5x - 1$

17. Scientists plotted data for two animal populations on a scatterplot: Population A, which they graphed along the x-axis, and Population B, which they graphed along the y-axis. The data showed a strong negative correlation. Which of the following statements is justified?

    A) The rise in Population A caused the decline in Population B.

    B) The decline in Population B caused the rise in Population A.

    C) Because the correlation is negative, there cannot be causation between the two populations.

    D) The rise in Population A is correlated to the decline in Population B, but causation is unknown.

18. If a scatterplot shows data points in the first quadrant of a coordinate plane that decrease very quickly at first, and then continue to decrease but at a much slower rate, then which of the following functions is the best model for the data?

    A) $f(x) = ax^2 + bx + c$, where $a > 0$

    B) $f(x) = ax^2 + bx + c$, where $a < 0$

    C) $f(x) = a(1 + r)^x$, where $r > 0$

    D) $f(x) = a(1 + r)^x$, where $r < 0$

19. When a baby is born, it has a small stomach and therefore only needs small amounts of breast milk or formula at a time. As the baby gets older, it needs more calories to grow, so it starts consuming more milk. At about 6 months, babies are able to eat solid foods and will get some of their calories from that. Accordingly, the child's need for milk starts to decrease, until it is no longer even necessary, which occurs at about one year of age. If data is collected on a typical infant's milk intake over the first year and plotted on a scatterplot, what kind of model would most likely match the data?

    A) Positive linear

    B) Negative linear

    C) Positive quadratic

    D) Negative quadratic

Extra Practice

20. Genji is compiling data relating snowfall to temperature where he lives. He records his data points in the form (temperature in degrees Fahrenheit, snowfall in inches). He plots the data on a scatterplot and draws a line of best fit, which indicates a strong negative correlation. He then remembers that his temperature gauge reads 10 degrees colder than it actually is. This means all of his data points are correct for the amount of snowfall, but the temperature readings are all lower than they should be. To correct the problem, he adds 10 degrees to all of his temperature readings and re-plots the data. What does this mean for his data?

A) The data is no longer necessarily correlated.

B) There is no change in the strength of correlation.

C) The rate of change for the line of best fit is less now.

D) The rate of change for the line of best fit is greater now.

21. A physics class is doing an experiment in order to write a function that models the height of a new super bouncy ball after each time that it bounces off the parking lot. The ball is thrown from the roof of the gym straight down to the parking lot pavement. The ball bounces to a height of 80 feet. The ball is allowed to bounce again, without anyone touching it, this time reaching a maximum height of 40 feet. It bounces again, reaching a height of 20 feet, and continues until it eventually stops bouncing. Which of the following functions could be used to model the height (H) of the ball after each time that it hits the pavement (b), until the ball stops bouncing.

A) $H(b) = \dfrac{80}{2^b}$

B) $H(b) = \dfrac{80}{2^{b-1}}$

C) $H(b) = 80 - 2b$

D) $H(b) = 80 - 2(b-1)$

22. The maximum value of the data shown in the scatterplot above occurs at $x = 25$. If the data is modeled using a quadratic regression and the correlation coefficient is 1.0, then what is the y-value when $x = 35$?

   A) 10

   B) 15

   C) 22

   D) 27

23. The figure above represents the trajectory of a t-shirt shot from a t-shirt cannon, from one end of a football field toward the other. The quadratic function $h(d) = -\dfrac{1}{10}(d-20)^2 + 45$ can be used to model the data. Based on the model, approximately how many feet farther did the t-shirt travel horizontally than it did vertically upward, assuming that no one caught the t-shirt and that it did not roll once it hit the ground? Round your answer to the nearest whole foot.

x	y
−3	−9.1
−1	−0.8
1	2.3
3	12.9
5	14.1
7	19.5

24. If Lynette uses a linear regression to model the data shown in the table, what is the correlation coefficient for the regression? Round your answer to two decimal places.

CHAPTER 7

Two-way Tables, Statistics, and Probability

CHAPTER OBJECTIVES

By the end of this chapter, you will be able to:

1. Use two-way tables to summarize data and calculate basic probabilities

2. Make inferences about population parameters based on sample data

3. Evaluate scenarios/reports to make inferences, justify conclusions, and determine appropriateness of data collection methods

SMARTPOINTS

Point Value	SmartPoint Category
50 Points	Statistics and Probability

TWO-WAY TABLES AND CHARTS/GRAPHS

Data can be represented in a multitude of ways. In this chapter we'll focus on a numerical approach (two-way table) and a pictorial one (chart or graph).

A two-way table is a table that contains data on two variables. This type of table can be used to make comparisons and determine whether relationships exist between the variables. You might see this data referred to as bivariate (two-variable) data.

If you're worried about having to learn a new topic, you need not be. You've likely encountered two-way tables in the past and just not known their formal name—if you've ever generated a spreadsheet, two-way tables should look familiar. Take a look at the following example that contains data on several antique book stores' sales to see what we mean.

	Bob's Books	Nalia's Novels	Tumiko's Tomes	Vladimir's Volumes	Total
Monday	14	7	15	12	48
Tuesday	8	13	15	13	49
Wednesday	10	13	12	14	49
Thursday	8	15	14	10	47
Friday	13	7	10	9	39
Total	53	55	66	58	232

Two-way tables contain a wealth of information: You can quickly determine how many books Nalia's Novels sold on Friday just by finding the appropriate cell in the table. You can also find quantities that are not explicitly written. For instance, you can determine numerous ratios: total books sold on Wednesday to total books sold on Thursday, Tumiko's Monday sales to Tumiko's total sales, and so on. You can also find percentages and probabilities.

> **✔ Note**
>
> Although two-way tables are generally easy to follow, they're also easy to misinterpret when you're in a rush. Take time to ensure that you've extracted the correct information for a given question.

Ratios and the like aside, you could be asked to make a prediction based on given data; that is, you'll need to extrapolate data to derive an answer. For instance, let's say the community in which these four shops are located has an annual antique appreciation week, and Nalia anticipates that her antique book sales will increase by 40% from the week for which the data is shown in the table. She sold 55 books that week, and 40% of 55 is 22. This means that if Nalia's prediction is true, she can expect to sell 55 + 22 = 77 books during antique appreciation week.

In addition to two-way tables, the SAT can also ask questions about charts and graphs, whether about the data itself or a prediction based on the data.

Take a look at the next few pages for sample questions involving two-way tables, charts, and graphs.

Use the table introduced at the beginning of this section to answer the following question.

1. Which of the four shops made the greatest fraction of its total sales on Tuesday?

   A) Bob's Books
   B) Nalia's Novels
   C) Tumiko's Tomes
   D) Vladimir's Volumes

Work through the Kaplan Method for Math step-by-step to solve this question. The following table shows Kaplan's strategic thinking on the left, along with suggested math scratchwork on the right.

Strategic Thinking	Math Scratchwork
Step 1: Read the question, identifying and organizing important information as you go Understanding what's being asked is the trickiest part of this question. You *do not* want the shop that sold the most books on Tuesday. Rather, you are solving for the shop whose Tuesday sales, as a fraction of the shop's total sales, were the greatest.	
Step 2: Choose the best strategy to answer the question Only two rows matter for this question: The Tuesday row and the Total row (*not* the Total column). Divide each shop's Tuesday sales by its total sales. The shop with the largest result is the correct answer. Because the fractions involve less manageable numbers, using a calculator to simplify the arithmetic is reasonable here. Nalia's Tuesday sales as a fraction of her total sales were highest.	need $\dfrac{Tuesday}{Total}$ B: $\dfrac{8}{53} \approx 0.1509$ N: $\dfrac{13}{55} \approx 0.2364$ T: $\dfrac{15}{66} \approx 0.2273$ V: $\dfrac{13}{58} \approx 0.2241$
Step 3: Check that you answered the *right* question You've identified the shop that had the highest fraction of its sales on Tuesday, so you're done. Choice (B) is correct.	

> ✔ **Expert Tip**
>
> If you're adept at quantitative comparison of fractions, you can omit the decimal conversion calculations (and save some time).

The question below requires the table used for question 1.

2. What fraction of the books sold on Monday, Wednesday, and Friday were sold at Tumiko's Tomes and Vladimir's Volumes?

   A) $\dfrac{9}{29}$

   B) $\dfrac{11}{32}$

   C) $\dfrac{9}{17}$

   D) $\dfrac{18}{31}$

Work through the Kaplan Method for Math step-by-step to solve this question. The following table shows Kaplan's strategic thinking on the left, along with suggested math scratchwork on the right.

Strategic Thinking	Math Scratchwork
Step 1: Read the question, identifying and organizing important information as you go You need to find how many books Tumiko and Vladimir sold on Monday, Wednesday, and Friday as a fraction of the total number of books all four shops sold on those days.	
Step 2: Choose the best strategy to answer the question Use the Monday, Wednesday, and Friday rows and the Tumiko, Vladimir, and Total columns (*not* the Total row). Add the number of books Tumiko and Vladimir sold on these three days, and then repeat the process with the total number of books all four shops sold on these days. Combine these values into a fraction.	Mon + Wed + Fri for T & V: (15 + 12) + (12 + 14) + (10 + 9) = 72 Mon + Wed + Fri total: 48 + 49 + 39 = 136 $\dfrac{72}{136}$

Strategic Thinking	Math Scratchwork
Step 3: Check that you answered the _right_ question	
None of the answer choices match the fraction you found, but don't panic. You just need to simplify. The GCF of 72 and 136 is 8, so the most simplified form of the fraction is $\frac{9}{17}$. Select (C) and you're done.	$\frac{72}{136} = \frac{9}{17}$

Now that you've seen how to use two-way tables, keep reading for more about what you can learn from them.

STATISTICS AND PROBABILITY

While there are entire high school and college courses devoted to the study of statistics, the SAT will (fortunately) only test you on a few basic statistical concepts. If you aren't a statistics fan, now is a great time to rethink your position: Statistics is a part of almost every major in college and can be used in a variety of careers. Using an example from high school, let's take a look at the sort of concepts the SAT expects you to be familiar with.

Suppose you took five tests in a world history class and earned scores of 85, 92, 85, 80, and 96. Descriptions of six fundamental statistics figures you can find for this data set follow:

- **Mean (also called average):** The sum of the values divided by the number of values. For your history class, the mean of your test scores is $\frac{85+92+85+80+96}{5} = \frac{438}{5} = 87.6$. At most schools, that's a B or B+.

- **Median:** The value that is in the middle of the set _when the values are arranged in ascending order_. The test scores in ascending order are 80, 85, 85, 92, and 96, making the median 85. Be careful: The SAT could give you a set of numbers that is not in order. Make sure you properly arrange them before determining the median.

- **Mode:** The value that occurs most frequently. The score that appears more than any other is 85 (twice vs. once), so it is the mode. If more than one value appears the most often, that's okay: A set of data can have multiple modes.

- **Range:** The difference between the highest and lowest values. From finding the median you know the highest and lowest scores are 96 and 80, respectively; so the range is 96 – 80 = 16.

- **Standard deviation:** A measure of how far a typical data point is from the mean. A low standard deviation means most values in the set are fairly close to the mean; a high standard deviation means there is much more spread in the data set. On the SAT, **You will need to know what standard deviation is, but you won't have to calculate it.**

- **Margin of error:** A description of the maximum expected difference between a true value for a data pool (e.g., mean) and a random sampling from the data pool. A lower margin of error is achieved by increasing the size of the data pool. **As with standard deviation, you will need to know what a margin of error is on the SAT, but you won't be asked to calculate one.**

Mean, median, and mode are referred to as measures of central tendency because they can be used to represent a typical value in the data set. Range, standard deviation, and margin of error are measures of spread because they show how much the data in a set vary.

> ✔ **Note**
>
> To find the median of a data set that contains an even number of terms, arrange the terms in ascending order, then find the average of the two middle terms.

On Test Day, you might also be asked to analyze the shape of data. The shape of a data set can be either symmetric or skewed (asymmetric). Many data sets have a head, where many data points are clustered in one area, and tails, where the number of data points slowly decreases to 0. Examining the tails will help you describe the shape of a data set. A data set is skewed in the direction of its longer tail.

Symmetric

The data are evenly spread out.
mean ≈ median

Skewed to the Left

The tail is longer on the left.
mean < median

Skewed to the Right

The tail is longer on the right.
mean > median

> ✔ **Expert Tip**
>
> When you have a group of evenly spaced terms (e.g., 2, 4, 6, 8, 10, 12), the mean and median will be identical. With this data set, the mean is
>
> $$\frac{2+4+6+8+10+12}{6} = \frac{42}{6} = 7, \text{ and}$$
>
> the median is $\frac{6+8}{2} = \frac{14}{2} = 7$. In addition, you can find the mean of a group of evenly spaced terms by taking the mean of the highest and lowest:
>
> $$\frac{12+2}{2} = \frac{14}{2} = 7.$$

It is possible to determine a data mean from a bar graph (also called a histogram). Suppose a teacher made a bar graph of student performance on a recent test like the one shown here.

To find the mean of these data, first determine the sum of terms and number of terms and then use the average formula. We see from the graph that 3 students scored 60, 9 scored 65, 11 scored 70, and so on. Add these up to make the sum of terms; then divide by the total number of students, which is the number of terms:

$$\frac{3(60)+9(65)+11(70)+13(75)+18(80)+15(85)+12(90)+8(95)+2(100)}{3+9+11+13+18+15+12+8+2} = \frac{7265}{91} = 79.8$$

The mean score on this test was 79.8.

A concept closely linked to statistics is probability. **Probability** is a fraction or decimal comparing the number of desired outcomes to the number of total possible outcomes. For instance, if you have a full deck of playing cards and want to know the probability of drawing an ace, you would compute

$\frac{\text{\# aces}}{\text{\# cards}} = \frac{4}{52} = \frac{1}{13} \approx 0.077$. To find the probability that an event will *not* happen, subtract the

probability that the event will happen from 1. In the ace example, this would be

$1 - \frac{\text{\# aces}}{\text{\# cards}} = 1 - \frac{4}{52} = \frac{48}{52} = \frac{12}{13} \approx 0.923$.

✔ **Note**

$$\text{Probability} = \frac{\text{\# desired outcomes}}{\text{\# total possible outcomes}}$$

You can also find the probability for a series of events. If you're asked for the probability of drawing an ace without replacement (the card does not go back in the deck) followed by a red nine,

multiply the probability of the first event by that of the second: $\frac{\text{\# aces}}{\text{\# cards}} \times \frac{\text{\# red nines}}{\text{\# cards} - 1} = \frac{4}{52} \times \frac{2}{51} = $

$\frac{8}{2652} \approx 0.003$.

"With replacement" means the item chosen, in this case a card, is returned to the original group (here, the deck). The number of possible outcomes in the denominator will stay constant. "Without replacement" indicates the item is not returned; the number of possible outcomes will change to reflect the new possible outcome count.

With a two-way table, you can find the probability that a randomly selected data value (be it a person, object, etc.) will fit a certain profile. In addition, you might be asked to calculate a conditional probability. Conditional probability questions are easy to spot, as the word *given* is usually present. The following is a two-way table summarizing a survey on water preference.

	Bottled	Carbonated	Tap	Total
Female	325	267	295	887
Male	304	210	289	803
Total	629	477	584	1,690

If asked for the probability of randomly selecting a female who prefers bottled water from all the participants of the original survey for a follow-up survey, you would calculate it using the same general formula as before: $\dfrac{\text{\# female bottled}}{\text{\# total}} = \dfrac{325}{1690} = \dfrac{5}{26} \approx 0.192$.

If asked for the probability of randomly selecting a female for the follow-up survey, given that the chosen participant prefers bottled water, the setup is a little different. The clause starting with "given" indicates your number of possible outcomes is the total participants who prefer bottled water, which is 629 and not the grand total of 1,690. Your calculation is now $\dfrac{\text{\# female bottled}}{\text{\# total bottled}} = \dfrac{325}{629} \approx 0.517$.

Conversely, if you need to find the probability of selecting someone who prefers bottled water for the follow-up survey, given that the chosen participant is female, the new number of possible outcomes is the female participant total (887). The calculation becomes $\dfrac{\text{\# bottled}}{\text{\# total females}} = \dfrac{325}{887} \approx 0.366$.

Take a look at the next few pages for some test-like questions involving two-way tables and probability.

Use the table below about a survey related to favorite video game genres for a group of high school students to answer the two questions that follow. Assume that every student had a favorite video game genre and that each student could only select one favorite.

	Freshmen	Sophomores	Juniors	Seniors	Total
First-person shooters	144	122	134	115	515
Strategy games	126	140	152	148	566
Role-playing games	120	117	153	148	538
Indie games	110	114	63	98	385
Total	500	493	502	509	2004

3. The research group that conducted the survey wants to select one sophomore and one senior at random for a follow-up survey. What is the probability that both students selected will prefer a type of video game other than strategy games?

A) $\dfrac{140}{493} + \dfrac{148}{509}$

B) $\dfrac{140}{493} \times \dfrac{148}{509}$

C) $\dfrac{353}{493} + \dfrac{361}{509}$

D) $\dfrac{353}{493} \times \dfrac{361}{509}$

There's no scratchwork for this question, but Kaplan's strategic thinking follows. Follow along as we reason through the question to get the correct answer.

Strategic Thinking
Step 1: Read the question, identifying and organizing important information as you go
You need to determine the probability that a sophomore and a senior selected at random will both prefer a video game genre other than strategy games.

Strategic Thinking
Step 2: Choose the best strategy to answer the question
The answer choices are unsimplified expressions, which means that you don't need to find the actual probability—you just need to set up the correct expression.
The word "both" in the question stem signals that you need to find the probability that one event AND another will both happen. To find the probability that more than one event will occur, multiply the individual probabilities together. This means that A and C, which feature addition rather than multiplication, are incorrect.
You can determine which of the remaining answer choices is correct without any number crunching. Of the 493 sophomores, 140 prefer strategy games. Choice B contains the probability $\frac{140}{493}$, which means it's incorrect—you want the probability of picking students who *don't* prefer strategy games.
Step 3: Check that you answered the *right* question
By process of elimination, you know that (D) must be correct.

The following question pertains to the table used in question 3.

4. The research group that conducted the survey wishes to see if there is a connection between the time a student spends playing video games and that student's grade point average (GPA). The school at which the initial survey was conducted was in Dallas, Texas; and the group decides to include three additional Dallas high schools in the follow-up study. Data produced from the follow-up study showed a moderately strong negative correlation between time spent playing video games and GPA. Based on these findings, which of the following is a valid conclusion?

    A) There is an association between the amount of time a high school student in Dallas spends playing video games and his/her GPA.

    B) There is an association between the amount of time a high school student anywhere in Texas spends playing video games and his/her GPA.

    C) An increase in the amount of time a high school student in Dallas spends playing video games causes a decrease in his/her GPA.

    D) An increase in the amount of time a high school student anywhere in Texas spends playing video games causes a decrease in his/her GPA.

There's no scratchwork for this question, but Kaplan's strategic thinking follows. Follow along as we reason through the question to get the correct answer.

Strategic Thinking
Step 1: Read the question, identifying and organizing important information as you go
You're asked to identify the valid conclusion (in other words, the true statement).
Step 2: Choose the best strategy to answer the question
Carefully examine each answer choice. You're told that there is a moderately strong correlation between time spent playing video games and GPA. However, because the study utilized students in Dallas only, no conclusions about the entire Texas high school population can be drawn. Eliminate B and D. To determine which of the two remaining answer choices is correct, carefully read each choice and compare it to the question stem. Although there is a correlation between time spent playing video games and GPA, the study did not conclude that one causes the other. Eliminate C.
Step 3: Check that you answered the *right* question
Choice (A) matches your analysis.

✔ Expert Tip

Look for key details—such as the study's population, location, and any results derived—in questions like this one. These details will help you quickly solve for the correct answer.

5. A fair coin is flipped five times. What is the probability that at least four of the five flips will be heads?

   A) $\frac{3}{16}$

   B) $\frac{3}{10}$

   C) $\frac{7}{10}$

   D) $\frac{13}{16}$

Work through the Kaplan Method for Math step-by-step to solve this question. The following table shows Kaplan's strategic thinking on the left, along with suggested math scratchwork on the right.

Strategic Thinking	Math Scratchwork
Step 1: Read the question, identifying and organizing important information as you go You need to find the probability that at least four out of five coin flips will land on heads.	

Strategic Thinking	Math Scratchwork
Step 2: Choose the best strategy to answer the question	
Use the fundamental probability formula: $$\text{probability} = \frac{\text{number of desired outcomes}}{\text{number of possible outcomes}}.$$	$p = \dfrac{\text{number desired}}{\text{number possible}}$
There are five coin flips. Each coin flip has two possible outcomes. $2^5 = 32$ possible outcomes.	# possible: $2 \times 2 \times 2 \times 2 \times 2 = 2^5 = 32$
You can find the number of outcomes that have at least four heads by writing out all of the possibilities. Work systematically to ensure you don't miss anything.	# desired: *HHHHH* *HHHHT* *HHHTH* *HHTHH* *HTHHH* *THHHH*
There are six desired outcomes that have at least four heads.	6 desired
Combine these two quantities in a fraction to represent the probability that at least four of the five coin flips will land on heads.	$\dfrac{6}{32} = \dfrac{3}{16}$
Step 3: Check that you answered the *right* question	
Of the 32 possible outcomes for five coin flips, six of these contain at least 4 heads. Choice (A) is equivalent to this finding and is therefore correct.	

Following is a sample Multi-Part Math question involving the concepts you've learned in this chapter. Remember to tackle this question one step at a time, and follow the Kaplan Method for Multi-Part Math Questions.

Questions 6 and 7 refer to the following information.

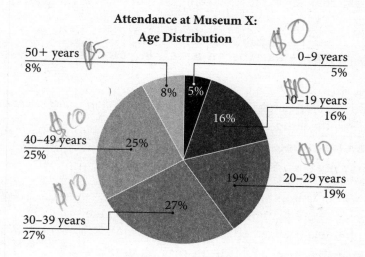

Attendance at Museum X:
Age Distribution

The pie graph above shows the age distribution of visitors to Museum X in 2014. Visitors aged 0-9 years get into Museum X for free, visitors aged 50 and older pay $5 for admission, and everyone else pays $10.

6. If 553 people aged 20 years and older visited Museum X in 2014, then approximately how many people visited Museum X in 2014?

7. Based on the pie graph and the result from the previous question, how much revenue did Museum X collect from tickets sold to people aged 40 and older in 2014?

Work through the Kaplan Method for Multi-Part Math Questions step-by-step to solve this question (for a review of this Method, see chapter 5). The following table shows Kaplan's strategic thinking on the left, along with suggested math scratchwork on the right.

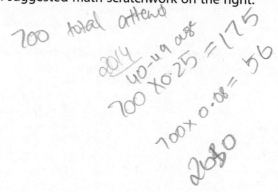

Strategic Thinking	Math Scratchwork
Step 1: Read the first part of the question, looking for clues The infographic shows the age distribution of visitors to Museum X in 2014. From the accompanying text you also learn the ticket prices based on age.	0-9: free 10-49: $10 50+: $5
Step 2: Identify and organize the information you need You're asked to find the total number of visitors to Museum X in 2014, given that 553 of the visitors were aged 20 and up.	need total # attendees
Step 3: Based on what you know, plan your steps to navigate the first part You know the *number* of visitors aged 20 and up. If you find the accompanying percent, you can figure out the total using the three-part percent formula you learned previously.	_____ % of total is 553
Step 4: Solve, step-by-step, checking units as you go You could add the percentages for the 20-29, 30-39, 40-49, and 50+ categories, but there's a faster route. Look at the sections of the pie graph for the two groups that are *not* 20 or older: 0-9 and 10-19. Those two groups represent 5% and 16% of the total, respectively. Subtract these values from 100% to find what percent of visitors were aged 20 and up. To find the total number of visitors, plug what you know into the three-part percent formula.	% not aged 20+: 5% + 16% = 21% % aged 20+: 100% − 21% = 79% total × 0.79 = 553 total = $\dfrac{553}{0.79}$ = 700
Step 5: Did I answer the *right* question? The question asks for the total number of visitors in 2014, which is 700.	

Part 1 is complete. Now on to Step 6: Repeat for the other parts. Kaplan's strategic thinking is on the left, along with suggested math scratchwork on the right.

Strategic Thinking	Math Scratchwork
Step 1: Read the second part of the question, looking for clues From part 1, you know the total number of visitors in 2014; nothing new is given in part 2.	*700 total attendees*
Step 2: Identify and organize the information you need Part 2 asks for the revenue from tickets sold to people aged 40 and older. The total number of visitors, which you learned from part 1, will help calculate this figure.	*$ from aged 40+: ?*
Step 3: Based on what you know, plan your steps to navigate the second part Because you already know the total number of visitors, you can calculate the number of visitors aged 40-49 and 50+ using the percentages given in the pie graph.	*find # of 40-49, 50+*
Step 4: Solve, step-by-step, checking units as you go Calculate the number of attendees in the 40-49 and 50+ age groups by taking 25% of 700 and 8% of 700, respectively. The 40-49 group paid $10 per ticket, and the 50+ group paid $5 per ticket. Use these facts to determine the revenue generated from these groups.	*# aged 40-49:* *700 x 0.25 = 175* *# aged 50+:* *700 x 0.08 = 56* *175 ppl paid $10/ticket* *56 ppl paid $5/ticket* *175 x $10 = $1,750* *56 x $5 = $280* *$1,750 + $280 = $2,030*
Step 5: Did I answer the *right* question? $2,030 was collected from the 40-49 and 50+ age groups; grid in 2030.	

As you saw, statistics and graphical analysis have powerful real-world applications.

✔ Note

It's easy to misread questions like #7 and use a part of the infographic other than the one you need. Take time to ensure that you know what you need to find.

WORD PROBLEMS

You're already well versed in deciphering SAT word problems, but word problems involving probability sometimes require you to use different skills. You'll need to use your analytical abilities to develop inferences and predictions, draw and justify logical conclusions, and evaluate the appropriateness of data collection techniques. Sometimes you'll need to consult a provided two-way table as you did for some earlier questions, and in other cases you'll just study the question stem to gather pertinent information. Perhaps the best part of these questions is the fact that they often require little or no actual mathematical calculation!

Here is a test-like sample question.

8. A local softball league has male and female members. If m is the average age of the males, f is the average age of the females, a is the overall average age, and 65 percent of the league's members are male, then which one of the following statements must be true about m, f, and a?

    A) If $m < f$, then $a > \dfrac{m+f}{2}$.

    B) If $m > f$, then $a < \dfrac{m+f}{2}$.

    C) If $m < f$, then $a < \dfrac{m+f}{2}$.

    D) $a = \dfrac{m+f}{2}$

There's no scratchwork for this question, but Kaplan's strategic thinking follows. Follow along as we reason through the question to get the correct answer.

Strategic Thinking
Step 1: Read the question, identifying and organizing important information as you go
The question asks you to identify the statement that is true. You're told that 65% of the league's members are male, and you're given the definition of three variables: m, f, and a.

Strategic Thinking

Step 2: Choose the best strategy to answer the question

Don't panic over the limited amount of information. Examine the answer choices to see if you can spot any useful patterns. Each answer choice makes a comparison between a (the overall average age) and $\frac{m+f}{2}$. If the male and female member counts were equal, then the overall average age would simply be the average of the male and female average ages, or $\frac{m+f}{2}$. However, because there are more males than females in the group, the overall average must be closer to the average male age than to the average female age. You don't know which of m or f is greater, so use a number line to visualize this information. There are two ways to do so. The first assumes that $m < f$; the second assumes that $m > f$:

The only choice consistent with the visualization is (C): when m is less than f, the value of a is less than the average age of both groups.

Step 3: Check that you answered the *right* question

Choice (C) matches your analysis.

✔ **Note**

For questions like this, think about what information is given or not given, the conclusion(s) you can draw from either, and answers you can eliminate based on said conclusion(s).

Now you'll have a chance to try a couple test-like problems in a scaffolded way. See if you can fill in the missing pieces and solve for the correct answer without a full explanation.

We've provided some guidance, but you'll need to fill in the missing parts of explanations or the step-by-step math in order to get to the correct answer. Don't worry—after going through the worked examples at the beginning of this section, these problems should be completely doable.

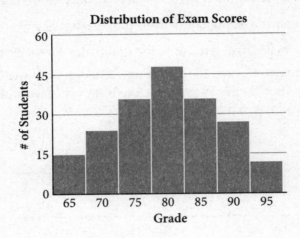

9. A history professor observes that the scores of a recent 20-question multiple choice exam are normally distributed as shown in the histogram above. However, she later discovers that 25% of the results were omitted from the distribution. Of the omitted scores, 80% are greater than what the professor thought the mean was; the rest are less. Assuming all new data points fit in the current histogram range, which of the following is most likely to occur upon adding the new scores to the data?

   A) The data will be skewed to the right.

   B) The data will be skewed to the left.

   C) The median will decrease.

   D) The range will decrease.

The following table can help you structure your thinking as you go about solving this more involved problem. The Kaplan strategic thinking is provided, as are bits of structured scratchwork. If you're not sure how to approach a question like this, start at the top and work your way down.

Strategic Thinking	Math Scratchwork
Step 1: Read the question, identifying and organizing important information as you go *What is the question asking you to do?* You need to determine the effect of adding extra data points, most of which are above the mean, to what was previously a normal (symmetric) distribution.	

Strategic Thinking	Math Scratchwork
Step 2: Choose the best strategy to answer the question *What will the distribution look like after the new data are added?* The question states that most of the new scores are above the mean. Draw a rough sketch of what the new distribution will look like. *What can you learn from the answer choices?* The choices mention skew, median, and range. Think about the effect the additions to the data set will have on each of these.	post-addition: direction of skew: _____ median shift: _____ range shift: _____
Step 3: Check that you answered the *right* question *Which answer contains an effect you found?* If you chose (B), congrats! You're correct.	_____

Now try two Multi-Part Math questions.

The following information pertains to questions 10 and 11.

	1	2	3	4	5	Total
Worker Placement	5	17	24	10	5	61
Bidding	3	12	28	8	3	54
Area Control	3	10	30	14	2	59

A small boutique sells board games online. The boutique specializes in worker placement, bidding, and area control board games. Any customer who purchases a game is invited to rate the game on a scale of 1 to 5. A rating of 1 or 2 is considered "bad," a rating of 3 is considered "average," and a rating of 4 or 5 is considered "good." The table above shows the distribution of average customer ratings of the board games sold by the boutique. For example, 24 of the worker placement games sold by the boutique have an average rating of 3.

10. According to the table, what percent of all the board games sold by the boutique received a rating of "bad"? Round your answer to the nearest tenth of a percent and ignore the percent sign.

11. The boutique decides to stop selling 50% of the board games that received a rating of "bad" to make room for promising new stock. Assuming no significant changes in ratings in the foreseeable future, what should the difference be between the percentages of board games with a rating of "bad" before and after this change? Round your answer to the nearest tenth of a percent and ignore the percent sign.

The following table can help you structure your thinking as you go about solving this more involved problem. The Kaplan strategic thinking is provided, as are bits of structured scratchwork. If you're not sure how to approach a question like this, start at the top and work your way down.

Strategic Thinking	Math Scratchwork
Step 1: Read the first part of the question, looking for clues *What useful information are you given?* You're provided a chart with data on the average ratings of board games sold by a boutique.	
Step 2: Identify and organize the information you need *What does part 1 ask you to find?* You're asked to find the percent of games that received a rating of "bad", meaning a rating of 1 or 2.	find # games with "bad" rating
Step 3: Based on what you know, plan your steps to navigate the first part *How many games received a rating of 1 or 2?* Examine the chart carefully, identifying the necessary data from each type of game. *What's the next step?* Add the figures to get the total number of games that received a rating of "bad."	worker placement 1: _____ games 2: _____ games bidding 1: _____ games 2: _____ games area control 1: _____ games 2: _____ games total: _____
Step 4: Solve, step-by-step, checking units as you go *How do you find the percent of games that received a rating of "bad"?* Use the values in the table to find the total number of games in these groups. Write the "bad" *part* over the *total* game count, and then convert to a percent.	_____ × 100 = _____%

Strategic Thinking	Math Scratchwork
Step 5: Did I answer the *right* question? *What percent of the games in these groups received a rating of "bad"?* If you got 28.7, you're correct!	_____

> ✔ **Note**
>
> You might see unusual jargon (such as "worker placement" and "area control" in this question) on Test Day; don't fret. This question only tests your ability to correctly interpret a two-way table and complete appropriate calculations.

Great job! Repeat for the second part. Kaplan strategic thinking is on the left, and bits of scratchwork guidance are on the right.

Strategic Thinking	Math Scratchwork
Step 1: Read the second part of the question, looking for clues *Any new information presented?* From part 1 you know the number (and percent) of games that received a rating of "bad."	# games with "bad" rating: _____; = _____ %
Step 2: Identify and organize the information you need *What does this question ask you to find? Will anything from the previous question help here?* You're asked for the difference between the percentages of games that received a "bad" rating before and after 50% of such games are removed from the store's inventory. Your answer from the previous question is key to this calculation.	"bad" % pre-removal: _____ % "bad" % post-removal: ?
Step 3: Based on what you know, plan your steps to navigate the second part *How do you determine the new "bad" percentage after the removal?* You know the store wants to get rid of 50% of the games that received a "bad" rating. You already know the current number with a "bad" rating, so finding the new "bad" game count is straightforward. Once there, determine the new "bad" percentage and subtract that from the original.	_____ × old "bad" count = new "bad" count → convert to % old "bad" % − new "bad" % = answer

Strategic Thinking	Math Scratchwork
Step 4: Solve, step-by-step, checking units as you go	
After the 50% reduction in "bad" games, how many games should have a "bad" rating? Reduce the original "bad" game count by 50%.	_____ % × old "bad" count = new "bad" count _____ × _____ = _____
What percent of remaining games will have a "bad" rating after the clearance?	new "bad" %: _____ × 100 = _____ %
Divide your new "bad" count by the total game count. Remember that when the number of "bad" games decreases, the total count decreases by the same amount. Write your results using a couple of decimal points to minimize rounding errors. *What's the difference between the two percents?* Subtract the new "bad" percent from the old "bad" percent.	old "bad" % – new "bad" %: _____ % – _____ % = _____ %
Step 5: Did I answer the *right* question?	
How do the two percents compare? Did you get 11.9? If so, you're absolutely correct!	% change: _____

Nice work! Now test what you've learned by taking a brief quiz.

Now that you've seen the variety of ways in which the SAT can test you on two-way tables, statistics, and probability, try the following questions to check your understanding. Give yourself 5 minutes to tackle the following 4 questions. Make sure you use the Kaplan Method for Math (and the Kaplan Method for Multi-Part Math Questions where appropriate) as often as you can. Remember, you want to emphasize speed and efficiency in addition to simply getting the correct answer.

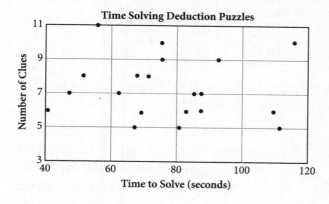

Time Solving Deduction Puzzles

Number of Clues

Time to Solve (seconds)

	Ceren	Han	Billy
Run 1	8.3	8.5	8.4
Run 2	7.7	8.0	8.0
Run 3	7.1	8.5	7.5
Run 4	6.6	7.8	9.0
Run 5	8.0	8.1	7.5
Run 6	6.6	7.5	7.2
Mean Score	7.38	8.07	7.93
Standard Deviation	0.73	0.39	0.67

12. Rolff recently completed a book of 20 deduction puzzles. The scatterplot above shows the time it took Rolff to solve a puzzle versus the number of clues it had. If a puzzle is selected at random from the book, what is the probability that it had fewer than six clues, took Rolff fewer than 100 seconds to solve, or both?

A) 10%

B) 15%

C) 85%

D) 90%

13. Ceren, Han, and Billy participated in a snowboarding competition. The scores for each of their six qualifying runs are in the table above. According to the data, which of the following is a valid conclusion?

A) Ceren had the smallest mean score, so her performance was the least consistent.

B) Han had the smallest standard deviation, so his performance was the most consistent.

C) Ceren had the largest standard deviation, so her performance was the most consistent.

D) Billy had the largest range in scores, so his performance was the least consistent.

Use the following information to answer questions 14 and 15.

	Scarves	Pairs of Mittens	Hats	Pairs of Socks	Total
Wilhelmina	7	2	24	19	52
Emanuel	8	2	9	14	33
Jose Raul	3	4	18	10	35
Alexandra	15	1	9	9	34
Total	33	9	60	52	154

Wilhelmina, Emanuel, Jose Raul, and Alexandra are in a knitting club. The table above shows the quantity of several different items each person has knitted over the lifetime of the club.

14. The four club members plan to knit hats to sell for Spirit Week at their college. They surveyed a group of students regarding their hat pattern preferences and found that 60% of those surveyed prefer solid-colored hats, 22% prefer stripes, and 18% prefer stars. The club anticipates that 1,800 students will each buy one hat. If the ratios in the table remain constant for Spirit Week hat production, how many solid-colored hats will Wilhelmina and Alexandra be responsible for knitting?

15. The knitting club plans to embroider a small, hidden emblem on the interior of 20% of the hats they make for Spirit Week; anyone who finds this emblem on their hat will win a free scarf. The four members will split up the making of the free scarves according to the ratios in the table. For how many winning hats and scarf prizes will Emanuel and Jose Raul be responsible?

Answers and Explanations for this chapter begin on page 872.

EXTRA PRACTICE

Required	Recommended
Questions 1–8	Questions 9–29

You may use your calculator for all questions in this section.

Questions 1 and 2 refer to the following information.
Numerous health studies have found that people who eat breakfast are generally healthier and weigh less than people who skip it. Although scientists are not certain as to the reason, it is generally believed that breakfast jumpstarts the metabolism and encourages a more regular consumption of calories throughout the day, instead of the calories being consumed in two big meals at lunch and dinner. The following table shows the results of a study related to this topic.

Breakfast Study Results

	Breakfast ≤1 time per week	Breakfast 2-4 times per week	Breakfast 5-7 times per week	Total
Within Healthy Weight Range	6	15	36	57
Outside Healthy Weight Range	38	27	9	74
Total	44	42	45	131

1. What percent of the participants who were outside a healthy weight range ate breakfast one or fewer times per week?

    A) 29.00%
    B) 51.35%
    C) 56.49%
    D) 86.36%

2. A large company that provides breakfast for all its employees wants to determine how many of them are likely to be within a healthy weight range, given that all the employees take advantage of the free breakfast all 5 weekdays. If the company has 3,000 employees, and assuming the participants in the study were a good representative sample, about how many of the employees are likely to be within a healthy weight range?

    A) 825
    B) 1,030
    C) 1,900
    D) 2,400

3. A shoe manufacturing company is thinking about introducing a new product designed to help athletes jump higher. The company conducts a marketing study by asking people outside community gymnasiums and sporting goods stores whether they would purchase such a product. Approximately 40% of 3,000 respondents said they would purchase these shoes over regular tennis shoes. Based on the study, the company concludes that 40% of shoe store customers shopping for tennis shoes would purchase their new product. Why is this not a valid conclusion?

A) The study was too small to draw any conclusions about the larger population.

B) The data from the survey does not represent the whole population because it was not conducted across the whole country.

C) The data from the survey likely underestimates the number of people interested in the new product because it only compared the new product to tennis shoes, not all types of shoes.

D) The data from the survey likely overestimates the number of people interested in the new product because the survey targeted respondents already interested in athletics.

Questions 4 and 5 refer to the following information.
At most colleges, students receive letter grades, which correspond to a GPA score, rather than a numerical grade, such as 92. The following figure shows the distribution of grades and corresponding GPA scores among students in a history class.

4. What is the mean history GPA for this class of students?

   A) 2.0

   B) 2.5

   C) 2.6

   D) 3.0

5. College professors sometimes use statistics to summarize class performance so that students will have an idea of how they are doing relative to the rest of the class. If this professor wants to report that at least half of the grades were a 3.0 or above, which measure of center should she use to describe the results?

   A) Mean

   B) Mode

   C) Mode or median

   D) Standard deviation

Questions 6 and 7 refer to the following information.

The amount of glucose, or sugar, in a person's blood is the primary indicator of diabetes. When a person fasts (doesn't eat) for eight hours prior to taking a blood sugar test, his/her glucose level should be below 100 mg/dL. A person is considered at risk for diabetes, but is not diagnosed as diabetic, when fasting glucose levels are between 100 and 125. If the level is above 125, the person is considered to have diabetes. The following table shows the ages and glucose levels of a group of diabetes study participants.

Diabetes Study Results

Age Group	<100 mg/dL	100-125 mg/dL	>125	Total
18-25	9	22	17	48
26-35	16	48	34	98
36-45	19	35	40	94
Older than 45	12	27	21	60
Total	56	132	112	300

6. According to the data, which age group had the smallest percentage of people with a healthy blood sugar level?

   A) 18-25

   B) 26-35

   C) 36-45

   D) Older than 45

7. Based on the table, if a single participant is selected at random from all the participants, what is the probability that he or she will be at risk for diabetes and be at least 36 years old?

   A) $\dfrac{7}{60}$

   B) $\dfrac{11}{25}$

   C) $\dfrac{31}{77}$

   D) $\dfrac{31}{150}$

8. On a used vehicle lot, 50% of the vehicles are cars, $\frac{3}{4}$ of which have automatic transmissions. Of the cars with automatic transmissions, $\frac{1}{3}$ have leather interiors. If a vehicle is chosen from the lot at random, what is the probability that it will be a car with an automatic transmission and a leather interior?

A) $\frac{1}{8}$

B) $\frac{1}{6}$

C) $\frac{1}{4}$

D) $\frac{1}{3}$

9. A United States senator is running for reelection and wants to know what the most important issue to the greatest number of people who might vote for him is. If his campaign hires a company to collect data by conducting a survey, which of the following samples should the company use?

A) United States voters

B) United States citizens

C) Voters in the senator's district

D) Citizens in the senator's district

10. An electronics manufacturer wants to know if customers would be interested in a detachable keyboard for their tablets and if so, what the most important features would be. The manufacturer partners with an electronics store to include copies of the survey with every purchase at that store for one week. Which of the following best explains why this random sample is unlikely to be a good representative sample of tablet owners' preferences for a detachable keyboard?

A) One week is likely not enough time to get a large enough sample.

B) Most people won't bother to send in the survey, which is likely to skew the results.

C) There is no way to verify whether the responders to the survey actually own a tablet.

D) The survey is biased because it was conducted through an electronics store, not the general population.

Reduction of Debt Schedule

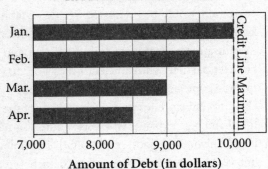

Amount of Debt (in dollars)

Final Trivia Round

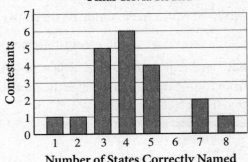

Number of States Correctly Named

11. A credit score is a number used by financial institutions to determine a person's financial health. One of the factors that affects a person's credit score is the percentage of credit available that he or she is currently utilizing. For example, a person with a credit line of $1,000 who has debt of $900 is utilizing 90% of his or her available credit. Ideally, a person should use no more than 25% of available credit. Charlie has been trying to pay down his debt to increase his credit score. Suppose Charlie has a credit line of $10,000. The graph above shows the amount of debt he is currently carrying on that credit line each month. If he continues to pay down this debt at the same rate, how many months from when Charlie reached his credit line maximum will it take him to reach 25% utilization?

A) 8

B) 15

C) 20

D) 24

12. In the final round of a trivia competition, contestants were asked to name as many states that begin with the letter M as they could in 15 seconds. The bar graph shows the number of states the contestants were able to name. How many contestants participated in the final round of this competition?

A) 6

B) 8

C) 14

D) 20

Appliance Sales

Number Sold

13. An appliance salesman sets a goal to sell an average of 6 appliances per day for the first two weeks of his new job. The dot plot shows the number he sold each day during the first 13 days. What is the minimum number of appliances he must sell on the 14th day in order to reach his goal?

A) 5

B) 6

C) 7

D) 8

14. Muscles, a membership-only gym, is hoping to open a new branch in a small city in Pennsylvania that currently has no fitness centers. According to their research, approximately 12,600 residents live within driving distance of the gym. Muscles sends out surveys to a sample of 300 randomly selected residents in this area (all of whom respond) and finds that 40 residents say they would visit a gym if one was located in their area. Based on past survey research, Muscles estimates that approximately 30% of these respondents would actually join the gym if they opened one in the area. Based on this information and the results of the sample survey, about how many residents should Muscles expect to join its new branch?

A) 134

B) 504

C) 1,680

D) 3,780

Quarterly Profits

	Branch A	Branch B	Branch C	Branch D
Q1	4.1	7.4	8.0	5.4
Q2	3.6	5.2	3.7	6.2
Q3	5.0	4.5	4.9	4.8
Q4	4.9	6.3	5.9	5.6
$\bar{x}$	4.4	5.85	5.625	5.5
s	0.67	1.27	1.82	0.58

15. A company affected by a downturn in the economy decides to close one of its four branches. The table shows each branch's quarterly profits in millions of dollars for 2014, along with the mean ($\bar{x}$) and the standard deviation (s) of the data. The accounting department recommends that the company's Board of Directors close either the store with the lowest average quarterly profits or the store that performs the least consistently. According to the data in the table, which branches will the accounting department recommend for closure to the board?

A) Branches A or C

B) Branches A or D

C) Branches B or C

D) Branches B or D

Country Music Festival Attendees

	Attendees
Entertainer A (Day 1)	1,280
Entertainer B (Day 2)	1,120
Entertainer C (Day 3)	1,600

16. Three well-known entertainers performed at a country music festival, one on each day. Tickets sold were valid for the full three-day period, and ticket holders were permitted to enter and leave as desired. The table above shows the number of people who attended each day of the festival. The host of the festival wants to know which performer was the most popular. If the host defines a performer's popularity rating as the ratio of the number of attendees on that performer's day to the combined number of attendees across all three days, then what was the most popular performer's popularity rating?

Questions 17 and 18 refer to the following information.

When people sleep, they experience various types of brain activity. Scientists have classified these types of activity into four sleep stages: 1, 2, 3, and 4 (also known as REM). Stage 3 is the only stage considered to be deep sleep. A person goes to a sleep clinic to have his/her sleeping brainwaves analyzed. A technician monitored the person's brainwaves in 15-minute intervals, for 8 continuous hours, and categorized them into one of the four stages. The bar graph below shows the results of the one-night study.

8-Hour Sleep Study Results

Sleep Stage

Each bar = 15 minutes

17. Based on the graph, how many minutes did the patient spend in non-deep sleep over the course of the entire night?

18. If one 15-minute time period is chosen at random, what is the probability that the patient was in deep sleep during that time?

Questions 19 and 20 refer to the following information.

The following table shows the number of houses in a development. The table categorizes the houses by type (single-family or townhouse) and by the number of bedrooms.

Development Houses

	2 Br	3 Br	4 Br	Total
Single-Family	5	19	34	58
Townhouse	24	42	30	96
Total	29	61	64	154

19. The homeowner's association partners with a local daycare center. The HOA has agreed to allow the daycare center to advertise in the development using flyers. In general, families with children typically reside in single-family homes or townhouses. These dwellings usually have 3 or more bedrooms. The daycare center has a limited budget and plans to concentrate its marketing efforts on only those homes and townhouses that have 3 or more bedrooms. What percent of the houses in the development should receive the flyer? Round to the nearest whole percent and ignore the percent sign when entering your answer.

20. In addition to sending out flyers, the daycare center decides to send out invitations for a free day of daycare, but determines that it would be too expensive to do this for all of the family residences in the development. Instead, it decides to market this benefit only to the two categories in the table with the most houses. If a house that already received a flyer is chosen at random to receive the second stage of the marketing, what is the probability that the house belongs to one of these two groups? Enter your answer as a decimal.

Questions 21 and 22 refer to the following information.

As part of its market research, a company sent out a survey to see how much consumers would be willing to pay for a certain product. The survey distinguished between a store brand version of the product and a brand name version, and people participating in the survey only received questions about one of the versions. A summary of the survey results is shown in the following bar graph.

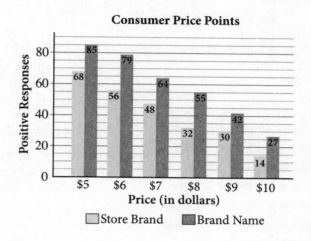

21. On average, how many more cents are consumers willing to pay for the brand name version of the product than the store brand version? Round your answer to the nearest cent.

22. If a consumer is chosen at random from all of the respondents, what is the probability that the consumer is willing to pay at least $8 for the product?

Cookies Baked

	Chocolate Chip	Oatmeal Raisin	Total
With Nuts		40	
Without Nuts			104
Total			186

23. Most animals give birth during a general time of year. This is because animals naturally breed so that their young will be born at the time of year when there will be an adequate food supply. The figure shows the number of live births of a jackrabbit native to California over the course of Year X. Based on the data, which of the following would be an appropriate conclusion?

A) In general, rabbits give birth during the spring months.

B) In general, rabbits give birth during the summer months.

C) In general, Californian jackrabbits give birth during the spring months.

D) In general, Californian jackrabbits give birth during the summer months.

24. A baker makes 186 cookies. Some are chocolate chip and some are oatmeal raisins, and both kinds are made with and without nuts, as shown in the table above. Because they are more popular, the baker made $\frac{2}{3}$ of the cookies chocolate chip. If a chocolate chip cookie is chosen at random, what is the probability that it will have nuts?

A) $\dfrac{21}{93}$

B) $\dfrac{21}{62}$

C) $\dfrac{41}{93}$

D) $\dfrac{21}{41}$

25. A bottled water company conducts a survey to find out how many bottles of water people consume per day. If a representative sample of 500 people is chosen without bias from a population estimated to be 50,000, which of the following accurately describes how the mean of the sample data relates to the estimated mean of the entire population?

A) The mean of the sample data is equal to the estimated mean of the population.

B) The mean of the sample data cannot be used to estimate the mean of the much larger population.

C) The mean of the sample data should be multiplied by 100 to get the estimated mean of the population.

D) The mean of the sample data should be multiplied by 1,000 to get the estimated mean of the population.

26. A fertilizer company conducted an experimental study to determine which of five compounds is most effective relative to helping soil retain nutrients. If, after application of the compounds, the fertilizer company only tested for nitrogen and potassium, which of the following is a valid conclusion?

A) The compound that is found to be the most effective will work for all nutrients in the soil.

B) The compound that is found to be the most effective will work only for nitrogen and potassium.

C) The study is clearly biased and therefore not significant relevant to determining which compound is most effective.

D) The study will only be able to produce results concerning the effects of the compounds on nitrogen and potassium.

Distribution of Fish Breeds

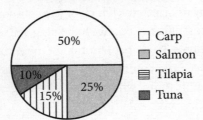

- ☐ Carp
- ▨ Salmon
- ▤ Tilapia
- ▰ Tuna

History Majors Declared at College X

Year	Number of History Majors
2010	225
2011	287
2012	162
2013	240
2014	s

27. Mercury poisoning is a dangerous overload of mercury within the body. A major source of mercury poisoning is consuming fish that contain mercury. Certain fish are more prone to having higher levels of mercury than others. The pie chart shows the distribution of four breeds of fish at a hatchery. The hatchery has approximately 6,000 fish. A biologist from the Centers for Disease Control and Prevention randomly tests 5% of each breed of fish for mercury content. Her findings are shown in the following table.

Mercury Content Test Results

Breed	Number of Fish with Dangerous Mercury Levels
Carp	11
Salmon	6
Tilapia	5
Tuna	8

Based on the biologist's findings, if a single salmon is randomly selected from those that were tested, what is the probability that this particular fish would have a dangerous mercury level?

A) 0.001

B) 0.004

C) 0.02

D) 0.08

28. The table above shows the number of history majors declared each year at a certain college from 2010 to 2014. If the median number of history majors declared for the five years was 225, what is the greatest possible value of s?

A) 161

B) 225

C) 239

D) 288

29. A Writer's Association sponsored a nation-wide convention for nonfiction writers. The association received 1,650 responses from members indicating that they were planning to attend the convention. The association sent a randomly generated follow-up email to 250 writers who were planning to attend and asked them about lunch preferences. Seventy-four said salads, 22 said pizza, 30 said pasta salad, 29 said grilled chicken, and the rest said sandwiches. Out of all of the writers planning to attend, about how many could the association expect to want sandwiches for lunch at the convention?

Passport to Advanced Math

BY THE END OF THIS UNIT, YOU WILL BE ABLE TO:

1. Simplify, solve, and rewrite equations involving polynomials, radicals, and exponents
2. Solve functions questions graphically and algebraically
3. Combine multiple functions
4. Solve quadratic equations with and without a calculator
5. Connect quadratic equations to features of a parabola

CHAPTER 8

Exponents, Radicals, Polynomials, and Rational Expressions

CHAPTER OBJECTIVES

By the end of this chapter, you will be able to:

1. Simplify, rewrite, and solve equations involving radicals and/or exponents
2. Perform arithmetic operations on polynomials
3. Simplify polynomial expressions

SMARTPOINTS

Point Value	SmartPoint Category
70 Points	Exponents

INTRODUCTION TO EXPONENTS AND RADICALS

We often turn to our calculators to solve difficult radical and exponent problems, especially in math-intensive classes. However, being too calculator dependent can cost you time and points on the SAT. Further, on the SAT, many radical and exponent problems are structured in such a way that your calculator can't help you, even if it is allowed.

This chapter will review many algebraic and arithmetic rules that you may have learned at some point but likely haven't used in a while. This chapter will reacquaint you with the formulas and procedures you'll need to simplify even the toughest expressions and equations on the SAT. We'll start with exponents.

Questions involving exponents often look intimidating, but when you know the rules governing them, you'll see that there are plenty of shortcuts. First, it's important to understand the anatomy of a term with an exponent. This term is comprised of two pieces: a base and an exponent (also called a power). The base is the number in larger type and is the value being multiplied by itself. The exponent, written in superscript, shows you how many times to multiply the base by itself.

$$Base \Rightarrow 3^4 \Leftarrow Exponent \text{ is the same as } 3 \times 3 \times 3 \times 3$$

The following table lists the rules you'll need to master to handle any exponent question you'll see on the SAT.

Rule	Example
When multiplying two terms with the same base, add the exponents.	$a^b \times a^c = a^{(b+c)} \rightarrow 4^2 \times 4^3 = 4^{2+3} = 4^5$
When dividing two terms with the same base, subtract the exponents.	$\dfrac{a^b}{a^c} = a^{(b-c)} \rightarrow \dfrac{4^3}{4^2} = 4^{3-2} = 4^1$
When raising a power to another power, multiply the exponents.	$(a^b)^c = a^{(bc)} \rightarrow (4^3)^2 = 4^{3 \times 2} = 4^6$; $(2x^2)^3 = 2^{1 \times 3} x^{2 \times 3} = 8x^6$
When raising a product to a power, apply the power to all factors in the product.	$(ab)^c = a^c \times b^c \rightarrow (2m)^3 = 2^3 \times m^3 = 8m^3$
Any term raised to the zero power equals 1.	$a^0 = 1 \rightarrow 4^0 = 1$
A base raised to a negative exponent can be rewritten as the reciprocal raised to the positive of the original exponent.	$a^{-b} = \dfrac{1}{a^b}$; $\dfrac{1}{a^{-b}} = a^b \rightarrow 4^{-2} = \dfrac{1}{4^2}$; $\dfrac{1}{4^{-2}} = 4^2$

Different things happen to different kinds of numbers when they are raised to powers greater than 1. Take a look at the following number line and table for a summary.

Quantity	Even Exponent Result	Odd Exponent Result	Example
w	positive, absolute value increases	negative, absolute value increases	$(-5)^2 = 25; (-5)^3 = -125$
-1	always 1	always -1	n/a
x	positive, absolute value decreases	negative, absolute value decreases	$\left(-\frac{1}{2}\right)^2 = \frac{1}{4}; \left(-\frac{1}{2}\right)^3 = -\frac{1}{8}$
0	always 0	always 0	n/a
y	positive, absolute value decreases	positive, absolute value decreases	$\left(\frac{1}{4}\right)^2 = \frac{1}{16}; \left(\frac{1}{4}\right)^3 = \frac{1}{64}$
1	always 1	always 1	n/a
z	positive, absolute value increases	positive, absolute value increases	$3^2 = 9; 3^3 = 27$

1. Which of the following expressions is equal to $\dfrac{z^{570} - z^{480}}{2z^{30}}$?

A) $\dfrac{z^{540} - z^{450}}{2}$

B) $\dfrac{z^{60}}{2}$

C) z^{30}

D) $\dfrac{z^{19} - z^{16}}{2}$

You might be tempted to try Picking Numbers to handle this question. However, if you try to plug in a number such as 2 for z, you'll quickly run into a problem, as most graphing calculators cannot handle numbers that large (2^{570} is over 150 places long and would not fit on a TI-84 calculator screen).

Instead, work through the Kaplan Method for Math and your knowledge of exponent rules to solve this question step-by-step. The following table shows Kaplan's strategic thinking on the left, along with suggested math scratchwork on the right.

Strategic Thinking	Math Scratchwork
Step 1: Read the question, identifying and organizing important information as you go *What do you need to find?* You need the simplified form of the expression.	
Step 2: Choose the best strategy to answer the question Exponent rules will help you. Be mindful that because the two z terms in the numerator have different exponents and are being subtracted, you cannot combine them into one term. Break the fraction into two pieces before applying exponent rules. Because your initial answer doesn't match any of the answer choices, you'll need to combine the two fractions back into one to reveal the correct answer.	$$\frac{z^{570} - z^{480}}{2z^{30}} = \frac{z^{570}}{2z^{30}} - \frac{z^{480}}{2z^{30}}$$ $$\frac{z^{570}}{2z^{30}} - \frac{z^{480}}{2z^{30}} = \frac{z^{570-30}}{2} - \frac{z^{480-30}}{2}$$ $$\frac{z^{540}}{2} - \frac{z^{450}}{2} = \frac{z^{540} - z^{450}}{2}$$
Step 3: Check that you answered the *right* question You've simplified as much as possible, so you're done. The correct choice is (A).	

2. Simplify the expression $2(-4j^3k^{-4})^{-3}$.

A) $-\dfrac{k^{12}}{512j^9}$

B) $-\dfrac{k^{12}}{32j^9}$

C) $-\dfrac{j^9}{32k^{12}}$

D) $-\dfrac{k^{12}}{128j^9}$

Use the Kaplan Method for Math to solve this question, working through it step-by-step. The following table shows Kaplan's strategic thinking on the left, along with suggested math scratchwork on the right.

Strategic Thinking	Math Scratchwork
Step 1: Read the question, identifying and organizing important information as you go You're asked to simplify the given expression.	
Step 2: Choose the best strategy to answer the question Use your exponent rules to quickly find the answer. Move the expression in parentheses to the denominator to make the exponent outside the parentheses positive. Once you've moved the parenthetical expression, distribute the exponent to each term it contains. You're not done yet. Look for terms you can cancel, and eliminate any remaining negative exponents by appropriately moving their respective terms.	$2(-4j^3k^{-4})^{-3}$ $\dfrac{2}{(-4j^3k^{-4})^3}$ $-\dfrac{2}{64j^9k^{-12}}$ $-\dfrac{k^{12}}{32j^9}$
Step 3: Check that you answered the *right* question Choice (B) matches your simplified expression.	

3. What is the value of $\dfrac{3^5 \times 27^3}{81^3}$?

$$\frac{3^5 \times 27^3}{81^3} \qquad \frac{3^5 \times (3^3)^3}{(3^4)^3}$$

$$\frac{3^5 \times 3^9}{3^{12}} = \frac{3^{14}}{3^{12}}$$

$$\boxed{3^2}$$

Work through the Kaplan Method for Math step-by-step to solve this question. The following table shows Kaplan's strategic thinking on the left, along with suggested math scratchwork on the right.

Strategic Thinking	Math Scratchwork
Step 1: Read the question, identifying and organizing important information as you go You're asked to find the value of the expression presented, which means you'll need to simplify it.	
Step 2: Choose the best strategy to answer the question Simplify the expression using exponent rules. You can't combine the bases or the exponents of the expression as written. However, $27 = 3^3$ and $81 = 3^4$, so rewrite the numerator and denominator to reflect these relationships. Add the exponents of the numbers in the numerator. Once finished, subtract the exponent of the number in the denominator.	$\dfrac{3^5 \times 27^3}{81^3}$ $\dfrac{3^5 \times (3^3)^3}{(3^4)^3} = \dfrac{3^5 \times 3^9}{3^{12}} = \dfrac{3^{14}}{3^{12}} = 3^2$
Step 3: Check that you answered the *right* question After simplification is complete, you'll get 9 as the correct answer.	9

✔ **Note**

A calculator could probably handle numbers the size of those in the previous question, but what if the question is in the non-calculator section? Knowing the exponent rules for Test Day is critical.

RADICALS

A radical is essentially a fractional exponent. You can think of addition and subtraction (and likewise multiplication and division) as opposites, and an exponent and radical are another opposite pair. Whenever you raise a term to the nth power, taking the nth root will return the original term. For instance, three to the fourth power is $3^4 = 3 \times 3 \times 3 \times 3 = 81$; take the fourth root of 81 (that is, determine the number that can be multiplied by itself four times to get 81) to get the original term: $\sqrt[4]{81} = \sqrt[4]{3 \times 3 \times 3 \times 3} = 3$.

Radicals can also be intimidating at first, but remembering the basic rules for radicals can make them much easier to tackle. The following table contains all the formulas you'll need to know to achieve "radical" success on the SAT!

Rule	Example
When a fraction is under a radical, you can rewrite it with two radicals: one containing the numerator and the other containing the denominator.	$\sqrt{\dfrac{a}{b}} = \dfrac{\sqrt{a}}{\sqrt{b}} \rightarrow \sqrt{\dfrac{4}{9}} = \dfrac{\sqrt{4}}{\sqrt{9}} = \dfrac{2}{3}$
Two factors under a single radical can be rewritten as separate radicals multiplied together.	$\sqrt{ab} = \sqrt{a} \times \sqrt{b} \rightarrow \sqrt{75} = \sqrt{25} \times \sqrt{3} = 5\sqrt{3}$
A radical can be rewritten using a fractional exponent.	$\sqrt{a} = a^{\frac{1}{2}}, \sqrt[3]{a} = a^{\frac{1}{3}} \rightarrow \sqrt{289} = 289^{\frac{1}{2}}$
When you have a fractional exponent, the numerator is the power to which the base is raised, and the denominator is the root to be taken.	$a^{\frac{b}{c}} = \sqrt[c]{a^b} \rightarrow 5^{\frac{2}{3}} = \sqrt[3]{5^2}$
When a number is squared, the original number can be positive or negative, but the square root of a number can only be positive.	If $a^2 = 81$, then $a = \pm 9$, BUT $\sqrt{81} = 9$ *only*

✔ **Note**

Note the difference between the printed square root sign and taking the square root yourself as you solve an equation. By definition, when printed, the square root of a number must be positive, but when you take the square root to solve for a variable, you will have two solutions: one positive, and one negative. For instance, by definition $\sqrt{4} = 2$. However, if you are solving $x^2 = 4$, x will have two solutions, so $x = \pm 2$.

Fractions in simplest form will never contain radicals in their denominators, but it's sometimes better to keep them through intermediate steps to make your math easier (and sometimes the radical is eliminated along the way). Once all manipulations are complete, the fraction can be rationalized to remove a remaining radical from the denominator by multiplying both the numerator and denominator by that same radical.

1. Original Fraction	2. Rationalization	3. Intermediate Math	4. Resulting Fraction
$\dfrac{x}{\sqrt{5}}$	$\dfrac{x}{\sqrt{5}} \times \dfrac{\sqrt{5}}{\sqrt{5}}$	$\dfrac{x\sqrt{5}}{\sqrt{5 \times 5}} = \dfrac{x\sqrt{5}}{\sqrt{25}} = \dfrac{x\sqrt{5}}{5}$	$\dfrac{x\sqrt{5}}{5}$
$\dfrac{14}{\sqrt{x^2+2}}$	$\dfrac{14}{\sqrt{x^2+2}} \times \dfrac{\sqrt{x^2+2}}{\sqrt{x^2+2}}$	$\dfrac{14\sqrt{x^2+2}}{\sqrt{(x^2+2)(x^2+2)}}$ $= \dfrac{14\sqrt{x^2+2}}{\sqrt{(x^2+2)^2}}$	$\dfrac{14\sqrt{x^2+2}}{x^2+2}$

Sometimes you'll have an expression such as $2+\sqrt{5}$ as a denominator. To rationalize this, multiply by its conjugate (found by negating the second term; in this case, the conjugate is $2-\sqrt{5}$).

As a rule of thumb, you likely won't see a radical in the denominator of an SAT question's answer choice, so you'll need to be comfortable with rationalizing and either eliminating them or moving them to the numerator.

> **✔ Note**
>
> When you rationalize a denominator, you are not changing the value of the expression; you're only changing the expression's appearance. Notice that in each case, you're multiplying by 1 (the multiplicative identity), because the numerator and the denominator of the fraction are the same.

Ready to take on a test-like question that involves radicals? Take a look at the following:

4. If $-1 < x < 0$ and a is a negative integer, then which of the following must be false?

A) $\sqrt{ax} = ax$

B) $\sqrt{ax} < ax$

C) $\left| x^3 \right| > |x|$

D) x^2 and x have opposite signs

There's no scratchwork for this question, but Kaplan's strategic thinking follows. Follow along as we reason through the question to get the correct answer.

Strategic Thinking
Step 1: Read the question, identifying and organizing important information as you go
You need to identify the statement that is always false.
Step 2: Choose the best strategy to answer the question
Because you're looking for the statement that is false for all values of a and x, all you need is one example of a statement being true to eliminate an answer choice. Start with the statements that appear easiest to verify first; D and C look pretty manageable. The square of a negative fraction is always positive, so D is always true; eliminate it. As you raise a negative fraction to higher powers, the absolute value of the result will decrease. This contradicts C regardless of the negative fraction you pick, so it is always false.
Step 3: Check that you answered the *right* question
Choice (C) is the only statement that is always false and is, therefore, correct.

✔ **Note**

Look at the Answers & Explanations for this chapter to see examples that confirm A and B are incorrect. Remember, you don't have to verify every answer choice unless you're unsure of the one you selected.

$-\dfrac{6}{3} = 2$

5. Which of the following represents $\dfrac{\sqrt[6]{x^{10}y^{12}}}{\sqrt[3]{x^{5}y^{6}}}$ written in simplest form?

   A) 1

   B) 2

   C) $x^2 y^3 \sqrt{x}$

   D) $xy^2 \sqrt[3]{x^2}$

$\dfrac{x^{\frac{10}{6}}\, y^{\frac{12}{6}}}{x^{\frac{5}{3}}\, y^{\frac{6}{3}}}$ OH!!

Work through the Kaplan Method for Math step-by-step to solve this question. The following table shows Kaplan's strategic thinking on the left, along with suggested math scratchwork on the right.

Strategic Thinking	Math Scratchwork
Step 1: Read the question, identifying and organizing important information as you go You must simplify the given expression.	
Step 2: Choose the best strategy to answer the question Attempting to combine the radicals as written is incorrect and will lead you to a trap answer. Rewrite each variable with a fractional exponent instead. When simplifying fractional exponents, remember "power over root." Once you have simplified, subtract the exponents for the x terms, and then repeat for the y terms.	$\dfrac{\sqrt[6]{x^{10}y^{12}}}{\sqrt[3]{x^{5}y^{6}}} = \dfrac{x^{\frac{10}{6}}\, y^{\frac{12}{6}}}{x^{\frac{5}{3}}\, y^{\frac{6}{3}}}$ $x^{\frac{10}{6}-\frac{5}{3}}\, y^{\frac{12}{6}-\frac{6}{3}} = x^{\frac{10}{6}-\frac{10}{6}}\, y^{\frac{12}{6}-\frac{12}{6}}$ $x^{0} y^{0}$
Step 3: Check that you answered the *right* question Any quantity raised to the zero power is equal to 1, which means (A) is correct.	$x^{0} y^{0} = 1$

POLYNOMIALS

By now you're used to seeing equations, exponents, and variables; another important topic you are sure to see on the SAT is polynomials. A polynomial is an expression comprised of variables, exponents, and coefficients, and the only operations involved are addition, subtraction, multiplication, division (by constant(s) *only*), and non-negative integer exponents. A polynomial can have one or multiple terms. The following table contains examples of polynomial expressions and non-polynomial expressions.

Polynomial	$23x^2$	$\dfrac{x}{5} - 6$	$y^{11} - 2y^6 + \dfrac{2}{3}xy^3 - 4x^2$	47
Not a Polynomial	$\dfrac{10}{z} + 13$	$x^3 y^{-6}$	$\dfrac{1}{x^{\frac{1}{2}}}$	$\dfrac{4}{y-3}$

✔ **Note**

Remember that constants such as 47 are considered polynomials; this is the same as $47x°$. Also, keep in mind that division by a constant is allowed, but division by a variable is not.

Identifying like terms is an important skill that will serve you well on Test Day. You can combine like terms as you did with linear expressions and equations (x terms with x terms, constants with constants) to simplify. To have like terms, the types of variables present and their exponents must match. For example, $2xy$ and $-4xy$ are like terms; x and y are present in both, and their corresponding exponents are identical. However, $2x^2y$ and $3xy$ are not like terms because the exponents on x do not match. When combining like terms, follow the order of operations as always, being particularly careful when distributing negative signs.

Like terms	$7x$, $3x$, $5x$	3, 15, 900	xy^2, $7xy^2$, $-2xy^2$
Not like terms	3, x, x^2	$4x$, $4y$, $4z$	xy^2, x^{2y}, $2xy$

A polynomial can be named based on its **degree**. For a single-variable polynomial, the degree is the highest power on the variable. For example, the degree of $3x^4 - 2x^3 + x^2 - 5x + 2$ is 4 because the highest power of x is 4. For a multi-variable polynomial, the degree is the highest sum of the exponents on any one term. For example, the degree of $3x^2y^2 - 5x^2y + x^3$ is 4 because the sum of the exponents in the term $3x^2y^2$ equals 4.

On Test Day you might be asked about the nature of the **zeros** or **roots** of a polynomial. Simply put, zeros are the x-intercepts of a polynomial's graph, which can be found by setting each factor of the polynomial equal to 0. For example, in the polynomial equation $y = (x + 6)(x - 2)^2$, you would have three equations: $x + 6 = 0$, $x - 2 = 0$, and $x - 2 = 0$ (because $x - 2$ is squared, that binomial appears twice in the equation). Solving for x in each yields -6, 2, and 2; we say that the equation has two zeros: -6 and 2. Zeros can have varying levels of **multiplicity**, which is the number of times that a factor appears in the polynomial equation. In the example above, $x + 6$ appears once in the equation, so its corresponding zero (-6) is called a **simple zero**. Because $x - 2$ appears twice in the equation, its corresponding zero (2) is called a **double zero**.

You can recognize the multiplicity of a zero from the polynomial's graph as well. Below is the graph of $y = (x + 6)(x - 2)^2$.

When a polynomial has a simple zero (multiplicity 1) or any zero with an odd multiplicity, its graph will cross the x-axis (as it does at $x = -6$ in the graph above). When a polynomial has a double zero (multiplicity 2) or any zero with an even multiplicity, it just touches the x-axis (as it does at $x = 2$ in the graph above).

Use your knowledge of like terms to solve the following test-like example.

6. If y is a polynomial equation that has a simple zero at $x = 4$ and a triple zero at $x = -4$, which of the following could be the factored form of y?

    A) $y = (x + 4)(2x - 8)^3$ $x = 4$

    B) $y = (x - 4)(3x + 12)$

    C) $y = 3(x + 4)(2x - 8)$

    D) $y = (2x + 8)^3(x - 4)$

There's no scratchwork for this question, but Kaplan's strategic thinking follows. Follow along as we reason through the question to get the correct answer.

Strategic Thinking
Step 1: Read the question, identifying and organizing important information as you go You need to determine which equation could be the factored form of the equation that contains the zeros described.
Step 2: Choose the best strategy to answer the question Adjectives such as "simple" and "triple" indicate how many times a zero's corresponding binomial is repeated in its polynomial equation. This means that you need one binomial raised to the first power and one raised to the third. You can eliminate B and C, both of which lack the third power exponent. The remaining answer choices each contain two binomial expressions: one with an exponent of 1 (remember, if no exponent is written, it is assumed to be 1) and one with an exponent of 3. Quick mental math reveals that both have 4 and −4 as zeros. You need the equation that has the 3 exponent on the binomial that gives $x = -4$ and the 1 exponent on the binomial that gives $x = 4$. Only (D) meets this requirement.
Step 3: Check that you answered the _right_ question Choice (D) is the only answer choice that satisfies the criteria in the question.

Adding and subtracting polynomials are straightforward operations, but what about multiplying and dividing them? These operations are a little tougher but (fortunately) are far from impossible.

Multiplying polynomials is just like multiplying ordinary numbers except you want to pay special attention to distribution and combining like terms. Take the expression $(3x^3 + 5x)(2x^2 + x - 17)$ as an example. All you need to do is distribute both terms in the first set of parentheses to each term in the second set. Distribute the $3x^3$ first, then repeat with $5x$:

$$
\begin{array}{ccc}
1 & 2 & 3 \\
\end{array}\qquad\qquad
\begin{array}{ccc}
4 & 5 & 6 \\
\end{array}
$$

$$(3x^3 + 5x)\quad(2x^2 + x - 17)\qquad (3x^3 + 5x)\quad(2x^2 + x - 17)$$

$$6x^5 + 3x^4 - 51x^3 \qquad\qquad 10x^3 + 5x^2 - 85x$$

The following table shows the product of each step.

1	2	3
$3x^3 \bullet 2x^2 = 6x^5$	$3x^3 \bullet x = 3x^4$	$3x^3 \bullet -17 = -51x^3$
4	**5**	**6**
$5x \bullet 2x^2 = 10x^3$	$5x \bullet x = 5x^2$	$5x \bullet -17 = -85x$

All that's left to do now is write out the expression and combine any like terms.

$$6x^5 + 3x^4 - \mathbf{51x^3} + \mathbf{10x^3} + 5x^2 - 85x$$

$$6x^5 + 3x^4 - 41x^3 + 5x^2 - 85x$$

RATIONAL EXPRESSIONS

A rational expression is simply a ratio (or fraction) of polynomials. In other words, it is a fraction with a polynomial as the numerator and another polynomial as the denominator. The rules that govern fractions and polynomials also govern rational expressions, so if you know these well, you'll be in good shape when you encounter one on Test Day.

There are a few important tidbits to remember about rational expressions; these are summarized here. They are also true for rational equations.

- For an expression to be rational, the numerator and denominator must both be polynomials.
- Like polynomials, rational expressions are also designated certain degrees based on the term with the highest variable exponent sum. For instance, the expression $\dfrac{1-2x}{3x^2+3}$ has a first-degree numerator and a second-degree denominator.
- Because rational expressions by definition can have polynomial denominators, they will often be undefined for certain values. For example, the expression $\dfrac{x-4}{x+2}$ is defined for all values of x except −2. This is because when $x = -2$, the denominator of the expression is 0, which would make the expression undefined.
- Factors in a rational expression can be cancelled when simplifying, but under no circumstances can you do the same with individual terms. Consider, for instance, the expression $\dfrac{x^2 - x - 6}{x^2 + 5x + 6}$.

  Many students will attempt to cancel the x^2, x, and 6 terms to give $\dfrac{1-1-1}{1+5+1} = \dfrac{-1}{7}$, which is *never* correct. Don't even think about trying this on Test Day.
- Like fractions, rational expressions can be proper or improper. A proper rational expression has a lower-degree numerator than denominator $\left(\text{e.g., } \dfrac{1-x}{x^2+3}\right)$, and an improper one has a

  higher-degree numerator than denominator $\left(\text{e.g., } \dfrac{x^2+3}{1-x}\right)$. The latter can be simplified using polynomial long division.

> **✔ Note**
>
> For those who are curious, the correct way to simplify $\dfrac{x^2 - x - 6}{x^2 + 5x + 6}$ is to factor, which you'll learn about
>
> in chapter 11. For now, know that this equals $\dfrac{(x+2)(x-3)}{(x+2)(x+3)}$. Cancel the $x + 2$ factors to get $\dfrac{(x-3)}{(x+3)}$.

7. Which of the following is equal to the expression $\dfrac{27m^4n^3 + 6mn^2}{18m^2n + 81m^5n^2}$, given $m \neq 0$ and $n \neq 0$?

   A) $\dfrac{n^2}{3m^2}$

   B) $\dfrac{3}{2}m^2n^2 + \dfrac{2}{27m^4}$

   C) $\dfrac{n}{3m}$

   D) $\dfrac{m}{3n}$

Work through the Kaplan Method for Math step-by-step to solve this question. The following table shows Kaplan's strategic thinking on the left, along with suggested math scratchwork on the right.

Strategic Thinking	Math Scratchwork
Step 1: Read the question, identifying and organizing important information as you go You're asked to identify the expression that equals the one given in the question.	
Step 2: Choose the best strategy to answer the question Start by looking for ways to simplify the expression; factoring should come to mind. You can factor a number and at least one m and one n out of both the numerator and denominator. Several terms cancel each other at this point. Note that the expressions in parentheses are identical by the commutative property of addition, so they can be cancelled. The GCF of the numerator and denominator is $3mn$; factor it out and cancel it to get your final expression.	$\dfrac{27m^4n^3 + 6mn^2}{18m^2n + 81m^5n^2} \rightarrow \dfrac{3mn^2(9m^3n+2)}{9m^2n(2+9m^3n)}$ $\dfrac{3mn^2}{9m^2n} \rightarrow \dfrac{3mn(n)}{3mn(3m)}$ $\dfrac{n}{3m}$

Strategic Thinking	Math Scratchwork
Step 3: Check that you answered the *right* question	
You've properly simplified the expression, so your work for this question is complete. Choice (C) is correct.	$\dfrac{n}{3m}$

You'll notice that the question indicated $m \neq 0$ and $n \neq 0$. This is because either of these values will create a denominator of 0, which makes the entire expression undefined. This becomes particularly important when dealing with rational equations, as they can have what are called **extraneous solutions**. Extraneous solutions are numbers that are found algebraically but do not solve the original equation (such as when they generate 0 in a denominator). Plug the solutions that you find back into the original equation to make sure that the denominator does not become 0.

> ✔ **Note**
>
> Extraneous solutions are solutions that cause the entire expression to become undefined. Look out for zeros in denominators and negatives under square roots.

MODELING REAL-WORLD APPLICATIONS USING POLYNOMIAL, RADICAL, AND RATIONAL EQUATIONS

Sometimes the test writers want to test your simplifying prowess by converting an expression into a "useful" form, as standard form is not always the most practical for use.

Let's say you and your friends want to enjoy a brisk fall day by going apple picking. To go apple picking, you must rent a basket for $20, and you'll be charged an additional $0.35 for each apple you pick. On top of that, a 9% sales tax will be added to your final bill. We could represent this scenario with the following equation:

$$c = 1.09 \times (0.35a + 20)$$

In this situation, c is the cost of your apple-picking experience and a is the number of apples you pick. You'll notice the 1.09 out in front of the parentheses ensures that sales tax is applied to your entire purchase, not just the apples or the rental. Now suppose you're asked to determine the true price of each additional apple; that is, how much more money will one extra apple cost you? We can't get that by just glancing at the equation, but distributing the 1.09 will help. When we do this, we arrive at a different equation for the same apple-picking experience:

$$c = 0.3815a + 21.8$$

Although this equation isn't as elegant or intuitive as our initial equation, it is much more useful for answering the question at hand. Now we can see how sales tax affects our fixed costs (basket rental) and our variable costs (each additional apple). The only term that matters here is the one that depends on the number of apples: Each additional apple will cost about $0.38 when tax is included.

Try the more challenging example that follows.

8. Laura and Donnie are researching mortgage options for a home purchase. They plan to apply for a 30-year $300,000 loan with a 3.375% annual interest rate, which they will pay off in monthly installments. They can calculate their monthly payment (m) using the formula $m = \dfrac{Pr}{1-(1+r)^{-N}}$, where P is the initial principal balance, r is the monthly interest rate expressed as a decimal, and N is the number of monthly payments that will be made over the life of the mortgage. How much will Laura and Donnie pay in mortgage payments over a six-month period? Round your answer to the nearest dollar.

Use the Kaplan Method for Math to solve this question, working through it step-by-step. The table below shows Kaplan's strategic thinking on the left, along with suggested math scratchwork on the right.

Strategic Thinking	Math Scratchwork
Step 1: Read the question, identifying and organizing important information as you go *What are you being asked to do here?* You're asked to find the amount of money Laura and Donnie will pay over six months for their mortgage.	

Strategic Thinking	Math Scratchwork
Step 2: Choose the best strategy to answer the question	initial annual rate: 0.03375
This is a wordy question. How can you break it apart?	$P = 300,000$
Use the Kaplan Strategy for Translating English into Math to wade through the words.	$r = \dfrac{0.03375}{12} = 0.0028125$
What should be done first?	$N = 12 \times 30 = 360$
The variables are already defined, and you're given an equation that relates them. Identify the values of the variables, and then calculate the monthly payment at 3.375% annual interest. Decimals are truncated in the scratchwork column for brevity, but don't round until you arrive at your final answer. Make sure you divide 0.03375 by 12 to convert it to the monthly interest rate.	$m = \dfrac{Pr}{1-(1+r)^{-N}}$ $m = \dfrac{300000 \times 0.0028125}{1-(1+0.0028125)^{-360}}$ $m = \dfrac{843.75}{1-(1.0028125)^{-360}}$
Are you finished?	$m = \dfrac{843.75}{0.6362}$
Not yet; the question asks for the amount paid over six months, not one month. Multiply m by 6 to get your final answer.	$m = 1,326.2886$ $1,326.2886 \times 6 = 7,957.7318$
Step 3: Check that you answered the *right* question	
How much will have been paid in mortgage costs after six months?	
Round to get 7958.	7958

> **✔ Note**
>
> Be particularly careful when calculating the monthly payments here; you're given an annual interest rate, but r is a monthly rate. Manipulate the annual rate accordingly.

Way to go! You just answered a question involving a real-life example of an exponential equation.

SOLVING A FORMULA OR EQUATION FOR A GIVEN VARIABLE

If you've ever taken a chemistry or physics course, you probably noticed that many real-world situations can't be represented by beautiful linear equations. There are frequently radicals, exponents, and fractions galore. Furthermore, these equations can seem to lack a logical arrangement. For example, the root-mean-square velocity for particles in a gas can be described by the following equation:

$$v = \sqrt{\left(\frac{3kT}{m}\right)}$$

In this equation, v represents the root-mean-square velocity, k is the Boltzmann constant, T is the temperature in degrees Kelvin, and m is the mass of one molecule of the gas. It's a great equation if you have k, T, and m and are looking for v. However, if you're looking for a different quantity, having that unknown buried among others (and under a radical to boot) can be unnerving, but unearthing it is easier than it appears. Let's say we're given v, k, and m but need to find T. First, square both sides to eliminate the radical to yield $v^2 = \frac{3kT}{m}$. Next, isolate T by multiplying both sides by m and dividing by $3k$: $\frac{mv^2}{3k} = T$.

At this point, you can plug in the values of m, v, and k to solve for T. Sometimes the SAT will have you do just that: Solve for the numerical value of a variable of interest. In other situations, you'll need to rearrange an equation so that a different variable is isolated. The same rules of algebra you've used all along apply. The difference: You're manipulating solely variables.

Now you'll have a chance to try a few more test-like questions. Some guidance is provided, but you'll need to fill in the missing parts of explanations or the step-by-step math to get to the correct answer. Don't worry—after going through the examples at the beginning of this chapter, these questions should be completely doable. If you're still struggling, review the worked examples in this chapter.

9. Special relativity is a branch of physics that deals with the relationship between space and time. The Lorentz term, a term that relates the change in time, length, and relativistic mass of a moving object, is given by the following formula:

$$\gamma = \frac{1}{\sqrt{1 - \frac{v^2}{c^2}}}$$

where v is the relative velocity of the object and c is the speed of light in a vacuum. Which of the following equations correctly represents the relative velocity in terms of the other variables?

A) $v = c\sqrt{\frac{1}{\gamma^2} - 1}$

B) $v = c\sqrt{1 - \gamma^2}$

C) $v = c\left(1 - \frac{1}{\gamma^2}\right)$

D) $v = c\sqrt{1 - \frac{1}{\gamma^2}}$

Use the scaffolding below as your map through the question. Strategic thinking is on the left, and bits of scratchwork are on the right. If you aren't sure where to start, answer the questions in italics, and fill in the blanks in the table as you work from top to bottom.

Strategic Thinking	Math Scratchwork
Step 1: Read the question, identifying and organizing important information as you go *What are you being asked to do here?* You need to identify the expression that equals relative velocity. Translation: solve the given equation for *v*.	

Strategic Thinking	Math Scratchwork
Step 2: Choose the best strategy to answer the question *There are several variables and weird symbols. How should this be solved?* Don't let the multiple variables intimidate you; just treat them as you would when manipulating a "friendlier" equation. Start by undoing the radical so you can get to what's underneath, and then isolate the correct variable.	$\gamma = \dfrac{1}{\sqrt{1 - \dfrac{v^2}{c^2}}}$ _____ = _____ _____ = _____ _____ = _____ _____ = _____ _____ = _____ _____ = _____
Step 3: Check that you answered the *right* question *Did you solve for the right term?* Did you get (D)? If so, you're absolutely correct!	

✔ **Note**

Don't panic over the unfamiliarity of the physics terms; just identify what you need to do (in this case, isolate *v* on one side of the equation).

10. Given that g and h are both positive, which of the following is equivalent to the expression $\sqrt[3]{g^6h^3 - 27g^4h^3}$?

   A) $\frac{1}{3}gh\sqrt[3]{g^2 - 27}$

   B) $gh\sqrt[3]{g^3 - 27g}$

   C) $g^2h - 3gh\sqrt[3]{g}$

   D) $g^2h - 3\sqrt[3]{g}$

Use the scaffolding that follows as your map through the question. Strategic thinking is on the left, and bits of scratchwork are on the right. If you aren't sure where to start, answer the questions in italics and fill in the blanks in the table as you work from top to bottom.

Strategic Thinking	Math Scratchwork
Step 1: Read the question, identifying and organizing important information as you go *What are you being asked to do here?* You need to simplify the given expression.	
Step 2: Choose the best strategy to answer the question *Can anything be factored out of the radicand?* Identifying the GCF should be your first step. Once this is complete, check to see whether any part of it can be "cube rooted" and placed outside the radical. *Is there any other factoring/simplification that can be done?* Double check to make sure no factoring was missed, and then look for a match in the answer choices. If you can't find one, try rewriting the expression.	GCF: _____ $\sqrt[3]{\underline{\quad}(\underline{\quad}-\underline{\quad})}$ $\underline{\quad}\sqrt[3]{\underline{\quad}(\underline{\quad}-\underline{\quad})}$ $\underline{\quad}\sqrt[3]{\underline{\quad}-\underline{\quad}}$
Step 3: Check that you answered the *right* question *Which choice matches your simplified expression?* If your answer is (B), congrats! You're correct.	_____

11. Human blood contains three primary cell types: red blood cells (RBC), white blood cells (WBC), and platelets. In an adult male, a single microliter (1×10^{-3} milliliters) of blood contains approximately 5.4×10^6 RBC, 7.5×10^3 WBC, and 3.5×10^5 platelets on average. What percentage of an adult male's total blood cell count is comprised of red blood cells?

   A)   1.30%

   B)   6.21%

   C)   60.79%

   D)   93.79%

Use the scaffolding that follows as your map through the question. Strategic thinking is on the left, and bits of scratchwork are on the right. If you aren't sure where to start, answer the questions in italics and fill in the blanks in the table as you work from top to bottom.

Strategic Thinking	Math Scratchwork
Step 1: Read the question, identifying and organizing important information as you go *What is the question asking?* You need to calculate the percent of an adult male's blood that is comprised of red blood cells.	
Step 2: Choose the best strategy to answer the question *Can you set up an equation?* Remember that a percentage is derived from a ratio that compares a partial quantity to a total quantity. Write an equation that compares the RBC count to the total blood cell count and solve. You can save time by using exponent rules instead of punching everything into your calculator. Note that the answer choices are fairly far apart. Compare the numerator and denominator of your simplified expression; you can estimate the resulting quantity and eliminate incorrect answers accordingly. *Am I finished?* Multiply the RBC fraction you found by 100 to convert it to a percent.	RBC % = _____ $\dfrac{\_\_\_}{\_\_\_ + \_\_\_ + \_\_}$ = _____ = _____ = _____ _____ × 100 = _____%
Step 3: Check that you answered the *right* question *What percent of an adult male's blood is comprised of red blood cells?* Did you get (D)? If so, you're absolutely correct!	____

✔ **Expert Tip**

You can do this question almost entirely without a calculator. Just use your exponent and scientific notation expertise.

Now that you've seen the variety of ways in which the SAT can test you on the topics in this chapter, try the following questions to check your understanding. Give yourself 3.5 minutes to tackle the following three questions. Make sure you use the Kaplan Method for Math as often as you can. Remember, you want to emphasize speed and efficiency in addition to simply getting the correct answer.

12. An object launched straight up into the air is said to have parabolic motion (because it goes up, reaches a maximum height, and then comes back down). The height (h) of a projectile at time t is given by the equation $h = \frac{1}{2}at^2 + v_0 t + h_0$, where a is the acceleration due to gravity and v_0 and h_0 are the object's initial velocity and initial height, respectively. Which of the following equations correctly represents the object's acceleration due to gravity in terms of the other variables?

A) $a = \dfrac{h - v_0 t - h_0}{t}$

B) $a = \dfrac{h - v_0 t - h_0}{2t^2}$

C) $a = \dfrac{2(h - v_0 t - h_0)}{t^2}$

D) $a = t\sqrt{2(h - v_0 t - h_0)}$

13. Which of the following expressions is equal to $\dfrac{3 + \sqrt{72}}{3 - \sqrt{72}}$?

A) $\dfrac{9 + 4\sqrt{2}}{-7}$

B) $\dfrac{9 + 2\sqrt{2}}{-7}$

C) $\dfrac{9}{-7}$

D) $1 + \dfrac{4\sqrt{2}}{9}$

14. Car dealerships often require car buyers to provide a down payment (money paid up front), which is a percent of a car's price. The down payment is deducted from the purchase price, and the buyer usually takes out a loan to pay for what is left. Teri is buying a car that costs $19,560. Her monthly car payment is given by $m = \dfrac{Pr}{1 - (1+r)^{-N}}$, where P is the initial loan balance, r is the monthly interest rate expressed as a decimal, and N is the number of payments to be made over the duration of the loan. If Teri wants to fully pay off the loan in five years at 1.5% annual interest and wishes to have a monthly payment of $200, what percent of the purchase price will she need for her down payment? Round your answer to the nearest whole percent.

Answers and Explanations for this chapter begin on page 884.

EXTRA PRACTICE

Required	Recommended
Questions 1–8	Questions 9–21

1. Which of the following expressions is equivalent to $-x^{\frac{1}{4}}$?

   A) $-\dfrac{1}{4x}$

   B) $-\dfrac{1}{x^4}$

   C) $-\sqrt[4]{x}$

   D) $\dfrac{1}{\sqrt[4]{-x}}$

2. If $\dfrac{7\sqrt{x}}{2} = 14$, what is the value of x?

   A) 2

   B) 4

   C) 16

   D) 49

$$\frac{4x+8y}{24x-12}$$

3. Which of the following is the simplified form of the rational expression above?

   A) $\dfrac{1}{6} - \dfrac{2y}{3}$

   B) $\dfrac{x+2y}{6x-3}$

   C) $\dfrac{x+2y}{2x-1}$

   D) $\dfrac{x+8y}{6x-12}$

4. What is the resulting coefficient of x when $-x + 6$ is multiplied by $2x - 3$?

   A) -15

   B) -2

   C) 9

   D) 15

5. What is the difference when $\dfrac{3x+7}{x-1}$ is subtracted from $\dfrac{8x-5}{x-1}$?

   A) $\dfrac{5x+2}{x-1}$

   B) $\dfrac{5x+2}{2x-1}$

   C) $\dfrac{5x-12}{x-1}$

   D) $\dfrac{-5x+12}{x-1}$

6. If $p(x)$ is a polynomial that has a simple zero at $x = -3$ and a double zero at $x = \dfrac{5}{4}$, which of the following could be the factored form of $p(x)$?

   A) $p(x) = 2(x+3)(5x-4)$

   B) $p(x) = (x+3)(5x-4)^2$

   C) $p(x) = 2(x+3)(4x-5)$

   D) $p(x) = (x+3)(4x-5)^2$

$$v = \frac{2\pi r}{T}$$

7. Uniform circular motion is used in physics to describe the motion of an object traveling at a constant speed in a circle. The speed of the object is called tangential velocity, and it can be calculated using the formula above, where r is the radius of the circle and T is the time is takes for the object to make one complete circle, called a period. Which of the following formulas could be used to find the length of one period if you know the tangential velocity and the radius of the circle?

A) $T = \dfrac{v}{2\pi r}$

B) $T = \dfrac{2\pi r}{v}$

C) $T = 2\pi r v$

D) $T = \dfrac{1}{2\pi r v}$

$$\sqrt{0.75} \times \sqrt{0.8}$$

8. Which of the following has the same value as the expression above?

A) $\dfrac{3}{5}$

B) $\dfrac{\sqrt{15}}{5}$

C) $\sqrt[4]{0.6}$

D) $\sqrt{1.55}$

9. Which of the following expressions is equivalent to $(27x^6 y^{12})^{\frac{1}{3}}$?

A) $3x^2 y^4$

B) $9x^2 y^4$

C) $\dfrac{27x^6 y^{12}}{3}$

D) $(27x^6 y^{12})^{-3}$

$$8 + \frac{\sqrt{2x+29}}{3} = 9$$

10. For what value of x is the equation above true?

A) -10

B) -2

C) 19

D) No solution

$$\frac{12x^3 y^2 - 9x^2 y}{6x^4 y + 18x^3 y^3}$$

11. Which of the following is equivalent to the expression above?

A) $\dfrac{4xy - 3}{x + 3y^2}$

B) $\dfrac{3x^2 y - 3xy}{x + 3y^2}$

C) $\dfrac{4xy - 3}{2x^2 + 6xy^2}$

D) $\dfrac{4xy - 9}{2x^2 + 18xy^3}$

12. If $30x^3 + 45x^2 - 10x$ is divided by $5x$, what is the resulting coefficient of x?

A) 6

B) 9

C) 25

D) 40

$$\sqrt{9m^5 n^2 - m^4 n^2}$$

13. Which of the following expressions is equivalent to the expression above, given that m and n are positive?

A) $3\sqrt{m}$

B) $3mn$

C) $3n\sqrt{m}$

D) $m^2 n\sqrt{9m - 1}$

$$T = 2\pi\sqrt{\frac{L}{g}}$$

14. The formula above was created by Italian scientist Galileo Galilei in the early 1600s to demonstrate that the time it takes for a pendulum to complete a swing, called its period (T), can be found using only the length of the pendulum, L, and the force of gravity, g. He proved that the mass of the pendulum did not affect its period. Based on the equation above, which of the following equations could be used to find the length of the pendulum given its period?

A) $L = \dfrac{gT}{2\pi}$

B) $L = \dfrac{gT^2}{4\pi^2}$

C) $L = \dfrac{T^2}{4\pi^2 g}$

D) $L = \dfrac{g}{4\pi^2 T^2}$

15. If $A = 4x^2 + 7x - 1$ and $B = -x^2 - 5x + 3$, then what is $\dfrac{3}{2}A - 2B$?

A) $4x^2 + \dfrac{31}{2}x - \dfrac{9}{2}$

B) $4x^2 + \dfrac{41}{2}x - \dfrac{15}{2}$

C) $8x^2 + \dfrac{31}{2}x - \dfrac{9}{2}$

D) $8x^2 + \dfrac{41}{2}x - \dfrac{15}{2}$

$$\sqrt{2} \times \sqrt[4]{2}$$

16. Which of the following is equivalent to the product given above?

A) $\sqrt[4]{8}$

B) $\sqrt[6]{2}$

C) $\sqrt[8]{2}$

D) $\sqrt[8]{4}$

$$\frac{\sqrt[3]{x} \cdot x^2 \cdot x^{\frac{5}{2}}}{\sqrt{x}}$$

17. If x^n is the simplified form of the expression above, what is the value of n?

18. If $12 + \dfrac{3\sqrt{x-5}}{2} = 18$, what is the value of x?

19. Which of the following is equivalent to the expression $4\sqrt[3]{ab^9}$?

   A) $4a^{\frac{1}{3}}b^3$

   B) $4a^3b^{\frac{1}{3}}$

   C) $4a^3b^{27}$

   D) $\dfrac{4}{a^{\frac{1}{3}}b^3}$

20. What is the sum of the polynomials $6a^2 - 17a - 9$ and $-5a^2 + 8a - 2$?

   A) $a^2 - 9a - 11$

   B) $a^2 - 25a - 7$

   C) $11a^2 - 9a - 11$

   D) $11a^2 - 25a - 7$

21. When simplified, $8^{\frac{4}{3}}$ is what number?

CHAPTER 9

Advanced Techniques for Polynomials and Rational Equations

CHAPTER OBJECTIVES

By the end of this section, you will be able to:

- Solve rational equations
- Simplify expressions using polynomial long division
- Find polynomial remainders

SMARTPOINTS

Point Value	SmartPoint Category
80 Points	Exponents

In the previous chapter, you were introduced to polynomials and rational expressions, as well as fundamental techniques for manipulating them. In this chapter, we'll take you through some advanced polynomial and rational expression/equation tactics so you'll be able to tackle the toughest math questions with confidence on Test Day.

MULTIPLICATION & DIVISION OF MULTI-TERM POLYNOMIALS

Adding and subtracting polynomials are straightforward, as are multiplication and division by a monomial (like $2x^3$ or $\frac{z}{15}$). But what happens when neither polynomial has only one term? Although the math takes more time, the process used is the same.

> ✔ **Note**
>
> Occasionally, you will see mention of techniques called *FOIL* and *factoring* in this chapter. FOIL is a mnemonic device used for multiplying two binomials; it is the same distribution process described above. Factoring is the reverse of FOIL. Both are discussed in more detail in chapter 11.

Mulitplying polynomial expressions was discussed previously, in chapter 8. Dividing polynomial expressions requires a different, more involved process called *polynomial long division*. Polynomial long division is just like regular long division except, as the name suggests, you use polynomials in place of numbers.

Suppose you want to divide $x^3 + 3x + 7$ by $x + 4$. You can set this up as a long division problem:

$$x+4 \overline{\smash{\big)}\, x^3 + 0x^2 + 3x + 7}$$

Notice that even though the dividend does not have an x^2 term, a placeholder is used to keep the terms organized. Because $0x^2$ is equal to 0, adding this placeholder term doesn't change the value of the polynomial. Start by dividing the first term of the dividend by the first term of the divisor to get x^2. Multiply the entire divisor by x^2 and subtract this product from the dividend.

$$
\begin{array}{r}
x^2 - 4x + 19 + \dfrac{-69}{x+4} \\
x+4 \overline{\smash{\big)}\, x^3 + 0x^2 + 3x + 7} \\
\underline{-(x^3 + 4x^2)} \\
-4x^2 + 3x + 7
\end{array}
$$

Continue by dividing the next term, $-4x^2$, by the first term of the divisor. Bring down leftover terms as needed. Multiply the quotient, $-4x$, by the entire divisor and then subtract.

$$\begin{array}{r} x^2 - 4x \\ x+4\overline{\smash{\big)}\ x^3 + 0x^2 + 3x + 7} \\ -\underline{(x^3 + 4x^2)} \\ -4x^2 + 3x + 7 \\ -\underline{(-4x^2 - 16x)} \\ 19x + 7 \end{array}$$

Finally, repeat this process with the $19x + 7$.

$$\begin{array}{r} x^2 - 4x + 19 \\ x+4\overline{\smash{\big)}\ x^3 + 0x^2 + 3x + 7} \\ -\underline{(x^3 + 4x^2)} \\ -4x^2 + 3x + 7 \\ -\underline{(-4x^2 - 16x)} \\ 19x + 7 \\ -\underline{(19x + 76)} \\ -69 \end{array}$$

When all is said and done, the quotient is $x^2 - 4x + 19$ with a remainder of -69; the remainder is written over the divisor in a separate term. Thus, the final answer is $x^2 - 4x + 19 - \dfrac{69}{x+4}$.

This is a topic many students tend to forget soon after it's tested in math class, so make sure you spend sufficient time brushing up on it.

> ✔ **Note**
>
> You can use polynomial long division to determine whether a binomial is a factor of a polynomial. If the remainder in the previous example had been 0, then $x + 4$ would have been a factor of the polynomial $x^3 + 3x + 7$.

SOLVING RATIONAL EQUATIONS

Rational equations are just like rational expressions except for one difference: They have an equal sign. They follow the same rules as rational expressions. The steps you take to solve the more friendly-looking linear equations apply to rational equations as well.

Before proceeding further, it is imperative that you have a full understanding of the rules and tips for simplifying rational expressions that were introduced in chapter 8, as well as a strong command of the Kaplan Strategy for Translating English into Math for questions involving application of rational equations.

A typical rational equation question that you're likely to see on Test Day involves rates. Recall from chapter 5 that distance is the product of rate and time ($d = rt$); this equation will serve you well when solving rational equations involving rates. In some cases, you may want to change d to W (for work), as some questions ask how long it will take to complete some kind of work or a specific task. The good news is that the math doesn't change. For example, you can calculate a combined rate by rewriting $W = rt$ as $r = \dfrac{W}{t}$ for each person (or machine) working on a job and then adding the rates together.

Here's an example: Suppose machine A can complete a job in 2 hours and machine B can do the same job in 4 hours. You want to know how long it will take to do this job if both machines work together. Their rates would be $r_A = \dfrac{W_A}{t_A} = \dfrac{1}{2}$ job per hour and $r_B = \dfrac{W_B}{t_B} = \dfrac{1}{4}$ job per hour, respectively.

The combined rate would be $\dfrac{3}{4}$ job per hour, which means $t_{total} = \dfrac{W_{total}}{r_{total}} = \dfrac{1}{\frac{3}{4}} = \dfrac{4}{3}$ hours. Thus, it will take $\dfrac{4}{3}$ hours to complete the job if A and B work together.

When solving rational equations, beware of **extraneous solutions**—solutions derived that don't satisfy the original equation. This happens when the derived solution causes 0 in the denominator of *any* of the terms in the equation (because division by 0 is not possible). Take the equation $\dfrac{1}{x+4} + \dfrac{1}{x-4} = \dfrac{8}{(x+4)(x-4)}$, for instance. After multiplying both sides by the common denominator $(x + 4)(x - 4)$, you have $(x - 4) + (x + 4) = 8$. Solving for x yields $x = 4$. However, when 4 is substituted for x, you get 0 in the denominator of both the second and third terms of the equation, so 4 is an extraneous solution. Therefore, this equation is said to have no solution.

You might be asked to solve and/or graph a rational equation. To do this, make note of any x-values that cause the equation to be undefined and then simplify the equation if necessary. When graphing rational equations, mark undefined values of x with open dots on the graph or, in more complex equations, with dashed lines (called *asymptotes*). For instance, the equation $y = \dfrac{x+6}{x+6} + 3$ can be simplified to $y = 1 + 3 = 4$, which is a horizontal line at $y = 4$ with one critical difference: an open dot when $x = -6$, as -6 causes the equation to be undefined.

> ✔ **Note**
>
> Whenever you encounter an equation with variables in a denominator or under a radical, after solving, make sure to check for extraneous solutions by plugging the values you found back into the original equation.

1. For how many distinct values of x is the expression $\dfrac{x-2}{(3x-6)(x^2-1)}$ undefined?

   A) 1

   B) 2

   C) 3

   D) 4

$$3\overparen{(x-2)}(x+1)(x-1)$$

Not all questions involving rational expressions or equations will ask you to simplify or solve for a variable. Questions like this one are designed to see if you can go beyond "plug-and-chug" and truly understand the nature of the expression.

There's no scratchwork for this question, but Kaplan's strategic thinking follows. Follow along as we reason through the question to get the correct answer.

Strategic Thinking
Step 1: Read the question, identifying and organizing important information as you go
You must determine the number of x-values that cause the given expression to be undefined.
Step 2: Choose the best strategy to answer the question
An expression is undefined when the denominator in one or more of the terms is 0. To determine when this occurs, you can set each factor in the denominator equal to 0 and solve: $3x - 6 = 0$ and $x^2 - 1 = 0$. The first equation yields $x = 2$; the second, $x = \pm 1$. The expression is undefined at -1, 1, and 2—three values in all.
Step 3: Check that you answered the *right* question
The expression is undefined when $x = -1$, 1, or 2. Choice (C) is correct.

> ✔ **Note**
>
> **When you're asked for distinct values, count each value only once. For example, if the denominator of an expression looks like $(x - 2)(x - 2)(x - 3)$, then 2 and 3 are the distinct values for which the expression is undefined, and there are two such values.**

2. Which value of x satisfies the equation $\dfrac{4}{x} + \dfrac{2}{x-8} = \dfrac{-2}{x^2-8x}$?

   A) -1

   B) 1

   C) 4

   D) 5

[handwritten work:]

$x(x-8)$

$x(x-8)$

$x(x-8)$

$4x - 32 + 2x = -2$

$6x - 32 = -2$

$+32 \quad +32$

$\dfrac{6x}{6} = \dfrac{30}{6}$

Work through the Kaplan Method for Math step-by-step to solve this question. The following table shows Kaplan's strategic thinking on the left, along with suggested math scratchwork on the right.

Strategic Thinking	Math Scratchwork
Step 1: Read the question, identifying and organizing important information as you go You're asked to determine which value of x satisfies the equation.	
Step 2: Choose the best strategy to answer the question Start by identifying a common denominator. By factoring x out of the denominator of the term on the right side of the equation, you'll see that the common denominator across all three terms is $x(x-8)$. Multiply the entire equation by this expression, then distribute properly and solve for x.	$x^2 - 8x \rightarrow x(x-8)$ $x(x-8)\left(\dfrac{4}{x} + \dfrac{2}{x-8} = \dfrac{-2}{x(x-8)}\right)$ $4(x-8) + 2x = -2$ $4x - 32 + 2x = -2$ $6x = 30$ $x = 5$
Step 3: Check that you answered the *right* question Because "no solution" is not a choice, you can be confident that 5 is not an extraneous solution. Choice (D) is therefore correct.	

Ready for a real-world example? Check out the following question.

3. Johanna, Elizabeth, and Dan are preparing a chemical intermediate for a research project. When working alone, either Johanna or Elizabeth can prepare the intermediate in six days. Dan can prepare the intermediate in four days if he works alone. How many days will it take the three of them to prepare the intermediate if they work together?

A) $\dfrac{5}{12}$

B) $\dfrac{7}{12}$

C) $\dfrac{12}{7}$

D) $\dfrac{12}{5}$

Work through the Kaplan Method for Math step-by-step to solve this question. The following table shows Kaplan's strategic thinking on the left, along with suggested math scratchwork on the right.

Strategic Thinking	Math Scratchwork
Step 1: Read the question, identifying and organizing important information as you go You're asked how long it will take the three colleagues to prepare an intermediate if they work together. A rate for each colleague is given.	

Strategic Thinking	Math Scratchwork
Step 2: Choose the best strategy to answer the question The question asks for a total time, so start by determining individual rates. Once you've done that, add them together to find the combined rate in terms of time. There is one intermediate to prepare (or one job to do), so use 1 for *W*. Once you have an equation, isolate *t*. Start by combining the fractions on the left side, then cross-multiply to solve for *t*.	$W = rt \rightarrow r = \dfrac{W}{t}$ J: 6 days to complete $\rightarrow$ $\dfrac{1}{6}$ completed per day E: 6 days to complete $\rightarrow$ $\dfrac{1}{6}$ completed per day D: 4 days to complete $\rightarrow$ $\dfrac{1}{4}$ completed per day t = time working together $\dfrac{1}{6} + \dfrac{1}{6} + \dfrac{1}{4} = \dfrac{1}{t}$ $\dfrac{2}{12} + \dfrac{2}{12} + \dfrac{3}{12} = \dfrac{1}{t}$ $\dfrac{7}{12} = \dfrac{1}{t}$ $7t = 12$ $t = \dfrac{12}{7}$
Step 3: Check that you answered the *right* question Working together, Johanna, Elizabeth, and Dan will need $\dfrac{12}{7}$ days to prepare the intermediate, which is (C).	

4. Which of the following is the graph of $y = \dfrac{2x^2 - 8}{x^2 - 4} + 1$?

$$\frac{2\,(x+2)(x-2)}{(x+2)(x-2)}$$

$$y = 2 + 1$$

A)

B)

C)

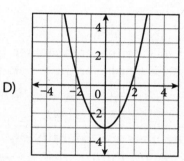

D)

There's no scratchwork for this question, but Kaplan's strategic thinking follows. Follow along as we reason through the question to get the correct answer.

Strategic Thinking
Step 1: Read the question, identifying and organizing important information as you go
You need to match the given equation to its graph.
Step 2: Choose the best strategy to answer the question
The equation is rational with variables in the denominator, so watch for values that yield a denominator of 0. Factoring the denominator reveals that both −2 and 2 cause a 0 denominator, so look for a graph that has open dots at $x = -2$ and $x = 2$. The graphs in C and D lack these, so eliminate them. When simplified, the equation is $y = \dfrac{2(x^2 - 4)}{x^2 - 4} + 1 = 2 + 1 = 3$, given that $x \neq -2, 2$. The graph in B is not a horizontal line, so eliminate it.
Step 3: Check that you answered the *right* question
Choice (A) contains the graph that corresponds to the given equation.

Let's try a polynomial long division question.

5. What is the remainder when $16a^2 + 3$ is divided by $4a + 2$?

    A) −7

    B) −1

    C) 1

    D) 7

Work through the Kaplan Method for Math step-by-step to solve this question. The following table shows Kaplan's strategic thinking on the left, along with suggested math scratchwork on the right.

Strategic Thinking	Math Scratchwork
Step 1: Read the question, identifying and organizing important information as you go You must find the remainder of $\dfrac{16a^2 + 3}{4a + 2}$.	
Step 2: Choose the best strategy to answer the question Write as a polynomial long division problem. Once it's set up, work carefully through each step until you get to the end.	$\begin{array}{r} 4a-2 \\ 4a+2\overline{\smash{\big)}\,16a^2+0a+3} \\ -(16a^2+8a) \\ \hline -8a+3 \\ -(-8a-4) \\ \hline 7 \end{array}$
Step 3: Check that you answered the *right* question You get 7 for the remainder, which is (D).	

6. Ankeet needs to back up a large quantity of financial data for his firm. He has access to two systems that can assist with the task. One system is three times as fast as the other. If Ankeet uses both systems together, the backup will be complete in twelve hours. If the equation $\frac{1}{h} + \frac{3}{h} = \frac{1}{12}$ represents the situation, what does $\frac{3}{h}$ represent?

A) The time, in hours, that it takes the faster system to complete the full data backup when working alone

B) The portion of the data backup that the faster system will complete in one hour

C) The time, in hours, that it takes the slower system to complete the full data backup when working alone

D) The portion of the data backup that the faster system will complete in three hours

There's no scratchwork for this question, but Kaplan's strategic thinking follows. Follow along as we reason through the question to get the correct answer.

Strategic Thinking
Step 1: Read the question, identifying and organizing important information as you go
You must determine the significance of $\frac{3}{h}$ in the given situation.
Step 2: Choose the best strategy to answer the question
The left side of the equation shows the sum of the two systems' task completion rates. A rate cannot also be a quantity of time, so eliminate A and C.
To determine which remaining choice is correct, think carefully. When the machines work together, they complete the job in 12 hours; put another way, they complete $\frac{1}{12}$ of the job in 1 hour. Because the right side of the equation represents the portion of the job that will be done in 1 hour, the terms on the left represent the portion of the job that is done by each system in 1 hour. The faster system is three times as fast as the other, so it will complete three times as much work. Therefore, $\frac{3}{h}$ is the portion of the job completed by the faster system in 1 hour.
Step 3: Check that you answered the *right* question
The portion of the job that the faster system will complete in one hour is $\frac{3}{h}$. Choice (B) is correct.

7. What are the solution(s) to the equation $\dfrac{x}{x+2} + \dfrac{2}{x+6} = \dfrac{-8}{(x+2)(x+6)}$?

   A) -2

   B) 2

   C) -2 and -6

   D) No solution

Work through the Kaplan Method for Math step-by-step to solve this question. The following table shows Kaplan's strategic thinking on the left, along with suggested math scratchwork on the right.

Strategic Thinking	Math Scratchwork
Step 1: Read the question, identifying and organizing important information as you go You're asked for the solution(s) to the equation.	
Step 2: Choose the best strategy to answer the question The first order of business is to eliminate the fractions. Remember the big no-no from chapter 8: NEVER divide a numerator by each term in the denominator. Instead, multiply both sides by a common denominator. Move all the terms to one side of the equation so that it is equal to 0. You've created a quadratic, so you can factor to solve it. Look for a pair of integers with a sum of 8 and a product of 12; the magic picks are 2 and 6. Split the two binomials into separate equations, set them equal to 0, and then solve. Be careful here. The question asks for the solutions, but you must plug them back into the equation (at least mentally) to make sure they're not extraneous: -2 causes $x+2$ to be 0, and -6 causes $x+6$ to be 0, so both solutions are extraneous. Therefore, the equation actually has no solution.	$((x+2)(x+6))\left(\dfrac{x}{x+2} + \dfrac{2}{x+6}\right)$ $= x(x+6) + 2(x+2)$ $= x^2 + 6x + 2x + 4$ $= x^2 + 8x + 4$ $((x+2)(x+6))\left(\dfrac{-8}{(x+2)(x+6)}\right)$ $= -8$ $x^2 + 8x + 4 = -8$ $x^2 + 8x + 12 = 0$ $(x+2)(x+6) = 0$ $x+2 = 0 \quad x+6 = 0$ $x = -2 \quad x = -6$
Step 3: Check that you answered the *right* question You've solved for x and determined that the solutions are extraneous. Choice (D) is the correct answer.	

✔ Note

Refer to chapter 11 for information on factoring.

8. What is the nature of the solutions to the equation $\dfrac{x}{x+1} - \dfrac{9}{x+2} = \dfrac{1}{(-1-x)(x+2)}$?

   A) One valid solution and one extraneous solution

   B) Two extraneous solutions

   C) Two valid solutions

   D) Infinitely many solutions

Work through the Kaplan Method for Math step-by-step to solve this question. The following table shows Kaplan's strategic thinking on the left, along with suggested math scratchwork on the right.

Strategic Thinking	Math Scratchwork
Step 1: Read the question, identifying and organizing important information as you go You must determine the nature of the solutions to the equation given.	

Strategic Thinking	Math Scratchwork
Step 2: Choose the best strategy to answer the question	
Before you multiply both sides by a trio of binomials, factor −1 out of (−1 − x) in the denominator of the right side. Then attach the negative sign to the 1 in the numerator. The common denominator now only has two binomials. Multiply both sides of the equation by the binomials. Watch the negative signs!	$\dfrac{1}{(-1-x)(x+2)} = \dfrac{-1}{(x+1)(x+2)}$ $((x+1)(x+2))\left(\dfrac{x}{x+1} - \dfrac{9}{x+2}\right)$ $= x(x+2) - 9(x+1)$ $= x^2 + 2x - 9x - 9$ $= x^2 - 7x - 9$ $((x+1)(x+2))\left(\dfrac{-1}{(x+1)(x+2)}\right)$ $= -1$
If you noticed this equation is a quadratic, great! Move everything to one side and then factor. You need a pair of numbers with a sum of −7 and a product of −8; the two numbers are 1 and −8. After writing the equation as the product of two binomials, separate them into two equations, set each one equal to 0 and solve for x. Remember to check for extraneous solutions. You'll find that 8 is valid, but −1 causes both x + 1 and −1 − x to be 0 and is therefore invalid.	$x^2 - 7x - 9 = -1$ $x^2 - 7x - 8 = 0$ $(x+1)(x-8) = 0$ $x+1=0 \quad x-8=0$ $x=-1 \quad x=8$
Step 3: Check that you answered the *right* question	
The equation has one valid solution (8) and one extraneous solution (−1), so (A) is correct.	

✔ **Note**

Beware of choice C! Whenever you have variables in the denominator, always check to make sure your solutions are not extraneous.

Now you'll have a chance to try a few more test-like questions. Some guidance is provided, but you'll need to fill in the missing parts of explanations or the step-by-step math to get to the correct answer. Don't worry—after going through the examples at the beginning of this chapter, these questions should be completely doable. If you're still struggling, review the worked examples in this chapter.

9. When $-7x^5 - 7x^4 - 6x^3 + 3x^2 + 9x$ is divided by $x^2 + x$, what is the product of the coefficients of the terms in the quotient and the constant?

Use the scaffolding below as your map through the question. Strategic thinking is on the left, and bits of scratchwork are on the right. If you aren't sure where to start, answer the questions in italics and fill in the blanks in the table as you work from top to bottom.

Strategic Thinking	Math Scratchwork
Step 1: Read the question, identifying and organizing important information as you go *What are you being asked to do here?* You need to divide the first polynomial by the second and then multiply the coefficients of the terms in the quotient and the constant together.	
Step 2: Choose the best strategy to answer the question *Can anything be factored out of the first polynomial?* Possibly, but it will likely use up time you don't have. Polynomial long division is a faster route. Fill in the blanks on the right to get to the answer. Don't stop after you're done dividing; keep in mind what the question asks.	$\underline{\quad}\,|\overline{\underline{\qquad\qquad}}$ $-(\quad-\quad)\underline{\qquad}$ $\qquad-(\quad-\quad)\underline{\qquad}$ $\qquad\qquad-(\quad-\quad)$ product: $\underline{\quad}$ x $\underline{\quad}$ x $\underline{\quad}$ $=\underline{\quad}$

Strategic Thinking	Math Scratchwork
Step 3: Check that you answered the *right* question *What's the product of the coefficients of the terms in the quotient and the constant?* If your answer is 378, congrats! You're right.	

10. A botanical garden is draining its lily pad pools for the winter using three pumps. The second pump is two times faster than the first pump, which is three times faster than the third. If the three pumps can completely drain the pools in four hours when working together, what expression could represent the portion of the draining that could be completed by the second pump in one hour?

A) $\dfrac{6}{x}$

B) $\dfrac{2}{x}$

C) $\dfrac{1}{4} - \dfrac{6}{x}$

D) $\dfrac{1}{4} - \dfrac{2}{x}$

Use the scaffolding below as your map through the question. Strategic thinking is on the left, and bits of scratchwork are on the right. If you aren't sure where to start, answer the questions in italics and fill in the blanks in the table as you work from top to bottom.

Strategic Thinking	Math Scratchwork
Step 1: Read the question, identifying and organizing important information as you go *What is the question asking?* You need to identify the expression that could represent the portion of the draining done by the second pump in one hour.	

Strategic Thinking	Math Scratchwork
Step 2: Choose the best strategy to answer the question *How do you determine which term corresponds to the second pump?* Don't assume that the terms related to the pumps are ordered 1-2-3 in the equation. Start by ordering the pumps in order of increasing drain speed. *What do you do after establishing the correct order?* Write the pump speeds as a ratio based on the information in the question stem. Use the second pump component of the ratio to derive an expression that represents the portion of the draining it completed in one hour.	speed: ____ < ____ < ____ ____ : ____ : ____ 2nd pump completes ____
Step 3: Check that you answered the *right* question *Which expression corresponds to the portion of the draining completed by the second pump in one hour?* Did you get (A)? If so, congrats! You're right.	

11. The area of a rectangle is equal to the product of its length and width. Suppose a rectangle has an area of $x^4 + 8x^3 + 9x^2 - 6x$, and its shorter side has length $x^2 + 2x$. If $x > 1$, for what value of x will one side of the rectangle be 25 units longer than the other side?

Use the following scaffolding as your map through the question. Strategic thinking is on the left, and bits of scratchwork are on the right. If you aren't sure where to start, answer the questions in italics and fill in the blanks in the table as you work from top to bottom.

Strategic Thinking	Math Scratchwork
Step 1: Read the question, identifying and organizing important information as you go *What is the question asking?* You need to find the value of x that will make one side of the rectangle 25 units longer than the other.	
Step 2: Choose the best strategy to answer the question *What's the connection between the two polynomials?* Because a rectangle's area is the product of its dimensions, you know $x^2 + 2x$ is a factor of $x^4 + 8x^3 + 9x^2 - 6x$. To find the expression that represents the longer side (and eventually the requested x-value), get ready for some polynomial long division. *What should you do after you find the expression for the longer side?* Set up an equation showing that the longer side is equal to the shorter side (which was given in the question) plus 25. Then solve for x.	___ ⟌ _____ $-(\ \ -\ \ )$ $-(\ \ -\ \ )$ $-(\ \ -\ \ )$ _____ = _____ +25 _____ = _____ $x =$ _____
Step 3: Check that you answered the *right* question *What value of x results in a longer side that is 25 more than the shorter side?* Did you get 7? If so, congrats! You're right.	

Now that you've seen the variety of ways in which the SAT can test you on advanced polynomial and rational expression/equations, try the following questions to check your understanding. Give yourself 3.5 minutes to tackle the following three questions. Make sure you use the Kaplan Method for SAT Math as often as you can. Remember, you want to emphasize speed and efficiency in addition to simply getting the correct answer.

12. Given the expression $3x^4 + 4x^3 - 6x - c$, where c is a constant, for what value of c will $\dfrac{3x^4 + 4x^3 - 6x - c}{x - 2}$ have no remainder?

14. What are the solution(s) to the equation $\dfrac{-4}{\sqrt{x} - 4} + \dfrac{\sqrt{x}}{\sqrt{x} + 3} = \dfrac{-24}{x - \sqrt{x} - 12}$?

   A)   4 only

   B)   36 only

   C)   4 and 36

   D)   No solution

Answers and Explanations are provided on page 895.

13. Isabel is planting new spring bulbs in her flowerbeds; she can plant 50 bulbs in 40 minutes. If her friend Richard helps her plant bulbs, then the number of bulbs she can plant in 40 minutes is increased by 44%. If Isabel has 120 bulbs to plant, which of the following equations would allow her to determine t, the time it will take to complete the job if Richard helps?

   A) $\dfrac{5}{4} + \dfrac{11}{10} = \dfrac{120}{t}$

   B) $\dfrac{5}{4} + \dfrac{11}{20} = \dfrac{120}{t}$

   C) $\dfrac{5}{4} + \dfrac{44}{t} = \dfrac{4}{3}$

   D) $\dfrac{5}{4} + \dfrac{22}{t} = \dfrac{4}{3}$

EXTRA PRACTICE

Required	Recommended
Questions 1–8	Questions 9–18

$$\frac{18x^4 + 27x^3 - 36x^2}{9x^2}$$

(handwritten: $2x^2 + 3x - 4$)

1. Which of the following is equivalent to the expression above?

   A) $2x^2 + 3x - 4$ *(circled)*

   B) $2x^2 + 3x - 6$

   C) $2x^4 + 3x^3 - 4x^2$

   D) $2x^6 + 3x^5 - 4x^4$

2. If $-2x^2 + 5x - 8$ is multiplied by $4x - 9$, what is the coefficient of x in the resulting polynomial?

   A) -77 *(circled)*

   B) -45

   C) -32

   D) -13

   (handwritten work:
   $(4x - 9)(-2x^2 + 5x - 8)$
   $-8x^3 + 20x^2 - 32x$
   $+ 18x^2 - 45x - 72$
   $-8x^3 + 38x^2 - 77x - 72 = 0$
)

3. An online business card printer charges a setup fee of $15 plus $0.02 per card, based on a minimum order of at least 100 cards. Assuming a customer orders at least 100 cards, which of the following represents the average cost per card, x, including the setup fee, before taxes and shipping costs?

   A) $C_{ave} = \dfrac{15 + 0.02}{x}$

   B) $C_{ave} = \dfrac{15}{x} + 0.02$

   C) $C_{ave} = 0.02x + 15$

   D) $C_{ave} = \dfrac{15}{x} + 0.02x$

4. Which of the following could be the graph of $y = \dfrac{3x - 6}{x - 2} + 1$?

   A)

   B)

   C)

   D)

$$\frac{6x^2 + 19x + 10}{2x + 5}$$

5. If $ax + b$ represents the simplified form of the expression above, then what is the value of $a + b$?

A) 2

B) 3

C) 5

D) 6

6. Which of the following expressions is equivalent to $25x^2y^4 - 1$?

A) $5(x^2y^4 - 1)$

B) $-5(xy^2 + 1)$

C) $(5xy - 1)(5xy + 1)$

D) $(5xy^2 - 1)(5xy^2 + 1)$

$$\frac{8x}{3(x-5)} + \frac{2x}{3x-15} = \frac{50}{3(x-5)}$$

7. What value(s) of x satisfy the equation above?

A) 0

B) 5

C) No solution

D) Any value such that $x \neq 5$

8. Given the equation $\dfrac{6}{x} = \dfrac{3}{k+2}$, and the constraints $x \neq 0$ and $k \neq -2$, what is x in terms of k?

A) $x = 2k + 4$

B) $x = 2k + 12$

C) $x = 2k - \dfrac{1}{4}$

D) $x = \dfrac{1}{4}k + 12$

9. Mail-order pharmacies typically use machines to count pills and dispense them into bottles, particularly pills that are pre-scribed on a regular basis by physicians, such as blood pressure medicine, choles-terol medicine, and diabetes medicine. Suppose a pharmacy has two pill counters that work in tandem (together). The first counter can finish separating a typical batch of blood pressure pills in 1 hour, and the second counter can finish the same batch in 40 minutes. How long should it take to finish a typical batch if both pill counters work together?

A) 18 minutes

B) 24 minutes

C) 36 minutes

D) 50 minutes

10. When $18x^2 + 24x - 10$ is divided by $3x + 5$, there is no remainder. What is the constant in the resulting quotient?

A) -2

B) $-\dfrac{1}{2}$

C) 0

D) 2

11. For all a and b, what is the sum of $(a - b)^2$ and $(a + b)^2$?

A) $2a^2$

B) $2a^2 - 2b^2$

C) $2a^2 + 2b^2$

D) $2a^2 + 4ab + 2b^2$

12. Which of the following best describes the solutions to the equation $\dfrac{3}{x-2} - \dfrac{12}{x^2-4} = 1$?

    A) No solution

    B) Two valid solutions

    C) Two extraneous solutions

    D) One valid solution and one extraneous solution

13. Which of the following is a factor of the polynomial $15x^4 + 107x^3 + 193x^2 + 17x - 12$?

    A) $3x - 5$

    B) $3x - 1$

    C) $3x + 1$

    D) $3x + 5$

14. Which of the following equations could have been used to generate the graph shown above?

    A) $y = \dfrac{x^2-4}{x+3}$

    B) $y = \dfrac{x^2-4}{x^2-9}$

    C) $y = \dfrac{x+2}{x^2-4} - 3$

    D) $y = \dfrac{2x^2-8}{x^2-4} - 5$

15. If $\dfrac{16}{7x+4} + A$ is equivalent to $\dfrac{49x^2}{7x+4}$, what is A in terms of x?

    A) $7x + 4$

    B) $7x - 4$

    C) $49x^2$

    D) $49x^2 + 4$

16. What is the remainder when $x^3 + 12$ is divided by $x + 2$?

17. Given the expression $2x^4 + 16x^3 + 34x^2 + 10x + k$ where k is a constant, for what value of k will $\dfrac{2x^4 + 16x^3 + 34x^2 + 10x + k}{x+4}$ have no remainder?

18. Marcia has two window air-conditioning units, one in each bedroom of her townhouse. Both bedrooms are upstairs and can be closed off from the rest of the townhouse by shutting a door at the top of the stairs. The first AC unit, an older model, can lower the temperature of the 260-square foot guest bedroom by 15 degrees Fahrenheit in 3 hours and 15 minutes. The second, a new energy-efficient model, can lower the temperature of the 300-square foot master bedroom by 15 degrees Fahrenheit in 2.5 hours. If Marcia closes the door at the top of the stairs, opens the bedroom doors, and lets both air conditioners work together to cool the two bedrooms, how many hours should it take to lower the temperature of both rooms by 15 degrees Fahrenheit? Do not round your answer.

CHAPTER 10

Functions & Function Notation

CHAPTER OBJECTIVES

By the end of this chapter, you will be able to:

1. Use function notation to answer questions containing equations, tables, and/or graphs

2. Interpret functions and functional statements that represent real-world scenarios

3. Combine functions properly using basic operations and compute compositions of functions correctly

4. Determine if a function is increasing, decreasing, or constant and correctly apply transformations to a given function or functions

SMARTPOINTS

Point Value	SmartPoint Category
70 points	Functions

FUNCTIONS & FUNCTION NOTATION

Functions act as rules that transform inputs into outputs, and they differ from equations in that each input must have only one corresponding output. For example, imagine a robot: every time you give it an apple, it promptly cuts that apple into three slices. The following table summarizes the first few inputs and their corresponding outputs.

Domain x: # apples given to robot	Range $f(x)$: # slices returned by robot
0	0
1	3
2	6
3	9

From the table you see that the output will always be triple the input, and you can express that relationship as the function $f(x) = 3x$ (read "f of x equals three x").

SAT questions, especially those involving real-world situations, might ask you to derive the equation of a function, so you'll need to be familiar with the standard forms. Following, for instance, is the standard form of a linear function:

$$f(x) = kx + f(0)$$ —initial value

The input, or **domain**, is the value represented by x. Sometimes the domain will be constrained by the question (e.g., x must be an integer). Other times, the domain could be defined by real-world conditions. For example, if x represents the time elapsed since the start of a race, the domain would need to exclude negative numbers. The output, or **range**, is the result of what you plug into the function and is represented by $f(x)$. The initial condition or **y-intercept** is represented by $f(0)$—the value of the function at the very beginning. If you think this looks familiar, you're absolutely right! It's just a dressed-up version of the standard $y = mx + b$ equation you've already seen. Take a look at the following table for a translation:

Linear Function Piece	What It Represents	Slope-Intercept Counterpart
$f(x)$	dependent variable or output	y
k	rate of change, slope	m
$f(0)$	y-intercept or initial quantity in a word problem	b

As you might have guessed, an exponential equation has a standard function notation as well. Here we've used g in place of f for visual clarity. Know that the letter used to represent a function (f, g, h, etc.) is sometimes arbitrarily chosen.

$$g(x) = g(0)(1+r)^x$$

Analogous to the linear standard function form, $g(x)$ has replaced y, and $g(0)$ has replaced $f(0)$. Recognizing that function notation is a variation of something you already know will go a long way toward reducing nerves on Test Day. You should also note that graphing functions is a straightforward process: In the examples above, just set the side on the right equal to y and enter into your graphing calculator.

✔ Note

A quick way to determine whether an equation is a function is to conduct the vertical line test: If a vertical line passes through the graph of the equation more than once at any time, the equation is not a function.

Below is an example of a test-like functions question.

1. The cube of x subtracted from the fourth root of the sum of three and the square of the product of two and x is less than $f(x)$. Which of the following correctly depicts the function described?

   A) $f(x) < \sqrt[4]{3+4x^2} - x^3$

   B) $f(x) > x^3 - \sqrt[4]{3+4x^2}$

   C) $f(x) > \sqrt[4]{3+4x^2} - x^3$

   D) $f(x) > \sqrt[4]{3+2x^2} - x^3$

Because there isn't any scratchwork required for a question like this, only the column containing Kaplan's strategic thinking is included. Follow along as we reason our way through this question.

Strategic Thinking
Step 1: Read the question, identifying and organizing important information as you go
The question asks for the function that correctly describes the situation presented.

Strategic Thinking
Step 2: Choose the best strategy to answer the question
This is an exercise in translating English into math, so utilize tactics from that Kaplan Strategy. Take each piece one at a time. "The cube of x" becomes x^3. "The fourth root of the sum of three and the square of the product of two and x" becomes $\sqrt[4]{3+(2x)^2}$; don't forget the parentheses around $2x$!
Read carefully when deciding how to combine these two pieces. "The cube of x" is being subtracted from "the fourth root . . . ," so the expression should now read $\sqrt[4]{3+(2x)^2}-x^3$. According to the question, this entire quantity is less than $f(x)$ (in other words, $f(x)$ is greater than . . .). The inequality should read $f(x)>\sqrt[4]{3+(2x)^2}-x^3$.
Your inequality isn't among the answer choices, but don't worry. The $(2x)^2$ can be simplified to $4x^2$; once you make the switch, you'll see a match.
Step 3: Check that you answered the *right* question
Choice (C) is the correct answer.

Once broken into simpler pieces, this function question became much easier. Read on for more information about other ways the SAT can test your knowledge of functions.

GRAPHICAL & TABULAR FUNCTION INTERPRETATION

The ability to interpret the graphs of functions will serve you well on Test Day (as well as in real life . . . even outside of math class!). Better yet, to interpret graphs of functions, you'll need to utilize the same skills you use to interpret "regular" equations on the coordinate plane, so this material shouldn't be completely foreign.

You know from the first part of this chapter that a function is merely a dressed-up equation, so translating from function to "regular" notation or vice versa is a straightforward process. Consider the following brief example.

Suppose you're asked to find the value of x for which $f(x) = 6$. Because $f(x)$ represents the output value, or range, translate this as "When does the y value equal 6?" To answer the question, find 6 on the y-axis, then trace over to the function (the line). Read the corresponding x value: It's –2, so when $f(x) = 6$, x must be –2.

The SAT might also present functions in the form of tables. These may or may not have an equation associated with them, but regardless, you'll need to be adept at extracting the information necessary to answer questions. Most of the time the table will have just two columns, one for the domain and another for the range.

✔ Note

Remember: A value of $f(x)$ corresponds to a location on the y-axis. A value of x corresponds to a location on the x-axis.

Now try a test-like example.

2. In the figure above, what is the value of $h(0) - 3(g(2) - f(2))$?

    A) −23
    B) −11
    C) $-\dfrac{11}{2}$
    D) $-\dfrac{3}{2}$

Work through the Kaplan Method for Math step-by-step to solve this question. The following table shows Kaplan's strategic thinking on the left, along with suggested math scratchwork on the right.

Strategic Thinking	Math Scratchwork
Step 1: Read the question, identifying and organizing important information as you go You're asked to determine the value of $h(0) - 3(g(2) - f(2))$. In other words, you need to find the y-value of function h when $x = 0$, the y-value of function g when $x = 2$, and the y-value of function f when $x = 2$. You then need to manipulate them as dictated in the given expression.	

Strategic Thinking	Math Scratchwork
Step 2: Choose the best strategy to answer the question Consider each value in the expression one at a time. Study the graph to determine the value of each function at the specified *x*-values. Plug each value into the original expression, and then follow the order of operations to simplify. Be careful as you do this, as it's easy to make careless mistakes, especially with negative signs.	 $h(0) - 3(g(2) - f(2))$ $4 - 3(8 - 3) = 4 - 3(5) = -11$
Step 3: Check that you answered the *right* question You found that the expression equals –11, which is (B).	

✔ **Note**

Watch your axis scales; like scatterplot questions, questions involving graphs of functions often contain trap answers for students who misread the axes.

Although this question would have been much simpler if the graph had labeled the points or given you an equation to plug values into, it wouldn't be testing your knowledge of functions if it did. Your ability to figure out what functions questions are actually asking you for is key to solving them correctly on Test Day.

Try out a tabular function interpretation question.

Day	Vote Count
3	21
4	35
5	53
6	75
7	101

3. Clara is one of five contest finalists in the running for a year's worth of college book expenses. The winner is the finalist with the highest number of votes on the contest host's website. Clara recorded her vote total each day of the contest; data for five days are in the table above. Which of the following represents Clara's vote count, v, as a function of time, t, in days?

A) $v(t) = 2t^2 + 3$

B) $v(t) = \dfrac{t^2}{2} + 3$

C) $v(t) = 2t^2 + 21$

D) $v(t) = \dfrac{t^2}{2} + 21$

Work through the Kaplan Method for Math step-by-step to solve this question. The following table shows Kaplan's strategic thinking on the left, along with suggested math scratchwork on the right.

Strategic Thinking	Math Scratchwork
Step 1: Read the question, identifying and organizing important information as you go The question is asking which function accurately depicts the relationship between time (t) and Clara's vote count (v). A table with data for selected days is given.	

Strategic Thinking	Math Scratchwork
Step 2: Choose the best strategy to answer the question Look for answer choices you can easily eliminate. From the table, you can tell that the rate of change of $v(t)$ is not constant and therefore not linear, but none of the choices are linear. However, the first table entry indicates Clara has 21 votes on day 3, and two choices have 21 as a y-intercept. The y-intercept is where $t = 0$; according to the table, $v(t) = 21$ at $t = 3$, not 0. Therefore, you can eliminate C and D. To evaluate the remaining choices, try plugging a pair of data points into the remaining choices. The point (4, 35) validates (A). To ensure (A) is the correct answer, you can repeat this process with B.	$v(3) = 21, v(0) \neq 21$ use (4, 35) A: $35 = 2 \times 4^2 + 3$ $35 = 2 \times 16 + 3$ $35 = 32 + 3$ $35 = 35$ B: $35 = \dfrac{1}{2} \times 4^2 + 3$ $35 = \dfrac{1}{2} \times 16 + 3$ $35 = 8 + 3$ $35 \neq 11$
Step 3: Check that you answered the *right* question The only function that fits the data is (A).	

As you saw, you won't always have to plug points into each answer choice; you can often reduce your work by eliminating blatantly incorrect answers first. This is crucial for saving time on the SAT and quickly getting to the correct answer.

> ✔ **Note**
>
> When you have only one answer choice remaining, it isn't necessary to evaluate it. If you've done your math correctly up until that point, you know the remaining answer choice *has* to be correct. However, if you're at all worried that you made a mistake earlier, check the remaining answer choice to validate your math.

REAL-WORLD APPLICATION OF FUNCTIONS

Because functions are equations, you have a great deal of flexibility in working with them. For example, order of operations (PEMDAS) and the basic rules of algebra apply to functions just as they do to equations. You learned in unit 1 that equations can represent real-world situations in convenient ways, and the same is true for functions.

For example, suppose a homeowner wants to determine the cost of installing a certain amount of carpet in her living room. In prose, this would quickly become awkward to handle, as a description would need to account for the cost per square foot, fixed installation fee, and sales tax to get the final cost. However, you can easily express this as a function.

Suppose that, in the homeowner example, carpet costs $0.86 per square foot, the installer charges a $29 installation fee, and sales tax on the total cost is 7%. Using your algebra and function knowledge, you can describe this situation in which the cost, c, is a function of square footage, f: $c = 1.07(0.86f + 29)$. In function notation, this becomes $c(f) = 1.07(0.86f + 29)$, where $c(f)$ is shorthand for "cost as a function of square footage." The following table summarizes the origin of each piece of the function.

English	Overall cost	Square footage	Material cost	Installation fee	Sales tax
Math	c	f	$0.86f$	29	1.07

> ✔ **Note**
>
> Why does a 7% tax translate to 1.07? Using 0.07 would only provide the sales tax due. Because the function is meant to express the total cost, 1.07 is used to retain the carpet cost and installation fee while introducing the sales tax. Think of it as 100% (the original price) + the 7% sales tax on top. In decimal form, $1 + 0.07 = 1.07$.

This test-like question will test your ability to write a function.

4. Each calendar year, a certain credit card gives cardholders 5% cash back on gasoline purchases up to $1,500 and 2% cash back on any amount spent on gasoline thereafter. If $g(x)$ and $e(x)$ represent cash back earned on gasoline purchases up to $1,500 and in excess of $1,500, respectively, which of the following sets of functions could be used to determine the amount of cash back earned at each tier?

A) $g(x) = 0.05x$, $0 \le x < 1,500$; $e(x) = 0.02(x - 1,500)$, $x \ge 1,500$

B) $g(x) = 0.05x$, $0 < x \le 1,500$; $e(x) = 0.02x$, $x > 1,500$

C) $g(x) = 0.05x$, $0 \le x \le 1,500$; $e(x) = 0.02(x - 1,500)$, $x > 1,500$

D) $g(x) = 0.05x$, $0 \le x \le 1,500$; $e(x) = 0.02(1,500 - x)$, $x > 1,500$

A word problem like this is a great time to reach for the Kaplan Strategy for Translating English into Math. The following table shows Kaplan's strategic thinking on the left, along with suggested math scratchwork on the right.

Strategic Thinking	Math Scratchwork
Step 1: Read the question, identifying and organizing important information as you go You're asked to find the functions that describe the situation given.	

Strategic Thinking	Math Scratchwork
Step 2: Choose the best strategy to answer the question Use the Kaplan Strategy for Translating English into Math to extract what you need. The question has already defined the variables for you. The function $g(x)$ represents cash back on gasoline purchases up to $1,500, which the question states is 5%. Therefore, a cardholder earns $0.05x$ on this portion of gasoline purchases. Because this rate applies only to the first $1,500, there is a restriction on the function domain: $0 \leq x \leq 1,500$. Eliminate A and B. The function $e(x)$ is used for cash back on gasoline purchases over $1,500. To account for this $1,500, you must subtract it from x. The difference is then multiplied by 0.02 to calculate the additional cash back for gasoline purchases beyond $1,500. Like $g(x)$, $e(x)$ has a domain restriction.	$g(x) = 5\%$ on gas up to $1,500$ $g(x) = 0.05x$, $0 \leq x \leq 1,500$ $e(x) = 2\%$ above $1,500$ $e(x) = 0.02(x - 1,500)$, $x > 1,500$
Step 3: Check that you answered the *right* question Choice (C) is the only choice with both of the functions you built. Watch out for choice A, which lacks the correct inequality symbols in the domain restrictions.	

Notice that even with a more difficult word problem, the Kaplan Strategy for Translating English into Math gets the job done.

MULTIPLE FUNCTIONS

There are several ways in which the SAT might ask you to juggle multiple functions simultaneously. Fortunately, the rules governing what to do are easy to understand. To start, we'll look at how to combine functions. This technique simply involves adding, subtracting, multiplying, and/or dividing the functions in play. Check out the following table for a synopsis of how to combine functions with the four basic operations (and make them look less intimidating).

When you see . . .	. . . convert it to:
$(f + g)(x)$	$f(x) + g(x)$
$(f - g)(x)$	$f(x) - g(x)$
$(fg)(x)$	$f(x) \times g(x)$
$\left(\dfrac{f}{g}\right)(x)$	$\dfrac{f(x)}{g(x)}$

lol T.T

You'll have a chance to solve a problem involving combined functions shortly.

A more challenging type of function combination you're apt to see is a **composition of functions** or **nested functions**. Questions involving a composition of functions require you to find the range of a function at a given value and plug that range into the domain of another function to get the final solution. A composition of functions would be written as $f(g(x))$, (f of g of x), or $(f \circ g)(x)$ (f follows $g(x)$). Remember PEMDAS. To tackle these questions, start with the innermost parentheses and work your way out. A hypothetical situation follows.

> ✔ **Note**
>
> You might see a composition of functions written as $(f \circ g)(x)$. Just remember that it's the same as $(f(g(x))$, and solve as you would normally, working from the inside outward.

If $f(x) = 8x$ and $g(x) = x + 3$, find the value of $f(g(1))$. Your steps are as follows:

1. Determine $g(1)$, the innermost function when $x = 1$.

2. By substituting 1 for x in $g(x)$, you can quickly see that $g(1) = 4$. Now use substitution. If $g(1) = 4$, then you can plug in a 4 every time you see a $g(1)$. Rewrite $f(g(1))$ as $f(4)$.

3. Find $f(4)$, the outer function when $x = 4$. Substituting 4 for x in function f, we quickly realize that our final answer must be 32.

> ✔ **Note**
>
> Note that $f(g(x))$ does *not* equal $g(f(x))$! Not only is interchanging these incorrect, but this practice might also lead you to a trap answer on Test Day.

On Test Day, you might see **piecewise functions**. A piecewise function is a function that is, literally, multiple pieces. What breaks a function into pieces are different rules that govern different parts of a function's domain. Following is an example of this.

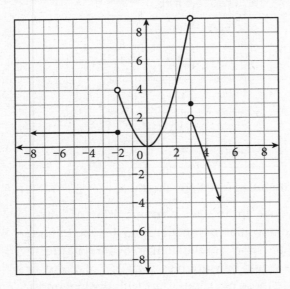

$$f(x) = \begin{cases} 1 & \text{if } x \leq -2 \\ x^2 & \text{if } -2 < x < 3 \\ 3 & \text{if } x = 3 \\ -3x + 11 & \text{if } x > 3 \end{cases}$$

In the function shown, the function behavior depends on the domain. Linear, quadratic, and even single point intervals are possible. We write each "rule" inside an open bracket; to the right is the domain interval for which the "rule" applies. An open dot indicates that a point is not included in that interval; a closed dot indicates one that is. Note the different inequality signs used depending on whether a dot is open or closed. For a single-point interval, an equal sign is used.

5. If $p(x) = x^2 - 4x + 8$ and $q(x) = x - 3$, what is the value of $\dfrac{q(p(5))}{p(q(5))}$?

A) 0

B) 0.4

C) 1

D) 2.5

Appearances can be deceiving. At first glance, this question looks tough, but the following table will clarify anything confusing. Kaplan's strategic thinking is on the left, along with suggested math scratchwork on the right.

Strategic Thinking	Math Scratchwork
Step 1: Read the question, identifying and organizing important information as you go You're asked for the value of $\dfrac{q(p(5))}{p(q(5))}$.	
Step 2: Choose the best strategy to answer the question The numerator and denominator look quite similar, so keep track of your calculations. Start with the numerator: Compute the innermost set of parentheses first, and then work your way outward. Repeat this process with the denominator. Once finished, combine the final values in the original expression.	$p(5) = 5^2 - 4 \times 5 + 8 = 13$ $q(13) = 13 - 3 = 10$ $q(p(5)) = 10$ $q(5) = 5 - 3 = 2$ $p(2) = 2^2 - 4 \times 2 + 8 = 4$ $p(q(5)) = 4$ $\dfrac{q(p(5))}{p(q(5))} = \dfrac{10}{4} = 2.5$
Step 3: Check that you answered the _right_ question You've correctly calculated the expression. The correct answer is (D).	

Below is another example of a real-world scenario involving functions. Recall that the notation $(f \circ g)(x)$ means that f and g are functions of x such that $f(x)$ is computed based on $g(x)$.

6. Everett works at an electronics store. His base salary is $1,000 per week, and he earns a 10% commission on any sales over his $4,000 per week goal. If Everett's commission (c) and sales in excess of $4,000 ($e$) are both functions of his overall sales (s), which of the following correctly describes Everett's total weekly pre-tax pay?

    A) $(c \circ e)(s + 1,000)$

    B) $(e \circ c)(s + 1,000)$

    C) $(e \circ c)(s) + 1,000$

    D) $(c \circ e)(s) + 1,000$

Because there isn't any scratchwork required for a question like this, only the column containing Kaplan's strategic thinking is included. Follow along as we reason our way through this question.

Strategic Thinking
Step 1: Read the question, identifying and organizing important information as you go
You need to identify the expression that correctly depicts Everett's total weekly pay.
Step 2: Choose the best strategy to answer the question
Consider each part of Everett's pay separately. To find Everett's commission, you must first determine the portion of his sales to use for the commission calculation. In other words, commission (c) depends on sales in excess of $4,000 ($e$). This means you'll have a composition of functions with c computed based on e, which translates to $(c \circ e)(s)$.
Everett earns $1,000 regardless of sales, so this figure is independent of functions c and e. It should be added on outside the functions. You can eliminate incorrect answer choices based on this information and the information above.
Step 3: Check that you answered the *right* question
The only match for your function is (D).

Handling multiple functions in the same question or equation is only slightly more involved than manipulating a single function. Be sure to read particularly carefully when the question is embedded in a real-world scenario.

RELATIONSHIPS BETWEEN FUNCTION VARIABLES AND FUNCTION TRANSFORMATIONS

When describing a graph of a function or an interval (a specific segment) of a function, the trend of the relationship between the *x* and *y* values while reading the graph from left to right is often important. Three terms you are sure to see in more difficult function questions are **increasing**, **decreasing**, and **constant**. Let's look carefully at what these terms mean and how they apply to SAT questions.

- **Increasing** functions have *y* values that *increase* as the corresponding *x* values increase.

- **Decreasing** functions have *y* values that *decrease* as the corresponding *x* values increase.

- **Constant** functions have *y* values that *stay the same* as the *x* values increase.

The SAT can ask about function trends in a variety of ways. The most basic would be to examine a function's interval and determine if the function is increasing, decreasing, or constant. Tougher questions might ask you to identify the trend and then explain what it means in the context of a real-life situation presented in the question, or to identify the effect a transformation would have on the trend of a function.

A function transformation occurs when a change is made to the function's equation or graph. Transformations include translations (moving a graph up/down, left/right), reflections (flips about an axis or other line), and expansions/compressions (stretching or squashing horizontally or vertically). How do you know which is occurring? The following table provides some rules for guidance when altering a hypothetical function $f(x)$.

Algebraic Change	Corresponding Graphical Change	Graph	Algebraic Change	Corresponding Graphical Change	Graph
$f(x)$	N/A—original function		$f(x + a)$	$f(x)$ moves left a units	
$f(x) + a$	$f(x)$ moves up a units		$f(x - a)$	$f(x)$ moves right a units	

Algebraic Change	Corresponding Graphical Change	Graph	Algebraic Change	Corresponding Graphical Change	Graph
$f(x) - a$	$f(x)$ moves down a units		$-f(x)$	$f(x)$ reflected over the x-axis (top-to-bottom)	
$f(-x)$	$f(x)$ reflected over the y-axis (left-to-right)		$af(x)$ $(0 < a < 1)$	$f(x)$ undergoes vertical compression	
$f(ax)$ $(0 < a < 1)$	$f(x)$ undergoes horizontal expansion		$af(x)$ $(a > 1)$	$f(x)$ undergoes vertical expansion	
$f(ax)$ $(a > 1)$	$f(x)$ undergoes horizontal compression				

If you forget what a particular transformation looks like, you can always plug in a few values for x and plot the points to determine the effect on the function's graph.

✔ **Expert Tip**

Adding or subtracting inside the parentheses of a function will always effect a horizontal change (e.g., shift left/right, horizontal reflection); if the alteration is outside, you're looking at a vertical change.

A function transformation question for you to try follows.

7. Given function $j(x)$, which of the following choices corresponds to a horizontal compression, reflection about the x-axis, and an upward shift?

A) $-j(2x) + 2$

B) $-j(2x + 2)$

C) $j(-2x) + 2$

D) $-j(\frac{1}{2}x) + 2$

Because there isn't any scratchwork required for a question like this, only the column containing Kaplan's strategic thinking is included. Follow along as we reason our way through this question.

Strategic Thinking
Step 1: Read the question, identifying and organizing important information as you go
You must determine which function shows the transformations specified in the question stem.
Step 2: Choose the best strategy to answer the question
Remember your transformation rules. A horizontal compression requires a variable coefficient greater than 1 (for example, $f(3x)$); D doesn't contain this, so eliminate it. A reflection about the x-axis (vertical) requires a negative sign before j. Eliminate C. An upward shift (also vertical) means the constant quantifying the shift must be outside the function argument parentheses. Of the remaining choices, (A) is the only function that satisfies the conditions in the question stem.
Step 3: Check that you answered the *right* question
The only matching function is (A).

Now you'll have a chance to try a few test-like problems in a scaffolded way. See if you can fill in the missing pieces and solve for the correct answer without a full explanation.

8. Joan is an entomologist (a scientist who studies insects) researching possible causes of honeybee disappearance. At the start of a recent study, she estimated the number of honeybees in a 50 mi² area to be 4.23×10^8 distributed among 7,050 hives. Joan discovered that the honeybee population in this area decreases by 35% every month. Assuming the rate of disappearance remains 35% every month, approximately how many honeybees will remain after one year?

   A) 340

   B) 1,430

   C) 2,406,000

   D) 116,166,000

The following table can help you structure your thinking as you go about solving this question. The Kaplan strategic thinking is provided, as are bits of structured scratchwork. If you're not sure how to approach a question like this, start at the top and work your way down.

Strategic Thinking	Math Scratchwork
Step 1: Read the question, identifying and organizing important information as you go *What are you being asked to find?* You need to determine the approximate number of honeybees remaining in Joan's study area after one year.	

Strategic Thinking	Math Scratchwork
Step 2: Choose the best strategy to answer the question *How can you find the requested information? Is there an equation you can use?* You bet! You're asked about the honeybee population, so zero in on information on the honeybee count and any rates of change, and ignore the rest. *What kind of change is this? What should the function look like?* A reduction of 35% each month means the exact number of honeybees lost will change over time, so you're looking at exponential decay. Add the values you know to create your function. *Am I done?* The question wants a value, so plug in the correct duration into your function to find the number of remaining honeybees. Watch your time units!	exponential change: $y = x_0(1 + r)^x$ $p(t) =$ honeybee pop. $t =$ time in _____ $p(t) = ($_____$)(1 +$ _____$)^t$ $p($__$) = ($_____$)($_____$)$_____ $=$ _____
Step 3: Check that you answered the *right* question *How many honeybees are left after one year?* If you picked (C), you'd be correct.	_____

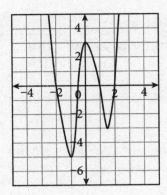

9. The graph of the function $a(x)$ is shown above. If $b(x) = \dfrac{1}{x}$, which of the following is a true statement about $(b \circ a)(x)$?

    A) $(b \circ a)(x)$ is defined for all real numbers.

    B) $(b \circ a)(x)$ is undefined for three real values of x.

    C) $(b \circ a)(x)$ is undefined for four real values of x.

    D) $(b \circ a)(x)$ is undefined for all real numbers.

The following table can help you structure your thinking as you go about solving this problem. The Kaplan strategic thinking is provided, as are bits of structured scratchwork. If you're not sure how to approach a question like this, start at the top and work your way down.

Strategic Thinking	Math Scratchwork
Step 1: Read the question, identifying and organizing important information as you go *What do you ultimately need to find?* You need to figure out when the composition of functions is undefined.	

Strategic Thinking	Math Scratchwork
Step 2: Choose the best strategy to answer the question *What does the composition notation indicate? What is function b doing to function a?* The range of one function is the domain of the other. *What value of a(x) would cause b(x) to be undefined? What should you look for on the graph to indicate this?* You'll notice there's an x in the denominator of b(x); think about what restriction this places on $b(x)$ and when this would make $(b \circ a)(x)$ undefined. *How many times does that value occur?* Examine the graph of $a(x)$ to determine this.	 $(b \circ a)(x) \rightarrow b(a(x))$ range of ____ = domain of ____ if $b(x) = \dfrac{1}{x}$, then $x \neq$ ____ $\rightarrow a(x) \neq$ ____ in $(b \circ a)(x)$ $a(x) =$ ____ at ____ places
Step 3: Check that you answered the *right* question When is $(b \circ a)(x)$ undefined? If you got (C), you're absolutely correct!	 _____

Now that you've seen the variety of ways in which the SAT can test you on functions, try the following questions to check your understanding. Give yourself 4.5 minutes to tackle the following three questions. Make sure you use the Kaplan Method for Math as often as you can. Remember, you want to emphasize speed and efficiency in addition to simply getting the correct answer.

10. The graph of $h(x) = \sin x$ is shown above. Which of the following correctly depicts the transformations effected in $\dfrac{h(2x)}{3} - 4$?

A)

B)

C)

D)

11. Briana is writing a 60-page paper for a law school class; she has a full outline of the paper and needs to convert it to prose. She estimates that she will average 45 words per minute while typing. If one page of prose contains approximately 500 words, which of the following correctly estimates the number of prose pages, p, remaining as a function of the number of minutes, m, that Briana types?

A) $p(m) = 60 - \dfrac{9m}{100}$

B) $p(m) = \dfrac{60 - 100}{9m}$

C) $p(m) = 60 - \dfrac{100}{9m}$

D) $p(m) = \dfrac{60 - 9m}{100}$

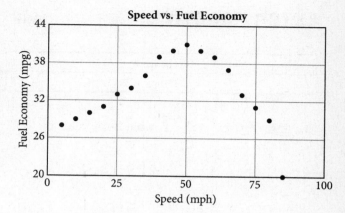

Speed vs. Fuel Economy

12. The graph above shows a compact car's fuel economy as a function of speed. Which of the following is true?

A) The rate of increase in fuel economy below 50 mph is greater than the rate of decrease in fuel economy above 50 mph.

B) The rate of increase in fuel economy below 50 mph is equal to the rate of decrease in fuel economy above 50 mph.

C) Fuel economy peaks at 50 mph, but nothing can be said about the rates of change in fuel economy above and below 50 mph.

D) The rate of increase in fuel economy below 50 mph is less than the rate of decrease in fuel economy above 50 mph.

Answers and Explanations for this chapter begin on page 906.

EXTRA PRACTICE

Required	Recommended
Questions 1–7	Questions 8–18

1. If $g(x) = -2x^2 + 7x - 3$, what is the value of $g(-2)$?

    A) –25

    B) –9

    C) –1

    D) 3

    $$= -2(-2)^2 + 7(-2) - 3$$
    $$= -2(4) + 7 \cdot 14 - 3$$
    $$= -8 - 14 - 3$$
    $$= -22 - 3 = -25$$

2. If $k(x) = 5x + 2$, what is the value of $k(4) - k(1)$?

    A) 15

    B) 17

    C) 19

    D) 21

    $$22 \qquad = 5 + 2$$
    $$= 7$$
    $$= 22 - 7$$
    $$= 15$$
    $$= 1$$

3. The graph of $f(x)$ is shown above. Which of the following represents the domain and range of the function?

    A) Domain: $f(x) \geq 4$; Range: all real numbers

    B) Domain: $f(x) \leq 4$; Range: all real numbers

    C) Domain: all real numbers; Range: $f(x) \geq 4$

    D) Domain: all real numbers; Range: $f(x) \leq 4$

4. If $g(x) = (x - 2)^2 - 5$, which of the following statements is true?

    A) The function $g(x)$ is increasing over the entire domain.

    B) The function $g(x)$ is decreasing over the entire domain.

    C) The function $g(x)$ is increasing for $x < 2$ and decreasing for $x > 2$.

    D) The function $g(x)$ is decreasing for $x < 2$ and increasing for $x > 2$.

5. A function is defined by the equation $f(x) = \dfrac{x^2}{4} - 11$. For this function, which of the following domain values corresponds to a range value of 14?

    A) –4

    B) 10

    C) 38

    D) 100

    $$14$$
    $$\frac{4}{56}$$
    $$\left(\frac{14}{1} = \frac{x^2}{4} - \frac{11}{1}\right)$$
    $$56 = x^2 - 44$$
    $$+44 \qquad +44$$
    $$100 = x^2$$
    $$\pm 10$$

6. The figure shows the function $p(x) = |x|$.
Which statement about the function is not true?

A) $p(0) = 0$

B) $p(-4) = 4$

C) $p(4) = -4$

D) The domain of $p(x)$ is all real numbers.

$$f(x) = \begin{cases} x^2 + 1, & \text{if } x \leq 0 \\ \dfrac{2x}{3} - 1, & \text{if } 0 < x \leq 3 \\ 4 - x, & \text{if } x > 3 \end{cases}$$

7. For the piecewise function $f(x)$ defined above, what is the value of $f(-3)$?

A) −3

B) 7

C) 10

D) −3, 7, and 10

8. The graph above shows Carmel's distance from home over a one-hour period, during which time he first went to the library, then went to the grocery store, and then returned home. Which of the following statements could be true?

A) The grocery store is about 5 miles from Carmel's house.

B) Carmel traveled a total of 7 miles from the time he left home until he returned.

C) The grocery store is 7 miles farther from Carmel's house than the library is.

D) Carmel spent 10 minutes at the library and 15 minutes at the grocery store.

9. Based on the figure above, what is the value of $f(-2) + g(2)$?

A) –3

B) 0

C) 3

D) 6

10. If the graph of a function $g(x)$ passes through the point $(5, 3)$, and $h(x)$ is defined as $h(x) = -g(x - 2) + 8$, through which point does the graph of $h(x)$ pass?

A) $(-3, 11)$

B) $(3, 5)$

C) $(7, 5)$

D) $(7, 11)$

11. If p is a function defined over the set of all real numbers and $p(x + 2) = 3x^2 + 4x + 1$, then which of the following defines $p(x)$?

A) $p(x) = 3x^2 - 7x + 3$

B) $p(x) = 3x^2 - 8x + 5$

C) $p(x) = 3x^2 + 16x + 9$

D) $p(x) = 3x^2 + 16x + 21$

12. A company uses the function $P(x) = 150x - x^2$ to determine how much profit the company will make when it sells 150 units of a certain product that sells for x dollars per unit. How much more profit per unit will the company make if it charges $25 for the product than if it charges $20?

13. The customer service department of a wireless cellular provider has found that on Wednesdays, the polynomial function $C(t) = -0.0815t^4 + t^3 + 12t$ approximates the number of calls received by any given time, where t represents the number of hours that have passed since the department opened at 7 AM. Based on this function, how many calls can be expected by 5 PM?

14. Which of the following does not represent the graph of a function?

A)

B)

C)

D)

15. A biologist is studying the effect of pollution on the reproduction of a specific plant. She uses the function $n(p)$ to represent these effects, where p is the number of seeds germinated by the test group of the plant over a given period of time. Which of the following lists could represent a portion of the domain for the biologist's function?

A) {... −150, −100, −50, 0, 50, 100, 150...}

B) {−150, −100, −50, 0, 50, 100, 150}

C) {0, 0.25, 0.5, 0.75, 1, 1.25, 1.5...}

D) {0, 20, 40, 60, 80...}

x	g(x)
−6	−3
−3	−2
0	−1
3	0
6	1

x	h(x)
0	6
1	−4
2	2
3	0
4	−2

16. Several values for the functions $g(x)$ and $h(x)$ are shown in the tables above. What is the value of $g(h(3))$?

A) −1

B) 0

C) 3

D) 6

17. If $f(x) = 3 - x$ and $g(x) = \dfrac{x^2}{2}$, which of the following is not in the range of $f(g(x))$?

A) −3

B) 0

C) 2

D) 4

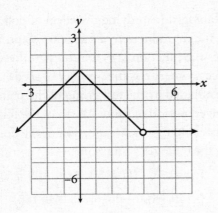

18. Which of the following piecewise functions could have been used to generate the graph above?

A) $g(x) = \begin{cases} -|x|, \text{if } x \le 4 \\ -3, \quad \text{if } x > 4 \end{cases}$

B) $g(x) = \begin{cases} -|x|, \text{if } x < 4 \\ x - 3, \text{if } x > 4 \end{cases}$

C) $g(x) = \begin{cases} -|x| + 1, \text{if } x < 4 \\ -3x, \quad \text{if } x > 4 \end{cases}$

D) $g(x) = \begin{cases} -|x| + 1, \text{if } x < 4 \\ -3, \quad \text{if } x > 4 \end{cases}$

CHAPTER 11

Quadratic Equations

CHAPTER OBJECTIVES

By the end of this chapter, you will be able to:

1. Solve quadratic equations via algebra, graphing, or the quadratic formula

2. Sketch the graph of a given quadratic equation

3. Identify how various components of a quadratic equation are significant to its graph or a real-world scenario

SMARTPOINTS

Point Value	SmartPoint Category
50 Points	Quadratics

INTRODUCTION TO QUADRATIC EQUATIONS

A quadratic equation or expression is simply one that contains a squared variable (x^2) as the highest-order term (also called highest-powered term). In standard form, a quadratic equation is written as $ax^2 + bx + c = 0$, where a, b, and c are constants. However, quadratics can be written in a variety of other forms as well, such as these:

$$x^2 - 9 = 0 \qquad 2r^2 - 8r + 10 = 4 \qquad 2(x-3)^2 = 8 \qquad (x-2)(x+3) = 6$$

> **Note**
>
> At first glance, the last equation might not look quadratic, but it is; it's merely masquerading as a product of binomials. You'll learn a strategy for unveiling its x^2 term shortly.

All quadratic equations will have 0, 1, or 2 real solutions. When you are asked to find the solutions of a quadratic, all you need to do is equate the variable to a constant. Solutions might also be called roots, x-intercepts, or zeros.

Before you can solve, however, there is a step you must always complete: **Set the equation equal to 0**. In other words, move everything to one side of the equation so that 0 is the only thing left on the other side. Once your quadratic equation is equal to 0, you can take one of three routes to determine how many solutions it has: **algebra**, **graphing**, or the **quadratic formula**. Read on for more information about these three techniques.

SOLVING QUADRATICS ALGEBRAICALLY

Algebra is often the most efficient way to work through quadratics, so getting comfortable with it is critical. We'll start with a technique that is highly useful for manipulating quadratics: FOIL. **FOIL is essential for putting a quadratic into standard form.**

> ✔ **Expert Tip**
>
> If you're really stuck on the algebra in a quadratics question, Picking Numbers can often help. Just remember that it might take more time than the algebra route, so use good judgment if you're in a bind—and remember that you can always skip the question and revisit it later.

FOIL

Whenever you see a pair of binomials on the SAT, your default algebra strategy should be FOIL, which stands for First, Outer, Inner, Last. This acronym helps ensure that you don't forget any terms when distributing. You multiply the first terms in each binomial together, then repeat with the outer, inner, and last terms. Then you add the four products together, combining like terms as needed. Here is a generic scheme for the FOIL procedure:

$$(a + b)(c + d) = ac + ad + bc + bd$$

(Binomial 1)(Binomial 2) = First + Outer + Inner + Last

It is often tempting to FOIL in your head, but this is risky: It is very easy to lose a negative sign or switch a pair of coefficients (and arrive at a trap answer). Show *all* of your work when using FOIL.

Factoring

Factoring, also known as reverse-FOIL, allows you to go from a quadratic to a product of two binomials. This is a very powerful tool; once you have a binomial pair, you're a few short algebraic steps away from the solution(s). The factoring process is demonstrated in the following table:

Step	Scratchwork
Starting point. Notice a, the coefficient in front of x^2, is equal to 1, a great condition for factoring!	$x^2 + 5x + 6 = 0 \rightarrow (x \pm ?)(x \pm ?) = 0$
1. What are the factors of c? Remember to include negatives.	factors of 6: 1 & 6, −1 & −6, 2 & 3, −2 & −3
2. Which factor pair, when added, equals b, the coefficient in front of x?	$2 + 3 = 5$
3. Write as a product of binomials.	$(x+2)(x+3) = 0$
4. Split the product of binomials into two equations set equal to 0.	$x+2=0, x+3=0$
5. Solve each equation.	$x=-2, x=-3$

Factoring is easiest when a is 1, so whenever possible, try to simplify your expression so that is the case. In addition, if you see nice-looking numbers (integers, simple fractions) in your answer choices, this is a clue that factoring is possible. If you're ever not sure that you've done your factoring correctly, go ahead and FOIL to check your work. You should get the expression you started with.

✔ **Note**

Sometimes the two factors you choose for your binomials will be identical. In this case, the quadratic will have only one real solution (because the two solutions are identical).

Completing the Square

For more difficult quadratics, you'll need to turn to a more advanced strategy: completing the square. In this process you'll create a perfect square trinomial, which has the form $(x+h)^2 = k$, where h

and k are constants. This route takes some practice to master but will pay dividends when you sail through the most challenging quadratics questions on Test Day. The following table illustrates the procedure along with a corresponding example.

Step	Scratchwork
Starting point.	$x^2 + 6x - 7 = 0$
1. Move the constant to the opposite side.	$x^2 + 6x = 7$
2. Divide b by 2, then square the quotient.	$b = 6; \left(\dfrac{b}{2}\right)^2 = \left(\dfrac{6}{2}\right)^2 = (3)^2 = 9$
3. Add the number from the previous step to both sides of the equation, then factor.	$x^2 + 6x + 9 = 7 + 9 \rightarrow (x+3)(x+3) = 16 \rightarrow$ $(x+3)^2 = 16$
4. Take the square root of both sides.	$\sqrt{(x+3)^2} = \pm\sqrt{16} \rightarrow x + 3 = \pm 4$
5. Split the equation in two and solve.	$x + 3 = 4, \ x + 3 = -4 \rightarrow x = 1, \ x = -7$

A note about completing the square: a needs to be 1 to use this process. You can divide the first term by a to convert the coefficient to 1, but if you start getting strange-looking fractions, it may be easier to use the quadratic formula instead.

Grouping

Although less commonly seen than other strategies, grouping is useful with the more challenging quadratics, especially those with a values greater than 1. You'll need two x terms to use this route. The goal of grouping is to identify the greatest common factor (GCF) of the first two terms, repeat for the second two terms, then finally combine the two GCFs into a separate binomial. Check out the following example if this seems murky.

Step	Scratchwork
Starting point.	$2x^2 - 7x - 15 = 0$
1. You need to split the x term in two; the sum of the new terms' coefficients must equal b, and their product must equal ac.	$a \times c = 2 \times -15 = -30, b = -7$ new x-term coefficients : 3 and -10 $2x^2 - 10x + 3x - 15 = 0$
2. What's the GCF of the first pair of terms?	GCF of $2x^2$ and $-10x$: $2x$
3. Factor out the GCFs.	$2x^2 - 10x + 3x - 15 = 0 \rightarrow$ $2x(x-5) + 3(x-5) = 0$

4. Factor out the newly formed binomial and combine the GCFs into another.	$2x(x-5)+3(x-5)=0 \rightarrow (2x+3)(x-5)=0$
5. Split into two equations and solve as usual.	$2x+3=0,\ x-5=0 \rightarrow x=-\dfrac{3}{2},\ x=5$

Straightforward Math

Sometimes you can get away with not having to FOIL or factor extensively, but you need to be able to spot patterns or trends. When you're missing an x term or constant, that's a good clue that straightforward math will work. Don't resort to complex techniques when some easy simplification will get the job done. Equations similar to the following examples are highly likely to appear on the SAT.

No Middle Term	No Last Term	Squared Binomial	
$x^2 - 9 = 0$	$x^2 - 9x = 0$	$(x-3)^2 = 9$	
$x^2 = 9$	$x(x-9) = 0$	$(x-3) = \pm\sqrt{9}$	
$x = \pm 3$	$x = 0, 9$	$(x-3) = \pm 3$	
		$x - 3 = 3$	$x - 3 = -3$
		$x = 6$	$x = 0$

✔ **Expert Tip**

You can also factor $x^2 - 9$ to get $(x + 3)(x - 3)$; this is called a difference of squares. Note that this only works when the terms are being subtracted.

Quadratic Formula

The quadratic formula can be used to solve any quadratic equation. However, because the math can often get complicated, use this as a last resort or when you need to find exact (e.g., not rounded; fractions and/or radicals intact) solutions.

The quadratic formula that follows outputs solutions to a quadratic equation, given values of a, b, and c from the equation of a parabola in standard form.

$$x = \frac{-b \pm \sqrt{b^2 - 4ac}}{2a}$$

The $\pm$ operator indicates you will use two equations to solve to get all potential solutions, so remember to compute both.

The expression under the radical ($b^2 - 4ac$) is called the discriminant, and its sign determines the number of real solutions. If this quantity is positive, there are two distinct real solutions; if it is equal to zero, there is just one distinct real solution; and if it's negative, then there are no real solutions.

> ✔ **Note**
>
> Being flexible and familiar with your strengths on Test Day is essential. By doing so, you can identify the path to the answer to a quadratics question that is the most efficient for you.

On the next few pages, you'll get to try applying some of these strategies to test-like SAT problems.

1. Which of the following is an equivalent form of the expression $(6 - 5x)(15x - 11)$?

   A) $-75x^2 + 35x - 66$

   B) $-75x^2 + 145x - 66$

   C) $90x^2 - 141x + 55$

   D) $90x^2 + 9x + 55$

Work through the Kaplan Method for Math step-by-step to solve this question. The following table shows Kaplan's strategic thinking on the left, along with suggested math scratchwork on the right.

Strategic Thinking	Math Scratchwork
Step 1: Read the question, identifying and organizing important information as you go You're asked to identify the quadratic expression equivalent to $(6 - 5x)(15x - 11)$.	
Step 2: Choose the best strategy to answer the question You have binomials in the question stem and standard form quadratics in the answer choices, so FOIL is the quickest route. Follow the standard FOIL procedure, and then simplify.	$(6 - 5x)(15x - 11)$ $(6)(15x) + (6)(-11) + (-5x)(15x) + (-5x)(-11)$ First + Outer + Inner + Last $90x - 66 - 75x^2 + 55x$ $-75x^2 + 145x - 66$

Strategic Thinking	Math Scratchwork
Step 3: Check that you answered the *right* question You correctly expanded the quadratic using FOIL and got an exact match for (B), the correct answer.	$-75x^2 + 145x - 66$

✔ **Expert Tip**

Although you could Pick Numbers here, remember you have only a few seconds to solve questions like this on Test Day. FOIL is much faster and should be your preferred method.

Although it's technically not a quadratic expression, the expression in the following question provides a chance to practice the strategies you've learned in this section.

2. Which of the following is equivalent to $\dfrac{x^2 - 10x + 25}{3x^2 - 75}$?

    A) $\dfrac{3(x-5)}{(x+5)}$

    B) $\dfrac{3(x+5)}{(x-5)}$

    C) $\dfrac{(x-5)}{3(x+5)}$

    D) $\dfrac{(x+5)}{3(x-5)}$

Work through the Kaplan Method for Math step-by-step to solve this question. The following table shows Kaplan's strategic thinking on the left, along with suggested math scratchwork on the right.

Strategic Thinking	Math Scratchwork
Step 1: Read the question, identifying and organizing important information as you go You need to identify which answer choice contains an expression equivalent to the one in the question stem.	

Strategic Thinking	Math Scratchwork
Step 2: Choose the best strategy to answer the question There are a few x^2 terms, so you should be thinking about quadratics and factoring. Also, whenever you're given a fraction, think about ways to cancel terms. Examine the numerator first: You can use the quadratic shortcut $a^2 - 2ab + b^2 = (a - b)^2$ to rewrite it. The denominator is more involved. Factor out a 3 first, and then factor the quadratic, which is a difference of squares. Lastly, cancel any factors that the numerator and denominator share.	$$\dfrac{x^2 - 10x + 25}{3x^2 - 75}$$ $$\dfrac{(x-5)(x-5)}{3(x^2 - 25)}$$ $$\dfrac{(x-5)\cancel{(x-5)}}{3(x+5)\cancel{(x-5)}}$$
Step 3: Check that you answered the *right* question The expression is now in simplest form, so you're done. Choice (C) is correct.	$$\dfrac{(x-5)}{3(x+5)}$$

✔ **Expert Tip**

Utilize the special quadratics, such as difference of squares, to eliminate factoring tasks and save time on Test Day.

3. Which of the following is a value of x that satisfies the equation $x^2 + 2x - 5 = 0$?

A) -1

B) $1 - \sqrt{6}$

C) $1 + \sqrt{6}$

D) $-1 - \sqrt{6}$

This question is full of radicals, but don't panic. You can use the Kaplan Method for Math to efficiently tackle this kind of question on Test Day. The following table shows Kaplan's strategic thinking on the left, along with suggested math scratchwork on the right.

Strategic Thinking	Math Scratchwork
Step 1: Read the question, identifying and organizing important information as you go The question asks for a solution to the given equation.	

Strategic Thinking	Math Scratchwork
Step 2: Choose the best strategy to answer the question The equation is a quadratic, so you have a few potential options. Because –5 does not have factors that add up to 2, you cannot factor or group. However, because the coefficient of x^2 is 1, completing the square is doable. We'll use that method here, but you can use the quadratic formula if you prefer.	$x^2 + 2x - 5 = 0$ $x^2 + 2x = 5$ $\left(\dfrac{b}{2}\right)^2 = \left(\dfrac{2}{2}\right)^2 = 1^2 = 1$ $x^2 + 2x + 1 = 5 + 1$ $(x + 1)^2 = 6$ $(x+1) = \sqrt{6}$ and $(x+1) = -\sqrt{6}$ $x = -1 \pm \sqrt{6}$
Step 3: Check that you answered the *right* question The question asks for one possible value of x, so you should expect to see one (but not both) of the possible values in the choices. Choice (D) contains one of these values.	$x = -1 + \sqrt{6}$ or $x = -1 - \sqrt{6}$

CONNECTIONS BETWEEN QUADRATICS AND PARABOLAS

A quadratic function is simply a quadratic equation set equal to y or $f(x)$ instead of 0. To solve one of these, you would follow the same procedure as before: Substitute 0 for y or $f(x)$, then solve using one of the three methods demonstrated (algebra, graphing, quadratic formula). Consider the graphical connection: When you set y equal to 0, you're really solving for x-intercepts.

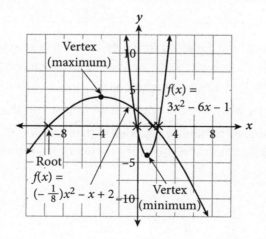

All quadratic functions will graph as parabolas (U-shaped), opening up or down. To determine whether a parabola will open up or down, examine the a value in your function's equation. If a is positive, the parabola will open upward; if *a* is negative, it will open downward. Take a look at the examples below to see this graphically.

Like quadratic equations, quadratic functions will have zero, one, or two real solutions, corresponding to the number of times a parabola crosses the *x*-axis. As you saw with previous examples, graphing is a powerful way to determine the number of solutions a quadratic function has.

Two Real Solutions	One Real Solution	No Real Solutions

There are three forms that a quadratic function can take: standard, factored, and vertex. Each is provided in the following table along with some helpful properties of each form.

Standard	Factored	Vertex
$y = ax^2 + bx + c$	$y = a(x - m)(x - n)$	$y = a(x - h)^2 + k$
y-intercept: *c*	Solutions are *m* and *n*	Vertex is (h, k)
In real-world contexts, starting quantity is *c*		Min/max function value (vertex) is *k*
Format used to solve via quadratic formula		

You've already seen standard and factored forms earlier in this chapter, but vertex form might be new to you. In vertex form, *a* is the same as the *a* from standard form, and *h* and *k* are the coordinates of the vertex (h, k). If a quadratic function is not in vertex form, you can still find the *x*-coordinate of the vertex by plugging the appropriate values into the equation $h = \frac{-b}{2a}$, which is also the equation for the axis of symmetry (see graph that follows). Once you determine *h*, plug this value into the quadratic function and solve for *y* to determine *k*, the *y*-coordinate of the vertex.

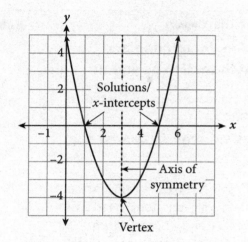

In addition to familiarity with the various forms a quadratic equation/function can take, you should have a foundational knowledge of the structure of a parabola. Some of the basic pieces you could be asked about on Test Day are shown here. You already know how to determine the solutions and vertex, and the axis of symmetry is straightforward. **The equation of the axis of symmetry of a parabola is $x = h$, where h is the x-coordinate of the vertex.**

✔ **Note**

The formula for a parabola's axis of symmetry is easy to remember: It's the quadratic formula without the radical component. If the x-intercepts are rational numbers, you can also determine the axis of symmetry by finding the midpoint, the point exactly halfway between.

Take some time to explore the questions on the next several pages to test your new wealth of quadratic knowledge.

A question like this next one could arise in either the calculator or the non-calculator section. Think critically about how you'd solve it in either case.

4.   What are the x-intercepts of the parabolic function $f(x) = 3x^2 - 2x - 8 = 0$?

A) $\dfrac{1}{3}$ and -25

B) $\dfrac{4}{3}$ and -2

C) $-\dfrac{4}{3}$ and 2

D) $-\dfrac{4}{3}$ and -2

Work through the Kaplan Method for Math step-by-step to solve this question. The following table shows Kaplan's strategic thinking on the left, along with suggested math scratchwork on the right.

Strategic Thinking	Math Scratchwork
Step 1: Read the question, identifying and organizing important information as you go You're given a quadratic in standard form and asked to find its x-intercepts.	
Step 2: Choose the best strategy to answer the question Because the coefficient of x^2 isn't 1, you can't easily factor. However, the grouping method will work. You'll need two numbers whose product is ac (–24) and whose sum is b (–2); the two magic numbers are –6 and 4. Rewrite the middle term using these numbers before you group, factor, and solve for x.	$f(x) = 3x^2 - 2x - 8 = 0$ $ac = 3 \times -8 = -24$ $b = -2$ $3x^2 - 6x + 4x - 8 = 0$ $3x(x - 2) + 4(x - 2) = 0$ $(3x + 4)(x - 2) = 0$ $(3x + 4) = 0 \text{ or } (x - 2) = 0$
Step 3: Check that you answered the *right* question The question asks for the x-intercepts of the equation, which is what you calculated. Select (C) and move on.	$x = -\dfrac{4}{3} \text{ or } x = 2$

✔ **Note**

If a question like this were in the calculator section, you could also solve it by graphing.

In one final type of quadratic-related problem, you may be asked to match a function to a graph or vice-versa. An example of this appears below; unfortunately, it is not likely to appear in the calculator section of the test.

5. The previous function is represented by the equation $f(x) = a(x - h)^2 + k$. Which of the following statements is NOT true?

    A) The value of a is negative.

    B) $f(x)$ is symmetrical across the line $y = 3$.

    C) The function $g(x) = \dfrac{2x}{3}$ intersects $f(x)$ at its vertex.

    D) The value of h is positive.

Because there isn't any scratchwork required for a question like this, only the column containing Kaplan's strategic thinking is included. Try to ask yourself similar questions as you work through questions like this on Test Day.

Strategic Thinking
Step 1: Read the question, identifying and organizing important information as you go
The equation given is in vertex form. You must pick the answer choice that is *not* true.
Step 2: Choose the best strategy to answer the question
Take control of this question—tackle everything in a strategic order. Choices A and D contain the simplest statements, so check them first. Choice A says that a is negative. For parabolas that open downward, a will always be negative, so this statement is true. Eliminate it. Choice D says that h is positive. Recall that when a parabola is written in vertex form, h represents the x-coordinate of the vertex. Because the vertex is (3, 2), h must indeed be positive. Choice D is therefore true, so eliminate it. Of the remaining answer choices, B is simpler: It involves the parabola's axis of symmetry, which you can quickly find. Because the x-coordinate of the vertex is 3, the axis of symmetry is the line $x = 3$. Choice B says that the axis of symmetry is $y = 3$ and is therefore false.
Step 3: Check that you answered the *right* question
Remember that you're looking for a false statement, not a true statement. Choice (B) is false, so you can select it confidently without even bothering to evaluate C.

✔ **Note**

Stay on the lookout for words such as "not" that are easily missed if you don't read the question stem carefully. This is especially true of questions testing more involved topics.

GRAPHING QUADRATICS ON A CALCULATOR

At this point, you've become quite an expert at working with quadratics on paper. In this part, we'll explore how you can use your calculator to efficiently graph quadratics. Calculators can be great time-savers *when you're allowed to use them*.

Graphing

All quadratics can be solved by graphing. That said, you might ask why you should bother learning all the aforementioned algebra gymnastics. There are a few reasons why graphing shouldn't be the first option you turn to:

- Remember, there's a non-calculator section on the SAT; graphing isn't an option here.

- Graphing is often slower because entering complex equations and then zooming to trace the graph(s) can be tedious.

- It is easy to accidentally mistype when you're being timed—a misplaced parenthesis or negative sign will likely lead to a trap answer choice.

However, if you have complicated algebra ahead (e.g., fractional coefficients), decimals in the answer choices, or time-consuming obstacles to overcome, graphing can be a viable alternative to solving quadratics algebraically. A set of straightforward steps for graphing on a calculator follows:

1. Manipulate your equation so that it equals 0.

2. Substitute $y =$ or $f(x) =$ for the 0.

3. Enter the function into your calculator.

4. Trace the graph to approximate the x-intercepts (usually the answer choices will be sufficiently different to warrant approximation over an exact value) or use your calculator's built-in capability to find the x-intercepts exactly.

Graphing on the TI-83/84

While on the home screen, press [Y=]. Then enter your function to be graphed. Press [GRAPH] and allow the function to plot. If you can't see everything or want to ensure there isn't something hiding, consider pressing [WINDOW] to set your own manual parameters or hitting [ZOOM] to quickly zoom in and out, among other quick options. If you want to simply investigate your graph, press [TRACE] and use the right and left arrow keys to move around on the graph. If you type in any x-value and press [ENTER], the y-value will be returned on screen.

Determining Solutions on the TI-83/84

Once you have your graph on screen, you're ready to find solutions. Press [2ND] [TRACE] to pull up the CALC menu, which has options for finding points of interest. Select option 2: ZERO by highlighting and pressing [ENTER]. You will be taken back to the graph. Use the arrow keys to move to the left of the *x*-intercept (zero) that you want to calculate. Once you are just to the left of only the zero you are interested in, press [**ENTER**]—this is called the Left Bound. Next, move to the right of that zero only, careful not to go past any others, and press [**ENTER**]—this is called the Right Bound. Finally, the calculator will ask you to "Guess," so move left or right to approximate this zero, and press [**ENTER**].

Because you've already set your quadratic equation equal to zero, you know the zeros that your calculator returns will be the solutions to the overall equation.

✔ **Note**

Take the time to get comfortable with your calculator functions regardless of what calculator you have. You can find great instructions and even video demonstrations on the Internet.

Next, you'll get to try a sample test-like problem that could be solved via graphing or the quadratic formula. Choose wisely. In almost every case, graphing will be faster, but familiarize yourself with the quadratic formula approach in case you encounter a problem like this in the non-calculator section.

6. Which are the real values of *x* that satisfy the equation $2x^2 - 5x - 2 = 0$?

    A) 1 and 4

    B) $-\dfrac{5}{4} + \dfrac{\sqrt{41}}{4}$ and $-\dfrac{5}{4} - \dfrac{\sqrt{41}}{4}$

    C) $\dfrac{5}{4} + \dfrac{\sqrt{41}}{4}$ and $\dfrac{5}{4} - \dfrac{\sqrt{41}}{4}$

    D) No real solutions

Work through the Kaplan Method for Math step-by-step to solve this question. The following table shows Kaplan's strategic thinking on the left, along with suggested math scratchwork on the right.

Strategic Thinking	Math Scratchwork
Step 1: Read the question, identifying and organizing important information as you go You need to identify the values of *x* that satisfy the given equation.	

Strategic Thinking	Math Scratchwork
Step 2: Choose the best strategy to answer the question When solving quadratics, you have three options: factor, graph, or use the quadratic formula. Attempting to factor is not wise, as the coefficients aren't factoring-friendly. Using a calculator would work, but it's likely to be messy: Two answer choices contain radicals, so you'd have to plug both solutions into the calculator and use the [TRACE] feature to see which ones approximately match the values you find. The quadratic formula, although a longer route, is actually the most efficient option for this question. Plug in your coefficients and constants appropriately. Labeling the equation will help keep the values of a, b, and c straight.	$$2x^2 - 5x - 2 = 0$$ $$a b c$$ $$x = \frac{-b \pm \sqrt{b^2 - 4ac}}{2a}$$ $$x = \frac{-(-5) \pm \sqrt{(-5)^2 - 4(2)(-2)}}{2(2)}$$ $$x = \frac{5 \pm \sqrt{25 - (-16)}}{4}$$ $$x = \frac{5 \pm \sqrt{41}}{4}$$ $$x = \frac{5}{4} + \frac{\sqrt{41}}{4} \text{ or } x = \frac{5}{4} - \frac{\sqrt{41}}{4}$$
Step 3: Check that you answered the *right* question The question asks for the solutions to the equation, so you're finished. Your match is (C).	$$x = \frac{5}{4} \pm \frac{\sqrt{41}}{4}$$

✔ **Note**

Note that in this question, the quadratic formula was the most efficient way to solve the question. Be prepared to use any of the quadratics tools at your disposal on Test Day.

Nicely done! Take a look at another example.

7. The equation $\frac{1}{4}(4x^2 - 8x - k) = 30$ is satisfied when $x = -5$ and when $x = 7$. What is the value of $2k$?

A) 40

B) 20

C) 0

D) −20

Although this question seems more complicated than others you've seen in this chapter, if you use the Kaplan Method for Math, you'll find the correct answer. The following table shows Kaplan's strategic thinking on the left, along with suggested math scratchwork on the right.

Strategic Thinking	Math Scratchwork
Step 1: Read the question, identifying and organizing important information as you go You're asked to find the value of $2k$.	
Step 2: Choose the best strategy to answer the question Notice that the equation in the question stem is not in standard form. Distributing the $\frac{1}{4}$ won't result in unmanageable fractions, so doing so won't cost you a lot of time. After distributing, set the equation equal to 0. The "normal" routes to the solutions (factoring, etc.) would be difficult to take here because of the presence of k. Instead, use the solutions to construct and FOIL two binomials. The quadratic expressions must be equal because they share the same solutions. Set them equal to each other, and then use algebra to solve for k.	$\frac{1}{4}(4x^2 - 8x - k) = 30$ $x^2 - 2x - \frac{k}{4} = 30$ $x^2 - 2x - \frac{k}{4} - 30 = 0$ $(x-7)(x+5) = 0$ $x^2 - 2x - 35 = 0$ $x^2 - 2x - \frac{k}{4} - 30 = x^2 - 2x - 35$ $-\frac{k}{4} = -5$ $-k = -20$ $k = 20$
Step 3: Check that you answered the *right* question Be careful! Many students will select B, but you're asked for $2k$. Multiply the value of k by 2, and select (A).	$k = 20$ $2k = 40$

As demonstrated, even the most daunting quadratics questions are made more straightforward by using the Kaplan Method for Math.

Now you'll have a chance to try a few more test-like questions. Use the scaffolding as needed as a guide through the question and to the right answer.

Some guidance is provided, but you'll need to fill in the missing parts of explanations or the step-by-step math in order to get to the correct answer. Don't worry—after going through the examples at the beginning of this chapter, these questions should be completely doable. If you're still struggling, review the worked examples in this chapter.

8. The height of a potato launched from a potato gun can be described as a function of elapsed time according to the following quadratic equation: $y(t) = -16t^2 + 224t + 240$. What is the sum of the potato's maximum height and the time it takes the potato to reach the ground?

   A) 15

   B) 240

   C) 1,024

   D) 1,039

Use the following scaffolding as your map through the question. If you aren't sure where to start, answer the questions in italics and fill in the blanks in the table as you work from top to bottom.

Strategic Thinking	Math Scratchwork
Step 1: Read the question, identifying and organizing important information as you go *What are you being asked to do here?* You're asked to find the sum of the maximum height and the time it takes the potato to hit the ground. The t^2 indicates a quadratic (and therefore a parabolic trajectory).	

Strategic Thinking	Math Scratchwork
Step 2: Choose the best strategy to answer the question	
How can you tackle this systematically? What component of the parabola would correspond to the maximum height?	$h = \dfrac{-b}{2a} = \rule{2cm}{0.4pt}$ $k = y(h)$
Because *a* (the t^2 coefficient) is negative, this parabola opens down, which means the maximum height would be at the vertex.	$k = -16(\_)^2 + 224x\_ + 240$ $k = \rule{4cm}{0.4pt}$
The vertex form of a parabola is f(x) = a(x − h)² + k. Which variable represents the height? What is the max height the potato will reach?	$O = \rule{4cm}{0.4pt}$ $O = (\rule{1.5cm}{0.4pt})(\rule{1.5cm}{0.4pt})$
Find *h*, then use it to find the maximum height.	$t = \rule{3.5cm}{0.4pt}$
What is the height of the potato when it hits the ground?	$t = \rule{3.5cm}{0.4pt}$
	sum = $\rule{2cm}{0.4pt}$ + $\rule{2cm}{0.4pt}$
When the potato hits the ground, its height will be zero. Translation: factor!	
What are the possible solutions for t? Which of these solutions doesn't make sense in the context of the question? Is there anything left to do?	
Remember, the question asks you for the sum of the potato's maximum height and the time it takes the potato to hit the ground.	
Step 3: Check that you answered the *right* question	
Did you calculate the sum of the maximum height and the time the potato spent in the air?	
If you came up with (D), you're absolutely correct.	$\rule{2cm}{0.4pt}$

9. If $ab > 0$, $b^2ac < 0$, *a* is a constant, and *b* and *c* are distinct *x*-intercepts of the function *f(x)*, then *f(x)* could equal which of the following?

   A) $5x^2 + 1$

   B) $(x - \sqrt{17})(x + \sqrt{24})$

   C) $(x - \sqrt{17})(x - \sqrt{24})$

   D) $(x + \sqrt{17})(x + \sqrt{24})$

Use the scaffolding that follows as your map through the question. If you aren't sure where to start, answer the questions in italics and fill in the blanks in the table as you work from top to bottom.

Strategic Thinking	Math Scratchwork
Step 1: Read the question, identifying and organizing important information as you go *What do you need to find?* You need to select the equation that satisfies the given properties of $f(x)$.	
Step 2: Choose the best strategy to answer the question *What can you deduce about a and b?* If $ab > 0$, then a and b are either both positive or both negative. *What can you deduce about c?* In the inequality $b^2ac < 0$, b^2 will be positive regardless of the sign of b. Therefore, either a or c is positive, and the other must be negative. *What must be true about the x-intercepts of f(x)?* The *x*-intercepts are b and c. Since b has the same sign as a, while c has the opposite sign as a, it follows that b and c also have opposite signs. *What does that imply?* The correct answer must be a function with one negative root and one positive root. Scan the functions to find the correct one. Ignore the complicated-looking numbers; all that matters are the signs!	$ab > 0$ a and b have _____ sign $b^2ac < 0$ a and c have _____ signs b and c are roots of $f(x)$ $f(x)$ has one _____ root and one _____ root A's roots are _____ B's roots are _____ C's roots are _____ D's roots are _____
Step 3: Check that you answered the *right* question *Do you need to go any further?* If you picked (B), then you got it!	_____

Now that you've seen the variety of ways in which the SAT can test you on quadratics, try the following questions to check your understanding. Give yourself 5 minutes to tackle the following four questions. Make sure you use the Kaplan Method for Math as often as you can. Remember, you want to emphasize speed and efficiency in addition to simply getting the correct answer.

10. If $4x - 12\sqrt{x} + 9 = 16$, then $10\sqrt{x} - 15 =$

   A) 20

   B) 25

   C) 30

   D) 35

11. How many times do the parabolas $f(x) = 3(x - 4)^2 + 4$ and $g(x) = (x + 5)^2 + 2x - 135$ intersect?

   A) Never

   B) Once

   C) Twice

   D) More than twice

12. What is positive difference between the x-intercepts of the parabola $g(x) = -2.5x^2 + 10x - 7.5$?

13. What is the axis of symmetry of the function $f(x) = -\dfrac{11}{3}x^2 + 17x - \dfrac{43}{13}$?

   A) $x = -\dfrac{102}{11}$

   B) $x = -\dfrac{51}{22}$

   C) $x = \dfrac{51}{22}$

   D) $x = \dfrac{102}{11}$

Answers and Explanations for this chapter begin on page 914.

EXTRA PRACTICE

Required	Recommended
Questions 1–8	Questions 9–31

1. Which of the following is equivalent to $(2a + 5b)(a - 3b)$?

    $2a^2 + 6ab + 5ab$
    $2a^2 - ab - 15b^2$

    A) $2a^2 - 2ab - 15b^2$

    B) $2a^2 - ab - 15b^2$

    C) $2a^2 + 2ab - 15b^2$

    D) $2a^2 + 11ab - 15b^2$

2. Which of the following are roots of the quadratic equation $(x + 3)^2 = 49$?

    $\sqrt{(x+3)^2} = \sqrt{49}$
    $x + 3 = \pm 7$
    $-3 \quad -3$
    $4, -10$

    A) $x = -10, x = 4$

    B) $x = -10, x = 10$

    C) $x = -4, x = 10$

    D) $x = 3 \pm 2\sqrt{13}$

3. The factored form of a quadratic equation is $y = (2x + 1)(x - 5)$, and the standard form is $y = x^2 - 3x - 5$. Which of the following statements accurately describes the graph of y?

    A) The x-intercepts are –1 and 5, and the y-intercept is –5.

    B) The x-intercepts are $-\dfrac{1}{2}$ and 5, and the y-intercept is –5.

    C) The x-intercepts are $-\dfrac{1}{2}$ and 5, and the y-intercept is 5.

    D) The x-intercepts are 1 and –5, and the y-intercept is –5.

4. What information does the value of c reveal when a quadratic equation is written in the form $y = ax^2 + bx + c$, assuming $a \neq 0$, $b \neq 0$, and $c \neq 0$?

    A) The solution (zero) of the equation

    B) The location of the graph's axis of symmetry

    C) The y-intercept of the graph of the equation

    D) The maximum or minimum value of the equation

5. Taylor fires a toy rocket from ground level. The height of the rocket with respect to time can be represented by a quadratic function. If the toy rocket reaches a maximum height of 34 feet, 3 seconds after it was fired, which of the following functions could represent the height, h, of the rocket t seconds after it was fired?

    A) $h(t) = -16(t - 3)^2 + 34$

    B) $h(t) = -16(t + 3)^2 + 34$

    C) $h(t) = 16(t - 3)^2 + 34$

    D) $h(t) = 16(t + 3)^2 + 34$

6. Which of the following could be the graph of
   the equation $y = x^2 + 2x - 8$?

A)

B)

C)

D)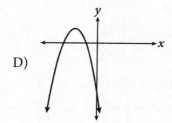

7. If $x^2 - 7x = 30$ and $x > 0$, what is the value of
   $x - 5$?

   A) 5

   B) 6

   C) 10

   D) 25

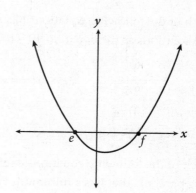

8. If e is half as far from the origin as f in the figure
   above, which of the following could be the factored form of the graph's equation?

   A) $y = (x - \frac{1}{2})(x + 1)$

   B) $y = (x - 1)(x + 2)$

   C) $y = (x - 1)(2x + 1)$

   D) $y = (x + \frac{1}{2})(2x + 1)$

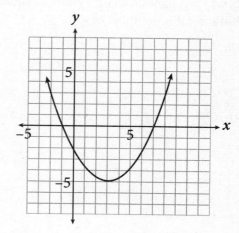

9. If $f(x) = ax^2 + bx + c$ represents the quadratic
   function whose graph is shown in the figure
   above, which of the following statements is
   NOT true?

   A) $a > 0$

   B) $b > 0$

   C) $c < 0$

   D) All of the statements are true.

10. Which of the following equations has the same solutions as the equation $40 - 6x = x^2$?

    A) $y = (x - 6)^2 - 40$

    B) $y = (x - 6)^2 + 40$

    C) $y = (x + 3)^2 - 49$

    D) $y = (x + 3)^2 + 49$

11. Which of the following equations could represent a parabola that has a minimum value of 5 and whose axis of symmetry is the line $x = -3$?

    A) $y = (x - 3)^2 + 5$

    B) $y = (x + 3)^2 + 5$

    C) $y = (x - 5)^2 + 3$

    D) $y = (x + 5)^2 - 3$

$$\begin{cases} y = 2x \\ 2x^2 + 2y^2 = 240 \end{cases}$$

12. If (x, y) is a solution to the system of equations above, what is the value of x^2?

    A) 24

    B) 40

    C) 120

    D) 576

Tyree's Punt

Time in Air (seconds)

13. Tyree punts a football into the air. The equation $h = -16t^2 + 60t$ represents the height of the ball in feet, t seconds after it was punted. The graph of part of the equation is shown in the figure above. If Craig punts a ball higher than Tyree did, which of the following equations could be use to find the height of Craig's punt?

    A) $h = -16(t^2 - 3t)$

    B) $h = -8t(2t - 9)$

    C) $h = -4(2t - 5)^2 + 48$

    D) $h = -4(2t - 6)^2 + 52$

14. What is the positive difference between the roots of the equation $y = \frac{1}{3}x^2 - 2x + 3$?

15. If $x = -5$ when $x^2 + 2xk + k^2 = 0$, what is the value of k?

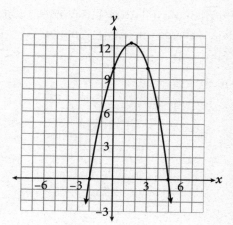

16. If the graph of $y = ax^2 + bx + c$ passes through the points $(-2, -10)$, $(0, 2)$, and $(4, 14)$, what is the value of $a + b + c$?

17. The factored form of a quadratic equation is $y = (2x - 3)(x + 5)$. What are the solutions to the equation?

A) $x = -5, x = \dfrac{2}{3}$

B) $x = -5, x = \dfrac{3}{2}$

C) $x = 5, x = -\dfrac{2}{3}$

D) $x = 5, x = -\dfrac{3}{2}$

18. Which of the following could be the equation of the graph shown?

A) $y = 2x + 10$

B) $y = -x^2 + \dfrac{3}{2}x + 10$

C) $y = -(x - 2)(x + 5)$

D) $y = -(x + 2)(x - 5)$

19. The following quadratic equations are all representations of the graph above. Which equation directly reveals the exact values of the x-intercepts of the graph?

A) $y = 4x^2 - x - 3$

B) $y = (4x + 3)(x - 1)$

C) $y = 4(x - 0.125)^2 - 3.0625$

D) $y + 3.0625 = 4(x - 0.125)^2$

20. Which of the following linear expressions divides evenly into $6x^2 + 7x - 20$?

    A) $3x - 10$

    B) $3x - 5$

    C) $3x - 4$

    D) $3x - 2$

$$\begin{cases} x + y = 4 \\ y = x^2 - 2x - 15 \end{cases}$$

21. If (a, b) and (c, d) represent the solutions to the system of equations above, and $a < c$, then which of the following statements is true?

    A) $a > 0$ and $c > 0$

    B) $a < 0$ and $c < 0$

    C) $a > 0$ and $c < 0$

    D) $a < 0$ and $c > 0$

22. If the equation of the axis of symmetry of the parabola given by $y = 3x^2 + 12x - 8$ is $x = m$, then what is the value of m?

    A) -8

    B) -4

    C) -2

    D) 0

23. Given that a, b, and c are all positive integers such that $ac > \dfrac{b^2}{4}$, how many times does the graph of the equation $y = ax^2 + bx + c$ cross the x-axis?

    A) 0

    B) 1

    C) 2

    D) There is not enough information to determine how many solutions the system has.

24. Given the equation $y = -(2x - 4)^2 + 7$, which of the following statements is not true?

    A) The vertex is $(4, 7)$.

    B) The y-intercept is $(0, -9)$.

    C) The parabola opens downward.

    D) The graph crosses the x-axis at least one time.

25. The x-coordinates of the solutions to a system of equations are 3.5 and 6. Which of the following could be the system?

    A) $\begin{cases} y = x + 3.5 \\ y = x^2 + 6 \end{cases}$

    B) $\begin{cases} y = 2x - 7 \\ y = -(x - 6)^2 \end{cases}$

    C) $\begin{cases} y = \dfrac{1}{2}x + 3 \\ y = -(x - 5)^2 + 7 \end{cases}$

    D) $\begin{cases} y = \dfrac{1}{2}x + 7 \\ y = -(x - 6)^2 + 3.5 \end{cases}$

26. If the quadratic equation $y = 3(x + 5)^2 + 12$ is rewritten in standard form, $y = ax^2 + bx + c$, what is the value of c?

27. If m and n are positive integers where n is 2 less than three times m, and the product of m and n is 176, what is the smaller of the two integers?

x	p(x)
−2	3
0	−3
2	−5
4	−3
6	3
8	13

28. The table above shows several points that lie on the graph of quadratic function $p(x)$. Based on the data in the table, what is $p(-4)$?

Questions 29-31 refer to the following information.

The following graph shows the paths of two bottle rockets that were fired straight up at the same time. The functions $h_1(t)$ and $h_2(t)$ represent the heights in feet of the rockets t seconds after they were fired off.

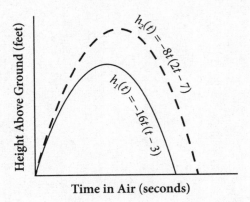

29. After 1 second in the air, how many feet higher was the second bottle rocket than the first?

30. How many seconds longer did it take the second rocket to reach its maximum height than the first rocket?

31. When written in the form $h(t) = -16t^2 + v_0 t + h_0$, the variable quantities v_0 and h_0 represent the initial velocity in feet per second of the rocket and the initial height in feet of the rocket, respectively. How much greater was the initial velocity in feet per second of the second rocket than the first?

Additional Topics in Math

BY THE END OF THIS UNIT, YOU WILL BE ABLE TO:

1. Solve geometry questions with lines, angles, triangles, and other complex shapes

2. Interpret 3-D figures and solve problems using formulas for volume and surface area

3. Use special right triangles and Pythagorean triplets to save time on Test Day

4. Solve problems involving imaginary and complex numbers

5. Interpret basic trigonometric functions and use them to solve problems with right triangles

CHAPTER 12

Imaginary Numbers

CHAPTER OBJECTIVES

By the end of this section, you will be able to:

1. Perform arithmetic operations on imaginary and complex numbers

2. Convert imaginary numbers into useful forms

3. Solve equations using imaginary numbers

SMARTPOINTS

Point Value	SmartPoint Category
10 Points	Imaginary Numbers

INTRODUCTION TO IMAGINARY NUMBERS

Until you reached more advanced math classes like Algebra 2 and Trigonometry, you were likely taught that it is impossible to take the square root of a negative number. There is some truth to this, as the result isn't a **real number**. What you'll get instead is an **imaginary number**.

To take the square root of a negative number, it is necessary to use i, which is defined in math as the square root of -1. Take $\sqrt{-49}$ as an example. To simplify this expression, rewrite $\sqrt{-49}$ as $\sqrt{-1} \times \sqrt{49}$, take the square root of -1 (which is by definition i), and then take the square root of 49, which is 7. The end result is $7i$.

> **✔ Note**
>
> Be particularly careful when multiplying two radicals that contain negative numbers. The first step is *always* to rewrite each quantity as the square root of the product of –1 and a positive number. Take the square root of –1 and then multiply the resulting expressions. For example, if you're asked to simplify $\sqrt{-16} \times \sqrt{-25}$, you must first rewrite the expression as $i\sqrt{16} \times i\sqrt{25}$, which becomes $4i \times 5i = 20i^2 = -20$. Combining the two radicals into one and canceling the negative signs to give $\sqrt{16 \times 25}$ is incorrect and will likely lead to a trap answer.

When a number is written in the form $a + bi$, where a is the real component and b is the imaginary component (and i is $\sqrt{-1}$), it is referred to as a **complex number**. The realm of complex numbers encompasses all numbers, including those that do not have an imaginary component (like 5, π, $\sqrt{2}$), in which case $b = 0$ (likewise, with a purely imaginary number, $a = 0$). You can add, subtract, multiply, and divide complex numbers just as you do real numbers. Things get slightly more challenging when you delve into exponents; the following table has more information on this.

Raising i to progressively higher powers yields a cycle:

When you have ...	i^1	i^2	i^3	i^4
... it becomes:	i	$\sqrt{-1} \times \sqrt{-1} = -1$	$i^2 \times i = -i$	$i^2 \times i^2 = -1 \times -1 = 1$

When you have an imaginary number with i raised to an exponent greater than 4, divide the exponent by 4. The remainder will dictate what the i component will become. For example, if you're asked to simplify $-4i^{44}$, start by dividing 44 by 4. The quotient is 11 with a remainder of 0, meaning $i^{44} = (i^4)^{11} = 1^{11}$. Therefore, the expression $-4i^{44}$ becomes -4. Take $15i^{63}$ as another example. Divide 63 by 4 to get 15 with a remainder of 3. This means that $i^{63} = (i^4)^{15}i^3 = 1^{15}i^3$. Because $i^3 = -i$, $15i^{63}$ becomes $-15i$.

In chapter 8, you learned about how to use the conjugate of an expression to rationalize a denominator; you can do this with complex numbers as well. Suppose you're asked to simplify the expression $\dfrac{21}{3+5i}$. The conjugate of $3 + 5i$ is $3 - 5i$, so you would multiply the expression by $\dfrac{3-5i}{3-5i}$ to get $\dfrac{21}{3+5i} \times \dfrac{3-5i}{3-5i} = \dfrac{21(3-5i)}{(3+5i)(3-5i)} = \dfrac{63-105i}{9-25i^2}$. You know $i^2 = -1$, so the expression simplifies to

$\dfrac{63-105i}{9-(25)(-1)} = \dfrac{63-105i}{34}$. To separate the complex expression into its real and imaginary compo-

nents, you can write each of the terms in the numerator over the denominator in separate fractions,

which yields $\dfrac{63}{34} - \dfrac{105}{34}i$.

Ready to try some test-like questions involving imaginary numbers? Check out the next few pages.

1. Which of the following is the correct simplification of the expression $(2i - 3) - (6 + 4i)$?
   (Note: $i = \sqrt{-1}$)

   A) $-9 - 2i$

   B) $-9 + 6i$

   C) $-7 - 4i$

   D) $3 + 6i$

Work through the Kaplan Method for Math step-by-step to solve this question. The following table shows Kaplan's strategic thinking on the left, along with suggested math scratchwork on the right.

Strategic Thinking	Math Scratchwork
Step 1: Read the question, identifying and organizing important information as you go You must correctly simplify the expression given.	
Step 2: Choose the best strategy to answer the question Use straightforward math to simplify. Distribute the negative sign and then combine like terms.	$(2i-3)-(6+4i)$ $2i-3-6-4i$ $-9-2i$
Step 3: Check that you answered the *right* question Choice (A) contains the correct simplification.	

✔ **Note**

Read carefully! Don't trust that both expressions in the parentheses have the real and imaginary components in the same order. Not checking the order means you risk falling for a trap answer.

2. Which of the following is equal to $(17 + 7i)(3 - 5i)$? (Note: $i = \sqrt{-1}$)

A) 16

B) 86

C) $16 - 64i$

D) $86 - 64i$

Work through the Kaplan Method for Math step-by-step to solve this question. The following table shows Kaplan's strategic thinking on the left, along with suggested math scratchwork on the right.

Strategic Thinking	Math Scratchwork
Step 1: Read the question, identifying and organizing important information as you go You need to correctly simplify the given expression.	
Step 2: Choose the best strategy to answer the question Use FOIL as you did with real binomials in chapter 11. Be careful when multiplying the two imaginary components together; i^2 will become -1.	$(17 \times 3) + (17 \times -5i)$ $+ (7i \times 3) + (7i \times -5i)$ $51 - 85i + 21i - 35i^2$ $51 - 64i - (35 \times -1)$ $86 - 64i$
Step 3: Check that you answered the _right_ question Choice (D) is equal to the original expression.	

3. Simplify the expression $\dfrac{6+\sqrt{-8}}{3+\sqrt{-18}}$.

A) $\dfrac{10}{9}$

B) $\dfrac{8}{3}$

C) $\dfrac{2}{9}-\dfrac{4\sqrt{2}}{9}i$

D) $\dfrac{10}{9}-\dfrac{4\sqrt{2}}{9}i$

Work through the Kaplan Method for Math step-by-step to solve this question. The following table shows Kaplan's strategic thinking on the left, along with suggested math scratchwork on the right.

Strategic Thinking	Math Scratchwork
Step 1: Read the question, identifying and organizing important information as you go You need to simplify the expression given.	
Step 2: Choose the best strategy to answer the question Use caution in the first couple steps. There's a negative under the radical in the denominator, as well as under the one in the numerator. Rewrite the expression with the negatives properly removed before rationalizing the denominator. No match in the answer choices? Look for a way to simplify your expression. Separate the real and imaginary components and then reduce the fractions.	$\dfrac{6+\sqrt{-8}}{3+\sqrt{-18}}=\dfrac{6+\sqrt{8}i}{3+\sqrt{18}i}$ denom. conj.: $3-\sqrt{18}i$ $\dfrac{6+\sqrt{8}i}{3+\sqrt{18}i}\times\dfrac{3-\sqrt{18}i}{3-\sqrt{18}i}$ $=\dfrac{(6\times3)+(6\times-\sqrt{18}i)+(3\times\sqrt{8}i)+(-\sqrt{8\times18}i^2)}{9-18i^2}$ $=\dfrac{18-6\sqrt{18}i+3\sqrt{8}i+\sqrt{144}}{9-18i^2}$ $=\dfrac{18-18\sqrt{2}i+6\sqrt{2}i+12}{9-(-18)}$ $=\dfrac{30-12\sqrt{2}i}{27}$ $=\dfrac{30}{27}-\dfrac{12\sqrt{2}}{27}i$ $=\dfrac{10}{9}-\dfrac{4\sqrt{2}}{9}i$

Strategic Thinking	Math Scratchwork
Step 3: Check that you answered the *right* question You've correctly simplified the expression in the question stem, so you're done! Choice (D) is correct.	

Great job persevering through that challenging question! As you saw, complex numbers follow the same rules of arithmetic that real numbers do.

✔ **Note**

Don't forget to take the square root of −1 before using FOIL. C is a trap answer designed to lure students who miss this critical step!

IMAGINARY NUMBERS, CONT.

Imaginary Solutions of Quadratics

Chapter 11 showed you how to determine a quadratic equation's real solutions using a variety of techniques, including factoring, completing the square, using the quadratic formula, and graphing. This chapter will expand your quadratics arsenal by showing you how to identify imaginary solutions via algebra.

Recall that the quadratic formula is $x = \dfrac{-b \pm \sqrt{b^2 - 4ac}}{2a}$ and that sign of the discriminant, $b^2 - 4ac$, dictates the nature of the solutions. When $b^2 - 4ac < 0$, the equation in question will have two imaginary solutions.

Computing Complex Numbers with a Calculator

You can use your TI-83/84 to simplify challenging complex number expressions more quickly than you can by hand.

Step 1: Press [MODE] and then scroll down to the row that starts with REAL. Highlight $a + bi$ and press [ENTER]. If you miss this step, you'll get an error message when you try to compute a complex expression.

```
NORMAL  SCI  ENG
FLOAT  0123456789
RADIAN  DEGREE
FUNC  PAR  POL  SEQ
CONNECTED  DOT
SEQUENTIAL  SIMUL
REAL  a+bi  re^0i
FULL  HORIZ  G-T
SET CLOCK01/01/01 12:04AM
```

Step 2: Exit the mode screen and punch in the expression you wish to simplify. Press [ENTER] when done. If you wish to convert decimal coefficients into fractions, press [MATH][ENTER][ENTER].

```
√(-4)
                    2i
(4-2i)/(4+2i)
                 .6-.8i
Ans▶Frac
              3/5-4/5i
```

✔ **Note**

Note that if you have an expression containing a fraction with imaginary components in the numerator and/or denominator, such as $\dfrac{4-2i}{4+2i}$, you need to be very careful with the order of operations. Enter the expression using parentheses; for the previous example, you would punch in (4 − 2*i*)/(4 + 2*i*).

4. What are the solutions to the equation $y = x^2 - 4x + 5$?

A) $5, -1$

B) $2 \pm i$

C) $2 \pm 3i$

D) $-2 \pm i$

$$2 \pm i$$
$$x^2 - 4x = 5$$
$$b = -$$
$$x^2 - 4x + 4 = -5 + 4$$
$$\sqrt{(x-2)^2} = \sqrt{-1}$$
$$x - 2 = \pm \sqrt{-1}$$

Work through the Kaplan Method for Math step-by-step to solve this question. The following table shows Kaplan's strategic thinking on the left, along with suggested math scratchwork on the right.

Strategic Thinking	Math Scratchwork
Step 1: Read the question, identifying and organizing important information as you go You're asked to identify the solutions (a.k.a. the x-intercepts) of the given equation.	
Step 2: Choose the best strategy to answer the question The x^2 term indicates a quadratic equation. Attempts to factor will reveal no pair of numbers that yields a product of 5 and a sum of -4; because the numbers are fairly small, try completing the square. (Note: To keep x on the left, we reversed the left and right sides of the equation.) Set the right side equal to 0 and subtract 5 from each side of the equation. Divide b (the coefficient of the x-term) by 2, square that result, and then add it to both sides. Rewrite the left side as a square of binomials and take the square root of both sides. Don't fret about the negative sign; this equation just has imaginary solutions. Replace $\sqrt{-1}$ with i and solve for x.	factors of 5: 1, 5; $-1, -5$ $x^2 - 4x + 5 = 0$ $x^2 - 4x = -5$ $b = -4 \rightarrow -2 \rightarrow 4$ $x^2 - 4x + 4 = -5 + 4$ $(x - 2)^2 = -1$ $x - 2 = \pm\sqrt{-1}$ $x = 2 \pm i$
Step 3: Check that you answered the *right* question You've found the (imaginary) solutions to the equation, so you're done! Choice (B) is correct.	

✔ Note

You can also answer this question using the quadratic formula, but it might take more time, especially if a question like this is in the non-calculator section. Additionally, if it's in the calculator section, you can graph the equation to make sure the solutions really are imaginary (the graph will not touch or intersect the x-axis).

Now you'll have a chance to try a test-like question. Some guidance is provided, but you'll need to fill in the missing parts of explanations or the step-by-step math in order to get to the correct answer. Don't worry—after going through the examples at the beginning of this chapter, this question should be completely doable. If you're still struggling, review the worked examples in this chapter.

Myriad students ask when they'd need to use imaginary numbers in the real world. One field that commonly uses them is electrical engineering, as demonstrated below. Note that electrical engineers use j to represent $\sqrt{-1}$, as i is used to represent a different quantity in their field.

5. The voltage of an alternating current circuit is given by the formula $E = I \times Z$, where E is voltage in volts, I is current in amps, and Z is impedance (a type of resistance encountered with alternating current) in ohms. If a certain circuit has a voltage of $38 + 18j$ volts and an impedance of $4 + 6j$ ohms, what is the current, in amps, that passes through the circuit? (Note: $j = \sqrt{-1}$)

    A) $\dfrac{11}{13} - 3j$

    B) $5 - 3j$

    C) $\dfrac{19}{2} + 3j$

    D) $44 + 300j$

Use the following scaffolding as your map through the question. If you aren't sure where to start, answer the questions in italics and fill in the blanks in the table as you work from top to bottom.

Strategic Thinking	Math Scratchwork
Step 1: Read the question, identifying and organizing important information as you go *What are you being asked to find? Is any helpful information provided?* You're asked to calculate the current of an alternating current circuit. The question provides an equation and the values of two of the variables in it.	

Strategic Thinking	Math Scratchwork
Step 2: Choose the best strategy to answer the question *How should you go about finding the answer?* You know the voltage and impedance, so all you need to do is plug those values into the given equation and solve for current (*I*). Once there, determine the conjugate of the denominator and use it to eliminate the imaginary component from the denominator. *The fraction is fully simplified, but it's not among the answer choices. Did I do a calculation incorrectly?* Not necessarily. Remember that complex numbers can be broken into their real and imaginary components. Do this with your fraction and simplify.	$E = I \times Z$ _____ $= I \times$ _____ $I = \dfrac{}{} \times \dfrac{}{}$ $I = \dfrac{}{}$ $I = \dfrac{}{}$ $I = \dfrac{}{}$ $I = \dfrac{}{}$ $I = \dfrac{}{} - \dfrac{}{} j$ $I = \dfrac{}{} - \dfrac{}{} j$
Step 3: Check that you answered the *right* question *Which answer choice is correct?* Did you get (B)? If so, you're right!	

Now that you've seen the variety of ways in which the SAT can test you on imaginary numbers, try the following questions to check your understanding. Give yourself 3 minutes to tackle the following 2 questions. Make sure you use the Kaplan Method for Math as often as you can. Remember, you want to emphasize speed and efficiency in addition to simply getting the correct answer.

6. Which of the following is not a solution to the equation $y = (x^4 + 84x^2 + 243)(x^2 + 5x - 36)$?

A) $-9i$

B) $-\sqrt{3}i$

C) $3i$

D) $9i$

7. When the complex number $(11+14i)^3$ is computed and written in the form $a + bi$ where a is the real component, b is the imaginary component, and $i = \sqrt{-1}$, what is the value of b?

Answers & Explanations for this chapter begin on page 928.

EXTRA PRACTICE

Required	Recommended
Questions 1–8	Questions 9–14

1. If $A = 3 + 5i$ and $B = -2 - i$, what is $2A - B$? (Note: $i = \sqrt{-1}$)

   A) $4 + 9i$

   B) $4 + 11i$

   C) $8 + 9i$

   D) $8 + 11i$

2. Which of the following is equivalent to $4i(5 - 7i)$? (Note: $i = \sqrt{-1}$)

   A) $-8i$

   B) $48i$

   C) $-28 + 20i$

   D) $28 + 20i$

3. Which of the following does not have the same value as i^3? (Note: $i = \sqrt{-1}$)

   A) i^{15}

   B) $i^5 \times i^4$

   C) $5i - 6i$

   D) $(2 + 3i) - (2 + 4i)$

4. What is the simplified form of $(4 + 3i)^2$? (Note: $i = \sqrt{-1}$)

   A) 7

   B) $7 + 24i$

   C) $16 + 15i$

   D) $25 + 24i$

5. What is the value of $\dfrac{\sqrt{-12}}{\sqrt{75}}$? (Note: $i = \sqrt{-1}$)

   A) $-\dfrac{2}{5}$

   B) $-\dfrac{4}{25}$

   C) $\dfrac{4}{25}i$

   D) $\dfrac{2}{5}i$

6. Which of the following is equivalent to $(3 + 2i)^4$? (Note: $i = \sqrt{-1}$)

   A) 97

   B) $-119 + 120i$

   C) $5 + 12i$

   D) $81 - 16i$

7. Which of the following represents $\dfrac{1}{3-i}$ written in the form $a + bi$? (Note: $i = \sqrt{-1}$)

   A) $\dfrac{3}{10} + \dfrac{1}{10}i$

   B) $\dfrac{1}{3} - \dfrac{1}{i}$

   C) $\dfrac{3}{8} + \dfrac{1}{8}i$

   D) $3 + i$

8. What value(s) of x satisfy the equation $x^2 + \dfrac{4}{25} = 0$? (Note: $i = \sqrt{-1}$)

   A) $\pm\dfrac{16}{625}i$

   B) $\pm\dfrac{4}{25}i$

   C) $\pm\dfrac{2}{5}i$

   D) $2 \pm 5i$

9. Which of the following has the same value as $i^{14} + i^{122}$? (Note: $i = \sqrt{-1}$)

   A) i^{136}

   B) $2i^2$

   C) $2i^{136}$

   D) $(1 + i)(1 - i)$

10. Which of the following shows $\left(2 + \sqrt{-9}\right)\left(-1 + \sqrt{-4}\right)$ written in the form $a + bi$? (Note: $i = \sqrt{-1}$)

    A) $-8 + i$

    B) $-8 - i$

    C) $4 + i$

    D) $4 - i$

11. What are the solutions over the complex number system to the equation $x^2 + 13 = 4x$? (Note: $i = \sqrt{-1}$)

    A) $-4 \pm 3i$

    B) $2 \pm 3i$

    C) $2 \pm 6i$

    D) $4 \pm 3i$

12. Which of the following is equivalent to the complex number $\dfrac{1}{4 - 2i} + (3 + i)$? (Note: $i = \sqrt{-1}$)

    A) $\dfrac{4 + i}{4 - 2i}$

    B) $\dfrac{4 - i}{4 + 2i}$

    C) $\dfrac{15 - 2i}{4 - 2i}$

    D) $\dfrac{15 + 2i}{4 + 2i}$

13. If $\dfrac{2 + i}{5 - i}$ is written in the form $a + bi$, what is the value of b? (Note: $i = \sqrt{-1}$)

14. The absolute value of a complex number $a + bi$ is defined as $\sqrt{a^2 + b^2}$. What is $|15 + 8i|$? (Note: $i = \sqrt{-1}$)

CHAPTER 13

Lines, Angles, and Triangles

CHAPTER OBJECTIVES

By the end of this chapter, you will be able to:

1. Apply the properties of lines and angles to solve geometry questions

2. Use the Pythagorean theorem, Pythagorean triplets, and special right triangles to answer questions involving triangles

3. Identify simple shapes within complex figures and use them to solve questions

SMARTPOINTS

Point Value	SmartPoint Category
30 Points	Geometry

LINES AND ANGLES

Lines and angles are the foundation of SAT geometry. Therefore, mastering their basic rules will make solving these questions, as well as related geometry questions, easier. With the knowledge you'll gain from this chapter, you can quickly identify geometric relationships, build upon the information given in the question, and often bypass complex algebra.

Familiarity with angle types will often unlock information that is not explicitly given in a question. This makes getting to the answer much easier on even the toughest geometry questions. First, let's take a look at the types of angles you should be able to recognize.

Angle Type	Angle Measurement	Example
Acute	Less than 90°	
Right	90°	
Obtuse	Between 90° and 180°	
Straight	180°	

More often than not, you'll work with multiple angles in a single question. Therefore, it's worth noting two likely familiar terms that involve working with two or more angles: complementary and supplementary angles. Two angles are **complementary** if their measures add up to 90°; if two angles' measures add up to 180°, the angles are **supplementary**.

✔ Note

Two angles need *not* be adjacent to be complementary or supplementary.

Intersecting lines create angles with special relationships you'll need to know as well. When two lines intersect, adjacent angles are supplementary, and **vertical** angles (two angles opposite a vertex) are equal, or **congruent**. Take a look at the following figure for an example.

The angles marked $a°$ and $b°$ are supplementary; therefore, $a + b = 180$. The angle marked $a°$ is vertical (and thus equal) to the one marked 60°, so $a = 60$. With this new information, you can find b: $a + b = 60 + b = 180$, so $b = 120$.

When two parallel lines are intersected by another line (called a **transversal**), all acute angles are equal, and all obtuse angles are equal. Additionally, **corresponding angles** are angles that are in the same position but on different parallel lines/transversal intersections; they are also equal. Furthermore, **alternate interior angles** and **alternate exterior angles** are equal. Alternate interior angles are angles that are positioned between the two parallel lines on opposite sides of the transversal, whereas alternate exterior angles are positioned on the outside of the parallel lines on opposite sides of the transversal. Consider the following figure:

- Line 1 and Line 2 are parallel and cut by transversal ℓ.

- Angles a, d, e, and h are obtuse and equal.

- Angles b, c, f, and g are acute and equal.

- Angle pairs (b and f), (c and g), (a and e), and (d and h) are corresponding angles.

- Angle pairs (a and h) and (b and g) are alternate exterior angles.

- Angle pairs (d and e) and (c and f) are alternate interior angles.

Now use your knowledge of lines and angles to tackle a test-like question.

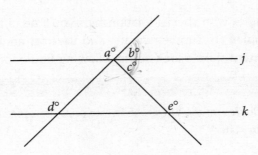

Note: Figure not drawn to scale.

1. In the figure above, if lines *j* and *k* are parallel, which of the following statements must be true?

   A) *a* = *e*

   B) *b* = *c*

   C) *d* = 180 − *c*

   D) *b* + *d* − *c* = *e*

✔ **Note**

"Figure not drawn to scale" means that you can't eyeball angles, line measurements, or relationships.

Work through the Kaplan Method for Math step-by-step to solve this question. The following table shows Kaplan's strategic thinking on the left, along with suggested math scratchwork on the right.

Strategic Thinking	Math Scratchwork
Step 1: Read the question, identifying and organizing important information as you go You're asked to find which answer choice contains a true statement. You're told that lines *j* and *k* are parallel. Two transversals are also drawn.	

Strategic Thinking	Math Scratchwork
Step 2: Choose the best strategy to answer the question Two parallel lines cut by a transversal yield four equal obtuse angles and four equal acute angles. In this figure, however, there are two transversals, so you must take care not to draw erroneous conclusions about two angles formed by different transversals. Angles from different transversals have nothing to do with each other. Identify relationships among the angles. Angles a and d are corresponding angles and are therefore equal. Angles a and b are supplementary, as are angles c and e. By extension, angles d and b are supplementary as well. However, note that angles a, b, and d have no relation to angles c and e, as the two groups are formed by different transversals. Now look for answers you can eliminate based on what you know. Choice A claims a relationship between a and e, which are formed by different transversals, so eliminate it. Similarly, because b and c are formed by different transversals, b is incorrect. Choice C is incorrect for the same reason: d and c are formed by different transversals.	$a = d$ $d + b = 180$ $c + e = 180$ $a + b = 180$ No relationships between $\{a, b, d\}$ and $\{c, e\}$
Step 3: Check that you answered the *right* question Choice (D) must be correct by process of elimination.	

> ✔ **Note**
>
> Choice (D) is correct because $b + d - c = e$ is equivalent to $b + d = e + c$. This is a true statement because b is supplementary to d and e is supplementary to c, making the two sums both equal to 180 and therefore each other as well.

TRIANGLES

Lines and angles form the basis of triangles—some of the most commonly occurring shapes on the SAT. Luckily, triangle questions usually don't involve a lot of complex algebra and are a great way to earn a few quick points on Test Day. A strong command of triangle properties will help you recognize and solve these questions quickly. Many seemingly difficult questions will become easier once you can confidently speak the language of triangles.

All triangles follow the rules listed here, regardless of the type of triangle, so take the time now to get comfortable with them. We've provided a sample figure to help you visualize the rules.

- The sum of the interior angles add up to 180°. In the triangle shown, $a + b + c = 180$.

- The exterior angle of a triangle is equal to the sum of the two opposite interior angles. In this example, $d = a + b = 180 - c$.

- A side opposite a greater angle is longer than a side opposite a smaller angle. For instance, if $a = 50$, $b = 60$, and $c = 70$, then $A < B < C$.

- Triangle Inequality theorem: The sum of two side lengths must be greater than the third side length, and the positive difference of two side lengths must be less than the third side length. For example, $A + B > C$ and $A - B < C$.

Up next is a sample question that tests your knowledge of these rules. Don't forget about the angle properties, either.

2. During a camping trip, Aundria and Annette decide to climb a mountain using two different routes to the top. Aundria takes the hiking route that travels 5 mi south, 6 mi east, 7 mi south, and 2 mi west to the summit; Annette uses the climbing route that starts at the same point as the hiking route but goes directly from there to the summit. Assuming vertical travel distance is not considered, about how many miles in all will the two travel?

A) 32.65

B) 33.42

C) 34.00

D) 34.42

Work through the Kaplan Method for Math step-by-step to solve this question. The following table shows Kaplan's strategic thinking on the left, along with suggested math scratchwork on the right.

Strategic Thinking	Math Scratchwork
Step 1: Read the question, identifying and organizing important information as you go You need to determine the total distance Aundria and Annette traveled.	
Step 2: Choose the best strategy to answer the question Draw a diagram to visualize the situation, and label it with what you know. Next, draw additional lines to reveal hidden shapes, such as right triangles. When you draw the right triangle, you'll also create a rectangle. Opposite sides of a rectangle are congruent, so you can transfer this information to the unknown pieces you drew.	Start 5 mi 6 mi 7 mi ★ 2 mi

Strategic Thinking	Math Scratchwork
Annette's route is the hypotenuse of the triangle. You know the lengths of the legs, so you can find the hypotenuse using the Pythagorean theorem. Read carefully! You need the sum of the two distances traveled. Add all the segments of Aundria's route together, and then add that number to Annette's total distance traveled.	Start 5 mi 6 mi 7 mi 7 mi 4 mi 2 mi Annette $$(5+7)^2 + 4^2 = c^2$$ $$c^2 = 144 + 16 = 160$$ $$c = \sqrt{160} = 4\sqrt{10}$$ Aundria $$5+6+7+2=20$$ total: $20 + 4\sqrt{10}$
Step 3: Check that you answered the *right* question The answer choices are in decimal form, so round your radical figure, add it to 20, and you're finished. The result matches (A).	32.65

✔ **Note**

Stay focused on what the question asks. Don't stop until you're sure you've found what you need.

THE PYTHAGOREAN THEOREM, PYTHAGOREAN TRIPLETS & SPECIAL RIGHT TRIANGLES

The Pythagorean theorem is one of the most fundamental equations in geometry, and it will be of great use to you on the SAT. Common Pythagorean triplets and special right triangle ratios that originate from this formula will also serve you well on Test Day.

The **Pythagorean theorem** is an important triangle topic that you are probably familiar with already. If you know any two lengths of a right triangle, you can use the Pythagorean theorem equation to find the missing side. It is expressed as $a^2 + b^2 = c^2$, where a and b are the shorter sides of the triangle (called legs) and c is the hypotenuse, which is always across from the right angle of the triangle.

> **✔ Note**
>
> The Pythagorean theorem can only be applied to right triangles.

Consider an example: A right triangle has a leg measuring 9 and a hypotenuse measuring 14. To find the missing leg, plug the known values into the Pythagorean theorem: $9^2 + b^2 = 14^2$. This simplifies to $81 + b^2 = 196$, which becomes $b^2 = 115$. Take the square root of both sides to get $b = \sqrt{115}$. Because no factors of 115 are perfect squares, $b = \sqrt{115}$ is the answer.

> **✔ Note**
>
> Wait to simplify radicals until you have your final answer. Leave answers in radical form unless a question says otherwise or the answer choices are written as decimals.

Because time is such a premium on the SAT, time-saving strategies are invaluable, and there are two that will come in handy on triangle questions. The first is knowing common **Pythagorean triplets**, which are right triangles that happen to have integer sides. These triangles show up *very* frequently on the SAT. The two most common are 3-4-5 and 5-12-13. Multiples of these (e.g., 6-8-10, 10-24-26) can also pop up, so watch out for them, as well. The beauty of these triplets is that if you see any two sides, you can automatically fill in the third without having to resort to the time-consuming Pythagorean theorem.

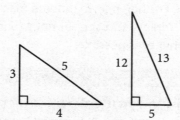

The second time-saving strategy involves recognizing **special right triangles**. Like Pythagorean triplets, special right triangles involve a ratio comparing a right triangle's legs and hypotenuse, but with these triangles, you only need to know one side in order to calculate the other two. These triangles are defined by their angles.

The ratio of the sides in a **45-45-90** triangle is $x : x : x\sqrt{2}$, where x is the length of each leg and $x\sqrt{2}$ is the length of the hypotenuse.

The ratio of the sides in a **30-60-90** triangle is $x : x\sqrt{3} : 2x$, where x is the shorter leg, $x\sqrt{3}$ is the longer leg, and $2x$ is the hypotenuse.

While the Pythagorean theorem can always be used to solve right triangle questions, it is not always the most efficient way to proceed. Further, many students make errors when simplifying radicals and exponents. The Pythagorean triplets and special right triangles allow you to save time and avoid those mistakes. Use them whenever possible!

> ✔ **Note**
>
> Although you will be given the special right triangle ratios on Test Day, you can save yourself time by memorizing them. That way you won't have to keeping flipping back to the formula page!

On Test Day you might also be asked to determine the area of a triangle. The area of a triangle can be determined using $A = \frac{1}{2}bh$, where b is the triangle base and h is the triangle height.

When you have a right triangle, you can use the legs as the base and the height. If the triangle isn't a right triangle, you'll need to draw the height in, as demonstrated in the figure shown. Remember that the height *must* be perpendicular to the base.

Similar triangles have the same angle measurements and proportional sides. In the figure below, $\triangle ABC$ and $\triangle DEF$ have the same angle measurements, so the side lengths can be set up as

the following proportion: $\dfrac{A}{D} = \dfrac{B}{E} = \dfrac{C}{F}$.

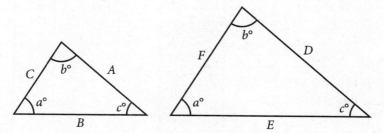

Drawing multiple heights in one triangle creates similar triangles, as shown in the diagram below. When you encounter a question like this, redrawing the similar triangles with their angles and sides in the same positions will help keep information in order.

Complex figures are also a recurring SAT geometry topic. A complex figure is not a shape such as a dodecahedron: Instead, a complex figure is usually a larger shape that is composed of multiple (familiar) shapes; these can be obvious or cleverly hidden. These figures can always be broken down into squares, rectangles, triangles, and/or circles. Although this chapter emphasizes triangles, you'll get plenty of practice with other figures over the next few questions. No matter how convoluted the figure, following the guidelines here will lead you to the correct answer on Test Day.

- Transfer information from the question stem to the figure. If a figure isn't provided, draw one!

- Break the figure into familiar shapes.

- Determine how one line segment can play multiple roles in a figure. For example, if a circle and triangle overlap correctly, the circle's radius might be the triangle's hypotenuse.

- Work from the shape with the most information to the shape with the least information.

A final note about triangles: You are likely to see triangle questions involving real-world situations. But don't fret: All you need to do is follow the Kaplan Strategy for Translating English into Math. Extract the geometry information you need, then solve!

Take a look at the next few pages for more test-like triangle questions.

3. Uwe has a rectangular field that he would like to split into two triangular fields—one for planting grain and one for planting vegetables—by building a fence from one corner of the field to the opposite corner. If the area of the field is 540 m² and the length of the field is 36 m, how many meters of fence will Uwe need?

Work through the Kaplan Method for Math step-by-step to solve this question. The following table shows Kaplan's strategic thinking on the left, along with suggested math scratchwork on the right.

Strategic Thinking	Math Scratchwork
Step 1: Read the question, identifying and organizing important information as you go You need to find the length of the fence (the diagonal of the rectangular field).	
Step 2: Choose the best strategy to answer the question Draw a figure to visualize the situation. Sketch the rectangle and label what you know. The area of a rectangle is the product of its length and width. Because you know the length and the area, you can find the width.	[diagram of rectangle with diagonal, labeled 36] $A = 540 = 36 \times h$ $h = 540 \div 36 = 15$

Strategic Thinking	Math Scratchwork
The diagonal of the rectangle is also the hypotenuse of a right triangle with legs of lengths 15 and 36. This is a multiple of the 5-12-13 Pythagorean triplet. Multiply 3 by 13 to find the length of the hypotenuse (and that of the diagonal of the rectangle).	$15 = 5 \times 3$ $36 = 12 \times 3$ diagonal $= 13 \times 3 = 39$
Step 3: Check that you answered the *right* question The question asks for the length of the fence, which is represented by the diagonal, so you're done. Grid in 39 and move on.	39

✔ **Note**

If you didn't recognize the multiple of the Pythagorean triplet, you could have used the Pythagorean theorem to find the length of the diagonal.

4. In the figure above, $\overline{AD}$ and $\overline{BC}$ are parallel. What is the value of x?

A) 60

B) 70

C) 80

D) 110

Work through the Kaplan Method for Math step-by-step to solve this question. The following table shows Kaplan's strategic thinking on the left, along with suggested math scratchwork on the right.

Strategic Thinking	Math Scratchwork
Step 1: Read the question, identifying and organizing important information as you go You're asked for the value of *x*.	
Step 2: Choose the best strategy to answer the question Look for familiar shapes within the given figure. There are three triangles present. Because $\overline{AD}$ and $\overline{BC}$ are parallel, *BFDA* is a trapezoid. Although *x* might seem far removed from the known angles, you can find it. It will just take more than one step. In $\triangle FDC$, only one angle is missing, so you can solve for it and fill it in easily. Note that $\angle DFC$ and $\angle BFG$ are vertical angles, so $\angle BFG$ is also 50°. At this point, you have two of the three angles in $\triangle BFG$, so you can solve for the third. $\angle FBG$ and $\angle BAD$ are corresponding angles (and are therefore congruent). You can now conclude that $x = 70$.	$m\angle DFC = 180° - 70° - 60°$ $= 50°$ $m\angle BFG = m\angle DFC = 50°$ $m\angle FBG = 180° - 50° - 60°$ $= 70°$ $m\angle BAD = x = m\angle FBG = 70°$
Step 3: Check that you answered the *right* question You're asked for *x*, so select (B), and you're done.	$x = 70$

5. In the figure above, *ABCD* is a rectangle and ∠*F* is a right angle. If $\overline{FD} = \overline{DC}$, $\overline{AB} = 6$, and the perimeter of rectangle *ABCD* is 30, then what is the length of $\overline{FA}$?

    A) 6
    B) $3\sqrt{5}$
    C) 8
    D) $5\sqrt{3}$

Work through the Kaplan Method for Math step-by-step to solve this question. The following table shows Kaplan's strategic thinking on the left, along with suggested math scratchwork on the right.

Strategic Thinking	Math Scratchwork
Step 1: Read the question, identifying and organizing important information as you go You need to find the length of $\overline{FA}$.	

Strategic Thinking	Math Scratchwork
Step 2: Choose the best strategy to answer the question Look for familiar shapes within the provided figure: There is a rectangle and a right triangle. You're told that $\overline{AB} = 6$ and $\overline{FD} = \overline{DC}$. Because $ABCD$ is a rectangle, $\overline{AB}$ must equal $\overline{DC}$, so $\overline{AB} = \overline{DC} = \overline{FD} = 6$. You're also told that the perimeter of rectangle $ABCD$ is 30. Because you know the length of two sides of the rectangle, you can find the other two. Unfortunately, with a hypotenuse of 9 and a leg of 6, $\triangle FAD$ isn't a Pythagorean triplet or special right triangle. Use the Pythagorean theorem to find the missing side. Although $\sqrt{45}$ isn't an answer choice, it doesn't mean you made an error. When your answer is a radical and you don't see it among the choices, that means you need to simplify the radical.	$\overline{AB} = 6,\ \overline{FD} = \overline{DC}$ $\overline{AB} = \overline{FD} = \overline{DC} = 6$ $30 = 6 + 6 + \overline{AD} + \overline{BC}$ $\overline{AD} + \overline{BC} = 18$ $\overline{AD} = \overline{BC} = 9$ $6^2 + FA^2 = 9^2$ $FA^2 = 81 - 36 = 45$ $FA = \sqrt{45}$ $\sqrt{45} = \sqrt{9} \times \sqrt{5} = 3\sqrt{5}$
Step 3: Check that you answered the *right* question You've provided what the question asks for, so (B) is correct.	

Now you'll have a chance to try a few more test-like questions. Use the scaffolding as needed as a guide through the question and to the right answer.

Some guidance is provided, but you'll need to fill in the missing parts of explanations or the step-by-step math in order to get to the correct answer. Don't worry—after going through the examples at the beginning of this chapter, these questions should be completely doable. If you're still struggling, review the worked examples in this chapter.

6. Given △ABC and △ABD above, what is the perimeter of △ACD?

A) $2\sqrt{6} - 2\sqrt{2}$

B) $4\sqrt{3}$

C) $4 + 2\sqrt{6} + 2\sqrt{2}$

D) $2\sqrt{6} + 6\sqrt{2}$

Use the following scaffolding as your map through the question. If you aren't sure where to start, answer the questions in italics and fill in the blanks in the table as you work from top to bottom.

Strategic Thinking	Math Scratchwork
Step 1: Read the question, identifying and organizing important information as you go *What are you being asked to find here?* You need to find the perimeter of △ACD.	

Strategic Thinking	Math Scratchwork
Step 2: Choose the best strategy to answer the question *How can you use the figure to get to the answer?* Look for unknown values that you can derive from the information in the question stem. For instance, you can find $\angle ACD$ from the two given angles. From there you can easily determine the measures of the angles in $\triangle ABC$. Fill in the blanks on the right as you go. *What do you notice about the two triangles?* Both $\triangle ABC$ and $\triangle ABD$ have special characteristics. Use these to determine the length of each missing side. Once again, update the figure on the right as you work. $\triangle ACD$ *isn't a special right triangle. How can you find $\overline{CD}$?* $\overline{BD}$ is the sum of $\overline{BC}$ and $\overline{CD}$. Subtract $\overline{BC}$ from $\overline{BD}$ to find $\overline{CD}$. Once you find all three sides of $\triangle ACD$, add them together to find its perimeter.	$m\angle ACD = \underline{\quad}° - \underline{\quad}° - \underline{\quad}°$ $= \underline{\quad}°$ $\triangle ABC:\ \underline{\quad} - \underline{\quad} - \underline{\quad}$ $\triangle ABD:\ \underline{\quad} - \underline{\quad} - \underline{\quad}$ $\overline{CD} = \underline{\quad} - \underline{\quad} = \underline{\quad}$ $P_{\triangle ACD} = \underline{\quad} + (\underline{\quad}) + \underline{\quad}$ $= \underline{\quad}$
Step 3: Check that you answered the *right* question *What is the perimeter of $\triangle ACD$?* If you got (C), you are correct!	$\underline{\quad}$

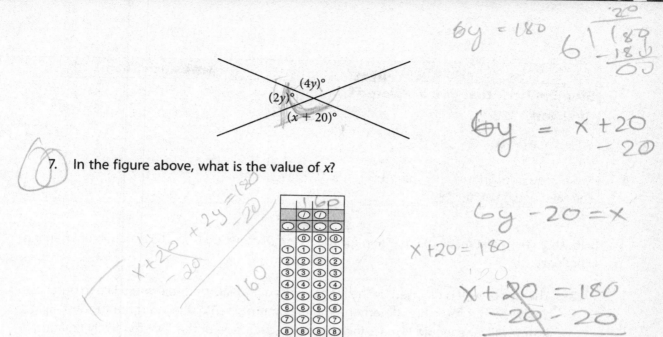

$6y = 180$ $6\overline{\smash{\big)}\,180}$

$6y = x + 20$
$\quad\quad -20$

$6y - 20 = x$

$x + 20 = 180$

$x + 20 = 180$
$\underline{-20 \quad -20}$
$\quad\quad\quad 160$

7. In the figure above, what is the value of *x*?

$x + 20 + 2y = 180$
$\quad\quad -20$
160

Use the following scaffolding as your map through the question. If you aren't sure where to start, answer the questions in italics and fill in the blanks in the table as you work from top to bottom.

Strategic Thinking	Math Scratchwork
Step 1: Read the question, identifying and organizing important information as you go *What are you being asked to find?* You need to find the value of *x*.	
Step 2: Choose the best strategy to answer the question *How can you use the figure to get to the answer?* A quick option is to solve for *y* using the fact that supplementary angles add up to 180°. You can then solve for *x* using the fact that vertical angles are equal.	supp. ___ + ___ = 180 ___ = 180 *y* = _____, 4*y* = _____ vertical _____ = _____ *x* = _____

Strategic Thinking	Math Scratchwork
Step 3: Check that you answered the *right* question *What is the value of x?* Make sure you grid in the value of *x*, not *y*. You're correct if you got 100!	——

Below is a real-world rectangle question for you to try. Don't worry if you have no picture framing experience.

8. The size of a TV is dictated by the length of its diagonal. Whitney would like to purchase a new TV but must first determine the maximum size TV she can mount on her living room wall. She would like a 3-inch space on each side of the TV, effectively creating a frame of empty space around the TV that is 3 inches wide on each side. If the rectangular wall space Whitney plans to use for her TV is 28.25 inches by 53 inches, what is the largest size TV (in inches) that she can fit on the wall? Round your answer to the nearest inch.

Use the following scaffolding as your map through the question. If you aren't sure where to start, answer the questions in italics and fill in the blanks in the table as you work from top to bottom.

Strategic Thinking	Math Scratchwork
Step 1: Read the question, identifying and organizing important information as you go *What do you ultimately need to find?* You're asked for the largest size TV Whitney can mount on her wall; in other words, you need to calculate the length of its diagonal..	

Strategic Thinking	Math Scratchwork
Step 2: Choose the best strategy to answer the question	

This is a geometry question presented in word form. What's a good route to consider?

Draw a figure! First, draw a rectangle to represent the wall space. Next, draw another rectangle inside the first to represent the TV. Label the diagram with the information the question provides.

How do you find the dimensions of the TV?

Subtract the width of the empty wall space from the given dimensions. Once there, use the Pythagorean theorem to find the diagonal of the TV area, and then subtract the area of the picture from it.

wall space: _____ × _____

TV space: _____ × _____

_____^{2} × _____^{2} = _____^{2}

_____ + _____ = _____

Step 3: Check that you answered the *right* question

What's the largest diagonal Whitney's TV can have?

If you got 52, you'd be correct!

Now that you've seen the variety of ways in which the SAT can test you on triangles, try the following questions to check your understanding. Give yourself 5 minutes to tackle the following four questions. Make sure you use the Kaplan Method for Math as often as you can. Remember, you want to emphasize speed and efficiency in addition to simply getting the correct answer.

Note: Figure not drawn to scale.

9. If the area of $\triangle ABC$ is $8\sqrt{3}$, what is the length of $\overline{AB}$?

A) 4

B) 6

C) 7

D) 8

Note: Figure not drawn to scale.

10. Four squares are inscribed inside each other as shown in the figure above. Each progressively larger square has a perimeter that is 4 cm greater than that of the previous square. If the innermost square has a perimeter of 4 cm, what is the probability of randomly selecting a point within one of the white regions?

Note: Figure not drawn to scale.

11. $\triangle ABC$ above has an area of 150 square units. If $\overline{AB} = \overline{AH} = 20$, then what is the length of $\overline{HG}$?

A) 5

B) 12

C) 16

D) 20

Note: Figure not drawn to scale.

12. In the figure above, lines j and k are parallel. What is the value of $\angle q$?

A) 50

B) 55

C) 75

D) 130

Answers and Explanations for this chapter begin on page 935.

EXTRA PRACTICE

Required	Recommended
Questions 1–8	Questions 9–23

1. If the length of side $\overline{AB}$ in the triangle above is 28 cm and the length of $\overline{BC}$ is 45 cm, what is the length in centimeters of $\overline{AC}$?

   A) 35

   B) 45

   C) 53

   D) 64

2. The sides of the triangle above have been extended as shown. What is the value in degrees of $\angle x - \angle y$?

   A) 3

   B) 6

   C) 87

   D) 180

3. The moon goes through several phases, such as new, crescent, quarter, and full. During the quarter phase, we see half the moon. During this phase, the sun (relative to Earth) forms a right angle with the moon as shown in the figure above. If the distance from Earth to the moon is approximately 240,000 miles, and the distance from the moon to the sun is approximately 91,674,000 miles, how many miles are between Earth and the sun?

   A) 84,042,000

   B) 88,434,000

   C) 91,674,000

   D) 8,404,180,000

Note: Figure not drawn to scale.

4. A company designs removable handicap access ramps as temporary measures for buildings to become compliant with the Americans with Disabilities Act (ADA). The particular ramp shown in the figure must be placed at a 30° angle, eight feet from the bottom step. About how long, in inches, is the ramp?

   A) 67

   B) 116

   C) 128

   D) 134

5. The longer leg of a right triangle is three times the length of the shorter leg. Given that the length of each leg is a whole number, which of the following could be the length of the hypotenuse?

   A) $\sqrt{40}$

   B) $\sqrt{47}$

   C) $\sqrt{55}$

   D) $\sqrt{63}$

6. A tourist ranch built the horse-riding trail shown in the figure. The trail takes a rider from the ranch to an old watering hole, then to a historic barn, and finally to a campsite where riders can spend the night. If a rider takes a horse on a direct path from the ranch to the campsite, how much shorter, in miles, would the trip be?

   A) 6

   B) 8

   C) 17

   D) 23

7. A geometry teacher drew a right triangle on the board and measured the lengths of the sides. Which of the following could NOT have been the lengths of the sides of the triangle she drew?

   A) 5 inches, 12 inches, 13 inches

   B) $\frac{1}{3}$ of a foot, $\frac{1}{4}$ of a foot, $\frac{1}{5}$ of a foot

   C) 9 cm, 40 cm, 41 cm

   D) $\frac{3}{4}$ of a foot, 1 foot, 15 inches

8. What is the value of *h* in the figure above?

   A) 3.5

   B) 7

   C) 12.5

   D) 14

9. In the figure above, if ∠*q* = 140, what is the value of ∠*r* − ∠*p*?

   A) 0

   B) 10

   C) 90

   D) 130

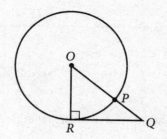

10. The radius of circle *O* shown in the figure is 1.5. If $\overline{RQ}$ = 2, what is the length of $\overline{PQ}$?

   A) 0.5

   B) 1

   C) 2.5

   D) 4

11. In the figure above, the diagonal of the rectangle has length *h*. What is the value of *h* in terms of *d*?

   A) *d*

   B) 4*d*

   C) $\sqrt{34d}$

   D) $d\sqrt{34}$

12. What is the area of the triangle shown in the
 figure?

   A) $18\sqrt{3}$

   B) $9+9\sqrt{3}$

   C) $9+18\sqrt{3}$

   D) $18+18\sqrt{3}$

13. The area of a right triangle is 35 square inches.
   If the longer leg is 3 inches longer than the
   shorter leg, what is the length of the hypotenuse in inches?

   A) 10

   B) $\dfrac{\sqrt{35}}{2}$

   C) $7\sqrt{10}$

   D) $\sqrt{149}$

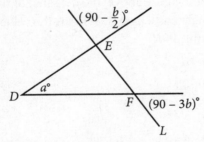

14. In the figure above, $\overline{EF}$ of $\triangle DEF$ is on line L.
   What is a in terms of b?

   A) $3b$

   B) $\dfrac{3b}{2}$

   C) $\dfrac{7b}{2}$

   D) $180 - b$

15. What is the measure in degrees of the smallest
   angle of a triangle that has sides of length
   $1.5, \dfrac{3\sqrt{3}}{2}$, and 3?

Note: Figure not drawn to scale.

16. A college has a sidewalk that cuts through a
   block of greenspace on the campus. To ensure
   student safety, the college decides to put lights
   along both sides of the sidewalk. If the lights
   should be placed 5 feet apart as shown in the
   figure, how many lights does the college need?

17. The figure above consists of 81 small squares, each with a side length of $\frac{1}{2}$ centimeter. What is the area in square centimeters of $\triangle XYZ$?

Questions 18 and 19 refer to the following information.

The capital of North Dakota is Bismarck, which is almost directly north of the capital of South Dakota, which is Pierre. An airplane leaving from Bismarck travels on a bearing of 120°, as shown in the figure below.

18. If the plane is 295 miles directly east of Pierre, how far apart are Bismarck and Pierre? Round your answer to the nearest mile.

19. If the plane flew at an average rate of 400 miles per hour, how many minutes had it been in the air when it was 295 miles from Pierre? Round your answer to the nearest whole minute.

20. In the figure above, $\overline{LM} = \overline{MN} = \overline{NO} = \overline{OL} = \overline{LN}$. What is the value of $b - c$?

    A) −30

    B) 0

    C) 10

    D) 30

21. Which angle has the smallest measure in the figure above?

    A) Angle A

    B) Angle B

    C) Angle C

    D) All three angles have equal measures.

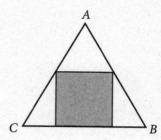

22. In the figure above, the shaded region is a square with an area of 12 square units, inscribed inside equilateral triangle ABC. What is the perimeter of triangle ABC?

    A) $18\sqrt{3}$

    B) $4 + \sqrt{3}$

    C) $4 + 6\sqrt{3}$

    D) $12 + 6\sqrt{3}$

23. If the vertices of a right triangle have coordinates (−6, 4), (1, 4), and (1, −2), what is the hypotenuse of the triangle?

    A) 7

    B) 8

    C) $\sqrt{85}$

    D) $5\sqrt{17}$

CHAPTER 14

Similarity, Congruence, and Proofs

CHAPTER OBJECTIVES

By the end of this section, you will be able to:

1. Use concepts and theorems about congruence and similarity to solve problems about lines, angles, and triangles

SMARTPOINTS

Point Value	SmartPoint Category
30 points	Geometry

LINE, ANGLE, & TRIANGLE THEOREMS

Many students ask why they need to learn how to do proofs when they take geometry. Although you will likely not need them in college (unless you're a math or computer science major), there is a fundamental skill that comes with constructing proofs: The ability to construct an argument effectively for a statement or position. This skill is critical in numerous situations and fields—for criminal cases in law, research proposals in science, treatment plans in medicine, and others—so it's a powerful tool to have in your skill set.

That being said, there's no question that proofs can be unnerving. The good news: You will *not* need to construct a complete proof on the SAT. The language of certain questions might still be slightly intimidating, but it will be far more manageable than a full-blown proof.

> ✔ **Note**
>
> Another reason not to fret a lot over this chapter: There are only two geometry questions on the entire SAT.

We covered basic theorems for lines, angles, and triangles in chapter 11. However, we did not always directly use the names of the theorems. To help you remember which theorem has what name (a skill you'll need to complete missing portions of proofs), we've summarized the essential ones in the following table. Notice that the converse of most of these theorems is also true.

Angle Theorem	Definition
Alternate Interior Angles	• If two parallel lines are cut by a transversal, the alternate interior angles are congruent. • If two lines are cut by a transversal and the alternate interior angles are congruent, the lines are parallel.
Alternate Exterior Angles	• If two parallel lines are cut by a transversal, the alternate exterior angles are congruent. • If two lines are cut by a transversal and the alternate exterior angles are congruent, the lines are parallel.
Corresponding Angles	• If two parallel lines are cut by a transversal, the corresponding angles are congruent. • If two lines are cut by a transversal and the corresponding angles are congruent, the lines are parallel.
Vertical Angles	• If two parallel lines are cut by a transversal, the vertical angles are congruent.

When part of a question stem links back to a theorem, you can use that theorem to infer new information about a problem, a technique that can get you closer to the answer.

In geometry class you probably saw quite a few triangles in your proof homework; we've provided the fundamentals in the next few tables.

Triangle Theorem	Definition
Triangle Sum and Exterior Angle Theorems	• Interior angles add up to 180°. • An exterior angle equals the sum of the two opposite interior angles.
Isosceles Triangle Theorems	• If two sides of a triangle are congruent, the angles opposite them are congruent. • If two angles of a triangle are congruent, the sides opposite them are congruent.
Triangle Inequality Theorem	• The sum of the lengths of any two sides of a triangle must be greater than the third side. • The difference of the lengths of any two sides of a triangle must be less than the third side.
Side-Angle Relationship	• In a triangle, the longest side is across from the largest angle. • In a triangle, the largest angle is across from the longest side.
Mid-Segment Theorem	• A triangle mid-segment (or midline) is parallel to one side of the triangle and joins the midpoints of the other two sides. • The mid-segment's length is half the length of the side to which it is parallel.

✔ Note

The Pythagorean theorem, $a^2 + b^2 = c^2$, might also appear in proof-type questions. Remember, the Pythagorean theorem only applies to right triangles.

You learned about similarity and congruence in chapter 11, and these two terms come up again in this chapter as well. Recall that two similar triangles have identical angles and proportional sides; two congruent triangles have identical angles and identical sides.

There are several theorems that can be used to prove two triangles are congruent; these are summarized in the following table. Make sure you are comfortable with all of them.

Triangle Congruence Theorem	Notation	Diagram
If three sides of one triangle are congruent to the corresponding sides of another triangle, then the two triangles are congruent.	SSS (side-side-side)	
If two sides and the included angle of one triangle are congruent to the corresponding parts of another triangle, then the two triangles are congruent.	SAS (side-angle-side)	
If two angles and the non-included side in one triangle are congruent to the corresponding parts of another triangle, then the two triangles are congruent.	AAS (angle-angle-side)	
If two angles and the included side of one triangle are congruent to the corresponding parts of another triangle, then the two triangles are congruent.	ASA (angle-side-angle)	
If the hypotenuse and leg of one right triangle are congruent to the corresponding parts of another right triangle, then the two triangles are congruent.	HL (hypotenuse-leg)	
An angle or line segment is congruent to itself.	Reflexive Property	
Corresponding parts of congruent triangles are congruent.	CPCTC	

✔ Note

There are two bogus congruence "theorems" to watch out for: AAA and SSA. Two triangles with identical angles are always similar, but they aren't necessarily congruent. If you have two triangles with two adjacent congruent sides and a congruent angle outside them, the third side can be two different lengths. SSA is valid only with right triangles, in which case you call it HL. Never use AAA.

Now that you've refreshed your memory, let's polish those skills with some practice questions. The next two questions are reminiscent of those in chapter 11, but the Strategic Thinking columns now use theorem names from the previous tables. Questions about proofs require you to think about the rules that govern line, angle, and triangle relationships, which means you'll need to be able to justify your conclusions when working through questions. Again, you will *not* need to write a full proof, but you must be able to draw conclusions based on geometry theorems.

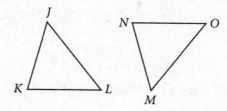

1. △JKL and △MNO are shown above. If $\overline{JK} \cong \overline{MN}$, ∠KJL ≅ ∠NMO, and $\overline{JL} \cong \overline{MO}$, then which theorem can be used to prove △JKL and △MNO are congruent?

    A) SAS

    B) ASA

    C) AAS

    D) SSS

There's no scratchwork for this question, but Kaplan's strategic thinking follows. Follow along as we reason through the question to get the correct answer.

Strategic Thinking
Step 1: Read the question, identifying and organizing important information as you go
The question asks you to identify the theorem that proves the two triangles are congruent.
Step 2: Choose the best strategy to answer the question
You know $\overline{JK} \cong \overline{MN}$, ∠KJL ≅ ∠NMO, and $\overline{JL} \cong \overline{MO}$, which you should mark on the figure using hash marks. Once you've marked the figure, you'll see that ∠KJL and ∠NMO are contained by two sets of congruent sides. Because the two angles are congruent, you can use the SAS theorem to prove the triangles are congruent.
Step 3: Check that you answered the *right* question
The triangles are congruent by SAS; therefore, (A) is correct.

✔ **Note**

Beware of choice B; it's the reverse of what you need. Work carefully to avoid misreading.

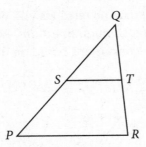

2. In the figure above, $\overline{ST}$ is a mid-segment of $\triangle PQR$. If $ST = 4x + 9$ and $PR = 16x + 6$, what is the length of $\overline{PR}$?

    A) 0.25
    B) 1.5
    C) 15
    D) 30

Work through the Kaplan Method for Math step-by-step to solve this question. The following table shows Kaplan's strategic thinking on the left, along with suggested math scratchwork on the right.

Strategic Thinking	Math Scratchwork
Step 1: Read the question, identifying and organizing important information as you go You must find the length of $\overline{PR}$.	
Step 2: Choose the best strategy to answer the question A triangle's mid-segment has a length that is half that of the side to which it is parallel. In other words, $ST = \frac{1}{2}PR$. You're given an expression for each segment, so plug in the expressions and solve for x.	$ST = \frac{1}{2}PR$ $4x+9 = \frac{1}{2}(16x+6)$ $-4x = -6$ $x = \frac{3}{2}$
The question asks for the length of $\overline{PR}$. Substitute the value you got for x back into the expression for PR and solve.	$16x\frac{3}{2}+6 = 30$
Step 3: Check that you answered the *right* question The correct choice is (D).	

✔ **Note**

You can also use a proportion to answer this question. Because the length of the mid-segment is half that of the side to which it is parallel, the two lengths are in the ratio 1:2. Use $\frac{4x+9}{16x+6} = \frac{1}{2}$ as your proportion.

3. $\triangle GRN$ and $\triangle YLW$ are similar, and the ratio of the length of $\overline{RN}$ to the length of $\overline{LW}$ is 2:3. Which of the following ratios must also be 2:3?

A) $m\angle NGR : m\angle WYL$

B) area of $\triangle GRN$: area of $\triangle YLW$

C) perimeter of $\triangle GRN$: perimeter of $\triangle YLW$

D) $GN : RN$

There's no scratchwork for this question, but Kaplan's strategic thinking follows. Follow along as we reason through the question to get the correct answer.

Strategic Thinking
Step 1: Read the question, identifying and organizing important information as you go
The question asks for the ratio that must also equal 2:3. You're told that $\triangle GRN$ and $\triangle YLW$ are similar and that the ratio of the length of $\overline{RN}$ to the length of $\overline{LW}$ is 2:3.
Step 2: Choose the best strategy to answer the question
Look for answers that you can easily eliminate. Corresponding angles of similar triangles are congruent (which means they are in a 1:1 ratio), so you can eliminate A. Corresponding sides of similar triangles are proportional, but two sides within the same triangle are not necessarily in the same proportion. Eliminate D.
Because each pair of corresponding sides of the two triangles are in the ratio 2:3, when the lengths of the sides of each are added up, the ratio of the sums (which are the perimeters) will also match this ratio. Try an example if you're not sure: If $\triangle GRN$ and $\triangle YLW$ are equilateral triangles with sides of 2 and 3, respectively, their perimeters are $2 + 2 + 2 = 6$ and $3 + 3 + 3 = 9$. The perimeter ratio is 6:9, which reduces to 2:3.
Step 3: Check that you answered the *right* question
Only (C) must be in the ratio 2:3.

As you saw on this question, trying out specific numbers can eliminate any doubt you have about your answer. The question does not specify whether the triangles must be equilateral, isosceles, etc., so you're welcome to use special triangles as long as they follow the rules set in the question.

✔ **Note**

If visualizing the triangles in your head is difficult, you can always draw them on a piece of scratch paper.

QUADRILATERAL THEOREMS

Quadrilaterals are four-sided figures, with interior angles that add up to 360°. You will likely not see a question solely about quadrilaterals; if a quadrilateral appears at all, it will likely contain hidden triangles. However, it is the properties of the quadrilateral that will allow you to deduce information about the triangles present, so make sure you know the basic properties of the most common quadrilaterals.

Given the high likelihood of a Test Day geometry problem containing hidden triangles, you should familiarize yourself with the types of quadrilaterals that are most likely to have useful triangles within.

Parallelogram Theorems	Properties
Parallelogram	• Both pairs of sides are parallel. • Both pairs of sides are congruent. • Both pairs of opposite angles are congruent. • An angle is supplementary to both angles adjacent to it. • The diagonals bisect each other.
Rhombus	• All of the properties of a parallelogram • All four sides are congruent. • Diagonals bisect angles and are perpendicular.
Rectangle	• All of the properties of a parallelogram • All angles are right angles. • Diagonals are congruent.
Square	• All of the properties of a parallelogram, rhombus, and rectangle • All sides are congruent.

A word of caution: Do not make any assumptions about a test figure that go beyond the information provided in the question. It's tempting to assume a quadrilateral is a rectangle or other more "friendly" shape, but unless this is proven or stated in the question (or indicated in the figure), don't do it!

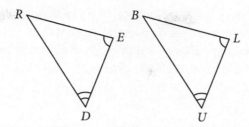

4. △*RED* and △*BLU* are shown above. Confirmation of which of the following facts will not prove that the two triangles are congruent?

    A) *RE = BL*

    B) *m∠DRE = m∠UBL*

    C) *DE = UL*

    D) Confirmation of any of the above will prove that the two triangles are congruent.

There's no scratchwork for this question, but Kaplan's strategic thinking follows. Follow along as we reason through the question to get the correct answer.

Strategic Thinking
Step 1: Read the question, identifying and organizing important information as you go
You must identify the statement that will *not* prove that the two triangles are congruent.
Step 2: Choose the best strategy to answer the question
Examine the hash marks. ∠*RDE* and ∠*BUL* are congruent, as are ∠*RED* and ∠*BLU*. To prove the triangles are congruent, you need to prove one pair of corresponding sides is congruent. This will allow you to use ASA or AAS. Proving the third pair of corresponding angles is congruent only allows you to conclude that the triangles are similar; you cannot conclude that they are congruent.
Step 3: Check that you answered the *right* question
Choice (B) confirms that the triangles are similar, but it doesn't confirm that they are congruent. It is therefore the correct answer.

Yet another math question with no calculations! Dare we say this is a silver lining to proof-type questions?

✔ **Note**

Remember that AAA is not a valid triangle congruence theorem! This is a typical trap waiting for less cautious students.

Now you'll have a chance to try a test-like question in a scaffolded manner. We've provided some guidance, but you'll need to fill in the missing parts of explanations or the step-by-step math to get to the correct answer. Don't worry—after going through the worked examples at the beginning of this section, this problem should be completely doable.

5. The diagram above shows a 40-foot flagpole and its shadow in relation to a nearby building that is 324 feet tall. If the flagpole's shadow is 50% longer than the flagpole itself, how far is the building from the flagpole?

The following table can help you structure your thinking as you go about solving this problem. The Kaplan strategic thinking is provided, as are bits of structured scratchwork. If you're not sure how to approach a question like this, start at the top and work your way down.

Strategic Thinking	Math Scratchwork
Step 1: Read the question, identifying and organizing important information as you go *What are you being asked to do here?* You're asked to find the distance between the building and the flagpole.	

Strategic Thinking	Math Scratchwork
Step 2: Choose the best strategy to answer the question *What kind of shapes are present?* You have a pair of similar triangles. Once you find the length of the flag-pole's shadow using the percentage given, you can use a proportion to find the distance between the building and the flagpole. *What should the proportion look like?* There are a couple different ways you can write your proportion. Follow the rules for assembling a proportion (see chapter 5 for a refresher), and you'll be in good shape. Don't forget to subtract the length of the shadow from the horizontal leg of the large triangle after solving the proportion!	flagpole shadow: ____ x ____ = ____ ____ = ____ ____ = ____ ____ = ____ ____ - ____ = ____
Step 3: Check that you answered the *right* question *How far is the building from the flagpole?* If you got 426 feet, congrats! You're correct.	

Now that you've seen the variety of ways in which the SAT can test you on similarity, congruence, and proofs, try the following questions to check your understanding. Give yourself 2 minutes to tackle the following two questions. Make sure you use the Kaplan Method for Math as often as you can. Remember, you want to emphasize speed and efficiency in addition to simply getting the correct answer.

Note: Figure not drawn to scale.

6. Given △*ABC* and △*XYZ* above, *m*∠*ABC* = *m*∠*XYZ* = 90°, $\overline{AC} \cong \overline{XZ}$, and any information that can be inferred based on these facts, which of the following is needed to prove △*ABC* and △*XYZ* are congruent?

    A) $\overline{BC} \cong \overline{YZ}$

    B) ∠*BAC* ≅ ∠*YXZ*

    C) $\overline{AB} \cong \overline{XY}$

    D) More than one of the above statements will prove the two triangles are congruent.

7. In the figure above, lines *j* and *k* are parallel. Which of the following must be true?

    A) △*VWX* ≅ △*ZYX*

    B) $\overline{VZ} \cong \overline{WY}$

    C) △*VWX* ~ △*ZYX*

    D) $\overline{VZ} \parallel \overline{WY}$

Answers & Explanations for this chapter begin on page 948.

EXTRA PRACTICE

Required	Recommended
Questions 1–8	Questions 9–18

1. Given the triangles shown above, if ∠*H* ≅ ∠*S*, $\overline{HA}$ ≅ $\overline{SU}$, and $\overline{HT}$ ≅ $\overline{SN}$, then which theorem can be used to prove Δ*HAT* ≅ Δ*SUN*?

   A) ASA

   B) SAS

   C) SSS

   D) HL

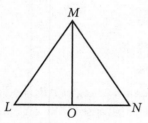

2. In Δ*LMN* above, $\overline{MO}$ ⊥ $\overline{LN}$. If $\overline{MO}$ bisects $\overline{LN}$, which statement cannot be proven?

   A) ∠*LOM* ≅ ∠*NOM*

   B) $\overline{LO}$ ≅ $\overline{ON}$

   C) $\overline{MO}$ ≅ $\overline{MN}$

   D) Δ*LMO* ≅ Δ*NMO*

3. Given that triangle *DOG* is congruent to triangle *CAT*, and that triangle *CAT* is congruent to triangle *HEN*, $\overline{OG}$ must be congruent to which of the following sides?

   A) $\overline{CA}$

   B) $\overline{CT}$

   C) $\overline{EN}$

   D) $\overline{HE}$

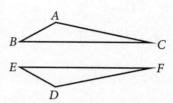

4. If ∠*A* ≅ ∠*D* and $\overline{AB}$ ≅ $\overline{DE}$ in the diagram above, what additional information is needed to prove Δ*ABC* ≅ Δ*DEF* by the ASA theorem?

   A) ∠*B* ≅ ∠*E*

   B) ∠*C* ≅ ∠*F*

   C) $\overline{AC}$ ≅ $\overline{DF}$

   D) $\overline{BC}$ ≅ $\overline{EF}$

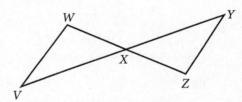

5. If triangles *VXW* and *YXZ* in the figure above are congruent, which statement cannot always be proven?

   A) $\overline{VW}$ ≅ $\overline{ZY}$

   B) $\overline{VX}$ ≅ $\overline{XZ}$

   C) ∠*WXV* ≅ ∠*ZXY*

   D) ∠*XVW* ≅ ∠*XYZ*

6. Triangle *BED* is similar to triangle *COT*. Triangle *COT* has side lengths of 8, 15, and 17. Which of the following could be the side lengths of triangle *BED*?

   A) 3, 4, 5

   B) 5, 12, 13

   C) 10, 17, 19

   D) 24, 45, 51

7. If $\triangle OLD \sim \triangle NEW$, and the ratio of the length of $\overline{OL}$ to $\overline{NE}$ is 7:4, which of the following ratios must also be equal to 7:4?

   A) $\overline{OD} : \overline{EW}$

   B) $\angle D : \angle W$

   C) area of $\triangle OLD$: area of $\triangle NEW$

   D) perimeter of $\triangle OLD$: perimeter of $\triangle NEW$

Note: Figure not drawn to scale.

8. Triangle *LOW* is shown in the figure above, where $\overline{HI}$ is the bisector of both $\overline{LO}$ and $\overline{OW}$. Given that $\overline{LW} = 30$ and $\overline{HI} = 4x - 1$, what is the value of *x*?

   A) 3.5

   B) 4

   C) 7.75

   D) 8

9. Two rectangles, *LION* and *PUMA*, are similar. Rectangle *LION* has a length of 86 and a width of 52. If the perimeter of rectangle *PUMA* is 69, what is its width?

   A) 13

   B) 17.25

   C) 26

   D) 34.5

Note: Figure not drawn to scale.

10. What is the area, in square units, of the triangle that is not similar to the other three?

    A) 120

    B) 270

    C) 288

    D) 384

11. Brigitte says triangles *ABC* and *XYZ* are congruent because $\angle A \cong \angle X$ and $\angle C \cong \angle Z$. All of the following pieces of information would make Brigitte correct, except which one?

    A) $\angle B \cong \angle Y$

    B) $\overline{AB} \cong \overline{XY}$

    C) $\overline{AC} \cong \overline{XZ}$

    D) $\overline{BC} \cong \overline{YZ}$

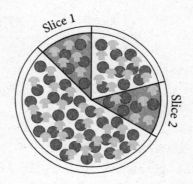

12. In the figure above, $\overline{AD} \perp \overline{BE}$, $\overline{AD}$ and $\overline{BE}$ intersect at C, and $\overline{AB} \parallel \overline{DE}$. Which theorem proves that $\triangle BAC \sim \triangle EDC$?

   A) AAA

   B) ASA

   C) SAS

   D) SSS

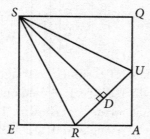

13. Square *SQAE* is shown above. Points *U* and *R* are midpoints of *QA* and *EA*, respectively, and *D* is the midpoint of *RU*. Which of the following correctly lists the sets of triangles that must be congruent in the figure?

   A) *RSD* and *USD* only

   B) *ESR*, *QSU*, *RSD*, and *USD*

   C) *ESR* and *QSU*; *RSD* and *USD*

   D) *ESR*, *QSU*, and *AUR*; *RSD* and *USD*

14. Four cuts are made from the center of a perfectly circular pizza to form Slice 1 and Slice 2. The arc lengths of the crusts of both slices are congruent. Which of the following statements regarding the two slices is true?

   A) The two slices may or may not be congruent, depending on the length of each side of each slice.

   B) The two slices may or may not be congruent, depending on the angle created by the cuts that were made.

   C) The two slices cannot be congruent because the side lengths of each slice cannot be the same length.

   D) The two slices must be congruent because the arc lengths are congruent and the side lengths of each slice are congruent.

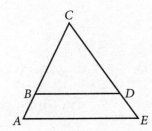

Note: Figure not drawn to scale.

15. In the figure above, $\overline{BD} \parallel \overline{AE}$ and $AB = 5$. If BC is three times AB and CD is 2 more than half AC, then what is the length of segment DE?

A) 3

B) 4

C) 5

D) 6

16. If $\triangle TIM \sim \triangle JOE$, $m\angle T = 40°$, and $m\angle I = 65°$, what is the measure of $\angle E$?

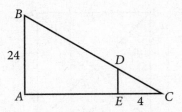

Note: Figure not drawn to scale.

17. In the figure above, $\overline{DE} \parallel \overline{AB}$ and $\overline{DE} \perp \overline{AC}$. If $AE = 28$, what is the length of BD?

18. Triangle *ANT* is similar to triangle *BUG*, which are both plotted on a coordinate plane (not shown). The vertices of triangle *ANT* are $A(3, 2)$, $N(3, -1)$, and $T(-1, -1)$. Two of triangle *BUG*'s vertices are $(-8, -3)$ and $(8, -3)$. If vertex *B* is in the same quadrant of the coordinate plane as vertex *A*, what is the *y*-coordinate of vertex *B*?

CHAPTER 15

Circles

CHAPTER OBJECTIVES

By the end of this section, you will be able to:

1. Apply theorems about circles to find arc lengths, angle measures, chord lengths, and areas of sectors

2. Create or use an equation with two variables to solve a problem about a circle in the coordinate plane

SMARTPOINTS

Point Value	SmartPoint Category
30 Points	Geometry

INTRODUCTION TO CIRCLES

You already know the SAT can ask a variety of questions about lines, angles, and triangles; it can also test you on your knowledge of circles. Keep reading for a refresher on these ubiquitous shapes.

Circle Anatomy & Basic Formulas

There are a number of circle traits you should know for Test Day. The good news: Most will already be familiar to you if you've taken geometry.

- **Radius (*r*):** The distance from the center of a circle to its edge
- **Chord:** A line segment that connects two points on a circle
- **Diameter (*d*):** A chord that passes through the center of a circle. The diameter is always the longest chord a circle can have and is twice the length of the radius.
- **Circumference (*C*):** The distance around a circle; the equivalent of a polygon's perimeter. Find this using the formula $C = 2\pi r = \pi d$.
- **Area:** the space a circle takes up, just like a polygon. A circle's area is found by computing $A = \pi r^2$.
- Every circle contains 360°. You'll find out more on this fact's utility shortly.

As the formulas demonstrate, the radius is often key to unlocking several other components of a circle. Therefore, your first step for many circle questions will be to find the radius.

Circles on the Coordinate Plane and Their Equations

You've learned how to use the radius, area, and circumference to describe circles in a variety of situations. However, when you have a circle on the coordinate plane, you can describe it with an equation. The equation of a circle in **standard form** is as follows:

$$(x - h)^2 + (y - k)^2 = r^2$$

> ✔ **Note**
>
> A circle is one of the four conic sections, which are made by slicing a double cone with a plane. The parabola is another conic section that you read about in chapter 10. The ellipse and hyperbola (with standard forms $\frac{(x-h)^2}{a^2} + \frac{(y-k)^2}{b^2} = 1$ and $\frac{(x-h)^2}{a^2} - \frac{(y-k)^2}{b^2} = 1$, respectively) will not be tested on the SAT. Watch out for them in trap answer choices, however!

The variables *x* and *y* are the independent and dependent variables, respectively, and *r* is the radius of the circle. The likely unfamiliar *h* and *k* are the *x*- and *y*-coordinates of the circle's center, respectively: (*h*, *k*).

You might also see what is referred to as **general form:**

$$x^2 + y^2 + Cx + Dy + E = 0$$

At first glance, this probably doesn't resemble a circle equation, but the fact that you have an x^2 term and a y^2 term with coefficients of 1 is your indicator that the equation does indeed graph as a circle. To convert to standard form, complete the square for the x terms, then repeat for the y terms.

> ✔ **Note**
>
> The x^2 and y^2 terms of a circle equation occasionally have coefficients other than 1. If this is the case, simply divide through to eliminate them.

> ✔ **Note**
>
> Refer to chapter 10 for a review of completing the square.

Circle Ratios: Arcs, Central Angles, & Sectors

The SAT can ask you about parts of circles as well. There are three partial components that can be made in a circle: arcs, central angles, and sectors. These circle pieces are frequently used in proportions with their whole counterparts, so the ability to set up ratios and proportions correctly is of utmost importance for these questions.

- An **arc** is part of a circle's circumference. Both chords and radii can cut a circle into arcs. The number of arcs present depends on how many chords and/or radii are present. If only two arcs are present, the smaller arc is called the **minor arc**, and the larger one is the **major arc**. If a diameter cuts the circle in half, the two formed arcs are called **semicircles**. An arc length can never be greater than the circle's circumference.

- When radii cut a circle into multiple (but not necessarily equal) pieces, the angle at the center of the circle contained by the radii is the **central angle**. As a full circle contains 360°, a central angle measure cannot be higher than this.

- Radii splitting a circle into pieces can also create **sectors**, which are parts of the circle's area. The area of a sector cannot be greater than its circle's total area.

Here's a summary of the ratios formed by these three parts and their whole counterparts.

$$\frac{\text{arc length}}{\text{circumference}} = \frac{\text{central angle}}{360°} = \frac{\text{sector area}}{\text{circle area}}$$

Notice that all of these ratios are equal. Intuitively, this should make sense: When you slice a pizza into four equal slices, each piece should have $\frac{1}{4}$ of the cheese, sauce, crust, and toppings. If you slice a circle into four equal pieces, the same principle applies: Each piece should have $\frac{1}{4}$ of the degrees, circumference, and area.

There are many theorems that govern circles and their additional associated lines; fortunately, only a handful of these might appear on the SAT. Familiarize yourself with the ones described in the next few paragraphs.

Inscribed Angle Theorem

An angle whose vertex is on the edge of the circle is called an **inscribed angle**. As this vertex moves along the edge, the measure of the inscribed angle remains constant as long as the minor arc created (in other words, isolated or **subtended** by the chords) does not change. When the chords that create an inscribed angle subtend the same minor arc that a pair of radii do, a special relationship appears: the central angle measure is twice that of the inscribed angle.

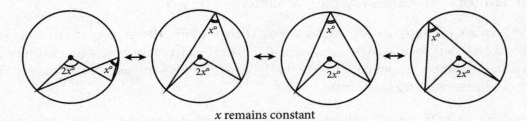

x remains constant

Arcs Formed from Parallel Chords

Another theorem states that two parallel chords will intercept two congruent arcs; see the following diagram for an example. The congruent arcs will be between the chords.

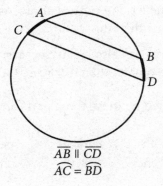

$\overline{AB} \parallel \overline{CD}$
$\overset{\frown}{AC} = \overset{\frown}{BD}$

Tangent Lines

You might have heard of the tangent function in trigonometry, but when talking about a line tangent to a circle, this is something quite different. A tangent line touches a circle at exactly one point and is perpendicular to a circle's radius at that point of contact. The following diagram demonstrates what this looks like.

The presence of a right angle opens up the opportunity to draw otherwise hidden shapes, so pay special attention to tangents when they're mentioned. They often come up in complex figure questions.

The problems on the next few pages will give you a chance to see how these properties of circles can be tested on the SAT.

1. An orange with a diameter of 2 inches is sitting on a counter. If the distance from the center of the orange to the edge of the counter is 10 inches, how far is it between the point where the orange sits on the counter to the counter edge?

   A) $4\sqrt{6}$ in.

   B) $3\sqrt{11}$ in.

   C) 10 in.

   D) $\sqrt{101}$ in.

Work through the Kaplan Method for Math step-by-step to solve this question. The following table shows Kaplan's strategic thinking on the left, along with suggested math scratchwork on the right.

Strategic Thinking	Math Scratchwork
Step 1: Read the question, identifying and organizing important information as you go You must calculate the distance between where the orange sits to the edge of the counter.	
Step 2: Choose the best strategy to answer the question Draw a cross-section of the orange on the counter; you'll see this is a circle with a tangent line. Draw in a perpendicular radius and a line from the center of the orange to the edge of the counter to reveal a right triangle. Use the Pythagorean theorem to calculate the distance requested.	 $1^2 + x^2 = 10^2$ $x^2 = 99$ $x = \sqrt{99}$
Step 3: Check that you answered the *right* question Simplify the radical; (B) is correct.	$\sqrt{99} = \sqrt{9 \times 11} = 3\sqrt{11}$

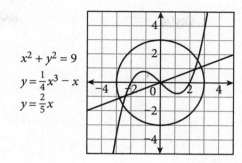

$x^2 + y^2 = 9$

$y = \frac{1}{4}x^3 - x$

$y = \frac{2}{5}x$

2. A system of three equations and their graphs in the *xy*-plane are shown above. How many solutions does the system have?

    A) 0

    B) 1

    C) 3

    D) 7

There's no scratchwork for this question, but Kaplan's strategic thinking follows. Follow along as we reason through the question to get the correct answer.

Strategic Thinking
Step 1: Read the question, identifying and organizing important information as you go
You're asked for the number of solutions for the given system of equations.
Step 2: Choose the best strategy to answer the question
Graphically, the solution to this system of equations is the point (or points) where *all three* graphs intersect. You're given the graphs of the equations, so don't waste valuable time trying to solve the system algebraically.
There are seven points of intersection in the *xy*-plane, but none of them is an intersection of *all three* graphs. Therefore, this system of equations has 0 solutions.
Step 3: Check that you answered the *right* question
Choice (A) is the correct answer.

✔ **Note**

Beware of choice D; you'll fall for this trap if you include the intersections involving only two graphs.

Note: Figure not drawn to scale.

3. The semicircle above has a radius of *r* inches, and chord $\overline{YZ}$ is parallel to diameter $\overline{WX}$. If the length of $\overline{YZ}$ is 25% shorter than the length of $\overline{WX}$, what is the greatest distance between $\overline{YZ}$ and $\overline{WX}$ in terms of *r*?

A) $\frac{1}{4}\pi r$

B) $\frac{3}{4}\pi r$

C) $\frac{\sqrt{2}}{4}r$

D) $\frac{\sqrt{7}}{4}r$

Work through the Kaplan Method for Math step-by-step to solve this question. The following table shows Kaplan's strategic thinking on the left, along with suggested math scratchwork on the right.

Strategic Thinking	Math Scratchwork
Step 1: Read the question, identifying and organizing important information as you go You need to determine the distance between the two chords in terms of *r*. You're told that $\overline{WX}$ is the diameter and that $\overline{YZ}$ is 25% smaller than $\overline{WX}$.	

Strategic Thinking	Math Scratchwork
Step 2: Choose the best strategy to answer the question Remember one of the simplest ways to uncover information in tough geometry questions: Draw additional lines. Start with an additional radius that extends from the center of the diameter of the semicircle to $\overline{YZ}$. Then add a line that represents the greatest distance between the two chords, which will create a right triangle. Label the new radius (which is the hypotenuse of the right triangle) as r. You know that YZ is 25% shorter than WX, so $YZ = \dfrac{3}{4}WX$. Analogously, because $r = \dfrac{1}{2}WX$, $\dfrac{3}{4}r = \dfrac{1}{2}YZ$. You now have two of the three sides of the right triangle and can solve for the third using the Pythagorean theorem.	$YZ = \dfrac{3}{4}WX$ $r = \dfrac{1}{2}WX \;\rightarrow\; \dfrac{3}{4}r = \dfrac{1}{2}YZ$ $\left(\dfrac{3}{4}r\right)^2 + x^2 = r^2$ $\dfrac{9}{16}r^2 + x^2 = r^2$ $x^2 = \dfrac{7}{16}r^2$ $x = \pm\dfrac{\sqrt{7}}{4}r$
Step 3: Check that you answered the right question A distance can't be negative, so (D) is the correct answer.	

✔ **Note**

Remember that helpful triangles are often hidden; drawing extra lines in figures can help uncover them.

$$x^2 + 6x + y^2 - 8y = 171$$

4. The equation of a circle in the *xy*-plane is shown above. What is the positive difference between the *x*- and *y*-coordinates of the center of the circle?

Work through the Kaplan Method for Math step-by-step to solve this question. The following table shows Kaplan's strategic thinking on the left, along with suggested math scratchwork on the right.

Strategic Thinking	Math Scratchwork
Step 1: Read the question, identifying and organizing important information as you go You need to determine the positive difference between the *x*- and *y*-coordinates of the center of the circle.	
Step 2: Choose the best strategy to answer the question You'll need to rewrite the equation in standard form to get what you need. The coefficients of the *x* and *y* terms are even, so consider completing the square for *x* and *y*. Divide *b* (from the *x* term) by 2 and square the result. Repeat for *y*. Factor properly to yield the equation in standard form. The center of the circle is (−3, 4); subtract −3 from 4 to get the positive difference.	$(x-h)^2 + (y-k)^2 = r^2$ $x^2 + 6x + y^2 - 8y = 171$ $x: b = 6 \rightarrow 3 \rightarrow 9$ $y: b = -8 \rightarrow -4 \rightarrow 16$ $x^2 + 6x + 9 + y^2 - 8y + 16 = 171 + 9 + 16$ $(x+3)^2 + (y-4)^2 = 196$ $4 - (-3) = 7$
Step 3: Check that you answered the *right* question The positive difference between the two coordinates is 7.	

It's quite likely you'll see questions that test you on multiple concepts on Test Day, so make sure you're comfortable working with several in one question.

Now you'll have a chance to try another test-like question. Some guidance is provided, but you'll need to fill in the missing parts of explanations or the step-by-step math to get to the correct answer. Don't worry—after going through the examples at the beginning of this chapter, this question should be completely doable. If you're still struggling, review the worked examples in this chapter and the additional questions further.

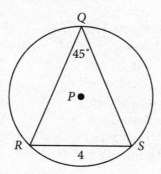

Note: Figure not drawn to scale.

5. In circle P above, $RS = 4$ and $\angle RQS$ measures 45°. What is the circumference of circle P?

   A) 4π

   B) $4\pi\sqrt{2}$

   C) 8π

   D) $8\pi\sqrt{2}$

Use the scaffolding that follows as your map through the question. If you aren't sure where to start, answer the questions in italics and fill in the blanks in the table as you work from top to bottom.

Strategic Thinking	Math Scratchwork
Step 1: Read the question, identifying and organizing important information as you go *What are you being asked to do here?* You need to find the circumference of circle *P*.	

Strategic Thinking	Math Scratchwork
Step 2: Choose the best strategy to answer the question *How can you use the shapes shown?* Pay attention to the note below the figure. The shapes are not drawn to scale, and although it looks like it, all the angles in the triangle are not 45° (they can't be because the sum wouldn't be 180°). You'll need to draw in a couple additional lines to reveal a more useful triangle. Once done, use your knowledge of subtended arcs to determine a special property of your new triangle. *How will the properties of this new triangle help you get to the answer?* The legs of your new triangle are radii of the circle, so they are congruent. Use this and the fact that $RS = 4$ to determine the radius and then the circumference of the circle.	 <u>Note</u>: Figure not drawn to scale. $\triangle$ _____ is a _____-_____-_____ triangle
Step 3: Check that you answered the *right* question *What is the circumference of circle* P? Did you get (B)? If so, you're absolutely right!	_____

Now that you've seen the variety of ways in which the SAT can test you on circles, try the following questions to check your understanding. Give yourself 2 minutes to tackle the following two questions. Make sure you use the Kaplan Method for Math as often as you can. Remember, you want to emphasize speed and efficiency in addition to simply getting the correct answer.

6. A circle is given by the equation $(x-3)^2 + (y+4)^2 = 25$. Which of the following equations does not represent a line that contains a diameter of this circle?

A) $y = \dfrac{4}{3}x - 8$

B) $y = -4$

C) $y = 3x - 5$

D) $x = 3$

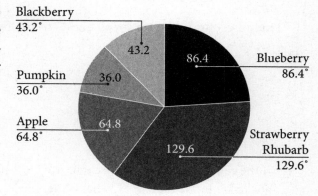

7. After a Thanksgiving gathering, John brought home several different kinds of pie in a 10-inch diameter pie tin; the portion of each is shown above. What is the area (in square inches) of the portion of leftover pie that is not strawberry rhubarb?

A) 9π

B) 16π

C) 36π

D) 64π

Answers & Explanations for this chapter begin on page 956.

EXTRA PRACTICE

Required	Recommended
Questions 1–8	Questions 9–18

 may use your calculator for all questions in this section.

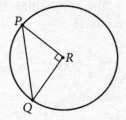

1. If the central angles in the circle shown above are in the ratio 4:3:2, what is the measure in degrees of the smallest angle?

   A) 40

   B) 60

   C) 72

   D) 80

2. What is the length, to the nearest inch, of an arc intercepted by a central angle of 135 degrees in a circle that has a radius of 12 inches?

   A) 9

   B) 16

   C) 21

   D) 28

3. What is the length of chord PQ in the figure above if the radius of the circle is 4 cm?

   A) 4

   B) $4\sqrt{2}$

   C) 8

   D) $8\sqrt{2}$

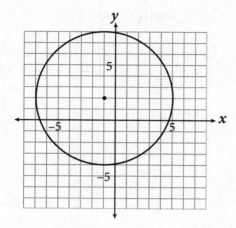

4. Which of the following represents the equation of the circle shown above?

A) $(x - 1)^2 + (y + 2)^2 = 6$

B) $(x + 1)^2 + (y - 2)^2 = 6$

C) $(x - 1)^2 + (y + 2)^2 = 36$

D) $(x + 1)^2 + (y - 2)^2 = 36$

5. If the area of the shaded sector in circle O is 14π square units, what is the radius of the circle?

A) 6

B) 8

C) 9

D) 12

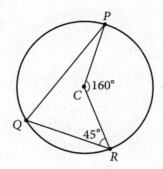

6. What is the measure of $\angle QPC$ in the figure above?

A) 25°

B) 30°

C) 35°

D) 40°

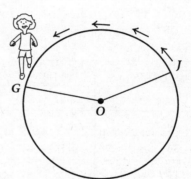

7. Cherie is jogging around a circular track. She started at point J and has jogged 200 yards to point G. If the radius of the track is 120 yards, what is the measure to the nearest tenth of a degree of minor angle JOG?

A) 95.5

B) 98.2

C) 102.1

D) 105.4

8. At 2:15, the short hand of an analog clock lines up exactly with the 11-minute tick mark, and the long hand lines up with the 15-minute tick mark. What central angle do the hands form at 2:15?

A) 18°

B) 20°

C) 24°

D) 28°

Age Range	Number of People
Under 16	880
16–35	560
36–55	120
Over 55	40

9. The table above represents the age distribution of people attending a waterpark one weekend. If Maurice wants to display the information in a pie graph, what should the degree measures of the angles in the pie graph be?

A) 8°, 24°, 140°, 188°

B) 8°, 32°, 127°, 193°

C) 9°, 27°, 126°, 198°

D) 9°, 36°, 122°, 193°

10. Which system of equations has no solution?

A) $\begin{cases} y = x \\ x^2 + y^2 = 25 \end{cases}$

B) $\begin{cases} y = x + 6 \\ x^2 + y^2 = 9 \end{cases}$

C) $\begin{cases} y = x - 4 \\ x^2 + y^2 = 16 \end{cases}$

D) $\begin{cases} y = x + 8 \\ x^2 + y^2 = 100 \end{cases}$

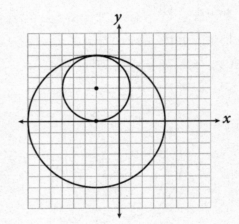

11. If the area of the smaller circle shown above is 144π square units, then what is the equation of the larger circle?

A) $(x + 2)^2 + y^2 = 36$

B) $(x + 2)^2 + (y - 3)^2 = 9$

C) $(x + 8)^2 + (y - 12)^2 = 144$

D) $(x + 8)^2 + y^2 = 576$

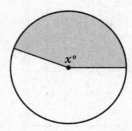

12. In the figure above, the ratio of the shaded area to the unshaded area is 4 to 5. What is the value of x?

    A) 135

    B) 145

    C) 160

    D) 170

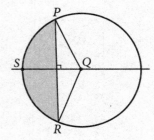

13. If the measure of $\angle PQR$ in the figure above is 120°, and the radius of the circle is 4 units, what is the area in square units of the shaded portion of the circle?

    A) $\dfrac{4\pi}{3} - 8\sqrt{3}$

    B) $\dfrac{5\pi}{3} - 4\sqrt{3}$

    C) $\dfrac{8\pi}{3} - 4\sqrt{3}$

    D) $\dfrac{16\pi}{3} - 4\sqrt{3}$

14. Earth makes one complete rotation about its axis every 24 hours, at a fairly constant rate. Through how many degrees would Quito, Ecuador, which lies on the Earth's equator, rotate from 12:00 noon on January 1 to 3:00 PM on January 2?

    A) 340°

    B) 370°

    C) 385°

    D) 405°

$$x^2 + y^2 + 8x - 20y = 28$$

15. What is the diameter of the circle given by the equation above?

    A) 12

    B) 24

    C) 28

    D) 56

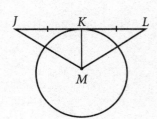

16. In the figure above, $\overline{JL}$ is tangent to circle M at point K. If the area of the circle is 36π, and $JL = 16$, what is the length of $\overline{LM}$?

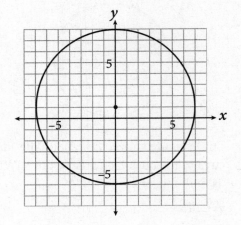

17. If the pattern above continues around the circle, what is the positive angle measure at point P?

18. If the equation of the circle shown above is written in the form $x^2 + y^2 + ax + by = c$, what is the value of $a + b + c$?

CHAPTER 16

3-D Shapes

CHAPTER OBJECTIVES

By the end of this section, you will be able to:

1. Solve problems using surface area and volume formulas

SMARTPOINTS

Point Value	SmartPoint Category
30 Points	Geometry

INTRODUCTION TO 3-D SHAPES

Over the last few chapters you learned about two-dimensional (2-D) shapes and how to tackle SAT questions involving them. In this chapter, you'll learn how to do the same for questions containing three-dimensional (3-D) shapes, also called solids. There are several different types of solids that might appear on Test Day—rectangular solids, cubes, cylinders, prisms, spheres, cones, pyramids—so it is critical that you be familiar with them.

The following is a diagram with the basic anatomy of a 3-D shape.

A **face** (or **surface**) is a 2-D shape that acts as one of the sides of the solid. Two faces meet at a line segment called an **edge**, and three faces meet at a single point called a **vertex**.

Keep reading for more on types of 3-D shapes and questions you could be asked about them.

Volume

Volume is the amount of 3-D space occupied by a solid. This is analogous to the area of a 2-D shape like a triangle or circle. You can find the volume of many 3-D shapes by finding the area of the base and multiplying it by the height. We've highlighted the base area components of the formulas in the following table with parentheses.

Rectangular Solid	Cube	Right Cylinder
$(l \times w) \times h$	$(s \times s) \times s = s^3$	$(\pi \times r^2) \times h$

✔ **Note**

Recall that a square is a special type of rectangle that has four equal sides. Likewise, a cube is a special type of rectangular solid whose edges (and faces) are all equal.

These three 3-D shapes are prisms. Almost all prisms on the SAT are right prisms; that is, all faces are perpendicular to those with which they share edges.

Following are some examples of less commonly seen prisms.

Triangular Prism	Hexagonal Prism	Decagonal Prism

Like the rectangular solids, cubes, and cylinders you saw earlier, these right prisms use the same general volume formula ($V = A_{base} \times h$).

> ✔ **Note**
>
> You might not be told explicitly the area of the base of a prism, in which case you'll need to rely on your two-dimensional geometry expertise to find it before calculating the volume.

More complicated 3-D shapes include the right pyramid, right cone, and sphere. The vertex of a right pyramid or right cone will always be centered above the middle of the base. Their volume formulas are similar to those of prisms, albeit with different coefficients.

> ✔ **Note**
>
> Some of these formulas might look daunting, but don't fret—you won't have to memorize them for Test Day. They'll be provided on the reference page at the beginning of each math section.

Right (Square) Pyramid	Right Cone	Sphere
$\frac{1}{3} \times (l \times w) \times h$	$\frac{1}{3} \times (\pi \times r^2) \times h$	$\frac{4}{3} \times \pi \times r^3$

> **✔ Note**
>
> A right pyramid can have any regular polygon as its base; the square variety is the one you're most likely to see. Also note that the vertex above the base of a right pyramid or cone is not necessarily formed by an intersection of exactly three faces like in prisms, but it is still a single point and is still called a vertex.

Surface Area

Surface area is the sum of the areas of all faces of a solid. You might liken this to determining the amount of wrapping paper needed to cover all faces of a solid.

To calculate the surface area of a solid, simply find the area of each face using your 2-D geometry skills, and then add them all together.

> **✔ Note**
>
> You won't be expected to know the surface area formulas for right pyramids, right cones, and spheres; they'll be provided if you need them. However, you could be asked to find the surface area of a prism, in which case you'll be given enough information to find the area of each surface of the solid.

You might think that finding the surface area of a solid with many sides, such as a 10-sided right octagonal prism, is a tall order. However, you can save time by noticing a vital trait: This prism has two identical octagonal faces and eight identical rectangular faces. Don't waste time finding the area of each of the 10 sides; find the area of one octagonal face and one rectangular face instead. Once complete, multiply the area of the octagonal face by 2 and the area of the rectangular face by 8, add the products together, and you're done! The same is true for other 3-D shapes such as rectangular solids (including cubes), other right prisms, and certain pyramids.

If you're ready to test your knowledge of 3-D shapes, check out the next few pages for some practice questions.

1. Desiree is making apple juice from concentrate. The cylindrical container of concentrate has a diameter of 7 cm and a height of 12 cm. To make the juice, the concentrate must be diluted with water so that the mix is 75% water and 25% concentrate. If Desiree wishes to store all of the prepared juice in one cylindrical pitcher that has a diameter of 10 cm, what must its minimum height be (rounded to the nearest centimeter)?

Work through the Kaplan Method for Math step-by-step to solve this question. The following table shows Kaplan's strategic thinking on the left, along with suggested math scratchwork on the right.

Strategic Thinking	Math Scratchwork
Step 1: Read the question, identifying and organizing important information as you go You need to find the minimum height of a pitcher with a diameter of 10 cm that can hold the entire amount of juice after it has been properly mixed.	
Step 2: Choose the best strategy to answer the question Before finding the height of the pitcher, you'll need to determine the volume of the juice after it has been mixed with the water. Determine the volume of concentrate Desiree has, and then multiply this amount by 4 (because the concentrate only makes up 25% of the new juice volume) to calculate the post-dilution volume. Use the volume formula again to find the minimum height of the juice pitcher.	$d_{conc} = 7 \rightarrow r_{conc} = 3.5$ $V_{conc} = \pi r^2 h$ $V_{conc} = \pi \times 3.5^2 \times 12$ $V_{conc} = 147\pi$ $\quad V_{dil} = 4 \times 147\pi = 588\pi$ $d_{pitcher} = 10 \rightarrow r_{pticher} = 5$ $588\pi = \pi \times 5^2 \times h$ $\quad h = \dfrac{588}{25} = 23.52$
Step 3: Check that you answered the *right* question Round to the nearest centimeter, and you're done!	24

2. A machine is filling boxes with baseballs in the 5 × 3 layout above. When the box is closed, each baseball fits in a cubic enclosure within the box with no space between the ball and the six walls containing it. If each baseball has a diameter of 8 cm, what volume of two of these filled boxes is empty space? Assume volume contributed by the box itself and the dividers inside the box is negligible.

    A) $3,840 - 640\pi$ cm^3

    B) $7,680 - 1,280\pi$ cm^3

    C) $15,360 - 2,560\pi$ cm^3

    D) $15,360 - 1,280\pi$ cm^3

Work through the Kaplan Method for Math step-by-step to solve this question. The following table shows Kaplan's strategic thinking on the left, along with suggested math scratchwork on the right.

Strategic Thinking	Math Scratchwork
Step 1: Read the question, identifying and organizing important information as you go You need to find the volume of the empty space inside two filled boxes. Note: before you start punching numbers into your calculator, take a peek at the answer choices—they are not completely simplified, so you'll want to jot down your calculations as you work.	

Strategic Thinking	Math Scratchwork
Step 2: Choose the best strategy to answer the question Identify the shapes present. The baseballs are spheres, and the box containing them is a rectangular prism. Use the proper volume formula for each calculation. Remember to account for the fact that each box holds 15 baseballs. Subtract the volume of the baseballs from that of the box to find the volume of empty space in one box.	$V_{sph} = \dfrac{4}{3}\pi r^3$, $r = 4$ cm $V_{rect} = lwh$ $V_{ball} = \dfrac{4}{3}\pi \times 4^3$ $\quad\ = \dfrac{4}{3}\pi \times 64$ $\quad\ = \dfrac{256}{3}\pi$ $\dfrac{256}{3}\pi \times 15 = 1{,}280\pi$ $V_{box} = (5 \times 8)\,(3 \times 8)\,(8)$ $\quad\ = 7{,}680$ diff. $= 7{,}680 - 1{,}280\pi$
Step 3: Check that you answered the _right_ question Double your result from the previous step to get the correct answer, (C).	$\times 2 = 15{,}360 - 2{,}560\pi$

3. Holly is designing a kaleidoscope for a friend's birthday gift. To make the body of the kaleidoscope, she plans to arrange six identical rectangular mirrors in the shape of a hexagon inside a right cylindrical casing that is open on both ends. A cross section of the interior is shown above. If the casing is 30.5 cm in length and has a surface area of 61π cm^2, what is the distance between the centers of two parallel mirrors?

A) $\sqrt{2}$ cm

B) $\dfrac{\sqrt{3}}{2}$ cm

C) $\sqrt{3}$ cm

D) 2 cm

Work through the Kaplan Method for Math step-by-step to solve this question. The following table shows Kaplan's strategic thinking on the left, along with suggested math scratchwork on the right.

Strategic Thinking	Math Scratchwork
Step 1: Read the question, identifying and organizing important information as you go You are asked to find the distance between the centers of two parallel mirrors in the casing.	

Strategic Thinking	Math Scratchwork
Step 2: Choose the best strategy to answer the question The figure is a cross section of a regular hexagonal prism inside a right cylinder. Use the quantities given (and your complex figure finesse) to map a route to the correct answer. Ever peel a label off a water bottle? The label is a rectangle wrapped around the bottle. Think of the casing the same way. The cylinder's height and circumference are the rectangle's length and width, respectively. Use these to find the circle's diameter. Drawing three diameters that each pass through two opposite vertices of the hexagon creates six equilateral triangles. The sides of each one are half the circle diameter, so they are all 1 cm. These are shown in the scratchwork column; the distance that you ultimately need to find is also drawn. Notice that the latter bisects two of the equilateral triangles, creating 30-60-90 triangles. The longer leg of each is half the distance you need to find; use the 30-60-90 ratio to calculate it.	$h = 30.5\ cm$ $SA\ of\ casing = h \times C = 61\pi\ cm^2$ $C = \dfrac{61\pi}{30.5} = 2\pi\ cm$ $C = \pi d \rightarrow d = 2\ cm$ $30\text{-}60\text{-}90: x : x\sqrt{3} : 2x$
Step 3: Check that you answered the *right* question Double the length of the longer leg of the 30-60-90 triangle to get $\sqrt{3}$ cm, which is (C).	$\dfrac{\sqrt{3}}{2} \times 2 = \sqrt{3}$

✔ **Note**

This question houses an easy opportunity to fall for a trap because you find half the distance you need during your calculations; remember to confirm that you've answered the right question.

4. The ratio of the lengths of two spheres' radii is 1:2. Which of the following ratios correctly compares their volumes?

A) $1:\frac{4}{3}$

B) 1:2

C) 1:4

D) 1:8

Work through the Kaplan Method for Math step-by-step to solve this question. The following table shows Kaplan's strategic thinking on the left, along with suggested math scratchwork on the right.

Strategic Thinking	Math Scratchwork
Step 1: Read the question, identifying and organizing important information as you go You need to determine the ratio of the volume of the two spheres. A ratio comparing their radii is given.	
Step 2: Choose the best strategy to answer the question Pick your own radii to make this question less abstract; just be sure they obey the given ratio. Compute the volumes of the corresponding spheres, and then use the volumes to write a second ratio, reducing as necessary.	$r_1 = 1, r_2 = 2$ $V = \frac{4}{3}\pi r^3$ $V_1 = \frac{4}{3}\pi \times 1^3 = \frac{4}{3}\pi$ $V_2 = \frac{4}{3}\pi \times 2^3 = \frac{32}{3}\pi$ $\frac{4}{3}\pi : \frac{32}{3}\pi \rightarrow 1:8$
Step 3: Check that you answered the *right* question You've found the ratio of the volume of the spheres, so you're done! Choice (D) is correct.	1:8

Remember that doubling a particular parameter of a 3-D shape does not always translate to the doubling of another! Do the necessary calculations instead of merely jumping to a conclusion.

Now you'll have a chance to try a test-like question. Use the scaffolding as needed as a guide through the question and to the correct answer.

Some guidance is provided, but you'll need to fill in the missing parts of explanations or the step-by-step math to get to the correct answer. Don't worry—after going through the examples at the beginning of this chapter, this question should be completely doable. If you're still struggling, review the worked examples in this chapter.

5. A basic megaphone is a truncated cone; that is, a cone with its apex (pointed end) removed. Suppose the openings (ends) of a megaphone have diameters of 2 inches and 10 inches. If the original cone from which the megaphone was created had a height of 20 inches, what is the volume inside the megaphone?

    A) 150π in.^{3}

    B) $165\frac{1}{3}\pi$ in.^{3}

    C) 496π in.^{3}

    D) $661\frac{1}{3}\pi$ in.^{3}

Use the following scaffolding as your map through the question. If you aren't sure where to start, answer the questions in italics and fill in the blanks in the table as you work from top to bottom.

Strategic Thinking	Math Scratchwork
Step 1: Read the question, identifying and organizing important information as you go *What are you being asked to find?* You're asked for the volume inside the megaphone.	

Strategic Thinking	Math Scratchwork
Step 2: Choose the best strategy to answer the question *What 3-D shapes are involved? How will this affect your calculations?* You have a small cone that was once part of a larger cone; you'll need to subtract the volume of the former from that of the latter to get the answer. *How can you find the height of the small cone?* A cone's diameter increases at a constant rate as the height increases, so you can use a proportion to find the height of the small cone. You will then have all the information you need to find the volumes of the two cones. Remember to convert the diameters to radii first. *Am I done?* Subtract the volume of the small cone from that of the large cone to determine the volume inside the megaphone.	$V_{cone} = \underline{\hspace{2cm}}$ $h_{sm}: \underline{\hspace{1.5cm}} = \underline{\hspace{1cm}}$ $\underline{\hspace{1.5cm}} = \underline{\hspace{1cm}}$ $\underline{\hspace{1.5cm}} = \underline{\hspace{1cm}}$ $V_{sm} = \underline{\hspace{0.5cm}} \times \underline{\hspace{0.5cm}} \times \underline{\hspace{0.5cm}} \times \underline{\hspace{0.5cm}}$ $= \underline{\hspace{1cm}}$ $V_{lg} = \underline{\hspace{0.5cm}} \times \underline{\hspace{0.5cm}} \times \underline{\hspace{0.5cm}} \times \underline{\hspace{0.5cm}}$ $= \underline{\hspace{1cm}}$ $V_{mp} = \underline{\hspace{1.5cm}} - \underline{\hspace{1cm}}$ $= \underline{\hspace{1cm}}$
Step 3: Check that you answered the *right* question *What is the volume inside the megaphone?* Did you get (B)? If so, you'd be right!	 $\underline{\hspace{2cm}}$

✔ **Note**

This is another question with opportunities to fall for trap answers. Be sure you use radii, not diameters; and confirm that you've used the correct formula in your calculations!

Now that you've seen the variety of ways in which the SAT can test you on 3-D shapes, try the following questions to check your understanding. Give yourself 3 minutes to tackle the following two questions. Make sure you use the Kaplan Method for Math as often as you can. Remember, you want to emphasize speed and efficiency in addition to simply getting the correct answer.

6. Before being released into the outside air, exhaust from a car passes through a catalytic converter. The converter is made of sheets of precious metals that are arranged in a honeycomb-type structure. As the exhaust passes through the space between the metal sheets, it is converted into carbon dioxide, water, and nitrogen via a chemical reaction. A close-up of a triangular prism honeycomb that is in some catalytic converters is shown above. If the side of one of the triangles is 4 mm and the honeycomb structure is 30 cm long, how many square millimeters of reaction surface does the interior of one of these prisms contribute?

7. Each edge of the cube shown above measures $2\sqrt{6}$ cm. What is the distance from a vertex of this cube to its center?

A) $\sqrt{6}$

B) $3\sqrt{2}$

C) $2\sqrt{6}$

D) $6\sqrt{2}$

Answers & Explanations for this chapter begin on page 965.

EXTRA PRACTICE

Required	Recommended
Questions 1–8	Questions 9–18

Note: Figure not drawn to scale.

1. What is the volume in cubic units of the solid shown above?

   A) 252π

   B) 588π

   C) $1,764\pi$

   D) $2,352\pi$

2. The Washington Monument in Washington, D.C., is the world's tallest obelisk-shaped building. The tall part of the monument is a rectangular prism-like shape that is wider at the bottom than it is at the top. At the very top of the monument, there is a regular pyramid with a square base that is 34.5 feet wide. If the volume of the pyramid top is 21,821.25 cubic feet, what is its height in feet?

   A) 6.1

   B) 18.3

   C) 55.0

   D) 210

3. The figure above represents a camping tent that will be sprayed using a water-proofing agent. If it takes 1 ounce of the agent to cover 3 square feet, how many ounces will it take to spray the entire tent, inside and outside, including the tent bottom and its front door flaps?

   A) 56

   B) 112

   C) 168

   D) 336

4. What is the volume of a cubical cardboard moving box that has a surface area of 1,176 square inches?

   A) 84 in.³

   B) 196 in.³

   C) 1,176 in.³

   D) 2,744 in.³

5. Alma pours water into a small cylindrical glass with a height of 6 inches and a diameter of 3 inches. The water fills the glass to the very top, so she decides to pour it into a bigger glass that is 8 inches tall and 4 inches in diameter. Assuming Alma doesn't spill any when she pours, how many inches high will the water reach in the bigger glass?

A) 1.5

B) 2.25

C) 3.375

D) 6.0

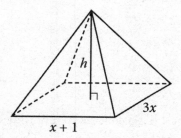

6. If the volume of the pyramid shown in the figure above can be represented by the function $V(x) = x^3 - x$, which of the following expressions represents the height?

A) x

B) $2x$

C) $x - 1$

D) $x - 3$

7. One of the three most expensive cheeses in the world is a Swedish cheese made from moose milk, which sells for about $500 a pound. Suppose a moose cheesemaker produces his cheese in rectangular blocks, each with a volume of 576 cubic inches. Customers or restaurants can buy this cheese in increments of $\frac{1}{8}$ blocks. One day, a customer buys $\frac{1}{8}$ of a block and a restaurant buys $\frac{1}{2}$ of a block. If the height of a cheese block is always 8 inches and the width is always 6 inches, what is the difference in the lengths of the two purchases?

A) 4.5 inches

B) 6 inches

C) 7.6 inches

D) 12 inches

8. A medical test tube is made up of a cylinder with a half-sphere on the bottom. The volume in square inches of the tube is $\frac{19}{12}\pi$. The diameter of the cylinder (and the half-sphere) is 1 inch. How tall in inches is the test tube?

A) 4.75

B) 5

C) 6

D) 6.5

Note: Figure not drawn to scale.

9. A solid wood cube is cut perfectly in half diagonally from corner to corner as shown above, to be used as chocks, which are wedges placed behind wheels of vehicles to prevent them from rolling. What is the volume in cubic inches of one of these chocks?

    A) 10

    B) 100

    C) 500

    D) 1,000

10. Two balls are filled with air. One has a volume of 36π and the other has a volume of 288π. What is the ratio of the balls' diameters?

    A) 1:2

    B) 1:3

    C) 1:4

    D) 1:8

11. The height of the cone shown above is 16 cm. If the top quarter of the cone's height is cut off and discarded, what will be the volume in cubic centimeters of the remaining solid?

    A) 192π

    B) 576π

    C) 756π

    D) 768π

12. Rupert has a collection of Blu-ray discs he wants to store in a cubical box with edges of length 10 inches. If each Blu-ray has dimensions 5 inches by 5 inches by $\frac{1}{4}$ inch, what is the maximum number of discs that can fit into the box?

    A) 60

    B) 80

    C) 120

    D) 160

16 in.

9 in.

24 in.

13. A pet store just decided to sell fish, so they purchased 50 of the fish tanks shown above to hold the fish. They need to fill the bottom two inches of each tank with sand, which comes in bags of 40 pounds. If 1 cubic inch of sand weighs about 2 ounces, how many bags of sand does the pet store need to buy?

A) 45

B) 68

C) 84

D) 125

14. The roof of a certain bell tower is in the shape of a square pyramid with a length and width of 20 feet and a slant height of 18 feet. The roof needs new shingles, which are 72 square inches in size. The shingles must overlap so that water doesn't leak between the seams. What is the minimum number of shingles needed to cover the roof, assuming 20% extra to account for the overlap?

A) 432

B) 518

C) 1,440

D) 1,728

15. A yogurt factory fills cylindrical containers 80% of the way to the top, putting 6 ounces of yogurt in each cup. The containers are 4 inches tall and 2.5 inches wide. Approximately how many cubic inches of space does one ounce of yogurt take up?

A) 2.1

B) 2.6

C) 3.3

D) 4.2

16. The opening of a perfectly circular sewer tunnel has a circumference of 8π. The tunnel has a volume of $2,048\pi$ cubic feet. How many feet long is the tunnel?

17. If a cube has side lengths of 10 cm, what is the ratio of the surface area to the volume of the cube? Write the ratio as a fraction.

18. The length, width, and height of a rectangular prism are in the ratio 4:2:1 (in that order). If the volume of the prism is 216 cubic inches, how many inches wide is the prism?

CHAPTER 17

Trigonometry

CHAPTER OBJECTIVES

By the end of this section, you will be able to:

- Use trigonometric ratios to calculate sides of right triangles
- Convert between degrees and radians
- Recognize symmetry and transformations between different types of trigonometric functions

SMARTPOINTS

Point Value	SmartPoint Category
10 Points	Trigonometry

INTRODUCTION TO TRIGONOMETRY

Although the word *trigonometry* comes from Greek words meaning "triangle" and "measure", some students fear the subject enough that they'd believe the word came from the Greek roots *trig*, meaning "designed," and *onometry*, meaning "to give high school students nightmares." Fortunately, any SAT trig questions you encounter won't be ludicrously difficult, and investing just a little time in studying this topic will give you a slight edge over your competition.

Trigonometric Ratios

You probably remember learning the acronym SOH-CAH-TOA, a mnemonic device for the sine, cosine, and tangent ratios. There are three other ratios (cosecant, secant, and cotangent) that you might see on Test Day as well, but fortunately, you won't have to memorize brand-new relationships for them. We've provided an example triangle below; check out the table beneath it for a summary of the six ratios and what each equals for $\angle CAB$.

Sine (sin)	Cosine (cos)	Tangent (tan)	Cosecant (csc)	Secant (sec)	Cotangent (cot)
$\dfrac{\text{opposite}}{\text{hypotenuse}}$	$\dfrac{\text{adjacent}}{\text{hypotenuse}}$	$\dfrac{\text{opposite}}{\text{adjacent}}$	$\dfrac{\text{hypotenuse}}{\text{opposite}}$	$\dfrac{\text{hypotenuse}}{\text{adjacent}}$	$\dfrac{\text{adjacent}}{\text{opposite}}$
$\dfrac{3}{5}$	$\dfrac{4}{5}$	$\dfrac{3}{4}$	$\dfrac{5}{3}$	$\dfrac{5}{4}$	$\dfrac{4}{3}$

> ✔ **Note**
>
> Related note: $\tan A = \dfrac{\sin A}{\cos A}$.

> ✔ **Note**
>
> Alternate mnemonic: Some Old Hag Cracked All Her Teeth On Asparagus.

The Unit Circle

Up until now you've likely been told that the trigonometric ratios are only applicable to right triangles; however, you can expand their utility to include angles greater than 90° by using the **unit circle**. The unit circle is a circle with a radius of 1 centered around the origin in the *xy*-plane. Below is such a circle containing an example triangle.

> ✔ **Note**
>
> An angle in the unit circle always begins with its radius on the positive side of the *x*-axis. As the angle measure increases, the radius moves counterclockwise through each quadrant. If you have a negative angle, the radius starts in the same spot but moves clockwise as the absolute value of the angle measure increases.

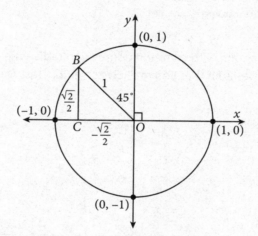

Suppose you were asked to determine sin 135° and cos 135°. Draw a radius at 135° (which is 45° past the *y*-axis in the second quadrant), and then add a vertical line from where the radius intersects the circle down to the *x*-axis. Because this radius (<u>OB</u>) is within the unit circle, its length is 1. Δ*OBC* is a

45-45-90 triangle, so each of its legs has a length of $\frac{\sqrt{2}}{2}$. This means $\sin 135° = \frac{\frac{\sqrt{2}}{2}}{1} = \frac{\sqrt{2}}{2}$. Note

that because <u>OC</u> lies on the negative part of the *x*-axis, you should use $-\frac{\sqrt{2}}{2}$ as the "measure" of

the adjacent side. Therefore, $\cos 135° = \frac{-\frac{\sqrt{2}}{2}}{1} = -\frac{\sqrt{2}}{2}$. Notice that if you were to label point *B* on

the unit circle, its (*x*, *y*) coordinates would correspond to (cos 135°, sin 135°).

Radians

Most geometry questions present angle measures in degrees. In trigonometry, however, you will encounter a different unit: the radian. The prospect of learning a new unit shouldn't scare you, though; just remember that $180° = \pi$ radians. For instance, if you're asked to convert $90°$ into radians, use this relationship as a conversion factor with the factor-label method (refer to chapter 5 to brush up): $90° \times \dfrac{\pi}{180°} = \dfrac{\pi}{2}$. Note that there isn't a symbol for radians, so $\dfrac{\pi}{2}$ in trigonometry is read as "$\dfrac{\pi}{2}$ radians." This conversion works in the opposite direction as well: to convert radians to degrees, multiply by $\dfrac{180°}{\pi}$.

> ✔ **Note**
>
> Most graphing calculators have both degree and radian modes. Make sure you're in the correct mode when working on trigonometry questions!

Here is a handy unit circle diagram with common degree and radian measures (and the coordinates of the ends of their respective radii) that you're likely to see on Test Day.

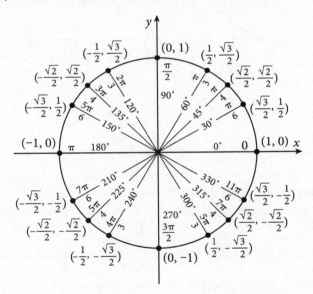

> ✔ **Note**
>
> The coordinates at a particular angle measure translate into the leg lengths of the triangle created when a vertical line is drawn from the end of the radius down (or up if you're in quadrant III or IV) to the x-axis. For example, at $60°$, the horizontal leg has a length of $\dfrac{1}{2}$, and the vertical leg has a length of $\dfrac{\sqrt{3}}{2}$.

Graphs of Trigonometric Functions

The SAT may ask you to recognize the graphs of the sine, cosine, and tangent functions, which are presented in the table below. Notice that sine and cosine oscillate (bounce back and forth) between −1 and 1.

Sine	Cosine	Tangent

> ✔ **Note**
>
> The sine and cosine functions have the same shape. Shifting the cosine function to the right by $\frac{\pi}{2}$ (90°) produces the sine function, and shifting the sine function to the left by $\frac{\pi}{2}$ produces the cosine function.

> ✔ **Note**
>
> The tangent function at all multiples of $x = \frac{\pi}{2}$ (90°) and $x = -\frac{\pi}{2}$ (−90°) is undefined. As a result, the graph of the tangent function has asymptotes at $x = \pm\frac{\pi}{2}, \pm\frac{3\pi}{2}, \pm\frac{5\pi}{2}$, etc.

Other Properties and Non-Right Triangles

The sine and cosine functions have a special relationship and are related to each other by the following identities:

- $\sin x = \cos(\frac{\pi}{2} - x)$
- $\cos x = \sin(\frac{\pi}{2} - x)$
- $\sin^2 x + \cos^2 x = 1$

For acute angles, the first two relationships tell you something special about complementary angles: the cosine of an acute angle is equal to the sine of the angle's complement and vice versa. To see some examples, look at the first quadrant of the unit circle: cos 30° = sin 60°, cos 45° = sin 45°, and cos 60° = sin 30°. Understanding how trig functions of complementary angles work can help you learn the unit circle.

The third relationship is called a Pythagorean identity because it is derived from the Pythagorean theorem.

> ✔ **Note**
>
> Note that $\sin^2(x)$ is NOT the same as $\sin(x^2)$! The former dictates that the sine of x is squared, but the latter indicates finding the sine of x^2. The exponent is written between the trigonometric function and the variable to eliminate this ambiguity.

Ready to test your SAT trigonometry knowledge? Check out the next several pages for some test-like questions.

1. If $\tan x = \dfrac{7}{24}$, then what is $\sin x$?

Work through the Kaplan Method for Math step-by-step to solve this question. The following table shows Kaplan's strategic thinking on the left, along with suggested math scratchwork on the right.

Strategic Thinking	Math Scratchwork
Step 1: Read the question, identifying and organizing important information as you go You need to find the value of $\sin x$.	
Step 2: Choose the best strategy to answer the question If $\tan x = \dfrac{7}{24}$, then the sides opposite and adjacent to angle x must be 7 and 24, respectively. Draw a diagram to reflect this. Because $\sin x = \dfrac{opp}{hyp}$, you'll need to solve for the hypotenuse length using the Pythagorean theorem. Once you calculate this, plug that value into the sine ratio.	$\tan x = \dfrac{opp}{adj}$, $\sin x = \dfrac{opp}{hyp}$ (diagram of right triangle with hyp, legs 7 and 24, angle x) $7^2 + 24^2 = hyp^2$ $49 + 576 = hyp^2$ $625 = hyp^2$ $25 = hyp$

Strategic Thinking	Math Scratchwork
Step 3: Check that you answered the *right* question The value of sin x is $\frac{7}{25}$. Grid in $\frac{7}{25}$ or .28.	$\sin x = \frac{7}{25}$

✔ **Expert Tip**

The triangle in this question is another Pythagorean triplet (7-24-25). Although the 7-24-25 is not as common as the 3-4-5 and 5-12-13, knowing it means you can skip a Pythagorean theorem calculation (and save a few seconds).

2. Which of the following is coterminal with 690°? (Coterminal angles are formed by radii that point to the same place on the unit circle.)

A) $-\frac{\pi}{4}$

B) $-\frac{\pi}{6}$

C) $\frac{\pi}{6}$

D) $\frac{\pi}{4}$

Work through the Kaplan Method for Math step-by-step to solve this question. The following table shows Kaplan's strategic thinking on the left, along with suggested math scratchwork on the right.

Strategic Thinking	Math Scratchwork
Step 1: Read the question, identifying and organizing important information as you go You need to determine the radian measure of an angle that is coterminal with 690°.	
Step 2: Choose the best strategy to answer the question Use the factor-label method (or a proportion) to make short work of this question. Start by subtracting 360° (one full circle) as many times as necessary to get the absolute value of the angle measure between 0° and 90°. Once there, convert to radians.	$690° - 360° - 360° = -30°$ $-30° \times \frac{\pi}{180°} = -\frac{30\pi}{180} = -\frac{\pi}{6}$

Strategic Thinking	Math Scratchwork
Step 3: Check that you answered the _right_ question	
Choice (B) is coterminal with 690°.	(B)

✔ **Expert Tip**

Subtracting 360° as many times as needed until the absolute value of the angle measure is between 0° and 90° will give you an easier number to work with, which is a nice strategy if you're in the no-calculator section. Also, if you're adept at recalling angle measures from the unit circle, you can simply derive the radian equivalent of 330° from memory.

3. If $HG = 6$ and $\cot G = \sqrt{3}$, then what is the area of circle P?

    A) $\dfrac{\pi}{4}$

    B) π

    C) $\dfrac{9\pi}{4}$

    D) 9π

Work through the Kaplan Method for Math step-by-step to solve this question. The following table shows Kaplan's strategic thinking on the left, along with suggested math scratchwork on the right.

Strategic Thinking	Math Scratchwork
Step 1: Read the question, identifying and organizing important information as you go	
You are asked to find the area of the circle.	

Strategic Thinking	Math Scratchwork
Step 2: Choose the best strategy to answer the question	
You can likely transfer information from one shape to the other here. The short leg of the right triangle is also the diameter of the circle. You know that cot $G = \sqrt{3}$. Recall that the cotangent ratio is $\dfrac{adj}{opp}$; therefore, cot $G = \dfrac{GF}{HF} = \dfrac{\sqrt{3}}{1}$.	$\cot G = \dfrac{adj}{opp} = \dfrac{GF}{HF} = \sqrt{3}$
If you thought ΔHFG is a 30-60-90 triangle, you'd be right! But be careful: you can't just assume that $HF = 1$ and $GF = \sqrt{3}$. You know the ratio, but that doesn't necessarily tell you the lengths of the sides. You also have to consider what you know about the hypotenuse, which is 6. Because the hypotenuse is twice the length of the shorter leg, $HF = 3$. The shorter leg is also the diameter of the circle, which means the radius is $\dfrac{3}{2}$. You can now find the area of the circle.	$\Delta HFG: 30\text{-}60\text{-}90$ $HF : GF : HG = 1 : \sqrt{3} : 2$ $HG = 6 \rightarrow HF = 3$ $d = 3 \rightarrow r = \dfrac{3}{2}$ $A = \pi r^2 = \pi(\dfrac{3}{2})^2 = \dfrac{9\pi}{4}$
Step 3: Check that you answered the *right* question	
You've found the area of the circle; your match is (C).	

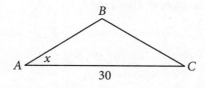

4.   If the area of ΔABC is 225 and $AB = 17$, then what is the value of cos x?

   A) $\dfrac{8}{17}$

   B) $\dfrac{8}{15}$

   C) $\dfrac{17}{30}$

   D) $\dfrac{15}{17}$

Work through the Kaplan Method for Math step-by-step to solve this question. The following table shows Kaplan's strategic thinking on the left, along with suggested math scratchwork on the right.

Strategic Thinking	Math Scratchwork
Step 1: Read the question, identifying and organizing important information as you go You're asked to calculate the value of cos *x*.	
Step 2: Choose the best strategy to answer the question The area of a triangle is half the product of the base and height, so draw in a height. Label the point at which the base and height intersect *D* to help keep things clear. Use the triangle area formula to find the height; you'll find that *BD* = 15. You now have two sides of a right triangle (Δ*ABD*), so you can find the third. You might recognize this as an 8-15-17 Pythagorean triplet; if not, use the Pythagorean theorem.	 $A = \dfrac{1}{2}bh$ $225 = \dfrac{1}{2} \times 30h$ $h = \dfrac{225}{15} = 15 = BD$ $AD^2 + 15^2 = 17^2$ $AD^2 = 17^2 - 15^2$ $AD^2 = 289 - 225$ $AD = \sqrt{64} = 8$
Step 3: Check that you answered the *right* question The question asks for cos *x*, not the length of any of the sides. Recall that cosine $= \dfrac{adjacent}{hypotenuse}$. Thus, $\cos x = \dfrac{AD}{AB} = \dfrac{8}{17}$, (A).	$\cos x = \dfrac{adj}{hyp} = \dfrac{8}{17}$

Now you'll have a chance to try another test-like question. Use the scaffolding as needed as a guide through the question and to the right answer.

Some guidance is provided, but you'll need to fill in the missing parts of explanations or the step-by-step math in order to get to the correct answer. Don't worry—after going through the examples at the beginning of this chapter, this question should be completely doable. If you're still struggling, review the worked examples in this chapter.

5. Which of the following is the graph of $f(x) = \cos(x + \pi)$?

Use the following scaffolding as your map through the question. If you aren't sure where to start, answer the questions in italics and fill in the blanks in the table as you work from top to bottom.

Strategic Thinking	Math Scratchwork
Step 1: Read the question, identifying and organizing important information as you go *What are you being asked to find?* You need to identify the graph of $f(x) = \cos(x + \pi)$.	
Step 2: Choose the best strategy to answer the question *What does the standard cosine function look like? What kind of transformation is being applied?* Within the domain shown in the answer choices, the standard cosine function has one maximum and two minima. This matches one of the choices, but it's not what you're looking for, so eliminate it. Adding a constant inside the parentheses with the variable results in a certain kind of shift in the graph of the function. Think about how this will alter the maximum and minima of the standard cosine function.	$\cos x$: max @ (___, ___) min @ (___, ___) and (___, ___) $\cos(x + \pi)$: min @ (___, ___) max @ (___, ___) and (___, ___)
Step 3: Check that you answered the *right* question *Which graph correctly depicts the given function?* Did you get (D)? If so, you're right.	___

Now that you've seen the variety of ways in which the SAT can test you on trigonometry, try the following questions to check your understanding. Give yourself 4 minutes to tackle the following three questions. Make sure you use the Kaplan Method for Math as often as you can. Remember, you want to emphasize speed and efficiency in addition to simply getting the correct answer.

6. If $\sin x = \cos(\frac{13\pi}{6})$, then which of the following could be the value of x?

   A) $-\frac{13\pi}{6}$

   B) $-\frac{\pi}{3}$

   C) $\frac{\pi}{3}$

   D) $\frac{13\pi}{6}$

7. Miguel measured the angle of elevation from the ground to the top of his tree-house and found it to be approximately 62°. If Miguel stood 10 feet from his tree-house when making the measurement, approximately how tall is the treehouse?

   A) 1.8 ft

   B) 8.8 ft

   C) 18.8 ft

   D) 22.8 ft

8. If $\sin x = \frac{1}{5}$, then which of the following statements must be true?

   A) $\cos^2 x = \frac{24}{25}$

   B) $\cos^2 x = \frac{1}{25}$

   C) $\cos^2 x = \frac{1}{5}$

   D) $\cos x = \frac{24}{25}$

Answers & Explanations for this chapter begin on page 975.

EXTRA PRACTICE

Required	Recommended
Questions 1–8	Questions 9–30

1. Which of the following represents a 120°
   angle given in radians?

   A) $\dfrac{2\pi}{3}$

   B) $\dfrac{3\pi}{4}$

   C) $\dfrac{5\pi}{6}$

   D) $\dfrac{11\pi}{12}$

2. If the measure, in radians, of one acute
   angle in a right triangle is $\dfrac{\pi}{3}$, what is the
   measure of the other acute angle?

   A) $\dfrac{\pi}{12}$

   B) $\dfrac{\pi}{6}$

   C) $\dfrac{\pi}{3}$

   D) $\dfrac{2\pi}{3}$

3. What is the length of minor arc *AB* shown
   in the figure above?

   A) $\dfrac{5\pi}{6}$

   B) $\dfrac{5\pi}{3}$

   C) $\dfrac{5\pi}{2}$

   D) 5π

4. Which of the following angles has the
   same trigonometric values as 450°?

   A) 30°

   B) 45°

   C) 60°

   D) 90°

5. The value of cos 30° is the same as which
   of the following?

   A) sin(−30°)

   B) cos(−60°)

   C) sin 60°

   D) cos 150°

6. In the triangle above, $\cos A = \dfrac{5}{13}$. What is sin A?

A) $\dfrac{5}{12}$

B) $\dfrac{8}{13}$

C) $\dfrac{5}{8}$

D) $\dfrac{12}{13}$

9. What is the measure in degrees of $\angle PQR$ shown above?

A) 105

B) 120

C) 135

D) 150

7. Which of the following is equivalent to $1 - \cos^2 x$, for any value of x?

A) $-1 + \cos^2 x$

B) $-\cos^2 x$

C) $\sin^2 x$

D) $1 - \sin^2 x$

10. Arc CD subtends a central angle that has a measure of 135° on circle O. If the length of $\overarc{CD}$ is $\dfrac{3\pi}{4}$, what is the radius of circle O?

A) 0.25

B) 0.5

C) 1

D) 1.5

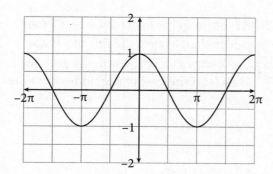

11. The cosine of which of the following angles is not equal to the cosine of the other three?

A) -120

B) -60

C) 120

D) 240

8. The graph above shows $y = \cos x$. What is the value of $\cos 90° + \cos 180°$?

A) -2

B) -1

C) 0

D) 1

12. If *MN* in the triangle above is equal to 1,000, and $\cos 47° \approx \dfrac{341}{500}$, what is the approximate length of side *LN*?

   A) 86

   B) 318

   C) 731

   D) 917

14. Based on the figure above, which of the following is true?

   A) $\sin 22.6° = \dfrac{5}{12}$

   B) $\sin 67.4° = \dfrac{5}{13}$

   C) $\cos 22.6° = \dfrac{5}{13}$

   D) $\cos 67.4° = \dfrac{5}{13}$

13. If the hypotenuse of the triangle shown above has length 24 units, what is the area in square units of the triangle?

   A) $72\sqrt{3}$

   B) $144\sqrt{3}$

   C) 288

   D) $288\sqrt{3}$

15. As shown in the figure above, a 17-foot ladder leans against the side of a house and makes a 65° angle with the ground. How far is the base of the ladder from the house?

   A) 6.29 feet

   B) 7.18 feet

   C) 15.41 feet

   D) 36.46 feet

16. If $\sin x = \cos\left(\dfrac{\pi}{6}\right)$, then which of the following could not be the value of x?

    A) $\dfrac{\pi}{3}$

    B) $\dfrac{2\pi}{3}$

    C) $\dfrac{5\pi}{3}$

    D) $\dfrac{7\pi}{3}$

17. If $N = 3\sin^2\theta + 3\cos^2\theta$, what is the value of N?

    A) $\dfrac{1}{3}$

    B) $\dfrac{2}{3}$

    C) 1

    D) 3

Note: Figure not drawn to scale.

18. The figure above shows a vertical pole with two cables that are connected to the pole and anchored into the ground. One of the cables is 20 feet long. What is the length of the other cable?

    A) 12.9 feet

    B) 14.8 feet

    C) 17.3 feet

    D) 26.9 feet

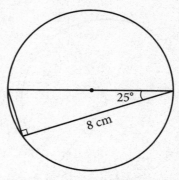

Note: Figure not drawn to scale.

19. What is the approximate area in square centimeters of the circle shown above?

    A) 28

    B) 50

    C) 55

    D) 61

20. It is given that $\sin\theta = k$, where θ is an angle measured in radians and $\dfrac{3\pi}{2} < \theta < 2\pi$. If $\sin\beta = k$, which of the following could be the value of β?

    A) $2\pi - \theta$

    B) $3\pi - \theta$

    C) $\pi + \theta$

    D) $\theta - \pi$

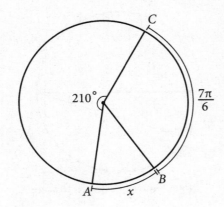

21. If the length of the radius of the circle

   shown above is 2, what is the value of x?

    A) $\dfrac{\pi}{6}$

    B) $\dfrac{\pi}{2}$

    C) $\dfrac{7\pi}{12}$

    D) $\dfrac{7\pi}{3}$

22. Which trigonometric function could be
    represented by the graph above?

    A) $y = \sin(x - \pi)$

    B) $y = \sin(x + \pi)$

    C) $y = \sin\left(x - \dfrac{\pi}{2}\right)$

    D) $y = \sin\left(x + \dfrac{\pi}{2}\right)$

23. Which of the following is equal to $\cos\left(\dfrac{\pi}{8}\right)$?

    A) $\sin\left(\dfrac{3\pi}{8}\right)$

    B) $\cos\left(\dfrac{7\pi}{8}\right)$

    C) $-\sin\left(\dfrac{\pi}{8}\right)$

    D) $-\cos\left(\dfrac{\pi}{8}\right)$

24. What is the value of $\cos 45° + \cos 60°$?

    A) -1

    B) $\dfrac{\sqrt{5}}{2}$

    C) $\dfrac{1 + \sqrt{2}}{2}$

    D) $\dfrac{\sqrt{2} + \sqrt{3}}{2}$

25. Which of the following is equivalent to
    $\dfrac{\tan\theta\cos^2\theta + \tan\theta\sin^2\theta}{\sin\theta}$?

    A) $\cos\theta$

    B) $\sin\theta$

    C) $\csc\theta$

    D) $\sec\theta$

26. If $\angle A$ has a measure of $\dfrac{7\pi}{4}$, what is the
    measure of $\angle A$ in degrees?

27. If $x = -\cos(11\pi)$, what is the value of x?

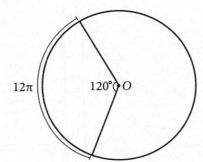

12π $120°$ O

28. What is the radius of circle O shown
 above?

29. The triangle shown above is a cross section
of a feeding trough that is 24 inches deep
and whose top is 36 inches across. If
$\cos x = B$, what is the value of B?

13

β

40

Note: Figure not drawn to scale.

30. If the area of the triangle shown above is
 240 square inches, what is $\tan \beta$?

Evidence-Based Reading and Writing

UNIT SIX

Reading

BY THE END OF THIS UNIT, YOU WILL BE ABLE TO:

1. Apply the Kaplan Method for Reading Comprehension

2. Identify many kinds of Reading Test questions and apply the appropriate strategies to correctly answer them

CHAPTER 18

The Kaplan Method for Reading Comprehension

CHAPTER OBJECTIVES

By the end of this chapter, you will be able to:

1. Read actively using the Kaplan Method for Reading Comprehension

2. Take efficient and organized notes on a passage

3. Answer questions using a Passage Map

SMARTPOINTS

Point Value	SmartPoint Category
Point Builder	The Kaplan Method for Reading Comprehension
Point Builder	Passage Mapping

THE KAPLAN METHOD FOR READING COMPREHENSION

Use the Kaplan Method for Reading Comprehension to analyze every SAT Reading passage and question you encounter, whether practicing, completing your homework, working on a Practice Test, or taking the actual exam on Test Day.

The Kaplan Method for Reading Comprehension consists of three steps:

Step 1: Read actively

Step 2: Examine the question stem

Step 3: Predict and answer

Let's take a closer look at each step.

✔ Remember

There are three Reading Test passage types: U.S. and World Literature, History/Social Studies, and Science.

Step 1: Read actively

Active reading means:

- Ask questions and take notes *as* you read the passage. Asking questions about the passage and taking notes is an integral part of your approach to acing the SAT Reading Test.

Some of the questions you might want to ask are:

- Why did the author write this word/detail/sentence/paragraph?
- Is the author taking a side? If so, what side is he or she taking?
- What are the tone and purpose of the passage?

Make sure you remember to:

- Identify the passage type.
- Take notes, circle keywords, and underline key phrases.

✔ Expert Tip

Questions will range from general to specific. By using clues in the question stem to identify what the question is looking for, you will be better able to complete Step 3 of the Kaplan Method for Reading Comprehension.

Step 2: Examine the question stem

This means you should:

- Identify keywords and line references in the question stem.

- Apply question type strategies as necessary.

Step 3: Predict and answer

This means you should:

- Predict an answer before looking at the answer choices, also known as "predict before you peek."

- Select the best match.

Predicting before you peek helps you:

- Eliminate the possibility of falling into wrong answer traps.

PASSAGE MAPPING

Step 1 of the Kaplan Method for Reading Comprehension dictates that you must take notes as you read the passage. We call these notes a Passage Map because they guide you through the passage and will lead you to the correct answers.

> **✔ On Test Day**
>
> A Passage Map should not replace the occasional underline or circle—it is important that you underline, circle, *and* take notes to create the most effective Passage Map.

Make sure you pay attention and take note of the following when you map the passage:

- The "why" or the central idea of the passage—in other words, the thesis statement

- Transitions or changes in direction in a passage's logic

- The author's opinions and other opinions the author cites

- The author's tone and purpose

While Passage Mapping may seem time-consuming at first, with practice it will become second nature by Test Day, and your overall Reading Test timing will greatly improve because you'll be spending less time searching the passage for answers to the questions.

SAT experts always map Reading Test passages. Look at the test-like excerpt and question on the next page. Make sure you spend some time looking over the sample Passage Map—these are the types of notes you should practice taking as you read Reading Test passages. Also, look at the questions an SAT expert would ask himself or herself and what kind of prediction he or she would make on Test Day when presented with a Reading Test question.

> **✔ Remember**
>
> The SAT Reading Test is an open-book test! The answer is always in the passage.

Strategic Thinking
Step 1: Read actively
Read the passage and the notes provided. Remember, a well-crafted Passage Map should summarize the central idea of each paragraph, as well as important topics or themes. Use your Passage Map to help you answer each question.

Question 1 is based on the following passage.

The following passage discusses how the evolution of ancient Greek society affected early Greek poetry.

The poems of the earliest Greeks, like those of other ancient societies, consisted of magical charms, mysterious predictions, prayers, and
Line traditional songs of work and war. These poems
5   were intended to be sung or recited, not written down, because they were created before the Greeks began to use writing for literary purposes. All that remains of these poems are fragments mentioned by later Greek writers. Homer, for example, quoted
10 an ancient work song for harvesters, and Simonides adapted the ancient poetry of ritual lamentation, songs of mourning for the dead, in his writing.

The different forms of early Greek poetry all had something in common: they described the
15 way of life of a whole people. Poetry expressed ideas and feelings that were shared by everyone in a community—their folktales, their memories of historical events, and their religious speculation. The poems were wholly impersonal, with little
20 emphasis on individual achievement. It never occurred to the earliest Greek poets to tell us their names or to try to create anything completely new.

In the "age of heroes," however, the content and purpose of Greek poetry changed. By this later
25 period, Greek communities had become separated into classes of rulers and ruled. People living in the same community, therefore, had different, even opposing, interests; they shared fewer ideas and emotions. The particular outlook of the warlike

30 upper class gave poetry a new content, one that focused on the lives of individuals. Poets were assigned a new task: to celebrate the accomplishments of outstanding characters, whether they were real or imaginary, rather than the activity and history of
35 the community.

In the heroic age, poets became singers of tales and performed long poems about the fates of warriors and kings. One need study only Homer's *The Iliad* and *The Odyssey*, which are recorded examples
40 of the epic poetry that was sung in the heroic age, to understand the influence that the upper class had on the poet's subject matter. Thus, the poetry of the heroic age replaced the folk poetry that had preceded it. In this era of heroic poetry, poets no longer
45 remained anonymous, and the poems themselves were decidedly less religious in character compared to earlier works.

Handwritten margin notes (left): DEAR FAN · Greek poetry · continuation · Early Greek poetry · Not written, H quoted · who · Poems re: entire society · AoH / later poetry · sentence structure · who · later When · continuation

Handwritten margin notes (right): Focused on indiv. · transition · Poet's role changed · Upper class: His epics singers. · Not anon. or relig. · comparison contrast · when who · continuation · Key words – continuation – contrast

Handwritten notes (bottom):
Notes
1 Early GP sang not written
2nd Early GP, way of poetry.
3 Early GP is anonymous
4th Early GP focus on real star
5th Later sppnd.

— heroic vs. folk
poets no longer remain anonymous · less religious in

Question	Strategic Thinking
1. The main purpose of the passage is to A) argue that earlier forms of Greek poetry were artistic and later forms were political. B) discuss how changes in ancient Greek society brought about changes in ancient Greek poetry. C) provide an example of how an ancient society's shift from an oral to a written tradition had positive and negative effects. D) show that artistic expression can be used either to build people into communities or separate people into classes.	**Step 2: Examine the question stem** Identify the key words and phrases in the question stem. The words "main purpose" indicate that you're looking for the central idea of the passage. Review the Passage Map to identify the central idea or main purpose of the passage. You can use the entire map to get a sense of the central idea of the passage. The notes are about Greek poetry and how it changed over time. **Step 3: Predict and answer** This passage begins by discussing early Greek poetry, then summarizes how and why it changed over time. Choice (B) matches this prediction.

✔ **Note**

Resist the temptation to reread large portions of the passage. Your Passage Map can help you predict and answer questions correctly without having to dive back into the text. Doing so will save you time on Test Day!

You have seen the kinds of notes SAT experts take and the critical thinking questions they ask themselves when they encounter Reading Test passages and questions.

Look at the Reading Test passage excerpt that follows. There are two questions associated with it. Since part of the passage has been mapped for you, your first step is to complete the Passage Map. Then, use the Kaplan Method for Reading Comprehension to answer the questions. Remember to look at the strategic thinking questions that have been laid out for you—some of the answers have been filled in, but you will have to fill in the answers to others.

Use your answers to the strategic thinking questions to select the correct answer, just as you will on Test Day.

Strategic Thinking

Step 1: Read actively

The passage below is partially mapped. Read the passage and the first part of the Passage Map. Then, complete the Passage Map on your own. Remember to focus on the central ideas of each paragraph as well as the central idea of the overall passage. Use your Passage Map as a reference when you're answering questions.

Questions 2-3 are based on the following passage.

The following passage discusses facts and speculation about a spy during the American Revolution.

Although he may not have been the first American spy, when Captain Nathan Hale uttered his famous final words, "I only regret that I have but one
Line life to lose for my country," he ensured that
5   he would long be remembered as the first patriotic martyr of the American Revolution. Even today, Hale's story serves as an inspiration for others who have chosen to enter the often deadly and thankless profession of covert intelligence gathering. Yet, as
10 it seems clear that the sacrifice Hale made in the autumn of 1776 will long be valued, relatively little is actually known about his fateful mission.
    Born in Connecticut in 1755 as the sixth child of Richard Hale, a prosperous farmer, Nathan's
15 childhood and education were rather accelerated. Nathan was only 14 years old when he entered Yale University as a freshman, just 18 when he graduated as one of the top students in his class, and not yet 20 when he enlisted in the militia in 1774. With
20 the whole country abuzz from military movements and with many joining the separatist cause, Nathan quickly became involved in the military organization of his hometown. Historical records indicate that, by the time news of the first battles of the war reached
25 Connecticut in 1775, Hale had already become an outspoken leader of the independence movement.

His subsequent commissioning as an officer in the Connecticut regiment is also well documented, but it is the events of 1776, when Hale began his secret
30 mission, that are largely unknown.
    It is known that Hale was indeed a spy and that he had been a member of the Knowlton Rangers, a small group of elite soldiers operating under what was called a "detached command," taking orders
35 directly from General George Washington. Historians also believe that it was Hale who accompanied a young sergeant named Stephen Hempstead on a mission involved with involving Washington's Long Island forces. But, perhaps due to chaos in New York
40 City created by the great fires that had been set in September of 1776, the precise details of Hale's mission and capture are unclear. Historical accounts pick up the story when he was taken before the commanding British General and, after honestly
45 providing his rank and name, was immediately condemned to death by hanging. There was no formal trial, but, according to the British, the papers Hale had on his person were damning enough, and the next morning he was hanged in an apple
50 orchard in the middle of Manhattan. Yet, despite the uncertainty surrounding Hale's story of espionage, a clear and undisputed written record verifies the young martyr's final words, for which he will likely be forever remembered and admired.

Don't get distracted by less important details. While there is a lot going on in this passage, your additions to the Passage Map should note Nathan Hale's role in the Revolutionary War and his ultimate fate. If you're stuck, review the example Passage Map in the Answers & Explanations for this chapter on page 988.

Handwritten margin notes:

NH = Am. spy during Rev. War

mission details unknown

bkgd & educ

Childhood accelerated

military bkgd: CT Reg

Officer well know not spy

career & legacy

Questions	Strategic Thinking
2. According to the passage, Hale received a commission in A) the independence movement. B) the Knowlton Rangers. C) the Long Island forces. D) the Connecticut regiment.	**Step 2: Examine the question stem** *What are the key words and phrases in the question stem?* "According to the passage," and "commission." "According to the passage" implies that the answer can be directly found in the passage. *What parts of your Passage Map are relevant?* Paragraph 2 discusses Hale's military background. Look at your Passage Map, particularly the notes for paragraph 2, to find information about Hale's "commission." **Step 3: Predict and answer** *What does the author say Hale received a commission in?* the Connecticut regiment *What answer choice matches this prediction?* D

Notes

ONH — US SPY ✓ → means important.

② Notes (Jerry)
Last paragraphs are about his career in the military and at the end, it talked about his legacy.

10/3/16

Questions	Strategic Thinking
3. The main purpose of the passage is to A) provide background information on Hale's secret mission to New York. B) discuss the history and development of covert operations during the War of Independence. C) suggest that Hale deserves the respect and admiration that he receives. D) challenge the relevance of Hale's quotation in light of the questions about his mission.	**Step 2: Examine the question stem** *What are the key words and phrases in the question stem?* Main purpose *What parts of your Passage Map are relevant?* **Step 3: Predict and answer** *What is the author's purpose?* *Which answer choice matches this prediction?* C

Now, try a test-like Reading Test passage on your own. Give yourself 5 minutes to read and map the passage and answer the questions.

Questions 4-5 are based on the following passage.

This passage discusses the cane toad's introduction to and effect on the Australian environment.

The cane toad, a large, brightly colored amphibian that can weigh more than a pound, was first introduced to the Australian continent by the sugar-
Line cane industry. The cane toad was a known predator
5 of the cane beetle, which had been devouring the sugarcane crops since the early 1900s. Australian farmers thought that by importing these toads from their native habitats in the Americas, they could effectively use the toads to feast on pests like the
10 cane beetle and eradicate the growing insect threat. So, in 1935, roughly 100 cane toads were carefully packed into crates and shipped to Australia. Upon their toads' arrival, the cane farmers eagerly brought them to a pond in the northeast province of Queensland.
15 Before long, the female cane toads had laid hundreds of thousands of eggs in elongated, gelatinous strings, and the farmers waited for their new predators to be born. As the eggs hatched, the pond became filled with great clouds of squirming,
20 wriggling tadpoles that, upon reaching maturity, were taken to the sugarcane fields and turned loose. The situation that resulted from this fateful release, however, did not coincide with the farmers' plan. In fact, the introduction of cane toads into the wild
25 in Australia has since been deemed nothing short of an ecological disaster.
Easily numbering well into the millions—an exact figure has been impossible to calculate— the cane toads soon dominated the landscape in
30 Queensland. Following their release, some of the toads descended as planned on the sugarcane crops and began to eat the beetles. However, they soon lost interest in their new habitat. For one thing, the mature cane beetles could fly away from their
35 predators, forcing these slow, fat toads to work very hard for their food. In addition, the fields were hot and dry and provided little sleeping shelter for

the newcomers, who generally prefer wet shade. These adverse conditions were not severe enough
40 to kill off the toads, but instead the toads began to look elsewhere for food and shelter. Nearby towns, full of lush gardens and well-watered lawns, were extremely inviting, and soon the toads had overrun entire residential areas. They covered the lawns,
45 filled the gardens, found shelter under flowerpots or on porches, and even began to eat bowls of food left outside for pets like cats and dogs.
Today, the people of Queensland hunt cane toads as if they were mosquitoes. But the toads
50 continue to spread south and west through Australia in staggering numbers. As for the sugarcane industry, just five years after the release of the toads, an effective insecticide spray became available, and the cane beetles were easily exterminated. Scien-
55 tists as well as the Australian government, however, continue to grapple with the cane toad problem.

4. All of the following are true EXCEPT

A) the cane toad was introduced to Australia to control the cane beetle.

B) the cane toad bred readily in Australia.

C) the introduction of the cane toad to Australia is considered an ecological disaster.

D) the cane toad quickly adapted to the conditions in the sugarcane fields.

5. The author would most likely agree with which of the following statements?

    A) Human intervention in a natural ecosystem always results in disaster.

    B) The introduction of a non-native species can have unfortunate effects on the local environment.

    C) The sugarcane farmers should have considered the potential risks before initiating their plan.

    D) A possible solution to this problem is the introduction of a natural predator of the cane toad.

Answers & Explanations for this chapter begin on page 988.

EXTRA PRACTICE

Required	Recommended
Questions 1–11	Questions 12–22

Questions 1-11 are based on the following passage and supplementary material.

The following passage describes the discovery of gold in California and the effects of that discovery on the United States.

People around the world unanimously agree that gold is a valuable mineral. Gold has been seen as a precious commodity by many cultures throughout
Line time, and Americans of the 1840s were no different.
5 When James W. Marshall, a carpenter and sawmill owner, discovered a gold nugget in the American River, California was forever changed. News of his discovery attracted thousands of immigrants from other parts of California, as well as other places around the United
10 States and the world.

In the Sierra Nevada, a mountain range that runs 400 miles through California, years of erosion caused by rainfall and the downhill flow of mountain streams loosened pieces of gold that had been embedded in
15 the solid rock formed over 100 million years ago. California is largely made of quartz previously found at the bottom of the Pacific Ocean. Underwater volcanoes melted the quartz into magma and pushed it up towards the surface, sometimes forming islands. Due to the
20 movements of the Earth's tectonic plates, these islands were pushed together and against the West Coast. This movement and accumulation of land over millions of years formed the area known as California. The gold that was dispersed across the sea floor became
25 concentrated and redistributed throughout the veins of quartz in the Sierra Nevada Mountains.

Marshall's discovery was quickly verified and publicized by the New York Herald in August of 1848. Current California residents of the time were able to
30 get to the gold fields first. Soon after, President James Polk confirmed the discovery in an address to Congress. His address prompted many Americans to move west,

as well as other fortune-seekers from around the world to immigrate to the United States. This influx of people
35 caused California's population to increase, as well as experience a change in demographics. The particular geologic makeup made California the prime location for mining gold. The Northern California city of San Francisco grew from 1,000 people in 1848 to more than
40 20,000 people in just two years. Because of the rapid population increase, the United States government incorporated the territory into the Union. California became the Union's 31st state in 1850, though it had only been acquired from Mexico two short years before. This
45 was the fastest any new territory has ever been given statehood in the history of the United States.

Americans from places east of California migrated via two very long and often dangerous paths. Some endured a six-month boat voyage, which departed from
50 New York City and sailed south as far as the tip of South America before heading north to California. The trip was so perilous that most Americans relocating to California opted to travel the famous Oregon Trail. Riding in covered wagons through dangerous conditions, trav-
55 elers who opted to move by land also had a six-month trip to endure. By 1850, the sheer number of people attempting the voyage inspired the creation of the Panama Railway. Built specifically to reduce travel time to California, the first transcontinental railroad decreased
60 the length of the trip by several months.

Forty-Niners came to California from many different countries around the globe, including China, Germany, Mexico, Turkey, France, and Ireland. The largest group of people to successfully
65 immigrate to California from abroad was the Chinese. Many did not intend to settle in the United States, but instead planned to return home

with their fortunes. While many did so, when gold grew scarce and the Chinese Exclusion Act was
70 passed in 1882, prohibiting Chinese immigration for 10 years, many immigrants instead put down roots in California. The result was the most ethnically diverse state in the Union by the middle of the 19th century.
75   Though the gold in California didn't last long after its discovery, the effects that it had on the population, including the number of people in the state, their ethnicities, and the way they travelled, have lasted to the modern day.

Percent Population Change, 1850–1860

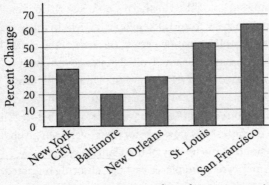

*Data for San Francisco are from the state census in 1852. The 1850 census data were destroyed in a fire.

Data from the *United States Bureau of the Census*.

1. The author includes the second paragraph primarily to

    A) illustrate why gold is such a valuable metal.

    B) show why California was a prime location for gold mining.

    C) explain why California became a state so rapidly.

    D) give scientific information about how gold is formed over time.

2. According to the passage, which of the following was a main cause of westward migration?

    A) President Polk's speech about the gold rush

    B) California's acceptance into the union as a state

    C) The development of new gold extraction techniques

    D) New immigration restrictions passed by the federal government

3. As used in line 34, "influx" most nearly means

    A) assault.

    B) movement.

    C) news.

    D) rush.

4. The passage suggests that which of the following was unusual about California's entry into the Union, as compared to that of other new states?

    A) It had more natural resources.

    B) It had a smaller population.

    C) It had less wealth.

    D) It had spent less time as a territory.

5. Which choice provides the best evidence for the answer to the previous question?

    A) Lines 27-28 ("Marshall's discovery … August 1848")

    B) Lines 32-34 ("His address … United States")

    C) Lines 44-46 ("This was … United States")

    D) Lines 68-72 ("While many … in California")

10/4/16

6. According to the passage, what was one result of the presence of many dangers on the journey to California?

   A) Expansion of the population across the entire country

   B) Increased wealth for those living along the Oregon Trail

   C) Decreased immigration to other parts of the country

   D) Improved transportation options between the East Coast and California

7. What can be inferred about immigrants who came to California?

   A) They were forbidden from returning home once California became a state.

   B) Migrating to California was more attractive for them than for other Americans.

   C) They came from more nations than did immigrants to other states.

   D) Most were escaping difficult political conditions at home rather than seeking fortune.

8. Which choice provides the best evidence for the answer to the previous question?

   A) Lines 61-64 ("Forty-Niners … and Ireland")

   B) Lines 64-66 ("The largest … the Chinese")

   C) Lines 68-72 ("While many … in California")

   D) Lines 72-74 ("The result … the 19th century")

9. As used in line 52, "perilous" most nearly means

   A) boring.

   B) exotic.

   C) dangerous.

   D) expensive.

10. The overall structure of the passage can be described as

    A) a history of gold in California, followed by a discussion of why gold is valuable.

    B) an analysis of why gold is important, followed by criticism of the politics surrounding gold.

    C) a list of the causes of a gold rush, followed by an analysis of the effects of gold on a region.

    D) a discussion of the benefits of the gold rush in California, followed by a list of consequences.

11. Based on the chart, which conclusion is best supported?

    A) The United States grew greatly from 1850 to 1860.

    B) San Francisco was the largest city in the United States in 1860.

    C) From 1850 to 1860, cities in the East lost population, while San Francisco gained population.

    D) Of all five cities, San Francisco gained the largest total number of people from 1850 to 1860.

Questions 12-22 are based on the following passage and supplementary material.

This passage details the history of Eleanor Roosevelt and how she changed the role of the First Lady of the United States.

Eleanor Roosevelt, wife of president Franklin Delano Roosevelt (FDR), forever altered the role of American First Lady and women in U.S. politics
Line in general. Dedicated, humble, and brave, Eleanor
5 Roosevelt powerfully shouldered the nation's burdens during the longest and arguably most difficult presidency America has yet seen. Her sustained commitment to social justice began long before her husband's presidency and endured
10 through the end of her life.

Born in 1884 to the brother of president Theodore Roosevelt, Eleanor's upbringing acquainted her with both politics and hardship. Having lost her parents in childhood, Eleanor was cared for by her grand-
15 mother in New York and was later sent to London for secondary schooling. After this education, Roosevelt returned to the States and became involved in humanitarian work, which would prove to be a lifelong engagement. At twenty years old she married
20 her distant cousin, Franklin Delano, with whom she would parent six children.

While Mrs. Roosevelt was a committed wife and mother, she was also heavily involved with the national and international crises that plagued her
25 generation. During World War I she volunteered in hospitals while supporting and partnering in her husband's political career. When FDR contracted polio in the early 1920s, she assumed much of his political responsibility, as he held a number of high-
30 profile government positions before his presidency. This quickly afforded her an increasing national influence. Eleanor Roosevelt fought diligently for women's empowerment and numerous other human rights issues. Her husband's presidency (1933 to 1945)
35 also oversaw both the Great Depression and World War II, two major national dilemmas with which Eleanor Roosevelt was intimately involved in addressing.

Before Eleanor Roosevelt, U.S. First Ladies had less political voice. Never before had a First Lady
40 hosted press conferences, let alone assumed significant portions of the public responsibilities of the presidency. But due to FDR's lasting illness and his wife's wisdom, eloquence, and powerful political presence, all of this was possible, and in many ways
45 essential, for his effective leadership.

Eleanor Roosevelt's concern for human rights aided her husband in his development of the New Deal, which was his legislative effort to alleviate the Great Depression. Mrs. Roosevelt catalyzed,
50 advocated for, oversaw, and in many ways sustained much of the New Deal programming. Through these programs she sought to equip and employ youth, protect labor rights, and mend racial injustices.

Eleanor travelled extensively, speaking publicly,
55 taking reports on relief programs, and visiting troops in wartime. Outside of direct political involvements, she taught and lectured in educational settings, aggressively fundraised for charitable causes, hosted countless social functions, and even
60 spearheaded a small furniture business to employ the jobless.

Many remember Eleanor Roosevelt best for her power with words. Ever an advocate for the rights of the disadvantaged, Roosevelt spoke and wrote
65 extensively. She published several books and even maintained a daily newspaper column for nearly thirty years.

FDR's declining health prevented him from completing his fourth elected presidential term. He
70 died in April of 1945, one month before the official end of Europe's involvement in World War II. This marked the end of Eleanor's time as First Lady, and in her grief she indicated an intent to absent herself from politics altogether. Yet her dedication to the
75 pursuit of world peace and human rights would prevail. Toward the end of that year she accepted President Truman's invitation to help represent the U.S. at the newly forming United Nations.

In serving the UN, Roosevelt drafted the Universal
80 Declaration of Human Rights. This document still holds paramount importance today; it sets a standard against which international justice is still principally measured. She soon became chair of the UN Human Rights Commission. Stateside, Roosevelt actively
85 bolstered the Civil Rights movement. She visited those imprisoned for nonviolent protest, spoke publicly for the cause, served on the boards of various organizations, and helped to catalyze the Justice Department's Civil Rights Division. Roosevelt's work
90 toward labor justice and women's equality in America also continued into her final years.

Eleanor Roosevelt died in 1962 at the age of 78 years old. Over a half-century later, this woman's legacy remains. Her wise words are cherished in
95 American hearts, her impact echoes throughout national and international human rights legislation, and her strength still empowers the powerless to

continue their efforts toward equality and justice. Roosevelt's perseverance, integrity, and accomplish-
100 ments forever render her one of the most well-loved and revered women in American history.

Unemployment Rates Over the Course of FDR's "New Deal" Programs

Adapted from HERB: Resources for Teachers and Bureau of Labor Statistics, "Graph of U.S. Unemployment Rate 1930-1945." ©2011 by American Social History Productions, Inc.

12. As used in line 5, "shouldered" most nearly means

   A) arranged.

   B) handled.

   C) refused.

   D) endured.

13. The passage most clearly reflects the author's

   A) admiration for Eleanor Roosevelt.

   B) regard for the accomplishments of Franklin D. Roosevelt.

   C) support for the expansion of women's roles in politics.

   D) uncertainty regarding the official role of the First Lady.

14. Which choice provides the best evidence for the answer to the previous question?

   A) Lines 22-25 ("While Mrs. Roosevelt . . . generation")

   B) Lines 34-37 ("Her husband's . . . addressing")

   C) Lines 39-42 ("Never before . . . presidency")

   D) Lines 99-101 ("Roosevelt's perseverance . . . American history")

15. The passage most strongly suggests that Eleanor Roosevelt

   A) modeled her political service on that of the women who had come before her.

   B) proved pivotal to the success of Franklin D. Roosevelt's presidency.

   C) was instrumental in winning suffrage and equal rights for women.

   D) would not have had such a lasting legacy had she not been First Lady.

16. Based on the passage, which choice best describes the focus of Eleanor Roosevelt's work?

   A) Expansion of health care and medical research

   B) Human rights and social justice

   C) Support for small business and entrepreneurship

   D) Wartime economic and political reform

17. The author most likely includes the detail in lines 25-26 ("During World War I . . . hospitals") to

    A) demonstrate Eleanor Roosevelt's expansion of the role of First Lady.

    B) prove the influence of Roosevelt in developing international human rights standards.

    C) show how Roosevelt worked closely with her husband on his policy agenda.

    D) support the idea that humanitarian work was a lifelong pursuit for Roosevelt.

18. The data in the graph most clearly support which conclusion related to the passage?

    A) Labor and other social unrest occurred in direct response to wartime economic cuts.

    B) President Roosevelt's policies helped ease hardship during the Great Depression.

    C) Volunteer efforts undertaken by Eleanor Roosevelt lessened suffering in cities.

    D) Women played a crucial role in the economic recovery of the nation during the war.

19. The passage suggests that Eleanor Roosevelt would most likely engage in what activity?

    A) Volunteer disaster response

    B) Political party campaigning

    C) Legal challenges to corporate monopolies

    D) Protests for tighter environmental regulations

20. Which choice provides the best evidence for the answer to the previous question?

    A) Lines 7-10 ("Her sustained commitment . . . end of her life")

    B) Lines 16-19 ("After this education . . . engagement")

    C) Lines 42-45 ("But due to . . . leadership")

    D) Lines 76-78 ("Toward the end . . . United Nations")

21. As used in line 60, "spearheaded" most nearly means

    A) invested in.

    B) advertised for.

    C) led development of.

    D) worked for.

22. Paragraph 9 most clearly supports the purpose of the whole passage by

    A) applauding the advances made in civil and human rights during Eleanor Roosevelt's lifetime.

    B) distinguishing Eleanor Roosevelt's legacy as independent from her husband's.

    C) emphasizing the importance of Eleanor Roosevelt's skills as an orator and a writer.

    D) showing the relationship between Eleanor Roosevelt's roles as First Lady and as diplomat.

CHAPTER 19

Reading Test Passage Types

 ## CHAPTER OBJECTIVES

By the end of this chapter, you will be able to:

1. Passage Map Reading Test passages, identifying keywords and central ideas across passage types

2. Determine the meaning of challenging vocabulary by using context

3. Predict an answer and find its match among the answer choices by using a Passage Map

4. Identify the three types of passages on the SAT Reading Test

SMARTPOINTS

Point Value	SmartPoint Category
Point Builder	U.S. and World Literature Passages
Point Builder	History/Social Studies Passages
Point Builder	Science Passages

OVERVIEW OF THE SAT READING TEST PASSAGE TYPES

SAT Reading Test Passage Distribution	
U.S. and World Literature	1 passage; 9 questions
History/Social Studies	2 passages OR 1 passage and 1 paired-passage set; 9–10 questions each
Science	2 passages OR 1 passage and 1 paired-passage set; 9–10 questions each

It is imperative that you use the Kaplan Method for Reading Comprehension for every passage on the SAT Reading Test. Doing so ensures that you spend your time efficiently and maximize your opportunity to earn points. However, just as the passages span different genres, your approaches will also vary from subject to subject. The approach for each type of Reading Test passage will be addressed in this chapter.

Before you learn passage-type specifics, take some time to do a quick review of the Kaplan Method for Reading Comprehension.

Step 1: Read actively

Step 2: Examine the question stem

Step 3: Predict and answer

Now, let's look at the specific passage types individually.

U.S. AND WORLD LITERATURE PASSAGES

There will be one U.S. and World Literature single passage on the SAT. It is different from the other passages because:

- There are multiple characters and, therefore, multiple opinions.

- The tone will be nuanced and derived from emotions rather than informative or explanatory.

As you read a U.S. and World Literature passage, you should:

1. Identify the characters and evaluate how the author describes them.

   - What do the characters want?

   - What are the characters doing?

   - Can you think of adjectives to describe each character?

2. Assess the characters' opinions of each other and themselves.

   - Do they like each other? Dislike each other?

- Why does each character make a particular decision or take a particular course of action?
- What do these decisions or actions tell you about a character?

3. Identify the themes of the story.

- What are the "turning points" in the passage?
- Is there a moral to the story?

F ↓ *For*   *A* *N* → *neutral*   *against*

✔ **Remember**

Because U.S. and World Literature passages have multiple characters with multiple opinions, remember to keep straight who said what.

Let's look at the following example of an abbreviated U.S. and World Literature passage and question set. After the mapped passage, the left column contains questions similar to those you'll see on the Reading Test on Test Day. The column on the right features the strategic thinking a test expert employs when approaching the passage and questions presented.

Strategic Thinking

Step 1: Read actively

Read the passage and the notes provided. Remember, a well-crafted Passage Map should summarize the central idea of each paragraph as well as important topics or themes. Use your Passage Map to help you answer each question.

Questions 1-2 are based on the following passage.

The following passage is an excerpt from English novelist and poet Thomas Hardy's Tess of the D'Urbervilles, *published in 1891.*

young girls working in fields

The women—or rather girls, for they were mostly young—wore drawn cotton bonnets with great flapping curtains to keep off the sun, and gloves to
Line prevent their hands being wounded by the stubble.
5 There was one wearing a pale pink jacket, another in a cream-coloured, tight-sleeved gown, another in a petticoat as red as the arms of a reaping-machine; and others, older in the brown-rough "wropper," or over-all—the old-established and most appropriate

wear bright colors inapprop., against trad.

10 dress of the field-woman, which the young ones were abandoning. This morning, the eye returns involuntarily to the girl in the pink cotton jacket, she being the most flexuous and finely drawn figure of them all. But her bonnet is pulled so far over her brow that
15 none of her face is disclosed while she binds, though

her complexion may be guessed from a stray twine or two of dark brown hair which extends below the curtain of her bonnet. Perhaps one reason why she seduces casual attention is that she never courts it,
20 though the other women often gaze around them.

girl in pink stands out bc she doesn't ask for attention

Her binding proceeds with clock-like monotony. From the sheaf last finished she draws a handful of ears, patting their tips with her left palm to bring them even. Then, stooping low, she moves forward, gather-

has a system for field work

25 ing the corn with both hands against her knees and pushing her left gloved hand under the bundle to meet the right on the other side, holding the corn in an embrace like that of a lover. She brings the ends of the bond together and kneels on the sheaf while she ties

field work = corn

30 it, beating back her skirts now and then when lifted by the breeze. A bit of her naked arm is visible between the buff leather of the gauntlet and the sleeve of her gown; and as the day wears on, its feminine smooth-ness becomes scarified by the stubble and bleeds.

YG in FLD
YG in pink
SO

becomes
dirty, less
feminine

35   At intervals she stands up to rest, and to retie her
disarranged apron, or to pull her bonnet straight.
Then one can see the oval face of a handsome young
woman with deep, dark eyes and long, heavy, cling-
ing tresses, which seem to clasp in a beseeching way

40 anything they fall against. The cheeks are paler, the
teeth more regular, the red lips thinner than is usual
in a country-bred girl.

can see face
when she rests;
doesn't look like
others

Questions	Strategic Thinking
1. The passage is best described as A) a psychological study of a character's personality. B) a sweeping portrait of nature in autumn. C) a drab rendering of a farmland routine. D) a gradual focusing on a single individual.	**Step 2: Examine the question stem** Identify the key words and phrases in the question stem. The phrase "passage is best described as" implies that you are looking for a description of the passage as a whole. Use your Passage Map notes to find the author's central theme. **Step 3: Predict and answer** The Passage Map notes from the end of the first paragraph through the end of the passage focus on one nameless young girl. Choice (D) is correct.
2. The activity described in lines 21-28 ("Her binding . . . of a lover") seems indicative of A) routine. B) memory. C) necessity. D) optimism.	**Step 2: Examine the question stem** Identify the key words and phrases in the question stem. The word "activity" and the line reference indicate you should look at your Passage Map notes surrounding those lines. **Step 3: Predict and answer** The Passage Map underlines the phrase "clock-like monotony" (line 21) and features the note "has a system for field work." In this context, "system" is synonymous with "routine." Choice (A) is correct.

HISTORY/SOCIAL STUDIES PASSAGES

The History/Social Studies portion of the SAT Reading Test will consist of either two single History/ Social Studies passages or one single History/Social Studies passage and one History/Social Studies paired-passage set. History/Social Studies passages are different from other passage types because:

- The passage will have a clearly stated topic, a well-defined scope, and a specific purpose.

- There will be at least one primary source passage that uses antiquated language.

Because History/Social Studies passages can be densely written, you need to:

1. Identify the topic and scope of the passage.

   - You can usually find the topic and scope in the first paragraph.

2. Identify the topic sentence of each succeeding paragraph.

   - What does this paragraph accomplish? Does it provide evidence to support a previous statement? Or does it introduce questions about an earlier claim?

3. Summarize the purpose of the passage.

   - Some common purposes include: to inform, to refute, to promote, to explore.

Let's look at the following example of an abbreviated History/Social Studies passage and question set. After the mapped passage, the left column contains questions similar to those you'll see on the Reading Test on Test Day. The column on the right features the strategic thinking a test expert employs when approaching the passage and questions presented. Note how a test expert can quickly condense the entire passage into a few words and use his or her Passage Map to ask questions that build a prediction for the correct answer.

Strategic Thinking
Step 1: Read actively
Read the passage and the notes provided. Remember, a well-crafted Passage Map should summarize the central idea of each paragraph as well as important topics or themes. Use your Passage Map to help you answer each question.

Questions 3-4 are based on the following passage.

The following passage is an excerpt from a speech by Canassatego, an Iroquois, as printed by Benjamin Franklin in the 1740s.

Iro: BF proposal = well-intentioned

We know that you highly esteem the kind of learning taught in those colleges, and that the maintenance of our young men, while with you, would
Line be very expensive to you. We are convinced, there-
5 fore, that you mean to do us good by your proposal,

and we thank you heartily. But you who are wise must know that different nations have different conceptions of things; and you will therefore not take it amiss if our ideas of this kind of education
10 happen not to be the same with yours. We have had some experience of it: several of our young people were formerly brought up at the colleges of the northern provinces; they were instructed in all

diff. people, diff. edu.

10/6/16

your sciences; but when they came back to us, they
15 were bad runners; ignorant of every means of living
in the woods; unable to bear either cold or hunger;
knew neither how to build a cabin, take a deer, or
kill an enemy; spoke our language imperfectly;
were therefore neither fit for hunters, warriors, or
20 counselors; they were totally good for nothing.

We are, however, not the less obliged by your kind
offer, though we decline accepting it: and to show
our grateful sense of it, if the gentlemen of Virginia
will send us a dozen of their sons, we will take great
25 care of their education, instruct them in all we
know, and make men of them.

Questions	Strategic Thinking
3. In lines 6-10 ("But . . . yours"), what general idea is the author most likely conveying? A) It can be a mistake to disagree on the purpose of education. B) What constitutes a useful education for one group of people may not be useful for another group of people. C) Although grateful for the opportunity to attend college, the author wishes to pursue a more practical course of study. D) Challenging wise men on their concept of education is best done on a national basis.	**Step 2: Examine the question stem** The key phrases in this question stem are the line reference, "general idea," and "most likely conveying." The Passage Map notes near the cited lines will help you answer this question. **Step 3: Predict and answer** The Passage Map near the cited lines notes that different people have different ideas about what constitutes an appropriate and complete education. Choice (B) matches this prediction.
4. The passage can best be described as A) an attempt to explain why the Iroquois could not accept such a generous offer. B) a desire to describe the benefits of promoting multiple points of view on a subject. C) an examination of the similarities and differences between two opposing concepts. D) an argument that the Iroquois' concept of education was superior to other concepts.	**Step 2: Examine the question stem** There are no key words or phrases in this question stem; the fact that there are no specific key words indicates this is a general question about the passage as a whole. Use the entire Passage Map to answer this question. **Step 3: Predict and answer** The central idea of the passage is that the author believes young Iroquois men need a specific kind of education to fully function within their society. Choice (D) matches this prediction.

SCIENCE PASSAGES

The SAT Reading Test will contain either two single Science passages or one single Science passage and one set of paired Science passages. Science passages differ from other passage types because:

- They often contain a lot of jargon and technical terms.

- They can utilize unfamiliar terms and concepts.

While Science passages can be tricky due to unfamiliar language, you will never need to employ knowledge outside of the passage when answering questions. Use the following strategy when approaching Science passages on the SAT:

1. Locate the central idea in the first paragraph.

2. Note how each paragraph relates to the central idea. Does the paragraph . . .

   - Explain?

   - Support?

   - Refute?

   - Summarize?

3. Don't be distracted by jargon or technical terms.

   - Unfamiliar terms will generally be defined within the passage or in a footnote.

Look at the test-like Science passage excerpt with a Passage Map and two questions that follow. See how an SAT test expert's Passage Map focuses on the central ideas of the passage and the location of key information, rather than on the information itself. After the mapped passage, the left column contains questions similar to those you'll see on the Reading Test on Test Day. The column on the right features the strategic thinking a test expert employs when approaching the passage and questions presented.

> ✔ **Remember**
>
> When you encounter more than one theory or idea, paraphrase each in as few words as possible in your Passage Map.

Strategic Thinking

Step 1: Read actively

Read the passage and the notes provided. Remember, a well-crafted Passage Map should summarize the central idea of each paragraph as well as important topics or themes. Use your Passage Map to help you answer each question.

Questions 5-6 are based on the following passage.

This passage details the regular journey of a group of green sea turtles from their feeding to breeding grounds.

Green sea turtles, shelled reptiles that plowed the oceans eons before mammals evolved, are known for their prodigious migrations. One group
Line of green sea turtles makes a regular journey from
5 feeding grounds near the Brazilian Coast to breeding beaches on Ascension Island, a barren, relatively predator-free island in the central equatorial Atlantic. Proverbially slow on land, these turtles cover the distance of more than 2,000 kilometers
10 in as little as two weeks. But how is this navigation of deep, featureless ocean accomplished? The sun's movements seem to provide the turtles with a navigational aid, but this is only part of the answer. In addition to possessing good eyesight, green
15 turtles appear to have an excellent sense of smell. In fact, the turtles may orient themselves by detecting traces of substances released from Ascension Island itself. Because Ascension Island lies in the midst of a major west-flowing ocean current,
20 scientists believe that chemical substances picked up from the islands would tend to flow westward toward the feeding grounds of the turtle. As a result, these substances may provide a scented chemical trail that the turtles are able to follow. A mathematical
25 model has been used to show that a concentration of substances delivered from Ascension Island to the turtles' feeding grounds, though diluted, would probably be sufficient to be sensed by the turtles.

The turtles' eyesight, meanwhile, may help direct
30 the turtles from their feeding grounds into the path of this chemical trail. It is an established fact that turtles are capable of distinguishing between different light densities. Turtles recognize at least four colors and are especially attuned to the color
35 red, because it often appears in their shell coloration. Researchers believe that these turtles swim east toward the rising sun at the beginning of their migration, changing course toward Ascension Island's beaches as soon as their route intersects the
40 scented path.

Margin notes:
- sea turtle migration = vast distance
- use smell to navigate
- smell bits of island chem.
- sight involved
- interaction btwn. sight & smell

Questions	Strategic Thinking
5. The main purpose of the last paragraph, lines 29-40, is to (A) connect two partial explanations for the turtles' navigational ability. B) describe how color perception depends upon the eye's ability to recognize different light densities. C) establish that color sensitivity and shell coloration are closely linked but not explained. D) argue that color perception is the main reason that sea turtles can navigate to Ascension Island.	**Step 2: Examine the question stem** The key words and phrase in the question stem are "main purpose" and the paragraph/line reference. The Passage Map notes from the last paragraph will help you answer this question. **Step 3: Predict and answer** The Passage Map notes for the last paragraph say that the turtles' eyesight helps them find the scented path discussed in paragraph 2. Choice (A) reflects these notes.
6. According to the passage, turtles' eyesight is especially sensitive to A) patterns of stars. B) the sun's movements. (C) the color red. D) the chemical trail.	**Step 2: Examine the question stem** The key words and phrases of this question stem are "according to the passage" and "turtles' eyesight." Your Passage Map notes about the turtles' eyesight will help you answer this question. **Step 3: Predict and answer** The turtles' eyesight is discussed in the third paragraph. The author says that turtles are sensitive to the color red: "Turtles recognize at least four colors and are especially attuned to the color red" (lines 33–35). Choice (C) matches this prediction.

You have now seen how to approach the three different Reading Test passage types on Test Day.

Look at the test-like Science passage excerpt that follows. There are two questions associated with it. Part of the Passage Map has been filled in for you, but you must complete it. Then, use the Kaplan Method for Reading Comprehension to answer the questions. As you map the passage and answer the questions, make sure to keep in mind the specifics for approaching SAT Science passages. Strategic thinking questions have been included to guide you—some of the answers have been filled in, but you will have to fill in the answers to others.

Use your answers to the strategic thinking questions to select the correct answer, just as you will on Test Day.

Strategic Thinking
Step 1: Read actively
The passage below is partially mapped. Read the passage and the first part of the Passage Map. Then, complete the Passage Map on your own. Remember to focus on the central ideas of each paragraph as well as the central idea of the overall passage. Use your Passage Map as a reference when you're answering questions.

Questions 7-8 are based on the following passage.

The following Science passage explains the forces of flight.

forces of flight

What do paper airplanes and large commercial airliners such as the Boeing 747 have in common? Plenty. Despite differences in size and weight, both
Line must make use of the same physical forces in order
5 to fly. The flight of any airplane results from the interaction of four different forces: thrust, drag, gravity, and lift.

thrust & drag

All of the forces acting on the airplane must balance each other in order for the plane to travel
10 along in steady horizontal flight. Thrust supplied by jet engines or propellers (or by a person's hand for a paper airplane) is the force that drives the airplane forward. The airplane cannot actually move any distance forward, however, unless the amount of
15 thrust is enough to overcome the force of drag.

impact on aircraft design

Drag is the air resistance that the plane encounters in flight. Just as the name indicates, air resistance has the effect of dragging the airplane backward as it moves through the air. Jet engines are designed
20 so that the airplane has the necessary thrust to overcome air resistance. Drag can be reduced if the airplane is streamlined—that is, constructed in such a way that air flows smoothly around it so that there is little friction at the airplane's surface.

25 To rise into the air, an airplane has to overcome the force of gravity, the downward pull that the Earth exerts on everything on or near its surface. The airplane accomplishes this feat with lift force, which acts in an upward direction opposite to
30 gravity. Lift is provided by the airplane's wings. The wings and wing flaps are shaped and angled so that air will flow more rapidly over them than under them. When air flows more rapidly over the wing tops, air pressure above the wings drops
35 in comparison with the air pressure below the wings. (This phenomenon is known to engineers as Bernoulli's principle.) When an airplane taxis down the runway (or when a paper airplane is released from a person's hand), the greater air pressure
40 below the wings pushes the wings upward, allowing the airplane to rise despite the pull of gravity. Once the plane is safely in the air, all four of the basic aerodynamic forces figure into the flight as well, whether it is the flight of a big jet or a paper
45 airplane.

10/7/16

Don't get distracted by less important details. While there is a lot going on in this passage, your additions to the Passage Map should have noted the final two forces (gravity and lift) as well as how planes take off. If you're stuck, review the example Passage Map in the Answers & Explanations for this chapter on page 997.

Questions	Strategic Thinking
7. As used in line 29, "acts" most nearly means A) behaves. B) works. C) portrays. D) pretends.	**Step 2: Examine the question stem** *What are the key words in the question stem?* The line reference, cited word, and "most nearly means" **Step 3: Predict and answer** *Read around the cited word. What synonym can you predict to replace "acts" in this context?* "Functions" or "works" *What answer choice matches this prediction?* _____
8. Which of the following does the passage imply about drag force? A) Drag is the most important physical force needed for flight. B) Drag increases when surface friction increases. C) Drag decreases as a function of increased thrust. D) Drag reduces wind speed and direction.	**Step 2: Examine the question stem** *What are the key words in the question stem?* "Drag force" *What parts of your Passage Map are relevant?* The notes, circled words, and underlined sections in paragraph 2, which is where drag force is introduced. **Step 3: Predict and answer** *What part of the passage discusses drag and drag force?* _____ _____ _____ *Which answer choice correctly reflects the passage's discussion of drag force?* _____

Now, try a test-like History/Social Studies Reading passage and question set on your own. Give yourself 6 minutes to read and map the passage and answer the questions.

Questions 9-12 are based on the following passage.

The following passage is an excerpt from Abraham Lincoln's second autobiography, published in a Pennsylvania newspaper in 1860.

I was born February 12, 1809, in Hardin County, Kentucky. My parents were both born in Virginia, of undistinguished families—second families,
Line perhaps I should say. My mother, who died in my
5 tenth year, was of a family of the name of Hanks, some of whom now reside in Adams, and others in Macon County, Illinois. My paternal grandfather, Abraham Lincoln, emigrated from Rockingham County, Virginia, to Kentucky about 1781 or 1782,
10 where a year or two later he was killed by the Indians, not in battle, but by stealth, when he was laboring to open a farm in the forest. His ancestors, who were Quakers, went to Virginia from Berks County, Pennsylvania. An effort to identify them with the
15 New England family of the same name ended in nothing more definite than a similarity of Christian names in both families, such as Enoch, Levi, Mordecai, Solomon, Abraham, and the like.
    My father, at the death of his father, was but
20 six years of age, and he grew up literally without education. He removed from Kentucky to what is now Spencer County, Indiana in my eighth year. We reached our new home about the time the state came into the Union. It was a wild region,
25 with many bears and other wild animals still in the woods. There I grew up. There were some schools, so called, but no qualification was ever required of a teacher beyond "readin', writin', and cipherin'" to the rule of three. If a straggler supposed to understand
30 Latin happened to sojourn in the neighborhood, he was looked upon as a wizard. There was absolutely nothing to excite ambition for education. Of course,

when I came of age I did not know much. Still, somehow I could read, write, and cipher to the rule
35 of three, but that was all. I have not been to school since. The little advance I now have upon this store of education I have picked up from time to time under the pressure of necessity.
    I was raised to farm work, which I continued till
40 I was twenty-two. At twenty-one I came to Illinois, Macon County. Then I got to New Salem, at that time in Sangamon, now in Menard, County, where I remained a year as a sort of clerk in a store.
    Then came the Black Hawk War, and I was
45 elected a captain of volunteers, a success which gave me more pleasure than any I have had since. I went the campaign, was elated, ran for the legislature the same year (1832), and was beaten—the only time I have ever been beaten by the people. The next and
50 three succeeding biennial elections I was elected to the legislature. I was not a candidate afterward. During this legislative period I had studied law, and removed to Springfield to practice it. In 1846 I was once elected to the lower house of Congress.
55 I was not a candidate for reelection. From 1849 to 1854, both inclusive practiced law more assiduously than ever before. Always a Whig in politics; and generally on the Whig electoral tickets, making active canvasses. I was losing interest in politics when
60 the repeal of the Missouri Compromise aroused me again. What I have done since then is pretty well known.
    If any personal description of me is thought desirable, it may be said I am, in height, six feet four
65 inches, nearly; lean in flesh, weighing on an average one hundred and eighty pounds; dark complexion, with coarse black hair and gray eyes. No other marks or brands recollected.

9. The author's stance is most similar to that of

    A) an ambitious politician campaigning for office.

    B) an education activist arguing for school reform.

    C) an accomplished storyteller spinning fanciful yarns.

    D) a common man describing his humble beginnings.

10. The author's central purpose for writing this passage is most likely to

    A) emphasize the influence his early education had on his later accomplishments.

    B) recount the important events that shaped his political philosophy.

    C) describe his life prior to his rise to national prominence.

    D) convey the idea that early hardship can strengthen an individual's character.

11. Based on the passage, which answer choice best describes the effect of the Black Hawk War on the author's life?

    A) It gave him an understanding of military tactics.

    B) It allowed him to escape the drudgery of working as a clerk.

    C) It launched his career into electoral politics.

    D) It informed his opinions on the necessity of the Civil War.

12. As used in line 38, "under the pressure of necessity" most nearly means

    A) when most convenient.

    B) when he needed to.

    C) whenever he could.

    D) when he was interested.

Answers & Explanations for this chapter begin on page 997.

EXTRA PRACTICE

Required	Recommended
Questions 1–10	Questions 11–21

Questions 1-10 are based on the following passage.

This passage is adapted from Guy de Maupassant's short story, "The False Gems," from The Entire Original Maupassant Short Stories.

Monsieur Lantin had met the young girl at a reception at the house of the second head of his department, and had fallen head over heels in love
Line with her.
5   Her simple beauty had the charm of angelic modesty, and the imperceptible smile which constantly hovered about the lips seemed to be the reflection of a pure and lovely soul.

Monsieur Lantin, then chief clerk in the
10 Department of the Interior, enjoyed a snug little salary of three thousand five hundred francs, and he proposed to this model young girl, and was accepted.

He was unspeakably happy with her. She governed his household with such clever economy that
15 they seemed to live in luxury.

He found fault with only two of her tastes: Her love for the theatre, and her taste for imitation jewelry.

After a time, Monsieur Lantin begged his wife to request some lady of her acquaintance to accompa-
20 ny her, and to bring her home after the theatre. She opposed this arrangement, at first; but, after much persuasion, finally consented, to the infinite delight of her husband.

Now, with her love for the theatre, came also the
25 desire for ornaments. Her costumes remained as before, simple, in good taste, and always modest; but she soon began to adorn her ears with huge rhinestones, which glittered and sparkled like real diamonds. Around her neck she wore strings of
30 false pearls, on her arms bracelets of imitation gold, and combs set with glass jewels.

Her husband frequently remonstrated with her, saying:

"My dear, as you cannot afford to buy real
35 jewelry, you ought to appear adorned with your beauty and modesty alone, which are the rarest ornaments of your sex."

But she would smile sweetly, and say:

"Look! are they not lovely? One would swear
40 they were real."

One evening, in winter, she had been to the opera, and returned home chilled through and through. The next morning she coughed, and eight days later she died of inflammation of the
45 lungs.

He wept unceasingly; his heart was broken as he remembered her smile, her voice, every charm of his dead wife.

Time did not assuage his grief. Everything in his
50 wife's room remained as it was during her lifetime; all her furniture, even her clothing, being left as it was on the day of her death. Here he was wont to seclude himself daily and think of her who had been his treasure—the joy of his existence.
55 But life soon became a struggle.

One morning, finding himself without a cent in his pocket, he resolved to sell something, and immediately the thought occurred to him of disposing of his wife's paste jewels, for he cherished in his
60 heart a sort of rancor against these "deceptions," which had always irritated him in the past. The very sight of them spoiled, somewhat, the memory of his lost darling.

To the last days of her life she had continued to
65 make purchases, bringing home new gems almost every evening, and he turned them over some time

before finally deciding to sell the heavy necklace, which she seemed to prefer, and which, he thought, ought to be worth about six or seven francs; for
70 it was of very fine workmanship, though only imitation.

He put it in his pocket, and started out in search of what seemed a reliable jeweler's shop. At length he found one, and went in, feeling a little ashamed
75 to expose his misery, and also to offer such a worthless article for sale.

"Sir," said he to the merchant, "I would like to know what this is worth."

The man took the necklace, examined it,
80 called his clerk, and made some remarks in an undertone; he then put the ornament back on the counter, and looked at it from a distance to judge of the effect.

Monsieur Lantin, annoyed at all these ceremo-
85 nies, was on the point of saying: "Oh! I know well enough it is not worth anything," when the jeweler said: "Sir, that necklace is worth from twelve to fifteen thousand francs; but I could not buy it, unless you can tell me exactly where it came from."
90 The widower opened his eyes wide and remained gaping, not comprehending the merchant's meaning. Finally he stammered: "You say—are you sure?"

Monsieur Lantin, beside himself with astonishment, took up the necklace and left the store.

1. As used in line 5, "angelic" most nearly means
   A) invisible.
   B) generous.
   C) genuine.
   D) innocent.

2. The author describes Monsieur Lantin's wife early in their marriage as
   A) wealthy.
   B) artistic.
   C) frugal.
   D) flighty.

3. The passage suggests that Lantin believed the jewels to be false because
   A) they did not have enough money to buy real jewels of this size.
   B) the theatregoers all wore elaborate costume jewelry.
   C) his wife preferred costume jewelry to real jewels.
   D) Madame Lantin was too concerned with modesty to wear real jewels.

4. Which choice provides the best evidence for the answer to the previous question?
   A) Lines 16-17 ("He found fault . . . jewelry")
   B) Lines 18-23 ("After a time . . . of her husband")
   C) Lines 24-29 ("Now, with her love . . . real diamonds")
   D) Lines 32-37 ("Her husband frequently . . . your sex")

5. Lines 46-54 ("He wept . . . joy of his existence") suggest that which of the following is true of Lantin?
   A) He holds a grudge due to his wife's spending.
   B) He is profoundly depressed after his wife's death.
   C) He idealized his wife and overlooked her flaws.
   D) He is resilient and will find happiness in the future.

6. Which choice provides the best evidence for the answer to the previous question?

    A) Lines 18-23 ("After a time . . . her husband")

    B) Lines 46-48 ("He wept unceasingly . . . his dead wife")

    C) Lines 64-71 ("To the last . . . only imitation")

    D) Lines 90-94 ("The widower opened . . . left the store")

7. As used in line 60, "rancor" most nearly means

    A) passion.

    B) prejudice.

    C) warning.

    D) bitterness.

8. The main purpose of lines 87-89 ("'Sir, that necklace is worth . . . where it came from'")
    is to

    A) offer a resolution to Lantin's crisis.

    B) foreshadow future happiness for Lantin.

    C) create a plot twist by suggesting a conflict.

    D) develop an antagonist character in the story.

9. The end of the passage suggests that which of the following was true of Madame Lantin?

    A) She was a notorious jewel thief.

    B) She accrued massive debts to purchase her jewels.

    C) She hid a substantial inheritance from her husband.

    D) She was not as virtuous as her husband believed.

10. What central theme does the excerpt communicate through Lantin's experiences?

    A) Appearances can be deceiving.

    B) People never appreciate what they have until it is gone.

    C) Beautiful things make for a rich life.

    D) A good reputation is easily damaged.

10/8/16

Questions 11-21 are based on the following passage.

The following passage details the antibody that produces peanut allergies and how scientists are using this information to develop a peanut that does not cause allergic reactions.

Peanuts can cause deadly allergic reactions in some people, and there is no real cure for peanut allergies. However, scientists may be working on
Line the next best thing to a cure: peanuts that do not
5 cause allergic reactions.

Allergic reactions start with the immune system, which normally works to keep us healthy. The immune system recognizes dangerous materials, such as poisons and viruses, and reacts to keep
10 the materials from harming the rest of the body. Some of these reactions, such as swelling of nose and throat tissues, keep the materials from moving farther through the body. Other reactions, such as producing mucus and coughing, help expel the
15 foreign materials. Unfortunately, too much swelling, mucus, or coughing make it hard to breathe and can even be life-threatening.

People who are allergic to peanuts produce an antibody called IgE that combines with a specific
20 part of the peanut protein. The IgE-protein complex then alerts the immune system and the reactions begin. Once the allergic person's throat starts swelling, that person will need immediate medical treatment to reduce the risk of injury or death.

25 People who are allergic to peanuts must avoid them, and avoiding peanuts can be very hard to do. Many popular fast foods contain peanuts or peanut oil, or have been made using machines that also handle peanuts. Some very sensitive people cannot
30 even be in the same room where peanuts are being eaten. This can be very difficult for children, and many allergic children cannot safely eat lunch in their own school cafeteria.

Some scientists wondered if they could find a
35 way to change the allergen, the part of the peanut protein that causes the allergic reaction, to keep

IgE from combining with it. They first needed to measure the amount of reaction caused by untreated peanuts. Measuring how much of an allergic
40 reaction the peanuts caused in people would not be safe, so they instead measured how much IgE combined with the peanut protein in a laboratory test. They found that frying and boiling peanuts reduced the amount of reaction, as compared to
45 raw peanuts. However, frying and boiling do not reduce the amount of antibody reaction to a safe amount, so scientists tried other treatments. Some of the treatments, such as high heat for long periods of time, changed the taste of the peanuts too much.

50 One treatment that showed promise was exposing the peanuts to very strong light. The light used by the scientists is similar to normal sunlight, but thousands of times stronger. By "pulsing" the light, or producing the light in short bursts, the scientists
55 hoped to avoid heating the peanuts to the point where the taste changed, while still deactivating the allergens in the peanuts.

In one experiment, the scientists exposed the peanuts to 3 pulses of light per second for dif-
60 ferent amounts of time. They then extracted the protein from the peanuts. To measure the amount of allergens left in the peanut protein, they coated a special plastic plate with the extracted protein. Next, they added blood plasma that contained the
65 IgE antibodies. When they washed the plasma off the plate, the IgE antibodies that combined with the allergen part of the protein remained stuck to the plate. They then added other chemicals that combined with the IgE antibodies and produced
70 a dark blue color; the darker the blue, the more IgE antibodies remained. Blood also contains very small amounts of other antibodies that will stick to the plate, so the same test on blood from a non-allergic person would still produce a small amount
75 of blue color. To account for this, the scientists used blood plasma that did not have any IgE antibodies as a negative control. They then compared the darkness of all of the samples to the darkness of the negative control.

80 From the results, it appears that the scientists can change the peanut allergens so that the reaction in an allergic person is about the same as in a non-allergic person. The next steps will be to test the peanuts on humans: first by testing for reactions

85 on the skin of allergic people, and finally by having allergic people eat the peanuts while being monitored for any reaction. Eventually, the scientists hope, they will have a treatment that will make a safe peanut, which will make eating a much safer

90 and simpler experience for many.

Results of allergen measurements for peanuts exposed to pulsed light for different amounts of time.

Adapted from Xingyu Zhao, "Effect of Pulsed Light on Allergenic Proteins of Shelled Whole Peanuts." ©2013.

11. As used in line 14, "expel" most nearly means

 A) dismiss.

B) eject.

C) emit.

D) separate.

12. The passage most strongly suggests that

A) exposure to peanut proteins can be potentially fatal for almost anyone.

B) a peanut allergy is caused by a compromised or weakened immune system.

C) anyone who wishes to avoid developing a peanut allergy should avoid all peanut products.

D) the body of a person allergic to peanuts sees the peanut protein as a dangerous invader.

13. Which choice provides the best evidence for the answer to the previous question?

A) Lines 6-10 ("Allergic reactions . . . body")

B) Lines 25-26 ("People who are . . . hard to do")

C) Lines 34-37 ("Some scientists . . . combining with it")

D) Lines 87-90 ("Eventually . . . for many")

14. Based on the information in the passage, how does an allergic reaction compare to a normal immune system response to a dangerous material?

   A) An allergic reaction is milder than a normal immune system response and is usually shorter in duration.

   B) A normal immune system response is characterized by the body's producing mucus and coughing, while an allergic reaction makes it difficult to breathe.

   C) A normal immune system response is milder than an allergic response, but the allergic response is triggered by a material that is dangerous.

   D) An allergic reaction is similar to a normal immune system response, but the response can be stronger and cause life-threatening symptoms.

15. According to paragraph 4, people with peanut allergies

   A) will likely encounter peanut allergens on a daily basis.

   B) are more likely to have other allergies than people without a peanut allergy.

   C) will prefer the taste of peanuts with deactivated allergens.

   D) have a difficult time avoiding peanut allergens.

16. Which choice provides the best evidence for the answer to the previous question?

   A) Lines 3-5 ("However, scientists . . . allergic reactions")

   B) Lines 31-33 ("This can be . . . school cafeteria")

   C) Lines 47-49 ("Some of the treatments . . . too much")

   D) Lines 80-83 ("From the results . . . a non-allergic person")

17. As used in line 56, "deactivating" most nearly means

   A) restricting.

   B) hindering.

   C) disabling.

   D) arresting.

18. It can be reasonably inferred from both the evidence in the passage and the data in the graph that

   A) of the peanuts tested, those exposed to pulses of light for the shortest periods of time contained the lowest amounts of the protein that acts as an allergen.

   B) of the peanuts tested, those exposed to pulses of light for the longest periods of time contained the lowest amounts of the protein that acts as an allergen.

   C) of the peanuts tested, those exposed to pulses of light for the longest periods of time contained the highest amounts of the protein that acts as an allergen.

   D) the amount of time a peanut was exposed to pulses of light had little to no effect on the amounts of the protein that acts an allergen.

19. According to the passage, why did scientists measure how much IgE combined with peanut protein in a lab test instead of measuring the allergic reaction in people?

    A) They could not find enough people allergic to peanuts to create a large enough sample.

    B) The lab tests gave more accurate and reliable data than experiments with people.

    C) It would be unsafe to provoke a potentially fatal allergic response in a person.

    D) The scientists conducted tests on people before the lab tests began.

20. Paragraphs 6 and 7 can best be described as

    A) a suggestion on how scientists can more productively study how people who are allergic to peanuts are affected by the IgE antibodies.

    B) a description of how some treatments of peanuts aimed at deactivating the allergens in peanuts affect the taste of the peanut.

    C) a summary of one method of treating peanuts scientists hope can reduce the allergic response in people who are allergic to peanuts.

    D) an explanation of how the chemical structure of peanuts can be altered by small genetic changes to the plant.

21. The purpose of the last paragraph is to

    A) describe the next steps scientists might take toward creating a safer environment for peanut allergy sufferers.

    B) persuade the reader to learn more about peanut allergies and how scientists are working to help those who suffer from allergies.

    C) explain how future experiments on peanut proteins could provide clues to helping people who suffer from other food allergies.

    D) summarize the results of the experiments on peanuts described in detail throughout the passage.

Final paragraph.

CHAPTER 20

Reading Closely

CHAPTER OBJECTIVES

By the end of this chapter, you will be able to:

1. Identify and answer questions that ask about explicit meanings within the passage
2. Identify and answer questions that ask about implicit meanings within the passage
3. Identify analogies and use analogical reasoning to answer test-like questions

SMARTPOINTS

Point Value	SmartPoint Category
20 Points	Detail
40 Points	Inference

DETAIL QUESTIONS

Detail questions ask about a specific part of the passage. Because your Passage Map should note only the *location* of key details rather than the details themselves, you will have to refer to the passage to answer these questions.

You can recognize Detail questions because they normally include line references or phrasing that directs you to a particular part of the passage.

When answering Detail questions:

- Read around the cited text to understand the context.

- Predict by rephrasing the relevant section in your own words.

- Eliminate any answer choices that do not match your prediction.

Also, make sure to read answer choices carefully. Watch out for negatives such as *not* and *no* that change an otherwise correct answer choice into the opposite of what you are looking for.

> ✔ **Expert Tip**
>
> **Watch out for misused details—details that are in the passage but do not answer the question.**

INFERENCE QUESTIONS: IMPLICIT MEANINGS

Implicit Meanings questions ask you to find something that must be true based on the passage but is not directly stated in the passage. The answer will be in the text, but you will need to read between the lines to find it.

To answer these questions efficiently and effectively, you must not only use your Passage Map but also fully utilize Step 3 of the Kaplan Method for Reading Comprehension: Predict and answer. If you need to review the Kaplan Method for Reading Comprehension, please turn to chapter 18.

There are two types of inferences that can be derived from questions asking about implicit meanings:

1. **Narrow Inferences** refer to specific parts of the passage. To answer these questions, find the relevant details and look for clues indicating how the author connects these details. Then, make a general prediction based on how the details are connected.

These questions will use phrasing such as:

- In lines xx-xx, the author implies that . . .

- The author strongly suggests that . . .

- It can be reasonably inferred that . . .

2. **Broad Inferences** ask about what can be inferred from the passage as a whole or what the author would generally agree with. To answer these questions, consider how the author's point of view limits the range of what could be true.

These questions will use phrasing such as:

- With which of the following statements would the author most likely agree?

- It can be inferred from the passage . . .

> ✔ **Expert Tip**
>
> An inference is NOT an opinion. It is a conclusion drawn from facts in the passage.

INFERENCE QUESTIONS: ANALOGICAL REASONING

Analogical Reasoning questions ask you to take ideas and information found in the passage and use an analogy to describe a new and parallel situation. In every Analogical Reasoning question, there is a strong connection between the two ideas. Identify that relationship and describe it in a short sentence.

You can recognize Analogical Reasoning questions because they normally include line references or phrasing such as "The situation described in line x is most comparable to . . ."

When answering Analogical Reasoning questions:

- Go to the cited lines and read around them to understand the context.

- Identify the relationship between the characters, the information, or the ideas cited in the question stem.

- Describe the relationship through characteristics (qualities that each idea possesses) and functions (roles played by each part).

- Look for the answer choice that describes a situation that is similar to the one in the passage.

Also, make sure to read answer choices carefully. Eliminate answer choices that include only one of the parts or have the parts in reverse order.

> ✔ **Remember**
>
> The question stem will describe the situation and tell you where to look for it in the passage. Always go back to the passage and find it.

Let's look at the following example of a test-like Science passage and question set. After the mapped passage, the left column contains questions similar to those you'll see on the Reading Test on Test Day. The column on the right features the strategic thinking a test expert employs when approaching the passage and questions presented. Pay attention to how a test expert varies his or her approach to the different question types.

Strategic Thinking
Step 1: Read actively
Read the passage and the notes provided. Remember, a well-crafted Passage Map should summarize the central idea of each paragraph as well as important topics or themes. Use your Passage Map to help you answer each question.

Questions 1-3 are based on the following passage.

This passage looks into the effects of and interactions between light and color and the resulting types of luminescence.

Atoms can be excited in many ways other than by absorbing a photon. The element phosphorous spontaneously combines with oxygen when
Line exposed to air. There is a transfer of energy to the
5 phosphorous electrons during this chemical reaction, which excites them to sufficiently high energy states so that they can subsequently emit light when dropping into a lower state. This is an example of what is termed chemiluminescence, the emission of
10 light as a result of chemical reaction.

A related effect is bioluminescence, when light is produced by chemical reactions associated with biological activity. Bioluminescence occurs in a variety of life forms and is more common in marine
15 organisms than in terrestrial or freshwater life. Examples include certain bacteria, jellyfish, clams, fungi, worms, ants, and fireflies. There is considerable diversity in how light is produced. Most processes involve the reaction of a protein with oxygen,
20 catalyzed by an enzyme. The protein varies from one organism to another, but all are grouped under the generic name luciferin. The enzymes are known as luciferase. Both words stem from the Latin *lucifer* meaning light-bearing. The various chemical steps

25 leading to bioluminescence are yet to be explained in detail, but in some higher organisms the process is known to be activated by the nervous system.

The firefly is best understood. Its light organ is located near the end of the abdomen. Within it luciferin
30 is combined with other atomic groups in a series of processes in which oxygen is converted into carbon dioxide. The sequence culminates when the luciferin is split off from the rest, leaving it in an excited state. The excess energy is released as a photon. The peak in the
35 emission spectrum lies between 550 and 600 nm depending on the type of luciferase. This flash produced by the simultaneous emission of many photons serves to attract mates, and females also use it to attract males of other species, which they devour.

40 Certain bacteria also produce light when stimulated by motion. This is why the breaking sea or a passing boat generates the greenish light seen in some bodies of water such as Phosphorescent Bay in Puerto Rico. Some fish have a symbiotic rela-
45 tionship with bacteria. The "flashlight fish" takes advantage of the light created by bacteria lodged beneath each eye. Certain other fish produce their own bioluminescence, which serves as identification. However, the biological advantage, if any, of
50 bioluminescence in some other organisms such as fungi remains a mystery.

[Margin notes:]

chemilum. def.

biolum. = common in marine life

how biolum. produces light

firefly → used for mating

bacteria & fish exs.

bio adv. of biolum unknown for some

Triboluminescence is the emission of light when one hard object is sharply struck against another. This contact, when atom scrapes against atom,
55 excites electrons and disrupts electrical bonds. Light is then created when the electrons find their way to lower states. Triboluminescence is not to be confused with the glow of small particles that may be broken off by the impact. Such "sparks" are seen
60 as a result of their high temperature. Light given off by hot objects is known as thermoluminescence, or incandescence.

Another form of thermoluminescence is the basis for dating ancient ceramic objects. Quartz and
65 other constituents of clay are continually irradiated by naturally occurring radioactive elements (e.g., uranium and thorium) and by cosmic rays. This produces defects in the material where electrons may be trapped. Heating pottery to 500°C releases
70 the trapped electrons, which can then migrate back to their original atoms, where on returning to an

atomic orbit they then emit a photon. The intensity of thermoluminescence is therefore a measure of the duration of irradiation since the time when the
75 pottery had been previously fired.

Excitation is also possible by other means. The passage of an electrical current (electrolumines-cence) is one. The impact of high-energy particles is another. The aurora borealis and its southern coun-
80 terpart the aurora australis, arise when a stream of high-energy particles from the sun enters the Earth's upper atmosphere and literally shatters some of the molecules in the air. This leaves their atoms in excited states, and the light subsequently given off
85 is characteristic of the atoms. Although the oxygen molecule, a major constituent of our atmosphere, has no emission in the visible spectrum, the oxygen atom can emit photons in either the red or green portions of the spectrum. Other atoms contribute
90 to light at other wavelengths.

tribolum. vs thermolum.

thermolum. = used for dating

aurora bo-realis

Questions	Strategic Thinking
1. The statement "the emission spectrum lies between 550 and 600 nm" in lines 34-35 most strongly suggests that the spectrum A) contains mostly ultraviolet light. B) requires special equipment to detect. C) is produced only by fireflies. D) is visible to a variety of insects.	**Step 2: Examine the question stem** The key words and phrases in this question stem are the cited phrase and "most strongly suggests." The cited lines are from paragraph 3, which your Passage Map notes details the example of the firefly. **Step 3: Predict and answer** The emission spectrum in the cited phrase refers to light produced by fireflies. This light is used to attract mates and prey. Therefore, you can infer that if insects are attracted to the spectrum, they must be able to see it. Choice (D) matches this prediction.

Questions	Strategic Thinking
2. According to the passage, "bioluminescence," line 11, is more often found A) with oxygen when exposed to the air. B) among terrestrial creatures. C) in marine life. D) in light given off by hot objects.	**Step 2: Examine the question stem** The key words and phrases in the question stem are "according to the passage," the quoted word, and its line reference. The Passage Map notes for the second paragraph, where the quoted word in the question stem ("bioluminescence") is first mentioned, will help you answer the question. **Step 3: Predict and answer** The first Passage Map note for paragraph 2 says that bioluminescence is common in marine life. Choice (C) matches this statement.
3. Which of the following situations most closely parallels the description of the excitation caused by the impact of high-energy particles in lines 76-85? A) A bowling ball striking bowling pins B) A raindrop hitting the pavement C) A prism reflecting light D) A goalie stopping a shot	**Step 2: Examine the question stem** The key words and phrases in the question stem are "most closely parallels" and the line numbers of the cited description. The Passage Map for the last paragraph will help you answer this question. **Step 3: Predict and answer** The last paragraph is about the excitation caused by the impact of high-energy particles. According to the passage, the "stream of high-energy particles . . . literally shatters some of the molecules in the air" (lines 80-83). Choice (A) is most similar to this description.

10/10/16.

You have now seen how to approach Detail questions and two kinds of Inference questions.

Look at the test-like History/Social Studies passage that follows. There are three questions associated with it—one of each kind reviewed in this chapter. Part of the passage has been mapped already. Your first step is to complete the Passage Map. Then, use the Kaplan Method for Reading Comprehension and the strategies discussed in this chapter to answer the questions. Strategic thinking questions have been included to guide you—some of the answers have been filled in, but you will have to fill in the answers to others.

Use your answers to the strategic thinking questions to select the correct answer, just as you will on Test Day.

Strategic Thinking

Step 1: Read actively

The passage below is partially mapped. Read the passage and the first part of the Passage Map. Then, complete the Passage Map on your own. Remember to focus on the central ideas of each paragraph as well as the central idea of the overall passage. Use your Passage Map as a reference when you're answering questions.

Questions 4-6 are based on the following passage.

The following passage describes findings regarding American colonists based on archeological explorations at Jamestown, Virginia.

Archaeological explorations at <u>Jamestown, Virginia</u>, have brought to light thousands of <u>colonial period artifacts</u> that were used by the Virginia
Line settlers from 1607 until 1699. A study of these
5 objects, which were buried under the soil at Jamestown for decades, reveals in many ways <u>how the English colonists lived on a small wilderness island over 300 years ago.</u> Artifacts unearthed include building materials and handwrought hardware,
10 kitchen utensils and fireplace accessories, furniture hardware, and many items relating to household and town industries.

These artifacts provide valuable information <u>concerning the everyday life and manners</u> of the
15 first Virginia settlers. Excavated artifacts reveal that the Jamestown colonists built their houses in the same style as those they knew in England, insofar

as local materials permitted. There were differences, (however,) for the settlers were in a land replete with
20 vast forests and untapped natural resources close at hand that they used to their advantage.

The Virginia known to the first settlers was a carpenter's paradise, and (consequently) the early buildings were the work of artisans in wood. The
25 first rude shelter, split-wood fencing, clapboard roof, puncheon floors, cupboards, benches, stools, and wood plows are all examples of skilled working with wood.

Timber at Jamestown was plentiful, so many
30 houses, especially in the early years, were of frame construction. During the first decade or two, <u>house construction reflected a primitive use of materials found ready at hand,</u> such as saplings for a sort of framing, and use of branches, leafage, bark, and
35 animal skins. During these early years, when the settlers were having such a difficult time staying alive, mud walls, wattle-and-daub, and coarse marsh-grass thatch were used. Out of these years

artif. show how col. lived

clues abt. life

ex's of woodwork-ing

early structures = primitive

of improvising, construction with squatted posts,
40 and later with studs, came into practice. There was
probably little thought of plastering walls during
the first two decades. When plastering was adopted,
clay, either by itself or mixed with oyster-shell lime,
was first used. The early floors were of clay, and
45 such floors continued to be used in the humbler
dwellings throughout the 1600s. It can be assumed
that most of the dwellings, or shelters, of the early
Jamestown settlers had a rough and primitive
appearance.
50   After Jamestown had attained some degree of
permanency, many houses were built of brick. It is
quite clear from documentary records and archeological remains that the colonists not only made
their own brick but also that the process, as well as
55 the finished products, followed closely the English
method. Four brick kilns were discovered on Jamestown Island during archeological explorations.
     While some of the handwrought hardware found
at Jamestown was made in the colony, most of it
60 was imported from England. Types of building
hardware unearthed include an excellent assort-
ment of nails, spikes, staples, locks, keys, hinges,
pintles, shutter fasteners, bolts, hasps, latches, door
knockers, door pulls, bootscrapes, gutter supports,
65 wall anchors, and ornamental hardware. In many

instances, each type is represented by several variet-
ies. It is believed that wooden hardware was used
on many of the early houses.
     A few glass windowpanes may have been made
70 in the Jamestown glass factory, which was built in
1608. Most of the window glass used in the colony,
however, was shipped from England. Many of the
early panes used were diamond-shaped pieces
known as "quarrels" and were held in place by
75 means of slotted lead strips known as "cames." The
window frames used in a few of the Jamestown
houses were handwrought iron casements. Most
of the humbler dwellings had no glass panes in the
windows. The window openings were closed by bat-
80 ten shutters, operated by hinges of wood, and fitted
with wooden fastening devices.
     Busy conquering a stubborn wilderness, the first
Jamestown settlers had only a few things to make
their homes cozy and cheerful. In most cases, their
85 worldly goods consisted of a few cooking utensils, a change of clothing, a weapon or two, and a
few pieces of handmade furniture. After the early
years of hardship had passed, the colonists began
to acquire possessions for more pleasant living; by
90 1650 the better houses were equipped with most of
the necessities of life of those times, as well as a few
luxuries of comfortable living.

Don't get distracted by less important details. While there is a lot going on in this passage, your additions to the Passage Map should have noted the evolution of building practices, bricks, furniture, and
glass. If you're stuck, review the example Passage Map in the Answers & Explanations for this chapter
on page 1007.

Questions	Strategic Thinking
4. The statement in lines 40-42 ("There was ...decades") suggests that the Jamestown colonists A) followed London fashions. B) lacked the resources to import the raw materials from England. C) focused their energies on survival, not on decoration. D) hesitated to build more permanent homes until bricks were available.	**Step 2: Examine the question stem** The key words and phrases in this question stem are the cited statement with its corresponding line numbers and the word "suggests." **Step 3: Predict and answer** *Read around the cited lines. Why was there "little thought of plastering walls during the first two decades" (lines 41-42)?* _____ _____ _____ _____ _____ _____ *Which answer choice matches this prediction?* _____

Questions	Strategic Thinking
5. All of the following are true about the Jamestown colonists EXCEPT A) some of them were skilled wood-workers. (B) they struggled to survive in the early decades. C) they made floors out of clay. D) they constructed most of their own hardware.	**Step 2: Examine the question stem** *What are the key words and phrases in this question stem?* _____ _____ _____ _____ *What parts of your Passage Map are relevant?* _____ _____ _____ _____ **Step 3: Predict and answer** *Is A mentioned in the passage? If so, where?* _____ *Is B mentioned in the passage? If so, where?* _____ *Is C mentioned in the passage? If so, where?* _____ *Is D mentioned in the passage? If so, where?* _____ *Which answer choice is not mentioned in the passage and is therefore correct?* _____

Questions	Strategic Thinking

6. The description of the Jamestown colonists' brick industry, as discussed in lines 50-57, is most comparable to
 	
  A) traditional weavers making cloth with imported cotton.
 	
  B) mountain climbers carrying all of their food and shelter on their expedition.
 	
  C) pioneer farmers bringing seeds and agricultural techniques to new lands.
 	
  D) an immigrant chef using local ingredients to make recipes from her homeland.
	Step 2: Examine the question stem
	
	What are the key words and phrases in this question stem?
	
	_____
	_____
	_____
	_____
	
	What parts of your Passage Map are relevant?
	
	_____
	_____
	_____
	_____
	
	Step 3: Predict and answer
	
	How do the cited lines describe the brick industry?
	
	_____
	_____
	_____
	_____
	_____
	
	Which answer choice is most similar to this process?
	
	_____

Now, use the strategies you learned about in this chapter to answer questions for a U.S. and World Literature passage. Give yourself 6 minutes to read and map the passage and answer the questions.

Questions 7-10 are based on the following passage.

The following passage is an excerpt from "The Murders in the Rue Morgue," a short story by Edgar Allan Poe published in 1841.

Our first meeting was at an obscure library in the Rue Montmartre, where the accident of our both being in search of the same very rare and
Line very remarkable volume, brought us into closer
5 communion. We saw each other again and again. I was deeply interested in the little family history which he detailed to me with all that candor which a Frenchman indulges whenever mere self is the theme. I was astonished too, at the vast extent of
10 his reading; and, above all, I felt my soul enkindled within me by the wild fervor, and the vivid freshness of his imagination. Seeking in Paris the objects I then sought, I felt that the society of such a man would be to me a treasure beyond price; and this
15 feeling I frankly confided to him. It was at length arranged that we should live together during my stay in the city; and as my worldly circumstances were somewhat less embarrassed than his own, I was permitted to be at the expense of renting, and
20 furnishing in a style which suited the rather fantastic gloom of our common temper, a time-eaten and grotesque mansion, long deserted through superstitions into which we did not inquire, and tottering to its fall in a retired and desolate portion of the
25 Faubourg St. Germain.

Had the routine of our life at this place been known to the world, we should have been regarded as madmen—although, perhaps, as madmen of a harmless nature. Our seclusion was perfect. We
30 admitted no visitors. Indeed the locality of our retirement had been carefully kept a secret from my own former associates; and it had been many years since Dupin had ceased to know or be known in Paris. We existed within ourselves alone.

35 It was a freak of fancy in my friend (for what else shall I call it?) to be enamored of the Night for her own sake; and into this bizarrerie, as into all his others, I quietly fell; giving myself up to his wild whims with a perfect abandon. The sable divinity would not
40 herself dwell with us always; but we could counterfeit her presence. At the first dawn of the morning we closed all the massy shutters of our old building; lighted a couple of tapers which, strongly perfumed, threw out only the ghastliest and feeblest of rays. By
45 the aid of these we then busied our souls in dreams— reading, writing, or conversing, until warned by the clock of the advent of the true Darkness. Then we sallied forth into the streets, arm and arm, continuing the topics of the day, or roaming far and wide
50 until a late hour, seeking, amid the wild lights and shadows of the populous city that infinity of mental excitement which quiet observation can afford.

At such times I could not help remarking and admiring (although from his rich ideality I had been
55 prepared to expect it) a peculiar analytic ability in Dupin. He seemed, too, to take an eager delight in its exercise—if not exactly in its display—and did not hesitate to confess the pleasure thus derived. He boasted to me, with a low chuckling laugh, that most
60 men, in respect to himself, wore windows in their bosoms, and was wont to follow up such assertions by direct and very startling proofs of his intimate knowledge of my own. His manner at these moments was frigid and abstract; his eyes were
65 vacant in expression; while his voice, usually a rich tenor rose into a treble which would have sounded petulantly but for the deliberateness and entire distinctness of the enunciation. Observing him in these moods, I often dwelt meditatively upon the old
70 philosophy of the Bi-Part soul, and amused myself with the fancy of a double Dupin—the creative and the resolvent.

7. The statement in lines 17-18 ("my worldly . . . his own") suggests that

   A) Dupin wishes his family history were different.

   B) the narrator was more self-confident about his own wealth.

   C) Dupin was less well-off than the narrator.

   D) the narrator led an exemplary life.

8. In the third paragraph, the relationship between the narrator and Dupin most closely parallels which of the following situations?

   A) Two scientists collaborating on a research project

   B) A professor instructing a new student

   C) An art student adapting a teacher's techniques in a new way

   D) A fan dressing and acting like a pop star

9. According to the passage, the narrator and Dupin met because they

   A) lived in the Rue Montmartre.

   B) wanted to find the same book.

   C) preferred the night to the day.

   D) enjoyed solitude.

10. The narrator would most likely agree with which of the following statements?

    A) Dupin understood other people's inner thoughts in ways the narrator could not comprehend.

    B) Dupin was a humorously eccentric character given to flights of fancy.

    C) Dupin enjoyed entertaining groups of other fashionable Parisians.

    D) Dupin represented an obscure aspect of French society that the narrator wished to study.

Answers & Explanations for this chapter appear on page 1007.

EXTRA PRACTICE

Required	Recommended
Questions 1–11	Questions 12–21

Questions 1-11 are based on the following passages and supplementary material.

The following passages detail different aspects of the United States National Parks System.

Passage 1

In the mid- to late nineteenth century, America legislated an idea that would come to be emulated worldwide: the National Parks System. Starting
Line with Yellowstone National Park in 1872, the United
5 States government sparked a national and international trend of setting aside treasured spaces for preservation, protection, and public enjoyment. Since then, over 400 national parks have been established in American states and territories, and
10 globally over a thousand parks are now protected by similar systems in their respective nations.

The United States National Park Service (NPS) is responsible for managing and protecting these parks. Set up by President Wilson in 1916, this
15 federal organization oversees budgeting, care, advocacy, and education for the country's parks. As a piece of legislation enacted in 1933, the NPS includes landmarks of historic and scientific significance in addition to those significant for their
20 sheer natural beauty or unique wildlife populations. There are now 84 million acres of United States national parkland (and water). Thousands of employees and millions of volunteers work with the NPS to accomplish its vast responsibilities. From
25 national monuments and battlegrounds, to the breathtaking vistas of the Great Smoky Mountains, Alaska's Glacier Bay, and even underwater snorkeling trails in the U.S. Virgin Islands, spaces marked with awe and meaning are preserved for the enjoy-
30 ment of generations to come.

Today, more than 275 million people visit America's national parks yearly. They come prepared to be amazed; the stunning beauty, powerful history, and inspiring intricacies of nature they en-
35 counter never disappoint. And America's great idea, in which over a hundred countries now participate, enables that amazement to be spread and shared across nations and generations. The National Park System teaches and invites people worldwide to
40 practice preservation in their daily lives by making choices to protect the earth's wonders and treasures.

Passage 2

John Muir, often called "Father of the National Park System," was America's most famous and influential naturalist. Born in 1838, he bore witness
45 to the establishment of the first national parks and the many visions, debates, and victories of the early environmentalist movement. Muir was a man of many talents. He began his career working in carriage production but soon chose a life of explor-
50 ing the nation's spectacular wilderness, traveling thousands of miles by foot and across oceans. From relative anonymity as a wayfarer, shepherd, and mill laborer, Muir would soon become a national hero whose widely read writings would drive govern-
55 ment policy makers to action.

When Muir encountered California's Yosemite Valley and the greater Sierra Nevada mountains, he immediately recognized their worth. He saw in them not only astounding scenic beauty, but also
60 crucial ecological significance. Over the rest of his life, he would advocate for their protection. Yet his interest would stretch far beyond the Sierras. Muir regularly traversed California's forested mountains and made a home in Yosemite Valley, but his
65 activism and wanderlust also drew him to other picturesque locations, such as Washington's Mount

Rainier and Alaska's coast and glaciers. He published hundreds of articles documenting his travels.
These invoked the wonder of the natural beauty he
70 witnessed, channeling that marvel into the hearts of
readers nationwide.

The political impact of Muir's life was immense.
His publications were elemental in persuading the
United States government to establish Yosemite,
75 Sequoia, the Grand Canyon, and Mount Rainier
as national parks. His relationship with Theodore
Roosevelt was foundational to the environmental
policies and gains made during Roosevelt's presidency; Muir's relentless advocacy for protecting the
80 Sierras catalyzed and empowered a movement that
would carry through the coming centuries. Much of
this advocacy manifested itself in Muir's founding
of a political activist organization called the Sierra
Club. Internationally this group was one of the first
85 of its kind, and it remains one of the nation's leading environmental organizations.

However, perhaps ever greater than Muir's
political accomplishments was his ideological
impact. His unforgettable philosophies about the
90 importance of nature reminded Americans that the
wild was worth cherishing and saving, even at the
expense of short-lived material gains for which it
might be exchanged. Muir's legacy has invited and
inspired billions of people worldwide to guard the
95 global ecosystem, and to go out and enjoy it all.

**Average Yearly Visitation to Popular
National Parks in America**

Years of Park Operation

Yearly Visitors (in millions)

Key
Grand Canyon National Park
Great Smoky Mountains National Park
Olympic National Park

1. As used in line 2, "emulated" most nearly
   means
   A) admired.
   B) feared.
   C) imitated.
   D) invented.

2. What is the most likely purpose of the
   second paragraph of Passage 1?
   A) To describe the impressive scale of
      the National Parks System
   B) To show that national parks have
      become popular despite early setbacks
   C) To argue that national parks are valu-
      able because of their aesthetic value
   D) To defend the existence of national
      parks against critics of their eco-
      nomic cost

3. What can be most strongly concluded
   about the United States National Parks
   System from Passage 1?
   A) It is more popular with visitors today
      than it was initially.
   B) Its accomplishments have historically
      been controversial.
   C) It is the most popular service provided
      by the American government.
   D) Its ideas about conservation have
      been influential internationally.

4. Which choice provides the best evidence
   for the answer to the previous question?
   A) Lines 14-16 ("Set up . . . country's
      parks")
   B) Lines 22-24 ("Thousands of . . . vast
      responsibilities")
   C) Lines 31-32 ("Today more than . . .
      yearly")
   D) Lines 35-38 ("And America's . . . and
      generations")

5. As used in line 65, "wanderlust" most likely means

    A) an interest in travel.

    B) an inability to concentrate.

    C) a love of diversity.

    D) a desire for the countryside.

6. What does the use of the word "channeling" in line 70 suggest about Muir's writings?

    A) They were focused on his spiritual connection with nature.

    B) They were emotionally moving to his readers.

    C) They were entertaining in a manner similar to television.

    D) They were strident and opinionated.

7. With which statement would the author of Passage 2 most likely agree?

    A) The preservation of the wilderness came at an economic cost.

    B) John Muir's contributions were largely unrecognized during his life.

    C) Many naturalists were important in creating the national parks system.

    D) The most important work John Muir did was in helping create government policy.

8. Which choice provides the best evidence for the answer to the previous question?

    A) Lines 73-76 ("His publications . . . national parks")

    B) Lines 76-81 ("His relationship . . . coming centuries")

    C) Lines 87-89 ("However . . . ideological impact")

    D) Lines 89-93 ("His unforgettable . . . exchanged")

9. How do the central ideas of the two passages primarily differ?

    A) Passage 1 describes the parks system generally, while Passage 2 focuses on its founding.

    B) Passage 1 argues that the parks system is underappreciated, while Passage 2 celebrates it as a national treasure beloved by many.

    C) Passage 1 focuses on the parks system's creation, while Passage 2 focuses on its structure.

    D) Passage 1 describes the idea of national parks, while Passage 2 focuses specifically on how the idea was applied in the United States.

10. The authors of both passages would most likely agree that the most important role of national parks is to

    A) preserve natural beauty so it can inspire visitors.

    B) allow city residents to escape polluted environments.

    C) instill a sense of patriotism in those who spend time there.

    D) help foster economic development through the use of public lands.

11. What conclusion can be drawn from the graph?

A) The population of the United States has doubled since 1930.

B) Olympic National Park is in a location difficult for most visitors to access.

C) The Great Smoky Mountains National Park has become less popular since its inception.

D) The Grand Canyon has consistently been a more popular destination than the Olympic National Park.

Questions 12-21 are based on the following passage.

This passage is adapted from Jane Austen's Sense and Sensibility.

Before the house-maid had lit their fire the next day, or the sun gained any power over a cold, gloomy morning in January, Marianne, only half dressed,
Line was kneeling against one of the window-seats for the
5 sake of all the little light she could command from it, and writing as fast as a continual flow of tears would permit her. In this situation, Elinor, roused from sleep by her agitation and sobs, first perceived her; and after observing her for a few moments with silent anxiety,
10 said, in a tone of the most considerate gentleness,
    "Marianne, may I ask-?"
    "No, Elinor," she replied, "ask nothing; you will soon know all."
    The sort of desperate calmness with which this
15 was said, lasted no longer than while she spoke, and was immediately followed by a return of the same excessive affliction. It was some minutes before she could go on with her letter, and the frequent bursts of grief which still obliged her, at intervals, to with-
20 hold her pen, were proofs enough of her feeling how more than probable it was that she was writing for the last time to Willoughby.
    At breakfast she neither ate, nor attempted to eat any thing; and Elinor's attention was then all
25 employed, not in urging her, not in pitying her, nor in appearing to regard her, but in endeavouring to engage Mrs. Jennings's notice entirely to herself.
    As this was a favourite meal with Mrs. Jennings, it lasted a considerable time, and they were just
30 setting themselves, after it, round the common working table, when a letter was delivered to Mari-anne, which she eagerly caught from the servant, and, turning of a death-like paleness, instantly ran out of the room. Elinor, who saw as plainly by this,
35 as if she had seen the direction, that it must come from Willoughby, felt immediately such a sickness at heart as made her hardly able to hold up her head, and sat in such a general tremour as made her fear it impossible to escape Mrs. Jennings's notice.
40 That good lady, however, saw only that Marianne had received a letter from Willoughby, which appeared to her a very good joke, and which she treated accordingly, by hoping, with a laugh, that she would find it to her liking. Of Elinor's distress,
45 she was too busily employed in measuring lengths of worsted for her rug, to see any thing at all; and calmly continuing her talk, as soon as Marianne disappeared, she said,
    "Upon my word, I never saw a young woman so
50 desperately in love in my life! MY girls were noth-ing to her, and yet they used to be foolish enough; but as for Miss Marianne, she is quite an altered creature. I hope, from the bottom of my heart, he won't keep her waiting much longer, for it is quite
55 grievous to see her look so ill and forlorn. Pray, when are they to be married?"
    Elinor, though never less disposed to speak than at that moment, obliged herself to answer such an attack as this, and, therefore, trying to smile,
60 replied, "And have you really, Ma'am, talked yourself into a persuasion of my sister's being engaged to Mr. Willoughby? I thought it had been only a joke, but so serious a question seems to imply more; and I must beg, therefore, that you will not deceive your-
65 self any longer. I do assure you that nothing would surprise me more than to hear of their being going to be married."

"For shame, for shame, Miss Dashwood! how can you talk so? Don't we all know that it must be
70 a match, that they were over head and ears in love with each other from the first moment they met? Did not I see them together in Devonshire every day, and all day long; and did not I know that your sister came to town with me on purpose to buy wedding
75 clothes? Come, come, this won't do. Because you are so sly about it yourself, you think nobody else has any senses; but it is no such thing, I can tell you, for it has been known all over town this ever so long. I tell every body of it and so does Charlotte."

80 "Indeed, Ma'am," said Elinor, very seriously, "you are mistaken. Indeed, you are doing a very unkind thing in spreading the report, and you will find that you have though you will not believe me now."

12. As used in line 57, "disposed" most nearly means

   A) capable.

   B) inclined.

   C) shed.

     permitted.

13. In line 33, the author describes Marianne as "turning of a death-like paleness" in order to emphasize

   A) her comical overreaction to an every-day event.

   B) the anxiety she feels about the letter's contents.

   C) the supernatural elements that surround the house.

   D) her knowledge that the letter contains news of illness.

14. The passage most strongly suggests which of the following about Elinor's feelings toward Marianne?

   A) Elinor feels protective of Marianne.

   B) Elinor is sad that they are not closer.

   C) Elinor is jealous of Marianne's success in life.

   D) Elinor considers them to be rivals in matters of love.

15. Which choice provides the best evidence for the answer to the previous question?

   A) Lines 14-17 ("The sort . . . excessive affliction")

   B) Lines 23-27 ("At breakfast . . . entirely to herself")

   C) Lines 53-55 ("I hope . . . ill and forlorn")

   D) Lines 62-65 ("I thought . . . any longer'")

16. Which statement does the passage most strongly suggest is true of Mrs. Jennings?

   A) She does not have many people with whom to talk.

   B) She knows the intimate details of Marianne's feelings.

   C) She is not very perceptive about the events around her.

   D) She has spoken to Willoughby more recently than Marianne has.

10/15/16

17. Which choice provides the best evidence for the answer to the previous question?

A) Lines 23-27 ("At breakfast . . . to herself")

B) Lines 28-34 ("As this was . . . of the room")

C) Lines 44-46 ("Of Elinor's . . . any thing at all")

D) Lines 49-50 ("Upon my word . . . in my life")

18. As used in line 61, "persuasion" most nearly means

A) argument.

B) belief.

C) excitement.

D) joke.

19. According to the passage, Mrs. Jennings believes that

A) Willoughby intends to marry Marianne.

B) Elinor is overreacting to Willoughby's letter.

C) Marianne loves someone other than Willoughby.

D) Elinor is mistaken about why Marianne is upset.

20. Based on the information in the passage, Marianne's situation can most directly be compared to that of

A) a stray cat who shows affection to strangers in hopes of being fed.

B) a person who cultivates charm in order to compensate for a lack of physical beauty.

C) a scientist working on an ambitious project in which only she has faith.

D) a worker who has not been hired for a job she was certain she would get.

21. What is the author's most likely purpose in providing the last paragraph of dialogue?

A) To help readers understand why Marianne is so upset

B) To demonstrate the degree of Elinor's concern about Marianne

C) To argue that Mrs. Jennings's understanding of the situation may be accurate

D) To persuade readers that Marianne is not entirely innocent

CHAPTER 21

Citing Textual Evidence and Determining Central Ideas & Themes

CHAPTER OBJECTIVES

By the end of this chapter, you will be able to:

1. Locate appropriate textual evidence to support the answer to a previous question

2. Summarize the passage or key information and ideas within the passage

3. Identify central ideas and themes of a passage to answer questions about central ideas and themes

SMARTPOINTS

Point Value	SmartPoint Category
20 Points	Global
70 Points	Command of Evidence

GLOBAL QUESTIONS

Global questions require you to both identify explicit and determine implicit central ideas or themes in a text. If you pay attention to the big picture—the author's central idea and purpose—while reading SAT Reading passages, you will be able to answer Global questions with little to no rereading of the passage. To fully understand the central ideas and themes of a passage, you must synthesize the different points the author makes with his or her thesis statement, which you should underline when Passage Mapping.

Global questions may also ask you to choose a correct summary of the passage as a whole or key information and ideas within the passage. When presented with this type of Global question, you can use your Passage Map, which is essentially a brief summary of what you have read.

> ### ✔ On Test Day
>
> The italicized portion at the beginning of an SAT Reading passage can be very helpful in determining the author's central ideas and themes. Make sure you take the time on Test Day to read this information—it orients you to the passage.

You can recognize Global questions because they typically do not reference line numbers or even individual paragraphs. To confidently answer Global questions, you need to not only identify the central idea or theme of the passage but also avoid choosing answers that summarize secondary or supplementary points.

Do note there is a slight difference between nonfiction and fiction passages. Science and History/Social Studies passages are nonfiction and will have a definite central idea and thesis statement; U.S. and World Literature passages are fiction and will have a central theme but no thesis statement.

> ### ✔ Remember
>
> History/Social Studies and Science passages on the SAT Reading Test are just well-written essays or article excerpts. You can normally find the thesis statement of a well-written piece at the end of the introductory paragraph.

COMMAND OF EVIDENCE QUESTIONS

A Command of Evidence question relies on your answer to the question that precedes it. These questions require you to identify the portion of the text that provides the best evidence for the conclusion you reached when selecting your answer to the previous question.

Kaplan's Strategy for Command of Evidence questions involves retracing your steps; that is, you must return to the previous question to ensure you answer the Command of Evidence question correctly. The question preceding a Command of Evidence question can be any other question type.

To answer Command of Evidence questions efficiently and correctly, employ the following Kaplan Strategy:

- When you see a question asking you to choose the best evidence to support your answer to the previous question, review how you selected that answer

- Avoid answers that provide evidence for incorrect answers to the previous question

- The correct answer will support why the previous question's answer is correct

✔ Expert Tip

You can recognize Command of Evidence questions easily. The question stem usually reads, "Which choice provides the best evidence for the answer to the previous question?" Furthermore, the answer choices are always line numbers with parentheses containing the first and last word of the intended selection. Answer choices are listed in the order they appear in the passage.

Command of Evidence questions ask that you cite the textual evidence that best supports a given claim or point. The given claim or point will be the correct answer choice to the previous question. Then, you will choose one of the four excerpts from the passage as the best evidence or support for that answer.

The first step to approaching a Command of Evidence question is to make sure you answered the previous question—no matter its type—correctly. If you answer the question preceding a Command of Evidence question incorrectly, you have a smaller chance of selecting the correct answer.

✔ Remember

There is no wrong answer penalty on the SAT, so even if you have no idea of how to approach a question, take your best guess and move on.

Let's look at the following example of a test-like U.S. and World Literature passage and question set. After the mapped passage, the left column contains questions similar to those you'll see on the Reading Test on Test Day. The column on the right features the strategic thinking a test expert employs when approaching the passage and questions presented. Pay attention to how a test expert varies his or her approach to the different question types.

10/12

Strategic Thinking

Step 1: Read actively

Read the passage and the notes provided. Remember, a well-crafted Passage Map should summarize the central idea of each paragraph as well as important topics or themes. Use your Passage Map to help you answer each question.

Questions 1-3 are based on the following passage.

The following is excerpted from Frederick Douglass's autobiographical Narrative of the Life of Frederick Douglass, An American Slave.

Mrs. helped FD read

His mistress had been severely reprimanded by her husband for helping Frederick Douglass learn to read. After all, the husband admonished, giving a
Line slave the knowledge to read was like giving the slave
5 access to thinking he or she was human. If you give the slaves an inch, they will take the ell.

Mr. = "slaves not human"

My mistress was, as I have said, a kind and tender-hearted woman; and in the simplicity of her soul she commenced, when I first went to live with

Mrs. = kind at first

10 her, to treat me as she supposed one human being ought to treat another. In entertaining upon the duties of a slaveholder, she did not seem to perceive that I sustained to her the relation of a mere chattel, and that for her to treat me as a human being

15 was not only wrong, but dangerously so. Slavery

BUT slavery hurt Mrs.

proved as injurious to her as it did to me. When I went there, she was a pious, warm, and tender-hearted woman. There was no sorrow or suffering for which she had not a tear. She had bread for

20 the hungry, clothes for the naked, and comfort for every mourner that came within her reach. Slavery soon proved its ability to divest her of these heavenly qualities. Under its influence, the tender heart

Mrs. became hard and mean

became stone, and the lamblike disposition gave

25 way to one of tiger-like fierceness. The first step in her downward course was in her ceasing to instruct me. She now commenced to practice her husband's precepts. She finally became even more violent in her opposition [to my learning to read] than her

30 husband himself. She was not satisfied with simply doing as well as he had commanded; she seemed anxious to do better. Nothing seemed to make her

more angry than to see me with a newspaper. She seemed to think that here lay the danger. I have had
35 her rush at me with a face made all up of fury, and snatch from me a newspaper, in a manner that fully revealed her apprehension. She was an apt woman;

Mrs. became as bad as Mr.

and a little experience soon demonstrated, to her satisfaction, that education and slavery were incom-
40 patible with each other.

From this time I was most narrowly watched. If I was in a separate room any considerable length of time, I was sure to be suspected of having a book, and was at once called to give an account of myself.
45 All this, however, was too late. The first step had been taken. Mistress, in teaching me the alphabet, had given me the inch, and no precaution could prevent me from taking the *ell.*

The plan which I adopted, and the one by which
50 I was most successful, was that of making friends of all the white children whom I met in the street. As

friends → teachers → full literacy

many of these as I could, I converted into teachers. With their kindly aid, obtained at different times and in different places, I finally succeeded
55 in learning to read. When I was sent on errands, I always took my book with me, and by going one part of my errand quickly, I found time to get a lesson before my return. I used also to carry bread with me, enough of which was always in the house,
60 and to which I was always welcome, for I was much better off in this regard than many of the poor

gave bread in exchg. for learning

white children in our neighborhood. This bread I used to bestow upon the hungry little urchins, who, in return, would give me that more valuable bread
65 of knowledge. I am strongly tempted to give the names of two or three of those children, as a testimonial of the gratitude and affection I bear

them; but prudence forbids;—not that it would injure me, but it might embarrass them; for it is al-
70 most a unpardonable offence to teach slaves to read in this Christian country. I used to talk this matter of slavery over with them. I would sometimes say

to them, I wished I could be as free as they would be when they got to be men. This used to trouble
75 them; they would express for me the liveliest sympathy, and console me with the hope that something would occur by which I might be free.

antislavery sentiment

Questions	Strategic Thinking
1. The main purpose of the passage is to A) emphasize the cruelty of slavery. B) refute the idea that education and slavery are incompatible. C) offer historical background to provide context for positions Douglass later espoused. D) describe the risks Douglass willingly took to learn to read.	**Step 2: Examine the question stem** Identify the keywords in the question stem. The words "main purpose" indicate that you will find the answer by using the entire Passage Map to summarize the central idea and purpose of the passage. **Step 3: Predict and answer** While the beginning of the passage discusses Douglass's relationship with his mistress, it is primarily about how Douglass learned to read despite his slave status. Choice (D) matches this prediction.
2. The statement in lines 15-16 ("Slavery proved … to me") suggests that A) the mistress and Douglass suffered equally from the institution of slavery. B) owning slaves destroyed the mistress's admirable human qualities. C) the mistress regretted the actions she was forced to take as a slave owner. D) Douglass pitied the mistress for the sacrifices she made.	**Step 2: Examine the question stem** Identify the keywords in the question stem: The line references and parenthetical quotation, as well as the phrase "suggests that." You can find your answer by using your Passage Map notes near lines 15-16, particularly those about the mistress, to answer the question. **Step 3: Predict and answer** In this section, the Passage Map notes about the mistress say that she was kind at first but slavery eventually was harmful to her as well because she became hard and mean. Choice (B) matches this prediction.

Questions	Strategic Thinking
3. Which choice provides the best evidence for the answer to the previous question? A) Lines 11-15 ("In entertaining … dangerously so") B) Lines 23-25 ("Under its … fierceness") C) Lines 41-44 ("If I … of myself") D) Lines 53-55 ("With their … to read")	**Step 2: Examine the question stem** This question stem indicates that you will need to choose the answer choice featuring the lines from the passage that best support your answer to the previous question. Use the Kaplan Strategy for Command of Evidence questions when you encounter this question stem. **Step 3: Predict and answer** You found the answer to the previous question—that owning slaves destroyed the mistress's admirable human qualities—by using the Passage Map notes surrounding the cited sentence in lines 15-16. The Passage Map says that the mistress became hard and mean. This is supported from line 21 through the end of the paragraph (line 40). Choice (B) is the only answer choice that falls within these lines and is therefore correct.

✔ Note

Remember the Kaplan Strategy for Command of Evidence questions: review how you selected the answer to the previous question and avoid answer choices that provide evidence for incorrect answer choices to it. The correct answer will support why the previous question's answer is correct.

You have now seen how to answer both Global and Command of Evidence questions.

Look at the test-like Science passage that follows. There are three questions associated with it. Part of the passage has been mapped already. Your first step is to complete the Passage Map. Then, use the Kaplan Method for Reading Comprehension and the strategies discussed in this chapter to answer the questions. Strategic thinking questions have been included to guide you—some of the answers have been filled in, but you will have to fill in the answers to others.

Use your answers to the strategic thinking questions to select the correct answer, just as you will on Test Day.

Strategic Thinking

Step 1: Read actively

The passage below is partially mapped. Read the passage and the first part of the Passage Map. Then, complete the Passage Map on your own. Remember to focus on the central ideas of each paragraph as well as the central idea of the overall passage. Use your Passage Map as a reference when you're answering questions.

Questions 4-6 are based on the following passage.

The following passage explains the challenges facing a population of trees and possible solutions.

Today, oaks are plagued with problems. There is lack of regeneration in populations of certain species. Pests such as the acorn weevil and the filbert
Line worm eat away at acorns and prevent germination.
5 By undermining the root systems of seedlings and saplings, ground squirrels, gophers, and other small mammals often prevent these young plants from reaching tree size. Severe diseases such as sudden oak death, kill many adult oaks. Many mature oaks
10 are having a tough time with fire suppression. In the past, with light surface fires, the oaks had been able to maintain a stronghold where other plants were not able to compete and died out. Now oaks are being toppled by trees that have a higher toler-
15 ance for shade and are not fire-resistant; earlier such trees would have been killed when Native Americans set fires.

oak problems: pests & disease, other trees

Given all of these challenges, the "old-growth" oaks—the large old valley oaks, Garry oaks, coast
20 live oaks, and canyon live oaks that have huge girth and large canopies—may become a thing of the past. These oaks in particular are important because there are often more terrestrial vertebrates living in mature oak stands than in seedling and sapling
25 areas. This prevalence of animals occurs because the large crowns of such oaks provide cover and feeding sites for a large variety of wildlife.

oaks may die out

The University of California has embarked on an ambitious and necessary research program called
30 the Integrated Hardwood Range Management Program to explore the significant causes of oak decline and offer varied solutions. These include

research into problems & solutions

investigating the use of grassing regimes that are compatible with oak seedling establishment, reveg-
35 etating sites with native grasses to facilitate better germination of oak seedlings, documenting insects and pathogens that attack oaks, and exploring the ways that native people managed oaks in the past. Scientists at the Pacific Northwest Research Station
40 in Olympia, Washington, and at Redwood National Park in northern California are reintroducing the burning practices of Native Americans. When used in Garry oak ecosystems, fires keep Douglas firs from encroaching on the oaks and promote
45 the growth of wildflowers that are important food plants. Further investigations about these fire practices may be essential in figuring out how to maintain oaks in the western landscape today, given that the fires address many of the factors that are
50 now causing oak decline—from how to eliminate insect pests of acorns to how to maintain an open structure in oak groves.

Nat. Am. approach

Ecological restoration, the traditional approach to woodland maintenance, refers to humans
55 intervening on a very limited time scale to bring back plants and animals known to have historically existed in an area. The decline of oaks, one of the most significant plants to Native Americans, shows us that humans may play an integral part in the
60 restoration of oak areas. While animals such as jays have been recognized as crucial partners in oak well-being, human actions through the eons may also have been key to the oaks' flourishing.

Sudden oak death, for example, although of
65 exotic origin, may be curtailed locally by thinning around coastal oaks and tan oaks and setting light surface fires, simulating ancient fire management

practices of Native Americans. Indigenous shrubs
and trees that grow in association with oaks
70 are hosts to the sudden oak death pathogen. By
limiting the growth of these shrubs, burning that
mimics earlier Native American ways may reduce
opportunities for disease agents to jump from
other plants to oak trees. With a more open envi-
75 ronment, it may be harder for sudden oak death to
spread.

The oak landscapes that we inherited, which
still bear the marks of former Native American
interactions, demand a new kind of restoration that
80 complements other forms of ecological restoration.
This new kind of restoration could be called ethnobotanical restoration, defined as reestablishing
the historic plant communities of a given area
and restoring indigenous harvesting, vegetation

85 management, and cultivation practices (seedbear-
ing, burning, pruning, sowing, tilling, and weeding)
necessary to maintain these communities in the
long term.

Thus, this kind of restoration is not only about
90 restoring plants but also about restoring the human
place within nature. Ethnobotanical restoration is
viewed not as a process that can be completed but
rather as a continuous interaction between people
and plants, as both of their fates are intertwined in
95 a region. Using oaks (through harvesting acorns
and making products from all parts of the tree) and
human intervention (by thinning tree populations
and lighting light fires) may offer us ways to benefi-
cially coexist while improving the long-term health
100 and well-being of the remarkable oak.

Don't get distracted by less important details. While there is a lot going on in this passage, your
additions to the Passage Map should note the views regarding human involvement in ecological
restoration as well as the definitions of unfamiliar terms like "ecological restoration" and "ethnobotanical restoration." If you're stuck, review the example Passage Map in the Answers & Explanations
for this chapter on page 1018.

Questions	Strategic Thinking
4. Throughout the passage, the author emphasizes that a key element in the restoration of the oak tree is (A) protecting the wildlife diversity found in the oaks' large crowns. B) preventing Douglas firs from encroaching on oak tree habitats. C) utilizing a continuous restoration process focused on human and oak interactions. D) curtailing sudden oak death by eliminating exotic pathogens.	**Step 2: Examine the question stem** *What are the key words and phrases in the question stem?* The key phrases in this question stem are "throughout the passage" and "a key element in the restoration of the oak tree." *What parts of your Passage Map are relevant?* The author begins to focus on the restoration of the oak tree in line 53. Look at your Passage Map notes from this point through the end of the passage to determine what the "key element" is. **Step 3: Predict and answer** *What can you predict?* The Passage Map notes from this point on focus on how humans can affect ecological restoration. *Which answer choice matches this prediction?* _____

Questions	Strategic Thinking
5. According to the passage, an important distinction between "ecological restoration" in line 53 and "ethnobotanical restoration" in lines 81-82 is that the latter	**Step 2: Examine the question stem**
	What are the key words and phrases in the question stem?
A) recreates ecosystems that accurately reflect historical uses of an area.	
	The keywords in this question stem are "according to the passage," which implies the answer will be directly stated in the text, as well as the two quoted phrases and the lines in which they appear.
B) aspires to reintegrate humans into the continuous maintenance of plant communities.	
C) intervenes for a limited time to restore an area to an earlier condition.	*What parts of your Passage Map are relevant?*
	Use your Passage Map near these lines to compare the two types of restoration.
D) uses fire suppression more effectively to reduce risks from a variety of factors.	
	Step 3: Predict and answer
	What is the primary difference between ecological restoration and ethnobotanical restoration?
	_____
	_____
	_____
	_____
	Which answer choice matches this prediction?
	_____

Questions	Strategic Thinking
6. Which choice provides the best evidence for the answer to the previous question? A) Lines 10-13 ("In the … died out") B) Lines 42-46 ("When used … plants") C) Lines 70-74 ("By limiting … trees") D) Lines 89-91 ("Thus, this … nature")	**Step 2: Examine the question stem** *What are the key words and phrases in the question stem?* _____ _____ _____ _____ _____ *What parts of your Passage Map are relevant?* _____ _____ _____ _____ **Step 3: Predict and answer** *What part of the passage supports your answer to the previous question?* _____ _____ _____ *Which answer choice matches this prediction?* _____

10/13

Now, use the strategies you learned about in this chapter to answer questions for a Science passage. Give yourself 5 minutes to read and map the passage and answer the questions.

Questions 7-11 are based on the following passage.

The following passage details findings from different eras of prenatal screening and the methods and experiments those findings prompted.

Screening newborns for rare genetic diseases is a relatively new practice that began approximately forty years ago. Prior to the advent of screening,
Line biomedical researchers and health professionals
5 were preoccupied with the most prominent causes of newborn mortality, such as diarrheal diseases, influenza, and other infectious diseases. By 1960, however, the infant mortality rate had dropped to less than three percent of live births from over
10 ten percent fifty years earlier. The declining rate was due, in part, to the widespread use of antibiotics; the development of vaccines, particularly the Salk and Sabin polio vaccines; improved nutrition; better education; and generally im-
15 proved sanitary practices. As infant mortality rates dropped, attention shifted to the etiology of rare diseases. The first major milestone in this focus shift occurred in 1962, when President Kennedy announced that the federal government would
20 begin exploring the problem of mental disability—until then, a largely ignored issue. He created the President's Panel on Mental Retardation to lead this exploration.

During roughly the same time period, a major
25 scientific breakthrough in the study of phenylke-tonuria, or PKU, was underway. In 1934, Dr. Asbjorn Folling of Norway first described the condition when he observed that some of his mentally disabled patients had phenylpyruvic acid
30 in their urine, a finding indicative of a deficiency in the enzyme that converts phenylalanine to tyrosine, a necessary component for protein synthesis. When this transformation does not occur, phenylalanine accumulates in the blood. High levels of phenylala-
35 nine are toxic to the developing brain of an infant

and cause mental retardation. At the time, the pre-ventive strategy was to reduce phenylalanine levels in the patient's diet. This approach had one serious drawback, though. Phenylalanine is an essential
40 amino acid necessary for proper growth, so defi-ciencies in it may also lead to mental retardation.

Despite this risk, the younger siblings of children with PKU were given diets low in phenylalanine from a very early age. The results were somewhat
45 encouraging and, in light of the beneficial evidence from this special diet, two therapeutically promis-ing research initiatives were launched. One was to devise a source of protein free of phenylalanine. The outcome was the infant formula Lofenalac, which is
50 still in use today. The other initiative was aimed at developing a method for detecting high phenylala-nine levels before damage to the developing brain could occur.

Dr. Robert Guthrie led the second initiative,
55 which yielded a breakthrough in the early 1960s. He developed a test to detect PKU before it became clinically symptomatic. The test consisted of a culture of *Bacillus subtilis* and B-2-thienylalanine, which inhibits the growth of the bacteria. Once
60 a blood sample from the newborn was added to this culture, the bacteria would leach the phenyl-alanine from the blood spot, overcome the inhibi-tion caused by the B-2-thienylalanine, and grow. Bacterial growth beyond a normal range indicated
65 elevated levels of phenylalanine and thus the pres-ence of PKU in the newborn.

The test was not perfect. Over the next few years, it produced quite a few false positives, and some children unnecessarily received low phenylala-
70 nine diets. To compound the problem, there was uncertainty about the amount of phenylalanine to cut from the diet; as a result, some healthy children developed mental disabilities because of the treat-ment. Nevertheless, PKU screening was generally

75 considered a success, and spurred questions about whether other diseases might be prevented through early detection. After further study it became clear that they could. By the late 1960s, newborn screening for rare genetic diseases had become a perma-
80 nent part of infant health care in the United States.

7. The passage most strongly suggests that prior to the research initiatives described in lines 42-53,

A) little research had been conducted on the causes of newborn mortality.

B) influenza research had yielded the most effective treatments.

C) a treatment for PKU was implemented, despite its inherent risks.

D) screening newborns for genetic diseases was a well-established practice.

8. Which choice provides the best evidence for the answer to the previous question?

A) Lines 1-3 ("Screening newborns … years ago")

B) Lines 6-7 ("such as … diseases")

C) Lines 32-34 ("When this … blood")

D) Lines 39-41 ("Phenylalanine … retardation")

9. This passage can best be described as

A) a brief history of biomedical research in the 20th century.

B) a description of how an important diagnostic tool grew out of an attempt to treat a specific disease.

C) an argument in support of genetic screening for rare diseases.

D) an essay questioning the ethical nature of using untested medical treatments.

10. According to the passage, which of the following contributed to the practice of screening newborns for rare genetic diseases?

A) Increased use of antibiotics

B) The development of Lofenalac

C) The false positives produced by Dr. Guthrie's test

D) The success of PKU screening

11. Which choice provides the best evidence for the answer to the previous question?

A) Lines 10-15 ("The declining … practices")

B) Lines 48-50 ("The outcome … today")

C) Lines 67-70 ("Over the … diets")

D) Lines 74-77 ("Nevertheless, PKU … detection")

Answers & Explanations for this chapter begin on page 1018.

EXTRA PRACTICE

Required	Recommended
Questions 1–11	Questions 12–21

Questions 1-11 are based on the following passage and supplementary material.

This passage describes how tree farms, widely thought to offer little support to wildlife, became home to a rare species of birds.

As our environment changes over time, certain species thrive while others become rarer. One such species is the small, difficult-to-find Swainson's
Line warbler. Scientists struggle to estimate the popula-
5 tion of this songbird because it is challenging to track. America's foremost wildlife artist, John James Audubon, attempted to describe the bird in the 1830s. Even then, it was considered uncommon. Some of the other birds studied by Audubon have
10 already become extinct, including the ivory-billed woodpecker. Others, such as the Allen's hummingbird, the spotted owl, and the osprey, are at increased risk of extinction due to their habitats disappearing. Against all odds, the Swainson's
15 warbler has held on by changing where it spends its summer seasons.

The Swainson's warbler has been at risk for extinction due to the specificity of its needs. During breeding season, summer, the bird tradition-
20 ally spends time in the southeastern United States forests and lowlands. It then migrates to subtropical locations in the winter, seeking the dry forests of Jamaica or other evergreen forests in Mexico and Cuba. The low population has been attributed to
25 the loss of these habitats due to the gradual conversion of hardwood forests into farmland, reservoirs, and urban or suburban areas. With numbers as low as 90,000 worldwide, the prognosis for the continued survival of the bird has been bleak.
30 Scientists have been studying the birds across the southern United States for more than two decades, but attempts to conserve the species have fallen

short due to a lack of understanding of their true habitat needs. Scientists tried to shift the Swainson's
35 warbler to national forests, public refuges, and private sanctuaries, but success was limited. Recently, though, researchers found that the population is increasing. Since the 1990s, Swainson's warblers have been doing what scientists attempted to do for
40 them: the birds have created new breeding grounds for themselves by moving into industrial pine plantations that have been planted in ten different states.

Millions of acres of industrial pine forests have been planted since the 1920s. Some of these planta-
45 tions are even located in the same areas that Swainson's warblers used to use for breeding grounds before the area's natural forests disappeared. With trees cut every 25 to 35 years, these plantations support a $200 billion industry that produces wood-
50 based goods from housing lumber to notebook paper. The pine plantations were once thought by scientists to offer little support to any wildlife. They do not make ideal habitats due to the even spacing of planted rows and the lack of diversity in tree
55 species. These plantations, though, happen to offer the Swainson's warbler two of the things they most require from their habitats.

When the pines at these tree farms reach about twenty feet high, they hit the one specific stage of
60 growth that appeals to the birds. This height creates high-density undergrowth that the birds rely on for protection during their breeding season. This point of the pine development best mimics the bird's traditional habitat. Before deforestation occurred in
65 the Southeastern United States, Swainson's warblers lived in thickets of cane or areas with dense vines and tangled undergrowth. At the pine plantations, the habitat lasts for about seven to eight years before the trees grow too tall to provide the birds the
70 coverage that they seek. The birds move on once the tangled undergrowth they prefer disappears.

The Swainson's warbler's secondary requirement that pine plantations can easily provide is space. A single breeding pair of the species requires between
75 10 and 20 acres of land. This large amount of space is one of the reasons why the species was so vulnerable to deforestation.

Today, pine plantations occupy some 40 million acres in the southern United States. Not all of
80 these acres are usable to the birds, though. When the cutting cycles and the amount of time the trees offer the type of undergrowth desirable to the Swainson's warblers are considered, it is estimated that approximately 10 million acres of pine
85 plantations are available to the birds at one time.

These numbers suggest that pine plantations will become the Swainson's warbler's primary habitat over time. The species owes its continued existence to its ability to adapt. While other species of warbler have dis-
90 appeared entirely due to the clearing of natural forests, the Swainson's warbler has remained flexible, shifting its behavior to ensure its own preservation.

Planted vs. Natural Pine Forests in the Southern U.S.

Adapted from *United States Geological Survey, Land Cover Trends Project.*

1. The central idea of the passage is primarily concerned with

   A)   the impact of deforestation on endangered birds throughout North America and the Caribbean.

   B)   how industrial pine plantations have affected the manufacturing of wood-based commercial goods.

   C)   how the population of the Swainson's warbler is recovering despite the destruction of the bird's natural habitat.

   D)   the ways in which scientists have struggled to increase populations of the Swainson's warbler.

2. The author refers to the Allen's hummingbird, spotted owl, and osprey in lines 11-12 to

   A)   contrast the habitat needs of the Swainson's warbler with that of other bird species.

   B)   illustrate the difficulties faced by conservationists attempting to protect threatened birds.

   C)   provide examples of other birds threatened by the disappearance of their habitats.

   D)   imply that more species of birds will find alternative habitats as deforestation continues.

3. Based on the information in the passage, conservation efforts to protect the Swainson's warbler have been unsuccessful because scientists have

   A)   been unable to track the Swainson's warbler population.

   B)   not had the resources to move the birds to new habitats.

   C)   not understood the bird's habitat needs.

   D)   been unable to get the birds to breed in captivity.

4. Which choice provides the best evidence for the answer to the previous question?

   A) Lines 4-6 ("Scientists struggle … track")

   B) Lines 18-21 ("During breeding … lowlands")

   C) Lines 30-34 ("Scientists have been … habitat needs")

   D) Lines 58-60 ("When the pines … birds")

5. As used in line 26, "conversion" most nearly means

   A) translation.

   B) destruction.

   C) variation.

   D) transformation.

6. Based on the information in the passage, the reader can infer that

   A) bird populations will continue to decrease if their natural habitats are destroyed.

   B) the Swainson's warbler's population will decrease again if more pine forests are not planted.

   C) the profitability of the pine forests is increased by the presence of the Swainson's warbler.

   D) populations of other endangered birds would increase if they moved to private sanctuaries.

7. Which choice provides the best evidence for the answer to the previous question?

   A) Lines 1-4 ("As our environment … warbler")

   B) Lines 11-14 ("Others, such as … disappearing")

   C) Lines 43-44 ("Millions of acres … 1920s")

   D) Lines 51-52 ("The pine plantations … wildlife")

8. The primary purpose of this passage is to

   A) argue that more must be done to protect endangered bird species.

   B) persuade readers to learn more about how they can help protect birds.

   C) summarize the ways that conservation groups have failed to protect endangered birds.

   D) explain how one threatened species of bird has adapted to its disappearing habitat.

9. The migration of the Swainson's warbler to industrial pine forests is most similar to which of the following?

   A) Beavers building dams using sticks and logs

   B) Spiders creating cobwebs in bushes and trees

   C) Aquatic animals creating artificial reefs from shipwrecks

   D) Raccoons foraging for food in garbage bins

10. As used in line 62, "point" most nearly means

    A) stage.

    B) purpose.

    C) detail.

    D) level.

11. Which of the following conclusions is supported by the information in the graph?

    A) The number of acres of pine plantation could soon surpass that of natural pine forests.

    B) Natural pine forests have been converted to pine plantations to provide habitats for birds.

    C) Natural pine forests will be completely replaced by pine plantations by the year 2050.

    D) Pine plantations produce more useable lumber per acre than natural pine forests.

10/14

Questions 12-21 are based on the following passage.

The following passage is adapted from Lucy Maud Montgomery's 1908 novel Anne of Green Gables. *This excerpt details a conversation between Anne, the young protagonist, and Marilla, Anne's guardian.*

"And what are your eyes popping out of your head about now?" asked Marilla, when Anne had just come in from a run to the post office. "Have
Line you discovered another kindred spirit?" Excitement
5 hung around Anne like a garment, shone in her eyes, kindled in every feature. She had come dancing up the lane, like a wind-blown sprite, through the mellow sunshine and lazy shadows of the August evening.
10 "No, Marilla, but oh, what do you think? I am invited to tea at the manse tomorrow afternoon! Mrs. Allan left the letter for me at the post office. Just look at it, Marilla. 'Miss Anne Shirley, Green Gables.' That is the first time I was ever called 'Miss.'
15 Such a thrill as it gave me! I shall cherish it forever among my choicest treasures."

"Mrs. Allan told me she meant to have all the members of her Sunday-school class to tea in turn," said Marilla, regarding the wonderful event very
20 coolly. "You needn't get in such a fever over it. Do learn to take things calmly, child."

For Anne to take things calmly would have been to change her nature. All "spirit and fire and dew," as she was, the pleasures and pains of life
25 came to her with trebled intensity. Marilla felt this and was vaguely troubled over it, realizing that the ups and downs of existence would probably bear hardly on this impulsive soul and not sufficiently understanding that the equally great capacity for
30 delight might more than compensate. Therefore Marilla conceived it to be her duty to drill Anne into a tranquil uniformity of disposition as impossible and alien to her as to a dancing sunbeam in one of the brook shallows. She did not
35 make much headway, as she sorrowfully admitted to herself. The downfall of some dear hope or plan plunged Anne into "deeps of affliction." The fulfillment thereof exalted her to dizzy realms of delight. Marilla had almost begun to despair of ever

40 fashioning this waif of the world into her model little girl of demure manners and prim deportment. Neither would she have believed that she really liked Anne much better as she was.

Anne went to bed that night speechless with
45 misery because Matthew had said the wind was round northeast and he feared it would be a rainy day tomorrow. The rustle of the poplar leaves about the house worried her, it sounded so like pattering raindrops, and the full, faraway roar of the gulf,
50 to which she listened delightedly at other times, loving its strange, sonorous, haunting rhythm, now seemed like a prophecy of storm and disaster to a small maiden who particularly wanted a fine day. Anne thought that the morning would never come.

55 But all things have an end, even nights before the day on which you are invited to take tea at the manse. The morning, in spite of Matthew's predictions, was fine and Anne's spirits soared to their highest. "Oh, Marilla, there is something in
60 me today that makes me just love everybody I see," she exclaimed as she washed the breakfast dishes. "You don't know how good I feel! Wouldn't it be nice if it could last? I believe I could be a model child if I were just invited out to tea every day. But
65 oh, Marilla, it's a solemn occasion too. I feel so anxious. What if I shouldn't behave properly? You know I never had tea at a manse before, and I'm not sure that I know all the rules of etiquette, although I've been studying the rules given in the Etiquette
70 Department of the Family Herald ever since I came here. I'm so afraid I'll do something silly or forget to do something I should do. Would it be good manners to take a second helping of anything if you wanted to VERY much?"

75 "The trouble with you, Anne, is that you're thinking too much about yourself. You should just think of Mrs. Allan and what would be nicest and most agreeable to her," said Marilla, hitting for once in her life on a very sound and pithy piece of
80 advice. Anne instantly realized this.

"You are right, Marilla. I'll try not to think about myself at all."

12. In lines 3-4, what is implied by Marilla's question, "'Have you discovered another kindred spirit?'"

    A) Anne is deeply spiritual.

    B) Anne is a sociable person.

    C) Anne seeks out adventures.

    D) Anne has a fear of strangers.

13. As used in line 79, "sound" most nearly means

    A) practical.

    B) clamor.

    C) ethical.

    D) secure.

14. Which choice best describes the relationship between Anne and Matthew?

    A) Anne does not trust Matthew's predictions.

    B) Anne is worried about Matthew's safety.

    C) Anne takes Matthew's statements seriously.

    D) Anne is uncertain about Matthew's intentions.

15. According to the passage, what does Marilla think is Anne's greatest challenge in life?

    A) Anne thinks about herself too much.

    B) Anne must learn to take things calmly.

    C) Anne needs to master the rules of etiquette.

    D) Anne worries too much about thing she cannot control.

16. As used in line 40, "fashioning" most nearly means

    A) preparing.

    B) constructing.

    C) styling.

    D) devising.

17. The fourth paragraph is important to the passage's progression of ideas because it

    A) explains the antagonistic relationship between Anne and Marilla.

    B) offers background information about Marilla's concerns about Anne.

    C) explains how Marilla has systematically changed Anne into a model child.

    D) provides a transition from Anne reading the letter to the following morning.

18. It can be inferred that the author

    A) is an omniscient third-person observer.

    B) allows the reader to know only Anne's inner thoughts.

    C) offers an objective perspective from within the story.

    D) is unaware of actions that take place elsewhere in the story.

19. The author's use of words such as "dancing" and "wind-blown" in line 7 implies that Anne is

    A) graceful and rhythmic.

    B) messy and disorganized.

    C) energetic and active.

    D) scatterbrained and confused.

20. The passage most strongly suggests that which of the following is true of Marilla?

    A) She hopes Anne will soon learn to admire Mrs. Allen.

    B) She believes Anne's "deeps of affliction" are dangerous.

    C) She has come to dislike Anne's overly excitable nature.

    D) She values calm and even-keeled responses to all situations.

21. Which choice provides the best evidence for the answer to the previous question?

A) Lines 20-21 ("'You needn't … child'")

B) Lines 25-30 ("Marilla felt … compensate")

C) Lines 42-43 ("Neither would … as she was")

D) Lines 75-80 ("The trouble … advice")

CHAPTER 22

Inferring Relationships and Vocab-in-Context Questions

CHAPTER OBJECTIVES

By the end of this chapter, you will be able to:

1. Identify explicitly stated cause-and-effect, compare-and-contrast, and sequenced relationships in a passage

2. Determine implicit cause-and-effect, compare-and-contrast, and sequenced relationships in a passage

3. Interpret words and phrases in context to answer test-like questions

SMARTPOINTS

Point Value	SmartPoint Category
40 Points	Inference
55 Points	Vocab-in-Context

INFERENCE QUESTIONS: EXPLICIT RELATIONSHIPS

Before we jump into the specifics about inferring relationships—explicit and implicit—let's look at different kinds of relationships that can exist in an SAT Reading passage.

Relationship questions ask about how two events, characters, or ideas are connected. The three most common relationship types are:

1. **Cause-and-Effect** relationships require you to identify an action or condition that brings about a predictable result. You can identify cause-and-effect relationships by the keywords *caused by*, *results in*, *because*, and *therefore*.

2. **Compare-and-Contrast** relationships highlight the similarities or differences between two items. Common compare-and-contrast keywords are *similar*, *different*, *despite*, and *like*.

3. **Sequential** relationships describe the chronology, or order, in which the items are arranged or occur. Keywords include *first*, *second*, *following*, and *after*.

Some Inference questions about relationships will ask about explicit relationships. Questions about explicit relationships will provide one part of the relationship and ask you to find the other part. In an Explicit Relationship question, the wording of the correct answer will be very similar to the wording of the passage.

✔ **Remember**

Don't forget Step 2 of the Kaplan Method for Reading Comprehension: examine the question stem.

INFERENCE QUESTIONS: IMPLICIT RELATIONSHIPS

Questions about implicit relationships, like those about explicit relationships, ask you to identify how items are connected. However, unlike explicit relationship questions, an Implicit Relationship question requires you to find a connection that may not be directly stated in the passage.

When answering Implicit Relationship questions, describe the relationship being tested in your own words by using keywords like *because*, *although*, and *in order to*.

✔ **Expert Tip**

Eliminating answer choices that are clearly wrong will help you answer even the toughest Implicit Relationship questions correctly.

VOCAB-IN-CONTEXT QUESTIONS

Vocab-in-Context questions require you to deduce the meaning of a word or phrase by using the context in which the word or phrase appears. You can recognize Vocab-in-Context questions because the wording of the question stem is often like this: "As used in line 7, 'clairvoyant' most nearly means…"

> ✔ **Expert Tip**
>
> Some Vocab-in-Context questions ask about infrequently used words that you don't know or that may not have a common meaning. Approach these questions exactly the same way you would any other Vocab-in-Context question—by using the Kaplan Strategy.

Kaplan's Strategy for Vocab-in-Context questions relies heavily on Step 3 of the Kaplan Method for Reading Comprehension: Predict and answer. If you need to review the Kaplan Method for Reading Comprehension, please turn to chapter 18.

To answer Vocab-in-Context questions efficiently and correctly, employ the following Kaplan Strategy:

- Pretend the word is a blank in the sentence
- Predict what word could be substituted for the blank
- Select the answer choice that best matches your prediction

> ✔ **Real-world Application**
>
> You can use the Kaplan Strategy for Vocab-in-Context questions outside of the test preparation context. It works for unfamiliar words that you come across when reading for school or for fun.

Let's look at the following example of a test-like, primary source History/Social Studies passage and question set. After the mapped passage, the left column contains questions similar to those you'll see on the Reading Test on Test Day. The column on the right features the strategic thinking a test expert employs when approaching the passage and questions presented. Pay attention to how a test expert varies his or her approach to the different question types.

> ✔ **Note**
>
> SAT passages often use primary source material, which means the language can seem antiquated to modern readers. Don't let that distract you from making a Passage Map focusing on the central ideas.

10/16

Strategic Thinking
Step 1: Read actively
Read the passage and the notes provided. Remember, a well-crafted Passage Map should summarize the central idea of each paragraph, as well as important topics or themes. Use your Passage Map to help you answer each question.

Questions 1-3 are based on the following passage.

The following passage is adapted from President Abraham Lincoln's Second Inaugural Address, delivered on March 4, 1865.

At this second appearing to take the oath of the Presidential office there is <u>less occasion for an extended address</u> than there was at the first. Then,
Line a statement somewhat in detail of a course to be
5 pursued seemed fitting and proper. (Now,) at the expiration of four years, during which public declarations have been constantly called forth on every point and phase of the great contest which still absorbs the attention and engrosses the energies
10 of the nation, <u>little that is new would be presented</u>. The progress of our arms, upon which all else chiefly depends, is as <u>well known to the public as to myself</u>, and it is, I trust, reasonably satisfactory and encouraging to all. With high hope for the future,
15 no prediction in regard to it is ventured.

On the occasion corresponding to this four years ago <u>all</u> thoughts were anxiously directed to an impending civil war. <u>All</u> dreaded it, <u>all</u> sought to avert it. (While) the inaugural address was being delivered
20 from this place, devoted altogether to *saving* the Union without war, urgent agents were in the city seeking to *destroy* it without war—seeking to dissolve the Union and divide effects by negotiation. Both parties deprecated war, (but) one of them would
25 *make* war rather than let the nation survive, and the other would *accept* war rather than let it perish, and the war came.

One-eighth of the whole population were black slaves, not distributed generally over the Union,
30 but localized in the southern part of it. These slaves constituted a peculiar and powerful interest. All knew that this interest was somehow the cause of

the war. <u>To strengthen, perpetuate, and extend this interest was the object for which the insurgents</u>
35 <u>would rend the Union, even by war</u>; while the (Government) claimed no right to do more than to restrict the territorial enlargement of it. <u>Neither party expected</u> for the war the magnitude or the duration which it has already attained. <u>Neither an-</u>
40 <u>ticipated</u> that the cause of the conflict might cease with or even before the conflict itself should cease. Each looked for an easier triumph, and a result less fundamental and astounding.

left margin notes:

1st & 2nd Alinaug. add.

public knows too

war about to happen but no one wanted it

bad guys made war to destroy Union; good guys accepted to save it

most slaves in South

slavery = cause of war

right margin notes:

goals of both sides

no one knew how big or how long war would be

no one wanted it

Questions	Strategic Thinking
1. Which choice best describes the differing attitudes of the insurgents and the government toward slavery? A) The insurgents wanted to preserve slavery's reach, while the government wanted to reduce it. B) The insurgents wanted to extend slavery's reach, while the government wanted to abolish the institution. C) The insurgents wanted to extend slavery's reach, while the government wanted to limit the expansion of slavery. D) The insurgents wanted to reduce slavery's reach, while the government wanted to preserve it.	**Step 2: Examine the question stem** Identify the key words and phrases in the question stem: "differing attitudes of the insurgents and the government toward slavery." The Passage Map note "goals of both sides" indicates that the answer will be found in the third paragraph. **Step 3: Predict and answer** According to the third paragraph, the insurgents wanted to "strengthen, perpetuate, and extend" slavery (line 33) and the government wanted to "restrict the territorial enlargement" of slavery (line 37). Choice (C) matches this prediction.
2. As used in line 34, "interest" most nearly means A) involvement. B) attention. C) claim. D) return.	**Step 2: Examine the question stem** The key words and phrases in this question stem are the cited word and "most nearly means." Use the Kaplan Strategy for Vocab-in-Context questions to answer question stems with this phrasing. **Step 3: Predict and answer** "Interest" is used three times in lines 31-34, but this question is asking about its third appearance. The context of "interest" in this sentence is related to the goals of the insurgents, who wanted to extend slavery. "Interest" could be replaced by "ownership" or "privilege." Choice (C) matches this prediction.

Questions	Strategic Thinking
3. The result referred to in lines 42-43 ("a result … astounding") was most likely caused by the A) magnitude of the war. B) the limitation of slavery. C) duration of the war. D) dissolution of the Union.	**Step 2: Examine the question stem** The key words and phrases in the question stem are the cited phrase and "most likely caused by." The Passage Map notes surrounding the cited lines will point toward the correct answer. **Step 3: Predict and answer** The Passage Map notes earlier in this paragraph cite that slavery was the cause of the war. Choice (B) matches this prediction.

10/17

You have now seen how to approach these question types on Test Day.

Look at the test-like U.S. and World Literature passage that follows. There are three questions associated with it—one of each kind reviewed in this chapter. Part of the passage has been mapped already. Your first step is to complete the Passage Map. Then, use the Kaplan Method for Reading Comprehension and the strategies discussed in this chapter to answer the questions. Strategic thinking questions have been included to guide you—some of the answers have been filled in, but you will have to fill in the answers to others.

Use your answers to the strategic thinking questions to select the correct answer, just as you will on Test Day.

Strategic Thinking
Step 1: Read actively
The passage below is partially mapped. Read the passage and the first part of the Passage Map. Then, complete the Passage Map on your own. Remember to focus on the central ideas of each paragraph as well as the central idea of the overall passage. Use your Passage Map as a reference when you're answering questions.

Questions 4-6 are based on the following passage.

The following passage is an excerpt from the preface of Moll Flanders (1722) by Daniel Defoe.

The world is so taken up of late with novels and romances, that it will be hard for a private history to be taken for genuine, where the names and other
Line circumstances of the person are concealed, and on
5 this account we must be content to leave the reader to pass his own opinion upon the ensuing sheet, and take it just as he pleases.

The author is here supposed to be writing her own history, and in the very beginning of her
10 account she gives the reasons why she thinks fit to conceal her true name, after which there is no occasion to say any more about that.

It is true that the original of this story is put into new words, and the style of the famous lady we here
15 speak of is a little altered; particularly she is made to tell her own tale in modester words than she told it at first, the copy which came first to hand having been written in language more like one still in Newgate than one grown penitent and humble, as
20 she afterwards pretends to be.

The pen employed in finishing her story, and making it what you now see it to be, has had no little difficulty to put it into a dress fit to be seen, and to make it speak language fit to be read. When
25 a woman debauched from her youth, nay, even being the offspring of debauchery and vice, comes to give an account of all her vicious practices, and even to descend to the particular occasions and circumstances by which she ran through in threescore
30 years, an author must be hard put to wrap it up so clean as not to give room, especially for vicious readers, to turn it to his disadvantage.

All possible care, however, has been taken to give no lewd ideas, no immodest turns in the new
35 dressing up of this story; no, not to the worst parts of her expressions. To this purpose some of the vicious part of her life, which could not be modestly told, is quite left out, and several other parts are very much shortened. What is left 'tis hoped will
40 not offend the chastest reader or the modest hearer; and as the best use is made even of the worst story, the moral 'tis hoped will keep the reader serious, even where the story might incline him to be otherwise. To give the history of a wicked life repented
45 of, necessarily requires that the wicked part should be make as wicked as the real history of it will bear,

Margin notes:

auth. to reader: story might not seem true

MF = autobio but not real ID

writing style altered to be tamer

MF story = dark

to illustrate and give a beauty to the penitent part, which is certainly the best and brightest, if related with equal spirit and life.

50 But as this work is chiefly recommended to those who know how to read it, and how to make the good uses of it which the story all along recommends to them, so it is to be hoped that such read-ers will be more pleased with the moral than the 55 fable, with the application than with the relation, and with the end of the writer than with the life of the person written of.

There is in this story abundance of delightful incidents, and all of them usefully applied. There is 60 an agreeable turn artfully given them in the relat-ing, that naturally instructs the reader, either one

way or other. The first part of her lewd life with the young gentleman at Colchester has so many happy turns given it to expose the crime, and warn all 65 whose circumstances are adapted to it, of the ruin-ous end of such things, and the foolish, thoughtless, and abhorred conduct of both the parties, that it abundantly atones for all the lively description she gives of her folly and wickedness.

70 Upon this foundation this book is recommended to the reader as a work from every part of which something may be learned, and some just and religious inference is drawn, by which the reader will have something of instruction, if he pleases to 75 make use of it.

Don't get distracted by less important details. While there is a lot going on in this passage, your additions to the Passage Map should show that Moll Flanders did eventually change and how the author thinks the reader should respond to the story. If you're stuck, review the example Passage Map in the Answers & Explanations for this chapter on page 1029.

Questions	Strategic Thinking
4. According to the passage, the narrator is concerned that readers may not believe the story because A) each reader is entitled to form his or her own opinion about the story. B) some parts of the story have been omitted. C) different readers will interpret the story in different ways. D) readers will assume that the story is a novel.	**Step 2: Examine the question stem** *What are the key words and phrases in this question stem?* The key phrases in the question stem are "Accord-ing to the passage" and "readers may not believe the story." The answer will be found in the passage. *What parts of your Passage Map are relevant?* The Passage Map notes for the first paragraph say that the story might not seem true, which corresponds to the question stem. The answer will be in the first paragraph. **Step 3: Predict and answer** *What can you predict?* The author is concerned that the readers might not believe the story because "the world is so taken up of late with novels and romances," which may cause many readers to believe that the story is fictional (lines 1-2). *Which answer choice matches this prediction?* _____

Questions	Strategic Thinking
5. Based on the passage, the narrator hopes that readers of the story will A) understand the reasons for omitting certain parts of the story. B) recognize the harm that a misguided reading might cause. C) use the moral of the story to improve their own lives. D) enjoy the story for the vividness of the characterizations.	**Step 2: Examine the question stem** *What are the key words and phrases in this question stem?* The key words in this question stem are the phrase "Based on the passage," which implies that the correct answer is not explicitly stated, and "narrator hopes." *What parts of the passage are relevant?* The narrator discusses his hopes for the reader in the final paragraph, which is where you will find the answer. **Step 3: Predict and answer** *What does the narrator specifically want the reader to take away from the story?* _____ _____ _____ _____ Which answer choice matches this prediction? _____

Questions	Strategic Thinking
6. As used in line 59, "usefully applied" most nearly means A) well written. B) consistent with the author's purpose. C) useful in the proper context. D) humorously recounted.	**Step 2: Examine the question stem** *What are the key words and phrases in this question stem?* _____ _____ _____ _____ *How can you find the answer?* _____ _____ _____ _____ **Step 3: Predict and answer** *What word or phrase can you substitute for the phrase in question?* _____ _____ _____ *Which answer choice matches this prediction?* _____

10/18

Now, use the strategies you learned in this chapter to answer questions about a Science passage. Give yourself 6 minutes to read and map the passage and answer the questions.

Questions 7-10 are based on the following passage.

The following passage is about the role chemistry plays in archeology.

Demonstrating that chemistry sometimes can inform history, researchers from the National Institute of Standards and Technology (NIST), Colorado
Line College and Mount Saint Mary's University in
5 Emmitsburg, Maryland, have shown that sensitive nondestructive evaluation (NDE) techniques can be used to determine the elemental composition of ancient coins, even coins that generally have been considered too corroded for such methods. Along
10 the way, the researchers' analysis of coins minted in ancient Judea has both raised new questions about who ruled the area and given insight into trading pat-terns and industry in the region.

Elemental and isotope analysis of the metals in
15 ancient artifacts sometimes can pinpoint the places where the metal was mined, because ores in a given region often have a unique composition. This can be combined with historical records of when mines in the area were operating to determine when the
20 coin was likely struck. The results not only help date the coin, but also offer insight into trade and power relationships in the region.

To compare the effectiveness of various non-destructive analytical methods with destructive
25 methods often used to determine the age and origin of ancient coins, the group studied coins minted by Kings Herod Agrippa I and Herod Agrippa II in what is modern day Palestine and Israel, during a biblically and historically significant period.

30 The vast numbers of a particular coin, a prutah, found in the archaeological record has led scholars to disagree about when they were struck and by whom. The provenance of the coin is important because it is used to establish dates for places and
35 events in the early years of Christianity and the onset of the Jewish War (66-70 CE) against the Romans and the Diaspora that followed.

To better establish whether the coins were minted by Agrippa I (41-45 CE) or Agrippa II
40 (after 61 CE), the team performed X-ray fluorescence and lead isotope analysis to fingerprint the ores used in the production of the coins. These NDE methods are not commonly used on corroded coins because the corrosion can affect the
45 results—in some cases making it difficult to get a result at all. The team showed that these problems could be overcome using polarizing optics and powerful new software for X-ray fluorescence analysis, combined with careful calibration of
50 the mass spectrometer using Standard Reference Materials from NIST.

The lead isotope analysis, performed at NIST, showed that the coins that had been attributed to Agrippa I were indeed from that era. More interest-
55 ingly, however, the group found that the copper from which the coins were made most likely came from mines that scholars thought hadn't been opened until a century later.

"All the archaeological evidence has thus far
60 suggested that the Romans had moved into Arabia in the second century CE," says Nathan Bower of Colorado College. "What this analysis shows is that the Romans may have reached the region earlier or found that these mines had already been
65 opened. Either way, our findings suggest that the Romans had a much closer relationship with this particular region than scholars had previously thought."

To follow up on their research, the group is
70 planning to perform more tests to determine if the mines in question may have been operating even earlier than their recent findings suggest.

7. As used in line 32, "struck" most nearly means

   A) made.

   B) hit.

   C) ignited.

   D) discovered.

8. The passage strongly suggests that the results of the lead isotope analysis on the ancient coins

   A) proved the value of an experimental method of analysis.

   B) were enhanced by the corrosion of the coins.

   C) established that the coins were minted by Agrippa II (after 61 CE).

   D) answered old questions and raised new ones.

9. According to the passage, the researchers chose to analyze a particular coin because

   A) it was less corroded than other coins of the same era.

   B) historians knew very little about the era during which it was minted.

   C) the metal used to mint the coin came from mines in Arabia.

   D) scholars disagreed about the origin of the coin.

10. As used in line 38, "establish" most nearly means

    A) ascertain.

    B) install.

    C) build.

    D) begin.

Answers & Explanations for this chapter appear on page 1029.

EXTRA PRACTICE

Required	Recommended
Questions 1–10	Questions 11–21

Questions 1-10 are based on the following passage.

The following passage is adapted from Around the World in Eighty Days *by Jules Verne.*

Phileas Fogg, having shut the door of his house at half-past eleven, and having put his right foot before his left five hundred and seventy-five times,
Line and his left foot before his right five hundred and
5 seventy-six times, reached the Reform Club. He repaired at once to the dining-room and took his place at the habitual table, the cover of which had already been laid for him. A flunkey handed him an uncut Times, which he proceeded to cut with a
10 skill which betrayed familiarity with this delicate operation. The perusal of this paper absorbed Phileas Fogg until a quarter before four, whilst the Standard, his next task, occupied him till the dinner hour. Dinner passed as breakfast had done,
15 and Mr. Fogg re-appeared in the reading-room and sat down to the Pall Mall[1] at twenty minutes before six. Half an hour later several members of the Reform came in and drew up to the fireplace. They were Mr. Fogg's usual partners at whist:[2]
20 Andrew Stuart, an engineer; John Sullivan and Samuel Fallentin, bankers; Thomas Flanagan, a brewer; and Gauthier Ralph, one of the Directors of the Bank of England.

"Well, Ralph," said Thomas Flanagan, "what
25 about that robbery?"

"Oh," replied Stuart, "the Bank will lose the money."

"On the contrary," broke in Ralph, "I hope we may put our hands on the robber. Skillful detectives
30 have been sent to all the principal ports of America and the Continent, and he'll be a clever fellow if he slips through their fingers."

"But have you got the robber's description?" asked Stuart.

35 "In the first place, he is no robber at all," returned Ralph, positively.

"What! a fellow who makes off with fifty-five thousand pounds, no robber?"

"No."

40 "Perhaps he's a manufacturer, then."

"The Daily Telegraph says that he is a gentleman."

It was Phileas Fogg, whose head now emerged from behind his newspapers, who made this
45 remark. A package of banknotes, to the value of fifty-five thousand pounds, had been taken from the principal cashier's table, that functionary being at the moment engaged in registering the receipt of three shillings and sixpence. Let it be observed that
50 the Bank of England reposes a touching confidence in the honesty of the public. There are neither guards nor gratings to protect its treasures; gold, silver, banknotes are freely exposed, at the mercy of the first comer. A keen observer of English customs
55 relates that, being in one of the rooms of the Bank one day, he had the curiosity to examine a gold ingot weighing some seven or eight pounds. He took it up, scrutinised it, passed it to his neighbour, he to the next man, and so on until the ingot, going from
60 hand to hand, was transferred to the end of a dark entry; nor did it return to its place for half an hour. Meanwhile, the cashier had not so much as raised his head. But in the present instance things had not gone so smoothly. The package of notes not being
65 found when five o'clock sounded from the ponderous clock in the "drawing office," the amount was passed to the account of profit and loss.

There were real grounds for supposing, as the Daily Telegraph said, that the thief did not belong
70 to a professional band. On the day of the robbery a well-dressed gentleman of polished manners, and

with a well-to-do air, had been observed going to
and fro in the paying room where the crime was
committed. A description of him was easily pro-
75 cured and sent to the detectives; and some hopeful
spirits, of whom Ralph was one, did not despair of
his apprehension. The papers and clubs were full
of the affair, and everywhere people were discussing the probabilities of a successful pursuit; and the
80 Reform Club was especially agitated, several of its
members being Bank officials.

   Ralph would not concede that the work of the
detectives was likely to be in vain, for he thought
that the prize offered would greatly stimulate their
85 zeal and activity. But Stuart was far from sharing
this confidence; and, as they placed themselves at
the whist-table, they continued to argue the matter.

   "I maintain," said Stuart, "that the chances are in
favour of the thief, who must be a shrewd fellow."
90 "Well, but where can he fly to?" asked Ralph.
"No country is safe for him."

   "Pshaw!"

   "Where could he go, then?"

   "Oh, I don't know that. The world is big enough."
95 "It was once," said Phileas Fogg, in a low tone.

[1] Pall Mall: a street in the city of Westminster, London
[2] Whist: a trick-taking card game. Modern derivatives include Hearts
and Spades.

1. As used in line 6, "repaired" most nearly means

   A) fixed.
   B) returned.
   C) stormed.
   D) proceeded.

2. The passage suggests that Phileas Fogg is a
   man who
   A) focuses on cultural activites.
   B) lives beyond his means.
   C) enjoys routine.
   D) keeps to himself.

3. Which choice provides the best evidence for
   the answer to the previous question?
   A) Lines 5-8 ("He repaired ... for him")
   B) Lines 8-11 ("A flunkey ... delicate
      operation")
   C) Lines 14-17 ("Dinner passed ... before six")
   D) Lines 29-32 ("Skillful detectives ... their
      fingers")

4. The passage suggests that Fogg
   A) keeps abreast of current events.
   B) is a political reformer.
   C) has strong opinions about crime.
   D) makes his living as a banker.

5. Which choice provides the best evidence for
   the answer to the previous question?
   A) Lines 8-11 ("A flunkey ... delicate
      operation")
   B) Lines 17-18 ("Half an hour ... the
      fireplace")
   C) Lines 29-32 ("Skillful detectives ... their
      fingers")
   D) Lines 43-45 ("It was ... this remark")

6. According to the passage, which statement
   about the Bank of England is true?
   A) The public has faith in the integrity of the
      Bank.
   B) The Bank has taken few precautions to
      guard against theft.
   C) The Bank has a history of money being
      stolen.
   D) The Bank has carefully managed public
      relations.

7. As used in line 47, "functionary" most nearly means

   A) official.

   B) money.

   C) servant.

   D) criminal.

8. The passage suggests that the thief was not part of a professional crime ring because

   A) the suspect acted alone.

   B) the Bank had never been burglarized before.

   C) the suspect was described as a gentleman.

   D) the Bank carefully screened the customers.

9. The purpose of line 95 ("'It was once,' … a low tone") is to

   A) create an ominous atmosphere at the table.

   B) foreshadow Fogg's ideas about the world.

   C) illustrate Fogg's proper demeanor and social skills.

   D) introduce the conflict of the plot.

10. What is the primary purpose of the passage?

    A) To illustrate the problems with theft at the Bank of England

    B) To examine the lives of wealthy men in England

    C) To introduce Phileas Fogg and his social circle at the Reform Club

    D) To parody the social customs of the upper class

10/19

Questions 11-21 are based on the following passages.

Passage 1 discusses possible uses of video games in designing educational materials. Passage 2 explores how elements of video games can be used in combatting deteriorating cognition in older adults.

Passage 1

Many teenagers have heard from their parents that playing too many video games can negatively affect their learning and socialization. Studies per-
Line formed in the 1990s supported this claim. Scientists
5 evaluated the content of popular video games and the amount of time children and teenagers were allowed to spend playing them. They eventually connected video games to anger issues, obesity, and addiction.

Studies showed that violent video games played
10 for long periods of time inadvertently mimicked a method of repetition long used by teachers to rein-force subject matter. The method of advancement in many violent video games involves winning a contest of some kind. This is also a method used in
15 the classroom and other settings familiar to chil-dren and teenagers. This method makes the content of the video games, including overall aggressive themes, easy to absorb.

Until recently, the only positive effect of play-
20 ing video games seemed to be an improvement in manual dexterity and computer literacy. These important upsides didn't seem to outweigh the negatives. A 2013 study by the National Academy of Sciences shows that the playing of fast-paced video
25 games can actually improve performance in areas like attention span, spatial navigation, cognition, reasoning, and memory. Researchers tested small pools of gamers and found that those who had a history of playing action-packed video games were
30 better at tasks such as pattern discrimination. They also found that the gamers excelled at conceptual-izing 3-D objects.

This new information could change the form that educational materials take. Content developers
35 hope that the new materials may inspire interest in the fields of engineering, math, and technology.

Educators can transform this data into classroom experiences that will not only cater to the current interests of students, but also use old patterns of
40 teaching in a new and more modern way.

Passage 2

As adults age, certain brain functions deterio-rate. Two of these important functions are cogni-tion and memory. This kind of decline can lead to an associated loss of well-being. The number of
45 adults affected by Alzheimer's disease or dementia is also on the rise. Researchers are racing to find ways for people to maintain brain health while aging. A recent study examined the effects of non-action video-game training on people experiencing
50 cognitive decline.

The study worked with small sample sizes of aging participants. Researchers found that that the use of video games can allow the adult brain to maintain some plasticity. Test subjects trained
55 their memories with games that featured patterned blocks, jigsaw puzzles, facial recognition, and other iterations requiring the recall of patterns. Test subjects who completed as few as twenty training sessions with these video games showed an increase
60 in attention span, alertness, and visual memory. They also showed a decrease in distraction. These results are encouraging, as they suggest that there may be ways to stave off mental decline and to help the elderly maintain functions needed for safe driv-
65 ing and other activities of daily living.

More tests need to be done in order to un-derstand the full potential of video games in the anti-aging market. There are several companies currently capitalizing on the success of these stud-
70 ies, and increasingly more games that promise increased cognitive function are sure to find their way to retailers soon.

11. The central idea of Passage 1 is primarily concerned with

    A) the effects of video games on teenagers who play popular violent video games.

    B) outdated methods used by teachers and content developers to interest students in science and engineering.

    C) how research about the effects of video games on gamers is being used to develop new teaching methods.

    D) how the impact that video games have had on children and teenagers has changed over the past few decades.

12. Which choice provides the best evidence for the answer to the previous question?

    A) Lines 4-7 ("Scientists evaluated … them")

    B) Lines 16-18 ("This method … absorb")

    C) Lines 19-21 ("Until recently … literacy")

    D) Lines 37-40 ("Educators … modern way")

13. Based on the information in the passage, studies performed in the 1990s support the claim that

    A) excessive video game playing can have a negative effect on teenagers.

    B) children who play video games are more likely to be interested in math and science.

    C) video games can improve performance in many areas related to success in education.

    D) teenagers who spend too much time playing violent video games become violent criminals.

14. As used in line 10, "inadvertently" most nearly means

    A) hastily.

    B) impulsively.

    C) unintentionally.

    D) imprudently.

15. According to the information presented in Passage 1, the content of video games is easily absorbed by teenagers because

    A) games are played for many hours a day on a daily basis.

    B) the games utilize methods used in the classroom to encourage retention.

    C) playing video games improves memory and increases cognitive functions.

    D) teenagers are predisposed to absorb material to which they are repeatedly exposed.

16. Based on the information in Passage 2, the reader can infer that

    A) elderly people who are able to ward off or reverse dementia may be able to live longer independently.

    B) video games could completely cure dementia and other age-related cognitive problems.

    C) playing board games for extended periods of time could have the same effect as playing video games.

    D) too much time spent playing video games would likely have a negative effect on cognition in aging populations.

17. Which choice provides the best evidence for the answer to the previous question?

    A) Lines 44-46 ("The number of … rise")

    B) Lines 48-50 ("A recent study … decline")

    C) Lines 61-65 ("These results … living")

    D) Lines 66-68 ("More tests … market")

18. As used in lines 41-42, "deteriorate" most nearly means

    A) adapt.

    B) restrict.

    C) transform.

    D) weaken.

19. The author of Passage 2 supports the central claim of the passage in paragraph 2 by

    A) explaining the results of preliminary research involving the elderly and video games.

    B) describing the physiological causes of memory loss and declining cognitive functions.

    C) listing ways that the elderly can reduce the cognitive effects of aging and Alzheimer's disease.

    D) giving details about the research methods used to study dementia in elderly populations.

20. The purpose of Passage 2 is to

    A) describe the potential of video games to help combat the deterioration of brain function in aging populations.

    B) explain how companies are reaching out to the elderly to increase video game markets.

    C) encourage the reader to play video games as a way to increase memory and attention span.

    D) support research that will increase the quality of life of people as they age and lose brain function.

21. Which generalization about video games does the evidence presented in both passages support?

    A) People who have trouble with memory loss and are easily distracted should avoid video games.

    B) Initial research conducted in the 1990s failed to uncover some of the benefits of playing video games.

    C) Video games could be part of a comprehensive approach to helping people cope with the effects of aging.

    D) Researchers in a diverse range of fields are looking to video games for solutions to problems.

CHAPTER 23

Rhetoric I

CHAPTER OBJECTIVES

By the end of this chapter, you will be able to:

1. Determine the author's purpose in a given passage

2. Determine the author's point of view in a given passage

3. Determine why the author used a certain word or phrase in a given passage

SMARTPOINTS

Point Value	SmartPoint Category
70 Points	Rhetoric

RHETORIC QUESTIONS: ANALYZING PURPOSE

Some Analyzing Purpose questions ask about the purpose of the passage as a whole. Every author has a reason for writing. To identify that reason—or purpose—ask these two questions:

- Why did the author write this passage?

- What does the author want the reader to think about this topic?

Other Analyzing Purpose questions will ask you to identify the purpose of part of a passage, usually one or more paragraphs. To answer this type of question, read around the cited portion, review your Passage Map, and ask these two questions:

- What is the function of this section?

- How does this section help achieve the author's purpose?

✔ Remember

Everything an author includes in a passage is there to help achieve his or her purpose in writing.

RHETORIC QUESTIONS: ANALYZING POINT OF VIEW

Rhetoric questions that ask you to analyze point of view require you to establish the author's perspective and how that perspective affects the content and the style of the passage. That is, you need to figure out not only what the author says but also how the author says it. Your Passage Map will help you determine the author's point of view.

When answering these types of questions, ask:

- Is the author's tone positive, negative, or neutral?

- Does the author want things to change or stay the same?

- Is the author addressing supporters or opponents?

✔ Expert Tip

As you study, practice asking these questions as you read every passage you encounter. The author is always trying to tell you something, so the more accustomed you are to asking these questions, the easier it will be for you to determine the author's point of view.

RHETORIC QUESTIONS: ANALYZING WORD CHOICE

Rhetoric questions about word choice ask about how a particular word or phrase affects your understanding of the author's purpose and point of view.

While these questions do focus on a word or phrase, do not confuse them with Vocab-in-Context questions. Vocab-in-Context questions ask about the meaning of a word or phrase; Analyzing Word Choice questions ask about the function of a word or phrase within the passage. That is, why did the author use this word or phrase?

If you want to review Vocab-in-Context questions, turn to chapter 22.

To answer Analyzing Word Choice questions, ask what the function of the cited word or phrase is. Common functions of words or phrases include:

- Setting a mood
- Conveying an emotion
- Building to a conclusion
- Calling to action
- Stating an opinion

> ✔ **Remember**
>
> **Correct answers to Analyzing Word Choice questions will always be in line with the author's overall purpose.**

Let's look at the following example of a test-like Science passage and question set. After the mapped passage, the left column contains questions similar to those you'll see on the Reading Test on Test Day. The column on the right features the strategic thinking a test expert employs when approaching the passage and questions presented. Pay attention to how a test expert varies his or her approach to the different question types.

Strategic Thinking

Step 1: Read actively

Read the passage and the notes provided. Remember, a well-crafted Passage Map should summarize the central idea of each paragraph as well as important topics or themes. Use your Passage Map to help you answer each question.

Questions 1-3 are based on the following passage.

This passage details the varying and changing scientific theories surrounding sunspots.

Astronomers noted more than 150 years ago that sunspots wax and wane in number in an 11-year cycle. Ever since, people have speculated
Line that the solar cycle might exert some influence on
5 the Earth's weather. In this century, for example, scientists have linked the solar cycle to droughts in the American Midwest. Until recently, however, none of these correlations has held up under close scrutiny.
10 One problem is that sunspots themselves are so poorly understood. Observations have revealed that the swirly smudges represent areas of intense magnetic activity where the sun's radiative energy has been blocked and that they are considerably cooler
15 than bright regions of the sun. Scientists have not been able, however, to determine just how sunspots are created or what effect they have on the solar constant (a misnomer that refers to the sun's total radiance at any instant).
20 The latter question, at least, now seems to have been resolved by data from the *Solar Maximum Mission* satellite, which has monitored the solar constant since 1980, the peak of the last solar cycle. As the number of sunspots decreased through 1986,
25 the satellite recorded a gradual dimming of the sun. Over the past year, as sunspots have proliferated, the sun has brightened. The data suggest that the sun is 0.1 percent more luminous at the peak of the solar cycle, when the number of sunspots is greatest,
30 than at its nadir, according to Richard C. Willson of the Jet Propulsion Laboratory and Hugh S. Hudson of the University of California at San Diego.

The data show that sunspots do not themselves make the sun shine brighter. Quite the contrary.
35 When a sunspot appears, it initially causes the sun to dim slightly, but then after a period of weeks or months islands of brilliance called faculas usually emerge near the sunspot and more than compensate for its dimming effect. Willson says faculas may rep-
40 resent regions where energy that initially was blocked beneath a sunspot has finally breached the surface.

Does the subtle fluctuation in the solar constant manifest itself in the Earth's weather? Some recent reports offer statistical evidence that it does, albeit
45 rather indirectly. The link seems to be mediated by a phenomenon known as the quasi-biennial oscillation (QBO), a 180-degree shift in the direction of stratospheric winds above the Tropics that occurs about every two years.
50 Karin Labitzke of the Free University of Berlin and Harry van Loon of the National Center for Atmospheric Research in Boulder, Colorado, were the first to uncover the QBO link. They gathered temperature and air-pressure readings from vari-
55 ous latitudes and altitudes over the past three solar cycles. They found no correlation between the solar cycle and their data until they sorted the data into two categories: those gathered during the QBO's west phase (when the stratospheric winds blow
60 west) and those gathered during its east phase. A remarkable correlation appeared: temperatures and pressures coincident with the QBO's west phase rose and fell in accordance with the solar cycle.

Building on this finding, Brian A. Tinsley of the
65 National Science Foundation discovered a statistical correlation between the solar cycle and the posi-

sunspot cycle & weather

sunspots = poorly understood

SMM = effects of spots on solar constant

initially, spots dim

eventually become much brighter

spots indirectly affect weather (QBO)

KL & HvL studied

QBO west phase = link to temp & pressure

tion of storms in the North Atlantic. The latitude of storms during the west phase of the QBO, Tinsley found, varied with the solar cycle: storms occurring
70 toward the peak of a solar cycle traveled at latitudes about six degrees nearer the Equator than storms during the cycle's nadir.

Labitzke, van Loon, and Tinsley acknowledge that their findings are still rather mysterious. Why
75 does the solar cycle seem to exert more of an influence during the west phase of the QBO than it does during the east phase? How does the 0.1 percent variance in solar radiation trigger the much

larger changes—up to six degrees Celsius in polar
80 regions—observed by Labitzke and van Loon? Van Loon says simply, "We can't explain it."

John A. Eddy of the National Center for Atmospheric Research, nonetheless, thinks these QBO findings as well as the *Solar Maximum Mission* data
85 "look like breakthroughs" in the search for a link between the solar cycle and weather. With further research, for example, into how the oceans damp the effects of solar flux, these findings may lead to models that have some predictive value. The next
90 few years may be particularly rich in solar flux.

Margin notes (handwritten):

BT → found link btwn. solar cycle & storms

findings mysterious → why west phase?

breakthroughs, but more research to be done

Questions	Strategic Thinking
1. The author's point of view can best be described as that of A) a meteorologist voicing optimism that the findings of recent solar research will improve weather forecasting. B) an astronomer presenting a digest of current findings to a review board of other astronomers. C) a science writer explaining the possible influence of a solar phenomenon on terrestrial weather patterns. D) a historian detailing the contributions to climate science made by the *Solar Maximum Mission*.	**Step 2: Examine the question stem** Identify the key words and phrases in the question stem: "The author's point of view." Any Passage Map notes about the author's viewpoint will help answer this question. However, the Passage Map doesn't note any specific view or opinion the author offers. **Step 3: Predict and answer** Because the author doesn't express his or her own opinions regarding the topic, the correct answer will accurately reflect the informative style and neutral tone of the passage as well as the passage's central idea. Choice (C) matches this prediction.

Questions	Strategic Thinking
2. The main purpose of the questions in paragraph 8 (lines 73-81) is to A) emphasize how little scientists know about the solar constant. B) explain more fully the mysterious nature of the scientists' findings. C) question the basis upon which these scientists built their hypotheses. D) express doubts about the scientists' interpretations of their findings.	**Step 2: Examine the question stem** Identify the key words and phrases in the question stem: "Main purpose of the questions" and "paragraph 8." Look at the Passage Map notes for paragraph 8 to answer this question. **Step 3: Predict and answer** The notes next to paragraph 8 say, "Findings mysterious → why west phase?" The correct answer will allude to the uncertainty that surrounds Labitzke, van Loon, and Tinsley's findings. Choice (B) matches this prediction.
3. The use of the quoted phrase "look like breakthroughs" in line 85 is primarily meant to convey the idea that A) new research into the solar cycle has allowed scientists to build models that predict changes in Earth's complex climate system. B) recent advances in scientific understanding of the link between the solar cycle and Earth's weather may yield useful models. C) despite the associated costs, space missions can make important discoveries that are worth the expense. D) although the QBO findings may seem conclusive, it is important to keep an open mind about alternative interpretations of the data.	**Step 2: Examine the question stem** Identify the key words and phrases in the question stem. The key words include not only the cited phrase and its line number but also "primarily meant to convey the idea." The correct answer will not restate the meaning of the cited phrase but its purpose within the passage. Look at the Passage Map notes surrounding "look like breakthroughs" in line 85. **Step 3: Predict and answer** The cited phrase is a quotation from an official at the National Center for Atmospheric Research. The note next to this part of the passage says that more research is required to fully comprehend any possible link between the solar cycle and weather. Choice (B) matches this prediction.

NIGGER   10/21

You have now seen how to approach these question types on Test Day.

Look at the test-like U.S. and World Literature passage that follows. Part of the passage has been mapped already. Your first step is to complete the Passage Map. Then, use the Kaplan Method for Reading Comprehension and the strategies discussed in this chapter to answer the questions. Strategic thinking questions have been included to guide you—some of the answers have been filled in, but you will have to fill in the answers to others.

Use your answers to the strategic thinking questions to select the correct answer, just as you will on Test Day.

Strategic Thinking
Step 1: Read actively
The passage below is partially mapped. Read the passage and the first part of the Passage Map. Then, complete the Passage Map on your own. Remember to focus on the central ideas of each paragraph as well as the central idea of the overall passage. Use your Passage Map as a reference when you're answering questions.

Questions 4-6 are based on the following passage.

The following is an excerpt from The Woman in White, *a novel by Wilkie Collins published in 1859 and considered to be one of the first novels of the mystery genre.*

P's face → smthg happened

Pesca's face and manner, on the evening when we confronted each other at my mother's gate, were more than sufficient to inform me that something
Line extraordinary had happened. It was quite useless,
5 however, to ask him for an immediate explanation. I could only conjecture, while he was dragging me in by both hands, that, knowing my habits, he had come to the cottage to make sure of meeting me that night and that he had some news to tell of an
10 unusually agreeable kind.

We both bounced into the parlor in a highly abrupt and undignified manner. My mother sat by the open window laughing and fanning herself. Pesca was one of her especial favorites, and his

Mom accepts 15 P's oddities

P = prof?

wildest eccentricities were always pardonable in her eyes. From the first moment she found out that the little Professor was deeply and gratefully attached to her son, she opened her heart to him unreservedly and took all his puzzling foreign peculiarities for

20 granted, without so much as attempting to understand any one of them.

S does not accept P bc of propriety

My sister Sarah, with all the advantages of youth, was, strangely enough, less pliable. She did full justice to Pesca's excellent qualities of heart, but
25 she could not accept him implicitly, as my mother accepted him, for my sake. Her insular notions of propriety rose in perpetual revolt against Pesca's constitutional contempt for appearances, and she was always more or less undisguisedly astonished
30 at her mother's familiarity with the eccentric little foreigner. I have observed, not only in my sister's case, but in the instances of others, that we of the young generation are nowhere near as hearty and impulsive as some of our elders. I constantly see
35 old people flushed and excited by the prospect of some anticipated pleasure which altogether fails to ruffle the tranquility of their serene grandchildren. Are we, I wonder, quite such genuine boys and girls now as our seniors were in their time? Has the great
40 advance in education taken rather too long a stride, and are we in these modern days just the least trifle in the world too well brought up?

elders = more excited by new things; youth = unaffected

kids = too well raised?

Detail
E
A

Without attempting to answer those questions decisively, I may at least record that I never saw my
45 mother and my sister together in Pesca's society without finding my mother much the younger woman of the two. On this occasion, for example, while the old lady was laughing heartily over the boyish manner in which we tumbled into the par-
50 lor, Sarah was perturbedly picking up the broken pieces of a teacup, which the Professor had knocked off the table in his precipitate advance to meet me at the door.

"I don't know what would have happened,
55 Walter," said my mother, "if you had delayed much longer. Pesca has been half mad with impatience, and I have been half mad with curiosity. The Professor has brought some wonderful news with him, in which he says you are concerned, and he has
60 cruelly refused to give us the smallest hint of it till his friend Walter appeared."

"Very provoking: it spoils the set," murmured Sarah to herself, mournfully absorbed over the ruins of the broken cup.
65 While these words were being spoken, Pesca, happily and fussily unconscious of the irreparable wrong which the crockery had suffered at

his hands, was dragging a large arm-chair to the opposite end of the room, so as to command us all
70 three, in the character of a public speaker addressing an audience. Having turned the chair with its back towards us, he jumped into it on his knees and excitedly addressed his small congregation of three from an impromptu pulpit.
75 "Now, my good dears," began Pesca, "listen to me. The time has come—I recite my good news— I speak at last."

"Hear, hear," said my mother, humoring the joke.

"The next thing he will break, Mamma," whis-
80 pered Sarah, "will be the back of the best arm-chair."

"Among the fine London Houses where I teach the language of my native country," said Pesca, "is one, mighty fine, in the big place called Portland. The golden Papa there, the mighty merchant, says 'I
85 have got a letter from my friend, the Mister, and he wants a recommend from me, of a drawing-master, to go down to his house in the country. Perhaps you know of a drawing master that I can recommend?'

"I address myself to the mighty merchant, and
90 I say, 'Dear sir, I have the man! The first and foremost drawing-master of the world!'"

Don't get distracted by less important details. While there is a lot going on in this passage, your additions to the Passage Map should note how the different characters interact with and regard each other. If you're stuck, review the example Passage Map in the Answers & Explanations for this chapter on page 1039.

Questions	Strategic Thinking
4. The central purpose of the first paragraph is to A) provide insight into the narrator's habits. B) demonstrate Pesca's disregard for the narrator's feelings. C) introduce the tone and setting of the passage. D) build suspense regarding the nature of the news Pesca has brought.	**Step 2: Examine the question stem** *What are the key words and phrases in this question stem?* The key words in this question stem are "central purpose" and "first paragraph." *What parts of your Passage Map are relevant?* The Passage Map notes for the first paragraph ("P's face → something happened"). Considering this information in the context of the entire passage will help answer this question. **Step 3: Predict and answer** *What can you predict?* The Passage Map note for the first paragraph highlights that Pesca is about to reveal something that has happened. The remainder of the passage describes how Pesca stalls and eventually relates the information to the other characters. *Which answer choice matches this prediction?* _____

Questions	Strategic Thinking
5. The description of Pesca and the narrator in lines 11-12 ("highly abrupt…manner") is primarily meant to A) illustrate the personalities of the narrator and Pesca. B) suggest that their behavior was inappropriate for the situation. C) portray Pesca as a bad influence on the narrator. D) provide a humorous contrast to the seriousness of the narrator's mother.	**Step 2: Examine the question stem** *What are the key words and phrases in this question stem?* The key words in this question stem include the cited description of Pesca and the narrator as well as the phrase "primarily meant to." *What parts of your Passage Map are relevant?* The Passage Map notes surrounding these lines will help determine the purpose of the description. The Passage Map note in the previous paragraph says that you could tell from Pesca's face that something had happened. Shortly after these lines, the Passage Map note says that the narrator's mother accepted Pesca's oddities. **Step 3: Predict and answer** *What does the cited phrase accomplish when viewed in the context of the entire passage?* _____ _____ _____ _____ *Which answer choice matches this prediction?* _____

Questions	Strategic Thinking
6. The narrator's stance is best described as that of A) an artist learning about a possible teaching job. B) a social historian chronicling generational changes produced by evolving social conventions. C) a young man eager to set out on his own, free of the strictures of his family. D) a careful observer describing the natures of two characters he knows well.	**Step 2: Examine the question stem** *What are the key words and phrases in the question stem?* _____ _____ _____ _____ _____ *What parts of your Passage Map are relevant?* _____ _____ _____ _____ _____ **Step 3: Predict and answer** *What is the narrator's overall tone and attitude?* _____ _____ _____ _____ *Which answer choice matches this prediction?* _____

Now, use the strategies you learned about in this chapter to answer questions about a History/Social Studies passage. Give yourself 6 minutes to read and map the passage and answer the questions.

Questions 7-9 are based on the following passage.

The following is adapted from Helen Keller's address to the American Association to Promote the Teaching of Speech to the Deaf at Mt. Airy, Philadelphia, Pennsylvania (July 8, 1896).

If you knew all the joy I feel in being able to speak to you today, I think you would have some idea of the value of speech to the deaf, and you

Line would understand why I want every little deaf
5   child in all this great world to have an opportunity to learn to speak. I know that much has been said and written on this subject, and that there is a wide difference of opinion among teachers of the deaf in regard to oral instruction. It seems very strange to
10 me that there should be this difference of opinion; I cannot understand how any one interested in our education can fail to appreciate the satisfaction we feel in being able to express our thoughts in living words. Why I use speech constantly, and I cannot
15 begin to tell you how much pleasure it gives me to do so. Of course I know that it is not always easy for strangers to understand me, but it will be by and by; and in the meantime I have the unspeakable happiness of knowing that my family and friends
20 rejoice in my ability to speak. My little sister and baby brother love to have me tell them stories in the long summer evenings when I am at home; and my mother and teacher often ask me to read to them from my favourite books. I also discuss the politi-
25 cal situation with my dear father, and we decide the most perplexing questions quite as satisfactorily to ourselves as if I could see and hear. So you see what a blessing speech is to me. It brings me into closer and tenderer relationship with those I love, and
30 makes it possible for me to enjoy the sweet companionship of a great many persons from whom I should be entirely cut off if I could not talk.

I can remember the time before I learned to speak, and how I used to struggle to express my

35 thoughts by means of the manual alphabet—how my thoughts used to beat against my fingertips like little birds striving to gain their freedom, until one day Miss Fuller opened wide the prison-door and let them escape. I wonder if she remembers how
40 eagerly and gladly they spread their wings and flew away. Of course, it was not easy at first to fly. The speech-wings were weak and broken, and had lost all the grace and beauty that had once been theirs; indeed, nothing was left save the impulse to fly,
45 but that was something. One can never consent to creep when one feels an impulse to soar. But, nevertheless, it seemed to me sometimes that I could never use my speech wings as God intended I should use them; there were so many difficulties
50 in the way, so many discouragements; but I kept on trying, knowing that patience and perseverance would win in the end. And while I worked, I built the most beautiful air-castles, and dreamed dreams, the pleasantest of which was of the time when I
55 should talk like other people; and the thought of the pleasure it would give my mother to hear my voice once more, sweetened every effort and made every failure an incentive to try harder the next time. So I want to say to those who are trying to
60 learn to speak and those who are teaching them: Be of good cheer. Do not think of today's failures, but of the success that may come tomorrow. You have set yourselves a difficult task, but you will succeed if you persevere; and you will find a joy in over-
65 coming obstacles—a delight in climbing rugged paths, which you would perhaps never know if you did not sometime slip backward—if the road was always smooth and pleasant. Remember, no effort that we make to attain something beautiful is ever
70 lost. Sometime, somewhere, somehow we shall find that which we seek. We shall speak, yes, and sing, too, as God intended we should speak and sing.

7. The author's use of the phrase in lines 35-37 ("how my ... freedom") is primarily meant to convey

    A) the frustration the author experienced before she could speak.

    B) that the author was unable to organize her ideas effectively when using the manual alphabet.

    C) the importance of patience when faced with difficult obstacles.

    D) the differences between written and oral communication.

8. The author's point of view can best be described as that of

    A) an adviser detailing the positive and negative aspects of a course of action.

    B) an educator outlining a new approach to teaching speech.

    C) a reformer using personal experience to persuade an audience.

    D) a student promoting the benefits of an experimental learning method.

9. The main purpose of the first paragraph is to

    A) encourage members of the audience to communicate with their friends and families.

    B) provide specific examples of ways in which the course of action the author advocates improved her quality of life.

    C) help the audience understand her experiences by using personal anecdotes.

    D) inspire other deaf students to persevere through the hardships they will encounter on their own journeys.

Answers & Explanations for this chapter begin on page 1039.

10/22

EXTRA PRACTICE

Required	Recommended
Questions 1–11	Questions 12–21

Questions 1-11 are based on the following passage.

The following passage explores the history and impact of public higher education in the United States.

Every year, hundreds of thousands of students graduate from U.S. public universities. Many of the largest and most elite schools in the nation fall into
Line the category of public, or state, institutions. Unlike
5 private universities, which generally operate independently from any government influence, public higher education was established through government legislation and is sustained through state or federal involvement in various ways. A look into
10 the history of U.S. public higher education can shed light on the changing ideals of the American story over the past century and a half.

America's earliest higher-education institutions, like Harvard, were initially developed by and for
15 clergy, or church workers. For 17th-century Puritans in America, church leadership was of utmost importance. At that time, clergy was the main profession for which college degrees were offered. But during the 18th and 19th centuries, paralleling
20 the onset of secular (and increasingly scientifically inclined) modern thought, the nation and government acknowledged the need for broader higher education opportunities. Philosophers and politicians alike were aware that well-educated citizens
25 were a vital element of a functional democracy. A better-informed voting population could secure a better political future. Moreover, with aims to advance the fields of technology and agriculture through higher education, legislators anticipated
30 potential economic improvements nationwide as well. It was in the nation's best interest to make college more accessible.

In 1862, President Lincoln signed the Morill Land-Grant Act. This was, in many ways, the force
35 behind the public university system. The Morill Act ensured that public land would be set aside for the establishment of universities across the country. The coming decades saw a massive increase in the opening of universities in the nation. Hundreds
40 of U.S. public universities began to operate. These schools received federal and state support, offered practical, accessible education, and sought, originally, to advance the fields of agriculture and mechanics. Soon these schools offered wide variet-
45 ies of subjects and specialties. These universities would be operated by their respective states, but all would adhere to certain broad federal regulations.

At the time, the government was seeking to mend racial injustices through legislation. To
50 this effect, a second Land Act was passed in 1890 in hopes of inhibiting discrimination in public universities. While at the time this did not accomplish the intended openness and diversity, it paved the way for the culture of diversity the
55 American university system enjoys today. Many public universities are now richly diverse, with regulations in place to accept students of any race, ethnicity, or socioeconomic status. In a similar vein, women—once a minority in colleges—increasingly
60 gained a strong presence in U.S. universities over the past 150 years. Women actually surpassed men in overall U.S. college attendance around the turn of the 21st century.

Since the legislation of the 19th century, public
65 universities have undergone momentous growth. The system has evolved to address and accommodate the nuances of 20th- and 21st-century American culture and development. Offering to in-state students some of the most affordable degree
70 programs in higher education, these schools have now graduated millions of undergraduate and

graduate students. Public universities also manage the majority of the nation's government-funded academic research initiatives. Featuring some of the
75 most competitive athletic programs in the world, as well as elite scholarship and arts programs, the U.S. public universities' accomplishments seem boundless. With schools in Alaska, Hawaii, and even U.S. territories like Puerto Rico and Guam, public
80 university impact reaches the farthest corners and populations of the nation. The state school system has been formative for American culture, philosophy, economics, medicine, politics, and much more.

The eminence of the U.S. public university net-
85 work stretches beyond the United States. Students travel from across the globe to study at the top programs. Cutting-edge schools like the University of Virginia (UVA) and University of California at Los Angeles (UCLA) receive continual international
90 attention for their accomplishments in scholarship and research. Programs, faculty, and students from these schools participate in the global conversation in significant ways, working toward a better future for the planet.

95 Given those early visions for a more robustly educated voting population, the enormity of the system that the Morill Act launched is remarkable. U.S. public universities have both shaped and employed many of America's greatest
100 thinkers. Considering their timeline and their accomplishments, these schools seem to reflect the post–Civil War history of diversity, liberty, creativity, and equal opportunity that in many ways distinguishes the American cultural identity.

1. In the second paragraph, the author uses the idea that educated citizens are necessary for a functioning democracy to

   A) show why an educated work force increased agricultural production.

   B) demonstrate the continued role of the clergy in American public life.

   C) explain why the government was playing a larger role in public education.

   D) emphasize the importance of technological innovation for the economy.

2. Which choice provides the best evidence for the answer to the previous question?

   A) Lines 17-18 ("At that time … were offered")

   B) Lines 19-23 ("But during … opportunities")

   C) Lines 25-27 ("A better-informed … political future")

   D) Lines 27-31 ("Moreover, with aims … nationwide as well")

3. The purpose of the third paragraph is to

   A) highlight an example of the government increasing access to public education.

   B) discuss initial technological advances in agriculture and mechanics.

   C) outline the effects of the Morill Land-Grant Act on the U.S. economy.

   D) explain the relationship between federal and state control of public universities.

4. In line 42, the author's use of the word "accessible" implies that

   A) public universities would expand course offerings to encompass a range of subjects.

   B) the likelihood that people with limited means could attend a university was increasing.

   C) agriculture and mechanics would receive the most federal and state support.

   D) President Lincoln supported passage of the Morill Land-Grant Act to expand education.

5. As used in line 47, "adhere" most nearly means

   A) resist.

   B) notice.

   C) acquiesce.

   D) comply.

6. Which of the following pieces of evidence would most strengthen the author's line of reasoning throughout the passage?

   A) Information about the ways in which private and public universities differ in paragraph 1

   B) An example of how the 17th-century clergy benefited from higher education in paragraph 2

   C) Statistics showing increased enrollment numbers of minority students in paragraph 4

   D) An example of a competitive public university athletic program in paragraph 5

7. In the fourth paragraph, the author uses the fact that more women than men now attend college to

   A) contrast the advances of women's rights with racial injustice in public universities.

   B) provide an example of how the land acts initially failed to stop discrimination.

   C) show that public universities have grown increasingly diverse over time.

   D) illustrate the challenges many people still face to attend public universities.

8. Which choice provides the best evidence for the answer to the previous question?

   A) Lines 49-52 ("To this effect … public universities")

   B) Lines 52-55 ("While at the time … enjoys today")

   C) Lines 55-58 ("Many public universities … status")

   D) Lines 58-61 ("In a similar vein … 150 years")

9. As used in line 67, "nuances" most nearly means

   A) eras.

   B) categories.

   C) circumstances.

   D) variations.

10. The passage's primary purpose is to

   A) summarize the accomplishments of U.S. public universities since the 19th century.

   B) explain the historical influence of religion on the development of the university system.

   C) discuss the relationship between U.S. higher education and the cultural values of the nation.

   D) summarize the historical effect of the Morill Land-Grant Act on United States public universities.

11. The fifth paragraph supports the central idea of the passage by

A) discussing how public university athletic programs have grown increasingly competitive.

B) providing evidence of the success of federal legislation meant to invest in public universities.

C) explaining that in-state tuition rates have increased enrollment in United States public universities.

D) noting that the U.S. public university system has expanded into U.S. territories.

Questions 12-21 are based on the following passage.

Adapted from "Young Goodman Brown" by Nathaniel Hawthorne, first published in 1835.

Young Goodman Brown came forth at sunset into the street at Salem village; but put his head back, after crossing the threshold, to exchange a parting
Line kiss with his young wife. And Faith, as the wife was
5 aptly named, thrust her own pretty head into the street, letting the wind play with the pink ribbons of her cap while she called to Goodman Brown.

"Dearest heart," whispered she, softly and rather sadly, when her lips were close to his ear, "prithee
10 put off your journey until sunrise and sleep in your own bed to-night. A lone woman is troubled with such dreams and such thoughts that she's afeard of herself sometimes. Pray tarry with me this night, dear husband, of all nights in the year."
15 "My love and my Faith," replied young Goodman Brown, "of all nights in the year, this one night must I tarry away from thee. My journey, as thou callest it, forth and back again, must needs be done 'twixt now and sunrise. What, my sweet, pretty wife, dost
20 thou doubt me already, and we but three months married?"

"Then God bless you!" said Faith, with the pink ribbons; "and may you find all well when you come back."
25 "Amen!" cried Goodman Brown. "Say thy prayers, dear Faith, and go to bed at dusk, and no harm will come to thee."

So they parted; and the young man pursued his way until, being about to turn the corner by the
30 meeting-house, he looked back and saw the head of Faith still peeping after him with a melancholy air, in spite of her pink ribbons.

"Poor little Faith!" thought he, for his heart smote him. "What a wretch am I to leave her on such an
35 errand! She talks of dreams, too. Methought as she spoke there was trouble in her face, as if a dream had warned her what work is to be done tonight. But no, no; 't would kill her to think it. Well, she's a blessed angel on earth; and after this one night I'll cling to
40 her skirts and follow her to heaven."

With this excellent resolve for the future, Goodman Brown felt himself justified in making more haste on his present evil purpose. He had taken a dreary road, darkened by all the gloomiest trees
45 of the forest, which barely stood aside to let the narrow path creep through, and closed immediately behind. It was all as lonely as could be; and there is this peculiarity in such a solitude, that the traveller knows not who may be concealed by the innumer-
50 able trunks and the thick boughs overhead; so that with lonely footsteps he may yet be passing through an unseen multitude.

Goodman Brown glanced fearfully behind as he said to himself, "What if the devil himself should be at
55 my very elbow!"

His head being turned back, he passed a crook of the road, and, looking forward again, beheld the figure of a man, in grave and decent attire, seated at the foot of an old tree. He arose at Goodman Brown's
60 approach and walked onward side by side with him.

"You are late, Goodman Brown," said he. "The clock of the Old South was striking as I came through Boston, and that is full fifteen minutes agone."

"Faith kept me back a while," replied the young
65 man, with a tremor in his voice, caused by the

sudden appearance of his companion, though not wholly unexpected.

It was now deep dusk in the forest, and deepest in that part of it where these two were journeying.
70 As nearly as could be discerned, the second traveller was about fifty years old, apparently in the same rank of life as Goodman Brown, and bearing a considerable resemblance to him, though perhaps more in expression than features. Still they might have been
75 taken for father and son. And yet, though the elder person was as simply clad as the younger, and as simple in manner too, he had an indescribable air of one who knew the world, and who would not have felt abashed at the governor's dinner table or in
80 King William's court, were it possible that his affairs should call him thither.

12. As used in line 70, "discerned" most nearly means

   A) perceived.

   B) tolerated.

   C) surmised.

   D) procured.

13. The passage most strongly suggests that which of the following is true of Goodman Brown's journey?

   A) Goodman Brown does not enjoy traveling alone with so much money and is scared.

   B) Brown is hiding the journey's true and sinister purpose from his innocent wife.

   C) Goodman Brown does not wish to go on this journey but is pressured to go by his wife.

   D) Brown may not return from the journey, and he is beginning to second-guess his actions.

14. Which choice provides the best evidence for the answer to the previous question?

   A) Lines 11-13 ("A lone woman … sometimes")

   B) Lines 35-37 ("Methought as she spoke … tonight")

   C) Lines 47-52 ("It was all as lonely … multitude")

   D) Lines 56-59 ("His head being … tree")

15. Which of the following is most strongly implied about Goodman Brown's relationship with the man he meets on the road?

   A) Goodman Brown is sure he has seen the strange man before but does not know where.

   B) The man by the road is helping Goodman Brown plan a crime during the trip.

   C) Goodman Brown is unsettled by the presence of the man by the side of the road.

   D) Goodman Brown does not know the stranger who joins him on his journey.

16. Which choice provides the best evidence for the answer to the previous question?

   A) Lines 59-60 ("He arose … him")

   B) Lines 64-67 ("Faith kept … unexpected")

   C) Lines 68-69 ("It was now deep … journeying")

   D) Lines 75-81 ("And yet, though he … thither")

17. The author's use of words such as "dreary," "darkened," and "lonely" in paragraph 8

    A) implies that Goodman Brown misses his wife and regrets his journey.

    B) creates a sense that Goodman Brown is about to do something wicked.

    C) foreshadows Goodman Brown's meeting his nemesis along the roadside.

    D) strengthens Faith's foreboding warning about the dangers on the road.

18. In line 54, what is the most likely reason that the author mentions "the devil himself"?

    A) To help the reader better understand that this story is of the fairy-tale genre

    B) To suggest that Goodman is superstitious and that his fears are driving him crazy

    C) To remind readers of Faith's claim that the road is notorious for robberies and disappearances

    D) To suggest that the forest is unsafe and to foreshadow a meeting with a dangerous figure

19. The greeting offered by the man on the road in lines 61-63 serves to support the claim that Goodman Brown

    A) and the man are heading to Boston.

    B) and the man already know one another.

    C) was supposed to wait at the Old South clock tower.

    D) is trying to delay whatever dark task lies ahead.

20. As used in line 79, "abashed" most nearly means

    A) boisterous.

    B) embarrassed.

    C) famished.

    D) frivolous.

21. Based on the passage, which choice offers the strongest possible connection between Goodman Brown and the man he meets?

    A) The man is an older relative of Goodman Brown.

    B) They are both representatives of the king.

    C) The man is Goodman Brown's twin brother.

    D) They are both competitors for Faith's love.

CHAPTER 24

10/23

Rhetoric II

CHAPTER OBJECTIVES

By the end of this chapter, you will be able to:

1. Evaluate both the overall and part-to-whole text structure of a given test-like passage

2. Distinguish between claims and counterclaims and evaluate the author's use of evidence to support either

3. Assess the soundness of the author's reasoning

SMARTPOINTS

Point Value	SmartPoint Category
70 Points	Rhetoric

RHETORIC QUESTIONS: ANALYZING TEXT STRUCTURE

Some Rhetoric questions on the SAT Reading Test will require you to analyze the structure of the passage. These questions tend to focus on the passage's form rather than its content.

✔ **Definition**

Form refers to a passage's style and rhetorical techniques. *Content* is what the work is telling you about. Analyzing Text Structure questions generally rely on your understanding of a passage's form.

The SAT Reading Test will ask about two kinds of text structures:

1. **Overall text structure** refers to how the information within a passage is organized. Some common text structures are cause-and-effect, compare-and-contrast, sequence, problem-and-solution, and description.

2. **Part-whole relationships** describe how a particular part of the passage (e.g., a sentence, quotation, or paragraph) relates to the overall text. When asked about a part-whole relationship, make sure you determine what function the part plays in the passage.

✔ **Expert Tip**

Include how a passage is structured in your Passage Map. Identifying the structure of the text will make it easier to understand and analyze its content.

RHETORIC QUESTIONS: ANALYZING ARGUMENTS

Other Rhetoric questions on the SAT Reading Test will ask you to analyze arguments within the text for both their form and content.

Questions that ask you to analyze a text's arguments vary in scope. There are three types of Analyzing Arguments questions. You may be asked to:

1. **Analyze claims and counterclaims.** A claim is not an opinion but rather the main point or thesis of a passage the author promotes. A counterclaim is the opposite of a claim—it will negate or disagree with the thesis or central idea of the passage.

2. **Assess reasoning.** The reasoning of a passage is composed of the statements offering support for claims and counterclaims. On the SAT, you may be asked whether an author's or character's reasoning is *sound*—that is, whether the argument is valid and the reasoning for the argument is true.

3. **Analyze evidence.** Evidence can be facts, reasons, statistics, and other information the author employs to *support* a claim or counterclaim. You will have to assess how this evidence is used and whether it is used successfully by recognizing logical traps and fallacies.

Let's look at the following example of a test-like U.S. and World Literature passage and question set. After the mapped passage, the left column contains questions similar to those you'll see on the Reading Test on Test Day. The column on the right features the strategic thinking a test expert employs when approaching the passage and questions presented. Pay attention to how a test expert varies his or her approach to the different question types.

Strategic Thinking
Step 1: Read actively
Read the passage and the notes provided. Remember, a well-crafted Passage Map should summarize the central idea of each paragraph as well as important topics or themes. Use your Passage Map to help you answer each question.

Questions 1-2 are based on the following passage.

The following is an adapted excerpt from Samuel Richardson's 1740 novel Pamela.

And one day he came to me, as I was in the summer-house in the little garden, at work with my needle, and Mrs. Jervis was just gone from me; and I
Line would have gone out; but he said, "Don't go, Pamela: I
5 have something to say to you; and you always fly me, when I come near you, as if you were afraid of me."

I was much out of countenance you may well think; and began to tremble, and the more when he took me by the hand; for no soul was near us.

10 "Lady Davers," said he, (and seemed, I thought, to be as much at a loss for words as I) "would have had you live with her; but she would not do for you what I am resolved to do, if you continue faithful and obliging. What say you, my girl?" said he, with
15 some eagerness; "had you not rather stay with me than go to Lady Davers?" He looked so, as filled me with fear; I don't know how; wildly, I thought.

I said, when I could speak, "Your Honour will forgive me; but as you have no lady for me to wait
20 upon, and my good lady has been now dead this twelvemonth, I had rather, if it would not displease you, wait upon Lady Davers, because—"

I was proceeding, and he said a little hastily, "Because you are a little fool, and know not
25 what's good for yourself. I tell you, I will make a gentlewoman of you, if you are obliging, and don't stand in your own light." And so saying, he put his arm about me, and kissed me.

Now, you will say, all his wickedness appeared
30 plainly. I struggled, and trembled, and was so be-numbed with terror, that I sunk down, not in a fit, and yet not myself; and I found myself in his arms, quite void of strength; and he kissed me two or three times, with frightful eagerness. At last I burst
35 from him, and was getting out of the summer-house; but he held me back, and shut the door.

I would have given my life for a farthing.* And he said, "I'll do you no harm, Pamela; don't be afraid of me."

40 I said, "I won't stay."

"You won't, do you know who you speak to?"

I lost all fear, and all respect, and said, "Yes, I do, sir, too well! Well may I forget that I am your servant, when you forget what belongs to a master." I
45 sobbed and cried most sadly. Said he: "Have I done you any harm?" "Yes, sir" said I, "the greatest harm in the world: You have taught me to forget myself, and what belongs to me; and have lessened the distance that fortune has made between us, by demean-
50 ing yourself, to be so free to a poor servant. Yet, sir, I will be bold to say, I am honest, though poor: And if you were a prince, I would not be otherwise than honest."

*farthing former British coin equaling ¼ of a penny

man accuses P of fear; wants to talk

live with him or Lady D?

P prefers Lady D bc she's a woman

man says he'll make P into woman → kisses her

P = does not like kiss; runs

P wants to leave man insults P

man = P's master; he insults her & pulls rank

P tells master that he took away her sense of self

Questions	Strategic Thinking
1. Over the course of the passage, the main focus of the narrative shifts from Pamela's A) curiosity about her master's motives to a fuller understanding of his purpose. B) fear in the presence of her master to disrespect for his actions. C) hopes for her future to her disappointment when she realizes the gravity of her situation. D) obligation to her master for providing her with a livelihood to the forgiveness she receives from him for fulfilling her duties.	**Step 2: Examine the question stem** Identify the key words and phrases in the question stem: "main focus of the narrative shifts." Looking at how the Passage Map notes change as the passage progresses will help you find the answer. **Step 3: Predict and answer** The first Passage Map note about Pamela says that she's afraid of her master. The note next to lines 48-51 highlights what Pamela says to her master when she stands up for herself. Choice (B) matches this prediction.
2. The passage most strongly suggests that Pamela believes which of the following A) Servants and masters differ only in their economic status, not in their basic human rights. B) Servants and masters may develop more equal relationships only if each retains an understanding of the distance between them. C) Masters are obligated to respect their servants despite the differences in social status. D) Servants are appropriately subordinate to their masters, who have the right to command them.	**Step 2: Examine the question stem** Identify the key words and phrases in the question stem: "most strongly suggests" and "Pamela believes." The Passage Map notes detailing Pamela's thoughts and reactions will lead you to the correct answer. **Step 3: Predict and answer** In the final paragraph (lines 42-53), Pamela stands up to her master's mistreatment of her. She admits that she is a "poor servant" (line 50), but defends herself, asserting that she is her own owner. Choice (A) matches this prediction.

You have now seen how to approach two kinds of Rhetoric questions: Analyzing Text Structure and Analyzing Arguments.

Look at the test-like History/Social Studies passage that follows. There are four questions associated with it. Part of the passage has been mapped already. Your first step is to complete the Passage Map. Then, use the Kaplan Method for Reading Comprehension and the strategies discussed in this chapter to answer the questions. Strategic thinking questions have been included to guide you—some of the answers have been filled in, but you will have to fill in the answers to others.

Use your answers to the strategic thinking questions to select the correct answer, just as you will on Test Day.

Strategic Thinking
Step 1: Read actively
The passage below is partially mapped. Read the passage and the first part of the Passage Map. Then, complete the Passage Map on your own. Remember to focus on the central ideas of each paragraph as well as the central idea of the overall passage. Use your Passage Map as a reference when you're answering questions.

Questions 3-6 are based on the following passage.

The following passage was written (on the last night of 1849) by Florence Nightingale. She was not only a pioneer in the profession of nursing but also one of the first European women to travel to Egypt (1849-1850) and keep a detailed journal of her letters and reflections of her journey.

My Dear People,

Yes, I think your imagination has hardly followed me through the place where I have been
Line spending the last night of the old year. Did you
5 listen to it passing away and think of me? Where
do you think I heard it sigh out its soul? In the dim
unearthly colonnades of Karnak, which stood and
watched it, motionless, silent, and awful, as they had
done for thousands of years, to whom, no doubt,
10 thousands of years seem but as a day. Would that
I could call up Karnak before your eyes for one
moment, but it "is beyond expression."
  No one could trust themselves with their
imagination alone there. Gigantic shadows spring
15 upon every side; "the dead are stirred up for thee to
meet thee at thy coming, even the chief ones of the
earth," and they look out from among the columns,
and you feel as terror-stricken to be there, miserable

imagination near Karnak?

K = impossible to describe

imagination runs wild → fear

intruder, among these mighty dead, as if you had
20 awakened the angel of the Last Day. Imagine six
columns on either side, of which the last is almost
out of sight, though they stand very near each other,
while you look up to the stars from between them,
as you would from a deep narrow gorge in the Alps,
25 and then, passing through 160 of these, ranged in
eight aisles on either side, the end choked up with
heaps of rubbish, this rubbish consisting of stones
twenty and thirty feet long, so that it looks like a
mountain fallen to ruin, not a temple. How art thou
30 fallen from heaven, oh Lucifer, son of the morning!
He did exalt his throne above the stars of God; for
I looked through a colonnade, and under the roof
saw the deep blue sky and star shining brightly; and
as you look upon these mighty ruins, a voice seems
35 continually saying to you, And seekest thou good
things for thyself? Seek them not, for is there ought
like this ruin? One wonders that people come back
from Egypt and live lives as they did before.
  Yet Karnak by starlight is not to me painful: we
40 had seen Luxor in the sunshine. I had expected
the temples of Thebes to be solemn, but Luxor was
fearful. Rows of painted columns, propylae, colossi,

details of Karnak = temple

10/24

and—built up in the Holy Place—mud [not even huts, but] unroofed enclosures chalked out, or
45 rather mudded out, for families, with their one oven and broken earthen vessel; and, squatting on the ground among the painted hieroglyphs, creatures with large nose-rings, the children's eyes streaming with matter, on which the mothers let the flies rest,
50 because "it is good for them," without an attempt to drive them off; tattooed men on the ground, with camels feeding out of their laps, and nothing but a few doura stalks strewed for their beds;—I cannot describe the impression it makes: it is as if one
55 were steering towards the sun, the glorious Eastern sun, arrayed in its golden clouds, and were to find,

on nearing it, that it were full—instead of glorified beings as one expected—of a race of dwarf cannibals, stained with blood and dressed in bones. The
60 contrast could not be more terrible than the savages of the Present in the temples of the Past at Luxor.

But Karnak by starlight is peace; not peace and joy, but peace—solemn peace. You feel like spirits revisiting your former world, strange and fallen to
65 ruins; but it has done its work, and there is nothing agonizing about it. Egypt should have no sun and no day, no human beings. It should always be seen in solitude and by night; one eternal night it should have, like Job's, and let the stars of the twilight be its
70 lamps; neither let it see the dawning of the day.

Don't get distracted by less important details. While there is a lot going on in this passage, your additions to the Passage Map should continue to note how the author perceives and describes what she experienced on her trip to Egypt. If you're stuck, review the example Passage Map in the Answers & Explanations for this chapter on page 1050.

Questions	Strategic Thinking
3. The statement in lines 37-38 ("One wonders … before") is primarily included to A) suggest that many people who visit Egypt overlook many of its important temples. B) express how profoundly Egypt has affected the author. C) emphasize how difficult it can be to understand someone else's experience. D) criticize travelers who do not experience Egypt in the same way the author did.	**Step 2: Examine the question stem** *What are the key words and phrases in this question stem?* The key words in this question stem are the cited statement and "primarily included to." *What parts of your Passage Map are relevant?* Looking at how the Passage Map notes surrounding the cited lines serve the passage as a whole will help you find the answer. **Step 3: Predict and answer** *What can you predict?* The Passage Map note next to the cited phrase should reveal that the author believes traveling to Egypt is a life-changing experience. *Which answer choice matches this prediction?*

Questions	Strategic Thinking
4. What is the most likely reason the author draws a distinction between the two cities in lines 39-40 ("Yet Karnak … sunshine")? A) To show that some ancient ruins have retained special relevance while others have reverted to everyday use B) To argue that Egyptian authorities should do more to protect Luxor C) To communicate how dreadful it was to find mundane activities in a place meant to hold great spiritual significance D) To demonstrate how much more difficult it is to describe Karnak than it is to describe Luxor	**Step 2: Examine the question stem** *What are the key words and phrases in this question stem?* The key words in this question stem are "the most likely reason," "distinction between the two cities," and the cited lines. **Step 3: Predict and answer** *What parts of your Passage Map are relevant?* Look at your Passage Map for notes about the author's contrast of the two cities. The author has a generally positive toward Karnak and a generally negative attitude toward Luxor. *What purpose does providing this contrast serve in the passage as a whole?* _____ _____ _____ _____ _____ _____ *Which answer choice matches this prediction?* _____

Questions	Strategic Thinking
5. Throughout the passage, the author employs which of the following techniques to convey her meaning? A) Physical descriptions interspersed with lyrical portrayals B) A series of analogies emphasizing the difference between past and present C) An extended metaphor evoking eternal truths (D) Expository prose describing a journey to Egypt	**Step 2: Examine the question stem** *What are the key words and phrases in this question stem?* The key words in the question stem are "throughout the passage" and "techniques." The answer to the question will be found by analyzing how the author conveys her meaning rather than what that meaning is. *What parts of your Passage Map are relevant?* Your Passage Map probably will not contain the answer, but it can guide you to the more important parts of the passage. **Step 3: Predict and answer** *What are the consistencies in the author's style and tone throughout the passage?* _____ _____ _____ _____ _____ *Which answer choice matches this prediction?* _____

Questions	Strategic Thinking
6. Does the author successfully support the claim that "Luxor was fearful" in lines 41-42? A) Yes, because seeing things in the sunshine can reveal more detail than seeing things by starlight. B) Yes, because the graphic descriptions of conditions in Luxor effectively convey the author's alarm. C) No, because without taking more time to learn about the inhabitants, the author may be misinterpreting the facts. D) No, because the evidence used to support the claim suggests that the inhabitants of Luxor were unfortunate, not frightening.	**Step 2: Examine the question stem** *What are the key words and phrases in the question stem?* _____ _____ _____ _____ *What parts of your Passage Map are relevant?* _____ _____ _____ _____ **Step 3: Predict and answer** *Does the author successfully support the claim in the cited line?* _____ *How does the author support, or not support, the claim?* _____ _____ _____ _____ *Which answer choice matches this prediction?* _____

Now, use the strategies you learned about in this chapter to answer questions for a Science passage. Give yourself 6 minutes to read and map the passage and answer the questions.

Questions 7-10 are based on the following passage.

This passage explores the differences in perception between humans and owls.

It's not difficult to believe that humans and animals perceive the world in different ways. As humans, sight is the sense with which we primarily interpret the
Line information around us, and other senses are gener-
5 ally subordinate. Our sense of survival is fortunately not dependent on our acute senses, or we would surely starve to death or be hunted into extinction. Owls, however, are masters of their senses, making such optimal use of their biological strengths that
10 we, by comparison, can best be described as wearing blindfolds and earplugs. Were an owl to attempt to hunt with our limited senses, it would most likely call us the lesser species, and possibly initiate attempts to label us as endangered.

15 As evidenced by our expression "owl-eyed," owls are known for their acute vision and all-seeing nature. Surprisingly, however, owls have a more limited range of view than humans. Whereas a human can see 180 degrees without turning his or
20 her head, an owl can only see 110 degrees under the same conditions. Owls have extremely well-developed eyes, but their structure is such that they are fixed in one position: an owl can look nowhere but straight ahead. They are farsighted, prevented
25 from seeing clearly anything within a few inches of their eyes; the popular image of a cartoon owl with reading glasses is not far removed from truth. Despite these limitations, however, owls maximize their advantages. Their sensitive eyes are very
30 effective at collecting and processing light, making them efficient night hunters. They can turn their heads almost completely around and nearly upside down, capitalizing on this range of movement to see over their own shoulders and directly
35 beneath themselves. They optimize their farsightedness to spot the minute movements of prey at great distances. With regard to auditory efficiency,

owls, like humans, hear a limited range of audible sounds. Within that range, however, they have
40 acute hearing at certain frequencies, helping them detect diminutive movements in the undergrowth. Some nocturnal species, such as the barn owl, have asymmetrical ear openings and disc-like facial feathers to facilitate the channeling and interpreta-
45 tion of sounds. They aggregate sensory information instantaneously to produce a mental map of their surroundings and location of possible prey.

Like owls, we use our senses to map the world around us, but there the similarities end. We cannot
50 understand the complex means by which the owl's hearing and sight work conjunctively to detect the subtle shifting of snow or leaves that signals food. The comparison itself is ludicrous, in fact, because our means for survival are so different: humans do
55 not live solitary lives, constantly alert to the movement of prey that determines whether we live or die. We do not think in the same way, if thought is even the right concept: we interpret information using extremely different cerebral processes, and we
60 can't know whether owls are even consciously aware of the complex workings of their brains. When I sit in the forest and study my environment, my world is interpreted with language. The owl's world is—well, it's impossible to tell, isn't it?

65 The owl may see the same forest we see, but he is aware of it in a completely different way. I admire the foliage and the rustling leaves, and listen to birdsong. He hears the soft rustle of a leaf and knows that a chipmunk moves thirty feet off to our
70 right, directly underneath the poplar tree. I can say that the owl thinks about the chipmunk, but not how, for I don't have the correct mental processes to describe the complex interpretations of sensory detail into impulse and action; I am governed by
75 words instead of instinct.

10/25

7. Which of the following statements supports the author's central argument?

   A) Owls are better adapted to survive than humans because owls are masters of their senses.

   B) Owls, as opposed to humans, overcome limitations by maximizing their advantages.

   C) Humans and owls evolved in differing environments, resulting in a variety of adaptations.

   D) Human brains and owl brains share few, if any, similarities in how sensory input is interpreted.

8. The author provides support for which of the following claims about owls?

   A) Their survival is not dependent on their acute senses.

   B) They do not live solitary lives.

   C) They maximize their advantages.

   D) They have a greater range of view than humans.

9. In line 42, the author refers to the barn owl in order to

   A) contrast the barn owl's hearing to human hearing.

   B) illustrate the range of evolutionary adaptations displayed by various species.

   C) imply that feathers are uniquely suited to channeling sound.

   D) provide an example of adaptation that improves the owl's ability to locate prey.

10. The structure of the passage can best be described as a

    A) comparison between humans and other animals using specific examples to illustrate similarities and differences.

    B) discussion of the evolutionary advantages afforded by differing adaptations to various environmental stimuli.

    C) philosophical discourse on the role of language and its limitations when discussing the acquisition of knowledge.

    D) hypothetical situation presented in the context of adaptive strategies employed by various species in response to environmental stress.

Answers & Explanations for this chapter begin on page 1050.

EXTRA PRACTICE

Required	Recommended
Questions 1–11	Questions 12–21

Questions 1-11 are based on the following passage.

This passage is adapted from Carrie Chapman Catt's 1917 "Address to the United States Congress." Catt served as president of the National American Woman Suffrage Association; the closing arguments of her speech are excerpted below.

Your party platforms have pledged woman suffrage. Then why not be honest, frank friends of our cause, adopt it in reality as your own,
Line make it a party program and "fight with us"? As
5 a party measure—a measure of all parties—why not put the amendment through Congress and the Legislatures? We shall all be better friends, we shall have a happier nation, we women will be free to support loyally the party of our choice, and we shall
10 be far prouder of our history.

"There is one thing mightier than kings and armies"—aye, than Congresses and political parties—"the power of an idea when its time has come to move." The time for woman suffrage has come.
15 The woman's hour has struck. If parties prefer to postpone action longer and thus do battle with this idea, they challenge the inevitable. The idea will not perish; the party which opposes it may. Every delay, every trick, every political dishonesty from now
20 on will antagonize the women of the land more and more, and when the party or parties which have so delayed woman suffrage finally let it come, their sincerity will be doubted and their appeal to the new voters will be met with suspicion. This is
25 the psychology of the situation. Can you afford the risk? Think it over.

We know you will meet opposition. There are a few "woman haters" left, a few "old males of the tribe," as Vance Thompson calls them, whose duty
30 they believe it to be to keep women in the places they have carefully picked out for them. Treitschke, made world famous by war literature, said some

years ago: "Germany, which knows all about Germany and France, knows far better what is good
35 for Alsace-Lorraine than that miserable people can possibly know." A few American Treitschkes we have who know better than women what is good for them. There are women, too ... But the world does not wait for such as these, nor does Liberty pause to
40 heed the plaint of men and women with a grouch. She does not wait for those who have a special interest to serve, nor a selfish reason for depriving other people of freedom. Holding her torch aloft, Liberty is pointing the way onward and upward and
45 saying to America, "Come."

To you the supporters of our cause, in Senate and House, and the number is large, the suffragists of the nation express their grateful thanks. This address is not meant for you. We are more truly
50 appreciative of all you have done than any words can express. We ask you to make a last, hard fight for the amendment during the present session. Since last we asked a vote on this amendment your position has been fortified by the addition
55 to suffrage territory of Great Britain, Canada, and New York.

Some of you have been too indifferent to give more than casual attention to this question. It is worthy of your immediate consideration—a ques-
60 tion big enough to engage the attention of our Allies in war time, is too big a question for you to neglect. . .

Gentlemen, we hereby petition you, our only designated representatives, to redress our griev-
65 ances by the immediate passage of the influence to secure its ratification in your own state, in order that the women of our nation may be endowed with political freedom that our nation may resume its world leadership in democracy.

70   Woman suffrage is coming—you know it. Will you, Honorable Senators and Members of the House of Representatives, help or hinder it?

1. What is Carrie Chapman Catt's purpose in giving this speech?

    A) To assert that women will vote for the party that supports their cause

    B) To demand more women candidates on political party tickets

    C) To persuade lawmakers to pass a law for women's right to vote

    D) To rally support for women's equal representation in Congress

2. What is the explicit meaning of the phrase in line 70 ("Woman suffrage … know it")?

    A) All women support woman suffrage.

    B) States have already approved woman suffrage.

    C) Women have always had the right to vote.

    D) Women will eventually gain the right to vote.

3. The phrase in lines 21-24 ("when the party … with suspicion") most nearly implies that

    A) women voters will not support lawmakers who do not support suffrage.

    B) women will not run for office because they do not trust politicians.

    C) women will vote more women into political office.

    D) women's influence on Congress will be minimal and is not a threat.

4. As used in line 64, "redress" most nearly means

    A) appeal.

    B) communicate.

    C) implement.

    D) remedy.

5. Catt most likely concludes her speech with a question in order to

    A) challenge lawmakers to investigate her claims.

    B) make clear that she is fair-minded and open to reason.

    C) open the matter of suffrage to debate.

    D) put responsibility for the choice on each lawmaker.

6. As used in line 20, "antagonize" most nearly means

    A) dishearten.

    B) embitter.

    C) humiliate.

    D) inhibit.

7. What counterclaim does Catt offer to the argument that some men and women still oppose suffrage?

    A) They are not voicing their opinions in Congress.

    B) They cannot stop the inevitable.

    C) They do have just cause for opposition.

    D) They have no legal basis for their claims.

8. Which choice provides the best evidence for the answer to the previous question?

    A) Lines 7-10 ("We shall all … our history")

    B) Lines 46-48 ("To you … grateful thanks")

    C) Lines 53-56 ("Since last … New York")

    D) Lines 58-62 ("It is worthy … to neglect")

9. Which choice most clearly reflects the inference expressed in lines 66-69 ("in order that ... in democracy")?

   A) No citizen in our democracy is free as long as women cannot vote.

   B) Other nations have demanded that our government grant woman suffrage.

   C) A nation needs more women in positions of leadership.

   D) Woman suffrage is essential to true democracy.

10. The stance that Catt takes is best described as that of

   A) a historian reflecting on historical events.

   B) an official campaigning for political office.

   C) an activist advocating for legislative reform.

   D) a reporter investigating a current controversy.

11. Which choice provides the best evidence for the answer to the previous question?

   A) Lines 11-14 ("There is one thing ... to move")

   B) Lines 27-29 ("There are a few ... calls them")

   C) Lines 53-56 ("Since last we ... New York")

   D) Lines 63-66 ("Gentlemen, we hereby ... own state")

Questions 12-21 are based on the following passage.

Adapted from "The Red House Mystery" by A.A. Milne, first published in 1922.

Whether Mark Ablett was a bore or not depended on the point of view, but it may be said at once that he never bored his company on the subject of his
Line early life. However, stories get about. There is always
5 somebody who knows. It was understood—and this, anyhow, on Mark's own authority—that his father had been a country clergyman. It was said that, as a boy, Mark had attracted the notice, and patron-age, of some rich old spinster of the neighbourhood,
10 who had paid for his education, both at school and university. At about the time when he was coming down from Cambridge, his father had died; leaving behind him a few debts, as a warning to his family, and a reputation for short sermons, as an example to
15 his successor. Neither warning nor example seems to have been effective. Mark went to London, with an allowance from his patron, and (it is generally agreed) made acquaintance with the money-lenders. He was supposed, by his patron and any others who
20 inquired, to be "writing"; but what he wrote, other than letters asking for more time to pay, has never been discovered. However, he attended the theatres and music halls very regularly—no doubt with a view to some serious articles in the "Spectator" on
25 the decadence of the English stage.

Fortunately (from Mark's point of view) his patron died during his third year in London, and left him all the money he wanted. From that moment his life loses its legendary character, and becomes more
30 a matter of history. He settled accounts with the money-lenders, abandoned his crop of wild oats to the harvesting of others, and became in his turn a pa-tron. He patronized the Arts. It was not only usurers who discovered that Mark Ablett no longer wrote for
35 money; editors were now offered free contributions as well as free lunches; publishers were given agree-ments for an occasional slender volume, in which the author paid all expenses and waived all royalties; promising young painters and poets dined with him;
40 and he even took a theatrical company on tour, play-ing host and "lead" with equal lavishness.

He was not what most people call a snob. A snob has been defined carelessly as a man who loves a lord; and, more carefully, as a mean lover of mean
45 things—which would be a little unkind to the peerage if the first definition were true. Mark had his vanities undoubtedly, but he would sooner have met an actor-manager than an earl; he would have spoken of his friendship with Dante—had that been
50 possible—more glibly than of his friendship with the Duke. Call him a snob if you like, but not the worst kind of snob; a hanger-on, but to the skirts of Art, not Society; a climber, but in the neighbourhood of Parnassus, not Hay Hill.
55   His patronage did not stop at the Arts. It also included Matthew Cayley, a small cousin of thirteen, whose circumstances were as limited as had been Mark's own before his patron had rescued him. He sent the Cayley cousin to school and Cambridge. His
60 motives, no doubt, were unworldly enough at first; a mere repaying to his account in the Recording Angel's book of the generosity which had been lavished on himself; a laying-up of treasure in heaven. But it is probable that, as the boy grew up, Mark's designs for
65 his future were based on his own interests as much as those of his cousin, and that a suitably educated Matthew Cayley of twenty-three was felt by him to be a useful property for a man in his position; a man, that is to say, whose vanities left him so little time for
70 his affairs.
        Cayley, then, at twenty-three, looked after his cousin's affairs. By this time Mark had bought the Red House and the considerable amount of land which went with it. Cayley superintended the
75 necessary staff. His duties, indeed, were many. He was not quite secretary, not quite land-agent, not quite business-adviser, not quite companion, but something of all four. Mark leant upon him and called him "Cay," objecting quite rightly in the
80 circumstances to the name of Matthew. Cay, he felt was, above all, dependable; a big, heavy-jawed, solid fellow, who didn't bother you with unnecessary talk—a boon to a man who liked to do most of the talking himself.

12. What is most likely true about Mark's father's successor?

    A) He made more money than Mark's father had.

    B) He was more popular than Mark's father.

    C) His sermons were long and boring.

    D) He took a great deal of interest in Mark's life.

13. Which choice provides the best evidence for the answer to the previous question?

    A) Lines 4-7 ("There is ... clergyman")

    B) Lines 5-11 ("It was ... university")

    C) Lines 11-15 ("At about the time ... successor")

    D) Lines 15-16 ("Neither ... been effective")

14. What can be inferred from the author's choice to place the word "writing" in quotation marks in line 20?

    A) People doubted that Mark was actually writing.

    B) Mark's writing was understood by many to be terrible.

    C) Mark's writing more closely resembled philosophy than entertainment.

    D) Mark was writing in secret but his acquaintances knew about his talent.

15. Why is the death of Mark's patron "fortunate" for him (line 26)?

    A) Mark becomes wealthy as a result.

    B) Mark and his patron do not like each other.

    C) Mark's patron disapproved of his writing.

    D) Mark felt pressure from his patron to start a career.

10/26

16. As used in line 33, "usurer" most nearly means

   A) employer.

   B) lender.

   C) relative.

   D) supporter.

17. As used in line 41, "lavishness" most nearly means

   A) diplomacy.

   B) enthusiasm.

   C) melodrama.

   D) skill.

18. Mark's acquaintances probably consider stories of his later life

   A) less respectable than when he had to work for his money.

   B) more interesting because of the lessons he has learned.

   C) less exciting than those of his earlier life in London.

   D) more scandalous than he is willing to admit.

19. Which choice provides the best evidence for the answer to the previous question?

   A) Lines 19-22 ("He was … discovered")

   B) Lines 28-30 ("From that … of history")

   C) Lines 46-51 ("Mark had … the Duke")

   D) Lines 51-54 ("Call him … Hay Hill")

20. "Parnassus" (line 54) is included in the passage to illustrate the idea of

   A) a place where the wealthy gather.

   B) an artistic community.

   C) a myth to which Mark can be compared.

   D) a place that does not really exist.

21. The tone of the last paragraph serves to

   A) suggest parallels between Matthew and Mark.

   B) surprise the reader with Matthew's capabilities.

   C) demonstrate the dramatic changes in Mark's character.

   D) mock Mark for the way he sees Matthew.

CHAPTER 25

Synthesis

 CHAPTER OBJECTIVES

By the end of this chapter, you will be able to:

1. Apply the Kaplan Strategy for Paired Passages to History/Social Studies and Science paired passages and question sets

2. Synthesize, compare, and contrast information from two different but related passages

3. Analyze quantitative information and infographics and combine information from infographics and text

4. Use the Kaplan Method for Infographics to answer questions about charts and graphs

SMARTPOINTS

Point Value	SmartPoint Category
Point Builder	The Kaplan Method for Infographics
50 Points	Synthesis

PAIRED PASSAGES

There will be exactly one set of Paired Passages on the SAT Reading Test. These passages will be either History/Social Studies passages or Science passages.

The Kaplan Strategy for Paired Passages helps you attack each pair you face by dividing and conquering, rather than simultaneously processing two different passages with 10–11 questions:

- Read Passage 1, then answer its questions
- Read Passage 2, then answer its questions
- Answer questions about both passages

By reading Passage 1 and answering its questions before moving on to Passage 2, you avoid falling into wrong answer traps that reference the text of Passage 2. Furthermore, by addressing each passage individually, you will have a better sense of the central idea and purpose of both passages, and this will help you answer questions that ask you to synthesize information.

> ✔ **Remember**
>
> Even though the individual passages are shorter in a Paired Passage set, you should still Passage Map both of them.

Questions in a Paired Passage set that ask about only one of the passages will be no different from questions you've seen and answered about single passages. Use the same methods and strategies you've been using to answer these questions.

Other questions in a Paired Passage set will ask you questions about both passages. You may be asked to identify similarities or differences between the passages or how the author of one passage may respond to a point made by the author of the other passage.

THE KAPLAN METHOD FOR INFOGRAPHICS

The SAT Reading Test will contain one or more passages and/or questions that include one or more infographics. Each infographic will convey or expand on information from or related to the passage.

The Kaplan Method for Infographics consists of three steps:

Step 1: Read the question

Step 2: Examine the infographic

Step 3: Predict and answer

Let's take a closer look at each step.

Step 1: Read the question

Assess the question stem for information that will help you zero in on the specific parts of the infographic that apply to the question.

Step 2: Examine the infographic

Make sure to:

- Circle parts of the infographic that relate directly to the question
- Identify units of measurement, labels, and titles

> **✔ Expert Tip**
>
> For more data-heavy infographics, you should also make note of any present variables or categories, trends in the data, or relationships between variables.

Step 3: Predict and answer

Just as in Step 3 of the Kaplan Method for Reading Comprehension, do not look at the answer choices until you've used the infographic to make a prediction.

Let's look at the following example of an abbreviated History/Social Studies Paired Passage set. After the mapped passage, the left column contains questions similar to those you'll see on the Reading Test on Test Day. The column on the right features the strategic thinking a test expert employs when approaching the passage and questions presented.

Strategic Thinking
Step 1: Read actively
Read the paired passages and the notes provided. Remember, a well-crafted Passage Map should summarize the central idea of each paragraph as well as important topics or themes. Use your Passage Map to help you answer each question.

Questions 1-3 are based on the following passages and supplementary material.

Passage 1 warns against society becoming preoccupied with the rehabilitation of criminals. Passage 2 discusses the merits of said rehabilitation.

Passage 1

Nowadays, you hear quite a bit of mealy-mouthed hogwash about diversion and rehabilitation of criminals. If we were to listen to
Line   the so-called experts, we would conclude as a soci-
5   ety that criminals are simply misunderstood, and that the only thing that separates good, law-abiding citizens from the worst scofflaws is an accident of birth. These pundits can quote all sorts of statistics and studies, but they seem to do so at the expense
10   of one simple fact: as a society, we must uphold the standards of right and wrong. If we lose track of this obligation to reward the just and punish the guilty, then it is not just the criminals who have lost their moral compass, but society itself.

criminal rehab = good?

can lose sight of punishing & moral standards

Passage 2

15   When a crime is committed in our society, we are always quick to cast blame. The politicians and pundits who profit from fear and anger will be quick to promote newer and harsher penalties nearly every time that a violent crime appears in
20   the national news, locking up the criminals for longer at greater expense to the taxpayers and society itself, and yet nothing changes. The root cause of the crime has not been addressed, and

rehab = less $$ and time alternative

in the rush to blame, nothing has been done to
25   prevent the next violent crime from occurring. For only a fraction of the money it takes to lock up an offender, we could intercede earlier on, mentoring at-risk kids and making sure that they have the educational opportunities that will
30   steer them away from crime. Instead of locking up criminals forever, we can give them the counseling and job training they need to become productive members of society. It is easy to blame, but changing things for the better requires
35   more.

focus on prevention

Education of Inmates

y-axis: Percentage of U.S. Inmate Population (0% to 80%)

	High School Graduates	High School Dropouts
Federal Inmates		
Jail Inmates		
Prison Inmates		

10/27

Questions	Strategic Thinking
1. The authors of both passages agree that A) the root causes of crime need to be addressed. B) society must uphold standards of right and wrong. (C) it is important for society to confront the problem of crime. D) diversion and rehabilitation can help criminals become productive members of society.	**Step 2: Examine the question stem** Identify the key words and phrases in the question stem: "authors of both passages agree." The correct answer will describe a point on which the authors of both passages agree. Look at the passages for similarities. **Step 3: Predict and answer** Both authors believe that the issue of crime needs to be addressed. Choice (C) matches this prediction.
2. One difference between the conclusions reached in the two passages is that unlike the author of Passage 1, the author of Passage 2 A) recommends lighter sentences for violent criminals. (B) argues that increasing educational opportunities can help reduce crime. C) blames politicians instead of pundits for the increase in criminal behavior. D) believes that individuals must be held accountable for their actions.	**Step 2: Examine the question stem** The key words and phrases in this question stem are "one difference between the conclusions" and "unlike the author of Passage 1, the author of Passage 2." The correct answer will focus on how the conclusion of Passage 2 differs from that of Passage 1. **Step 3: Predict and answer** The author of Passage 1 concludes, "we must uphold the standards of right and wrong" (lines 10-11). The author of Passage 2 concludes that we should make sure there are more "educational opportunities that will steer [at-risk kids] away from crime" (lines 29-30). Choice (B) matches this prediction.

Questions	Strategic Thinking
3. Based on the graph, if society adapted the practices outlined in Passage 2, the percentage of high school dropouts in inmate populations would most likely A) decrease. B) increase. C) remain the same. D) fall below that of high school graduates.	**Step 1: Read the question** Assess the question for information on what part of the infographic to focus on: the bars that represent the percentage of high school dropouts in inmate populations. The bars that represent the percentage of high school graduates can be ignored for the sake of this question. **Step 2: Examine the infographic** The unit of measurement on the *y*-axis is the percentage of the inmate population. The labels on the *x*-axis are different kinds of inmates: federal, jail, and prison. The key also provides labels for the two different categories: high school graduates and high school dropouts. The title of the graph is "Education of Inmates." **Step 3: Predict and answer** If the practices in Passage 2 were adopted, the percentage of high school dropouts in inmate populations would decrease. Choice (A) matches this prediction.

Strategic Thinking

Step 1: Read actively

The paired passage set below is partially mapped. Read the first passage and its Passage Map. Then, complete the Passage Map for the second passage on your own. Remember to focus on the central ideas of each paragraph as well as the central idea of the overall passage. Use your Passage Map as a reference when you're answering questions.

Questions 4-6 are based on the following passages and supplementary material.

Passage 1 describes how scientists study stem cells and possible uses. Passage 2 discusses the potential risks of stem cell research.

Passage 1

how SCs work, why powerful

Stem cells truly are science's miracle cure. These undifferentiated cells have not yet chosen what type of cell to become, and can be nudged into becom-
Line ing whatever type of cell is needed to help a sick
5 patient. Stem cells can be used to replace damaged cells in a person who has a degenerative disease or a serious injury.

embryonic > adult SCs

Scientists obtain stem cells primarily from discarded embryos. True, they can also be obtained
10 from the blood or organs from healthy adults, but these stem cells, while showing some usefulness, are not as adaptable as embryonic stem cells. Embryonic stem cells are incredibly helpful and can mean a revolutionary change in quality of life for patients
15 suffering from debilitating diseases such as Parkinson's or Alzheimer's. Someday, stem cells could even eliminate the need for human test subjects in

w/o emb. SCs, research = slower

drug tests. Without the use of embryonic stem cells, though, that could take an immeasurably longer
20 amount of time to become a reality.

SC research should continue

With stem cell research, the benefits for living, breathing, sentient people outweigh any debate regarding the origins of the cells themselves. In this age of scientific enlightenment, we must always ask
25 ourselves: What action can best benefit humanity? By answering, we see clearly that stem cell research must continue.

Passage 2

We stand at an important crossroads in scientific progress. We have the capability now to improve

30 humanity in ways never thought possible, but at what cost? At what point must progress bow before conscience? Just because we can, is it true that we should?

Stem cell research has the potential to be an
35 enormous boon to the medical industry. The advance of diseases can be assuaged or halted completely through this remarkable new medicine. But scientists assault the dignity of life when they use embryonic stem cells for their work. By taking
40 cells from discarded embryos, we begin treading on a slippery slope. It is all too easy to transition from using discarded embryos to creating embryos solely for the purpose of stem cell medicine.

Since stem cells can be obtained from healthy
45 adults with no cost to life, this is the path on which we should be progressing. These stem cells, safely obtained, can have a significant positive impact on the lives of patients.

Stem Cell Research Support and Opposition

Don't get distracted by less important details. Your Passage Map for Passage 2 should note the author's views on the ethics surrounding embryonic stem cell research. If you're stuck, review the example Passage Map in the Answers & Explanations for this chapter on page 1061.

Questions	Strategic Thinking
4. Which assumption do the authors of both passages share? A) Embryonic stem cells have greater potential than adult stem cells. B) The medical benefits of stem cell research outweigh any ethical concerns. C) Stem cell research could provide enormous benefits to humanity. D) The medical benefits of stem cell research must be weighed against ethical concerns.	**Step 2: Examine the question stem** *What are the key words and phrases in this question stem?* The key words and phrases in this question stem are "assumption" and "both passages share." The correct answer will describe an assumption both authors make. **Step 3: Predict and answer** *What can you predict?* The authors of both passages claim that stem cell research is potentially beneficial. Which answer choice matches this prediction?
5. The authors of the passages disagree most strongly on which issue? A) The sources of stem cells available to researchers B) The value of stem cell research to medical science C) The adaptability of adult stem cells D) The ethics of using embryonic stem cells	**Step 2: Examine the question stem** *What are the key words and phrases in this question stem?* The key words and phrases in this question stem are "disagree most strongly." You will find the correct answer by finding the biggest difference between the two different opinions. **Step 3: Predict and answer** *What is the central idea of Passage 1?* _____ _____ *What is the central idea of Passage 2?* _____ _____ *What is the biggest difference between these central ideas?* _____ _____ *Which answer choice matches this prediction?* _____

Questions	Strategic Thinking
6. What claim about stem cell research is supported by the graph? A) Between 2003 and 2005, support for stem cell research increased more than opposition to stem cell research decreased. B) Between 2004 and 2006, support for stem cell research decreased and then increased. C) Between 2005 and 2007, opposition to stem cell research increased more than support for stem cell research decreased. D) Between 2006 and 2008, opposition to stem cell research decreased and then increased.	**Step 1: Read the question** *What are the key words and phrases in this question stem?* The question stem does not offer any information about what part of the infographic will provide the answer. **Step 2: Examine the infographic** *What are the units of measurement, labels, or titles of the infographic?* _____ _____ _____ _____ _____ _____ **Step 3: Predict and answer** *What can you predict?* Because this question stem is general and does not provide information on what part of the graph to look at, it is difficult to make a prediction. Evaluate each answer choice. *Look at A. Did support for stem cell research increase more than opposition to stem cell research decreased between 2003 and 2005? How do you know?* No, because the increase of support and the decrease of opposition are equal, according to the graph. (You can determine they're equal by counting the number of boxes each line spans.) *Look at B. Did support for stem cell research decrease and then increase between 2004 and 2006? How do you know?* _____ _____ _____ _____ _____ _____

10/28

Questions	Strategic Thinking
	Look at C. Did opposition to stem cell research increase more than support for stem cell research decreased between 2005 and 2007? How do you know?
	_____
	_____
	_____
	_____
	_____
	_____
	Look at D. Did opposition to stem cell research decrease and then increase between 2006 and 2008? How do you know?
	_____
	_____
	_____
	_____
	_____
	_____
	What is the correct answer?
	_____

Now, use the strategies you learned about in this chapter to answer questions for a History/Social Studies Paired Passage set. Give yourself 8 minutes to read and map the passages and answer the questions.

Questions 7-9 are based on the following passages and supplementary material.

The following passages reflect on the Machnovschina, an anarchist peasant uprising in the Ukraine active from approximately 1917 to 1922 under the leadership of Nestor Makhno. During their brief and turbulent history, the Makhnovshchina (also known as Makhnovists) fought against the Central Powers, the White Army, and the Red Army, their sometimes ally that eventually turned on them and defeated them. The first passage discusses the relationship between the Makhnovists and their supporters, while the second discusses the differences between the Makhnovists on the outskirts of the emerging Soviet Union and the Bolsheviks who controlled it.

Passage 1

Even had the Ukrainian civilians wanted to ignore the sectarianism of their time and remain neutral, they did not have that luxury—the turmoil
Line was too absolute, the excitement and terror of
5   revolutionary upheaval too absolutely compelling. Even for the most isolated of peasants, political impartiality was impossible. From the beginning, there was a bond among revolutionary intellectuals, civilians, and military leaders.
10   The causes of civil unrest compounded. Adding to the burden of uncounted years of economic and political subjugation under a quasi-feudal system[1] was the added pressure of an invading Austro-Hungarian army. Meanwhile, Russia was in a state
15   of chaos, and the Bolsheviks[2] were rapidly consolidating power in a system that promised equality and the rule of the proletariat. There was no central authority to organize them (Russia had all but given up the Ukraine to the invading Central Powers[3]),
20   and the traditional power of the rich landlords had collapsed with the Czarist government. There was no status quo and no safe choice.
     Faced with this state of affairs, many Ukrainian peasants chose to organize themselves within
25   the Makhnovshchina. Educated in the field and trained behind the plow, they were now charged with the task of organizing and defending a new

society under conditions of tremendous adversity. Although the Makhnovshchina was an anarchist,
30   revolutionary movement, it was one that emerged out of necessity. It was a way for peasants to join together for mutual aid, revolutionary intellectuals to explore the possibility of a society without central authority, and generals to attempt to secure the rights
35   of the Ukrainian people to self-determination.

Passage 2

The revolutionary period in Russian history is a classic example of the conflicts between the programs of dogmatic, rigid leaders and the desires and needs of ordinary people. One of the best
40   examples of this is the struggle between the Bolsheviks and the Makhnovshchina. Not only did the word "revolution" mean very different things to the Kremlin[4] bureaucrats and the Ukrainian partisans, but the reality of the revolution was very different
45   as well. This fact was noted by one anonymous soldier who, beginning his career as a Kremlin guard, eventually became a member of the Makhnovist army. He noted that "conditions could not have been more different between the two camps.
50   In the one, decisions were based on the political theories of Marx[5] and Lenin,[6] theories which were never doubted or questioned in the least. In the other, theories were even more important—debated vigorously and openly—but only after the day's
55   work had been done and the important decisions had been made based on the needs of the community for food, freedom, and self-defense."
     Although the Kremlin's approach might seem like harmless intellectualism, it had disastrous con-
60   sequences that the anonymous soldier couldn't have forseen. As the Bolshevik Party gained increasing power, it began to control the official view of events with a systematic paranoia unprecedented in history. If the events differed from the official view, the

65 events themselves (and those who participated in them) were deemed the enemy.

The wartime writings of Leon Trotsky[7] are the best indication of this trend. He alternately characterized the Makhnovists as heroes and traitors depending
70 on the current needs of the Bolsheviks. When he required Makhnovists to fight alongside the Red Army,[8] he portrayed them as courageous heroes and valiant fighters, but when he did not, they suddenly became traitors and enemies of the revolu-
75 tion. In 1920, as the Makhnovshchina and the Red Army united to fight against a powerful White Army[9] campaign, Trotsky wrote:

"The working class of the Ukraine can never, and especially not in conditions of tremendous military
80 danger, allow particular units sometimes to fight in our ranks and sometimes to stab us in the back.[+] Waging war against the world's exploiters, the workers' and peasants' Red Army says: 'Who is not with me is against me, and whoever is with me is to
85 remain in my ranks and not leave them till the end.'"

The Ukranian partisans, even as peasants and workmen, were painted as the servants of foreign aristocrats bent on undermining the revolu- tion. Even though Bolshevik presence had been
90 weak in the Ukraine, Trotsky still saw fit to portray himself as the representative of "the working class of the Ukraine" and the Makhnovists as loyal to the working class only to the degree that they recog- nized Red Army authority.

[1] Serfdom had only been abolished in 1861, and many traces of it remained.
[2] The Bolsheviks were the Communist party that established the Soviet Union.
[3] The Central Powers were Germany, Austria-Hungary, the Ottoman Empire, and Bulgaria. During World War I (which took place from 1914 to 1918), they were fighting against the Allies—France, Russia, Great Britain, and the United States. During the period in question, the Austro-Hungarian Army was occupying much of the Ukraine.
[4] The Russian capital building which, at the time, was occupied by the Bolshevik Party
[5] Karl Marx, the ideological founder of Communism
[6] Vladimir Ilyich Lenin, the leader of the Bolsheviks
[7] Leon Trotsky, one of the leaders of the Bolsheviks
[8] The Bolshevik Army
[9] A conservative army opposed to the revolutionary movements in Russia
[+] The previous alliance between the Makhnovshchina and the Red Army had been broken when the Bolsheviks attacked and devastated the unsuspecting anarchists in a surprise attack.

Proportion of Seats in the Russian Constituent Assembly, 1918

52.4% — SRs, Left SRs, Bolsheviks, Makhnovists, Kadets, Nationality Parties, Other; 12.2%; 24.7%; 5.6%

7. The author of Passage 2 would most likely characterize the Bolsheviks' promise described in Passage 1 as

A) the reason the Makhnovischina fought alongside the Red Army.

B) based on theories that had been openly debated.

C) an example of the Bolsheviks' attempt to control the official view of events.

D) inspired by Trotsky's wartime writings.

8. The authors of both passages would most likely agree that

A) the Bolshevik and Makhnovischina leaders shared many fundamental principles.

B) the Austro-Hungarian army posed the greatest threat to the Ukranian peasants.

C) the Makhnovischina were servants of foreign aristocrats.

D) the Makhnovischina was composed of peasants, intellectuals, and soldiers.

9. It can be reasonably inferred from Passage 2 and the graphic that the Bolsheviks

    A) wielded political power disproportionate to their voting power.

    B) needed to form coalitions to realize their revolutionary promise.

    C) represented a loyal opposition to the ruling SR group.

    D) allied with the Makhnovischina only when necessary to form a majority.

Answers & Explanations for this chapter appear on page 1061.

EXTRA PRACTICE

Required	Recommended
Questions 1–11	Questions 12–22

Questions 1-11 are based on the following passages and supplementary material.

Passage 1 is about how scientists use radioisotopes to date artifacts and remains. Passage 2 discusses the varying problems with radioactive contaminants.

Passage 1

Archaeologists often rely on measuring the amounts of different atoms present in an item from a site to determine its age. The identity of an atom
Line depends on how many protons it has in its nucleus;
5 for example, all carbon atoms have 6 protons. Each atom of an element, however, can have a differ-ent number of neutrons, so there can be several versions, or isotopes, of each element. Scientists name the isotopes by the total number of protons
10 plus neutrons. For example, a carbon atom with 6 neutrons is carbon-12 while a carbon atom with 7 neutrons is carbon-13.

Some combinations of protons and neutrons are not stable and will change over time. For example,
15 carbon-14, which has 6 protons and 8 neutrons, will slowly change into nitrogen-14, with 7 protons and 7 neutrons. Scientists can directly measure the amount of carbon-12 and carbon-14 in a sample or they can use radiation measurements to calculate these
20 amounts. Each atom of carbon-14 that changes to nitrogen-14 emits radiation. Scientists can measure the rate of emission and use that to calculate the total amount of carbon-14 present in a sample.

Carbon-14 atoms are formed in the atmosphere
25 at the same rate at which they decay. Therefore, the ratio of carbon-12 to carbon-14 atoms in the atmosphere is constant. Living plants and animals have the same ratio of carbon-12 to carbon-14 in their tissues because they are constantly taking in
30 carbon in the form of food or carbon dioxide. After the plant or animal dies, however, it stops taking in

carbon and so the amount of carbon-14 atoms in its tissues starts to decrease at a predictable rate.

By measuring the ratio of carbon-12 to carbon-14
35 in a bone, for example, a scientist can determine how long the animal the bone came from has been dead. To determine an object's age this way is called "car-bon-14 dating." Carbon-14 dating can be performed on any material made by a living organism, such as
40 wood or paper from trees or bones and skin from animals. Materials with ages up to about 50,000 years old can be dated. By finding the age of several objects found at different depths at an archeological dig, the archeologists can then make a timeline for the layers
45 of the site. Objects in the same layer will be about the same age. By using carbon dating for a few objects in a layer, archeologists know the age of other objects in that layer, even if the layer itself cannot be carbon dated.

Passage 2

50 Radioactive materials contain unstable atoms that decay, releasing energy in the form of radiation. The radiation can be harmful to living tissue because it can penetrate into cells and damage their DNA. If an explosion or a leak at a nuclear power plant releases
55 large amounts of radioactive materials, the sur-rounding area could be hazardous until the amount of radioactive material drops back to normal levels. The amount of danger from the radiation and the amount of time until the areas are safe again depends
60 on how fast the materials emit radiation.

Scientists use the "half-life" of a material to indicate how quickly it decays. The half-life of a material is the amount of time it takes for half of a sample of that material to decay. A mate-
65 rial with a short half-life decays more quickly

10|29

than a material with a long half-life. For example, iodine-131 and cesium-137 can both be released as a result of an accident at a nuclear power plant. Iodine-131 decays rapidly, with a half-life of 8 days.
70 Cesium-137, however, decays more slowly, with a half-life of 30 years.

If an accident releases iodine-131, therefore, it is a short-term concern. The amount of radiation emitted will be high but will drop rapidly. After
75 two months, less than one percent of the original iodine-131 will remain. An accidental release of cesium-137, however, is a long-term concern. The amount of radiation emitted at first will be low but will drop slowly. It will take about 200 years
80 for the amount of cesium-137 remaining to drop below one percent. The total amount of radiation emitted in both cases will be the same, for the same amount of initial material. The difference lies in whether the radiation is all released rapidly at high
85 levels in a short time, or is released slowly at low levels, over a long time span.

Decay of Carbon-14

This data is from the *Journal of Research of the National Bureau of Standards*, Vol. 64, No. 4, April 1951, pp. 328 – 333.

1. Based on the information in Passage 1, which of the following could be dated using carbon-14 dating?

    A) An iron pot found in a cave

    B) A rock at the bottom of a quarry

    C) An arrowhead made from bone

    D) The remains of a house made from stone

2. Which choice provides the best evidence for the answer to the previous question?

    A) Lines 10-12 ("For example … carbon-13")

    B) Lines 27-30 ("Living plants … dioxide")

    C) Lines 30-33 ("After the plant … rate")

    D) Lines 38-41 ("Carbon-14 dating … animals")

3. As used in line 25, "decay" most nearly means

    A) yield.

    B) deteriorate.

    C) discharge.

    D) circulated.

4. Which statement best describes the relationship between carbon-12 and carbon-14 in living tissue?

    A) There is more carbon-14 than carbon-12.

    B) There is more carbon-12 than carbon-14.

    C) The ratio of carbon-12 to carbon-14 is constant.

    D) The ratio of carbon-12 to carbon-14 fluctuates greatly.

5. Which choice provides the best evidence for the answer to the previous question?

    A) Lines 13-14 ("Some combinations …time")

    B) Lines 24-25 ("Carbon-14 atoms … decay")

    C) Lines 27-30 ("Living plants … carbon dioxide")

    D) Lines 30-33 ("After the plant … rate")

6. In Passage 2, the author refers to an accident that results in the release of iodine-131 as a "short-term concern" (line 73) because the initial amount of radiation released is

    A) low but will drop slowly.

    B) high but will drop quickly.

    C) low and will drop quickly.

    D) high and will drop slowly.

7. Based on the information in Passage 2, living tissue exposed to radioactive material can

   A) be destroyed by high levels of heat caused by the radiation.

   B) become radioactive itself and damage surrounding tissue.

   C) suffer injury when the cell's components are damaged.

   D) be killed by extra protons released by the radioactive material.

8. As used in line 75, "original" most nearly means

   A) earliest.

   B) unique.

   C) unusual.

   D) critical.

9. According to Passage 2, scientists use the half-life of radioactive material to determine the

   A) amount of danger posed by radiation immediately following a nuclear accident.

   B) likelihood of a nuclear accident involving the release of radioactive material at any given location.

   C) amount of radiation contained in a sample of iodine-131 or cesium-137 used in nuclear reactions.

   D) length of time that must pass until an area is safe after the release of radioactive material.

10. Which generalization about the study of physics is supported by both passages?

    A) The study of atomic and nuclear physics can have many applications in a variety of fields.

    B) The study of physics has helped revolutionize how archaeologists study artifacts.

    C) Scientists use physics to keep people and wildlife safe following a nuclear accident.

    D) Scientists use different concepts to date ancient items and assess danger from nuclear accidents.

11. Based on the graph and the information in the passages, which statement is accurate?

    A) Carbon-14 has a half-life of about 5,400 years.

    B) The half-life of carbon-14 is similar to that of cesium-137.

    C) The half-life of iodine-131 is greater than that of cesium-137.

    D) All radioactive materials have a half-life of 30 to 5,400 years.

Questions 12-22 are based on the following passages.

Passage 1 tells the story behind the writing of the United States national anthem. Passage 2 discusses how the prevalence, use, and value of the United States national anthem have changed over time.

Passage 1

The story behind "The Star-Spangled Banner," America's national anthem, begins with the War of 1812. This war, which began just three decades after
Line the Revolution, was again waged between American
5 and British forces for various reasons, including trade interference. Stakes were high: this was one of America's earliest opportunities to solidify its status as a sovereign nation equal to other world powers. Moreover, many Americans feared that the
10 nation might forfeit its hard-earned liberty were the British to defeat them.

Britain's involvement was limited in the war's first two years due to conflict at home, where Napoleon's army had attacked. But in the summer of 1814,
15 after the conflict with France had mostly subsided, Britain's focus turned to the American theater, which up to this point had been merely a distraction. In August of that year, the British sent an invading force that quickly defeated a smaller American force that
20 was ill-equipped and poorly trained. Later that night, the British Army invaded Washington, setting fire to several buildings, including the president's home and the Capitol. A few weeks later, on September 12th, British infantry troops tried to overtake Baltimore,
25 but America's defenses prevailed. The next morning, Britain's navy began a heavy bombardment of Baltimore's Fort McHenry, located at the mouth of Baltimore's harbor.

Some American men, including lawyer Francis
30 Scott Key, happened to be aboard a British ship in the harbor that same day. These men had come to peacefully request a captive friend's release—a request that, to their fortune, was granted. But the British detained them on the ship until the attack
35 on McHenry had run its course. From this vantage point, Key and his companions witnessed Fort McHenry's bombard-ment: twenty-five rain-drenched hours of rockets, explosions, and gunfire.

Through the night, Key waited in grim expectation
40 that the morning would reveal a white flag raised over the fort, symbolizing McHenry's surrender. But instead, by dawn's light he saw the American flag. McHenry had endured; British forces were already retreating. Moved by the sight, Key began
45 to write, on the back of a letter he was carrying, the words that would become America's national anthem.

This event marked a turning point in America's favor; within months, the war would be over. The
50 War of 1812 would list among the less significant wars in United States history, by many accounts. But Francis Scott Key's eloquent description of the flag—and the brave victory it represented—would become a lasting emblem of American patriotism.

Passage 2

55 America's National Anthem began as a poem titled "The Defence of Fort McHenry." Its melody came from the British tune, "Anacreon in Heaven." Written on September 14, 1814, and distributed shortly thereafter, the song enjoyed almost instant
60 popularity. A Baltimore theater housed its first public performance about a month after its writing. Following this, a music shop printed the song under the enduring title "The Star-Spangled Banner."

Over the next century, the song gained increasing
65 value in the hearts of Americans, growing especially popular during the Civil War. Around the 1890s, the military began playing the song for ceremonial uses. At the time of World War I, when patriotic music again served as a crucial ideological refuge for
70 America's people, "The Star-Spangled Banner" began to be treated by the military as the national anthem. Also around this time, the anthem was played in its first baseball game: a Cubs versus Red Sox game in which the song surprised and moved the crowds
75 during the seventh-inning stretch. The effect made national headlines, and, in each game to follow during that series, the anthem was played, meeting an equally enthusiastic reception. This launched the tradition of the national anthem's now near-ubiquitous pres-
80 ence at major American sporting events.

In 1931, Congress and President Hoover passed the bill to officially designate the song as America's national anthem. It had long since distinguished itself from other patriotic songs and held special signifi-
85 cance in American hearts, but now it would remain the nation's staple celebratory score. Today, the song is taught to children in schools, used in various ceremonies, printed in many church hymnals and community songbooks, and sung collectively at
90 sporting events, including those featuring American participation internationally, such as World Cup Soccer games or the opening ceremonies of the Olympics. The anthem's final words about those over whom the flag waves ("O'er the land of the free / and the home
95 of the brave") remind Americans of the liberty for which the country was established, and the courage of those who fought for it.

12. What is the author of Passage 1's overall purpose?
   A) Analyzing the impact of the War of 1812
   B) Describing the reasons for the War of 1812
   C) Explaining the origins of the national anthem
   D) Evaluating the legacy of the national anthem

13. The author of Passage 1 most likely includes the information in lines 6-11 ("Stakes were high... defeat them") in order to
   A) call attention to the reasons for going to war.
   B) emphasize the role of Francis Scott Key in defending the nation.
   C) explain the symbolism featured in the anthem.
   D) show the significance of the outcome of the war.

14. As used in line 22, "prevailed" most nearly means
   A) entrenched.
   B) floundered.
   C) persuaded.
   D) succeeded.

15. The information in paragraph 4 of Passage 1 most clearly suggests that Francis Scott Key wrote the national anthem to
   A) call public attention to the bombardment of American forces.
   B) honor the act of American fortitude that he witnessed.
   C) denounce critics of the War of 1812.
   D) inspire the defenders of Fort McHenry.

16. Which choice provides the best evidence for the answer to the previous question?
   A) Line 39 ("Through the night ... expectation")
   B) Lines 40-41 ("morning ... the fort")
   C) Lines 43-44 ("British forces ... retreating")
   D) Lines 44-45 ("Moved by ... to write")

17. The author of Passage 1 would most likely agree with which of the following statements?

   A) The national anthem grew out of an incidental war but gained importance as a result of government propaganda during later wars.

   B) The national anthem captured the triumph of the United States in defending its sovereignty and might during the War of 1812.

   C) The national anthem would have gone unnoticed if it were not for its popular resonance with an American people steeped in British musical tradition.

   D) The national anthem rallied support for the defense of Fort McHenry and helped sustain American forces through the War of 1812.

18. Why does the author of Passage 2 most likely begin with lines 55-57 ("America's National Anthem . . . 'Anacreon in Heaven'")?

   A) To show that Key did not set out to write the national anthem

   B) To give credit to the influence of British tradition in American culture

   C) To highlight the poetic devices that Key used in the writing of the national anthem

   D) To demonstrate that the national anthem describes a specific event, not American patriotism

19. As used in line 79, "near-ubiquitous" most nearly means

   A) commonplace.

   B) controversial.

   C) intermittent.

   D) offensive.

20. In line 94-95, the author quotes "The Star-Spangled Banner" primarily to

   A) demonstrate the lyrical mastery of Francis Scott Key.

   B) explain the symbolism of the American flag in the national anthem.

   C) recall the specific events of the War of 1812.

   D) show how the lyrics of the national anthem reflect American patriotism.

21. How does the information in Passage 2 most enhance the content of Passage 1?

   A) It describes the lasting legacy of the national anthem.

   B) It emphasizes the patriotic nature of the national anthem.

   C) It explores the origins of the national anthem in the War of 1812.

   D) It explains how Key's words became the national anthem.

22. Which choice provides the best evidence for the answer to the previous question?

   A) Lines 58-60 ("Written . . . popularity")

   B) Lines 68-71 ("At the time . . . anthem")

   C) Lines 86-90 ("Today . . . events")

   D) Lines 93-96 ("The anthem's . . . established")

Expression of Ideas

BY THE END OF THIS UNIT, YOU WILL BE ABLE TO:

1. Apply the Kaplan Method for Writing & Language

2. Evaluate the effectiveness and clarity of a given passage

3. Identify proper and effective language use

4. Utilize the standard conventions of usage in written English

CHAPTER 26

The Kaplan Methods for Writing & Language and Infographics

CHAPTER OBJECTIVES

By the end of this chapter, you will be able to:

1. Identify issues in a passage and select the correct answer by applying the Kaplan Method for Writing & Language

2. Identify and analyze quantitative information and infographics

3. Synthesize information from infographics and text

SMARTPOINTS

Point Value	SmartPoint Category
Point Builder	The Kaplan Method for Writing & Language
Point Builder	The Kaplan Method for Infographics
10 Points	Quantitative

THE KAPLAN METHOD FOR WRITING & LANGUAGE

The Kaplan Method for Writing & Language is the method you will use to boost your score on the Writing & Language Test. By understanding what the question is looking for, how it relates to the passage, and what questions you should ask yourself on Test Day, you will maximize the number of points you earn. Use the Kaplan Method for Writing & Language for every SAT Writing & Language Test passage and question you encounter, whether practicing, completing your homework, working on a Practice Test, or taking the actual exam on Test Day.

The Kaplan Method for Writing & Language has three steps:

Step 1: Read the passage and identify the issue

- If there's an infographic, apply the Kaplan Method for Infographics

Step 2: Eliminate answer choices that do not address the issue

Step 3: Plug in the remaining answer choices and select the most correct, concise, and relevant one

✔ On Test Day

The SAT will expect you to be able to recognize errors in organization, pronouns, agreement, comparisons, development, sentence structure, modifiers, verbs, wordiness, style, tone, and syntax.

Let's take a closer look at each step.

Step 1: Read the passage and identify the issue

This means:

- Rather than reading the whole passage and then answering all of the questions, you can answer questions as you read because they are mostly embedded in the text itself.

- When you see a number, stop reading and look at the question. If you can answer it with what you've read so far, do so. If you need more information, keep reading for context until you can answer the question.

Step 2: Eliminate answer choices that do not address the issue

Eliminating answer choices that do not address the issue:

- Increases your odds of getting the correct answer by removing obviously incorrect answer choices.

Step 3: Plug in the remaining answer choices and select the most correct, concise, and relevant one

Correct, concise, and relevant means that the answer choice you select:

- Makes sense when read with the correction.
- Is as short as possible while retaining the information in the text.
- Relates well to the passage overall.

Answer choices should not:

- Change the intended meaning of the original sentence, paragraph, or passage
- Introduce new grammatical errors, even if the answer choice in question resolves the initial issue in the passage

You will see four Writing & Language passages on Test Day, each of which will have 11 questions. When you encounter a Writing & Language question, use the Kaplan Method, asking yourself a series of strategic thinking questions.

By asking these strategic thinking questions, you will be able to select the correct answer choice more easily and efficiently. Pausing to ask questions may seem like it takes a lot of time, but it actually saves you time by preventing you from weighing the four answer choices against each other. Better to ask questions that lead you directly to the correct answer than to debate which of four answers seems the least incorrect.

Let's look at the following example of the Kaplan Method for Writing & Language in action in a short test-like passage. The left column contains text and a question similar to what you'll see on the Writing & Language Test on Test Day. The column on the right features the strategic thinking a test expert employs when approaching the passage and question presented.

Question	Strategic Thinking
A 2005 report from the United States Department of Agriculture estimates that the cost of raising a child from birth until age seventeen is approximately $500,000. This cost includes housing, food, clothing, transportation, health care, child care, and education and does, of course, vary considerably. However, with the average cost of having and raising a child set at half a million dollars, and with additional children in the family raising that financial expenditure accordingly, it becomes clear that parenthood should not be entered into lightly. Even for families that plan for children, there may be costs for which they are unprepared. For instance, if a woman chooses to spend the first years of her child's life as a full-time mother and homemaker, she can lose career momentum and end up making a substantially lower salary than a woman with the same background who maintains consistent employment. While these factors should in no way be construed as a recommendation against having children, ❶ if you're planning a family, be ready.	**Step 1: Read the passage and identify the issue** The underlined phrase is grammatically correct. When there is no apparent grammatical issue, check style, tone, and syntax. The tone of the underlined portion is much more informal than the tone of the overall passage, as evidenced by the use of the second person ("you"). **Step 2: Eliminate answer choices that do not address the issue** Eliminate A because there is a tone issue in the underlined portion. Eliminate B and D because they still use the second person (it's implied in B with the imperative mood of the verb "think"). **Step 3: Plug in the remaining answer choices and select the most correct, concise, and relevant one** Choice (C) is the only answer choice left and is therefore correct.

1. A) NO CHANGE
      B) but think about the problems it might cause.
      C) they speak to the need for responsible family planning and financial preparation.
      D) make sure you understand what you're getting into.	

THE KAPLAN METHOD FOR INFOGRAPHICS

The SAT Writing & Language Test will contain one or more passages and/or questions that include one or more infographics. Each infographic will convey or expand on information from the passage.

The Kaplan Method for Infographics has three steps:

Step 1: Read the question
Step 2: Examine the infographic
Step 3: Predict and answer

Let's examine these steps a bit more closely.

Step 1: Read the question

Assess the question stem for information that will help you zero in on the specific parts of the infographic that apply to the question.

Step 2: Examine the infographic

Make sure to:

- Circle parts of the infographic that relate directly to the question

- Identify units of measurement, labels, and titles

Step 3: Predict and answer

Just as in Step 3 of the Kaplan Method for Reading Comprehension, do not look at the answer choices until you've used the infographic to make a prediction. Even though the Kaplan Method for Writing & Language does not ask you to predict before you peek, make sure to do so when presented with an infographic question on the SAT Writing & Language Test.

No matter how many infographics you see on the Writing & Language Test on Test Day, make sure you use the Kaplan Method for Infographics for each one so that you maximize your score by answering the associated questions correctly.

SAT experts ask themselves the questions outlined in the previous section as well as other questions that are more specific to the infographic and the passage it accompanies. Remember, infographics vary in format—there can be tables, graphs, charts, and so on—so be flexible when you ask yourself these critical-thinking questions.

As always, asking questions and taking time to assess the given information before answering the test question will increase your chances of selecting the correct answer.

Let's look at how to apply the Kaplan Method for Infographics. This infographic would either represent data described in the passage or present new data that expand on what the passage is about.

The left column contains an infographic similar to the ones you'll see on the Writing & Language Test on Test Day. The column on the right features the strategic thinking a test expert employs when approaching the question and infographic presented.

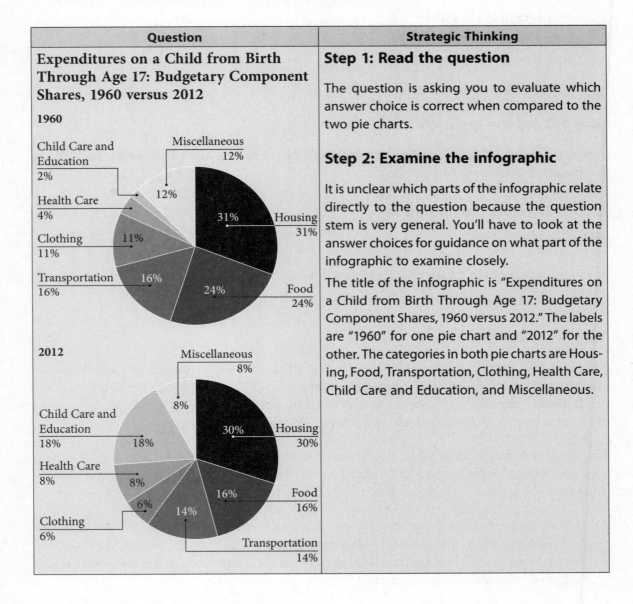

Question	Strategic Thinking
Expenditures on a Child from Birth Through Age 17: Budgetary Component Shares, 1960 versus 2012	**Step 1: Read the question** The question is asking you to evaluate which answer choice is correct when compared to the two pie charts. **Step 2: Examine the infographic** It is unclear which parts of the infographic relate directly to the question because the question stem is very general. You'll have to look at the answer choices for guidance on what part of the infographic to examine closely. The title of the infographic is "Expenditures on a Child from Birth Through Age 17: Budgetary Component Shares, 1960 versus 2012." The labels are "1960" for one pie chart and "2012" for the other. The categories in both pie charts are Housing, Food, Transportation, Clothing, Health Care, Child Care and Education, and Miscellaneous.

Question	Strategic Thinking
2. Which claim about the cost of raising children is supported by the two pie charts? A) Between 1960 and 2012, the percent of a budget spent on food increased. B) Between 1960 and 2012, the percent of a budget spent on health care decreased. C) Between 1960 and 2012, the percent of a budget spent on transportation experienced the greatest decrease. D) Between 1960 and 2012, the percent of a budget spent on child care and education experienced the greatest increase.	**Step 3: Predict and answer** The percent of a budget spent on food did not increase from 1960 to 2012, as A claims. Rather, it decreased from 24% to 16%. Eliminate A. The percent of a budget spent on health care did not decrease from 1960 to 2012, as B claims. Rather, it increased from 4% to 8%. Eliminate B. The percent of a budget spent on transportation decreased from 16% in 1960 to 14% in 2012. This was not the greatest decrease, as C claims; the decrease of the percent of a budget spent on food was greater. Eliminate C. The percent of a budget spent on child care and education increased from 2% in 1960 to 18% in 2012. This is the greatest increase, as D claims. Choice (D) is correct.

You have seen what kinds of strategic thinking questions SAT experts ask themselves when they encounter Writing & Language Test questions.

Look at the Writing & Language passage excerpt below. There are three questions associated with it. Use the Kaplan Method for Writing & Language to answer the questions. But remember to look at the guiding questions that have been laid out for you—some of the answers have been filled in, but you will have to fill in the answers to others.

Use your answers to the strategic thinking questions to select the correct answer, just as you will on Test Day.

Questions 3-5 are based on the following passage.

Industrial Progress

Is industrial progress a mixed blessing? **3** <u>Hundred years</u> ago, this question was seldom asked. Science and industry were flooding the world with products that made life easier. But today we know that many industrial processes create pollution that can destroy our environment. Industries produce toxic waste, discharging harmful chemicals directly into lakes, rivers, and the air. One of the results of this pollution that must be managed in order to protect our ecosystems is acid rain.

Air, clouds, and rain containing acids caused by industrial pollution can have terrible effects. Acid droplets in the air can be inhaled, causing illness. From clouds, these acid droplets fall as rain. If natural chemical processes in soils do not deactivate the acids, these acids can accumulate and kill both plant and animal life. In some parts of the Northeast and Midwest, 10 percent of all lakes show dangerous acid levels. In eastern mountains in the United States, large forest tracts have been lost at elevations where trees are regularly bathed in acidic clouds.

Acid rain is caused by industrial processes that release compounds of nitrogen and sulfur. **4** <u>These pollutants</u> combine with clean air, the results are nitric and sulfuric acids. The main components of acid rain **5** <u>is</u> oxides of nitrogen and sulfur dioxide, which are emitted by oil- and coal-burning power plants. To reduce acid rain, emissions from these plants, particularly sulfur dioxide, must be reduced. One way is to install machines that remove sulfur dioxide from a plant's emissions. Another is to build new plants modeled on currently experimental designs that produce less sulfur dioxide.

Questions	Strategic Thinking
3. A) NO CHANGE B) A hundred years, give or take, C) One hundred years D) Hundred years or so	**Step 1: Read the passage and identify the issue** *What is the issue?* As written, the underlined portion uses the incorrect form of a number, which is an error in idiom construction. **Step 2: Eliminate answer choices that do not address the issue** *What answer choice(s) can you eliminate?* _____ _____ _____ **Step 3: Plug in the remaining answer choices and select the most correct, concise, and relevant one** *What is the answer?* _____
4. A) NO CHANGE B) Because these pollutants C) When these pollutants D) Where these pollutants	**Step 1: Read the passage and identify the issue** *What is the issue?* While there is nothing necessarily incorrect about the underlined portion, if you keep reading the entire sentence it belongs to, you'll see that it is is a run-on. **Step 2: Eliminate answer choices that do not address the issue** *What answer choice(s) can you eliminate?* _____ _____ _____ **Step 3: Plug in the remaining answer choices and select the most correct, concise, and relevant one** *What is the answer?* _____

Questions	Strategic Thinking
5. A) NO CHANGE B) are *(circled)* C) was D) were	**Step 1: Read the passage and identify the issue** *What is the issue?* The singular verb "is" does not agree with its subject, "the main components." You need a plural verb in the present tense. **Step 2: Eliminate answer choices that do not address the issue** *What answer choice(s) can you eliminate?* _____ _____ _____ **Step 3: Plug in the remaining answer choices and select the most correct, concise, and relevant one** *What is the answer?* _____

Now, try a test-like Writing & Language passage and infographic on your own. Give yourself 5 minutes to read the passage and answer the questions.

Questions 6-13 are based on the following passage and supplementary material.

Jupiter

As the fifth planet from the Sun, and by far the most massive in our solar system at 318 times the mass of Earth, Jupiter has **6** fascinated and intrigued scientists for centuries. In fact, it was the initial discovery of this massive, gaseous planet that marked the first time astronomers considered the possibility that the movement of other planets was not centered around the earth. More specifically, when Jupiter was first viewed from Earth by the Italian astronomer Galileo in 1610, four large moons were also spotted in orbit around this enormous planet. It was these moons, now known as the Galilean moons, that provided important evidence for Galileo's outspoken support of Copernicus's heliocentric theory of planetary **7** movement. Because these moons seemed to revolve around a planet other than Earth.

The first close look at Jupiter came in 1973, when the unmanned NASA probe *Pioneer 10* completed a successful **8** flyby, and it collected important data regarding the planet's chemical composition and interior structure. **9** After completing its mission to Jupiter, *Pioneer 10* became the first spacecraft to leave the Solar System. Designated as one of the gas planets—along with Saturn, Uranus, and Neptune—Jupiter is composed of about 90 percent hydrogen and 10 percent helium and has no solid surface, only varying densities of gas. In fact, very little is known about the interior of Jupiter. What is visible when looking at a gas planet like Jupiter is really only the tops of clouds making up the outermost atmosphere, and probes have been able to penetrate only about 90 miles below this layer. However, after analyzing traces of water and minerals

6. A)   NO CHANGE
    B)   fascinated
    C)   intrigued, and fascinated
    D)   fascinated intriguing

7. A)   NO CHANGE
    B)   movement. These
    C)   movement. Although
    D)   movement because

8. A)   NO CHANGE
    B)   flyby and it collected
    C)   flyby, and collecting
    D)   flyby and collected

9. The author is considering omitting the underlined sentence. Should the sentence be kept or omitted?

    A)   It should be kept because it adds an interesting detail about the *Pioneer 10* mission.

    B)   It should be kept because it provides support for the claim that the mission was successful.

    C)   It should be omitted because it shifts the focus of the passage from Jupiter to the *Pioneer 10* mission.

    D)   It should be omitted because it does not include information about when *Pioneer 10* left the solar system.

collected from Jupiter's atmosphere, scientists believe that the planet has a core of rocky material amounting to a mass perhaps as much as 15 times that of Earth.

⑩ Jupiter is like other gaseous planets. Jupiter has high-velocity winds that blow in wide bands of latitude, each moving in an alternate direction. Slight chemical and temperature changes between these bands, and the resulting chemical reactions, are probably responsible for the array of vibrant colors that dominate the planet's appearance. ⑪ Measurement taken by a number of probes indicate that the powerful winds moving these bands can reach speeds exceeding 400 miles per hour and likely extend thousands of miles below Jupiter's outer atmosphere.

Yet perhaps the most fascinating characteristic of this planet is the rotational speed of the entire globe of gas itself. While Earth takes 24 hours to make a full revolution, Jupiter completes a full revolution ⑫ in less time, an amazingly short period of time for a planet with a diameter roughly 11 times that of ⑬ ours. How Jupiter is able to rotate so fast is just one of many mysteries that scientists continue to explore in their efforts to understand our largest neighbor.

10. A) NO CHANGE
    B) Like other gaseous planets,
    C) Jupiter is like other gaseous planets,
    D) Jupiter, like other gaseous planets,

11. A) NO CHANGE
    B) A measurement
    C) The measurement
    D) Measurements

12. Which choice most accurately reflects the data found in the table?
    A) NO CHANGE
    B) in half that time
    C) in fewer than 10 Earth hours
    D) in more time than all the other planets

13. A) NO CHANGE
    B) our own planet
    C) our own
    D) our own planet's

Planets in Our Solar System				
Planet	Period of Revolution Around the Sun (1 planetary year)	Period of Rotation (1 planetary day)	Mass (kg)	Diameter (miles)
Mercury	87.96 Earth days	58.7 Earth days	3.3×10^{23}	3,031 miles
Venus	224.68 Earth days	243 Earth days	4.87×10^{24}	7,521 miles
Earth	365.26 days	24 hours	5.98×10^{24}	7,926 miles
Mars	686.98 Earth days	24.6 Earth hours	6.42×10^{23}	4,222 miles
Jupiter	11.862 Earth years	9.84 Earth hours	1.90×10^{27}	88,729 miles
Saturn	29.456 Earth years	10.2 Earth hours	5.69×10^{26}	74,600 miles
Uranus	84.07 Earth years	17.9 Earth hours	8.68×10^{25}	32,600 miles
Neptune	164.81 Earth years	19.1 Earth hours	1.02×10^{26}	30,200 miles
Pluto (a dwarf planet)	247.7 Earth years	6.39 Earth days	1.29×10^{22}	1,413 miles

Answers & Explanations for this chapter begin on page 1072.

EXTRA PRACTICE

Required	Recommended
Questions 1–11	Questions 12–22

Questions 1-11 are based on the following passage.

Physical Therapy Careers: Health Care in Motion

Physical therapy is a health care field that is **1** concurrently rated by the U.S. Bureau of Labor Statistics as one of today's best career choices. Featuring considerable variety in work environments, patient relationships, and job activity levels, the work of a physical therapist has the potential to be highly motivating and satisfying. **2** And current projections indicate that this particular field of physical therapy should grow significantly over the next decade and continue to be one of the more flexible—not to mention enjoyable and fun—jobs in health care.

1. A) NO CHANGE
   B) consistently
   C) unusually
   D) finally

2. A) NO CHANGE
   B) And current projections indicate that the field should grow significantly over the next several years and the next decade and remain one of the more flexible—not to mention enjoyable—jobs in health care.
   C) And current projections and predictions by the Bureau of Labor indicate that the field should grow significantly over the next decade and remain one of the more flexible and even enjoyable—jobs in the health care industry.
   D) Current projections indicate that the field should grow significantly over the next decade and remain one of the more flexible and enjoyable jobs in health care.

[3] After completing a bachelor's degree (and specific science-related prerequisites), students must obtain a Doctor of Physical Therapy (DPT) degree. This program typically lasts three years. All graduates of DPT programs must then pass the National Physical Therapy Examination. After the exam, they must complete any additional requirements for licensure in the state in which they intend to practice. Once licensed by the state, physical therapists (PTs) are equipped to begin their careers.

3. Which choice most effectively establishes the main topic of the second paragraph?

A) A license is required to practice as a physical therapist, even in a foreign country.

B) Those pursuing careers in physical therapy must undergo the appropriate education and licensure processes.

C) Requirements vary from state to state to practice physical therapy, just as they do for physicians and physicians' assistants.

D) Physical therapists must pass a national exam that covers a wide range of material.

4 **5** <u>PTs work with a broad range of patients in a wide variety of settings such as hospitals or private clinics.</u> Some clientele, for example, are elderly or ill. Other patients include athletes ranging from elite

4. Which choice best supports the topic sentence of paragraph 3?

A) PTs must demonstrate their willingness to spend long hours on the job.

B) Still others include people who have been injured at work.

C) The clientele pay for their physical therapy services according to their ability, so some PTs earn more than others.

D) No special license is required to work with patients who are professional athletes, but some states may require additional courses to work with students.

5. A) NO CHANGE

B) PTs work with a broad range of patients, in a wide variety of settings some work in hospitals, while others work in private clinics.

C) PTs work with a broad range of patients; in a wide variety of settings. Some work in hospitals; others in private clinics.

D) PTs work with a broad range of patients: The variety of settings, includes hospitals and private clinics.

professionals and college sports stars to middle school sports teams. ❻ And some kinds of PTs have personal, long-term patient relationships, while others focus on research or testing most of the time and occasionally interact with patients only minimally.

❼ [1] A physical therapist primarily works with patients who have suffered motion loss from illness or injury. The goal is to restore mobility

6. (A) NO CHANGE
    B) Some PTs have personal, long-term patient relationships, while others, who focus on research or testing, have minimal interaction with patients.
    C) Some PTs have personal, long-term patient relationships; others interact with patients only minimal and focus on research or testing.
    D) And some kinds of PTs have personal, long-term patient relationships. Others focus on research or testing and interact with patients only minimally.

7. A) NO CHANGE
    B) A physical therapist primarily works with patients. They have suffered motion loss from illness or injury. And the therapist's goal is to restore mobility. While managing and limiting pain.
    C) A physical therapist, whose goal is to restore mobility and manage pain primarily works with patients who have suffered motion loss or illness or injury.
    D) A physical therapist primarily works with patients who have suffered motion loss from illness or injury to restore mobility while managing and limiting pain.

while managing and limiting pain. **8** [2] <u>This job often involves long-term planning, creatively personalized application, and patience, in addition to highly refined medical knowledge.</u> [3] In many cases, physical therapists invite and rely on patients to participate actively in their own recovery. [4] This interpersonal and **9** <u>collaborative</u> aspect of physical therapy is often essential to the medical work itself. [5] For example, recovering athletes must often commit to long-term conditioning programs before returning to their sports. [6] Surgery or medication alone isn't always enough to restore full mobility; many PT patients must relearn their muscle use and work hard to increase flexibility. [7] PTs determine the course of action and coach their patients through the steps to recovery. **10**

[1] The horizon for employment rates in physical therapy is exceptionally bright. [2] The Bureau of Labor Statistics predicts that the coming decade will see a 36% growth in PT jobs. [3] This means that there should be a need for over 70,000 new PTs nationwide. [4] Physical therapist assistants (PTAs) will also be needed. [5] For those willing to commit the time and effort to become experts in physical therapy, the possibilities and quality of work environment are among the most desirable in health care, and considering projected employment rates, such a career seems to be an especially prudent choice. **11**

8. A) NO CHANGE
   B) This job often involves long-term planning and patience, creative personalized application, and highly refined medical knowledge.
   C) This job often involves long-term planning, creative personalized application and patience, in addition to highly refined medical knowledge.
   D) This job often involves long-term planning, creatively personal application and patience, as well as highly refined medical knowledge.

9. A) NO CHANGE
   B) concentrated
   C) planned
   D) consolidated

10. The logical sequence of the sentences in this paragraph is best when sentence 2 is placed
    A) before sentence 1.
    B) after sentence 3.
    C) after sentence 5.
    D) at the end of the paragraph.

11. Which sentence could be removed in order to improve the focus of this paragraph?
    A) Sentence 1
    B) Sentence 2
    C) Sentence 3
    D) Sentence 4

Questions 12-22 are based on the following passage and supplementary material.

The Pony Express: Not a Tame Ride

The 19th century saw the Civil War, the California Gold Rush, and the migration of thousands of people to the West along the Oregon Trail. With these events came **12** the really great and strong need for communication between the original colonies and the new state of California.

13 William H. Russell, Alexander Majors, and William B. Waddell brought about the solution to this need by creating Leavenworth & Pike's Peak Express Company, which later became known as the Pony Express.

The Pony Express was a system of riders that ran 2,000 miles from St. Joseph, Missouri, to Sacramento, California. Riders, who carried mail in leather satchels, changed every 75 to 100 miles. They changed horses every 10 to 15 miles. **14** When the Pony Express was its largest, it had a lot of riders who were paid for their services.

12. A) NO CHANGE
    B) the very strong and real need
    C) the need
    D) the strong and real need

13. A) NO CHANGE
    B) William H. Russell
       Alexander Majors and
       William B. Waddell
    C) William H. Russell
       Alexander Majors, and
       William B. Waddell
    D) William H. Russell,
       Alexander Majors, and,
       William B. Waddell

14. Which choice most effectively revises the underlined sentence?

    A) When the Pony Express was at its largest, it was a very glamorous job.

    B) At its largest, the Pony Express had over 150 riders of all ages and they were paid.

    C) When the Pony Express peaked, it employed a lot of riders and the youngest one was named Bronco Charlie Miller.

    D) At its peak, the Pony Express employed over 180 riders who ranged in age from 11 to 50 years old, and earned $50 a month.

Riders changed horses or took a short break at relay posts, or stations: small, simple cabins, with dirt floors and a few stalls for the horses. Riders could get small meals at the ⑮ stations, they usually consisted of dried fruit, cured meats, pickles, coffee, and cornmeal. At some bigger stations, known as "home stations," riders were able to enjoy a more relaxed meal, perhaps chat with other riders, and get some sleep.

The relay posts were also a source of employment. Each housed a station keeper who was responsible for having horses saddled and ready when a rider arrived, as well as for logging ⑯ accurate records of arrival and departure times. The job of a station keeper was not an easy one. ⑰ The stations were located in remote areas, had little access to resources, and were being unprotected from attacks by Native Americans.

⑱ Riders often rode through rough, unfamiliar terrain; were exposed to harsh weather; and were susceptible to attack by hostile Native Americans.

15. A) NO CHANGE
    B) stations they usually consisted
    C) stations. They usually consisted
    D) stations yet they usually consisted

16. A) NO CHANGE
    B) lengthy
    C) sorrowful
    D) agreeable

17. A) NO CHANGE
    B) stations were located in remote areas, had little access to resources, and were unprotected
    C) stations were being located in remote areas, had little access to resources, and were unprotected
    D) stations were located in remote areas, having little access to resources, and were unprotected

18. Which choice most effectively establishes the main topic of the paragraph?
    A) The riders' routes were fraught with danger of many kinds.
    B) The Pony Express helped tie California with the rest of the country.
    C) The Pony Express was not successful financially.
    D) Some of the riders died while trying to deliver the mail.

As a result of these challenges, only one mail delivery was lost during the Pony Express's 19 months of operation.

Shortly after the first riders of the Pony Express set out on April 3, 1860, Congress approved a bill funding the construction of a transcontinental telegraph line in March, 1860. The result of this bill was the creation of the Overland Telegraph Company of California and the Pacific Telegraph Company of Nevada. Once they were fully ㉑ invented on October 24, 1861, the Pony Express was no longer needed. Two days later, the Pony Express announced its closure.

Although its existence was a short one, the Pony Express played an important role in the development of the Pacific Coast. It remains an icon of the Wild West.

History of the Pony Express

January–March 1860 ➤	Russell, Majors, and Waddell establish Pony Express mail service.
April 3, 1860 ➤	First riders leave St. Joseph, Missouri, and Sacramento, California.
June 8, 1860 ➤	Congress authorizes building of transcontinental telegraph line.
October 24, 1861 ➤	East and West coasts connected by telegraph line.
October 26, 1861 ➤	Pony Express discontinued.

19. A) NO CHANGE
    B) Despite
    C) However
    D) For instance

20. Which choice completes the sentence with accurate data based on the timeline?
    A) NO CHANGE
    B) funding the construction of a transcontinental telegraph line on June 8, 1860
    C) funding the construction of a transcontinental telegraph line on October 24, 1861
    D) funding the construction of a transcontinental telegraph line in January, 1860

21. A) NO CHANGE
    B) breached
    C) operational
    D) contrasted

22. Which choice most effectively combines the sentences at the underlined portion?
    A) the Pacific Coast, since it remains
    B) the Pacific Coast, however, it remains
    C) the Pacific Coast, that it remains
    D) the Pacific Coast and remains

CHAPTER 27

Passage Types & Organization

CHAPTER OBJECTIVES

By the end of this chapter, you will be able to:

1. Distinguish between the three different Writing & Language text types

2. Organize a text's information and ideas into the most logical order

3. Evaluate whether transition words, phrases, or sentences are used effectively to introduce, conclude, or connect information and ideas, and revise the text to improve these transitions when necessary

SMARTPOINTS

Point Value	SmartPoint Category
Point Builder	Writing & Language Text Types
50 Points	Organization

WRITING & LANGUAGE TEXT TYPES

This chapter builds on the Kaplan Method for Writing & Language, which you can review in chapter 26.

Writing & Language Text Types	
1–2 Argumentative texts	Author will advocate a point, idea, or proposal
1–2 Informative/Explanatory texts	Author will explain, describe, or analyze a topic in order to impart information without necessarily advocating
1 Nonfiction Narrative text	Author will use a story-like approach to convey information or ideas

Recognizing the text type of a Writing & Language passage lets you focus on the questions as they relate to the passage's general purpose. Although an author will have specific goals beyond the general purpose of the passage, knowing what the overarching aim of the passage is will help you answer questions more efficiently and accurately.

> ✔ **Remember**
>
> The SAT rewards critical thinking in context. Pay attention to the text type to answer Writing & Language questions more efficiently.

Let's look at three short Writing & Language passage excerpts (without errors) and see how an SAT expert identifies the text type of each. The left column features the passage excerpt, while the column on the right demonstrates the strategic thinking a test expert employs when identifying Writing & Language text types.

Passages	Strategic Thinking
As if malpractice suits and unnecessary bankruptcies were not enough of a problem, lawyers have chosen to increase the burden that they place on society by engineering an excess of increasingly ridiculous product warnings. Why else would a box of Midol be marketed with the cautionary note that consumers with prostate problems should not purchase the tablets? Or a cup of coffee be emblazoned with a notice that "THIS PRODUCT MAY BE HOT"? Anyone with common sense will not need to be warned about these possibilities, and anyone WITHOUT common sense is probably not going to be stopped by a warning label from undertaking a foolish course of action anyway. So honestly, in the long run, the only ones who benefit from these warnings are the lawyers who are paid hundreds of dollars an hour to compose them.	The phrases "ridiculous product warnings," "anyone with common sense," and "foolish course of action"—plus the rhetorical questions in the passage—indicate that the tone of the passage is incredulous, cynical, and mocking. The author is mocking the "excess of increasingly ridiculous product warnings." The author says that "the only ones who benefit from these warnings are the lawyers who are paid hundreds of dollars an hour to compose them." The text type of this passage excerpt is therefore Argumentative.
It is amazing how little the structure of the American public school system has changed since its inception. Students still change classes according to bells, even though the bell system originated during the days of factories. School is still not in session during the summer, although most students will not use that time to work on farms. Although class and school sizes have varied widely and the curriculum has certainly become varied, the actual system remains surprisingly similar to the way it once was. Despite these idiosyncrasies, however, the American public school system continues to educate the children of this country in a fair and equitable fashion. Without the established structure, the chaotic nature of school would severely inhibit learning.	In the first sentence of the passage, the author establishes the topic of the passage. The keywords "although" and "despite" later in the passage suggest that the author is reporting on various aspects of the public school system. The text type of this passage excerpt is therefore Informative/Explanatory.

Passages	Strategic Thinking
I still remember the magic of walking home under the cold, brittle blue sky, watching the sun strike the glittering blanket laid down by that first snowfall. The world dripped with frosting, and everything was pure and silent. I breathed deeply, enjoying the sting of the icy air in my nostrils, and set off through the trees, listening to the muffled crunch of my footsteps and the chirps of the waking birds. Later, the cars and schoolchildren and mundane lives would turn the wonderland back into dingy slush; the hush would be interrupted by horns and shouts. Indeed for now, the sparkling, cloistered world was mine alone. I smiled, and for a moment, my mind was still.	This passage is different from the previous two passages because it is written in the first person, as evidenced by the author's use of personal pronouns like "I." The text type of this passage is therefore a Nonfiction Narrative.

ORGANIZATION

Organization questions require you to assess the logic and coherence of a Writing & Language passage. These questions differ in scope: You might be asked to organize the writing at the level of the sentence, the paragraph, or even the entire passage.

There are two kinds of Organization questions:

1. Logical Sequence

- These questions ask you to reorder the sentences in a paragraph or paragraphs in a passage to ensure that information and ideas are logically conveyed.

- When rearranging sentences or paragraphs, begin by determining which sentence or paragraph most logically introduces the paragraph or the passage, respectively.

2. Introductions, Conclusions, and Transitions

- These questions task you with improving the beginning or ending of a passage or paragraph, making sure that the transition words, phrases, or sentences are being used effectively not only to connect information and ideas but also to maintain logical structure.

- While introductions and conclusions focus on the beginning and ending of a passage or paragraph, respectively, transitions are a bit more complicated. It's important to identify what two ideas the transition is linking and how it is doing so. Common types and examples of transitions are listed in the following chart.

Contrast Transitions	Cause-and-Effect Transitions	Continuation Transitions
although	as a result	**Providing an example**
but	because	for example
despite	consequently	for instance
even though	since	**Showing emphasis**
however	so	certainly
in contrast	therefore	in fact
nonetheless	thus	indeed
on the other hand		that is
rather than		**Showing a parallel relationship**
though		also
unlike		furthermore
while		in addition
yet		and
		moreover

✔ **Remember**

Organization questions require you to not only improve grammar and style but also ensure that these elements accurately express the author's logic and reasoning.

Let's look at how an SAT expert approaches Organization questions in the test-like Writing & Language passage excerpts you saw earlier in this chapter. The left column features the passage excerpt and question, while the column on the right demonstrates the strategic thinking a test expert employs when answering Organization questions.

Passages & Questions	Strategic Thinking
① As if malpractice suits and unnecessary bankruptcies were not enough of a problem, lawyers have chosen to increase the burden that they place on society by engineering an excess of increasingly ridiculous product warnings. Why else would a box of Midol be marketed with the cautionary note that consumers with prostate problems should not purchase the tablets? Or a cup of coffee be emblazoned with a notice that "THIS PRODUCT MAY BE HOT"? Anyone with common sense will not need to be warned about these possibilities, and anyone WITHOUT common sense is probably not going to be stopped by a warning label from undertaking a foolish course of action anyway. So honestly, in the long run, the only ones who benefit from these warnings are the lawyers who are paid hundreds of dollars an hour to compose them.	**Step 1: Read the passage and identify the issue** The underlined segment contains the introductory sentence, which introduces the passage's topic of the ridiculousness of product warnings. The author concludes that lawyers are the only people who benefit from product warnings because they are paid to write them.
1. Which answer choice most effectively establishes the main topic of the paragraph? (A) NO CHANGE B) Each year, effective product warning labels help countless people avoid serious injuries resulting from their use of consumer products. C) In recent years, a coalition of lawyers and consumer safety advocates has successfully campaigned to require companies to include safety warnings on product labels. D) Product safety warnings are necessary to protect consumers who thoughtlessly use products without first thinking about the possible risks involved.	**Step 2: Eliminate answer choices that do not address the issue** Eliminate B because the author does not believe the product warnings are "effective." Eliminate C because the author mentions the lawyers only in a negative light. Eliminate D because the author does not believe product safety warnings are "necessary." **Step 3: Plug in the remaining answer choices and select the most correct, concise, and relevant one** Choice (A) is the only answer choice left and is therefore correct.

Passages & Questions	Strategic Thinking
[1] It is amazing how little the structure of the American public school system has changed since its inception. [2] Students still change classes according to bells, even though the bell system originated during the days of factories. [3] School is still not in session during the summer, although most students will not use that time to work on farms. [4] Although class and school sizes have varied widely and the curriculum has certainly become varied, the actual system remains surprisingly similar to the way it once was. [5] Despite these idiosyncrasies, however, the American public school system continues to educate the children of this country in a fair and equitable fashion. [6] Without the established structure, the chaotic nature of school would severely inhibit learning. [2]	**Step 1: Read the passage and identify the issue** Sentence 4 is about the fact that even though there have been educational changes over the years, the school system itself has actually not changed that much. It is not properly placed within the paragraph.
2. In order for this paragraph to be cohesive, sentence 4 should be placed A) where it is now. B) before sentence 1. C) after sentence 1. D) after sentence 6.	**Step 2: Eliminate answer choices that do not address the issue** Eliminate A because sentence 4's location is incorrect as is. Eliminate B because sentence 4 is not an appropriate introduction to the paragraph. Eliminate D because sentence 4 is not an appropriate conclusion to the paragraph. **Step 3: Plug in the remaining answer choices and select the most correct, concise, and relevant one** Choice (C) contains the correct placement of sentence 4 within the paragraph.

Passages & Questions	Strategic Thinking
I still remember the magic of walking home under the cold, brittle blue sky, watching the sun strike the glittering blanket laid down by that first snowfall. The world dripped with frosting, and everything was pure and silent. I breathed deeply, enjoying the sting of the icy air in my nostrils, and set off through the trees, listening to the muffled crunch of my footsteps and the chirps of the waking birds. Later, the cars and schoolchildren and mundane lives would turn the wonderland back into dingy slush; the hush would be interrupted by horns and shouts. ③ Indeed for now, the sparkling, cloistered world was mine alone. I smiled, and for a moment, my mind was still.	**Step 1: Read the passage and identify the issue** The underlined word is a continuation transition showing emphasis. It is incorrect as written because the sentence preceding it discusses what will happen to the snow while this sentence discusses what the snow is like now. A contrast transition would be more correct in this context.

3. A) NO CHANGE
    B) But
    C) Consequently
    D) In fact
	Step 2: Eliminate answer choices that do not address the issue
	
	Eliminate C and D because they are not contrast transitions.
	
	Step 3: Plug in the remaining answer choices and select the most correct, concise, and relevant one
	
	Choice (B) is the only contrast transition among the answer choices and is therefore correct.

You have seen the ways in which the SAT tests you on Organization in Writing & Language passages and the way an SAT expert approaches these types of questions.

Look at the Writing & Language passage excerpt that follows. There are three questions associated with it. Use the Kaplan Method for Writing & Language to answer the questions. Remember to look at the strategic thinking questions that have been laid out for you—some of the answers have been filled in, but you will have to fill in the answers to others.

Use your answers to the strategic thinking questions to select the correct answer, just as you will on Test Day.

Questions 4-6 are based on the following passage.

Earthquakes

[1]

The recent devastating earthquakes in China, Haiti, Chile, Mexico, and elsewhere have many wondering if this earthquake activity is unusual.

[2]

"While the number of earthquakes is within the normal range, this does not diminish the fact that there has been extreme devastation and loss of life in heavily populated areas," said USGS Associate Coordinator for Earthquake Hazards Dr. Michael Blanpied. 4

[3]

Scientists say 2010 is not showing signs of unusually high earthquake activity. Since 1900, an average of 16 magnitude 7 or greater earthquakes—the size that seismologists define as major—have occurred worldwide each year. Some years have had as few as 6, as in 1986 and 1989, while 1943 had 32, with considerable variability from year to year.

[4]

With six major earthquakes striking in the first four months of this year, 2010 is well within the normal range. From April 15, 2009, to April 14, 2010, there have been 18 major earthquakes, a number also well within the expected variation.

[5]

[1] What will happen next? [2] It is unlikely that any of these aftershocks will be stronger than the earthquakes experienced so far, but structures damaged in the previous events could be further damaged and should be treated with caution. [3] Beyond the ongoing aftershock sequences, earthquakes in recent months have not raised the likelihood of future major earthquakes; that likelihood has not decreased, either. [4] Aftershocks will continue in the regions around each of this year's major earthquakes sites. [5] Large earthquakes will continue to occur just as they have in the past. 5

[6]

Though the recent earthquakes are not unusual, they are a stark reminder that earthquakes can produce disasters when they strike populated areas—especially areas where the buildings have not been designed to withstand strong shaking. What can you do to prepare? Scientists cannot predict the timing of specific earthquakes. 6 However, families and communities can improve their safety and reduce their losses by taking actions to make their homes, places of work, schools, and businesses as earthquake-safe as possible.

Questions	Strategic Thinking

4. In order for this passage to be cohesive, paragraph 2 should be placed
 	
    A)   where it is now.
    (B)   after paragraph 3.
    C)   after paragraph 4.
    D)   after paragraph 5.
	Step 1: Read the passage and identify the issue
	
	What is the Organization issue?
	
	Paragraph 2 is not properly placed within the passage.
	
	What is the content of paragraph 2?
	
	A quotation from a USGS official about how, despite the fact that the number of earthquakes is normal for the area, the loss and devastation suffered in populated regions is still profound.
	
	What two topics does this paragraph connect?
	
	The frequency of earthquakes and the damage caused by earthquakes.
	
	Step 2: Eliminate answer choices that do not address the issue
	
	What answer choice(s) can you eliminate?
	
	_____
	_____
	_____
	_____
	_____
	
	Step 3: Plug in the remaining answer choices and select the most correct, concise, and relevant one
	
	What is the correct answer? _____

Questions	Strategic Thinking

5. In order for this paragraph to be cohesive, sentence 4 should be placed
 	
   A) where it is now.
   B) before sentence 1.
   C) before sentence 2.
   D) after sentence 2.
	Step 1: Read the passage and identify the issue
	
	What is the Organization issue?
	
	Sentence 4 is not properly placed within the paragraph.
	
	What is the content of sentence 4?
	
	It explains what will happen next in the regions that have suffered earthquakes.
	
	Where in the paragraph does this sentence belong (beginning, middle, end)? Why?
	
	In the beginning, because the sentence discusses the immediate future while the paragraph ends with a reference to the far future.
	
	Step 2: Eliminate answer choices that do not address the issue
	
	What answer choice(s) can you eliminate?
	_____
	_____
	_____
	_____
	_____
	
	Step 3: Plug in the remaining answer choices and select the most correct, concise, and relevant one
	
	What is the correct answer? _____

Questions	Strategic Thinking
6. Which choice most effectively concludes the paragraph? A) NO CHANGE B) However, earthquake forecasting employs methods to assess the general earthquake hazard in a particular area. C) However, researchers have studied dogs to determine their ability to sense an impending earthquake. D) However, undersea earthquakes produce low-frequency sound waves that can arrive minutes before the associated tsunami wave.	**Step 1: Read the passage and identify the issue** *What is the Organization issue?* The question is asking whether the underlined sentence is an appropriate conclusion for the paragraph. *What is the content of the paragraph?* Earthquakes are normal, yet unpredictable. *All of the answer choices begin with the transition "however." What does this transition indicate?* _____ _____ _____ _____ _____ _____ _____ **Step 2: Eliminate answer choices that do not address the issue** *What answer choice(s) can you eliminate?* _____ _____ _____ _____ _____ **Step 3: Plug in the remaining answer choices and select the most correct, concise, and relevant one** *What is the correct answer?* _____

Now, try a test-like Writing & Language passage and question set on your own. Give yourself 5 minutes to read the passage and answer the questions. While most of the questions will pertain to Organization, some will touch on other grammatical issues tested on the SAT Writing & Language Test.

Questions 7-14 are based on the following passage.

The Internet and Conversation

[1]

Internet speak is often maligned as vacuous in its reliance on acronyms and abbreviations, but **7** this is far from universal. On certain discussion boards, you can witness opinions stated and arguments debated with an eloquence that people rarely use when speaking, freely sharing knowledge just for the joy of it. An online Renaissance music discussion group that I participate in has a library of original articles that are the product of a master's thesis. The author gained no monetary reward for the information (which he made available for free) and receives little praise for it outside the community that shares his interest. He does it because he is passionate about the music, and that inspires him to share what he knows with anyone who wants to learn.

[2]

[1] In part, this has to do with my habit of observing the world from my bedroom. [2] As a child, I was frequently ill and forced to stay in. [3] Although my health is much better now, **8** I still go out much less than most people. [4] After all, I have everything I need inside. [5] Everyone can be everywhere they want when they want, and every social situation feels completely comfortable and natural. [6] From my room, I have access to people all over the world. [7] I can talk about medieval literature with a friend in China and later collaborate on a piece of music with a synthesizer virtuoso in Spain. [8] There is no need for awkward introductions or a graceful exit—people feel free to launch right into what they want to talk about and, when they are done, just sign off with a "g2g," or "got to go."
[9] Everything is **9** succinct and to the point. **10**

7. A) NO CHANGE
    B) these are
    C) this reliance is
    D) empty chatter is

8. Which choice provides the best transition within the paragraph?
    A) NO CHANGE
    B) I still remember those long afternoons cooped up inside
    C) I am still careful to eat well and get plenty of rest
    D) I regret not being able to play outdoors with other children

9. A) NO CHANGE
    B) succinct
    C) succinctly stated and to the point
    D) succinct, brief, and to the point

10. In order for this paragraph to be cohesive, sentence 5 should be placed
    A) where it is now.
    B) before sentence 4.
    C) after sentence 7.
    D) after sentence 8.

[3]

For as long as I can remember, conversation **11** had always struck me as a strange chimera, something that is half two minds exchanging sophisticated ideas and **12** at the same time two dogs barking at each other. I do not find the banalities of small talk comforting, but boring and idiotic. **13** When I can dispense with it altogether and proceed right to substantive dialogue, it is almost like flying. I can be talking with the closest of friends or a mere acquaintance with a shared interest. Either way, the kinship is there. I don't feel myself included by smiles, pats on the back, or eye contact so much as by the willingness of a partner to share my ideas or gift me with thoughts of his own. There is nothing more ingratiating than intellectual passion. **14**

11. A) NO CHANGE
    B) has
    C) would have
    D) have

12. A) NO CHANGE
    B) similar to
    C) frequently like
    D) half

13. A) NO CHANGE
    B) Now
    C) Later
    D) Where

14. Which choice places the paragraphs of this passage in the most logical order?
    A) NO CHANGE
    B) 1, 3, 2
    C) 3, 1, 2
    D) 3, 2, 1

Answers & Explanations for this chapter begin on page 1079.

EXTRA PRACTICE

Required	Recommended
Questions 1–11	Questions 12–33

Questions 1-11 are based on the following passage.

Inside Looking Out: Post-Impressionism

Post-Impressionism was an artistic movement that took place between 1886 and 1892 and **1** produces some of the world's foremost artists. Post-Impressionism emerged as one of the many different artistic styles created in response to the Impressionist movement, which focused on creating realistic representations of human perceptions. **2** Next, Impressionists sought to **3** restate nature in their work. They used small, controlled brush strokes in an effort to capture how the human eye sees light. Post-Impressionism was radically different. Artists of this time focused more on self-discovery than anything else. Instead of looking out on a landscape and **4** attempt to paint exactly what they saw, they turned their eyes inward. They interpreted subjects through their own **5** unique vision, which included their personal experiences and emotions. This change influenced the course of all art created since.

1. A) NO CHANGE
    B) produced
    C) was producing
    D) will produce

2. A) NO CHANGE
    B) For example
    C) Consequently
    D) However

3. A) NO CHANGE
    B) obscure
    C) photocopy
    D) replicate

4. A) NO CHANGE
    B) attempting
    C) was attempted
    D) is attempting

5. A) NO CHANGE
    B) single
    C) cautious
    D) acceptable

[6] Paul Cezanne and Georges Seurat used shape and color to describe their worlds rather than mimic them. Their work acted as a bridge between Impressionist art and the more abstract subcategories of Post-Impressionism. Two such subcategories were Cubism and Abstract Expressionism. [7] Cubism was created by Spanish painter Pablo Picasso and French painter Georges Braque. It featured geometric shapes used to construct conceptual portraits. Both of these artists rejected traditional views on modeling nature and people, as well as classical techniques. Abstract Expressionism used color instead of geometric figures, and artists like Jackson Pollock and Willem de Kooning covered their canvases with color and indistinct forms. Abstract Expressionists aimed to express deep emotional themes. The work of Paul Gauguin and Vincent van Gogh is also considered to be Abstract Expressionism,

6. Which sentence would most effectively establish the central idea if added to the paragraph?

A) Among the Impressionist artists were Claude Monet, Pierre-Auguste Renoir, and Edgar Degas.

B) Modern artists are well versed in many different kinds of styles thanks to the many artists of the past.

C) Artists in the Post-Impressionist era employed a wide range of methods when creating their art.

D) Prior to the Impression-ist and Post-Impressionist eras, artists painted in a much more realistic style.

7. Which choice most effectively combines the sentences at the underlined portion?

A) NO CHANGE

B) Created by Spanish painter Pablo Picasso and French painter Georges Braque, Cubism featured geometric shapes.

C) Cubism was created by Spanish painter Pablo Picasso and French painter Georges Braque so it featured geometric shapes.

D) Cubism was created by Spanish painter Pablo Picasso and French painter Georges Braque, but it featured geometric shapes.

as 8 they both prioritized the depiction of their memories and emotions over observations that could be made with the eye. Never before had such an emphasis on individualism taken precedence over classical technique, a change that laid the foundation for art in the 20th century and beyond. 9

[1] These artists worked and created during the same time period and movement. [2] However, they had varying worldviews and techniques. [3] Today, we can get to know the souls of some of the world's greatest artists by visiting ❿ they're Post-Impressionist work in museums around the world. [4] These differences cumulatively succeeded in breaking from the natural guidelines of Impressionism to create something entirely new that dramatically influenced all artists who came after them. [5] In the words of Edvard Munch, another Post-Impressionist painter, "Nature is not only all that is visible to the eye . . . it also includes the inner pictures of the soul." 11

8. A) NO CHANGE
   B) it
   C) you
   D) we

9. Which sentence provides evidence to effectively support the central idea of the paragraph?

   A) Some Impressionist artists, such as Renoir, painted images of children, flowers, and social gatherings.

   B) Degas often painted ballet dancers at the barre as well as molding sculptures of them.

   C) Art is often viewed as a window into the minds and experiences of artists as they lived their lives.

   D) To transfer their emotions to their canvases, Post-Impressionist artists sometimes used violent gestures to apply paint.

10. A) NO CHANGE
    B) their
    C) they are
    D) there

11. For the sake of the cohesion of this paragraph, sentence 3 should be placed

    A) where it is now.
    B) after sentence 1.
    C) before sentence 5.
    D) after sentence 5.

Questions 12-22 are based on the following passage and supplementary material.

Putting Microbes to Work for Us

[1]

The decline of the world's supply of fossil fuels is a growing concern. With increasingly more countries becoming dependent on fossil fuels for transportation, home heating, and powering engines, the 12 failing of this finite resource has the potential to cause major disruption around the globe. To combat this issue, scientists are researching alternative energy sources. 13 Used to produce biofuel are living things or the waste of living things, and biofuel is one such alternative.

12. A) NO CHANGE
    B) wilting
    C) depletion
    D) obstruction

13. A) NO CHANGE
    B) Biofuel is produced from living things or the waste of living things, and is one such alternative.
    C) Living things or the waste of living things are used in producing the one such alternative known as biofuel.
    D) One such alternative is biofuel, produced from living things or from the waste of living things.

[2]

14 Ethanol is created from plants such as corn, sugar cane, soybeans, and rice. While ethanol is a viable energy **15** source, its use has been met with several challenges. These have limited its development as a quality alternative to traditional fossil fuels. One roadblock is that it is expensive to produce. The plant must be first broken down into sugars and then fermented by microbes into a final useable product. It cannot be distributed by pipeline because it can pick up impurities along the way, so it must be transported by truck, train, or barge. Additionally, very large areas of cropland must be dedicated to growing these plants in order to produce enough ethanol to be designated for commercial use. This raises ethical questions because it means farmers are growing food sources earmarked solely for fuel when there are many people around the world in **16** horrible

14. Which of the following would most effectively establish the central idea of the paragraph if used at the beginning of the paragraph?

   A) Until recently, the primary focus of biofuel development has been ethanol.

   B) A variety of food crops can be used to produce ethanol.

   C) Many farmers have begun to grow corn for ethanol rather than food.

   D) Converting corn to ethanol is a complicated and expensive process.

15. A) NO CHANGE
   B) source, its'
   C) source, it's
   D) source, it is

16. A) NO CHANGE
   B) dire
   C) grim
   D) grieving

need of food. 17 In addition, countries such as Brazil are decimating rain forests in order to grow sugar cane for ethanol production.

[3]

Once ethanol is produced, it is limited in its use as a commercial fuel. Therefore, it must be heavily refined and then blended with petroleum-based fuels in order to be used. 18

17. Based on the graph, which sentence could be added to strengthen this paragraph?

A) In recent years, the price of corn has increased as the percentage of corn produced for ethanol has stayed the same.

B) In recent years, the price of corn has stayed the same as the percentage of corn produced for ethanol has decreased.

C) In recent years, the price of corn has increased as the percentage of corn produced for ethanol has increased.

D) In recent years, the price of corn has decreased as the percentage of corn produced for ethanol has increased.

18. Which sentence could be added to this paragraph to provide support for the central idea?

A) Standard internal combustion engines, such as those in cars, cannot run on ethanol alone.

B) Most fuel sold for automobiles in the United States contains a blend of ethanol and gasoline.

C) Ethanol has been used as an energy source in the United States for over 200 years.

D) Although most often used to power automobiles, ethanol can be used to power other engines.

[4]

19 The fossil fuels we rely on today for energy are finite. By researching alternate energy resources, including fuel produced by bacteria and other microbes, we can become less dependent on nonrenewable sources.

[5]

Researchers in the United Kingdom 20 had been developing a new kind of biofuel that addresses several of the issues hindering ethanol use. They have extracted genes from different species of bacteria and inserted them into *E. coli* bacteria. Once this process is complete, the *E. coli* can then perform the same metabolic functions of the donor 21 bacteria, this enables it to absorb fat molecules, convert these molecules to hydrocarbons, and then excrete the hydrocarbons as a waste product. The hydrocarbons produced by the genetically modified *E. coli* are the same as those found in commercial fossil fuels. 22 Finally, the newly created hydrocarbon molecules are interchangeable with the hydrocarbon molecules found in petroleum-based diesel fuels. This allows them to be used in a typical diesel engine, without any blending or refining.

19. To improve the cohesion of this passage, paragraph 4 should be placed

A) where it is now.

B) before paragraph 2.

C) before paragraph 3.

D) after paragraph 5.

20. A) NO CHANGE

B) have developed

C) had developed

D) were developing

21. A) NO CHANGE

B) bacteria; and this enables it

C) bacteria. This enables it

D) bacteria this enables it

22. A) NO CHANGE

B) Therefore,

C) For example,

D) Also,

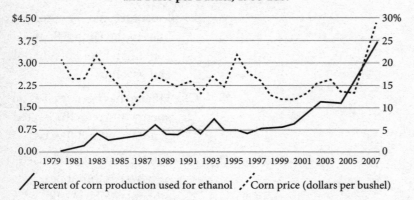

Percentage of U.S. Corn Used to Produce Ethanol and Price per Bushel, 1980-2007

Percent of corn production used for ethanol   ⋰ Corn price (dollars per bushel)

Questions 23-33 are based on the following passage.

The Science of Us

In 1908, heavy rains flooded the land near the town of Folsom, New Mexico, in the southwestern United States. In one washed-out arroyo, cowboy George McJunkin noticed a **23** tier of bones sticking out of the exposed earth. He recognized them as looking like bison bones, **24** and much larger than bison of that time.

25 The Folsom site was remote, and therefore, difficult for the scientists to reach. Prior to the investigation of the Folsom site, it was believed that humans had been in North America only since approximately 5,000 years before the present day. But projectile points found embedded between the ribs of the bison remains suggested that humans had hunted the animal. Using carbon dating techniques, the bones were determined to be approximately 12,000 years old.

23. A) NO CHANGE
    B) layer
    C) assemblage
    D) shroud

24. A) NO CHANGE
    B) so that
    C) although
    D) therefore

25. A) NO CHANGE
    B) Radiocarbon dating was first used to estimate the age of plants and animals in the late 1960s.
    C) Located in Union County, Folsom is a virtual ghost town except for its museum established in 1966.
    D) The site wasn't excavated until 1927, but what was discovered there rewrote the history of modern humans in the Americas.

This important discovery analysis was the work of archaeologists. Archaeology is the study of human history through material remains. **26** From fossils uncovered in remote parts of the world to buildings still standing in Europe and America, archaeology analyzes physical sites and artifacts to understand human culture.

    27 [1] Archaeology is a cross-disciplinary science in that it incorporates chemistry, geology, and biology. [2] Chemistry is used when artifacts, such as bones, are dated by analyzing their chemical makeup. [3] Biology comes into play when human and animal remains **28** are discovered: archaeologists can apply what they know about people to tell them what happened to people of the past, such as the impact of a species going extinct. [4] Geology is essential to archaeology because the composition of the earth at a historic site, such as a Roman coliseum or tribal burial site, can tell us a lot about the time period when the site was erected and used.

26. A) NO CHANGE
     B) From fossils excavated and uncovered in remote, unknown parts of the world to buildings still standing in Europe and America, archaeology analyzes physical sites and artifacts to understand human culture.
     C) From fossils uncovered in remote parts of the world to homes, playhouses, arenas, and buildings of all kinds still standing in Europe and America, archaeology analyzes physical sites and artifacts to understand human culture.
     D) From fossils uncovered in remote parts of the world to buildings still standing in Europe and America, archaeology analyzes the excavated physical sites, materials found, and artifacts to understand human culture.

27. To enhance the logical sequence of paragraph 4, sentence 4 should be placed
     A) where it is now.
     B) before sentence 1.
     C) after sentence 1.
     D) before sentence 3.

28. A) NO CHANGE
     B) are discovered archaeologists
     C) are discovered, archaeologists
     D) are discovered . . . archaeologists

Human history is extensive and varied, so archaeology has many **(29)** parts. Prehistoric archaeology focuses on cultures that did not have written language—*prehistoric* means prior to that which is recorded by historical record. **(30)** There is also classical archaeology, which centers mainly on Greek and Roman ruins, and biblical archaeology. Which explores sites described in the Bible. Maritime archaeology studies ship-

29. A) NO CHANGE
    B) divisions
    C) categories
    D) subfields

30. A) NO CHANGE
    B) There is also classical archaeology, which centers mainly on Greek and Roman ruins, and biblical archaeology, which explores sites described in the Bible.
    C) There is also classical archaeology; which centers mainly on Greek and Roman ruins and biblical archaeology, which explores sites described in the Bible.
    D) There is also classical archaeology, which centers mainly on Greek and Roman ruins. And biblical archaeology, which explores sites described in the Bible.

wrecks that provide clues to the culture and the people who built and sailed the ships. 31

The importance of archaeology to humankind's understanding of itself cannot be overstated. Without the scientists who 32 carefully dig, preserved, and interpreted sites around the world, we would not know all that we do about the Incas, Egyptians, and Native Americans. Archaeologists are like translators of the story of human existence on Earth, from the language of 33 innate material into the language of life.

31. Which sentence adds supporting information to paragraph 5?

A) Written language changed how all cultures recorded historic events in their individual societies.

B) Greek and Roman ruins are more popular as tourist destinations than the sites described in the Bible.

C) There is also a whole branch of underwater archaeology in which cities and harbors that are now submerged are studied.

D) Some archaeologists consider the temples of ancient Greece to be easier to excavate than the ruins of ancient Rome.

32. A) NO CHANGE

B) dug, preserve, and interpret

C) digs, preserving, and interprets

D) dug, preserved, and interpreted

33. A) NO CHANGE

B) inert

C) inept

D) adept

CHAPTER 28

Development

 ## CHAPTER OBJECTIVES

By the end of this chapter, you will be able to:

1. Evaluate the effectiveness and clarity of a passage's arguments, information, and ideas and determine whether a revision is necessary for the passage to be clear and effective

2. Evaluate information and ideas intended to support claims or points in the passage

3. Identify elements in the passage that are not relevant to the passage's topic and purpose

SMARTPOINTS

Point Value	SmartPoint Category
40 Points	Development

PROPOSITION

Proposition questions ask about how well a writer uses language—arguments, information, and ideas—to express the central purpose of a passage or part of a passage.

You will be asked to add, revise, or retain portions of the passage to communicate key ideas, claims, counterclaims, and topic sentences most clearly and effectively.

To answer Proposition questions, you need to identify the topic and purpose of the passage and focus on the writer's point of view. Ask questions such as:

- What is the central idea of the passage?
- Why did the author write the passage?
- What does the author think about the subject?
- What is the author's tone?

> ✔ **Remember**
>
> The writer's point of view will be consistent throughout the passage. If the writer supports a certain issue, the correct answer choices will reflect this support and how the author effectively communicates it.

SUPPORT

Support questions test issues related to information and ideas presented by the writer. You will be asked to evaluate the effectiveness of the facts and details employed by the writer to support claims made in the passage.

Support questions may ask you to keep, change, or add a detail or example. A Support question could ask about an example used to support a central argument or simply a minor detail used to weaken a point made by the author.

To answer Support questions, look around the underlined portion for a clue indicating what kind of support is required. If the example supports a central idea or claim, ask if the example strengthens the author's central idea. Eliminate answer choices that don't fit the context or have a negative or trivial effect on the central idea.

FOCUS

Focus questions require you to assess whether portions of the passage include only the information and ideas relevant to the author's topic and purpose. You may be asked to add, change, or omit text.

You can recognize relevant information and ideas by making sure they match the rest of the passage's topic, scope, and purpose.

> ✔ **Remember**
>
> *Topic* is what the passage is about. *Scope* is the aspect of the broader topic that is the center of the author's focus. *Purpose* is the author's reason for writing.

When answering Focus questions, identify whether the text in question fits the topic, scope, and purpose of the entire passage.

Let's look at the following Writing & Language passage and questions. After the passage, there are two columns. The left column contains test-like questions. The column on the right features the strategic thinking a test expert employs when approaching the passage and questions presented.

Questions 1-4 are based on the following passage.

Dr. Barry Marshall

For hundreds of years, the medical community and conventional wisdom held that ulcers were caused by stress. Strong gastric juices would sometimes burn sores through the lining of the stomach or intestines, causing widely varied symptoms, including internal bleeding, inflammation, and stomach pain. Doctors reasoned that if patients with ulcers changed their daily habits to reduce the level of tension in their lives, altered their diets to avoid foods that would irritate the stomach, and took medicine to moderate the amount of stomach acid, these ulcers would heal. Although the problem often recurred, no one seriously questioned why. ❶ This medical advice remained standard for generations, until Dr. Barry Marshall came along.

Beginning in the 1980s, Marshall, an Australian physician, hypothesized that at least some ulcers were caused by bacteria that often lie dormant in the human stomach. The international medical community scoffed. It was common knowledge, or so Marshall's colleagues believed, that no microbes could survive for long in the highly acidic environment of the stomach. ❷ At medical conferences, the veteran, well-known Marshall was regarded as at best, a maverick, and at worst, a quack. Over several years, he and his fellow researcher, Dr. J. Robin Warren, attempted to isolate and identify the bacteria that caused ulcers. As is the case with many medical discoveries, their breakthrough came about partly by accident, when they left a culture growing in the lab overnight. ❸

After this, to further prove his point, Dr. Marshall took a bold step. Although hospitals frown on such potentially dangerous actions, the doctor experimented on himself by deliberately drinking a flask of the bacteria. Over a two-week period, Marshall developed vague, though not disabling, symptoms, and medical tests showed evidence of ulcers and infection. Other researchers' studies later confirmed that Marshall's and Warren's findings apply to about 90% of all ulcers, which can now be cured by a short course of antibiotics instead of being temporarily managed by antacids.

In 2005, Marshall's bold move earned him and Warren the Nobel Prize in Medicine. ❹

Questions	Strategic Thinking
1. (A) NO CHANGE B) This medical advice remains the standard today, despite Dr. Barry Marshall's recent efforts. C) This medical advice remained the standard for generations, until Dr. Barry Marshall developed a cure for the stomach ulcer. D) This medical advice remained standard for generations despite a lack of evidence. That is, until Dr. Barry Marshall proved it with scientific experiments.	**Step 1: Read the passage and identify the issue** The issue is Proposition: The underlined portion is the concluding sentence of a paragraph and should therefore provide a claim central to the passage as a whole. **Step 2: Eliminate answer choices that do not address the issue** Eliminate B because it is untrue according to the rest of the passage. Eliminate C and D because they distort the supporting details provided in the remainder of the passage. **Step 3: Plug in the remaining answer choices and select the most correct, concise, and relevant one** Choice (A) is the only remaining answer choice and is therefore correct.

Questions	Strategic Thinking
2. A) NO CHANGE B) At medical conferences, the young, unknown Marshall was regarded as at best, a maverick, and at worst, a quack. C) At medical conferences, the young, unknown Marshall was regarded as friendly and sociable at after-hours networking events. D) Dr. Marshall mostly avoided medical conferences and symposia.	**Step 1: Read the passage and identify the issue** The issue is Focus because the underlined sentence provides details about Dr. Marshall's character that you need to make sure fit the tone, scope, and purpose of the passage. **Step 2: Eliminate answer choices that do not address the issue** Eliminate A because the surrounding text does not support that Marshall was "veteran" and "well-known." Eliminate C and D because they are irrelevant to the passage as a whole. **Step 3: Plug in the remaining answer choices and select the most correct, concise, and relevant one** Choice (B) is the only remaining answer choice and is therefore correct.

Questions	Strategic Thinking
3. Which additional detail is most appropriate to include at this point in the passage? A) Dr. Marshall was a well-organized man and valued a neat workspace; the misplaced petri dish was almost certainly Dr. Warren's fault. B) The following morning, Marshall and Warren found a vibrant culture of a theretofore overlooked bacteria that they soon realized was an important suspect in the formation of ulcers. C) Marshall's and Warren's research was supported by grants, and by that point they were nearing the exhaustion of their funds. D) What Marshall and Warren discovered in their lab the next day brought them closer to finding the link between bacteria, ulcers, and stress.	**Step 1: Read the passage and identify the issue** The issue is Support. The question stem asks for the answer choice that includes an "appropriate" detail for this point in the passage. Details should support the passage's central idea. **Step 2: Eliminate answer choices that do not address the issue** The preceding paragraph is about Dr. Marshall's first hypothesis, his career and partnership, and the fact that his and Dr. Warren's breakthrough was an accident. Eliminate A because it does not describe why the discovery was accidental. Eliminate C because it does not relate to the discovery. Eliminate D because it is too general. **Step 3: Plug in the remaining answer choices and select the most correct, concise, and relevant one** Choice (B) is the only remaining answer choice and is therefore correct.

Questions	Strategic Thinking
4. Which choice most effectively concludes the passage? A) Dr. Marshall brought his wife to the Nobel Prize ceremony, and she was very proud to witness the public celebration of his work. B) Both of their careers flourished from this point forward, with each earning a tenured, endowed faculty position at a prestigious university. C) Sadly, since 2005, Marshall's and Warren's work has been neglected by the medical and scientific communities, and our understanding of ulcers has not progressed since that time. D) Their important advance, like many other scientific discoveries in history, was a combination of experimentation, persistence, and luck.	**Step 1: Read the passage and identify the issue** The issue is Proposition because the question asks for an effective conclusion for the overall passage. An effective conclusion should contain a summary of the author's central idea and argument. **Step 2: Eliminate answer choices that do not address the issue** Eliminate A and B because they are only details. Eliminate C because it goes beyond the scope of the passage by talking about events since 2005. **Step 3: Plug in the remaining answer choices and select the most correct, concise, and relevant one** Choice (D) is the only remaining answer choice and is therefore correct.

You have seen the ways in which the SAT tests you on Development on the Writing & Language Test and how an SAT expert approaches these types of questions.

Look at the Writing & Language passage excerpt that follows. There are four questions associated with it. Use the Kaplan Method for Writing & Language to answer the questions. Remember to look at the strategic thinking questions that have been laid out for you—some of the answers have been filled in, but you will have to fill in the answers to others.

Use your answers to the strategic thinking questions to select the correct answer, just as you will on Test Day.

Questions 5-8 are based on the following passage.

Human Skin

The skin is the human body's largest organ. An adult's skin comprises between 15 and 20 percent of the total body weight. Each square centimeter has 6 million cells, 5,000 sensory points, 100 sweat glands, and 15 sebaceous glands. The outer layer, the epidermis, consists of rows of cells about 12 to 15 deep and is between .07 and .12 millimeters thick (the thickness of a piece of paper). This top layer **5** has already been studied by countless scientists, and few new discoveries or insights are likely to occur. One square inch of skin contains up to 4.5 m of blood vessels, which have as one of their functions the regulation of body temperature. The skin varies in thickness from .5 mm on the eyelids to 4 mm or more on the palms and the soles.

The skin forms a protective barrier against the action of physical, chemical, and bacterial agents on the deeper tissues and contains the special nerve organs for the various sensations commonly grouped as the sense of touch. The body replaces its skin every month, and because the skin constitutes the first line of defense against dehydration, infection, injuries, and extreme temperatures, **6** the skin detoxifies harmful substances with many of the same enzymatic processes the liver uses.

Skin is constantly being regenerated. A cell is born in the lower layer of the skin, called the dermis, which is supplied with blood vessels and nerve endings. For the next two weeks, the cell migrates upward until it reaches the bottom portion of the epidermis, which is the outermost skin layer. The cell then flattens out and continues moving toward the surface until it dies and is shed.

The most important property of the skin is that it provides our sense of touch. All other senses have a definite key organ that can be studied, but the skin is spread over the entire body and cannot be as easily studied. Receptors located at the ends of nerve fibers are used to detect stimuli and convert them into neural impulses to be sent to the brain through the peripheral and central nervous systems. The sense of touch is actually recorded in the dermis (skin) and passed on to the central nervous system.

The most important job of the skin is to protect the inside of the body; it acts like a "shock absorber." If a body falls, the skin protects all of the internal organs. When the skin is broken, **7** there is an elaborate repair system that relies primarily on blood cells, which clot the breach, fight infection, and initiate healing. The skin also acts as a thermostat to regulate body temperature. **8**

Questions	Strategic Thinking
5. A) NO CHANGE B) has already been studied by countless scientists. C) is mainly composed of dead cells and thus is not of great interest to scientists. D) is mainly composed of dead cells and these are constantly being replaced by newer cells.	**Step 1: Read the passage and identify the issue** *What is the issue?* Focus. The underlined portion consists of details in the middle of a paragraph. **Step 2: Eliminate answer choices that do not address the issue** *What is this paragraph about?* It introduces the topic of the passage—human skin—and contains many details about said organ. *What answer choice(s) can you eliminate?* _____ _____ _____ _____ **Step 3: Plug in the remaining answer choices and select the most correct, concise, and relevant one** *What is the answer?* _____

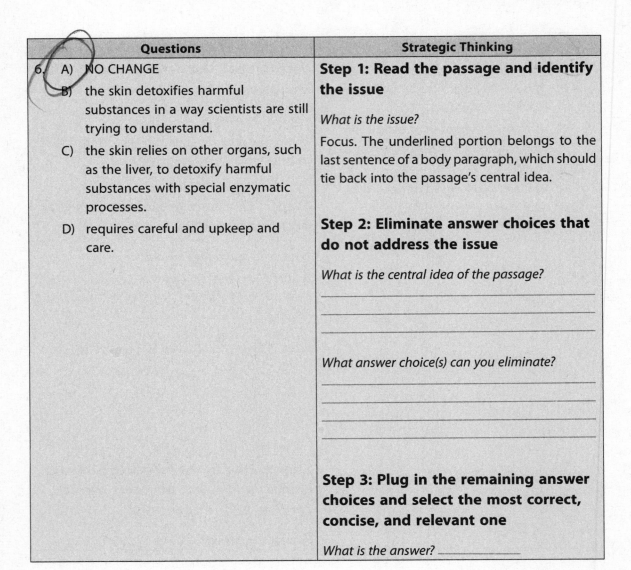

Questions	Strategic Thinking
6. A) NO CHANGE B) the skin detoxifies harmful substances in a way scientists are still trying to understand. C) the skin relies on other organs, such as the liver, to detoxify harmful substances with special enzymatic processes. D) requires careful and upkeep and care.	**Step 1: Read the passage and identify the issue** *What is the issue?* Focus. The underlined portion belongs to the last sentence of a body paragraph, which should tie back into the passage's central idea. **Step 2: Eliminate answer choices that do not address the issue** *What is the central idea of the passage?* _____ _____ _____ *What answer choice(s) can you eliminate?* _____ _____ _____ _____ **Step 3: Plug in the remaining answer choices and select the most correct, concise, and relevant one** *What is the answer?* _____

Questions	Strategic Thinking
7. A) NO CHANGE B) immediate medical attention is necessary to protect the internal organs. C) it has its own defense system that immediately goes into repair mode. D) there is an elaborate repair system that relies primarily on red and white blood cells, which clot the breach, fight infection, and initiate healing.	**Step 1: Read the passage and identify the issue** *What is the issue?* Support. *How do you know?* _____ _____ _____ **Step 2: Eliminate answer choices that do not address the issue** *What is the paragraph to which the underlined portion belongs about?* _____ _____ _____ *What answer choice(s) can you eliminate?* _____ _____ _____ _____ **Step 3: Plug in the remaining answer choices and select the most correct, concise, and relevant one** *What is the answer?* _____

Questions	Strategic Thinking
8. Which choice most effectively concludes the passage? A) It is no exaggeration to say that skin is among the most important organs—without it, a body simply cannot continue living. B) Since skin covers the body and is easily visible, it is no wonder that its color and decoration have important cultural meanings. C) However, more important organs do indeed exist and likely deserve more scientific attention than the skin. D) Without the skin's properties, most importantly the sense of touch, life would hardly be worth living.	**Step 1: Read the passage and identify the issue** *What is the issue?* _____ *How do you know?* _____ _____ _____ **Step 2: Eliminate answer choices that do not address the issue** *What would effectively conclude the passage?* _____ _____ _____ *What answer choice(s) can you eliminate?* _____ _____ _____ _____ **Step 3: Plug in the remaining answer choices and select the most correct, concise, and relevant one** *What is the answer?* _____

Now, try a test-like Writing & Language passage on your own. Give yourself 5 minutes to read the passage and answer the questions.

Questions 9-16 are based on the following passage.

James Polk

For much of his distinguished career, James Knox Polk followed in the footsteps of Andrew Jackson.[1] [9] In fact, "Young Hickory's"

9. Which detail is most appropriate to include at this point in the passage?

A) Like the fiery Jackson, Polk was born in North Carolina and moved to Tennessee to begin a political career.

B) Both men were fiery, aggressive personalities who hailed from North Carolina and later moved to Tennessee to begin their political careers.

C) Like the fiery Jackson, Polk was born in North Carolina and moved to Tennessee, but unlike Jackson, he did not fight in the War of 1812.

D) Polk, like Jackson, had antipathy toward the Native Americans of the southeastern United States, and his efforts to remove them defined his career.

policies were very similar to Jackson's: both men favored lower taxes, championed the frontiersmen, farmers, and workers, and neither was afraid to indulge in Tennessee whisky. Polk, however, did not share Jackson's rather fierce temperament but was instead known for remaining soft-spoken even as he worked energetically toward his goals. Although history will likely always remember the frontier persona of Andrew Jackson, it was Polk who did much more to shape the course of American history.

11 From an early age, Polk suffered ill health that would turn out to be a lifelong affliction. Despite his physical shortcomings, he was an able student and graduated from the University of North Carolina with honors in 1818. Two years later, Polk was admitted to the bar, and in 1823,

10. A) NO CHANGE

   B) while they agreed on little regarding taxes or the suffrage of frontiersmen, farmers, and workers, both men were known to indulge in Tennessee whisky.

   C) both men favored lower taxes, championed the frontiersmen, farmers, and workers, and opposed the controversial Bank of the United States.

   D) both men favored lower taxes, championed the frontiersmen, farmers, and workers, and yet they could not agree on the controversial Bank of the United States.

11. Which choice most effectively introduces this paragraph?

   A) The Polk family was poor—James's father had emigrated from Scotland and arrived in the U.S. South penniless.

   B) James Polk's parents tried to discourage the draw of politics and law, instead urging their eldest son to become a farmer.

   C) Polk married his wife, Sarah Childress, in 1823.

   D) Polk was born in Mecklenburg, North Carolina, in 1795 as the oldest of 10 children.

⓬ <u>he married Sarah Childress, the daughter of a prominent planter and merchant from Murfreesboro.</u> From there, he was elected to the U.S. House of Representatives in 1825, serving until 1839. **⓭** <u>Polk was also Speaker of the House from 1835 to 1839.</u>

12. A) NO CHANGE

    B) he married Sarah Childress.

    C) he was elected as governor of Tennessee.

    D) he was elected to the Tennessee House of Representatives.

13. A) NO CHANGE

    B) Polk was also Speaker of the House from 1835 to 1839, an experience that made him wary of wading deeper into national politics.

    C) Polk was also Speaker of the House from 1835 to 1839, a post that catapulted him to a position of prominence in politics.

    D) Polk was also Speaker of the House from 1835 to 1839, an experience that left his already strained constitution exhausted and forced him into a temporary retirement.

After he left Congress to serve as governor of Tennessee in 1839, it became clear that Polk's political aspirations were high indeed. During the 1844 presidential campaign, **14** <u>a young Abraham Lincoln threw his support behind Whig Henry Clay instead of the Democratic ex-President Martin van Buren.</u> Both men, as part of their platforms, opposed expansionist policies, and neither intended to annex the independent state of Texas or the Oregon Territory. **15** <u>Polk, spurred on by Jackson's advice, recognized</u> that neither candidate had correctly surmised the feelings of the people, so he publicly announced that, as president, he would do his utmost to acquire Texas and Oregon. Polk was the first political "dark horse" in American politics, coming out of nowhere to win the Democratic nomination and the election.

As the eleventh President of the United States, **16** <u>Polk pursued an agenda of diverse issues.</u> First, he reached an agreement with England that divided the Oregon Territory, carving out the present-day states of Washington and Oregon. Polk also quickly annexed Texas and provoked war with Mexico to acquire California and the New Mexico territory. While these triumphs were somewhat diminished by controversy from abolitionists who opposed the spread of slavery into new territories, under Polk's leadership the dream of "manifest destiny" became a reality, and the United States fully extended its borders from the Atlantic to the Pacific.

[1] Seventh U.S. President from 1829 to 1837 and War of 1812 hero often referred to as "Old Hickory"

14. A) NO CHANGE
    B) the leading Democratic candidate was ex-President Martin van Buren, and the Whig candidate was Henry Clay.
    C) the issue of slavery's expansion into new territories began its long stint as the most divisive issue to plague national politics.
    D) both the leading Democratic candidate, ex-President Martin van Buren, and the Whig candidate, Henry Clay, sought to campaign under the banner of "Manifest Destiny" and territorial expansion.

15. A) NO CHANGE
    B) Polk, against Jackson's advice, recognized
    C) Polk recognized
    D) Polk, against the wishes of his advisors, recognized

16. A) NO CHANGE
    B) Polk worked tirelessly to expand the borders of the nation.
    C) Polk worked to reign in unchecked expansion of the frontiers.
    D) Polk stopped at nothing short of war to expand the borders of the nation.

Answers & Explanations for this chapter begin on page 1088.

EXTRA PRACTICE

Required	Recommended
Questions 1–11	Questions 12–22

Questions 1-11 are based on the following passage and supplementary material.

Reefs at Risk

1 [1] Coral reefs contain more than one quarter of all marine life and help reduce storm damage to coastal lands. [2] 2 <u>Ultimately</u>, about ten percent of the world's coral reefs have been destroyed and 3 <u>about sixty percent of the remaining reefs are in danger.</u> [3] Many people enjoy

1. For the sake of focus, which sentence should be deleted from this paragraph?
   A) Sentence 1
   B) Sentence 3
   C) Sentence 6
   D) Sentence 8

2. A) NO CHANGE
   B) Unfortunately,
   C) Consequently,
   D) Inevitably,

3. A) NO CHANGE
   B) threats have been made to sixty percent of remaining reefs.
   C) more than 6 in 10 reefs have faced threats of some kind or another
   D) about sixty percent of the remaining reefs have experienced danger

snorkeling and fishing near coral reefs. [4] ❹ <u>A coral reef is formed by a community of very small plants and animals. [5] These plants and animals are known as algae and polyps.</u> [6] The algae use sunlight to produce their own food for energy and growth. [7] The polyps eat other small animals that come to feed on the algae. [8] They also make a hard substance, called limestone, which eventually builds up to form a reef.

The health of a coral reef depends on having clean water and sunlight, but human activities can threaten these ❺ <u>basic</u> resources. Oil or chemical spills in the water near the reefs can harm the polyps, and chemical runoff into streams from mines and farms can also destroy the polyps and algae.

6 People who fish for a living often use explosives to catch the many fish that are attracted to coral reefs, causing significant damage. Boats also destroy reefs with their anchors, and tourists who swim in coral reefs often break coral off to keep as a souvenir.

Development along a coast, such as cutting down trees and building roads or parking lots, ❼ <u>increased</u> the amount of dirt and sand that washes into the ocean and settles on the bottom. This covers the coral and blocks sunlight. Without sunlight, the algae cannot grow, and in turn, the polyps lack the energy needed to produce limestone and build up the reef.

4. A) NO CHANGE
   B) Very small plants and animals, known as algae and polyps, make up the community that forms a coral reef.
   C) A coral reef is formed by a community of very small plants and animals called algae and polyps.
   D) Known as algae and polyps, very small plants and animals form a community that is called a coral reef.

5. A) NO CHANGE
   B) elusive
   C) committed
   D) vital

6. Which sentence can be added to this paragraph to most effectively establish its central idea?
   A) Fishing and boating are popular sports near coral reefs.
   B) People who participate in activities near coral reefs often cause damage.
   C) Boats are dangerous to the health of coral reefs.
   D) Coral reefs are fragile, and people should be careful around them.

7. A) NO CHANGE
   B) increases
   C) increasing
   D) increase

8 [1] Marine biologists have found that small crabs living in coral reefs can help prevent the damage caused by coastal development. [2] They remove particles of dirt and sand that settle on the coral and **9** stop sunlight. [3] The crabs also eat some of the polyps, which **10** would probably suggest that the crabs might also be a threat to the coral. [4] The crabs help the coral survive **11** . [5] The crabs living on the coral have a steady source of food, and the reef provides the crabs with shelter from predators. [6] However, when the biologists removed crabs from sections of coral, less coral survived than in the sections where the crabs remained.

The destruction of coral reefs does not have to continue. Recognizing the part that local animals, such as crabs, can play to reduce the amount of damage will help to slow the loss of coral reefs and may provide better ways to protect them.

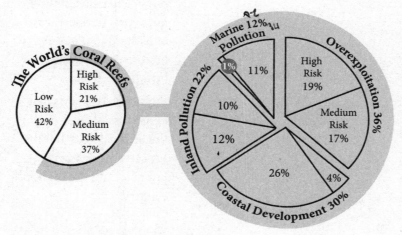

Almost 60% of the world's coral reefs are at high or medium risk of destruction.

Adapted from Wheeling Jesuit University/NASA-supported Classroom of the Future, "Exploring the Environment: Coral Reefs."

8. For the sake of cohesion in this paragraph, sentence 6 should be placed

   A) where it is now.

   B) before sentence 1.

   C) after sentence 2.

   D) before sentence 4.

9. A) NO CHANGE

   B) hinder

   C) obstruct

   D) cover

10. A) NO CHANGE

    B) would suggest

    C) maybe suggests

    D) almost certainly suggests

11. What could be added to this sentence to provide more support for the central idea of the paragraph?

    A) but benefit from the relationship as well

    B) but are one of millions of animals that live in coral reefs

    C) and can be very large or very small in size

    D) and are found on coral reefs all over the world

Questions 12-22 are based on the following passage.

The Power of the PA

[12] In 1960s America, there were not enough doctors to meet the primary care needs of patients nationwide. Due to the shortage, and in hopes of improving health care and its accessibility, educators sought to establish alternatives to medical school that would effectively equip other health care workers to share more of the physicians' workload. Their project altered health care history: the physician assistant (PA) was born. In 1967, the first PA program [13] launched at Duke University, notable for its education and sports programs. The coming decades saw the field develop into what is considered today to be one of the most desirable and quickly growing careers in the country.

12. Which choice most effectively establishes the main topic of the paragraph?

   A) Today, physician assistants are vital members of any health care system, but it hasn't always been that way.

   B) For many years, doctors and educators struggled to find a role for the high number of incoming medical students.

   C) The difference between physician assistants and nurse practitioners was often hard to quantify, but then came a shift in health care needs.

   D) Physician assistants had long played a vital role in the medical field, but the PA career didn't become popular until the mid-20th century.

13. A) NO CHANGE

   B) launched at Duke University, noted for its education programs.

   C) launched at the renowned Duke University.

   D) launched at Duke University.

[1] Becoming a PA is simpler than becoming a physician, which usually takes over nine years of higher education and training. [2] Those seeking acceptance into PA programs typically study science or health as undergraduates. [3] Once practicing, PAs are required to maintain proficiency through continued education and a recertification exam every ten years. [4] They also usually ⓮ obtain some health-related work experience before applying. [5] ⓯ Once accepted to a program, most students will be in their programs for about twenty-seven months. [6] Schooling involves both classroom and field study, and students undergo hundreds of hours in clinical training rotations in order to gain a breadth of supervised experience. [7] Today there are over one hundred and seventy accredited PA programs, most of which award masters degrees to graduates. [8] After graduation, ⓰ graduates must complete one final step: passing the national licensure exam. ⑰

While physicians can work ⓲ anonymously, PAs always work under the supervision of physicians. But like nurse practitioners, another primary care alternative that emerged from the 1960s, PAs can do much of the work commonly expected of a physician. PAs are trained and qualified to meet with, examine, treat, diagnose, and counsel patients. They can prescribe medication, interpret lab data, and help physicians with surgical procedures. ⓳ In many ways, PAs lighten the workload for physicians on their teams. This enables clinics, hospitals, and other health care systems to run more efficiently and meet patient needs with greater accuracy and timeliness.

Physician assistants enjoy various options in terms of where they can practice. Almost every field of medicine has positions for those PAs who specialize accordingly. Also, depending on the needs of the physicians ⓴ under which PAs work, as well as the particular limitations that might be imposed by a specific state, the requirements and responsibilities of the job can vary.

14. A) NO CHANGE
    B) accrue
    C) perceive
    D) formulate

15. A) NO CHANGE
    B) Once accepted
    C) Once they begin
    D) Once programs accept them

16. A) NO CHANGE
    B) physicians
    C) PAs
    D) candidates

17. For the sake of cohesion in this paragraph, sentence 3 should be placed
    A) where it is now.
    B) after sentence 5.
    C) before sentence 7.
    D) after sentence 8.

18. A) NO CHANGE
    B) defensively
    C) autonomously
    D) fundamentally

19. A) NO CHANGE
    B) On the other hand
    C) For example
    D) First of all

20. A) NO CHANGE
    B) where PAs work
    C) under whom PAs work
    D) who work under PAs

The past half-century saw the career of physician assistant rise from nascence to become a highly sought-after and still rapidly growing addition to American health care. Projections indicate that within the next decade, the number of employed PAs should increase significantly. **㉑** <u>I believe PAs are an ever-increasing presence</u> in health care and a powerful influence on the medical world for the better. **22**

21. A) NO CHANGE
    B) PAs are an ever-increasing presence
    C) Doctors believe PAs are an ever-increasing presence
    D) You can believe that PAs are an ever-increasing presence

22. What fact is omitted from this paragraph that would help support the author's claims?
    A) The number of PAs hired over the last half-century
    B) The expected PA-to-patient ratio over the next decade
    C) The number of PA positions compared to the number of nurse practitioner positions
    D) The specific rate at which PAs will be employed over the next decade

CHAPTER 29

Effective Language Use

CHAPTER OBJECTIVES

By the end of this chapter, you will be able to:

1. Revise the text as needed to improve the exactness or content appropriateness of word choice or eliminate wordiness and redundancy

2. Improve the consistency of style and tone with the passage's purpose, as necessary

3. Evaluate the use of sentence structure to accomplish the intended rhetorical purpose of a passage

SMARTPOINTS

Point Value	SmartPoint Category
50 Points	Effective Language Use

PRECISION

On the SAT, precision refers to the exactness and accuracy of the author's choice of words, also known as diction. Precision questions will ask you to revise a text as needed to improve the exactness or content appropriateness of the author's word choice.

Word choice is important because being precise in language use allows an author to effectively and precisely convey his or her thoughts, including the thesis and central arguments.

SAT Precision questions mostly test your knowledge of correct word choice in context. These questions are very similar to the Reading Test's Vocab-in-Context questions, which you can review in chapter 22.

> ✔ **Expert Tip**
>
> One common way in which precision is tested is through incorrect pronoun use. Remember to use *who* and *whom* when referring to people; use *that* or *which* to refer to any other nouns.

CONCISION

Remember the third step of the Kaplan Method for Writing & Language: Plug in the remaining answer choices and select the most clear, concise, and relevant one. You must use not only the correct words to convey your ideas but also as few words as possible.

Concision questions will require you to revise text to improve the economy of word choice by eliminating wordiness and redundancy. The SAT tests concision by presenting you with unnecessarily long and complex structures or redundant usage—or sometimes both.

> ✔ **On Test Day**
>
> The shortest answer will not always be the correct one; the portion of the passage in question needs to be grammatically correct and retain the intended meaning.

Unnecessarily long and complex structure implies that a sentence uses more words than necessary to make its point, even though it may be grammatically correct. Not every long underlined segment will be a Concision question; sometimes it takes a lot of words to convey meaning. Nevertheless, when a long selection is underlined, you should ask, "Are all of these words necessary? Is there a more concise way to say the same thing?"

Another aspect of concision is redundancy. Redundancy errors occur when two words in the sentence have essentially the same meaning in context or when the meaning of one word is implicit in the meaning of another.

STYLE AND TONE

SAT Style and Tone questions ask you to revise a text to ensure consistency of style and tone or to reflect the author's purpose. You must also confirm that the text's style and tone match its subject and format.

Style and Tone questions will sometimes have question stems that correspond to small numbers in boxes within the passage. Other times, these questions will not have question stems. In the case of the latter, you must determine if the underlined segment matches the general tone of the passage or if one of the other choices is more appropriate in context.

> ✔ **Expert Tip**
>
> If you spot a Style and Tone question at the beginning of a passage, read the passage through before answering it so you can determine overall tone first.

SYNTAX

Questions about syntax will ask you to assess whether different sentence structures accomplish an author's intended rhetorical purpose. In narratives or prose, syntax can enhance intended meaning and contribute toward tone.

> ✔ **Definition**
>
> Syntax refers to the arrangement of words and phrases within a sentence. It dictates how words from different parts of speech are assembled to convey a complete thought.

Sophisticated and academic writing like the kind you'll see on the SAT employs varied kinds of syntax. One way in which syntax is categorized is by sentence type. The following table portrays the four sentence types classified by the clauses they contain.

> ✔ **Definition**
>
> A clause is a part of a sentence containing a subject and a predicate verb.

Sentence Type	Description	Example
Simple	Contains a single, independent clause	I don't like cats.
Compound	Contains two independent clauses that are joined by a coordinating conjunction (e.g., *but*, *or*, *and*, *so*)	I don't like cats, and my sister doesn't like dogs.
Complex	Contains an independent clause plus one or more dependent clauses (a dependent clause starts with a coordinating conjunction such as *that*, *because*, *while*, *although*, *where*, *if*)	I don't like cats that scratch the furniture.
Compound-Complex	Contains three or more clauses (of which at least two are independent and one is dependent)	I don't like cats, and my sister doesn't like dogs because they bark.

Let's look at the following Writing & Language passage and questions. After the passage, there are two columns. The left column contains test-like questions. The column on the right features the strategic thinking a test expert employs when approaching the passage and questions presented.

Questions 1-4 are based on the following passage.

Modern Readers

Judging by the types of novels that typically receive the top rankings on contemporary "best seller" lists, one would be wise to conclude that the modern book consumer does not enjoy reading ancient mythology. Seemingly, such antiquated stories hold little relevance to the concerns of the modern age. It is a literature not for the **1** distracted reader immersed in his "everyday" cares but for a more imaginative audience with more universal tastes.

To even begin **2** to understand or comprehend this issue, we must understand what it is that most readers seek out in the works they read. What is it in a book—a novel, for example—that causes them to continue turning the pages? The answer can be a bit slippery. Is it the psychological realism of the characters? Is it the drama of the events they encounter? Is it the modern author's consciousness of his position as author and the relationship—distant or intimate, serious or playful—that he develops with his readers?

The obvious answer is that it is all of these things. The defining features of the modern story are its complexity and ambivalence. Narrators are not always reliable. Loyalties are often fleeting, and even a character's central motives may undergo a transformation before the story is done. There is no neat conclusion, no definitive redemption or damnation, and not always even a clear message. In this confusion and dislocation, the modern reader sees his own life reflected, complete with all of its **3** complexity and ambivalence.

In a complex world where the disparate lives of alienated individuals still manage to affect each other on a daily basis, there is a paradoxical credulity extended towards anything murky and unclear. Far from the cosmopolitan savant he would like us to believe he is (to say nothing of the author who writes for him), the modern reader is only able to take comfort in his own confusion. When, for example, George and Jane finish their fairy-tale courtship and suddenly find themselves unable to live together, the contemporary pop intellectual will **4** nod his head sagely, and he will think about the relationships in his own life that he didn't understand either.

What escapes the minds of the masses is that, taken past a certain point, realism is not art. Neither unsatisfying conclusions, nor irritating characters, nor obscure motives are indications of the literary talents of the author. The older, mythic characters may be drawn with a broad brush, and may possess a simplicity and singularity of purpose that finds no parallel in day-to-day life, but that simplicity is not a sign of an author lacking in subtlety. Rather, a purposeful author will have purposeful characters. Whether the story is meant to illustrate moral principles, explore character types, or simply entertain, a quality work of art must have a purpose.

Questions	Strategic Thinking
1. A) NO CHANGE B) prosaic C) voracious D) modern	**Step 1: Read the passage and identify the issue** The issue is Word Choice, or Precision. **Step 2: Eliminate answer choices that do not address the issue** Eliminate A because while the "distracted" reader may be "immersed in his cares," "distracted" does not directly contrast the "more imaginative audience with more universal tastes," as indicated by the use of the word "but." Eliminate C because a "voracious" reader is one who reads an enormous amount, not an ordinary amount. Eliminate D because the reader's era has nothing to do with the sentence. **Step 3: Plug in the remaining answer choices and select the most correct, concise, and relevant one** Choice (B) is the only remaining answer choice and is therefore correct.

Questions	Strategic Thinking
2. A) NO CHANGE B) to understand or to comprehend C) to understand and comprehend D) to understand	**Step 1: Read the passage and identify the issue** The issue is Redundancy or Concision because "understand" and "comprehend" have the same meaning. **Step 2: Eliminate answer choices that do not address the issue** Eliminate A because the underlined portion is redundant as written. Eliminate B and C because they do not correct the redundancy issue. **Step 3: Plug in the remaining answer choices and select the most correct, concise, and relevant one** Choice (D) is the only remaining answer choice and is therefore correct.
3. A) NO CHANGE B) ambivalence C) complexity D) ambivalent complexity	**Step 1: Read the passage and identify the issue** The issue is Style and Tone. The style and tone of the passage are authoritative and academic. **Step 2: Eliminate answer choices that do not address the issue** The author uses the underlined phrase previously in the second sentence of the paragraph: "The defining features of the modern story are its complexity and ambivalence." Eliminate B and C because they both remove one of the previously used words. Eliminate D because even though it is more concise, it alters the intended meaning. **Step 3: Plug in the remaining answer choices and select the most correct, concise, and relevant one** Choice (A) is the only remaining answer choice and is therefore correct.

Questions	Strategic Thinking
4. Which choice most effectively combines the sentences at the underlined portion? A) NO CHANGE B) nod his head sagely. He will think about C) nod his head sagely, thinking about D) nod his head sagely, be thinking about	**Step 1: Read the passage and identify the issue** The issue is Syntax. **Step 2: Eliminate answer choices that do not address the issue** Eliminate A because as written, the underlined portion creates a run-on sentence. Eliminate B because it separates the underlined portion into two sentences, which, while grammatically correct, is not the most effective combination because it places distance between the joined content of the two parts. Eliminate D because it is grammatically incorrect. **Step 3: Plug in the remaining answer choices and select the most correct, concise, and relevant one** Choice (C) is the only remaining answer choice and is therefore correct.

You have seen the ways in which the SAT tests you on Effective Language Use on the Writing & Language Test and how an SAT expert approaches these types of questions.

Look at the Writing & Language passage excerpt that follows. There are four questions associated with it. Use the Kaplan Method for Writing & Language to answer the questions. Remember to look at the strategic thinking questions that have been laid out for you—some of the answers have been filled in, but you will have to fill in the answers to others.

Use your answers to the strategic thinking questions to select the correct answer, just as you will on Test Day.

Questions 5-8 are based on the following passage.

Military Nurses

During the American Civil War, Miss Dorothea Dix was in charge of organizing the volunteer nurses who assisted the Union Army. The nurses chosen by Dix were all women, preferably plain ones, and had to dress simply in order to serve. Dorothea Dix's volunteers were the first famous nurses in United States history, but on both the Union and Confederate sides, **5** other health care professionals there that few people knew about were male nurses. However, as the nineteenth century progressed, nursing became increasingly considered "women's work," until, at the turn of the 20th century, female nurses began to organize, unofficially excluding men. The American Nursing Association was formed in 1917, and men were officially not permitted to join until 1930.

One of the **6** major victories of the female-dominated nursing community was to have men **7** denied admission to and excluded from military nursing. Although traditionally, non-volunteer military nurses had been exclusively male, in 1901 the United States Army Nurse Corps was formed, and only women could serve. **8** It is amazing to even think that men couldn't work as military nurses until after the Korean War. Today, depending on the branch of service, anywhere between 35% and 70% of military nurses are men; this is in sharp contrast to the civilian world, where an average of 6% of American nurses are men.

Questions	Strategic Thinking
5. A) NO CHANGE B) few people knew there were other health care professionals about: male nurses C) some health care professionals were male nurses that few people knew about D) there were other health care professionals that few people knew about: male nurses	**Step 1: Read the passage and identify the issue** *What is the issue?* The issue is Syntax because as written, the sentence is hard to follow due to the placement of the words. **Step 2: Eliminate answer choices that do not address the issue** *What answer choice(s) can you eliminate?* Eliminate A, B, and C because they do not correct the Syntax error. **Step 3: Plug in the remaining answer choices and select the most correct, concise, and relevant one** *What is the correct answer?* _____
6. A) NO CHANGE B) first triumphs C) undisputed wins D) finest achievements	**Step 1: Read the passage and identify the issue** *What is the issue?* Word choice, or Precision. *What does the underlined phrase indicate? Does it fit the context of the passage? Why or why not?* Notice, C and D both mean the same thing as A. Since there can't be three correct answers on the SAT, this should assist you in eliminating several possibilities. **Step 2: Eliminate answer choices that do not address the issue** *What answer choice(s) can you eliminate?* _____ _____ **Step 3: Plug in the remaining answer choices and select the most correct, concise, and relevant one** *What is the correct answer?* _____

Questions	Strategic Thinking
7. A) NO CHANGE B) denied to and excluded from C) excluded from D) denied and excluded from	**Step 1: Read the passage and identify the issue** *What is the issue?* Redundancy, or Concision. *Why is the underlined portion redundant?* _____ _____ _____ _____ _____ **Step 2: Eliminate answer choices that do not address the issue** *What answer choice(s) can you eliminate?* _____ _____ _____ _____ **Step 3: Plug in the remaining answer choices and select the most correct, concise, and relevant one** *What is the correct answer?* _____

Questions	Strategic Thinking
8. A) NO CHANGE B) It was not until after the Korean War that men could once more work as military nurses. C) In this day and age, it is nearly inconceivable that it took until after the Korean War before men could once more exercise their right to work as military nurses. D) Not until after the Korean War could men once more take up the noble calling to serve as military nurses.	**Step 1: Read the passage and identify the issue** *What is the issue?* Style and Tone. *What are the style and tone of the passage?* _____ _____ _____ _____ *Does the underlined portion match the style and tone of the passage? Why or why not?* _____ _____ _____ _____ **Step 2: Eliminate answer choices that do not address the issue** *What answer choice(s) can you eliminate?* _____ _____ _____ _____ _____ **Step 3: Plug in the remaining answer choices and select the most correct, concise, and relevant one** *What is the correct answer?* _____

Now, try a test-like Writing & Language passage on your own. Give yourself 5 minutes to read the passage and answer the questions.

Questions 9-16 are based on the following passage.

Genetically Modified Organisms

Although biotechnology companies and the chronically naïve ⑨ imagine that there is no danger to be feared from genetically modified foods, they overlook a plethora of evidence indicating that we may be gambling with our very lives by continuing to ⑩ interfere and tamper with nature to create these "Frankenfoods." Potential problems range from the relatively minor—increased possibilities of allergic reactions to certain foods, for instance—to the potentially devastating—the complete skewing of the balance of an ecosystem. All of these factors should be carefully considered before ⑪ we choose to risk so much for the possibility of a better tomato.

For example, the cultivation of insect-resistant plants could lead to the reduction or even destruction of certain insect species that naturally feed on those plants. A change in the insect population could have a disastrous impact on ⑫ certain bird species. They rely on the affected insects as their food source. And alterations in the balance of the bird population could have further-reaching consequences, all the way up the food chain. An ecosystem is a delicate thing, and the ripple created by genetically altering one variety of soybean ⑬ will translate into a shock wave of unforeseen repercussions in the long term.

9. A) NO CHANGE
   B) insist
   C) hope
   D) think

10. A) NO CHANGE
    B) thoughtlessly interfere and casually tamper
    C) interfere by casually tampering
    D) tamper

11. A) NO CHANGE
    B) we as a society
    C) those of us who comprise society
    D) the citizens making up our population

12. Which choice most effectively combines the sentences at the underlined portion?
    A) NO CHANGE
    B) certain bird species that rely on the affected insects
    C) certain bird species relying on the affected insects
    D) certain bird species, and they rely on the affected insects

13. A) NO CHANGE
    B) must
    C) would
    D) could

14 The actual impact on the genetically modified organisms themselves, and on those who consume foods produced from genetically modified organisms, also remains to be seen. Some studies have indicated that certain genetically modified foods had negative effects on the digestive systems and cardiac health of rats that consumed those foods in high quantities; although human studies have not been performed, the possibility that tampering with an organism's genetic structure could cause far-reaching health consequences for the people who eat genetically modified foods must be confronted.

14. A) NO CHANGE

B) What also remains to be seen, on both the genetically modified organisms themselves and on those who consume foods produced from genetically modified organisms, is the actual impact.

C) Remaining to be seen is the actual impact on genetically modified organisms themselves and those who consume genetically modified organisms.

D) The actual impact remains to be seen on genetically modified organisms themselves and those who consume genetically modified organisms.

And arguments about the potential for genetic engineering to end world hunger by maximizing the quantity and quality of food grown around the world are based on an **15** essential fallacy: people do not starve because there is a lack of food. People starve because it is more profitable to let food go to waste than to distribute it to the world's impoverished and famine-stricken regions. We have plenty of farmland sitting fallow and plenty of food rotting in warehouses. Many of the agribusinesses arguing that genetically modified foods can solve world hunger are the same companies that accept government subsidies now to limit their production of crops in order to avoid flooding the market. These companies are primarily concerned with profit, and whatever lip service they pay to global well-being, the driving force behind genetically modified organisms and foods is profit, not people. **16** In conclusion, the benefits and risks of any new technology must be carefully considered before implementing that technology.

15. A) NO CHANGE
     B) harmful delusion
     C) fanciful illusion
     D) fundamental untruth

16. A) NO CHANGE
     B) It would be nice if we could trust the very companies that could benefit most from the creation of genetically modified organisms.
     C) Unfortunately, those companies affect so many aspects of modern life that we have no choice but to trust them.
     D) Why would we trust our own well-being and that of the planet to companies recklessly pursuing money at the risk of Mother Earth?

Answers & Explanations for this chapter begin on page 1095.

EXTRA PRACTICE

Required	Recommended
Questions 1–11	Questions 12–22

Questions 1-11 are based on the following passage.

Long History, Short Poem: The Haiku

1 Of the many forms poetry can take, triolet, ballad, ode, and epigram, to name a few, none is quite as briefly beautiful as the Japanese haiku. With a **2** complex history and a challenging structure, the haiku is as popular as it is difficult to master. Composed of only three lines and 17 or fewer syllables, haiku have been written by some of the world's most prominent poets.

1. A) NO CHANGE
    B) Of the many forms poetry can take—triolet, ballad, ode, and epigram, to name a few—none is quite as briefly beautiful as the Japanese haiku.
    C) Of the many forms poetry can take, triolet, ballad, ode and epigram to name a few—none is quite as briefly beautiful as the Japanese haiku.
    D) Of the many forms poetry can take: triolet, ballad, ode, and epigram to name a few, none is quite as briefly beautiful as the Japanese haiku.

2. A) NO CHANGE
    B) controversial
    C) brief
    D) difficult

[3] [1] Pre-Buddhist and early Shinto ceremonies included narrative poems called "uta," or songs. [2] These songs were written about common activities like planting and prayer. [3] The most popular "uta" were "waka," or songs featuring 31 syllables broken into five different lines. [4] Later, the "waka" format was distilled into the 5-7-5-7-7 syllables-per-line format that is still used and recognized today. [5] During the same time period, writers played word games. [6] The syllabic 5-7-5-7-7 structure would remain throughout the work, adhering to the guidelines used in ceremonies and royal court proceedings. [7] They would compose lines of poetry, alternating turns, until long strings of text called "renga" were created. [8] It was not until the 15th and 16th centuries that writers of "renga" broke with tradition and shortened the form, writing "hokku," meaning "first verse." [9] ④ <u>This name changed into "haiku" over time.</u> [5]

3. Which sentence should be inserted before sentence 1 in order to introduce the topic of the paragraph?

    A) Although the format remained unknown to Americans until the 1950s, haiku dates back as early as the seventh century.

    B) The art of haiku includes specific rules about how lines are to be structured, but these rules are difficult to pin down.

    C) Despite its difficult reputation and the years it takes to master, haiku is highly entertaining.

    D) Haiku is a Japanese poetic art form and many poets enjoy the challenge of writing a poem within its rules.

4. A) NO CHANGE

    B) Omit the sentence

    C) Nobody is quite sure when it became known as "haiku."

    D) These days, we know this word as "haiku."

5. For the sake of the cohesion of this paragraph, sentence 7 should be placed

    A) where it is now.

    B) before sentence 2.

    C) before sentence 6.

    D) after sentence 8.

6 Previously, hokku master Matsunaga Teitoku began teaching renga in an attempt to ignite a classical renaissance. He founded a writing school where he taught Matsuo Basho, who is now known as one of Japan's most famous writers. Basho traveled throughout Japan writing about nature and his travels.

It is through Basho's many poems that 7 haiku came to be known as being pretty tied up with nature and the seasons. 8 Basho influenced many students of verse over the course of his lifetime and was declared the saint of the haiku in the Shinto religion.

6. A) NO CHANGE
   B) However
   C) In the next century
   D) As a result

7. A) NO CHANGE
   B) haiku transformed into a mode of artistic expression that was irreversibly intertwined with the themes of
   C) haiku became popular because it was seen as having something to do with
   D) haiku developed its common association with

8. Which sentence, if added here, would provide the best support for this paragraph?
   A) However, haiku can be used to communicate many other ideas as well, from love to humor.
   B) His words emphasized contentment and solitary contemplation, ideals linked to Japanese religions.
   C) Basho's poetic influence continues to be felt even now in the work of several modern poets.
   D) For example, a Basho haiku might focus on a frog or on the coming of spring.

It was not until 1827 that the hokku was renamed haiku by Masaoka Shiki. **9** Shiki was a poet, and he most famously shrank the structure of the haiku to its current format of 5-7-5. His work **10** helped Western writers like e. e. cummings and Ezra Pound, but haiku did not become the easily recognizable, popular type of poetry that it is today until writers like Allen Ginsberg and Jack Kerouac popularized it.

These writers were taken by **11** the brevity of the form, but it provided them a new, challenging form of expression while enabling them to share full ideas in such a short form. Both Japanese and American poets continue to use the structures to create snapshots of beauty and calm.

9. A) NO CHANGE
   B) Shiki was a poet who also shrank the structure of the haiku to the current 5-7-5 format.
   C) Shiki was the poet who shrank the structure of the haiku to its current 5-7-5 format.
   D) Shiki was the poet who was also known for shrinking the structure of the haiku to its current format of 5-7-5.

10. A) NO CHANGE
    B) inspired
    C) aided
    D) started

11. A) NO CHANGE
    B) the brevity of the form, it
    C) the brevity of the form, and it
    D) the brevity of the form, as it

Questions 12-22 are based on the following passage and supplementary material.

Tesla Lights Up the World

[1] Nikola Tesla, born in 1856, was an Austrian electrical engineer who worked for a telegraph company in Budapest before immigrating to the United States to join Thomas Edison's company in New York. [2] The two engineers did not work well together, and Tesla moved on to work with George Westinghouse, another engineer and inventor, at the Westinghouse Electric & Manufacturing Company in 1885. [3] **12** During his time there, Tesla invented the alternating current system, or what we know in our homes as AC power. [4] Several years later, Tesla made the first successful wireless energy transfer. [5] Reportedly, Tesla slept little and often occupied himself with games, such as chess and billiards. **13**

[1] The Westinghouse Electric Company was quick to put Tesla's invention to work. [2] They **14** implemented the use of alternating current during the World Colombian Exposition in **15** 1897, with fantastic results. [3] It was more efficient than Edison's earlier energy transfer system, the direct current (DC) system, as well as more effective. [4] Edison knew, though, that the DC system was difficult to transmit over long distances. [5] He didn't, however, believe that Tesla's

12. A) NO CHANGE
    B) Tesla, while there, invented the AC power system we know in our homes, more formally called the alternating current system.
    C) Tesla invented the alternating current system during his time there, also known in our homes as AC power.
    D) When he worked there, the alternating current system, or what we know in our homes as AC power, was invented by him.

13. Which sentence, if omitted, would improve the focus of this paragraph?
    A) Sentence 1
    B) Sentence 2
    C) Sentence 4
    D) Sentence 5

14. A) NO CHANGE
    B) encouraged
    C) invoked
    D) developed

15. Which choice completes the sentence with accurate data based on the timeline at the end of the passage?
    A) NO CHANGE
    B) 1882
    C) 1890
    D) 1893

AC system was a credible threat to the dominance he and his company held over the electrical market of the time because of his invention of the lightbulb. [6] **16** But it is Tesla's system that moves power from a main grid across long distances.

[1] Tesla went on to develop the technology that is now used in X-rays, as well as radio and remote controls. [2] Some of his inventions even worked together, expanding his influence on the world and history. [3] Tesla paired his AC system with his understanding of physics to invent an electric motor. [4] Developing the AC system was only the beginning for Tesla, though. [5] To do so, he used his knowledge of magnetism to create a closed system in which a motor could turn without disruption or the use of manpower. [6] The motor generated a stable current that had been lacking in earlier attempts to transition industry to AC power. [7] With Tesla's motor, though, AC power systems could be broadly used in manufacturing and beyond. **17 18**

16. Which choice most effectively conveys the central idea of the paragraph?
    A) NO CHANGE
    B) However, bulbs alone do not light our homes; it is Tesla's system that moves power from one grid across long distances to the fixtures we use every day.
    C) Later, Tesla developed a system that allows us to use lightbulbs every day.
    D) We now use Edison's bulbs every day; we can thank Tesla for inventing the system that moves power from one grid across distances to those fixtures.

17. Which sentence would provide the best transition from the previous paragraph if placed before sentence 1?
    A) Sentence 2
    B) Sentence 4
    C) Sentence 6
    D) Sentence 7

18. Based on the timeline, "In 1883," would be most appropriately added to the beginning of which of the following?
    A) Paragraph 1, sentence 2
    B) Paragraph 2, sentence 1
    C) Paragraph 3, sentence 3
    D) Paragraph 4, sentence 3

[1] Tesla's inventions are not only a part of our daily lives, but they continue **19** to be expanded upon to create new advances in science and technology. [2] **20** Tesla's approach to energy transmission, as well as his invention of the radio, including antenna and other recognizable aspects, has allowed leaps and bounds to be made in wireless communications, such as radio broadcasting. [3] Edison may have invented the lightbulb, **21** but Tesla was an inventor bent on bringing electricity to the people, seeking no fame or fortune. [4] The reach of his technology goes even as far as the mobile phone. [5] Although long gone, Tesla remains **22** a pathfinder on the edge of miraculous invention.

Tesla's Inventions

1882 ➤ Rotating Magnetic Field—A rotating field that enabled alternating current to power a motor.

1883 ➤ AC Motor—The rotating magnetic field was put into practice in this motor, which spun without a mechanical aid.

1890 ➤ Tesla Coil—A coil that enables transformers to produce extremely high voltages.

1893 ➤ Tesla and Westinghouse display their AC current systems at the Columbian Exposition in Chicago.

1897 ➤ Radio—Tesla invented the radio, including antennae, tuners, and other pieces we're familiar with.

19. Which of the following provides the most concise revision without altering the author's intended meaning?

   A) to necessitate

   B) to be developed into

   C) to inspire scientists to make

   D) to lead to

20. Which supporting detail is least essential to sentence 2?

   A) That Tesla invented the radio

   B) That Tesla's invention of the radio included the "antenna and other recognizable aspects"

   C) That Tesla's invention of the radio allowed further innovation in wireless communications

   D) That radio broadcasting is a kind of wireless communication

21. A) NO CHANGE

   B) but Tesla, seeking no fame or fortune, was an inventor bent on bringing electricity to the people

   C) but seeking no fame or fortune, Tesla was an inventor bent on bringing electricity to the people

   D) but Tesla was an inventor bent on seeking no fame or fortune, bringing electricity to the people

22. A) NO CHANGE

   B) an explorer

   C) a champion

   D) a pioneer

Standard English Conventions

BY THE END OF THIS UNIT, YOU WILL BE ABLE TO:

1. Recognize correct and incorrect instances of conventions of usage and punctuation

2. Correct errors in sentence structure

CHAPTER 30

Sentence Structure

CHAPTER OBJECTIVES

By the end of this chapter, you will be able to:

1. Recognize and correct grammatically incomplete or substandard sentences
2. Recognize and correct inappropriate grammatical shifts in the construction of verb and pronoun phrases

SMARTPOINTS

Point Value	SmartPoint Category
40 Points	Sentence Formation
5 Points	Shifts in Construction

RUN-ONS AND FRAGMENTS

Run-ons and fragments create grammatically incomplete sentences. There are specific rules governing complete sentences, and the SAT requires that you know them.

A complete sentence must have a subject and a predicate verb in an independent clause that expresses a complete thought. If any one of these elements is missing, the sentence is a fragment. You can recognize a fragment because the sentence will not make sense as written because it lacks one of the three components:

- John running down the street. (lacks a predicate verb)

- Because Martha led the team in assists. (does not express a complete thought)

- Practiced the piano every day. (needs a subject)

> ✔ **Definition**
>
> The **predicate** is the part of the sentence that describes what the **subject** *does* (action), *is* (being), or *has* (condition); the **predicate verb** is the main verb in the sentence.

If a sentence has more than one independent clause, the clauses must be properly joined. Otherwise, the sentence is a run-on:

- I know English now, I didn't know it before I came to America.

To Correct a Run-On	Example
Use a semicolon.	I know English now**;** I didn't know it before I came to America.
Make one clause dependent.	**Although** I know English now, I didn't know it before I came to America.
Add a FANBOYS conjunction: *For, And, Nor, But, Or, Yet, So.*	I know English now, **but** I didn't know it before I came to America.

SUBORDINATION AND COORDINATION

Subordination and coordination questions focus on the relationship between clauses. On the SAT, you will be asked to determine the best way to link clauses to most effectively express the writer's intent.

COORDINATE CLAUSES

Coordinate clauses are independent clauses that can stand on their own and express a complete thought. When two or more independent clauses are properly joined, they form a compound sentence.

Two independent clauses are *coordinated* by using a comma and the conjunction *and*:

- *The class was interesting, and we prepared thoroughly for each session.* (Equal emphasis on the two ideas suggests that the class would have been interesting whether or not we prepared and that we would have prepared whether or not the class was interesting.)

SUBORDINATE CLAUSES

A subordinate clause cannot stand on its own and make sense. Combining a subordinate clause with an independent clause by using a connecting word forms a complex sentence. In a complex sentence, the independent clause expresses the central idea of the sentence and the subordinate clause provides additional support that modifies or clarifies the central idea.

The central idea of the sentence is changed depending upon which clause is *subordinated*:

- *Because the class was interesting,* we prepared thoroughly for each session. (The main emphasis is on our preparation. The subordinate clause gives the reason for our thoroughness.)
- The class was interesting *because we prepared thoroughly for each session.* (The main emphasis is on the class. The subordinate clause explains why it was interesting.)

PARALLELISM

Parallelism questions on the SAT test your ability to revise sentences to create parallel structure. Items in a series, list, or compound must be parallel in form. Series, lists, and compounds may contain nouns, adjectives, adverbs, or verb forms.

Check for parallelism if the sentence contains:

A list	Before you leave, you should **charge your phone, clean your room**, and **find your car keys**.	3 verb phrases
A compound	**Swimming** and **biking** provide aerobic exercise.	2 gerund verb forms
A correlative	It is necessary not only **to prepare** thoroughly, but also **to listen** carefully.	2 infinitive verb forms
A comparison	Your **homework** is just as important as your **class participation**.	2 nouns
Related nouns	**Students** who complete all of their **homework assignments** will receive **higher grades**.	3 related plural nouns

MODIFIERS

A modifier is a word or a group of words that describes, clarifies, or provides additional information about another part of the sentence. Modifier questions on the SAT Writing & Language Test require you to identify the part of a sentence being modified and use the appropriate modifier in the proper place. Modifiers should be close to the words they modify.

Modifier	Function	Example
Adjective	A single word modifier that describes a noun or pronoun	Amanda bought the **maroon** love seat from the **garage** sale.
Adverb	A single word modifier that describes a verb, an adjective, or another adverb	Ian **carefully** walked over the **rapidly** melting ice.
Modifying phrase	Modifying phrases and clauses must be properly placed to correctly modify another part of the sentence.	**Wanting to do well on her exams**, Sasha devoted extra time to her studies.

Use context clues in the passage to identify the correct placement of a modifier.

A misplaced modifier can cause confusion:

- The restaurant provides carryout meals to its diners **in recyclable containers**.

Who or what is in the containers? The context of the sentence suggests that the meals are in the containers. When the modifier is placed near what it modifies, the meaning is clarified:

- The restaurant provides carryout meals **in recyclable containers** to its diners.

Modifier placement can change the meaning of a sentence:

- The waiter **just** described the dinner specials. (The sentence is about **when** the action took place.)
- **Just** the waiter described the dinner specials. (The sentence is about **who** took the action.)
- The waiter described **just** the dinner specials. (The sentence is about **what** was acted upon.)

VERB TENSE, MOOD, AND VOICE

On the SAT Writing & Language Test, you will be asked to identify and replace unnecessary shifts in verb tense, mood, and voice. Because these shifts may occur within a single sentence or among different sentences, you will need to read around the underlined portion to identify the error.

In questions about shifts in construction, the underlined segment must logically match the tense, mood, and voice in other parts of the sentence.

Verb tense places the action or state being described by the verb into a place in time: **present**, **past**, or **future**. Each tense has three forms: **simple**, **progressive**, and **perfect**.

> ✔ **On Test Day**
>
> Shifts in verb tense are grammatically incorrect unless warranted by the context of the sentence or passage.

	Present	Past	Future
Simple: Actions that simply occur at some point in time	She studies diligently every day.	She studied two extra hours before her math test.	She will study tomorrow for her French test.
Progressive: Actions that are ongoing at some point in time	She is studying today for her math test tomorrow.	She was studying yesterday for a French test today.	She will be studying tomorrow for her physics test next week.
Perfect: Actions that are completed at some point in time	She has studied diligently every day this semester.	She had studied two extra hours before her math test yesterday.	She will have studied each chapter before her physics test next week.

Grammatical **moods** are classifications that indicate the attitude of the speaker.

	Description	Example
Indicative Mood	Used to make a statement or ask a question	Snow **covered** the moonlit field.
Imperative Mood	Used to give a command or make a request	Please **return** your library books.
Subjunctive Mood	Used to express hypothetical outcomes	If I **do** my homework, I will score well on the test.

The **voice** of a verb describes the relationship between the action expressed by the verb and the subject.

	Description	Example
Active	The subject is the agent or doer of the action.	The carpenter **hammered** the nail.
Passive	The subject is the target of the action.	The nail **was hammered** by the carpenter.

✔ **Expert Tip**

On the SAT, the active voice is preferred over the passive voice.

PRONOUN PERSON AND NUMBER

Pronouns replace nouns in sentences. They must agree with the noun they are replacing in person and number. The SAT will test your ability to recognize and correct inappropriate shifts in pronoun usage. To learn more about pronoun clarity and pronoun-antecedent agreement on the SAT, turn to chapter 30.

Pronoun Person and Number			
Person	Refers to	Singular Pronouns	Plural Pronouns
First person	the person speaking	I, me, my	we, us, our
Second person	the person spoken to	you, your	you, your
Third person	the person or thing spoken about	he, she, it, him, her, his, hers, its	they, them, theirs
Indefinite	a nonspecific person or group	anybody, anyone, each, either, every-one, someone, one	both, few, many, several

Let's look at the following Writing & Language passage and questions. After the passage, there are two columns. The left column contains test-like questions. The column on the right features the strategic thinking a test expert employs when approaching the passage and questions presented.

Questions 1-3 are based on the following passage.

SMOMS

At 69 Condotti Street in Rome sits what is believed by many to be the smallest country in the world—and it is not Vatican City. The Sovereign Military and Hospitaller Order of St. John of Jerusalem of Rhodes and of Malta, or SMOM, is an ancient order of knights well known for its humanitarian activities. The order's headquarters in Rome—at a mere 6,000 square meters, or about one acre—is considered an independent state by at least 75 nations. How SMOM got to Rome is a story almost a millennium old, spanning as many places as the order's official name suggests.

SMOM began in 1099, during the First Crusade, as a large-scale military conflict pitting Christian armies against the Muslim rulers of what is now Israel. The order's task was to protect and defend Christian pilgrims traveling to Jerusalem as well as ❶ providing a hospital for their care. Though it began as a religious order, SMOM developed into a military knighthood as well, due to the volatile political situation.

Because of the ongoing conflict between Muslims and Christians, the order was forced to move a number of times. The Muslims overran Jerusalem in the 1170s, forcing SMOM to relocate first to the Mediterranean island of Cyprus and then to the nearby island of Rhodes. The Ottoman Turks seized Rhodes in 1522, forcing SMOM to move again, this time to Malta. ❷ Then Napoleon drives the order from Malta in 1798, and the island fell into British hands soon after. SMOM wandered from city to city in Italy, finally establishing its current headquarters in 1834.

Today, SMOM is a knighthood and a religious order but no longer actively combats Muslims, as it did in the past. Instead, SMOM concentrates on caring for humanitarian needs regardless of ❸ creed. Establishing hospitals and charities in all corners of the world. Its many activities include vaccination programs, refugee relief, and philanthropic works to combat deadly diseases such as leprosy and malnutrition.

Because of the order's dual role, the Vatican has always recognized—and continues to recognize—SMOM as an independent nation and its headquarters in Rome as the sovereignty of SMOM. Seventy-five countries recognize the order as a country, although the United States and Great Britain do not. SMOM coins its own money, mints its own stamps, and issues its own passports. The order is a Permanent Observer in the United Nations and enjoys membership in other international organizations as well. Although not physically important anymore, SMOM continues its more than 90-year mission of helping the sick of every nation from its base in the smallest country on Earth.

Questions	Strategic Thinking
1. A) NO CHANGE (B) to provide C) providing them D) ensuring availability of	**Step 1: Read the passage and identify the issue** The underlined verb ("providing") is not parallel to the verbs used earlier in the sentence ("to protect and defend"). **Step 2: Eliminate answer choices that do not address the issue** Eliminate A, C, and D because they do not correct the parallelism error. **Step 3: Plug in the remaining answer choices and select the most correct, concise, and relevant one** Choice (B) is correct.
2. A) NO CHANGE B) Then Napoleon is driving (C) Napoleon drove D) Napoleon drives	**Step 1: Read the passage and identify the issue** The verb in the underlined portion is in a different tense from the other verbs in this paragraph. A writer can shift verb tense only when there is a logical reason to do so. In this instance, the writer does not have a reason to switch tenses: the earlier verbs are in the simple past tense, which indicates that the action occurred at some point in the past. **Step 2: Eliminate answer choices that do not address the issue** Eliminate A, B, and D because they are not in the simple past tense. **Step 3: Plug in the remaining answer choices and select the most correct, concise, and relevant one** Choice (C) is correct.

Questions	Strategic Thinking

3. A) NO CHANGE
   (B) creed, establishing
   C) creed establishing
   D) creed; establishing
	Step 1: Read the passage and identify the issue
	
	The second sentence in the underlined portion is a fragment because it is missing a predicate verb.
	
	Step 2: Eliminate answer choices that do not address the issue
	
	Eliminate C because it creates a run-on sentence. Eliminate D because it does not correct the sentence fragment.
	
	Step 3: Plug in the remaining answer choices and select the most correct, concise, and relevant one
	
	Choice (B) is correct.

You have seen the ways in which the SAT tests you on Sentence Structure in Writing & Language passages and the way an SAT expert approaches these types of questions.

Look at the Writing & Language passage excerpt that follows. There are three questions associated with it. Use the Kaplan Method for Writing & Language to answer the questions. Remember to look at the strategic thinking questions that have been laid out for you—some of the answers have been filled in, but you will have to fill in the answers to others.

Use your answers to the strategic thinking questions to select the correct answer, just as you will on Test Day.

Questions 4-6 are based on the following passage.

The Sun

It is perhaps impossible to overestimate the impact of the Sun on our planet Earth. Functioning like a great thermonuclear reactor situated roughly 100 million miles away, the Sun provides essentially all of Earth's heat in the form of radiant energy, without which there would be no light, warmth, plants, or animals. In addition, with a core temperature of nearly 30 million degrees Fahrenheit, the Sun affects all of Earth's natural phenomena, including all weather and atmospheric movement. Even the energy sources we use daily to fuel our cars and heat our homes, resources like oil and coal harvested from deep within the Earth's crust, were produced by the power of the Sun acting upon living organisms millions of years ago. Yet, **4** while its ability to provide heat and light can be easily felt by simply lying out on a beach or gazing up into a brilliant blue sky, closer inspection of the Sun's dynamic surface through special telescopes has revealed activity capable of affecting Earth in less obvious ways.

Technically classified by scientists as a yellow dwarf star and thought to be approximately 4 billion years old, the Sun's constantly changing surface is actually quite stormy, but it is not the visually dramatic gas particle eruptions that constitute the Sun's most volatile surface activity. Instead, **5** they are the seemingly static black spots that pepper the surface, referred to by scientists as sunspots, that are the true storms. At roughly half the Sun's surface temperature of 10,300 degrees Fahrenheit, sunspots are by far the coolest areas of the Sun, which is why they appear darker than the hotter plasma that surrounds them. And, although in telescopic images these spots appear as little more than tiny black specks, they can be more than 19,000 miles across—wide enough to fit two Earths with orbiting moons.

Historical records show that these spots were first viewed by telescope as early as 1610, but scientists today still know relatively little about them. Almost always seen in pairs, sunspots are thought to be **6** powerfully created by magnetic fields that keep heat from flowing up to the Sun's surface. Scientists have also noticed that these spots seem to erupt and fade in 11-year cycles, manifesting incessant change that is thought to affect the Sun's luminosity and, in turn, Earth's climate. In addition, studies have shown that the charged particles released by sunspots can react with Earth's magnetic field and disrupt satellite communications, radio broadcasts, and even cell phone calls. As scientists continue to carefully observe such occurrences, referred to as space weather, they gain a greater understanding of the powerful ability of the Sun to impact our lives.

Questions	Strategic Thinking
4. (A) NO CHANGE B) when C) with D) because	**Step 1: Read the passage and identify the issue** *What part of speech is underlined?* A subordinating conjunction. *What does a subordinating conjunction do?* It helps to join an independent clause with a dependent clause. **Step 2: Eliminate answer choices that do not address the issue** *What answer choice(s) can you eliminate?* _____ _____ _____ _____ _____ **Step 3: Plug in the remaining answer choices and select the most correct, concise, and relevant one** *What is the correct answer?* _____

Questions	Strategic Thinking
5. A) NO CHANGE B) they are not C) we are D) it is	**Step 1: Read the passage and identify the issue** *What is the issue?* Pronoun consistency. *What pronoun is used in the sentence before the one to which the underlined portion belongs?* "It." *To what does the underlined pronoun refer?* _____ _____ **Step 2: Eliminate answer choices that do not address the issue** *What answer choice(s) can you eliminate?* _____ _____ _____ _____ _____ **Step 3: Plug in the remaining answer choices and select the most correct, concise, and relevant one** *What is the correct answer?* _____

Questions	Strategic Thinking
6. A) NO CHANGE B) created by powerful magnetic C) powerful created by magnetic D) strongly created by magnetic	**Step 1: Read the passage and identify the issue** *What is the issue?* Modifier placement and form. *What type of modifier is included in the underlined segment?* _____ _____ _____ *What should the adverb ("powerfully") logically modify?* _____ _____ *Based on what the adverb ("powerfully") should logically modify, what part of speech should it be?* _____ _____ _____ **Step 2: Eliminate answer choices that do not address the issue** *What answer choice(s) can you eliminate?* _____ _____ _____ _____ _____ **Step 3: Plug in the remaining answer choices and select the most correct, concise, and relevant one** *What is the correct answer?* _____

Now, try a test-like Writing & Language passage on your own. Give yourself 5 minutes to read the passage and answer the questions.

Questions 7-14 are based on the following passage.

Sergei Eisenstein

Considered the father of the montage—a popular cinematic technique that involves a rapid succession of shots, often superimposed— **7** one of the principal architects of the modern movie was the Russian director Sergei Eisenstein. Although his career was not particularly prolific—he completed only seven feature-length films— Eisenstein's work contains a clarity and sharpness of composition that make the depth of his plots and the powerful complexity of his juxtaposed images easily accessible to most **8** viewers, in fact, few filmmakers were more instrumental in pushing the envelope of the established, conservative nineteenth-century Victorian theatre than Eisenstein, whose films helped to usher in a new era of abstract thought and expression in art.

Born in 1898 in what is now the independent nation of Latvia, Eisenstein grew up in affluence as the son of a successful architect. Following in his father's footsteps, he studied at the Institute of Civil Engineering in Petrograd. After the Bolshevik Revolution of 1917, however, Eisenstein was pushed out of academics **9** and into the service of the Red Army as an engineer. When the Russian Civil War ended, Eisenstein sought to leave his work for the new Soviet state behind him. He quickly found employment in show business as a set designer for a prominent Moscow theatre, but the new communist government **10** was likely to remain a heavy influence throughout his career.

7. A) NO CHANGE
   B) Sergei Eisenstein, the Russian director, was one of the principal architects of the modern movie
   C) the Russian director Sergei Eisenstein was one of the principal architects of the modern movie
   D) one of the principal architects of the modern movie was Sergei Eisenstein, the Russian director

8. A) NO CHANGE
   B) viewers. In fact
   C) viewers—in fact
   D) viewers in fact

9. A) NO CHANGE
   B) nor
   C) or
   D) as far as

10. A) NO CHANGE
    B) remained
    C) did likely remain
    D) remains

It was with ⑪ <u>Eisenstein's</u> feature debut, a film entitled *Statchka* released in 1924, that Eisenstein introduced moviegoers to the montage. Expanding upon a complex theory of biomechanics—the study of the mechanical forces at work within a particular body or organ—Eisenstein's first montage consisted of a powerful sequence of conflicting images that were able to abbreviate time spans in the film while introducing new metaphors and allusions to the storyline. Essentially, Eisenstein sought to use the montage to create a ● ⑫ <u>regressive emotional effect that was greater than the sum of the individual shots</u>. It was with this enormously successful technique that Eisenstein's work caught the eye of the new Communist Party leaders in Moscow, who saw in his cinematic style a film for the ⑬ <u>"common man." And</u> a chance to use his skills as a propaganda tool for the state.

Eisenstein's second and third films, ⑭ <u>the enormously famous 1925 hit *Battleship Potemkin* and the 1927 celebration of the October Revolution, *Oktibr*</u>, still widely considered to be masterpieces, were commissioned by party officials in an attempt to use Eisenstein's mass appeal to disseminate Soviet propaganda. As a result, these achievements have been frequently criticized for their lack of artistic integrity. Yet, in the end, regardless of politics, Eisenstein's films continue to have an undeniably significant and lasting impact on filmmakers.

11. A) NO CHANGE
    B) Sergei Eisenstein's
    C) its
    D) his

12. A) NO CHANGE
    B) regressive that was greater than the sum of the individual shots
    C) detrimental emotional effect that was greater than the sum of the individual shots
    D) cumulative emotional effect that was greater than the sum of the individual shots

13. A) NO CHANGE
    B) "common man," and
    C) "common man" and
    D) "common man." And

14. A) NO CHANGE
    B) the enormously famous 1925 hit and the 1927 celebration of the October Revolution, *Battleship Potemkin* and *Oktibr*
    C) the famously enormous 1925 hit *Battleship Potemkin* and the 1927 celebration of the October Revolution, *Oktibr*
    D) the 1925 film *Battleship Potemkin* and the 1927 film *Oktibr*

Answers & Explanations for this chapter appear on page 1103.

EXTRA PRACTICE

Required	Recommended
Questions 1–11	Questions 12–22

Questions 1-11 are based on the following passage.

The Experts of Visual Communication

1 The digital explosion of the past two decades has resulted in decreased costs of devices for the average consumer. From early cave painters and the intricate craftspeople of ancient worlds to the vast, magnificent artwork that has emerged across countless generations and cultures, art accomplishes fascinating measures of human communication. In today's world, the **2** prominent arena in which art and communication meet is graphic design. The digital age has seen an explosion of media and connectivity. This offers an ever-growing platform for art, through graphic design, to deliver ideas and messages.

1. A) NO CHANGE
    B) Throughout history, visual art has contested verbal communication in its power to convey meaning.
    C) In recent times, cell phone and tablet use have rendered the desktop computer nearly obsolete.
    D) Because of the increasing use of wireless communication, new laws will be needed to regulate usage.

2. A) NO CHANGE
    B) obscure
    C) inconspicuous
    D) distinguished

Incorporating creativity, communication knowledge, and technological expertise, graphic designers fashion messages for the public eye. Their work is peppered throughout Western life. **③** Business logos; billboard advertisements; website layouts, T-shirt designs; and even the decorated cardboard of cereal boxes and coffee cups feature graphic design. In a culture increasingly wired for visual communication, graphic designers are the artists of today's media. **④** They create and craft the medium and formats, visual images, and symbols that add vibrancy and color to this world and shape the way information is passed, transmitted, and received.

3. A) NO CHANGE

    B) Business logos, billboard advertisements—website layouts, T-shirt designs, and even the decorated cardboard of cereal boxes and coffee cups feature graphic design.

    C) Business logos and billboard advertisements and website layouts, T-shirt designs, and even the decorated cardboard of cereal boxes and coffee cups feature graphic design.

    D) Business logos, billboard advertisements, website layouts, T-shirt designs, and even the decorated cardboard of cereal boxes and coffee cups feature graphic design.

4. A) NO CHANGE

    B) They create and craft the medium and formats, visual images, and symbols that add color to this world and shape the way information is passed, transmitted, and received.

    C) They craft the formats, images, and symbols that color this world and shape the way information is passed and received.

    D) They create the formats, visual images, and symbols that add color to this world and shape the way information is passed, transmitted, and received.

[1] How do these powerful innovators navigate a career path? [2] Most begin by studying graphic design in a bachelor's degree program. [3] Here they build skills through highly interactive class settings to teach expertise. [4] These programs are heavily project-based mirroring the sort of experience professional work will entail. [5] Once students have graduated, these portfolios are essential for the job search, revealing an artist's excellence and creative potential. [6] Students gradually compile design portfolios to showcase their best work. 6

Job competition for graphic designers is rigorous, but graphic design features a variety of professional options. Some will work in design studios. ❼ Here they team with other graphic designers, taking

5. A) NO CHANGE
   B) hone
   C) fulfill
   D) discipline

6. To enhance the logical sequence of paragraph 3, sentence 6 should

   A) remain where it is.
   B) be placed after sentence 2.
   C) be placed after sentence 3.
   D) be placed after sentence 4.

7. A) NO CHANGE
   B) Here they team with other graphic designers; taking on projects for external clients.
   C) Here they team with other graphic designers. Taking on projects for external clients.
   D) Here they team with other graphic designers—taking on projects for external clients.

on projects for external clients. Others work "in-house" for businesses that staff their own graphic designers to create media on a more consistent basis. Those with more entrepreneurial inclinations can work as freelance graphic designers, doing their own networking and contracting. 8

9 Because the demand for graphic designers continues, the highly competitive job market gives some prospective artists pause. The trope

8. Which sentence provides supporting details when added to paragraph 4?

A) Often, graphic designers are encouraged by employers to obtain a master's degree.

B) Some graphic designers return to the university to pursue business administration degrees.

C) Increasingly, graphic designers are taking their skills online and transferring them to website and web application design, which is another growing field for tech-minded artists.

D) Graphic designers often earn less as freelancers than their counterparts who are employed by design studios.

9. A) NO CHANGE
   B) Although
   C) Since
   D) Consequently,

of the "struggling artist" holds true, it seems, even in this visually dominant generation. **10** <u>Most graphic designers find their careers not only satisfying, but also one of invigoration.</u> Perhaps, for those brave artists who follow this career path, the thrill and beauty of the work yields enough motivation and inspiration to persevere and succeed. **11**

10. A) NO CHANGE

B) Most graphic designers find their careers satisfying, in addition to being vigorous.

C) Most graphic designers find their careers not only satisfying, but also invigorating.

D) Most graphic designers find their careers to be not only one of satisfaction, but also invigorating.

11. Which sentence adds relevant information to paragraph 5?

A) Graphic designers experience creative opportunities not offered by other careers.

B) This visually dominant generation spends more on entertainment than any previous age group.

C) Perseverance is vital to a successful career, but luck plays an important factor, too.

D) Graphic designers, along with physical therapists, experience the most competitive job markets.

Questions 12-22 are based on the following passage.

Musical Enjoyment: Better in Numbers?

Music is many things to many ⓬ people: a mode of expression, an escape, or a way to understand life experiences. Although its prominence in global culture has stayed the same, music has changed considerably since its prehistoric invention. ⓭ Music has evolved from a primarily group-enjoyed art form into one consumed mostly on an individual basis.

Researchers have no way of knowing who first invented music, ⓮ but educated guesses can be made about the purposes it served. It is hypothesized that in the Prehistoric Era, early humans used sounds like

12. A) NO CHANGE
    B) people, a mode of expression, an escape, or a way
    C) people; a mode of expression; an escape; or a way
    D) people: a mode of expression or an escape or a way

13. A) NO CHANGE
    B) Music has evolved from an art form that has been primarily enjoyed by groups
    C) Music has evolved from a group art form
    D) Primarily, music as a group art form has evolved

14. A) NO CHANGE
    B) but they can make educated guesses about the purposes it served
    C) but educated guesses of the purposes it served have been made
    D) but educated guesses are made about the purposes it served

hand clapping and foot stomping to create rhythmic repetition.

15 For instance, art in both Stone Age cave paintings and later

Persian cave paintings shows examples of people using handmade

instruments to create music in a group setting. The sounds produced

were an early form of communication. The use of music as a tool

opened early humans **16** up to one another. Advancing social bonding

even in an age before common languages.

17 In ancient Egypt, musicians were appointed to play for specific

gods. In addition to enhancing religious ceremonies, music was used

in the royal court. Gifted musicians were hired to honor the pharaoh

15. A) NO CHANGE
    B) Similarly
    C) For example
    D) In other words

16. Which choice most effectively combines the sentences at the underlined portion?

    A) up to one another while advancing
    B) up to one another; this advanced
    C) up to one another, advancing
    D) up to one another, a tool advancing

17. Which sentence creates the most cohesive transition from the previous paragraph?

    A) More recent examples show music primarily becoming a source of entertainment.
    B) Music became a notable social bonding tool among wealthy and aristocratic circles.
    C) Music from Egypt traveled to America and helped convey the importance of social bonding.
    D) Further examples throughout history show the development of music as a social bonding tool.

and impress guests of the royal family. In American history, music has been used as a vehicle for storytelling. At the time of the Underground Railroad, music was used to deliver messages to groups of people trying to escape slavery. Directions were embedded **18** <u>in lyrics that were well-known to many</u>. Although these examples are very different, they highlight how music was used to encourage social bonding.

[1] With the **19** <u>advent</u> of headphones in 1910, music was changed from an inherently social experience to a personal one. [2] Based on Thomas Edison's discovery of sound created by electrical signals, Nathaniel Baldwin created the first headset that could amplify sound. [3] This invention has been greatly improved upon since. [4] Instead of music being primarily used in group settings, it became a highly individual form of entertainment. [5] While this is seen as a positive departure, studies link the use of headphones to feelings of isolation and decreased personal satisfaction. [6] With music becoming more portable than ever, headphones have enabled people to listen to music in almost any situation, including on their way to work, at the workplace, and at home while their families listen to their own choice of music. **20**

18. A) NO CHANGE
    B) in lyrics that included references to famous abolitionists
    C) in popular lyrics, hiding helpful instructions in plain sight
    D) in lyrics that were typically banned by plantation owners

19. A) NO CHANGE
    B) enhancement
    C) prevalence
    D) prohibition

20. For the sake of cohesion in this paragraph, sentence 5 should be placed
    A) where it is now.
    B) after sentence 2.
    C) before sentence 4.
    D) after sentence 6.

21 <u>Psychologists' and sociologists'</u> hypothesize that the shift in music from a social to an individual enjoyment contributes to a high number of people reporting feelings of loneliness in recent studies. While the long-term psychological effects of this shift will take time to analyze, it is already apparent that humans are less connected in their enjoyment of something we have shared throughout history. 22

21. A) NO CHANGE

    B) Psychologists and sociologists'

    C) Psychologist's and sociologist's

    D) Psychologists and sociologists

22. Which answer choice, when inserted into this paragraph, would most help support the author's claims?

    A) The number of people reporting feelings of loneliness in recent studies

    B) Which psychologists and sociologists are making these claims

    C) The specific differences in the ways humans have shared music over time

    D) Which long-term psychological effects may be related to using headphones

CHAPTER 31

Conventions of Usage

CHAPTER OBJECTIVES

By the end of this chapter, you will be able to:

1. Recognize and correct errors in pronoun clarity, grammatical agreement, and logical comparison

2. Distinguish among commonly confused possessive determiners, contractions, and adverbs

3. Recognize and correct incorrectly constructed idioms and frequently misused words

SMARTPOINTS

Point Value	SmartPoint Category
50 Points	Usage

PRONOUNS

A pronoun is ambiguous if its antecedent is either missing or unclear. On the SAT, you must be able to recognize either situation and make the appropriate correction. When you see an underlined pronoun, make sure you can find the specific noun to which it refers.

Missing Antecedent

- When the flight arrived, *they* told the passengers to stay seated until the plane reached the gate. (The pronoun "they" does not have an antecedent in this sentence.)

- When the flight arrived, *the flight crew* told the passengers to stay seated until the plane reached the gate. (Replacing the pronoun with a specific noun clarifies the meaning.)

Unclear Antecedent

- Martha asked Mia to drive Samantha to the airport because *she* was running late. (The pronoun "she" could refer to any of the three people mentioned in the sentence.)

- Because Martha was running late, she asked Mia to drive Samantha to the airport. (By rearranging the sentence, the pronoun "she" unambiguously refers to Martha.)

> ✔ **Definition**
>
> The **antecedent** is the noun that the pronoun replaces or stands in for another part of the sentence. To identify the **antecedent** of a pronoun, check the nouns near the pronoun. Substitute those nouns for the pronoun to see which one makes sense.

AGREEMENT

Pronoun-Antecedent Agreement

Pronouns must agree with their antecedents not only in person and number, but also in gender. Only third-person pronouns make a distinction based on gender.

Gender	Example
Feminine	Because Yvonne had a question, *she* raised her hand.
Masculine	Since *he* had lots of homework, Justin started working right away.
Neuter	The rain started slowly, but then *it* became a downpour.
Unspecified	If a traveler is lost, *he* or *she* should ask for directions.

Pronoun-Case Agreement

There are three pronoun cases:

1. Subjective case: The pronoun is used as the subject.

2. Objective case: The pronoun is used as the object of a verb or a preposition.

3. Possessive case: The pronoun expresses ownership.

Subjective Case	I, you, she, he, it, we, you, they, who
Objective Case	me, you, her, him, it, us, you, them, whom
Possessive Case	my, mine, your, yours, his, her, hers, its, our, ours, their, theirs, whose

✔ **Expert Tip**

When there are two pronouns or a noun and a pronoun in a compound structure, drop the other noun to confirm which case to use. For example: *Tom and me walk into town.* Would you say, "Me walk into town"? No, you would say, "I walk into town." Therefore, the correct case is subjective and the original sentence should read *Tom and I walk into town.*

✔ **Remember**

Use "who" when you would use "he" or "she." Use "whom" when you would use "him" or "her."

Subject-Verb Agreement

A verb must agree with its subject noun in person and number:

- Singular: A **stamp sticks** to an envelope.

- Plural: **Stamps stick** to envelopes.

The noun closest to a verb may not be its subject: *The **chair** with the cabriole legs **is** an antique.* The noun closest to the verb in this sentence ("is," which is singular) is "legs," which is plural. However, the verb's subject is "chair," so the sentence is correct as written.

Only the conjunction *and* forms a compound subject requiring a plural verb form:

- Danny **and** Jared **are** in the fencing club.

- **Either** Danny or Jared **is** in the fencing club.

- **Neither** Danny nor Jared **is** in the fencing club.

Noun-Number Agreement

Related nouns must be consistent in number:

- *Students* applying for college must submit their *applications* on time. (The sentence refers to multiple students, and they all must submit applications.)

FREQUENTLY CONFUSED WORDS

The English language contains many pairs of words that sound alike but are spelled differently and have different meanings.

ACCEPT/EXCEPT: To *accept* is to take or receive something that is offered: *Dad said he would accept my apology for putting a dent in his new car, but then he grounded me for two weeks.* To *except* is to leave out or exclude: *The soldier was excepted from combat duty because he had poor field vision.* Except is usually used as a preposition that signifies "with the exception of, excluding": *When the receptionist found out that everyone except him had received a raise, he demanded a salary increase as well.*

AFFECT/EFFECT: To *affect* is to have an influence on something: *Al refused to let the rain affect his plans for a picnic, so he sat under an umbrella and ate potato salad.* To *effect* is to bring something about or cause something to happen: *The young activist received an award for effecting a change in her community.* An *effect* is an influence or a result: *The newspaper article about homeless animals had such an effect on Richard that he brought home three kittens from the shelter.* Most often, *affect* is used in its verb form, and *effect* is used in its noun form.

AFFLICT/INFLICT: To *afflict* is to torment or distress someone or something. It usually appears as a passive verb: *Jeff is afflicted with severe migraine headaches.* To *inflict* is to impose punishment or suffering on someone or something: *No one dared displease the king, for he was known to inflict severe punishments on those who upset him.*

ALLUSION/ILLUSION: An *allusion* is an indirect reference to something, a hint: *I remarked that Sally's boyfriend was unusual looking; this allusion to his prominent tattoos did not please Sally.* An *illusion* is a false, misleading, or deceptive appearance: *A magician creates the illusion that something has disappeared by hiding it faster than the eye can follow it.*

EMIGRATE/IMMIGRATE: To *emigrate* is to leave one country for another country. It is usually used with the preposition *from*: *Many people emigrated from Europe in search of better living conditions.* To *immigrate* is to enter a country to take up permanent residence there. It is usually used with the preposition *to*: *They immigrated to North America because land was plentiful.*

EMINENT/IMMINENT: Someone who is *eminent* is prominent or outstanding: *The eminent archeologist Dr. Wong has identified the artifact as prehistoric in origin.* Something that is *imminent* is likely to happen soon or is impending: *After being warned that the hurricane's arrival was imminent, beachfront residents left their homes immediately.*

LAY/LIE: To *lay* is to place or put something down, and this verb usually does have a "something"— a direct object—following it: *Before she begins her pictures, Emily lays all of her pencils, brushes, and paints on her worktable to avoid interruptions while she draws and paints.* One form, *laid*, serves as the simple past and the past participle of *lay*. To *lie* is to recline, to be in a lying position or at rest. This verb never takes a direct object: you do not lie anything down. The simple past form of *lie* is *lay*; the past participle is *lain*. Notice that the past form of *lie* is identical with the present form of *lay*. This coincidence complicates the task of distinguishing the related meanings of *lay* and *lie*: *Having laid the picnic cloth under the sycamore, they lay in the shady grass all last Sunday afternoon.*

LEAVE/LET: To *leave* is to depart, to allow something to remain behind after departing, or to allow something to remain as it is. One irregular verb form, *left*, serves as the simple past and the past participle: *I boarded my plane and it left, leaving my baggage behind in Chicago.* When *leave* is used in the third sense—to allow something to remain as it is—and followed by *alone*, this verb does overlap with *let*: *If parents leave* (or *let*) *a baby alone with a new toy, she will understand it as quickly as if they demonstrated how the toy works.* To *let* is to allow or to rent out. These are the verb's core meanings, but it also combines with several different prepositions to produce various specific senses. *Let* is irregular. One form serves as present tense, past tense, and past participle. *The French border police would not let the Dutch tourist pass without a passport.*

RAISE/RISE: *Raise* is a regular verb that means to lift up or to cause to rise or grow, and it usually has a direct object: you *raise* dumbbells, roof beams, tomato plants, or livestock. *The trade tariff on imported leather goods raised the prices of Italian shoes.* To *rise* is to get up, to go up, or to be built up. This verb never takes a direct object: you do not *rise* something. The past and past participle forms are irregular; *rose* is the simple past tense, while *risen* is the past participle. *Long-distance commuters must rise early and return home late.*

SET/SIT: The difference between *set* and *sit* is very similar to the difference between *lay* and *lie* and between *raise* and *rise*. To *set* is to put or place something, to settle or arrange it. But *set* takes on other specific meanings when it combines with several different prepositions. *Set* is an irregular verb in that one form serves as present tense, past tense, and past participle. *Set* usually takes a direct object: you *set* a ladder against the fence, a value on family heirlooms, or a date for the family reunion: *The professor set the students' chairs in a semicircle in order to promote open discussion.* To *sit* is to take a seat or to be in a seated position, to rest somewhere, or to occupy a place. This verb does not usually take a direct object, although you can say: *The usher sat us in the center seats of the third row from the stage.* The irregular form *sat* serves as past tense and past participle. This verb does not typically take a direct object. *The beach house sits on a hill at some distance from the shoreline.*

Other pairs of words do not sound alike at all but have similar meanings that are often confused:

AMONG/BETWEEN: The preposition *among* refers to collective arrangements; that is, use it when referring to three or more people or items. *The soccer team shared a whole case of water among themselves.* *Between* is also a preposition but is used in the presence of only two people or items: *Amy and Tonia split the tasks between them.*

AMOUNT/NUMBER: *Amount* is used in reference to mass nouns (also known as uncountable nouns): *The amount of bravery displayed was awe-inspiring. Number* is used in reference to countable nouns: *The recipe calls for a specific number of chocolate chips.*

FEWER/LESS: *Fewer* should be used when referring to countable objects and concepts: *Diana's yard has fewer squirrels than mine. Less* should be used only with a grammatically singular noun: *Diana's yard has less wildlife than mine.* One common misuse of *less* is a sign you probably encounter frequently at the supermarket: The *10 items or less* sign should actually be *10 items or fewer*, because the items are countable.

MANY/MUCH: *Many* modifies things that can be counted, such as plural nouns: *Samantha has many awards in her collection. Much*, on the other hand, modifies things that cannot be counted, often singular nouns: *Jim has much more money than I do.*

The SAT will also test your ability to correctly use and identify possessive pronouns, contractions, and adverbs:

ITS/IT'S: *Its* is a possessive pronoun like *his* and *hers*: *The rare book would be worth more if its cover weren't ripped. It's* is a contraction that can mean *it is*, *it has*, or *it was*: *It's been a long time since I last saw you.*

THEIR/THEY'RE/THERE: *Their* is a possessive form of the pronoun *they*: *The players respected their coach. They're* is a contraction of *they are*: *The students say they're planning to attend college. There* is used to introduce a sentence or indicate a location: *There was no water in the well when we arrived there.*

THEIRS/THERE'S: *Theirs* is the possessive plural form of the pronoun *they*: *The careless bikers admitted the fault was theirs. There's* is a contraction of *there is* or *there has*: *There's been a lot of rain this summer.*

WHOSE/WHO'S: *Whose* is a possessive pronoun used to refer to people or things: *Whose phone is ringing? Who's* is a contraction of *who is* or *who has*: *Who's planning to join us for dinner?*

COMPARISONS

The SAT will test your ability to recognize and correct improper comparisons. There are three rules governing correct comparisons:

1. Compare Logical Things

   The **price of tea** has risen sharply, while **coffee** has remained the same.

   This sentence incorrectly compares *the price of tea* to *coffee*. The sentence should read: *The* **price of tea** *has risen sharply, while the* **price of coffee** *has remained the same.*

2. Use Parallel Structure

   I prefer **hiking** *rather than* **to read**.

   This sentence uses the gerund verb form (*hiking*) then switches to the infinitive verb form (*to read*). To correct the sentence, make sure the verb forms are consistent: *I prefer* **to hike** *rather than* **to read**.

3. Structure Comparisons Correctly

   Some students are **better** *in reading* **than** *they are in math.*
   Other students are **as** *good in math* **as** *they are in reading.*

   Both of these sentences are correctly structured: the first with the use of *better . . . than,* and the second with the use of *as . . . as.*

When comparing like things, use adjectives that match the number of items being compared. When comparing two items or people, use the comparative form of the adjective. When comparing three or more items or people, use the superlative form.

Comparative	Superlative
Use when comparing two items.	Use when comparing three or more items.
better	best
more	most
newer	newest
older	oldest
shorter	shortest
taller	tallest
worse	worst
younger	youngest

IDIOMS

An **idiom** is a combination of words that must be used together to convey either a figurative or literal meaning. Idioms are tested in four ways on the SAT:

1. Proper Preposition Usage in Context

   *The three finalists will compete **for** the grand prize: an all-inclusive cruise to Bali.*
   *Roger will compete **against** Rafael in the final round of the tournament.*
   *I will compete **with** Deborah in the synchronized swimming competition.*

2. Verb Forms

   *The architect likes **to draft** floor plans.*
   *The architect enjoys **drafting** floor plans.*

3. Idiomatic Expressions

   Idiomatic expressions refer to words or phrases that must be used together to be correct.

   *Simone will **either** continue sleeping **or** get up and get ready for school.*
   ***Neither** the principal **nor** the teachers will tolerate tardiness.*
   *This fall, Shari is playing **not only** soccer **but also** field hockey.*

4. Implicit Double Negatives

   Some words imply a negative and therefore cannot be paired with an explicit negative.

   *Janet **cannot hardly** wait for summer vacation.*

   This sentence is incorrect as written. It should read: *Janet **can hardly** wait for summer vacation.*

Frequently Tested Prepositions	Idiomatic Expressions	Words That Can't Be Paired with Negative Words
at	as . . . as	barely
by	between . . . and	hardly
for	both . . . and	scarcely
of	either . . . or	
on	just as . . . so too	
to	neither . . . nor	
with	not only . . . but also	

Let's look at the following example of the Kaplan Method for Writing & Language in action in a short test-like passage. The left column contains text and a question similar to what you'll see on the Writing & Language Test on Test Day. The column on the right features the strategic thinking a test expert employs when approaching the passage and question presented.

Questions 1-4 are based on the following passage.

Akira Kurosawa

What do samurai,[1] cowboys, shogun,[2] gangsters, peasants, and William Shakespeare all have in common? These are just some of the varied influences on the work of Akira Kurosawa (1910–1998), a Japanese film director considered by movie critic Leonard Maltin to be "one of the undisputed giants of cinema." Over his career, Kurosawa's unique blend of Western themes and Eastern settings made him arguably the ❶ more important Japanese filmmaker in history.

Kurosawa's style reflects his own experiences. As a young man, he studied Western art and literature, deciding to be a painter. However, World War II led Kurosawa to film; he acted as an assistant director of wartime propaganda films in Tokyo. After Japan's surrender in 1945, he took the lessons he learned in Tokyo and began making his own films— ❷ work that took the values and traditions of the West and reinterpreted them with a Japanese sensibility, using distinctly Japanese settings and characters.

The most famous example of Kurosawa's style is his 1954 film *Seven Samurai*. Although the setting is medieval Japan, with peasants and samurai, its story is influenced by Western films: a group of villagers, terrorized by local bandits, turn to seven down-on-their-luck yet good-hearted samurai for their protection. Like movie cowboys, the samurai are romantic heroes, sure of their morals and battling clear forces of evil. This contrasts with the traditional Japanese version of a samurai as a noble and often distant symbol of Japan's imperial heritage. To ❸ him, the film's samurai were distinctly human characters, with both a conscience and the will to act to correct the wrongs around them.

Although Kurosawa's films enjoyed—and still enjoy—a lofty reputation in the West, Japanese audiences have regarded his work with suspicion. By using Western ideals and themes—even reinterpreting Western authors such as William Shakespeare and Fyodor Dostoyevsky—Kurosawa is regarded by many critics and moviegoers in his home country as ❹ neither original nor particularly Japanese. They see his using Japanese culture as mere "window dressing" applied to what were essentially foreign stories. Ironically, it was Kurosawa's success that opened the door for other, more "Japanese" directors, such as Yasujiro Ozu and Kenji Mizoguchi, to gain a wider audience.

Regardless of the criticism, Kurosawa's effect on Western filmmaking is beyond dispute. Ironically, Kurosawa's films have influenced the very same American movie genres that Kurosawa admired so much. *Seven Samurai* became the basis for the American Western epic *The Magnificent Seven*. *Yojimbo,* another story of a samurai for hire, strongly influenced the film *A Fistful of Dollars*. Other genres benefited from Kurosawa's work as well; *Rashomon,* a crime story told from different points of view, has influenced almost every crime movie since. Finally, *The Hidden Fortress,* about two peasants escorting a princess during a war, became George Lucas's expressed basis for the science fiction masterpiece *Star Wars*.

[1] samurai: noble warriors of medieval Japan, similar to European knights
[2] shogun: military dictators of Japan from 1603 to 1868

Questions	Strategic Thinking
1. A) NO CHANGE B) important C) most important (circled) D) least important	**Step 1: Read the passage and identify the issue** The issue is Comparisons. The underlined portion contains the word "more," which is an adjective used to compare two items. **Step 2: Eliminate answer choices that do not address the issue** Eliminate A because more than two items are being compared. Eliminate B because it eliminates the comparison. Eliminate D because it changes the meaning of the sentence. **Step 3: Plug in the remaining answer choices and select the most correct, concise, and relevant one** Choice (C) is the only remaining answer choice and is therefore correct.
2. A) NO CHANGE B) works (circled) C) working D) idea	**Step 1: Read the passage and identify the issue** The issue is Noun Agreement because the underlined word (a singular noun) is a synonym for the word that precedes the dash: "films" (a plural noun). **Step 2: Eliminate answer choices that do not address the issue** Eliminate A because the singular "work" does not agree with the plural "films." Eliminate C because "working" is a verb, not a noun. Eliminate D because it changes the author's meaning. **Step 3: Plug in the remaining answer choices and select the most correct, concise, and relevant one** Choice (B) is the only remaining answer choice and is therefore correct.

Questions	Strategic Thinking
3. A) NO CHANGE B) them C) Kurosawa D) the samurai	**Step 1: Read the passage and identify the issue** The issue is Pronoun Clarity. The underlined pronoun's antecedent is unclear. **Step 2: Eliminate answer choices that do not address the issue** The most likely antecedent of the underlined pronoun "him" is Akira Kurosawa. Eliminate A because it is ambiguous as written. Eliminate B because even though the pronoun is plural, it is still ambiguous. Eliminate D because the pronoun does not refer to "the samurai." **Step 3: Plug in the remaining answer choices and select the most correct, concise, and relevant one** Choice (C) is the only remaining answer choice and is therefore correct.
4. A) NO CHANGE B) either C) never D) both	**Step 1: Read the passage and identify the issue** The issue is Idioms because the underlined word is part of an idiomatic expression. **Step 2: Eliminate answer choices that do not address the issue** "Neither...nor" is a common idiomatic expression. Eliminate B, C, and D because the sentence later uses the word "nor," which means "neither" must precede it. **Step 3: Plug in the remaining answer choices and select the most correct, concise, and relevant one** Choice (A) is the only remaining answer choice and is therefore correct.

You have seen the ways in which the SAT tests you on Usage in Writing & Language passages and the way an SAT expert approaches these types of questions.

Look at the Writing & Language passage excerpt that follows. There are four questions associated with it. Use the Kaplan Method for Writing & Language to answer the questions. Remember to look at the strategic thinking questions that have been laid out for you—some of the answers have been filled in, but you will have to fill in the answers to others.

Use your answers to the strategic thinking questions to select the correct answer, just as you will on Test Day.

Questions 5-8 are based on the following passage.

Opossum

Commonly seen rooting through the trash or slipping down a sewer grate, the opossum is actually one of North America's ❺ best animals. While its rodent-like body seems unremarkable at first glance, the opossum is actually closely related to the kangaroo and is the only marsupial native to this continent. Indeed, like all female marsupials, the female opossum has a pouch for carrying and nursing her young. After a 12-day gestation period, thought to be the shortest of any marsupial, between 5 and 25 blind and hairless babies instinctively crawl the two inches from the birth canal to the pouch. Upon arrival, they quickly attach themselves to a nipple, drawing constant nourishment from the mother for more than two months.

The distinctive features of the opossum go beyond its surprising relation to the kangaroo. ❻ It boasts an incredible array of 50 razor-sharp teeth, the most of any mammal in the world. The opossum is also among the most primitive of animals, having lived during the time of the dinosaurs. It has survived for millions of years by adapting to diverse habitats—including dense urban areas—and food supplies. Opossums eat beetles and even earthworms as well as tree roots, eggs, vegetables, and fruit. Today, many opossums that live in areas densely populated by humans survive on garbage and small mice. Opossums thrive in fields and woodlands, but they can also survive by digging a nest under a building or deck.

Of course, the opossum does have vulnerabilities. Its average three-year life span is not unusual for its size, typically between two and three feet long. What is unusual is that opossums continue growing throughout their lifetimes. Such a state of constant development is linked with metabolic limitations ❼ in the amount of food and energy that can be stored within the opossum's body, requiring that ready food sources be available year-round. In addition, opossums are highly susceptible to the cold, making it rather common to see opossums with frostbitten ears and tails. Nevertheless, opossums have displayed amazing resilience over the years, often surviving attacks from intimidating predators like dogs and even hawks. While the opossum's first reaction when threatened is to begin running to the nearest tree, ❽ their primary defense is a nervous system reaction that, when sensing danger, throws the opossum's body into a catatonic state that dramatically slows its heart rate. The opossum will then begin to drool and appear dead, another trait that only adds to the fascinating nature of these animals.

Questions	Strategic Thinking
5. A) NO CHANGE B) most unusual C) better D) abnormal (circled)	**Step 1: Read the passage and identify the issue** *What is the issue?* Comparisons. The underlined word is a superlative adjective, used to compare three or more items. **Step 2: Eliminate answer choices that do not address the issue** *What answer choice(s) can you eliminate?* _____ _____ _____ _____ **Step 3: Plug in the remaining answer choices and select the most correct, concise, and relevant one** *What is the answer?* _____
6. A) NO CHANGE (circled) B) They C) The kangaroo D) The opossum	**Step 1: Read the passage and identify the issue** *What is the issue?* Pronoun clarity. The underlined word is a pronoun that begins a sentence. **Step 2: Eliminate answer choices that do not address the issue** *To what does the underlined pronoun refer?* _____ _____ *What answer choice(s) can you eliminate?* _____ _____ _____ _____ **Step 3: Plug in the remaining answer choices and select the most correct, concise, and relevant one** *What is the answer?* _____

Questions	Strategic Thinking
7. (A) NO CHANGE (B) with C) on D) for	**Step 1: Read the passage and identify the issue** *What is the issue?* Idioms. The underlined word is a preposition, so the question is likely testing proper preposition usage in context. **Step 2: Eliminate answer choices that do not address the issue** *What answer choice(s) can you eliminate?* _____ _____ _____ _____ **Step 3: Plug in the remaining answer choices and select the most correct, concise, and relevant one** *What is the answer?* _____
8. (A) NO CHANGE B) there C) its D) his	**Step 1: Read the passage and identify the issue** *What is the issue?* Pronoun-antecedent agreement. The underlined word is a pronoun in the middle of a sentence. **Step 2: Eliminate answer choices that do not address the issue** *What is the underlined pronoun's antecedent?* _____ _____ *What answer choice(s) can you eliminate?* _____ _____ _____ _____ **Step 3: Plug in the remaining answer choices and select the most correct, concise, and relevant one** *What is the answer?* _____

Now, try a test-like Writing & Language passage on your own. Give yourself 5 minutes to read the passage and answer the questions.

Questions 9-16 are based on the following passage.

The Hindenburg

Today, airships are seen mostly as advertisements hovering in the sky over sporting events. Such companies as Goodyear®, Metropolitan Life®, and Fuji Film® have all made use of "blimps" in this way. But before World War II, **9** blimps—as well as other lighter-than-air vehicles—were used as modes of transportation. One in particular, the German airship *Hindenburg*, changed the fate of airships forever. In spectacular fashion, the *Hindenburg* revealed the downside of the use of airships in transportation.

Airships enjoyed many advantages in the early twentieth century, and the *Hindenburg* was considered one of a kind. When the 804-foot *Hindenburg* was launched in 1936, it was the **10** large airship in the world. Like most airships of the period, the *Hindenburg* was built with a solid frame that encased a simple balloon filled with a light gas—in this case, hydrogen. In an age when airplanes could not carry more than 10 passengers at a time, **11** they could initially carry 50 passengers, a capacity that was later upgraded to 72.

Despite these advantages, the *Hindenburg* was hampered by many of the same drawbacks as other airships. Tickets to fly in the *Hindenburg* were not affordable for most people. The massive amount of fuel needed to not only fill the balloon **12** and to power **13** it's propellers made this airship very expensive to operate. Even with all of that fuel, the *Hindenburg* flew at a mere 76 miles per hour—a snail's pace considering that it was used for transatlantic passenger service. Because an airship is essentially a balloon with an engine, it is extremely vulnerable to air currents and stormy weather, and the *Hindenburg* was no different.

9. A) NO CHANGE
   B) the blimp
   C) the airship
   D) airplanes

10. A) NO CHANGE
    B) largest
    C) big
    D) larger

11. A) NO CHANGE
    B) it
    C) the *Hindenburg*
    D) he

12. A) NO CHANGE
    B) but also
    C) and also
    D) nor

13. A) NO CHANGE
    B) its
    C) it is
    D) their

The *Hindenburg's* fate, however, rested by the most dangerous characteristic of these airships: hydrogen gas is extremely flammable. Any spark or flame that came near the gas could cause a horrific explosion, which is exactly what happened. On May 6, 1937, as the *Hindenburg* was landing in Lakehurst, New Jersey, it suddenly burst into flames, killing 36 of the 97 passengers and crew on board. This explosion, which ultimately destroyed the airship, was believed to have been caused by a discharge of electricity in the air, which reacted with a small leak in the balloons.

However, when the disaster occurred, the airship was already obsolete as a mode of transportation. By the 1940s, commercial airplanes had advanced in development far beyond the airship's capacity. Today, airplanes cost much less to operate and fly at more than seven times the speed of the *Hindenburg*, and airline tickets are far more affordable. The airship thus became outdated as a mode of passenger service and acquired **16** their modern-day role as an advertising platform.

14. A) NO CHANGE
    B) in
    C) on
    D) with

15. A) NO CHANGE
    B) blimps
    C) hydrogen
    D) balloon

16. A) NO CHANGE
    B) its
    C) it's
    D) they're

Answers & Explanations for this chapter begin on page 1110.

EXTRA PRACTICE

Required	Recommended
Questions 1–11	Questions 12–22

Questions 1-11 are based on the following passage and supplementary material.

Batteries Out in the Cold

Many people have trouble starting their cars on a cold winter morning. In a cold car, the engine turns over more slowly, ❶ <u>since</u> it sometimes does not turn over at all. Car owners may ❷ <u>credit</u> their cold engines, but the real problem is a cold battery.

 [1] A motor is generally connected to its circuit by using a battery. [2] When a motor is hooked up in a circuit with a battery, electrons move through the circuit, creating a current. [3] Likewise, decreasing the number of electrons moving will decrease the amount of power available. [4] Increasing the number of electrons moving increases the current and so increases the amount of power available to the motor.

1. A) NO CHANGE
    B) and
    C) but
    D) yet

2. A) NO CHANGE
    B) criticize
    C) accuse
    D) blame

3. To enhance the logical sequence of paragraph 2, sentence 3 should be placed
    A) where it is now.
    B) before sentence 1.
    C) before sentence 2.
    D) after sentence 4.

4 5 <u>A typical car battery, uses lead, and sulfuric acid.</u> At the negative pole, lead reacts with sulfate ions in the solution around it to form lead sulfate, giving off electrons. At the positive pole, lead oxide

4. Which choice most effectively establishes the main topic of the paragraph?

   A) Electrons move through a battery as a result of two chemical reactions occurring within the battery, one at each pole.

   B) Sulfuric acid can cause burns to the skin, eyes, lungs, and digestive tract, and severe exposure can result in death.

   C) In a direct current circuit, one pole is always negative, the other pole is always positive, and the electrons flow in one direction only.

   D) Lead sulfate is toxic by inhalation, ingestion, and skin contact; repeated exposure may lead to anemia, kidney damage, and other serious health issues.

5. A) NO CHANGE

   B) A typical car battery uses lead, and sulfuric acid.

   C) A typical car battery, uses lead and sulfuric acid.

   D) A typical car battery uses lead and sulfuric acid.

6 would have reacted with sulfate ions, hydrogen ions, and electrons in the same solution to also form lead sulfate, taking in electrons. The electrons produced at the negative pole flow through the **7** boundary to the positive pole, providing an electric current in the circuit.

8 A battery charger uses the same reactions, but in reverse. As the current flows in the opposite direction, supplied by house current or a generator, the lead sulfate at the positive pole reacts to change back to lead oxide.

Temperature affects the speed of chemical reactions in two ways. For a chemical reaction to happen, the reactants must collide with enough energy to get the reaction going. As the temperature increases, the motion of the reactants increases. The increased motion of the reactants increases the **9** practicality that they will collide and therefore increases the rate of reaction. The amount of energy in the reactants also increases as temperature increases.

6. A) NO CHANGE
   B) did react
   C) reacts
   D) reacted

7. A) NO CHANGE
   B) cycle
   C) circuit
   D) path

8. Which sentence adds supporting information to paragraph 4?

   A) Lead oxide, sometimes called litharge, is an inorganic compound with a formula including lead and oxygen.

   B) At the same time, the lead sulfate at the negative pole reacts to change back to lead metal.

   C) The difference between a house current and a generator is that the generator converts mechanical energy to electrical energy for use in an external circuit.

   D) Using a battery charger incorrectly can be dangerous since a car battery contains chemicals that produce hydrogen, a potentially volatile gas.

9. A) NO CHANGE
   B) way
   C) question
   D) probability

This makes it more likely that any two colliding reactants will have enough energy to react, and so ❿ its rate of reaction increases.

Low temperatures have the opposite effect from high temperatures. The chemicals in the battery react more slowly at low temperatures, due both to fewer collisions and less energetic collisions, so fewer electrons move through the circuit. A cold battery takes longer to charge and often cannot provide enough energy to start a car. A cold car that will not start will need either additional power from another car to get the motor moving or a source of heat to warm up the battery and speed up the chemical reactions. Research conducted by FleetCarma in Waterloo, Ontario, demonstrates that ⓫ colder temperatures negatively affect the distance electric cars can travel.

Average Range of Electric Cars as a Function of Temperature

Adapted from research published by FleetCarma, Waterloo, Ontario.

10. A) NO CHANGE
    B) it's
    C) their
    D) they're

11. Which choice completes the sentence with accurate data based on the graph?
    A) NO CHANGE
    B) the number of kilometers an electric car can travel declines as the outside temperature increases.
    C) temperatures below 15°C make it extremely difficult to start an electric car.
    D) once the electric car's battery has an alternate heat source by which to start, the distance the car can travel is greatly increased.

Questions 12-22 are based on the following passage and supplementary material.

Pearl Harbor

On December 7, 1941, Japanese fighter planes attacked the American naval base at Pearl Harbor near Honolulu, Hawaii, sinking or damaging 19 ships and destroying 169 planes. More than 2,400 soldiers, sailors, and marines died in the attack, and another 1,178 were wounded. The next day President Franklin D. Roosevelt **12** hinted the United States' entrance into World War II by asking Congress to declare war on Japan.

Japan and the U.S. had been in a standoff for years. In 1937, Japan had declared war on China, seeking to expand into Chinese territory and secure its import markets. The U.S. had responded by placing bans on Japanese exports and imposing other trade embargoes. **13** But Japan had not capitulated; instead, it had strengthened its expansionist aims.

[1] Although the conflict with Japan **14** was being understood to be dangerous, because of the great distance across the Pacific Ocean, it did not seem likely that Japan would attack the United States. [2] American intelligence officials thought that if Japan did attack, it would hit a European colony in the South Pacific, such as Singapore. [3] Nearly the entire Pacific Fleet was moored around Ford Island in the harbor, and hundreds of airplanes were grounded at nearby airfields. [4] Pearl Harbor was a large open target. **15**

12. A) NO CHANGE
    B) signaled
    C) mimicked
    D) communicated

13. A) NO CHANGE
    B) But Japan had not capitulated; rather,
    C) And Japan had not capitulated; in fact,
    D) However, Japan had not capitulated; furthermore,

14. A) NO CHANGE
    B) was understanding
    C) was understood
    D) was being and understood

15. Which sentence, if inserted before sentence 3, would offer the strongest support for sentence 2?
    A) This had been true in multiple previous conflicts with other nations as well.
    B) But Japan had a history of surprising its enemies.
    C) After decades of isolationism, the American navy was impressive.
    D) Therefore, Pearl Harbor was not heavily defended.

The Japanese plan was **16** simple; destroy the Pacific Fleet. That way, the Americans would not be able to fight back as Japan's armed forces spread across the South Pacific. **17** On December 7, after they had been making plans and practicing for months and months, the Japanese launched their attack.

The attack began around **18** 8:00 o'clock AM, with Japanese planes dropping bombs and raining bullets. Torpedoes and huge **19** bombs, some weighing over a ton and a half, destroyed the battleships USS *Arizona* and USS *Oklahoma*, each of which had hundreds of sailors trapped inside. In all, eight battleships **20** put up with heavy damage. Dry docks and airfields were likewise destroyed.

16. A) NO CHANGE
    B) simple: destroy
    C) simple destroy
    D) simple, destroy

17. A) NO CHANGE
    B) On December 7, after months of planning and practice, the Japanese launched their attack.
    C) On December 7, after they had for months and months been practicing, the Japanese launched their attack.
    D) On December 7, after months of planning as well as a voluminous amount of practice, the Japanese launched their attack.

18. A) NO CHANGE
    B) 8:00 o'clock AM in the morning
    C) 8:00 AM in the morning,
    D) 8:00 AM,

19. A) NO CHANGE
    B) bombs, some weighed
    C) bombs, some were weighing
    D) bombs, some weigh

20. A) NO CHANGE
    B) lost
    C) sustained
    D) tolerated

21 In a December 8 radio address, President Roosevelt said, "I believe I interpret the will of the Congress and of the people when I assert that we will not only defend ourselves to the uttermost, but will make very certain that this form of treachery shall never endanger us again." In a sense, the Japanese plan had backfired. Japanese hopes had been to get trade sanctions lifted; instead, the U.S. entered a war that would **22** end in Japan's defeat and occupation by a foreign power.

Timeline of WWII Events

1939 Germany invades Poland

1941 (June) Germans invade Soviet Union; (Dec.) Japan attacks Pearl Harbor

1944 D-Day invasion occurs

1940 France surrenders to Germany; Battle of Britain begins

1943 Allies defeat Japan at Guadalcanal

1945 (May) Germany surrenders; (Aug.)Atomic bombs dropped; Japan surrenders

21. Which choice most effectively establishes the main topic of this paragraph?

A) The Pearl Harbor attack united the American people around the long-contentious issue of Japanese aggression: there was widespread determination to go to war.

B) The United States had been very reluctant to go to war; in fact, it had long been considered an isolationist nation.

C) President Roosevelt had been an extremely popular president so far; he had implemented new programs to pull the United States out of the Great Depression.

D) Japan and the United States might have avoided war if their leaders had managed to come to a diplomatic solution; instead, the conflict had simmered for years.

22. Which choice most effectively establishes the main topic of this paragraph?

A) NO CHANGE

B) end two years later after a long and brutal battle on Guadalcanal

C) prove to be Japan's last military battle for four long years

D) cost it millions of lives before Germany's surrender allowed an American victory

CHAPTER 32

Conventions of Punctuation

CHAPTER OBJECTIVES

By the end of this chapter, you will be able to:

1. Recognize and correct inappropriate uses of punctuation within and at the end of sentences

2. Identify and correct inappropriate uses of possessive nouns

3. Recognize and omit unnecessary punctuation

SMARTPOINTS

Point Value	SmartPoint Category
30 Points	Punctuation

END-OF-SENTENCE AND WITHIN-SENTENCE PUNCTUATION

The SAT Writing & Language Test will require you to identify and correct inappropriate use of ending punctuation that deviates from the intent implied by the context. You will also have to identify and correct inappropriate colons, semicolons, and dashes when used to indicate breaks in thought within a sentence.

You can recognize Punctuation questions because the underlined portion of the text will include a punctuation mark. The answer choices for the question will move that punctuation mark around or replace it with another punctuation mark.

Use **commas** to:

- Separate independent clauses connected by a FANBOYS conjunction (*For, And, Nor, But, Or, Yet, So*)

- Separate an introductory phrase from the rest of the sentence

- Set off three or more items in a series or list

When you see an underlined **comma**, ask:

- Can the comma be replaced by a **period** or a **semicolon**?

Use **semicolons** to:

- Join two independent clauses when a FANBOYS conjunction is not present

- Separate items in a series or list if those items already include commas

Use **colons** to:

- Introduce and/or emphasize a short phrase, quotation, explanation, example, or list

Use **dashes** to:

- Indicate a hesitation or a break in thought

When you see an underlined **colon** or **dash**, ask:

- Has the author shifted gears by introducing or explaining something or breaking his or her thought process?

Let's look at the following example of the Kaplan Method for Writing & Language in action in a short test-like passage. The left column contains text and a question similar to what you'll see on the Writing & Language Test on Test Day. The column on the right features the strategic thinking a test expert employs when approaching the passage and question presented.

Questions 1-2 are based on the following passage.

Sir Edmund Hilary

In the late spring of 1953, New Zealand mountaineer Sir Edmund Hillary and Nepalese Sherpa Tenzing Norgay became the first men to walk on the top of the world. After a grueling expedition that spanned several ❶ months. They had finally reached the summit of Mount Everest. This was the mountain the Tibetan people called "Mother of the Universe," but despite its maternal nomenclature, it had already claimed the lives of George Mallory and Andrew Irvine before Hillary and Norgay finally conquered its icy peak. The mountain's siren call continues to lure mountaineers to this day. But climbing Mount Everest may be easier than answering the question posed by decades of non-climbers: Why? Perhaps Mallory said it best in 1923 before his ill-fated ❷ climb; "Because it is there."

Questions	Strategic Thinking
1. A) NO CHANGE B) months, and they C) months; they D) months, they (circled)	**Step 1: Read the passage and identify the issue** The underlined segment includes a period, but the sentence before the period is a fragment. **Step 2: Eliminate answer choices that do not address the issue** Eliminate A because as written, the sentence before the period is a fragment. Eliminate B because it creates a run-on. Eliminate C because it does not correct the original error. **Step 3: Plug in the remaining answer choices and select the most correct, concise, and relevant one** Choice (D) is correct.
2. A) NO CHANGE B) climb: "Because it is there." (circled) C) climb. "Because it is there." D) climb "Because it is there."	**Step 1: Read the passage and identify the issue** The underlined segment includes a semicolon, which is used incorrectly because it is not joining two independent clauses or separating items containing commas in a series or list. It is supposed to be providing emphasis. **Step 2: Eliminate answer choices that do not address the issue** Eliminate C because it creates two separate sentences, which changes the author's intended meaning. Eliminate D because it removes punctuation altogether, creating a new error. **Step 3: Plug in the remaining answer choices and select the most correct, concise, and relevant one** Choice (B) is correct.

POSSESSIVE NOUNS AND PRONOUNS

Possessive nouns and pronouns indicate who or what possesses another noun or pronoun. Each follows different rules, and the SAT will test both. These questions require you to identify both the singular and plural forms.

You can spot errors in possessive noun and pronoun construction by looking for:

- Two nouns in a row

- Context clues

- Pronouns with apostrophes

- Words that sound alike

Possessive Nouns		
Singular	sister's	My oldest *sister's* soccer game is on Saturday.
Plural	sisters'	My two older *sisters'* soccer games are on Saturday.

Questions about possessive pronouns often require you to watch out for contractions and sound-alike words.

Possessive Pronouns and Words to Watch Out For	
Its = possessive	It's = it is
Their = possessive	There = location/place
Whose = possessive	Who's = who is/who has

Let's look at the following example of the Kaplan Method for Writing & Language in action in a short test-like passage. The left column contains text and a question similar to what you'll see on the Writing & Language Test on Test Day. The column on the right features the strategic thinking a test expert employs when approaching the passage and question presented.

Questions 3-4 are based on the following passage.

Literary Theory

Sometimes, being overeducated about literary theory and criticism can have detrimental effects on one's reading. In some cases, before one even opens a book, one might have certain expectations as to ❸ it's literary genre, its cultural and historical significance, its symbolism, its author's life and times, and other matters. One can therefore lose out on the experience of entering a world for the first time, where every ❹ sight, sound, and taste is eternally new, where the book is forever in the process of forming itself. When one brings preconceived notions and generalizations to a book, the book is petrified in time and space.

Questions	Strategic Thinking

3. A) NO CHANGE
    B) its
    C) it is
    D) the
	Step 1: Read the passage and identify the issue
	
	The underlined apostrophe suggests there is a grammatical issue. "It's" is a contraction meaning "it is," but the sentence requires a possessive pronoun.
	
	Step 2: Eliminate answer choices that do not address the issue
	
	Eliminate A, C, and D because they are not possessive pronouns.
	
	Step 3: Plug in the remaining answer choices and select the most correct, concise, and relevant one
	
	Choice (B) is correct.

4. A) NO CHANGE
    B) sight, sound, taste
    C) sight, and sound, and taste
    D) sight sound and taste
	Step 1: Read the passage and identify the issue
	
	The underlined portion contains a series. Commas should be used to set off three or more items in a series or list. These commas should be placed after every item in the series. A series or list should include the word "and" following the comma before the last item.
	
	Step 2: Eliminate answer choices that do not address the issue
	
	Eliminate B, C, and D because they do not feature proper series or list construction.
	
	Step 3: Plug in the remaining answer choices and select the most correct, concise, and relevant one
	
	Choice (A) is correct.

NONRESTRICTIVE/PARENTHETICAL ELEMENTS AND UNNECESSARY PUNCTUATION

Use **commas**, **dashes**, or **parentheses** to set off parenthetical or nonrestrictive information in a sentence.

✔ **Definition**

Parenthetical or nonrestrictive information includes words or phrases that aren't essential to the sentence structure or content. Sometimes, however, this information is explanatory.

The SAT will also ask you to recognize instances of unnecessary punctuation, particularly **commas**.

Do not use a comma to:

- Separate a subject from its predicate
- Separate a verb from its object or its subject, or a preposition from its object
- Set off restrictive elements
- Precede a dependent clause that comes after an independent clause
- Separate adjectives that work together to modify a noun

✔ **Expert Tip**

To determine if information is nonessential, read the sentence without the information. If the sentence still makes sense without the omitted words, then those words need to be set off with punctuation.

Let's look at the following example of the Kaplan Method for Writing & Language in action in a short test-like passage. The left column contains text and a question similar to what you'll see on the Writing & Language Test on Test Day. The column on the right features the strategic thinking a test expert employs when approaching the passage and question presented.

Questions 5-6 are based on the following passage.

Chimpanzees and Language

Many linguistic researchers are excited about the possibility of humans using language to communicate with chimpanzees, our close cousins in the animal world. Some scientists believe that chimpanzees, and in particular Bonobo chimpanzees, may have the comprehension skills of two-and-a-half-year-old children. With dedicated **5** training, the scientists claim these chimpanzees are able to understand complicated **6** sentences, and to communicate on an advanced level with human beings. In a recent and rather astonishing episode, for example, a Bonobo chimpanzee pressed symbols on a special keyboard in order to tell her trainers about a fight between two chimpanzees in a separate facility.

Questions	Strategic Thinking
5. A) NO CHANGE (B) training, the scientists claim, these C) training the scientists claim these D) training the scientists claim, these	**Step 1: Read the passage and identify the issue** The underlined segment includes a comma that precedes nonessential information that the scientists claim the content of the sentence to be true. The nonessential information ("the scientists claim") is separated from the rest of the sentence by only one comma before it, rather than one comma before it and one after it. **Step 2: Eliminate answer choices that do not address the issue** Eliminate C because it removes all punctuation. Eliminate D because it makes the sentence grammatically incorrect. **Step 3: Plug in the remaining answer choices and select the most correct, concise, and relevant one** Choice (B) is correct.
6. A) NO CHANGE (B) sentences and to communicate C) sentences: to communicate D) sentences and communicating	**Step 1: Read the passage and identify the issue** The comma used in the underlined portion is incorrect. The phrase "and to communicate" placed after the comma forms a compound with "to understand complicated sentences," which precedes it. No punctuation is necessary when two phrases are joined by "and," thus forming a compound. **Step 2: Eliminate answer choices that do not address the issue** Eliminate C because it incorrectly replaces the comma with a colon. Eliminate D because it introduces a parallelism error. **Step 3: Plug in the remaining answer choices and select the most correct, concise, and relevant one** Choice (B) is correct.

You have seen the ways in which the SAT tests you on Punctuation in Writing & Language passages and the way an SAT expert approaches these types of questions.

Look at the Writing & Language passage excerpt that follows. There are four questions associated with it. Use the Kaplan Method for Writing & Language to answer the questions. Remember to look at the strategic thinking questions that have been laid out for you—some of the answers have been filled in, but you will have to fill in the answers to others.

Use your answers to the strategic thinking questions to select the correct answer, just as you will on Test Day.

Questions 7-10 are based on the following passage.

Bebop Jazz

For a jazz musician in New York City in the early 1940s, the most interesting place to spend the hours between midnight and dawn was probably a Harlem nightclub called Minton's. After finishing their jobs at other clubs, young musicians like **7** Charlie Parker, Dizzy Gillespie, Kenny Clarke, Thelonious Monk would gather at Minton's and have jam sessions, or informal performances featuring lengthy group and solo improvisations. The all-night sessions resulted in the birth of modern jazz as these African-American artists together forged a new sound, known as bebop.

Unlike swing, the enormously popular jazz played in the 1930s, bebop was not dance music. It was often blindingly fast, incorporating tricky, irregular rhythms and discordant sounds that jazz audiences had never heard before. Earlier jazz, like practically all of Western music up to that time, used an eight-note scale. Bebop, in contrast, was based on a 12-note **8** scale. Thereby, it opened up vast new harmonic opportunities for musicians.

The musicians who pioneered bebop shared two common elements: a vision of the new music's possibilities and astonishing improvisational skill—the ability to play or compose a musical line on the spur of the moment. After all, **9** improvisation, within the context of a group setting, is the essence of jazz, which has been described as the musical experience of the passing moment. Parker, perhaps the greatest instrumental genius jazz has known, was an especially brilliant improviser. He often played twice as fast as the rest of the band, but his solos were always in rhythm and exquisitely shaped, revealing a harmonic imagination that enthralled his listeners.

Like many revolutions, unfortunately, the bebop movement encountered heavy resistance. Opposition came from older jazz musicians initially, but also, later and more lastingly, from a general public alienated by the ❿ music's complexity and sophistication. Furthermore, due to the government ban on recording that was in effect during the early years of World War II (records were made of vinyl, a petroleum product that was essential to the war effort), the creative ferment that first produced bebop remains largely undocumented today.

Questions	Strategic Thinking
7. A) NO CHANGE B) Charlie Parker; Dizzy Gillespie; Kenny Clarke; and Thelonious Monk C) Charlie Parker and Dizzy Gillespie, and Kenny Clarke and Thelonious Monk D) Charlie Parker, Dizzy Gillespie, Kenny Clarke, and Thelonious Monk	**Step 1: Read the passage and identify the issue** *Are there any clues suggesting a grammatical issue?* Yes, the underlined portion contains a series. *What kind of punctuation is used to set off three or more items in a series or list?* Commas. *Where should these punctuation marks be placed?* After every item. *Is there anything else a series or list should include? If so, what?* A series or list should include the word "and" following the comma before the last item. **Step 2: Eliminate answer choices that do not address the issue** *What answer choice(s) can you eliminate?* _____ _____ _____ _____ _____ **Step 3: Plug in the remaining answer choices and select the most correct, concise, and relevant one** *What is the correct answer?* _____

Questions	Strategic Thinking
8. A) NO CHANGE B) scale, and thereby opening up C) scale, opening up D) scale, thereby opening up	**Step 1: Read the passage and identify the issue** *What punctuation does the underlined segment include?* A period. *What is the issue?* _____ _____ _____ _____ _____ _____ **Step 2: Eliminate answer choices that do not address the issue** *What answer choice(s) can you eliminate?* _____ _____ _____ _____ _____ **Step 3: Plug in the remaining answer choices and select the most correct, concise, and relevant one** *What is the correct answer?* _____

Questions	Strategic Thinking
9. (A) NO CHANGE B) improvisation within the context of a group setting is the essence C) improvisation within the context of a group setting, is the essence D) improvisation, within the context of a group setting is the essence	**Step 1: Read the passage and identify the issue** *What punctuation does the underlined segment include?* Two commas surrounding the phrase "within the context of a group setting." *What purpose do two commas surrounding a phrase within a sentence serve?* _____ _____ _____ _____ *Is the information set off by the commas in the underlined portion nonessential? Why or why not?* _____ _____ _____ _____ _____ **Step 2: Eliminate answer choices that do not address the issue** *What answer choice(s) can you eliminate?* _____ _____ _____ _____ _____ **Step 3: Plug in the remaining answer choices and select the most correct, concise, and relevant one** *What is the correct answer?* _____

Questions	Strategic Thinking
10. A) NO CHANGE B) musics C) musics' D) music	**Step 1: Read the passage and identify the issue** *What punctuation does the underlined segment include?* _____ *What is this type of punctuation used for?* _____ _____ _____ _____ _____ **Step 2: Eliminate answer choices that do not address the issue** *What answer choice(s) can you eliminate?* _____ _____ _____ _____ _____ **Step 3: Plug in the remaining answer choices and select the most correct, concise, and relevant one** *What is the correct answer?* _____

Now, try a test-like Writing & Language passage on your own. Give yourself 5 minutes to read the passage and answer the questions.

Questions 11-18 are based on the following passage.

Mauritius

⓫ Although, most of the products we buy today are made abroad in well-known places like Mexico and China, a quick check of many clothing labels will reveal the name of a country that might not be so ⓬ familiar. It's Mauritius. Named in honor of Prince Maurice of Nassau by the Dutch who colonized it in 1638, this small island in the Indian Ocean has a complicated history influenced by several international powers. Since gaining independence in 1968, Mauritius has emerged as a stable democracy with one of Africa's highest per capita ⓭ incomes. Mauritius is considered a significant player in the modern global economy of the Southern Hemisphere.

Yet Mauritius was not always so conspicuous. The island itself, situated 1,200 miles off the east coast of Africa, covers only about 2,000 square kilometers. As recently as the tenth century, it was completely uninhabited by humans, although it was likely known to Arab and Malay sailors of this period. The Portuguese landed in 1511, and with this initial visit, Mauritius gained its first taste of distinction through the discovery of an unlikely creature: the dodo bird. Early Portuguese accounts of encounters with this large, slow-moving bird on the island suggest that the dodo did not recognize humans as ⓮ predators, making the dodo even easier to catch for food. As a result, by the mid-1600s, the entire dodo population had been wiped out.

Soon after the disappearance of the dodo, the Portuguese presence was replaced by that of the Dutch. Roughly 80 years of Dutch control brought waves of ⓯ traders, planters, and slaves; indentured laborers, merchants, and artisans, ⓰ who's collective arrival brought international recognition to Mauritius.

11. (A) NO CHANGE
    B) Although most
    C) Although; most
    D) Most

12. A) NO CHANGE
    B) familiar, and it's Mauritius
    C) familiar: Mauritius
    (D) familiar named Mauritius

13. A) NO CHANGE
    B) incomes; Mauritius is
    C) incomes, and is
    (D) incomes and is

14. (A) NO CHANGE
    B) predators and made
    C) predators by making
    D) predators making

15. A) NO CHANGE
    B) traders, planters and slaves, indentured laborers, merchants and artisans
    C) traders, planters, slaves, indentured laborers, merchants, artisans
    (D) traders, planters, slaves, indentured laborers, merchants, and artisans

16. A) NO CHANGE
    (B) whose collective arrival
    C) their collective arrival
    D) the collective arrival of whom

In 1715, the island again changed hands, this time to the French, and in 1810, with a successful invasion during the Napoleonic Wars, the British became the fourth European power to rule the island. Yet it was during this period of changing ❼ colonial powers—Mauritius was traded like a commodity, that the demographics of the island began to experience important changes with great political ramifications.

By the time slavery was abolished in 1835, for example, the remaining Franco-Mauritian elites were outnumbered by the growing Indian population, the Creoles who could trace their roots back to island's sugarcane plantations, and the Muslim community originating from present-day Pakistan. And with these demographic changes came political change. The first step toward self-rule came with the legislative elections of 1947, and in March of 1968, an official constitution was adopted. Today, Mauritius peacefully balances the diversity of its multicultural society and flourishes in international ❽ trade through its advantageous geographic location and large labor force.

17. A) NO CHANGE
B) colonial powers—Mauritius was traded like a commodity that
C) colonial powers—Mauritius was traded like a commodity—that
D) colonial powers, Mauritius was traded like a commodity that

18. A) NO CHANGE
B) trade, through
C) trade through,
D) trade; through

Answers & Explanations for this chapter appear on page 1118.

EXTRA PRACTICE

Required	Recommended
Questions 1–11	Questions 12–22

Questions 1-11 are based on the following passage and supplementary material.

Feeling the Burn of Lactic Acid

As a person works a muscle excessively or for a long period of time, that person will most likely feel a burning sensation. Coaches and trainers often encourage ❶ they're athletes to exercise until they "feel the burn" because that is an indication that the muscle is working hard. Some people ❷ bond the burning feeling with "burning" calories, but the burning sensation has nothing to do with the energy released during exercise; ❸ first, it is caused by chemicals that form when muscles use more oxygen than they have available.

    ❹ The muscles cannot use the glucose directly, however; they can use only adenosine triphosphate (ATP), which is a molecule formed when cells break down glucose. First, the muscle cells break the six-carbon glucose into two three-carbon molecules of pyruvic acid. This makes two ATP molecules available for the muscle cells to use.

1. A) NO CHANGE
   B) their
   C) it's
   D) its

2. A) NO CHANGE
   B) equate
   C) acquaint
   D) observe

3. A) NO CHANGE
   B) instead
   C) although
   D) consequently

4. Which sentence, if added to the beginning of this paragraph, would effectively establish the central idea?

   A) Blood brings the energy muscles need to move in the form of glucose.

   B) Adenosine triphosphate (ATP) is a molecule that is found in all living cells.

   C) Glucose is a carbohydrate that is absorbed into the blood during digestion.

   D) Muscles are made of soft tissue and require an external energy source to move.

When enough oxygen is available, the cells ❺ <u>then continues</u> to break the pyruvic acid down in a series of steps, each of which produces more ATP. The full cycle releases another 34 ATP molecules, as well as carbon dioxide and water, from one molecule of glucose.

When a cell breaks down glucose without oxygen present, however, it can only accomplish the first step. Even this step will halt, unless the cell converts the pyruvic acid formed into lactic acid. The longer we exercise without enough oxygen, the more lactic acid we build up in our muscle tissues. You are probably familiar with the discomfort acetic ❻ <u>acid found in vinegar, causes</u> when it comes in contact with a cut; lactic acid ❼ <u>annoys</u> muscle tissues in a similar way, causing a burning sensation.

❽ [1] Lactic acid does not form during normal daily activities because our muscles have a small store of ATP available, which is easily replenished as it is used. [2] More intense activity, however, quickly uses up that ❾ <u>store once the store</u> is used up, and if the level of oxygen needed for the activity is greater than the amount reaching the muscles, lactic acid starts to build up. [3] The buildup of lactic acid occurs most quickly while engaging in so-called power sports, such as sprinting. [4] After we stop exercising, ❿ <u>you</u> continue to breathe harder in order to

5. A) NO CHANGE
   B) did continue
   C) continue
   D) continued

6. A) NO CHANGE
   B) acid, found in vinegar, causes
   C) acid found, in vinegar, causes
   D) acid found in vinegar causes

7. A) NO CHANGE
   B) rubs
   C) hurts
   D) irritates

8. Which sentence provides the least support for the central idea of paragraph 4?
   A) Sentence 1
   B) Sentence 2
   C) Sentence 3
   D) Sentence 4

9. A) NO CHANGE
   B) store once, the store
   C) store; once the store
   D) store: once the store

10. A) NO CHANGE
    B) we
    C) they
    D) them

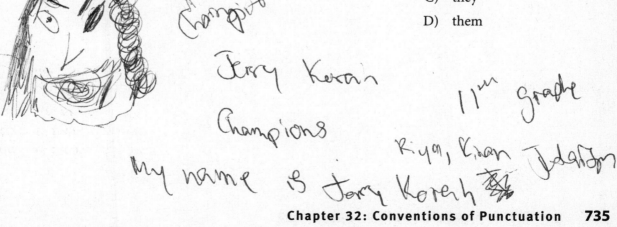

get enough oxygen to convert the lactic acid back to pyruvic acid, to be used in the normal cycle once again. [5] As a result, lactic acid does not return to normal immediately after we stop exercising. [11]

Concentration of Lactic Acid in Blood Before, During, and After Exercise (5-minute fast run)

Based on data from Journal of Sport Sciences, 28(9) pp. 975-982.

11. Based on the information in the graph, which sentence could be added to the end of this paragraph to conclude the passage?

A) Lactic acid concentration peaks at eight minutes then begins to drop.

B) At 28 minutes, lactic acid concentration is half of what it is during exercise.

C) We continue to "feel the burn" for about 40 minutes after we stop.

D) Lactic acid concentration declines steadily when exercise stops.

Questions 12-22 are based on the following passage and supplementary material.

The Brooklyn Bridge: The Eighth Wonder of the World

As one of New York City's most iconic landmarks, the Brooklyn Bridge spans 5,989 feet across the East River. Connecting the boroughs of Brooklyn (Kings County) and Manhattan, this bridge was a fantastic marvel of engineering **⑫** when it was completed in 1883, just years after the Golden Gate Bridge. The Brooklyn Bridge was the longest suspension bridge of **⑬** its time. It was dubbed the "8th Wonder of the World." Its construction, **⑭** consequently, was riddled with problems from the very start.

12. Which choice completes the sentence with accurate data based on the table?

   A) NO CHANGE
   B) when it was completed in 1883, several years before the Tower Bridge in London, England, was built.
   C) when it was completed in 1883, two years after the Tower Bridge in London, England, was built.
   D) when it was completed in 1883, the same year that the Golden Gate Bridge was built.

13. Which choice most effectively combines the sentences at the underlined portion?

   A) its time, however, it was dubbed
   B) its time, and it was dubbed
   C) its time, was dubbed
   D) its time, it was dubbed

14. A) NO CHANGE
   B) as a result
   C) for example
   D) however

Residents of Brooklyn had **15** watched for a bridge to connect them with Manhattan, as the frozen East River was **16** absolutely so impossible to cross during the winter. The dream would finally come to fruition, when New York legislators approved John Augustus Roebling's plan for a suspension bridge over the East River. Roebling had a successful reputation as a designer of suspension bridges, and the Brooklyn Bridge would be **17** their biggest feat yet, as both the suspension bridge with the longest span (1,600 feet from tower to tower) and as the first steel-cabled suspension bridge.

Roebling would never see his design completed; in fact, he would never even see construction begin. Just before construction was about to start in 1867, Roebling was the victim of a **18** special accident; a boat **19** was smashing into his foot, and he succumbed to tetanus. His son, Washington Roebling, took over the project.

15. A) NO CHANGE
    B) longed
    C) fought
    D) went

16. A) NO CHANGE
    B) absolutely impossible
    C) impossible
    D) so impossible

17. A) NO CHANGE
    B) its
    C) her
    D) his

18. A) NO CHANGE
    B) exceptional
    C) common
    D) freak

19. A) NO CHANGE
    B) smashing
    C) smashed
    D) was smashed

20 The first task was for workers to excavate the riverbed in order to anchor the two towers of the bridge to the bedrock below. To accomplish this, bottomless wooden boxes called caissons were sunk into the depths of the river. Once inside, workers would begin the laborious task of removing mud and boulders. To get down into the caissons, workers traveled in airlocks filled with compressed air, which prevented water **21** from entering, if the workers ascended to the surface and left the compressed air too quickly, they would suffer from the debilitating condition known as "caisson disease," or "the bends." Over 100 workers experienced caisson disease, and many others died or were injured from construction-related accidents. The cement-filled caissons remain under the towers of the bridge today.

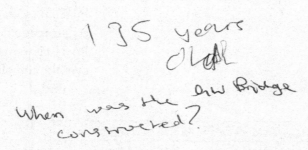

135 years old

When was the new bridge constructed?

20. Which choice most effectively establishes the central idea of the paragraph?
    A) Designs for the Brooklyn Bridge included a promenade above the traffic.
    B) The conditions inside the caissons were so terrible that workmen could stay there only for two hours.
    C) The towers were built of limestone, granite, and cement that came from a village called Rosendale in upstate New York.
    D) The building of the bridge was a monumental and often dangerous undertaking.

21. A) NO CHANGE
    B) from entering. If the workers ascended
    C) from entering if the workers ascended
    D) from entering, since if the workers ascended

Washington Roebling himself suffered from the bends and was partially paralyzed for the rest of his life. Determined to remain part of the project now supervised by his wife, Emily, he watched the construction continue with a telescope. 22 In May, 1883, more than a dozen years after construction began, Emily Roebling was given the first ride over the completed Brooklyn Bridge. She was followed by 150,300 people on that opening day. Despite the setbacks, Manhattan and Brooklyn were finally connected.

22. Which choice most effectively revises the underlined sentence?

A) In 1883, many years after construction began, Emily Roebling was given a ride over the completed Brooklyn Bridge.

B) In May 1883, many years after construction began, Emily Roebling was given the first ride over the completed Brooklyn Bridge.

C) On May 24, 1883, 14 years after construction began, Emily Roebling was given the first ride over the completed Brooklyn Bridge.

D) In 1883, 14 years after construction began, Emily Roebling was given a ride over the completed Brooklyn Bridge.

Bridges of the World			
Bridge Name & Location	**Date Completed**	**Length**	**Largest Single Span**
Akashi Kaikyo Bridge, Japan	1998	12,828 feet	6,527 feet
Brooklyn Bridge, New York	1883	5,989 feet	1,595 feet
Golden Gate Bridge, San Francisco	1937	8,981 feet	4,200 feet
Tower Bridge, London	1894	880 feet	200 feet

PART THREE

The Essay

UNIT NINE

The Essay

CHAPTER 33

The Kaplan Method for the SAT Essay

CHAPTER OBJECTIVES

By the end of this chapter, you will be able to:

1. Apply the Kaplan Method for the SAT Essay to produce a clear analysis of a source text

SMARTPOINTS

Point Value	SmartPoint Category
Point Builder	The Kaplan Method for the SAT Essay

THE SAT ESSAY IS OPTIONAL. SHOULD YOU WRITE IT?

One of the biggest changes for the 2016 SAT is the fact that the Essay Test is now optional. If you don't want to spend 50 minutes writing an essay, you certainly don't have to. You are free to leave after the final multiple choice section of the test.

However, just because you can leave without completing the Essay Test doesn't mean that you should. If you can state with 100 percent certainty that the colleges to which you are applying do not require the essay component of the SAT, feel free to omit it on Test Day. However, if you are unsure, or don't yet have a finalized list of colleges, Kaplan recommends you complete the Essay Test for the following reasons:

First, consider the fact that the SAT is not an exam you can take in bits and pieces. If you want to take the Essay Test at a later date, you'll have to sit through the entire SAT again. That can translate to a lot of unnecessary stress during your senior year.

Second, if the colleges you apply to don't require you to take the Essay Test, they won't negatively judge you if you do. There is nothing to lose by completing the essay. You might get a great score and add a few more possibilities to your list of potential schools.

Finally, while the Essay Test question on the new SAT will be challenging, it is also standardized. That means you can learn how to write a high-scoring essay by putting in some time, effort, and willingness to practice. This chapter is a great place to start.

THE KAPLAN METHOD FOR THE SAT ESSAY

The SAT Essay, while optional, presents you with a challenge: to read and understand a high-quality source text and write an essay analyzing the author's argument in 50 minutes. By using the Kaplan Method for the SAT Essay, you will be able to make the most out of those 50 minutes and produce a high-scoring written response to a previously published, sophisticated source.

The Kaplan Method for the SAT Essay consists of four steps:

Step 1: Read the source text, taking notes on how the author uses:

- Evidence to support claims

- Reasoning to develop ideas and to connect claims and evidence

- Stylistic or persuasive elements to add power to the ideas expressed

Step 2: Develop an outline of the features you will analyze in your response

Step 3: Write your essay

Step 4: Check your essay for mistakes in grammar, spelling, and clarity

Let's take a closer look at each step.

Step 1: Read the source text, taking notes on how the author uses:

- **evidence to support claims**

- **reasoning to develop ideas and to connect claims and evidence**

- **stylistic or persuasive elements to add power to the ideas expressed**

What is the source text?

The source text for the SAT essay will consist of a passage that is very similar to the passages you'll see in the Reading Test. It will typically be 500–750 words and will deal with topics of general interest in the arts, sciences, and public life. In many cases, the passages will be biased in favor of the author's argument.

While the source text changes from test to test, the directions and essay prompt remain similar. Spend more time reading and understanding the text—the prompt will likely be very similar to other prompts that you've encountered.

What kinds of notes should I take?

The notes you take while reading the source text are similar to those you would take when creating a Passage Map on the Reading Test (see chapter 18). However, these notes will focus on how the author connects central ideas and important details.

Your notes should focus on:

- evidence to support claims (e.g., cited data or statistics, or authoritative sources that support the author's argument)

- reasoning to develop ideas and make connections (e.g., the author explains his logic for using a specific piece of evidence to support a specific claim)

- stylistic or persuasive elements to add power to the ideas expressed (e.g., using figurative language, irony, metaphor, and other elements to appeal to emotions)

In addition to taking notes in the margins of the passage, it is also helpful to underline and circle the following:

- central ideas

- important details

- errors of fact or interpretation

- textual evidence (quotations, paraphrases, or both)

You should spend approximately 10 minutes on Step 1.

Step 2: Develop an outline of the features you will analyze in your response

Why do I need an outline?

Creating an outline before you write your essay is a huge time-saver, which is essential when you have only 50 minutes to complete the SAT Essay Test. Spending the first part of the allotted time effectively (i.e., reading and taking notes on the source text and creating an outline) will lead to a well-organized, more convincing essay. You'll also find that organizing your thoughts ahead of time will enable you to write much more quickly!

What should I put in my outline?

Kaplan has created an efficient and effective template to outline the SAT Essay. The template consists of tasks you should complete and questions you should ask before you begin writing. You do not need to answer the questions in complete sentences—sketch out your notes and use abbreviations that you understand.

The six questions for each body paragraph may seem like a lot, but answering these questions before you write will make the writing itself that much easier.

Using the template will prevent you from encountering a writing or thinking block. With the template and the Kaplan Method, you will know what you want to write about the source text and not waste any time.

The Kaplan Template for the SAT Essay can be found on page 750.

You should spend approximately 8 minutes on Step 2.

> ✔ **On Test Day**
>
> You will not be able to bring these questions with you to Test Day. Therefore, it is important that you memorize the gist and logical flow of the questions well before Test Day so that asking these questions is second nature to you when you sit down to write your essay.

Step 3: Write your essay

After you have read and analyzed the source text, your next goal is to write a cohesive essay that demonstrates your use and command of standard written English. To demonstrate your proficiency, you must:

- Provide your own precise central claim
- Use a variety of sentence structures
- Employ precise word choice
- Maintain a constant and appropriate style and tone

You should spend approximately 30 minutes on Step 3.

Step 4: Check your essay for mistakes in grammar, spelling, and clarity

While a few grammar and spelling mistakes won't drastically harm your SAT Essay score, setting aside some time to proofread can help you catch careless errors that you can easily correct, thereby increasing your Writing score on the SAT Essay.

You should spend the remaining 2 minutes on Step 4.

THE KAPLAN TEMPLATE FOR THE SAT ESSAY

Introductory Paragraph:

To demonstrate that you understand the source text, **paraphrase the author's central idea or claim:** _____

_____

_____

_____

> ✔ **Definition**
>
> Features are the key elements of the essay that you marked in your notes. They could include stylistic techniques, like irony, or data, like statistics, used to bolster a claim.

List the three features you will analyze in your essay.

1. Feature #1

2. Feature #2

3. Feature #3

Body Paragraph Feature #1: _____

Where does the author use this feature? _____

What example(s) of this feature can you cite from the source text (direct quotations or paraphrases)?
_____

_____

_____

How does this example interrelate with the author's central claim? _____
_____

_____

How does this feature affect the author's audience? _____
_____

_____

Does achieving this effect help build the author's argument? Why or why not? _____
_____

_____

_____

What are the function of this feature and example in the overall text? _____
_____

_____

Body Paragraph Feature #2: _____

Where does the author use this feature? _____

What example(s) of this feature can you cite from the source text (direct quotations or paraphrases)?
_____
_____
_____

How does this example interrelate with the author's central claim? _____
_____
_____

How does this feature affect the author's audience? _____
_____
_____

Does achieving this effect help build the author's argument? Why or why not? _____
_____
_____
_____

What are the function of this feature and example in the overall text? _____
_____
_____

Body Paragraph Feature #3: _____

Where does the author use this feature? _____

What example(s) of this feature can you cite from the source text (direct quotations or paraphrases)?
_____
_____
_____

How does this example interrelate with the author's central claim? _____
_____
_____

How does this feature affect the author's audience? _____
_____
_____

Does achieving this effect help build the author's argument? Why or why not? _____
_____
_____

What are the function of this feature and example in the overall text? _____
_____
_____

Conclusion:

What is the author's overall purpose for writing this passage? _____
_____
_____

What is the author's central argument or claim? _____
_____
_____

How did the author build his or her argument or claim? <u>By using Feature #1, Feature #2, and Feature #3.</u>

THE SAT ESSAY PROMPT

As mentioned previously in this chapter, the SAT Essay source text will change from administration to administration, but the prompt will remain largely the same in both format and wording.

Become familiar with the idea behind the prompt and assignment as soon as you can so that on Test Day, you will be able to focus on reading, analyzing, and writing, rather than figuring out what the prompt is asking you to accomplish.

The generic SAT Essay prompt is as follows:

As you read the passage below, consider how [the author] uses

- evidence, such as facts or examples, to support claims.

- reasoning to develop ideas and to connect claims and evidence.

- stylistic or persuasive elements, such as word choice or appeals to emotion, to add power to the ideas expressed.

Source Text Will Appear Here

Write an essay in which you explain how [the author] builds an argument to persuade [his/her] audience that [author's claim]. In your essay, analyze how [the author] uses one or more of the features listed previously (or features of your own choice) to strengthen the logic and persuasiveness of [his/her] argument. Be sure your analysis focuses on the most relevant aspects of the passage.

Your essay should not explain whether you agree with [the author's] claims, but rather explain how [the author] builds an argument to persuade [his/her] audience.

SAT ESSAY SCORING RUBRIC

There are three different scores for the SAT Essay: Reading, Analysis, and Writing. Each category will be scored on a scale of 1 to 4. The scores you receive will range from 2 to 8, as they will be the scores of two raters.

The raters will use the following rubric to determine each area score.

	1	2
Reading	• Demonstrates **little or no comprehension** of the source text • Fails to show an understanding of the text's central idea(s), and may include only details without reference to central idea(s) • May contain numerous errors of fact and/or interpretation with regard to the text • Makes little or no use of textual evidence	• Demonstrates **some comprehension** of the source text • Shows an understanding of the text's central idea(s) but not of important details • May contain errors of fact and/or interpretation with regard to the text • Makes limited and/or haphazard use of textual evidence
Analysis	• Offers **little or no analysis or ineffective analysis** of the source text and demonstrates **little to no understanding** of the analytical task • Identifies without explanation some aspects of the author's use of evidence, reasoning, and/or stylistic and persuasive elements, and/or feature(s) of the student's own choosing • Numerous aspects of analysis are unwarranted based on the text • Contains little or no support for claim(s) or point(s) made, or support is largely irrelevant • May not focus on features of the text that are relevant to addressing the task • Offers no discernible analysis (e.g., is largely or exclusively summary)	• Offers **limited analysis** of the source text and demonstrates only **partial understanding** of the analytical task • Identifies and attempts to describe the author's use of evidence, reasoning, and/or stylistic and persuasive elements, and/or feature(s) of the student's own choosing, but merely asserts rather than explains their importance • One or more aspects of analysis are unwarranted based on the text • Contains little or no support for claim(s) or point(s) made • May lack a clear focus on those features of the text that are most relevant to addressing the task
Writing	• Demonstrates **little or no cohesion** and **inadequate skill** in the use and control of language • May lack a clear central claim or controlling idea • Lacks a recognizable introduction and conclusion; does not have a discernible progression of ideas • Lacks variety in sentence structures; sentence structures may be repetitive; demonstrates general and vague word choice; word choice may be poor or inaccurate; may lack a formal style and objective tone • Shows a weak control of the conventions of standard written English and may contain numerous errors that undermine the quality of writing	• Demonstrates **little or no cohesion** and **limited skill** in the use and control of language • May lack a clear central claim or controlling idea or may deviate from the claim or idea • May include an ineffective introduction and/or conclusion; may demonstrate some progression of ideas within paragraphs but not throughout • Has limited variety in sentence structures; sentence structures may be repetitive; demonstrates general or vague word choice; word choice may be repetitive; may deviate noticeably from a formal style and objective tone • Shows a limited control of the conventions of standard written English and contains errors that detract from the quality of writing and may impede understanding

	3	4
Reading	• Demonstrates **effective comprehension** of the source text • Shows an understanding of the text's central idea(s) and important details • Is free of substantive errors of fact and interpretation with regard to the text • Makes appropriate use of textual evidence	• Demonstrates **thorough comprehension** of the source text • Shows an understanding of the text's central idea(s) and most important details and how they interrelate • Is free of errors of fact or interpretation with regard to the text • Makes skillful use of textual evidence
Analysis	• Offers an **effective analysis** of the source text and demonstrates an **understanding** of the analytical task • Competently evaluates the author's use of evidence, reasoning, and/or stylistic and persuasive elements, and/or feature(s) of the student's own choosing • Contains relevant and sufficient support for claim(s) or point(s) made • Focuses primarily on those features of the text that are most relevant to addressing the task	• Offers an **insightful analysis** of the source text and demonstrates a **sophisticated understanding** of the analytical task • Offers a thorough, well-considered evaluation of the author's use of evidence, reasoning, and/or stylistic and persuasive elements, and/or feature(s) of the student's own choosing • Contains relevant, sufficient, and strategically chosen support for claim(s) or point(s) made • Focuses consistently on those features of the text that are most relevant to addressing the task
Writing	• Is **mostly cohesive** and demonstrates **effective use and control** of language • Includes a central claim or implicit controlling idea • Includes an effective introduction and conclusion; demonstrates a clear progression of ideas both within paragraphs and throughout the essay • Has variety in sentence structures; demonstrates some precise word choice; maintains a formal style and objective tone • Shows a good control of the conventions of standard written English and is free of significant errors that detract from the quality of writing	• Is **cohesive** and demonstrates a **highly effective use and command** of language • Includes a precise central claim • Includes a skillful introduction and conclusion; demonstrates a deliberate and highly effective progression of ideas both within paragraphs and throughout the essay • Has a wide variety of sentence structures; demonstrates a consistent use of precise word choice; maintains a formal style and objective tone • Shows a strong command of the conventions of standard written English and is free or virtually free of errors

Look at the test-like source text and prompt that follows. Notice what kinds of notes an SAT expert takes in the margins of the passage. Then, look at how the SAT expert answers the Kaplan Template questions for the introduction and one of the body paragraphs of his own essay and uses those answers to write those sections.

As you read the passage below, consider how Tony Blair uses

- evidence, such as facts or examples, to support claims.

- reasoning to develop ideas and to connect claims and evidence.

- stylistic or persuasive elements, such as word choice or appeals to emotion, to add power to the ideas expressed.

Adapted from British Prime Minister Tony Blair's speech to American citizens following 9/11/2001.

The only purpose of being in politics is to strive for the values and ideals we believe in: freedom, justice, what we Europeans call solidarity but you might call respect for and help for others. These are the decent democratic values we all avow. But alongside the values we know we need a hard-headed pragmatism—a realpolitik—required to give us any chance of translating those values into the practical world we live in.

juxt. btwn. Euro & aud. (U.S.)

The same tension exists in the two views of international affairs. One is utilitarian: each nation maximizes its own self-interest. The other is utopian: we try to create a better world. Today I want to suggest that more than ever before those two views are merging.

ev: util. vs utop. views

I advocate an enlightened self-interest that puts fighting for our values right at the heart of the policies necessary to protect our nations. Engagement in the world on the basis of these values, not isolationism from it, is the hard-headed pragmatism for the 21st century.

Why? In part it is because the countries and people of the world today are more interdependent than ever. In truth, it is very rare today that trouble in one part of the globe remains limited in its effect. Not just in security, but in trade and finance—witness the crisis of 1998 which began in Thailand and ended in Brazil—the world is interlocked.

rhet. ?

ev: 1998 crisis

This is heightened by mass communications and technology. In Queen Victoria's time, reports of battles came back weeks or months after they were won or lost. Today we see them enacted live on the BBC, Sky or CNN. Their very visibility, immediate and in Technicolor, inflames feelings that can spread worldwide across different ethnic, religious, and cultural communities.

ev: Queen Vic. time's reports vs today's

So today, more than ever, "their" problem becomes "our" problem. Instability is contagious and, again today, more than ever, nations, at least most of them, crave stability. That's for a simple reason. Our people want it, because without it, they can't do business and prosper. What brings nations together—what brought them together post–September 11—is the international recognition that the world needs order. Disorder is the enemy of progress.

quotes → irony

The struggle is for stability, for the security within which progress can be made. Of course, countries want to protect their territorial integrity but few are into empire-building. This is especially true of democracies whose people vote for higher living standards and punish governments who don't deliver them. For 2,000 years Europe fought over territory.

ex: 2000 year Eur. fight

Today boundaries are virtually fixed. Governments and people know that any territorial ambition threatens stability, and instability threatens prosperity.

And of course the surest way to stability is through the very values of freedom, democracy and justice. Where these are strong, the people push for moderation and order. Where they are absent, regimes act unchecked by popular accountability and pose a threat; and the threat spreads.

logic & results

So the promotion of these values becomes not just right in itself but part of our long-term security and prosperity. We can't intervene in every case. Not all the wrongs of the world can be put right, but where disorder threatens us all, we should act.

Like it or not, whether you are a utilitarian or a utopian, the world is interdependent. One consequence of this is that foreign and domestic policy are ever more closely interwoven.

what prompted speech

It was September 11 that brought these thoughts into sharper focus. Watching the horror unfold, imagining the almost unimaginable suffering of the thousands of innocent victims of the terror and carnage, the dominant emotion after the obvious feelings of revulsion, sympathy and anger was determination.

juxt. "imagining… unimaginable"

The guts and spirit of the people of New York and America in the aftermath of that terrible day were not just admirable, they were awesome. They were the best riposte to the terrorists that humanity could give and you should be very proud of that. I want you to know too that the British people were with you from the first moment, and we will always be with you at times like those. We are not half-hearted friends and we never will be. But the determination must be not just to pursue those responsible and bring them to justice but to learn from September 11. There is a real danger we forget the lessons of September 11. Human beings recover from tragedy and the memory becomes less fraught. That is a healthy part of living. But we should learn from our experience.

praising aud.

promises

The <u>most obvious lesson is indeed our</u> interdependence. For a time our world stood still. Quite apart from our security, the shock impacted on economic confidence, on business, on trade, and it is only now, with the terrorist network on the run, that confidence is really returning. <u>Every nation in the world</u> felt the reverberation of that fateful day. And that <u>has been well illustrated</u> by the role which the United Nations—under Kofi Annan's excellent leadership—has played since September 11.

ex: U.N. & Kofi A.
global effects of 9/11

So if we didn't know it before, we know now: <u>these events and our response to them</u> shape the fate <u>not of one nation but of one world</u>.

For America, it has laid bare the reality. American power affects the world <u>fundamentally</u>. It is there. It is real. It is never irrelevant. It can affect the world for good, or for bad. Stand aside or engage; it never fails to affect.

short sentences

You know I want it engaged. Under President Bush, I am confident it will be and for good. But if that's what I and many others want, it comes at a price for us too. It means we don't shirk our responsibility. It means that when America is fighting for those values, then, however tough, we fight with her. No grandstanding, no offering implausible but impractical advice from the comfort of the touchline, no wishing away the hard not the easy choices, but working together, side by side.

personification of America

Write an essay in which you explain how Tony Blair builds an argument to persuade his audience that imbuing the world with values must be approached pragmatically and universally. In your essay, analyze how Blair uses one or more of the features listed above (or features of your own choice) to strengthen the logic and persuasiveness of his argument. Be sure your analysis focuses on the most relevant aspects of the passage.

Your essay should not explain whether you agree with Blair's claims, but rather explain how Blair builds an argument to persuade his audience.

Now that you've seen what kinds of notes a test expert takes for the SAT Essay source text, look at how he or she does some analysis by using the Kaplan Template to create an outline.

While the following example includes full sentences and quotations from the source text, please know that you should use shorthand and ellipses on Test Day; it's not your outline that's evaluated, but your actual essay.

Introductory Paragraph:

To demonstrate that you understand the source text, **paraphrase the author's central idea or claim**: Because the 21st-century world is interdependent, all nations must fight together for the values of freedom, democracy, and justice.

List the three features you will analyze in your essay.

1. Irony
2. Historical Evidence
3. Juxtaposition

Body Paragraph #1: Irony

Where does the author use this feature?

In the beginning of the sixth paragraph.

What example(s) of this feature can you cite from the source text (direct quotations or paraphrases)?

The use of quotation marks around the words "their" and "our." Also: "Like it or not, whether you are a utilitarian or a utopian, the world is interdependent."

How does this example interrelate with the author's central claim?

By using quotation marks, Blair is suggesting that there is no real difference between "their" problem and "our" problem. The "us versus them" mentality is no more because of the "international recognition that the world needs order."

How does this feature affect the author's audience?

By pointing out the silliness of the "us versus them" mentality, Blair makes his audience realize that different countries with different ideologies can still work together to fight the same battles to achieve the same goals.

Does achieving this effect help build the author's argument? Why or why not?

Yes, because it reinforces a lack of divide and that the world is "interdependent."

What is the function of this feature and example in the overall text?

To serve as a rhetorical reminder or example that one nation's tragedy affects many other nations: "For a time our world stood still . . . Every nation in the world felt the reverberation of that fateful day."

Now, look at how these notes translate into the first two paragraphs of a high-scoring student response to the SAT Essay.

In his speech to American citizens after the events of September 11, 2001, British Prime Minister Tony Blair asserted that because of the interdependent state of the world in the 21st century, all nations must band together in the fight for the values of freedom, democracy, and justice. Blair effectively conveys this argument by using irony, relevant historical examples as evidence, and juxtaposition.

In the beginning of the sixth paragraph, Blair uses quotation marks around the words "their" and "our," stating, "So today, more than ever, "their" problem becomes "our" problem." By using quotation marks around these opposing plural pronouns, Blair reveals the irony of the terms in the 21st-century global context. There is no "their" and no "our"—the preconceived notion of an "us versus them" mentality no longer applies to the interdependent state of the world. Blair supports this implication by emphasizing that there is an "international recognition that the world needs order." By highlighting the impracticality of the "us versus them" mentality, Blair convinces his audience that different countries must unite in order to achieve common goals, reinforcing his recurring characterization of the world as "interdependent." The use of irony through the quotation marks serves as a rhetorical reminder or example that one nation's tragedy (like 9/11) is not isolated: "it can affect the world for good, or for bad."

You have seen the kinds of notes SAT experts take and the strategic thinking questions they ask while planning their responses to the SAT Essay source text.

Based on the prompt on pages 756-758, use the Kaplan Template questions to plan an additional body paragraph for the response essay. You may use one of the other two features mentioned on page 759 (Historical Evidence or Juxtaposition) or come up with one of your own to answer the questions for the template.

Body Paragraph Feature: _____

Where does the author use this feature? _____

What example(s) of this feature can you cite from the source text (direct quotations or para-phrases)? _____
_____
_____
_____

How does this example interrelate with the author's central claim? _____
_____
_____
_____

How does this feature affect the author's audience? _____
_____
_____
_____

Does achieving this effect help build the author's argument? Why or why not? _____
_____
_____
_____
_____

What are the function of this feature and example in the overall text? _____
_____
_____
_____

Now, use your answers to the Kaplan Template questions you completed on page 761 to write a full body paragraph on the lines that follow. Give yourself 8 minutes to write the paragraph.

_____
_____
_____
_____
_____
_____
_____
_____
_____
_____
_____
_____
_____
_____
_____
_____
_____
_____
_____
_____
_____
_____
_____
_____
_____
_____
_____
_____
_____

EXTRA PRACTICE

Required	Recommended
Practice Essay on p. 763	

As you read the passage below, consider how Emmeline Pankhurst uses

- evidence, such as facts or examples, to support claims.

- reasoning to develop ideas and to connect claims and evidence.

- stylistic or persuasive elements, such as word choice or appeals to emotion, to add power to the ideas expressed.

Adapted from "Freedom or Death," a speech delivered by Emmeline Pankhurst on November 13, 1913, in Hartford, Connecticut

Mrs. Hepburn, ladies, and gentlemen:

Tonight I am not here to advocate woman suffrage. American suffragists can do that very well for themselves. I am here as a soldier who has temporarily left the field of battle in order to explain what civil war is like when civil war is waged by women. I am here as a person who, according to the law courts of my country, it has been decided, is of no value to the community at all: and I am adjudged because of my life to be a dangerous person.

Now, first of all I want to make you understand the inevitableness of revolution and civil war, even on the part of women, when you reach a certain stage in the development of a community's life. It is quite easy for you to understand the desirability of revolution if I were a man. If an Irish revolutionary had addressed this meeting, and many have addressed meetings all over the United States during the last twenty or thirty years, it would not be necessary for that revolutionary to explain the need of revolution beyond saying that the people of his country were denied—and by people, meaning men—were denied the right of self-government. That would explain the whole situation. If I were a man and I said to you, "I come from a country which professes to have representative institutions and yet denies me, a taxpayer, an inhabitant of the country, representative rights," you would at once understand that that human being, being a man, was justified in the adoption of revolutionary methods to get representative institutions. But since I am a woman it is necessary in the twentieth century to explain why women have adopted revolutionary methods in order to win the rights of citizenship.

You see, in spite of a good deal that we hear about revolutionary methods not being necessary for American women, we women, in trying to make our case clear, always have to make as part of our argument, and urge upon men in our audience the fact—a very simple fact—that women are human beings. I want to put a few political arguments before you—not arguments for the suffrage, because I said when I opened, I didn't mean to do that—but arguments for the adoption of militant methods in order to win political rights.

Suppose the men of Hartford had a grievance, and they laid that grievance before their legislature, and the legislature obstinately refused to listen to them, or to remove their grievance, what would be the proper and the constitutional and the practical way of getting their grievance removed? Well, it is perfectly obvious at the next general election, when the legislature is elected, the men of Hartford would turn out that legislature and elect a new one: entirely change the personnel of an obstinate legislature.

But let the men of Hartford imagine that they were not in the position of being voters at all, that they were governed without their consent being obtained, that the legislature turned an absolutely deaf ear to their demands, what would the men of Hartford do then? They couldn't vote the legislature out. They would have to make a choice of two evils: they would either have to submit indefinitely to an unjust state of affairs, or they would have to rise up and adopt some of the antiquated means by which men in the past got their grievances remedied. We know what happened when your forefathers decided that they must have representation for taxation, many, many years ago. When they felt they couldn't wait any longer, when they laid all the arguments before an obstinate British government that they could think of, and when their arguments were absolutely disregarded, when every other means had failed, they began by the tea party at Boston, and they went on until they had won the independence of the United States of America. That is what happened in the old days.

It is perfectly evident to any logical mind that when you have got the vote, you can get out of any legislature whatever you want, or, if you cannot get it, you can send them about their business and choose other people who will be more attentive to your demands, But, it is clear to the meanest intelligence that if you have not got the vote, you must either submit to laws just or unjust, administration just or unjust, or the time inevitably comes when you will revolt against that injustice and use violent means to put an end to it.

Write an essay in which you explain how Emmeline Pankhurst builds an argument to persuade her audience that violent as well as nonviolent protest tactics are necessary and justifiable to gain political rights for women. In your essay, analyze how Pankhurst uses one or more of the listed features (or features of your own choice) to strengthen the logic and persuasiveness of her argument. Be sure that your analysis focuses on the most relevant features of the passage.

Your essay should not explain whether you agree with Pankhurst's claims, but rather explain how Pankhurst builds an argument to persuade her audience.

_____

_____

_____

_____

_____

_____

_____

_____

_____

_____

_____

_____

_____

_____

_____

_____

_____

_____

_____

_____

_____

_____

_____

_____

_____

_____

_____

_____

_____

_____

_____

_____

_____

_____

_____

_____

_____

CHAPTER 34

Reading, Analyzing, and Writing the SAT Essay

CHAPTER OBJECTIVES

By the end of this chapter, you will be able to:

1. Identify the source text's central ideas and important details and how the two interrelate

2. Evaluate the author's use of evidence, reasoning, and/or stylistic and persuasive elements

3. Understand the standards by which the technical aspects of your written response will be evaluated

Point Value	SmartPoint Category
4 Points	Reading
4 Points	Analysis
4 Points	Writing

THE SAT ESSAY: READING

One of the three scores you'll receive on the SAT Essay is the Reading score. Graded on a scale of 1 to 4 by two different readers for a total score of 2 to 8, the Reading score is based on:

- Your understanding of the source text
- Your comprehension of the source text's central ideas, important details, and their interrelationship
- The accuracy of your interpretation of the source text
- Your use of textual evidence to demonstrate your understanding of the source text

Your ability to achieve a high Reading score depends on how well you accomplish Step 1 of the Kaplan Method for the SAT Essay:

Step 1: Read the source text, taking notes on how the author uses:
- **evidence to support claims**
- **reasoning to develop ideas and to connect claims and evidence**
- **stylistic or persuasive elements to add power to the ideas expressed**

For an in-depth review of the Kaplan Method for the SAT Essay, please read chapter 33.

Central Ideas

The **central idea** of a text is the key point the author wants to make. The central idea is also often referred to as the text's theme or thesis. Here are some questions to help you pinpoint a text's central idea:

- What is the author's central idea or claim?
- Why did the author write this passage?
- What is the tone of the passage?
- What is this passage primarily about?

> ✔ **Expert Tip**
>
> Do not confuse a text's topic and its central idea. The topic can usually be stated in 1–2 words, while the central idea is a longer statement. A well-written sentence describing the central idea does more than announce the topic; it also identifies the specific angle or facet of the topic being addressed.

Important Details

While a source text will inevitably be full of details, the **important details** are those that support or explain the author's central idea. Authors often use certain structural clues or keywords to highlight important details. The following chart lists common categories of keywords and examples.

List	to begin with, first, secondly, next, then, finally, most important, also, for instance, in fact, for example, another
Chronology	on (date), not long after, now, as, before, after, when
Compare-and-Contrast	however, but, as well as, on the other hand, not only . . . but also, either . . . or, while, although, unless, similarly, yet
Cause-and-Effect	because, since, therefore, consequently, as a result, this led to, so that, nevertheless, accordingly, if . . . then, thus

If you're unsure if a detail is important when reading a source text, it probably isn't. Always ask: "Does this detail support or enhance the author's central idea? How?"

Let's look at the following test-like source text excerpt. After the annotated passage, there is a series of questions and answers an SAT expert would ask to determine the text's central idea and important details.

Adapted from Hayakawa, S.I. *Language in Thought and Action* (Fifth Edition). New York: Harcourt Brace & Company, 1991.

The following passage is excerpted from a book that examines language and its necessity in ensuring survival in society.

Names that are "loaded" tend to influence behavior toward those to whom they are applied. Currently, the shop doorways and freeway underpasses of American cities are sheltering tens of thousands of people who have no work and no homes. These people used to be referred to as "bums"—a word that suggests not only a lack of employment but a lack of desire to work, people who are lazy, satisfied with little, and who have no desire to enter the mainstream of the American middle class or subscribe to its values. Thus to think of these people as "bums" is to think that they are only getting what they deserve. With the search for new names for such people—"street people," "homeless," "displaced persons"—we may find new ways of helping these individuals.

. . . One other curious fact needs to be recorded about the words we apply to such hotly debated issues as race, religion, political heresy, and economic dissent. Every reader is acquainted with people who, according

central idea: names lead to behavior

ex. of "bums" connotation

if rename, better help?

to their own flattering descriptions of themselves, "believe in being frank" and like to "tell it like it is." By "telling it like it is," such people usually mean calling anything or anyone by the term which has the strongest and most disagreeable affective connotations. Why people should pin medals on themselves for "candor" for performing this nasty feat has often puzzled me. Sometimes it is necessary to violate verbal taboos as an aid to clearer thinking, but, more often, to insist upon "telling it like it is" is to provide our minds with a greased runway down which we may slide back into unexamined and reactive patterns of evaluation and behavior.

"candor" does
not = being
mean but many
think it does

What is the author's central idea or claim? Names or labels, especially those with negative connotations, can lead to negative behavior or beliefs.

Why did the author write this passage? To demonstrate how language, even on the level of word or name choice, can affect society and influence people's attitudes toward others.

What is the tone of this passage? Appalled or indignant.

What is this passage mostly about? How negative names can affect our actions and the excuses people use to continue to be politically incorrect.

What is the most important detail in the first paragraph? The example of the connotations of the word "bums."

How does this detail serve the author's central idea? The example supports the idea that the connotation of a word used to label a group of people can color how most of society views that group and how that view may be skewed.

What is the most important detail in the second paragraph? The author's assertion that when most people "tell it like it is," they call "anything or anyone by the term which has the strongest and most disagreeable affective connotations," thereby allowing society to "slide back into unexamined and reactive patterns of evaluation and behavior."

How does this detail serve the author's central idea? It discusses how the more generalized theory behind why people use derogatory labels causes negative societal behavior.

THE SAT ESSAY: ANALYSIS

One of the three scores you'll receive on the SAT Essay is the Analysis score. Graded on a scale of 1 to 4 by two different readers for a total score of 2 to 8, the Analysis score is based on:

- Your analysis of the source text and understanding of the analytical task

- Your evaluation of the author's use of evidence, reasoning, and/or stylistic and persuasive elements, and/or features of your own choosing

- Your support for the claims or points you make in your response

- Your focus on features of the text that are most relevant to addressing the task

The SAT Essay prompt dictates that you analyze one or more features the author uses to strengthen the logic and persuasiveness of his or her argument. The Kaplan Template for the SAT Essay detailed in chapter 33 suggests that you pick three features to discuss in your response. Because the source text is different for every administration of the SAT, the three features you pick to analyze will depend on the source text.

Commonly Used Features and Styles

- **Allusion:** A literary, historical, religious or mythological reference

- **Appeals to authority, emotion, or logic:** Rhetorical arguments in which the speaker claims to be an authority or expert in a field, attempts to play upon the emotions, or appeals to the use of reason.

- **Diction:** The specific word choice an author uses to persuade or convey tone, purpose, or effect

- **Didactic:** Writing or speech that has an instructive purpose or lesson, often associated with a dry, pompous presentation, regardless of its innate value to the audience

- **Hyperbole:** Overstatement characterized by exaggerated language, usually to make a point or draw attention

- **Irony (ironic):** The contrast between what is stated explicitly and what is really meant. The intended meaning is often the opposite of what is stated, often suggesting light sarcasm. Irony is used for many reasons, often to create poignancy or humor.

- **Juxtaposition:** The location of one thing adjacent to or juxtaposed with another to create an effect, reveal an attitude, or accomplish some other purpose

- **Rebuttal/refutation:** An argument technique wherein opposing arguments are anticipated and countered

- **Rhetorical question:** A question that is asked simply for the sake of stylistic effect and is not expected to be answered

- **Symbolism:** Use of a person, place, thing, event, or pattern that figuratively represents or "stands for" something else. Often the thing or idea represented is more abstract or general than the symbol, which is concrete.

You can choose to analyze any of the aforementioned features in your SAT Essay response; however, make sure to select features that are easily found within the source text and that the author uses to further his or her argument. If you cannot answer the questions posed in the Kaplan Template for the SAT Essay, pick another feature.

Let's look at the following test-like source text excerpt. After the annotated passage, the left column contains the features used in the excerpt. The column on the right describes how those features are used.

Adapted from Jonathan Swift's *A Modest Proposal*, written in 1729.

In the following passage, the narrator is proposing an idea "For Preventing the Children of Poor People From Being a [Burden] to Their Parents."

I shall now therefore humbly propose my own thoughts, which I hope will not be liable to the least objection.

I have been assured by a very knowing American of my acquaintance in London that a young healthy child well nursed is at a year old a most delicious, nourishing, and wholesome food, whether stewed, roasted, baked, or boiled; and I make no doubt that it will equally serve in a fricassee or a ragout.*   — appeal to authority

I do therefore humbly offer it to public consideration that of the hundred and twenty thousand children already computed†, twenty thousand may be reserved for breed, whereof only one-fourth part be males; which is more than we allow to sheep, black cattle, or swine; and my reason is that these children are seldom the fruits of marriage, a circumstance not much regarded by our savages; therefore one male will be sufficient to serve four females. That the remaining hundred thousand may, at a year old, be offered in sale to the persons of quality and fortune through the kingdom; always advising the mother to let them suck plentifully in the last month, so as to render them plump and fat for a good table. A child will make two dishes at an entertainment for friends; and when the family dines alone, the fore or hind quarter will make a reasonable dish, and seasoned with a little pepper or salt will be very good boiled on the fourth day, especially in winter.   — audience = public / compare boys to livestock / children as food!!

I have reckoned upon a medium that a child just born will weigh twelve pounds, and in a solar year, if tolerably nursed, will increase to twenty-eight pounds.   — stats/logic/math

I grant this food will be somewhat dear, and therefore very proper for landlords, who, as they have already devoured most of the parents, seem to have the best title to the children.

*a spicy meat stew
†that is, the number of children annually born to Irish parents who cannot support them

Feature	How It's Used
Appeal to authority	The author cites his "very knowing American" acquaintance in London who claims that "a young healthy child well nursed is at a year old a most delicious, nourishing, and wholesome food."
Diction	The author's repetitive use of the word "humbly" in the first and third paragraphs implies that his proposal is a modest one (thereby reinforcing the title of the essay). This further contributes to the irony of the passage because the proposal is anything but modest.
Irony	The author says he believes the solution to the crisis is to start using children as livestock, but is not seriously suggesting cannibalism as an answer.

THE SAT ESSAY: WRITING

Just as the SAT Writing & Language Test assesses your knowledge of expression of ideas and for conformity to the conventions of standard written English grammar, usage, and punctuation by having you revise and edit texts, so too does the SAT Essay Test by having you craft an original response. Therefore, the stronger your mastery of the writing and grammar concepts outlined in Unit 7: Expression of Ideas and Unit 8: Standard English Conventions, the better able you will be to earn a high Writing score on the SAT Essay.

One of the three scores you'll receive on the SAT Essay is the Writing score. Graded on a scale of 1 to 4 by two different readers for a total score of 2 to 8, the Writing score is based on:

- Your use of a central claim
- Your use of effective organization and progression of ideas
- Your use of varied sentence structures
- Your employment of precise word choice
- Your ability to maintain a consistent and appropriate style and tone
- Your command of the conventions of standard written English

Grammar Tips for the SAT Essay

1. **Avoid Sentence Fragments and Run-on Sentences.** Technically, a sentence fragment has no independent clause. A run-on sentence has two or more independent clauses that are improperly connected.

2. **Use Commas Correctly.** When using the comma, follow these guidelines:

- Use commas to separate items in a series. If more than two items are listed in a series, they should be separated by commas.

- Do not place commas before the first element of a series or after the last element.

- Use commas to separate two or more adjectives before a noun; do not use a comma after the last adjective in the series.

- Use commas to set off parenthetical clauses and phrases. A parenthetical expression is one that is not necessary to the central idea of the sentence.

- Use commas after most introductory phrases.

- Use commas to separate independent clauses (clauses that could stand alone as complete sentences) connected by coordinate conjunctions such as *and*, *but*, *not*, *yet*.

3. **Use Semicolons Correctly.** Follow these guidelines for correct semicolon usage:

- A semicolon may be used instead of a coordinate conjunction such as *and*, *or*, or *but* to link two closely related independent clauses.

- A semicolon may also be used between independent clauses connected by words like *therefore*, *nevertheless*, and *moreover*.

4. **Use Colons Correctly.** When you see a colon, it means "something's coming." Follow these rules for correct colon usage:

- In formal writing, the colon is used only as a means of signaling that what follows is a list, definition, explanation, or concise summary of what has gone before. The colon usually follows an independent clause, and it will frequently be accompanied by a reinforcing expression like *the following*, *as follows*, or *namely*, or by an explicit demonstrative like *this*.

- Be careful not to put a colon between a verb and its direct object.

- Context will occasionally make clear that a second independent clause is closely linked to its predecessor, even without an explicit expression. Here, too, a colon is appropriate, although a period will always be correct too.

5. **Use Apostrophes Correctly.** Follow these guidelines to correct apostrophe usage:

- Use the apostrophe with contracted forms of verbs to indicate that one or more letters have been eliminated in writing. Generally, though, you should try to avoid contractions when writing your SAT Essay response.

- Use the apostrophe to indicate the possessive form of a noun.

- The apostrophe is used to indicate possession only with nouns; in the case of pronouns, there are separate possessives for each person and number, with the exception of the neutral *one*, which forms its possessive by adding an apostrophe and an *s*.

6. **Pay Attention to Subject-Verb Agreement.** Singular subjects and plural subjects take different forms of the verb in the present tense. Usually, the difference lies in the presence or absence of a final *s*, but sometimes the difference is more radical. You can usually trust your ear to give you the correct verb form. However, certain situations may cause difficulty, such as:

- when the subject and verb are separated by a number of words.

- when the subject is an indefinite pronoun.

- when the subject consists of more than one noun.

7. **Use Modifiers Correctly.** In English, the position of a word within a sentence often establishes the word's relationship to other words in the sentence. This is especially true with modifying phrases. Modifiers, like pronouns, are generally connected to the nearest word that agrees with the modifier in person and number. If a modifier is placed too far from the word it modifies (the referent), the meaning may be lost or obscured. Avoid ambiguity by placing modifiers as close as possible to the words they are intended to modify.

8. **Use Pronouns Correctly.** A pronoun is a word that replaces a noun in a sentence. Every time you write a pronoun—*he, him, his, she, her, it, its, they, their, that,* or *which*—be sure there can be absolutely no doubt what its antecedent is. The antecedent is the particular noun a pronoun refers to or stands for. Careless use of pronouns can obscure your intended meaning.

9. **Pay Attention to Parallelism.** Matching constructions must be expressed in parallel form. It is often rhetorically effective to use a particular construction several times in succession in order to provide emphasis. The technique is called parallel construction, and it is effective only when used sparingly. If your sentences are varied, a parallel construction will stand out. If your sentences are already repetitive, a parallel structure will further obscure your meaning.

Style Tips for the SAT Essay

1. **Write succinctly.**

   - Do not use several words when one word will do.

   - If you have something to say, just say it.

2. **Write assertively.**

   - Avoid overuse of qualifiers.

   - You don't need to overly clarify your opinion.

   - Put verbs in the active voice whenever possible.

3. **Write clearly.**

   - Try not to begin sentences with *there is, there are, it would be, it could be, it can be,* or *it is.*

   - Avoid vague references, indirect language, and general wordiness. Choose specific, descriptive words.

   - Avoid clichés, which are overused expressions. Always substitute more specific language for a cliché.

   - Limit your use of jargon.

   - Avoid using slang and colloquialisms.

Let's look at the following examples of how to correct the aforementioned style and grammar issues. The left column contains the issue. The column in the middle features an incorrect sentence. The column on the right demonstrates how to rewrite the sentence correctly.

Issue	Incorrect	Correct
Needless Qualification	This rather serious breach of etiquette may possibly shake the very foundations of the diplomatic community	This serious breach of etiquette may shake the foundations of the diplomatic community.
Filling Up Space	Which idea of the author's is more in line with what I believe? This is a very interesting question. . . .	The author's beliefs are similar to mine.
Needless Self Reference	I am of the opinion that air pollution is a more serious problem than the government has led us to believe.	Air pollution is a more serious problem than the government has led us to believe.
Weak Openings	There are several reasons why Andre and his brother will not share an apartment.	Andre and his brother will not share an apartment for several reasons.
Vagueness	Chantal is highly educated.	Chantal has a master's degree in business administration.

Remember Step 1 of the Kaplan Method for the SAT Essay: Read the source text, taking notes on how the author uses:

- Evidence to support claims

- Reasoning to develop ideas and to connect claims and evidence

- Stylistic or persuasive elements to add power to the ideas expressed

Read the test-like source text excerpt and accompanying notes. Then, use the Kaplan Template for the SAT Essay to plan your introduction and first body paragraph.

Adapted from David Foster Wallace's "Tense Present: Democracy, English, and the Wars over Usage." *Harper's Magazine*, April 2001.

The following passage is excerpted from a monthly journal of literature, politics, culture, and the arts.

My own humble opinion is that some of the cultural and political realities of American life are themselves racially insensitive and elitist and offensive and unfair, and that tiptoeing around these realities with euphemistic doublespeak is not only hypocritical but toxic to the project of ever actually changing them. Such tiptoeing has of course now achieved the status of a dialect—one powerful enough to have turned the normal politics of the Usage Wars sort of inside out.

    I refer here to Politically Correct English (PCE). Although it's common to make jokes about PCE, be advised that Politically Correct English's various pre- and proscriptions are taken very seriously *indeed* by colleges and corporations and government agencies, whose own institutional dialects now evolve under the beady scrutiny of a whole new kind of Language Police.

    From one perspective, the history of PCE evinces a kind of irony. That is, the same ideological principles that informed the original sixties-era rejections of traditional authority and traditional inequality have now actually produced a far more inflexible tradition or complexity backed by the threat of real-world sanctions (termination, litigation) for those who fail to conform. This is sort of funny in a dark way, maybe, and most criticism of PCE seems to consist in making fun of its trendiness or vapidity. This reviewer's own opinion is that prescriptive PCE is not just silly but confused and dangerous.

    Usage is always political, of course, but it's complexly political. With respect, for instance, to political change, usage conventions can function in two ways: on the one hand they can be a *reflection* of political change, and on the other they can be an *instrument* of political change. These two functions are different and have to be kept straight. Confusing them—in particular, mistaking for political efficacy what is really just a language's political symbolism—enables the bizarre conviction

cliché

juxt. of colloquial & academic

some think PCE = joke

others think PCE = serious

appeal to authority

explains irony of PCE

colloquial makes his opinion clear

instrument vs reflection of pol. change

that America ceases to be elitist or unfair simply because Americans stop using certain vocabulary that is <u>historically associated with elitism and unfairness</u>. This is PCE's central fallacy—that a society's mode of expression is productive of its attitudes rather than a product of those attitudes.

central argument

Now, move on to Step 2: Develop an outline of the features you will analyze in your response.

Introductory Paragraph:

To demonstrate that you understand the source text, **paraphrase the author's central idea or claim**:

_____

_____

_____

List the three features you will analyze in your essay.

1. _____

2. _____

3. _____

Body Paragraph #1: _____

Where does the author use this feature?

_____

What example(s) of this feature can you cite from the source text (direct quotations or paraphrases)?

_____

_____

_____

How does this example interrelate with the author's central claim?

_____

_____

_____

How does this feature affect the author's audience?

_____

_____

_____

Does achieving this effect help build the author's argument? Why or why not?

_____

_____

_____

What is the function of this feature and example in the overall text?

_____

_____

_____

Now, use your answers to the Kaplan Template questions you completed on pages 780-781 to complete Steps 3 and 4 of the Kaplan Method for the SAT Essay: Write your essay and check your essay for mistakes in grammar, spelling, and clarity. Give yourself 8 minutes to write the introduction and first body paragraph.

_____
_____
_____
_____
_____
_____
_____
_____
_____
_____
_____
_____
_____
_____
_____
_____
_____
_____
_____
_____
_____
_____
_____
_____
_____
_____
_____
_____
_____
_____
_____
_____

Answers & Explanations for this chapter begin on page 1131.

EXTRA PRACTICE

Required	Recommended
Practice Essay on p. 786	

As you read the passage below, consider how Vice President Agnew uses

- evidence, such as facts or examples, to support claims.

- reasoning to develop ideas and to connect claims and evidence.

- stylistic or persuasive elements, such as word choice or appeals to emotion, to add power to the ideas expressed.

Adapted from Vice President Spiro Agnew's 1969 speech "Television News Coverage."

Tonight I want to discuss the importance of the television news medium to the American people. No nation depends more on the intelligent judgment of its citizens. No medium has a more profound influence over public opinion. So, nowhere should there be more conscientious responsibility exercised than by the news media.

Monday night a week ago, President Nixon delivered the most important address of his Administration, one of the most important of our decade. His subject was Vietnam. My hope, as his at that time, was to rally the American people to see the conflict through to a lasting and just peace in the Pacific. For 32 minutes, he reasoned with a nation that has suffered almost a third of a million casualties in the longest war in its history.

When the President completed his address—an address, incidentally, that he spent weeks in the preparation of—his words and policies were subjected to instant analysis and querulous criticism. The audience of 70 million Americans was inherited by a small band of network commentators and self-appointed analysts, the majority of whom expressed in one way or another their hostility to what he had to say.

It was obvious that their minds were made up in advance. Those who recall the fumbling and groping that followed President Johnson's dramatic disclosure of his intention not to seek another term have seen these men in a genuine state of nonpreparedness. This was not it.

One commentator twice contradicted the President's statement about the exchange of correspondence with Ho Chi Minh.[1] Another challenged the President's abilities as a politician. A third asserted that the President was following a Pentagon line. Others, by the expressions on their faces, the tone of their questions, and the sarcasm of their responses, made clear their sharp disapproval.

To guarantee in advance that the President's plea for national unity would be challenged, one network trotted out Averell Harriman for the occasion.

All in all, Mr. Harriman offered a broad range of gratuitous advice challenging and contradicting the policies outlined by the President of the United States. Where the President had issued a call for unity, Mr. Harriman was encouraging the country not to listen to him.

Now every American has a right to disagree with the President of the United States and to express publicly that disagreement. But the President of the United States has a right to communicate directly with the people who elected him, and the people of this country have the right to make up their own minds.

When Winston Churchill rallied public opinion to stay the course against Hitler's Germany, he didn't have to contend with a gaggle of commentators raising doubts about whether he was reading public opinion right, or whether Britain had the stamina to see the war through. When President Kennedy rallied the nation in the Cuban missile crisis, his address to the people was not chewed over by a roundtable of critics who disparaged the course of action he'd asked America to follow.

At least 40 million Americans every night, it's estimated, watch the network news. Seven million of them view ABC, the remainder being divided between NBC and CBS. According to Harris polls and other studies, for millions of Americans the networks are the sole source of national and world news.

Now how is this network news determined? A small group of anchormen, commentators, and executive producers settle upon the 20 minutes or so of film and commentary that's to reach the public. This selection is made from the 90 to 180 minutes that may be available. Their powers of choice are broad.

They decide what 40 to 50 million Americans will learn of the day's events in the nation and in the world. These men can create national issues overnight. They can make or break by their coverage and commentary a moratorium on the war. They can elevate men from obscurity to national prominence within a week. They can reward some politicians with national exposure and ignore others.

The views of the majority of this fraternity do *not*—and I repeat, not—represent the views of America. Not only did the country receive the President's speech more warmly than the networks, but so also did the Congress of the United States.

Yesterday, the President was notified that 300 individual Congressmen and 50 Senators of both parties had endorsed his efforts for peace. As with other American institutions, perhaps it is time that the networks were made more responsive to the views of the nation and more responsible to the people they serve.

---

[1] Ho Chi Minh—president of North Vietnam, the enemy of the U.S. in the Vietnam War

Write an essay in which you explain how Vice President Agnew builds an argument to persuade his audience of the inappropriate way in which network news covered a presidential address. In your essay, analyze how Agnew uses one or more of the listed features (or features of your own choice) to strengthen the logic and persuasiveness of his argument. Be sure that your analysis focuses on the most relevant features of the passage.

Your essay should not explain whether you agree with Agnew's claims, but rather explain how he builds an argument to persuade his audience.

PART FOUR

Review

CHAPTER 35

Putting It All Together

KAPLAN METHOD FOR MATH

Step 1: Read the question, identifying and organizing important information as you go

Step 2: Choose the best strategy to answer the question

Step 3: Check that you answered the *right* question

Step 1: Read the question, identifying and organizing important information as you go

- **What information am I given?** Take a few seconds to jot down the information you are given and try to group similar items together.

- **Separate the question from the context.** Word problems may include information that is unnecessary to solve the question. Feel free to discard any unnecessary information.

- **How are the answer choices different?** Reading answer choices carefully can help you spot the most efficient way to solve an SAT math question. If the answer choices are decimals, then painstakingly simplifying your final answer as a fraction is a waste of time; you can just use your calculator instead.

- **Should I label or draw a diagram?** If the question describes a shape or figure but doesn't provide one, sketch a diagram so you can see the shape or figure and add notes to it. If a figure is provided, take a few seconds to label it with information from the question.

Step 2: Choose the best strategy to answer the question

- **Look for patterns.** Every SAT math question can be solved in a variety of ways, but not all strategies are created equally. To finish all of the questions, you'll need to solve questions as *efficiently* as possible. If you find yourself about to do time-consuming math, take a minute to look for time-saving shortcuts.

- **Pick numbers or use straightforward math.** While you can always solve an SAT math question with what you've learned in school, doing so won't always be the fastest way. On questions that describe relationships between numbers (such as percentages) but don't actually use numbers, you can often save time on Test Day by using techniques such as Picking Numbers instead of straightforward math.

Step 3: Check that you answered the *right* question

- When you get the final answer, **resist the urge to immediately bubble in the answer.** Take a moment to:

  - Review the question stem
  - Check units of measurement
  - Double-check your work

- The SAT will often ask you for quantities such as $x + 1$ or the product of x and y. Be careful on these questions! They often include tempting answer choices that correspond to the values of x or y individually. There's no partial credit on the SAT, so take a moment at the end of every question to make sure you're answering the right question.

KAPLAN METHOD FOR MULTI-PART MATH QUESTIONS

Step 1: Read the first part of the question, looking for clues

Step 2: Identify and organize the information you need

Step 3: Based on what you know, plan your steps to navigate the first part

Step 4: Solve, step-by-step, checking units as you go

Step 5: Did I answer the *right* question?

Step 6: Repeat for remaining questions, incorporating results from the previous parts

Step 1: Read the first part of the question, looking for clues

- **Focus all your energy here** instead of diluting it over the whole question; solving a Multi-Part Math question in pieces is far simpler. Further, you may need the results from earlier parts to solve subsequent ones. Don't even consider the later parts of the question until you've solved the first part.

- **Watch for hints** about what you'll need to use or how to solve. Underlining key quantities is often helpful to separate what you need from extraneous prose.

Step 2: Identify and organize the information you need

- **What information am I given?** Jot down key notes, and group related quantities to develop your strategy.

- **What am I solving for?** This is your target. As you work your way through subsequent steps, keep your target at the front of your mind. This will help you avoid unnecessary work (and subsequent time loss). You'll sometimes need to tackle these problems from both ends, so always keep your goal in mind.

Step 3: Based on what you know, plan your steps to navigate the first part

- **What pieces am I missing?** Many students become frustrated when faced with a roadblock such as missing information, but it's an easy fix. Sometimes you'll need to do an intermediate calculation to elucidate the missing piece or pieces of the puzzle.

Step 4: Solve, step-by-step, checking units as you go

- **Work quickly but carefully,** just as you've done on other SAT math questions.

Step 5: Did I answer the *right* question?

- As is the case with the Kaplan Method for Math, **make sure your final answer is the requested answer**.
- Review the first part of the question.
- Double-check your units and your work.

Step 6: Repeat for remaining questions, incorporating results from the previous parts

Now take your results from the first part and think critically about how they fit into the subsequent parts. Previous results won't always be applicable, but when they are, they often lead to huge time savings.

KAPLAN METHOD FOR READING COMPREHENSION

Step 1: Read actively

Step 2: Examine the question stem

Step 3: Predict and answer

Step 1: Read actively

Active reading means:
- Ask questions and take notes *as* you read the passage. Asking questions about the passage and taking notes is an integral part of your approach to acing the SAT Reading Test.

Some of the questions you might want to ask are:
- Why did the author write this word/detail/sentence/paragraph?
- Is the author taking a side? If so, what side is he or she taking?
- What are the tone and purpose of the passage?

Make sure you remember to:
- Identify the passage type.
- Take notes, circle keywords, and underline key phrases.

Step 2: Examine the question stem

This means you should:
- Identify keywords and line references in the question stem.
- Apply question-type strategies as necessary.

Step 3: Predict and answer

This means you should:
- Predict an answer before looking at the answer choices, also known as "predict before you peek."
- Select the best match.

Predicting before you peek helps you:
- Eliminate the possibility of falling into wrong answer traps.

THE KAPLAN METHOD FOR INFOGRAPHICS

Step 1: Read the question
Step 2: Examine the infographic
Step 3: Predict and answer

Step 1: Read the question

- Assess the question stem for information that will help you zero in on the specific parts of the infographic that apply to the question.

Step 2: Examine the infographic

- Circle parts of the infographic that relate directly to the question.
- Identify units of measurement, labels, and titles.

Step 3: Predict and answer

- Do not look at the answer choices until you've used the infographic to make a prediction.

KAPLAN METHOD FOR WRITING & LANGUAGE

Step 1: Read the passage and identify the issue

- If there's an infographic, apply the Kaplan Method for Infographics

Step 2: Eliminate answer choices that do not address the issue
Step 3: Plug in the remaining answer choices and select the most correct, concise, and relevant one

Step 1: Read the passage and identify the issue

This means:
- Rather than reading the whole passage and then answering all of the questions, you can answer questions as you read because they are mostly embedded in the text itself.
- When you see a number, stop reading and look at the question. If you can answer it with what you've read so far, do so. If you need more information, keep reading for context until you can answer the question.

Step 2: Eliminate answer choices that do not address the issue

Eliminating answer choices that do not address the issue:
- Increases your odds of getting the correct answer by removing obviously incorrect answer choices

Step 3: Plug in the remaining answer choices and select the most correct, concise, and relevant one

Correct, concise, and relevant means that the answer choice you select:
- Makes sense when read with the correction
- Is as short as possible while retaining the information in the text
- Relates well to the passage overall

Answer choices should not:
- Change the intended meaning of the original sentence, paragraph, or passage
- Introduce new grammatical errors, even if the answer choice in question resolves the initial issue in the passage

KAPLAN METHOD FOR THE SAT ESSAY

Step 1: Read the source text, taking notes on how the author uses:
- Evidence to support claims
- Reasoning to develop ideas and to connect claims and evidence
- Stylistic or persuasive elements to add power to the ideas expressed

Step 2: Develop an outline of the features you will analyze in your response
Step 3: Write your essay
Step 4: Check your essay for mistakes in grammar, spelling, and clarity

Step 1: Read the source text, taking notes on how the author uses:

- **Evidence to support claims**
- **Reasoning to develop ideas and to connect claims and evidence**
- **Stylistic or persuasive elements to add power to the ideas expressed**

Your notes should focus on:

- Evidence to support claims (e.g., cited data or statistics, or authoritative sources that support the author's argument)

- Reasoning to develop ideas and make connections (e.g., the author explains his logic for using a specific piece of evidence to support a specific claim)

- Stylistic or persuasive elements to add power to the ideas expressed (e.g., using figurative language, irony, metaphor, and other elements to appeal to emotions)

In addition to taking notes in the margins of the passage, it is also helpful to underline and circle the following:

- central ideas

- important details

- errors of fact or interpretation

- textual evidence (quotations, paraphrases, or both)

You should spend approximately 10 minutes on Step 1.

Step 2: Develop an outline of the features you will analyze in your response

Creating an outline before you write your essay is a huge time-saver, which is essential when you have only 50 minutes to complete the SAT Essay Test. Spending the first part of the allotted time effectively (i.e., reading and taking notes on the source text and creating an outline) will lead to a well-organized, more convincing essay. You'll also find that organizing your thoughts ahead of time will enable you to write much more quickly!

You should spend approximately 8 minutes on Step 2.

Step 3: Write your essay

After you have read and analyzed the source text, your next goal is to write a cohesive essay that demonstrates your use and command of standard written English. To demonstrate your proficiency, you must:

- Provide your own precise central claim

- Use a variety of sentence structures

- Employ precise word choice

- Maintain a constant and appropriate style and tone

You should spend approximately 30 minutes on Step 3.

Step 4: Check your essay for mistakes in grammar, spelling, and clarity

While a few grammar and spelling mistakes won't drastically harm your SAT Essay score, setting aside some time to proofread can help you catch careless errors that you can easily correct, thereby increasing your Writing score on the SAT Essay.

You should spend the remaining 2 minutes on Step 4.

KAPLAN STRATEGY FOR TRANSLATING ENGLISH INTO MATH

- Define any variables, choosing letters that make sense
- Break sentences into short phrases
- Translate each phrase into a mathematical expression
- Put the expressions together to form an equation

KAPLAN STRATEGY FOR COMMAND OF EVIDENCE QUESTIONS

- When you see a question asking you to choose the best evidence to support your answer to the previous question, review how you selected that answer
- Avoid answers that provide evidence for incorrect answers to the previous question
- The correct answer will support why the previous question's answer is correct

KAPLAN STRATEGY FOR VOCAB-IN-CONTEXT QUESTIONS

- Pretend the word is a blank in the sentence
- Predict what word could be substituted for the blank
- Select the answer choice that best matches your prediction

KAPLAN STRATEGY FOR PAIRED PASSAGES

- Read Passage 1, then answer its questions
- Read Passage 2, then answer its questions
- Answer questions about both passages

SAT READING TEST PRACTICE

Questions 1-11 are based on the following passage and supplementary material.

The following passage discusses the interactions between sickle cell disease and malaria and their implications.

Sickle cell disease affects millions of people throughout the world, and it affects about 1 in 500 African Americans. It is the most common inherited
Line blood disorder in America. The disease causes severe
5 illness and shortens a person's life span if not treated. However, it is much more common than other disorders because it also has a surprising helpful side effect.

Sickle cell disease is caused by a small mutation in
10 a gene that carries the instructions to make hemo-globin, the protein in red blood cells that helps carry oxygen. Hemoglobin, like all proteins, is made from amino acids strung together like a chain in a certain sequence. The gene's instructions indicate which
15 amino acids to include and their sequence in the hemoglobin chain. The mutation in the gene changes the instructions and substitutes a different amino acid at one point in the sequence, thereby changing the properties of the hemoglobin protein. The hemo-
20 globin then tends to stick together and form long, thin structures. The structures grow long enough to push the red blood cell out of shape, forming a curved sickle-like shape that gives the disease its name.
25 The sickle-shaped red blood cells wear out faster than normal red blood cells, so a person with the disease often has a low red blood cell count. With fewer red blood cells, that person does not get enough oxygen in the blood, causing weakness and exhaus-
30 tion. The cells also tend to get stuck in the smaller blood vessels, causing pain and tissue damage.

We each receive two copies of the hemoglobin gene, one from each parent. A person with sickle cell disease receives the sickle cell gene from both
35 parents and consequently produces no normal

hemoglobin. A person who receives only one sickle cell gene will produce both normal and abnormal hemoglobin. This person will not have sickle cell disease but will carry the gene for it. Red blood cells
40 in people who carry the gene do not normally form the sickle shape. Carriers turn out to have an unusual advantage over people who have two normal copies of the gene: they are better able to survive malaria.

Malaria is a disease caused by a parasite that
45 invades red blood cells. It can be deadly, especially in young children. People who survive malaria infections gain a certain amount of immunity against future infections. After a few infections, their immune system is able to recognize and
50 destroy the parasites. When a parasite invades a red blood cell of a carrier, the cell forms the sickle shape. Since the sickle-shaped cells wear out rapidly, the parasite is destroyed with the cell soon after invading. The immune system removes the
55 worn out cells and recognizes the parasite, so it starts to attack the parasite even before it invades the red blood cells. The carrier is then more likely to survive the infection and also gains resistance to future infections.
60 It is therefore not surprising that the gene for sickle cell anemia is found mainly in people whose ancestors come from parts of the world in which malaria is common. People living in these areas have an increased chance of survival if they are carriers
65 of the sickle cell gene and so are more likely to live long enough to pass the gene on to their children. Therefore, although people with two copies of the gene were likely to die of the disease before they could pass it on, the gene still became common
70 because of the benefit to the carriers. Because modern medicine has treatments for both malaria and sickle cell disease, neither disease is as dangerous as it once was. Scientists hope to wipe out malaria in the future. The gene for sickle cell disease, however,
75 being a part of the human gene pool, will persist.

Malaria Parasites in Blood of Children Living in a High-Malaria Area

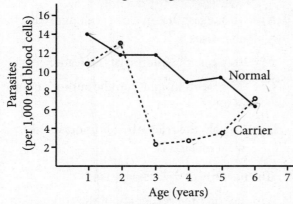

Adapted from Lucio Luzzatto, "Sickle Cell Anemia and Malaria."

1. The central idea of the passage is that sickle cell disease and malaria are

   A) both serious conditions that are untreatable.

   B) likely to be wiped out in the future.

   C) related in an unexpected way.

   D) similar to one another in the way they develop.

2. The passage most strongly suggests that which of the following is true?

   A) Malaria is often the result of poor nutrition.

   B) Sickle cell disease can be caught through exposure to it.

   C) Malaria is found in the southern states of the United States.

   D) Sickle cell disease is a major threat for African Americans.

3. Which choice provides the best evidence for the answer to the previous question?

   A) Lines 1-3 ("Sickle cell ... African Americans")

   B) Lines 9-12 ("Sickle cell ... carry oxygen")

   C) Lines 25-27 ("The sickle-shaped red ... cell count")

   D) Lines 44-46 ("Malaria ... young children")

4. As used in line 9, "mutation" most nearly means

   A) failure.

   B) change.

   C) structure.

   D) process.

5. According to the passage, which of the following is most likely true?

   A) It is better to have one sickle cell gene than to have two.

   B) It is difficult to understand the relationship between sickle cell disease and malaria.

   C) People who suffer from malaria are also sickle cell gene carriers.

   D) People who have sickle cell disease have higher rates of malaria.

6. Which choice provides the best evidence for the answer to the previous question?

   A) Lines 6-8 ("However, it is ... side effect")

   B) Lines 21-24 ("The structures ... its name")

   C) Lines 38-41 ("This person ... sickle shape")

   D) Lines 36-39 ("A person ... gene for it")

7. Which claim in the passage is supported by the graphic?

    A) Children are more likely to develop malaria than adults are.

    B) Carriers of the sickle cell gene are prone to getting other diseases.

    C) Children should receive treatment for sickle cell disease as early as three years old.

    D) Carriers of the sickle cell gene are less likely to get malaria.

8. As used in line 75, "pool" most nearly means

    A) puddle.

    B) lake.

    C) group.

    D) team.

9. According to the passage, why do people with sickle cell disease often have a low red blood cell count?

    A) They are more easily exposed to the malaria parasite.

    B) They have two copies of the hemoglobin gene.

    C) Sickle cell blood cells are inherited from parents.

    D) Sickle cell blood cells wear out faster than normal red blood cells.

10. Why does the author use the word "surprising" in line 7?

    A) To suggest that malaria is an unpredictable disease

    B) To pique the interest of the reader

    C) To give an insight into the author's point of view

    D) To help the reader better understand what malaria is

11. The purpose of this passage is to

    A) instruct the reader about the connection between sickle cell disease and malaria.

    B) explain how red blood cells are affected by sickle cell disease.

    C) show that malaria and sickle cell disease are usually diagnosed easily.

    D) discuss the differences in treatment for sickle cell disease and malaria.ment for sickle cell disease and malaria.

SAT MATH TEST PRACTICE

$$\frac{3(n-2)+5}{4} = \frac{11-(7-n)}{6}$$

1. In the equation above, what is the value of n?

   A) $-\dfrac{1}{11}$

   B) $\dfrac{5}{11}$

   C) 1

   D) $\dfrac{11}{7}$

2. A cell phone tower has a safety light to warn airplanes of its location. It blinks once every 3.5 seconds. If $f(m)$ is the number of times the light blinks over the course of m minutes, which of the following equations defines f?

   A) $f(m) = 2.5m$

   B) $f(m) = \dfrac{3.5m}{60}$

   C) $f(m) = \dfrac{60m}{3.5}$

   D) $f(m) = 210m$

3. A school is hosting a teacher's professional development luncheon. Attending teachers can choose one of two different meals: a veggie burger or a roast beef sandwich. The catering company charges $4.50 per veggie burger and $6.25 per roast beef sandwich. If 56 teachers ordered lunch and the school's total bill was $308, which of the following systems of equations could be used to find the number of teachers who ordered a veggie burger, v, and the number who ordered a roast beef sandwich, r?

   A) $\begin{cases} v+r=308 \\ 4.5v+6.25r=56 \end{cases}$

   B) $\begin{cases} v+r=56 \\ 4.5v+6.25r=308 \end{cases}$

   C) $\begin{cases} v+r=56 \\ 4.5v+6.25r=\dfrac{308}{2} \end{cases}$

   D) $\begin{cases} 2(v+r)=56 \\ 4.5v+6.25r=308 \end{cases}$

4. A store is running a sale, discounting merchandise by a specific percentage. Margo purchases a coffee maker with an original price of $62.00. After the sale discount, she gets an additional 10% off for using her store credit card. She ends up paying $41.85, not including tax. What was the amount of the original sale discount?

   A) 15%

   B) 22.5%

   C) 25%

   D) 32.5%

5. If $f(x) = x^2 + \dfrac{5}{2}$ and $g(x) = \dfrac{x}{4} - 1$, what is the value of $(f \cdot g)(6)$

   A) 2.75

   B) 3

   C) 3.5

   D) 8.625

6. Which of the following are the roots of the equation $x^2 + 4x + 7 = 0$?

   A) $-4 \pm i\sqrt{3}$

   B) $-4 \pm \sqrt{3}$

   C) $-2 \pm i\sqrt{3}$

   D) $-2 \pm 2i\sqrt{3}$

7. For how many distinct values of x is the expression $\dfrac{x-3}{(x+1)(x^2-9)}$ undefined?

   A) 1

   B) 2

   C) 3

   D) 4

8. The area of the triangle shown above is given by the expression $3x^2 - 5x - 12$. Which of the following expressions is equivalent to h?

   A) $x - 3$

   B) $2x - 6$

   C) $4x - 6$

   D) $4x - 12$

	Laptops	Tablets	Smartphones	Total
In-Store Fix	21	17	9	47
Further Analysis	35	29	14	78
Send Off for Repair	16	12	5	33
Total	72	58	28	158

9. An electronics store offers repairs on its electronic devices, such as laptops and tablets. Customers bring in their devices, and a technician does one of the following: an immediate, in-store fix; sets it aside for further analysis; or sends it off to the store's repair center. The table above shows the store's actions on all items for the month of January. What fraction of laptops and tablets did the store's technician send off for repair?

   A) $\dfrac{33}{158}$

   B) $\dfrac{14}{79}$

   C) $\dfrac{14}{65}$

   D) $\dfrac{65}{79}$

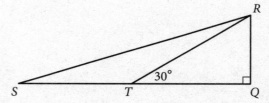

10. In the figure above, the length of $\overline{QR}$ is 4, and T is the midpoint of $\overline{QS}$. What is the length of $\overline{RS}$?

    A) 4

    B) $2\sqrt{3}$

    C) $2\sqrt{13}$

    D) $4\sqrt{13}$

SAT WRITING & LANGUAGE TEST PRACTICE

Questions 1-11 are based on the following passage.

Murals: The Large-Scale Paintings Remain Symbols of Hope

[1] A mural is a painting done on a wall or ceiling in such a way that it becomes a part of the architecture of the building on which it is painted. Murals are distinct from all other types of pictorial art, or art in which the artist **2** attempts to create a picture of something. The addition of a mural to a building renders the artwork three-dimensional. Murals are still as popular an art form as they were in ancient civilizations, although the techniques for painting them have evolved over time.

Cave paintings are considered the **3** worlds first murals. The earliest prehistoric examples can be found in caves throughout France and Spain, where the paintings show several different species of animals depicted on the walls. Like most early cave paintings, humans were not

1. Which sentence should be added to the beginning of paragraph 1 to best state the passage's central idea?

   A) Murals are often referred to as the "art of the common man," as they were used exclusively in public places.

   B) A once-ignored art form, murals have recently found a home in many buildings and monuments around the world.

   C) Murals have changed over time, but one thing has remained the same—the inclusion of human figures accomplishing great feats.

   D) Murals have been used across civilizations and centuries to share ideas and messages with the masses in an artistic manner.

2. A) NO CHANGE
   B) attempt
   C) are attempting
   D) have attempted

3. A) NO CHANGE
   B) world is
   C) worlds'
   D) world's

④ entailed in these paintings. Artists preferred to use the medium to present things surrounding them. This is still common today.

Murals were also the artwork of choice ⑤ in ancient classical civilizations such as Ancient Egypt. Murals were painted on the inside of tombs in Egypt, depicting the life of the entombed. Ancient ⑥ Romans nearly used murals on the walls of all of their buildings, and remnants of these murals can be seen in ⑦ towns, like Pompeii and Ostia in Italy. The Romans used murals to decorate the insides of their buildings, depicting columns and landscaped patios as a way of artificially opening the interiors of their homes and public houses. Murals remained a popular art form through the Renaissance as well as the Baroque period.

[1] In the times of the ancient Greeks and Romans, color pigments were mixed into hot beeswax and applied to walls or ceilings while the color mixture was still hot. [2] This was called encaustic painting. [3] It was not until the 16th century that oil paints were used for murals, though this proved problematic as oil paints ⑧ decline easily under

4. A) NO CHANGE
    B) patronized
    C) depicted
    D) transposed

5. A) NO CHANGE
    B) in the classical civilization
    C) prior to classical civilizations
    D) in classical civilizations

6. A) NO CHANGE
    B) Romans used murals on the walls of nearly all their buildings
    C) Romans used murals on the walls of all their buildings nearly
    D) Romans used murals nearly on the walls of all their buildings

7. A) NO CHANGE
    B) towns like Pompeii and Ostia in Italy
    C) towns, like Pompeii and Ostia, in Italy
    D) towns—like Pompeii and Ostia in Italy

8. A) NO CHANGE
    B) provoke
    C) deteriorate
    D) permeate

certain conditions. [4] In other areas, egg yolks or egg whites were used instead of beeswax in a technique called tempera painting. **9**

The uses of murals have also evolved over time. Murals were once used as educational tools, **10** painting on church walls to educate illiterate attendees. This form of visual art remains an important form of communication, and is sometimes used for political purposes, drawing attention to social issues or supporting various ideals. In Mexico, murals were painted to give hope to those in downtrodden communities after the Mexican Revolution. The common thread seems to be that murals serve to bring people together, offering a common message that all community members can understand and support. **11**

9. For the sake of cohesion of this paragraph, sentence 4 should be placed

A) where it is now.

B) before sentence 1.

C) before sentence 2.

D) after sentence 2.

10. A) NO CHANGE

B) painted

C) paint

D) paints

11. Which of these details would best support the author's claims in this paragraph?

A) The rate of decline in the use of murals to spread political ideas

B) An instance of a politician opposing the use of murals in public spaces

C) The names of artists who created murals in Mexico during the revolution

D) A specific example of a church wall mural that helped educate the masses

COUNTDOWN TO TEST DAY

The Week Before the Test

- Finish up any required homework assignments, including online quizzes.

- Focus your additional practice on the question types and/or subject areas in which you usually score highest. Now is the time to sharpen up your best skills, not cram new information.

- Make sure you are registered for the test. Remember, Kaplan cannot register you. If you missed the registration deadlines, you can request Waitlist Status on the test maker's website, collegeboard.org.

- Confirm the location of your test site. Never been there before? Make a practice run to make sure you know exactly how long it will take to get from your home to your test site. Build in extra time in case you hit traffic on the morning of the test.

- Get a great night's sleep the two days before the test.

The Day Before the Test

- Review the Kaplan Methods and Strategies, as well as the ReKap pages.

- Put new batteries in your calculator.

- Pack your backpack or bag for Test Day with the following items:
  - Photo ID
  - Registration slip or printout
  - Directions to your test site location
  - Five or more sharpened no. 2 pencils (no mechanical pencils)
  - Pencil sharpener
  - Eraser
  - Calculator
  - Extra batteries
  - Non-prohibited timepiece
  - Tissues
  - Prepackaged snacks, like granola bars
  - Bottled water, juice, or sports drink
  - Sweatshirt, sweater, or jacket

Night Before the Test

- No studying!

- Do something relaxing that will take your mind off the test, like watching a movie or playing video games with friends.

- Set your alarm to wake up early enough so that you won't feel rushed.

- Go to bed early, but not too much earlier than you usually do. You want to fall asleep quickly, not spend hours tossing and turning.

Morning of the Test

- Dress comfortably and in layers. You need to be prepared for any temperature.
- Eat a filling breakfast, but don't stray too far from your usual routine. If you normally aren't a breakfast eater, don't eat a huge meal, but make sure you have something substantial.
- Read something over breakfast. You need to warm up your brain so you don't go into the test cold. Read a few pages of a newspaper, magazine, or novel.
- Get to your test site early. There is likely to be some confusion about where to go and how to sign in, so allow yourself plenty of time, even if you are taking the test at your own school.
- Leave your cell phone at home or in your car's glovebox. Many test sites do not allow them in the building.
- While you're waiting to sign in or be seated, read more of what you read over breakfast to stay in reading mode.

During the Test

- Be calm and confident. You're ready for this!
- Remember that while the SAT is a three-hour marathon (or four if you opt to do the essay), it is also a series of shorter sections. Focus on the section you're working on at that moment; don't think about previous or upcoming sections.
- Use the Kaplan Methods and Strategies as often as you can.
- Don't linger too long on any one question. Mark it and come back to it later.
- Can't figure out an answer? Try to eliminate some choices and guess strategically. Remember, there is no penalty for a wrong answer, so even if you can't eliminate any choices, you should take a guess.
- There will be plenty of questions you CAN answer, so spend your time on those first!
- Maintain good posture throughout the test. It will help you stay alert.
- If you find yourself losing concentration, getting frustrated, or stressing about the time, stop for 30 seconds. Close your eyes, put your pencil down, take a few deep breaths, and relax your shoulders. You'll be much more productive after taking a few moments to relax.
- Use your breaks effectively. During the five-minute breaks, go to the restroom, eat your snacks, and get your energy up for the next section.

After the Test

- Congratulate yourself! Also, reward yourself by doing something fun. You've earned it.
- If you got sick during the test or if something else happened that might have negatively affected your score, you can cancel your scores by the Wednesday following your test date.

Request a score cancellation form from your test proctor, or visit the test maker's website for more information. If you have questions about whether you should cancel your scores, call 1-800-KAP-TEST.

- Your scores will be available online approximately three to four weeks after your test and will be mailed to you in approximately six weeks.

- Email your instructor or tutor with your SAT scores. We want to hear how you did!

PART FIVE

Answers & Explanations

CHAPTER 2

PREPARE

1. D
Difficulty: Medium

Category: Heart of Algebra / Linear Equations

Strategic Advice: Simplify as much as possible, then isolate the variable.

Getting to the Answer: Begin by combining like terms on both sides of the equation. Once complete, solve for z.

$$\frac{4+z-(3+2z)}{6}=\frac{-z-3(5-2)}{7}$$

$$\frac{1-z}{6}=\frac{-z-9}{7}$$

$$7-7z=-6z-54$$

$$-z=-61$$

$$z=61$$

(D) is correct.

2. B
Difficulty: Easy

Category: Heart of Algebra / Linear Equations

Strategic Advice: Straightforward math works well on simple equations like this one.

Getting to the Answer: Combine like terms, then solve for y.

$$3y+2y-4=-25$$

$$5y-4=-25$$

$$5y=-21$$

$$y=-\frac{21}{5}$$

Choice (B) is correct.

3. C
Difficulty: Easy

Category: Heart of Algebra / Linear Equations

Strategic Advice: Before choosing the "cannot be determined" option, check to see if the y terms will cancel.

Getting to the Answer: Divide both sides by 3, then combine like terms. The y terms will drop out, leaving one equation with one variable. Once there, solve for x as usual.

$$3(y-8)+3(6x+2)=24+3y$$

$$y-8+6x+2=8+y$$

$$-8+6x+2=8$$

$$-6+6x=8$$

$$6x=14$$

$$x=\frac{14}{6}=2.33$$

Your answers are in decimal form, so don't waste time trying to reduce $\frac{14}{6}$; just plug it into your calculator. (C) is the correct answer.

4. A
Difficulty: Medium

Category: Heart of Algebra / Linear Equations

Strategic Advice: Wordy questions call for the Kaplan Strategy for Translating English into Math.

Getting to the Answer: Use the route labels for your variables, then break off phrases from the question stem for translation into math. "Route A is 1.5 times longer than Route B" becomes $A=1.5B$, and "[Route A is] $\frac{3}{4}$ the length of Route C" becomes $A=\frac{3}{4}C$. You're told C is 3 km, so plug this into the second equation to solve for A; you'll find $A=\frac{9}{4}=2.25$ km.

Plug this value into the first equation to get B: $2.25 = 1.5B \rightarrow B = \dfrac{2.25}{1.5} = 1.5$ km. But you're not done yet! Subtract B from A to get your answer, 0.75 km, which matches (A).

5. B

Difficulty: Medium

Category: Heart of Algebra / Linear Equations

Strategic Advice: No real math acrobatics here, but the Kaplan Method for Math will still prove useful.

Getting to the Answer: You're asked to identify the line that the one described in the question stem will never intersect. Lines that never intersect are parallel and therefore have identical slopes, so start by finding the slope of the line whose two coordinate pairs are given. You'll find $m = \dfrac{1 - 0}{0 - (-\frac{2}{5})} = \dfrac{1}{\frac{2}{5}} = \dfrac{5}{2}$;

C and D have negative slopes, so eliminate them. Next, find the slopes of A and B. No need to use the slope formula; counting units on the graphs will be faster. The slope of A is $\dfrac{2}{5}$, and the slope of B is $\dfrac{5}{2}$. Therefore, (B) is correct.

6. A

Difficulty: Easy

Category: Heart of Algebra / Linear Equations

Strategic Advice: Don't get bogged down by the prose; zero in on what you need to answer the question posed.

Getting to the Answer: The last two sentences of the question stem are all you need to answer this; you need the equation of the line shown. Start by finding the slope of the line by picking a pair of points, such as $(40, 0)$ and $(65, 100)$: $m = \dfrac{100 - 0}{65 - 40} = \dfrac{100}{25} = 4$.

B and C have slopes other than 4, so eliminate them. A and D have y-intercepts of –160 and 40, respectively. According to the graph, 40 cannot be the y-intercept because the line does not intersect the y-axis at 40. Therefore, the answer must be (A).

7. C

Difficulty: Medium

Category: Heart of Algebra / Linear Equations

Strategic Advice: Think carefully about the general importance of the slope of a line.

Getting to the Answer: A line's slope is always a rate of change of some sort, so you can eliminate B and D. Now turn to A and C; the way they describe the relationship between exam performance and time spent on the exam is different. The graph indicates time spent on the exam is the independent variable, so exam performance depends on it. The only choice that correctly describes this relationship is (C).

PRACTICE

8. D

Difficulty: Hard

Category: Heart of Algebra / Linear Equations

Strategic Advice: Mind the order in which the changes to the graph occur.

Getting to the Answer: The question states that the downward shift of 2 units occurs first, making the new y-intercept $-\dfrac{3}{2}$. A reflection over the x-axis follows, which changes the y-intercept to $\dfrac{3}{2}$ and makes the slope $\dfrac{7}{4}$. The only graph that correctly depicts these changes is (D). Beware C; this results from a reflection over the *y*-axis, not the *x*-axis. The graphs below visualize each change.

1)

2)

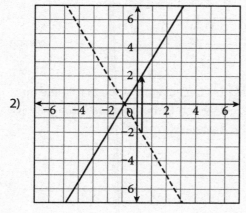

9. C
Difficulty: Medium

Category: Heart of Algebra / Linear Equations

Strategic Advice: Look closely; buried in the text are two sets of coordinates you can use.

Getting to the Answer: The question states that admission was $2 when the admission charge was first implemented and increased to $2.50 after 3 years, making your coordinates (0, 2) and (3, 2.5). The slope of the line passing through these is $m = \dfrac{2.5 - 2}{3 - 0} = \dfrac{0.5}{3} = \dfrac{1}{6}$. Eliminate A and D. Because the admission fee started at $2, 2 is the *y*-intercept, so the full equation is $y = \dfrac{c}{6} + 2$. (C) is correct.

Because the question says "three years ago," it's tempting to use (–3, 2) and (0, 2.5) as your coordinates. Think about what that would mean: The first admission charge would be $2.50, as it's impossible to have a negative year. This contradicts the question stem, so B is incorrect.

PERFORM

10. A
Difficulty: Easy

Category: Heart of Algebra / Linear Equations

Strategic Advice: Think about what happens to the slope of a line if you're merely moving the line around the coordinate plane.

Getting to the Answer: Any shift of a line, whether it's up, down, left, right, or some combination thereof, will never change the line's slope. The slope will remain –5, which is (A).

11. 36
Difficulty: Medium

Category: Heart of Algebra / Linear Equations

Strategic Advice: That you're asked to find an expression rather than a variable value means there's likely a shortcut.

Getting to the Answer: Start by eliminating the fractions. A common multiple of 4 and 3 is 12, so multiply both sides of the equation by that. Once the fractions are gone, manipulate the equation until you have $2c + \dfrac{9}{2}y$ isolated.

$$12\left(\frac{3}{4}y = 6 - \frac{1}{3}c\right)$$
$$9y = 72 - 4c$$
$$4c + 9y = 72$$
$$2c + \frac{9}{2}y = 36$$

Grid in 36, the correct answer.

12. A

Difficulty: Hard

Category: Heart of Algebra / Linear Equations

Strategic Advice: Don't panic over the presence of m. Just solve for y, then think about what kind of graph it can have.

Getting to the Answer: Start by distributing m on the right, then move all terms to the left.

$$x - y = m(2x + y)$$
$$x - y = 2mx + my$$
$$x - 2mx - y - my = 0$$

Continue by factoring out x and y, then move any terms without y back to the right.

$$x(1 - 2m) + y(-1 - m) = 0$$
$$y(-1 - m) = -x(1 - 2m)$$

Divide by $(-1-m)$, then factor out -1 from the denominator and cancel.

$$y = \frac{-x(1-2m)}{(-1-m)} = \frac{-x(1-2m)}{-(1+m)} = \frac{x(1-2m)}{(1+m)}$$

Don't worry about how messy the right side looks yet; for now, you just need to realize that it's merely x multiplied by a complicated coefficient. Because the equation is now solved for y, you have an equation of a line: the big coefficient is the slope, and because there's no added (or subtracted) constant, the y-intercept is 0. You can eliminate B (not a line) and D ($b \neq 0$) based on this.

Examine the remaining choices more closely: They only differ in slope sign. To determine which is correct, pick a value for m between 0 and $\frac{1}{2}$ (but not 0 or $\frac{1}{2}$ themselves), and plug it into the slope expression. If $k = \frac{1}{4}$, for instance, then the slope would be $\frac{(1 - 2 \times \frac{1}{4})}{(1 + \frac{1}{4})} = \frac{(1 - \frac{1}{2})}{\frac{5}{4}} = \frac{1}{2} \times \frac{4}{5} = \frac{2}{5}$, which

is a positive value. Because the slope of this line must be positive, (A), which is the only remaining choice with a positive slope, is correct.

EXTRA PRACTICE

1. C
Difficulty: Easy

Category: Heart of Algebra / Linear Equations

Strategic Advice: Look at the variables in each equation. When written in exponent form (no radicals and no variables in the denominator of a fraction), in which equation would all the exponents be 1?

Getting to the Answer: You can eliminate D right away because the exponent on x is 2. When written in exponent form, the other equations look like:

Choice A: $y = 3x^{-1}$ (not linear because of the -1 power)

Choice B: $x^{\frac{1}{2}} + y = 0$ (not linear because of the $\frac{1}{2}$ power)

Choice (C): $\frac{1}{2}x - \frac{5}{8}y = 11$ (linear)

2. B
Difficulty: Easy

Category: Heart of Algebra / Linear Equations

Strategic Advice: For the equations, look at the exponents on the variables. Are they all 1? For the table, check to see if the change in the y-values compared to the change in the x-values is constant for each pair of values.

Getting to the Answer: The table in (B) does not represent a linear relationship because the x-values change by +4 each time, while the y-values change by -10 then -8 then $+8$ then $+10$. A linear relationship has a constant rate of change, which means it is either always increasing or always decreasing, and by the same amount. This data clearly changes direction and is therefore not linear, so (B) is correct.

3. A
Difficulty: Easy

Category: Heart of Algebra / Linear Equations

Strategic Advice: Write the equation in words first and then translate from English into math.

Getting to the Answer: The total cost, c, is the weight of the potatoes in pounds, p, multiplied by the sale price because the purchase is made on Friday: $\$0.90 \times (100 - 30)\% = 0.9 \times 0.7 = 0.63$. This gives the first part of the expression: $0.63p$. Now, add the cost of two cantaloupes, $3.50 \times 2 = 7$, to get the equation $c = 0.63p + 7$, which is (A).

You could also Pick Numbers to answer this question—pick a number for the weight of the potatoes and calculate how much they would cost (on sale) and add the cost of two cantaloupes. Then find the equation that gives the same amount when you substitute the number you picked.

4. C
Difficulty: Easy

Category: Heart of Algebra / Linear Equations

Strategic Advice: The total cost of the two kinds of items is the cost of the paintbrushes multiplied by the number purchased plus the cost of the canvases multiplied by the number purchased. Because a canvas cost "6 times" the cost of a paintbrush, a canvas costs $6(\$1.50) = \$9$.

Getting to the Answer:
Total cost of paintbrushes: $1.50 \times p$ or $1.5p$
Total cost of canvases: $9 \times c$ or $9c$
Sum of both: $9c + 1.5p$
Therefore, (C) is correct.

5. D

Difficulty: Easy

Category: Heart of Algebra / Linear Equations

Strategic Advice: Think about whether 0.004 is a constant in the equation or a coefficient that is multiplied by the independent variable.

Getting to the Answer: The total bill consists of a flat tax (the local impact fee) and some part (or percent) of the market value of the volume of gas extracted. The local impact fee is a one-time fee that does not depend on the amount of gas extracted and therefore should not be multiplied by v. This means that 50,000 is the local impact fee. The other expression in the equation, $0.004v$, represents the severance tax times the market value of the volume of gas extracted (which the question tells you is v). Therefore, 0.004 could represent the amount of the severance tax as a percentage (0.4%), which is (D).

6. C

Difficulty: Easy

Category: Heart of Algebra / Linear Equations

Strategic Advice: Try to picture in your head what "increase in property values starts to slow down" would look like. It doesn't say the values start to decrease, but rather that the increase is not as fast.

Getting to the Answer: An increasing line (one with a positive slope) indicates increasing property values. The steepness of the line (the actual *value* of the slope) indicates how fast the values are increasing. The second line segment in the graph (between $t = 8$ and $t = 16$) still shows a positive slope, but one that is less steep than the first segment, so the increase in property values starts to slow down at $t = 8$, which is the year $2014 + 8 = 2022$, (C).

7. B

Difficulty: Easy

Category: Heart of Algebra / Linear Equations

Strategic Advice: Read the axis labels carefully. The y-intercept is the point at which $x = 0$, which means the number of songs purchased is 0.

Getting to the Answer: The y-intercept is $(0, 20)$. This means the cost is $20 before buying any songs, and therefore most likely represents a flat membership fee for joining the service, which means (B) is correct.

8. D

Difficulty: Medium

Category: Heart of Algebra / Linear Equations

Strategic Advice: Let x be the number of surfboards Jon sells in a month. Write a linear equation that represents the scenario and then solve for x.

Getting to the Answer: Sales must equal expenses for the store to break even. Jon's sales are equal to the selling price ($120) times the number of surfboards he sells (x), so write $120x$ on one side of the equal sign. His monthly expenses are his fixed expenses ($3,600) plus the amount he paid for each surfboard ($80) times the number of surfboards (x), so write $3,600 + 80x$ on the other side of the equal sign. Then, solve for x.

$$120x = 3,600 + 80x$$
$$40x = 3,600$$
$$x = 90$$

Therefore, (D) is correct.

9. A

Difficulty: Medium

Category: Heart of Algebra / Linear Equations

Strategic Advice: This question has multiple fractions, so clear the $\frac{8}{5}$ by multiplying both sides of the equation by its reciprocal, $\frac{5}{8}$. Then, because the answers are given in decimal form, change the other fraction to a decimal by dividing the numerator by the denominator.

Getting to the Answer:

$$\frac{8}{5}\left(x+\frac{33}{12}\right)=16$$

$$\frac{5}{8}\cdot\left[\frac{8}{5}\left(x+\frac{33}{12}\right)\right]=\frac{5}{8}\cdot16$$

$$x+2.75=10$$

$$x=7.25$$

Choice (A) is correct.

10. D

Difficulty: Medium

Category: Heart of Algebra / Linear Equations

Strategic Advice: Take a quick peek at the answer choices. The equations are given in slope-intercept form, so start by finding the slope.

Getting to the Answer: Find the slope by substituting two pairs of values from the table (try to pick easy ones if possible) into the slope formula, $m=\frac{y_2-y_1}{x_2-x_1}$. Keep in mind that the projected number of pounds sold *depends* on the price, so the price is the independent variable (x) and the projected number is the dependent variable (y). Using the points (1.2, 15,000) and (2, 5,000), the slope is:

$$m=\frac{5{,}000-15{,}000}{2-1.20}$$

$$m=\frac{-10{,}000}{0.8}$$

$$m=-12{,}500$$

This means you can eliminate A and B because the slope is not correct. Don't let B fool you—the projected number of pounds sold goes *down* as the price goes *up*, so there is an inverse relationship, which means the slope must be negative. To choose between C and (D), you could find the *y*-intercept of the line, but this is a fairly time-intensive process. Instead, choose the easiest pair of values from the table, (2, 5,000), and substitute into C and (D) only. Choice (D) is correct because 5,000 = −12,500(2) + 30,000 is a true statement.

11. C

Difficulty: Medium

Category: Heart of Algebra / Linear Equations

Strategic Advice: It takes too much time to think about and then compare each answer choice to the scenario. Instead, figure out what each part of the equation most likely represents, and look for the answer choice that matches.

Getting to the Answer: Because the equation represents the balance if Henry deposits his paycheck for *x* weeks, then his paycheck amount must be multiplied by the number of weeks he works. The only two factors in the equation being multiplied are 360 and *x*, so 360 must be the amount of his paycheck. This means you can eliminate A and D. The other number in the equation, −126.13, is a constant, which represents a starting amount. Because the constant is negative, Henry must have had a negative balance in his account before setting up the direct deposit, which means he had overdrawn the account. Thus, (C) is correct.

12. B
Difficulty: Medium

Category: Heart of Algebra / Linear Equations

Strategic Advice: There is not a lot of information to go on here, so start by determining the relationship between the number given in the question, 54,000, and the number in the equation, 2,250.

Getting to the Answer: Because $54,000 \div 2,250 = 24$ and there are 24 hours in a day, 2,250 is the number of pages the press can print in 1 hour. If the press can print 2,250 in 1 hour, then it can print 2,250 times x in x hours. This means the function $f(x) = 2,250x$ represents the number of pages the press can print in x hours, which means (B) is correct.

13. A
Difficulty: Medium

Category: Heart of Algebra / Linear Equations

Strategic Advice: In this scenario, both the flat fee for serving the food and the per-person rate are likely to be fixed amounts (determined by the catering company), while the number of people attending Nadim's party is likely to be a variable amount.

Getting to the Answer: The total cost is the dependent variable and is calculated by multiplying the per person rate by the number of people attending and then adding the flat serving fee. So the total cost is represented by y. Because the flat serving fee and the per person rate are likely to be fixed amounts, they should be represented by numbers in the equations, 300 and 11, respectively. The total cost depends on the number of people attending, so the number of people is the independent variable and is most likely represented by x. Therefore, (A) is correct.

14. A
Difficulty: Medium

Category: Heart of Algebra / Linear Equations

Strategic Advice: A line with an undefined slope is a vertical line (a horizontal line has a slope of 0 because it is flat), so look for an equation that represents a vertical line.

Getting to the Answer: Start with the first equation. If $x = 3$ is the only thing you have to go on, choose a few points with an x-coordinate of 3, such as (3, 0), (3, 1), and (3, 2). Plot these points and draw a line through them to see that the graph is a vertical line and therefore has an undefined slope. There is no need to check the other equations. Choice (A) is correct.

15. C
Difficulty: Medium

Category: Heart of Algebra / Linear Equations

Strategic Advice: Use the graph to identify the y-intercept and the slope of the line, and then write an equation in slope-intercept form, $y = mx + b$. Once you have your equation, look for the answer choice that matches.

Getting to the Answer: The line crosses the y-axis at (0, −4) so the y-intercept (b) is −4. The line rises vertically 1 unit for every 3 units that it runs to the right, so the slope (m) is $\frac{1}{3}$. The equation of the line is $y = \frac{1}{3}x - 4$, which matches (C).

You could also graph each of the answer choices in your calculator to see which one matches the given graph, but this is not the most time-efficient strategy. You also have to be very careful when entering fractions—to graph (C), for example, you would enter $(1/3)x - 4$.

16. B

Difficulty: Medium

Category: Heart of Algebra / Linear Equations

Strategic Advice: Quickly scan the answer choices—they are written as inequalities, so you'll need to translate them into something that makes more sense to you. Use the fact that "< 0" means *negative* and "> 0" means *positive*.

Getting to the Answer: When a linear equation is written in the form $y = mx + b$, the variable m represents the slope of the line and b represents the y-intercept of the line. Look at the graph—the line is decreasing (going down from left to right), so the slope is negative ($m < 0$). This means you can eliminate C and D. Now look at the y-intercept—it is above the x-axis and is therefore positive ($b > 0$), which means (B) is correct.

17. A

Difficulty: Medium

Category: Heart of Algebra / Linear Equations

Strategic Advice: There are no axis labels or numbers on the graph, so quickly skim the answer choices to get the right context.

Getting to the Answer: Regardless of the scenario presented or the missing axis labels, the slope of the line tells you the answer. The line is decreasing from left to right, so it has a negative slope. This means there is an inverse relationship between the amount of algae and the number of fish. In other words, as one increases, the other must decrease, so (A) must be correct.

18. B

Difficulty: Medium

Category: Heart of Algebra / Linear Equations

Strategic Advice: You could find the unit rate by calculating the slope of the line using two of the points shown on the graph, but it may be quicker to simply read the answer from the graph.

Getting to the Answer: The x-axis represents the number of lightbulbs, so find 1 on the x-axis and trace up to where it meets the graph of the line. The y-value is somewhere between $1 and $2, so the only possible correct answer choice is $1.80.

Finding the slope should result in the same answer—the graph rises 9 units and runs 5 units from one point to the next, so the slope is $\frac{9}{5}$, or 1.80, which means (B) is correct.

19. C

Difficulty: Hard

Category: Heart of Algebra / Linear Equations

Strategic Advice: Let v represent the number of visits. The question asks when the two memberships will cost the same, so write an equation that sets the total membership costs equal to each other.

Getting to the Answer: The first membership type costs $325 for unlimited visits, so write 325 on one side of the equal sign. The second type costs $8 per visit (not including the first 5 visits), or $8(v - 5)$, plus a flat $125 enrollment fee, so write $8(v - 5) + 125$ on the other side of the equal sign. Use inverse operations to solve for v.

$$325 = 8(v - 5) + 125$$
$$325 = 8v - 40 + 125$$
$$240 = 8v$$
$$30 = v$$

Choice (C) is correct.

20. D

Difficulty: Hard

Category: Heart of Algebra / Linear Equations

Strategic Advice: When solving a linear equation that has no solution, the variable terms will cancel out and you will be left with a false statement that consists of two numbers that are not equal to each other.

Getting to the Answer: First, check to see if the variables cancel out. In A and B, they don't, so eliminate these choices. To decide between C and (D), check the constant after both sides of the equation have been simplified. If the constants are equal, then the equation has an infinite number of solutions (because a number is always equal to itself). If they are not equal, then the equation has no solution. Choice (D) is correct because:

$$6\left(\frac{2}{3}x+5\right)=4x+5$$
$$4x+30=4x+5$$
$$30\neq 5$$

21. D
Difficulty: Hard

Category: Heart of Algebra / Linear Equations

Strategic Advice: When solving a linear equation that has infinitely many solutions, the variable terms will cancel out leaving a number that is equal to itself (which is always true).

Getting to the Answer: Start by simplifying both sides of the equation using the distributive property.

$$2\left(x-\frac{5}{2}\right)=c\left(\frac{4}{5}x-2\right)$$
$$2x-5=\frac{4c}{5}x-2c$$

Because the constant terms must be equal, set $-5=-2c$ and solve for c to get $c=\frac{5}{2}$, which means (D) is correct.

If this were a Grid-in question, you could check your answer by setting the two variable terms equal to each other and solving for c—the result is the same.

22. B
Difficulty: Hard

Category: Heart of Algebra / Linear Equations

Strategic Advice: Do not automatically assume that an equation has *no solution* or *infinite solutions* just because those choices are given as possible answers. This question can be simplified quite a bit by clearing the fractions first. To do this, multiply both sides of the equation by the least common denominator, 12. Then solve for h using inverse operations.

Getting to the Answer:

$$\frac{1}{4}(10h)-\frac{3}{2}(h+1)=-\frac{2}{3}\left(\frac{9}{2}h\right)+6$$
$$12\left[\frac{1}{4}(10h)\right]-12\left[\frac{3}{2}(h+1)\right]=12\left[-\frac{2}{3}\left(\frac{9}{2}h\right)\right]+12[6]$$
$$3(10h)-18(h+1)=-4(9h)+72$$
$$30h-18h-18=-36h+72$$
$$12h-18=-36h+72$$
$$48h=90$$
$$h=\frac{90}{48}=\frac{15}{8}$$

Choice (B) is correct.

23. B
Difficulty: Hard

Category: Heart of Algebra / Linear Equations

Strategic Advice: The key to answering this question is determining how many jumps land across each line. If Vera gets 7 jumps total and x jumps land over the farther line, the rest, or $7-x$, must land over the closer line.

Getting to the Answer: Try writing the expression in words first: points per farther line (10) times number of jumps landing over the farther line (x), plus points per closer line (5) times number of jumps landing over the closer line ($7-x$). Now, translate the words to numbers, variables, and operations: $10x + 5(7-x)$. This is not one of the answer choices, so simplify the expression by distributing the 5 and then combining like terms: $10x + 5(7 - x) = 10x + 35 - 5x = 5x + 35$, so the function is $f(x) = 5x + 35$, making (B) correct.

24. D
Difficulty: Hard

Category: Heart of Algebra / Linear Equations

Strategic Advice: Consider each choice systematically.

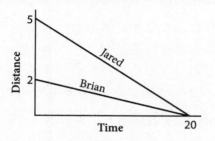

Getting to the Answer: Use the numbers to help you evaluate each statement. It took Brian and Jared each 20 minutes to bike home so A and B are false. Jared biked 5 miles in 20 minutes, while Brian only biked 2 miles in 20 minutes; their rates are not the same, so C is false. This means (D) must be true. Jared starts out farther away than Brian, so Jared must have biked at a faster rate to arrive home in the same amount of time.

25. B
Difficulty: Hard

Category: Heart of Algebra / Linear Equations

Strategic Advice: You aren't given any numbers in this question, so make some up. Sketch a quick graph of any simple linear equation that has a positive y-intercept (because it is given that $b > 0$). Then, change the sign of the y-intercept and sketch the new graph on the same coordinate plane.

Getting to the Answer: Pick a simple equation that you can sketch quickly, such as $y = x + 3$, and then change the sign of b. The new equation is $y = x - 3$. Sketch both graphs. The second line is

shifted down 3 units, twice, or $b \times 2$ units. If you're not convinced, try another pair of equations. Choice (B) is correct.

26. D
Difficulty: Hard

Category: Heart of Algebra / Linear Equations

Strategic Advice: Compare the differences in the two lines to the statements in the answer choices. Pay careful attention to which line represents before the law (the solid line) and which represents after the law (the dashed line).

Getting to the Answer: The y-intercept of both lines is the same. The key difference between the lines is their slopes. The solid line (pre-law) has a steeper slope, while the dashed line has a more gradual slope, so you can eliminate C. The slope of each line is negative (falling from left to right), so even after the proposed law is implemented, the population is still expected to decline, which means you can eliminate B. Because the dashed line's slope is more gradual, the decline in the population is slowing down (decelerating, not accelerating), so you can eliminate A. This means (D) is correct.

27. 18
Difficulty: Medium

Category: Heart of Algebra / Linear Equations

Strategic Advice: Clear the fractions first by multiplying both sides of the equation by 8. Then solve for x using inverse operations.

Getting to the Answer:

$$\frac{7}{8}(n-6)=\frac{21}{2}$$

$$8\left[\frac{7}{8}(n-6)\right]=8\left[\frac{21}{2}\right]$$

$$7(n-6)=4(21)$$

$$7n-42=84$$

$$7n=126$$

$$n=18$$

28. 1/4

Difficulty: Medium

Category: Heart of Algebra / Linear Equations

Strategic Advice: Start by finding the equation of each line using their slopes and y-intercepts, and then compare the equations.

Getting to the Answer: First, determine the equation for line A. Remember that slope is equal to rise over run, so count the change in y and the change in x from one point on the line to the next. The slope is $\frac{2}{1}$, or just 2. Next, find the y-intercept: -12. Now find the equation for line B: the slope is $\frac{1}{2}$ and the y-intercept is -3. So the equations are:

Line A: $y=2x-12$

Line B: $y=\frac{1}{2}x-3$

Don't be tempted to say $k = 4$. Notice that the numbers in the equation for line A are larger, so k must be a fraction, $\frac{1}{4}$.

$$\frac{1}{4}(2x-12)\rightarrow\frac{1}{2}x-3$$

29. C

Difficulty: Easy

Category: Heart of Algebra / Linear Equations

Strategic Advice: Don't let this fairly simple question fool you. Just because 5 and -5 are opposites, this does not mean the value on the right-hand side of the equals sign will be the opposite of 11.

Getting to the Answer: Solve for x, then substitute that value into the second equation for x and simplify.

$$2x + 5 = 11$$

$$2x = 6$$

$$x = 3$$

$$2x - 5 = 2(3) - 5 = 6 - 5 = 1$$

Therefore, (C) is correct.

You might also recognize that $2x - 5$ is 10 less than $2x + 5$, so you could find the answer by subtracting 10 from 11.

30. B

Difficulty: Easy

Category: Heart of Algebra / Linear Equations

Strategic Advice: Don't let questions that involve fractions intimidate you. To make the numbers easier to work with, clear the fraction by multiplying both sides of the equation by the denominator, 2.

Getting to the Answer:

$$2\cdot\left[\frac{3}{2}(x+7)\right]=6\cdot2$$

$$3(x+7)=12$$

$$3x+21=12$$

$$3x=-9$$

$$x=-3$$

Choice (B) is correct.

31. C
Difficulty: Easy

Category: Heart of Algebra / Linear Equations

Strategic Advice: When writing a linear equation to represent a real-world scenario, a flat rate is a constant while a unit rate is always multiplied by the independent variable. You can identify the unit rate by looking for words like *per* or *for each*.

Getting to the Answer: Because the amount Andrew gets paid per day, $120, is a flat rate that doesn't depend on the number of cruises he books, 120 should be the constant in the equation. This means you can eliminate B and D. The clue "per" tells you to multiply $25 by the number of cruises he books (*c*), so the equation is *pay* = 25 × *number of cruises* + 120, or *d* = 25*c* + 120, making (C) correct.

32. A
Difficulty: Easy

Category: Heart of Algebra / Linear Equations

Strategic Advice: Think about whether 250 is a constant in the equation or a coefficient that is multiplied by the independent variable.

Getting to the Answer: The total amount donated consists of a flat donation and an additional amount per mile. The flat amount is a one-time donation that does not depend on the number of miles walked and therefore should not be multiplied by the number of miles. This means that 250 is the flat donation. The other expression in the equation, 100*x*, represents the amount donated per mile (100) times the number of miles walked (*x*), thus (A) is correct.

33. B
Difficulty: Easy

Category: Heart of Algebra / Linear Equations

Strategic Advice: Look for two points on the line that hit the intersection of two grid lines. Then count the rise (or the fall if the line is decreasing) and the

run as you move from one point to the next (always left to right). The slope is the change in the *y*-values (rise or fall) over the change in the *x*-values (run).

Getting to the Answer: Start at the *y*-intercept, (0, 5), and move to the point (3, 3). The line moves down 2 units and to the right 3 units, so the slope is $-\frac{2}{3}$, making (B) correct.

34. A
Difficulty: Medium

Category: Heart of Algebra / Linear Equations

Strategic Advice: The rate of change (or slope) of a linear relationship is constant, so find the rate and apply it to the missing value.

Getting to the Answer: Choose any two points (preferably ones with the nicest numbers) from the table and substitute them into the slope formula. Using the points (0, 8) and (3, 7), the slope is $\frac{7-8}{3-0} = \frac{-1}{3}$. This means that for every 3 units the *x*-value increases, the *y*-value decreases by 1, so to get from *x* = 3 to *x* = 9, decrease the *y*-value by 1, two times: 7 − 1 − 1 = 5, making (A) correct.

35. D
Difficulty: Medium

Category: Heart of Algebra / Linear Equations

Strategic Advice: Use the information in the question to write your own expression, and then look for the answer choice that matches. Simplify your expression only if you don't find a match.

Getting to the Answer: Be careful on this question! If a couple earns $50 *per half-hour* that they dance, then they earn 50 × 2 = $100 *per hour*. Multiply this amount times the number of hours (not including the first 3 hours). This can be expressed as 100(*h* − 3). This is not one of the answer choices, so simplify by distributing the 100 to get 100*h* − 300, which is (D).

If you're struggling with the algebra, try Picking Numbers. Pick a number of hours a pair might dance, like 5. They don't earn anything for the first 3 hours, but they earn $50 per half-hour for the last 2 hours, which is 50 × 4 half-hours = $200. Now, find the expression that gives you an answer of $200 when $h = 5$ hours: $100(5) - 300 = 500 - 300 = 200$.

36. A
Difficulty: Hard

Category: Heart of Algebra / Linear Equations

Strategic Advice: Although you could try plugging values from the table into the equations, some of the answer choices may be traps. For example, B works for the first pair of values in the table, but not for any of the other pairs of values, so it is not correct.

Getting to the Answer: The question tells you that the functions are all linear, so start by finding the rate of change (the slope, m) using any two pairs of values from the table and the slope formula. Next, substitute the slope and any pair of values from the table, such as (10, 34), into the equation $f(x) = mx + b$, and solve for b. Finally, use the value of m and b to write the function.

$$m = \frac{y_2 - y_1}{x_2 - x_1}$$

$$m = \frac{64 - 34}{30 - 10} = \frac{30}{20} = 1.5$$

You can stop right there! Since only Choice (A) has a slope of 1.5, it must be the correct answer.

37. B
Difficulty: Hard

Category: Heart of Algebra / Linear Equations

Strategic Advice: As written, the equation doesn't tell you a lot about the graph, but you should notice that there are no exponents on the variables, which means the exponents are all equal to 1. This means the equation is linear and the graph must be a line, so you can eliminate D right away (it is an absolute value equation, not a linear equation). To choose

the correct line, rearrange the equation so that it is in slope-intercept form, $y = mx + b$.

Getting to the Answer: To write the equation in slope-intercept form, you'll need to first collect the y-terms on the left side of the equation. Rearranging the equation results in the following:

$$y = ay + ax + x + 1$$
$$y - ay = ax + x + 1$$
$$y(1 - a) = x(a + 1) + 1$$
$$y = \frac{(a + 1)}{(1 - a)}x + \frac{1}{1 - a}$$

This manipulation reveals a linear equation with a slope of $\frac{(a + 1)}{(1 - a)}$ and a y-intercept of $\frac{1}{1 - a}$. It is given in the question that $a > 1$, so the quantity $a + 1$ is positive, and $1 - a$ is negative, resulting in a negative slope $\left(\frac{+\#}{-\#} = -\# \right)$ and a negative y-intercept $\left(\frac{1}{-\#} = -\# \right)$. Of the choices given, only the graph in (B) satisfies these conditions.

38. A
Difficulty: Hard

Category: Heart of Algebra / Linear Equations

Strategic Advice: Try to describe the scenario in words first: if a car is more efficient, it can travel a greater distance on less gas. A less efficient car will use more gas to travel the same distance. In other words, the change in gas compared to the change in distance is greater for a less efficient car. Graphically, this means the slope is steeper for the less efficient car.

Getting to the Answer: Look for the graph where the line representing the less efficient car (i) has a steeper slope (more gas per distance) than the line representing the efficient car (e), which is the graph in (A). Note that C and D don't represent gas mileage at all—in C, the cars aren't travelling anywhere because the distance isn't changing; in D, no gas is being used even though the distance is changing.

39. 6

Difficulty: Medium

Category: Heart of Algebra / Linear Equations

Strategic Advice: Decimals can be messy, especially without a calculator, so clear the decimals by multiplying each term by 100—this moves the decimal two places to the left, resulting in an equation with only integer values.

Getting to the Answer:

$$0.55x - 1.04 = 0.35x + 0.16$$
$$100(0.55x - 1.04) = 100(0.35x + 0.16)$$
$$55x - 104 = 35x + 16$$
$$20x = 120$$
$$x = 6$$

40. 12

Difficulty: Medium

Category: Heart of Algebra / Linear Equations

Strategic Advice: The place where the line crosses the y-axis is the y-intercept, or b when the equation is written in slope-intercept form, $y = mx + b$.

Getting to the Answer: Rewrite the equation in slope-intercept form using inverse operations. To make the numbers easier to work with, clear the fraction by multiplying each term by 2.

$$\frac{3}{2}y - 2x = 18$$
$$2 \cdot \left[\frac{3}{2}y - 2x\right] = 2 \cdot 18$$
$$3y - 4x = 36$$
$$3y = 4x + 36$$
$$y = \frac{4}{3}x + 12$$

The y-intercept is 12.

Because the y-intercept of a graph is always of the form $(0, y)$, you could also substitute 0 for x and solve for y.

41. 70

Difficulty: Hard

Category: Heart of Algebra / Linear Equations

Strategic Advice: Because 40 pounds is not shown on the graph, you need more information. In a real-world scenario, the y-intercept of a graph usually represents a flat fee or a starting amount. The slope of the line represents a unit rate, such as the cost per pound to airmail the box.

Getting to the Answer: The y-intercept of the graph is 10, so the flat fee is \$10. To find the cost per pound (the unit rate), substitute two points from the graph into the slope formula. Using the points $(0, 10)$ and $(4, 16)$, the cost per pound is $\frac{16-10}{4-0} = \frac{6}{4} = 1.5$, which means it costs \$1.50 per pound to airmail a box. The total cost to airmail a 40-pound box is $\$10 + 1.50(40) = \$10 + \$60 = \$70$.

CHAPTER 3

PREPARE

1. B

Difficulty: Easy

Category: Heart of Algebra / Linear Equations

Strategic Advice: Don't just use substitution: Check to see if one of the equations can be easily manipulated for use with another method.

Getting to the Answer: Start by combining like terms in the second equation, then use combination to solve for x. No additional manipulation is necessary to eliminate the y terms.

$$
\begin{array}{r}
28x - 5y = 36 \\
+ \quad 15x + 5y = 50 \\
\hline
43x = 86 \\
x = 2
\end{array}
$$

Choice (B) is correct.

2. D

Difficulty: Medium

Category: Heart of Algebra / Linear Equations

Strategic Advice: The question states that there is no solution; use that to your advantage. Also keep in mind what the question is asking, as it requests something other than k.

Getting to the Answer: A system of equations with no solution means that the two equations have identical x coefficients and identical y coefficients and are equal to two different constants. First, rearrange the second equation to $-kx + 6y = -42$ so that variables and constants are properly aligned with those of the first equation. Divide both sides by -2 to get $\frac{k}{2}x - 3y = 21$. The coefficient of x in the

first equation is 5, so $\frac{k}{2} = 5$. Therefore, k must be 10. The question asks for $2k$, so multiply by 2 to get $2k = 20$, which is (D).

3. 9/2 or 4.5

Difficulty: Medium

Category: Heart of Algebra / Linear Equations

Strategic Advice: Substitution will get you the answer, but there's a faster route.

Getting to the Answer: Clear the fractions from the first equation by multiplying it by 4, then set up to solve using combination.

$$
\begin{array}{r}
x + 8y = 11 \\
+ \quad -x - 6y = 7 \\
\hline
2y = 18 \\
y = 9
\end{array}
$$

Take half of 9 to get $\frac{9}{2}$, then grid in 9/2 or 4.5.

4. D

Difficulty: Easy

Category: Heart of Algebra / Linear Equations

Strategic Advice: If you're not asked for an individual variable, look for a shortcut.

Getting to the Answer: The question asks for $b + c$, so don't waste your time finding the variables individually. After rearranging the equations so that variables and constants are aligned, you can add them together:

$$
\begin{array}{r}
-2b + 7c = 15 \\
+3b - 6c = 2 \\
\hline
b + c = 17
\end{array}
$$

This matches choice (D).

5. A

Difficulty: Medium

Category: Heart of Algebra / Linear Equations

Strategic Advice: Another wordy question means another chance to use the Kaplan Strategy for Translating English into Math.

Getting to the Answer: First, define your variables logically: t for tiny pandas, g for giant pandas. You're given the cost of each, as well as the number of each sold and the total revenue generated. Next, write the system of equations that represents the information given:

$$t + g = 29$$
$$3.5t + 14g = 217$$

Multiplying the top equation by −14 allows you to solve for t by combination:

$$-14t - 14g = -406$$
$$+ \quad 3.5t + 14g = 217$$
$$\overline{\quad -10.5t = -189 \quad}$$
$$t = 18$$

Solving for t gives 18, which eliminates B and C. Plugging this value back into the first equation allows you to find g, which is 11. (A) is the only choice with these values.

6. C

Difficulty: Medium

Category: Heart of Algebra / Linear Equations

Strategic Advice: Word problems that do not require you to actually solve a system of equations are a quick way to earn points; just follow the Kaplan Strategy for Translating English into Math.

Getting to the Answer: Since you're given the variables (r for resident and n for nonresident), the only thing left for you to do here is break the wording apart into phrases and translate into math. Residents pay \$421 in fees ($421r$), and nonresidents pay \$879 in fees ($879n$). Add together both student types to get the first equation: $r + n = 1{,}980$. Piece together the fee amounts into your second equation, which will be $421r + 879n = 1{,}170{,}210$. Only (C) contains both of those equations.

PRACTICE

7. A

Difficulty: Medium

Category: Heart of Algebra / Linear Equations

Strategic Advice: Use the Kaplan Strategy for Translating English into Math to make sense of the prose.

Getting to the Answer: First, define your variables: w for wooden and c for crystal are good choices. Breaking apart the question, you know the jewelry artist bought 127 beads total. You're also told each wooden bead costs \$0.20 ($0.2w$) and each crystal bead costs \$0.50 ($0.5c$), as well as the fact that she spent \$41 total. You'll have two equations: one relating the number of wooden beads and crystal beads, and a second relating the costs associated with each.

$$w + c = 127$$
$$0.2w + 0.5c = 41$$

Either combination or substitution is a good choice for solving this system. Both are shown here:

Combination

$$-0.5(w + c = 127) \rightarrow -0.5w - 0.5c = -63.5$$
$$-0.5w - 0.5c = -63.5$$
$$+ \quad 0.2w + 0.5c = 41$$
$$\overline{\quad -0.3w = -22.5 \quad}$$
$$w = 75$$
$$75 + c = 127 \rightarrow c = 52$$

Substitution

$$w + c = 127 \rightarrow c = 127 - w$$
$$0.2w + 0.5(127 - w) = 41$$
$$0.2w + 63.5 - 0.5w = 41$$
$$-0.3w = -22.5$$
$$w = 75$$
$$75 + c = 127 \rightarrow c = 52$$

Be careful here: The question asks for the difference in amount spent on each type of bead, not the difference in quantity of each type. Multiply the bead counts by the correct pricing to get $15 for the wooden beads and $26 for the crystal beads. Take the difference to get $11, which is (A).

8. 59

Difficulty: Medium

Category: Heart of Algebra / Linear Equations

Strategic Advice: Once again, you're asked for an expression instead of a variable; utilize the same tactics you've used for similar questions.

Getting to the Answer: Start by rearranging the two equations so that variables and constants are aligned:

$$x + y = -15$$
$$\frac{x}{2} + \frac{5y}{2} = 37$$

Clear out the fractions, and then combine:

$$2\left(\frac{x}{2} + \frac{5y}{2} = 37\right) \rightarrow x + 5y = 74$$
$$\begin{array}{r} x + y = -15 \\ + x + 5y = 74 \\ \hline 2x + 6y = 59 \end{array}$$

You're done! Grid in 59 and move on.

PERFORM

9. B

Difficulty: Hard

Category: Heart of Algebra / Linear Equations

Strategic Advice: A system of equations with infinitely many solutions describes a single line. Therefore, the equations are dependent, and correct manipulation of one will yield the other.

Getting to the Answer: Because q is the x coefficient in the second equation, look for a way to make the y coefficient equal to the one in the first equation. This can be done by multiplying the second equation by -9: $-9(qx - \frac{y}{3} = -2) \rightarrow -9qx + 3y = 18$. The y-terms and constants of the second equation now match those of the first; all that's left is to set the x coefficients equal to each other and solve for q: $-9q = 6 \rightarrow q = -\frac{6}{9} = -\frac{2}{3}$. (B) is correct.

10. 3/17

Difficulty: Medium

Category: Heart of Algebra / Linear Equations

Strategic Advice: Don't be intimidated by the bigger numbers; the rules of systems of equations still apply. Mind what the question asks, too.

Getting to the Answer: Using combination will make life easier. A common multiple of 5 and 12, the x coefficients, is 60, so multiply by the appropriate factors, remembering to make one of them negative:

$$-5(12x + 15y = 249) \rightarrow -60x - 75y = -1,245$$
$$12(5x + 13y = 124) \rightarrow 60x + 156y = 1,488$$

Combine as usual:

$$\begin{array}{r} -60x - 75y = -1,245 \\ + 60x + 156y = 1,488 \\ \hline 81y = 243 \\ y = 3 \end{array}$$

Don't stop yet; you need x so you can determine $\dfrac{y}{x}$. Substitute 3 for y in one of the original equations:

$$5x + 13(3) = 124$$
$$5x + 39 = 124$$
$$5x = 85$$
$$x = 17$$

Plug your x- and y-values into the expression you need, $\dfrac{y}{x}$, to get $\dfrac{3}{17}$. Grid in 3/17.

11. C

Difficulty: Hard

Category: Heart of Algebra / Linear Equations

Strategic Advice: You can write equations to represent profits generated from each pizza type.

Getting to the Answer: You're told The Works sells for $17 each and that its ingredients cost the pizzeria $450 per week. This means profit generated by this pizza's sales are represented by the equation $y = 17x - 450$. Profits from The Hawaiian are analogous: Each one sells for $13, but the pizzeria loses $310 to pay for ingredients each week. Therefore, profits from this pizza are represented by $y = 13x - 310$. To determine where profits from one pizza overtake the other, set the two equations equal to each other and solve:

$$17x - 450 = 13x - 310$$
$$4x = 140$$
$$x = 35$$

Although ingredients for The Works cost more, the pizza's higher price tag means its profits will eventually surpass those of The Hawaiian. This will occur after the pizzeria sells 35 of each, making (C) correct. Beware D; 145 is the y-value when $x = 35$.

EXTRA PRACTICE

1. D

Difficulty: Easy

Category: Heart of Algebra / Systems of Linear Equations

Strategic Advice: The word "and" in this question tells you that you're dealing with a system of equations.

Whenever a question involves a system, quickly compare the two equations. Sometimes, writing the equations vertically gives you a clue about how to solve it.

$$\begin{cases} 2x - 3y = 14 \\ 5x + 3y = 21 \end{cases}$$

This system is already set up perfectly to solve using elimination by addition (also known as combination) because the y-terms ($-3y$ and $3y$) are opposites.

Getting to the Answer: Add the two equations to cancel $-3y$ and $3y$. Then solve the resulting equation for x. Remember, the question only asks for the value of x, so you don't need to substitute x back into the equation and solve for y.

$$\begin{array}{r} 2x - 3y = 14 \\ + 5x + 3y = 21 \\ \hline 7x = 35 \\ x = 5 \end{array}$$

Choice (D) is correct.

2. C

Difficulty: Medium

Category: Heart of Algebra / Systems of Linear Equations

Strategic Advice: Because x has a coefficient of 1 in the second equation, solve the system using substitution. Before you select your answer, make

sure you found the right quantity (the difference of x and y).

Getting to the Answer: First, solve the second equation for x and substitute the result into the first equation and solve for y.

$$x - 5y = 2$$
$$x = 2 + 5y$$
$$4(2 + 5y) + 3y = 14 - y$$
$$8 + 20y + 3y = 14 - y$$
$$8 + 23y = 14 - y$$
$$24y = 6$$
$$y = \frac{6}{24} = \frac{1}{4}$$

Next, substitute this value back into $x = 2 + 5y$ and simplify.

$$x = 2 + 5\left(\frac{1}{4}\right)$$
$$x = \frac{8}{4} + \frac{5}{4}$$
$$x = \frac{13}{4}$$

Finally, subtract $x - y$ to find the difference.

$$\frac{13}{4} - \frac{1}{4} = \frac{12}{4} = 3$$

3. C

Difficulty: Medium

Category: Heart of Algebra / Systems of Linear Equations

Strategic Advice: Skim the answer choices. They are talking about systems with no solution and infinite solutions. Picture the graphs of both.

Getting to the Answer: Graphically, a system of linear equations that has no solution consists of two parallel lines that will never intersect. They have the same slope but different y-intercepts. A system of linear equations that has infinite solutions is actually the same line, just represented in different ways. Graphically, one line would sit on top of the other, intersecting itself an infinite number of times. These lines would have the same slope *and* the same y-intercept. Without additional information, it is not possible to determine whether the system that Charlie graphed has no solutions or an infinite number of solutions. Therefore, the solution to Charlie's system of equations depends on the y-intercepts of the lines and (C) is correct.

4. C

Difficulty: Medium

Category: Heart of Algebra / Systems of Linear Equations

Strategic Advice: If the graphs intersect at (–3, 1), then the solution to the system is $x = -3$ and $y = 1$. This means you can substitute these values into both equations and go from there.

Getting to the Answer: Substitute the values of x and y into each equation and solve for h and k. Then, divide k by h.

$$hx - 4y = -10 \qquad kx + 3y = -15$$
$$h(-3) - 4(1) = -10 \qquad k(-3) + 3(1) = -15$$
$$-3h - 4 = -10 \qquad -3k + 3 = -15$$
$$-3h = -6 \qquad -3k = -18$$
$$h = 2 \qquad k = 6$$

So, $\dfrac{k}{h} = \dfrac{6}{2} = 3$, making (C) correct.

5. D

Difficulty: Hard

Category: Heart of Algebra / Systems of Linear Equations

Strategic Advice: The easiest way to answer this question is to think about how the graphs of the equations would look. Graphically, a system of linear equations that has no solution indicates two parallel lines, or in other words, two lines that have the same slope but different y-intercepts.

Getting to the Answer: In a system with no solutions, the x- and y-coefficients must be the same. The two y-coefficients are $-\dfrac{2}{3}$ and -8. To make $-\dfrac{2}{3}$ equal -8, multiply by 12. Then $\dfrac{1}{2}x$ becomes $6x$. Since the other x-coefficient is a, it must be that $a = 6$.

6. C

Difficulty: Hard

Category: Heart of Algebra / Systems of Linear Equations

Strategic Advice: Create a system of linear equations where x represents the number of packs with 8 plates and y represents the number of packs with 12 plates. Before selecting your final answer, make sure you are answering the right question (how many plates would a customer have who bought all of the packs of 12).

Getting to the Answer: The first equation should represent the total number of *packs*, each with 8 or 12 plates, or $e + t = 54$. The second equation should represent the total number of *plates*. Because e represents packs with 8 plates and t represents packs with 12 plates, the second equation should be $8e + 12t = 496$. Now solve the system using substitution (or combination if it is faster for you). Solve the first equation for either variable and substitute the result into the second equation.

$$e + t = 546$$
$$e = 54 - t$$
$$8(54 - t) + 12t = 496$$
$$432 - 8t + 12t = 496$$
$$432 + 4t = 496$$
$$4t = 64$$
$$t = 16$$

So 16 packs have 12 plates. The question asks about packs of 12, so you don't need to find the value of e. But you are not done yet. The problem asks how many *plates* a customer would buy if he or she buys all of the packs of 12 the store has, not just the *number of packs.* The customer would buy 16 × 12 = 192 plates, which is (C).

7. D

Difficulty: Hard

Category: Heart of Algebra / Systems of Linear Equations

Strategic Advice: A system of linear equations has infinitely many solutions if both lines in the system have the same slope and the same *y*-intercept (in other words, they are the same line).

Getting to the Answer: When a system has infinitely many solutions, the *x*- and *y*-coefficients of the two equations must be the same. Use the *x*-coefficients here: To turn $\frac{1}{2}$ into 3, multiply by 6. So *c* becomes 6*c*, and 6*c* = −6. Thus *c* = −1.

Choice (D) is correct.

8. 8

Difficulty: Hard

Category: Heart of Algebra / Systems of Linear Equations

Strategic Advice: The solution to the system is the point that both tables will have in common, but the tables, as given, do not share any points. You could use the data to write the equation of each line and then solve the system, but this will use up valuable time on Test Day. Instead, whenever data is presented in a table, look for patterns that can be extended.

Getting to the Answer: In the table on the left, the *x*-values increase by 2 each time and the *y*-values decrease by 2. In the table on the right, the *x*-values increase by 4 each time and the *y*-values increase by 1. Use these patterns to continue the tables.

Equation 1		Equation 2	
x	**y**	**x**	**y**
−2	6	−8	−8
0	4	−4	−7
2	2	0	−6
4	0	4	−5
6	−2	**8**	**−4**
8	**−4**	12	−3

The point (8, −4) satisfies both equations, so the *x*-coordinate of the solution to the system is 8.

9. B

Difficulty: Easy

Category: Heart of Algebra / Systems of Linear Equations

Strategic Advice: The solution to a system of linear equations represented graphically is the point of intersection. If the lines do not intersect, the system has no solution.

Getting to the Answer: According to the graph, the lines intersect, or cross each other, at (6, 3). The question asks for the *y*-coordinate of the solution, which is 3, making (B) correct.

10. A

Difficulty: Medium

Category: Heart of Algebra / Systems of Linear Equations

Strategic Advice: Read the axis labels carefully. Each grid-line represents 2 units.

Getting to the Answer: The solution to a system of equations shown graphically is the point of intersection. The two lines intersect at (−6, −6), so *A* + *B* = −6 + (−6) = −12, which means (A) is correct.

11. C

Difficulty: Medium

Category: Heart of Algebra / Systems of Linear Equations

Strategic Advice: Write a system of equations with c = the cost of the chair in dollars and s = the cost of the sofa in dollars.

Getting to the Answer: Translate from English into math to write two equations: a sofa costs $50 less than three times the cost of the chair, or $s = 3c - 50$; together, a sofa and a chair cost $650, so $s + c = 650$.

The system is:

$$\begin{cases} s = 3c - 50 \\ s + c = 650 \end{cases}$$

The top equation is already solved for s, so substitute $3c - 50$ into the second equation for s.

$$3c - 50 + c = 650$$
$$4c - 50 = 650$$
$$4c = 700$$
$$c = 175$$

Be careful—that's not the answer! The chair costs $175 so the sofa costs $3(175) - 50 = 525 - 50 = \$475$. This means the sofa costs $475 - \$175 = \$300$ more than the chair. Therefore, (C) is correct.

12. A

Difficulty: Hard

Category: Heart of Algebra / Systems of Linear Equations

Strategic Advice: Create a system of linear equations where x represents the number of rows with 20 seats and y represents the number of rows with 24 seats. Before selecting your final answer, make sure you are answering the right question (how many rows have 24 seats).

Getting to the Answer: The first equation should represent the total *number of rows*, each with 20 or 24 seats, or $s + l = 16$. The second equation should represent the total *number of seats*. Because s represents rows with 20 seats and l represents rows with 24 seats, the second equation should be $20s + 24l = 348$. Now solve the system using substitution. Solve the first equation for either variable and substitute the result into the second equation.

$$s + l = 16$$
$$s = 16 - l$$
$$20(16 - l) + 24l = 348$$
$$320 - 20l + 24l = 348$$
$$320 + 4l = 348$$
$$4l = 28$$
$$l = 7$$

So 7 rows have 24 seats, which means (A) is correct. This is what the question asks for, so you don't need to find the value of s.

CHAPTER 4

PREPARE

1. A
Difficulty: Easy

Category: Heart of Algebra / Inequalities

Strategic Advice: Use the Kaplan Strategy for Translating English into Math to quickly find the answer to this question.

Getting to the Answer: The question has defined the variables for you (r and g). The bowling alley charges $6.50 for shoe and ball rental and $3.75 per game. Sales tax is 6.325% (0.06325 in decimal form). Rental and game costs are given by $6.5r$ and $3.75g$, respectively. To incorporate sales tax into the total cost, multiply the sum of $6.5r$ and $3.75g$ by 1.06325 (not 0.06325, which gives the cost of sales tax only). The question asks for an inequality that represents the amount that the group can spend, which can be no more than $7 \times 20 = 140$; therefore, the correct inequality is $1.06325(6.5r + 3.75g) \leq 140$. This matches (A).

2. C
Difficulty: Easy

Category: Heart of Algebra / Inequalities

Strategic Advice: Rewrite the inequality in slope-intercept form and then identify which half-plane should be shaded.

Getting to the Answer: Subtract $5x$ from both sides of the inequality, divide both sides by -10, and flip the inequality symbol to yield $y < \frac{1}{2}x - \frac{3}{5}$. Eliminate A and D because they have positive y-intercepts. The "less than" symbol indicates that the half-plane below the line should be shaded, making (C) the correct answer.

You can also pick a pair of coordinates, such as those of the origin, to plug into the inequality to confirm your choice. If the coordinates of the point satisfy the inequality, then the point will lie in the shaded region. In this case, the origin should not be in the shaded region (0 is not greater than $0 + \frac{3}{5}$), confirming that (C) is correct.

3. $0 \leq x + y \leq \frac{5}{3}$
Difficulty: Medium

Category: Heart of Algebra / Inequalities

Strategic Advice: Look for a way to use combination to get $x + y$ instead of solving for the variables individually or manipulating the inequalities into slope-intercept form.

Getting to the Answer: If you look closely, you'll see that the x term coefficients sum to 1, as do the y term coefficients. Therefore, you can add the two inequalities together as they are to reveal $x + y$:

$$\frac{1}{2}x + \frac{1}{3}y \leq \frac{2}{3}$$
$$+\frac{1}{2}x + \frac{2}{3}y \leq 1$$
$$\overline{\qquad\qquad\qquad}$$
$$x + y \leq \frac{5}{3}$$

You can't choose a negative number for a Grid-in, so use a number between 0 and $\frac{5}{3}$, inclusive.

4. B
Difficulty: Easy

Category: Heart of Algebra / Inequalities

Strategic Advice: Rewrite the inequalities in slope-intercept form. Once complete, determine whether each line should be solid or dashed and which half-plane (above or below the line) should be shaded for each.

Getting to the Answer: The correct graph should have a dashed line with a positive slope ($y < 3x - 2$) and a solid line with a negative slope $\left(y \geq -\frac{1}{9}x + \frac{7}{3}\right)$; eliminate C. According to the inequality symbols, the half-plane above the solid line and the half-plane below the dashed line should be shaded; the only match is (B).

PRACTICE

5. A
Difficulty: Medium

Category: Heart of Algebra / Inequalities

Strategic Advice: Use the Kaplan Strategy for Translating English into Math to piece together an inequality.

Getting to the Answer: The question states that n represents the number of overnight stays. The cost of hotel accommodations for a trip without the discount card is $180 per night, or $180n$. If a customer purchases the discount card, accommodations would equal the cost of the card plus $120 per night, or $720 + 120n$. Combine these in an inequality, remembering which way the inequality symbol should be oriented. You want the cost with the discount card to be less than the cost without the card, so the inequality is $720 + 120n < 180n$. Solving for n gives $n > 12$; a traveler must stay in hotels in the network more than 12 days for the discount card to be a better deal. Choice (A) is the correct answer.

PERFORM

6. $0 \leq h < 3.5$
Difficulty: Hard

Domain: Heart of Algebra / Inequalities

Strategic Advice: Resist autopilot! Instead of solving two inequalities separately, look for a series of quick manipulations to convert $\frac{4}{3}h + \frac{1}{6}$ to $12h - 4$.

Getting to the Answer: Start by multiplying the entire inequality by 9 to yield $-27 < 12h + \frac{3}{2} < 9$. Next, subtract $\left(\frac{3}{2}+4\right)$ from all parts of the inequality (converting the fraction component to a decimal will make this step easier), which will become $-32.5 < 12h - 4 < 3.5$. Because Grid-in answers cannot be negative, pick a value that is greater than or equal to 0 but less than 3.5.

Note that you could also solve the inequality for h and then manipulate the answer so that it looks like the expression in the question, but this strategy is likely to take much longer.

7. C
Difficulty: Medium

Domain: Heart of Algebra / Inequalities

Strategic Advice: Use the Kaplan Strategy for Translating English into Math to assemble a system of inequalities.

Getting to the Answer: The question has defined the variables for you (t_s and p_s, t_z and p_z). You know that tops and pants cost $35 and $60 each, respectively. In addition, the question states that Sarah and Zena must sell an average of 75 items each (which means that together they must sell at least 150 items, regardless of who sells more) and that their total sales must be at least $6,000. The sum of the four item counts must meet or exceed 150, so the first inequality is $t_s + p_s + t_z + p_z \geq 150$. Revenue from the sale of tops is $35(t_s + t_z)$, and revenue from the sale of pants is $60(p_s + p_z)$. The minimum revenue required to earn the bonus is $6,000, so the second inequality is $35(t_s + t_z) + 60(p_s + p_z) \geq 6,000$. (C) is the only choice that contains both inequalities.

EXTRA PRACTICE

1. A

Difficulty: Easy

Category: Heart of Algebra / Inequalities

Strategic Advice: You solve an inequality just like an equation. The only difference is that if you multiply or divide both sides by a negative number (usually in the last step of the solution), you must reverse (flip) the inequality symbol.

Getting to the Answer: Take a second to study the inequality. Distributing the fraction will yield messy calculations. Instead, multiply both sides of the inequality by 5 to clear the fraction. Then, use inverse operations to isolate the variable:

$$\cancel{5} \times \left[\frac{1}{\cancel{5}}(7 - 3b) \right] > 5 \times 2$$
$$7 - 3b > 10$$
$$-3b > 3$$
$$b < -1$$

Notice that the inequality symbol was reversed because the last step in the solution required dividing by -3. The correct answer is (A).

2. C

Difficulty: Easy

Category: Heart of Algebra / Inequalities

Strategic Advice: When matching the solution of an inequality to a number line, check the number, the dot (open or solid), and the direction of the shading.

Getting to the Answer: Solve the inequality by first distributing the 2 and then using inverse operations.

$$2(4x - 1) > 5x + 13$$
$$8x - 2 > 5x + 13$$
$$8x > 5x + 15$$
$$3x > 15$$
$$x > 5$$

Now, find the number line that matches. Because x is greater than (but *not* equal to) 5, the dot should be open, and the graph should be shaded to the right of 5. This is called a *strict* inequality because the numbers in the solution are strictly greater than 5. This means (C) is correct.

3. B

Difficulty: Easy

Category: Heart of Algebra / Inequalities

Strategic Advice: Choose the best strategy to answer the question. Substituting each answer choice into both inequalities will use up valuable time on Test Day. Instead, solve each inequality for n and then eliminate incorrect answer choices.

Getting to the Answer:

First inequality: $n - 3 > 8$ so $n > 11$. This means you can eliminate A because 11 is not greater than itself.

Second inequality: $n + 1 < 14$ so $n < 13$. This means you can eliminate C and D because neither 13 nor 14 is less than 13. The number 12 is the only answer choice that is both greater than 11 and less than 13, so (B) is correct.

4. B

Difficulty: Medium

Category: Heart of Algebra / Inequalities

Strategic Advice: Understanding connections between graphing and algebra will earn you points on Test Day. This question tests your knowledge of how the graph of an inequality in two dimensions looks.

Getting to the Answer: Quickly skim the first answer choice to see that you'll need to decide whether the boundary line is dashed or solid, whether it rises or falls from left to right, and which half-plane should be shaded. The inequality symbol tells you two of these—the symbol does not have an equal sign, so the line should be dashed; the symbol represents *less than*, so the half-plane *below* the line should be shaded. This means either A or B must be correct. To decide which one, recall that when a line is written in the form $y = mx + b$, the variable m represents the slope of the line. Here, $m = -2$, so the line is decreasing, which means it falls from left to right, making (B) correct.

5. D

Difficulty: Medium

Category: Heart of Algebra / Inequalities

Strategic Advice: You don't have time to try each symbol in the equation. Instead, look at the dot (open or solid?) and the direction of the shading (left or right?).

Getting to the Answer: There is a solid dot at 6, which means the sign must be $\geq$ or $\leq$, so you can eliminate A and B. Next, look at the shading. The graph is shaded to the left of the dot. This means the graph shows $x \leq 6$, but be careful—there is a negative coefficient (-1) in front of the x-term, so the inequality will be reversed at some point in the solution. This means the original inequality sign, before you reverse it, should be $\geq$, which is (D). You can check your answer by solving the inequality using the sign you chose. If you chose correctly, your answer should match the graph.

6. C

Difficulty: Medium

Category: Heart of Algebra / Inequalities

Strategic Advice: The best way to answer this question is to pretend you are the person paying for your power. How much less would you pay for *one* kWh of power at Company D than at Company B? If you used 530 kWh, how much would this be? If you used 730 kWh, how much would this be?

Getting to the Answer: Based on the data in the table, a consumer would pay $17.4 - 14.8 = 2.6$ cents (or 0.026) less for one kWh of power at Company D than at Company B. If she used 530 kWh per month, she would pay $530(0.026) = \$13.78$ less at Company D. If she used 730 kWh, she would pay $730(0.026) = \$18.98$ less. So, the consumer would pay somewhere between \$13.78 and \$18.98 less per month, which can be expressed as the compound inequality $13.78 \leq x \leq 18.98$, which matches (C).

7. B

Difficulty: Medium

Category: Heart of Algebra / Inequalities

Strategic Advice: The intersection (overlap) of the two shaded regions is the solution to the system of inequalities. Check each point to see whether it lies in the region where the shading overlaps. Be careful—you are looking for the point that is *not* a solution to the system.

Getting to the Answer: Choices A and C clearly lie in the overlap so you can eliminate them. Choice D, which is the point $(6, -3)$, lies on a boundary line, and because the line is solid, the point *is* included in the solution region. The only point that does not lie within the overlap is (B). To check this, plug $(1, -1)$ into the first inequality:

$$y < \frac{3}{5}x - 2$$

$$-1 < \frac{3}{5}(1) - 2$$

$$-1 \not< -\frac{7}{5}$$

Choice (B) is correct because -1 is not less than $-\frac{7}{5}$.

8. C

Difficulty: Medium

Category: Heart of Algebra / Inequalities

Strategic Advice: Use the Kaplan Method for Translating from English into Math. The clue "holds a maximum" means it can hold exactly that much or less, so use the symbol $\leq$ throughout.

Getting to the Answer: The cargo container can hold a maximum of 50 microwaves, so the first inequality is $m \leq 50$. This means you can eliminate A. The container can hold a maximum of 15 refrigerators, so the second inequality is $r \leq 15$. The third inequality deals with the size of each appliance. The cargo container can hold m microwaves multiplied by the size of the microwave, 6 cubic feet; it can hold r refrigerators multiplied by the size of the refrigerator, 20 cubic feet; and it can hold a maximum of 300 cubic feet total. Put these together to write the final inequality: $6m + 20r \leq 300$, which is (C).

9. C

Difficulty: Medium

Category: Heart of Algebra / Inequalities

Strategic Advice: A question like this is purely conceptual. The only time a system of inequalities has *no solution* (no overlap at all) is when the boundary lines are parallel and the shading is in opposite directions (above the upper boundary line and below the lower boundary line).

Getting to the Answer: The boundary lines must be parallel, so the slope of the second line must be equal to the slope of the first line, which is 2. This means you can eliminate A and B. The inequality symbol $<$ (in the first inequality) tells you that the half-plane *below* the boundary line is shaded, which means the half-plane *above* the second boundary line must be shaded. Therefore, the correct symbol is greater than ($>$). Choice (C) is correct.

10. D

Difficulty: Hard

Category: Heart of Algebra / Inequalities

Strategic Advice: Before immediately trying to solve for k, notice that $-6k + 8$ is simply $3k - 4$ multiplied by -2. So, multiply each of the other parts of the inequality by -2 also.

Getting to the Answer: Don't forget to flip the inequality symbols because you are multiplying by a negative number.

$$-2\left[-\frac{2}{5} < 3k - 4 < \frac{6}{7}\right]$$

$$\frac{4}{5} > -6k + 8 > -\frac{12}{7}$$

Now, you don't need to solve for k because the question is asking about $-6k + 8$, but it does help to rewrite the inequality from smallest to largest: $-\frac{12}{7} < -6k + 8 < \frac{4}{5}$. So, any value greater than $-\frac{12}{7}$ but less than $\frac{4}{5}$ is a possible value, but be careful—you are looking for the number that is *not* a possible value. This means you are looking for a number that is *less* than $-\frac{12}{7}$ or *greater* than $\frac{4}{5}$. Choice (D) is correct because $\frac{4}{3} > \frac{4}{5}$.

11. D

Difficulty: Hard

Category: Heart of Algebra / Inequalities

Strategic Advice: The solution to a system of inequalities is where the shading overlaps. The first inequality is ready to graph, but the second is not, so start by rewriting the second inequality in slope intercept form ($y = mx + b$). Then draw a sketch of the two lines.

Getting to the Answer: Don't forget to reverse the inequality symbol when you divide by -3.

$$2x - 3y \geq 12$$
$$-3y \geq -2x + 12$$
$$y \leq \frac{2}{3}x - 4$$

Now, compare the lines. Because the slopes are the same $\left(\frac{2}{3}\right)$ and the y-intercepts are different (1 and −4), the boundary lines are parallel and never intersect. Don't answer too quickly—the answer is *not* "no solution"! The solution set revolves around the shading, not the boundary lines, so draw a quick sketch of the system.

The region between the two boundary lines is shaded in both directions, so (D) is correct.

12. 8
Difficulty: Medium

Category: Heart of Algebra / Inequalities

Strategic Advice: Translate from English into math to create an inequality where h represents the number of hours of overtime Marco must work.

Getting to the Answer: Marco gets paid a daily wage plus an hourly rate for overtime. So, his weekly pay is his daily rate ($80) times 5 days, plus the number of hours of overtime he works (h) times his overtime rate ($15). If he wants to make *at least* $520, which means that much or more, the inequality is $(80 \times 5) + 15h \geq 520$. Solve for h.

$$400 + 15h \geq 520$$
$$15h \geq 120$$
$$h \geq 8$$

Marco must work at least 8 hours of overtime to make $520 or more this week.

13. 2
Difficulty: Medium

Category: Heart of Algebra / Inequalities

Strategic Advice: If (a, b) is a solution to the system, then a is the x-coordinate of any point in the region where the shading overlaps, and b is the corresponding y-coordinate.

Getting to the Answer: When $a = 0$ (or $x = 0$), the maximum possible value for b lies on the upper boundary line, $y < 2x + 3$. It looks like the y-coordinate is 3, but to be sure, substitute $x = 0$ into the equation and simplify. You can use $=$ in the equation, instead of the inequality symbol, because you are finding a point on the boundary line.

$$y = 2(0) + 3$$
$$y = 3$$

The point on the boundary line is (0, 3). The boundary line is dashed (because the inequality is strictly less than), so (0, 3) is *not* a solution to the system. This means 2 is the greatest possible *integer* value for b when $a = 0$.

CHAPTER 5

PREPARE

1. A
Difficulty: Easy

Category: Problem Solving and Data Analysis / Rates, Ratios, Proportions, and Percentages

Strategic Advice: Map out your route from starting units to end units, being mindful of the fact that you have area units.

Getting to the Answer: Your starting quantity is in ft^3, and your desired quantity should be in m^3. The only conversion factor you need is 1 m $\approx$ 3.28 ft. Setting up your route to m^3, you get $\dfrac{700 \text{ ft}^3}{1} \times \dfrac{1 \text{ m}}{3.28 \text{ ft}} \times \dfrac{1 \text{ m}}{3.28 \text{ ft}} \times \dfrac{1 \text{ m}}{3.28 \text{ ft}} = \dfrac{700}{(3.28)^3}\text{m} \approx$ 19.84 m^3, which matches (A).

2. 150
Difficulty: Easy

Category: Problem Solving and Data Analysis / Rates, Ratios, Proportions, and Percentages / Multi-Part Math

Strategic Advice: Identify the units of the starting and desired quantities, then use the given relationships (and those you already know) to plan a route to the answer.

Getting to the Answer: The starting quantity is 2.43 TB, and you need to convert this to hours. Using the correct conversion factors, your calculation is as follows:

$$2.43 \text{ TB} \times \dfrac{10^6 \text{ MB}}{1 \text{ TB}} \times \dfrac{1 \text{ s}}{4.5 \text{ MB}} \times \dfrac{1 \text{ min}}{60 \text{ s}} \times \dfrac{1 \text{ h}}{60 \text{ min}} = 150 \text{ h}$$

3. 103
Difficulty: Medium

Strategic Advice: Find the new rate using your percentage expertise, then convert with the factor-label method.

Getting to the Answer: Using the percent three-part formula, you'll find the New York team's software is $1.4 \times 4.5 = 6.3$ MB/s; analogously, Boston's team's software contributes $0.8 \times 4.5 = 3.6$ MB/s:
$$2.43 \text{ TB} \times \dfrac{10^6 \text{ MB}}{1 \text{ TB}} \times \dfrac{1 \text{ s}}{14.4 \text{ MB}} \times \dfrac{1 \text{ min}}{60 \text{ s}} \times \dfrac{1 \text{ h}}{60 \text{ min}} = 46.875 \text{ h}.$$
Subtract this value from the original 150 h to get 103.125 h; rounding to the nearest hour gives 103.

4. B
Difficulty: Medium

Category: Problem Solving and Data Analysis / Rates, Ratios, Proportions, and Percentages

Strategic Advice: Look for a way to consolidate the two given ratios into one, and ensure you provide the ratio requested.

Getting to the Answer: The first paint can has a red:blue (R:B) ratio of 25:60; and the second can's ratio, yellow:blue:white (Y:B:W), is 30:70:15. Reduce the ratios to make the math easier. R:B becomes 5:12, and Y:B:W becomes 6:14:3. These cannot be combined as they are, so you need a common factor to link them. Blue is the term common to both ratios; look for a small common multiple of the blue components, 12 and 14. Using 84 as the common multiple, determine factors that, when multiplied by the ratios, turn both blue components into 84. For R:B, the calculation is $7 \times (5:12) = 35:84$. Repeating for Y:B:W, you get $6 \times (6:14:3) = 36:84:18$. The combined ratio R:B:Y:W becomes 35:84:36:18, making R:W 35:18. The question asks for the ratio of white to red, so flip your ratio to get 18:35, which is (B).

5. C
Difficulty: Easy

Category: Problem Solving and Data Analysis / Rates, Ratios, Proportions, and Percentages

Strategic Advice: Finding 10% of 240 will reduce the number of calculations you'll need to do.

Getting to the Answer: You know Kristina will make 240 oz of each juice blend; 10% of 240 oz is 24 oz. Because each desired percentage is a multiple of 10, you only need to multiply 24 by the appropriate number to get the juice volume for each blend. Therefore, 20% is 48 oz, 40% is 96 oz, 50% is 120 oz, 60% is 144 oz, and 80% is 192 oz. The sum of these five volumes is 600 oz, but you're not done yet. Divide by the volume of one juice bottle, 32 oz, to get 18.75 bottles. Round up to 19; the correct answer is (C).

6. 59

Difficulty: Medium

Category: Problem Solving and Data Analysis / Rates, Ratios, Proportions, Percentages

Strategic Advice: It's easy to switch on autopilot and do five separate cost increase calculations, but you can get away with just one (and subsequently save time).

Getting to the Answer: First, determine the total increase from 2014-15 through 2019-20: $15, 564 − $12, 192 = $3, 372$. Dividing $3,372 by 5 (the number of increases) gives $674.40, the average increase per year. To find what portion of this amount is fees, determine 8.75% of $674.40: $0.0875 \times \$674.40 = \$59.01$. Rounded to the nearest dollar, the correct answer is 59.

7. 44

Difficulty: Medium

Strategic Advice: Determine the total increase over the entire period (including the extension), and use this to find the percent increase in cost.

Getting to the Answer: Three academic years will pass after the end of the initial five year increase period (2020-21, 2021-22, 2022-23), so multiply the average yearly increase you found in part 1 by 3 to get $\$674.40 \times 3 = \$2, 023.20$. Add this to $3,372, the increase through 2019-20, to get the total increase over this entire period, which is $5,395.20. Divide this by the pre-increase implementation cost (from 2014-15), and multiply this result by 100 to find the percent change: $\frac{\$5395.20}{\$12192} \times 100 = 44.252\%$. Round to 44.

PRACTICE

8. C
Difficulty: Easy

Category: Problem Solving and Data Analysis / Rates, Ratios, Proportions, and Percentages

Strategic Advice: You have a couple rates, but you need to manipulate them slightly before using them in the DIRT equation.

Getting to the Answer: Start by changing the given rates to unit rates. For the 5-second interval, $r_5 = 1$ car per 5 s = 0.2 cars/s. The 8-second interval becomes $r_8 = 1$ car per 8 s = 0.125 cars/s. Next, convert the time window into seconds to match your rates: $3 \text{ h} \times \dfrac{60 \text{ min}}{1 \text{ h}} \times \dfrac{60 \text{ h}}{1 \text{ min}} = 10{,}800$ s. Now you can use the DIRT equation to find the number of cars allowed through at each interval.

5 seconds: $d_5 = 0.2$ cars/s $\times$ 10,800 s $= 2{,}160$ cars
8 seconds: $d_8 = 0.125$ cars/s $\times$ 10,800 s $= 1{,}350$ cars

Subtracting these gives $2{,}160 - 1{,}350 = 810$ more cars, which is (C).

9. D
Difficulty: Hard

Category: Problem Solving and Data Analysis / Rates, Ratios, Proportions, and Percentages

Strategic Advice: Read carefully to ensure you do your calculations correctly and in the order specified.

Getting to the Answer: Murray starts with $75,400 per year. The first deduction is the 20% 401(k) contribution. Using the percent three-part formula, you'll find Murray has $0.8 \times \$75{,}400 = \$60{,}320$ left. He pays $150 per month for insurance, which is $1,800 per year. This leaves $58,520 pre-tax. Taxes are trickier, so work carefully. State taxes are easy; just take 4.5% of the pre-tax total: $0.045 \times \$58{,}520 = \$2{,}633.40$.

Federal taxes involve three separate calculations as follows:

$$10\% \text{ bracket: } 0.1 \times \$9{,}225 = \$922.50$$
$$15\% \text{ bracket: } 0.15 \times (\$37{,}450 - \$9{,}226) = \$4{,}233.60$$
$$25\% \text{ bracket: } 0.25 \times (\$58{,}520 - \$37{,}451) = \$5{,}267.25$$

Adding up all of Murray's tax liability gives $13,056.75. Subtract this from his pre-tax total to get $45,463.25. Don't stop yet! The question asks for Murray's biweekly pay. Divide $45,463.25 by 26, the number of pay periods in one year, to get $1,748.59. (D) is the correct choice.

10. 7/16
Difficulty: Hard

Category: Problem Solving and Data Analysis / Rates, Ratios, Proportions, and Percentages / Multi-Part Math

Strategic Advice: The question asks for a fraction, a relative quantity, so don't panic about not having exact dimensions for the squares. Pick your own instead.

Getting to the Answer: Start by labeling each square for clarity.

Pick a side length for square 1; 1 in. is an excellent choice. This means its area is 1 in.^{2} If the square edges are 0.5 in. apart, that means square 2 has a side length of $1 + 0.5 + 0.5 = 2$ in., square 3 has a side length of $2 + 0.5 + 0.5 = 3$ in., and so on. This translates to areas of 1, 4, 9, 16, 25, 36, 49, and 64 (all in.^{2}). But don't forget you need to subtract the square within each to get the true areas! You'll get the following:

$$\text{sq. 1 (gray)} = 1 \text{ in.}^2$$
$$\text{sq. 2 (black)} = 2^2 - 1 = 3 \text{ in.}^2$$
$$\text{sq. 3 (gray)} = 3^2 - 4 = 5 \text{ in.}^2$$
$$\text{sq. 4 (black)} = 4^2 - 9 = 7 \text{ in.}^2$$
$$\text{sq. 5 (gray)} = 5^2 - 16 = 9 \text{ in.}^2$$
$$\text{sq. 6 (black)} = 6^2 - 25 = 11 \text{ in.}^2$$
$$\text{sq. 7 (gray)} = 7^2 - 36 = 13 \text{ in.}^2$$
$$\text{sq. 8 (black)} = 8^2 - 49 = 15 \text{ in.}^2$$

After a few calculations you might start to see a pattern; if so, great! You can shave off a few seconds of number crunching. Now add up the gray squares to get 28, then divide by the area of the whole plate (64) to get $\frac{28}{64} = \frac{7}{16}$. Grid in 7/16, then move to part 2.

11. 10/9

Difficulty: Medium

Strategic Advice: You've already done most of the work for this part; look closely at your work for the first part to see what you can reuse.

Getting to the Answer: Finding the large plate black fraction is easy; just subtract the large plate gray fraction from 1 to get $\frac{9}{16}$. Because the small plate is just a smaller version of the large plate with only four squares, you can use your calculations for squares 1-4 from part 1 here. Squares 1 and 3 (gray) comprise 6 in.^{2}, and squares 2 and 4 (black) comprise 10 in.^{2}. This means the small plate black fraction is $\frac{10}{16} = \frac{5}{8}$. To find how many times more black glaze is on the small plate, divide the small plate black fraction by its large plate counterpart: $\frac{5}{8} \div \frac{9}{16} = \frac{5}{8} \times \frac{16}{9} = \frac{10}{9}$. Grid in 10/9, and you're done!

PERFORM

12. A

Difficulty: Easy

Category: Problem Solving and Data Analysis / Rates, Ratios, Proportions, and Percentages

Strategic Advice: Convert all four rates into the same units before comparing.

Getting to the Answer: You might think you should convert each price into cost per banana, but a closer look reveals that all but one price already uses weight. Save time by converting the units into cost per pound; the order will be no different than if you did cost per banana. Use the banana-pound relationship to convert each price into cost per pound. FoodCo's price is already per pound, so no work is needed there. Bob's charges $0.29 per banana, which becomes $\frac{\$0.29}{1 \text{ banana}} \times \frac{1 \text{ banana}}{\frac{1}{3} \text{ lb}} = \frac{\$0.87}{1 \text{ lb}}$. Acme's price is $1.50 for 2 lb or $0.75 per pound. The deal at Stu's means you pay $1.95 for 4 lb, which is $0.4875 per pound. Therefore, the correct order is Bob's, Acme, FoodCo, Stu's; which matches (A).

13. 18.2

Difficulty: Easy

Category: Problem Solving and Data Analysis / Rates, Ratios, Proportions, and Percentages

Strategic Advice: Start by drawing a diagram to make sense of the situation.

Getting to the Answer: The ziplines make up hypotenuses of two right triangles. Because the two zipline setups are proportional, the triangles are similar.

You can use a proportion to solve for the length of the kids' zipline: $\dfrac{10}{26} = \dfrac{3}{x}$. Solving for x gives 7.8 m. But you're not done yet! The question asks for the difference in zipline length, so subtract 7.8 from 26 to get 18.2, the correct answer.

14. 166
Difficulty: Medium

Category: Problem Solving and Data Analysis / Rates, Ratios, Proportions, and Percentages / Multi-Part Math

Strategic Advice: Identify the units of your start and end quantities, then string together the proper conversion factors.

Getting to the Answer: You know Mark will drive 960 miles over the course of his trip, and you need to determine what he should budget for fuel. The full conversion is as follows:

$960 \text{ mi} \times \dfrac{1 \text{ gal}}{40 \text{ mi}} \times \dfrac{3.785 \text{ L}}{1 \text{ gal}} \times \dfrac{1.20 \text{ GBP}}{1 \text{ L}} \times \dfrac{1.52 \text{ USD}}{1 \text{ GBP}} =$ 165.69 USD. Round to 166 per the question instructions.

15. 17
Difficulty: Medium

Strategic Advice: Determine Mark's fuel cost with the offer, then compare it to the original.

Getting to the Answer: If you stopped your calculations in part 1 after the gallon-to-liter conversion, you would find that Mark will use 90.84 L of fuel. At the new fuel price, Mark would pay 90.84 × 0.75 = 68.13 GBP for fuel. Add the 30 GBP cost for the rate reduction to get 98.13 GBP. Use the GBP-USD conversion to get 149.15 USD. Subtracting this from 166 gives 16.85, which is rounded to 17.

EXTRA PRACTICE

1. A
Difficulty: Easy

Category: Problem Solving and Data Analysis / Rates, Ratios, Proportions, and Percentages

Strategic Advice: When a question involves several rates, break it into separate, manageable pieces and deal with each in turn.

Getting to the Answer: When the car is driven off the lot, it immediately loses $12,000 in value, regardless of how far it is driven, so the after-purchase value is $35,000 – $12,000 = $23,000. The first 50,000 miles *reduce* the car's value by $0.15 each, or 50,000(–$0.15) = –$7,500. Now the car's value is $23,000 – $7,500 = $15,500. Any miles driven over 50,000 reduce the value by $0.10 per mile, and the car is driven for 92,000 miles, which is 42,000 over 50,000. This means the car depreciates another 42,000(–0.10) = –$4,200. The value of the car after being driven 92,000 miles is $15,500 – $4,200 = $11,300, which matches (A).

2. D
Difficulty: Easy

Category: Problem Solving and Data Analysis / Rates, Ratios, Proportions, and Percentages

Strategic Advice: To answer a question that says "directly proportional," set two ratios equal to each other and solve for the missing amount. Don't forget—match the units in the numerators and in the denominators on both sides of the proportion.

Getting to the Answer: Because the first rate is given in minutes, write 1 hour as 60 minutes. Let t equal the number of topics the teacher can cover

in a 60-minute period. S_____ _____ solve for t:

$$\frac{9 \text{ topics}}{45 \text{ minutes}} = \frac{t \text{ topics}}{60 \text{ minutes}}$$

$$9(60) = 45(t)$$

$$540 = 45t$$

$$12 = t$$

Choice (D) is correct.

3. C
Difficulty: Easy

Category: Problem Solving and Data Analysis / Rates, Ratios, Proportions, and Percentages

Strategic Advice: It can be confusing to decide which operation to perform when dealing with conversions, especially when the conversions involve decimals. Think about how your answer should look first. A person weighs *less* on the moon, so he or she should weigh *more* on Earth. This means your answer must be greater than 29, so you can eliminate A right away.

Getting to the Answer: The easiest way to convert the units and keep them straight is to set up a proportion.

$$\frac{0.166 \text{ lb on moon}}{1 \text{ lb on Earth}} = \frac{29 \text{ lb on moon}}{p \text{ lb on Earth}}$$

$$29(1) = 0.166p$$

$$\frac{29}{0.166} = \frac{0.166p}{0.166}$$

$$174.7 \approx p$$

The man weighs about 175 pounds on Earth. Choice (C) is correct.

4. A
Difficulty: Easy

Category: Problem Solving and Data Analysis / Rates, Ratios, Proportions, and Percentages

Strategic Advice: Whenever multiple rates are given, pay very careful attention to the units. As you read the question, decide how and when you will need to convert units. Use the factor label method as needed.

Getting to the Answer: The answer choices are given in hours and minutes, so start by converting the given typing rate from words per second to words per minute:

$$\frac{3.75 \text{ words}}{1 \text{ second}} \times \frac{60 \text{ seconds}}{1 \text{ minutes}} = \frac{225 \text{ words}}{1 \text{ minute}}$$

Next, find the number of words in the 25-page transcript:

$$\frac{675 \text{ words}}{1 \text{ page}} \times 25 \text{ pages} = 16,875 \text{ words}$$

Finally, let m be the number of minutes it takes the court reporter to type the whole transcript. Set up a proportion and solve for m.

$$\frac{225 \text{ words}}{1 \text{ minute}} = \frac{16,875 \text{ words}}{m \text{ minutes}}$$
$$225m = 16,875$$
$$m = 75$$

Because 75 minutes is not an answer choice, convert it to hours and minutes: 75 minutes = 1 hour, 15 minutes, making (A) the correct answer.

5. C
Difficulty: Medium

Category: Problem Solving and Data Analysis / Rates, Ratios, Proportions, and Percentages

Strategic Advice: Don't let the three-way ratio scare you. You can solve this problem just like any other ratio question.

Getting to the Answer: Set up an equation using *parts*: 35 parts of the vote were for Taft, 41 parts were for Roosevelt, and 63 parts were for Wilson.

You don't know how big a part is, so call it x. Now, write and solve an equation:

$$35x + 41x + 63x = 208,500$$
$$139x = 208,500$$
$$x = 1,500$$

Look back at the ratio—35 parts of the vote were for Taft, so the number of votes cast for Taft was $35(1,500) = 52,500$, which matches (C).

6. B
Difficulty: Medium

Category: Problem Solving and Data Analysis / Rates, Ratios, Proportions, and Percentages

Strategic Advice: This is a typical proportion question. Use words first to write the proportion. Then translate from English into math.

Getting to the Answer: Let n equal the number of people tested. Set up a proportion and solve for n. Be sure to match the units in the numerators and in the denominators on both sides of the proportion.

$$\frac{\text{false positives}}{\text{number tested}} = \frac{\text{false positives}}{\text{number tested}}$$
$$\frac{6}{3,500} = \frac{27}{n}$$
$$6n = 27(3,500)$$
$$6n = 94,500$$
$$n = 15,750$$

This means (B) is correct.

7. C
Difficulty: Medium

Category: Problem Solving and Data Analysis / Rates, Ratios, Proportions, and Percentages

Strategic Advice: Think about this question for a few seconds before you start, and make a plan for solving it. The question is asking for the discounted hourly rate, which is the rate *after* the one free hour and *after* the 10 hours at the $30 rate. Make sure you subtract these numbers from the total number of hours of tutoring the client paid for before you find the discounted rate.

Getting to the Answer: Start with the hours. The client received 25 hours of tutoring, of which 1 hour was free. So, the client paid for 24 hours of tutoring. The first 10 hours were at a different rate than the discounted rate, so subtract these to find that the client paid the discounted rate for 24 − 10 = 14 hours. Now look at the money: The first 10 hours the client was actually billed for cost $30 per hour for a total of $300, so subtract this from the total amount paid to get $664 − $300 = $364. This is the amount charged for the 14 discounted hours. Divide this amount by the number of hours billed at the discounted rate to get $364 ÷ 14 = $26 per hour, making (C) the correct choice.

8. D
Difficulty: Medium

Category: Problem Solving and Data Analysis / Rates, Ratios, Proportions, and Percentages

Strategic Advice: You can use the formula Percent = $\frac{Part}{Whole}$ × 100% to answer this question. But be careful—you have been given several pieces of information, so you'll need to be organized.

Getting to the Answer: First, find the number of people at each location who responded favorably using the formula. Start with the first location: 125 × 0.224 = 28. Move on to the second location: 272 × 0.375 = 102. Next, find the total number of people that were surveyed at both locations (125 + 272 = 397) and the total number who responded favorably (28 + 102 = 130). Finally, find the percent of people who responded favorably by using the formula one more time:

$$397 \times \text{Percent} = 130 \times 100\%$$
$$\text{Percent} = 130 \div 397 \times 100\%$$
$$\text{Percent} = 0.3274 \times 100\%$$
$$\text{Percent} = 32.7\%$$

Of all the people surveyed, about 32.7% responded favorably, making (D) the correct answer.

9. A
Difficulty: Medium

Category: Problem Solving and Data Analysis / Rates, Ratios, Proportions, and Percentages

Strategic Advice: Let the units in this question guide you to the solution. The cooking rates of the ovens are given in pounds per hour, but the question asks about the number of ounces each oven can cook in 10 minutes, so convert pounds per hour to ounces per minute. Use the factor-label method.

Getting to the Answer: Start by converting pounds to ounces. There are 16 ounces in one pound, so 3 pounds is 48 ounces and 4.5 pounds is 72 ounces. Now convert the hours to minutes:

Oven at 350°:

$$\frac{48 \text{ oz}}{1 \text{ hr}} \times \frac{1 \text{ hr}}{60 \text{ min}} \times 10 \text{ min} = 8 \text{ oz}$$

Oven at 450°:

$$\frac{72 \text{ oz}}{1 \text{ hr}} \times \frac{1 \text{ hr}}{60 \text{ min}} \times 10 \text{ min} = 12 \text{ oz}$$

In 10 minutes, the oven at 450° can cook 12 − 8 = 4 ounces more than the oven at 350°, making (A) the correct answer.

10. B
Difficulty: Medium

Category: Problem Solving and Data Analysis / Rates, Ratios, Proportions, and Percentages

Strategic Advice: Before you start, think about where this question is. It is not near the beginning of the homework, so it is probably not an easy problem. This means it won't be as simple as converting 20°C to degrees Fahrenheit using the formula.

Getting to the Answer: The question says temperatures can vary by 20°C during a single day. This is not the same as saying the temperature itself is 20°, so you can't just convert the temperature to Fahrenheit. You aren't given exact numbers, just a range, so you'll need to pick some convenient numbers for yourself. You might know (or can tell from the formula) that 0°C is equal to 32°F. So pick 0°C and 20°C. Convert each of these to Fahrenheit and then find the difference.

$$F = \frac{9}{5}(C) + 32$$

$$F_{at\,0} = \frac{9}{5}(0) + 32$$

$$= 0 + 32$$

$$= 32$$

$$F_{at\,20} = \frac{9}{5}(20) + 32$$

$$= 36 + 32$$

$$= 68$$

0°C = 32°F and 20°C = 68°F, which means a change in temperature of 20°C is equivalent to a change of 68° − 32° = 36°F, which is (B).

You could also recognize from the formula that Fahrenheit measurements are exactly $\frac{9}{5}$ of Celsius measurements, so you could multiply 20 by $\frac{9}{5}$ to arrive at 36 as well.

11. B
Difficulty: Medium

Category: Problem Solving and Data Analysis / Rates, Ratios, Proportions, and Percentages

Strategic Advice: Don't let all the technical words in this question overwhelm you. Solve it step-by-step examining the units as you go. Use the factor label method to help you stay organized.

Getting to the Answer: *Step 1:* Determine the number of megabytes the company can upload in 1 evening (4 hours):

$$\frac{12\ \text{MB}}{1\ \text{sec}} \times \frac{60\ \text{sec}}{1\ \text{min}} \times \frac{60\ \text{min}}{1\ \text{hr}} \times \frac{4\ \text{hr}}{1\ \text{evening}} = \frac{172{,}800\ \text{MB}}{1\ \text{evening}}$$

Step 2: Convert this amount to gigabytes (because the information about the scans is given in gigabytes, not megabytes):

$$172{,}800\ \text{MB} \times \frac{1\ \text{GB}}{1{,}024\ \text{MB}} = 168.75\ \text{GB}$$

Step 3: Each video file is about 4.5 gigabytes, so divide by 4.5 to determine how many videos the company can upload to the cloud using its internet service provider: 168.75 ÷ 4.5 = 37.5 videos. Remember, you should round this number down to 37, because the question asks for the maximum number the company can upload and it cannot complete the 38th video upload in the time allowed. The correct answer is (B).

12. D
Difficulty: Hard

Category: Problem Solving and Data Analysis / Rates, Ratios, Proportions, and Percentages

Strategic Advice: The key to answering this question is translating from English into math. Start by assigning a variable to what you're looking for.

Getting to the Answer: Let m be the number of months the customer has subscribed to the service. The first month costs a dollars and the remaining months $(m - 1)$ are charged at a rate of b dollars per month. So, the total charge for the service so far is $a + b(m - 1)$. Set this equal to the amount the customer has paid and solve for m. Note that you're not going to get a nice number answer, because the question doesn't give you the actual rates.

$$a + b(m-1) = 108.60$$

$$a + bm - b = 108.60$$

$$bm = 108.60 - a + b$$

$$m = \frac{108.60 - a + b}{b}$$

The expression for m matches the one in (D).

13. D

Difficulty: Hard

Category: Problem Solving and Data Analysis / Rates, Ratios, Proportions, and Percentages

Strategic Advice: Draw a chart or diagram detailing the various price reductions for each two weeks.

Getting to the Answer:

Length of Time on Market	% of Most Recent Price	Resulting Price
List Price	–	$200,000.00
After 2 weeks	100% – 5% = 95%	$190,000.00
After 4 weeks	100% – 5% = 95%	$180,500.00
After 6 weeks	100% – 3% = 97%	$175,085.00
After 8 weeks	100% – 3% = 97%	$169,832.45

You can stop here because the item was sold after 9 weeks and the next price reduction would have been at 10 weeks, so the selling price was $169,832.45, which is (D).

14. B

Difficulty: Hard

Category: Problem Solving and Data Analysis / Rates, Ratios, Proportions, and Percentages

Strategic Advice: Pay careful attention to the units. You need to convert all of the dimensions to inches, and then find the scale factor. You'll have to start with the skull because it's the only part of the T-rex for which you know both the actual length and the model length. Before selecting your answer, make sure you found the right quantity (the difference between the scale model's length and its height).

Getting to the Answer: There are 12 inches in one foot, so Sue's skull length was $12 \times 5 = 60$ inches and the model skull is $3 \times 12 = 36 + 1.5 = 37.5$ inches. Find the scale factor by writing this as a fraction. Multiply both numbers by 10 to get rid of the decimal and then simplify the ratio:

$$\frac{37.5}{60} = \frac{375}{600} = \frac{5}{8}$$

This means the scale factor is $\frac{5}{8}$. You might be tempted to now find the scale model's length and height by multiplying 40 and 13 by $\frac{5}{8}$, but this would waste valuable time. Because the model is a $\frac{5}{8}$ scale model, the difference between the model's length and height will be exactly $\frac{5}{8}$ of the difference between Sue's actual length and height, which is $40 - 13 = 27$ feet. Multiply 27 by $\frac{5}{8}$ to find that the difference between the length and height of the model should be 16.875 feet, or 16 feet, 10.5 inches, which matches (B).

15. C

Difficulty: Medium

Category: Problem Solving and Data Analysis / Rates, Ratios, Proportions, and Percentages

Strategic Advice: This is another question where the units can help you find the answer. Use the number of employees to find the total number of miles driven to find the total number of gallons of gas used. Then you can write an equation, with r equal to the reimbursement rate, and set it equal to the amount of total reimbursements paid.

Getting to the Answer:

$$126 \text{ employees} \times \frac{12,250 \text{ mi}}{\text{employee}} = 1,543,500 \text{ mi}$$

$$1,543,500 \text{ mi} \times \frac{1 \text{ gal of gas}}{22.5 \text{ miles}} = 68,600 \text{ gal}$$

$$68,600r = \$96,040.00$$
$$r = \$1.40$$

The reimbursement rate was $1.40 per gallon, which is (C).

16. 14
Difficulty: Easy

Category: Problem Solving and Data Analysis / Rates, Ratios, Proportions, and Percentages

Strategic Advice: Identify the information you are given and figure out what you still need to answer the question—you need to know how long each person took to read their book.

Getting to the Answer: You know the length of Betsy's book and the rate at which she reads. You need to know how many minutes she reads.

$$\frac{116 \text{ pg}}{1 \text{ book}} \times \frac{1.5 \text{ min}}{1 \text{ pg}} = 116 \times 1.5 = 174$$

It takes Betsy 174 minutes to read her book. You know Raymond starts reading at 8:30 AM and reads until 11:38 AM, which is 11:38 − 8:30 = 3 hours, 8 minutes, or 188 minutes. It takes Raymond 188 − 174 = 14 minutes longer to read his book.

17. 4
Difficulty: Easy

Category: Problem Solving and Data Analysis / Rates, Ratios, Proportions, and Percentages

Strategic Advice: Lining up the units so that they cancel nicely is the key to answering this question.

Getting to the Answer: Katrina already knows how much cardboard she needs; she just doesn't have the amount in the proper units. All this question is asking you to do is convert 576 *square* inches to *square* feet.

$$\frac{576 \text{ in.}^2}{1} \times \frac{1 \text{ ft}}{12 \text{ in.}} \times \frac{1 \text{ ft}}{12 \text{ in.}} = \frac{576}{144} \text{ ft}^2 = 4 \text{ ft}^2$$

18. 540
Difficulty: Medium

Category: Problem Solving and Data Analysis / Rates, Ratios, Proportions, and Percentages

Strategic Advice: Break the questions into steps. First, find how long it took the employee to collect samples from one house, and then use that amount to find how long it should take the employee to collect samples from all of the houses.

Getting to the Answer: The employee *started* the 1st house at 9:00 and the 6th house at 10:00, so it took him 1 hour, or 60 minutes, to collect samples from 5 houses. This gives a unit rate of 60 ÷ 5 = 12 minutes per house. Multiply the unit rate by the number of houses in the subdivision (45) to get 12 × 45 = 540 minutes to collect samples from all the houses.

19. 1000
Difficulty: Medium

Category: Problem Solving and Data Analysis / Rates, Ratios, Proportions, and Percentages

Strategic Advice: The distance on the students' maps is 2.5 inches, but you can't just multiply this by the scale because the maps the students have are $\frac{1}{4}$ the size of the wall map, so the scale isn't the same. You must first determine how long 2.5 inches on the student map is on the wall map.

Getting to the Answer: If the student map is $\frac{1}{4}$ the size of the wall map, then 2.5 inches on the student map would be 2.5 × 4 = 10 inches on the wall map. Now set up a proportion to find the actual distance between the cities using the scale of the wall map:

$$\frac{1}{100} = \frac{10}{x}$$
$$x = 1,000$$

The correct answer is 1000.

20. 76.5

Difficulty: Medium

Category: Problem Solving and Data Analysis / Rates, Ratios, Proportions, and Percentages

Strategic Advice: This question is tricky. The interest (after being rounded down) is added to the account at the end of each year. The next year, the new, higher amount is the amount that will earn interest.

Getting to the Answer: Start by multiplying the principal by the interest rate:

$$1,500 \times 0.01 = 15$$

Now add this to the principal:

$$1,500 + 15 = 1,515$$

This is the amount that will earn interest in the next year. Repeat this process for 4 more years. Multiply the principal by the interest rate, round the interest down to the nearest cent, and then add it to the principal to use for the next year's calculation.

Year two:
$$1,515 \times 0.01 = 15.15$$
$$1,515 + 15.15 = 1,530.15$$
Year three:
$$1,530.15 \times 0.01 = 15.3015 \rightarrow 15.30$$
$$1,530.15 + 15.30 = 1,545.45$$
Year four:
$$1,545.45 \times 0.01 = 15.4545 \rightarrow 15.45$$
$$1,545.45 + 15.45 = 1,560.90$$
Year five:
$$1,560.90 \times 0.01 = 15.609 \rightarrow 15.60$$
$$1,560.90 + 15.60 = 1,576.50$$

Over five years, the account earned $1,576.50 − $1,500 = $76.50 in interest. Enter this as 76.5.

Be careful here—you might be tempted to use the exponential function $f(5) = 1,500(1.01)^5$ to arrive at the answer more quickly. However, the question specifically states that the interest is rounded down to the nearest whole cent each year, which changes the answer by just a couple of cents.

21. 40

Difficulty: Hard

Category: Problem Solving and Data Analysis / Rates, Ratios, Proportions, and Percentages

Strategic Advice: Start by determining what the question is asking. You need to find the net change in the power allocated to Grid 1 over the course of a day. To do this, you need to know how much the grid was allocated at the beginning of the day and how much at the end.

Getting to the Answer: You aren't given a concrete starting point (or units of power), so simply pick a starting number. The best number to use when dealing with percents is 100. First, find how much power the grid was allocated after the first 20% increase: $100 \times 1.2 = 120$. Next, find the amount after the 10% decrease: $120 \times 0.9 = 108$. Finally, find the amount after the last 30% increase: $108 \times 1.3 = 140.4$, which is $140.4 - 100 = 40.4$ more than it started the day with. To find the percent change, use the formula $\text{Percent change} = \dfrac{\text{Amount of change}}{\text{Original amount}}$ to get $\dfrac{40.4}{100} = 0.404$. Rounded to the nearest whole percent, this is 40 percent.

22. 50

Difficulty: Medium

Category: Problem Solving and Data Analysis / Rates, Ratios, Proportions, and Percentages

Strategic Advice: Break this problem into short steps. Step one: Find the total number of drips needed to deliver 800 mL of medication. Step two: Divide this by the number of hours, 8, over which the meds will be delivered. Step three: Divide the result by 60 to convert the rate to drips per minute.

Getting to the Answer: *Step one*: Find the total number of drips needed by multiplying the amount of medication prescribed, 800 mL, by the number of drips needed to deliver 1 mL: $800 \times 30 = 24,000$ drips.

Step two: Divide this number by 8 to find how many drips per hour are needed: 24,000 ÷ 8 = 3,000 drips per hour.

Step three: Divide this by 60 (because there are 60 minutes in one hour) to convert drips per hour to drips per minute: 3,000 ÷ 60 = 50 drips per minute.

23. 10.5

Difficulty: Medium

Category: Problem Solving and Data Analysis / Rates, Ratios, Proportions, and Percentages

Strategic Advice: Questions that involve distance, rate, and time can almost always be solved using the DIRT formula, Distance = Rate × Time.

Getting to the Answer: For each of the three friends, you know how long they traveled and their rate. Use the formula to find the distance for each one. But be careful—the rates are given in miles per hour, which means you must use hours, not minutes, for the times.

Andrea:
30 minutes = 0.5 hours
Distance = 3 × 0.5 = 1.5 miles
Kellan:
45 minutes = 0.75 hours
Distance = 14 × 0.75 = 10.5 miles
Joelle:
15 minutes = 0.25 hours
Distance = 35 × 0.25 = 8.75 miles

Kellan lives the farthest away at 10.5 miles. An important note here—the question did not tell you to round and the entire answer fits in the grid, so you MUST grid the answer in as 10.5. However, had you gotten an answer like 10.57 (which wouldn't fit in the grid), then you could either round to 10.6 or truncate (cut off) the answer at 10.5 because it would still fill the entire grid.

24. 731

Difficulty: Hard

Category: Problem Solving and Data Analysis / Rates, Ratios, Proportions, and Percentages

Strategic Advice: When answering questions that share information, you can almost always save yourself some time by using amounts you found in the first question to answer the second one. You will need to find the total amount of time Kellan was travelling, and then subtract that from his arrival time.

Getting to the Answer: In the previous question, you already found that Andrea's house is 1.5 miles from the restaurant. Use the DIRT formula to determine how long Kellan walked with Andrea:

$$1.5 = 2.5 \times \text{time}$$
$$1.5 = 2.5t$$
$$0.6 = t$$

They walked for 0.6 hours, or 60 × 0.6 = 36 minutes. Now calculate how long Kellan biked. Again, you have the distance and the rate, so you need to use the formula to find the time:

$$12 = 15 \times \text{time}$$
$$12 = 15t$$
$$0.8 = t$$

Kellan biked for 0.8 hours, or 60 × 0.8 = 48 minutes. So Kellan traveled for a total of 36 + 48 = 84 minutes, or 1 hour, 24 minutes. Don't forget that they arrived 5 minutes early, or at 8:55. So Kellan must have left his house at 8:55 − 1 hour = 7:55 − 24 minutes = 7:31 AM. Enter this as 731.

25. 660

Difficulty: Easy

Category: Problem Solving and Data Analysis / Rates, Ratios, Proportions, and Percentages

Strategic Advice: Break this question into short steps. Find the amount of the hostess share for one evening. Multiply this by the number of evenings per week, 5, and then the number of weeks, 4. Do this for each restaurant, and then subtract to find the difference.

Getting to the Answer:

Restaurant A:
0.07 × $1,100 = $77
$77 × 5 = 385
$385 × 4 = $1,540

Restaurant B:
0.04 × $1,100 = $44
$44 × 5 = $220
$220 × 4 = $880

Mia would make $1,540 – $880 = $660 more at Restaurant A.

26. 75
Difficulty: Hard

Category: Problem Solving and Data Analysis / Rates, Ratios, Proportions, and Percentages

Strategic Advice: This question requires multiple steps and multiple formulas, so make a plan before you dive in. The formula for percent increase is
$$\text{Percent increase} = \frac{\text{Final amount} - \text{Original amount}}{\text{Original amount}}.$$
This tells you that you need the final amount in tips that Restaurant B needs to bring in to be equal to Restaurant A, which will depend on the amount in tips Restaurant A brings in. You'll need to use the percent formula (Percent × Whole = Part) to determine what amount would be required at 4% for the hostess share to be equal.

Getting to the Answer: The hostess tip share for one evening at Restaurant A is $1,100 × 0.07 = $77. Use this amount to find the final amount of tips, *t*, Restaurant B needs:

$$0.04 \times t = 77$$
$$0.04t = 77$$
$$t = \$1,925$$

Now use the percent increase formula:

$$\text{Percent increase} = \frac{1,925 - 1,100}{1,100}$$
$$= \frac{825}{1,100}$$
$$= 0.75$$

The percent increase needed is 75%. Per the question's instructions, enter this as 75 (not .75).

27. 45.5
Difficulty: Medium

Category: Problem Solving and Data Analysis / Rates, Ratios, Proportions, and Percentages

Strategic Advice: Use the formula, Percent = $\frac{\text{Part}}{\text{Whole}} \times 100$. You'll need to do some preliminary calculations to find the *whole*.

Getting to the Answer: The *part* of the budget represented by the textbook is $24.99. The total cost of all the supplies (or the *whole*) is 1 textbook ($24.99) + 5 notebooks (5 × $3.78 = $18.90) + 20 pencils (20 × $0.55 = $11.00) = $54.89. Now use the formula:

$$\text{Percent} = \frac{24.99}{54.89} \times 100$$
$$= 0.45527 \times 100$$
$$= 45.527$$

Before you grid in your answer, make sure you followed the directions—round to the nearest tenth of a percent and ignore the percent sign, which is 45.5.

28. 100
Difficulty: Hard

Category: Problem Solving and Data Analysis / Rates, Ratios, Proportions, and Percentages

Strategic Advice: This question contains several steps. Be careful—there are lots of calculations that involve decimals, and you shouldn't round until the very end.

Getting to the Answer: Start with the total cost of the year's supplies: $988.02. After taking inventory,

Bridget knows she has used $713.57 worth of supplies, which means she should have $988.02 – $713.57 = $274.45 worth of supplies left. From the previous question, you know that 1 textbook, 5 notebooks, and 20 pencils together cost $54.89, which means Bridget has $274.45 ÷ $54.89 = 5 sets of the initial supplies left. Don't grid in this amount because you're not finished yet! The question asks for the *number of pencils* left. According to the table, each order (set) contains 20 pencils, so there should be 5 × 20 = 100 pencils left.

29. C
Difficulty: Easy

Category: Problem Solving and Data Analysis / Rates, Ratios, Proportions, and Percentages

Strategic Advice: Be sure to answer the right question. This question asks for the number (not the percent) of customers who are totally or somewhat satisfied.

Getting to the Answer: According to the pie graph, 25% of the customers are totally dissatisfied and 15% are somewhat dissatisfied. So, 100% – 25% – 15% = 60% of the customers are totally or somewhat satisfied. Thus, the *number* of customers that are totally or somewhat satisfied is 60% of 240, or 0.6 × 240 = 144 customers, making (C) correct.

30. B
Difficulty: Easy

Category: Problem Solving and Data Analysis / Rates, Ratios, Proportions, and Percentages

Strategic Advice: The total budget can be represented by 100%, so start with that. Before you select an answer, check that you answered the right question (the amount of the general contractor's fee).

Getting to the Answer: The percent of the budget spent on the contractor's fee is 100% – 20% – 55% – 10% = 15%. You're told that the estimate for materials is $5,200, which represents 20% of the total budget.

Let x be the total amount of the budget in dollars. Then 20% of x is $5,200, or $0.2x = 5,200$. Solve this equation for x.

$$0.2x = 5,200$$
$$x = 26,000$$

The total budget is $26,000. The contractor's fee represents 15% of this amount, or 0.15 × $26,000 = $3,900, which means (B) is correct.

31. C
Difficulty: Medium

Category: Problem Solving and Data Analysis / Rates, Ratios, Proportions, and Percentages

Strategic Advice: You are given a lot of numbers in this question. Break the question into short steps. Before you move on, check that you answered the right question (the number of LED bulbs that were *not* defective).

Getting to the Answer:

Step 1: Find the number of LED bulbs produced. A total of 12,500 of both kinds of bulbs were produced. The ratio of LED to CFL is 2:3, so two parts LED plus three parts CFL equals 12,500. Write this as $2x + 3x = 12,500$. Simplify and solve this equation to find that $x = 2,500$. Multiply this amount by 2 (because two parts were LED bulbs): 2,500 × 2 = 5,000.

Step 2: Use that number to find the number of LED bulbs that were defective: 3% of 5,000 or 5,000 × 0.03 = 150 defective LEDs.

Step 3: Find the number of LED bulbs that were not defective: 5,000 – 150 = 4,850.

Choice (C) is correct.

32. B
Difficulty: Medium

Category: Problem Solving and Data Analysis / Rates, Ratios, Proportions, and Percentages

Strategic Advice: Find the percent increase using this formula: % increase = $\dfrac{\text{amount of increase}}{\text{original amount}}$. Then apply the same percent increase to the animal population in 2000.

Getting to the Answer: The amount of increase is 7,200 − 6,400 = 800, so the percent increase is $\dfrac{800}{6,400} = 0.125 = 12.5\%$ between 1950 and 2000. If the total percent increase over the next 50 years is the same, the animal population should be about 7,200 × 1.125 = 8,100. Choose (B) and move on to the next question.

33. D
Difficulty: Medium

Category: Problem Solving and Data Analysis / Rates, Ratios, Proportions, and Percentages

Strategic Advice: There are a lot of parts to this question, so make sure your answer satisfies all of the guidelines given in the bulleted list as well as the criteria set forth in the question itself (includes as many row lengths as possible).

Getting to the Answer: Start with the smallest possible row length, 20 feet. The next length must be at least 20% larger, so multiply by 1.2 to get 24 feet. But 24 is not the next row length because each row length must be evenly divisible by the width of each seat, 2.5. The next highest number that is evenly divisible by 2.5 is 25, so 25 is the next row length. You must always use the next highest number up because rounding down would make the subsequent length less than 20% longer than the row in front of it. Now multiply 25 by 1.2 to get 30 feet. This number is evenly divisible by 2.5, so it is the third row length. Continue this process until you reach the maximum length allowed, 90 feet.

$$20 \times 1.2 = 24 \rightarrow 25$$
$$25 \times 1.2 = 30 \rightarrow 30$$
$$30 \times 1.2 = 36 \rightarrow 37.5$$
$$37.5 \times 1.2 = 45 \rightarrow 45$$

$$45 \times 1.2 = 54 \rightarrow 55$$
$$55 \times 1.2 = 66 \rightarrow 67.5$$
$$67.5 \times 1.2 = 81 \rightarrow 82.5$$
$$82.5 \times 1.2 = 99 \rightarrow \text{Too long}$$

The possible row lengths are 25, 30, 37.5, 45, 55, 67.5, and 82.5, which means (D) is correct.

34. D
Difficulty: Hard

Category: Problem Solving and Data Analysis / Rates, Ratios, Proportions, and Percentages

Strategic Advice: Read the question, organizing important information as you go. You need to find the ratio of lionfish to seahorses. You're given two ratios: eels to lionfish and eels to seahorses.

Getting to the Answer: Both of the given ratios contain eels, but the eel amounts (5 and 2) are not identical. To directly compare them, find a common multiple (10). Multiply each ratio by the factor that will make the number of eels equal to 10.

$$\text{Eels to Lionfish: } (5{:}2) \times (2{:}2) = 10{:}4$$
$$\text{Eels to Seahorses: } (2{:}3) \times (5{:}5) = 10{:}15$$

Now that the number of eels needed are the same in both ratios, you can merge the two ratios to compare lionfish to seahorses directly: 4:10:15. So the proper ratio of lionfish to seahorses is 4:15, which is (D).

35. 9.88
Difficulty: Easy

Category: Problem Solving and Data Analysis / Rates, Ratios, Proportions, and Percentages

Strategic Advice: Make sure you read the question carefully. It says the 5% clothing discount is applied *before* any other discounts, so you much subtract this first.

Getting to the Answer: If the student receives a 5% discount, this means she pays 95%, so don't waste time multiplying the amount of her check by 0.05 and then subtracting. Instead, just multiply the amount of her check by 0.95 to get $13.00 × 0.95 = $12.35. Then, apply the student discount using the same strategy. The student discount is 20% (which means she paid 80%), so she paid $12.35 × 0.8 = $9.88, not including tax.

36. 3.89
Difficulty: Medium

Category: Problem Solving and Data Analysis / Rates, Ratios, Proportions, and Percentages

Strategic Advice: Calculate the discount for each person. Make sure you answer the right question. It asks for the total amount they *save*, not the total amount they *pay*.

Getting to the Answer: This question asks about the *savings*, not about what each person pays, so this time, you *should* multiply by the discount amounts (either 20% or 5%) to save time. Calculate Sharon's military discount first: $16.25 × 0.2 = $3.25 saved. Now, Damien's discount for participating in the clothing drive: $12.80 × 0.05 = $0.64 saved. Add the two amounts to find that together they saved $3.25 + $0.64 = $3.89.

37. 11.5
Difficulty: Medium

Category: Problem Solving and Data Analysis / Rates, Ratios, Proportions, and Percentages

Strategic Advice: This question involves a proportion and a unit conversion. You may be tempted to divide the number of steps by the number of feet in Jordan's stride (because the number of steps is already very large), but this isn't correct. To be safe, start by writing a proportion comparing feet and steps.

Getting to the Answer: Let f represent the number of feet Jordan ran. There are 2.5 feet to every 1 of Jordan's steps and he took 24,288 steps.

$$\frac{2.5 \text{ feet}}{1 \text{ step}} = \frac{f \text{ feet}}{24,288 \text{ steps}}$$
$$f = 2.5(24,288)$$
$$f = 60,720$$

Jordan ran 60,720 feet. Now convert this to miles. There are 5,280 feet in one mile, so divide to get 60,720 ÷ 5,280 = 11.5 miles. Don't forget—if the question doesn't tell you to round and the answer will fit in the grid, don't round! Enter the answer as 11.5.

You could also use the factor label method to answer this question:

$$24,288 \text{ steps} \times \frac{2.5 \text{ ft}}{1 \text{ step}} \times \frac{1 \text{ mi}}{5,280 \text{ ft}} = 11.5 \text{ miles}$$

38. 18.5
Difficulty: Easy

Category: Problem Solving and Data Analysis / Rates, Ratios, Proportions, and Percentages

Strategic Advice: Again, don't be tempted to either multiply or divide until you're sure which operation is correct. Let k represent the number of kilometers and set up and solve a proportion.

Getting to the Answer:

$$\frac{1 \text{ km}}{0.62 \text{ mi}} = \frac{k \text{ km}}{11.5 \text{ mi}}$$
$$11.5 = 0.62k$$
$$\frac{11.5}{0.62} = k$$
$$18.5483 = k$$

The question tells you to round to the nearest tenth of a kilometer, so enter the answer as 18.5.

CHAPTER 6

PREPARE

1. B
Difficulty: Easy

Category: Problem Solving and Data Analysis / Scatterplots

Strategic Advice: Use a line of best fit to determine whether a correlation exists.

Getting to the Answer: Draw a line of best fit through the data points. You'll see that as farm size increases, the number of farms decreases, which indicates a negative correlation. The majority of the data points are fairly close to the line of best fit, which means the correlation is strong. Therefore, (B) must be correct.

2. C
Difficulty: Easy

Category: Problem Solving and Data Analysis / Scatterplots

Strategic Advice: Identify the type of growth/ decay occurring to determine the type of equation you need.

Getting to the Answer: Because the no-show count and group size do not change, you can assume Tracy's account balance will increase at a constant rate, indicating a linear equation. You can therefore eliminate A and B. Identify the last class Tracy missed, and draw a line of best fit through that and any points after it. Extend the line to the y-axis; you'll see the y-intercept is 11. Of the remaining choices, only (C) has this y-intercept, so it must be correct.

3. B
Difficulty: Medium

Category: Problem Solving and Data Analysis / Scatterplots

Strategic Advice: Address each piece of the question individually. Pay attention to the axis labels when interpreting the infographic.

Getting to the Answer: The 2001 formula plot has a slight curve that straightens as wind speed increases. Extend the line to reflect this trend; once complete, draw a straight line from 40 mph on the x-axis to the extended 2001 formula plot (a straight edge such as a piece of scratch paper will help). Then draw a horizontal line from the intersection of the 2001 formula line and the vertical line to the y-axis; you'll see that the corresponding wind chill is −30°F. C and D have different wind chill values, so eliminate them.

The horizontal line that you drew to find the wind chill factor intersects a data point on the 1939 formula plot. Draw a vertical line from that point to the x-axis; you'll find that in 1939, a wind speed of approximately 15 mph would yield a wind chill of −30°F. Therefore, the correct answer is (B).

PRACTICE

4. C
Difficulty: Easy

Category: Problem Solving and Data Analysis / Scatterplots

Strategic Advice: Examine the equation to determine the type of plot it will produce.

Getting to the Answer: When the exponent in an equation is a variable, the graph of the equation is exponential, so eliminate choices A and B. To distinguish between the remaining choices, pick an easy-to-use value to plug into the given equation for x (e.g., 0). You'll see that when $x = 0$, y should equal 5, which matches the graph in (C).

5. 2

Difficulty: Medium

Category: Problem Solving and Data Analysis / Scatterplots / Extended Thinking

Strategic Advice: You're asked for a rate; this means finding the slope of the line of best fit.

Getting to the Answer: Start by picking a pair of points, preferably where the line of best fit passes through a gridline intersection to minimize error. The points (50, 20) and (100, 40) are good choices. Determine the slope: $m = \dfrac{y_2 - y_1}{x_2 - x_1} = \dfrac{40 - 20}{100 - 50} = \dfrac{20}{50} = \dfrac{2}{5}$. Don't grid in $\dfrac{2}{5}$, though. Remember what you're being asked: You need the road clearing duration increase for a 5% increase in snowpack water content, not 1%. Multiply $\dfrac{2}{5}$ by 5, which yields 2.

6. 99.2

Difficulty: Medium

Strategic Advice: The slope you derived in the previous part will aid you here.

Getting to the Answer: The line of best fit on the scatterplot intersects the y-axis at (0, 0). Therefore, the equation of the line of best fit is $y = \dfrac{2}{5}x$. Plug 248 in for x and solve for y:

$$y = \frac{2}{5} \times 248$$

$$y = \frac{496}{5} = 99.2$$

The road clearing time at 248% snowpack water content will take 99.2 days.

PERFORM

7. A

Difficulty: Easy

Category: Problem Solving and Data Analysis / Scatterplots

Strategic Advice: Translate English to Math to make quick work of this question.

Getting to the Answer: The question asks for a rate of change, which means you'll need the slope of the line of best fit. Pick a pair of points to use in the slope formula, such as (1998, 20) and (2012, 90):

$m = \dfrac{y_2 - y_1}{x_2 - x_1} = \dfrac{90 - 20}{2012 - 1998} = \dfrac{70}{14} = 5$. (A) is correct.

8. A

Difficulty: Easy

Category: Problem Solving and Data Analysis / Scatterplots

Strategic Advice: Identify the type of change described in the question to narrow down your choices.

Getting to the Answer: If the number of smartphone users increases by 35% each year, then the amount of the increase is variable (because it's 35% of a bigger number each time), indicating nonlinear (exponential) growth. Eliminate C and D. Recall that when assembling an exponential growth model, r (the rate) must be in decimal form. Therefore, the number raised to the power of x should be $1 + 0.35$ or 1.35. (A) is the only choice that fits these criteria.

9. D

Difficulty: Medium

Category: Problem Solving and Data Analysis / Scatterplots

Strategic Advice: Compare each statement to the infographic one at a time, eliminating true statements as you work.

Getting to the Answer: Start with A: According to the infographic, Strain 1's OD600 was always higher than that of Strain 2, which is consistent with the statement. Eliminate A. B states that Strain 2's growth rate overtook Strain 1's at hour 50, which is consistent with the infographic; eliminate it. C requires math, so skip it for now. (D) states that Strain 1's growth rate was greater than Strain 2's. Although Strain 1's growth rate was greater for part of the monitored period, it is not greater for the entire period (because the slope of Strain 1's curve is not steeper than that of Strain 2's curve for every line segment on the graph), which makes (D) false and, therefore, correct.

EXTRA PRACTICE

1. C

Difficulty: Easy

Category: Problem Solving and Data Analysis / Scatterplots

Strategic Advice: Correlation means that there is a discernible relationship between two or more variables. A positive correlation means that as one variable increases, so does the other variable. A negative correlation means that as one variable increases, the other decreases. The closer the relationship is, the stronger the correlation.

Getting to the Answer: Take a quick peek at the answer choices and picture or draw a sketch of each one. *Linear* indicates that the data follows the path of a straight line. *Positive* means rising from left to right. Finally, *strong* means the relationship is a close one, but not perfect, so the data points should be fairly close to, but not exactly on, the line; choice (C) is correct.

2. A

Difficulty: Easy

Category: Problem Solving and Data Analysis / Scatterplots

Strategic Advice: A line with a downward slant has a negative slope, so you can immediately eliminate C and D. To choose between (A) and B, recall that slope is a ratio that compares vertical change (rise) to horizontal change (run).

Getting to the Answer: Mark the bordered area using equal measures and then estimate the slope of a line drawn through the center of the points as shown.

The line appears to fall 3 units and run 1 unit, so a good estimate for the slope is –3, making (A) correct. Note that you could also use what you know about slope to answer the question—lines that have fractional slopes, between –1 and 1, are not steep lines, which means B can't be correct.

3. C

Difficulty: Easy

Category: Problem Solving and Data Analysis / Scatterplots

Strategic Advice: A regression equation is the equation of the line (or curve) that best fits the data. A *linear* regression is used to model data that follows the path of a straight line.

Getting to the Answer: In the equation given, a represents the slope of the linear regression (the line of best fit), so you are looking for data that is linear (looks like a line) and is decreasing, or falling from left to right ($a < 0$ means a is negative). You can eliminate A and D because the data is not linear (A is quadratic and D is exponential). You can also eliminate B because the data is increasing (rising from left to right). This means (C) is correct.

4. A

Difficulty: Easy

Category: Problem Solving and Data Analysis / Scatterplots

Strategic Advice: When an exponential equation is written in the form $y = x_0(1 + r)^x$, x_0 gives the y-intercept of the equation's graph. To answer this question, you need to think about what the y-intercept would represent in the context described.

Getting to the Answer: Whenever time is involved in a relationship that is modeled by an equation or a graph, it is always the independent variable and therefore graphed on the x-axis. Therefore, for this question, population would be graphed on the y-axis, so x_0 most likely represents the population when the time elapsed was zero, or in other words, in the year that Adriana was born, making (A) correct.

5. D

Difficulty: Medium

Category: Problem Solving and Data Analysis / Scatterplots

Strategic Advice: A line that "represents the trend of the data" is another way of saying best-fit line.

Getting to the Answer: The trend of the data is clearly linear because the path of the dots does not turn around or curve, so draw a best-fit line on the graph. Remember, about half of the points should be above the line and half below.

Seat Belt Use in England (1983-2009)

Years After Seat Belt Law Enacted

If you draw your best-fit line all the way to the *y*-axis, you'll save yourself a step by finding the *y*-intercept just by looking at the scatterplot. For this graph, it's about 25. This means you can eliminate B and C. To choose between A and (D), find the approximate slope using two points that lie on (or very close to) the best-fit line. You can use the *y*-intercept, (0, 25), as one of the points to save time and estimate the second, such as (21, 80). Use the slope formula to find the slope:

$$m = \frac{y_2 - y_1}{x_2 - x_1} = \frac{80 - 25}{21 - 0} = \frac{55}{21} = 2.62$$

The result is very close to the slope in (D), making it the correct answer.

6. A

Difficulty: Medium

Category: Problem Solving and Data Analysis / Scatterplots

Strategic Advice: Examine the graph, paying careful attention to units and labels. The average rate of change is the same as the slope of the best-fit line. The data is decreasing (going down from left to right) so you can immediately eliminate C and D.

Getting to the Answer: Find the slope of the best-fit line using the slope formula, $m = \frac{y_2 - y_1}{x_2 - x_1}$, and any two points that lie on (or very close to) the line. Using the two points (5, 14) and (10, 8), the average rate of change is about $\frac{8 - 14}{10 - 5} = \frac{-6}{5} = -1.2$, which matches (A).

7. A

Difficulty: Medium

Category: Problem Solving and Data Analysis / Scatterplots

Strategic Advice: Determine whether the predicted change in the interest rate is a common difference (linear function) or a common ratio (exponential function), or if it changes direction (quadratic or polynomial function).

Getting to the Answer: The company predicts that every six months, the Federal Reserve will *raise* rates by 0.25 percentage points. Interest rates are already expressed as percentages, so raising the rates by 0.25 percentage points means *adding* a quarter of a percent every six months. It does not mean it will increase *by* 0.25% every six months. The function therefore involves a common difference, so the best model would be a linear function, which is (A).

8. C
Difficulty: Medium

Category: Problem Solving and Data Analysis / Scatterplots

Strategic Advice: It is a good idea to familiarize yourself with statistics vocabulary before Test Day. "Correlation" simply means relationship. The word "weak" refers to the strength of the relationship (how close the data lies to the line of best fit), which has no effect on slope.

Getting to the Answer: Be careful not to confuse slope and strength. The fact that a data set shows a weak correlation does not give you any information about the magnitude of the slope. This means you can eliminate A and B. Also, keep in mind that the terms "weak" and "negative" are not related, but rather are two independent descriptors of the correlation. So the fact that the rate of change is negative has nothing to do with the strength of the correlation. In a weak correlation, the data points will loosely follow the line of best fit, making (C) the correct answer.

9. B
Difficulty: Medium

Category: Problem Solving and Data Analysis / Scatterplots

Strategic Advice: Sometimes, a question looks easier than it actually is, and deserves a second read once you've skimmed the answer choices. Remember, correlation does not prove causation, and as a general rule, conclusions can only be drawn about the population studied, not about all populations.

Getting to the Answer: The data points are scattered and do not form any discernible pattern. This means there is no correlation, which is another way of saying the two variables aren't related, so you can eliminate D. You can also eliminate C because the HR representative *is* able to draw a conclusion—that there is no relationship. To choose between A and (B), recall that when you analyze data from a

given population (the employees at that particular company), you can only draw conclusions about that population, not about employee populations in general. Therefore, (B) is correct.

10. C
Difficulty: Easy

Category: Problem Solving and Data Analysis / Scatterplots

Strategic Advice: The value of r^2 describes how well a certain type of regression line (also called a trend line or line of best fit) fits a data set. The closer r^2 is to 1, the better the fit. Ensure you've answered the right question before moving on.

Getting to the Answer: You need not know specific data points in order to answer this question, so you can immediately eliminate D. The question asks for the regression line type that is least (not most) appropriate, so look for the one with the lowest r^2 value. The exponential regression line has the lowest r^2 value (0.623), so (A) is the correct answer.

11. 3
Difficulty: Easy

Category: Problem Solving and Data Analysis / Scatterplots

Strategic Advice: Percent error gives the deviation of an actual value from an expected value. Graphically, this is determined by how far from the line of best fit the data point sits.

Getting to the Answer: You don't need to find the percent error of every point (or even a single point) to answer this question. Instead, you just need to understand that the point with the greatest percent error from the mean of the data is the point that is farthest from the line of best fit. Use the gridlines on the graph to find the point. The point (9, 3) is 4 full gridlines away from the line of best fit, which is farther than any other data point. The question asks for the *y*-value of this point, so the correct answer is 3.

12. 18

Difficulty: Medium

Category: Problem Solving and Data Analysis / Scatterplots

Strategic Advice: Because the y-value of the graph when x = 3,400 is not shown, this is a question for which a mathematical solution is necessary; extending the line of best fit will not provide an accurate enough answer.

Getting to the Answer: The equation of the model is given as $y = -\dfrac{1}{200}x + 35$. Miles over recommended servicing are graphed along the x-axis, so substitute 3,400 for x to find the answer: $y = -\dfrac{1}{200}(3,400) + 35 = -17 + 35 = 18$ miles per gallon.

13. 2

Difficulty: Easy

Category: Problem Solving and Data Analysis / Scatterplots

Strategic Advice: Being able to read information from an infographic is an important skill, and will surely earn you points on Test Day.

Getting to the Answer: Examine the graph, including the axis labels and numbering. Each vertical gridline represents 5 eggs, so look to see how many data points are more than a complete grid space away from the line of best fit. Only 2 are more than 5 away—the first data point and the one between 30 and 35 weeks, making 2 the correct answer.

14. 57

Difficulty: Medium

Category: Problem Solving and Data Analysis / Scatterplots

Strategic Advice: This is a Grid-in question, so you can't just use the graph to estimate the y-value

when x = 36. Instead, you need to find the equation of the line of best fit, and then substitute 36 for x and simplify. However, if you are running out of time on Test Day, at least take a guess based on the line of best fit—at x = 36, the y-value looks like it is either 56 or 57.

Getting to the Answer: First, determine the equation of the line of best fit. Start with the slope—you could pick two points on the line and use the slope formula, or you could count the rise and the run. The latter is easier in this question. Beginning at the point (0, 75), the line falls 5 units and runs 10 units to the first point on the line, so the slope is $\dfrac{-5}{10} = -\dfrac{1}{2}$. This means that the equation looks like $y = -\dfrac{1}{2}x + b$. Next, find the y-intercept. You can see clearly from the graph that it is approximately 75.

The equation is $y = -\dfrac{1}{2}x + 75$. Now, substitute 36 for x and simplify to find y:

$$y = -\frac{1}{2}(36) + 75$$
$$y = -18 + 75$$
$$y = 57$$

The correct answer is 57 (which, by the way, was one of the two guesses).

15. 15

Difficulty: Hard

Category: Problem Solving and Data Analysis / Scatterplots

Strategic Advice: Percent error shows the deviation of an actual value from an expected value. The formula for percent error is $\dfrac{|\text{Expected Value} - \text{Actual Value}|}{\text{Expected Value}}$.

To find the expected value, you'll need to use the equation of the line of best fit that you found in the previous question, which is often the case when questions are grouped together as a set.

Getting to the Answer: Substitute 20 for *x* in the equation for the line of best fit and simplify to find the expected number of eggs:

$$y = -\frac{1}{2}(20) + 75$$
$$y = -10 + 75$$
$$y = 65$$

The farmer's flock laid 55 eggs, so the percent error is: $\dfrac{|65 - 55|}{65} = \dfrac{10}{65} \approx 0.15 = 15\%$

16. D

Difficulty: Easy

Category: Problem Solving and Data Analysis / Scatterplots

Strategic Advice: Knowing where the *y*-intercept of the best-fit line falls will help you eliminate answer choices.

Getting to the Answer:

The best-fit line intercepts the *y*-axis below the *x*-axis, and is therefore negative, so you can eliminate B and C (the *y*-intercept is +1 for each of those lines). Now, look at the slope of the line you drew. The line rises along the *y*-axis slightly faster than it runs along the *x*-axis, so the slope must be slightly greater than 1, making (D) correct. If you have trouble choosing between A and (D), you could also graph each equation in your calculator to see which one is a better match for the line you drew. Use a viewing window that is approximately the same as in the graph. Here, the viewing window would be $-2 \leq x \leq 5$ and $-2 \leq y \leq 7$.

17. D

Difficulty: Medium

Category: Problem Solving and Data Analysis / Scatterplots

Strategic Advice: In statistics, correlation alone does *not* prove causation.

Getting to the Answer: The fact that the two variables are strongly correlated, whether it be negatively or positively, only shows that there is a relationship between the variables. It does not indicate whether the change in one variable caused the change in the other. For example, Population A might thrive in wet climates, while Population B does not, and in the years studied, rainfall may have increased, which caused the changes in the populations. This means (D) is the correct answer.

18. D

Difficulty: Medium

Category: Problem Solving and Data Analysis / Scatterplots

Strategic Advice: Try drawing a quick graph (or at least visualizing a graph) that matches the description in the question (decreases quickly at first and then at a much slower rate). The shape and direction of the curve should tell you which type of model to choose.

Getting to the Answer: The question doesn't say anything about the data points changing direction at any time, so you can eliminate A and B—they are both quadratic functions, which always turn around at their vertex. To choose between C and (D), skim through the question again. The data is decreasing, or getting smaller. In an exponential function, when the rate (*r*) is greater than 0, as in C, the function is an exponential growth model, which increases, not decreases, and therefore cannot be correct. This means (D) is correct. When the rate (*r*) is less than 0, the function is an exponential decay model, which matches the description of the data.

19. D

Difficulty: Medium

Category: Problem Solving and Data Analysis / Scatterplots

Strategic Advice: Think about the information given and imagine plotting it on a scatterplot. You are comparing the amount of breast milk or formula consumed by a typical baby with the age of that baby. Start with the fact that at 0 years, the baby needs 0 ounces of milk and at 1 year, the baby also needs 0 ounces.

Getting to the Answer: According to the question, the amount of milk a typical baby needs starts at 0 ounces and increases until it peaks at about 6 months of age. Then the amount of milk needed decreases until one year of age, when it becomes 0 ounces again. This means the shape of the data would look like an upside down parabola, which would match a negative quadratic model, making (D) correct. (Note: a negative absolute value model could also be used, depending on whether the rates of increase and decrease are constant, but that is not one of the answer choices.)

20. B

Difficulty: Medium

Category: Problem Solving and Data Analysis / Scatterplots

Strategic Advice: This question would be easier if you had an infographic to look at. You could sketch a quick graph, although it will save you time if you just think logically about what happens to the data points and the line of best fit.

Getting to the Answer: The amount of snowfall is recorded on the y-axis, so the y-values of the data points stay the same. The x-values of the points all shift to the right 10 units (because Genji adds 10 degrees to each of the temperature readings). This means that all the data points stay in the same place vertically, but shift horizontally, resulting in

the same rate of change, so you can eliminate C and D. The line of best fit would also still look the same, just shifted to the right. This means the strength of correlation does not change, as the points will still be the same distance away from the (now moved) line of best fit, making (B) correct.

21. B

Difficulty: Hard

Category: Problem Solving and Data Analysis / Scatterplots

Strategic Advice: When presented with a "series" of data, making a chart helps. In this question, the chart should include the number of bounces and the height after the bounce. You can then look for patterns that may tell you which function to pick, or at the very least, which functions to eliminate.

Getting to the Answer:

Bounce Number (b)	Height After Bounce (H(b))
1	80
2	40
3	20
4	10

Look for a pattern: the heights are decreasing by a common ratio each time $\left(\dfrac{1}{2}\right)$, so an exponential function will be the best match. This means you can eliminate C and D (which are linear functions). To choose between A and (B), evaluate each function at $b = 1$ and see what happens.

Choice A: $H(1) = \dfrac{80}{2^1} = \dfrac{80}{2} = 40$. The height should be 80 after the first bounce, so eliminate this choice.

Choice B: $H(1) = \dfrac{80}{2^{1-1}} = \dfrac{80}{2^0} = \dfrac{80}{1} = 80$. Choice (B) is correct.

If you're not convinced (or if both results had been 80), move on to $b = 2$ and evaluate each function again, until you are able to eliminate one of them.

22. D

Difficulty: Hard

Category: Problem Solving and Data Analysis / Scatterplots

Strategic Advice: This question requires a conceptual understanding of modeling data and properties of quadratic functions. When a regression model has a correlation coefficient of 1.0, it means that the model exactly fits the data. This tells you that you can use what you know about quadratic functions to answer the question.

Getting to the Answer: The graph of a quadratic function is symmetric with respect to its axis of symmetry. The axis of symmetry passes through the x-value of the vertex, which also happens to be where the maximum (or minimum) of the function occurs. The question tells you this value—it's $x = 25$. Because 35 is $35 - 25 = 10$ units to the right of the axis of symmetry, you know that the y-value will be the same as the point that is 10 units to the left of the axis of symmetry. This occurs at $x = 25 - 10 = 15$. Read the y-value from the graphing calculator screenshot to find the answer, which is 27. Therefore, (D) is correct.

23. 84

Difficulty: Hard

Category: Problem Solving and Data Analysis / Scatterplots

Strategic Advice: Make sure you read the axis labels and the question carefully. The vertical height is given in feet, while the horizontal distance is given in yards.

Getting to the Answer: The question asks for the difference between the horizontal and upward vertical distance the t-shirt traveled. Horizontally, the t-shirt started at 0 yards and stopped when its height was once again 0 (when it hit the ground). Use your calculator to find the rightmost x-intercept of the graph; the result is 41.21 yards, or 123.63 feet. (Note that you could also set the equation equal

to 0 and solve it algebraically, by expanding the equation and then either completing the square or using the quadratic formula, but this would be very time-consuming.) Calculating the upward vertical distance requires more thought. According to the graph (and the equation), the t-shirt's peak height is 45 feet, but it started at 5 vertical feet (not 0), making the net upward distance traveled 40 feet. Subtract to find the difference: $123.63 - 40 = 83.63$ feet, which, rounded to the nearest whole foot, is 84 feet.

24. .98

Difficulty: Hard

Category: Problem Solving and Data Analysis / Scatterplots

Strategic Advice: If you are familiar with the equation for calculating a correlation coefficient, then you are sure to recognize that a question like this would take entirely too long to answer by hand. It is one of those questions (which you may or may not see on Test Day) that should convince you to get to know some of the statistics features of your graphing calculator.

Getting to the Answer: Instructions are provided for the TI-83/84 series of calculators. To find the correlation coefficient (r), first press [STAT]. Select 1:Edit and enter the data given in the table. Press [STAT] again and the [CALC] menu at the top of the screen. Select 4:LinReg and press enter. You should see the following:

$y = ax + b$

$a = 2.832857143$

$b = .8176190476$

$r^2 = .9652019383$

$r = .9824469137$

Rounded to two decimal places, the correct answer is .98.

If you have a different graphing calculator, make sure to look up the appropriate procedure in your calculator's manual.

THIS PAGE INTENTIONALLY LEFT BLANK

CHAPTER 7

PREPARE

1. B
Difficulty: Easy

Category: Problem Solving and Data Analysis / Statistics and Probability

Strategic Advice: Focus on the rows of the table that you need, and block out the rest.

Getting to the Answer: The trickiest part of this question is understanding what is being asked. What you need is the shop that had the most Tuesday sales *as a fraction of its total sales*. For each shop, divide the number of books it sold on Tuesday by the number of books it sold all week. You can use your calculator to speed up this step.

$$\text{Bob's Books: } \frac{\text{Tuesday total}}{\text{weekly total}} = \frac{8}{53} \approx 0.1509$$

$$\text{Nalia's Novels: } \frac{\text{Tuesday total}}{\text{weekly total}} = \frac{13}{55} \approx 0.2364$$

$$\text{Tumiko's Tomes: } \frac{\text{Tuesday total}}{\text{weekly total}} = \frac{15}{66} \approx 0.2273$$

$$\text{Vladimir's Volumes: } \frac{\text{Tuesday total}}{\text{weekly total}} = \frac{13}{58} \approx 0.2241$$

The greatest portion of Tuesday sales belongs to Nalia's Novels, so (B) is correct.

2. C
Difficulty: Medium

Category: Problem Solving and Data Analysis / Statistics and Probability

Strategic Advice: When pulling data from the table, make sure you use the correct columns and rows.

Getting to the Answer: Add the number of books sold by Tumiko and Vladimir on Monday, Wednesday, and Friday; then divide the result by the total number of books sold on those days.

Tumiko's and Vladimir's M/W/F sales: $(15 + 12) + (12 + 14) + (10 + 9) = 72$

Total M/W/F sales: $48 + 49 + 39 = 136$

Divide Tumiko's and Vladimir's M/W/F sales by total M/W/F sales to get $\frac{72}{136}$, which simplifies to $\frac{9}{17}$. Choice (C) is correct.

3. D
Difficulty: Medium

Category: Problem Solving and Data Analysis / Statistics and Probability

Strategic Advice: The answer choices are unsimplified expressions rather than simple values. Don't waste time performing unnecessary calculations!

Getting to the Answer: To find the probability of two events occurring, calculate and then multiply the individual probabilities. The word "both" in the question is your clue that you will need to multiply the individual probabilities. The probability of choosing a sophomore who doesn't prefer strategy games is $\frac{493-140}{493} = \frac{353}{493}$, and the probability of choosing a senior who doesn't prefer strategy games is $\frac{509-148}{509} = \frac{361}{509}$. This means the probability of both occurring is $\frac{353}{493} \times \frac{361}{509}$. Don't do any more math; this is as far as you need to go! Choice (D) is correct.

4. A
Difficulty: Medium

Category: Problem Solving and Data Analysis / Statistics and Probability

Strategic Advice: Don't be intimidated by the verbose nature of this question. Look for key details, and think about the conclusions that you can draw based only on what's given.

Getting to the Answer: The question stem states that the study only utilized high school students in Dallas; consequently, you cannot assume that the findings will apply to all of Texas. Eliminate B and D. Although you know that the study found a correlation between video game time and GPA, there is no evidence to support one directly causing the other. You can therefore eliminate C, leaving (A) as the correct answer.

5. A
Difficulty: Hard

Category: Problem Solving and Data Analysis / Statistics and Probability

Strategic Advice: Pay attention to numeric keywords such as "at least" to make sure you don't count the wrong items when setting up the probability formula.

Getting to the Answer: Start with the fundamental probability formula: $P = \dfrac{\text{number desired}}{\text{number possible}}$. There are five coin flips, each with two possibilities, so the total number of outcomes is $2 \times 2 \times 2 \times 2 \times 2 = 2^5 = 32$. Because at least four of the five flips must be heads, simply writing out all desired outcomes won't take much time.

$$H\,H\,H\,H\,H$$
$$H\,H\,H\,H\,T$$
$$H\,H\,H\,T\,H$$
$$H\,H\,T\,H\,H$$
$$H\,T\,H\,H\,H$$
$$T\,H\,H\,H\,H$$

There are six outcomes for which at least four of the flips are heads, so the answer is $\dfrac{6}{32} = \dfrac{3}{16}$. Choice (A) is correct.

6. 700
Difficulty: Easy

Category: Problem Solving and Data Analysis / Statistics and Probability / Multi-Part Math

Strategic Advice: Identify the pieces of the pie graph you need, and then convert from the percent to the total.

Getting to the Answer: You know from the infographic that 21% (5% + 16%) of the visitors were *not* aged 20 or older. This means that 100% − 21% = 79% were aged 20+. Given that the number of visitors aged 20+ was 553, use the three-part percent formula to calculate the total:

$$\text{total} \times 79\% = 553$$
$$\text{total} = \frac{553}{0.79} = 700$$

7. 2030
Difficulty: Medium

Strategic Advice: Part of your calculations were done in the previous question; use that to save time.

Getting to the Answer: From part 1 you know that the total number of visitors in 2014 was 700. According to the infographic, 25% of all the visitors were aged 40-49, and 8% were aged 50+. This means that $0.25 \times 700 = 175$ attendees were aged 40-49, and $0.08 \times 700 = 56$ were aged 50+. The visitors aged 40-49 paid $175 \times \$10 = \$1,750$ for their tickets, and the visitors aged 50+ paid $56 \times \$5 = \$280$ for their tickets. The total revenue for the two groups was therefore $\$1,750 + \$280 = \$2,030$. Grid in 2030.

8. C
Difficulty: Hard

Category: Problem Solving and Data Analysis / Statistics and Probability

Strategic Advice: No math is required for this question, but you do need to think critically about averages.

Getting to the Answer: You know that m is the average age of the males, f is the average age of the females, a is the overall average, and 65% of the members are males. Because there are more males than females, the overall average age must be closer to the male average than to the female average. In other words, a is closer to m than to f. The expression $\dfrac{m+f}{2}$ appears in all of the choices. This is the average of *m* and *f*. You don't know which of *m* or *f* is greater, so there are two ways to visualize all of this information on a number line. The first assumes that $m < f$; the second assumes that $m > f$:

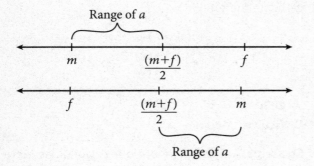

Examine the top number line carefully to see that the only choice consistent with the visualization is (C): when *m* is less than *f*, the value of *a* is less than the average age of both groups.

PRACTICE

9. B
Difficulty: Medium

Category: Problem Solving and Data Analysis / Statistics and Probability

Strategic Advice: You need to have an understanding of data shapes and normal distribution in order to answer this question.

Getting to the Answer: The professor starts with a normal distribution; when the new data are added, the distribution changes:

Added more data here.

The new distribution is skewed to the left (in the direction of the graph's tail, not in the direction of its biggest bump), and the median has increased. Although the range of the new data alone might be smaller than the original set, when all data are combined, the range will not have changed from the original data. The correct answer is (B).

10. 28.7
Difficulty: Easy

Category: Problem Solving and Data Analysis / Statistics and Probability / Multi-Part Math

Strategic Advice: Remember which ratings are considered "bad" when doing your calculations, and make sure your work reflects this.

Getting to the Answer: To be considered "bad," a game must have a rating of 1 or 2. Begin by counting the number of "bad" games. There are $5 + 3 + 3 = 11$ games with a rating of 1 and $17 + 12 + 10 = 39$ games with a rating of 2. That's a total of $11 + 39 = 50$ games. Divide this by the total number of games and multiply by 100: $\frac{50}{61+54+59} \times 100 = 28.7\%$. Grid in 28.7.

11. 11.9
Difficulty: Medium

Strategic Advice: The total game count will decrease after the games' removal; keep this in mind when working toward the answer.

Getting to the Answer: You know from part 1 that 50 games are "bad." Reducing this number by 50% is the same as halving it, meaning there will be 25 remaining "bad" games after the removal. Subtract this from the original total game count ($61 + 54 + 59 = 174$) to get the new total, which is 149. Divide the new "bad" count by this total, and then multiply by 100 as you did before: $\frac{25}{149} \times 100 = 16.8\%$. Subtracting the new percentage from the old one gives $28.7\% - 16.8\% = 11.9\%$. Grid in 11.9.

PERFORM

12. D
Difficulty: Medium

Category: Problem Solving and Data Analysis / Statistics and Probability

Strategic Advice: Consider finding the probability of *not* selecting one of the puzzles specified, as there will be fewer dots to count. You can then subtract that probability from 1.

Getting to the Answer: There are only three puzzles that *didn't* take Rolff fewer than 100 seconds to solve. Of these, 2 do *not* have fewer than 6 clues. Therefore, the probability that the conditions *won't* be met is $\frac{2}{20} = 0.1$. This isn't what you're asked to find, so don't stop yet. Subtract 0.1 from 1 to get 0.9. Multiply this by 100 to get 90%; (D) is correct.

13. B
Difficulty: Easy

Category: Problem Solving and Data Analysis / Statistics and Probability

Strategic Advice: Remember the difference between mean and standard deviation: the former is a measure of center; the latter, a measure of spread.

Getting to the Answer: The four answers all involve consistency, which means the explanation should involve standard deviation. Based on this, you can eliminate A and D. Higher consistency means lower standard deviation (and vice versa); the only choice that reflects this—and correctly represents the data in the table—is (B).

14. 594
Difficulty: Medium

Category: Problem Solving and Data Analysis / Statistics and Probability / Multi-Part Math

Strategic Advice: Identify Wilhelmina and Alexandra's hat contributions from the table, and then extrapolate to find how many solid-colored hats they should knit for Spirit Week.

Getting to the Answer: According to the table, Wilhelmina will be responsible for $\frac{24}{60}$ of the hats, and Alexandra will knit $\frac{9}{60}$ of them. The knitting club needs to knit 1,800 hats total, 60% of which should be solid-colored per the survey results. This means that $0.6 \times 1,800 = 1,080$ hats should be solid-colored. Add together the fractions for Wilhelmina and Alexandra to get $\frac{33}{60}$. Multiplying this by the total number of solid-colored hats will yield the number that Wilhelmina and Alexandra will knit: $\frac{33}{60} \times 1,080 = 594$.

15. 282
Difficulty: Medium

Strategic Advice: Read carefully; you're asked about the two other club members' Spirit Week production here, and the question is not limited to solid-colored hats.

Getting to the Answer: Work through this one step at a time. 20% of 1,800 hats = 360 hats with emblems and therefore 360 prize scarves.

The two boys make $\frac{27}{60}$ of the 360 hats = 162 hats.

The two boys make $\frac{11}{33} = \frac{1}{3}$ of the 360 scarves = 120 scarves. They are responsible for $162 + 120 = 282$ of these items.

Answers & Explanations

EXTRA PRACTICE

1. B
Difficulty: Easy

Category: Problem Solving and Data Analysis / Statistics and Probability

Strategic Advice: Don't spend too much time reading the description of the study. Focus on the information provided in the table.

Getting to the Answer: The question only asks about participants who were outside a healthy weight range, so focus on this row: 38 out of the 74 participants who were outside a healthy weight range ate breakfast one or fewer times per week. This represents $\frac{38}{74} = .51351$, or 51.35%, which matches (B).

2. D
Difficulty: Medium

Category: Problem Solving and Data Analysis / Statistics and Probability

Strategic Advice: Using the results of a sample study to make predictions about a larger population almost always involves multiplying the total number in the population by a percentage.

Getting to the Answer: The question asks about employees who eat breakfast every weekday, so focus on the "5-7 times per week" column in the table. Assuming the participants in the study were a good representative sample, 36 out of 45, or 80%, of the 3,000 employees are likely to be within a healthy weight range. Multiply 0.8 × 3,000 to arrive at 2,400, which is (D).

3. D
Difficulty: Easy

Category: Problem Solving and Data Analysis / Statistics and Probability

Strategic Advice: When considering the validity of a study, always look for possible sources of bias. In other words, look for things that might skew the results in either direction.

Getting to the Answer: Because the shoe is specifically targeted toward athletes, but is sold in regular shoe stores, conducting the survey outside gyms and sporting goods stores is likely to skew the results. The respondents are already interested in athletics and so are likely to respond more positively than the average shoe store shopper. Therefore, the data from the survey likely overestimates the number of people interested in the new product, making (D) the correct answer.

4. B
Difficulty: Easy

Category: Problem Solving and Data Analysis / Statistics and Probability

Strategic Advice: The mean of a set of numbers is the same as the average, which is the sum of the numbers divided by the amount of numbers.

Getting to the Answer: Use the graph to find the sum of the GPA values, and then calculate the mean. Read the graph carefully—each gridline represents one student. To save time, multiply the frequency in each category by the GPA value and then divide by the total number of students: $(10 \times 4) + (36 \times 3) + (28 \times 2) + (8 \times 1) + (2 \times 0) = 212 \div 84 = 2.523$, or about 2.5, which is (B).

5. C
Difficulty: Easy

Category: Problem Solving and Data Analysis / Statistics and Probability

Strategic Advice: Think about what each term means: The mean of a data set is the average; the mode is the most commonly occurring data point; the median is the data point in the center when arranged in order from least to greatest; and the standard deviation is a description of how far the data points, as a whole, vary from the mean.

Getting to the Answer: You can eliminate D right away because standard deviation is a measure of spread, not a measure of center. You can also eliminate A because you calculated the mean in the previous question, and it was 2.5, which is less than 3.0. To choose between B and (C), you only need to find the median, because the mode is included in both answer choices. You don't have to list out all 84 scores and find the one in the center; instead, think about it logically. There are 10 + 36 = 46 grades that were a 4.0 or a 3.0, which is more than half of 84, so the median is 3.0. This means either the mode or the median could be used, making (C) correct.

6. B
Difficulty: Medium

Category: Problem Solving and Data Analysis / Statistics and Probability

Strategic Advice: You do not need to use all of the information presented in the table to find the answer. Read the question carefully to make sure you use only what you need.

Getting to the Answer: To calculate the percentage of people in each age group with a healthy blood sugar level (<100), divide the number of people in *that* age group with a healthy blood sugar level by the total number of participants in *that* age group. Choice (B) is correct because 16 ÷ 98 ≈ 0.1633 = 16.33%, which is a lower percentage than in the other age groups (18-25 = 18.75%, 36-45 = 20.21%, and Older than 45 = 20%).

7. D
Difficulty: Hard

Category: Problem Solving and Data Analysis / Statistics and Probability

Strategic Advice: This question requires you to read the table carefully. The first criterion is fairly straightforward—you're looking for a participant with a blood sugar level in the 100-125 range, so focus on that column in the table. The second criterion is a bit trickier—*at least 36 years old* means 36 years old or older, so you'll need to use the values in the rows for 36-45, and Older than 45.

Getting to the Answer: Of the 300 participants, there were 35 in the 36-45 age group who were considered at risk, and 27 in the Older than 45 age group, resulting in a total of 35 + 27 = 62 out of 300 participants. The probability of randomly selecting one participant from either of these two groups is $\frac{62}{300}$, which reduces to $\frac{31}{150}$, or (D).

8. A
Difficulty: Medium

Category: Problem Solving and Data Analysis / Statistics and Probability

Strategic Advice: You aren't given the number of vehicles on the lot, but you don't need this information to answer the question because it is asking for a probability, which is a fraction.

Getting to the Answer: Don't neglect the 50% at the beginning of the question just because it is presented in a different form. Instead, convert 50% to a fraction $\left(\frac{1}{2}\right)$ and then think logically—the final probability is $\frac{1}{3}$ of $\frac{3}{4}$ of $\frac{1}{2}$. In math, "of" means multiply, so the probability of randomly choosing a vehicle that is a car with an automatic transmission and a leather interior is $\frac{1}{2} \times \frac{3}{4} \times \frac{1}{3} = \frac{1}{8}$. This means (A) is correct.

9. C
Difficulty: Medium

Category: Problem Solving and Data Analysis / Statistics and Probability

Strategic Advice: A good representative sample is not only random, but also a good representation of the population in question. Here, the senator wants to know about the people who might vote for him.

Getting to the Answer: If the senator is only concerned about people who might vote for him, then the survey only needs to focus on people who can vote. Not all citizens can or choose to vote. Additionally, not everyone in the entire country votes for every senator, so he only needs to focus on voters in his district, making (C) correct.

10. C
Difficulty: Medium

Category: Problem Solving and Data Analysis / Statistics and Probability

Strategic Advice: A good representative sample is not only random, but also a good representation of the population in question. Here, the population in question is tablet owners.

Getting to the Answer: Not everyone who shops at an electronics store owns a tablet. Customers who bought other items, such as laptops, TVs, or MP3 players are likely to make up at least a portion of the surveys distributed with customers' purchases. This means that, despite being randomly selected, the sample is unlikely to be a good representative sample because there is no way to verify whether the responders to the survey actually own a tablet. Therefore, (C) is correct.

11. B
Difficulty: Medium

Category: Problem Solving and Data Analysis / Statistics and Probability

Strategic Advice: Read infographics carefully. Look for patterns in the data that may help you answer the question.

Getting to the Answer: According to the graph, Charlie has been paying down his debt at a rate of

$500 per month. To reach 25% utilization, he needs to get down to $10,000 × 0.25 = $2,500, which means he needs to pay off $10,000 − $2,500 = $7,500. To do this it would take $7,500 ÷ $500 = 15 months, making (B) the correct answer.

12. D
Difficulty: Medium

Category: Problem Solving and Data Analysis / Statistics and Probability

Strategic Advice: Look carefully at the infographic's axes. The number of states correctly named is plotted along the horizontal axis, while the frequency (or number of contestants) is plotted along the vertical axis.

Getting to the Answer: Look at the vertical axis—the frequency tells you the number of contestants who named each number of states. This means 1 contestant named only 1 state, 1 contestant named 2 states, 5 contestants named 3 states, and so on. To answer the question, add all the frequencies to find the total number of contestants: $1 + 1 + 5 + 6 + 4 + 0 + 2 + 1 = 20$, which is (D).

13. D
Difficulty: Medium

Category: Problem Solving and Data Analysis / Statistics and Probability

Strategic Advice: Understanding how averages and sums are connected is the key to answering a question like this. If the average of 14 numbers is 6, then the sum of the 14 numbers must be 84 (because $84 \div 14 = 6$).

Getting to the Answer: Use the dot plot to find the total number of appliances the salesman has already sold. Then, subtract this amount from 84. The salesman has already sold $3(2) + 4(3) + 5 + 6(3) + 7 + 8 + 10(2) = 76$ appliances, so he needs to sell $84 − 76 = 8$ appliances on the 14th day to reach his goal. This means (D) is correct.

14. B

Difficulty: Hard

Category: Problem Solving and Data Analysis / Statistics and Probability

Strategic Advice: Work through a question like this one step at a time. Start by using the sample survey to find the percentage of respondents that say they would join a gym if one were located in their area.

Getting to the Answer: According to the sample survey, $\frac{40}{300}$ *say* they would join the gym. But the gym estimates that only 30% of these respondents would *actually* join, so multiply 40 by 30% to find that the gym can expect $\frac{12}{300} = 0.04 = 4\%$ of the respondents to join Muscles. Multiply this by the total number of residents: $12{,}600 \times 0.04 = 504$ residents, so (B) is correct.

15. A

Difficulty: Medium

Category: Problem Solving and Data Analysis / Statistics and Probability

Strategic Advice: Don't let all the numbers in the table intimidate you. You're not expected to calculate anything. All the information you need is already provided for you in the table, so quickly skim the answer choices to see what you're interested in.

Getting to the Answer: The keywords in the question are *average* and *consistently*. The average is the mean and the consistency relates to how spread out each branch's profits are. First, find the branch with the lowest mean profit. This is Branch A, so you can eliminate choices C and D. Standard deviation is a measure of spread, so now focus on that row only. Think about what standard deviation tells you. A lower standard deviation indicates that profits are less spread out and therefore more consistent. Likewise, a higher standard deviation indicates that profits are more spread out and therefore less consistent. Notice the opposite nature of this relationship:

lower standard deviation = more consistent; higher standard deviation = less consistent. Choice (A) is correct because the standard deviation of Branch C's quarterly profits is the *highest*, which means it performed the *least* consistently.

16. 2/5 or .4

Difficulty: Easy

Category: Problem Solving and Data Analysis / Statistics and Probability

Strategic Advice: Read the question carefully. You may not agree with the host's method of determining which entertainer is the most popular (because they did not account for weather, people attending on multiple days, etc.), but your job is to use the definition of "popularity rating" to answer the question.

Getting to the Answer: Take a second to think about the quickest way to answer the question—you're not asked to find the popularity rating of each performer and then compare them. Based on the host's definition, you can pick the most popular performer by simply looking at the numbers in the table. More people attended on day 3, so find the popularity rating for Entertainer C: 1,600 people attended on that day out of a total of $1{,}280 + 1{,}120 + 1{,}600 = 4{,}000$ festival goers, so Entertainer C's popularity rating is $\frac{1{,}600}{4{,}000} = \frac{2}{5}$, or .4.

17. 300

Difficulty: Easy

Category: Problem Solving and Data Analysis / Statistics and Probability

Strategic Advice: Read the graph carefully, including the key at the bottom indicating that each bar represents 15 minutes.

Getting to the Answer: The question states that only stage 3 is considered *deep* sleep, and the question asks how much time was spent in *light* sleep. You could count all of the bars that don't represent stage 3, but it would be faster to count the bars that do and subtract. There are 12 bars that represent stage 3, which means the person spent $12 \times 15 = 180$ minutes in deep sleep. The study was for 8 hours, or 480 minutes, so the person spent $480 - 180 = 300$ minutes in light sleep.

18. 3/8 or .375
Difficulty: Medium

Category: Problem Solving and Data Analysis / Statistics and Probability

Strategic Advice: Remember, probability compares the number of desired outcomes (here, the number of 15-minute periods with a sleep stage of 3) with the total number of possible outcomes (here, the total number of 15-minute periods over the course of the 8 hours).

Getting to the Answer: The opening paragraph tells you that the total amount of sleep is 8 hours. In the previous question, you calculated that 180 minutes, or 3 hours are spent in deep sleep. Therefore, the probability would be $\dfrac{3 \text{ hours}}{8 \text{ hours}}$ or $\dfrac{3}{8}$.

19. 81
Difficulty: Easy

Category: Problem Solving and Data Analysis / Statistics and Probability

Strategic Advice: Read the question carefully, identifying the information from the table that you will need. You only need to be concerned with the "Total" row for this question.

Getting to the Answer: There are sixty-one 3-bedroom houses and sixty-four 4-bedroom houses, so there are $61 + 64 = 125$ total houses in the development that have 3 or more bedrooms. There are 154 houses in all, which means that $125 \div 154 = 0.8117$ or approximately 81% of all the houses should receive flyers.

20. .608
Difficulty: Medium

Category: Problem Solving and Data Analysis / Statistics and Probability

Strategic Advice: Sometimes, a question requires more concentration than calculation. In this question, you need to first identify the two categories in the table to which the daycare center will send the invitation. Once you do that, the rest is easy.

Getting to the Answer: The categories to which the daycare center plans to send an invitation are limited to the 3- and 4-bedroom houses (because those are the ones that already received the flyer), so focus on those two columns. The two categories with the most houses are Townhouses/3-bedroom and Single-Family/4-bedroom, with a total of $42 + 34 = 76$ houses. You determined in the previous question that there were 125 houses to which the daycare sent flyers, so the probability of randomly selecting one from the two specified groups is $\dfrac{76}{125} = .608$.

21. 15
Difficulty: Medium

Category: Problem Solving and Data Analysis / Statistics and Probability

Strategic Advice: Think about what the infographic shows: dollar amounts that consumers are willing to pay for the store brand version versus the brand name version and the numbers of corresponding consumers (given by the heights of the bars). The question asks *on average* how many more cents consumers are willing to pay, so you will need to find a weighted average for each version of the product.

Getting to the Answer: Start with the store brand. Multiply each dollar amount by the height of the corresponding bar:

$$5 \times 68 = 340$$
$$6 \times 56 = 336$$
$$7 \times 48 = 336$$
$$8 \times 32 = 256$$
$$9 \times 30 = 270$$
$$10 \times 14 = 140$$

Next, add them all together: $1,678. Now, divide this number by the total number of respondents (68 + 56 + 48 + 32 + 30 + 14 = 248): 1,678 ÷ 248 = 6.766, which means *on average* consumers are willing to pay $6.77 for the store brand version of the product. Repeat this process for the brand name version.

$$5 \times 85 = 425$$
$$6 \times 79 = 474$$
$$7 \times 64 = 448$$
$$8 \times 55 = 440$$
$$9 \times 42 = 378$$
$$10 \times 27 = 270$$

Add them all together to get 2,435, and divide by the number of respondents (85 + 79 + 64 + 55 + 42 + 27 = 352) to arrive at 2,435 ÷ 352 = 6.917, or $6.92. *On average*, consumers are willing to pay $6.92 – $6.77 = $0.15, or 15 more cents for the brand name version than the store brand version.

> **✔ Note**
>
> The preceding calculation can be quite time-consuming. If you are familiar with the weighted average formula, consider using it!
>
> Weighted Average = $w_1x_1 + w_2x_2 + w_3x_3 \dots$
>
> Remember, w represents the percent occurrence (in decimal form) of each value, and x represents each value.

22. 1/3 or .333
Difficulty: Hard

Category: Problem Solving and Data Analysis / Statistics and Probability

Strategic Advice: In this question, you need to calculate a probability, which means you need to know the total (all the respondents in the survey) and the portion (respondents who are willing to pay at least $8) about which the question asks.

Getting to the Answer: First, find the number of respondents willing to pay at least $8 (which means $8 or more). Be careful—the question doesn't specify store brand or brand name, so use both versions of the product:

$$32 + 55 + 30 + 42 + 14 + 27 = 200$$

Now, find the total number of people in the survey. Again, the question doesn't specify store brand or brand name. You know from the previous question that 248 people responded to the store brand survey and 352 responded to the name brand survey, for a total of 600 respondents. This means the probability that a randomly chosen respondent is willing to pay at least $8 is $\frac{200}{600}$ or $\frac{1}{3}$.

23. C
Difficulty: Easy

Category: Problem Solving and Data Analysis / Statistics and Probability

Strategic Advice: When drawing a conclusion based on an infographic, be sure to consider both the data shown in the graphic and the information given in the question itself, especially when the graphic does not have a title that answers the information in question.

Getting to the Answer: The question states that the data was collected in California about jackrabbits, so any conclusion drawn can only be generalized to that particular geographic region and to that breed of rabbit. California is in the Northern Hemisphere, so its spring months are March, April, and May. According to the data, the California jackrabbit gives birth mostly during those months, so (C) is correct.

24. B
Difficulty: Medium

Category: Problem Solving and Data Analysis / Statistics and Probability

Strategic Advice: The table is not complete, so your first step is to fill in the missing values. Start with what you know and work from there. It may not be necessary to complete the entire table, but rather only what you need to answer the question.

Getting to the Answer: You know there are 186 cookies total and that 104 are without nuts, which means 186 – 104 = 82 have nuts. Because you already know that 40 of those cookies are oatmeal raisin, this mean 82 – 40 = 42 are chocolate chip. You also know that $\frac{2}{3}$ of the total number of cookies are chocolate chip, which means there are $\frac{2}{3} \times 186 = 124$ chocolate chips cookies, total, so you can fill this number in the "Total" row of that column. You do not need to fill in any more of the table because the question only asks about chocolate chips cookies with nuts. There are 124 chocolate chip cookies total and 42 of them have nuts, so the probability of randomly choosing one with nuts is $\frac{42}{124}$, or $\frac{21}{62}$, which matches (B).

25. A
Difficulty: Medium

Category: Problem Solving and Data Analysis / Statistics and Probability

Strategic Advice: When making inferences regarding population parameters, the parameter does not change from the sample data to the population.

Getting to the Answer: As long as a sample is both representative and without bias, inferences can be drawn from the sample data to the population from which the sample was taken. In this example, if the mean number of bottles of water consumed per person each day was 2.5, then it can be assumed that the average number consumed in the general population is also 2.5, so the means are equal, and (A) is the correct answer.

26. D
Difficulty: Medium

Category: Problem Solving and Data Analysis / Statistics and Probability

Strategic Advice: When answering a question about an experimental study, try to think logically about what the results of the study could indicate.

Getting to the Answer: The wording in this question implies that the population for the study includes all nutrients. However, the study only tests for nitrogen and potassium, so the sample was limited. You can eliminate A and B because all nutrients were not included in the sample, so you can't say anything about them, one way or the other. The compounds may or may not help the soil retain other types of nutrients, and you certainly don't know which of the five would produce the best results. You can eliminate C because the question doesn't tell you anything about the data collection methods, so you can't determine whether or not the study was biased. This means that choice (D) is correct—the study will only be able to produce results concerning the effects of the compounds on the soil retaining nitrogen and potassium.

27. D

Difficulty: Hard

Category: Problem Solving and Data Analysis / Statistics and Probability

Strategic Advice: The biggest challenge in answering this question is being able to synthesize (determine importance, organize, and analyze) the different pieces of information given. The first step is determining how the information in the pie graph relates to the information in the table. Be patient and try to think one step at a time.

Getting to the Answer: The probability that one randomly selected salmon from those that were tested would have a dangerous level of mercury is equal to the number of salmon that had dangerous mercury levels divided by the total number of salmon that were tested. This means you only need two numbers to answer this question. One of those numbers is in the table—Six salmon had dangerous mercury levels. Finding the other number is the tricky part. Use information from the question stem and the pie graph. The biologist tested 5% of the total number of each breed of fish, or 5% of 25% of 6,000 fish. Multiply $0.05 \times 0.25 \times 6,000 = 75$ salmon were tested. This means the probability is $\frac{6}{75} = 0.08$, which matches (D).

28. B

Difficulty: Medium

Category: Problem Solving and Data Analysis / Statistics and Probability

Strategic Advice: The median is the middle number in a series of numbers. Arrange the number of history majors from least to greatest, making sure that 225 is in the middle. Use s to balance out the number of history majors on either side of 225.

Getting to the Answer: Because there are two numbers above the median (240 and 287), there must be two numbers below the median, 162 and s:

s, 162, 225, 240, 287
or
162, s, 225, 240, 287

Because s could be on either side of 162, it could be anything less than or equal to 225. Its greatest possible value is therefore 225, which is (B).

29. 627

Difficulty: Medium

Category: Problem Solving and Data Analysis / Statistics and Probability

Strategic Advice: When making inferences about populations based on sample data, find the percent of the sample data that matches the given criteria and multiply by the number in the population.

Getting to the Answer: Of the 250 writers in the sample, $250 - 74 - 22 - 30 - 29 = 95$ writers said they would like sandwiches for lunch. This represents $\frac{95}{250} = 0.38$, or 38%. Multiply $0.38 \times 1,650$ to arrive at 627 writers that want sandwiches for lunch.

CHAPTER 8

PREPARE

1. A
Difficulty: Easy

Category: Passport to Advanced Math / Exponents

Strategic Advice: Remember your exponent rules and what they do and do not allow.

Getting to the Answer: You can't simplify the expression as it's written, so break it into two fractions first. You can then subtract the exponents of the z terms in each fraction. Once finished, combine the two new fractions back into one. The work for these steps is shown here.

$$\frac{z^{570} - z^{480}}{2z^{30}} = \frac{z^{570}}{2z^{30}} - \frac{z^{480}}{2z^{30}}$$

$$\frac{z^{570}}{2z^{30}} - \frac{z^{480}}{2z^{30}} = \frac{z^{570-30}}{2} - \frac{z^{480-30}}{2}$$

$$\frac{z^{540}}{2} - \frac{z^{450}}{2} = \frac{z^{540} - z^{450}}{2}$$

(A) is the correct answer.

2. B
Difficulty: Easy

Category: Passport to Advanced Math / Exponents

Strategic Advice: Work with each component of the expression one at a time to minimize the chance of careless errors.

Getting to the Answer: Move the expression in parentheses to the denominator to make the sign of the exponent outside positive; do not change the signs of the exponents inside the parentheses. Next, distribute the exponent as usual. Divide the 2 into

−64, and move k^{-12} back to the numerator. Work for all steps is shown below.

$$2(-4j^3k^{-4})^{-3}$$

$$\frac{2}{(-4j^3k^{-4})^3}$$

$$\frac{\cancel{2}}{-\cancel{64}\,j^9k^{-12}}$$

$$-\frac{k^{12}}{32j^9}$$

Choice (B) is the correct answer.

3. 9
Difficulty: Medium

Category: Passport to Advanced Math / Exponents

Strategic Advice: If you don't immediately see an obvious simplification route, look for links between different parts of the expression to help with rewriting it.

Getting to the Answer: Notice that $27 = 3^3$ and $81 = 3^4$. You can therefore rewrite the given expression as $\frac{3^5 \times (3^3)^3}{(3^4)^3}$, which becomes $\frac{3^5 \times 3^9}{3^{12}} = \frac{3^{14}}{3^{12}}$. Subtract the exponents to get 3^2, which becomes 9, the correct answer.

4. C
Difficulty: Medium

Category: Passport to Advanced Math / Exponents

Strategic Advice: Focus on the statements that appear easiest to verify first, and fight the urge to automatically lunge for the answer that "looks" false. Remember, you only need one example of a statement being true to eliminate it.

Getting to the Answer: D doesn't involve any math, so examine that one first. When a negative fraction is squared, the sign of the result is positive, so D is incorrect. Try C next; a you raise a negative fraction to higher powers, the absolute value of the result will decrease. This contradicts the inequality in (C) regardless of the value you pick for x, so it is the correct answer.

Picking Numbers is a quick route for checking A and B. Suppose $x = -\frac{1}{4}$ and $a = -4$: ax would equal 1, and $\sqrt{ax}$ would also equal 1, making A a true statement using these values. If $x = -\frac{1}{4}$ and $a = -16$, ax would equal 4, and $\sqrt{ax}$ would equal 2, which makes B true using these values.

5. A
Difficulty: Hard

Category: Passport to Advanced Math / Exponents

Strategic Advice: You can't simplify an expression that has different roots (in this case, third and sixth). Rewrite the expression with fraction exponents first, and then use exponent rules to simplify it.

Getting to the Answer: The rule for fraction exponents is "power over root"; use this to rewrite the expression.

$$\frac{\sqrt[6]{x^{10}y^{12}}}{\sqrt[3]{x^5y^6}} = \frac{x^{\frac{10}{6}}y^{\frac{12}{6}}}{x^{\frac{5}{3}}y^{\frac{6}{3}}}$$

When dividing like bases, subtract the exponents. Find common denominators as needed.

$$x^{\frac{10}{6}-\frac{5}{3}}y^{\frac{12}{6}-\frac{6}{3}} = x^{\frac{10}{6}-\frac{10}{6}}y^{\frac{12}{6}-\frac{12}{6}} = x^0y^0$$

Any number raised to the zero power becomes 1, so the expression becomes $1 \times 1 = 1$. (A) is correct.

6. D
Difficulty: Medium

Category: Passport to Advanced Math / Exponents

Strategic Advice: Remember how multiplicity of zeros works: the number of times a zero's corresponding binomial factor appears in a polynomial

equation dictates whether it is a simple zero, a double zero, etc.

Getting to the Answer: You're told that y has two zeros: one simple and one triple. This means you need one binomial expression raised to the first power and one raised to the third (because the latter is repeated three times). Eliminate B and C. Now examine the remaining choices; mental math reveals that they both have 4 and −4 as roots. The binomial leading to $x = -4$ should be raised to the third power, and the one that yields $x = 4$ should be raised to the first. Only (D) meets this criterion.

7. C
Difficulty: Medium

Category: Passport to Advanced Math / Exponents

Strategic Advice: Factor and cancel as much as you can, remembering the rules of simplifying rational expressions as you do so (meaning no canceling terms that are added or subtracted!).

Getting to the Answer: Start by factoring out the GCF of the two terms in the numerator, and then repeat with the denominator. The expressions left in both sets of parentheses are identical (once you apply the commutative property of addition), so you can cancel them.

$$\frac{27m^4n^3 + 6mn^2}{18m^2n + 81m^5n^2} = \frac{3mn^2(9m^3n + 2)}{9m^2n(2 + 9m^3n)}$$

Once here, you'll see that the GCF of the new numerator and denominator is $3mn$. Factor this out and cancel.

$$\frac{3mn^2}{9m^2n} = \frac{3mn(n)}{3mn(3m)}$$

The simplified expression is $\frac{n}{3m}$, which matches (C).

8. 7958

Difficulty: Medium

Category: Problem Solving and Data Analysis / Exponents

Strategic Advice: Word problems are always great opportunities to use the Kaplan Strategy for Translating English into Math. You'll have decimals early on and throughout your calculations, but do not round until the very end.

Getting to the Answer: The nice thing about this question is that some of the steps have been done for you: You already know your variables and are given an equation that relates them. All you need to do is plug in the appropriate values. You're told that $P = 300{,}000$, $r = \dfrac{0.03375}{12} = 0.0028125$ (because r is the monthly interest rate, not the annual rate), and $N = 12 \times 30 = 360$. Plug these values into the formula $m = \dfrac{Pr}{1-(1+r)^{-N}}$, and then solve for m as shown below.

$$m = \frac{300000 \times 0.0028125}{1-(1+0.0028125)^{-360}}$$

$$m = \frac{843.75}{1-(1.0028125)^{-360}}$$

$$m = \frac{843.75}{0.6362}$$

$$m = 1{,}326.2886$$

Don't stop yet! The question asks for the amount paid for the mortgage after six months, so multiply 1,326.2886 by 6 to get 7,957.7318. Round to 7958, and you're done!

Note that if you rounded 1,326.29 to 1,326, your answer would be off. Avoid rounding until you have your final answer!

PRACTICE

9. D

Difficulty: Hard

Category: Passport to Advanced Math / Exponents

Strategic Advice: Don't stress over wordiness or bizarre science jargon in questions like this. All you need to do is solve for the correct variable.

Getting to the Answer: Relative velocity is represented by v, so that's the variable you need to isolate. The manipulation sequence is shown here.

$$\gamma = \frac{1}{\sqrt{1-\dfrac{v^2}{c^2}}}$$

$$\gamma\sqrt{1-\frac{v^2}{c^2}} = 1$$

$$\sqrt{1-\frac{v^2}{c^2}} = \frac{1}{\gamma}$$

$$1-\frac{v^2}{c^2} = \frac{1}{\gamma^2}$$

$$-\frac{v^2}{c^2} = \frac{1}{\gamma^2}-1$$

$$v^2 = -c^2\left(\frac{1}{\gamma^2}-1\right)$$

$$v = c\sqrt{1-\frac{1}{\gamma^2}}$$

The correct answer is (D).

10. B

Difficulty: Medium

Category: Passport to Advanced Math / Exponents

Strategic Advice: Resist the urge to break the expression into two separate radicals; it will likely lead you to an incorrect answer! Look for a common factor instead.

Getting to the Answer: The GCF of the two expressions under the radical is $g^4 h^3$; factoring this out yields $\sqrt[3]{g^4 h^3 (g^2 - 27)}$. You can now pull a g and an h out from under the radical to obtain $gh\sqrt[3]{g(g^2 - 27)}$, which cannot be further simplified except for redistribution of g, which yields $gh\sqrt[3]{g^3 - 27g}$, making (B) correct. Note that $\sqrt[3]{g^3 - 27g}$ *does not* become $g - 3\sqrt[3]{g}$, as you cannot split the expression into two radicals.

11. D

Difficulty: Medium

Category: Passport to Advanced Math / Exponents

Strategic Advice: If you look closely, you'll notice you can do most of the math without a calculator by manipulating the exponents. For example, to convert 7.5×10^3 to a product of 10^6 and another number, move the decimal point in 7.5 three places to the left (the number of times you want to increase the exponent on 10), and write "$\times 10^6$" after it.

Getting to the Answer: Start by setting up a ratio that compares RBC count to total blood cell count. Manipulate the quantities to make all the exponents the same, factor out 10^6, and then add the quantities in parentheses together. Once there, you can use exponent rules to simplify your equation. Divide through and multiply by 100 to get the RBC component as a percentage. Work is shown here.

$$RBC = \frac{5.4 \times 10^6}{5.4 \times 10^6 + 7.5 \times 10^3 + 3.5 \times 10^5}$$

$$RBC = \frac{5.4 \times 10^6}{5.4 \times 10^6 + 0.0075 \times 10^6 + 0.35 \times 10^6}$$

$$RBC = \frac{5.4 \times 10^6}{10^6 (5.4 + 0.0075 + 0.35)}$$

$$RBC = \frac{5.4}{5.7575}$$

Note that the answer choices are, for the most part, far apart. Because 5.4 is relatively close to 5.7575, you can conclude with confidence that the correct answer is likely close to 100%. Therefore, (D) is the correct answer. If this question is in the calculator section, you can plug the numbers into your calculator to check:

$$\% \, RBC = \frac{5.4}{5.7575} \times 100 \approx 93.79\%$$

Choice (D) is still correct.

PERFORM

12. C

Difficulty: Medium

Category: Passport to Advanced Math / Exponents

Strategic Advice: Don't attempt to combine several steps when manipulating the equation; it's very easy for a small error to go unnoticed if you do so.

Getting to the Answer: Begin by moving all terms that don't contain an a to one side of the equation. Once there, multiply both sides by 2 to eliminate the fraction, and then divide by t^2 to isolate a. The manipulation sequence is shown here.

$$h = \frac{1}{2}at^2 + v_0 t + h_0$$

$$h - v_0 t - h_0 = \frac{1}{2}at^2$$

$$at^2 = 2(h - v_0 t - h_0)$$

$$a = \frac{2(h - v_0 t - h_0)}{t^2}$$

(C) is the correct answer.

13. A

Difficulty: Hard

Category: Passport to Advanced Math / Exponents

Strategic Advice: Remember to distribute properly when multiplying expressions.

Getting to the Answer: Start by simplifying the radicals: 72 is the product of 2 and 36, so $\sqrt{72} = 6\sqrt{2}$. You can then factor 3 out of the numerator and denominator to yield $\dfrac{3(1+2\sqrt{2})}{3(1-2\sqrt{2})}$. Cancel the 3s, and you're left with $\dfrac{1+2\sqrt{2}}{1-2\sqrt{2}}$. You can't leave a radical in the denominator, so you'll need to rationalize it. The conjugate of the denominator is $1+2\sqrt{2}$, so multiply the entire expression by $\dfrac{1+2\sqrt{2}}{1+2\sqrt{2}}$, and then simplify as usual (think FOIL):

$$\frac{1+2\sqrt{2}}{1-2\sqrt{2}} \times \frac{1+2\sqrt{2}}{1+2\sqrt{2}}$$

$$\frac{1+2\sqrt{2}+2\sqrt{2}+8}{(1-2\sqrt{2})(1+2\sqrt{2})}$$

$$\frac{1+2\sqrt{2}+2\sqrt{2}+8}{1+2\sqrt{2}-2\sqrt{2}-8}$$

$$\frac{9+4\sqrt{2}}{-7}$$

This expression matches (A).

14. 41

Difficulty: Hard

Category: Passport to Advanced Math / Exponents

Strategic Advice: This is the same formula you used in a previous question in this chapter; you're just looking for a different variable this time.

Getting to the Answer: Like in question 8, you're given all the variables you need and an equation that relates them. All you need to do is plug the given values into the correct locations ($m = 200$, $r = \dfrac{0.015}{12}$, $N = 60$) and solve for what's missing (P in this case). Decimals are truncated for brevity here, but no rounding was done until the final step.

$$m = \frac{Pr}{1-(1+r)^{-N}}$$

$$200 = \frac{P \times \dfrac{0.015}{12}}{1-\left(1+\dfrac{0.015}{12}\right)^{-60}}$$

$$200 = \frac{0.00125P}{1-(1+0.00125)^{-60}}$$

$$200 = \frac{0.00125P}{1-(1.00125)^{-60}}$$

$$200 = \frac{0.00125P}{1-0.9278}$$

$$14.4426 = 0.00125P$$

$$P = 11,554.0987$$

Subtract P from the total price (19,560) to obtain Teri's down payment. Divide this by 19,560 and multiply by 100 to arrive at 40.93%. Rounded properly, the correct answer is 41.

EXTRA PRACTICE

1. C

Difficulty: Easy

Category: Passport to Advanced Math / Exponents

Strategic Advice: A variable that has a fraction exponent can be written as a radical expression by writing the numerator as the power of the radicand and denominator as the degree of the root. You can remember this using the phrase "power over root." For example, $x^{\frac{2}{3}} = \sqrt[3]{x^2}$.

Getting to the Answer: Follow the standard order of operations—deal with the exponent first, and then attach the negative sign (because a negative in front of an expression means multiplication by –1). The variable x is being raised to the $\frac{1}{4}$ power, so rewrite the term as a radical expression with 4 as the degree of the root and 1 as the power to which the radicand, x, is being raised.

$$x^{\frac{1}{4}} = \sqrt[4]{x^1} = \sqrt[4]{x}$$

Now attach the negative to arrive at the correct answer, $-\sqrt[4]{x}$, which is (C).

2. C

Difficulty: Easy

Category: Passport to Advanced Math / Exponents

Strategic Advice: Solve equations containing radical expressions the same way you solve any other equation: isolate the variable using inverse operations.

Getting to the Answer: To get rid of the fraction, multiply both sides of the equation by 2. Then, divide by 7 to isolate the radical. Finally, square both sides to get rid of the radical and isolate x.

$$2 \cdot \left(\frac{7\sqrt{x}}{2} = 14 \right)$$
$$7\sqrt{x} = 28$$
$$\sqrt{x} = 4$$
$$(\sqrt{x})^2 = 4^2$$
$$x = 16$$

This means (C) is correct. You could also work backwards to answer this question, but only if you're comfortable finding square roots without a calculator.

3. B

Difficulty: Easy

Category: Passport to Advanced Math / Exponents

Strategic Advice: When you're asked to simplify a rational expression, look for common factors that can be divided out of the numerator and the denominator. If you find any common factors, you can cancel them. Keep in mind that you cannot cancel individual terms.

Getting to the Answer: Factor a 4 from the numerator and the denominator, and then cancel the $\frac{4}{4}$.

$$\frac{4x + 8y}{24x - 12}$$
$$= \frac{\cancel{4}(1x + 2y)}{\cancel{4}(6x - 3)}$$
$$= \frac{x + 2y}{6x - 3}$$

This matches (B).

4. D

Difficulty: Easy

Category: Passport to Advanced Math / Exponents

Strategic Advice: Distribute each term in the first factor to each term in the second factor (FOIL). Be careful with the signs.

Getting to the Answer:

$$(-x + 6)(2x - 3) = -x(2x - 3) + 6(2x - 3)$$
$$= -2x^2 + 3x + 12x - 18$$
$$= -2x^2 + 15x - 18$$

Be careful—the question asks for the coefficient of x, not x^2, so the answer is 15, which is (D).

5. C

Difficulty: Easy

Category: Passport to Advanced Math / Exponents

Strategic Advice: When the denominators of rational expressions are the same, you can combine the numerators and keep the same denominator, just like you do when adding or subtracting plain fractions.

Getting to the Answer: First, write the question as a subtraction problem. Pay careful attention to which expression is being subtracted.

$$\frac{8x-5}{x-1} - \frac{3x+7}{x-1}$$

The terms in the expression have the same denominator, $x - 1$, so their numerators can be subtracted. Simply combine like terms and keep the denominator the same. Don't forget to distribute the negative to both $3x$ and 7.

$$\frac{8x-5}{x-1} - \frac{3x+7}{x-1} = \frac{8x-5-3x-7}{x-1} = \frac{5x-12}{x-1}$$

The reduced expression matches (C).

6. D

Difficulty: Medium

Category: Passport to Advanced Math / Exponents

Strategic Advice: A *double zero* occurs in a polynomial when a factor is repeated, or in other words, squared. For example, the factor $(x - a)$ produces a simple zero at $x = a$, while $(x - b)^2$ produces a double zero at $x = b$. Graphically, this means that the polynomial *crosses* the axis at $x = a$, but just *touches* the x-axis (and then turns around) at $x = b$.

Getting to the Answer: The polynomial has a simple zero at $x = -3$, which corresponds to a factor of $(x + 3)$. The double zero at $x = \dfrac{5}{4}$ results from a repeated (squared) factor, so you can eliminate A and C. To choose between B and (D), set each factor equal to 0, and then use inverse operations to solve for x (mentally if possible). Choice (D) is correct because:

$$4x - 5 = 0$$
$$4x = 5$$
$$x = \frac{5}{4}$$

7. B

Difficulty: Medium

Category: Passport to Advanced Math / Exponents

Strategic Advice: Don't let all the scientific terminology intimidate you. All you need to do is to solve the equation for T using inverse operations.

Getting to the Answer: Start by getting T out of the denominator of the fraction. To do this, multiply both sides of the equation by T, and then divide both sides by v.

$$v = \frac{2\pi r}{T}$$
$$T \times (v) = \left(\frac{2\pi r}{\cancel{T}}\right) \times \cancel{T}$$
$$Tv = 2\pi r$$
$$T = \frac{2\pi r}{v}$$

Choice (B) is the correct answer.

8. B

Difficulty: Medium

Category: Passport to Advanced Math / Exponents

Strategic Advice: This question would probably be fairly easy if you were allowed to use a calculator. Keep in mind, however, that radicals can definitely show up on the No-calculator section of the test.

Getting to the Answer: Chances are that the test makers do not expect you to multiply decimals and then take a square root. Rather, the decimals are likely to have fairly common fraction equivalents that will multiply together nicely. Start with that:

$$\sqrt{0.75} \times \sqrt{0.8} = \sqrt{\frac{3}{4}} \times \sqrt{\frac{4}{5}} = \sqrt{\frac{3}{\cancel{4}} \times \frac{\cancel{4}}{5}} = \sqrt{\frac{3}{5}} = \frac{\sqrt{3}}{\sqrt{5}}$$

Don't forget—you're not allowed to leave a radical in the denominator of a fraction, so you need to rationalize the denominator. To do this, multiply the top and bottom of the fraction by the radical in the bottom. The result is $\frac{\sqrt{3}}{\sqrt{5}} \times \frac{\sqrt{5}}{\sqrt{5}} = \frac{\sqrt{15}}{5}$, which matches (B).

9. A

Difficulty: Medium

Category: Passport to Advanced Math / Exponents

Strategic Advice: You could rewrite the fraction exponent using a radical, find the largest perfect cube that divides into each factor, and bring the cube roots outside the radical. However, writing 27 as 3^3 and then using rules of exponents is most likely the faster route. Don't forget—when you raise an exponent to an exponent, you multiply the exponents.

Getting to the Answer:

$$(27x^6 y^{12})^{\frac{1}{3}}$$

$$= 3^{3 \times \frac{1}{3}} x^{6 \times \frac{1}{3}} y^{12 \times \frac{1}{3}}$$

$$= 3x^2 y^4$$

Choice (A) is correct.

10. A

Difficulty: Medium

Category: Passport to Advanced Math / Exponents

Strategic Advice: Solve equations containing radical expressions the same way you solve any other equation: isolate the variable using inverse operations. Try not to be concerned by how many parts there are to the equation in this question. Perform one inverse operation at a time, working your way toward getting the variable out of the radical and then by itself.

Getting to the Answer: Start by subtracting 8 from both sides of the equation, and then multiply by 3. Then, square both sides to remove the radical.

$$8 + \frac{\sqrt{2x+29}}{3} = 9$$

$$\frac{\sqrt{2x+29}}{3} = 1$$

$$\sqrt{2x+29} = 3$$

$$2x + 29 = 9$$

Now you have a simple linear equation that you can solve using more inverse operations: subtract 29 and divide by 2 to find that $x = -10$. Be careful—just because the equation started with a radical and the answer is negative, does not mean that *No solution* is the correct answer. If you plug −10 into the expression under the radical, the result is a positive number, which means −10 is a perfectly valid solution. Therefore, (A) is correct.

11. C

Difficulty: Medium

Category: Passport to Advanced Math / Exponents

Strategic Advice: Look for a common factor that can be divided out of the numerator and the denominator. If you find one, you can cancel it. It will save time if you look for the greatest common factor.

Getting to the Answer: Factor out the GCF of *both* the numerator and the denominator. Then cancel what you can. In this expression, the GCF is $3x^2y$.

$$\frac{12x^3y^2-9x^2y}{6x^4y+18x^3y^3}$$
$$=\frac{3x^2y(4xy-3)}{3x^2y(2x^2+6xy^2)}$$
$$=\frac{4xy-3}{2x^2+6xy^2}$$

This matches (C).

12. B
Difficulty: Medium

Category: Passport to Advanced Math / Exponents

Strategic Advice: Look closely at the dividend and the divisor. The divisor, $5x$, can be divided into each term in the dividend evenly, which means you don't need to use polynomial long division. Just divide each term by $5x$ and leave the signs the same.

Getting to the Answer: You could divide each term mentally, but it may be safer to write each term over $5x$, and then use rules of exponents to simplify.

$$\frac{30x^3}{5x}+\frac{45x^2}{5x}-\frac{10x}{5x}=6x^2+9x-2$$

The question asks for the coefficient of x, so the correct answer is 9, which is (B).

13. D
Difficulty: Medium

Category: Passport to Advanced Math / Exponents

Strategic Advice: Just as with rational expressions, factoring out the GCF of the terms is a great way to start a question like this.

Getting to the Answer: The GCF of the terms under the radical is m^4n^2. Factor this out and see if you can take the square root of anything:

$$\sqrt{9m^5n^2-m^4n^2}=\sqrt{m^4n^2(9m-1)}$$
$$=m^2n\sqrt{9m-1}$$

The result matches (D).

14. B
Difficulty: Medium

Category: Passport to Advanced Math / Exponents

Strategic Advice: This is another question that involves a science formula and, although interesting to learn about, may use up valuable time on Test Day. To save time, skim the first couple of sentences and look for the actual question near the end. Chances are that you'll either be plugging a value into the formula, or solving the formula for a specific variable.

Getting to the Answer: The question asks you to solve the equation for L. Use inverse operations to accomplish the task: divide both sides of the equation by 2π and then square both sides. You'll need to apply the exponent to all the terms on the left side of the equation, including the π:

$$T=2\pi\sqrt{\frac{L}{g}}$$
$$\frac{T}{2\pi}=\sqrt{\frac{L}{g}}$$
$$\left(\frac{T}{2\pi}\right)^2=\left(\sqrt{\frac{L}{g}}\right)^2$$
$$\frac{T^2}{4\pi^2}=\frac{L}{g}$$

Finally, multiply both sides by g to remove g from the denominator and isolate L.

$$L=\frac{gT^2}{4\pi^2}$$

The correct answer is (B).

15. D
Difficulty: Hard

Category: Passport to Advanced Math / Exponents

Strategic Advice: When adding and subtracting long polynomials, writing the problem vertically will help you stay organized.

Getting to the Answer: Multiply each term in the first expression by $\frac{3}{2}$ and each term in the second expression by -2. Then add the two polynomials by writing them vertically and combining like terms.

$$\frac{3}{2}A = \frac{3}{2}\left(4x^2 + 7x - 1\right) = 6x^2 + \frac{21}{2}x - \frac{3}{2}$$
$$-2B = -2\left(-x^2 - 5x + 3\right) = 2x^2 + 10x - 6$$

$$6x^2 + \frac{21}{2}x - \frac{3}{2}$$
$$+\ 2x^2 + \frac{20}{2}x - \frac{12}{2}$$
$$\overline{8x^2 + \frac{41}{2}x - \frac{15}{2}}$$

This means (D) is correct.

16. A
Difficulty: Hard

Category: Passport to Advanced Math / Exponents

Strategic Advice: It is not possible to add, subtract, multiply, or divide radicals that represent roots of different degrees (such as a square root and a cube root) when they are written in radical form. Instead, you must write the radicals using fraction exponents and then use rules of exponents to combine the terms. Keep in mind that this is a non-calculator question.

Getting to the Answer: Write each radical using a fraction exponent, and then use the rule $a^x \times a^y = a^{x+y}$ to answer the question.

$$\sqrt{2} \times \sqrt[4]{2} = 2^{\frac{1}{2}} \times 2^{\frac{1}{4}}$$
$$= 2^{\frac{1}{2}+\frac{1}{4}}$$
$$= 2^{\frac{2}{4}+\frac{1}{4}}$$
$$= 2^{\frac{3}{4}}$$

The answers are written in radical, so convert back to radicals using the saying "power over root." The result is $\sqrt[4]{2^3} = \sqrt[4]{8}$, which is (A).

17. 10/3
Difficulty: Hard

Category: Passport to Advanced Math / Exponents

Strategic Advice: Rewrite the radicals as fraction exponents: $\sqrt[3]{x} = x^{\frac{1}{3}}$ and $\sqrt{x} = x^{\frac{1}{2}}$.

Getting to the Answer: Write each factor in the expression in exponential form. Then use the rules of exponents to simplify the expression. Add the exponents of the factors that are being multiplied and subtract the exponent of the factor that is being divided:

$$\frac{\sqrt[3]{x} \cdot x^{\frac{5}{2}} \cdot x}{\sqrt{x}} = \frac{x^{\frac{1}{3}} \cdot x^{\frac{5}{2}} \cdot x^1}{x^{\frac{1}{2}}} = x^{\frac{1}{3}+\frac{5}{2}+\frac{1}{1}-\frac{1}{2}} = x^{\frac{2}{6}+\frac{15}{6}+\frac{6}{6}-\frac{3}{6}}$$
$$= x^{\frac{20}{6}} = x^{\frac{10}{3}}.$$

The question states that n is the power of x, so the value of n is $\frac{10}{3}$.

You can check your answer by choosing a value for x and plugging the original expression into your calculator and comparing it to the result when you plug the same value for x into the reduced expression.

18. 21

Difficulty: Hard

Category: Passport to Advanced Math / Exponents

Strategic Advice: The math itself is not difficult in this question. However, there are a lot of operations in the equation, so there will be a lot of steps to solving it. Be patient, carefully performing one step at a time.

Getting to the Answer: Solve this radical equation the same way you would solve any other equation: isolate the variable using inverse operations.

$$12 + \frac{3\sqrt{x-5}}{2} = 18 \qquad \text{Subtract 12.}$$

$$\frac{3\sqrt{x-5}}{2} = 6 \qquad \text{Multiply by 2.}$$

$$3\sqrt{x-5} = 12 \qquad \text{Divide by 3.}$$

$$\sqrt{x-5} = 4 \qquad \text{Square both sides.}$$

$$x-5 = 16 \qquad \text{Add 5.}$$

$$x = 21$$

The correct answer is 21. This is a Grid-in question, so if you have time it wouldn't hurt to check your answer by plugging 21 back into the original equation.

19. A

Difficulty: Easy

Category: Passport to Advanced Math / Exponents

Strategic Advice: A radical expression can be written using a fraction exponent by writing the degree of the root in the denominator of the fraction. The numerator of the fraction represents the power on the number or variable inside the radical. The phrase "power over root" works when converting in either direction.

Getting to the Answer: Write each factor in the expression in exponential form and use the rules of exponents to simplify the expression. The number 4 is simply being multiplied by the variables. The

power of a under the radical is 1 and the root is 3, so the exponent on a is $\frac{1}{3}$ (power over root). The power of b is 9 and the root is 3, so the exponent on b is $\frac{9}{3} = 3$ (power over root). This means $4\sqrt[3]{ab^9} = 4 \cdot a^{\frac{1}{3}} b^{\frac{9}{3}} = 4a^{\frac{1}{3}}b^3$, which matches (A).

20. A

Difficulty: Easy

Category: Passport to Advanced Math / Exponents

Strategic Advice: Add polynomial expressions by combining like terms. Be careful of the signs of each term. It may help to write the sum vertically (like you would with big numbers), lining up the like terms.

Getting to the Answer:

$$\begin{array}{r} 6a^2 - 17a - 9 \\ + \; -5a^2 + 8a - 2 \\ \hline a^2 - 9a - 11 \end{array}$$

The correct answer is (A).

21. 16

Difficulty: Hard

Category: Passport to Advanced Math / Exponents

Strategic Advice: Because this is a non-calculator question, you need to rewrite the exponent in a way that makes it easier to evaluate.

Getting to the Answer: Use the rules of exponents to rewrite $\frac{4}{3}$ as a unit fraction raised to a power. Then write the expression in radical form and simplify.

$$8^{\frac{4}{3}} = (8^{\frac{1}{3}})^4$$
$$= (\sqrt[3]{8})^4$$
$$= 2^4$$
$$= 2 \times 2 \times 2 \times 2$$
$$= 16$$

CHAPTER 9

PREPARE

1. C

Difficulty: Easy

Category: Passport to Advanced Math / Exponents

Strategic Advice: The question only asks you to determine how many values of x result in the expression being undefined so don't waste time trying to simplify the expression as a whole.

Getting to the Answer: A rational expression is undefined when one or more of its terms has a denominator that is equal to 0. Break the denominator into two equations and set each one equal to 0: $3x - 6 = 0$, $x^2 - 1 = 0$. Solving the first yields $x = 2$, and solving the second yields $x = \pm 1$. The expression is undefined at -1, 1, and 2; three values in all. (C) is the correct answer.

2. D

Difficulty: Easy

Category: Passport to Advanced Math / Exponents

Strategic Advice: Factor the denominator on the right side to help you find the common denominator.

Getting to the Answer: Factor an x out of $x^2 - 8x$ to get $x(x - 8)$. On the left side of the equation, x and $(x - 8)$ are the denominators; putting them together gives a common denominator across the entire equation. Distribute, then solve for x.

$$x(x-8)\left(\frac{4}{x} + \frac{2}{x-8} = \frac{-2}{x(x-8)}\right)$$

$$4(x - 8) + 2x = -2$$
$$4x - 32 + 2x = -2$$
$$6x = 30$$
$$x = 5$$

"No solution" is not an answer choice, so there's no need to check whether 5 is extraneous. Choice (D) is correct.

3. C

Difficulty: Medium

Category: Passport to Advanced Math / Exponents

Strategic Advice: Determine the rate at which each colleague works, then add them together to get the combined rate.

Getting to the Answer: You're told that either Johanna or Elizabeth can complete the preparation in six days if working alone. Use the equation $r = \dfrac{W}{t}$ to find that Johanna and Elizabeth each has a rate of $\dfrac{1}{6}$ of the preparation per day. Likewise, Dan can complete the preparation in four days, which is the same as $\dfrac{1}{4}$ of the preparation per day. Add these together, set them equal to $\dfrac{1}{t}$ (the rate for the whole task), and solve for t.

$$\frac{1}{6} + \frac{1}{6} + \frac{1}{4} = \frac{1}{t}$$
$$\frac{2}{12} + \frac{2}{12} + \frac{3}{12} + \frac{1}{t}$$
$$\frac{7}{12} = \frac{1}{t}$$
$$7t = 12$$
$$t = \frac{12}{7}$$

The correct answer is (C).

4. A

Difficulty: Medium

Category: Passport to Advanced Math / Exponents

Strategic Advice: Identify all x-values that cause the equation to be undefined. Then simplify the equation to determine the shape of its graph.

Getting to the Answer: Set the denominator $(x^2 - 4)$ equal to 0 and then solve for x to get $x = \pm 2$. The graph should have open dots at these x-values, so eliminate C and D, which are continuous graphs with no open dots. Now simplify the original equation: Factor 2 out of the numerator to get $y = \dfrac{2(x^2 - 4)}{x^2 - 4} + 1$ and then cancel the $x^2 - 4$ factors to get $y = 2 + 1 = 3$. The graph should be a horizontal line with open dots at $x = \pm 2$; (A) is the only graph that satisfies both criteria.

5. D

Difficulty: Easy

Category: Passport to Advanced Math / Exponents

Strategic Advice: Nothing tricky here; just use polynomial long division.

Getting to the Answer: Divide $16a^2 + 3$ by $4a + 2$ as shown below, being careful when subtracting to avoid losing a negative sign.

$$
\begin{array}{r}
4a - 2 \\
4a + 2 \overline{\smash{\big)}\, 16a^2 + 0a + 3} \\
\underline{-(16a^2 + 8a)} \\
-8a + 3 \\
\underline{-(-8a - 4)} \\
7
\end{array}
$$

Choice (D) is correct.

6. B

Difficulty: Hard

Category: Passport to Advanced Math / Exponents

Strategic Advice: Remember the equation $W = rt$ and the additive nature of rates.

Getting to the Answer: The two systems working in tandem can complete the backup task in 12 hours; this is the same as saying they complete $\dfrac{1}{12}$ of the task in 1 hour. Because this is a rate for completing the whole task, you can add the individual rates of the systems together and set the sum equal to $\dfrac{1}{12}$. Translation: $\dfrac{1}{h}$ and $\dfrac{3}{h}$ are rates, not times, so you can eliminate A and C. If $\dfrac{1}{12}$ is the amount of the task completed in 1 hour with both systems working together, and the faster system is triple the speed of the other, then $\dfrac{3}{h}$ must represent the portion that the faster system completes in 1 hour. Therefore, (B) is the correct choice.

7. D

Difficulty: Medium

Category: Passport to Advanced Math / Exponents

Strategic Advice: Eliminate the fractions first. Also, remember to check for extraneous solutions before selecting your answer.

Getting to the Answer: Multiply both sides of the equation by the common denominator, $(x + 2)(x + 6)$, to eliminate the fractions. Once complete, solve for x as usual via factoring.

$$x(x + 6) + 2(x + 2) = -8$$
$$x^2 + 8x + 4 = -8$$
$$x^2 + 8x + 12 = 0$$
$$(x + 2)(x + 6) = 0$$
$$x + 2 = 0 \quad x + 6 = 0$$
$$x = -2 \quad x = -6$$

Take another look at the denominators in the original equation. The equation is undefined when x is -2 or -6, which are the values that you found for your solutions. This means both are extraneous, so the equation has no solution. The correct answer is (D).

8. A

Difficulty: Medium

Category: Passport to Advanced Math / Exponents

Strategic Advice: Find a way to rewrite the denominator of the right side of the equation so that the math is less tricky.

Getting to the Answer: Factor -1 out of the denominator on the right side; the fraction will become $\dfrac{-1}{(x+1)(x+2)}$. Multiply through by a common denominator as usual and then solve for x via factoring.

$$x(x + 2) - 9(x + 1) = -1$$
$$x^2 - 7x - 9 = -1$$
$$x^2 - 7x - 8 = 0$$
$$(x + 1)(x - 8) = 0$$
$$x + 1 = 0 \quad x - 8 = 0$$
$$x = -1 \quad x = 8$$

Once again, check for extraneous solutions. The equation is undefined when x is -1 or -2, so one of the solutions is extraneous, and the other is valid. (A) is correct.

PRACTICE

9. 378

Difficulty: Medium

Category: Passport to Advanced Math / Exponents

Strategic Advice: This is a straightforward polynomial long division question with a slight twist at the end; don't stop prematurely.

Getting to the Answer: Start by executing polynomial long division.

$$
\require{enclose}
\begin{array}{r}
-7x^3 - 6x + 9 \\
x^2 + x \enclose{longdiv}{-7x^5 - 7x^4 - 6x^3 + 3x^2 + 9x} \\
\underline{-(-7x^5 - 7x^4)} \\
0x^4 - 6x^3 + 3x^2 + 9x \\
\underline{-(-6x^3 - 6x^2)} \\
9x^2 + 9x \\
\underline{-(9x^2 + 9x)} \\
0
\end{array}
$$

Now multiply the coefficients of the terms in the quotient and the constant to get $-7 \times -6 \times 9 = 378$.

10. A

Difficulty: Medium

Category: Passport to Advanced Math / Exponents

Strategic Advice: Keep in mind which pump you're looking for and how its speed compares to that of the other two.

Getting to the Answer: Start by arranging the pumps in order of increasing drain speed; you'll get P3 < P1 < P2. You're told that the second pump is twice as fast as the first and that the first is three times as fast as the third. You can turn the words into a ratio: If the speed of the third pump is $\dfrac{1}{x}$, then the speed of the first pump is $\dfrac{1}{x} \times 3 = \dfrac{3}{x}$, and the speed of the second pump must be $\dfrac{3}{x} \times 2 = \dfrac{6}{x}$. The term $\dfrac{6}{x}$ matches (A).

11. 7

Difficulty: Hard

Category: Passport to Advanced Math / Exponents

Strategic Advice: A rectangle's area is the product of its dimensions. If you know the area and one dimension, you can divide the former by the latter to get the second dimension.

Getting to the Answer: Start by dividing $x^4 + 8x^3 + 9x^2 - 6x$ by $x^2 + 2x$ via polynomial long division; the work for this is shown here.

$$
\begin{array}{r}
x^2 + 6x - 3 \\
x^2 + 2x \overline{\smash{\big)}\ x^4 + 8x^3 + 9x^2 - 6x} \\
\underline{-(x^4 + 2x^3)} \\
6x^3 + 9x^2 - 6x \\
\underline{-(6x^3 + 12x^2)} \\
-3x^2 - 6x \\
\underline{-(-3x^2 - 6x)} \\
0
\end{array}
$$

Be careful; the question asks for something less conventional. To determine when the dimensions are 25 units apart, add 25 to the smaller dimension and set that expression equal to the other dimension. Solve for x.

$$x^2 + 2x + 25 = x^2 + 6x - 3$$
$$-4x = -28$$
$$x = 7$$

The dimensions are 25 units apart when x is 7.

PERFORM

12. 68

Difficulty: Medium

Category: Passport to Advanced Math / Exponents

Strategic Advice: Don't bother with trial and error; it will take far too long. Use polynomial long division and your reasoning skills instead.

Getting to the Answer: The work for dividing the two expressions is shown here.

$$
\begin{array}{r}
3x^3 + 10x^2 + 20x + 34 \\
x - 2 \overline{\smash{\big)}\ 3x^4 + 4x^3 + 0x^2 - 6x - c} \\
\underline{-(3x^4 - 6x^3)} \\
10x^3 + 0x^2 - 6x - c \\
\underline{-(10x^3 - 20x^2)} \\
20x^2 - 6x - c \\
\underline{-(20x^2 - 40x)} \\
34x - c \\
\underline{-(34x - 68)} \\
-c + 68
\end{array}
$$

To make sure there is no remainder, you must add -68, which means c must be 68.

13. B

Difficulty: Hard

Category: Passport to Advanced Math / Exponents

Strategic Advice: The mention of a task being completed in a certain amount of time should make you think of rates.

Getting to the Answer: Adding Isabel and Richard's rates will yield the combined rate of the two working together. Using $r = \dfrac{W}{t}$, if W is defined as one planted bulb, Isabel's rate is $\dfrac{50}{40}$ bulbs per minute. In 40 minutes, Richard can plant 44%

of Isabel's bulb count, or $\dfrac{0.44 \times 50}{40} = \dfrac{22}{40}$ bulbs per minute. To complete the whole job, the two must plant 120 bulbs, so their combined rate for the whole job (not per minute) is $\dfrac{120}{t}$. Because $\dfrac{50}{40}$ and $\dfrac{22}{40}$ are not numbers that appear in the answer choices, reduce them to $\dfrac{5}{4}$ and $\dfrac{11}{20}$, respectively, and combine all the terms into a single equation to get $\dfrac{5}{4} + \dfrac{11}{20} = \dfrac{120}{t}$. Choice (B) is correct.

14. C
Difficulty: Hard

Category: Passport to Advanced Math / Exponents

Strategic Advice: This is not a true rational equation because of all the radicals floating around, but don't let them intimidate you. Just follow the same solving procedure you've used for rational equations.

Getting to the Answer: Begin by exploring options for factoring the denominator of the right side; look for a pair of numbers with a sum of -1 and a product of -12 to help you write the equation as a product of two binomials. You'll find that -4 and 3 are what you need, making the common denominator $(\sqrt{x} - 4)(\sqrt{x} + 3)$. Multiply both sides of the equation by this common denominator to eliminate the fractions, then solve for x.

$$-4(\sqrt{x} + 3) + \sqrt{x}(\sqrt{x} - 4) = -24$$
$$-4\sqrt{x} - 12 + x - 4\sqrt{x} = -24$$
$$x - 8\sqrt{x} + 12 = 0$$
$$(\sqrt{x} - 2)(\sqrt{x} - 6) = 0$$
$$\sqrt{x} - 2 = 0 \quad \sqrt{x} - 6 = 0$$
$$x = 4 \qquad x = 36$$

Remember to plug both solutions back into the original equation to check for extraneous solutions. Neither 4 nor 36 results in a 0 denominator, so both are valid solutions, making (C) correct.

EXTRA PRACTICE

1. A

Difficulty: Easy

Category: Passport to Advanced Math / Exponents

Strategic Advice: Find the greatest common factor of both the numerator and the denominator, which in this question happens to be the denominator. Factor out the GCF from the numerator and denominator and then cancel what you can.

Getting to the Answer: The GCF is $9x^2$.

$$\frac{18x^4 + 27x^3 - 36x^2}{9x^2} = \frac{\cancel{9x^2}(2x^2 + 3x - 4)}{\cancel{9x^2}}$$
$$= 2x^2 + 3x - 4$$

This matches (A). As an alternate method, you could split the expression up and reduce each term, one at a time.

$$\frac{18x^4 + 27x^3 - 36x^2}{9x^2} = \frac{18x^4}{9x^2} + \frac{27x^3}{9x^2} - \frac{36x^2}{9x^2}$$
$$= 2x^2 + 3x - 4$$

2. A

Difficulty: Easy

Category: Passport to Advanced Math / Exponents

Strategic Advice: Carefully multiply each term in the first factor by each term in the second factor. Then find the x-terms and add their coefficients. To save time, you do not need to simplify the other terms in the expression.

Getting to the Answer:

$$(-2x^2 + 5x - 8)(4x - 9)$$
$$= -2x^2(4x - 9) + 5x(4x - 9) - 8(4x - 9)$$
$$= -8x^3 + 18x^2 + 20x^2 - \underline{45x - 32x} + 72$$

The coefficient of x in the product is $-45 - 32 = -77$, which means (A) is correct.

3. B

Difficulty: Easy

Category: Passport to Advanced Math / Exponents

Strategic Advice: When asked to match an equation to a real-world scenario, Picking Numbers is often the strategy that will get you to the answer the quickest, especially when the answer choices look fairly complicated.

Getting to the Answer: Choose a number of cards to order (at least 100)— let's say 200 cards. Work the scenario out using your calculator: $15 setup fee + 200(0.02) = $19. The question asks about the average cost *per card*, so divide this amount by 200 to get $0.095 per card. Now, plug 200 into each of the equations for x, looking for the same result.

Choice A: $C_{ave} = \dfrac{15 + 0.02}{200} = 0.0751 \rightarrow$ No match.

Choice (B): $C_{ave} = \dfrac{15}{200} + 0.02 = 0.095 \rightarrow$ Match!

Check the remaining answer choices for completeness, but you'll see that only (B) is a match for the correct answer.

4. D

Difficulty: Medium

Category: Passport to Advanced Math / Exponents

Strategic Advice: Identify all x-values that cause the equation to be undefined and then simplify the equation to determine the shape of its graph.

Getting to the Answer: When x is 2, the denominator is 0 (and the equation is undefined), so the graph should have an open dot at $x = 2$. This means you can eliminate A, which is a continuous graph with no open dots and C, which has an open dot at x = −2. Next, simplify the original equation by factoring 3 from the numerator and cancelling common factors:

$$y = \frac{3\cancel{(x-2)}}{\cancel{x-2}} + 1$$
$$y = 3 + 1$$
$$y = 4$$

The graph is a horizontal line at $y = 4$ with an open dot at (2, 4), which matches (D).

5. C

Difficulty: Medium

Category: Passport to Advanced Math / Exponents

Strategic Advice: A fraction is the same as division, so you can use polynomial long division to simplify the expression.

Getting to the Answer:

$$\begin{array}{r} 3x+2 \\ 2x+5{\overline{\smash{\big)}\,6x^2+19x+10}} \\ \underline{-\left(6x^2+15x\right)} \\ 4x+10 \\ \underline{-\left(4x+10\right)} \\ 0 \end{array}$$

The simplified expression is $3x + 2$, so $a + b = 3 + 2 = 5$, which is (C). As an alternate method, you could factor the numerator of the expression, and cancel common factors.

$$\frac{6x^2+19x+10}{2x+5} = \frac{\cancel{(2x+5)}(3x+2)}{\cancel{(2x+5)}} = 3x+2$$

Use whichever method gets you to the correct answer in the shortest amount of time.

6. D

Difficulty: Medium

Category: Passport to Advanced Math / Exponents

Strategic Advice: Sometimes, the structure of an expression provides a huge clue as to how to factor it. In this question, notice that each term is a perfect square and there is a minus sign between the terms.

Getting to the Answer: Use the difference of squares rule, $a^2 - b^2 = (a - b)(a + b)$, to rewrite the expression. If you can't mentally determine what a and b are, write each term as the square of something:

$$25x^2y^4 - 1 = (5xy^2)^2 - 1^2$$
$$= (5xy^2 - 1)(5xy^2 + 1)$$

This matches (D).

7. C

Difficulty: Medium

Category: Passport to Advanced Math / Exponents

Strategic Advice: Whenever you're solving a rational equation, start by examining the denominators. In this question, recognizing that $3(x - 5)$ is the factored form of $3x - 15$ (which means the denominators are equivalent) will save you a bit of time.

Getting to the Answer: Because the denominators are the same (just written in different forms), multiplying both sides of the equation by $3x - 15$ will immediately clear all the fractions, the result of which is a much easier equation to solve:

$$8x + 2x = 50$$
$$10x = 50$$
$$x = 5$$

Because there are variables in the denominator, you must check the solution to make sure it is not extraneous.

When $x = 5$, each of the denominators is equal to 0, and division by 0 is not possible. Therefore, there is no solution to the equation, making (C) the correct answer.

8. A

Difficulty: Medium

Category: Passport to Advanced Math / Exponents

Strategic Advice: You won't always get a nice number answer when solving equations. In this question, there are two variables, and you're asked to solve for one of them *in terms of* the other.

Getting to the Answer: There are two variables and only one equation, but you still solve it the same way you would any other equation. Because there is only one term on each side of the equal sign, cross-multiplying is probably the quickest route to the solution. Don't forget—you want to get x by itself on one side of the equation.

$$\frac{6}{x} = \frac{3}{k+2}$$
$$6(k+2) = 3x$$
$$6k + 12 = 3x$$
$$\frac{6k}{3} + \frac{12}{3} = \frac{3x}{3}$$
$$2k + 4 = x$$

Switch x to the left side of the equation and the result matches (A).

9. B

Difficulty: Medium

Category: Passport to Advanced Math / Exponents

Strategic Advice: You can solve almost every *work* problem using the formula $W = rt$ or some manipulation of this formula, such as $r = \frac{W}{t}$ or

$t = \frac{W}{r}$. If two or more machines (or people) are working together, start by finding their combined rate and go from there. (Note: W is often 1 because many questions ask about completing *a job*, which is the same as *one job*.)

Getting to the Answer: The first pill counter can complete one batch in 1 hour, so its rate is $r = \frac{1}{1} = 1$ batch per hour. The second pill counter can complete one batch in 40 minutes (or $\frac{40}{60} = \frac{2}{3}$ hours), so its rate is $r = \frac{1}{\frac{2}{3}} = \frac{3}{2}$ batches per hour. Working together, the combined rate is $1 + \frac{3}{2} = \frac{2}{2} + \frac{3}{2} = \frac{5}{2}$ batches per hour. Use this combined rate in the formula for time to arrive at $t_{combined} = \frac{W}{r_{combined}} = \frac{1}{\frac{5}{2}} = \frac{2}{5}$ hours, which is equivalent to $\frac{2}{5} \times \overset{12}{\cancel{60}} = 24$ minutes. This means (B) is correct.

10. A

Difficulty: Medium

Category: Passport to Advanced Math / Exponents

Strategic Advice: The constant in an equation is the term without a variable. Thinking logically about a question like this one will save you a bit of time on Test Day.

Getting to the Answer: While you could use long division or factoring to find the quotient and then identify the constant, it is quicker to simply recognize that when a polynomial with a constant is divided by another polynomial with a constant, and there is no remainder, you can simply divide the constants to find the resulting constant of the quotient. Just be careful to use the correct signs. Because $-10 \div 5 = -2$, the constant in the resulting quotient is -2, which is (A).

11. C

Difficulty: Medium

Category: Passport to Advanced Math / Exponents

Strategic Advice: Whenever a binomial is squared (or raised to any power), you should rewrite it as repeated multiplication and expand it. Do this for both binomials and combine like terms to find the sum.

Getting to the Answer:

$(a - b)^2 + (a + b)^2$
$= [(a - b)(a - b)] + [(a + b)(a + b)]$
$= (a^2 - ab - ba + b^2) + (a^2 + ab + ba + b^2)$
$= (a^2 - 2ab + b^2) + (a^2 + 2ab + b^2)$
$= 2a^2 + 2b^2$

12. D

Difficulty: Hard

Category: Passport to Advanced Math / Exponents

Strategic Advice: Solving a rational equation almost always involves finding a common denominator and then multiplying all the terms by that denominator to clear the fractions. An extraneous solution is one that results in a 0 denominator.

Getting to the Answer: Factor the denominator in the second term to find that the common denominator for all three terms is $(x - 2)(x + 2)$. Multiply each term in the equation by the common denominator (in factored form or the original form, whichever is more convenient) to clear the fractions. Then solve the resulting equation for x:

$$(x-2)(x+2)\left(\frac{3}{x-2}\right) - (x^2-4)\left(\frac{12}{x^2-4}\right) = 1(x^2-4)$$

$$3(x+2) - 12 = x^2 - 4$$
$$3x + 6 - 12 = x^2 - 4$$
$$3x - 6 = x^2 - 4$$
$$0 = x^2 - 3x + 2$$
$$0 = (x-1)(x-2)$$

Set each factor equal to 0 to find that the potential solutions are $x = 1$ and $x = 2$. But wait, these are only *potential* solutions because the original equation was a rational equation. When x is 2, the denominators in both terms on the left side are equal to 0, so 2 is an extraneous solution, which means (D) is correct.

13. C

Difficulty: Hard

Category: Passport to Advanced Math / Exponents

Strategic Advice: You will not be expected to factor a fourth-degree polynomial like the one in this question, so there must be another way to approach the solution. This is a *long* polynomial, so think *long* division.

Getting to the Answer: Factors of polynomials must divide evenly into the polynomial, which means there is no remainder. In polynomial long division, the only time there is no remainder is when the *constant* in the factor divides evenly into the *constant* in the polynomial. This means you can eliminate A and D (because 5 does not divide evenly into 12). To decide between B and C, use long division. Start with C because it has all positive values, which means faster calculations and fewer potential mistakes:

$$3x+1 \overline{\smash{\big)}\ \begin{array}{r} 5x^3 + 34x^2 + 53x - 3 \\ 15x^4 + 107x^3 + 193x^2 + 17x - 12 \end{array}}$$
$$\underline{-(15x^4 + 5x^3)}$$
$$102x^3 + 193x^2 + 17x - 12$$
$$\underline{-(102x^3 + 34x^2)}$$
$$159x^2 + 17x - 12$$
$$\underline{-(159x^2 + 53x)}$$
$$-36x - 12$$
$$\underline{-(-36x - 12)}$$
$$0$$

Good news! You don't have to check B because $3x + 1$ is indeed a factor of the polynomial, making (C) correct.

14. D
Difficulty: Hard

Category: Passport to Advanced Math / Exponents

Strategic Advice: When graphs have holes in them (open dots), you can be sure that the equation will be either a rational equation or a piecewise equation. For rational equations, the number of holes corresponds to the number of values of x that produce a 0 denominator. There are two holes in this graph, so the degree of the denominator must be at least 2. This means you can eliminate A right away.

Getting to the Answer: Now, examine the graph more closely. The holes occur at $x = -2$ and $x = 2$, which means the denominator must equal 0 when x is -2 and when x is 2. This doesn't happen in B, so eliminate this choice (the denominator is -5 when $x = -2$ and when $x = 2$). To decide between C and D, simplify each equation to determine the shape of its graph. You're looking for the horizontal line $y = -3$. All of the factors in C don't cancel out, so the graph is not a horizontal line. (D) is correct because simplifying the equation results in the following:

$$y = \frac{2x^2 - 8}{x^2 - 4} - 5$$
$$y = \frac{2\,\cancel{(x^2 - 4)}}{\cancel{x^2 - 4}} - 5$$
$$y = 2 - 5$$
$$y = -3$$

15. B
Difficulty: Hard

Category: Passport to Advanced Math / Exponents

Strategic Advice: Don't let the wording confuse you on a question like this. Because the question states that the expressions are equivalent, set up the equation $\dfrac{16}{7x + 4} + A = \dfrac{49x^2}{7x + 4}$ and solve for A.

Getting to the Answer: Start by subtracting the first term from both sides of the equation to isolate A. Then, simplify if possible (usually by cancelling common factors). The denominators of the rational terms are the same, so they can be combined.

$$\frac{16}{7x + 4} + A = \frac{49x^2}{7x + 4}$$
$$A = \frac{49x^2}{7x + 4} - \frac{16}{7x + 4}$$
$$A = \frac{49x^2 - 16}{7x + 4}$$
$$A = \frac{\cancel{(7x + 4)}(7x - 4)}{\cancel{7x + 4}}$$
$$A = 7x - 4$$

The correct answer is (B).

16. 4
Difficulty: Medium

Category: Passport to Advanced Math / Exponents

Strategic Advice: To find a remainder, you must use polynomial long division (or synthetic division if you happen to know that nifty technique).

Getting to the Answer: Don't forget to set up the dividend with 0 placeholders for all missing terms.

$$x+2 \overline{)\,x^3+0x^2+0x+12} \quad \begin{array}{c} x^2 - 2x + 4 \end{array}$$

$$\underline{-(x^3+2x^2)}$$
$$-2x^2+0x$$
$$\underline{-(-2x^2-4x)}$$
$$4x+12$$
$$\underline{-(4x+8)}$$
$$4$$

The remainder is the number left over at the bottom, which is 4.

17. 8
Difficulty: Medium

Category: Passport to Advanced Math / Exponents

Strategic Advice: Don't bother with trial and error; it will take far too long. Use polynomial long division and your reasoning skills instead.

Getting to the Answer: The work for dividing the two expressions is shown.

$$x+4 \overline{)\,2x^4+16x^3+34x^2+10x+k} \quad \begin{array}{c} 2x^3+ 8x^2+ 2x + 2 \end{array}$$

$$\underline{-(2x^4+8x^3)}$$
$$8x^3+34x^2+10x+k$$
$$\underline{-(8x^3+32x^2)}$$
$$2x^2+10x+k$$
$$\underline{-(2x^2+8x)}$$
$$2x+k$$
$$\underline{-(2x+8)}$$
$$k-8$$

To make sure there is no remainder, k must be 8.

18. 2.8
Difficulty: Hard

Category: Passport to Advanced Math / Exponents

Strategic Advice: This is another example of a *work* problem, so you'll need to use the formula $W = rt$ or some manipulation of this formula, such as $r = \dfrac{W}{t}$ or $t = \dfrac{W}{r}$.

Getting to the Answer: The first unit can cool 260 square feet in 3 hours and 15 minutes, or 3.25 hours. The second unit can cool 300 square feet in 2.5 hours. The question asks how long it would take for both units to cool $260 + 300 = 560$ square feet. So set up a rational expression comparing the square feet (the amount of work) and the corresponding time for each unit and set the sum equal to the combined square feet and corresponding time (which you don't know, so call it h):

$$\frac{260}{3.25}+\frac{300}{2.5}=\frac{560}{h}$$

Find the unit rate for each term to make the numbers easier to work with. Then cross-multiply and solve for h.

$$\frac{80}{1}+\frac{120}{1}=\frac{560}{h}$$
$$\frac{200}{1}=\frac{560}{h}$$
$$200h=560$$
$$h=\frac{560}{200}=2.8$$

The question tells you not to round, so enter 2.8 and you're done.

CHAPTER 10

PREPARE

1. C
Difficulty: Easy

Category: Passport to Advanced Math / Functions & Function Notation

Strategic Advice: Ready your English-math translation skills for this question.

Getting to the Answer: Examine each piece of the question stem individually. "The cube of x" becomes x^3, and "the fourth root of the sum of three and the square of the product of two and x" becomes $\sqrt[4]{3+(2x)^2}$. The former is subtracted from the latter, so the right side of your inequality should be $\sqrt[4]{3+(2x)^2} - x^3$. The question states that this quantity is less than $f(x)$; after simplifying the radicand, you'll have $f(x) > \sqrt[4]{3+4x^2} - x^3$. (C) is correct.

2. B
Difficulty: Easy

Category: Passport to Advanced Math / Functions & Function Notation

Strategic Advice: Interpret each function's graph carefully to ensure you pick the correct points.

Getting to the Answer: Start with $h(0)$; according to the graph, $h(0) = 4$. Repeat with $g(x) (= 8)$ and $f(x) (= 3)$. Manipulate these values as instructed: $4 - 3(8 - 3) = 4 - 15 = -11$. (B) is correct.

3. A
Difficulty: Medium

Category: Passport to Advanced Math / Functions & Function Notation

Strategic Advice: Reduce the amount of work required by determining the y-intercept of the function.

Getting to the Answer: The table indicates that Clara had 21 votes on day 3, not at the start of the contest. This means that C and D are incorrect. To determine whether (A) or B is correct, pick a point to try in both functions.

$$(A): 35 = 2 \times 4^2 + 3$$
$$35 = 2 \times 16 + 3$$
$$35 = 32 + 3$$
$$35 = 35$$
$$B: 35 = \frac{1}{2} \times 4^2 + 3$$
$$35 = \frac{1}{2} \times 16 + 3$$
$$35 = 8 + 3$$
$$35 \neq 11$$

(A) is correct.

4. C
Difficulty: Medium

Category: Passport to Advanced Math / Functions & Function Notation

Strategic Advice: There's a lot going on in this question. Use the Kaplan Strategy for Translating English Into Math to help you keep everything organized.

Getting to the Answer: Variables have been defined for you, so there's no work to do there. Consider the functions one at a time. The function $g(x)$ represents 5% cash back on gasoline purchases up to $1,500, which translates to $g(x) = 0.05x$. A cardholder only gets 5% on purchases up to $1,500, so the function domain is restricted to $0 \leq x \leq 1,500$. Similarly, $e(x)$ represents 2% cash back. However, this is for purchases past $1,500, so the function must involve subtracting 1,500 from x. Multiplying the difference by 0.02 means $e(x) = 0.02(x - 1,500)$ with the domain restricted to $x > 1,500$. Only choice (C) contains both functions.

5. D

Difficulty: Easy

Category: Passport to Advanced Math / Functions & Function Notation

Strategic Advice: Read carefully; it's easy to make a mistake with such similar expressions in the numerator and denominator.

Getting to the Answer: Find the numerator and denominator separately:

$$p(5) = 5^2 - 4 \times 5 + 8 = 13$$
$$q(p(5)) = q(13) = 13 - 3 = 10$$
$$q(5) = 5 - 3 = 2$$
$$p(q(5)) = p(2) = 2^2 - 4 \times 2 + 8 = 4$$

Then combine properly:

$$\frac{q(p(5))}{p(q(5))} = \frac{10}{4} = 2.5$$

The correct answer is (D).

6. D

Difficulty: Medium

Category: Passport to Advanced Math / Functions & Function Notation

Strategic Advice: Think about the order in which the two functions must be computed to obtain Everett's pay.

Getting to the Answer: The question implies that Everett's commission depends on his sales over $4,000, which means your composition of functions should read $(c \circ e)(s)$. Because Everett's $1,000 base salary is independent of his sales, it should not be in the function argument (inside the parentheses with s). Therefore, the correct function is $(c \circ e)(s) + 1,000$, which is (D).

7. A

Difficulty: Medium

Category: Passport to Advanced Math / Functions & Function Notation

Strategic Advice: Read the transformation sequence carefully before selecting an answer.

Getting to the Answer: A horizontal compression requires the domain variable (x here) to have a coefficient greater than 1; eliminate D, which does not contain a coefficient greater than 1. A reflection about the x-axis (vertical) requires a negative sign before the function variable (j in this question). Eliminate C. An upward shift means the constant quantifying the shift must be outside the function argument parentheses. Only (A) contains all three transformations.

PRACTICE

8. C

Difficulty: Hard

Category: Passport to Advanced Math / Functions & Function Notation

Strategic Advice: Beware extraneous information; focus on what will get you to the answer.

Getting to the Answer: You're told the honeybee population decreases 35% each month; this means exponential decay is occurring, so use $y = x_0 (1 + r)^x$ as your function template. Set p as the honeybee population and t as the time in months; watch the sign of r. Your function should be $p(t) = (4.23 \times 10^8)(0.65)^t$. Now plug in the time in months:

$p(12) = (4.23 \times 10^8)(0.65)^{12} \approx 2,406,028$. The correct answer is (C).

9. C

Difficulty: Medium

Category: Passport to Advanced Math / Functions & Function Notation

Strategic Advice: Think critically: Once you realize that b follows a, you know that this composition of functions is really taking the reciprocal of $a(x)$.

Getting to the Answer: Remember how to translate function notation into something useful: $(b \circ a)(x)$ means $b(x)$ follows $a(x)$ (in other words, $b(a(x))$). You can rewrite this as $\dfrac{1}{a(x)}$, which you should recognize as the reciprocal of $a(x)$. This new function will be undefined anywhere that $a(x) = 0$. Looking at the graph, you can see that a(x) crosses the x-axis four times, making choice (C) correct.

PERFORM

10. B

Difficulty: Hard

Category: Passport to Advanced Math / Functions & Function Notation

Strategic Advice: Don't panic about this involving a trigonometric function; the standard transformation rules apply.

Getting to the Answer: The easiest transformation to identify is the −4 downward shift. Eliminate C and D, as neither contains this shift. Both A and (B) contain a vertical expansion, but the difference is subtle, so hone in on the transformed function's horizontal compression effected by the 2 in parentheses. Choice (B) has a compressed sine graph, so it is correct.

11. A

Difficulty: Hard

Category: Passport to Advanced Math / Functions & Function Notation

Strategic Advice: Determine how many prose pages Briana can type per minute, then assemble your function accordingly.

Getting to the Answer: Use the two given rates to determine Briana's typing rate in pages per minute. She types 45 words per minute, which becomes

$$\frac{45 \text{ words}}{1 \text{ min}} \times \frac{1 \text{ page}}{500 \text{ words}} = \frac{45 \text{ pages}}{500 \text{ min}} = \frac{9 \text{ pages}}{100 \text{ min}}.$$

Multiplying this rate by m gets you the number of pages typed after m minutes, which can then be subtracted from the starting page count (60) to get the number of pages Briana has left to type. The function should read $p(m) = 60 - \dfrac{9m}{100}$, which matches (A).

12. D

Difficulty: Medium

Category: Passport to Advanced Math / Functions & Function Notation

Strategic Advice: Use your knowledge of function increases and decreases.

Getting to the Answer: Examine the graph. A peak in fuel economy at 50 mph is obvious, but what else can be said? A closer look at the increase below 50 mph and the decrease below 50 mph reveals a critical detail: that the decreasing part of the graph is steeper than the increase. This means the rate of decrease is faster than the rate of increase. This corresponds to (D).

EXTRA PRACTICE

1. A
Difficulty: Easy

Category: Passport to Advanced Math / Functions & Function Notation

Strategic Advice: Understanding function notation will serve you well on Test Day. The notation $g(-2)$ means the value of the function when $x = -2$.

Getting to the Answer: Substitute -2 for x and simplify. Don't forget to use the correct order of operations as you work:

$$\begin{aligned} g(-2) &= -2(-2)^2 + 7(-2) - 3 \\ &= -2(4) + (-14) - 3 \\ &= -8 - 14 - 3 \\ &= -25 \end{aligned}$$

Choice (A) is correct.

2. A
Difficulty: Easy

Category: Passport to Advanced Math / Functions & Function Notation

Strategic Advice: The notation $k(x)$ is read k of x and means the range value (output) of the function that corresponds to a given domain value (input). So $k(4)$ means the output value of the function when 4 is substituted for the input (x), and $k(1)$ means the output value of the function when 1 is substituted for the input (x).

Getting to the Answer: Substitute 4 and 1 into the function, one at a time, and then subtract the results.

$$\begin{aligned} k(4) &= 5(4) + 2 = 20 + 2 = 22 \\ k(1) &= 5(1) + 2 = 5 + 2 = 7 \\ & \quad 22 - 7 = 15 \end{aligned}$$

Choice (A) is correct. Caution—this is not the same as subtracting $4 - 1$ and then substituting 3 into the function!

3. D
Difficulty: Medium

Category: Passport to Advanced Math / Functions & Function Notation

Strategic Advice: To determine the domain, look at the x-values. To determine the range, look at the y-values.

Getting to the Answer: For the domain, the graph is continuous (no holes or gaps in the graph) and has arrows on both sides, so the domain is all real numbers. This means you can eliminate A and B. For the range, the function's maximum (the vertex) is located at $(-3, 4)$, which means the highest possible y-value of $f(x)$ is 4. The graph is continuous and opens downward, so the range of the function is $y \leq 4$, which is the same as $f(x) \leq 4$, making (D) correct.

4. D
Difficulty: Medium

Category: Passport to Advanced Math / Functions & Function Notation

Strategic Advice: Draw a quick sketch of the equation (or graph it in your graphing calculator).

Getting to the Answer: Based on the equation, the graph is a parabola that opens upward with a vertex of $(2, -5)$. A parabola changes direction at the x-coordinate of its vertex. This is all the information you need to answer the question. You can immediately eliminate A and B. To choose between C and (D), take a closer look at the sketch. To the left of 2 (or $x < 2$), the parabola is decreasing, and to the right of 2 (or $x > 2$), it is increasing. This makes (D) correct.

5. B

Difficulty: Medium

Category: Passport to Advanced Math / Functions & Function Notation

Strategic Advice: When finding values associated with function notation, you almost always have to decide whether you're plugging something in for x or solving for x.

Getting to the Answer: In this question, you are given a range value (14), which means $f(x) = 14$, and you are asked for the corresponding domain value (x-value). This means you are solving for x, not substituting for x. Set the function equal to 14 and solve using inverse operations:

$$14 = \frac{x^2}{4} - 11$$
$$25 = \frac{x^2}{4}$$
$$100 = x^2$$
$$\pm 10 = x$$

Negative 10 is not one of the answer choices, so (B) is correct.

6. C

Difficulty: Medium

Category: Passport to Advanced Math / Functions & Function Notation

Strategic Advice: Use the properties of the absolute value function to quickly hone in on the right answer.

Getting to the Answer: The function graphed is the absolute value function, and you can see that all values in its range are positive. That makes the negative value in (C) impossible. Because you're looking for the statement that is NOT true, you can safely conclude that (C) is correct.

7. C

Difficulty: Medium

Category: Passport to Advanced Math / Functions & Function Notation

Strategic Advice: Piecewise functions look intimidating, but they are usually very simple functions—they're just written in pieces. Your job is to figure out which piece of the function you need to use to answer the question.

Getting to the Answer: The right-hand side of each piece of the function tells you what part of the domain (which x-values) goes with that particular expression. In this function, only values of x that are less than or equal to zero go with the top expression, values of x greater than zero and less than or equal to 3 go with the middle expression, and values of x that are greater than 3 go with the bottom expression. Because –3 is less than 0, plug it into the top expression and simplify:

$$f(-3) = (-3)^2 + 1$$
$$= 9 + 1$$
$$= 10$$

This matches (C).

8. D

Difficulty: Medium

Category: Passport to Advanced Math / Functions & Function Notation

Strategic Advice: Pay careful attention to the axis labels as you read the answer choices. Time is graphed on the x-axis, and distance is graphed on the y-axis.

Getting to the Answer: Compare each answer choice to the graph, eliminating false statements as you go.

Choice A: Carmel went to the library first, so the library (not the grocery store) is about 5 miles from his home. Eliminate this choice.

Choice B: Carmel traveled 7 miles away from his home (between $t = 0$ minutes and $t = 30$ minutes), but then also traveled 7 miles back (between $t = 45$ minutes and $t = 60$ minutes), so he traveled a total of 14 miles. Eliminate this choice.

Choice C: When Carmel reached the library, he was 5 miles from home; when he reached the grocery store, he was 7 miles from home. This means the grocery store must be $7 - 5 = 2$ miles farther away. Eliminate this choice.

Choice (D) must be correct. Carmel is the same distance from home (5 miles) between $t = 15$ minutes and $t = 25$ minutes, so he spent 10 minutes at the library. He is stopped once again (at the grocery store) between $t = 30$ minutes and $t = 45$ minutes, so he spent 15 minutes at the grocery store.

9. C
Difficulty: Medium

Category: Passport to Advanced Math / Functions & Function Notation

Strategic Advice: Graphically, the notation $f(-2)$ means the y-value when x is -2. Pay careful attention to which graph is which. It may help to draw dots on the graph.

Getting to the Answer: Find $x = -2$ along the horizontal axis, trace up to the graph of $f(x)$, and draw a dot on the graph. Do the same for $g(2)$, as shown below:

Now, read the y-coordinates from the graph and subtract: $f(-2)$ is 6 and $g(2)$ is -3, so $f(-2) + g(2) = 6 + (-3) = 3$, which is (C).

10. C
Difficulty: Medium

Category: Passport to Advanced Math / Functions & Function Notation

Strategic Advice: Transformations that are grouped with the x in a function shift the graph horizontally and therefore affect the x-coordinates of points on the graph. Transformations that are not grouped with the x shift the graph vertically and therefore affect the y-coordinates of points on the graph. Remember, horizontal shifts are always the reverse of what they look like. When working with multiple transformations, follow the same order of operations as always—parentheses first, then multiply and divide, then add and subtract.

Getting to the Answer: Start with the parentheses: $(x - 2)$. This shifts the graph right 2 units, so add 2 to the x-coordinate of the given point: $(5, 3) \rightarrow (5 + 2, 3) = (7, 3)$. Next, apply the negative in front of g because it represents multiplication. The negative is not grouped with the x, so multiply the y-coordinate by -1 to get $(7, 3(-1)) \rightarrow (7, -3)$. Finally, the $+8$ is not grouped with x, so add 8 to the y-coordinate: $(7, -3) \rightarrow (7, -3 + 8) = (7, 5)$, which matches (C).

You could also plot the point on a coordinate plane, perform the transformations (right 2, reflect vertically over the x-axis, and then up 8), to find the new point. The result will be the same.

11. B
Difficulty: Hard

Category: Passport to Advanced Math / Functions & Function Notation

Strategic Advice: The key to answering this question is to have a conceptual understanding of function notation. Here, the input $(x + 2)$ has already been substituted and simplified in the given function. Your job is to determine what the function would have looked like had x been the input instead.

Getting to the Answer: To keep things organized, let $u = x + 2$, the old input. This means $x = u - 2$. Substitute this into p and simplify:

$$p(u - 2) = 3(u - 2)^2 + 4(u - 2) + 1$$
$$= 3(u^2 - 4u + 4) + 4u - 8 + 1$$
$$= 3u^2 - 12u + 12 + 4u - 8 + 1$$
$$= 3u^2 - 8u + 5$$

Because we defined x as $u - 2$, this means $p(u) = 3u^2 - 8u + 5$.

When working with function notation, you evaluate the function by substituting a given input value for the variable in the parentheses. Here, if the input value is x, then $p(x) = 3x^2 - 8x + 5$, which means (B) is correct.

12. 3.5 or **3.50**
Difficulty: Medium

Category: Passport to Advanced Math / Functions & Function Notation

Strategic Advice: This is a fairly straightforward question, but be careful to check that you answered the right question (how much more profits *per unit* at a selling price of $25 than at $20).

Getting to the Answer: Start by evaluating the function at $x = 25$ and at $x = 20$. Make sure you follow the correct order of operations as you simplify.

$$P(25) = 150(25) - (25)^2$$
$$= 3,750 - 625$$
$$= 3,125$$
$$P(20) = 150(20) - (20)^2$$
$$= 3,000 - 400$$
$$= 2,600$$

The question asks how much more profit *per unit* the company makes, so find the difference in the amounts of profit and divide by the number of units (150) to get $\dfrac{3,125 - 2,600}{150} = \dfrac{525}{150} = \$3.50$, or 3.5.

13. 305
Difficulty: Medium

Category: Passport to Advanced Math / Functions & Function Notation

Strategic Advice: Always pay careful attention to what the variable in a function represents, especially in questions that deal with real-world scenarios. In this question, t does *not* represent the time, so don't find $C(5)$. Rather, you need to start by finding the number of hours that pass between 7 AM and 5 PM.

Getting to the Answer: Because there are 10 hours between 7 AM and 5 PM, evaluate the function at $t = 10$. Make sure you follow the correct order of operations as you simplify.

$$C(t) = -0.0815t^4 + t^3 + 12t$$
$$C(10) = -0.0815(10)^4 + (10)^3 + 12(10)$$
$$= -0.0815(10,000) + 1,000 + 120$$
$$= -815 + 1,000 + 120$$
$$= 305$$

14. C
Difficulty: Easy

Category: Passport to Advanced Math / Functions

Strategic Advice: A function, by definition, only has one output for every input. When you're given graphs to consider, use the vertical line test to see if the graph represents a function.

Getting to the Answer: If a vertical line intersects a graph more than one time, then the graph has more than one output for a given input and is therefore *not* a function. The graph in (C) fails the test, so it is not a function.

15. D

Difficulty: Easy

Category: Passport to Advanced Math / Functions

Strategic Advice: The domain of a function represents the possible values of *x*, or the input values. In this function, *x* is represented by *p*, which is the number of seeds germinated by the plants over a given period of time.

Getting to the Answer: This is a real-world scenario so you cannot simply use rules of functions to determine the domain. Because there cannot be a negative number of seeds germinated, or a fraction of a seed germinated, the list in (D) is the only one that could represent a portion of the function's domain.

16. A

Difficulty: Medium

Category: Passport to Advanced Math / Functions

Strategic Advice: The notation (*g*(*h*(*x*)) indicates a composition of two functions which can be read "*g* of *h* of *x*." It means that the output when *x* is substituted in *h*(*x*) becomes the input for *g*(*x*).

Getting to the Answer: First, use the table on the right to find that *h*(3) is 0. This is your new input. Now, use the table on the left to find *g*(0), which is –1, making (A) the correct answer.

17. D

Difficulty: Hard

Category: Passport to Advanced Math / Functions

Strategic Advice: Sometimes, a question requires thought rather than brute force. Here, you need to grasp that when dealing with compositions, the range of the inner function becomes the domain of the outer function, which in turn produces the range of the composition.

Getting to the Answer: In the composition $f(g(x))$, the function $g(x) = \dfrac{x^2}{2}$ is the inner function. Every value of *x*, when substituted into this function, will result in a nonnegative value (because the result of squaring a number is always a positive number). This means the smallest possible range value of *g*(*x*) is 0. Now look at *f*(*x*). Substituting large positive values of *x* in the function will result in large negative numbers. Consequently, substituting the smallest value from the range of *g*, which is 0, results in the largest range value for the composition, which is 3 – 0 = 3. Because 4 > 3, it is not in the range of $f(g(x))$. Therefore, (D) is correct.

18. D

Difficulty: Hard

Category: Passport to Advanced Math / Functions

Strategic Advice: Graphing piecewise functions can be tricky. Try describing the graph in words first, and then find the matching function. Use words like "to the left of" (which translates as *less than*) and "to the right of" (which translates as *greater than*).

Getting to the Answer: First notice that there is a hole in the graph at *x* = 4. This means you can eliminate A right away because the inequality symbol in the top piece would include the endpoint at 4. To choose between the remaining answers, think about parent functions and transformations. To the left of *x* = 4, the graph is an absolute value function that has been reflected vertically across the *x*-axis and then shifted up one unit. This means either C or (D) must be correct. Now look to the right of *x* = 4—the graph is a horizontal line, which means a line that has a slope of 0. The slope of the line in C is negative 3, so it can't be correct. This means (D) is correct. (The equation of a horizontal line always looks like *y* = *b*, or in this case, *g*(*x*) = –3.)

CHAPTER 11

PREPARE

1. B
Difficulty: Easy

Category: Passport to Advanced Math / Quadratics

Strategic Advice: Whenever you see binomials, think FOIL. Here, no rearranging is necessary, so you can go right into it!

Getting to the Answer: FOIL the binomials $(6 - 5x)$ $(15x - 11)$: First, Outer, Inner, Last. First: $(6)(15x) = 90x$. Outer: $(6)(-11) = -66$. Inner: $(-5x)(15x) = -75x^2$. Last: $(-5x)(-11) = 55x$. Add all the terms together and combine like terms: $90x - 66 - 75x^2 + 55x = -75x^2 + 145x - 66$. The correct answer is (B)

2. C
Difficulty: Easy

Category: Passport to Advanced Math / Quadratics

Strategic Advice: Unless you are asked to match a graph, you should try to factor quadratics. Whenever you have a fraction containing quadratics, something will usually cancel out.

Getting to the Answer: To factor the numerator and denominator into binomials, you should first factor out a 3 in the denominator to make that quadratic a bit simpler. Then use the quadratic shortcuts on the numerator and denominator to reveal an $x - 5$ term that will cancel out:

$$\frac{x^2 - 10x + 25}{3x^2 - 75} = \frac{(x-5)(x-5)}{3(x^2 - 25)}$$

$$= \frac{(x-5)(x-5)}{3(x-5)(x+5)} = \frac{(x-5)}{3(x+5)}$$

The correct answer is (C).

3. D
Difficulty: Medium

Category: Passport to Advanced Math / Quadratics

Strategic Advice: When something doesn't factor cleanly, consider completing the square or using the quadratic formula.

Getting to the Answer: Factoring won't work here. However, the coefficient of x^2 is 1, so try completing the square:

$$x^2 + 2x - 5 = 0$$
$$x^2 + 2x = 5$$
$$\left(\frac{b}{2}\right)^2 = \left(\frac{2}{2}\right)^2 = 1^2 = 1$$
$$x^2 + 2x + 1 = 5 + 1$$
$$(x+1)^2 = 6$$
$$x + 1 = \pm\sqrt{6}$$
$$x = -1 \pm \sqrt{6}$$

Choice (D) matches one of the two possible values of x, so it's the correct answer.

4. C
Difficulty: Medium

Category: Passport to Advanced Math / Quadratics

Strategic Advice: The x-coordinates of a function are the values of x that make the function equal 0.

Getting to the Answer: Set the equation equal to zero. Direct factoring is impossible because the coefficient of x^2 isn't 1, but you can use the grouping technique. Identify two numbers whose product is ac and whose sum is b

$$3x^2 - 2x - 8 = 0$$
$$3x^2 - 6x + 4x - 8 = 0$$
$$3x(x - 2) + 4(x - 2) = 0$$
$$(3x + 4)(x - 2) = 0$$
$$(3x + 4) = 0 \text{ or } (x - 2) = 0$$
$$x = -\frac{4}{3} \text{ or } x = 2$$

The answer is (C).

5. B

Difficulty: Medium

Category: Passport to Advanced Math / Quadratics

Strategic Advice: Use your knowledge of parabolas to evaluate each choice systematically.

Getting to the Answer: Keep in mind that the question asks for the statement that's false, so eliminate the true choices as you go. The parabola opens downward, so the *a* term should be negative. Eliminate A. The parabola's vertex is in quadrant I, so *h* and *k* are both positive. That makes choice D true as well; eliminate it. The axis of symmetry is *x* = *h*, so *x* = 3. Choice B, however, claims that the axis of symmetry is *y* = 3—a common mistake. The line *y* = 3 is horizontal, and a horizontal line cannot be the axis of symmetry for *any* parabolic function. (B) is false and is therefore the correct answer.

C is a true statement because the line $g(x) = \dfrac{2x}{3}$ passes through the point (3, 2), which is indeed the vertex of *f*(*x*).

6. C

Difficulty: Hard

Category: Passport to Advanced Math / Quadratics

Strategic Advice: When factoring, grouping, and completing the square are all unavailable, it's time to whip out the quadratic formula!

Getting to the Answer: Plug values carefully into the quadratic formula to solve for *x*.

$$2x^2 - 5x - 2 = 0$$

$$x = \frac{-b \pm \sqrt{b^2 - 4ac}}{2a}$$

$$x = \frac{-(-5) \pm \sqrt{(-5)^2 - 4(2)(-2)}}{2(2)}$$

$$x = \frac{5 \pm \sqrt{25 - (-16)}}{4}$$

$$x = \frac{5 \pm \sqrt{41}}{4}$$

$$x = \frac{5}{4} + \frac{\sqrt{41}}{4} \text{ or } x = \frac{5}{4} - \frac{\sqrt{41}}{4}$$

The answer is (C).

7. A

Difficulty: Hard

Category: Passport to Advanced Math / Quadratics

Strategic Advice: Most students see only the quadratic and start solving. Think about how the *x*-values can help you find the answer.

Getting to the Answer: First, rearrange to get the quadratic equal to zero.

$$\frac{1}{4}(4x^2 - 8x - k) = 30$$

$$x^2 - 2x - \frac{k}{4} = 30$$

$$x^2 - 2x - \frac{k}{4} - 30 = 0$$

Next, create binomials and FOIL.

$$(x - 7)(x + 5) = 0$$

$$x^2 - 2x - 35 = 0$$

Finally, set the two equations equal to each other and solve for *k*:

$$x^2 - 2x - \frac{k}{4} - 30 = x^2 - 2x - 35$$

$$-\frac{k}{4} = -5$$

$$-k = -20$$

$$k = 20$$

$$2k = 40$$

Here's the catch: you are not asked for *k*; you are asked for 2*k*, which is 40. The answer is (A).

PRACTICE

8. D

Difficulty: Hard

Category: Passport to Advanced Math / Quadratics

Strategic Advice: Work through this systematically. Find the maximum height of the potato, then find the time it takes the potato to hit the ground.

Getting to the Answer: The x-coordinate of the vertex is given by $h = \dfrac{-b}{2a} = \dfrac{-224}{2(-16)} = 7$. Plug this into the function to get the y-coordinate: $k = y(7) = -16(7)^2 + 224(7) + 240 = 1,024$. Next, calculate how long it takes for the potato to hit the ground. This will occur when $y(t) = 0$. Plug in and factor to solve:

$$-16t^2 + 224t + 240 = 0$$
$$t^2 - 14(t) - 15 = 0$$
$$(t - 15)(t + 1) = 0$$
$$t = 15 \text{ or } t = -1$$

Since time can't be negative, $t = 15$. Don't forget that you were asked for the sum of the height and the time, not for either of the raw values. The sum of 15 and 1,024 is 1,039, choice (D).

9. B

Difficulty: Medium

Category: Passport to Advanced Math / Quadratics

Strategic Advice: Use number properties to avoid doing any actual math.

Getting to the Answer: If $ab > 0$, then a and b are either both positive or both negative. In the inequality $b^2ac < 0$, you can ignore the b^2 term because it will be positive regardless of the sign of b. This implies that either a or c is positive, and the other is negative. The x-intercepts are b and c. Since b has the same sign as a, while c has the opposite sign as a, it follows that b and c have opposite signs.

The correct answer must therefore be a function with one negative root and one positive root. Scan the functions to find the correct one. Ignore the complicated-looking numbers—all that matter are the signs! (B) is correct.

PERFORM

10. A

Difficulty: Hard

Category: Passport to Advanced Math / Quadratics

Strategic Advice: When a quadratic looks impossible, see if you can use one of the quadratic shortcuts. The presence of 4, 9, and 16—all perfect squares—is a big clue!

Getting to the Answer: Observe that $4x - 12\sqrt{x} + 9$ is an instance of the quadratic shortcut $(a - b)^2 = a^2 - 2ab + b^2$. Use the shortcut to factor the equation, then finish the problem with substitution.

$$4x - 12\sqrt{x} + 9 = 16$$
$$(2\sqrt{x} - 3)^2 = 16$$
$$2\sqrt{x} - 3 = 4$$

Now go after $10\sqrt{x} - 15 : 10\sqrt{x} - 15 = 5(2\sqrt{x} - 3) = 5(4) = 20$.

The correct answer is (A).

11. B

Difficulty: Medium

Category: Passport to Advanced Math / Quadratics

Strategic Advice: To find where two functions intersect, set them equal to each other, then solve.

Getting to the Answer: Neither of the functions is presented in standard form, so make this question a little easier by simplifying each one before setting them equal to each other.

$f(x) = 3(x - 4)^2 + 4 = 3(x^2 - 8x + 16) + 4 = 3x^2$
$- 24x + 48 + 4 = 3x^2 - 24x + 52$

$g(x) = (x + 5)^2 + 2x - 135 = x^2 + 10x + 25 + 2x$
$- 135 = x^2 + 12x - 110$

$$f(x) = g(x)$$
$$3x^2 - 24x + 52 = x^2 + 12x - 110$$
$$2x^2 - 36x + 162 = 0$$
$$x^2 - 18x + 81 = 0$$

Notice that this is a quadratic shortcut:

$$x^2 - 18x + 81 = (x - 9)^2 = 0$$
$$x = 9$$

Note that the question asks how many intersection points there are, *not* what the points are. Since there is only one solution for x, there must be only one point of intersection, which is (B). Don't waste time plugging 9 back in!

12. 2
Difficulty: Easy

Category: Passport to Advanced Math / Quadratics

Strategic Advice: An x-intercept of a function is a point at which the y-coordinate equals 0.

Getting to the Answer: Set the equation equal to zero, simplify, and factor.

$$g(x) = -2.5x^2 + 10x - 7.5$$
$$0 = -2.5x^2 + 10x - 7.5$$
$$0 = x^2 - 4x + 3$$
$$0 = (x - 1)(x - 3)$$
$$x = 1 \text{ or } 3$$

Recall that the question asks for the *difference* between the x-intercepts, not for the x-intercepts themselves. The difference between 3 and 1 is 2.

13. C
Difficulty: Medium

Category: Passport to Advanced Math / Quadratics

Strategic Advice: Fraction-laden equations are often simpler than they look; they still follow the same rules that any other equation does.

Getting to the Answer: An axis of symmetry splits the parabola in half and travels through the vertex. You have a formula to find *h* instantly. All you have to do is plug and chug to get your answer—just be careful with the fractions and negatives.

$$x = -\frac{b}{2a}$$
$$x = -17 \div 2\left(\frac{-11}{3}\right)$$
$$x = -17 \div \frac{-22}{3}$$
$$x = -17 \times \frac{-3}{22}$$
$$x = \frac{51}{22}$$

The correct answer is (C).

EXTRA PRACTICE

1. B
Difficulty: Easy

Category: Passport to Advanced Math / Quadratics

Strategic Advice: To multiply two binomials, distribute each term in the first set of parentheses to each term in the second set. You can also think FOIL.

Getting to the Answer: Multiply $2a$ by each term in the second factor and then multiply $5b$ by each term. Combine like terms if possible.

$$
\begin{aligned}
(2a+5b)(a-3b) &= 2a(a-3b)+5b(a-3b)\\
&= 2a(a)+2a(-3b)+5b(a)+5b(-3b)\\
&= 2a^2-6ab+5ab-15b^2\\
&= 2a^2-ab-15b^2
\end{aligned}
$$

Choice (B) is correct.

2. A
Difficulty: Easy

Category: Passport to Advanced Math / Quadratics

Strategic Advice: *Roots* are the same as *solutions* to an equation, so you need to solve the equation for x. Taking the square root of a quantity is the inverse operation of squaring it, and both sides of this equation are already perfect squares, so take their square roots. Then solve the resulting equations. Remember, there will be two equations to solve.

Getting to the Answer:

$$
\begin{aligned}
(x+3)^2 &= 49\\
\sqrt[2]{(x+3)^2} &= \pm\sqrt{49}\\
x+3 &= \pm 7
\end{aligned}
$$

Now simplify each equation: $x + 3 = -7$, or $x = -10$; and $x + 3 = 7$, or $x = 4$, so (A) is correct.

If you didn't recognize that you could use square rooting to solve the equation, you could also expand the left side, then subtract 49, factor the resulting equation, and set the factors equal to 0. This is a perfectly fine way to solve the equation, but it takes considerably longer.

3. B
Difficulty: Easy

Category: Passport to Advanced Math / Quadratics

Strategic Advice: Use the factored form to find the x-intercepts and the standard form to find the y-intercept.

Getting to the Answer: Using the first equation, set each of the factors equal to 0 and solve for x to find that the x-intercepts are $-\frac{1}{2}$ and 5. This means you can eliminate A and D. From the standard form of the equation, you can see that the y-intercept is -5 because $0^2 - 3(0) - 5 = -5$, so (B) is correct.

4. C
Difficulty: Easy

Category: Passport to Advanced Math / Quadratics

Strategic Advice: Being able to make connections between equations and graphs is a valuable skill. The pieces of a quadratic equation written in standard form give you lots of information about its graph. For example, finding the value of $\frac{-b}{2a}$ (the quadratic formula without the radical part) tells you where the axis of symmetry occurs.

Getting to the Answer: This question is asking about c, which is the only constant term in the equation. If you substitute 0 for x, the equation becomes $y = a(0)^2 + b(0) + c$, or just $y = c$. This means the point $(0, c)$ will be on the graph, which is the y-intercept, making (C) correct.

5. A

Difficulty: Medium

Category: Passport to Advanced Math / Quadratics

Strategic Advice: When a question doesn't provide a lot of information to go on, it most likely involves something conceptual. In this question, you are being tested on whether you can relate a maximum value given in a real-world scenario to the vertex of a parabola and use that vertex to choose the corresponding quadratic equation.

Getting to the Answer: The answer choices all look very similar, so think logically to eliminate a couple. A rocket goes *up*, hits a maximum height, and then comes *down*. This tells you that the graph will be an upside-down parabola, which means the equation should have a negative sign in front. Eliminate C and D. To choose between A and B, you need to recall what the *vertex form* of a quadratic looks like and what it tells you. When a quadratic equation is written in the form $y = a(x - h)^2 + k$, the vertex of the graph is (h, k). The h tells you *where* the maximum (or minimum) occurs, and the k tells you *what* the maximum (or minimum) value is. Here, the maximum height of 34 feet occurs at 3 seconds, so k is 34 and h is 3. Substitute these values into vertex form to find that the correct equation is $y = -16(x - 3)^2 + 34$. Translate this to function language ($h(t) = y$ and $t = x$) to arrive at the answer: $h(t) = -16(t - 3)^2 + 34$, which is (A).

6. A

Difficulty: Medium

Category: Passport to Advanced Math / Quadratics

Strategic Advice: Use what you know about the different forms of a quadratic equation to choose the correct graph.

Getting to the Answer: The equation is given in standard form, so right away you know the y-intercept is the constant term (c), which is -8. This means you can eliminate B and C. The squared term in the equation has a positive coefficient (1), so the

parabola must open upward. This means D can't be correct. The only remaining choice is (A), which is correct. You could also write the equation in factored form, $y = (x + 4)(x - 2)$, to see that the x-intercepts are -4 and 2, which also match the graph in (A).

7. A

Difficulty: Medium

Category: Passport to Advanced Math / Quadratics

Strategic Advice: When finding solutions to a quadratic equation, always start by rewriting the equation to make it equal 0 (unless both sides of the equation are already perfect squares). Then, take a peek at the answer choices—if they are all nice numbers, then factoring is probably the quickest method for solving the equation. If the answers include messy fractions or square roots, then using the quadratic formula may be a better choice.

Getting to the Answer: To make the equation equal 0, subtract 30 from both sides to get $x^2 - 7x - 30 = 0$. The answer choices are all integers, so factor the equation. Look for two numbers whose product is -30 and whose sum is -7. The two numbers are -10 and 3, so the factors are $(x - 10)$ and $(x + 3)$. Set each factor equal to 0 and solve to find that $x = 10$ and $x = -3$. The question states that $x > 0$, so x must equal 10. Before selecting an answer, don't forget to check that you answered the right question—the question asks for the value of $x - 5$, not just x, so the correct answer is $10 - 5 = 5$, which means (A) is correct.

If this question appeared in the calculator section of the test, you could also graph the equation in your graphing calculator and use the "zero" function to find the solutions.

8. C

Difficulty: Medium

Category: Passport to Advanced Math / Quadratics

Strategic Advice: Examine the graph—there are no gridlines and no numbers along the axes.

This means that arriving at the correct answer will require some thought.

Getting to the Answer: According to the graph, one x-intercept is to the left of the y-axis, and the other is to the right. This tells you that one value of x is positive, while the other is negative, so you can immediately eliminate D (both factors have the same sign). To choose between the remaining equations, find the x-intercepts by setting each factor equal to 0 and solving for x. In A, the x-intercepts are $\frac{1}{2}$ and -1, but that would mean that e is *twice* as far from the origin as f, not *half* as far, so eliminate A. In B, the x-intercepts are 1 and -2. Again, that would mean that e is twice as far from the origin as f, not half as far, so eliminate B. This means (C) must be correct. The x-intercepts are 1 and $-\frac{1}{2}$, which fits the criterion that e is half as far from the origin as f.

9. B
Difficulty: Medium

Category: Passport to Advanced Math / Quadratics

Strategic Advice: There are no coefficients (numbers) in the equation, so you'll need to think about how the values of a, b, and c affect the graph.

Getting to the Answer: Compare each statement to the graph to determine whether it is true, eliminating choices as you go. Remember, you are looking for the statement that is *not* true. The parabola opens upward, so the value of a must be positive, which means you can eliminate A because it *is* true (> 0 means positive). The value of b is the tricky one, so skip it for now, and consider C. When written in standard form, the value of c tells you the y-intercept. According to the graph, the y-intercept is below the x-axis and is therefore negative, so $c < 0$ is true. Eliminate C. Unfortunately, this means you'll need to consider B. Based on the equation alone, it is not easy to determine whether b is positive or negative, so you'll need to think outside the box. The trick for finding the x-coordinate of the vertex of a parabola

is to calculate $\frac{-b}{2a}$ (the quadratic formula without the radical part). In the graph, the x-coordinate of the vertex is 3, so set the formula equal to 3, solve for b, and see what happens.

$$\frac{-b}{2a} = \frac{3}{1}$$
$$-b = 6a$$
$$b = -6a$$

You have already determined that a is positive (because the parabola opens upward), so b must be negative. This means b is less than 0, not greater, making (B) correct.

10. C
Difficulty: Medium

Category: Passport to Advanced Math / Quadratics

Strategic Advice: Equations that are equivalent have the same solutions, so you are looking for the equation that is simply written in a different form. You could expand each of the equations in the answer choices, but unless you get lucky, this will use up quite a bit of time.

Getting to the Answer: The answer choices are written in vertex form, so use the method of completing the square to convert the equation in the question to the same form. First, write the equation in standard form: $y = x^2 + 6x - 40$. Move the 40 to the other side to temporarily get it out of the way. Then, complete the square on the right-hand side, by finding $\left(\frac{b}{2}\right)^2 = \left(\frac{6}{2}\right)^2 = 3^2 = 9$, and adding the result to both sides of the equation.

$$y = x^2 + 6x - 40$$
$$y + 40 = x^2 + 6x$$
$$y + 40 + 9 = x^2 + 6x + 9$$
$$y + 49 = x^2 + 6x + 9$$

Next, factor the right-hand side of the equation (which should be a perfect square trinomial) and rewrite it as a square.

$$y + 49 = (x + 3)(x + 3)$$
$$y + 49 = (x + 3)^2$$

Finally, solve for y to get $y = (x + 3)^2 - 49$, which makes (C) correct.

11. B
Difficulty: Medium

Category: Passport to Advanced Math / Quadratics

Strategic Advice: When a quadratic equation is written in the form $y = a(x - h)^2 + k$, the minimum value (or the maximum value if $a < 0$) is given by k, and the axis of symmetry is given by the equation $x = h$.

Getting to the Answer: The question states that the minimum of the parabola is 5, so look for an equation where k is 5. You can eliminate C and D because k is 3 in C and –3 in D. The question also states that the axis of symmetry is $x = -3$, so h must be –3. Be careful—this is tricky. The equation in A is not correct because the vertex form of a parabola has a negative before the h, so $(x - 3)$ would produce an axis of symmetry at $x = 3$, not –3. This means (B) is correct.

You could also graph each equation in your graphing calculator to see which one matches the criteria given in the question, but this is likely to use up valuable time on Test Day.

12. A
Difficulty: Medium

Category: Passport to Advanced Math / Quadratics

Strategic Advice: Even though one of the equations in this system isn't linear, you can still solve the system using substitution.

Getting to the Answer: You already know that y is equal to $2x$, so substitute $2x$ for y in the second equation. Don't forget that when you square $2x$, you must square both the coefficient and the variable. Also, be careful—there are a lot of 2s floating around, so pay careful attention as you plug in values.

$$2x^2 + 2y^2 = 240$$
$$x^2 + y^2 = 120$$
$$x^2 + (2x)^2 = 120$$
$$x^2 + 4x^2 = 120$$
$$5x^2 = 120$$
$$x^2 = 24$$

The question asks for the value of x^2, not x, so there is no need to take the square root of 24 to find the value of x. Choice (A) is correct.

13. B
Difficulty: Hard

Category: Passport to Advanced Math / Quadratics

Strategic Advice: Pay careful attention to what the question is asking. You are looking for a quadratic equation that produces a maximum value that is greater than the one shown in the graph. Take a peek at the answer choices—C and D are given in vertex form, so consider those first. If neither is correct, then you'll need to think about the question in a different way.

Getting to the Answer: The maximum value shown in the graph is about 56 or 57 feet. When a quadratic equation is written in vertex form, $y = a(x - h)^2 + k$, the maximum value is given by k, so check C and D first because they will be the easiest to compare to the graph. In C, k is 48, which is not greater than 56 or 57 and therefore not correct. In D, k is 52, which is also not greater than 56 or 57. This means either A or (B) must be correct. You now have two options—you could expand the equation in each answer choice and then complete the square to find the vertex, or you could expand the equations, find the x-coordinate of the vertex using the formula $x = \frac{-b}{2a}$, and then plug in the result to find the *y*-value. Completing the square usually takes a bit of time, so the second option is probably the quicker route to take. Expanding A, you get $h = -16t^2 + 48t$ with $a = -16$ and $b = 48$. The *x*-coordinate of the vertex is $\dfrac{-48}{2(-16)} = \dfrac{-48}{-32} = 1.5$. Substituting this back into the equation, the *y*-value of the vertex (which is the maximum value of the function) is $-16(1.5)^2 + 48(1.5) = 36$, which is not greater than 56 or 57, so (B) must be correct. Don't waste valuable time checking, but if you use the same strategy, you'll find that the maximum height of the equation in (B) is 81 feet.

14. 0

Difficulty: Medium

Category: Passport to Advanced Math / Quadratics

Strategic Advice: To find the roots of an equation, you need to set it equal to 0, factor it, and then solve. Whenever the leading coefficient is a fraction, factoring becomes very messy. Luckily, you can clear the fraction the same way you do when solving equations (multiply both sides of the equation by the denominator of the fraction).

Getting to the Answer:

$$0 = \frac{1}{3}x^2 - 2x + 3$$

$$3(0) = 3\left(\frac{1}{3}x^2 - 2x + 3\right)$$

$$0 = x^2 - 6x + 9$$

$$0 = (x - 3)(x - 3)$$

The equation only has one unique solution ($x = 3$), so the positive difference between the roots is actually 0.

15. 5

Difficulty: Hard

Category: Passport to Advanced Math / Quadratics

Strategic Advice: Before you plug -5 in for *x*, which creates messy numbers, factor the given equation.

Getting to the Answer:

$$x^2 + 2xk + k^2 = 0$$

$$(x + k)(x + k) = 0$$

$$(x + k)^2 = 0$$

Now plug in -5 for *x* and solve for *k*:

$$(-5 + k)^2 = 0$$

$$\sqrt[2]{(-5 + k)^2} = \pm\sqrt{0}$$

$$-5 + k = 0$$

$$k = 5$$

16. 6.5 or 13/2

Difficulty: Hard

Category: Passport to Advanced Math / Quadratics

Strategic Advice: This is a tough question with no real shortcuts. The highest power of *x* in the equation is 2, so the equation is quadratic. Writing quadratic equations can be tricky and time-consuming. If you know the roots, you can use factors to write the equation. If you don't know the roots, you need to create a system of equations to find the coefficients of the variable terms.

Getting to the Answer: You don't know the roots of this equation, so start with the point that has the nicest values (0, 2) and substitute them into the equation, $y = ax^2 + bx + c$.

$$2 = a(0)^2 + b(0) + c$$

$$2 = c$$

Now your equation looks like $y = ax^2 + bx + 2$. Next, use the other two points to create a system of two equations in two variables.

$(-2, -10) \rightarrow -10 = a(-2)^2 + b(-2) + 2 \rightarrow -12 = 4a - 2b$

$(4, 14) \rightarrow 14 = a(4)^2 + b(4) + 2 \rightarrow 12 = 16a + 4b$

You now have a system of equations to solve. None of the variables has a coefficient of 1, so use elimination to solve the system. If you multiply the top equation by 2, the *b*-terms will eliminate each other.

$$2[4a - 2b = -12] \rightarrow 8a - 4b = -24$$
$$16a + 4b = 12 \rightarrow \underline{16a + 4b = 12}$$
$$24a = -12$$
$$a = -\frac{1}{2}$$

Now, find *b* by substituting the value of *a* into either of the original equations. Using the bottom equation, you get this:

$$16\left(-\frac{1}{2}\right) + 4b = 12$$
$$-8 + 4b = 12$$
$$4b = 20$$
$$b = 5$$

The value of $a + b + c$ is $-\frac{1}{2} + 5 + 2 = 6\frac{1}{2}$. You can't enter a mixed number, so grid in your answer as the decimal number 6.5 or the improper fraction 13/2.

17. B

Difficulty: Easy

Category: Passport to Advanced Math / Quadratics

Strategic Advice: Whenever a quadratic (or any polynomial) equation is given in factored form, to find the solutions set each of the factors equal to 0 and solve for the variable using inverse operations.

Getting to the Answer:

$$2x - 3 = 0 \qquad x + 5 = 0$$
$$2x = 3 \qquad\qquad x = -5$$
$$x = \frac{3}{2}$$

The solutions are $x = -5$ and $x = \frac{3}{2}$, making (B) correct.

18. D

Difficulty: Easy

Category: Passport to Advanced Math / Quadratics

Strategic Advice: Take a peek at the answer choices. Some are written in standard form and some in factored form. Factored form tells you the *x*-intercepts, so examine C and (D) first to see if they match the graph.

Getting to the Answer: The graph is a parabola, so you can eliminate A right way (the equation is linear, not quadratic). The *x*-intercepts of the graph are –2 and 5, so the factors of this quadratic must be $(x + 2)$ and $(x - 5)$. The parabola opens downward, so there should be a negative sign in front of the factors. The correct equation is $y = -(x + 2)(x - 5)$. Don't let C fool you—those factors would produce *x*-intercepts of +2 and –5. If you're not convinced, set each factor equal to 0 and solve for *x*. Therefore, (D) is correct.

19. B

Difficulty: Medium

Category: Passport to Advanced Math / Quadratics

Strategic Advice: Quadratic equations can be written in several different forms, each of which reveals something special about the graph. For example, the vertex form of a quadratic equation $(y = a(x - h)^2 + k)$ gives the minimum or maximum value of the function (it's *k*), while the standard form $(y = ax^2 + bx + c)$ reveals the *y*-intercept (it's *c*).

Getting to the Answer: The factored form of a quadratic equation reveals the solutions to the equation, which graphically represent the *x*-intercepts. Choice (B) is the only equation written in factored form and therefore must be correct. You can set each factor equal to 0 and quickly solve to find that the *x*-intercepts of the graph are $x = -\frac{3}{4}$ and $x = 1$, which agree with the graph.

20. C

Difficulty: Medium

Category: Passport to Advanced Math / Quadratics

Strategic Advice: Understanding that in algebra "divides evenly" means "is a factor" is the key to answering this question. You could use polynomial long division, but in most cases, factoring is quicker.

Getting to the Answer: The leading coefficient of the equation is not 1, so you'll need to use the *AC method* and grouping to factor the equation. Multiply *a* times *c* (6×-20) and then look for two factors of that product whose sum is equal to the coefficient of the middle term. Break the middle term ($7x$) into two terms using the numbers you found, and then factor by grouping. The product is -120 and the two factors of -120 that add up to 7 are 15 and -8.

$$6x^2 + 7x - 20 = 6x^2 + 15x - 8x - 20$$
$$= (6x^2 + 15x) - (8x + 20)$$
$$= 3x(2x + 5) - 4(2x + 5)$$
$$= (2x + 5)(3x - 4)$$

So, $3x - 4$ divides evenly into the expression, making (C) correct.

21. D

Difficulty: Medium

Category: Passport to Advanced Math / Quadratics

Strategic Advice: Take a peek at the answer choices—they are really just describing the sign of the *x*-coordinates of the solutions. This means you don't need to find the exact values of the solutions. Instead, draw a quick sketch of the system (or graph it in your calculator), and translate < 0 as *negative* and > 0 as *positive*.

Getting to the Answer: The top equation is a line and the bottom equation is a parabola. Write the linear equation in slope-intercept form and the quadratic equation in factored form to make them easy

to sketch: $x + y = 4 \rightarrow y = -x + 4$ and $y = x^2 - 2x - 15 \rightarrow (x - 5)(x + 3)$. A quick sketch is all you need—don't waste valuable time labeling things. The line has a *y*-intercept of 4 and a negative slope, and the parabola opens upward and crosses the *x*-axis at 5 and -3. The sketch looks like:

The solutions to the system are the points where the graphs intersect. The question tells you that $a < c$, so (a, b) must be the point on the left and (c, d) is the point on the right. Look at the *x*-values: *a* is to the left of the *y*-axis so it must be negative (or $a < 0$), and *c* is to the right of the *y*-axis so it must be positive (or $c > 0$). This means (D) is correct.

22. C

Difficulty: Medium

Category: Passport to Advanced Math / Quadratics

Strategic Advice: The axis of symmetry of a parabola always passes through the *x*-coordinate of the parabola's vertex. The trick for finding the *x*-coordinate of the vertex is to calculate $\dfrac{-b}{2a}$ (the quadratic formula without the radical part).

Getting to the Answer: In the equation, $a = 3$ and $b = 12$, so the equation of the axis of symmetry is $x = \dfrac{-(12)}{2(3)} = \dfrac{-12}{6} = -2$. In the question, the equation is $x = m$, so *m* must be -2, which makes (C) correct.

23. A

Difficulty: Hard

Category: Passport to Advanced Math / Quadratics

Strategic Advice: You may have to dig deep to answer to this question. You could try Picking Numbers, just make sure you meet all the criteria given in the question, including that $ac > \dfrac{b^2}{4}$.

Getting to the Answer: The quantity under the radical in the quadratic formula ($b^2 - 4ac$) is called the discriminant because it tells you what kind of solutions to expect. If $b^2 - 4ac = 0$, then the equation has exactly one unique real solution and the graph just touches the x-axis at that value. If $b^2 - 4ac > 0$, then the equation has two real solutions and the graph crosses the x-axis twice. If $b^2 - 4ac < 0$, then the equation has two imaginary solutions (because the square root of a negative number is imaginary) and does not cross the x-axis at all. Now, take a look at the criteria given in the question: $ac > \dfrac{b^2}{4}$. Notice that there is an ac, a b^2, and a 4, so try to manipulate the inequality to make it look like the discriminant:

$$ac > \frac{b^2}{4}$$
$$\frac{ac}{1} > \frac{b^2}{4}$$
$$4ac > b^2$$
$$0 > b^2 - 4ac$$
$$b^2 - 4ac < 0$$

This means the solutions are imaginary and the graph does not cross the x-axis at all, therefore (A) is correct.

24. A

Difficulty: Hard

Category: Passport to Advanced Math / Quadratics

Strategic Advice: To answer this question, you need to recall just about everything you've learned about quadratic graphs. Be careful—the equation looks like vertex form, $y = a(x - h)^2 + k$, but it's not quite there because of the 2 inside the parentheses.

Getting to the Answer: You could rewrite the equation in vertex form, but this would involve squaring the quantity in parentheses and then completing the square, which will take quite a bit of time. So, skip A for now and compare each of the other answer choices to the equation. Don't forget, you are looking for the statement that is *not* true.

Choice B: Substitute 0 for x and simplify to find that the y-intercept is indeed (0, −9).

Choice C: There is a negative in front of the equation, so the parabola *does* open downward.

Choice D: Look at the equation as a transformation of the parent function $y = x^2$. The parabola has been shifted to the right, moved up 7 units, and flipped upside down. Picture this in your head—it has to cross the x-axis at least one time.

This means (A) must be correct. As it turns out, the vertex is (2, 7), not (4, 7).

25. C

Difficulty: Hard

Category: Passport to Advanced Math / Quadratics

Strategic Advice: Trying to answer this question algebraically will take entirely too much time. You are not expected to solve each system. Instead, think about it graphically. The solution to a system of equations is the point(s) where their graphs intersect, so graph each pair of equations in your graphing calculator and look for the ones that intersect at $x = 3.5$ and $x = 6$, both of which happen to be positive values and would lie to the right of the x-axis.

Getting to the Answer: The graphs of the equations in A and B don't intersect at all, so you can eliminate both answers right away. The graphs in (C) *do* intersect, and both points of intersection are to the right of the x-axis, so (C) could be correct, but check D just in case. The graphs don't intersect at all, so (C) is correct.

A note of caution here—just because the solutions were given as 3.5 and 6, that does *not* mean that either number has to appear in one or both of the equations.

26. 87
Difficulty: Easy

Category: Passport to Advanced Math / Quadratics

Strategic Advice: There is no trick to this question. You just need to do the algebra to convert one form to another. Don't forget—when you square a quantity, you can't just square the terms inside the parentheses. Instead, you must multiply the quantity by itself and use FOIL to expand it.

Getting to the Answer:

$$y = 3(x+5)^2 + 12$$
$$= 3(x+5)(x+5) + 12$$
$$= 3(x^2 + 5x + 5x + 25) + 12$$
$$= 3(x^2 + 10x + 25) + 12$$
$$= 3x^2 + 30x + 75 + 12$$
$$= 3x^2 + 30x + 87$$

The question asks for the value of c, so grid in 87.

27. 8
Difficulty: Medium

Category: Passport to Advanced Math / Quadratics

Strategic Advice: Start by translating from English into math. You have two statements to translate, so chances are you'll be solving a system of equations. Before you select your answer, make sure you found what the question is asking for (the smaller of the two integers).

Getting to the Answer: Translate "n is 2 less than three times m" as $n = 3m - 2$. Translate "the product of m and n is 176" as $mn = 175$. Use substitution to solve the equations simultaneously:

$$n = 3m - 2$$
$$mn = 176$$
$$m(3m - 2) = 176$$
$$3m^2 - 2m - 176 = 0$$
$$(3m + 22)(m - 8) = 0$$

Setting each factor equal to 0 and solving results in $m = -\frac{22}{3}$ and $m = 8$. The question states that m and n are positive integers, so $m = 8$. This means $n = 3(8) - 2 = 22$. The smaller of the two integers is 8.

28. 13
Difficulty: Medium

Category: Passport to Advanced Math / Quadratics

Strategic Advice: Don't waste valuable time trying to find the equation for the function. The question states that the function is quadratic, so use what you know about the graphs of parabolas to answer the question.

Getting to the Answer: Notice that the x-values in the table increase by two each time. To find $p(-4)$, you just need to imagine adding one extra row to the top of the table. Now, think about symmetry—you can see from the points in the table that $(2, -5)$ is the vertex of the parabola. The points $(0, -3)$ and $(4, -3)$ are equidistant from the vertex, as are the points $(-2, 3)$ and $(6, 3)$. This means the point whose x-value is -4 should have the same y-value as the last point in the table $(8, 13)$. So, $f(-4) = 13$.

29. 8
Difficulty: Easy

Category: Passport to Advanced Math / Quadratics

Strategic Advice: Whenever you're given the equation for a function, you can evaluate it at any given value by substituting that value for the variable.

Getting to the Answer: The variable t represents the number of seconds after the rockets were fired, so find $h_2(1)$ and $h_1(1)$ and subtract. To make the calculations easier, simplify each equation first.

$h_2(t) = -8t(2t - 7) = -16t^2 + 56t$
$h_2(1) = -16(1)^2 + 56(1) = -16 + 56 = 40$
$h_1(t) = -16t(t - 3) = -16t^2 + 48t$
$h_1(1) = -16(1)^2 + 48(1) = -16 + 48 = 32$

So, after 1 second the second rocket was 40 – 32 = 8 feet higher.

30. 0.25 or 1/4
Difficulty: Hard

Category: Passport to Advanced Math / Quadratics

Strategic Advice: A quadratic function reaches its maximum (or minimum) value at its vertex. Don't do rework—you've already written each equation in standard form, so use the formula $x = \dfrac{-b}{2a}$ to find the x-coordinate of the vertex for each function.

Getting to the Answer:

$h_2(t)$: $a = -16$ and $b = 56$, so $x = \dfrac{-56}{2(-16)} = \dfrac{-56}{-32} = \dfrac{7}{4}$.
This means the second rocket reaches its maximum height at 1.75 seconds.

$h_1(t)$: $a = -16$ and $b = 48$, so $x = \dfrac{-48}{2(-16)} = \dfrac{-48}{-32} = \dfrac{3}{2}$.
This means the first rocket reaches its maximum height at 1.5 seconds.

So, it took the second rocket 1.75 – 1.5 = 0.25 seconds longer to reach its maximum height.

If you are comfortable using your graphing calculator (which could save quite a bit of time), you could graph each equation and use the "maximum" function on the calculator.

31. 8
Difficulty: Medium

Category: Passport to Advanced Math / Quadratics

Strategic Advice: This question is testing whether you can interpret an equation. If you look carefully, it tells you that the coefficient of the x-term from each equation is all you need. Again, don't do rework—you've already written each equation in standard form.

Getting to the Answer: The standard form for the second rocket is $h_2(t) = -16t^2 + 56t$, so the initial velocity was 56 feet per second. The standard form for the first rocket is $h_1(t) = -16t^2 + 48t$, so the initial velocity was 48 feet per second. The second rocket's initial velocity was 56 – 48 = 8 more feet per second than the first rocket's.

CHAPTER 12

PREPARE

1. A
Difficulty: Easy

Category: Additional Topics in Math / Imaginary Numbers

Strategic Advice: Read the expression carefully; the real and imaginary components of the two binomials aren't in the same order.

Getting to the Answer: Distributing the negative sign inside the second set of parentheses yields $2i - 3 - 6 - 4i$. Combine like terms to obtain $-9 - 2i$, which makes (A) correct.

2. D
Difficulty: Medium

Category: Additional Topics in Math / Imaginary Numbers

Strategic Advice: Two binomials being multiplied together means you can use FOIL.

Getting to the Answer: Use FOIL to expand the binomial and simplify.

$$(17 + 7i)(3 - 5i)$$
$$(17 \times 3) + (17 \times -5i) + (7i \times 3) + (7i \times -5i)$$
$$51 - 85i + 21i - 35i^2$$
$$51 - 64i - (35 \times -1)$$
$$86 - 64i$$

Choice (D) is correct.

3. D
Difficulty: Hard

Category: Additional Topics in Math / Imaginary Numbers

Strategic Advice: Determine the conjugate of the denominator to remove i from the fraction denominator.

Getting to the Answer: Rewrite the negative radicands as imaginary numbers. The conjugate of $3 + \sqrt{18}i$ is $3 - \sqrt{18}i$; multiply the numerator and denominator by this to remove i from the denominator. Use FOIL to expand the binomials and then combine like terms to simplify. Separate the real and imaginary components and reduce as needed. The steps for this sequence are shown here:

$$\frac{6 + \sqrt{8}i}{3 + \sqrt{18}i} \times \frac{3 - \sqrt{18}i}{3 - \sqrt{18}i}$$

$$= \frac{(6 \times 3) + (6 \times -\sqrt{18}i) + (3 \times \sqrt{8}i) + (-\sqrt{8} \times 18 i^2)}{9 - 18i^2}$$

$$= \frac{18 - 6\sqrt{18}i + 3\sqrt{8}i + \sqrt{144}}{9 - 18i^2}$$

$$= \frac{18 - 18\sqrt{2}i + 6\sqrt{2}i + 12}{9 - (-18)}$$

$$= \frac{30 - 12\sqrt{2}i}{27}$$

$$= \frac{30}{27} - \frac{12\sqrt{2}}{27}i$$

$$= \frac{10}{9} - \frac{4\sqrt{2}}{9}i$$

Choice (D) is the correct answer.

4. B
Difficulty: Medium

Category: Additional Topics in Math / Imaginary Numbers

Strategic Advice: Before resorting to the quadratic formula, look for an alternate solving technique if straight factoring doesn't work.

Getting to the Answer: The number 5 doesn't have a pair of factors that sum to -4, so use completing the square. Start by setting the equation equal to 0 and then subtracting 5 from both sides. Half of b (-4) is -2; squaring this gives 4. Rewrite the trinomial as a square of binomials, take the square root of both sides, and solve for x. The steps for this sequence are shown here:

$$x^2 - 4x + 5 = 0$$
$$x^2 - 4x = -5$$
$$x^2 - 4x + 4 = -5 + 4$$
$$(x - 2)^2 = -1$$
$$x - 2 = \pm\sqrt{-1}$$
$$x = 2 \pm i$$

Choice (B) is the correct answer.

PRACTICE

5. B
Difficulty: Hard

Category: Additional Topics in Math / Imaginary Numbers

Strategic Advice: Plug the two values you know into the given equation and then solve for the one whose value is missing.

Getting to the Answer: Plug in $38 + 18j$ for E and $4 + 6j$ for Z. Then rearrange the equation so that I is isolated. Multiply the numerator and denominator by the latter's conjugate and then use FOIL. Combine like terms and reduce fractions as needed. The steps for this sequence are shown below.

$$I = \frac{38 + 18j}{4 + 6j} \times \frac{4 - 6j}{4 - 6j}$$

$$I = \frac{(38 \times 4) + (38 \times -6j) + (18j \times 4) + (18j \times -6j)}{16 - 36j^2}$$

$$I = \frac{152 - 228j + 72j - 108j^2}{16 - (-36)}$$

$$I = \frac{152 - 156j - (-108)}{52}$$

$$I = \frac{260 - 156j}{52}$$

$$I = \frac{260}{52} - \frac{156}{52}j = 5 - 3j$$

Choice (B) is the correct answer.

PERFORM

6. C
Difficulty: Medium

Category: Additional Topics in Math / Imaginary Numbers

Strategic Advice: Plugging in each choice will cost you precious time. Instead, factor the trinomials to find the solutions.

Getting to the Answer: Factoring the first trinomial yields $(x^2 + 81)(x^2 + 3)$, and factoring the second gives $(x + 9)(x - 4)$. Set each expression equal to 0 and solve for x; you'll get $x = \pm 9i, \pm\sqrt{3}i, -9, 4$. (C) is the only choice that is not in this list of values, so it is correct.

7. 2338
Difficulty: Easy

Category: Additional Topics in Math / Imaginary Numbers

Strategic Advice: Instead of spending time going through each distribution step by hand, use your calculator to snag this point more quickly.

Getting to the Answer: Set your TI-83/84 to $a + bi$ mode (or the equivalent if you have a different calculator) and then compute $(11 + 14i)^3$. The result is $-5,137 + 2,338i$. The question asks for b, the coefficient of the imaginary component, so grid in 2338.

EXTRA PRACTICE

1. D
Difficulty: Easy

Category: Additional Topics in Math / Imaginary Numbers

Strategic Advice: You can add and subtract complex numbers, and multiples of complex numbers, the same way you add and subtract binomials—combine like terms.

Getting to the Answer: Substitute the given expressions for A and B, distribute, and then combine like terms. Be careful of the negative signs.

$$2A - B = 2(3 + 5i) - (-2 - i)$$
$$= 2(3) + 2(5i) - (-2) - (-i)$$
$$= 6 + 10i + 2 + i$$
$$= 8 + 11i$$

This matches (D).

2. D
Difficulty: Easy

Category: Additional Topics in Math / Imaginary Numbers

Strategic Advice: The definition of i is given as $i = \sqrt{-1}$. If you square both sides of this definition, you arrive at a more useful form:

$$(i)^2 = \left(\sqrt{-1}\right)^2 \rightarrow i^2 = -1 \cdot$$

Getting to the Answer: Distribute the $4i$ and then substitute -1 for i^2:

$$4i(5 - 7i) = 4i(5) - 4i(7i)$$
$$= 20i - 28i^2$$
$$= 20i - 28(-1)$$
$$= 20i + 28$$

Switch the terms so that the real part is first $(28 + 20i)$ to find that (D) is correct.

3. B
Difficulty: Easy

Category: Additional Topics in Math / Imaginary Numbers

Strategic Advice: Knowing the cycle of i when it is raised to powers will save you time on Test Day. The first four are $i^1 = i$; $i^2 = -1$ (by definition); $i^3 = i^2 \times i = -i$; $i^4 = i^2 \times i^2 = -1 \times -1 = 1$. The pattern repeats over and over (i, -1, $-i$, 1, i, -1, $-i$, 1, …).

Getting to the Answer: You know from the primary cycle that i^3 is $-i$, so you're looking for the expression that does *not* equal $-i$. You can tell from just looking at C that the expression *does* equal $-i$, so eliminate C right away. Choice D is also fairly quick to evaluate: $2 - 2 = 0$ and $3i - 4i = -i$, so eliminate D as well. To decide between A and B, you'll have to use the power pattern. For A, divide 15 by 4 (the number of terms in the primary cycle) to get 3 with a remainder of 3. This means that $i^{15} = (i^4)^3 \times i^3 = (1)^3 \times -i = -i$. Eliminate A; hence (B) must be correct. To check (which isn't necessary), $i^5 \times i^4 = i^9 = (i^4)^2 \times i = 1 \times i = i$.

4. B
Difficulty: Medium

Category: Additional Topics in Math / Imaginary Numbers

Strategic Advice: Just as with a binomial, raising a complex number written in the form $a + bi$ requires writing it out as repeated multiplication and using FOIL.

Getting to the Answer: After multiplying the expressions, substitute -1 for i^2 and then combine like terms.

$$(4+3i)^2 = (4+3i)(4+3i)$$
$$= 16+12i+12i+9i^2$$
$$= 16+24i+9(-1)$$
$$= 7+24i$$

This matches (B).

5. D
Difficulty: Medium

Category: Additional Topics in Math / Imaginary Numbers

Strategic Advice: Use the definition of i to simplify the numerator by writing the quantity under the radical as a product of -1 and 12.

Getting to the Answer: Factor a -1 out of 12 and look for other perfect squares that can be divided out of both the numerator and the denominator.

$$\frac{\sqrt{-12}}{\sqrt{75}} = \frac{\sqrt{-1\times4\times3}}{\sqrt{25\times3}} = \frac{2i\sqrt{3}}{5\sqrt{3}} = \frac{2}{5}i$$

Choice (D) is correct.

6. B
Difficulty: Medium

Category: Additional Topics in Math / Imaginary Numbers

Strategic Advice: You will not be expected to raise a complex number like the one in this question to the fourth power by hand. That's a clue that you should be able to use your calculator.

Getting to the Answer: The definition of i has been programmed into all graphing calculators, so you can perform basic operations on complex numbers using the calculator (in the calculator section of the test). Enter the expression as follows: $(3 + 2i)^4$. On the TI83/84 calculators, you can find i on the button with the decimal point.

After you enter the expression, the calculator should return $-119 + 120i$, which is (B).

7. A
Difficulty: Medium

Category: Additional Topics in Math / Imaginary Numbers

Strategic Advice: Because $i = \sqrt{-1}$, it isn't considered "proper" to leave i in the denominator of a fraction (just as you shouldn't leave a radical in the denominator). Use the same strategy you learned for rationalizing the denominator of a radical expression to rationalize a complex number (by multiplying by the conjugate).

Getting to the Answer: The conjugate of $3 - i$ is $3 + i$, so multiply the expression by $\frac{3+i}{3+i}$:

$$\frac{1}{3-i} \times \frac{3+i}{3+i} = \frac{3+i}{(3-i)(3+i)}$$
$$= \frac{3+i}{9+3i-3i-i^2}$$
$$= \frac{3+i}{9-(-1)}$$
$$= \frac{3+i}{10}$$

This isn't one of the answer choices, so split the number into its real part and its imaginary part by writing each of the terms in the numerator over 10. The result is $\frac{3}{10} + \frac{1}{10}i$, which matches (A).

8. C
Difficulty: Medium

Category: Additional Topics in Math / Imaginary Numbers

Strategic Advice: Now that you've been introduced to imaginary numbers, be on the lookout for quadratic equations that have complex solutions. This is a new twist, but you can still use the strategies you previously learned for solving quadratics.

Getting to the Answer: Notice that both terms are perfect squares. This is a clue that "square rooting" is probably the most direct solution. Move the constant to the right of the equal sign and then take the square root of both sides. Use the definition of i if necessary.

$$x^2 + \frac{4}{25} = 0$$
$$x^2 = -\frac{4}{25}$$
$$x = \pm\sqrt{\frac{-4}{25}}$$
$$x = \pm\frac{\sqrt{-1 \times 4}}{\sqrt{25}}$$
$$x = \pm\frac{2}{5}i$$

A perfect match for (C)!

9. B

Difficulty: Medium

Category: Additional Topics in Math / Imaginary Numbers

Strategic Advice: A question like this requires patience and an understanding of how the powers of i cycle. Whenever you're evaluating a high power of i, divide the power by 4 and let the remainder point you to the correct answer.

Getting to the Answer: Recall the power pattern for i: i, -1, $-i$, 1, and repeat. Divide 14 by 4, which yields 3 with a remainder of 2. This means $i^{14} = (i^4)^3 \times i^2 = 1 \times -1 = -1$. Repeat this process for i^{122} to get $i^{122} = (i^4)^{30} \times i^2 = 1 \times -1 = -1$. The sum is therefore $-1 + -1 = -2$, which means you're looking for an expression that has the same value. Choices B and C should look tempting (because of the 2), so start with them. In (B), you know $i^2 = -1$ and $2(-1) = -2$, so this is the correct answer.

10. A

Difficulty: Hard

Category: Additional Topics in Math / Imaginary Numbers

Strategic Advice: Each of the factors in this product has two terms, so they behave like binomials. This means you can use FOIL to find the product. To avoid messy numbers, simplify the two radicals first using the definition of i.

Getting to the Answer: Write each of the numbers under the radicals as a product of -1 and the number, take the square roots, and then FOIL the resulting expressions.

$$\left(2+\sqrt{-9}\right)\left(-1+\sqrt{-4}\right) = \left(2+\sqrt{-1\times9}\right)\left(-1+\sqrt{-1\times4}\right)$$
$$= (2+3i)(-1+2i)$$
$$= -2+4i-3i+6i^2$$
$$= -2+i+6(-1)$$
$$= -8+i$$

Choice (A) is correct.

11. B

Difficulty: Hard

Category: Additional Topics in Math / Imaginary Numbers

Strategic Advice: Take a peek at the answer choices—they're all complex numbers. This means factoring is out of the question, so think quadratic formula!

Getting to the Answer: Before you can use the quadratic formula, the equation must equal 0, so move all the terms to the left side of the equal sign; the quadratic (written in standard form) becomes $x^2 - 4x + 13 = 0$. Now, jot down the values you'll need: $a = 1$, $b = -4$, and $c = 13$.

$$x = \frac{-b \pm \sqrt{b^2 - 4ac}}{2a}$$

$$= \frac{-(-4) \pm \sqrt{(-4)^2 - 4(1)(13)}}{2(1)}$$

$$= \frac{4 \pm \sqrt{16 - 52}}{2}$$

$$= \frac{4 \pm \sqrt{-36}}{2}$$

$$= \frac{4 \pm \sqrt{-1 \times 36}}{2}$$

$$= \frac{4 \pm 6i}{2}$$

$$= \frac{\cancel{2}(2 \pm 3i)}{\cancel{2}}$$

The final answer is $2 \pm 3i$, which matches (B).

12. C
Difficulty: Hard

Category: Additional Topics in Math / Imaginary Numbers

Strategic Advice: Take a peek at the answer choices—the denominator in each one is the same as the denominator in the expression in the question. This means you're not trying to rationalize the expression but rather simply adding the two terms. Fractions with complex numbers are no different from any other fraction. You must find a common denominator before adding them.

Getting to the Answer: Find a common denominator by multiplying the second term by $4 - 2i$. As always, you're given that $\sqrt{-1} = i$, but a more useful fact is that $i^2 = -1$, so be sure to make this substitution as you work. Once you've found the common denominator, you can simply add like terms.

$$\frac{1}{4 - 2i} + (3 + i) = \frac{1}{4 - 2i} + \frac{3 + i}{1}$$

$$= \frac{1}{4 - 2i} + \frac{3 + i}{1}\left(\frac{4 - 2i}{4 - 2i}\right)$$

$$= \frac{1}{4 - 2i} + \frac{12 - 6i + 4i - 2i^2}{4 - 2i}$$

$$= \frac{1}{4 - 2i} + \frac{12 - 2i - 2(-1)}{4 - 2i}$$

$$= \frac{1 + 12 - 2i + 2}{4 - 2i}$$

$$= \frac{15 - 2i}{4 - 2i}$$

This matches (C).

13. 7/26
Difficulty: Medium

Category: Additional Topics in Math / Imaginary Numbers

Strategic Advice: To find the value of b, you'll need to rationalize the denominator so you can split the complex number into its real part and its imaginary part.

Getting to the Answer: Multiply the numerator and the denominator of the expression by the conjugate of $5 - i$, which is $5 + i$. Then, FOIL and simplify.

$$\frac{2 + i}{5 - i} = \frac{2 + i}{5 - i} \times \left(\frac{5 + i}{5 + i}\right)$$

$$= \frac{(2 + i)(5 + i)}{(5 - i)(5 + i)}$$

$$= \frac{10 + 2i + 5i + i^2}{25 + 5i - 5i - i^2}$$

$$= \frac{10 + 7i + (-1)}{25 - (-1)}$$

$$= \frac{9 + 7i}{26}$$

$$= \frac{9}{26} + \frac{7}{26}i$$

The coefficient of the imaginary part is represented by b, so the correct answer is 7/26.

14. 17

Difficulty: Medium

Category: Additional Topics in Math / Imaginary Numbers

Strategic Advice: Don't let this "new" definition intimidate you. All you're asked to do is to find the square root of the sum of a^2 and b^2. You don't even have to involve the i at all.

Getting to the Answer:

$$|15 + 8i| = \sqrt{15^2 + 8^2}$$
$$= \sqrt{225 + 64}$$
$$= \sqrt{289}$$
$$= 17$$

There is nothing else to do—the answer is 17.

CHAPTER 13

PREPARE

1. D

Difficulty: Medium

Category: Additional Topics in Math / Geometry

Strategic Advice: Pay attention to which angles are formed by which transversal. Angles formed by different transversals are not necessarily related.

Getting to the Answer: The left transversal forms angles *a*, *b*, and *d*. From the figure you know *a* and *d* are corresponding (and therefore equal) angles. Together, angles *a* and *b* form a straight line, so they are supplementary; because *a* and *d* are equal, *b* and *d* are also supplementary. The other transversal forms *c* and *e*, which are supplementary. Consider angles *a*, *b*, and *d* as belonging to Group 1 and angles *c* and *e* as belonging to Group 2. None of the angles in Group 1 are necessarily equal, supplementary, or in any way related to any of the angles in Group 2 because they are formed by different transversals. For this reason, A, B, and C are incorrect, as they all try to relate angles from two different groups. That leaves (D), which is correct.

If you're not fully confident that (D) is correct, remember that *b* and *d* are supplementary, as are *c* and *e*. Therefore, $b + d = e + c = 180$. Rearrange the equation to yield $b + d - c = e$.

2. A

Difficulty: Medium

Category: Additional Topics in Math / Geometry

Strategic Advice: Draw a diagram to visualize the situation. If you don't immediately see any helpful angles or shapes, add additional lines.

Getting to the Answer: After drawing a diagram of Aundria and Annette's routes to the summit and labeling it with the information given, look for a way to uncover a right triangle with additional lines. Once complete, use the rectangle you created to fill in the lengths of the new segments. The completed diagram is shown here:

Use the Pythagorean theorem to calculate the distance Annette will travel:

$$(5+7)^2 + 4^2 = c^2$$

$$c^2 = 144 + 16 = 160$$

$$c = \sqrt{160} = 4\sqrt{10}$$

But you're not done yet! The question asks you to find the total distance the two women travel. Aundria travels $5 + 6 + 7 + 2 = 20$ mi; together, she and Annette will travel $20 + 4\sqrt{10}$ mi, which is approximately 32.65 mi. Choice (A) is correct.

3. 39

Difficulty: Easy

Category: Additional Topics in Math / Geometry

Strategic Advice: Draw a diagram to visualize the situation in the question.

Getting to the Answer: Start by drawing Uwe's field and the fence he plans to build:

You know the length and the area of the field. Use these to find the width:

$$A = lw$$

$$540 = 36w$$

$$w = 15$$

Now you know that the fence is the hypotenuse of a right triangle with legs 15 and 36. Before turning to the Pythagorean theorem, look for a Pythagorean triplet to lessen the required work. Indeed, this is a 5-12-13 triangle multiplied by 3. Therefore, the hypotenuse—and meters of fence needed—is $13 \times 3 = 39$.

4. B

Difficulty: Medium

Category: Additional Topics in Math / Geometry

Strategic Advice: Don't panic if you don't see how to get the answer right away. Fill in the figure with what you know, and identify what else you can determine from there. You'll arrive at the answer in just a few steps.

Getting to the Answer: In $\triangle FDC$, only one angle is missing, so you can solve for it and fill it in: $m\angle DFC = 180° - 70° - 60° = 50°$. Because $\angle DFC$ and $\angle BFG$ are vertical angles, $m\angle BFG = m\angle DFC = 50°$. At this point, you have two of the three angles in $\triangle BFG$, so you can solve for the third: $m\angle FBG = 180° - 50° - 60° = 70°$. Because $\overline{AD}$ and $\overline{BC}$ are parallel, $\angle FBG$ and $\angle BAD$ are corresponding angles (and are therefore equal). You can now conclude that $\angle x = 70°$, which matches (B).

5. B

Difficulty: Easy

Category: Additional Topics in Math / Geometry

Strategic Advice: Look for simpler shapes, and determine what you know about those first.

Getting to the Answer: You're told that $\overline{AB} = 6$. Because $ABCD$ is a rectangle, $\overline{AB}$ must equal $\overline{DC}$, so $\overline{DC} = 6$. The question states that $\overline{FD} = \overline{DC}$, so $\overline{FD}$ is 6, too. You're told that the perimeter of rectangle $ABCD$ is 30. Thus, $30 = \overline{AB} + \overline{BC} + \overline{CD} + \overline{AD} = 6 + 6 + \overline{BC} + \overline{AD}$ and $\overline{BC} + \overline{AD} = 30 - 6 - 6 = 18$. Because $\overline{BC} = \overline{AD}$ and $9 + 9 = 18$, $\overline{BC}$ and $\overline{AD}$ must each equal 9. Use the Pythagorean theorem to find $\overline{FA}$:

$$6^2 + \overline{FA}^2 = 9^2$$

$$\overline{FA}^2 = 81 - 36$$

$$\overline{FA} = \sqrt{45}$$

Finally, simplify the radical to get your answer: $\sqrt{45} = \sqrt{9} \times \sqrt{5} = 3\sqrt{5}$. (B) is correct.

PRACTICE

6. C

Difficulty: Hard

Category: Additional Topics in Math / Geometry

Strategic Advice: Look for hidden special right triangles to help you find the answer, and add new information to your diagram as you find it.

Getting to the Answer: Start by finding $\angle ACD$ from the two given angles: $m\angle ACD = 180° - 15° - 30° = 135°$. Because $\angle ACB$ is supplementary to $\angle ACD$, $\angle ACB$ measures 45°. $\triangle ABC$ is a right triangle, so its missing angle ($\angle BAC$) is also 45°, making $\triangle ABC$ a 45-45-90 triangle. This means $\angle BAD$ is 60°; therefore, $\triangle ABD$ is a 30-60-90 triangle.

Knowing that you have two special right triangles will allow you to unlock the unknown side lengths. $\overline{AC}$ is the hypotenuse of the 45-45-90 triangle (side ratio: $x:x:x\sqrt{2}$), so $\overline{AB}$ and $\overline{BC}$ (the two legs) must be $2\sqrt{2}$ (solve the equation $4=x\sqrt{2}$ to find this). $\overline{AB}$ is also the shorter leg of the 30-60-90 triangle (side ratio: $x:x\sqrt{3}:2x$), so $\overline{BD}$ (longer leg) is $2\sqrt{6}$, and $\overline{AD}$ (hypotenuse) is $4\sqrt{2}$. Don't stop just yet; remember which perimeter you need. Take the difference of $\overline{BD}$ and $\overline{BC}$ to determine $\overline{CD}$, which is $2\sqrt{6}-2\sqrt{2}$. You now have all three sides of $\triangle ACD$, so add them together to get your answer: $P_{ACD}=4+(2\sqrt{6}-2\sqrt{2})+4\sqrt{2}$. This simplifies to $4+2\sqrt{6}+2\sqrt{2}$, making (C) correct.

The completed diagram is shown here:

7. 100

Difficulty: Easy

Category: Additional Topics in Math / Geometry

Strategic Advice: Use your knowledge of supplementary and vertical angles to systematically solve for y and then x.

Getting to the Answer: Because supplementary angles sum to $180°$, $2y+4y=180$. Simplification yields $y=30$. Don't stop here: the question wants x, not y. Shift your focus to the vertical angles. The angle marked $4y$ is vertical to the one marked $x+20$, so $4y=x+20$. Plugging in 30 for y yields $x=4(30)-20=120-20=100$. The correct answer is 100.

8. 52

Difficulty: Medium

Category: Additional Topics in Math / Geometry

Strategic Advice: If the question doesn't give you a figure, draw one. Making a figure saves time and helps you steer clear of traps.

Getting to the Answer: First, draw a rectangle to represent the wall space. Next draw another rectangle inside the first to represent the TV. Label the diagram with the information the question provides.

To find the dimensions of the TV, subtract 6 from the length and width of the wall space. Note that many students might erroneously subtract only 3 inches from each dimension, yielding TV dimensions of 25.2550. However, the space adds 3 inches on all four sides of the TV, so you should actually subtract 6 inches from the length and width of the wall space. Therefore, the correct TV dimensions are 22.25×47.

With the TV dimensions in hand, you can use the Pythagorean theorem to determine the size (a.k.a. the diagonal) of the largest TV that Whitney can fit in this wall space:

$$a^2 + b^2 = c^2$$

$$22.25^2 + 47^2 = c^2$$

$$495.0625 + 2,209 = c^2$$

$$2,704.0625 = c^2$$

$$52.001 \approx c$$

Grid in 52.

PERFORM

9. D
Difficulty: Medium

Category: Additional Topics in Math / Geometry

Strategic Advice: Use the 30-60-90 triangle ratio, and don't forget to answer the question posed.

Getting to the Answer: The sides of a 30-60-90 triangle are in the ratio $x : x\sqrt{3} : 2x$, so label the triangle accordingly:

The area of a triangle is $A = \frac{1}{2}bh$, and you're told that the area of this triangle is $8\sqrt{3}$. Use this to solve for x:

$$8\sqrt{3} = \frac{1}{2}(x)(x\sqrt{3}) = \frac{1}{2}x^2\sqrt{3}$$

$$16 = x^2$$

$$x = 4$$

This matches A, but A is a trap! You just solved for x, which is the length of $\overline{CB}$. The question asks for the length of $\overline{AB}$, not $\overline{CB}$. Because $\overline{CB}$ is twice $\overline{AB}$, the correct answer is 8, which is (D).

10. 3/8 or .375
Difficulty: Hard

Category: Additional Topics in Math / Geometry

Strategic Advice: Three of the four squares have a smaller square within them. Take this into account when doing your calculations.

Getting to the Answer: The question states that each progressively larger square has a perimeter that is 4 cm greater than that of the previous square. Therefore, each progressively larger square will also have a side length that is 1 cm greater than that of the previous square. Use this fact to determine the area of each square; the following table summarizes the change in side length and area moving outward from the innermost square.

	S1 (innermost)	S2	S3	S4 (outermost)
Side length	1	2	3	4
Area	1	4	9	16

Next, determine the area of the white and black regions. When calculating these, remember to account for the area taken up by the square inscribed within. Square 1 contains 1 cm² white space, Square 2 contains $4 - 1 = 3$ cm² black space, Square 3 contains $9 - 4 = 5$ cm² white space, and Square 4 contains $16 - 9 = 7$ cm² black space. The question asks for the probability of randomly selecting a point in one of the white regions, which is $\frac{1+5}{16} = \frac{6}{16} = \frac{3}{8}$. Grid in $\frac{3}{8}$ or .375.

11. B
Difficulty: Medium

Category: Additional Topics in Math / Geometry

Strategic Advice: With complex figures, keep in mind that it might take more than one calculation or step to get to the answer.

Getting to the Answer: Given the area of $\triangle ABC$ and the length of the base AB, you can find its height, $CB : 150 = \frac{1}{2}(20)CB = 10CB \rightarrow CB = 15$. This means that $\triangle ABC$ is a 3-4-5 triangle with dimensions scaled up by a factor of 5, so the hypotenuse $(\overline{AC})$ must be $5 \times 5 = 25$. Next, turn your attention to the smaller triangle, $\triangle AGH$. You're told that the hypotenuse of this triangle, $\overline{AH}$, is 20. Because $\triangle ABC$ and $\triangle AGH$ are similar triangles, their corresponding sides must be proportional.

$$\frac{AH}{AC} = \frac{HG}{CB}$$

$$\frac{20}{25} = \frac{HG}{15}$$

$$300 = 25HG$$

$$\overline{HG} = 12$$

Choice (B) is the correct answer.

12. A

Difficulty: Hard

Category: Additional Topics in Math / Geometry

Strategic Advice: Extend the existing lines to reveal helpful hidden angles and triangles.

Getting to the Answer: Because j and k are parallel, the two other segments are actually transversals. Extend them to visualize the rest of the associated angles. We've labeled a few angles to aid in the explanation; you need not do the same on Test Day.

The angles marked $a°$ and $150°$ are supplementary, so $a = 180° - 150° = 30°$. The angles marked $b°$ and $20°$ are alternate interior angles (and therefore equal), so $b = 20$. Notice that the angles marked $a°$, $b°$, and $c°$ are all in the same triangle; consequently, their sum is $180°$. Therefore, $c = 180 - 30 - 20 = 130$. Because the angles marked $c°$ and $q°$ are supplementary, $q = 180 - 130 = 50$. (A) is therefore correct.

EXTRA PRACTICE

1. C
Difficulty: Easy

Category: Additional Topics in Math / Geometry

Strategic Advice: Don't immediately assume you need to use trig to answer this question (although it is possible). Instead, keep in mind that the SAT is more likely to test your knowledge of right triangles, so start by determining whether triangle *ABC* is a right triangle.

Getting to the Answer: The sum of the angles of every triangle is 180 degrees. Subtract the angle measures given from 180 to find that angle *B* equals $180 - 51.5 - 38.5 = 90$ degrees. This means the triangle is a right triangle. Because *B* is the right angle, side *AC* must be the hypotenuse. Use the Pythagorean theorem to find its length:

$$a^2 + b^2 = c^2$$

$$28^2 + 45^2 = c^2$$

$$784 + 2{,}025 = c^2$$

$$2{,}809 = c^2$$

$$53 = c$$

This makes (C) the correct answer.

2. B
Difficulty: Easy

Category: Additional Topics in Math / Geometry

Strategic Advice: The sum of the interior angle measures of every triangle is 180°. To figure out the value of *x*, begin by filling in the angle measures for the triangle.

Getting to the Answer: The angle vertical to the 48° angle is also 48°, and the angle supplementary to the 135° angle has a measure of $180° - 135° = 45°$.

Now that you know two of the angles in the triangle, you can calculate the measure of the third angle, *y*, by subtracting from 180 to get $180 - 48 - 45 = 87°$. The angle with measure *x*° is supplementary to angle *y*, so $87 + x = 180°$. Thus, $x = 93°$, which means that $x - y = 93 - 87 = 6$, which is (B).

3. C
Difficulty: Easy

Category: Additional Topics in Math / Geometry

Strategic Advice: From the question, you know that the triangle formed by Earth, the moon, and the sun is a right triangle. This means you can use the Pythagorean theorem to find the missing side, which is the hypotenuse.

Getting to the Answer: You can divide both numbers by 1,000 to reduce the number of zeros and make them more manageable.

$$a^2 + b^2 = c^2$$

$$240^2 + 91{,}674^2 = c^2$$

$$57{,}600 + 8{,}404{,}122{,}276 = c^2$$

$$8{,}404{,}179{,}876 = c^2$$

$$91{,}674.31 = c$$

Don't forget to multiply the result by 1,000 (because you divided by 1,000 earlier). There are approximately 91,674,000 miles between Earth and the sun, which matches (C).

4. D
Difficulty: Easy

Category: Additional Topics in Math / Geometry

Strategic Advice: Two of the angles in the triangle have degree measures 30 and 90, which means the third angle must measure 60 degrees. This means you are dealing with a special right triangle and can use the 30-60-90 shortcut.

Getting to the Answer: In a 30-60-90 triangle, the sides are always in the ratio $x : x\sqrt{3} : 2x$ (short leg : long leg : hypotenuse). The only length you know is the long leg—the side represented by the ground and the width of the bottom two steps. The ramp is to be placed 8 feet, or 96 inches, from the bottom step, and the steps themselves account for an additional 20 inches, which means this leg of the triangle is 116 inches long. Use the ratio to determine that you need to divide by $\sqrt{3}$ to find the length of the shorter leg, and then multiply the result by 2 to find the length of the hypotenuse, which represents the ramp.

$$116 \div \sqrt{3} = 66.97$$
$$66.97 \times 2 = 133.95$$

The result is about 134 inches, which matches (D).

5. A

Difficulty: Medium

Category: Additional Topics in Math / Geometry

Strategic Advice: Start by translating from English into math. Because one leg of the triangle is three times as long as the other, let x and $3x$ represent the lengths.

Getting to the Answer: Use the Pythagorean theorem to find the hypotenuse.

$$a^2 + b^2 = c^2$$
$$x^2 + (3x)^2 = c^2$$
$$x^2 + 9x^2 = c^2$$
$$10x^2 = c^2$$
$$\sqrt{10x^2} = c$$

Although you can't find a numerical value for c, you do know that the number under the radical must be a multiple of 10, so (A) is correct.

6. A

Difficulty: Medium

Category: Additional Topics in Math / Geometry

Strategic Advice: Many geometry questions require adding lines to the figure given. If you're not sure where to get started on a question like this, see if you can add a line to make a right triangle or other familiar figure.

Getting to the Answer: Start by connecting the ranch to the campsite. Then draw in a horizontal line and a vertical line to form a right triangle.

The length of one leg of the triangle is 15 miles, the distance from the watering hole to the barn. The length of the other leg is $6 + 2 = 8$ miles, the distance from the ranch to the watering hole and then from the barn to the campsite. The two legs of the right triangle are 8 and 15. You might recognize the Pythagorean triplet, 8, 15, 17, but if you don't, you can always rely on the Pythagorean theorem:

$$8^2 + 15^2 = c^2$$
$$64 + 225 = c^2$$
$$289 = c^2$$
$$\sqrt{289} = \sqrt{c^2}$$
$$17 = c$$

The actual trail is $6 + 15 + 2 = 23$ miles long. The direct route is 17 miles, so the direct route is $23 - 17 = 6$ miles shorter, making (A) the correct answer.

7. B

Difficulty: Medium

Category: Additional Topics in Math / Geometry

Strategic Advice: Lengths that represent Pythagorean triplets form right triangles. Convert any fractional measurements or mixed units to inches so that you can look for Pythagorean triplets.

Getting to the Answer: Choice A is a Pythagorean triplet, so you can eliminate it right away. Don't let (B) fool you—3, 4, 5 is a Pythagorean triplet but $\frac{1}{3}, \frac{1}{4}, \frac{1}{5}$ is not. (If you're not convinced, try these numbers in the Pythagorean theorem).

Choice (B): $\frac{1}{3}$ foot = 4 inches, $\frac{1}{4}$ foot = 3 inches, and $\frac{1}{5}$ foot = 2.4 inches. Keep this choice for now.

Choice C: The numbers 9, 40, and 41 represent a Pythagorean triplet so eliminate this choice.

Choice D: $\frac{3}{4}$ foot = 9 inches, 1 foot = 12 inches, 15 inches = 15 inches. The numbers 9, 12, 15 are 3 times the numbers 3, 4, 5, so they represent a Pythagorean triplet Eliminate D.

This means (B) must be correct. You could also use the Pythagorean theorem to verify your answer.

8. D

Difficulty: Medium

Category: Additional Topics in Math / Geometry

Strategic Advice: Pay careful attention to labels on a diagram, including tick marks that indicate congruence.

Getting to the Answer: Because one angle of the triangle measures 90°, and the two legs are congruent (notice the tick marks), this is a 45-45-90 triangle. The side lengths of a 45-45-90 triangle are in the ratio $s:s:s\sqrt{2}$, where s represents the length of a leg and $s\sqrt{2}$ represents the length of the hypotenuse. (Don't forget—the formula page provides this information.) Don't be too hasty in choosing

your answer—it's not 7. Set up an equation using the ratio and the length of the side ($7\sqrt{2}$) to find h:

$$\begin{aligned} h &= s\sqrt{2} \\ &= 7\sqrt{2} \times \sqrt{2} \\ &= 7\sqrt{4} \\ &= 7(2) \\ &= 14 \end{aligned}$$

The length of the hypotenuse is 14, so (D) is correct.

9. C

Difficulty: Medium

Category: Additional Topics in Math / Geometry

Strategic Advice: If you're not sure how to start a question like this, look for vertical angles and supplementary angles in the figure and fill in their measures. Remember, vertical angles have equal measures, supplementary angles add up to 180°, and the sum of the interior angles of a triangle is also 180°.

Getting to the Answer: Line L forms a right triangle with the x- and y-axes, so one of the interior angles of the triangle has a measure of 90°. You know that $\angle q = 140°$, and angles p and q form a straight line, which means they are supplementary. So $\angle p$ must equal 180° − 140° = 40°. One of the interior angles of the triangle is vertical to $\angle p$, so it also equals 40°. Now find the last angle measure inside the triangle by subtracting: 180° − 90° − 40° = 50°. This angle is supplementary to angle r, so $r = 180° − 50° = 130°$. This means that $\angle r - p° = 130° - 40° = 90°$, making (C) the correct choice.

10. B

Difficulty: Medium

Category: Additional Topics in Math / Geometry

Strategic Advice: Be on the lookout for Pythagorean triplets such as 3-4-5 right triangles, as well as multiples of Pythagorean triplets.

Getting to the Answer: You've been given two side lengths of a right triangle; the shorter leg ($\overline{OR}$, which is a radius of the circle) is 1.5, and the longer leg ($\overline{RQ}$) is 2. If you mentally double these values, you should recognize that triangle ORQ is a 3-4-5 right triangle in which the 3-4-5 ratio has been cut in half, resulting in side lengths of 1.5, 2, and 2.5. This means the length of $\overline{OQ}$ is 2.5. Segment OP is a radius, so it must be equal in length to $\overline{OR}$, which is 1.5. Because $\overline{PQ} = \overline{OQ} - \overline{OP}$, the length of $\overline{PQ}$ is 2.5 − 1.5 = 1, making (B) correct.

11. D

Difficulty: Medium

Category: Additional Topics in Math / Geometry

Strategic Advice: This question is fairly straightforward—use the Pythagorean theorem to find h. The tricky part is the algebra, so simplify each term carefully as you work through the solution.

Getting to the Answer: The sides $3d$, $5d$, and h form a right triangle, so plug these values into the Pythagorean theorem, and then solve for h. Be careful—when you square $3d$ and $5d$, you must square the coefficient and the variable.

$$a^2 + b^2 = c^2$$
$$(3d)^2 + (5d)^2 = h^2$$
$$9d^2 + 25d^2 = h^2$$
$$34d^2 = h^2$$
$$\sqrt{34d^2} = h$$
$$d\sqrt{34} = h$$

Choice (D) is correct.

12. B

Difficulty: Hard

Category: Additional Topics in Math / Geometry

Strategic Advice: Always look for 45-45-90 and 30-60-90 triangles on Test Day.

Getting to the Answer: First, find the measure of the missing angle in the triangle: 180 − 105 − 45 = 30 degrees. Now, draw the height of the triangle up from B to a point, D, on $\overline{AC}$; this creates two right triangles.

Triangle ABD is a 45-45-90 triangle, so its side lengths are in the ratio $s : s : s\sqrt{2}$. Because $\overline{AB}$ is the hypotenuse, set up an equation using the ratio of the sides:

$$6 = s\sqrt{2}$$
$$\frac{6}{\sqrt{2}} = s$$
$$\frac{6}{\sqrt{2}}\left(\frac{\sqrt{2}}{\sqrt{2}}\right) = s$$
$$\frac{6\sqrt{2}}{2} = s$$
$$3\sqrt{2} = s$$

Triangle BDC is a 30-60-90 triangle, so its side lengths are in the ratio of $x : x\sqrt{3} : 2x$. You just found the dimensions of the shorter leg, $3\sqrt{2}$, so multiply it by $\sqrt{3}$ to find the length of the longer leg ($\sqrt{3} \times 3\sqrt{2} = 3\sqrt{6}$). Now, find the length of AC, which is the base of the triangle, by adding $\overline{AD}$ to $\overline{DC}$: $3\sqrt{2} + 3\sqrt{6}$. Finally, use the area formula, $A = \frac{1}{2}bh$, to find the area of the whole triangle:

$$A = \frac{1}{2}(3\sqrt{2} + 3\sqrt{6})(3\sqrt{2})$$
$$= \frac{1}{2}(18 + 9\sqrt{12})$$
$$= \frac{1}{2}(18 + 18\sqrt{3})$$
$$= 9 + 9\sqrt{3}$$

Choice (B) is correct.

13. D

Difficulty: Hard

Category: Additional Topics in Math / Geometry

Strategic Advice: You'll need to use several formulas to answer this question: area of a triangle, reverse FOIL (factoring), and the Pythagorean theorem. Be patient and take it one step at a time.

Getting to the Answer: In a right triangle, one leg is the base and the other is the height. Use x and $x + 3$ to represent the lengths of these two legs (because the question states that one leg is 3 inches longer than the other). Use the area formula and set the equation equal to the given area:

$$35 = \frac{1}{2}(x)(x+3)$$

$$2(35) = \cancel{2}\left(\frac{1}{\cancel{2}}(x)(x+3)\right)$$

$$70 = (x)(x+3)$$

$$70 = x^2 + 3x$$

Now, subtract 70 to make the equation equal 0 and then factor it. The factors are $(x + 10)$ and $(x - 7)$, which means $x = -10$ and $x = 7$. Lengths cannot be negative, so the shorter leg must have a length of 7. This means the longer leg has a length of $7 + 3 = 10$. Now use the Pythagorean theorem to find the length of the hypotenuse.

$$a^2 + b^2 = c^2$$

$$7^2 + 10^2 = c^2$$

$$49 + 100 = c^2$$

$$149 = c^2$$

$$\sqrt{149} = \sqrt{c^2}$$

$$\sqrt{149} = c$$

Choice (D) is correct.

14. C

Difficulty: Hard

Category: Additional Topics in Math / Geometry

Strategic Advice: The two most useful geometry properties you can memorize are that the interior angles of a triangle and supplementary angles both sum to 180°.

Getting to the Answer: Remember, vertical angles formed by intersecting lines are congruent. This means the angle with the measure $90 - \frac{b}{2}$ is congruent to the interior angle of the triangle vertical to it. Likewise, the angle with the measure $90 - 3b$ is vertical to the other interior angle of the triangle. To find a in terms of b, set the sum of triangle DEF's angles equal to 180° and solve for a:

$$a + \left(90 - \frac{b}{2}\right) + (90 - 3b) = 180$$

$$a - \frac{b}{2} - 3b = 0$$

$$a = 3b + \frac{b}{2}$$

$$a = \frac{6b}{2} + \frac{b}{2}$$

$$a = \frac{7b}{2}$$

This matches (C).

15. 30

Difficulty: Medium

Category: Additional Topics in Math / Geometry

Strategic Advice: Write the given lengths of the sides as a ratio (shortest to longest), $1.5: \frac{3\sqrt{3}}{2}:3$. Try to manipulate this ratio so that it looks like one you're familiar with.

Getting to the Answer: Clear the fraction by doubling each part of the ratio to get $3:3\sqrt{3}:6$. Notice that each part of the ratio is divisible by 3, so divide a 3 out. The result is $1 : \sqrt{3} : 2$, which should look very familiar by now. The triangle is a 30-60-90 triangle, which means the measure of the smallest angle is 30 degrees.

16. 28
Difficulty: Medium

Category: Additional Topics in Math / Geometry

Strategic Advice: Whenever you see a right triangle with whole number dimensions, you can bet you are probably going to use the Pythagorean theorem.

Getting to the Answer: Use the Pythagorean theorem to find the length of the diagonal shown in the figure.

$$a^2 + b^2 = c^2$$
$$42^2 + 56^2 = c^2$$
$$1{,}764 + 3{,}136 = c^2$$
$$4{,}900 = c^2$$
$$\sqrt{4{,}900} = \sqrt{c^2}$$
$$70 = c$$

The length of the sidewalk is 70 feet. Now, divide by 5 to get $70 \div 5 = 14$, but be careful—this is not the answer. The college plans to put the lights on *both* sides of the sidewalk, so they actually need $14 \times 2 = 28$ lights.

17. 2
Difficulty: Medium

Category: Additional Topics in Math / Geometry

Strategic Advice: The triangle shown is not pretty. Sketch in a line directly down from Z and directly across from X until the two lines meet to form a right triangle. Call this point W.

Getting to the Answer: The area of a triangle can be found using the formula $A = \frac{1}{2}bh$. Let $\overline{XY}$ be the base. It spans 2 squares on the grid, which measure $\frac{1}{2}$ centimeter each, so $\overline{XY} = 1$. Now, the height is $\overline{ZW}$. Count the number of units: there are 8, which means the height of the triangle is 4 units. Substitute these numbers into the area formula and simplify: $A = \frac{1}{2}(1)(4) = 2$ square centimeters.

18. 170
Difficulty: Medium

Category: Additional Topics in Math / Geometry

Strategic Advice: When there doesn't seem to be much information to go on in a question, look for information that might be hidden, such as the presence of a 30-60-90 triangle.

Getting to the Answer: The bearing of 120°, as shown in the figure, means 120° east of north. The bearing extends into the second quadrant. Each quadrant is 90°, which means the angle created by the bearing in the second quadrant is 120° – 90° = 30°. This means the angle inside the triangle is 90° – 30° = 60°. Hence, the triangle is a 30-60-90 triangle, which has side lengths in the ratio $x : x\sqrt{3} : 2x$. You know the longer leg, 295, so divide by $\sqrt{3}$ to find the length of the shorter leg, which represents the distance between Bismarck and Pierre: $295 \div \sqrt{3} = 170.318$, which rounds to 170 miles.

19. 51

Difficulty: Hard

Category: Additional Topics in Math / Geometry

Strategic Advice: You can often use the information you found in the first part of an extended response question to solve the second part.

Getting to the Answer: To find the amount of time the plane was in the air, you'll need to know how far it had flown. In the previous question, you found the length of the shorter side of the triangle, 170 miles. The airplane's path is represented by the hypotenuse of the triangle. To find its length, use the Pythagorean theorem or simply multiply the length of the shorter leg by 2 (because it's a 30-60-90 triangle) to get $170 \times 2 = 340$ miles. Now, use the formula Distance = Rate × Time and solve for time:

$$340 = 400t$$
$$\frac{340}{400} = t$$
$$0.85 = t$$

Be careful—this isn't the answer! The rate was given in miles per hour, so the plane had been in the air 0.85 hours, which is equal to $0.85 \times 60 = 51$ minutes.

20. B

Difficulty: Easy

Category: Additional Topics in Math / Geometry

Strategic Advice: Think about how the sides of the two triangles in the figure are related. If they are all the same length, what kinds of triangles are they? What angles does that type of triangle have?

Getting to the Answer: Because $LM = MN = NL$, triangle LMN is an equilateral triangle. In an equilateral triangle, each of the three interior angles has a measure of 60 degrees. Thus, $c = 60$. Because $NO = OL = LN$, triangle NOL is also an equilateral triangle, and $b = 60$. Therefore, $b - c = 60 - 60 = 0$, which is (B).

21. C

Difficulty: Medium

Category: Additional Topics in Math / Geometry

Strategic Advice: In a triangle, the angle across from the shortest side will have the smallest measure. Use the coordinate grid to figure out which side is the shortest.

Getting to the Answer: Point B has the same x-coordinate as C and the same y-coordinate as A, so its coordinates are (3, 3). The length of AB is 5 and the length of BC is 6, so AB is the shortest side. This means the angle opposite it, which is C, has the smallest measure, making (C) correct.

22. D

Difficulty: Hard

Category: Additional Topics in Math / Geometry

Strategic Advice: Start with what you know about the shaded square. Because its area is 12, each side must be $\sqrt{12} = 2\sqrt{3}$. Jot this down because you'll need it later.

Getting to the Answer: Triangle ABC is an equilateral triangle, so each of its interior angles measures 60 degrees. This means that the two vertical sides of the square each represent the longer leg of a 30-60-90 triangle (the small white triangles on the sides). This leg has a length of $2\sqrt{3}$, making the short legs 2 each. You now have the length of the base of the large equilateral triangle: $2 + 2\sqrt{3} + 2 = 4 + 2\sqrt{3}$. Therefore, each side of the large equilateral triangle has length $4 + 2\sqrt{3}$. The perimeter is the sum of all three sides, so multiply by three to get $12 + 6\sqrt{3}$, making (D) correct.

23. C

Difficulty: Medium

Category: Additional Topics in Math / Geometry

Strategic Advice: Whenever you're given coordinates in a geometry question, start by drawing a quick sketch.

Getting to the Answer: After drawing a sketch, you can see that the triangle is a right triangle. Subtract the coordinates to find the lengths of the legs and use the Pythagorean theorem to find the length of the hypotenuse. To find the length of the horizontal leg, subtract the x-coordinates: $1 - (-6) = 7$. To find the length of the vertical leg, subtract the y-coordinates: $4 - (-2) = 6$. The leg lengths are 6 and 7. Substitute these values into the Pythagorean theorem to find the length of the hypotenuse:

$$a^2 + b^2 = c^2$$
$$6^2 + 7^2 = c^2$$
$$36 + 49 = c^2$$
$$85 = c^2$$
$$\sqrt{85} = \sqrt{c^2}$$
$$\sqrt{85} = c$$

Choice (C) is correct.

CHAPTER 14

PREPARE

1. A

Difficulty: Easy

Category: Additional Topics in Math / Geometry

Strategic Advice: It's easy to misread if you're in a rush. Examine each piece of information (and the answer choices) carefully as you analyze the question. Mark up the diagram to keep congruent sides and congruent angles organized.

Getting to the Answer: You're given two pairs of congruent sides and a pair of congruent angles. Notice that $\angle KJL$ and $\angle NMO$ are contained by two sets of congruent sides. This indicates that the triangles are congruent by SAS, which is (A).

2. D

Difficulty: Medium

Category: Additional Topics in Math / Geometry

Strategic Advice: Knowing that $\overline{ST}$ is a mid-segment provides information vital to finding the answer. Think about how it relates to the rest of the triangle.

Getting to the Answer: The length of a triangle's mid-segment is always half that of the side to which it is parallel. Therefore, $ST = \frac{1}{2}PR$. Plug in the correct expression for each segment length and solve:

$$4x + 9 = \frac{1}{2}(16x + 6)$$
$$4x + 9 = 8x + 3$$
$$-4x = -6$$
$$x = \frac{3}{2}$$

The question asks for the length of $\overline{PR}$, so you're not done yet. Substituting $\frac{3}{2}$ for x yields $16 \times \frac{3}{2} + 6 = 30$, making (D) correct. You can also use the proportion $\frac{4x+9}{16x+6} = \frac{1}{2}$ to solve for x and then the requested length.

3. C

Difficulty: Medium

Category: Additional Topics in Math / Geometry

Strategic Advice: Remember the rules that govern similar triangles; eliminate answers that violate them.

Getting to the Answer: Similar triangles have congruent (not proportional) angles, so eliminate A. The question does not state anything about how the sides of one triangle relate to each other, so you cannot conclude that the ratio $GN : RN$ is 2:3. Eliminate D. Picking side lengths for the triangles will help eliminate the final incorrect answer: If $\triangle GRN$ has sides of 2, then its perimeter is $2 + 2 + 2 = 6$. $\triangle YLW$ would have sides of 3 and a perimeter of $3 + 3 + 3 = 9$. The ratio of the perimeters is 6:9, which simplifies to 2:3. (C) is therefore correct.

If you're uncertain, pick dimensions to find the area. If $\triangle GRN$ and $\triangle YLW$ are isosceles right triangles with legs measuring 2 and 3, respectively, the corresponding areas are $\frac{1}{2} \times 2 \times 2 = 2$ and $\frac{1}{2} \times 3 \times 3 = 4.5$. This does not match the given 2:3 ratio, so D cannot be correct.

4. B

Difficulty: Medium

Category: Additional Topics in Math / Geometry

Strategic Advice: Identify the corresponding congruent pieces of the two triangles. Then use your knowledge of triangle congruence theorems to determine what additional pieces can be used to prove the triangles are congruent.

Getting to the Answer: The two triangles have two pairs of corresponding congruent angles. Assuming you confirm the proper corresponding sides are congruent, you can conclude that the triangles are congruent by ASA or AAS. However, you cannot conclude the same by confirming the remaining corresponding angle pair is congruent; remember that this only confirms that the triangles are similar. Choice (B) is therefore correct.

PRACTICE

5. 426
Difficulty: Medium

Category: Additional Topics in Math / Geometry

Strategic Advice: The figure contains a pair of similar triangles. Use the ratio within them to determine the requested length.

Getting to the Answer: The shadow cast by the flagpole is 50% longer than the flagpole itself; that is, $1.5 \times 40 = 60$ ft. Use this in conjunction with the lengths provided to determine the distance from the building to the end of the flagpole's shadow.

$$\frac{40}{324} = \frac{60}{x}$$
$$\frac{10}{81} = \frac{60}{x}$$
$$10x = 4,860$$
$$x = 486$$

Subtract the length of the flagpole's shadow from 486 to obtain 426, the distance from the building to the flagpole. Grid in 426.

PERFORM

6. D
Difficulty: Easy

Category: Additional Topics in Math / Geometry

Strategic Advice: Choice D implies that there could be more than one way to prove the triangles are congruent. Test each statement instead of merely selecting the first one that works.

Getting to the Answer: Start with choice A: $\overline{BC}$ and $\overline{YZ}$ are two corresponding legs. Combined with the information in the question stem, if these are congruent, then $\triangle ABC$ and $\triangle XYZ$ would be congruent by HL. Move to choice B: If $\angle BAC \cong \angle YXZ$, then $\triangle ABC$ and $\triangle XYZ$ must be congruent by AAS. Because both choices would prove the two triangles are congruent, (D) must be the correct answer. (If you're curious about choice C: $\overline{AB}$ and $\overline{XY}$ make up the other pair of corresponding legs. If congruent, then $\triangle ABC$ and $\triangle XYZ$ would be congruent by HL.)

7. C
Difficulty: Medium

Category: Additional Topics in Math / Geometry

Strategic Advice: You're told lines j and k are parallel; think about what that means about the other two lines.

Getting to the Answer: Because lines j and k are parallel, the two other lines are transversals that create several special angle pairs. $\angle WVX$ and $\angle YZX$ are alternate interior angles and therefore congruent; the same is true of $\angle VWX$ and $\angle ZYX$. $\angle VXW$ and $\angle ZXY$ are vertical angles, so they are congruent. This means that $\triangle VWX$ and $\triangle ZYX$ share three pairs of corresponding congruent angles; consequently, you can conclude that the triangles are similar. However, no information on the lengths of either triangle's sides is given, so you cannot conclude that the triangles are congruent. There is also no evidence to support that $\overline{VZ}$ and $\overline{WY}$ are parallel or perpendicular. (C) is therefore correct.

EXTRA PRACTICE

1. B

Difficulty: Easy

Category: Additional Topics in Math / Geometry

Strategic Advice: When answering triangle congruence questions that involve a diagram, mark up the diagram so you can visualize how the parts of the triangles are related.

Getting to the Answer: Because $\overline{HA} \cong \overline{SU}$, draw a single tick mark on each of those sides to show that they are congruent to one another. Do the same for $\overline{HT} \cong \overline{SN}$ using two tick marks. Mark angles *H* and *S* in a similar fashion. Your sketch might look like this:

You can see that you have two pairs of congruent sides and their included angle. The SAS, or Side Angle Side, theorem states that these triangles must be congruent, making (B) correct.

2. C

Difficulty: Easy

Category: Additional Topics in Math / Geometry

Strategic Advice: Take a quick peek at the answers. All of them deal with congruence, so look at the figure to determine which parts of the two triangles are congruent. Marking up the diagram is an excellent habit to get into.

Getting to the Answer: The question tells you that $\overline{MO} \perp \overline{LN}$, so $\angle LOM \cong \angle NOM$ because both angles must be 90°; eliminate choice A. The question also states that $\overline{MO}$ bisects $\overline{LN}$, which means by definition that $\overline{LO} \cong \overline{ON}$, so eliminate B as well. Side $\overline{MO}$ is shared between the two triangles and is equal to itself by the Reflexive Property. However, it cannot

be congruent to side $\overline{MN}$ because the hypotenuse of a right triangle is always longer than both legs. This means (C) is correct (because it cannot be proven). Don't waste valuable time checking D unless you're not sure of your answer. ($\triangle LMO \cong \triangle NMO$ can be proven using SAS.)

3. C

Difficulty: Easy

Category: Additional Topics in Math / Geometry

Strategic Advice: Corresponding parts of congruent triangles are congruent. The order of the letters in the congruence statements tells you which parts of the triangles are corresponding parts.

Getting to the Answer: Because triangle *DOG* is congruent to *CAT* and *CAT* is congruent to *HEN*, then *DOG* must also be congruent to *HEN* by the Transitive Property of Equality. This means the corresponding parts of any of these three triangles are congruent. The corresponding part to $\overline{OG}$ of triangle *CAT* is $\overline{AT}$, and the corresponding part of triangle *HEN* is $\overline{EN}$. Only $\overline{EN}$ is listed as an answer choice, so (C) is correct.

4. A

Difficulty: Easy

Category: Additional Topics in Math / Geometry

Strategic Advice: The ASA, or Angle Side Angle, theorem states that when two angles and their included side of two triangles are congruent, then the triangles are congruent. Mark the figure so you can see which sides and which angles are congruent to each other.

Getting to the Answer: Your diagram should now look like this:

Now, be careful—more than one answer choice might prove that the triangles are congruent, but you are specifically looking for the piece of information that proves congruence using ASA, so you are looking for the *other angle* that makes the side *the included side* given in each triangle, which are angles *B* and *E*. This means (A) is correct.

5. B
Difficulty: Medium

Category: Additional Topics in Math / Geometry

Strategic Advice: Mark up the figure to show which sides and which angles are congruent. Remember, corresponding parts of congruent triangles are congruent. Use the order of the letters in the congruence statement to help you determine which sides and which angles are corresponding parts.

Getting to the Answer:

Now compare your sketch to the answer choices. The only one that is not necessarily true is $\overline{VX} \cong \overline{XZ}$, making (B) correct.

6. D
Difficulty: Medium

Category: Additional Topics in Math / Geometry

Strategic Advice: You might recognize the Pythagorean triplet 8, 15, and 17, which tells you that triangle *COT* is a right triangle. But be careful—all right triangles are not necessarily similar to each other, so you are not simply looking for another Pythagorean triplet.

Getting to the Answer: Corresponding sides of similar triangles are proportional. This is the same as saying the larger triangle is a scaled-up version of the smaller triangle. So, you're looking for the same ratio of sides (8:15:17), multiplied by a scale factor. This means (D) is correct because each side length of *COT* has been scaled up by a factor of 3.

7. D
Difficulty: Medium

Category: Additional Topics in Math / Geometry

Strategic Advice: Corresponding sides of similar triangles are proportional, and corresponding angles are congruent.

Getting to the Answer: You can eliminate B immediately because corresponding angles of similar triangles are congruent, so they are in a 1:1 ratio. You can also eliminate A, because $\overline{OD}$ would be proportional to $\overline{NW}$, not $\overline{EW}$. Evaluating C might get complicated, so skip it for now. Because the side lengths of the two triangles are proportional, when you find the sum of the side lengths (the perimeter), this number will be in the same proportion. You can check this by assigning numbers that are in the ratio 7:4 and finding the perimeter of each triangle:

$$OL = 7 \text{ and } NE = 4$$

$$LD = 14 \text{ and } EW = 8$$

$$OD = 21 \text{ and } NW = 12$$

Perimeter of triangle $OLD = 7 + 14 + 21 = 42$

Perimeter of triangle $NEW = 4 + 8 + 12 = 24$

$$42{:}24 = 7{:}4$$

This means (D) is correct.

8. B
Difficulty: Medium

Category: Additional Topics in Math / Geometry

Strategic Advice: With questions like this, always think about the information given and what that information must *mean* for the rest of the figure. You are told that $\overline{HI}$ is the bisector of $\overline{LO}$ and $\overline{OW}$.

This tells you two things: 1) The definition of *bisector* tells you that that $\overline{HI}$ divides both $\overline{LO}$ and $\overline{OW}$ exactly in half, and 2) a straight line connecting the midpoints of two sides of a triangle is parallel to the third side, so $\overline{HI}$ is parallel to $\overline{LW}$.

Getting to the Answer: Because $\overline{HI}$ is parallel to $\overline{LW}$, angles L and H must be congruent (they are corresponding angles), and angles W and I must be congruent (they are also corresponding angles). Angle O is shared by both triangles and is equal to itself by the Reflexive Property. This means the side lengths of the two triangles are different, but the corresponding angles are the same, so the triangles are similar. Side lengths of similar triangles are in proportion to one another. You are given the side lengths of $\overline{LW}$ and $\overline{HI}$. Because I is the midpoint of $\overline{OW}$, $\overline{OI}$ is half as long as $\overline{OW}$. The same is true for the other side. So the sides are in the ratio 1:2. Use this ratio to set up a proportion and solve for x:

$$\frac{1}{2} = \frac{4x - 1}{30}$$
$$30 = 2(4x - 1)$$
$$30 = 8x - 2$$
$$32 = 8x$$
$$4 = x$$

The correct answer is (B).

9. A

Difficulty: Medium

Category: Additional Topics in Math / Geometry

Strategic Advice: Just like triangles, corresponding sides of similar quadrilaterals are proportional. This means the perimeters of similar quadrilaterals are also proportional and in the same proportion as each pair of corresponding side lengths.

Getting to the Answer: Find the perimeter of rectangle *LION* and compare it to the perimeter of *PUMA*. *LION* has a perimeter of $86 + 86 + 52 + 52 = 276$.

Therefore, the ratio of the perimeter of *LION* to the perimeter of *PUMA* is 276:69, which reduces to 4:1. This tells you that the width of *LION* is 4 times greater than the width of *PUMA*, which means *PUMA*'s width is $52 \div 4 = 13$, making (A) correct.

10. D

Difficulty: Medium

Category: Additional Topics in Math / Geometry

Strategic Advice: Not all right triangles are similar—the corresponding sides must be in the same proportions. Three of the triangles are similar and one is not. You are looking for the one that is *not* similar.

Getting to the Answer: All four triangles are right triangles, so you can't immediately eliminate any of the choices. Because they are all right triangles, try simplifying the side lengths of the smallest one to look for a Pythagorean triplet. Then see if you can identify scaled-up versions of that one. The second triangle is the smallest with side lengths of 10, 24, and 26. If you divide each of these lengths by 2, you get the common Pythagorean triplet 5, 12, 13. Notice that if you triple these numbers, you get the first triangle; likewise, if you quadruple the numbers, you get the third triangle. The last triangle with side lengths of 24, 32, and 40 is *not* a scaled-up version of a 5, 12, 13 triangle, so it is the one that is not similar. Now, find its area. Remember the area of a triangle is $A = \frac{1}{2}bh$, and in right triangles, the base and height are the leg lengths.

$$A = \frac{1}{2}(24)(32)$$
$$A = \frac{1}{2}(768)$$
$$A = 384$$

This means (D) is correct.

11. A

Difficulty: Easy

Category: Additional Topics in Math / Geometry

Strategic Advice: Congruent triangles have angle measures that are congruent *and* side lengths that are congruent.

Getting to the Answer: The information that Brigitte has, $\angle A \cong \angle X$ and $\angle C \cong \angle Z$, tells you that two of the three pairs of corresponding angles are congruent. The key to answering this question is the fact that the third pair of angles is also congruent is only enough information to prove *similarity*. You must know that at least one pair of corresponding sides is congruent. This means (A) is correct and you don't even need to examine the other choices.

12. A

Difficulty: Medium

Category: Additional Topics in Math / Geometry

Strategic Advice: With questions like this, always think about how the information given applies to the rest of the figure. Mark up the figure as you think through it.

Getting to the Answer: Because AD and BE are perpendicular and intersect at C, they create right angles, so $m\angle BCA = 90°$ and $m\angle ECD = 90°$, which means these two angles are congruent. Because AB is parallel to DE, and these are intersected by AD, the alternate interior angles are congruent, which means $\angle BAC \cong \angle EDC$. The same is true for angles ABC and DEC because BE intersects the two parallel lines as well. This means that all three pairs of corresponding angles have equal measures, so the triangles are similar by the AAA theorem, which is (A).

13. C

Difficulty: Medium

Category: Additional Topics in Math / Geometry

Strategic Advice: Start by marking up the figure with what you know.

Getting to the Answer: Because *SQAE* is a square, you know each of the four sides are congruent to one another. Because points *U* and *R* are midpoints of their respective sides, *QU*, *UA*, *ER*, and *RA* must all be congruent to one another. Finally, because *D* is the midpoint of *RU*, the lengths of *RD* and *DU* must be congruent. All four corners of the square, by definition, are 90°. Angle *D* of both *RSD* and *USD* are shown to be right angles as well. Now, compare the answer choices to what you know. Triangles *RSD* and *USD* must be congruent by the SAS theorem. So you can't eliminate A yet. But you can eliminate B because there is no evidence to prove that triangles *RSD* and *USD* are congruent to triangles *ESR* and *QSU*. Now look at C. Triangles *ESR* and *QSU* must be congruent by the SAS theorem, and you've already determined that *RSD* and *USD* are congruent, so you can't eliminate this choice. However, you can now eliminate A, because more than just *RSD* and *USD* are congruent. Finally, check D. Triangle *AUR* has two legs with equal lengths. This is not true of *ESR* and *QSU* (which have one leg that is half the length of the other leg), which means D is false and (C) is therefore correct.

14. D

Difficulty: Medium

Category: Additional Topics in Math / Geometry

Strategic Advice: Although the focus of this question is congruence, you'll need to rely on your knowledge of circles as well.

Getting to the Answer: Because each cut is made from the center, each side of Slice 1 and Slice 2 is a radius of the circle, and all radii of a circle are congruent. Therefore, both pairs of corresponding sides are congruent. The arc lengths (edges of the crust) are also congruent, which means the central angle that subtends these arcs must be congruent. Now think SAS—the two slices must be congruent, making (D) correct.

15. B

Difficulty: Hard

Category: Additional Topics in Math / Geometry

Strategic Advice: There are two triangles in this fig-ure, *ACE* and *BCD*. Because $\overline{BD}$ is parallel to $\overline{AE}$, angles *A* and *B* must be congruent (they are corresponding angles), and angles *D* and *E* must be congruent (they are also corresponding angles). Angle *C* is shared by both triangles and is equal to itself by the Reflexive Property. This means the side lengths of the two triangles are different, but the angles are the same, so the triangles are similar by AAA. Side lengths of similar triangles are in proportion to one another.

Getting to the Answer: You know the two triangles are similar, so set up a proportion using their side lengths. You'll need to translate from English into math as you go: $AB = 5$ and *BC* is three times that or 15. This means $AC = 5 + 15 = 20$. *CD* is 2 more than half *AC* or $20 \div 2 = 10 + 2 = 12$. Now you know three side lengths, so you can set up and solve a proportion:

$$\frac{BC}{AC} = \frac{DC}{EC}$$
$$\frac{15}{20} = \frac{12}{EC}$$
$$15EC = 240$$
$$EC = 16$$

This is the length of side *EC*, but the question asks for the length of segment *DE*, which is $EC - CD$, or $16 - 12 = 4$. This makes (B) the correct choice.

16. 75

Difficulty: Easy

Category: Additional Topics in Math / Geometry

Strategic Advice: Corresponding angles of similar triangles are congruent. The sum of the measures of the internal angles of a triangle is 180 degrees.

Getting to the Answer: Because triangle *TIM* is similar to triangle *JOE*, $m\angle T = m\angle J$, $m\angle I = m\angle O$,

and $m\angle M = m\angle E$. This means that if you find the measure of angle *M*, then you'll have your answer. The measure of angle *M* is $180 - 40 - 65 = 75$ degrees, which means the measure of angle *E* is also 75 degrees.

17. 35

Difficulty: Hard

Category: Additional Topics in Math / Geometry

Strategic Advice: Start by determining whether there is a relationship between triangles *ABC* and *EDC*.

Getting to the Answer: The two triangles share a common angle, *C*. It is given that $\overline{DE} \perp \overline{AC}$, so angle *DEC* is a right angle. Because $\overline{DE} \parallel \overline{AB}$, $\overline{BA}$ is also per-pendicular to $\overline{AC}$, making angle *BAC* another right angle. Finally, because $\overline{AB}$ and $\overline{DE}$ are parallel lines intersected by a transversal (side *BC*), angles *ABD* and *EDC* are also congruent. This means the two triangles are similar by AAA. Now, start with what you know and find what you can. The length of *AE* is 28, which means the length of *AC* is $28 + 4 = 32$. The length of *EC* is 4, which means that the side lengths of triangle *ABC* are 8 times the side lengths of triangle *EDC*. Now use this to find *DE*: $24 \div 8 = 3$. You might now recognize the Pythagorean triplet 3-4-5, but you could also use the Pythagorean theorem to find that $DC = 5$. Multiply this by 8 to find *BC*: $5 \times 8 = 40$. Be careful—this isn't the answer. The ques-tion asks for the length of *BD*, which is $40 - 5 = 35$.

18. 9

Difficulty: Hard

Category: Additional Topics in Math / Geometry

Strategic Advice: Corresponding sides of similar triangles are proportional. Draw a quick sketch to find as many side lengths as you can, find the ratio of the sides between the two triangles, and use that ratio to find the missing vertex.

Getting to the Answer: Plot all the points given in the question, labeling them as you go so you don't get confused (especially because you won't have graph paper). You know that *A* and *B* are in the same quadrant, which means the triangles are both oriented the same way. So make your sketch accordingly.

Once you have plotted *ANT* and the base of *BUG*, you can determine that the ratio of the triangles is 1:4 (the base of *ANT* has a length of 4 and the base of *BUG* has a length of 16). To determine where you should put *B*, find the length of side *AN* and then multiply by 4. The length of the vertical side of *BUG* is 12. Because one vertex is at (8, –3), vertex *B* must be 12 vertical units above that point, or (8, 9). The *y*-coordinate of *B* is 9.

CHAPTER 15

PREPARE

1. B
Difficulty: Easy

Category: Additional Topics in Math / Geometry

Strategic Advice: Draw a diagram to visualize the situation.

Getting to the Answer: A cross section of the orange sitting on the counter is shown; you'll notice the orange is tangent to the counter and that a right triangle is present.

Plug the values from your diagram into the Pythagorean theorem: $1^2 + x^2 = 10^2$. Solving for x yields $x = \sqrt{99} = \sqrt{9 \times 11} = 3\sqrt{11}$, which makes (B) correct.

2. A
Difficulty: Easy

Category: Additional Topics in Math / Geometry

Strategic Advice: You need a solution for the entire system of equations, so look for points at which the graphs of *all three* equations intersect.

Getting to the Answer: There are seven points of intersection in the *xy*-plane shown, but none of them is an intersection of all three graphs. Therefore, this system of equations has 0 solutions, which makes (A) correct.

3. D
Difficulty: Hard

Category: Additional Topics in Math / Geometry

Strategic Advice: Draw additional lines (such as those that create hidden triangles) in the figure to glean more information.

Getting to the Answer: Draw in a radius from the center of the circle (on the diameter of the semicircle) to $\overline{YZ}$ and a line that represents the greatest distance between $\overline{YZ}$ and $\overline{WX}$ to form a right triangle.

Because YZ is 25% less than WX, $YZ = \dfrac{3}{4}WX$. In addition, $\dfrac{1}{2}WX = r$; therefore, $\dfrac{1}{2}YZ = \dfrac{3}{4}r$. Plug the known quantities into the Pythagorean theorem and solve for x:

$$\left(\frac{3}{4}r\right)^2 + x^2 = r^2$$

$$\frac{9}{16}r^2 + x^2 = r^2$$

$$x^2 = \frac{7}{16}r^2$$

$$x = \pm\frac{\sqrt{7}}{4}r$$

(D) is the correct answer.

4. 7
Difficulty: Hard

Category: Additional Topics in Math / Geometry

Strategic Advice: Rewrite the given equation for the circle in standard form to get what you need to answer the question (the coordinates of the center).

Getting to the Answer: Start by completing the square for each of the variables. You'll need to add $+9$ for x and $+16$ for y. Rewrite as two separate squares of binomials. Here are the steps:

$$(x-h)^2 + (y-k)^2 = r^2$$

$$x^2 + 6x + y^2 - 8y = 171$$

$$x : b = 6 \rightarrow 3 \rightarrow 9$$

$$y : b = -8 \rightarrow -4 \rightarrow 16$$

$$x^2 + 6x + 9 + y^2 - 8y + 16 = 171 + 9 + 16$$

$$(x+3)^2 + (y-4)^2 = 196$$

The coordinates of the center of the circle are $(-3, 4)$. The positive difference (and correct answer) is $4 - (-3) = 7$.

PRACTICE

5. B
Difficulty: Medium

Category: Additional Topics in Math / Geometry

Strategic Advice: Use your subtended arcs and hidden shapes expertise to uncover a useful triangle.

Getting to the Answer: Start by drawing in $\overline{PR}$ and $\overline{PS}$ as shown here.

Because the angle formed by $\overline{PR}$ and $\overline{PS}$ subtends the same arc as the angle formed by $\overline{QR}$ and $\overline{QS}$, $\angle RPS$ must be twice $\angle RQS$, which is $45° \times 2 = 90°$. In addition to being legs of $\triangle PRS$, $\overline{PR}$ and $\overline{PS}$ are radii, so they are congruent, which makes $\triangle PRS$ a 45-45-90 triangle. Therefore, the radius of circle P is $\dfrac{4}{\sqrt{2}} = 2\sqrt{2}$, and the circumference is $2\pi \times 2\sqrt{2} = 4\pi\sqrt{2}$, which makes (B) correct.

PERFORM

6. C
Difficulty: Medium

Category: Additional Topics in Math / Geometry

Strategic Advice: Use your knowledge of circle equations to quickly arrive at the answer.

Getting to the Answer: According to the equation, the center of the circle is $(3, -4)$; any line that contains a diameter of the circle must pass through this point. The lines with equations $x = 3$ and $y = -4$ pass through this point, so you can eliminate B and D. Plug the coordinates of the center of the circle into the remaining choices:

Choice A:

$$-4 = \frac{4}{3} \times 3 - 8$$

$$-4 = 4 - 8$$

$$-4 = -4$$

Choice (C):

$$-4 = 3 \times 3 - 5$$

$$-4 = 9 - 5$$

$$-4 \neq 4$$

(C) contains the only equation that does not pass through the center of the circle, so it is the correct answer.

7. B

Difficulty: Medium

Category: Additional Topics in Math / Geometry

Strategic Advice: Read carefully; you're asked for information on the portion that is *not* strawberry rhubarb.

Getting to the Answer: The diagram includes the measures of central angles, and you're told that the pie tin has a diameter of 10 inches (which means the radius is 5 inches and the area is 25π square inches). Therefore, you can set up a proportion to determine the area of non–strawberry rhubarb pie:

$$\frac{\text{central angle}}{360°} = \frac{\text{sector area}}{\text{circle area}}$$

$$\frac{360 - 129.6}{360} = \frac{x}{25\pi}$$

$$5{,}760\pi = 360\pi$$

$$x = 16\pi$$

The portion of leftover pie that is not strawberry rhubarb is 16π square inches, which makes (B) correct.

EXTRA PRACTICE

1. D
Difficulty: Easy

Category: Additional Topics in Math / Geometry

Strategic Advice: Whenever you're given a ratio, you can set up an equation. Sometimes the equation takes the form of a proportion, and sometimes it takes the form of "sum of the parts equals the whole." In this question, the *whole* is the total number of degrees in a circle, which is 360.

Getting to the Answer: You know the relative size of each of the parts in this question. You don't know the exact size of one part, so call it *x*. Now, set up an equation:

$$4x + 3x + 2x = 360$$
$$9x = 360$$
$$x = 40$$

Beware the trap answer! The question doesn't ask for the value of *x* but rather for the measure of the smallest angle, which is represented by 2*x*. The correct answer is 2(40) = 80, which is (D).

2. D
Difficulty: Easy

Category: Additional Topics in Math / Geometry

Strategic Advice: Use the relationship $\frac{\text{arc length}}{\text{circumference}} = \frac{\text{central angle}}{360°}$ to answer this question. To help you remember this relationship, just think $\frac{\text{partial distance}}{\text{whole distance}} = \frac{\text{partial angle}}{\text{whole angle}}$.

Getting to the Answer: The unknown in this question is the arc length, so call it *l*. You need to find the circumference of the circle before you set up the relationship. The question tells you that the radius is 12 inches, so use the formula $C = 2\pi r$ to

find that the circumference is $2\pi(12) = 24\pi$. You also know that the central angle has a measure of 135 degrees, so you're ready to set up and solve the relationship:

$$\frac{\text{arc length}}{\text{circumference}} = \frac{\text{central angle}}{360°}$$
$$\frac{l}{24\pi} = \frac{135}{360}$$
$$360l = 3,240\pi$$
$$l = \frac{3,240}{360}\pi$$
$$l = 9\pi$$

The answer choices are not given in terms of π, so multiply 9 times π to arrive at 28.2743, or about 28 inches, which makes (D) the correct answer.

3. B
Difficulty: Easy

Category: Additional Topics in Math / Geometry

Strategic Advice: Look carefully at triangle *PQR*. It is a right triangle that has two congruent legs (because each leg is a radius of the circle), which means it is a 45-45-90 triangle.

Getting to the Answer: Recall (or check the formula page at the beginning of the test) that the sides of a 45-45-90 right triangle are always in the ratio $s:s:s\sqrt{2}$. Each leg of the triangle is a radius of the circle, which is given as 4. Side *PQ* is the hypotenuse of the triangle, so it must have length $4\sqrt{2}$, which is (B).

4. D
Difficulty: Easy

Category: Additional Topics in Math / Geometry

Strategic Advice: If you're not sure how to start a question with a circle in it, look for the radius. The equation of circle takes the form $(x - h)^2 + (y - k)^2 =$

r^2, where (h, k) is the center of the circle and r is the length of the radius.

Getting to the Answer: To find the equation of a circle, you need the radius and the x- and y-coordinates of the center point. Look at the figure—the center has coordinates $(-1, 2)$. From the center, you can count horizontally or vertical to circle to find that its radius is 6. This means the equation is $(x - (-1))^2 + (y - 2)^2 = 6^2$, or $(x + 1)^2 + (y - 2)^2 = 36$, which matches the equation in (D).

5. A
Difficulty: Medium

Category: Additional Topics in Math / Geometry

Strategic Advice: Use the relationship $\dfrac{\text{area of sector}}{\text{area of circle}} = \dfrac{\text{central angle}}{360°}$ to answer this question. To help remember this relationship, just think $\dfrac{\text{partial area}}{\text{whole area}} = \dfrac{\text{partial angle}}{\text{whole angle}}$.

Getting to the Answer: The unknown in this question is the radius, which you can find by first finding the area of the whole circle and then by using the equation for area of a circle $A = \pi r^2$. You have everything you need to find the area of the circle:

$$\frac{\text{area of sector}}{\text{area of circle}} = \frac{\text{central angle}}{360°}$$
$$\frac{14\pi}{A} = \frac{140}{360}$$
$$5{,}040\pi = 140A$$
$$36\pi = A$$

Now, solve for r using $A = \pi r^2$:

$$36\pi = \pi r^2$$
$$36 = r^2$$
$$\pm 6 = r$$

The radius can't be negative, so the correct answer is 6, which is (A).

6. C
Difficulty: Medium

Category: Additional Topics in Math / Geometry

Strategic Advice: This question is like a puzzle. You'll need to work through it step-by-step, using properties of circles and quadrilaterals.

Getting to the Answer: Angle QPC is one angle of a quadrilateral, so you can subtract the measures of the other three angles from 360° to answer the question. However, you're only given one of those angles, so you'll have to use properties of circles to find the other two. Angle PQR is an inscribed angle that intercepts the same arc ($\overset{\frown}{PR}$) as the 160° central angle, which means the measure of $\angle PQR$ is half that, or 80°. The obtuse angle in the quadrilateral at the center completes a full circle with the 160° central angle, so its measure is $360° - 160° = 200°$. Now you have all the angles you need:

$$m\angle QPR = 360° - (200 + 45 + 80)°$$
$$= 360° - 325°$$
$$= 35°$$

This means (C) is correct.

7. A
Difficulty: Medium

Category: Additional Topics in Math / Geometry

Strategic Advice: Distance around *part* of a circle is the same as arc length, so use the relationship $\dfrac{\text{arc length}}{\text{circumference}} = \dfrac{\text{central angle}}{360°}$ to answer the question.

Getting to the Answer: The unknown in the relationship is the central angle, so call it a. Before you can fill in the rest of the equation, you need to find the circumference of the circle: $C = 2\pi r = 2\pi(120) = 240\pi$. Now you're ready to solve for a:

$$\frac{\text{arc length}}{\text{circumference}}=\frac{\text{central angle}}{360°}$$

$$\frac{200}{240\pi}=\frac{a}{360}$$

$$\frac{200\times360}{240\pi}=a$$

$$95.5\approx a$$

Be careful when you enter this expression into your calculator—you need to put 240π in parentheses so that the calculator doesn't divide by 240 and then multiply by π. If entered correctly, the result is about 95.5 degrees, which matches (A).

8. C

Difficulty: Medium

Category: Additional Topics in Math / Geometry

Strategic Advice: The key to solving a question like this is in thinking logically before diving into the math calculations.

Getting to the Answer: An analog clock has 12 hours marked off, each of which has 5 tick marks representing minutes, for a total of $12\times5=60$ tick marks. There are 360° in a circle, so each tick mark represents $360\div60=6°$. At 2:15, the hands of the clock are 4 tick marks apart $(15-11)$, so the angle between them is $4\times6=24°$, which is (C).

9. C

Difficulty: Medium

Category: Additional Topics in Math / Geometry

Strategic Advice: The sections of a pie graph represent the percent of the data that fits in a given category. To determine the angles for the sections, you need to find the corresponding percent of the degrees in the circle.

Getting to the Answer: Start by finding the percent of the data that each age group represents. The total number of people who attended the waterpark was $880+560+120+40=1,600$. To find the percent

represented by each age group, divide the number in that age group by 1,600:

Under 16: $\frac{880}{1,600}=0.55$; *16–35*: $\frac{560}{1,600}=0.35$;

36–55: $\frac{120}{1,600}=0.075$; *Over 55*: $\frac{40}{1,600}=0.025$

Now, multiply each percent by the number of degrees in a circle (360):

Under 16: $0.55\times360=198$; *16–35*: $0.35\times360=126$;

36–55: $0.075\times360=27$; *Over 55*: $0.025\times360=9$

The correct angle measures are 9°, 27°, 126°, and 198°, which matches (C).

10. B

Difficulty: Medium

Category: Additional Topics in Math / Geometry

Strategic Advice: You would not be expected to algebraically solve four systems of equations on Test Day for one question—there simply isn't enough time. This means there must be another way to answer this question. Think graphing!

Getting to the Answer: Take a peek at the answer choices—each one contains a line that is already written in slope-intercept form and a circle that has its center at the origin. Drawing a quick sketch will get you to the answer much quicker than trying to solve the systems algebraically. If the line and the circle don't intersect, then the system has no solution.

Choice A: Choice (B):

Eliminate A.   No solution

There is no need to go any further; choice (B) is correct because the graphs do not intersect.

11. D

Difficulty: Hard

Category: Additional Topics in Math / Geometry

Strategic Advice: To find the equation of a circle, you need the radius and the x- and y-coordinates of the center point. Then, you can use the standard equation: $(x - h)^2 + (y - k)^2 = r^2$, where (h, k) is the center of the circle and r is the length of the radius.

Getting to the Answer: Be careful—choice B is a trap! Sometimes finding the center and the radius from a graph is not as straightforward as you may think. This graph has no number labels on it, so you'll need to use the information given in the question about the smaller circle to determine the value of each grid line:

$$A = \pi r^2$$
$$144\pi = \pi r^2$$
$$144 = r^2$$
$$\pm 12 = r$$

The radius can't be negative, so it must be 12. There are only 3 grid lines between the center of the smaller circle and its edge, so each grid line must be equal to 4 units. This means the center of the larger circle is $(-8, 0)$ and its radius is $6 \times 4 = 24$. Therefore, the equation is $(x - (-8))^2 + (y - 0)^2 = 24^2$, or when simplified, $(x + 8)^2 + y^2 = 576$, making (D) the correct answer.

12. C

Difficulty: Hard

Category: Additional Topics in Math / Geometry

Strategic Advice: In this question, you're given a part-to-part ratio (shaded:unshaded) that you need to convert into a part-to-whole ratio (shaded:whole circle). Remember that the ratio between the interior angle of a sector and 360° is the same as the ratio

between the area of that sector and the area of the whole circle.

Getting to the Answer: Because the ratio of the shaded area to the unshaded area is 4:5, the ratio of the shaded area to the entire circle is $4:(4 + 5) = 4:9$. This ratio is the same as the ratio of the interior angle of the shaded sector to 360°, or x:360. Set up a proportion using these ratios:

$$\frac{4}{9} = \frac{x}{360}$$
$$360(4) = 9x$$
$$1{,}440 = 9x$$
$$160 = x$$

Choice (C) is correct.

13. D

Difficulty: Hard

Category: Additional Topics in Math / Geometry

Strategic Advice: Don't answer this question too quickly—the shaded portion is *not* the same as the sector because the triangular part at the center is not shaded. However, you'll need to find the area of the sector, and then *subtract* the area of the triangle.

Getting to the Answer: To find the area of the sector, you'll need the area of the whole circle: $A = \pi r^2 = \pi(4)^2 = 16\pi$. Now use the formula:

$$\frac{\text{area of sector}}{\text{area of circle}} = \frac{\text{central angle}}{360°}$$
$$\frac{A_{sector}}{16\pi} = \frac{120}{360}$$
$$A_{sector} = \frac{120 \times 16\pi}{360}$$
$$A_{sector} = \frac{16\pi}{3}$$

Time-saving tip: You could actually determine the answer right now—it's (D). The first term in each expression has a π in it, which means it must represent the area of the sector. The second term does not, so it must represent the area of the triangle. Choice (D) is the only one that correctly gives the area of the sector.

In case you really want to know . . . To find the area of the triangle, notice that triangle *PQR* is formed by two radii and a chord. The height of the triangle represents the shorter leg of each of the smaller triangles inside *PQR*. The small triangles are congruent, and because ∠*PQR* has a measure of 120°, each of the small triangles is a 30-60-90 triangle. The radius of the circle, which is the hypotenuse of each small triangle, is 4, so the shorter leg (the height) is half that (2), and the longer leg (half the base of *PQR*) is $2\sqrt{3}$, making the base of *PQR* $4\sqrt{3}$. The area of triangle *PQR* is $\frac{1}{\cancel{2}}\left(4\sqrt{3}\right)\left(\cancel{2}\right)=4\sqrt{3}$.

14. D
Difficulty: Medium

Category: Additional Topics in Math / Geometry

Strategic Advice: You'll need to think logically to answer this question. It doesn't really matter that Quito lies on the equator. Because Earth makes a complete rotation about its axis in 24 hours, any point on its surface must rotate through 360 degrees in that time.

Getting to the Answer: Quito rotates 360 degrees in the 24 hours from noon on January 1 to noon on January 2. There are 3 hours between noon on January 2 and 3:00 PM on January 2, so it rotates an additional $\frac{3}{24}\times360=45$ degrees, for a total of 360 + 45 = 405 degrees, which matches (D).

15. B
Difficulty: Hard

Category: Additional Topics in Math / Geometry

Strategic Advice: When the equation of a circle is in the form $(x-h)^2+(y-k)^2=r^2$, the *r* represents the length of the radius. To get the equation into this form, complete the square. Then you can double *r* to find the diameter.

Getting to the Answer: You already have an x^2 and a y^2 in the given equation and the coefficients of *x* and *y* are even, so completing the square is fairly straightforward—there are just a lot of steps. Start by grouping the *x*'s and *y*'s together. Then, take the coefficient of the *x*-term and divide it by 2, square it, and add it to the two terms with *x* variables. Do the same with the *y* term. Don't forget to add these amounts to the other side of the equation as well. This creates a perfect square of *x* terms and *y* terms, so take the square root of each.

$$x^2 + y^2 + 8x - 20y = 28$$
$$x^2 + 8x + y^2 - 20y = 28$$
$$(x^2 + 8x + 16) + (y^2 - 20y + 100) = 28 + 16 + 100$$
$$(x + 4)^2 + (y - 10)^2 = 144$$

The equation tells you that r^2 is 144, which means that the radius is 12 and the diameter is twice that, or 24, which is (B).

16. 10
Difficulty: Medium

Category: Additional Topics in Math / Geometry

Strategic Advice: The key to this question is that the radius of a circle is perpendicular to a tangent line—a line that touches a curve at a point without crossing over—at that point. Once you draw the crucial right angle in, just proceed step-by-step until you have enough information to apply the Pythagorean theorem or (if you've been studying your Kaplan tips) your knowledge of Pythagorean triplets.

Getting to the Answer:

$$A = \pi r^2$$
$$36\pi = \pi r^2$$
$$36 = r^2$$
$$6 = r$$

So, $KM = 6$. You also know that $JL = 16$, and the tick marks on the figure indicate congruence, so KL equals half that, or 8.

With $KM = 6$ and $KL = 8$, apply the Pythagorean theorem:

$$c^2 = a^2 + b^2$$
$$c^2 = 36 + 64$$
$$c^2 = 100$$
$$c = 10$$

You may have also noticed that this is a multiple of a 3:4:5 Pythagorean triplet, making it a 6:8:10 triplet, which means 10 is the correct answer.

17. 315
Difficulty: Medium

Category: Additional Topics in Math / Geometry

Strategic Advice: Whenever a question mentions a pattern, you need to find that pattern and apply it to whatever you're looking for.

Getting to the Answer: Notice that each line closest to an axis is 30° from that axis, and that each line between those lines is exactly half way between them, or 15° past the first line. For example, 45° is halfway between 30° and 60°, and it is 15° more than 30°. Now, apply the pattern. Start at 240°; move 30° more to get to the y-axis, which yields 270°; move 30° more to get to the first line after the y-axis, which yields 300°; finally, add 15° to arrive at P and the correct answer, which is 315°.

18. 46
Difficulty: Hard

Category: Additional Topics in Math / Geometry

Strategic Advice: Knowing how to write the equation of a circle will earn you points on Test Day. You'll also need to be able to algebraically expand that equation. Don't forget—when you square a binomial, you should write it as repeated multiplication and use FOIL.

Getting to the Answer: First, find the center and the radius of the circle: Each grid line represents one unit on the graph, so the center is (0, 1) and the radius is 7. Substitute these values into the equation for a circle, $(x - h)^2 + (y - k)^2 = r^2$, and then simplify until the equation looks like the one given in the question:

$$(x - 0)^2 + (y - 1)^2 = 7^2$$
$$x^2 + (y - 1)(y - 1) = 49$$
$$x^2 + y^2 - 2y + 1 = 49$$
$$x^2 + y^2 - 2y = 48$$

There is no x term, so $a = 0$. The coefficient of y is -2 and $c = 48$, so $a + b + c = 0 + (-2) + 48 = 46$.

CHAPTER 16

PREPARE

1. 24

Difficulty: Easy

Category: Additional Topics in Math / Geometry

Strategic Advice: Determine the volume of concentrate and the volume of the juice after it has been diluted with water. You can then find the dimensions of the pitcher that is needed.

Getting to the Answer: The diameter of the can of concentrate is 7 cm, making the radius 3.5 cm. Plug this and the given height into the volume formula: $V_{conc} = \pi \times 3.5^2 \times 12 = 147\pi$ cm^3. Desiree must dilute the concentrate to 25%; multiply the concentrate volume by 4 (because the concentrate comprises 25% of the new amount of juice, and 25% $\times$ 4 = 100%) to obtain the final volume of juice, which is 588π cm^3. The diameter of the juice pitcher is 10 cm, which makes the radius 5 cm. Use the volume formula again to obtain the minimum height of the pitcher:

$$V_{dil} = 588\pi = \pi \times 5^2 \times h$$
$$h = \frac{588}{25} = 23.52 \text{ cm}$$

Rounded properly, the correct answer is 24.

2. C

Difficulty: Medium

Category: Additional Topics in Math / Geometry

Strategic Advice: You have two 3D shapes in play: a rectangular prism and a sphere. Also, remember that the question asks for the volume of the empty space inside two boxes, not one.

Getting to the Answer: Start by finding the volume of the box, and then calculate the volume of one baseball.

$$V_{box} = (5 \times 8)(3 \times 8)(8) = 7{,}680 \text{ cm}^3$$

$$V_{ball} = \frac{4}{3}\pi \times 4^3 = \frac{4}{3}\pi \times 64 = \frac{256}{3}\pi$$

Multiplying the volume of one ball by 15 yields 1,280π cm^3, the total volume of all the baseballs in one box. You're asked for the volume of the empty space inside two boxes, so double the volumes and subtract: 15,360 $-$ 2,560π cm^3 is your final answer, which matches (C).

3. C

Difficulty: Hard

Category: Additional Topics in Math / Geometry

Strategic Advice: Identify the 3D shapes present, and draw additional lines on the figure to uncover helpful hidden triangles.

Getting to the Answer: Imagine cutting open the cylindrical casing and flattening it out; you'd get a rectangle. Its area is 61π cm^2 and its length is the height of the cylinder, which is 30.5 cm. Dividing the area by the length gives a width of 2π cm, which is also the circumference of the circular cross section of the kaleidoscope. Divide 2π by π to get the diameter, which is 2 cm. Add three diameters to the figure as shown to create six equilateral triangles, and then draw in the distance you're asked to find. The distance between the centers of two parallel mirrors bisects the equilateral triangles, creating 30-60-90 triangles; a close-up of one of these is also shown in the following figure.

Using the ratio $x : x\sqrt{3} : 2x$, you'll find that the longer leg (which is half the distance you need) is $\dfrac{\sqrt{3}}{2}$. Doubling this quantity yields $\sqrt{3}$, which matches (C).

4. D

Difficulty: Easy

Category: Additional Topics in Math / Geometry

Strategic Advice: Pick a pair of manageable numbers to represent the radii when doing your calculations.

Getting to the Answer: Suppose the first sphere has a radius of 1 and the second sphere has a radius of 2. That means the volume of the first sphere is $\dfrac{4}{3}\pi \times 1^3 = \dfrac{4}{3}\pi$, and the volume of the second sphere is $\dfrac{4}{3}\pi \times 2^3 = \dfrac{32}{3}\pi$. The ratio of the volumes is therefore $\dfrac{4}{3}\pi : \dfrac{32}{3}\pi$, which simplifies to 1:8, making (D) the correct answer.

You can also use r and $2r$ in your volume calculations: the corresponding volumes would be $\dfrac{4}{3}\pi r^3$ and $\dfrac{4}{3}\pi(2r)^3 = \dfrac{32}{3}\pi r^3$. The r^3 and $\dfrac{4}{3}\pi$ components cancel, leaving 1:8 as the ratio.

PRACTICE

5. B

Difficulty: Hard

Category: Additional Topics in Math / Geometry

Strategic Advice: Remember to take the truncated piece of the original cone into account when calculating the volume inside the megaphone.

Getting to the Answer: The original cone has a height of 20 in. and a diameter of 10 in. (therefore, the radius is 5 in.), so its volume is $\dfrac{1}{3}\pi \times 5^2 \times 20 = \dfrac{500}{3}\pi$ in.² You can use a proportion to solve for the height of the small cone that was truncated using the radii of both cones and height of the original cone: $\dfrac{x}{20} = \dfrac{1}{5} \rightarrow$ $x = 4$ in. Therefore, the volume of the small cone is $\dfrac{1}{3}\pi \times 1^2 \times 4 = \dfrac{4}{3}\pi$ in.² Subtract this from the volume of the original cone to find the volume inside the megaphone: $\dfrac{500}{3}\pi - \dfrac{4}{3}\pi = \dfrac{496}{3}\pi$ in.³ This becomes $165\dfrac{1}{3}\pi$ in.³, which is (B).

PERFORM

6. 3600

Difficulty: Medium

Category: Additional Topics in Math / Geometry

Strategic Advice: Don't get bogged down by the prose; identify the shape present, extract the relevant quantities, and start working toward the answer.

Getting to the Answer: You're told that the 3D shape in question is a triangular prism (without its triangular end faces) and that you need to find the area of the interior of its three faces. The question states that the honeycomb structure—and therefore the length of one of the prism's rectangular faces—is 30 cm. Multiply this by the rectangle width, which is the same as the side of one of the triangles, to find the area of one rectangular face (remember to convert the rectangle length to millimeters before computing): $A = 300 \times 4 = 1,200$ mm^2. Multiplying this value by 3 yields 3,600 mm^2, the area contributed by all three rectangular faces of one prism. Grid in 3600.

7. B

Difficulty: Hard

Category: Additional Topics in Math / Geometry

Strategic Advice: Add additional lines to the figure to uncover hidden shapes.

Getting to the Answer: A diagonal drawn across the bottom face of the cube reveals a 45-45-90 triangle. The length of the diagonal (which is the hypotenuse of the triangle) is $2\sqrt{6} \times \sqrt{2} = 2\sqrt{12}$ cm.

Do you see another right triangle you can use along with the Pythagorean theorem?

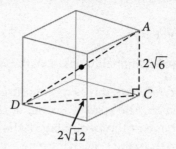

$$AC^2 + CD^2 = AD^2$$

$$(2\sqrt{6})^2 + (2\sqrt{12})^2 = AD^2$$

$$24 + 48 = AD^2$$

$$AD = \sqrt{72} = 6\sqrt{2}$$

The length of the diagonal from vertex to vertex is $6\sqrt{2}$, but you only need half that distance, so divide by 2 to yield $3\sqrt{2}$, the distance from a vertex to the center of the cube. (B) is your match.

EXTRA PRACTICE

1. B
Difficulty: Easy

Category: Additional Topics in Math / Geometry

Strategic Advice: This is a straight computation question. The solid is a cone, so check the formula page at the beginning of the test and substitute the values given into the appropriate volume formula, $V = \frac{1}{3}\pi r^2 h$.

Getting to the Answer: Be careful—the diagram shows the diameter, but you need to use the radius in the formula, so divide the diameter by 2.

$$V = \frac{1}{3}\pi (7)^2 (36)$$
$$V = \pi (49)(12)$$
$$V = 588\pi$$

This makes (B) the correct answer.

2. C
Difficulty: Easy

Category: Additional Topics in Math / Geometry

Strategic Advice: Don't forget to refer to the formula page provided for you on Test Day rather than relying on your memory. The volume of a pyramid is given by $V = \frac{1}{3}lwh$. Here, the base is a square, so both the length and the width are equal to 34.5 feet.

Getting to the Answer: You're looking for the height of the pyramid, so substitute all the other values into the formula and solve for h:

$$V = \frac{1}{3}lwh$$
$$21{,}821.25 = \frac{1}{3}(34.5)(34.5)h$$
$$65{,}463.75 = 1{,}190.25h$$
$$55 = h$$

Therefore, the height of the pyramid top is 55 feet, which matches (C).

3. B
Difficulty: Medium

Category: Additional Topics in Math / Geometry

Strategic Advice: In a question like this, you're looking for surface area (not volume) because you would spray the faces of the tent (not the space inside the tent). If you check the formula page, you'll notice that there are no surface area formulas for 3-D shapes. This means you need to decompose the figure into 2-D shapes. Pay careful attention to the dimensions of each shape.

Getting to the Answer: The bottom of the tent is a rectangle: $A = lw = (9)(6) = 54$; the two sides of the tent are also rectangles, but one of the dimensions is different than the bottom: $2A = 2(lw) = 2(9)(5) = 90$; the front and back of the tent are triangles: $2A_{triangle} = 2\left(\frac{1}{2}bh\right) = bh = (6)(4) = 24$. Thus, the total surface area of the tent is $54 + 90 + 24 = 168$ square feet. You're not done: both the inside and outside of the tent need to be sprayed, so double the surface area to get 336 square feet. And finally, 1 ounce can cover 3 square feet, so divide 336 by 3 to arrive at the final answer, 112 ounces of the waterproofing agent, which is (B).

4. D
Difficulty: Easy

Category: Additional Topics in Math / Geometry

Strategic Advice: To find the volume of a cubical box, you need to know the length of a side.

You can find this using the information given about the surface area of the box. The surface area of a cube equals 6 times the area of one face, or $6s^2$, where s is the length of a side.

Getting to the Answer: Substitute the given surface area into the formula and solve for s:

$$6s^2 = 1{,}176$$
$$s^2 = 196$$
$$s = 14$$

Thus, the length of a side of the cube is 14 inches. The volume of a cube is given by $V = lwh$ (or $V = s^3$ because the sides are all equal in length), so the volume of the moving box is 14^3, or 2,744 cubic inches, making (D) correct.

5. C
Difficulty: Medium

Category: Additional Topics in Math / Geometry

Strategic Advice: First, think logically: After it's poured into the larger glass, the volume of the water in the glass will still be the same as the volume when it was in the smaller glass. The volume of a cylinder equals the area of its base times its height, or $V = \pi r^2 h$. Be careful—the question gives you the diameters of the glasses, not the radii.

Getting to the Answer: Find the volume of the water in the smaller glass. Then, substitute this volume into a second equation where the height is unknown and solve for h.

$$V = \pi r^2 h$$
$$V = \pi (1.5)^2(6)$$
$$V = \pi (2.25)(6)$$
$$V = 13.5\pi$$
$$13.5\pi = \pi(2)^2 h$$
$$13.5\pi = \pi 4h$$
$$3.375 = h$$

The water will reach 3.375 inches high in the bigger glass, which is (C).

6. C
Difficulty: Medium

Category: Additional Topics in Math / Geometry

Strategic Advice: The formula for finding the volume of a pyramid with a rectangular base is $V = \frac{1}{3}lwh$. Start by substituting what you know into the formula.

Getting to the Answer: You know the volume is represented by $x^3 - x$. You also know the length is $x + 1$ and the width is $3x$.

$$V = \frac{1}{3}lwh$$
$$x^3 - x = \frac{1}{3}(x+1)(3x)h$$

Multiply both sides of the equation by 3 to clear the fraction, but don't multiply anything else just yet. First, look for a pattern.

$$3x^3 - 3x = (x+1)(3x)h$$

Notice that if you divide both sides of the equation by the width, $3x$, you'll be left with $x^2 - 1$ on the left side and $(x + 1)$ times h on the right side. The difference of squares rule tells you that the factors of $x^2 - 1$ are $x + 1$ and $x - 1$. This means the height of the pyramid must be represented by $x - 1$. Therefore, (C) is correct.

7. A
Difficulty: Medium

Category: Additional Topics in Math / Geometry

Strategic Advice: The cheese block purchases have the same height and width, so the block must be cut according to length. Find the original length of the entire block using the formula for volume of a rectangular solid, $V = lwh$, and then solve for length.

Getting to the Answer:

$$V = lwh$$

$$576 = (l)(6)(8)$$

$$12 = l$$

Don't stop here—the question asks for the difference in the two lengths. The customer bought $\frac{1}{8}$ block, which is equal to $(12)\left(\frac{1}{8}\right) = 1.5$ inches. The restaurant bought $\frac{1}{2}$ block, which is equal to $(12)\left(\frac{1}{2}\right) = 6$ inches. The difference in the lengths is $6 - 1.5 = 4.5$ inches, which is (A).

8. D

Difficulty: Hard

Category: Additional Topics in Math / Geometry

Strategic Advice: Try setting this problem up in words first, and then translate from English into Math: The volume of the test tube is equal to the volume of the cylinder plus the volume of the half-sphere. Use the formulas from the formula page to write an equation. Then, solve for the height.

Getting to the Answer: The diameter of the cylinder (and the half-sphere) is 1 inch, so the radius of each is $\frac{1}{2}$ inch.

$$V_{tube} = V_{cylinder} + \frac{1}{2}V_{sphere}$$

$$\frac{19}{12}\pi = \pi r^2 h + \frac{1}{2}\left(\frac{4}{3}\pi r^3\right)$$

$$\frac{19}{12}\pi = \pi\left(\frac{1}{2}\right)^2 h + \frac{2}{3}\pi\left(\frac{1}{2}\right)^3$$

$$\frac{19}{12}\pi = \frac{1}{4}\pi h + \frac{2}{3}\left(\frac{1}{8}\pi\right)$$

$$\frac{19}{12}\pi - \frac{1}{12}\pi = \frac{1}{4}\pi h$$

$$\frac{3}{2}\pi = \frac{1}{4}\pi h$$

$$6 = h$$

Finally, add 6 to the height created by the half sphere (its radius) to get $6 + 0.5 = 6.5$ inches, which matches (D).

9. C

Difficulty: Medium

Category: Additional Topics in Math / Geometry

Strategic Advice: A wedge shape is an unfamiliar solid, so you shouldn't try to calculate the volume directly. You are told that the solid is half of a cube. Now imagine the other half lying on top of the solid, forming a complete cube.

Getting to the Answer:

The question tells you that the hypotenuse is $10\sqrt{2}$. Notice that this diagonal with length $10\sqrt{2}$ and two of the cube's edges form an isosceles right triangle, or in other words, a 45-45-90 degree triangle. In a 45-45-90 triangle, the hypotenuse is $\sqrt{2}$ times the length of a leg, so the legs have length 10. Thus, the volume of the whole cube is $10 \times 10 \times 10 = 1,000$, and the volume of the chock is half that, or 500 cubic inches, which is (C).

10. A

Difficulty: Medium

Category: Additional Topics in Math / Geometry

Strategic Advice: Find the diameter of each ball using the volume formula. Be careful—the formula gives the radius, not the diameter, so after you solve for r, be sure to double it to find each diameter.

Getting to the Answer:

Smaller ball:

$$V = \frac{4}{3}\pi r^3$$

$$36\pi = \frac{4}{3}\pi r^3$$

$$36 = \frac{4}{3}r^3$$

$$27 = r^3$$

$$3 = r$$

$$d = 6$$

Larger ball:

$$288\pi = \frac{4}{3}\pi r^3$$

$$288 = \frac{4}{3}r^3$$

$$216 = r^3$$

$$6 = r$$

$$d = 12$$

The ratio of the diameters is 6:12 or 1:2, making (A) the correct choice.

11. C

Difficulty: Hard

Category: Additional Topics in Math / Geometry

Strategic Advice: Don't be too quick to answer a question like this. You can't simply find three-fourths of the volume of the cone because the top is considerably smaller than the bottom. Instead, you'll need to find the volume of the whole cone and subtract the volume of the top piece that is being discarded.

Getting to the Answer: The figure shows a right triangle inside the cone. The height of the cone is the longer leg the triangle, 16. The hypotenuse is given as 20. You might recognize this as a multiple of a Pythagorean triplet, 3-4-5, or in this case 12-16-20. This means the radius of the original cone is 12. Substitute this into the formula for volume:

$$V = \frac{1}{3}\pi r^2 h$$

$$V = \frac{1}{3}\pi (12)^2 (16)$$

$$V = 768\pi$$

To determine the dimensions of the top piece, use similar triangles.

One quarter of the height is $16 \div 4 = 4$, resulting in a 3-4-5 triangle, making the height 4 and the radius 3.

$$V = \frac{1}{3}\pi (3)^2 (4)$$

$$V = 12\pi$$

Thus, the volume of the remaining solid is $768\pi - 12\pi = 756\pi$, which is (C).

12. D

Difficulty: Medium

Category: Additional Topics in Math / Geometry

Strategic Advice: There are two ways to approach this question—but only because both shapes (the storage box and the discs) are rectangular prisms and the dimensions match up nicely (two rows of two discs will exactly fill one layer in the box with no extra space left over). One strategy is to find the volume of the storage box and divide by the volume of each disc. Another strategy is to find how many discs Rupert can fit in length, then in width, then in height, and multiply. The second approach must be used when the shapes are different and when the dimensions don't match up just right.

Getting to the Answer:

Strategy 1: The volume of a rectangular prism (or a cube) is given by the formula $V = l \times w \times h$, so the volume of the storage box is $10 \times 10 \times 10 = 1,000$ cubic units. The volume of each disc is $5 \times 5 \times \dfrac{1}{4} = 6.25$. The number of discs that can fit in the box is $1,000 \div 6.25 = 160$ discs, which is (D).

Strategy 2: The box has dimensions 10 inches by 10 inches by 10 inches. Because each disc is 5 inches in length, he can fit $10 \div 5 = 2$ rows of discs along the length of the box. Each disc is 5 inches in width, so he can fit $10 \div 5 = 2$ rows of discs along the width of the box. Finally, each disc is $\dfrac{1}{4}$ inch tall, so he can fit $10 \div \dfrac{1}{4} = 10 \times 4 = 40$ rows of discs along the depth of the box. Multiply to find that Rupert can fit $2 \times 2 \times 40 = 160$ Blu-ray discs in the box.

13. B
Difficulty: Medium

Category: Additional Topics in Math / Geometry

Strategic Advice: You'll need to make a plan to answer a question like this: You need to find the volume of the sand needed for one tank, multiply this by 50 tanks, determine the total weight (in ounces) of the sand based on the volume, convert that amount to pounds, and finally, divide by the number of pounds in one bag. Phew!

Getting to the Answer: Take it one step at a time! The volume of sand in one tank (only two inches of the height) will be $V = 24 \times 9 \times 2 = 432$ cubic inches, which means the volume of sand in all 50 tanks will be $50 \times 432 = 21,600$ cubic inches. Each cubic inch of sand weighs about 2 ounces, so the weight of all the sand will be $2 \times 21,600 = 43,200$ ounces. There are 16 ounces in one pound, so the weight of the sand in pounds is $43,200 \div 16 = 2,700$. Finally, each bag contains 40 pounds of sand, so the pet store needs to buy $2,700 \div 40 = 67.5$, or about 68 bags of sand. This means (B) is the correct answer.

14. D
Difficulty: Hard

Category: Additional Topics in Math / Geometry

Strategic Advice: Don't let this real-world scenario fool you. You aren't being asked to calculate the surface area or the volume of the pyramid. You only need to calculate the area of the four triangular faces, which is where the shingles will go. Drawing a sketch will help you visualize this and keep the dimensions straight.

Getting to the Answer: Use the formula for area of a triangle, $A = \dfrac{1}{2}bh$. The base of each triangular face is 20 feet and the height is the slant height of the pyramid, 18 feet, so the area of one side of the roof is $\dfrac{1}{2}(20)(18) = 180$. There are four sides, so the total area to be covered is $4(180) = 720$ square feet. Be careful—this is the area in square *feet* and the shingle size is given in square inches. Convert the square feet to square inches by multiplying 720 by 144

(12 inches × 12 inches). Then, divide the result by 72 to see how many shingles are needed: 720 × 144 = 103,680 ÷ 72 = 1,440. Finally, add 20% to this amount to account for the overlap in the shingles: 1,440 × 1.2 = 1,728 shingles, which is (D).

15. B
Difficulty: Hard

Category: Additional Topics in Math / Geometry

Strategic Advice: You need to think about a question like this logically: 6 ounces of yogurt takes up 80% of the volume of the container. The question is asking how much volume (space) does 1 ounce of yogurt take up, so you'll need to find 80% of the volume and divide by 6.

Getting to the Answer: Find the volume of the container using the formula for volume of a cylinder, $V = \pi r^2 h$. The question gives you the width, or diameter of the container, so divide by 2 to get the radius.

$$V = \pi(1.25)^2(4)$$

$$V = \pi(1.5625)(4)$$

$$V = 6.25\pi$$

The factory only fills the cup 80% of the way up, so multiply the container volume by 0.8 to find that the actual volume of the yogurt is $6.25\pi \times 0.8 = 5\pi$, or about 15.708 cubic inches. Divide this by 6 ounces to determine that 1 ounce takes up approximately 2.6 cubic inches of space, which matches (B).

16. 128
Difficulty: Easy

Category: Additional Topics in Math / Geometry

Strategic Advice: Sometimes, you have to search through the information given in a question to find what you need. The volume of a cylinder is given by the formula $V = \pi r^2 h$. You're told what V is and you're looking for h, so the radius of the tunnel must be given somehow in the question.

Getting to the Answer: The question tells you that the circumference of the opening (which is a circle) is 8π, so substitute this value in the formula for circumference and solve for r.

$$C = 2\pi r$$

$$8\pi = 2\pi r$$

$$4 = r$$

You now have everything you need to find h, which in this case is the length of the tunnel:

$$2,048\pi = \pi(4)^2(h)$$

$$2,048 = 16h$$

$$128 = h$$

The tunnel is 128 feet long.

17. 6/10 or 3/5
Difficulty: Medium

Category: Additional Topics in Math / Geometry

Strategic Advice: Find the surface area and the volume of the cube. If you can't remember the formula for surface area of a cube ($6s^2$, where s is the length of a side), you can find the area of one face and multiply the result times the number of faces, 6.

Getting to the Answer:

Surface area	Volume
$A = 6s^2$	$V = s^3$
$A = 6(10)^2$	$V = (10)^3$
$A = 600$	$V = 1,000$

The ratio of the surface area to the volume is 600:1,000, which reduces to 6:10 $\left(\dfrac{6}{10}\right)$, or 3:5 $\left(\dfrac{3}{5}\right)$.

18. 6

Difficulty: Hard

Category: Additional Topics in Math / Geometry

Strategic Advice: Use the formula for volume of a rectangular solid, $V = lwh$, to write an equation. Because the dimensions are given as the ratio 4:2:1, let the length, width, and height be represented by $4x$, $2x$, and $1x$.

Getting to the Answer: Substitute the expressions into the formula and solve for x.

$$216 = (4x)(2x)(1x)$$

$$216 = 8x^3$$

$$27 = x^3$$

$$3 = x$$

The width was represented by $2x$ so multiply to find that the width is $2(3) = 6$ inches.

CHAPTER 17

PREPARE

1. 7/25 or .28
Difficulty: Easy

Category: Additional Topics in Math / Geometry

Strategic Advice: Recall that $\tan x = \dfrac{\text{opp}}{\text{adj}}$. Draw a picture with the given lengths added to make finding the answer easier.

Getting to the Answer: The triangle described in the question stem is shown here.

Remember that $\sin x = \dfrac{\text{opp}}{\text{hyp}}$, so use the Pythagorean theorem to calculate the length of the hypotenuse.

$$7^2 + 24^2 = \text{hyp}^2$$
$$49 + 576 = \text{hyp}^2$$
$$625 = \text{hyp}^2$$
$$25 = \text{hyp}$$

You can now plug the length of the hypotenuse into the sine ratio to obtain your answer:

$\sin x = \dfrac{7}{25}$. Grid in 7/25 or .28.

You could also find the answer by making use of the fact that this triangle is a 7-24-25 Pythagorean triplet, thus bypassing the Pythagorean theorem.

2. B
Difficulty: Medium

Category: Additional Topics in Math / Geometry

Strategic Advice: Subtracting 360° or 2π radians from an angle measure results in an angle that is coterminal to the original angle (because you simply rotated the angle one full circle); use this fact to find a less cumbersome angle measure for your calculations.

Getting to the Answer: Subtract 360° from 690° twice to obtain −30°. Once here, convert to radians using the factor-label method: $-30° \times \dfrac{\pi}{180°} = -\dfrac{30\pi}{180} = -\dfrac{\pi}{6}$. (B) is therefore correct. Note that you could also subtract 360° just once (to get a measure below 360°), obtain 330°, and then convert to $\dfrac{11\pi}{6}$ radians. Because $\dfrac{11\pi}{6}$ is not an answer choice, you would subtract 2π to obtain $-\dfrac{\pi}{6}$. However, the fractions involved might be tough to simplify if you're in the no-calculator section.

3. C
Difficulty: Hard

Category: Additional Topics in Math / Geometry

Strategic Advice: Trigonometric ratios are just that: ratios. Remember that a ratio does not necessarily contain absolute measurements.

Getting to the Answer: Recall that cotangent is the reciprocal of tangent: $\text{cotangent} = \dfrac{\text{adjacent}}{\text{opposite}}$. Because $\cot G = \dfrac{\sqrt{3}}{1}$, the ratio GF:HF (adj:opp) is $\sqrt{3}$:1. This is part of the 30-60-90 triangle ratio, so HF:GF:HG = 1 : $\sqrt{3}$: 2. Note, however, that this is not a guarantee that 1, $\sqrt{3}$, and 2 are the correct lengths (and the question stem confirms this by stating that HG = 6). You can use the fact that HG = 6 to determine the factor by which the ratio is multiplied to obtain the actual side lengths. You know from the 30-60-90 triangle ratio $(x : x\sqrt{3} : 2x)$ that $2x = 6$, so $x = 3$. Therefore, the length of the shorter leg must be $3 \times 1 = 3$.

This is also the length of the diameter of the circle, so the radius is $\frac{3}{2}$. You can now find the area of the circle: $A = \pi r^2 = \pi\left(\frac{3}{2}\right)^2 = \frac{9\pi}{4}$. Choice (C) is the correct answer.

4. A

Difficulty: Medium

Category: Additional Topics in Math / Geometry

Strategic Advice: If a right triangle isn't presented in a trigonometry question, draw one!

Getting to the Answer: Begin by drawing a height in the triangle:

Next, find the length of BD using the triangle area formula:

$$A = \frac{1}{2}bh$$

$$225 = \frac{1}{2} \times 30h$$

$$h = \frac{225}{15} = 15 = BD$$

You now have two sides of a right triangle ($\triangle ABD$), so you can find the third easily. You might recognize $\triangle ABD$ as an 8-15-17 Pythagorean triplet, but if you don't, you can still use the Pythagorean theorem:

$$AD^2 + 15^2 = 17^2$$

$$AD^2 = 17^2 - 15^2$$

$$AD^2 = 289 - 225$$

$$AD = \sqrt{64} = 8$$

You can now find $\cos x$: $\frac{\text{adjacent}}{\text{hypotenuse}} = \frac{8}{17}$, which is (A).

PRACTICE

5. D

Difficulty: Medium

Category: Additional Topics in Math / Geometry

Strategic Advice: When it comes to transformations, trigonometric functions follow the same rules as "regular" functions.

Getting to the Answer: Recall the graph of the "plain" cosine function within the given domain $\left(-\frac{3\pi}{2} \text{ to } \frac{3\pi}{2}\right)$: it has a maximum at $(0, 1)$ and minima at $(-\pi, -1)$ and $(\pi, -1)$. Eliminate A. Because π is being added inside the parentheses with the variable, the result is a horizontal shift of π radians to the left. The maximum of the cosine function will become a minimum, and its minima will become maxima. The only choice that depicts these changes is (D).

PERFORM

6. C

Difficulty: Medium

Category: Additional Topics in Math / Geometry

Strategic Advice: The sine and cosine are cofunctions; that is, $\sin x = \cos\left(\frac{\pi}{2} - x\right)$ and $\cos x = \sin\left(\frac{\pi}{2} - x\right)$. Use these relationships to get to the answer.

Getting to the Answer: First, subtract 2π from $\frac{13\pi}{6}$ to obtain a more recognizable angle: $\frac{13\pi}{6} - 2\pi = \frac{13\pi}{6} - \frac{12\pi}{6} = \frac{\pi}{6}$. The equation in the question stem becomes $\sin x = \cos\left(\frac{\pi}{6}\right)$. Combining this with the relationship mentioned above yields $\sin x = \cos\left(\frac{\pi}{6}\right) = \cos\left(\frac{\pi}{2} - x\right)$. This new equation implies that $\frac{\pi}{6}$ and $\frac{\pi}{2}-x$ are equal, so you can write another equation with them and solve for x:

$$\frac{\pi}{6}=\frac{\pi}{2}-x$$

$$x=\frac{\pi}{2}-\frac{\pi}{6}$$

$$x=\frac{\pi}{3}$$

Choice (C) is the correct answer.

7. C

Difficulty: Easy

Category: Additional Topics in Math / Geometry

Strategic Advice: Draw a diagram to visualize the situation and what you need to do to find the answer.

Getting to the Answer: Start by drawing a diagram.

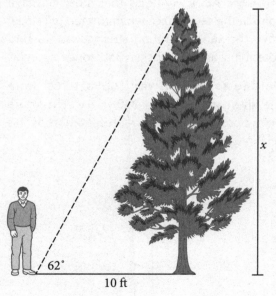

The question asks for the height of the treehouse; call this quantity x. The trigonometric

ratio that relates all of the values in the diagram is tangent, so set up an equation and solve for x:

$$\tan 62°=\frac{x}{10} \rightarrow x=10 \tan 62°\approx10\times1.88=18.8$$

Choice (C) is correct.

8. A

Difficulty: Medium

Category: Additional Topics in Math / Geometry

Strategic Advice: When an SAT question features sines or cosines being squared, consider using the identity $sin^2 x+cos^2 x = 1$, if possible.

Getting to the Answer: It might be tempting to draw a triangle, use the Pythagorean theorem, work out the cosine, and square it; but using the aforementioned trigonometric identity is much faster. Given that $\sin x=\frac{1}{5}$:

$$\sin^2 x+\cos^2 x=1$$

$$\left(\frac{1}{5}\right)^2+\cos^2 x=1$$

$$\cos^2 x=1-\frac{1}{25}=\frac{24}{25}$$

Choice (A) is the correct answer.

EXTRA PRACTICE

1. A
Difficulty: Easy

Category: Additional Topics in Math / Trigonometry

Strategic Advice: Use the conversion $180° = \pi$ to convert between degrees and radians. Write the conversion as a ratio, with degrees in the denominator so they cancel.

Getting to the Answer: The radian equivalent of 120 degrees is: $120° \times \dfrac{\pi}{180°} = \dfrac{120\pi}{180} = \dfrac{2\pi}{3}$, which is (A).

2. B
Difficulty: Easy

Category: Additional Topics in Math / Trigonometry

Strategic Advice: Recall that the sum of the acute angles in a right triangle is $180° - 90° = 90°$. Convert this to radians to find the measure of the missing angle.

Getting to the Answer: The sum of the acute angles, in radians, is $90° \times \dfrac{\pi}{180°} = \dfrac{90\pi}{180} = \dfrac{\pi}{2}$. Subtract the known angle to find the other angle: $\dfrac{\pi}{2} - \dfrac{\pi}{3} = \dfrac{3\pi}{6} - \dfrac{2\pi}{6} = \dfrac{\pi}{6}$. This matches (B).

3. C
Difficulty: Easy

Category: Additional Topics in Math / Trigonometry

Strategic Advice: Regardless of whether a central angle is given in degrees or in radians, you can use the relationship between the angle and the whole circle to find the length of the arc: $\dfrac{\text{central angle}}{\text{whole circle}} = \dfrac{\text{arc length}}{\text{circumference}}$. In radians, a full circle has an angle measure of 2π.

Getting to the Answer: Start by finding the circumference of the circle so you can fill in the proportion: $C = 2\pi r = 2\pi(3) = 6\pi$. Now, use the proportion to find the length of arc AB:

$$\frac{\text{central angle}}{\text{whole circle}} = \frac{\text{arc length}}{\text{circumference}}$$

$$\frac{\frac{5\pi}{6}}{2\pi} = \frac{AB}{6\pi}$$

$$\frac{5\pi}{6} \times 6\pi = 2\pi(AB)$$

$$5\pi^2 = 2\pi(AB)$$

$$\frac{5\pi}{2} = AB$$

Choice (C) is correct.

4. D
Difficulty: Easy

Category: Additional Topics in Math / Trigonometry

Strategic Advice: Angles that are coterminal (land in the same place when rotated full circle) have the same trigonometric values. To find coterminal angles, subtract 360° (one full circle).

Getting to the Answer: Subtract 360° from the given angle: $450° - 360° = 90°$. The figure below provides a visual representation of this relationship:

A 90° angle has the same trigonometric values as a 450° angle, making (D) correct.

5. C

Difficulty: Easy

Category: Additional Topics in Math / Trigonometry

Strategic Advice: Complementary angles have a special relationship relative to trig values: the cosine of an acute angle is equal to the sine of the angle's complement and vice versa.

Getting to the Answer: Because only one of the answers can be correct, look for the simplest relationship (complementary angles): 60° is complementary to 30°, so cos 30° = sin 60°, which means (C) is correct.

6. D

Difficulty: Medium

Category: Additional Topics in Math / Trigonometry

Strategic Advice: Mark up the triangle with what you know and then use SOH CAH TOA: $\sin = \dfrac{\text{opp}}{\text{hyp}}$ and $\cos = \dfrac{\text{adj}}{\text{hyp}}$.

Getting to the Answer: You're given that $\cos A = \dfrac{5}{13}$, so label the side adjacent to angle A (the leg that touches it) 5 and the hypotenuse 13. You might recognize these side lengths as part of the Pythagorean triplet 5, 12, 13. If not, use the Pythagorean theorem to find that the side opposite of angle A has length 12.

$$\sqrt{13^2 - 5^2} = 12$$

Now, use the definition of sine: $\sin A = \dfrac{\text{opp}}{\text{hyp}} = \dfrac{12}{13}$, which is (D).

7. C

Difficulty: Easy

Category: Additional Topics in Math / Trigonometry

Strategic Advice: Whenever a question involves a trig function that is squared, think of the Pythagorean Identity: $\sin^2 x + \cos^2 x = 1$.

Getting to the Answer: A simple manipulation of the identity gives you the answer. Jot down the identity and then subtract $\cos^2 x$ from both sides so it looks like the expression in the question:

$$\sin^2 x + \cos^2 x = 1$$
$$\sin^2 x = 1 - \cos^2 x$$

The correct answer is (C).

8. B

Difficulty: Medium

Category: Additional Topics in Math / Trigonometry

Strategic Advice: The values along the horizontal axis (the angle measures) are given in radians, but the angles in the question are given in degrees. Knowing common angle equivalents (radians/degrees) will save you time on Test Day, as will knowing the unit circle. However, you can also use the conversion $180° = \pi$ to convert the angle measures before reading the graph.

Getting to the Answer: Convert each of the angles to radians and then read the corresponding y-values on the graph.

$$\cos 90° = \cos\left(90° \times \frac{\pi}{180°}\right) = \cos\left(\frac{\pi}{2}\right) = 0$$

$$\cos 180° = \cos\left(180° \times \frac{\pi}{180°}\right) = \cos(\pi) = -1$$

The sum is $0 + (-1) = -1$, which is (B).

9. D

Difficulty: Medium

Category: Additional Topics in Math / Trigonometry

Strategic Advice: The measure of an angle that is composed of two adjacent angles is the sum of the two adjacent angle measures.

Getting to the Answer: The answers are given in degrees, and it's easier to add degrees than radians, so convert each angle measure to degrees and then find the sum. Use the conversion $180° = \pi$ with π written in the denominator so that it will cancel.

$$\frac{\cancel{\pi}}{4} \times \frac{180°}{\cancel{\pi}} = 45°$$

$$\frac{7\cancel{\pi}}{\cancel{12}^2} \times \frac{\overset{30}{\cancel{180}}°}{\cancel{\pi}} = \frac{210°}{2} = 105°$$

The measure of $\angle PQR$ is $45° + 105° = 150°$, which matches (D).

10. C

Difficulty: Medium

Category: Additional Topics in Math / Trigonometry

Strategic Advice: When given an arc length and a central angle, use the relationship $\frac{\text{central angle}}{\text{whole circle}} = \frac{\text{arc length}}{\text{circumference}}$ to find whatever is missing. In this question, the radius of the circle is missing, so use the proportion to find the circumference, and then work backward to find the radius.

Getting to the Answer: Fill in the proportion with what you know:

$$\frac{135°}{360°} = \frac{\dfrac{3\pi}{4}}{C}$$

$$135C = \frac{3\pi}{4} \times 360$$

$$135C = 270\pi$$

$$C = 2\pi$$

Now, use the formula for circumference to find that $2\pi r = 2\pi$, so $r = 1$. The radius of the circle is 1, which is (C).

11. B

Difficulty: Medium

Category: Additional Topics in Math / Trigonometry

Strategic Advice: When you're not asked to find a specific value, drawing a quick sketch to determine which quadrant each angle lies in may provide enough information to answer the question.

Getting to the Answer: Sketch each angle on a unit circle. It doesn't have to be perfect—you just need to know which quadrant the angle falls in.

Three of the angles (120°, 240°, and −120°) fall to the left of the y-axis (in Quadrants II and III) and therefore have a cosine value that is negative. The angle in (B) falls to the right of the vertical axis (in Quadrant IV) and therefore has a cosine value that is positive. This means (B) is correct because $\cos(-60°)$ cannot have the same value as the other three angles.

12. C

Difficulty: Medium

Category: Additional Topics in Math / Trigonometry

Strategic Advice: You can't always identify the side lengths of a right triangle based solely on a trig ratio. You need to know one of the sides to make sure the proportions are correct.

Getting to the Answer: Start by adjusting the given trig ratio to match the given side length, 1,000. The cosine of an angle is defined as $\cos x = \dfrac{\text{adj}}{\text{hyp}}$. According to the figure, the hypotenuse has length 1,000 (which is 500 × 2) so scale the trig ratio up by a factor of 2. This tells you that the adjacent side ($\overline{ML}$) has length 341 × 2 = 682. Now you know two sides of the right triangle and can use the Pythagorean theorem to find the missing side:

$$682^2 + b^2 = 1,000^2$$
$$b^2 = 1,000,000 - 465,124$$
$$b^2 = 534,876$$
$$b \approx 731.35$$

The length of side LN is approximately 731, which is (C).

13. A

Difficulty: Medium

Category: Additional Topics in Math / Trigonometry

Strategic Advice: When the measure of an angle in a triangle is given in radians, convert it to degrees so you'll have a better idea of what you're looking at.

Getting to the Answer: Use the relationship 180° = π to convert the angle:

$$\frac{\cancel{\pi}}{3} \times \frac{180°}{\cancel{\pi}} = 60°$$

Now you know the triangle is a 30-60-90 triangle, which has sides that are in the ratio $x : x\sqrt{3} : 2x$. The hypotenuse is $2x = 24$, so $x = 12$ and $x\sqrt{3} = 12\sqrt{3}$. This means the base and height of the triangle are 12 and $12\sqrt{3}$, and the area of the triangle is $\dfrac{1}{2}(12\sqrt{3})(12) = 72\sqrt{3}$, which is (A).

14. D

Difficulty: Medium

Category: Additional Topics in Math / Trigonometry

Strategic Advice: Whenever trig values are given as fractions, think SOH CAH TOA: $\sin x = \dfrac{\text{opposite}}{\text{hypotenuse}}$, $\cos x = \dfrac{\text{adjacent}}{\text{hypotenuse}}$, and $\tan x = \dfrac{\text{opposite}}{\text{adjacent}}$. It's also a good idea to fill in missing sides and angles when questions involve right triangles.

Getting to the Answer: Fill in the missing parts of the triangle. Use the Pythagorean theorem to find the missing leg length, and use properties of triangles to find the missing angle.

Sine and cosine both involve the hypotenuse (13), so you can eliminate A right away because it doesn't have a 13 in it. Next, quickly compare each answer choice to the trig ratios given by SOH CAH TOA. Sine is opposite over hypotenuse; in B, the side opposite the 67.4° angle has length 5 (not 12), so eliminate B. Cosine is adjacent over hypotenuse; in C, the side adjacent to the 22.6° angle has length 12 (not 5), so eliminate C. This means (D) must be correct. The side adjacent to the 67.4° angle has length 5 and the hypotenuse has length 13, so $\cos 67.4° = \dfrac{5}{13}$.

15. B
Difficulty: Medium

Category: Additional Topics in Math / Trigonometry

Strategic Advice: When the angle given in a real-world scenario is not 30°, 45°, or 60° (or some multiple of one of those), you can bet you're going to use trig to answer the question.

Getting to the Answer: Focus on the triangle—the side you're trying to find is *adjacent* to the angle you've been given, and you also know the length of the *hypotenuse*. This tells you to use cosine to answer the question. Make sure you calculator is set to "degree" mode before evaluating the cosine of the angle.

$$\cos A = \frac{\text{adj}}{\text{hyp}}$$
$$\cos 65° = \frac{x}{17}$$
$$17\cos 65° = x$$
$$7.18 \approx x$$

The base of the ladder is about 7.18 feet from the house, which is (B).

16. C
Difficulty: Medium

Category: Additional Topics in Math / Trigonometry

Strategic Advice: Before trying to recall specific values from the unit circle, check the sign (positive or negative) of the trig values involved. And be careful—you're looking for the one that could *not* be the value of x.

Getting to the Answer: The angle given $\left(\dfrac{\pi}{6}\right)$ is in the first quadrant, so its cosine is positive.

The question states that sin x is equal to the cosine of $\dfrac{\pi}{6}$, so x be must an angle for which the sine is positive, which means it must lie in the first or second quadrant (above the x-axis). This means you're looking for the angle that is *not* in one of those quadrants, which is (C): $\dfrac{5\pi}{3}$ is in the fourth quadrant and therefore has a negative sine value. (The angles in A and B meet this criterion because each one is less than π. The angle in D also meets the criterion because $\dfrac{7\pi}{3} - 2\pi = \dfrac{7\pi}{3} - \dfrac{6\pi}{3} = \dfrac{\pi}{3}$, which is in the first quadrant.)

17. D
Difficulty: Medium

Category: Additional Topics in Math / Trigonometry

Strategic Advice: Whenever a question involves a trig function that is squared, think of the Pythagorean identity: $\sin^2 x + \cos^2 x = 1$. Note that any variable can be used in place of x; the Greek θ is one that you are likely to see in trig questions.

Getting to the Answer: No substitutions or complicated manipulations are required to answer this question. Simply factor the 3 out and see what's left:

$$N = 3\sin^2 \theta + 3\cos^2 \theta$$
$$= 3(\sin^2 \theta + \cos^2 \theta)$$
$$= 3(1) = 3$$

$N = 3$, making (D) correct.

18. B
Difficulty: Medium

Category: Additional Topics in Math / Trigonometry

Strategic Advice: Although one of the small triangles is a 30-60-90 triangle, you don't have any information about any of its sides (yet), so you'll have to start with the other triangle.

Getting to the Answer: Use a trig function to find the height of the pole (since it is shared by both triangles), and then use another trig function to find the length of the other cable (or you can use what you know about 30-60-90 triangles). The pole is opposite the 40° angle, and you know the length of the hypotenuse, so use sine. Make sure your calculator is set to "degree" mode.

$$\sin A = \frac{\text{opp}}{\text{hyp}}$$

$$\sin 40° = \frac{x}{20}$$

$$20 \sin 40° = x$$

$$12.856 \approx x$$

Beware of the trap answer—A is the height of the pole, not the length of the other cable! In the other triangle, the pole is opposite the 60° angle, and you *want* the length of the hypotenuse, so use sine again.

$$\sin 60° = \frac{12.856}{x}$$

$$x \sin 60° = 12.856$$

$$x = \frac{12.856}{\sin 60°} \approx 14.844$$

The answers are rounded to one decimal place, so the correct length is about 14.8 feet, which is (B).

19. D

Difficulty: Medium

Category: Additional Topics in Math / Trigonometry

Strategic Advice: To find the area of a circle, you need to know the length of the radius. In

this question, you can find the diameter of the circle using a trig function, divide the diameter by 2, and then use the area formula.

Getting to the Answer: The diameter of the circle is also the hypotenuse of the inscribed right triangle. You're given the length of the side adjacent to the 25° angle, so use cosine.

$$\cos A = \frac{\text{adj}}{\text{hyp}}$$

$$\cos 25 = \frac{8}{x}$$

$$x \cos 25° = 8$$

$$x = \frac{8}{\cos 25°} \approx 8.827$$

Divide the diameter by 2 to find that the radius is approximately 4.414, and the area is $\pi(4.414)^2$, or about 61 square centimeters, which is (D).

20. B

Difficulty: Hard

Category: Additional Topics in Math / Trigonometry

Strategic Advice: Try to determine how angles θ and β are related, based on their corresponding sine values. Then, determine the quadrant in which angle β must lie, given the parameters of angle θ $\left(\frac{3\pi}{2} < \theta < 2\pi \right)$.

Getting to the Answer: If an angle with measure θ such that $\frac{3\pi}{2} < \theta < 2\pi$ is drawn on a unit circle, its terminal side will fall in Quadrant IV, and sin θ = *k* will be a negative value (because sine represents the *y*-value of the point that intersects the unit circle). If sin β = *k* also (and *k* is negative), then the terminal side of β must land in either of Quadrants III or IV (because sine is negative in those quadrants). Choose an easy radian measure (in Quadrant IV) for angle θ, such as $\frac{5\pi}{3}$. Try each answer choice to see which one results in an angle that lies in the third or fourth quadrant:

Choice A: $2\pi - \dfrac{5\pi}{3} = \dfrac{6\pi}{3} - \dfrac{5\pi}{3} = \dfrac{\pi}{3}$, which is in Quadrant I, can be eliminated.

Choice (B): $3\pi - \dfrac{5\pi}{3} = \dfrac{9\pi}{3} - \dfrac{5\pi}{3} = \dfrac{4\pi}{3}$, which is in Quadrant III, is correct.

No need to check the others, but just in case you're not sure …

Choice C: $\pi + \dfrac{5\pi}{3} = \dfrac{3\pi}{3} + \dfrac{5\pi}{3} = \dfrac{8\pi}{3} = \dfrac{8\pi}{3} - \dfrac{6\pi}{3} = \dfrac{2\pi}{3}$, which is in Quadrant II, can be eliminated.

Choice D: $\dfrac{5\pi}{3} - \pi = \dfrac{5\pi}{3} - \dfrac{3\pi}{3} = \dfrac{2\pi}{3}$, which is in Quadrant II, can be eliminated.

21. B
Difficulty: Hard

Category: Additional Topics in Math / Trigonometry

Strategic Advice: Together, arcs AB, BC, and CA make up the entire circumference of the circle, which is $2\pi r = 2\pi(2) = 4\pi$. Use the central angle given (210°) to find the length of arc CA, and then subtract the sum of BC and CA from 4π to find the value of x.

Getting to the Answer: Use the relationship between the central angle and the whole circle to find the length of arc CA:
$$\dfrac{\text{central angle}}{\text{whole circle}} = \dfrac{\text{arc length}}{\text{circumference}}.$$

$$\dfrac{210°}{360°} = \dfrac{CA}{4\pi}$$
$$\dfrac{7}{12} = \dfrac{CA}{4\pi}$$
$$28\pi = 12(CA)$$
$$\dfrac{7\pi}{3} = CA$$

Now, subtract the two arc lengths from the circumference of the circle to find the value of x:

$$x = 4\pi - \dfrac{7\pi}{6} - \dfrac{7\pi}{3}$$
$$= \dfrac{24\pi}{6} - \dfrac{7\pi}{6} - \dfrac{14\pi}{6}$$
$$= \dfrac{3\pi}{6} = \dfrac{\pi}{2}$$

The correct answer is (B).

22. D
Difficulty: Medium

Category: Additional Topics in Math / Trigonometry

Strategic Advice: When trying to match a graph to an equation, always take a peek at the answer choices. In this question, each choice involves a horizontal shift of the sine curve, so your job is to determine how much the graph has been shifted and in which direction. Don't forget—horizontal shifts are backward of what they look like.

Getting to the Answer: Think about a few key points on a standard sine curve: (0, 0), $\left(\dfrac{\pi}{2}, 1\right)$, ($\pi$, 0), and $\left(\dfrac{3\pi}{2}, -1\right)$. Now, look for the corresponding points on the graph—(0, 1), $\left(\dfrac{\pi}{2}, 0\right)$, ($\pi$, −1), and $\left(\dfrac{3\pi}{2}, 0\right)$. The sequence of points has been shifted to the left by $\dfrac{\pi}{2}$, so the correct equation is $y = \sin\left(x + \dfrac{\pi}{2}\right)$, which matches (D).

23. A
Difficulty: Medium

Category: Additional Topics in Math / Trigonometry

Strategic Advice: Complementary angles have a special relationship relative to trig values: The cosine of an acute angle is equal to the sine of the angle's complement and vice versa. Because only one of the answers can be correct, look for the simplest relationship (complementary angles). If that doesn't work, you'll need to rely on your knowledge of the unit circle.

Getting to the Answer: The angle measures are given in radians, so you're looking for an angle that, when added to $\frac{\pi}{8}$, gives $\frac{\pi}{2}$ (because $\frac{\pi}{2} = 90°$). Because $\frac{3\pi}{8} + \frac{\pi}{8} = \frac{4\pi}{8} = \frac{\pi}{2}$, the two angles, $\frac{\pi}{8}$ and $\frac{3\pi}{8}$ are complementary angles, which means (A) is correct.

24. C
Difficulty: Medium

Category: Additional Topics in Math / Trigonometry

Strategic Advice: If you come across a question like this on Test Day, it is likely to be in the no-calculator section of the test, so you'll need to rely on your knowledge of the unit circle, as well as some algebra skills.

Getting to the Answer: The cosine of 45° is $\frac{\sqrt{2}}{2}$ and the cosine of 60° is $\frac{1}{2}$. Finding the sum of these values is fairly straightforward since they have the same denominator—simply add the numerators and write the sum over 2 to get $\frac{\sqrt{2}+1}{2}$, which is the same as $\frac{1+\sqrt{2}}{2}$, which is (C).

25. D
Difficulty: Hard

Category: Additional Topics in Math / Trigonometry

Strategic Advice: You will not need to know a ton of trig identities on Test Day, but more likely only the Pythagorean Identity and the definitions of the trig ratios. That's all you need

to answer this question, along with a bit of algebraic manipulation.

Getting to the Answer: You should notice two things about the numerator of the expression: There's a tangent in each term (so it can be factored out) and there are squared trig functions. Start with that:

$$\frac{\tan\theta\cos^2\theta + \tan\theta\sin^2\theta}{\sin\theta} = \frac{\tan\theta(\cos^2\theta + \sin^2\theta)}{\sin\theta}$$
$$= \frac{\tan\theta(1)}{\sin\theta}$$
$$= \frac{\tan\theta}{\sin\theta}$$

Now, take a peek at the answer choices—each one is a single trig function, which means something in the result above must cancel. Use the trig ratios that you learned (SOH CAH TOA) to simplify your answer:

$$\frac{\tan\theta}{\sin\theta} = \frac{\dfrac{\text{opposite}}{\text{adjacent}}}{\dfrac{\text{opposite}}{\text{hypotenuse}}}$$
$$= \frac{\text{opposite}}{\text{adjacent}} \times \frac{\text{hypotenuse}}{\text{opposite}}$$
$$= \frac{\text{hypotenuse}}{\text{adjacent}}$$

Cosine is $\frac{\text{adj}}{\text{hyp}}$, and secant is the reciprocal of cosine, so the correct answer is (D).

26. 315
Difficulty: Easy

Category: Additional Topics in Math / Trigonometry

Strategic Advice: Use the conversion 180° = π with π written in the denominator so that it will cancel.

Getting to the Answer:

$$\frac{7\cancel{\pi}}{4} \times \frac{180°}{\cancel{\pi}} = 315°$$

The correct answer is 315.

27. 1
Difficulty: Medium

Category: Additional Topics in Math / Trigonometry

Strategic Advice: Knowing the basics of the unit circle and how to find coterminal angles will go a long way on Test Day. To find coterminal angles for which trig values are more easily recalled, you can subtract 2π as many times as you need to (because 2π is one full circle), which is equivalent to subtracting multiples of 2π.

Getting to the Answer: Start by "reducing" 11π to a more manageable angle measure: $11\pi - 5(2\pi) = 11\pi - 10\pi = \pi$. Now, apply our unit circle knowledge: $\cos(11\pi) = \cos(\pi) = -1$. The question states that $x = -\cos(11\pi)$, so don't forget to multiply by -1. The correct answer is $-(-1) = 1$.

28. 18
Difficulty: Medium

Category: Additional Topics in Math / Trigonometry

Strategic Advice: When you know the measure of a central angle and the corresponding arc length, you can find the circumference of the circle, and from that, you can find the radius.

Getting to the Answer: Use the relationship $\frac{\text{central angle}}{\text{whole circle}} = \frac{\text{arc length}}{\text{circumference}}$ to find the circumference of the circle.

$$\frac{120°}{360°} = \frac{12\pi}{C}$$
$$\frac{1}{3} = \frac{12\pi}{C}$$
$$C = 3(12\pi)$$
$$C = 36\pi$$

Now, use the formula for circumference to find that $2\pi r = 36\pi$, so $r = 18$. The radius of the circle is 18.

29. 3/5 or .6
Difficulty: Medium

Category: Additional Topics in Math / Trigonometry

Strategic Advice: Because trig functions typically apply to right triangles, drawn in an altitude and label what you know.

Getting to the Answer: You know the trough is 24 inches deep and 36 inches across the top. Because the given angles have equal measures ($x°$), the triangle is isosceles and the altitude bisects the top. Your figure should look like this:

You're given that $B = \cos x$, and the cosine of an angle involves the hypotenuse, so you need to find the length of the hypotenuse using the Pythagorean theorem:

$$18^2 + 24^2 = c^2$$
$$324 + 576 = c^2$$
$$900 = c^2$$
$$30 = c$$

Finally, $\cos x = \frac{\text{adj}}{\text{hyp}} = \frac{18}{30} = \frac{3}{5}$. Grid in 3/5 or .6.

30. 12/5 or **2.4**

Difficulty: Hard

Category: Additional Topics in Math / Trigonometry

Strategic Advice: Draw the height of the triangle to get an idea of which side lengths you need. Use the information given about the area of the triangle to find its height.

Getting to the Answer: Find the height of the triangle and add it to the figure.

$$A = \frac{1}{2}bh$$

$$240 = \frac{1}{2}(40)h$$

$$240 = 20h$$

$$12 = h$$

After you find the height, you might recognize the 5, 12, 13 Pythagorean triplet, which gives you another side of the triangle that contains β.

Note: Figure not drawn to scale.

Now use SOH CAH TOA: $\tan \beta = \dfrac{\text{opp}}{\text{adj}} = \dfrac{12}{5}$. Grid in 12/5 or 2.4.

CHAPTER 18

PREPARE

1. B
Difficulty: Medium

Category: Reading / Global

Strategic Advice: Review your Passage Map to find the general connection among the paragraphs. Be careful to stay within the scope of the passage.

Getting to the Answer: The passage begins with poems of the "earliest Greeks" and ends with the poetry of the "heroic age." The author attributes the differences in the poetry to the changes in Greek society between those two times. The author's tone is informational, offering no judgment on the poetry of the different periods. Predict that the main purpose is to discuss how societal changes affected poetry. Choice (B) matches this prediction.

PRACTICE

The following passage discusses facts and speculation about a spy during the American Revolution.

Although he may not have been the first American spy, when Captain Nathan Hale uttered his famous final words, "I only regret that I have but one
Line life to lose for my country," he ensured that
5 he would long be remembered as the first patriotic martyr of the American Revolution. Even today, Hale's story serves as an inspiration for others who have chosen to enter the often deadly and thankless profession of covert intelligence gathering. Yet, as
10 it seems clear that the sacrifice Hale made in the autumn of 1776 will long be valued, relatively little is actually known about his fateful mission.

NH = Am. spy during Rev. War.

mission details unknown

Born in Connecticut in 1755 as the sixth child of Richard Hale, a prosperous farmer, Nathan's
15 childhood and education were rather accelerated. Nathan was only 14 years old when he entered Yale University as a freshman, just 18 when he graduated as one of the top students in his class, and not yet 20 when he enlisted in the militia in 1774. With
20 the whole country abuzz from military movements and with many joining the separatist cause, Nathan quickly became involved in the military organization of his hometown. Historical records indicate that, by the time news of the first battles of the war reached
25 Connecticut in 1775, Hale had already become an outspoken leader of the independence movement. His subsequent commissioning as an officer in the Connecticut regiment is well documented, but it is the events of 1776, when Hale began his secret
30 mission, that are largely unknown.

bkgd & educ

military bkgd: CT Reg

It is known that Hale was indeed a spy and that he had been a member of the Knowlton Rangers, a small group of elite soldiers operating under what was called a "detached command," taking orders
35 directly from General George Washington. Historians also believe that it was Hale who accompanied a young sergeant named Stephen Hempstead on a mission involved with involving Washington's Long Island forces. But, perhaps due to chaos in New York
40 City created by the great fires that had been set in September of 1776, the precise details of Hale's mission and capture are unclear. Historical accounts pick up the story when he was taken before the commanding British General and, after honestly
45 providing his rank and name, was immediately condemned to death by hanging. There was no formal trial, but, according to the British, the papers Hale had on his person were damning enough, and the next morning he was hanged in an apple
50 orchard in the middle of Manhattan. Yet, despite the uncertainty surrounding Hale's story of espionage, a clear and undisputed written record verifies the young martyr's final words, for which he will likely be forever remembered and admired.

elite unit of soldiers: KR

mission still unclear

executed by Brit.

2. D

Difficulty: Medium

Category: Reading / Detail

Strategic Advice: Look at your Passage Map to find the important details you noted.

Getting to the Answer: Your Passage Map should note that paragraph 2 details Hale's military background. Review that paragraph to find the details of Hale's commission. In the last sentence, the author writes that Hale received a commission in the Connecticut regiment, or (D).

3. C

Difficulty: Medium

Category: Reading / Global

Strategic Advice: To answer a Global question, use your Passage Map to summarize the passage.

Getting to the Answer: Overall, the passage presents Hale and his history in a positive tone. In the first paragraph, the author states that Hale continues to be an inspiration, and in the final paragraph, the author suggests that there are good reasons Hale is remembered and admired. Predict that the author's purpose is to describe Hale in a positive way. Choice (C) matches this prediction. Be careful. While we'd like to know more about Hale's secret mission to New York, that detail is still unknown, making A out-of-scope and incorrect.

PERFORM

This passage discusses the cane toad's introduction to and effect on the Australian environment.

The cane toad, a large, brightly colored amphibian that can weigh more than a pound, was first introduced to the Australian continent by the sugar-
Line cane industry. The cane toad was a known predator
5 of the cane beetle, which had been devouring the sugarcane crops since the early 1900s. Australian farmers thought that by importing these toads from their native habitats in the Americas, they could effectively use the toads to feast on pests like the
10 cane beetle and eradicate the growing insect threat. So, in 1935, roughly 100 cane toads were carefully packed into crates and shipped to Australia. Upon their toads' arrival, the cane farmers eagerly brought them to a pond in the northeast province of Queensland.
15 Before long, the female cane toads had laid hundreds of thousands of eggs in elongated, gelatinous strings, and the farmers waited for their new predators to be born. As the eggs hatched, the pond became filled with great clouds of squirming,
20 wriggling tadpoles that, upon reaching maturity, were taken to the sugarcane fields and turned loose. The situation that resulted from this fateful release, however, did not coincide with the farmers' plan. In fact, the introduction of cane toads into the wild
25 in Australia has since been deemed nothing short of an ecological disaster.

Easily numbering well into the millions—an exact figure has been impossible to calculate— the cane toads soon dominated the landscape in
30 Queensland. Following their release, some of the toads descended as planned on the sugarcane crops and began to eat the beetles. However, they soon lost interest in their new habitat. For one thing, the mature cane beetles could fly away from their
35 predators, forcing these slow, fat toads to work very hard for their food. In addition, the fields were hot and dry and provided little sleeping shelter for the newcomers, who generally prefer wet shade. These adverse conditions were not severe enough
40 to kill off the toads, but instead the toads began to look elsewhere for food and shelter. Nearby towns, full of lush gardens and well-watered lawns, were extremely inviting, and soon the toads had overrun entire residential areas. They covered the lawns,
45 filled the gardens, found shelter under flowerpots or on porches, and even began to eat bowls of food left outside for pets like cats and dogs.

Today, the people of Queensland hunt cane toads as if they were mosquitoes. But the toads
50 continue to spread south and west through Aus-

Margin notes:

why Aus. farmers brought c.t.

toads released into fields

turned into disaster

A LOT of toads

c.t. ate other things, moved to lawns and gardens

toad takeover

today = c.t. hunted

tralia in staggering numbers. As for the sugarcane industry, just five years after the release of the toads, an effective insecticide spray became available, and the cane beetles were easily exterminated. Scien-
55 tists as well as the Australian government, however, continue to grapple with the cane toad problem.

4. D

Difficulty: Medium

Category: Reading / Detail

Strategic Advice: When presented with an EXCEPT question, use your Passage Map to locate the details in the answer choices. Eliminate an answer choice when you find its referenced detail.

Getting to the Answer: The first paragraph describes the reason the cane toad was introduced. Eliminate A. Paragraph 2 tells you that the toads bred rapidly and successfully; eliminate B. The last sentence in paragraph 2 calls the introduction of the cane toad "an ecological disaster" (line 26), so you can eliminate C. Thus, (D) is correct.

5. B

Difficulty: Hard

Category: Reading / Inference

Strategic Advice: Use your Passage Map to narrow the range of possible answers and paraphrase what the author would agree with.

Getting to the Answer: The passage describes the cause of a problem: the introduction of the cane toad. The passage then describes the effects of that introduction: a huge environmental disaster. Predict that the author would agree that the new species harmed the environment. You can eliminate answer choices that go beyond the scope of this prediction. The author's main focus is on the cause of the problem and the negative effect that resulted. Choice (B) is correct.

EXTRA PRACTICE

The following passage describes the discovery of gold in California and the effects of that discovery on the United States.

People around the world unanimously agree that gold is a valuable mineral. Gold has been seen as a precious commodity by many cultures throughout
Line time, and Americans of the 1840s were no different.
5 When James W. Marshall, a carpenter and sawmill owner, discovered a gold nugget in the American River, California was forever changed. News of his discovery attracted thousands of immigrants from other parts of California, as well as other places around the United
10 States and the world.

In the Sierra Nevada, a mountain range that runs 400 miles through California, years of erosion caused by rainfall and the downhill flow of mountain streams loosened pieces of gold that had been embedded in
15 the solid rock formed over 100 million years ago. California is largely made of quartz previously found at the bottom of the Pacific Ocean. Underwater volcanoes melted the quartz into magma and pushed it up towards the surface, sometimes forming islands. Due to the
20 movements of the Earth's tectonic plates, these islands were pushed together and against the West Coast. This movement and accumulation of land over millions of years formed the area known as California. The gold that was dispersed across the sea floor became
25 concentrated and redistributed throughout the veins of quartz in the Sierra Nevada Mountains.

Marshall's discovery was quickly verified and publicized by the New York Herald in August of 1848. Current California residents of the time were able to
30 get to the gold fields first. Soon after, President James Polk confirmed the discovery in an address to Congress. His address prompted many Americans to move west, as well as other fortune-seekers from around the world to immigrate to the United States. This influx of people
35 caused California's population to increase, as well as experience a change in demographics. The particular geologic makeup made California the prime location for mining gold. The Northern California city of San

topic = CA gold in 1940s

how CA & gold came to be

pop. explosion

why CA became state

Francisco grew from 1,000 people in 1848 to more than
40 20,000 people in just two years. <u>Because of the rapid population increase, the United States government incorporated the territory into the Union.</u> (California) became the Union's 31st state in 1850, though it had only been acquired from Mexico two short years before. This
45 was the <u>fastest any new territory has ever been given statehood in the history of the United States.</u>

2 ways to CA

Americans from places east of California migrated via two very long and often dangerous paths. Some endured a <u>six-month boat voyage,</u> which departed from
50 New York City and sailed south as far as the tip of South America before heading north to California. The trip was so perilous that most Americans relocating to California opted to travel the famous <u>Oregon Trail.</u> Riding in covered wagons through dangerous conditions, trav-
55 elers who opted to move by land also had a six-month trip to endure. By 1850, the sheer number of people attempting the voyage inspired the creation of the Panama Railway. Built specifically to reduce travel time to California, the first transcontinental railroad decreased
60 the length of the trip by several months.

Forty-Niners came to California from many different countries around the globe, including China, Germany, Mexico, Turkey, France, and

not just Amer.

Ireland. The largest group of people to successfully
65 immigrate to California from abroad was the Chinese. Many did not intend to settle in the United States, but instead planned to return home with their fortunes. While many did so, when gold grew scarce and the <u>Chinese Exclusion Act was
70 passed in 1882,</u> prohibiting Chinese immigration for 10 years, many immigrants instead put down roots in California. The <u>result was the most ethnically diverse state in the Union by the middle of the 19th century</u>.

CA gold effects → today

75 Though the gold in California didn't last long after its discovery, the <u>effects that it had on the population, including the number of people in the state, their ethnicities, and the way they travelled, have lasted to the modern day</u>.

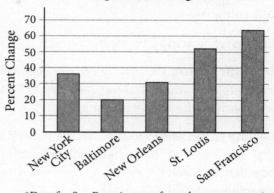

Percent Population Change, 1850-1860

*Data for San Francisco are from the state census in 1852. The 1850 census data were destroyed in a fire.

Data from the *United States Bureau of the Census*.

1. B
Difficulty: Medium

Category: Reading / Rhetoric

Strategic Advice: Look at your notes for the second paragraph. Why does the author include it?

Getting to the Answer: The passage provides geological information to make a point about why gold was so easily mined in California. Choice (B) correctly identifies this information.

2. A
Difficulty: Easy

Category: Reading / Detail

Strategic Advice: One main cause of migration is listed in the passage. Review your notes to find the answer.

Getting to the Answer: The passage states that President Polk's "address to Congress … prompted many Americans to move west" (lines 31-32). Choice (A) conveys this meaning.

3. D

Difficulty: Medium

Category: Reading / Vocab-in-Context

Strategic Advice: Read the referenced line and the sentences around it. Then, use context clues to determine the word's meaning.

Getting to the Answer: The passage suggests that there was an overwhelming increase in population. Choice (D), "rush," conveys this meaning.

4. D

Difficulty: Hard

Category: Reading / Inference

Strategic Advice: Note what the passage states about California's statehood: California entered into the Union despite a surprising fact.

Getting to the Answer: The passage states that "California became the Union's 31st state in 1850, though it had only been acquired from Mexico two short years before" (lines 42-44). It can be inferred, then, that most states had spent longer as territories before being admitted into the Union. Choice (D) is correct.

5. C

Difficulty: Medium

Category: Reading / Command of Evidence

Strategic Advice: Carefully reread the part of the passage that addresses statehood. Identify the specific claims it makes.

Getting to the Answer: The passage states that the United States incorporated California "though it had only been acquired from Mexico two short years before" (lines 43-44). Choice (C) is correct because it explicitly identifies what was unusual about California's statehood process.

6. D

Difficulty: Medium

Category: Reading / Inference

Strategic Advice: Skim quickly to find the information describing the cause stated in the question. Then, read closely to locate the effects of that cause.

Getting to the Answer: The passage states explicitly that the creation of the Panama Railway was built in response to the needs of migrants to California. Choice (D) is correct.

7. C

Difficulty: Hard

Category: Reading / Inference

Strategic Advice: Determine what the passage states about immigrant groups. Consider what can be concluded with certainty about them.

Getting to the Answer: The passage notes that California was very ethnically diverse by the middle of the 19th century. This suggests that immigrants to California came from more places than did immigrants to other states. Choice (C) is correct.

8. D

Difficulty: Medium

Category: Reading / Command of Evidence

Strategic Advice: Review your answer to the previous question. Look for information about California immigration from the passage.

Getting to the Answer: The passage states that California was "the most ethnically diverse state in the Union by the middle of the 19th century" (lines 72-74). This provides evidence for the assertion that immigrants to California came from more nations than did immigrants to other states. Choice (D), therefore, provides the strongest evidence and is correct.

9. C

Difficulty: Easy

Category: Reading / Vocab-in-Context

Strategic Advice: Consider the structure of the sentence. What is the relationship between the nature of the voyage and the choice to travel the Oregon Trail?

Getting to the Answer: The passage states that both routes to California were "very long and often dangerous" (line 48). "Perilous," therefore, is likely to mean "dangerous." Choice (C) is correct.

10. C

Difficulty: Hard

Category: Reading / Rhetoric

Strategic Advice: Review each paragraph and try to identify its main point. Then, assess the answer choices.

Getting to the Answer: The initial paragraphs discuss why gold is important and why it was concentrated in California. It then analyzes the effects of its discovery there. Choice (C) accurately assesses the structure of the passage.

11. A

Difficulty: Medium

Category: Reading / Synthesis

Strategic Advice: Read the chart carefully. Pay particular attention to what the *y*-axis represents.

Getting to the Answer: The population change of all cities for the period from 1850 to 1860 was positive. In other words, all cities gained population, though some gained more than others. Choice (A) is correct, as it correctly identifies that all cities gained in population during this period.

This passage details the history of Eleanor Roosevelt and how she changed the role of the First Lady of the United States.

Eleanor Roosevelt, wife of president Franklin Delano Roosevelt (FDR), forever altered the role of American First Lady and women in U.S. politics
Line in general. Dedicated, humble, and brave, Eleanor
5 Roosevelt powerfully shouldered the nation's burdens during the longest and arguably most difficult presidency America has yet seen. Her sustained commitment to social justice began long before her husband's presidency and endured
10 through the end of her life.

Born in 1884 to the brother of president Theodore Roosevelt, Eleanor's upbringing acquainted her with both politics and hardship. Having lost her parents in childhood, Eleanor was cared for by her grand-
15 mother in New York and was later sent to London for secondary schooling. After this education, Roosevelt returned to the States and became involved in humanitarian work, which would prove to be a lifelong engagement. At twenty years old she married
20 her distant cousin, Franklin Delano, with whom she would parent six children.

While Mrs. Roosevelt was a committed wife and mother, she was also heavily involved with the national and international crises that plagued her
25 generation. During World War I she volunteered in hospitals while supporting and partnering in her husband's political career. When FDR contracted polio in the early 1920s, she assumed much of his political responsibility, as he held a number of high-
30 profile government positions before his presidency. This quickly afforded her an increasing national influence. Eleanor Roosevelt fought diligently for women's empowerment and numerous other human rights issues. Her husband's presidency (1933 to 1945)
35 also oversaw both the Great Depression and World War II, two major national dilemmas with which Eleanor Roosevelt was intimately involved in addressing.

Before Eleanor Roosevelt, U.S. First Ladies had less political voice. Never before had a First Lady
40 hosted press conferences, let alone assumed

v. important

early life

political involvement

ER changed role of 1st Lady

significant portions of the public responsibilities of the presidency. But due to FDR's lasting illness and his wife's wisdom, eloquence, and powerful political presence, all of this was possible, and in many ways
45 essential, for his effective leadership.

New Deal

Eleanor Roosevelt's concern for human rights aided her husband in his development of the New Deal, which was his legislative effort to alleviate the Great Depression. Mrs. Roosevelt catalyzed,
50 advocated for, oversaw, and in many ways sustained much of the New Deal programming. Through these programs she sought to equip and employ youth, protect labor rights, and mend racial injustices.

Eleanor travelled extensively, speaking publicly,
55 taking reports on relief programs, and visiting troops in wartime. Outside of direct political involvements, she taught and lectured in educational settings, aggressively fundraised for charitable causes, hosted countless social functions, and even
60 spearheaded a small furniture business to employ the jobless.

Many remember Eleanor Roosevelt best for her power with words. Ever an advocate for the rights of the disadvantaged, Roosevelt spoke and wrote
65 extensively. She published several books and even maintained a daily newspaper column for nearly thirty years.

FDR died.

FDR's declining health prevented him from completing his fourth elected presidential term. He
70 died in April of 1945, one month before the official end of Europe's involvement in World War II. This marked the end of Eleanor's time as First Lady, and in her grief she indicated an intent to absent herself from politics altogether. Yet her dedication to the
75 pursuit of world peace and human rights would prevail. Toward the end of that year she accepted

ER joined U.N.

President Truman's invitation to help represent the U.S. at the newly forming United Nations.

In serving the UN, Roosevelt drafted the Universal
80 Declaration of Human Rights. This document still holds paramount importance today; it sets a standard against which international justice is still principally

work at U.N.

measured. She soon became chair of the UN Human Rights Commission. Stateside, Roosevelt actively

85 bolstered the Civil Rights movement. She visited those imprisoned for nonviolent protest, spoke publicly for the cause, served on the boards of various organizations, and helped to catalyze the Justice Department's Civil Rights Division. Roosevelt's work
90 toward labor justice and women's equality in America also continued into her final years.

Eleanor Roosevelt died in 1962 at the age of 78 years old. Over a half-century later, this woman's legacy remains. Her wise words are cherished in
95 American hearts, her impact echoes throughout national and international human rights legislation, and her strength still empowers the powerless to continue their efforts toward equality and justice. Roosevelt's perseverance, integrity, and accomplish-
100 ments forever render her one of the most well-loved and revered women in American history.

accomplished beyond role of 1st Lady

Unemployment Rates Over the Course of FDR's "New Deal" Programs

Adapted from HERB: Resources for Teachers and Bureau of Labor Statistics, "Graph of U.S. Unemployment Rate 1930-1945." ©2011 by American Social History Productions, Inc.

12. B
Difficulty: Easy

Category: Reading / Vocab-in-Context

Strategic Advice: The correct answer will flow naturally in place of the original word or phrase and maintain the meaning of the sentence.

Getting to the Answer: The text states that Eleanor Roosevelt "shouldered the nation's burdens" (lines 5-6). This means that she took responsibility for addressing, or handling, those burdens, as reflected by (B).

13. A
Difficulty: Medium

Category: Reading / Rhetoric

Strategic Advice: Consider the author's point of view throughout the passage. The correct answer will be supported by the central idea of the text as well as by the passage's supporting details.

Getting to the Answer: The central idea of the passage focuses on Roosevelt's many achievements both as First Lady and in supporting human rights. The final paragraph summarizes her impact and showcases the respect that the author has for Roosevelt, as indicated in (A).

14. D
Difficulty: Medium

Category: Reading / Command of Evidence

Strategic Advice: The correct answer will provide information and use rhetoric to support the central idea and tone of the answer to the previous question.

Getting to the Answer: The answer to the previous question asserts that the author holds admiration for Eleanor Roosevelt. Choice (D) identifies Eleanor Roosevelt as the object of love and reverence, and identifies the attributes (perseverance, integrity, and accomplishments) that merit admiration.

15. B
Difficulty: Hard

Category: Reading / Inference

Strategic Advice: The correct answer will make sense in the larger context of the passage and will be supported by specific textual evidence.

Getting to the Answer: The passage notes that Eleanor Roosevelt "aided her husband in his development of the New Deal" (lines 47-48), Franklin Roosevelt's key legislative policy. Further evidence asserts that Eleanor Roosevelt's contributions were "essential" (line 45) to President Roosevelt's "effective leadership" (line 45), as indicated in (B).

16. B
Difficulty: Medium

Category: Reading / Detail

Strategic Advice: The correct answer will be clearly stated in one or more lines from the text.

Getting to the Answer: The text repeatedly discusses Roosevelt's advocacy for social justice work and human rights reform, as indicated in (B).

17. D
Difficulty: Hard

Category: Reading / Rhetoric

Strategic Advice: The correct answer will reflect the direct intent of the information in the passage and will be supported by evidence throughout the text.

Getting to the Answer: Although the passage as a whole explores various contributions made by Eleanor Roosevelt, the excerpted line focuses on her humanitarian efforts during World War I, prior to her husband's rise to the presidency and her ascent to the role of First Lady. Therefore, (D) is correct, as it demonstrates that her humanitarian efforts began early in her life, a point argued throughout the passage.

18. B

Difficulty: Hard

Category: Reading / Synthesis

Strategic Advice: The correct answer will be supported by and will connect information shown in the graph and expressed in the passage.

Getting to the Answer: The data in the graph show declining unemployment during the Great Depression following the passage of President Roosevelt's New Deal policies. The passage suggests that the New Deal policies made up President Roosevelt's signature effort to ease the troubles of the Great Depression, as stated in (B). The passage further suggests that Eleanor Roosevelt proved crucial to this important effort.

19. A

Difficulty: Medium

Category: Reading / Inference

Strategic Advice: The correct answer will reflect Eleanor Roosevelt's ideas, actions, and sentiments as expressed in the passage.

Getting to the Answer: The passage focuses largely on the social justice, human rights, and humanitarian efforts of Eleanor Roosevelt, which would make her most likely to engage in (A).

20. B

Difficulty: Easy

Category: Reading / Command of Evidence

Strategic Advice: The correct answer will provide direct support for the answer to the previous question by connecting central ideas or themes.

Getting to the Answer: The answer to the previous question states that Eleanor Roosevelt would be most likely to volunteer in a disaster response effort, a humanitarian undertaking. Choice (B) is correct, as it states that Eleanor Roosevelt made humanitarian work a lifelong pursuit.

21. C

Difficulty: Easy

Category: Reading / Vocab-in-Context

Strategic Advice: The correct answer will reflect the specific meaning of the original word or phrase in the larger context of the sentence.

Getting to the Answer: The text states that Eleanor Roosevelt "spearheaded a small furniture business" (line 60). This suggests that she led the growth of the business, as reflected by (C).

22. B

Difficulty: Hard

Category: Reading / Rhetoric

Strategic Advice: The correct answer will reflect the main idea of the paragraph and will identify its role within the larger passage.

Getting to the Answer: The paragraph examines the contributions of Eleanor Roosevelt not only as First Lady but also as an individual before, during, and after her husband's presidency. Choice (B) emphasizes the accomplishments that Eleanor Roosevelt made following her husband's presidency.

CHAPTER 19

PREPARE

1. D
Difficulty: Easy

Category: Reading / Global

Strategic Advice: When asked for a description of the passage as a whole, think about the author or narrator's structural flow.

Getting to the Answer: This passage begins with a general description of many women performing agricultural labor. However, in the middle of the first paragraph, the narrator says, "the eye returns involuntarily" to the young girl in the pink jacket. The next two paragraphs describe her actions and features further. Choice (D) is correct.

2. A
Difficulty: Medium

Category: Reading / Inference

Strategic Advice: Remember that the SAT Reading Test is an open-book exam: The answer is always in the passage.

Getting to the Answer: According to the narrator, the girl works with "clock-like monotony" (line 21). Furthermore, she continues to work like this "as the day wears on" (line 33) and until her hands become "scarified" (line 34). Thus, the work is repetitive and ongoing to the point of physical damage. This suggests that the work is "routine," making (A) the correct answer.

3. B
Difficulty: Medium

Category: Reading / Rhetoric

Strategic Advice: This question asks you to identify the role that a particular part of a passage plays. Focus on the author's reason for writing the passage and think about how the cited section helps achieve that purpose.

Getting to the Answer: Reread the cited section and review your Passage Map. The author's central idea is to contrast differing ideas about education and explain why his ideas are different from those of his audience. Predict that different people can have different ideas about education. Choice (B) matches that prediction.

4. D
Difficulty: Easy

Category: Reading / Global

Strategic Advice: To summarize the central idea of a passage, review the key ideas you noted in your Passage Map. Even when you can't make a specific prediction, you can paraphrase the central ideas.

Getting to the Answer: Use your paraphrased summary to make a general prediction before looking at the answer choices. In this passage, the author begins by thanking his audience for their offer to educate the Iroquois youth. However, he swiftly shifts to a comparison of the two concepts of education, discussing a college education only in terms of how useless it is in comparison to the Iroquois concept. He concludes by making a reciprocal offer to the audience and promises that the result will be to "make men of them" (line 26). Predict that the author does not like the non-Iroquois way. Choice (D) matches your prediction.

5. A

Difficulty: Medium

Category: Reading / Rhetoric

Strategic Advice: Some Rhetoric questions will ask you to analyze the purpose of a portion of a passage in relation to the whole passage.

Getting to the Answer: The central idea of the passage is that turtles can navigate long distances using sight and smell. Review the final paragraph and your Passage Map notes to predict that the author describes how those two senses work in tandem to help turtles navigate to Ascension Island. Choice (A) matches your prediction.

6. C

Difficulty: Medium

Category: Reading / Detail

Strategic Advice: For a question this straightforward, the answer will be directly stated in the passage.

Getting to the Answer: Turtles' eyesight is discussed in the third paragraph, which establishes that the turtles can follow the rising sun toward the east because their eyes are especially sensitive to the color red. Choice (C) is correct.

PRACTICE

The following Science passage explains the forces of flight.

What do paper airplanes and large commercial airliners such as the Boeing 747 have in common? Plenty. Despite differences in size and weight, both
Line must make use of the same physical forces in order
5 to fly. The flight of any airplane results from the interaction of four different forces: thrust, drag, gravity, and lift.

forces of flight

All of the forces acting on the airplane must balance each other in order for the plane to travel
10 along in steady horizontal flight. Thrust supplied by jet engines or propellers (or by a person's hand for a paper airplane) is the force that drives the airplane forward. The airplane cannot actually move any distance forward, however, unless the amount of
15 *thrust* is enough to overcome the force of *drag*. Drag is the air resistance that the plane encounters in flight. Just as the name indicates, air resistance has the effect of dragging the airplane backward as it moves through the air. Jet engines are designed
20 so that the airplane has the necessary thrust to overcome air resistance. Drag can be reduced if the airplane is streamlined—that is, constructed in such a way that air flows smoothly around it so that there is little friction at the airplane's surface.

thrust & drag

impact on aircraft design

25 To rise into the air, an airplane has to overcome the force of gravity, the downward pull that the Earth exerts on everything on or near its surface. The airplane accomplishes this feat with lift force, which acts in an upward direction opposite to
30 gravity. Lift is provided by the airplane's wings. The wings and wing flaps are shaped and angled so that air will flow more rapidly over them than under them. When air flows more rapidly over the wing tops, air pressure above the wings drops
35 in comparison with the air pressure below the wings. (This phenomenon is known to engineers as Bernoulli's principle.) When an airplane taxis down the runway (or when a paper airplane is released from a person's hand), the greater air pressure
40 below the wings pushes the wings upward, allowing the airplane to rise despite the pull of gravity. Once the plane is safely in the air, all four of the basic aerodynamic forces figure into the flight as well, whether it is the flight of a big jet or a paper
45 airplane.

gravity & lift

pressure moves plane

all 4 forces play role

7. B

Difficulty: Medium

Category: Reading / Vocab-in-Context

Strategic Advice: When you see the phrase "most nearly means" and a cited word or phrase, pretend that word or phrase is blank and predict a synonym for it.

Getting to the Answer: Read the sentence without "acts" (line 29) and ask what "lift force" does. Predict that it functions or works. Choice (B) is correct.

8. B

Difficulty: Medium

Category: Reading / Inference

Strategic Advice: Review your Passage Map notes regarding drag. Remember to be wary of answer choices that are outside the scope of the passage.

Getting to the Answer: Paragraph 2 provides details about drag, specifically that it is "the air resistance that the plane encounters in flight" (lines 16-17). At the end of the paragraph, the author writes that drag decreases when "there is little friction at the airplane's surface" (lines 23-24). Choice (B) reflects the relationship between drag and friction and is therefore correct.

PERFORM

The following passage is an excerpt from Abraham Lincoln's second autobiography, published in a Pennsylvania newspaper in 1860.

AL birth & family

    I was born February 12, 1809, in Hardin County, Kentucky. My parents were both born in Virginia, of undistinguished families—second families, perhaps I should say. My mother, who died in my
Line
5 tenth year, was of a family of the name of Hanks, some of whom now reside in Adams, and others in

Macon County, Illinois. My paternal grandfather, Abraham Lincoln, emigrated from Rockingham County, Virginia, to Kentucky about 1781 or 1782,
10 where a year or two later he was killed by the Indians, not in battle, but by stealth, when he was laboring to open a farm in the forest. His ancestors, who were Quakers, went to Virginia from Berks County, Pennsylvania. An effort to identify them with the
15 New England family of the same name ended in nothing more definite than a similarity of Christian names in both families, such as Enoch, Levi, Mordecai, Solomon, Abraham, and the like.

    My father, at the death of his father, was but
20 six years of age, and he grew up literally without education. He removed from Kentucky to what is now Spencer County, Indiana in my eighth year. We reached our new home about the time the state came into the Union. It was a wild region,
25 with many bears and other wild animals still in the woods. There I grew up. There were some schools, so called, but no qualification was ever required of a teacher beyond "readin', writin', and cipherin'" to the rule of three. If a straggler supposed to understand
30 Latin happened to sojourn in the neighborhood, he was looked upon as a wizard. There was absolutely nothing to excite ambition for education. Of course, when I came of age I did not know much. Still, somehow I could read, write, and cipher to the rule
35 of three, but that was all. I have not been to school since. The little advance I now have upon this store of education I have picked up from time to time under the pressure of necessity.

    I was raised to farm work, which I continued till
40 I was twenty-two. At twenty-one I came to Illinois, Macon County. Then I got to New Salem, at that time in Sangamon, now in Menard, County, where I remained a year as a sort of clerk in a store.

    Then came the Black Hawk War, and I was
45 elected a captain of volunteers, a success which gave me more pleasure than any I have had since. I went the campaign, was elated, ran for the legislature the same year (1832), and was beaten—the only time I have ever been beaten by the people. The next and
50 three succeeding biennial elections I was elected

father & move to KY

school = v. basic

early jobs

ran for office

to the legislature. I was not a candidate afterward. During this legislative period I had <u>studied law</u>, and removed to Springfield to practice it. In 1846 I was once elected to the lower house of Congress.

55 I was not a candidate for reelection. From 1849 to 1854, both inclusive practiced law more assiduously than ever before. Always a Whig in politics; and generally on the Whig electoral tickets, making active canvasses. I was losing interest in politics when

60 the repeal of the Missouri Compromise aroused me again. <u>What I have done since then is pretty well known.</u>

If any personal description of me is thought desirable, it may be said I am, in height, six feet four

65 inches, nearly; lean in flesh, weighing on an average one hundred and eighty pounds; dark complexion, with coarse black hair and gray eyes. No other marks or brands recollected.

MO Comp. got interested

tone = humble

9. D

Difficulty: Medium

Category: Reading / Rhetoric

Strategic Advice: When a question asks you to identify the author's stance, think about the author's point of view.

Getting to the Answer: The author begins by referring to his parents' families as "undistinguished" (line 3) and keeps the focus of the passage on the simplicity of his life and circumstances. Predict that the author sees himself as an ordinary person who grew up without many advantages. Choice (D) matches your prediction.

10. C

Difficulty: Medium

Category: Reading / Global

Strategic Advice: To summarize the central purpose of the passage, review the key ideas you noted in your Passage Map. If you can't make a specific prediction, you can still paraphrase the central ideas.

Getting to the Answer: While the author does spend a good deal of the passage discussing education, this is not his reason for writing. The overall purpose of the passage is to provide his own history, which shifts from his modest childhood to his national importance, which is underscored by the phrase "What I have done since then is pretty well known" (lines 61-62). Choice (C) is correct.

11. C

Difficulty: Hard

Category: Reading / Inference

Strategic Advice: If you are not provided with a line reference, use your Passage Map to locate the part of the passage to which the question stem refers.

Getting to the Answer: The question asks about the effect of the Black Hawk War, which is first mentioned in the beginning of paragraph 4. The overall topic of paragraph 4 is the author's campaigns and subsequent elections, suggesting a connection between the war and the author's political career. Choice (C) is correct.

12. B

Difficulty: Medium

Category: Reading / Vocab-in-Context

Strategic Advice: When you see the phrase "most nearly means" and a cited line, pretend the word or phrase is a blank and predict the meaning of the word or phrase in context.

Getting to the Answer: Read the lines surrounding the cited phrase. The author says that he has not been to school since his childhood but "picked up" (line 37) the "little advance…upon this store of education" (lines 36-37) "under the pressure of necessity" (line 38). Predict that the phrase means that he learned when he had to, or when it was necessary. Choice (B) is correct.

EXTRA PRACTICE

This passage is adapted from Guy de Maupas-
sant's short story, "The False Gems," from The
Entire Original Maupassant Short Stories.

Monsieur Lantin had met the young girl at a
reception at the house of the second head of his
department, and had fallen head over heels in love

L in love with
girl

Line with her.

5   Her simple beauty had the charm of angelic
modesty, and the imperceptible smile which
constantly hovered about the lips seemed to be the
reflection of a pure and lovely soul.

Monsieur Lantin, then chief clerk in the
10 Department of the Interior, enjoyed a snug little
salary of three thousand five hundred francs, and he
proposed to this model young girl, and was accepted.

married girl

He was unspeakably happy with her. She governed his household with such clever economy that
15 they seemed to live in luxury.

He found fault with only two of her tastes: Her love
for the theatre, and her taste for imitation jewelry.
After a time, Monsieur Lantin begged his wife to

L got out of
theater

request some lady of her acquaintance to accompa-
20 ny her, and to bring her home after the theatre. She
opposed this arrangement, at first; but, after much
persuasion, finally consented, to the infinite delight
of her husband.

Now, with her love for the theatre, came also the
25 desire for ornaments. Her costumes remained as
before, simple, in good taste, and always modest;

wife: fake
jewelry

but she soon began to adorn her ears with huge
rhinestones, which glittered and sparkled like real
diamonds. Around her neck she wore strings of
30 false pearls, on her arms bracelets of imitation gold,
and combs set with glass jewels.

Her husband frequently remonstrated with her,

L argues abt.
jewels

saying:

"My dear, as you cannot afford to buy real
35 jewelry, you ought to appear adorned with your
beauty and modesty alone, which are the rarest
ornaments of your sex."

But she would smile sweetly, and say:
"Look! are they not lovely? One would swear
40 they were real."

One evening, in winter, she had been to the
opera, and returned home chilled through and
through. The next morning she coughed, and
eight days later she died of inflammation of the
45 lungs.

He wept unceasingly; his heart was broken as he
remembered her smile, her voice, every charm of
his dead wife.

wife died; L
devastated

Time did not assuage his grief. Everything in his
50 wife's room remained as it was during her lifetime;
all her furniture, even her clothing, being left as
it was on the day of her death. Here he was wont

preserved
her memory

to seclude himself daily and think of her who had
been his treasure—the joy of his existence.

But life soon became a struggle.

hard times →
had to sell
jewels

55   One morning, finding himself without a cent in
his pocket, he resolved to sell something, and immediately the thought occurred to him of disposing
of his wife's paste jewels, for he cherished in his
60 heart a sort of rancor against these "deceptions,"
which had always irritated him in the past. The very
sight of them spoiled, somewhat, the memory of his
lost darling.

To the last days of her life she had continued to
65 make purchases, bringing home new gems almost
every evening, and he turned them over some time
before finally deciding to sell the heavy necklace,
which she seemed to prefer, and which, he thought,
ought to be worth about six or seven francs; for
70 it was of very fine workmanship, though only
imitation.

He put it in his pocket, and started out in search
of what seemed a reliable jeweler's shop. At length
he found one, and went in, feeling a little ashamed

jeweler
appraised

75 to expose his misery, and also to offer such a worthless article for sale.

"Sir," said he to the merchant, "I would like to
know what this is worth."

The man took the necklace, examined it,
80 called his clerk, and made some remarks in an
undertone; he then put the ornament back on the

counter, and looked at it from a distance to judge of the effect.

jewels = real 85

Monsieur Lantin, annoyed at all these ceremonies, was on the point of saying: "Oh! I know well enough it is not worth anything," when the jeweler said: "Sir, that necklace is worth from <u>twelve to fifteen thousand francs</u>; but I could not buy it, unless you can tell me exactly where it came from."

90

The widower opened his eyes wide and remained gaping, not comprehending the merchant's meaning. Finally he stammered: "You say—are you sure?"

L = stunned

Monsieur Lantin, beside himself with astonishment, took up the necklace and left the store.

1. D
Difficulty: Medium

Category: Reading / Vocab-in-Context

Strategic Advice: Use context clues and tone to help determine the meaning of the word. Create a mental picture of what is being described by using the surrounding text. Finally, make sure the answer choice does not alter the meaning of the sentence when inserted.

Getting to the Answer: The paragraph in which the word appears describes the girl as "simple" (line 5) and "pure" (line 8), and as having a "lovely soul" (line 8). Therefore, (D) is correct. "Angelic" means "innocent" in this context.

2. C
Difficulty: Medium

Category: Reading / Detail

Strategic Advice: Skim the passage to locate descriptions of Lantin's wife at the beginning of their marriage.

Getting to the Answer: Paragraphs 3 and 4 describe the Lantins' "snug" (line 10) income and attribute their luxurious lifestyle to Lantin's wife's "clever economy" (line 14). Choice (C) is correct. "Frugal" describes someone who is thrifty and economical.

3. A
Difficulty: Medium

Category: Reading / Inference

Strategic Advice: Look for Lantin's thoughts and statements about the jewels. Use this as evidence of his attitude.

Getting to the Answer: The Lantins are described as making a "snug" (line 10) salary, and Madame Lantin has to be very economical. Later in the passage, Lantin mentions that they "cannot afford" (line 34) to buy real jewelry. Choice (A) is correct because Lantin clearly believes they cannot afford real gems.

4. D
Difficulty: Easy

Category: Reading / Command of Evidence

Strategic Advice: Review your answer to the previous question. Decide which lines of text give a reason that Lantin would believe the gems to be false.

Getting to the Answer: Choice (D) offers the best support. In these lines, Lantin explicitly states they cannot afford real jewelry.

5. B
Difficulty: Medium

Category: Reading / Inference

Strategic Advice: Reread the text, looking for evidence to support each of the answer choices. Examine Lantin's thoughts and statements for clues about characterization.

Getting to the Answer: This section of the passage describes Lantin's intense mourning for his wife, which suggests a deep unhappiness. Choice (B) is correct.

6. B

Difficulty: Medium

Category: Reading / Command of Evidence

Strategic Advice: Review your answer to the previous question. Read each choice and figure out which one provides specific support for that answer.

Getting to the Answer: Choice (B) provides the best support. These lines show that Lantin is overcome with grief. They indicate that his sadness is long-term, as time does not alter the extent of his grief.

7. D

Difficulty: Easy

Category: Reading / Vocab-in-Context

Strategic Advice: Use context clues from the target sentence and surrounding sentence. Predict the meaning of the word and look for a match in the answer choices.

Getting to the Answer: Lantin views the jewels as "deceptions" (line 60) and speaks of the irritation her jewels caused him. Looking at the jewels also negatively affects his memory of his wife. Choice (D) provides a suitably negative word and makes sense in the context of the rest of the paragraph.

8. C

Difficulty: Medium

Category: Reading / Rhetoric

Strategic Advice: Contrast this sentence with what has already occurred in the passage. Analyze the new information it provides and the response it provokes when you read it.

Getting to the Answer: The sentence calls into question the reliability of everything we have learned about Madame Lantin. Although she and her husband were not wealthy, Madame Lantin has somehow acquired a very expensive piece of jewelry. Choice (C) is correct. The author uses this sentence to create an unresolved conflict. Lantin does not know how his wife obtained the jewels, and the sentence suggests the answer might call his wife's virtue into question.

9. D

Difficulty: Hard

Category: Reading / Inference

Strategic Advice: Review the end of the excerpt. Think about what this text might suggest broadly. Don't speculate by choosing an overly specific answer.

Getting to the Answer: The correct answer will provide a logical conclusion about Madame Lantin based on what you have learned about her throughout the passage. Her husband idealized her but has discovered she has been dishonest and hidden things from him. Choice (D) provides a reasonable conclusion that a reader can make about Madame Lantin.

10. A

Difficulty: Hard

Category: Reading / Global

Strategic Advice: Ask yourself what purpose the author has in writing the passage. What main point does the majority of the excerpt support?

Getting to the Answer: The events in the passage show that Lantin judges his wife for her love of costume jewelry. After her death, he finds that her jewels are real. Both the "paste" jewels that turn out to be real and Lantin's realization that his wife had provided for him after her death with her collection of jewels support the idea that appearances can be deceiving. Choice (A) best describes the central theme the author develops throughout the excerpt.

The following passage details the antibody that produces peanut allergies and how scientists are using this information to develop a peanut that does not cause allergic reactions.

peanuts &
allergies

Peanuts can cause deadly allergic reactions in some people, and there is no real cure for peanut allergies. However, scientists may be working on
Line the next best thing to a cure: peanuts that do not
5 cause allergic reactions.

Allergic reactions start with the immune system, which normally works to keep us healthy. The immune system recognizes dangerous materials, such as poisons and viruses, and reacts to keep
immune
syst. resp.
vs allergic
rxn.
10 the materials from harming the rest of the body. Some of these reactions, such as swelling of nose and throat tissues, keep the materials from moving farther through the body. Other reactions, such as producing mucus and coughing, help expel the
15 foreign materials. Unfortunately, too much swelling, mucus, or coughing make it hard to breathe and can even be life-threatening.

peanuts & IgE

People who are allergic to peanuts produce an antibody called IgE that combines with a specific
20 part of the peanut protein. The IgE-protein complex then alerts the immune system and the reactions begin. Once the allergic person's throat starts swelling, that person will need immediate medical treatment to reduce the risk of injury or death.

tough to
avoid peanuts
25 People who are allergic to peanuts must avoid them, and avoiding peanuts can be very hard to do. Many popular fast foods contain peanuts or peanut oil, or have been made using machines that also handle peanuts. Some very sensitive people cannot
30 even be in the same room where peanuts are being eaten. This can be very difficult for children, and many allergic children cannot safely eat lunch in their own school cafeteria.

change
allergen?
Some scientists wondered if they could find a
35 way to change the allergen, the part of the peanut protein that causes the allergic reaction, to keep IgE from combining with it. They first needed to measure the amount of reaction caused by untreated peanuts. Measuring how much of an allergic
details of
experiments
40 reaction the peanuts caused in people would not

be safe, so they instead measured how much IgE combined with the peanut protein in a laboratory test. They found that frying and boiling peanuts reduced the amount of reaction, as compared to
45 raw peanuts. However, frying and boiling do not reduce the amount of antibody reaction to a safe amount, so scientists tried other treatments. Some of the treatments, such as high heat for long periods of time, changed the taste of the peanuts too much.

light
treatment
promising
50 One treatment that showed promise was exposing the peanuts to very strong light. The light used by the scientists is similar to normal sunlight, but thousands of times stronger. By "pulsing" the light, or producing the light in short bursts, the scientists
55 hoped to avoid heating the peanuts to the point where the taste changed, while still deactivating the allergens in the peanuts.

details
of light
experiment
In one experiment, the scientists exposed the peanuts to 3 pulses of light per second for dif-
60 ferent amounts of time. They then extracted the protein from the peanuts. To measure the amount of allergens left in the peanut protein, they coated a special plastic plate with the extracted protein. Next, they added blood plasma that contained the
IgE
antibodies
= blue
65 IgE antibodies. When they washed the plasma off the plate, the IgE antibodies that combined with the allergen part of the protein remained stuck to the plate. They then added other chemicals that combined with the IgE antibodies and produced
70 a dark blue color; the darker the blue, the more IgE antibodies remained. Blood also contains very small amounts of other antibodies that will stick to the plate, so the same test on blood from a non-allergic person would still produce a small amount
75 of blue color. To account for this, the scientists used blood plasma that did not have any IgE antibodies as a negative control. They then compared the darkness of all of the samples to the darkness of the negative control.

promising
results; test
humans next
80 From the results, it appears that the scientists can change the peanut allergens so that the reaction in an allergic person is about the same as in a non-allergic person. The next steps will be to test the peanuts on humans: first by testing for reactions
85 on the skin of allergic people, and finally by

having allergic people eat the peanuts while being monitored for any reaction. Eventually, the scientists hope, they will have a treatment that will make a safe peanut, which will make eating a much safer and simpler experience for many.

90

Results of allergen measurements for peanuts exposed to pulsed light for different amounts of time.

Adapted from Xingyu Zhao, "Effect of Pulsed Light on Allergenic Proteins of Shelled Whole Peanuts." ©2013.

11. B

Difficulty: Easy

Category: Reading / Vocab-in-Context

Strategic Advice: Read the sentence again and replace "expel" with each of the answer choices. Look for the answer choice that is the best substitute for "expel" in the sentence without changing the meaning.

Getting to the Answer: Choice (B) is correct because in this context, "eject" means almost the same thing as "expel."

12. D

Difficulty: Medium

Category: Reading / Inference

Strategic Advice: Avoid answers that go too far or are not supported by direct evidence in the passage.

Getting to the Answer: In paragraph 2, the author describes how a typical immune system response looks when the body recognizes

a dangerous material. The author goes on to explain in paragraph 3 that a particular protein found in peanuts is responsible for triggering the immune system response in people allergic to peanuts. Choice (D) is correct.

13. A

Difficulty: Hard

Category: Reading / Command of Evidence

Strategic Advice: Find each of the answer choices in the passage. The correct answer should provide direct support for the answer to the previous question.

Getting to the Answer: In paragraph 2, the author describes what causes a reaction in the immune system. Choice (A) is correct because this sentence describes what causes the immune system to react—a material it considers dangerous.

14. D

Difficulty: Medium

Category: Reading / Inference

Strategic Advice: Skim the passage and find the paragraph that describes the normal immune system response and an allergic reaction. Summarize each in your head and use those summaries to make a prediction.

Getting to the Answer: Paragraph 2 includes information about what a normal immune system response looks like, as well as details about allergic reactions and what makes them dangerous. Choice (D) is correct because it best summarizes the differences between a normal immune system response and an allergic reaction.

15. D

Difficulty: Medium

Category: Reading / Detail

Strategic Advice: Review your notes for paragraph 4 to predict an answer to the question.

Getting to the Answer: In paragraph 4, the author explains why people who have peanut allergies simply avoid allergens. The author also describes the difficulties people who are allergic to peanuts experience in trying to avoid allergens. Choice (D) is correct.

16. B
Difficulty: Medium

Category: Reading / Command of Evidence

Strategic Advice: Use your approach to answering the previous question to guide your selection of a Command of Evidence question's correct answer.

Getting to the Answer: Choice (B) is correct. This text tells you that allergens are so common that children cannot avoid them, even at school.

17. C
Difficulty: Medium

Category: Reading / Vocab-in-Context

Strategic Advice: Read the sentence again and replace "deactivating" with each of the answer choices.

Getting to the Answer: When you consider the overall meaning of the sentence, (C) is correct. In this context, "disabling" means almost the same thing as "deactivating."

18. B
Difficulty: Medium

Category: Reading / Synthesis

Strategic Advice: Carefully evaluate the data in the graph. Refer back to the passage and find where the author discusses the information presented in the graph.

Getting to the Answer: In paragraph 7, the author describes the experiment that produced the data presented in the graph. The information

in paragraph 7 and the data in the graph support (B) as the correct answer.

19. C
Difficulty: Easy

Category: Reading / Detail

Strategic Advice: Skim the passage to find the part that describes the lab tests. Eliminate answer choices that are not explicitly stated in the text.

Getting to the Answer: In lines 40-41, the author states that it would "not be safe" to measure allergic reactions caused in people. Choice (C) is correct.

20. C
Difficulty: Medium

Category: Reading / Rhetoric

Strategic Advice: Read paragraph 6 again and identify the main topic and author's purpose in including this paragraph.

Getting to the Answer: Paragraph 6 introduces the method used by scientists to conduct the experiment described in paragraph 7. It is a summary of this method, and therefore (C) is correct.

21. A
Difficulty: Medium

Category: Reading / Rhetoric

Strategic Advice: Read the last paragraph again. Think about the central idea of the paragraph and how it relates to the central idea of the entire passage.

Getting to the Answer: In the preceding paragraphs, the author describes experiments that have already taken place. In the final paragraph, the author describes what scientists might do next. Choice (A) is correct.

CHAPTER 20

PREPARE

1. D
Difficulty: Hard

Category: Reading / Inference

Strategic Advice: An inference is not an opinion, but a conclusion drawn from facts. Use the facts of the passage to decide which answer choice provides a logical conclusion.

Getting to the Answer: The cited lines refer to the light fireflies produce to send signals. Therefore, the light must be visible. Choice (D) is correct.

2. C
Difficulty: Easy

Category: Reading / Detail

Strategic Advice: Answer Detail questions by reading around the cited text until you find the information that answers the question.

Getting to the Answer: Paragraph 2 contains information about bioluminescence. Read around the cited lines to find the detail you need: "Bioluminescence occurs in a variety of life forms and is more common in marine organisms than in terrestrial or freshwater life" (lines 13-15). This matches (C).

3. A
Difficulty: Hard

Category: Reading / Inference

Strategic Advice: Situations that are similar or parallel are analogous.

Getting to the Answer: The relationship described by the cited lines features "high-

energy particles" (line 78) that impact and shatter the "molecules of the air" (line 83). An analogous relationship would involve a powerful object smashing into and dispersing a group of other objects. Choice (A) reflects this scenario.

PRACTICE

The following passage describes findings regarding American colonists based on archeological explorations at Jamestown, Virginia.

Archaeological explorations at Jamestown, Virginia, have brought to light thousands of colonial period artifacts that were used by the Virginia settlers from 1607 until 1699. A study of these
5 objects, which were buried under the soil at Jamestown for decades, reveals in many ways how the English colonists lived on a small wilderness island over 300 years ago. Artifacts unearthed include building materials and handwrought hardware,
10 kitchen utensils and fireplace accessories, furniture hardware, and many items relating to household and town industries.

These artifacts provide valuable information concerning the everyday life and manners of the
15 first Virginia settlers. Excavated artifacts reveal that the Jamestown colonists built their houses in the same style as those they knew in England, insofar as local materials permitted. There were differences, however, for the settlers were in a land replete with
20 vast forests and untapped natural resources close at hand that they used to their advantage.

The Virginia known to the first settlers was a carpenter's paradise, and consequently the early buildings were the work of artisans in wood. The
25 first rude shelter, split-wood fencing, clapboard roof, puncheon floors, cupboards, benches, stools, and wood plows are all examples of skilled working with wood.

Timber at Jamestown was plentiful, so many
30 houses, especially in the early years, were of frame construction. During the first decade or two, house construction reflected a primitive use of materials

artif. show how col. lived

clues abt. life

ex's of woodworking

early structures = primitive

energy
focused on
survival

found ready at hand, such as saplings for a sort of
framing, and use of branches, leafage, bark, and
35 animal skins. During these early years, when the
settlers were having such a difficult time staying alive, mud walls, wattle-and-daub, and coarse
marsh-grass thatch were used. Out of these years
of improvising, construction with squatted posts,
40 and later with studs, came into practice. There was
probably little thought of plastering walls during
the first two decades. When plastering was adopted,
clay, either by itself or mixed with oyster-shell lime,
was first used. The early floors were of clay, and
45 such floors continued to be used in the humbler
dwellings throughout the 1600s. It can be assumed
that most of the dwellings, or shelters, of the early
Jamestown settlers had a rough and primitive
appearance.

50   After Jamestown had attained some degree of
permanency, many houses were built of brick. It is

brick
process sim.
to England

quite clear from documentary records and archeological remains that the colonists not only made
their own brick but also that the process, as well as
55 the finished products, followed closely the English
method. Four brick kilns were discovered on Jamestown Island during archeological explorations.
     While some of the handwrought hardware found
at Jamestown was made in the colony, most of it

hardware
from
England

60 was imported from England. Types of building
hardware unearthed include an excellent assort-
ment of nails, spikes, staples, locks, keys, hinges,
pintles, shutter fasteners, bolts, hasps, latches, door
knockers, door pulls, bootscrapes, gutter supports,
65 wall anchors, and ornamental hardware. In many
instances, each type is represented by several variet-
ies. It is believed that wooden hardware was used
on many of the early houses.

glass

     A few glass windowpanes may have been made
70 in the Jamestown glass factory, which was built in
1608. Most of the window glass used in the colony,
however, was shipped from England. Many of the
early panes used were diamond-shaped pieces
known as "quarrels" and were held in place by
75 means of slotted lead strips known as "cames." The
window frames used in a few of the Jamestown

houses were handwrought iron casements. Most
of the humbler dwellings had no glass panes in the
windows. The window openings were closed by bat-
80 ten shutters, operated by hinges of wood, and fitted
with wooden fastening devices.

     Busy conquering a stubborn wilderness, the first
Jamestown settlers had only a few things to make
their homes cozy and cheerful. In most cases, their
85 worldly goods consisted of a few cooking utensils, a change of clothing, a weapon or two, and a
few pieces of handmade furniture. After the early
years of hardship had passed, the colonists began
to acquire possessions for more pleasant living; by
90 1650 the better houses were equipped with most of
the necessities of life of those times, as well as a few
luxuries of comfortable living.

after hardship,
gained luxuries

4. C
Difficulty: Easy

Category: Reading / Inference

Strategic Advice: The phrase "the statement…
suggests" signals that this is an Inference question. Find the relevant details and look for clues
indicating how the author connects them.

Getting to the Answer: Read around the cited
text. In the previous two sentences, the author
discusses the hardships the colonists faced in
the early years. Focus on the reasons they didn't
think about plastering during the early years.
Predict that the colonists were too busy trying
to stay alive. Choice (C) matches your prediction.

5. D
Difficulty: Easy

Category: Reading / Detail

Strategic Advice: When presented with an
EXCEPT question, use your Passage Map to
locate the cited details. When you find one of
the cited details in the passage, eliminate that
answer choice.

Getting to the Answer: The third paragraph describes Virginia as a "carpenter's paradise" (line 23) and says the wooden artifacts were skillfully made. Eliminate A. Paragraph 4 describes how the settlers had "a difficult time staying alive" (lines 36-37); eliminate B. In the fourth paragraph, you learn that the colonists made floors from clay, allowing you to eliminate C. The sixth paragraph says that most of the hardware was imported, which directly contradicts (D).

6. D
Difficulty: Medium

Category: Reading / Inference

Strategic Advice: The phrase "...most comparable to..." indicates that this is an Analogical Reasoning Inference question. Identify the relationship between the ideas.

Getting to the Answer: The description of the brick industry implies that the colonists made bricks with local materials using techniques they brought with them from England. The relationship is one of local materials formed using imported methods. Choice (D) reflects this relationship.

PERFORM

The following passage is an excerpt from "The Murders in the Rue Morgue," a short story by Edgar Allan Poe published in 1841.

Our first meeting was at an obscure library in the Rue Montmartre, where the accident of our both being in search of the same very rare and
Line very remarkable volume, brought us into closer
5 communion. We saw each other again and again. I was deeply interested in the little family history which he detailed to me with all that candor which a Frenchman indulges whenever mere self is the theme. I was astonished too, at the vast extent of
10 his reading; and, above all, I felt my soul enkindled

within me by the wild fervor, and the vivid freshness of his imagination. Seeking in Paris the objects I then sought, I felt that the society of such a man would be to me a treasure beyond pride; and this
15 feeling I frankly confided to him. It was at length arranged that we should live together during my stay in the city; and as my worldly circumstances were somewhat less embarrassed than his own, I was permitted to be at the expense of renting, and
20 furnishing in a style which suited the rather fantastic gloom of our common temper, a time-eaten and grotesque mansion, long deserted through superstitions into which we did not inquire, and tottering to its fall in a retired and desolate portion of the
25 Faubourg St. Germain.

Had the routine of our life at this place been known to the world, we should have been regarded as madmen—although, perhaps, as madmen of a harmless nature. Our seclusion was perfect. We
30 admitted no visitors. Indeed the locality of our retirement had been carefully kept a secret from my own former associates; and it had been many years since Dupin had ceased to know or be known in Paris. We existed within ourselves alone.
35 It was a freak of fancy in my friend (for what else shall I call it?) to be enamored of the Night for her own sake; and into this bizarrerie, as into all his others, I quietly fell; giving myself up to his wild whims with a perfect abandon. The sable divinity would not
40 herself dwell with us always; but we could counterfeit her presence. At the first dawn of the morning we closed all the massy shutters of our old building; lighted a couple of tapers which, strongly perfumed, threw out only the ghastliest and feeblest of rays. By
45 the aid of these we then busied our souls in dreams— reading, writing, or conversing, until warned by the clock of the advent of the true Darkness. Then we sallied forth into the streets, arm and arm, continuing the topics of the day, or roaming far and wide
50 until a late hour, seeking, amid the wild lights and shadows of the populous city that infinity of mental excitement which quiet observation can afford.

At such times I could not help remarking and admiring (although from his rich ideality I had been

narrator impressed w/ other's imag.

seem like madmen

char's name revealed: Dupin

emphasis = darkness

ventured outside when dark

auth admired D's analytic ability

55 prepared to expect it) <u>a peculiar analytic ability in</u> <u>Dupin.</u> He ⟨seemed⟩ too, to take an eager delight in its exercise—if not exactly in its display—and did not hesitate to confess the pleasure thus derived. He boasted to me, with a low chuckling laugh, that most

60 men, in respect to himself, wore windows in their bosoms, and was wont to follow up such assertions by direct and very startling proofs of his intimate knowledge of my own. <u>His manner at these</u> <u>moments was frigid and abstract; his eyes were</u>

65 <u>vacant in expression; while his voice, usually a rich</u> <u>tenor rose into a treble which would have sounded</u> <u>petulantly but for the deliberateness and entire</u> <u>distinctness of the enunciation.</u> Observing him in these moods, I often dwelt meditatively upon the old

70 philosophy of the Bi-Part soul, and amused myself with the fancy of a double Dupin—the creative and the resolvent.

other-worldly

narr → does D. have 2 selves?

7. C
Difficulty: Medium

Category: Reading / Inference

Strategic Advice: The word "suggests" and the line reference indicate that this is an Inference question. Determine which answer choice can be concluded based on the information in the passage.

Getting to the Answer: Read around the cited section. Substituting "because" for "as" clarifies that this is a cause-and-effect relationship. The cause is Dupin's "embarrassed" circumstances (line 18), and the effect is that the narrator paid for everything. Predict that the narrator had more money than Dupin. Choice (C) is correct.

8. D
Difficulty: Hard

Category: Reading / Inference

Strategic Advice: The phrase "closely parallels" is a clue that this is an Analogical Reasoning Inference question. To identify how the ideas are connected, describe the relationship.

Getting to the Answer: In the third paragraph, the narrator states that he followed Dupin's lead in everything, indicating that the narrator is subordinate to Dupin. Look for the answer choice that describes a relationship in which one side of the relationship is subordinate to the other. Although C might be tempting, the student acts independently in the second half of the passage. Choice (D) is correct.

9. B
Difficulty: Medium

Category: Reading / Detail

Strategic Advice: Because this question does not provide a line reference, use your Passage Map to locate the relevant text. Then, paraphrase the detail.

Getting to the Answer: Locate the details about how and where the narrator met Dupin. In the first sentence, the narrator mentions first meeting Dupin in a library while searching for a rare book. Predict that they were looking for the same book. Choice (B) is correct.

10. A
Difficulty: Hard

Category: Reading / Inference

Strategic Advice: "Most likely agree" signals a broad or open-ended Inference question. Summarize the passage to zero in on statements with which the narrator would most likely agree.

Getting to the Answer: The passage focuses on the ways the narrator becomes involved with Dupin. The final paragraph discusses Dupin's ability see into other people's inner thoughts: "windows in their bosoms" (lines 60-61). The passage ends with the narrator's speculating on how Dupin could do so. Choice (A) is correct.

EXTRA PRACTICE

The following passages detail different aspects of the United States National Parks System.

Passage 1

In the mid- to late nineteenth century, America legislated <u>an idea that would come to be emulated worldwide: the National Parks System</u>. Starting
Line with Yellowstone National Park in 1872, the United
5   States government sparked a <u>national and inter-national trend</u> of setting aside treasured spaces for preservation, protection, and public enjoyment. Since then, over 400 national parks have been established in American states and territories, and
10 globally over a thousand parks are now protected by similar systems in their respective nations.

The United States National Park Service (NPS) is responsible for managing and protecting these parks. <u>Set up by President Wilson in 1916</u>, this
15 federal organization oversees budgeting, care, advocacy, and education for the country's parks. As a piece of legislation enacted in 1933, the NPS includes landmarks of historic and scientific signifi-cance in addition to those significant for their
20 sheer natural beauty or unique wildlife popula-tions. There are now 84 million acres of United States national parkland (and water). Thousands of employees and millions of volunteers work with the NPS to accomplish its vast responsibilities. From
25 national monuments and battlegrounds, to the breathtaking vistas of the Great Smoky Mountains, Alaska's Glacier Bay, and even underwater snorkel-ing trails in the U.S. Virgin Islands, spaces marked with awe and meaning are preserved for the <u>enjoy-</u>
30 <u>ment of generations to come</u>.

Today more than 275 million people visit America's national parks yearly. They come pre-pared to be amazed; the stunning beauty, powerful history, and inspiring intricacies of nature they en-
35 counter never disappoint. And <u>America's great idea</u>, in which over a hundred countries now participate, enables that amazement to be spread and shared across nations and generations. The National Park

Left margin annotations for Passage 1:
U.S. idea of nat'l parks

NPS history

scope of NPS

millions appreciate lessons of parks

System teaches and invites people worldwide to
40 practice preservation in their daily lives by making choices to protect the earth's wonders and treasures.

Right margin annotation: parks teach preservation

Passage 2

John Muir, often called "Father of the National Park System," was America's most famous and influential naturalist. Born in 1838, he bore witness
45 to the establishment of the first national parks and the many visions, debates, and victories of the early environmentalist movement. Muir was a man of many talents. He began his career working in car-riage production but soon chose a life of explor-
50 ing the nation's spectacular wilderness, traveling thousands of miles by foot and across oceans. From relative anonymity as a wayfarer, shepherd, and mill laborer, Muir would soon become a <u>national hero whose widely read writings would drive govern-</u>
55 <u>ment policy makers to action</u>.

When Muir encountered California's Yosemite Valley and the greater Sierra Nevada mountains, he immediately recognized their worth. He saw in them not only astounding scenic beauty, but also
60 <u>crucial ecological significance</u>. Over the rest of his life, he would advocate for their protection. Yet his interest would stretch far beyond the Sierras. Muir regularly traversed California's forested moun-tains and made a home in Yosemite Valley, but his
65 activism and wanderlust also drew him to other picturesque locations, such as Washington's Mount Rainier and Alaska's coast and glaciers. He pub-lished hundreds of articles documenting his travels. These invoked the wonder of the natural beauty he
70 witnessed, channeling that marvel into the hearts of readers nationwide.

<u>The political impact of Muir's life was immense</u>. His publications were elemental in persuading the United States government to establish Yosemite,
75 Sequoia, the Grand Canyon, and Mount Rainier as national parks. His relationship with Theodore Roosevelt was foundational to the environmental policies and gains made during Roosevelt's presi-dency; Muir's relentless advocacy for protecting the
80 Sierras catalyzed and empowered a movement that

Right margin annotations for Passage 2:
JM = father of NPS

JM – start in CA, focus on ecol.

wrote abt. nat. beauty

political impact: TR

started SC

would carry through the coming centuries. Much of this advocacy manifested itself in Muir's founding of a political activist organization called the <u>Sierra Club</u>. Internationally this group was one of the first
85 of its kind, and it remains one of the nation's leading environmental organizations.

ideo > pol. accomps.

However, perhaps ever greater than Muir's political accomplishments was his <u>ideological impact</u>. His unforgettable philosophies about the
90 importance of nature reminded Americans that the wild was worth cherishing and saving, even at the expense of short-lived material gains for which it might be exchanged. Muir's legacy has invited and inspired billions of people worldwide to guard the
95 global ecosystem, and to go out and enjoy it all.

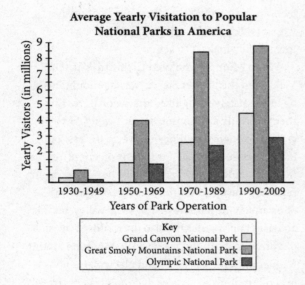

Average Yearly Visitation to Popular National Parks in America

Yearly Visitors (in millions) / Years of Park Operation

Key
Grand Canyon National Park
Great Smoky Mountains National Park
Olympic National Park

1. C
Difficulty: Medium

Category: Reading / Vocab-in-Context

Strategic Advice: Look for context clues to help you determine the meaning of unknown words. Read the rest of the paragraph to get a better idea of the relationship between America's national parks and the rest of the world.

Getting to the Answer: The last sentence of the paragraph states that "globally over a thousand parks are now protected by similar systems" (lines 10-11). The idea that originated in the United States later became popular worldwide. Choice (C), "imitated," is correct.

2. A
Difficulty: Medium

Category: Reading / Rhetoric

Strategic Advice: As you take notes, identify the general idea of each paragraph in the passage in your own words. Compare your notes to each choice to find the correct answer.

Getting to the Answer: The second paragraph provides the reader with statistics about the scale of the National Parks System, including the diversity of the parks, the number of employees required to manage the system, and the number of acres the system includes. Choice (A) correctly summarizes the purpose of this paragraph.

3. D
Difficulty: Medium

Category: Reading / Inference

Strategic Advice: Look for specific textual evidence in the passage that may support each answer choice. The correct answer will be concluded directly from the passage.

Getting to the Answer: The passage mentions the international influence of the United States National Parks System several times. Other answer choices are not supported by evidence. Only (D) is directly found within the passage.

4. D

Difficulty: Medium

Category: Reading / Command of Evidence

Strategic Advice: Review your answer to the previous question. Then, choose the textual evidence that best supports that conclusion.

Getting to the Answer: According to the passage, "over a hundred countries now participate" (line 36) in a national parks system. Choice (D) provides direct evidence for the passage's assertion that America's national parks idea has been influential internationally.

5. A

Difficulty: Easy

Category: Reading / Vocab-in-Context

Strategic Advice: Break the word down into its component parts to determine the correct answer.

Getting to the Answer: "Wander" suggests travel and "lust" suggests a positive interest. Looking at the context, "his activism and wanderlust also drew him to other picturesque locations" (lines 64-66), an interest in travel is the most logical choice.

6. B

Difficulty: Hard

Category: Reading / Rhetoric

Strategic Advice: Consider why the word "channeling" is used instead of an alternative word. What meaning does it add that a more general word like "communicating" does not?

Getting to the Answer: The context of the sentence suggests that Muir's writings were powerful. They seem to have captured the "marvel" (line 70) of the wilderness and transmitted it directly to readers, making them feel it, too.

"Channeling" emphasizes the way the power of his writing took the emotion he felt and communicated it directly and powerfully to readers. Choice (B) successfully captures this idea.

7. A

Difficulty: Hard

Category: Reading / Detail

Strategic Advice: Consider the passage as a whole. Are there any answers you can immediately eliminate as being obviously incorrect?

Getting to the Answer: The passage consistently states that John Muir was hugely influential during his lifetime, so B can be eliminated. It does acknowledge, however, that the preservation of such vast amounts of wilderness did come at an economic cost, though the passage suggests that this cost was worthwhile. Choice (A) is correct.

8. D

Difficulty: Medium

Category: Reading / Command of Evidence

Strategic Advice: Test each possible answer choice against your selection for the preceding question. Which piece of evidence most directly supports the previous answer choice?

Getting to the Answer: The passage states that conserving the wilderness was worthwhile, "even at the expense of short-lived material gains" (lines 91-92). This suggests that there was an economic cost to Muir's preservation goals. Choice (D) is correct, as it directly connects the parks system to ideas of money.

9. A

Difficulty: Hard

Category: Reading / Synthesis

Strategic Advice: Use your Passage Map to summarize each passage. Then, find the answer choice that best matches your ideas.

Getting to the Answer: Passage 1 describes the American National Parks System in general, focusing on its creation, its size, and its parks' diversity. Passage 2 focuses specifically on the importance of John Muir and his influence on conservation. Choice (A) correctly summarizes these differences.

10. A
Difficulty: Easy

Category: Reading / Synthesis

Strategic Advice: Evaluate how each passage describes the national parks. What do the word choices suggest about the purpose and value of the parks?

Getting to the Answer: Both passages use words like "awe" (line 29) and "wonder" (line 69) to discuss the national parks. Clearly, the authors of both passages agree that the main value of national parks is to preserve natural beauty for visitors. Choice (A) correctly reflects this idea.

11. D
Difficulty: Easy

Category: Reading / Synthesis

Strategic Advice: Carefully study the *x*- and *y*-axes to determine what trends can be inferred from the graph.

Getting to the Answer: According to the graph, visits to all five parks have increased from 1930 to 2010. No conclusions can be drawn about why parks have been more or less popular during these periods. However, the graph does show that during each period, the Grand Canyon has received more visitors than has Olympic National Park. Choice (D) is the only

answer choice that can be definitely concluded from the chart.

This passage is adapted from Jane Austen's Sense and Sensibility.

Before the house-maid had lit their fire the next day, or the sun gained any power over a cold, gloomy morning in January, <u>Marianne</u>, only half dressed,
Line was kneeling against one of the window-seats for the
5 sake of all the little light she could command from it, and writing as fast as a continual flow of tears would permit her. In this situation, <u>Elinor, roused from sleep by her agitation and sobs, first perceived her</u>; and after observing her for a few moments with silent anxiety,
10 said, in a tone of the most considerate gentleness,
  "Marianne, may I ask-?"
  "No, Elinor," she replied, "ask nothing; you will soon know all."
  The sort of desperate calmness with which this
15 was said, lasted no longer than while she spoke, and was immediately followed by a return of the same excessive affliction. It was some minutes before she could go on with her letter, and the frequent bursts of grief which still obliged her, at intervals, to with-
20 hold her pen, were proofs enough of her feeling how more than probable it was that she was <u>writing for the last time to Willoughby.</u>
  At breakfast she neither ate, nor attempted to eat any thing; and Elinor's attention was then all
25 employed, not in urging her, not in pitying her, nor in appearing to regard her, but in endeavouring to engage <u>Mrs. Jennings's</u> notice entirely to herself.
  As this was a favourite meal with Mrs. Jennings, it lasted a considerable time, and they were just
30 setting themselves, after it, round the common working table, when a letter was delivered to Mari- anne, which she eagerly caught from the servant, and, turning of a death-like paleness, instantly ran out of the room. Elinor, who saw as plainly by this,
35 as if she had seen the direction, that it must come from Willoughby, <u>felt immediately such a sickness at heart as made her hardly able to hold up her head</u>, and sat in such a general tremour as made her

M = very upset; E. inquires

M overcome; writing to W... last time?

E distracts Mrs. J

M receives letter from W; E is con- cerned

fear it impossible to escape Mrs. Jennings's notice.

40 That good lady, however, saw only that Marianne had received a letter from Willoughby, which appeared to her a very good joke, and which she treated accordingly, by hoping, with a laugh, that she would find it to her liking. Of Elinor's distress,

45 she was too busily employed in measuring lengths of worsted for her rug, to see any thing at all; and calmly continuing her talk, as soon as Marianne disappeared, she said,

"Upon my word, I never saw a young woman so

50 desperately in love in my life! MY girls were nothing to her, and yet they used to be foolish enough; but as for Miss Marianne, she is quite an altered creature. I hope, from the bottom of my heart, he won't keep her waiting much longer, for it is quite

55 grievous to see her look so ill and forlorn. Pray, when are they to be married?"

Elinor, though never less disposed to speak than at that moment, obliged herself to answer such an attack as this, and, therefore, trying to smile,

60 replied, "And have you really, Ma'am, talked yourself into a persuasion of my sister's being engaged to Mr. Willoughby? I thought it had been only a joke, but so serious a question seems to imply more; and I must beg, therefore, that you will not deceive your-

65 self any longer. I do assure you that nothing would surprise me more than to hear of their being going to be married."

"For shame, for shame, Miss Dashwood! how can you talk so? Don't we all know that it must be

70 a match, that they were over head and ears in love with each other from the first moment they met? Did not I see them together in Devonshire every day, and all day long; and did not I know that your sister came to town with me on purpose to buy wedding

75 clothes? Come, come, this won't do. Because you are so sly about it yourself, you think nobody else has any senses; but it is no such thing, I can tell you, for it has been known all over town this ever so long. I tell every body of it and so does Charlotte."

80 "Indeed, Ma'am," said Elinor, very seriously, "you are mistaken. Indeed, you are doing a very unkind thing in spreading the report, and you will find that you have though you will not believe me now."

12. B
Difficulty: Medium

Category: Reading / Vocab-in-Context

Strategic Advice: Consider each word carefully. The most common meaning for a word is not necessarily the correct one.

Getting to the Answer: Elinor, "though never less disposed to speak" (line 57), nonetheless speaks in this paragraph. The correct answer should be something like "eager," since Elinor is not eager to speak. Plugging in each of the answer choices will reveal which fits best. Choice (B) is similar to "eager," so it is correct.

13. B
Difficulty: Medium

Category: Reading / Rhetoric

Strategic Advice: Read the lines around this phrase. Look for clues that suggest what is making her react as she does.

Getting to the Answer: Marianne is clearly expecting bad news in the letter, as she runs out of the room before even opening it. Choice (B) is correct: she is driven by her anxiety.

14. A
Difficulty: Easy

Category: Reading / Inference

Strategic Advice: Look for clues about Elinor's behavior toward Marianne. What does this suggest about their relationship?

Getting to the Answer: Elinor seems almost as upset by what is upsetting Marianne as Marianne herself is. The sisters are clearly very close, and Elinor's words to Mrs. Jennings make clear that Elinor is trying to prevent Mrs. Jennings from doing further damage to Marianne by spreading rumors. Choice (A) is correct, as it reflects the sisters' close relationship.

15. B

Difficulty: Medium

Category: Reading / Command of Evidence

Strategic Advice: Review the answer to the previous question. Consider which of the answer choices provides the clearest sense of Elinor's feelings toward Marianne.

Getting to the Answer: Elinor's feelings toward Marianne are protective. This is demonstrated by the lines that show Elinor's trying to distract Mrs. Jennings from noticing Marianne's distress. Choice (B) is correct; it is a clear illustration of Elinor's protective feelings.

16. C

Difficulty: Easy

Category: Reading / Inference

Strategic Advice: Determine what Mrs. Jennings thinks is happening. Does it differ in any way from what is actually happening?

Getting to the Answer: Mrs. Jennings appears not to have noticed Marianne's distress over Willoughby. She remarks on how much the two of them seem to be in love, despite Marianne's altered behavior. Choice (C) is correct because it shows that Mrs. Jennings is not perceptive enough to notice what is happening.

17. C

Difficulty: Medium

Category: Reading / Command of Evidence

Strategic Advice: Review the answer to the previous question. Notice what Mrs. Jennings says or does to support your conclusion about her.

Getting to the Answer: Mrs. Jennings is not very perceptive. The passage states that she "was too busily employed . . . to see any thing at all" (lines 45-46) and then observes that

Marianne and Willoughby are likely to be married. Choice (C) is correct, as it offers an instance of Mrs. Jennings's failure to notice the events around her.

18. B

Difficulty: Medium

Category: Reading / Vocab-in-Context

Strategic Advice: Consider the context of this line. Notice what Elinor is suggesting about Mrs. Jennings.

Getting to the Answer: Elinor is surprised that Mrs. Jennings has "'talked [herself] into a persuasion'" (lines 60-61) that Marianne and Willoughby are to be married. Other context clues make clear that this is what Mrs. Jennings believes will happen, so the correct answer will mean something like "belief." Choice (B), therefore, is correct.

19. A

Difficulty: Easy

Category: Reading / Detail

Strategic Advice: Read the passage closely to find the answer stated explicitly.

Getting to the Answer: Both Elinor and Mrs. Jennings state that Mrs. Jennings believes Willoughby and Marianne are to be married soon. Choice (A) is correct.

20. D

Difficulty: Hard

Category: Reading / Inference

Strategic Advice: In your own words, describe Marianne's situation. Then, read the answer choices to see what situation is analogous.

Getting to the Answer: Marianne is upset because of a letter that has come from a man everybody believes she will marry. The correct answer should relate to unexpected disappointment. Choice (D) is correct: It conveys a sense of disappointment after high expectations have not been met.

21. B

Difficulty: Medium

Category: Reading / Inference

Strategic Advice: Consider what would be lost from the passage if this paragraph were not included.

Getting to the Answer: Elinor and Mrs. Jennings have argued over the events taking place. The final paragraph shows Elinor trying to convince Mrs. Jennings that she is "doing a very unkind thing" (lines 81-82) by spreading rumors of Marianne's marriage, rumors that will likely humiliate her. Elinor is not simply explaining why she believes Mrs. Jennings is wrong, but trying to stop her from causing Marianne additional pain. Choice (B) is correct because it is the only answer choice that conveys this meaning.

CHAPTER 21

PREPARE

1. D
Difficulty: Easy

Category: Reading / Global

Strategic Advice: After you read a passage, use your Passage Map to quickly paraphrase the author's reason for writing the passage. Keep your focus on the passage as a whole, not one specific part.

Getting to the Answer: The author describes how his introduction to the alphabet initiated changes in his mistress and her treatment of him. He continues to describe how he secretly continued to learn to read, despite the likely consequences if he were discovered. Predict that the main purpose is to describe a process undertaken by Douglass. Choice (D) matches this prediction.

2. B
Difficulty: Medium

Category: Reading / Inference

Strategic Advice: The phrase "strongly suggests" and the cited text indicate that this is an Inference question about an explicit cause-and-effect relationship. Determine whether the cited lines act as the cause or effect and predict what the missing part of the relationship is.

Getting to the Answer: The cited statement informs the reader that slavery caused injury to both Douglass and his mistress; this is the effect. Rephrase the question stem: What was the cause of slavery's injurious effect on the mistress? In the sentences following the cited portion, Douglass describes a variety of good qualities his mistress possessed when he first met her. Douglass then relates how, as a result

of owning slaves, her positive qualities were replaced by negative qualities. Predict that Douglass's mistress started out as a good person, and owning slaves turned her into a bad person. Choice (B) matches this prediction.

3. B
Difficulty: Medium

Category: Reading / Command of Evidence

Strategic Advice: Answering Command of Evidence questions correctly depends on your answer to the previous question. Use the prediction you made to answer the previous question to form your prediction for this question.

Getting to the Answer: To answer the previous question, you predicted that Douglass's mistress started out as a good person and turned into a bad person. This question asks you to provide evidence that she turned into a bad person. Choice (B) conveys how the mistress changed for the worse.

PRACTICE

The following passage explains the challenges facing a population of trees and possible solutions.

Today, oaks are plagued with problems. There is lack of regeneration in populations of certain species. Pests such as the acorn weevil and the filbert
Line worm eat away at acorns and prevent germination.
5 By undermining the root systems of seedlings and saplings, ground squirrels, gophers, and other small mammals often prevent these young plants from reaching tree size. Severe diseases, such as sudden oak death, kill many adult oaks. Many mature oaks
10 are having a tough time with fire suppression. In the past, with light surface fires, the oaks had been able to maintain a stronghold where other plants were not able to compete and died out. Now oaks are being toppled by trees that have a higher toler-
15 ance for shade and are not fire-resistant; earlier such trees would have been killed when Native Americans set fires.

oak problems: pests & disease, other trees

Given all of these challenges, the "old-growth" oaks—the large old valley oaks, Garry oaks, coast
20 live oaks, and canyon live oaks that have huge girth and large canopies—may become a thing of the past. These oaks in particular are important because there are often more terrestrial vertebrates living in mature oak stands than in seedling and sapling
25 areas. This prevalence of animals occurs because the large crowns of such oaks provide cover and feeding sites for a large variety of wildlife.

The University of California has embarked on an ambitious and necessary research program called
30 the Integrated Hardwood Range Management Program to explore the significant causes of oak decline and offer varied solutions. These include investigating the use of grassing regimes that are compatible with oak seedling establishment, reveg-
35 etating sites with native grasses to facilitate better germination of oak seedlings, documenting insects and pathogens that attack oaks, and exploring the ways that native people managed oaks in the past. Scientists at the Pacific Northwest Research Station
40 in Olympia, Washington, and at Redwood National Park in northern California are reintroducing the burning practices of Native Americans. When used in Garry oak ecosystems, fires keep Douglas firs from encroaching on the oaks and promote
45 the growth of wildflowers that are important food plants. Further investigations about these fire practices may be essential in figuring out how to maintain oaks in the western landscape today, given that the fires address many of the factors that are
50 now causing oak decline—from how to eliminate insect pests of acorns to how to maintain an open structure in oak groves.

Ecological restoration, the traditional approach to woodland maintenance, refers to humans
55 intervening on a very limited time scale to bring back plants and animals known to have historically existed in an area. The decline of oaks, one of the most significant plants to Native Americans, shows us that humans may play an integral part in the
60 restoration of oak areas. While animals such as jays have been recognized as crucial partners in oak

well-being, human actions through the eons may also have been key to the oaks' flourishing.

Sudden oak death, for example, although of
65 exotic origin, may be curtailed locally by thinning around coastal oaks and tan oaks and setting light surface fires, simulating ancient fire management practices of Native Americans. Indigenous shrubs and trees that grow in association with oaks
70 are hosts to the sudden oak death pathogen. By limiting the growth of these shrubs, burning that mimics earlier Native American ways may reduce opportunities for disease agents to jump from other plants to oak trees. With a more open envi-
75 ronment, it may be harder for sudden oak death to spread.

The oak landscapes that we inherited, which still bear the marks of former Native American interactions, demand a new kind of restoration that
80 complements other forms of ecological restoration. This new kind of restoration could be called eth- nobotanical restoration, defined as reestablishing the historic plant communities of a given area and restoring indigenous harvesting, vegetation
85 management, and cultivation practices (seedbear- ing, burning, pruning, sowing, tilling, and weeding) necessary to maintain these communities in the long term.

Thus, this kind of restoration is not only about
90 restoring plants but also about restoring the human place within nature. Ethnobotanical restoration is viewed not as a process that can be completed but rather as a continuous interaction between people and plants, as both of their fates are intertwined in
95 a region. Using oaks (through harvesting acorns and making products from all parts of the tree) and human intervention (by thinning tree populations and lighting light fires) may offer us ways to benefi- cially coexist while improving the long-term health
100 and well-being of the remarkable oak.

oaks may die out

research into problems & solutions

Nat. Am. approach

ecol rest = limited human intervention

new view: humans may help

sudden oak death

ethnobot. rest = uses humans

restore human role = help the oak

4. C

Difficulty: Medium

Category: Reading / Global

Strategic Advice: Even when you can't make a specific prediction, summarize the author's central idea by reviewing your Passage Map.

Getting to the Answer: The author begins by listing the problems plaguing oak trees and continues by describing possible solutions to each of the problems. Common to each of the solutions is the requirement that humans actively participate in an ongoing process. The author concludes the passage by describing this kind of participation as "ethnobotanical restoration" (line 81–82). Predict that humans need to participate actively in efforts to restore oaks. Choice (C) matches this prediction.

5. B

Difficulty: Medium

Category: Reading / Detail

Strategic Advice: Use your Passage Map to locate cited phrases. Rephrase what each phrase means.

Getting to the Answer: The author describes ecological restoration as a process that is completed in a very short time and ethnobotanical restoration as a process that seeks to restore ongoing human interaction with plant communities. Choice (B) is correct.

6. D

Difficulty: Easy

Category: Reading / Command of Evidence

Strategic Advice: To answer this question, use the prediction you made to answer the previous question.

Getting to the Answer: To answer the previous question, you needed to recognize that the main difference between the two types of restoration is that while ecological restoration takes place over a short period of time and can be completed, ethnobotanical restoration requires long-term involvement by humans in the natural process of maintaining historic plant communities. Choice (D) is correct.

PERFORM

The following passage details findings from different eras of prenatal screening and the methods and experiments those findings prompted.

Screening newborns for rare genetic diseases is a relatively new practice that began approximately forty years ago. Prior to the advent of screening,
Line biomedical researchers and health professionals
5 were preoccupied with the most prominent causes of newborn mortality, such as diarrheal diseases, influenza, and other infectious diseases. By 1960, however, the infant mortality rate had dropped to less than three percent of live births from over
10 ten percent fifty years earlier. The declining rate was due, in part, to the widespread use of antibiotics; the development of vaccines, particularly the Salk and Sabin polio vaccines; improved nutrition; better education; and generally im-
15 proved sanitary practices. As infant mortality rates dropped, attention shifted to the etiology of rare diseases. The first major milestone in this focus shift occurred in 1962, when President Kennedy announced that the federal government would
20 begin exploring the problem of mental disability— until then, a largely ignored issue. He created the President's Panel on Mental Retardation to lead this exploration.

During roughly the same time period, a major
25 scientific breakthrough in the study of phenylke-tonuria, or PKU, was underway. In 1934, Dr. Asbjorn Folling of Norway first described

early yrs, docs focused on common killers of newborns

success– look @ rare diseases

JFK → mental disability prg.

found
cause of
PKU

the condition when he observed that some of his
mentally disabled patients had phenylpyruvic acid
30 in their urine, a finding indicative of a deficiency in
the enzyme that converts phenylalanine to tyrosine,
a necessary component for protein synthesis. When
this transformation does not occur, phenylalanine
accumulates in the blood. High levels of phenylala-
35 nine are toxic to the developing brain of an infant
and cause mental retardation. At the time, the pre-
ventive strategy was to reduce phenylalanine levels
in the patient's diet. This approach had one serious
drawback, though. Phenylalanine is an essential
40 amino acid necessary for proper growth, so defi-
ciencies in it may also lead to mental retardation.

high &
low phen.
cause
problems

Despite this risk, the younger siblings of children
with PKU were given diets low in phenylalanine
from a very early age. The results were somewhat
45 encouraging and, in light of the beneficial evidence
from this special diet, two therapeutically promising research initiatives were launched. One was to
devise a source of protein free of phenylalanine. The
outcome was the infant formula Lofenalac, which is
50 still in use today. The other initiative was aimed at
developing a method for detecting high phenylalanine levels before damage to the developing brain
could occur.

possible
sol'n: phen-
free formula

Dr. Robert Guthrie led the second initiative
55 which yielded a breakthrough in the early 1960s.
He developed a test to detect PKU before it became
clinically symptomatic. The test consisted of a
culture of *Bacillus subtilis* and B-2-thienylalanine,
which inhibits the growth of the bacteria. Once
60 a blood sample from the newborn was added to
this culture, the bacteria would leach the phenylalanine from the blood spot, overcome the inhibi-
tion caused by the B-2-thienylalanine, and grow.
Bacterial growth beyond a normal range indicated
65 elevated levels of phenylalanine and thus the presence of PKU in the newborn.

possible
sol'n: early
detection

Dr G found
test

The test was not perfect. Over the next few years,
it produced quite a few false positives, and some
children unnecessarily received low phenylala-
70 nine diets. To compound the problem, there was
uncertainty about the amount of phenylalanine to

some
problems
w/ test...

cut from the diet; as a result, some healthy children
developed mental disabilities because of the treatment. Nevertheless, PKU screening was generally
75 considered a success, and spurred questions about
whether other diseases might be prevented through
early detection. After further study, it became clear
that they could. By the late 1960s, newborn screening for rare genetic diseases had become a perma-
80 nent part of infant health care in the United States.

overall =
very useful

other
screenings

7. C
Difficulty: Medium

Category: Reading / Inference

Strategic Advice: The phrase "most strongly
suggests" and the clue word "prior" indicate
that this is an Inference question asking about
an explicit relationship. Review your Passage
Map to understand how the author connects
certain ideas to each other.

Getting to the Answer: The word "prior" and
the cited lines indicate that the relationship is
sequential. First, the low phenylalanine diet,
which was implemented despite its risks, proved
beneficial. Then, the research initiatives began
because of the benefits associated with the diet.
Predict that the diet was prescribed in spite of
those negative outcomes. Choice (C) matches
this prediction.

8. D
Difficulty: Medium

Category: Reading / Command of Evidence

Strategic Advice: When answering a Command
of Evidence question, find the cited lines that
most closely support the prediction you made
to answer the previous question.

Getting to the Answer: You predicted that the
diet was prescribed in spite of the drawbacks.
Compare each of the answer choices to your
prediction. Only (D) describes the drawbacks
associated with the special diet.

9. B

Difficulty: Medium

Category: Reading / Global

Strategic Advice: Use your Passage Map to quickly summarize the passage. Maintain focus on the general context of each paragraph. Concentrate on the central ideas in each paragraph, not on specific details.

Getting to the Answer: The author introduces the passage by discussing the practice of screening newborns and concludes the passage by describing genetic screening as "a permanent part of infant health care" (lines 79–80). Throughout the passage, the author focuses on the process that brought about the use of genetic screening. Choice (B) is correct.

10. D

Difficulty: Easy

Category: Reading / Detail

Strategic Advice: "According to the passage" indicates that this is a Detail question. Use your Passage Map to locate the referenced details.

Getting to the Answer: Locate each referenced detail and determine why the author included that detail. Choice A is mentioned as a contributor to the decline in the infant mortality rate and can be eliminated. Eliminate B because Lofenalac was developed to treat PKU. Eliminate C because it discusses problems with the test. Choice (D) is correct because the general success of the test showed the potential of screening tests.

11. D

Difficulty: Medium

Category: Reading / Command of Evidence

Strategic Advice: To answer a Command of Evidence question, find the cited lines that most closely support the answer choice you selected in the previous question.

Getting to the Answer: Return to the place in the passage that provided the answer to the previous question. Check to see if one of the answer choices to this question includes the detail you found for the previous question. Choice (D) is correct.

EXTRA PRACTICE

This passage describes how tree farms, widely thought to offer little support to wildlife, became home to a rare species of birds.

As our environment changes over time, certain species thrive while others become rarer. One such species is the small, difficult-to-find Swainson's
Line warbler. Scientists struggle to estimate the popula-
5 tion of this songbird because it is challenging to track. America's foremost wildlife artist, John James Audubon, attempted to describe the bird in the 1830s. Even then, it was considered uncommon. Some of the other birds studied by Audubon have
10 already become extinct, including the ivory-billed woodpecker. Others, such as the Allen's hummingbird, the spotted owl, and the osprey, are at increased risk of extinction due to their habitats disappearing. Against all odds, the Swainson's
15 warbler has held on by changing where it spends its summer seasons.

The Swainson's warbler has been at risk for extinction due to the specificity of its needs. During breeding season, summer, the bird tradition-
20 ally spends time in the southeastern United States forests and lowlands. It then migrates to subtropical locations in the winter, seeking the dry forests of Jamaica or other evergreen forests in Mexico and Cuba. The low population has been attributed to
25 the loss of these habitats due to the gradual conversion of hardwood forests into farmland, reservoirs, and urban or suburban areas. With numbers as low as 90,000 worldwide, the prognosis for the continued survival of the bird has been bleak.

SW = uncommon, hard to track

Aud. studied SW

why SW = vulnerable

habitats disappearing

30   Scientists have been studying the birds across the
southern United States for more than two decades,
but attempts to conserve the species have fallen
short due to a lack of understanding of their true
habitat needs. Scientists tried to shift the Swainson's

need to truly understand habitat

35 warbler to national forests, public refuges, and private sanctuaries, but success was limited. Recently,
though, researchers found that the population is
increasing. Since the 1990s, Swainson's warblers
have been doing what scientists attempted to do for

birds made their own new habitat

40 them: the birds have created new breeding grounds
for themselves by moving into industrial pine plantations that have been planted in ten different states.
    Millions of acres of industrial pine forests have
been planted since the 1920s. Some of these planta-

SW uses pine plantations used in industry

45 tions are even located in the same areas that Swainson's warblers used to use for breeding grounds
before the area's natural forests disappeared. With
trees cut every 25 to 35 years, these plantations support a $200 billion industry that produces wood-

50 based goods from housing lumber to notebook
paper. The pine plantations were once thought by
scientists to offer little support to any wildlife. They
do not make ideal habitats due to the even spacing of planted rows and the lack of diversity in tree

55 species. These plantations, though, happen to offer
the Swainson's warbler two of the things they most
require from their habitats.
    When the pines at these tree farms reach about
20 feet high, they hit the one specific stage of

60 growth that appeals to the birds. This height creates
high-density undergrowth that the birds rely on for
protection during their breeding season. This point

ideal conditions for birds → undergrowth

of the pine development best mimics the bird's
traditional habitat. Before deforestation occurred in

65 the Southeastern United States, Swainson's warblers
lived in thickets of cane or areas with dense vines
and tangled undergrowth. At the pine plantations,
the habitat lasts for about seven to eight years before the trees grow too tall to provide the birds the

70 coverage that they seek. The birds move on once the
tangled undergrowth they prefer disappears.
    The Swainson's warbler's secondary requirement
that pine plantations can easily provide is space. A
single breeding pair of the species requires between

75 10 and 20 acres of land. This large amount of
space is one of the reasons why the species was so
vulnerable to deforestation.

birds need space → acres

    Today, pine plantations occupy some 40 mil-
lion acres in the southern United States. Not all of
80 these acres are usable to the birds, though. When the
cutting cycles and the amount of time the trees
offer the type of undergrowth desirable to the
Swainson's warblers are considered, it is estimated
that approximately 10 million acres of pine

only some plantations = useful

85 plantations are available to the birds at one time.
    These numbers suggest that pine plantations will
become the Swainson's warbler's primary habitat over
time. The species owes its continued existence to its
ability to adapt. While other species of warbler have dis-

90 appeared entirely due to the clearing of natural forests,
the Swainson's warbler has remained flexible, shifting its
behavior to ensure its own preservation.

pine will become primary habitat

Planted vs. Natural Pine Forests in the Southern U.S.

Adapted from *United States Geological Survey, Land Cover Trends Project.*

1. C

Difficulty: Medium

Category: Reading / Global

Strategic Advice: Think about the central idea of the passage. Eliminate answer choices such as A and D that contain supporting details for the central idea. The correct answer will be an idea that is supported by all of the details in the passage.

Getting to the Answer: This passage is mostly about how the Swainson's warbler population has begun to recover after its natural habitat was reduced by deforestation. Choice (C) is correct.

2. C

Difficulty: Hard

Category: Reading / Rhetoric

Strategic Advice: Review your notes for the first paragraph. Consider the central idea of the paragraph and how it relates to the central idea of the passage. Select the answer choice that most accurately describes the purpose this sentence serves in the passage.

Getting to the Answer: The author mentions these other species of birds to give examples of other animals that are at risk because their habitats have been destroyed, which matches (C).

3. C

Difficulty: Medium

Category: Reading / Inference

Strategic Advice: Review your paragraph 3 notes. How did scientists attempt to preserve the population of the Swainson's warbler? The correct answer should paraphrase your own idea.

Getting to the Answer: In lines 30–36 of paragraph 3, the author explains that previous attempts at conservation have been unsuccessful because scientists did not understand what the birds need in a habitat. This matches (C).

4. C

Difficulty: Medium

Category: Reading / Command of Evidence

Strategic Advice: Locate each of the answer choices in the passage. The correct answer should provide direct support for the answer to the previous question.

Getting to the Answer: In paragraph 3, the author describes why previous conservation efforts by scientists have failed. Choice (C) is correct.

5. D

Difficulty: Medium

Category: Reading / Vocab-in-Context

Strategic Advice: Replace "conversion" in the sentence with each of the answer choices. Consider which word makes the most sense in context.

Getting to the Answer: In this sentence, "transformation" can replace "conversion" without changing the overall meaning. Choice (D) is correct.

6. A

Difficulty: Hard

Category: Reading / Inference

Strategic Advice: Look for the answer choice that is directly supported by the evidence in the text. Eliminate answer choices that are related to the main topic but go too far, such as D.

Getting to the Answer: In paragraph 1, the author discusses the risk of extinction of other birds due to a decrease in their habitats. Choice (A) is correct because it is most directly supported by the evidence in the passage.

7. B

Difficulty: Medium

Category: Reading / Command of Evidence

Strategic Advice: Use your reasoning for answering the previous question to figure out where in the passage the best evidence for that answer will come from.

Getting to the Answer: The details in paragraph 1 provide the most direct support for the idea that more birds will become extinct if their habitats continue to disappear. Choice (B) is correct.

8. D
Difficulty: Easy

Category: Reading / Global

Strategic Advice: Consider the central idea of the passage and the message conveyed by the information included. Select the answer that most closely explains what the author wants to relate to the reader.

Getting to the Answer: This passage is mostly about how the Swainson's warbler has adapted after losing much of its natural habitat. The author's purpose is to explain how this happened, (D).

9. C
Difficulty: Hard

Category: Reading / Inference

Strategic Advice: Think about the process undertaken in each of the answer choices and compare it to the Swainson's warbler's migrating to a new, man-made habitat.

Getting to the Answer: The migration of the Swainson's warbler to pine forests planted by humans is most similar to aquatic animals making new homes from shipwrecks. In both instances, animals have taken something created by humans and made it into a home. Choice (C) is correct.

10. A
Difficulty: Medium

Category: Reading / Vocab-in-Context

Strategic Advice: Eliminate answer choices such as B and D that are synonyms for "point" but do not make sense in context.

Getting to the Answer: In this sentence, the author is describing the stage of development that most closely resembles the bird's natural habitat. This matches (A).

11. A
Difficulty: Medium

Category: Reading / Synthesis

Strategic Advice: Consider only the information presented in the graph. The correct answer will be directly supported by the data.

Getting to the Answer: The graph shows that over the decade, the number of acres of pine plantations has grown steadily while that of natural pine forests has declined. The conclusion that the number of acres of pine plantations could soon surpass that of natural pine forests is supported by the data presented in the graph. Choice (A) is correct.

The following passage is adapted from Lucy Maud Montgomery's 1908 novel Anne of Green Gables. *This excerpt details a conversation between Anne, the young protagonist, and Marilla, Anne's guardian.*

"And what are your eyes popping out of your head about now?" asked Marilla, when Anne had just come in from a run to the post office. "Have
Line you discovered another kindred spirit?" Excitement   *A = excited*
5 hung around Anne like a garment, shone in her eyes, kindled in every feature. She had come dancing up the lane, like a wind-blown sprite, through the mellow sunshine and lazy shadows of the August evening.

10 "No, Marilla, but oh, what do you think? I am invited to tea at the manse tomorrow afternoon! Mrs. Allan left the letter for me at the post office. Just look at it, Marilla. 'Miss Anne Shirley, Green Gables.' That is the first time I was ever called 'Miss.'
15 Such a thrill as it gave me! I shall cherish it forever among my choicest treasures."

A invited for tea, called Miss

"Mrs. Allan told me she meant to have all the members of her Sunday-school class to tea in turn," said Marilla, regarding the wonderful event very
20 coolly. "You needn't get in such a fever over it. Do learn to take things calmly, child."

M puts a damper on

For Anne to take things calmly would have been to change her nature. All "spirit and fire and dew," as she was, the pleasures and pains of life
25 came to her with trebled intensity. Marilla felt this and was vaguely troubled over it, realizing that the ups and downs of existence would probably bear hardly on this impulsive soul and not sufficiently understanding that the equally great capacity for
30 delight might more than compensate. Therefore Marilla conceived it to be her duty to drill Anne into a tranquil uniformity of disposition as impossible and alien to her as to a dancing sunbeam in one of the brook shallows. She did not
35 make much headway, as she sorrowfully admitted to herself. The downfall of some dear hope or plan plunged Anne into "deeps of affliction." The fulfillment thereof exalted her to dizzy realms of delight. Marilla had almost begun to despair of ever
40 fashioning this waif of the world into her model little girl of demure manners and prim deportment. Neither would she have believed that she really liked Anne much better as she was.

A is typically lively

M tries to calm to make life easier for A

M not very successful

Anne went to bed that night speechless with
45 misery because Matthew had said the wind was round northeast and he feared it would be a rainy day tomorrow. The rustle of the poplar leaves about the house worried her, it sounded so like pattering raindrops, and the full, faraway roar of the gulf,
50 to which she listened delightedly at other times, loving its strange, sonorous, haunting rhythm, now seemed like a prophecy of storm and disaster to a small maiden who particularly wanted a fine day. Anne thought that the morning would never come.

A worried about rain

55 But all things have an end, even nights before the day on which you are invited to take tea at the manse. The morning, in spite of Matthew's predictions, was fine and Anne's spirits soared to their highest. "Oh, Marilla, there is something in
60 me today that makes me just love everybody I see," she exclaimed as she washed the breakfast dishes. "You don't know how good I feel! Wouldn't it be nice if it could last? I believe I could be a model child if I were just invited out to tea every day. But
65 oh, Marilla, it's a solemn occasion too. I feel so anxious. What if I shouldn't behave properly? You know I never had tea at a manse before, and I'm not sure that I know all the rules of etiquette, although I've been studying the rules given in the Etiquette
70 Department of the Family Herald ever since I came here. I'm so afraid I'll do something silly or forget to do something I should do. Would it be good manners to take a second helping of anything if you wanted to VERY much?"

A very excited, even when doing dishes

A prepares & frets re: manners

75 "The trouble with you, Anne, is that you're thinking too much about yourself. You should just think of Mrs. Allan and what would be nicest and most agreeable to her," said Marilla, hitting for once in her life on a very sound and pithy piece of
80 advice. Anne instantly realized this.

M tells A to think about others

"You are right, Marilla. I'll try not to think about myself at all."

A agrees, tries to be selfless

12. B
Difficulty: Easy

Category: Reading / Inference

Strategic Advice: Reread the excerpt for clues that reveal Anne's previous behavior and her personality traits.

Getting to the Answer: Marilla specifically asks Anne whether she has found "another" kindred spirit, implying that Anne has previously rushed home excited about having made a new friend. This is a clue that Anne is a sociable, friendly person. Choice (B) is correct.

13. A

Difficulty: Medium

Category: Reading / Vocab-in-Context

Strategic Advice: Read the sentence and paragraph for context clues and determine which usage of the selected word best fits the author's intention.

Getting to the Answer: The passage implies that Marilla offers Anne helpful advice, so of the various meanings of the word "sound," (A) is correct.

14. C

Difficulty: Medium

Category: Reading / Inference

Strategic Advice: Read the context clues in the passage that relate to Matthew's and Anne's interactions. Examine what these clues suggest about their relationship.

Getting to the Answer: Anne goes to bed "speechless with misery" (lines 44–45) because Matthew predicts it will rain the next day. Anne's reaction shows that she takes Matthew's predictions seriously, so (C) is correct.

15. B

Difficulty: Easy

Category: Reading / Detail

Strategic Advice: Reread the entire passage and evaluate which of the four answer choices indicates the greatest challenge Anne will face in life.

Getting to the Answer: Marilla explicitly states that Anne's trouble is that she is "thinking too much about" (line 76) herself, which is choice A. However, this advice is intended for the specific situation at hand, the tea party, rather than Anne's greater challenge of learning to take things calmly, which will affect her entire life. Thus, (B) is correct.

16. B

Difficulty: Hard

Category: Reading / Vocab-in-Context

Strategic Advice: Predict a word that could replace the word in the question stem, then find its closest match among the answer choices.

Getting to the Answer: The passage states that Marilla hopes to actively change Anne from her current state and mold her into one of her own designs. Thus, of the various uses of the word "fashioning," (B) is correct.

17. B

Difficulty: Medium

Category: Reading / Rhetoric

Strategic Advice: After reading the entire passage, reread the paragraph in question and determine what role it plays in the progression of ideas within the passage.

Getting to the Answer: Paragraph 4 explains Marilla's feelings about Anne's personality traits, describes how she hoped to temper them, and says that she failed to do so, while also telling the reader that she likes Anne the way she is. Choice (B) best represents these ideas.

18. A

Difficulty: Medium

Category: Reading / Rhetoric

Strategic Advice: After reading the entire passage, evaluate the depth of the author's participation in the passage and how many perspectives the author introduces. Use this information to determine the correct answer.

Getting to the Answer: The author reveals the inner thinking of both Anne and Marilla while taking no active part in the passage, so (A) is correct.

19. C
Difficulty: Medium

Category: Reading / Rhetoric

Strategic Advice: Read the sentence and determine how the selected words shape the reader's image of Anne. Then select the answer choice that most accurately reflects this tone and image.

Getting to the Answer: The passage states that Anne runs home and implies that she is excited. Thus, the correct answer is (C), which supports the image of Anne as energetic.

20. D
Difficulty: Easy

Category: Reading / Inference

Strategic Advice: After reading the entire passage, evaluate how Marilla is presented in the passage and determine which answer choice is the most accurate.

Getting to the Answer: Throughout the passage, Marilla asks Anne to remain calm, coolly responds to Anne, and hopes to fashion Anne into a demure model child. Therefore, (D) is correct.

21. A
Difficulty: Medium

Category: Reading / Command of Evidence

Strategic Advice: To answer Command of Evidence questions, start by looking at the part of the passage that helped you answer the previous question.

Getting to the Answer: Throughout the passage, Marilla asks Anne to remain calm and coolly responds to Anne, and the quotation noted in lines 20–21 shows Marilla doing this; thus, (A) is correct.

CHAPTER 22

PREPARE

1. C

Difficulty: Medium

Category: Reading / Inference

Strategic Advice: When you see the phrase "which choice best describes" and the question stem provides both sides of the relationship, look for the answer choice that joins the two sides correctly.

Getting to the Answer: Locate the discussion regarding the insurgents and the government. Paraphrase what each side wanted. Predict that the insurgents wanted more slavery while the government wanted slavery to remain unchanged. Choice (C) matches your prediction.

2. C

Difficulty: Medium

Category: Reading / Vocab-in-Context

Strategic Advice: When you see the phrase "most nearly means" and a cited line, predict a word to substitute for the word in question.

Getting to the Answer: Read the sentence without "interest" and determine the author's intended meaning. Predict that the slave-owning states felt they had a right to own slaves. Choice (C) expresses the same idea.

3. B

Difficulty: Hard

Category: Reading / Inference

Strategic Advice: A relationship clue word in the question stem indicates that you should ask how items are related to each other.

Getting to the Answer: The question stem describes an unanticipated result and asks you to identify the cause. Read around the cited lines until you understand what the cause was. Earlier in the paragraph, Lincoln claims that the cause of the war was slavery, later stating that neither side thought slavery "might cease" (line 40). Predict that the referenced result is the end of slavery, (B).

PRACTICE

The following passage is an excerpt from the preface of Moll Flanders *(1722) by Daniel Defoe.*

The world is so taken up of late with novels and romances, that it will be hard for a private history to be taken for genuine, where the names and other
Line circumstances of the person are concealed, and on
5 this account we must be content to leave the reader to pass his own opinion upon the ensuing sheet, and take it just as he pleases.

The author is here supposed to be writing her own history, and in the very beginning of her
10 account she gives the reasons why she thinks fit to conceal her true name, after which there is no occasion to say any more about that.

It is true that the original of this story is put into new words, and the style of the famous lady we here
15 speak of is a little altered; particularly she is made to tell her own tale in modester words than she told it at first, the copy which came first to hand having been written in language more like one still in Newgate than one grown penitent and humble, as
20 she afterwards pretends to be.

The pen employed in finishing her story, and making it what you now see it to be, has had no little difficulty to put it into a dress fit to be seen, and to make it speak language fit to be read. When
25 a woman debauched from her youth, nay, even being the offspring of debauchery and vice, comes to give an account of all her vicious practices, and even to descend to the particular occasions and circumstances by which she ran through in threescore
30 years, an author must be hard put to wrap it up so

Margin notes:

auth. to reader: story might not seem true

MF = autobio but not real ID

writing style altered to be tamer

MF story = dark

clean as not to give room, especially for <u>vicious readers</u>, to turn it to his disadvantage.

    All possible care, (however,) has been taken to give no lewd ideas, no immodest turns in the new
35 dressing up of this story; no, not to the worst parts of her expressions. <u>To this purpose</u> some of the vicious part of her life, which could not be modestly told, is quite left out, and several other parts are very much shortened. What is left 'tis hoped will
40 not offend the chastest reader or the modest hearer; and as the best use is made even of the worst story, the moral 'tis hoped will keep the reader serious, even where the story might incline him to be otherwise. <u>To give the history of a wicked life</u> repented
45 of, necessarily requires that the wicked part should be make as wicked as the real history of it will bear, to illustrate and give a beauty to the penitent part, which is certainly the best and brightest, if related with equal spirit and life.
50   (But) as this work is <u>chiefly recommended to those who know how to read it</u>, and how to make the good uses of it which the story all along recommends to them, so it is to be hoped that such readers will be more pleased with the moral than the
55 fable, with the application than with the relation, and with the end of the writer than with the life of the person written of.
    <u>There is in this story abundance of delightful incidents, and all of them usefully applied.</u> There is
60 an agreeable turn artfully given them in the relating, that naturally instructs the reader, either one way or other. The first part of her lewd life with the young gentleman at Colchester has so many happy turns given it to expose the crime, and warn all
65 whose circumstances are adapted to it, of the ruinous end of such things, and the foolish, thoughtless, and abhorred conduct of both the parties, that it abundantly atones for all the lively description she gives of her folly and wickedness.
70   Upon this foundation this book is recommended to the reader as a work from every part of which something may be learned, and some just and religious inference is drawn, by which the reader will have something of instruction, if he pleases to
75 make use of it.

Left margin notes:

MF = changed ways later in life

auth's request: focus on how MF is good

how lewdness can be beneficial

reader should learn from MF's story

4. D

Difficulty: Medium

Category: Reading / Inference

Strategic Advice: The phrase "According to the passage" and a relationship clue word indicate that you should ask yourself how items are being related.

Getting to the Answer: The clue word "because" suggests that this is a cause-and-effect relationship. Find the reference to the narrator's concern and reread the section. Predict that the recent popularity of novels encourages readers to believe what they read is fictional. This prediction matches (D).

5. C

Difficulty: Medium

Category: Reading / Inference

Strategic Advice: Open-ended Inference questions about relationships (explicit or implicit) require you to describe the relationship in your own words.

Getting to the Answer: Because the question stem is essentially asking about why the narrator wrote the story described in the passage and not the passage itself, focus on what the narrator says about the purpose of the story. By paraphrasing the narrator's intent stated in the final paragraph, you can predict that the narrator thinks readers can learn good things from the story. Choice (C) matches this prediction.

6. B

Difficulty: Medium

Category: Reading / Vocab-in-Context

Strategic Advice: When answering Vocab-in-Context questions, focus on synonyms for the word in question, not on a specific definition.

Getting to the Answer: Read the sentence without "usefully applied" and ask what the narrator is trying to convey. Throughout the passage, the narrator returns to the idea that the story is written not to relate "wicked" tales but to provide readers with an opportunity to learn from the lessons found in the story. Predict that the narrator is reaffirming the purpose for writing such stories. Choice (B) matches your prediction.

PERFORM

The following passage is about the role chemistry plays in archeology.

Demonstrating that chemistry sometimes can inform history, researchers from the National Institute of Standards and Technology (NIST), Colorado
Line College and Mount Saint Mary's University in
5 Emmitsburg, Maryland, have shown that sensitive nondestructive evaluation (NDE) techniques can be used to determine the elemental composition of ancient coins, even coins that generally have been considered too corroded for such methods. Along
10 the way, the researchers' analysis of coins minted in ancient Judea has both raised new questions about who ruled the area and given insight into trading patterns and industry in the region.

Elemental and isotope analysis of the metals in
15 ancient artifacts sometimes can pinpoint the places where the metal was mined, because ores in a given region often have a unique composition. This can be combined with historical records of when mines in the area were operating to determine when the
20 coin was likely struck. The results not only help date the coin, but also offer insight into trade and power relationships in the region.

To compare the effectiveness of various nondestructive analytical methods with destructive
25 methods often used to determine the age and origin of ancient coins, the group studied coins minted by Kings Herod Agrippa I and Herod Agrippa II in what is modern day Palestine and Israel, during a biblically and historically significant period.

margin notes:
chemistry (NDE) → new q's abt. history

chem. shows where metal is from

chem + history → insight into trade & power

study to determine non-destructive vs destructive analysis

30 The vast numbers of a particular coin, a prutah, found in the archaeological record has led scholars to disagree about when they were struck and by whom. The provenance of the coin is important because it is used to establish dates for places and
35 events in the early years of Christianity and the onset of the Jewish War (66-70 CE) against the Romans and the Diaspora that followed.

To better establish whether the coins were minted by Agrippa I (41-45 CE) or Agrippa II
40 (after 61 CE), the team performed X-ray fluorescence and lead isotope analysis to fingerprint the ores used in the production of the coins. These NDE methods are not commonly used on corroded coins because the corrosion can affect the
45 results—in some cases making it difficult to get a result at all. The team showed that these problems could be overcome using polarizing optics and powerful new software for X-ray fluorescence analysis, combined with careful calibration of
50 the mass spectrometer using Standard Reference Materials from NIST.

The lead isotope analysis, performed at NIST, showed that the coins that had been attributed to Agrippa I were indeed from that era. More interest-
55 ingly, however, the group found that the copper from which the coins were made most likely came from mines that scholars thought hadn't been opened until a century later.

"All the archaeological evidence has thus far
60 suggested that the Romans had moved into Arabia in the second century CE," says Nathan Bower of Colorado College. "What this analysis shows is that the Romans may have reached the region earlier or found that these mines had already been
65 opened. Either way, our findings suggest that the Romans had a much closer relationship with this particular region than scholars had previously thought."

To follow up on their research, the group is
70 planning to perform more tests to determine if the mines in question may have been operating even earlier than their recent findings suggest.

margin notes:
scholars disagree abt. coin's origin

origin = used to establish timeline

method used in research

corrosion affects results

solution to corrosion issues

results of the research: mines existed earlier than they thought

quote abt findings: Romans & region coins minted in

next steps in research

7. A

Difficulty: Medium

Category: Reading / Vocab-in-Context

Strategic Advice: Remember to avoid common meanings when answering Vocab-in-Context questions.

Getting to the Answer: Read the sentence without "struck" and rephrase what the author means. Predict that the author is referring to when the coins were minted. Choice (A) is correct.

8. D

Difficulty: Medium

Category: Reading / Inference

Strategic Advice: To answer Inference questions that are not about specific parts of the passage, find the author's thesis and look for the answer choice that is consistent with it.

Getting to the Answer: Use your Passage Map to locate the thesis. The author states in the first sentence that science can help us learn about history. Lead isotope analysis is presented as an example of how science "can inform" (lines 1-2) history. In the first paragraph, the author states that this analysis has raised questions, and in paragraph 6, the author indicates that the analysis answered questions about when the analyzed coins were made. Therefore, (D) is correct.

9. D

Difficulty: Medium

Category: Reading / Inference

Strategic Advice: The phrase "according to the passage" and a relationship keyword in the question stem signal an Inference question.

Getting to the Answer: The relationship keyword "because" indicates a cause-and-effect relationship, so identify why the researchers

chose the coin in question. Predict that if the scientists' technique could help answer historians' questions, then historians would recognize the value of the technique. Choice (D) is correct.

10. A

Difficulty: Easy

Category: Reading / Vocab-in-Context

Strategic Advice: The phrase "most nearly means" and a cited line indicate a Vocab-in-Context question.

Getting to the Answer: Read the sentence without "establish" and think of a synonym that can replace it. Predict that because scientists wanted to determine facts through their research, they wanted to determine who made the coins. Choice (A) matches your prediction.

EXTRA PRACTICE

The following passage is adapted from Around the World in Eighty Days *by Jules Verne.*

Phileas Fogg, having shut the door of his house at half-past eleven, and having put his right foot before his left five hundred and seventy-five times, and his left foot before his right five hundred and seventy-six times, reached the Reform Club. He repaired at once to the dining-room and took his place at the habitual table, the cover of which had already been laid for him. A flunkey handed him an uncut Times, which he proceeded to cut with a skill which betrayed familiarity with this delicate operation. The perusal of this paper absorbed Phileas Fogg until a quarter before four, whilst the Standard, his next task, occupied him till the dinner hour. Dinner passed as breakfast had done, and Mr. Fogg re-appeared in the reading-room and sat down to the Pall Mall¹ at twenty minutes before six. Half an hour later several members of

usual routine

PF = creature of habit

day in the life of PF

PF's friends

the Reform came in and drew up to the fireplace. They were Mr. Fogg's usual partners at whist:[2]

20 Andrew Stuart, an engineer; John Sullivan and Samuel Fallentin, bankers; Thomas Flanagan, a brewer; and Gauthier Ralph, one of the Directors of the Bank of England.

"Well, Ralph," said Thomas Flanagan, "what

25 about that robbery?"

recent robbery @ bank

"Oh," replied Stuart, "the Bank will lose the money."

"On the contrary," broke in Ralph, "I hope we may put our hands on the robber. Skillful detectives

30 have been sent to all the principal ports of America and the Continent, and he'll be a clever fellow if he slips through their fingers."

"But have you got the robber's description?" asked Stuart.

35 "In the first place, he is no robber at all," returned Ralph, positively.

"What! a fellow who makes off with fifty-five thousand pounds, no robber?"

"No."

40 "Perhaps he's a manufacturer, then."

robber = unusual

"The Daily Telegraph says that he is a gentleman."

It was Phileas Fogg, whose head now emerged from behind his newspapers, who made this

45 remark. A package of banknotes, to the value of fifty-five thousand pounds, had been taken from the principal cashier's table, that functionary being at the moment engaged in registering the receipt of three shillings and sixpence. Let it be observed that

details about robbery

50 the Bank of England reposes a touching confidence in the honesty of the public. There are neither guards nor gratings to protect its treasures; gold, silver, banknotes are freely exposed, at the mercy of the first comer. A keen observer of English customs

55 relates that, being in one of the rooms of the Bank one day, he had the curiosity to examine a gold ingot weighing some seven or eight pounds. He took it up, scrutinised it, passed it to his neighbour, he to the next man, and so on until the ingot, going from

60 hand to hand, was transferred to the end of a dark

entry; nor did it return to its place for half an hour. Meanwhile, the cashier had not so much as raised his head. But in the present instance things had not gone so smoothly. The package of notes not being

65 found when five o'clock sounded from the ponderous clock in the "drawing office," the amount was passed to the account of profit and loss.

There were real grounds for supposing, as the Daily Telegraph said, that the thief did not belong

70 to a professional band. On the day of the robbery a well-dressed gentleman of polished manners, and with a well-to-do air, had been observed going to and fro in the paying room where the crime was committed. A description of him was easily pro-

75 cured and sent to the detectives; and some hopeful spirits, of whom Ralph was one, did not despair of his apprehension. The papers and clubs were full of the affair, and everywhere people were discussing the probabilities of a successful pursuit; and the

80 Reform Club was especially agitated, several of its members being Bank officials.

newspaper → thief = unusual, not common criminal

Ralph would not concede that the work of the detectives was likely to be in vain, for he thought that the prize offered would greatly stimulate their

85 zeal and activity. But Stuart was far from sharing this confidence; and, as they placed themselves at the whist-table, they continued to argue the matter.

different opinions on robbery being solved

"I maintain," said Stuart, "that the chances are in favour of the thief, who must be a shrewd fellow."

90 "Well, but where can he fly to?" asked Ralph. "No country is safe for him."

"Pshaw!"

"Where could he go, then?"

"Oh, I don't know that. The world is big enough."

95 "It was once," said Phileas Fogg, in a low tone.

Stuart → thief will escape

PF → world not big anymore

[1] Pall Mall: a street in the city of Westminster, London
[2] Whist: a trick-taking card game. Modern derivatives include Hearts and Spades

1. D

Difficulty: Medium

Category: Reading / Vocab-in-Context

Strategic Advice: Locate context clues to help determine the meaning of the word. Predict a meaning for the word and then match it to the closest answer choice.

Getting to the Answer: The sentence describes Fogg arriving at the club and going to his usual table. A good prediction might be "went." Be careful of answer choices that offer alternate meanings for the target word. Look for the nearest match in the answers. Choice (D) fits with the tone and context of the sentence.

2. C

Difficulty: Medium

Category: Reading / Inference

Strategic Advice: Review the descriptions of Phileas Fogg and his actions in your Passage Map. Summarize what the beginning of the passage says about Fogg.

Getting to the Answer: Paragraph 1 describes Fogg counting out his steps on his way to the club. Upon arriving at the club, Fogg goes to his "habitual table" (line 7) and performs a routine series of actions. Choice (C) is correct, as the details in paragraph 1 depict a man who likes to keep to a set routine.

3. A

Difficulty: Medium

Category: Reading / Command of Evidence

Strategic Advice: Review your answer to the previous question. Locate the answer choice that directly supports the conclusion you drew to answer the previous question.

Getting to the Answer: Choice (A) is correct. It provides the best support for the idea that

Phileas Fogg is a man of habit and routine. The word "habitual" (line 7) and the fact that his table was prepared ahead of time for him suggest that Fogg followed this routine regularly.

4. A

Difficulty: Medium

Category: Reading / Inference

Strategic Advice: Review the answer choices. Skim your Passage Map for evidence that would prove one of the answer choices.

Getting to the Answer: Fogg reads the newspaper at the beginning of the passage. He chimes in with a comment on the robbery the other men are discussing based on the information he learned in the paper. Therefore, (A) is correct.

5. D

Difficulty: Easy

Category: Reading / Command of Evidence

Strategic Advice: Review your answer to the previous question. Decide which lines of text show Fogg's understanding of current events.

Getting to the Answer: Choice (D) is correct. In these lines, Fogg interjects with additional information about a crime that is a current event.

6. B

Difficulty: Medium

Category: Reading / Detail

Strategic Advice: Locate the portion of the text that discusses the bank. Draw a logical conclusion about the Bank of England based on the text and predict an answer.

Getting to the Answer: The passage describes the lack of security measures at the bank that led to a theft in broad daylight. The text references a lack of guards or protective gratings. Choice (B) is correct.

7. A

Difficulty: Easy

Category: Reading / Vocab-in-Context

Strategic Advice: Find context clues in the target sentence. Predict the meaning of the word and look for a match in the answer choices.

Getting to the Answer: "Functionary" (line 47) refers back to the "principal cashier" (line 47) mentioned earlier in the sentence. Pay attention to the tone and specific context clues to help you choose between two related answer choices such as "official" and "servant." Choice (A) is correct; it provides a suitably neutral word that could substitute for "principal cashier."

8. C

Difficulty: Medium

Category: Reading / Inference

Strategic Advice: Find the part of the passage that describes the thief. Locate sentences that focus on a description of the suspect. Summarize the details in a one-sentence description.

Getting to the Answer: Lines 70-74 ("On the day ... crime was committed") describe the suspect as a gentleman. Choice (C) is correct because the passage suggests that the police do not believe the man to be a professional thief due to the description of his appearance and demeanor.

9. B

Difficulty: Hard

Category: Reading / Rhetoric

Strategic Advice: Reread the cited line. Concentrate on how the sentence impacts the text surrounding it.

Getting to the Answer: Examining the surrounding text shows that this comment occurs during a discussion about the thief being on the run. Fogg has silently listened to the conversation to this point, but now quietly interjects. This suggests that Fogg will have more to say about the topic; (B) is correct.

10. C

Difficulty: Hard

Category: Reading / Rhetoric

Strategic Advice: Think about the passage as a whole. Use one sentence to predict the purpose of this passage. Make sure the tone of the answer choice matches the tone of the passage.

Getting to the Answer: The excerpt provides a brief character sketch of Phileas Fogg and establishes the dynamics of his friendships at the Reform Club. Choice (C) is correct; it accurately identifies the purpose of the excerpt.

Passage 1 discusses possible uses of video games in designing educational materials. Passage 2 explores how elements of video games can be used in combatting deteriorating cognition in older adults.

Passage 1

Many teenagers have heard from their parents that <u>playing too many video games can negatively affect their learning and socialization</u>. <u>Studies per-</u>
Line <u>formed in the 1990s supported this claim.</u> Scientists
5 evaluated the content of popular video games and the amount of time children and teenagers were allowed to spend playing them. They (eventually) connected video games to anger issues, obesity, and addiction.

Studies showed that violent video games played
10 for long periods of time inadvertently mimicked a method of repetition long used by teachers to reinforce subject matter. The method of advancement in many violent video games involves winning a contest of some kind. <u>This is also a method used in</u>
15 <u>the classroom and other settings familiar to children and teenagers.</u> This method makes the content of the video games, including overall aggressive themes, easy to absorb.

sci. study: VG's can have neg. affects

violent VG's similar to teaching methods: repetition & winning

Until recently, the only positive effect of play-
20 ing video games seemed to be an improvement
in manual dexterity and computer literacy. These
important upsides didn't seem to outweigh the
negatives. A 2013 study by the National Academy of
Sciences shows that the playing of fast-paced video
25 games can actually improve performance in areas
like attention span, spatial navigation, cognition,
reasoning, and memory. Researchers tested small
pools of gamers and found that those who had a
history of playing action-packed video games were
30 better at tasks such as pattern discrimination. They
also found that the gamers excelled at conceptual-
izing 3-D objects.

This new information could change the form
that educational materials take. Content developers
35 hope that the new materials may inspire interest
in the fields of engineering, math, and technology.
Educators can transform this data into classroom
experiences that will not only cater to the current
interests of students, but also use old patterns of
40 teaching in a new and more modern way.

Passage 2

As adults age, certain brain functions deteriorate. Two of these important functions are cognition and memory. This kind of decline can lead to
an associated loss of well-being. The number of
45 adults affected by Alzheimer's disease or dementia
is also on the rise. Researchers are racing to find
ways for people to maintain brain health while
aging. A recent study examined the effects of non-
action video-game training on people experiencing
50 cognitive decline.

The study worked with small sample sizes of
aging participants. Researchers found that that
the use of video games can allow the adult brain
to maintain some plasticity. Test subjects trained
55 their memories with games that featured patterned
blocks, jigsaw puzzles, facial recognition, and other
iterations requiring the recall of patterns. Test
subjects who completed as few as twenty training
sessions with these video games showed an increase
60 in attention span, alertness, and visual memory.
They also showed a decrease in distraction. These

some pros of VG's emerging

playing VG's can improve some brain function

VG's have potential to shape new edu. methods

cog. and mem. decline with age

non-action VG's may help slow cog. decline

sci. study → VG's help maintain brain flexibility

↑functions; ↓distraction

results are encouraging, as they suggest that there
may be ways to stave off mental decline and to help
the elderly maintain functions needed for safe driv-
65 ing and other activities of daily living.

More tests need to be done in order to understand the full potential of video games in the
anti-aging market. There are several companies
currently capitalizing on the success of these stud-
70 ies, and increasingly more games that promise
increased cognitive function are sure to find their
way to retailers soon.

promising but more tested needed

11. C
Difficulty: Medium

Category: Reading / Global

Strategic Advice: Review your notes about
the passage's central ideas. The correct answer
will include an idea that is supported by all of
the evidence presented in the passage. Avoid
answer choices like A that refer to only one idea
presented in the passage.

Getting to the Answer: All of the details presented in the passage are related to the idea that
research about the effects of video games on
those who play them is being used to develop
new educational tools and methods. Choice (C)
is correct.

12. D
Difficulty: Medium

Category: Reading / Command of Evidence

Strategic Advice: Locate each answer choice
in the passage. Consider which lines from the
passage most directly support the central idea
of the passage, which you identified in the previous question.

Getting to the Answer: The central idea of
the passage is related to how research about
video games is affecting the development of
new methods of teaching. Choice (D) provides
the most direct support for the answer to the
previous question.

13. A

Difficulty: Easy

Category: Reading / Detail

Strategic Advice: Use your Passage Map to find the paragraph that discusses studies performed in the 1990s. The correct answer will be stated explicitly in the passage.

Getting to the Answer: In paragraph 1, the author states that studies performed in the 1990s confirmed what parents had long said: that too many videos games can have a negative impact on learning and socialization in teenagers. Choice (A) is correct.

14. C

Difficulty: Medium

Category: Reading / Vocab-in-Context

Strategic Advice: Replace the tested word with each of the answer choices. The correct answer will be a synonym that makes sense in the context of the sentence, paragraph, and passage.

Getting to the Answer: In paragraph 2, the author explains that certain video games simulate a repetition method used in the classroom but indicates that this was not intentional on the part of the game developers. Choice (C) is correct because "inadvertently" most nearly means "unintentionally" in this context.

15. B

Difficulty: Medium

Category: Reading / Inference

Strategic Advice: Review your Passage Map notes from paragraph 2. Identify the cause-and-effect relationship the author describes.

Getting to the Answer: In paragraph 2, the author explains that when played for extended periods of time, video games mimic methods used in the classroom to teach children information. This is what makes it easier for game players to absorb the content of the games. Choice (B) is correct.

16. A

Difficulty: Hard

Category: Reading / Inference

Strategic Advice: The correct answer will not be stated directly in the text but should be supported by the evidence presented. Avoid answers like B and D that go too far.

Getting to the Answer: In paragraph 2, the author asserts that the findings of the research described suggest that those elderly persons who are able to prevent mental decline could better maintain the functions they need to operate independently, such as driving. Choice (A) is correct.

17. C

Difficulty: Medium

Category: Reading / Command of Evidence

Strategic Advice: The answer to the previous question will not be directly stated in the lines in the answer choice to this question. Rather, the correct answer to this question will provide the strongest support for your answer to the previous question.

Getting to the Answer: In the previous question, you inferred from the information in the passage that people who are able to put off the cognitive effects of aging might be able to live longer independently. Choice (C) provides the strongest support for this inference.

18. D

Difficulty: Medium

Category: Reading / Vocab-in-Context

Strategic Advice: Reread the target sentence and predict your own definition for the cited word. Then, evaluate the answer choices to find the closest match to your prediction.

Getting to the Answer: In this context, "deteriorate" most nearly means "get worse" or "weaken." Choice (D) is correct.

19. A

Difficulty: Medium

Category: Reading / Rhetoric

Strategic Advice: Review your notes from paragraph 2. Consider how the information presented in this paragraph supports the central claim presented by the author in the overall passage.

Getting to the Answer: Passage 2 is mostly about how researchers are considering the potential of video games in treating dementia and other age-related cognitive problems. In paragraph 2, the author explains the results of preliminary research involving the elderly and video games. Choice (A) is correct.

20. A

Difficulty: Medium

Category: Reading / Rhetoric

Strategic Advice: Consider the overall message the author is conveying through the information presented in the passage. The author's purpose will not be directly stated but will be supported by the evidence presented.

Getting to the Answer: In Passage 2, the author describes how video games can potentially help elderly people who are experiencing cognitive decline due to aging. Choice (A) is correct.

21. D

Difficulty: Medium

Category: Reading / Synthesis

Strategic Advice: The correct answer will be supported by the information in both passages. Avoid answers like B and C that refer only to information presented in one of the passages.

Getting to the Answer: Both passages discuss how video games are being used by researchers in different fields. Choice (D) is correct.

CHAPTER 23

PREPARE

1. C
Difficulty: Medium

Category: Reading / Rhetoric

Strategic Advice: Use your Passage Map to summarize the author's tone and purpose. Look for key words that indicate the author's opinion.

Getting to the Answer: A good summary of the author's tone and purpose would be: "Do the solar constant and sunspots affect Earth's weather? Research suggests that they do, but does not explain how. Although questions remain, scientists think the data could be useful." The tone of the passage is informative, and key words are used to illustrate the connections between the data collected and the scientific understanding gained. Predict that the author's purpose is to inform the reader about an aspect of scientific research and the results of that research. Choice (C) is correct.

2. B
Difficulty: Medium

Category: Reading / Rhetoric

Strategic Advice: To answer questions about the role of a cited section in the context of the entire passage, focus on how the cited section helps the author achieve his overall purpose for writing the passage.

Getting to the Answer: Review your Passage Map notes for paragraph 8. The author explains that the scientists don't fully understand their findings. The author uses the questions in the paragraph to illustrate the areas of the research that the scientists don't understand. Choice (B) is correct.

3. B
Difficulty: Easy

Category: Reading / Rhetoric

Strategic Advice: Questions about the purpose of a particular phrase are really asking about how that phrase helps the author achieve his or her overall purpose.

Getting to the Answer: Think about the cited phrase in the context of the author's purpose to inform the reader about solar constant research and its potential applications. Predict that even without a full understanding of the interactions between solar cycles and Earth's climate, the solar constant research might soon have practical uses. Choice (B) is correct.

PRACTICE

The following is an excerpt from The Woman in White, *a novel by Wilkie Collins published in 1859 and considered to be one of the first novels of the mystery genre.*

Pesca's face and manner, on the evening when we confronted each other at my mother's gate, were more than sufficient to inform me that <u>something</u>
Line <u>extraordinary had happened</u>. It was quite useless,
5 however, to ask him for an immediate explanation. I could only conjecture, while he was dragging me in by both hands, that, knowing my habits, he had come to the cottage to make sure of meeting me that night and that <u>he had some news to tell of an</u>
10 <u>unusually agreeable kind</u>.
    We both bounced into the parlor in a highly abrupt and undignified manner. My mother sat by the open window laughing and fanning herself. Pesca was one of her especial favorites, and his
15 wildest eccentricities were always pardonable in her eyes. From the first moment she found out that the little Professor was deeply and gratefully attached to her son, she opened her heart to him unreservedly and took <u>all his puzzling foreign peculiarities</u> for

[margin notes: P's face → smthg happened; Mom accepts P's oddities; P = prof?]

S does not accept P bc of propriety

elders = more excited by new things; youth = unaffected

kids = too well raised?

Mom acted younger than sis w/ P

M&P – great news! Excited!

S obsessed with cup

20 granted, without so much as attempting to understand any one of them.

My sister Sarah, with all the advantages of youth,
was, strangely enough, less pliable. She did full
justice to Pesca's excellent qualities of heart, but
25 she could not accept him implicitly, as my mother
accepted him, for my sake. Her insular notions of
propriety rose in perpetual revolt against Pesca's
constitutional contempt for appearances, and she
was always more or less undisguisedly astonished
30 at her mother's familiarity with the eccentric little
foreigner. I have observed, not only in my sister's
case, but in the instances of others, that we of the
young generation are nowhere near as hearty and
impulsive as some of our elders. I constantly see
35 old people flushed and excited by the prospect of
some anticipated pleasure which altogether fails to
ruffle the tranquility of their serene grandchildren.
Are we, I wonder, quite such genuine boys and girls
now as our seniors were in their time? Has the great
40 advance in education taken rather too long a stride,
and are we in these modern days just the least trifle
in the world too well brought up?

Without attempting to answer those questions
decisively, I may at least record that I never saw my
45 mother and my sister together in Pesca's society
without finding my mother much the younger
woman of the two. On this occasion, (for example,)
while the old lady was laughing heartily over the
boyish manner in which we tumbled into the par-
50 lor, Sarah was perturbedly picking up the broken
pieces of a teacup, which the Professor had knocked
off the table in his precipitate advance to meet me
at the door.

"I don't know what would have happened,
55 Walter," said my mother, "if you had delayed much
longer. Pesca has been half mad with impatience,
and I have been half mad with curiosity. The Professor has brought some wonderful news with him,
in which he says you are concerned, and he has
60 cruelly refused to give us the smallest hint of it till
his friend Walter appeared."

"Very provoking: it spoils the set," murmured
Sarah to herself, mournfully absorbed over the
ruins of the broken cup.

65 While these words were being spoken, Pesca,
happily and fussily unconscious of the irreparable wrong which the crockery had suffered at
his hands, was dragging a large arm-chair to the
opposite end of the room, so as to command us all
70 three, in the character of a public speaker addressing an audience. Having turned the chair with its
back towards us, he jumped into it on his knees and
excitedly addressed his small congregation of three
from an impromptu pulpit.

75 "Now, my good dears," began Pesca, "listen to
me. The time has come—I recite my good news—
I speak at last."

"Hear, hear," said my mother, humoring the joke.

"The next thing he will break, Mamma," whis-
80 pered Sarah, "will be the back of the best arm-chair."

"Among the fine London Houses where I teach
the language of my native country," said Pesca, "is
one, mighty fine, in the big place called Portland.
The golden Papa there, the mighty merchant, says 'I
85 have got a letter from my friend, the Mister, and he
wants a recommend from me, of a drawing-master,
to go down to his house in the country. Perhaps you
know of a drawing master that I can recommend?'

"I address myself to the mighty merchant, and
90 I say, "Dear sir, I have the man! The first and foremost drawing-master of the world!'"

P addresses group

P jests

P needs drawing master to travel

P volunteers someone

4. C

Difficulty: Medium

Category: Reading / Rhetoric

Strategic Advice: Use your Passage Map to
identify how this paragraph helps the narrator
achieve his overall purpose for the passage.

Getting to the Answer: This paragraph provides context for the rest of the passage. The
narrator describes Pesca's expressive nature, his
understanding of Pesca, and the reason for the
subsequent events in the passage. Predict that
this paragraph sets the stage for understanding
how Pesca's character will impact the rest of
the story. Choice (C) matches your prediction.

5. A

Difficulty: Medium

Category: Reading / Rhetoric

Strategic Advice: To understand why a narrator chooses a particular word or phrase, focus on the author's purpose for writing the passage. The cited section will work to accomplish that purpose.

Getting to the Answer: Throughout the paragraph, the narrator describes why his mother finds Pesca so pleasing. This introductory wording sets the stage by describing Pesca as undignified. This feature of his personality is a great match for (A).

6. D

Difficulty: Medium

Category: Reading / Rhetoric

Strategic Advice: Focus on how the narrator sees the characters and events to understand the author's point of view.

Getting to the Answer: U.S. and World Literature passages focus on the relationships between main characters. Here, the main characters are the narrator, his mother, his sister, and Pesca. The narrator doesn't describe the interaction between the two women, focusing instead on the reaction that each woman has to Pesca's actions. Predict that the author wants to create a sketch of each woman by using those different responses. Choice (D) is correct.

PERFORM

The following is adapted from Helen Keller's address to the American Association to Promote the Teaching of Speech to the Deaf at Mt. Airy, Philadelphia, Pennsylvania (July 8, 1896).

If you knew all the joy I feel in being able to speak to you today, I think you would have some

idea of the value of speech to the deaf, and you
Line would understand why I want every little deaf
5   child in all this great world to have an opportunity
to learn to speak. I know that much has been said
and written on this subject, and that there is a wide
difference of opinion among teachers of the deaf in
regard to oral instruction. It seems very strange to
10   me that there should be this difference of opinion;
I cannot understand how any one interested in our
education can fail to appreciate the satisfaction we
feel in being able to express our thoughts in living
words. Why I use speech constantly, and I cannot
15   begin to tell you how much pleasure it gives me to
do so. Of course I know that it is not always easy
for strangers to understand me, but it will be by and
by; and in the meantime I have the unspeakable
happiness of knowing that my family and friends
20   rejoice in my ability to speak. My little sister and
baby brother love to have me tell them stories in the
long summer evenings when I am at home; and my
mother and teacher often ask me to read to them
from my favourite books. I also discuss the politi-
25   cal situation with my dear father, and we decide the
most perplexing questions quite as satisfactorily to
ourselves as if I could see and hear. So you see what
a blessing speech is to me. It brings me into closer
and tenderer relationship with those I love, and
30   makes it possible for me to enjoy the sweet companionship of a great many persons from whom
I should be entirely cut off if I could not talk.

I can remember the time before I learned to
speak, and how I used to struggle to express my
35   thoughts by means of the manual alphabet—how
my thoughts used to beat against my fingertips like
little birds striving to gain their freedom, until one
day Miss Fuller opened wide the prison-door and
let them escape. I wonder if she remembers how
40   eagerly and gladly they spread their wings and flew
away. Of course, it was not easy at first to fly. The
speech-wings were weak and broken, and had lost
all the grace and beauty that had once been theirs;
indeed, nothing was left save the impulse to fly,
45   but that was something. One can never consent
to creep when one feels an impulse to soar. But,

Margin notes:

HK → joy of speech, shared with deaf

all want ability to speak

uses speech to tell stories, read, argue, etc.

cut off from world until Ms F showed speech

struggled at first

nevertheless, it seemed to me sometimes that I could never use my speech wings as God intended I should use them; there were so many difficulties

hard to not succeed; kept trying

50 in the way, so many discouragements; (but) I kept on trying, knowing that patience and perseverance would win in the end. And while I worked, I built the most beautiful air-castles, and dreamed dreams, the pleasantest of which was of the time when I

55 should talk like other people; and the thought of the pleasure it would give my mother to hear my voice once more, sweetened every effort and made every failure an incentive to try harder the next time. (So) I want to say to those who are trying to

those struggling to speak: it gets better.

60 learn to speak and those who are teaching them: Be of good cheer. <u>Do not think of today's failures, but of the success that may come tomorrow</u>. You have set yourselves a difficult task, but you will succeed if you persevere; and you will find <u>a joy in over-</u>

65 <u>coming obstacles</u>—a delight in climbing rugged paths, which you would perhaps never know if you did not sometime slip backward—if the road was always smooth and pleasant. <u>Remember, no effort that we make to attain something beautiful is ever</u>

results will be worth it

70 <u>lost</u>. Sometime, somewhere, somehow we shall find that which we seek. We shall speak, yes, and sing, too, as God intended we should speak and sing.

7. A
Difficulty: Medium

Category: Reading / Rhetoric

Strategic Advice: Review your Passage Map and identify the author's purpose for writing the passage. Ask how the cited phrase helps the author achieve that purpose.

Getting to the Answer: This passage focuses on the author's experience of overcoming the obstacles between her and the ability to speak, the results that her success made possible, and her belief that others should have the same opportunity. By showing how difficult expression was before she could speak, the author emphasizes the benefits she received because she fought so hard. Predict that the phrase

highlights how hard expressing herself was before she could speak. Choice (A) matches your prediction.

8. C
Difficulty: Medium

Category: Reading / Rhetoric

Strategic Advice: To answer questions about an author's point of view, use your Passage Map to summarize the author's purpose for writing the passage. Ask who would express that point of view.

Getting to the Answer: In the first paragraph, the author describes a difference of opinion among teachers who work with deaf students and then states her position on the issue. She thinks that other deaf people should have the chance to learn to speak. Additionally, she makes it clear that she is not an outside observer of a disability, but someone who struggled to overcome adversity. Predict that the author seeks to ensure that other deaf people have access to the same oral instruction that she received. Choice (C) is correct.

9. B
Difficulty: Medium

Category: Reading / Rhetoric

Strategic Advice: Review your Passage Map and identify the author's purpose not only for the overall passage but also for the cited section.

Getting to the Answer: The author begins the passage by stating her position: All deaf children should have the opportunity to learn to speak. She then acknowledges that not everyone shares that opinion. To persuade those who disagree with her, she provides specific examples from her own experience to support her position and to sway those who disagree. Choice (B) is correct.

EXTRA PRACTICE

The following passage explores the <u>history and impact of public higher education</u> in the United States.

Every year, hundreds of thousands of students graduate from U.S. public universities. Many of the largest and most elite schools in the nation fall into
Line the category of public, or state, institutions. Unlike
5 private universities, which generally operate independently from any government influence, public higher education was established through government legislation and is sustained through state or federal involvement in various ways. <u>A look into</u>
10 <u>the history of U.S. public higher education can shed light on the changing ideals of the American story over the past century and a half.</u>

America's earliest higher-education institutions, like Harvard, were initially developed by and for
15 clergy, or church workers. For 17th-century Puritans in America, church leadership was of utmost importance. At that time, clergy was the main profession for which college degrees were offered. But during the 18th and 19th centuries, paralleling
20 the onset of secular (and increasingly scientifically inclined) modern thought, the nation and government acknowledged the <u>need for broader higher education opportunities</u>. Philosophers and politicians alike were aware that well-educated citizens
25 were a vital element of a functional democracy. A better-informed voting population could secure a better political future. Moreover, with aims to advance the fields of technology and agriculture through higher education, legislators anticipated
30 potential economic improvements nationwide as well. It was in the nation's best interest to make college more accessible.

In 1862, <u>President Lincoln</u> signed the <u>Morill Land-Grant Act.</u> This was, in many ways, the force
35 behind the public university system. The Morill Act ensured that public land would be set aside for the establishment of universities across the country. The coming decades saw a massive increase in the

opening of universities in the nation. Hundreds
40 of U.S. public universities began to operate. These schools received federal and state support, offered practical, accessible education, and sought, originally, to advance the fields of agriculture and mechanics. Soon these schools offered wide variet-
45 ies of subjects and specialties. These universities would be operated by their respective states, but all would adhere to certain broad federal regulations.

At the time, the government was seeking to mend racial injustices through legislation. To
50 this effect, a <u>second land act</u> was passed in 1890 in hopes of inhibiting discrimination in public universities. While at the time this did not accomplish the intended openness and diversity, <u>it paved the way for the culture of diversity</u> the
55 American university system enjoys today. Many public universities are now richly diverse, with regulations in place to accept students of any race, ethnicity, or socioeconomic status. In a similar vein, women—once a minority in colleges—increasingly
60 gained a strong presence in U.S. universities over the past 150 years. Women actually surpassed men in overall U.S. college attendance around the turn of the 21st century.

Since the legislation of the 19th century, public
65 universities have undergone <u>momentous growth</u>. The system has evolved to address and accommodate the nuances of 20th- and 21st-century American culture and development. Offering to in-state students some of the most affordable degree
70 programs in higher education, these schools have now graduated millions of undergraduate and graduate students. Public universities also manage the majority of the nation's government-funded academic research initiatives. Featuring some of the
75 most competitive athletic programs in the world, as well as elite scholarship and arts programs, the U.S. public universities' <u>accomplishments seem boundless</u>. With schools in Alaska, Hawaii, and even U.S. territories like Puerto Rico and Guam, public
80 university impact reaches the farthest corners and populations of the nation. The state school system

public colleges → tied closely to gov't & USA

early schools = religious

wanting to advance in tech. prompted public univ.

Lincoln & M L-G Act → public land for univ.

2nd act later pushed for diversity

growth in schools; affordable

gov't research, athletics, and more

impact on
others

has been formative for American culture, philosophy, economics, medicine, politics, and much more.

The eminence of the U.S. public university net-
85 work stretches beyond the United States. Students
travel from across the globe to study at the top programs. Cutting-edge schools like the University of
Virginia (UVA) and University of California at Los
Angeles (UCLA) receive continual international

attracts
global
attention

90 attention for their accomplishments in scholarship
and research. Programs, faculty, and students from
these schools participate in the global conversation
in significant ways, working toward a better future
for the planet.

95   Given those early visions for a more robustly
educated voting population, the enormity of
the system that the Morill Act launched is

reflect values
of U.S.
identity

remarkable. U.S. public universities have both
shaped and employed many of America's greatest
100 thinkers. Considering their timeline and their
accomplishments, <u>these schools seem to reflect
the post–Civil War history of diversity, liberty,
creativity, and equal opportunity</u> that in many ways
distinguishes the American cultural identity.

1. C
Difficulty: Hard

Category: Reading / Rhetoric

Strategic Advice: The correct answer will
reflect a specific position supported in both the
second paragraph and the passage as a whole.

Getting to the Answer: The author is citing political and economic reasons to explain why the government "acknowledged the need" (line 22) for
educated citizens. Choice (C) is correct.

2. B
Difficulty: Medium

Category: Reading / Command of Evidence

Strategic Advice: The correct choice should
support your answer to the previous question.
Consider which choice best shows a clear relationship to your answer.

Getting to the Answer: Choice (B) is correct
because it explicitly states that the government
saw the "need for broader higher education
opportunities" (lines 22–23).

3. A
Difficulty: Medium

Category: Reading / Rhetoric

Strategic Advice: Summarize the paragraph
and think about what the author would want
the reader to know after reading it.

Getting to the Answer: The Morill Act was
an early example of the federal government's
desire to increase enrollment at public universities. Choice (A) is correct.

4. B
Difficulty: Medium

Category: Reading / Rhetoric

Strategic Advice: The author's choice of words
is deliberate. Read the sentence carefully and
think about what the author is suggesting when
he uses the word "accessible."

Getting to the Answer: The passage notes that
public universities received federal and state
support. This means the universities could then
function at a lower cost and could enable more
students to attend. Choice (B) is correct.

5. D
Difficulty: Easy

Category: Reading / Vocab-in-Context

Strategic Advice: Use context clues to help
you predict the meaning of the word as it is
used in the sentence.

Getting to the Answer: The last sentence in
paragraph 3 contrasts the fact that although
universities would be operated by states, they

would still need to follow, or comply with, federal regulations because they received federal support. Choice (D) is correct.

6. C
Difficulty: Hard

Category: Reading / Rhetoric

Strategic Advice: A central theme of the passage is that expansion of public universities has impacted American culture. Consider which of these pieces of evidence best supports that theme.

Getting to the Answer: In paragraph 4, the author describes how public universities have gradually become more diverse, offering educational opportunities to many people who would not have otherwise had them in previous years. This has had a significant impact on American culture. Choice (C) is correct.

7. C
Difficulty: Medium

Category: Reading / Rhetoric

Strategic Advice: Think about why the author would want to include this fact. Look for the answer that is accurately reflected in the context of the paragraph.

Getting to the Answer: The paragraph's central idea is that the student populations of public universities have grown increasingly diverse. Choice (C) is correct because it provides support for this idea.

8. B
Difficulty: Easy

Category: Reading / Command of Evidence

Strategic Advice: Look for the choice that offers support for the answer to the previous question. There should be a clear relationship between the correct choice and the previous answer.

Getting to the Answer: Choice (B) clearly states that public universities are diverse today, even though the 1890 Land Act did not increase diversity when it was passed. This corresponds to the answer to the previous question.

9. D
Difficulty: Easy

Category: Reading / Vocab-in-Context

Strategic Advice: Predict the meaning of the word with context clues from the sentence and paragraph. Use each choice in the sentence to figure out which one makes the most sense.

Getting to the Answer: The second sentence of paragraph 5 states that the public university system "has evolved," which implies it has done so in response to change or variations in American culture over time. Choice (D) is correct.

10. C
Difficulty: Hard

Category: Reading / Rhetoric

Strategic Advice: Consider what the passage is about overall and what the author wants the reader to learn, rather than an idea that is mentioned only in passing or in support of the passage's purpose.

Getting to the Answer: The author has written a brief history of public higher education in the United States. In both the introduction and conclusion, the author connects the evolution of the public university system with generally accepted ideals and cultural values, such as diversity and liberty. Choice (C) is correct.

11. B

Difficulty: Medium

Category: Reading / Rhetoric

Strategic Advice: Consider the central idea of the passage that you identified in a previous question and the central idea in the fifth paragraph.

Getting to the Answer: The passage is primarily about the way in which U.S. higher education has reflected American cultural identity. Federal legislation often reflects the values of the nation as a whole. The fifth paragraph summarizes some contemporary examples of previous legislative efforts. Choice (B) is correct.

Adapted from "Young Goodman Brown" by Nathanial Hawthorne, first published in 1835.

GB & wife F

Young Goodman Brown came forth at sunset into the street at Salem village; but put his head back, after crossing the threshold, to exchange a parting
Line kiss with his young wife. And Faith, as the wife was
5 aptly named, thrust her own pretty head into the street, letting the wind play with the pink ribbons of her cap while she called to Goodman Brown.

"Dearest heart," whispered she, softly and rather sadly, when her lips were close to his ear, "prithee
10 put off your journey until sunrise and sleep in your own bed to-night. A lone woman is troubled with such dreams and such thoughts that she's afeard of herself sometimes. Pray tarry with me this night, dear husband, of all nights in the year."

F to GB "don't leave!"

15 "My love and my Faith," replied young Goodman Brown, "of all nights in the year, this one night must I tarry away from thee. My journey, as thou callest it, forth and back again, must needs be done 'twixt now and sunrise. What, my sweet, pretty wife, dost

GB – have to go tonight.

20 thou doubt me already, and we but three months married?"

"Then God bless you!" said Faith, with the pink ribbons; "and may you find all well when you come back."

25 "Amen!" cried Goodman Brown. "Say thy prayers, dear Faith, and go to bed at dusk, and no harm will come to thee."

So they parted; and the young man pursued his way until, being about to turn the corner by the

F said to see him go

30 meeting-house, he looked back and saw the head of Faith still peeping after him with a melancholy air, in spite of her pink ribbons.

"Poor little Faith!" thought he, for his heart smote him. "What a wretch am I to leave her on such an

GB has to go. Vows to never leave again

35 errand! She talks of dreams, too. Methought as she spoke there was trouble in her face, as if a dream had warned her what work is to be done tonight. But no, no; 't would kill her to think it. Well, she's a blessed angel on earth; and after this one night I'll cling to
40 her skirts and follow her to heaven."

With this excellent resolve for the future, Goodman Brown felt himself justified in making more haste on his present evil purpose. He had taken a dreary road, darkened by all the gloomiest trees

GB on evil purpose?

45 of the forest, which barely stood aside to let the narrow path creep through, and closed immediately behind. It was all as lonely as could be; and there is this peculiarity in such a solitude, that the traveller knows not who may be concealed by the innumer-
50 able trunks and the thick boughs overhead; so that with lonely footsteps he may yet be passing through an unseen multitude.

Goodman Brown glanced fearfully behind as he said to himself, "What if the devil himself should be at

scared of the devil

55 my very elbow!"

His head being turned back, he passed a crook of the road, and, looking forward again, beheld the figure of a man, in grave and decent attire, seated at the foot of an old tree. He arose at Goodman Brown's

GB meets a man

60 approach and walked onward side by side with him.

"You are late, Goodman Brown," said he. "The clock of the Old South was striking as I came through Boston, and that is full fifteen minutes agone."

"Faith kept me back a while," replied the young

GB late

65 man, with a tremor in his voice, caused by the sudden appearance of his companion, though not wholly unexpected.

It was now deep dusk in the forest, and deepest in that part of it where these two were journeying.
70 As nearly as could be discerned, the second traveller was about fifty years old, apparently in the same rank of life as Goodman Brown, and bearing a considerable resemblance to him, though perhaps more in expression than features. Still they might have been
75 taken for father and son. And yet, though the elder person was as simply clad as the younger, and as simple in manner too, he had an indescribable air of one who knew the world, and who would not have felt abashed at the governor's dinner table or in
80 King William's court, were it possible that his affairs should call him thither.

GB and man look similar

Old man sophisticated

12. A

Difficulty: Hard

Category: Reading / Vocab-in-Context

Strategic Advice: Read the sentence for context clues to understand the author's intention. Then replace the author's word with those in the answer choices to see which word's definition correctly reflects the sentence's meaning.

Getting to the Answer: "Perceived" is the best match for "discerned," as both words reflect Goodman Brown's observing the stranger's appearance and making judgments based on these observations. Thus, (A) is correct.

13. B

Difficulty: Medium

Category: Reading / Inference

Strategic Advice: Review your Passage Map to assess how Goodman Brown feels about his journey, particularly compared to what he tells his wife about the trip.

Getting to the Answer: Goodman Brown wonders if his wife had a dream about his trip's true "evil purpose" (line 43) but he is relieved to discover she hasn't. This means she knows nothing of the truth of his journey. Therefore, (B) is correct.

14. B

Difficulty: Easy

Category: Reading / Command of Evidence

Strategic Advice: Review each answer choice to assess its purpose in the passage and determine which best supports the correct answer to the previous question.

Getting to the Answer: Goodman Brown is hiding the true purpose of the journey from his wife and, as stated in (B), he fears that a dream told her of his purpose. He is later relieved when he discovers this is not true. Therefore, (B) is correct.

15. C

Difficulty: Medium

Category: Reading / Inference

Strategic Advice: Review your Passage Map for clues to assess how Goodman Brown feels about the man who joins him. Then, determine which answer choice accurately depicts the relationship between the two.

Getting to the Answer: Goodman Brown's voice trembles when he speaks to the man who appears by the side of the road, but the appearance is described as "not wholly unexpected" (lines 66–67), meaning Brown knows the man but is still unsettled. While Brown describes his trip as having an "evil purpose," no crime is discussed. Therefore, (C) is correct.

16. B

Difficulty: Easy

Category: Reading / Command of Evidence

Strategic Advice: Review each of the cited lines to determine what they reflect about Goodman's relationship with the man on the road and ascertain which answer choice best supports the correct answer from the previous question.

Getting to the Answer: Choice (B) is correct as it shows Goodman Brown's trembling in reply to the man's greeting while also acknowledging that the strange man's appearance was not wholly unexpected.

17. B
Difficulty: Medium

Category: Reading / Rhetoric

Strategic Advice: Review how the words in paragraph 8 help the reader understand the author's intention. Compare that intention to what you learned in the rest of the passage to determine which answer choice correctly describes why the author used those specific words.

Getting to the Answer: Goodman Brown is clearly hiding the journey's "evil purpose" from his wife, so the dark description of the forest he passes through helps heighten the feeling that Brown is about to do something wicked. Thus, (B) is correct.

18. D
Difficulty: Medium

Category: Reading / Rhetoric

Strategic Advice: Review the purpose of the cited lines in relation to the rest of the passage. Then, determine which answer choice correctly describes the author's intention in using those words.

Getting to the Answer: The author already describes the forest as a dark and foreboding place, but he also mentions specific figures that would frighten Goodman Brown, hinting at other possible entities waiting in the forest. Choice (D) is correct because the work is not a fairy tale as mentioned in choice A, the author

doesn't mention Goodman's going crazy as stated in choice B, and there is no mention of any robberies by Faith, as stated in C.

19. B
Difficulty: Hard

Category: Reading / Rhetoric

Strategic Advice: Review the cited lines and determine what claim about Goodman Brown this detail supports, especially in relation to what you already know about Brown.

Getting to the Answer: The man says he passed through Boston, but there is no other detail to support a claim that the two men are going there now, as noted in A. No evidence is provided to indicate that Brown was supposed to wait at the clock tower either, as is stated in C. And, while Brown is late, he has never hinted at any intended delay, as D implies. The only claim that is supported by the greeting is that the man and Brown know one another, as the man calls out Brown's name. Thus, (B) is correct.

20. B
Difficulty: Medium

Category: Reading / Vocab-in-Context

Strategic Advice: Read the sentence for clues to understand the author's intention. Predict a synonym to replace the selected word and see which of the answer choices best matches your synonym.

Getting to the Answer: "Embarrassed" and "abashed" both mean to feel out of place in a certain setting, which the stranger would not feel according to the sentence; (B) is correct.

21. A
Difficulty: Easy

Category: Reading / Inference

Strategic Advice: Review the passage for statements relating to Goodman's relationship with the man on the road and determine which answer choice offers the most logical statement.

Getting to the Answer: The man is described as older than Goodman, with a greater aura of wisdom. His expressions bear "a considerable resemblance" (lines 72–73) to Goodman's, enough that "they might have been taken for father and son" (lines 74–75). It is logical to assume that the man could be related to Brown; therefore, (A) is correct.

CHAPTER 24

PREPARE

1. B

Difficulty: Medium

Category: Reading / Rhetoric

Strategic Advice: Review your Passage Map to understand how the focus shifts over the course of the passage. Restate in one or two words what the focus is in the beginning of the passage and what the focus is at the end of the passage.

Getting to the Answer: The passage is written from the point of view of Pamela, who expresses her fear of the master in the beginning of the passage. By the middle of the passage, her fear has transformed into disrespectful anger at her master's actions. Predict that Pamela starts out afraid, but then loses her fear and respect for the master. Choice (B) matches your prediction.

2. A

Difficulty: Hard

Category: Reading / Rhetoric

Strategic Advice: In a U.S. and World Literature passage, identify what the characters think of each other and what they think about themselves.

Getting to the Answer: This question asks you to infer what Pamela thinks. For most of the passage, Pamela is subservient to her master; she asks for forgiveness and calls him "Your Honour" in line 18. However, in the final paragraph, Pamela defends herself. She says to her master that he has done her "the greatest harm in the world" (lines 46-47) because he has taught her "to forget herself, and what belongs to" (lines 47-48) her. Therefore, while Pamela recognizes the economic discrepancies that exist between her and

her master, she still likely believes that servants and masters do not differ in their basic human rights. Choice (A) is correct.

PRACTICE

The following passage was written (on the last night of 1849) by Florence Nightingale. She was not only a pioneer in the profession of nursing but also one of the first European women to travel to Egypt (1849-1850) and keep a detailed journal of her letters and reflections of her journey.

My Dear People,

Yes, I think your imagination has hardly followed me through the place where I have been
Line spending the last night of the old year. Did you
5 listen to it passing away and think of me? Where
do you think I heard it sigh out its soul? In the dim
unearthly colonnades of Karnak, which stood and
watched it, motionless, silent, and awful, as they had
done for thousands of years, to whom, no doubt,
10 thousands of years seem but as a day. Would that
I could call up Karnak before your eyes for one
moment, but it "is beyond expression."

No one could trust themselves with their
imagination alone there. Gigantic shadows spring
15 upon every side; "the dead are stirred up for thee to
meet thee at thy coming, even the chief ones of the
earth," and they look out from among the columns,
and you feel as terror-stricken to be there, miserable
intruder, among these mighty dead, as if you had
20 awakened the angel of the Last Day. Imagine six
columns on either side, of which the last is almost
out of sight, though they stand very near each other,
while you look up to the stars from between them,
as you would from a deep narrow gorge in the Alps,
25 and then, passing through 160 of these, ranged in
eight aisles on either side, the end choked up with
heaps of rubbish, this rubbish consisting of stones
twenty and thirty feet long, so that it looks like a
mountain fallen to ruin, not a temple. How art thou
30 fallen from heaven, oh Lucifer, son of the morning!
He did exalt his throne above the stars of God; for

Imagination near Karnak?

K = impossible to describe

Imagination runs wild → fear

details of Karnak = temple

I looked through a colonnade, and under the roof saw the deep blue sky and star shining brightly; and as you look upon these mighty ruins, a voice seems
35 continually saying to you, And seekest thou good things for thyself? Seek them not, for is there ought like this ruin? One wonders that people come back from Egypt and live lives as they did before.

Yet Karnak by starlight is not to me painful: we
40 had seen Luxor in the sunshine. I had expected the temples of Thebes to be solemn, but Luxor was fearful. Rows of painted columns, propylae, colossi, and—built up in the Holy Place—mud [not even huts, but] unroofed enclosures chalked out, or
45 rather mudded out, for families, with their one oven and broken earthen vessel; and, squatting on the ground among the painted hieroglyphs, creatures with large nose-rings, the children's eyes streaming with matter, on which the mothers let the flies rest,
50 because "it is good for them," without an attempt to drive them off; tattooed men on the ground, with camels feeding out of their laps, and nothing but a few doura stalks strewed for their beds;—I cannot describe the impression it makes: it is as if one
55 were steering towards the sun, the glorious Eastern sun, arrayed in its golden clouds, and were to find, on nearing it, that it were full—instead of glorified beings as one expected—of a race of dwarf cannibals, stained with blood and dressed in bones. The
60 contrast could not be more terrible than the savages of the Present in the temples of the Past at Luxor.

But Karnak by starlight is peace; not peace and joy, but peace—solemn peace. You feel like spirits revisiting your former world, strange and fallen to
65 ruins; but it has done its work, and there is nothing agonizing about it. Egypt should have no sun and no day, no human beings. It should always be seen in solitude and by night; one eternal night it should have, like Job's, and let the stars of the twilight be its
70 lamps; neither let it see the dawning of the day.

Margin annotations (left column):
trip to Egy. changes you

FN does not find K painful

describes people as different; does not approve

K = peaceful, spirits

at one with solitude at night

3. B
Difficulty: Easy

Category: Reading / Rhetoric

Strategic Advice: Questions about why an author includes a section in a passage require you to identify how it fits into the passage as a whole.

Getting to the Answer: The author concentrates, throughout the passage, on how much Egypt has affected her. The cited section is not so much about the lack of effect Egypt has had on the other people mentioned, but more about the great effect Egypt has had on the author. Choice (B) is correct.

4. C
Difficulty: Medium

Category: Reading / Rhetoric

Strategic Advice: Authors often use contrast to make a point or strengthen an argument. Reread around the cited lines and paraphrase the main points the author makes about the ideas being contrasted.

Getting to the Answer: To answer this question, you must compare the author's experiences in Karnak and Luxor. The author describes Karnak in lofty, ethereal language filled with references to the eternal. The author expects to find the same thing in Luxor—"I had expected the temples of Thebes to be solemn..." (lines 40–41)—but finds something completely different: "but Luxor was fearful" (lines 41–42). Predict that the comparison between the two cities highlights the author's negative reaction to the conditions at Luxor. Choice (C) matches your prediction.

5. A

Difficulty: Medium

Category: Reading / Rhetoric

Strategic Advice: Questions concerning the overall structure of a text require you to think about how the author presents the central ideas and builds the main argument.

Getting to the Answer: Review your Passage Map and look for patterns in how the author expresses the important ideas in the passage. In the second paragraph, the author shifts between the real and the imagined: "Gigantic shadows spring up on every side … 'the dead are stirred up for thee to meet…'" (lines 14–16). This shift between the real and the imagined continues in the third paragraph: "Rows of painted … golden clouds" (lines 42–56). Predict that the author mixes real descriptions with imaginative descriptions, which matches (A).

6. B

Difficulty: Medium

Category: Reading / Rhetoric

Strategic Advice: When a question gives you a "Yes, because" or "No, because" option, answer the question in two steps. First, determine whether the answer is "Yes" or "No" and eliminate the other two choices. Second, answer the "because" part of the question.

Getting to the Answer: Read around the cited claim and determine whether the evidence supports it. Review your notes about the third paragraph. The details that the author includes about Luxor provide adequate support for the claim she makes. Eliminate C and D. To answer the "because" question, paraphrase the support the author provided for the claim: conditions seemed dire. Choice (B) is correct.

PERFORM

This passage explores the differences in perception between humans and owls.

It's not difficult to believe that humans and animals perceive the world in different ways. As humans, sight is the sense with which we primarily interpret the
Line information around us, and other senses are gener-
5 ally subordinate. Our sense of survival is fortunately not dependent on our acute senses, or we would surely starve to death or be hunted into extinction. Owls, however, are masters of their senses, making such optimal use of their biological strengths that
10 we, by comparison, can best be described as wearing blindfolds and earplugs. Were an owl to attempt to hunt with our limited senses, it would most likely call us the lesser species, and possibly initiate attempts to label us as endangered.
15   As evidenced by our expression "owl-eyed," owls are known for their acute vision and all-seeing nature. Surprisingly, however, owls have a more limited range of view than humans. Whereas a human can see 180 degrees without turning his or
20 her head, an owl can only see 110 degrees under the same conditions. Owls have extremely well-developed eyes, but their structure is such that they are fixed in one position: an owl can look nowhere but straight ahead. They are farsighted, prevented
25 from seeing clearly anything within a few inches of their eyes; the popular image of a cartoon owl with reading glasses is not far removed from truth. Despite these limitations, however, owls maximize their advantages. Their sensitive eyes are very effective at collecting and processing light, mak-
30 ing them efficient night hunters. They can turn their heads almost completely around and nearly upside down, capitalizing on this range of movement to see over their own shoulders and directly
35 beneath themselves. They optimize their farsightedness to spot the minute movements of prey at great distances. With regard to auditory efficiency, owls, like humans, hear a limited range of audible sounds. Within that range, however, they have

[margin notes:]
humans use sight

owls use all senses

acute vision, but have to turn their heads

eyes = fixed & farsighted

process light, night hunters

can turn their heads all around

limited sounds, but better at hearing many frequencies

40 acute hearing at certain frequencies, helping them detect diminutive movements in the undergrowth. Some nocturnal species, such as the barn owl, have asymmetrical ear openings and disc-like facial feathers to facilitate the channeling and interpreta-
45 tion of sounds. They aggregate sensory information instantaneously to produce a mental map of their surroundings and location of possible prey.

   Like owls, we use our senses to map the world around us, but there the similarities end. We cannot

owls make complex map

50 understand the complex means by which the owl's hearing and sight work conjunctively to detect the subtle shifting of snow or leaves that signals food. The comparison itself is ludicrous, (in fact,) because our means for survival are so different: humans do
55 not live solitary lives, constantly alert to the movement of prey that determines whether we live or die. We do not think in the same way, if thought is

need to think this way bc solitary

even the right concept: we interpret information using extremely different cerebral processes, and we
60 can't know whether owls are even consciously aware of the complex workings of their brains. When I sit in the forest and study my environment, my world is interpreted with language. The owl's world is— well, it's impossible to tell, isn't it?

65   The owl may see the same forest we see, but

aware of forest in different way than humans

he is aware of it in a completely different way. I admire the foliage and the rustling leaves, and listen to birdsong. He hears the soft rustle of a leaf and knows that a chipmunk moves thirty feet off to our
70 right, directly underneath the poplar tree. I can say that the owl thinks about the chipmunk, but not how, for I don't have the correct mental processes to describe the complex interpretations of sensory detail into impulse and action; I am governed by
75 words instead of instinct.

7. D
Difficulty: Medium

Category: Reading / Rhetoric

Strategic Advice: Use your Passage Map to answer questions concerning the central argument in a passage. Review the first paragraph

to determine the author's thesis. Think about what must be true for the claim to be correct.

Getting to the Answer: The author begins with the claim that "humans and animals perceive the world in different ways" (lines 1–2). Predict that the assumption must have to do with how our brains work in different ways, which matches (D).

8. C
Difficulty: Medium

Category: Reading / Rhetoric

Strategic Advice: To answer a Rhetoric question that asks about support for a claim, use your Passage Map to locate the claims the author makes and the support the author provides. Make a general prediction about the claims the author supports and then find the answer choice that matches.

Getting to the Answer: The author claims that owls and humans have adapted to their environments in different ways. Since this question asks about owls, focus on the claims the author makes about them. Predict that the author provides support for the claim that owls have effectively adapted to their environment. In the second paragraph, the author provides several examples of ways owls successfully adapted. Choice (C) is correct.

9. D
Difficulty: Easy

Category: Reading / Rhetoric

Strategic Advice: When you see the phrase "in order to" and a cited line, identify how the cited detail fits into the overall structure of the passage.

Getting to the Answer: Overall, the passage compares the differences between the sensory adaptations of owls and humans. Read around the cited line and paraphrase why the author mentions barn owls. Predict that barn owl hearing is an example of how owls have adapted to improve their ability to hunt. Choice (D) matches your prediction.

10. A

Difficulty: Medium

Category: Reading / Rhetoric

Strategic Advice: Review your Passage Map, focusing on how the author presents the information in the passage.

Getting to the Answer: In paragraph 1, the author compares human perception to that of other animals, specifically owls. The author then discusses different ways in which owls and humans use their respective sensory apparatuses. Predict that the passage is structured by comparing the differences between how owls and humans perceive the world. Choice (A) is correct.

EXTRA PRACTICE

This passage is adapted from Carrie Chapman Catt's 1917 "Address to the United States Congress." Catt served as president of the National American Woman Suffrage Association; the closing arguments of her speech are excerpted below.

aud = congress

   Your party platforms have pledged woman suffrage. Then why not be honest, frank friends of our cause, adopt it in reality as your own,

auth: give suff. now

Line make it a party program and "fight with us"? As
5 a party measure—a measure of all parties—why not put the amendment through Congress and the Legislatures? We shall all be better friends, we shall have a happier nation, we women will be free to support loyally the party of our choice, and we shall
10 be far prouder of our history.

   "There is one thing mightier than kings and armies"—aye, than Congresses and political parties—"the power of an idea when its time has come

to move." The time for woman suffrage has come.
15 The woman's hour has struck. If parties prefer to postpone action longer and thus do battle with this idea, they challenge the inevitable. The idea will not perish; the party which opposes it may. Every delay, every trick, every political dishonesty from now
20 on will antagonize the women of the land more and more, and when the party or parties which have so delayed woman suffrage finally let it come, their sincerity will be doubted and their appeal to the new voters will be met with suspicion. This is
25 the psychology of the situation. Can you afford the risk? Think it over.

   We know you will meet opposition. There are a few "woman haters" left, a few "old males of the tribe," as Vance Thompson calls them, whose duty
30 they believe it to be to keep women in the places they have carefully picked out for them. Treitschke, made world famous by war literature, said some years ago: "Germany, which knows all about Germany and France, knows far better what is good
35 for Alsace-Lorraine than that miserable people can possibly know." A few American Treitschkes we have who know better than women what is good for them. There are women, too … But the world does not wait for such as these, nor does Liberty pause to
40 heed the plaint of men and women with a grouch. She does not wait for those who have a special interest to serve, nor a selfish reason for depriving other people of freedom. Holding her torch aloft, Liberty is pointing the way onward and upward and
45 saying to America, "Come."

   To you the supporters of our cause, in Senate and House, and the number is large, the suffragists of the nation express their grateful thanks. This address is not meant for you. We are more truly
50 appreciative of all you have done than any words can express. We ask you to make a last, hard fight for the amendment during the present session. Since last we asked a vote on this amendment your position has been fortified by the addition
55 to suffrage territory of Great Britain, Canada, and New York.

ideas > parties

give suffrage or lose votes

haters gonna hate!

America will not wait for haters to catch up

thanks suffragists for their work

suffrage = major issue

Some of you have been too indifferent to give more than casual attention to this question. It is worthy of your immediate consideration—a ques-
60 tion big enough to engage the attention of our Allies in war time, is too big a question for you to neglect…

Gentlemen, we hereby petition you, our only designated representatives, to redress our griev-
call to action 65 ances by the immediate passage of the influence to secure its ratification in your own state, in order that the women of our nation may be endowed with political freedom that our nation may resume its world leadership in democracy.

suff. will happen with or without gov't
70 Woman suffrage is coming—you know it. Will you, Honorable Senators and Members of the House of Representatives, help or hinder it?

1. C
Difficulty: Medium

Category: Reading / Rhetoric

Strategic Advice: The correct answer will be clearly stated within the text and will reflect the tone and intent of the author.

Getting to the Answer: The introduction to the passage states that Carrie Chapman Catt speaks on behalf of the National American Woman Suffrage Association. In the first paragraph, she asks lawmakers to support a constitutional amendment. The context of the surrounding paragraph makes clear that the amendment would grant women suffrage, rendering (C) correct.

2. D
Difficulty: Easy

Category: Reading / Detail

Strategic Advice: The correct answer will clearly restate—or have the same meaning as—the excerpted line.

Getting to the Answer: The excerpted line states, "Woman suffrage is coming" (line 70), which means that women will gain the right to vote, eventually, as expressed in (D).

3. A
Difficulty: Medium

Category: Reading / Inference

Strategic Advice: The correct answer will reflect the underlying or implied meaning of the excerpted line and the context of the surrounding text.

Getting to the Answer: The excerpted line states that suffrage will happen and women will gain the vote. It goes on to explain that as voters, women will not trust those who practiced dishonest and devious tactics (as expressed in the previous line). The concluding lines of the paragraph suggest a threat to the politicians' power. Taken together, these lines imply that women voters, when they gain the vote, will not vote for politicians who opposed their right to suffrage, as stated in (A).

4. D
Difficulty: Medium

Category: Reading / Vocab-in-Context

Strategic Advice: The correct answer will correctly replace the original word and retain the meaning of the original sentence.

Getting to the Answer: The text states that Catt and her supporters want congressional lawmakers to "redress our grievances" (lines 64–65), meaning to set right—or to remedy—the ills committed against women. Choice (D) reflects this meaning.

5. D
Difficulty: Hard

Category: Reading / Rhetoric

Strategic Advice: The correct answer will relate directly to the meaning of the question that Catt poses and to the main purpose of the passage as a whole.

Getting to the Answer: Catt's speech aims to win support for a constitutional amendment granting woman suffrage. Throughout the speech, she tries to persuade lawmakers to choose suffrage. She concludes by asking lawmakers whether they will help or hinder suffrage. Her final question puts responsibility on each lawmaker for his personal, individual choice on the matter, making (D) correct.

6. B

Difficulty: Medium

Category: Reading / Vocab-in-Context

Strategic Advice: The correct answer will reflect the specific meaning of the word in context of the surrounding sentence and text.

Getting to the Answer: The text states that "Every delay, every trick, every political dishonesty from now on will antagonize the women of the land more and more" (lines 18–21). The surrounding text suggests that women will only become more resolved to their purpose as a result of delay, as well as more angry— or bitter—with politicians who forestall them, making (B) correct.

7. B

Difficulty: Medium

Category: Reading / Rhetoric

Strategic Advice: The correct answer will be supported by evidence within the text.

Getting to the Answer: Catt acknowledges that opposition to woman suffrage remains, but she dismisses the opposition as "woman haters" (line 28) and "old males of the tribe" (lines 28–29), suggesting that they are dated and ineffectual. She goes on to state that the world will not slow down for this opposition and that the cause of liberty will continue, implying that suffrage will happen despite the opposition.

The suggestion is that suffrage is unavoidable, as stated in (B). In the previous paragraph, Catt also refers to suffrage as "inevitable" (line 17).

8. C

Difficulty: Medium

Category: Reading / Command of Evidence

Strategic Advice: The correct answer will provide evidence, either in reasoning or in fact, to support the claim in the answer to the previous question.

Getting to the Answer: The answer to the previous question asserts that woman suffrage is inevitable. Evidence to support this claim would show that suffrage is advancing, as demonstrated by (C).

9. D

Difficulty: Medium

Category: Reading / Inference

Strategic Advice: The correct answer will reflect the implied meaning of the excerpted line without assuming too much or distorting the context of the text.

Getting to the Answer: The excerpted line states that once women have the political freedom granted by suffrage, then the nation will resume its leadership in democracy. The implication is that the nation is not a leader in democracy as long as it denies women the right to vote. Therefore, (D) is correct.

10. C

Difficulty: Easy

Category: Reading / Rhetoric

Strategic Advice: The correct answer will reflect both the position of the author and the purpose expressed in the text.

Getting to the Answer: In the passage, Catt gives a speech in which she appeals to legislators to enact a constitutional amendment, or legislative reform, to grant women suffrage. She is speaking as a political activist. The correct answer is (C).

11. D

Difficulty: Medium

Category: Reading / Command of Evidence

Strategic Advice: The correct answer will provide evidence, either in reasoning or in fact, to support the specific position of the answer to the previous question.

Getting to the Answer: The answer to the previous question states that Catt is an activist appealing for legislative reform. Choice (D) is correct because in this line, Catt directly appeals to legislators to secure passage of the reform to which she refers earlier in the speech.

Adapted from "The Red House Mystery" by A.A. Milne, first published in 1922.

Whether Mark Ablett was a bore or not depended on the point of view, but it may be said at once that he never bored his company on the subject of his
Line early life. However, stories get about. There is always
5 somebody who knows. It was understood—and this, anyhow, on Mark's own authority—that his father had been a country clergyman. It was said that, as a boy, Mark had attracted the notice, and patronage, of some rich old spinster of the neighbourhood,
10 who had paid for his education, both at school and university. At about the time when he was coming down from Cambridge, his father had died; leaving behind him a few debts, as a warning to his family, and a reputation for short sermons, as an example to
15 his successor. Neither warning nor example seems to have been effective. Mark went to London, with an allowance from his patron, and (it is generally agreed) made acquaintance with the money-lenders. He was supposed, by his patron and any others who
20 inquired, to be "writing"; but what he wrote, other

MA = preacher's son

College paid for
Father died

MA in London. Supposed to write, but just tourist

than letters asking for more time to pay, has never been discovered. However, he attended the theatres and music halls very regularly—no doubt with a view to some serious articles in the "Spectator" on
25 the decadence of the English stage.

Fortunately (from Mark's point of view) his patron died during his third year in London, and left him all the money he wanted. From that moment his life loses its legendary character, and becomes more
30 a matter of history. He settled accounts with the money-lenders, abandoned his crop of wild oats to the harvesting of others, and became in his turn a patron. He patronized the Arts. It was not only usurers who discovered that Mark Ablett no longer wrote for
35 money; editors were now offered free contributions as well as free lunches; publishers were given agreements for an occasional slender volume, in which the author paid all expenses and waived all royalties; promising young painters and poets dined with him;
40 and he even took a theatrical company on tour, playing host and "lead" with equal lavishness.

He was not what most people call a snob. A snob has been defined carelessly as a man who loves a lord; and, more carefully, as a mean lover of mean
45 things—which would be a little unkind to the peerage if the first definition were true. Mark had his vanities undoubtedly, but he would sooner have met an actor-manager than an earl; he would have spoken of his friendship with Dante—had that been
50 possible—more glibly than of his friendship with the Duke. Call him a snob if you like, but not the worst kind of snob; a hanger-on, but to the skirts of Art, not Society; a climber, but in the neighbourhood of Parnassus, not Hay Hill.
55 His patronage did not stop at the Arts. It also included Matthew Cayley, a small cousin of thirteen, whose circumstances were as limited as had been Mark's own before his patron had rescued him. He sent the Cayley cousin to school and Cambridge. His
60 motives, no doubt, were unworldly enough at first; a mere repaying to his account in the Recording Angel's book of the generosity which had been lavished on himself; a laying-up of treasure in heaven. But it is probable that, as the boy grew up, Mark's designs for
65 his future were based on his own interests as much

Patron died and left MA everything

Became patron himself

Vain, but got along with creatives more than nobility

Sent cousin to school

as those of his cousin, and that a suitably educated Matthew Cayley of twenty-three was felt by him to be a useful property for a man in his position; a man, that is to say, whose vanities left him so little time for
70 his affairs.

Cayley, then, at twenty-three, looked after his

C looked after MA's affairs

cousin's affairs. By this time Mark had bought the Red House and the considerable amount of land which went with it. Cayley superintended the
75 necessary staff. His duties, indeed, were many. He was not quite secretary, not quite land-agent, not quite business-adviser, not quite companion, but something of all four. Mark leant upon him and called him "Cay," objecting quite rightly in the
80 circumstances to the name of Matthew. Cay, he felt was, above all, dependable; a big, heavy-jawed, solid

C very dependable

fellow, who didn't bother you with unnecessary talk—a boon to a man who liked to do most of the talking himself.

12. C
Difficulty: Medium

Category: Reading / Inference

Strategic Advice: The correct answer will be supported directly by the passage.

Getting to the Answer: The passage states that Mark's father left behind "a reputation for short sermons, as an example for his successor" (lines 14–15). However, it then states, "neither warning nor example seems to have been effective" (lines 15–16). In other words, his successor gave long sermons. Choice (C) is correct.

13. D
Difficulty: Medium

Category: Reading / Command of Evidence

Strategic Advice: Carefully review the part of the passage that discusses Mark's father's successor.

Getting to the Answer: The passage discusses Mark's father's successor in the context of his father's death. Mark's father has left an "example" of short sermons for his successor, but "neither warning nor example seems to have been effective" (lines 15–16). This suggests that Mark's father's successor did *not* follow his example of giving short sermons. Choice (D) is correct.

14. A
Difficulty: Hard

Category: Reading / Inference

Strategic Advice: Consider the purpose of quotation marks in general. Why would the author find it important to draw the reader's attention to the word by using quotation marks?

Getting to the Answer: The word "writing" is quoted in order to underscore the fact that it is dialogue. It is Mark who has used the word. The passage goes on to state that "what he wrote . . . has never been discovered" (lines 20–22). In other words, the only reason to believe that writing has taken place is Mark's word; other people have their doubts. Choice (A) is correct.

15. A
Difficulty: Easy

Category: Reading / Detail

Strategic Advice: The correct answer is directly stated in the passage.

Getting to the Answer: The passage states, "his patron died . . . and left him all the money he wanted" (lines 26–28). This directly supports the idea that he is now wealthy. Choice (A) is correct.

16. B

Difficulty: Medium

Category: Reading / Vocab-in-Context

Strategic Advice: Consider the topic of the paragraph in which the cited word appears. Then, predict a synonym for this word based on the topic and context of the paragraph.

Getting to the Answer: Earlier in the paragraph, the passage states, "he settled accounts with the money-lenders" (lines 30–31). The sentence to which the word in question belongs asserts that it was "not only usurers who discovered that Mark Ablett no longer wrote for money" (lines 33–35). "Money-lender," then, seems to be a synonym for "usurer." Choice (B) is correct.

17. B

Difficulty: Medium

Category: Reading / Vocab-in-Context

Strategic Advice: Consider the usual meaning of "lavish." How might it be applied more figuratively here?

Getting to the Answer: "Lavish" usually means something like "elaborate" or "sumptuous," depending on the context. Here, it is used to describe how Mark "play[s] host and 'lead'" (lines 40–41). It seems to be used to describe how Mark enjoys his theater company with enthusiasm and relish. Choice (B) is correct.

18. C

Difficulty: Medium

Category: Reading / Inference

Strategic Advice: Identify how the passage characterizes Mark's life. Then, read the answer choices to see how others view it.

Getting to the Answer: The passage characterizes Mark's early life in London as an exciting and irresponsible period. Later, he inherits money, settles his accounts, and becomes financially responsible. Compared with his earlier life, his later one was less exciting. Choice (C) is correct.

19. B

Difficulty: Medium

Category: Reading / Command of Evidence

Strategic Advice: Reread each answer choice. Identify the sentence that directly supports your answer to the previous question about the different periods of Mark's life.

Getting to the Answer: Only (B) makes a direct distinction between these two periods of Mark's life. When he inherits money, "his life loses its legendary character, and becomes more a matter of history" (lines 28–30). In other words, his earlier life in London is more like a legend, or myth. His later life is less exciting.

20. B

Difficulty: Hard

Category: Reading / Inference

Strategic Advice: Reread the sentence to find the analogy. It will be explicitly stated in the passage. Then, consider why the passage draws the comparison it does.

Getting to the Answer: Mark is described as "a hanger-on, but to the skirts of Art, not Society" (lines 52–53). "Art" is being compared with "Parnassus," and "Society" with "Hay Hill." Each appears to be a neighborhood associated with these ideas. Choice (B) is correct.

21. D

Difficulty: Hard

Category: Reading / Rhetoric

Strategic Advice: Identify the narrator's attitude toward Mark in the last paragraph.

Getting to the Answer: The tone of the last paragraph is one of mock-seriousness. On the surface, it appears to take Mark's ideas about himself and his place in the world seriously. But when read closely, the passage seems to characterize Mark as a pompous and arrogant man who finds Matthew useful because he doesn't steal attention from himself. Matthew "didn't bother you with unnecessary talk—a boon to a man who liked to do most of the talking himself" (lines 82–84). Choice (D) correctly identifies that the passage is subtly making fun of Mark.

CHAPTER 25

PREPARE

1. C

Difficulty: Medium

Category: Reading / Synthesis

Strategic Advice: To find similarities between paired passages, keep in mind the central idea, topic, and scope of each passage.

Getting to the Answer: Both passages focus on crime and society. Although the authors don't agree on how a society should deal with the issue of crime, they both argue that the issue needs to be addressed. Choice (C) is correct.

2. B

Difficulty: Medium

Category: Reading / Synthesis

Strategic Advice: Use the question stem to identify which parts of the two passages you're being asked to compare or contrast.

Getting to the Answer: Summarize what each author concludes. The author of Passage 1 suggests that strict standards must be upheld. The author of Passage 2 argues that addressing the root causes of crime will provide better societal outcomes. Predict that better education can help reduce crime. Choice (B) matches that prediction.

3. A

Difficulty: Easy

Category: Reading / Synthesis

Strategic Advice: Read the question closely. Identify how the question stem asks you to combine the information in the passage and the graphic.

Getting to the Answer: Because you are asked to infer a trend in the data based on Passage 2, paraphrase what the author of Passage 2 thinks would happen if the root causes of crime were addressed. Predict that the author thinks that greater educational opportunities would reduce crime. Applying that prediction to the graphic suggests that the percentage of high school dropouts in inmate populations would decrease. Choice (A) is correct.

PRACTICE

Passage 1 describes how scientists study stem cells and possible uses. Passage 2 discusses the potential risks of stem cell research.

Passage 1

Stem cells truly are science's miracle cure. These undifferentiated cells have not yet chosen what type of cell to become, and can be nudged into becom-
Line ing whatever type of cell is needed to help a sick
5   patient. Stem cells can be used to replace damaged cells in a person who has a degenerative disease or a serious injury.

how SCs work, why powerful

Scientists obtain stem cells primarily from discarded embryos. True, they can also be obtained
10   from the blood or organs from healthy adults, but these stem cells, while showing some usefulness, are not as adaptable as embryonic stem cells. Embryonic stem cells are incredibly helpful and can mean a revolutionary change in quality of life for patients
15   suffering from debilitating diseases such as Parkinson's or Alzheimer's. Someday, stem cells could even eliminate the need for human test subjects in drug tests. Without the use of embryonic stem cells, though, that could take an immeasurably longer
20   amount of time to become a reality.

embryonic > adult SCs

w/o emb. SCs, research = slower

With stem cell research, the benefits for living, breathing, sentient people outweigh any debate regarding the origins of the cells themselves. In this age of scientific enlightenment, we must always ask
25   ourselves: What action can best benefit humanity? By answering, we clearly see that stem cell research must continue.

SC research should continue

Passage 2

*ethics of emb.
SC use →
how far is
too far?*

We stand at an important crossroads in scientific progress. We have the capability now to improve
30 humanity in ways never thought possible, but at what cost? At what point must progress bow before conscience? Just because we can, is it true that we should?

Stem cell research has the potential to be an
35 enormous boon to the medical industry. The advance of diseases can be assuaged or halted completely through this remarkable new medicine.

*ethics easy
to disregard*

But scientists assault the dignity of life when they use embryonic stem cells for their work. By taking
40 cells from discarded embryos, <u>we begin treading on a slippery slope</u>. It is all too easy to transition from

*auth. op.: emb.
made just for
research = bad*

using discarded embryos to creating embryos solely for the purpose of stem cell medicine.

Since stem cells can be obtained from healthy
45 adults with no cost to life, <u>this is the path on which</u>

*use adult
SCs instead*

<u>we should be progressing</u>. These stem cells, safely obtained, can have a significant positive impact on the lives of patients.

Stem Cell Research Support and Opposition

- - - Opposition   ——— Support

4. C

Difficulty: Medium

Category: Reading / Synthesis

Strategic Advice: Synthesis questions ask you to find similarities and differences between paired passages. Compare the different points of view, focusing on how the authors agree and disagree.

Getting to the Answer: This question asks you to identify the way in which the authors think alike. To find the correct answer, compare your summaries of the passages. The author of Passage 1 maintains that stem cell research can provide benefits and recommends using stem cells regardless of the source. The author of Passage 2 agrees that stem cell research can provide benefits but argues that using adult stem cells is the course to follow. Both authors agree that stem cell research has benefits. Choice (C) is correct.

5. D

Difficulty: Hard

Category: Reading / Synthesis

Strategic Advice: To make a strong prediction when faced with a general question, focus on the central idea, topic, and scope of each passage.

Getting to the Answer: Harder Synthesis questions will require you to identify not only how the authors agree or disagree but also why they agree or disagree. What these authors disagree on is easy to identify: They disagree about which type of stem cells should be used in the research. Now, ask why they disagree. The author of Passage 1 thinks that the benefits are defined solely by the physical improvements possible, and the author of Passage 2 thinks that the benefits of stem cell research must be considered in terms of the moral as well as the physical results. Choice (D) is correct.

6. C

Difficulty: Medium

Category: Reading / Synthesis

Strategic Advice: Look for trends in the data. Evaluate the categories and time frames mentioned in the answer choices.

Getting to the Answer: This question asks you to compare changes in data between two categories—support for and opposition to—over different time periods. Count the number of squares up or down each line moves as it moves two squares over. Compare the changes on the graph to the changes described in each answer choice and eliminate answer choices that don't match. When you check the time frame of 2005 to 2007, note that opposition to stem cell research increased about one full square, and support for stem cell research decreased about one half of a square. This matches the changes in the data described in (C).

PERFORM

The following passages reflect on the Machnovschina, an anarchist peasant uprising in the Ukraine active from approximately 1917 to 1922 under the leadership of Nestor Makhno. During their brief and turbulent history, the Makhnovshchina (also known as Makhnovists) fought against the Central Powers, the White Army, and the Red Army, their sometimes ally that eventually turned on them and defeated them. The first passage discusses the relationship between the Makhnovists and their supporters, while the second discusses the differences between the Makhnovists on the outskirts of the emerging Soviet Union and the Bolsheviks who controlled it.

Passage 1

Even had the Ukrainian civilians wanted to ignore the sectarianism of their time and remain neutral, they did not have that luxury—the turmoil
Line was too absolute, the excitement and terror of
5 revolutionary upheaval too absolutely compelling. Even for the most isolated of peasants, political impartiality was impossible. From the beginning, there was a bond among revolutionary intellectuals, civilians, and military leaders.

10 The causes of civil unrest compounded. Adding to the burden of uncounted years of economic and political subjugation under a quasi-feudal system[1] was the added pressure of an invading Austro-

from beg.: bond among diff people

many causes of civil unrest

Hungarian army. Meanwhile Russia was in a state
15 of chaos, and the Bolsheviks[2] were rapidly consolidating power in a system that promised equality and the rule of the proletariat. There was no central authority to organize them (Russia had all but given up the Ukraine to the invading Central Powers[3]),
20 and the traditional power of the rich landlords had collapsed with the Czarist government. There was no status quo and no safe choice.

Faced with this state of affairs, many Ukrainian peasants chose to organize themselves within the Makhnovshchina. Educated in the field and
25 trained behind the plow, they were now charged with the task of organizing and defending a new society under conditions of tremendous adversity. Although the Makhnovshchina was an anarchist,
30 revolutionary movement, it was one that emerged out of necessity. It was a way for peasants to join together for mutual aid, revolutionary intellectuals to explore the possibility of a society without central authority, and generals to attempt to secure the rights
35 of the Ukrainian people to self-determination.

A-H army invasion

Bolsh. organizing but no central auth.

Uk. peasants → Makh.

anarchist but necessary

Passage 2

The revolutionary period in Russian history is a classic example of the conflicts between the programs of dogmatic, rigid leaders and the desires and needs of ordinary people. One of the best examples of this is the struggle between the Bol-
40 sheviks and the Makhnovshchina. Not only did the word "revolution" mean very different things to the Kremlin[4] bureaucrats and the Ukrainian partisans, but the reality of the revolution was very different
45 as well. This fact was noted by one anonymous soldier who, beginning his career as a Kremlin guard, eventually became a member of the Makhnovist army. He noted that "conditions could not have been more different between the two camps.
50 In the one, decisions were based on the political theories of Marx[5] and Lenin,[6] theories which were never doubted or questioned in the least. In the other, theories were even more important—debated vigorously and openly—but only after the day's
55 work had been done and the important decisions

Makh vs Bolsh

diff. in theory (accepted vs debated)

had been made based on the needs of the community for food, freedom, and self-defense."

Although the Kremlin's approach might seem like harmless intellectualism, it had disastrous con-
60 sequences that the anonymous soldier couldn't have forseen. As the Bolshevik Party gained increasing power, it began to control the official view of events with a systematic paranoia unprecedented in history. If the events differed from the official view, the
65 events themselves (and those who participated in them) were deemed the enemy.

The wartime writings of Leon Trotsky[7] are the best indication of this trend. He alternately characterized the Makhnovists as heroes and traitors depending
70 on the current needs of the Bolsheviks. When he required Makhnovists to fight alongside the Red Army[8], he portrayed them as courageous heroes and valiant fighters, but when he did not, they suddenly became traitors and enemies of the revolu-
75 tion. In 1920, as the Makhnovshchina and the Red Army united to fight against a powerful White Army[9] campaign, Trotsky wrote:

"The working class of the Ukraine can never, and especially not in conditions of tremendous military
80 danger, allow particular units sometimes to fight in our ranks and sometimes to stab us in the back.[+] Waging war against the world's exploiters, the workers' and peasants' Red Army says: 'Who is not with me is against me, and whoever is with me is to
85 remain in my ranks and not leave them till the end.'"

The Ukranian partisans, even as peasants and workmen, were painted as the servants of foreign aristocrats bent on undermining the revolution. Even though Bolshevik presence had been
90 weak in the Ukraine, Trotsky still saw fit to portray himself as the representative of "the working class of the Ukraine" and the Makhnovists as loyal to the working class only to the degree that they recognized Red Army authority.

[1] Serfdom had only been abolished in 1861, and many traces of it remained.

[2] The Bolsheviks were the Communist party that established the Soviet Union.

[3] The Central Powers were Germany, Austria-Hungary, the

Margin annotations (left column):

Bolsh. propaganda (line 60)

either w/ or against Bolsh. (line 65)

ex. of prop.: LT changed tack based on Makh. actions

LT → quote

all or nothing

Uk. partisans → neg portrayal; Makh. only loyal if respect for Red Army

---

Ottoman Empire, and Bulgaria. During World War I (which took place from 1914 to 1918), they were fighting against the Allies—France, Russia, Great Britain, and the United States. During the period in question, the Austro-Hungarian Army was occupying much of the Ukraine.

[4] The Russian capital building which, at the time, was occupied by the Bolshevik Party

[5] Karl Marx, the ideological founder of Communism

[6] Vladimir Ilyich Lenin, the leader of the Bolsheviks

[7] Leon Trotsky, one of the leaders of the Bolsheviks

[8] The Bolshevik Army

[9] A conservative army opposed to the revolutionary movements in Russia

[+] The previous alliance between the Makhnovshchina and the Red Army had been broken when the Bolsheviks attacked and devastated the unsuspecting anarchists in a surprise attack.

Proportion of Seats in the Russian Constituent Assembly, 1918

- ■ SRs
- ■ Left SRs
- ■ Bolsheviks
- ■ Makhnovists
- ■ Kadets
- ■ Nationality Parties
- ■ Other

7. C

Difficulty: Medium

Category: Reading / Synthesis

Strategic Advice: To answer Synthesis questions, focus on the similarities and differences between the passages. Identify what the authors agree and disagree on.

Getting to the Answer: This question stem asks what the author of Passage 2 thinks about a promise made by the Bolsheviks. Review your Passage Map to determine that the author of Passage 2 holds a negative view of the Bolsheviks. Predict that the author of Passage 2 would view the Bolsheviks' promise in a negative light. Choice (C) is correct.

8. D

Difficulty: Medium

Category: Reading / Synthesis

Strategic Advice: Synthesis questions that ask what the authors agree on require you to identify the similarities in each author's purpose for writing the passage.

Getting to the Answer: Although each passage focuses on a different aspect of the Makhnovischina, they both describe the Makhnovischina as a group formed to provide mutual aid, intellectual freedom, and military defense. Choice (D) is correct.

9. A

Difficulty: Hard

Category: Reading / Synthesis

Strategic Advice: Read the question stem closely to identify what it asks you to look for.

Getting to the Answer: Because the question stem asks what can be inferred by looking at Passage 2 and the data in the pie chart in tandem, base your interpretation of that data on the negative viewpoint that the author of Passage 2 expresses regarding the Bolsheviks. Predict that the author thinks that the Bolsheviks gained power at the expense of others. When the data in the pie chart are viewed from that perspective, it can be inferred that the Bolsheviks were stronger than their proportion of seats on the assembly would suggest. Choice (A) is correct.

EXTRA PRACTICE

Passage 1 is about how scientists use radioisotopes to date artifacts and remains. Passage 2 discusses the varying problems with radioactive contaminants.

Passage 1

Archaeologists often rely on measuring the amounts of different atoms present in an item from a site to determine its age. The identity of an atom

Line depends on how many protons it has in its nucleus;
5 for example, all carbon atoms have 6 protons. Each atom of an element, however, can have a different number of neutrons, so there can be several versions, or isotopes, of each element. Scientists name the isotopes by the total number of protons
10 plus neutrons. For example, a carbon atom with 6 neutrons is carbon-12 while a carbon atom with 7 neutrons is carbon-13.

Some combinations of protons and neutrons are not stable and will change over time. For example,
15 carbon-14, which has 6 protons and 8 neutrons, will slowly change into nitrogen-14, with 7 protons and 7 neutrons. Scientists can directly measure the amount of carbon-12 and carbon-14 in a sample or they can use radiation measurements to calculate these
20 amounts. Each atom of carbon-14 that changes to nitrogen-14 emits radiation. Scientists can measure the rate of emission and use that to calculate the total amount of carbon-14 present in a sample.

Carbon-14 atoms are formed in the atmosphere
25 at the same rate at which they decay. Therefore the ratio of carbon-12 to carbon-14 atoms in the atmosphere is constant. Living plants and animals have the same ratio of carbon-12 to carbon-14 in their tissues because they are constantly taking in
30 carbon in the form of food or carbon dioxide. After the plant or animal dies, however, it stops taking in carbon and so the amount of carbon-14 atoms in its tissues starts to decrease at a predictable rate.

By measuring the ratio of carbon-12 to carbon-14
35 in a bone, for example, a scientist can determine how long the animal the bone came from has been dead. To determine an object's age this way is called "carbon-14 dating." Carbon-14 dating can be performed on any material made by a living organism, such as
40 wood or paper from trees or bones and skin from animals. Materials with ages up to about 50,000 years old can be dated. By finding the age of several objects found at different depths at an archeological dig, the archeologists can then make a timeline for the layers
45 of the site. Objects in the same layer will be about the same age. By using carbon dating for a few objects in a layer, archeologists know the age of other objects in that layer, even if the layer itself cannot be carbon dated.

definition of isotope & examples

all atoms of one element have same # protons, diff. # neutrons

ways to measure decay

carb-14 atom decay = predictable

how carb-14 dating is used → timelines based on layers

Passage 2

50   <u>Radioactive materials</u> contain unstable atoms that decay, releasing energy in the form of radiation. The radiation can be <u>harmful to living tissue</u> because it can <u>penetrate into cells and damage their DNA</u>. If an explosion or a leak at a nuclear power plant releases

55   large amounts of radioactive materials, the surrounding area could be hazardous until the amount of radioactive material drops back to normal levels. <u>The amount of danger from the radiation and the amount of time until the areas are safe again depends</u>

60   <u>on how fast the materials emit radiation.</u>

    Scientists use the "half-life" of a material to indicate <u>how quickly it decays</u>. The half-life of a material is the <u>amount of time it takes for half of a sample of that material to decay</u>. A mate-

65   rial with a short half-life decays more quickly than a material with a long half-life. For example, iodine-131 and cesium-137 can both be released as a result of an accident at a nuclear power plant. Iodine-131 decays rapidly, with a half-life of 8 days.

70   Cesium-137, however, decays more slowly, with a half-life of 30 years.

    If an accident releases iodine-131, therefore, it is a short-term concern. The amount of radiation emitted will be high but will drop rapidly. After

75   two months, less than one percent of the original iodine-131 will remain. An accidental release of cesium-137, however, is a long-term concern. The amount of radiation emitted at first will be low but will drop slowly. It will take about 200 years

80   for the amount of cesium-137 remaining to drop below one percent. The total amount of radiation emitted in both cases will be the same, for the same amount of initial material. <u>The difference lies in whether the radiation is all released rapidly at high</u>

85   <u>levels in a short time, or is released slowly at low levels, over a long time span.</u>

Margin notes:
why radiation = harmful

danger depends rate of rad. release

half-life use and definition

half-life = faster decay

cesium-137 = bigger concern than iodine-131

danger comes down to how fast rad. is released

Decay of Carbon-14

This data is from the *Journal of Research of the National Bureau of Standards*, Vol. 64, No. 4, April 1951, pp. 328 – 333.

1. C
Difficulty: Hard

Category: Reading / Inference

Strategic Advice: Use your Passage Map to find a description of what materials can be dated using carbon-14 dating. Pay close attention to your notes for paragraph 4.

Getting to the Answer: In paragraph 4, the author states that carbon-14 dating can be used on materials made by a living organism. An arrowhead made from a bone is constructed of such material, (C).

2. D
Difficulty: Hard

Category: Reading / Command of Evidence

Strategic Advice: Locate each of the answer choices in the passage. The correct answer should provide direct support for the answer to the previous question.

Getting to the Answer: In paragraph 4, the author describes the process for carbon-14 dating. Choice (D) is correct because this sentence provides a direct description of the materials that can be dated using carbon-14 dating.

3. B

Difficulty: Medium

Category: Reading / Vocab-in-Context

Strategic Advice: Replace "decay" in the sentence with each of the answer choices. Consider which word makes the most sense in context.

Getting to the Answer: The previous paragraph discusses how scientists measure the rate of emission to calculate the amount of carbon-14 in a sample. "Emission" means release; therefore, the amount of carbon-14 is becoming smaller if the atoms are releasing it. In this sentence, therefore, "decay" most nearly means to decrease, which matches "deteriorate," (B).

4. C

Difficulty: Easy

Category: Reading / Inference

Strategic Advice: Look at your notes for paragraph 3. Summarize the ratio of carbon-12 to carbon-14 in living tissue in your own words. Look for the answer choice that most closely matches your prediction.

Getting to the Answer: In paragraph 3, the author explains that the ratio of carbon-12 to carbon-14 is constant. Choice (C) is correct.

5. C

Difficulty: Medium

Category: Reading / Command of Evidence

Strategic Advice: Review what part of the passage you used to predict an answer for the previous question.

Getting to the Answer: In paragraph 3, the author explains why the rate of carbon-12 to carbon-14 remains constant in the tissues of living plants and animals. Choice (C) is correct.

6. B

Difficulty: Medium

Category: Reading / Detail

Strategic Advice: Read around the cited lines. The author directly states why a release of iodine-131 is not cause for long-term concern.

Getting to the Answer: In paragraph 3, the author explains that the initial release of radiation from an accident involving iodine-131 will be high, but the level of radiation will drop quickly. Choice (B) is correct.

7. C

Difficulty: Medium

Category: Reading / Detail

Strategic Advice: Use your Passage Map to find the information about how exposure to radiation affects living tissue.

Getting to the Answer: In paragraph 1, the author explains that radiation is harmful to living tissue because it can cause damage to the cells' DNA, which matches (C).

8. A

Difficulty: Easy

Category: Reading / Vocab-in-Context

Strategic Advice: Eliminate answer choices such as B and C that are synonyms for "original" but do not make sense in context. Select the word that can replace "original" in the sentence without changing the meaning of the sentence.

Getting to the Answer: The previous paragraph explains how scientists use "half-life" to determine how quickly material decays. If the material is decaying, then "original" refers to the first, or earliest, material. Choice (A) is correct.

9. D

Difficulty: Medium

Category: Reading / Detail

Strategic Advice: Review your notes for the first part of Passage 2. Try to put into your own words how scientists use half-life calculations of radioactive materials. Look for the answer that most closely matches your idea.

Getting to the Answer: In paragraph 1, the author explains that the level of danger posed by radiation released during a nuclear accident depends on how quickly radiation is released. In paragraph 2, the author discusses how the half-life of radioactive material is used to determine how long a material will emit radiation. Choice (D) is correct because it most clearly paraphrases the information in the passage about how scientists use half-life calculations.

10. A

Difficulty: Hard

Category: Reading / Synthesis

Strategic Advice: The central idea will be supported by all of the evidence presented in both passages. Avoid answers such as B and C that are supported only by the evidence in one passage.

Getting to the Answer: Choice (A) is correct because this statement is a generalization about the study of physics supported by both passages: Passage 1 discusses the application of atomic and nuclear physics in archeology while Passage 2 details how scientists apply atomic and nuclear physics to studies of radioactivity.

11. A

Difficulty: Hard

Category: Reading / Synthesis

Strategic Advice: Consider the information in the passages about half-life and how it relates to the data presented in the chart.

Getting to the Answer: The definition of "half-life" is given in Passage 2. The half-life of a material is the amount of time it takes for half of that material to decay. The graph shows that about 50 percent of carbon-14 remains after 5,400 years. Choice (A) is correct.

Passage 1 tells the story behind the writing of the United States national anthem. Passage 2 discusses how the prevalence, use, and value of the United States national anthem have changed over time.

Passage 1

The story behind "The Star-Spangled Banner," America's national anthem, begins with the War of 1812. This war, which began just three decades after
Line the Revolution, was again waged between American
5 and British forces for various reasons, including trade inter-ference. Stakes were high: this was one of America's earliest opportunities to solidify its status as a sovereign nation equal to other world powers. Moreover, many Americans feared that the
10 nation might forfeit its hard-earned liberty were the British to defeat them.

Britain's involvement was limited in the war's first two years due to conflict at home, where Napoleon's army had attacked. But in the summer of 1814,
15 after the conflict with France had mostly subsided, Britain's focus turned to the American theater, which up to this point had been merely a distraction. In August of that year, the British sent an invading force that quickly defeated a smaller American force that
20 was ill-equipped and poorly trained. Later that night, the British Army invaded Washington, setting fire to several buildings, including the president's home and the Capitol. A few weeks later, on September 12th, British infantry troops tried to overtake Baltimore,
25 but America's defenses prevailed. The next morning, Britain's navy began a heavy bombardment of Baltimore's Fort McHenry, located at the mouth of Baltimore's harbor.

Some American men, including lawyer Francis
30 Scott Key, happened to be aboard a British ship in the harbor that same day. These men had come to peacefully request a captive friend's release—a

SSB origin

*War of 1812 →
high stakes
for U.S.*

*Brit. involve-
ment limited
until 1814*

Brit. victories

FSK detained

request that, to their fortune, was granted. (But) the British detained them on the ship until the attack
35 on McHenry had run its course. From this vantage point, Key and his companions witnessed Fort McHenry's bombard-ment: twenty-five rain-drenched hours of rockets, explosions, and gunfire.

Through the night, Key waited in grim expectation
40 that the morning would reveal a white flag raised over the fort, symbolizing McHenry's surrender. (But instead,) by dawn's light he saw the American flag. McHenry had endured; British forces were already retreating. Moved by the sight, Key began
45 to write, on the back of a letter he was carrying, the words that would become America's national anthem.

This event marked a turning point in America's favor; within months, the war would be over. The
50 War of 1812 would list among the less significant wars in United States history, by many accounts. (But) Francis Scott Key's eloquent description of the flag—and the brave victory it represented—would become a lasting emblem of American patriotism.

Passage 2

55 America's National Anthem began as a poem titled "The Defence of Fort McHenry." Its melody came from the British tune, "Anacreon in Heaven." Written on September 14, 1814, and distributed shortly thereafter, the song enjoyed almost instant
60 popularity. A Baltimore theater housed its first public performance about a month after its writing. Following this, a music shop printed the song under the enduring title "The Star-Spangled Banner." (Over the next century,) the song gained increasing
65 value in the hearts of Americans, growing especially popular during the Civil War. Around the 1890s, the military began playing the song for ceremonial uses. At the time of World War I, when patriotic music again served as a crucial ideological refuge for
70 America's people, "The Star-Spangled Banner" began to be treated by the military as the national anthem.

(margin notes, left column:)
@ end of McHenry, FSK wrote what became SSB

origin of SSB

how SSB became nat. anthem

military use

(Also around this time,) the anthem was played in its first baseball game: a Cubs versus Red Sox game in which the song surprised and moved the crowds
75 during the seventh-inning stretch. The effect made national headlines, and, in each game to follow during that series, the anthem was played, meeting an equally enthusiastic reception. This launched the tradition of the national anthem's now near-ubiquitous pres-
80 ence at major American sporting events.

(In 1931,) Congress and President Hoover passed the bill to officially designate the song as America's national anthem. It had long since distinguished itself from other patriotic songs and held special signifi-
85 cance in American hearts, (but now) it would remain the nation's staple celebratory score. (Today,) the song is taught to children in schools, used in various ceremonies, printed in many church hymnals and community songbooks, and sung collectively at
90 sporting events, including those featuring American participation internationally, such as World Cup Soc-cer games or the opening ceremonies of the Olympics. The anthem's final words about those over whom the flag waves ("O'er the land of the free / and the home
95 of the brave") remind Americans of the liberty for which the country was established, and the courage of those who fought for it.

(margin notes, right column:)
used in sports

1931: SSB officially nat. anthem

SSB today

why SSB important

War of 1812 vs SSB; SSB more famous

12. C

Difficulty: Medium

Category: Reading / Rhetoric

Strategic Advice: Review your Passage Map for paragraph 1. Paraphrase what you think the central idea is before reading the answer choices. Then, predict what the rest of the passage will be about.

Getting to the Answer: The author begins by referencing "the story behind 'The Star-Span-gled Banner,' American's national anthem" (lines 1–2). The remainder of the paragraph explores where that story begins: the War of 1812. Choice (C) is correct.

13. D

Difficulty: Medium

Category: Reading / Rhetoric

Strategic Advice: Reread around the cited lines and consider their role in the complete paragraph. The reason for including the lines will reflect their role and purpose in relation to the other information.

Getting to the Answer: The paragraph introduces the topic of the passage, which is the story behind the national anthem. It then relates the origin of that story in the War of 1812 and provides context for the war. These lines show the significance of the war for the American people and the importance of its outcome, which gives added weight to the poem that would become the national anthem. Choice (D) is correct.

14. D

Difficulty: Easy

Category: Reading / Vocab-in-Context

Strategic Advice: Read the complete sentence in which the cited word appears. Predict a definition before reviewing the answer choices. Compare your prediction with the answer choices and select the one that most nearly reflects the meaning you identified.

Getting to the Answer: The line states that "America's defense prevailed" against an attack by the British. In this context, the term most nearly means that America's defense succeeded in resisting attack, making choice (D) correct.

15. B

Difficulty: Medium

Category: Reading / Inference

Strategic Advice: Review your notes and the cited lines. Then, paraphrase their meaning and significance. Select the answer choice that best reflects why and how Key came to write the national anthem.

Getting to the Answer: Paragraph 4 demonstrates that Key expected Fort McHenry to fall to British forces. He was surprised by American perseverance and, as a result, was inspired to write the national anthem in response to the Americans' survival during the nightlong British bombardment. Choice (B) is correct.

16. D

Difficulty: Medium

Category: Reading / Command of Evidence

Strategic Advice: Review your answer to the previous question and your notes on the referenced paragraph. Identify the phrase that most clearly supports the conclusion identified in the previous question.

Getting to the Answer: Lines 44–45 ("Moved by … to write") clearly explain why Key wrote the words that would become the national anthem: The author says Key was moved by the "sight," which, if you read the previous sentence, is that "by dawn's light he saw the American flag" (lines 42–43). The first sentence of the paragraph reveals that Key had been expecting a white flag, indicating surrender. Choice (D) is correct.

17. B

Difficulty: Hard

Category: Reading / Rhetoric

Strategic Advice: Think about the author's overall tone and purpose to predict what point of view he or she might hold about the national anthem and its origins. Compare your conclusion with the answer choices.

Getting to the Answer: The passage begins by explaining the national anthem originated during the War of 1812. Choice (B) is correct because it reflects that the anthem was written to capture the triumph of the United States during a key event of the War of 1812.

18. A

Difficulty: Easy

Category: Reading / Rhetoric

Strategic Advice: Reread the cited lines and review your notes for Passage 2. Consider the placement of the lines in relation to the rest of the passage and how the lines prepare you to interpret subsequent content.

Getting to the Answer: The cited lines lay the foundation for the rest of the passage, which describes how Francis Scott Key's poem came to be the official national anthem known as "The Star-Spangled Banner." Choice (A) is correct because the cited lines state clearly that Key first wrote his words as a poem, not as a song or an anthem.

19. A

Difficulty: Easy

Category: Reading / Vocab-in-Context

Strategic Advice: The correct answer will make the most sense in place of the existing phrase.

Getting to the Answer: Lines 75–80 discuss how the national anthem had begun to increase in popularity and appear regularly in sporting events. The implication in the referenced sentence is that the singing of the national anthem has become a "tradition" and, therefore, commonplace. Choice (A) is correct.

20. D

Difficulty: Medium

Category: Reading / Inference

Strategic Advice: Consider how the quotation reflects the specific rhetoric and purpose of the complete sentence. The correct answer will relate the words of the quotation to the rest of the sentence.

Getting to the Answer: The text explains that these lyrics "remind Americans of the liberty for which the country was established, and the courage of those who fought for it" (lines 93–95). The author draws a parallel between "land of the free" and "the liberty for which the country was established," and between "home of the brave" and "the courage of those who fought for it." Choice (D) is correct.

21. D

Difficulty: Medium

Category: Reading / Synthesis

Strategic Advice: Review your notes for both passages. Identify what each passage offers to your understanding of the national anthem. The correct answer will reflect the specific contribution of Passage 2.

Getting to the Answer: Both passages discuss the legacy, patriotism, and origins of the national anthem. Only Passage 2 traces the events that led to Key's words being officially adopted as the national anthem in 1931. Choice (D) is correct.

22. B

Difficulty: Medium

Category: Reading / Command of Evidence

Strategic Advice: Predict what type of information would most support your answer to the previous question. Then, select the answer choice that most closely matches your prediction.

Getting to the Answer: Lines 68–71 ("At the time … national anthem") demonstrates one way in which the words written by Francis Scott Key gained popularity over time in the United States. The lines show the evolution of the poem during World War I. Choice (B) is correct.

CHAPTER 26

PREPARE

1. C
Difficulty: Medium

Category: Writing & Language / Effective Language Use

Strategic Advice: Be alert to sudden changes in tone and style within a passage. Describe the style in a word or two and look for the answer choice that is most similar.

Getting to the Answer: The overall tone of this passage can be described as formal. Reread the underlined segment. The shift to the second person pronoun makes the tone in the underlined section much less formal. Plug in the remaining choices to find the answer choice that matches the formal tone in the rest of the passage. Choice (C) matches well.

2. D
Difficulty: Medium

Category: Writing & Language / Quantitative

Strategic Advice: Look for trends in the data. Compare the categories that the answer choices mention.

Getting to the Answer: This question asks you to compare changes in data on two pie charts. Make sure to note which chart represents which year. Note the change in each of the answer choices. Eliminate choices that are incorrect. Eliminate A because the percent of a budget spent on food has dropped, not risen. Eliminate B because the percent of a budget spent on healthcare has risen, not dropped. Choice C can be eliminated because the percent of a budget spent on food has dropped more than the percent of a budget spent on transportation. Choice (D) is correct.

PRACTICE

3. C
Difficulty: Medium

Category: Writing & Language / Effective Language Use

Strategic Advice: Consider how you would refer to a number in a different context. Would you say you fell in love "hundred days" ago?

Getting to the Answer: "Hundred" refers to a digit (ones digit, tens digit, hundreds digit, etc.), whereas "one hundred" is an actual number. In order to begin the sentence in an idiomatically correct way, it is necessary to use the full number, "one hundred." Choice (C) matches well.

4. C
Difficulty: Medium

Category: Writing & Language / Sentence Formation

Strategic Advice: If there is no obvious error in the underlined segment, keep reading until you can identify the issue.

Getting to the Answer: The underlined portion is correctly used as the subject of an independent clause. However, because the clause after the comma is also independent, the sentence is a run-on. Since you are not given the option to fix the comma splice, look for the answer choice that makes the first clause dependent without introducing another error. Choice (C) correctly subordinates the first clause by beginning the sentence with "when."

5. B

Difficulty: Easy

Category: Writing & Language / Usage

Strategic Advice: Subjects and verbs must agree in person and number. Singular third person subjects take singular third person verbs, and plural third person subjects take plural third person verbs. The closest noun to an underlined verb may not be its subject.

Getting to the Answer: Read around the underlined portion until you can identify the subject of the underlined verb. Remember, a noun that is the object of a preposition cannot be the subject of a sentence. In this sentence, the subject is the plural noun "components" and needs a plural verb. Choice (B) is correct.

PERFORM

6. B

Difficulty: Medium

Category: Writing & Language / Effective Language Use

Strategic Advice: Using two words that mean the same thing is redundant. Look for the answer choice that creates the most concise sentence.

Getting to the Answer: As written, the sentence uses a compound predicate made up of "fascinated and intrigued." Because both words convey the same idea, namely that scientists found Jupiter to be very interesting, using one is sufficient. Choice (B) concisely conveys the idea.

7. D

Difficulty: Medium

Category: Writing & Language / Sentence Formation

Strategic Advice: Read around an underlined period and check to make sure that each clause forms a complete sentence.

Getting to the Answer: Because the second clause is a fragment, it needs to be properly connected to the previous sentence with either subordination or punctuation. Choice B provides punctuation that corrects the fragment but does not form an effective sentence. Since the information in the second clause explains why the moons of Jupiter provided evidence for a theory, the second clause needs to be combined with the previous sentence. Choice (D) joins the clause to the sentence.

8. D

Difficulty: Easy

Category: Writing & Language / Sentence Formation

Strategic Advice: Compare underlined verbs with related verbs. Related verbs forms need to be parallel.

Getting to the Answer: The verbs "completed" and "collected" form a compound predicate and need to be parallel in form. As written, the underlined section unnecessarily reintroduces the subject. Join the two verbs without punctuation. Choice (D) is correct.

9. C

Difficulty: Easy

Category: Writing & Language / Development

Strategic Advice: If you have the option to omit a sentence, think carefully about the author's topic. If the underlined portion strays from the topic, omit it.

Getting to the Answer: The author's topic is Jupiter. The underlined portion adds information about *Pioneer 10* that is irrelevant to the topic. Choice (C) correctly omits the sentence for this reason.

10. B

Difficulty: Medium

Category: Writing & Language / Effective Language Use

Strategic Advice: If an underlined segment does not contain a grammatical error, check for other kinds of errors tested on the SAT.

Getting to the Answer: As written, the underlined portion is a complete sentence. Reread that sentence in the context of the following sentence. They sound choppy together and create a wordiness issue. Because the underlined sentence provides information about Jupiter, it can be incorporated into the next sentence. Choice (B) forms a modifying phrase that effectively introduces the subject of the sentence.

11. D

Difficulty: Medium

Category: Writing & Language / Usage

Strategic Advice: Related nouns must be consistent in number. Check other nouns around an underlined noun to make sure they agree.

Getting to the Answer: The underlined noun is related to the noun phrase "number of probes." Because there was more than one probe, there was more than one measurement. Choice (D) correctly makes the underlined noun plural.

12. C

Difficulty: Medium

Category: Writing & Language / Quantitative

Strategic Advice: When you see a question with an infographic, remember to use the Kaplan Method for Infographics.

Getting to the Answer: The sentence to which the underlined portion belongs is comparing Earth's rotational speed to that of Jupiter's. The relevant information is how much faster Jupiter rotates. Look in the third column of the table for that data. Compare the information you find with the answer choices. Choice (C) provides accurate and relevant information.

13. D

Difficulty: Medium

Category: Writing & Language / Usage

Strategic Advice: A pronoun's antecedent must be clear and unambiguous. Always identify the antecedent of an underlined pronoun.

Getting to the Answer: The underlined possessive pronoun could refer to a number of things: our diameter, Earth's diameter, and Earth's rotational speed. Reread the sentence to determine what the author means. The sentence compares the diameter of Jupiter to the diameter of Earth. Look for the answer choice that makes that comparison clear. Choice (D) is correct.

EXTRA PRACTICE

1. B

Difficulty: Medium

Category: Writing & Language / Effective Language Use

Strategic Advice: Read the entire paragraph to determine if a career in physical therapy is rated as a good career choice by the Bureau of Labor Statistics.

Getting to the Answer: "Evenly" means level or flat, and "unusually" means not common. "Finally" implies that physical therapy was not a good career choice in the past. Choice (B) is correct because it means with regularity.

2. D

Difficulty: Medium

Category: Writing & Language / Effective Language Use

Strategic Advice: Read the sentence and determine how it can be more concise.

Getting to the Answer: As written, the text begins with a conjunction and uses a dash to indicate an unnecessary break in thought. Choice (D) eliminates both problems, creating a more direct sentence.

3. B
Difficulty: Medium

Category: Writing & Language / Development

Strategic Advice: Read the entire paragraph to identify what its focus is.

Getting to the Answer: Choices A, C, and D each offer a partial list of those components. Only (B) is complete.

4. B
Difficulty: Hard

Category: Writing & Language / Development

Strategic Advice: Read the entire paragraph to determine the pattern of the evidence. Most sentences include descriptions of the types of patients a PT will encounter.

Getting to the Answer: Since (B) is the only sentence that supports the topic sentence, it is the correct answer.

5. A
Difficulty: Easy

Category: Writing & Language / Punctuation

Strategic Advice: Read the sentence and determine whether it is grammatically complete. To form a grammatically complete sentence, you must have an independent clause after the semicolon.

Getting to the Answer: Choices B, C, and D all have excessive punctuation. Choice (A) is correct.

6. B
Difficulty: Medium

Category: Writing & Language / Sentence Formation

Strategic Advice: Read the sentence to determine how to improve its clarity. Consider whether the modifiers are correctly placed near the nouns or verbs they modify.

Getting to the Answer: The use of the modifier "minimally" at the end of the sentence is awkward. Choice (B) correctly moves the modifier next to the word it modifies: "interaction." It also removes the conjunction "And" at the beginning of the sentence.

7. D
Difficulty: Medium

Category: Writing & Language / Effective Language Use

Strategic Advice: Read the sentences and determine what words can be eliminated.

Getting to the Answer: As written, the text uses short, choppy sentences. Choice (D) combines the two sentences effectively to improve the economy of word choice.

8. B
Difficulty: Hard

Category: Writing & Language / Sentence Formation

Strategic Advice: Read the sentence and examine the order of the details. Reorganize the sentence so that it is clear and smooth.

Getting to the Answer: As written, the text contains coordinated ideas without regard to their grammatical form. Choice (B) correctly rearranges the ideas so that the three main ideas are nouns combined with "and" instead of "in addition to."

9. A

Difficulty: Easy

Category: Writing & Language / Effective Language Use

Strategic Advice: Read the sentence and determine the function of the word in the sentence.

Getting to the Answer: "Concentrated" means clustered or gathered together, "planned" means to arrange beforehand, and "consolidated" means brought together in a single whole. Only (A) means working together intellectually.

10. D

Difficulty: Hard

Category: Writing & Language / Organization

Strategic Advice: Read the paragraph and determine if the sequence of events is logical. For the paragraph to be logical, the examples need to build upon one another.

Getting to the Answer: Sentence 5 does not offer a proper conclusion to the paragraph, but sentence 2 gives a good summation. Choice (D) correctly moves the summative sentence to conclude the paragraph.

11. D

Difficulty: Medium

Category: Writing & Language / Development

Strategic Advice: Closely read the paragraph to find the central idea. Then, determine which sentence does not match the content.

Getting to the Answer: The evidence regarding physical therapy assistants does not connect with the main idea of this paragraph, which centers on the benefits of choosing to become a certified physical therapist. Choice (D) is correct.

12. C

Difficulty: Easy

Category: Writing & Language / Effective Language Use

Strategic Advice: Watch out for choices, like B, which are extremely wordy. It is better to be as direct and simple as possible.

Getting to the Answer: Additional adjectives do not add more meaning to this content. Choice (C) is the most concise and effective way of stating the information in the passage.

13. A

Difficulty: Medium

Category: Writing & Language / Punctuation

Strategic Advice: Study the words in a series and see where a comma might need to be inserted or eliminated.

Getting to the Answer: Recall that the SAT requires lists of three to have commas after the first two items in the list, not just after the first item. Choice (A) is correct.

14. D

Difficulty: Hard

Category: Writing & Language / Development

Strategic Advice: To find the best answer choice, look for the sentence that has the most relevant details presented in a clear and concise way.

Getting to the Answer: Choice (D) has the most relevant details about what the Pony Express was like when it was at its peak.

15. C

Difficulty: Medium

Category: Writing & Language / Sentence Formation

Strategic Advice: Be careful of inappropriate transition words when relating sentences to one another.

Getting to the Answer: Choice (C) divides the two thoughts into two complete sentences by adding a period and capitalizing the first word of the second sentence.

16. A

Difficulty: Easy

Category: Writing & Language / Effective Language Use

Strategic Advice: The context of the sentence suggests which word would have the correct connotation. Check each word to see how it fits with the context.

Getting to the Answer: Only (A) fits with the context of the sentence. The other choices are unlikely.

17. B

Difficulty: Medium

Category: Writing & Language / Sentence Formation

Strategic Advice: Verbs within a sentence should be parallel. Check to see if this is true here.

Getting to the Answer: The correct choice, (B), has all the verbs in the same form.

18. A

Difficulty: Hard

Category: Writing & Language / Development

Strategic Advice: To find the central idea of a paragraph, identify important details and summarize them in a sentence. Then, find the choice that is the closest to your summary. Do not choose a detail rather than a central idea.

Getting to the Answer: The paragraph mostly discusses the challenges riders faced, so (A) most accurately sums up the central idea of the paragraph.

19. B

Difficulty: Medium

Category: Writing & Language / Organization

Strategic Advice: Look for the relationship between this sentence and the previous one. This will help you choose the appropriate transition word. Read the word into the sentence to ensure that it makes sense.

Getting to the Answer: Choice (B) shows the relationship between the two sentences by emphasizing that the riders could overcome these challenges.

20. B

Difficulty: Medium

Category: Writing & Language / Quantitative

Strategic Advice: The graphic gives specific information about when events relating to the Pony Express took place. Interpret it to choose the correct answer choice.

Getting to the Answer: Choice (B) is the only one that accurately reflects the information in the timeline.

21. C

Difficulty: Medium

Category: Writing & Language / Effective Language Use

Strategic Advice: The context of the sentence suggests which word would have the best fit. Check each word to see how it fits with the context.

Getting to the Answer: Choice (C) best fits the context of the sentence.

22. D
Difficulty: Medium

Category: Writing & Language / Effective Language Use

Strategic Advice: Watch out for answer choices that may have incorrect transition words.

Getting to the Answer: Choice (D) joins the sentences concisely and correctly by using the conjunction "and."

CHAPTER 27

PREPARE

1. A
Difficulty: Medium

Category: Writing & Language / Organization

Strategic Advice: Make sure introductory sentences correctly portray the intended logic and scope of the entire paragraph.

Getting to the Answer: This sentence is correct as written. The author introduces the central idea that lawyers are responsible for an excess of product warnings. In the balance of the paragraph, the author argues that many product warnings are unnecessary and ineffective for consumers and beneficial only to the lawyers who write them. Choice (A) is correct.

2. C
Difficulty: Hard

Category: Writing & Language / Organization

Strategic Advice: When reordering a sentence within a paragraph, pay attention to any transition key words to help you determine what should logically precede or follow the sentence.

Getting to the Answer: Sentence 4 begins with the contrast transition "although" and describes aspects of schools that have changed. The sentence concludes with the comment that some aspects of the school system have remained the same. Therefore, sentence 4 should follow a sentence that discusses how schools have changed and precede a sentence that discusses the unchanged aspects of the school system. Choice (C) is correct.

3. B
Difficulty: Medium

Category: Writing & Language / Organization

Strategic Advice: Make sure introductory transitions logically connect the information and ideas in the sentences before and after.

Getting to the Answer: In the sentence before the underlined transition, the author acknowledges that the specialness of the day will later return to normal. In the sentences following the transition, the author puts aside thoughts of the coming noise and slush to enjoy the first snowfall. By using a contrast transition, (B) correctly indicates that the author still inhabits the quiet world of the first snowfall.

PRACTICE

4. C
Difficulty: Hard

Category: Writing & Language / Organization

Strategic Advice: An effective body paragraph can provide evidence to support the author's central idea or introduce a change in the focus of the passage.

Getting to the Answer: This paragraph begins with the transition word "while" and establishes a contrast between the number of recent earthquakes and the damage that those earthquakes can cause. The passage also shifts focus from a discussion of earthquake frequency to one of earthquake damage. Therefore, placing this paragraph between the two discussions in paragraph 4 and paragraph 5 makes the most sense. Choice (C) is correct.

5. C

Difficulty: Medium

Category: Writing & Language / Organization

Strategic Advice: When reordering a sentence within a paragraph, identify the information in the sentence and locate where in the paragraph that information is discussed.

Getting to the Answer: The topic of sentence 4 is aftershocks. Aftershocks are also discussed in sentence 2. However, in sentence 2 the pronoun "these" indicates that aftershocks have been previously discussed in the paragraph. Before sentence 2 is the logical place for sentence 4. Choice (C) is correct.

6. A

Difficulty: Easy

Category: Writing & Language / Organization

Strategic Advice: Don't answer questions that ask about the conclusion of a paragraph until you have read the entire paragraph.

Getting to the Answer: The paragraph focuses on the damage that earthquakes can cause and ways to improve safety in the event of an earthquake. Although the sentence preceding the concluding sentence mentions earthquake predictions, it does so in the context of how to prepare for these natural disasters. Therefore, the final sentence needs to discuss preparations, not predictions. Choice (A) provides a logical conclusion to the paragraph.

PERFORM

7. D

Difficulty: Medium

Category: Writing & Language / Usage

Strategic Advice: A pronoun is ambiguous when its antecedent is either missing or unclear.

Getting to the Answer: To find the antecedent for the underlined pronoun, read the previous sentence and think about the focus of the paragraph. The previous sentence has more than one possible antecedent—vacuous "Internet speak," "reliance," or "acronyms and abbreviations." However, in the context of the passage, "empty chatter," or (D), is the clearest and most relevant antecedent.

8. A

Difficulty: Medium

Category: Writing & Language / Organization

Strategic Advice: To answer questions about effective transitions within a paragraph, identify the focus of the paragraph both before and after the transition.

Getting to the Answer: The first part of the paragraph discusses the reasons the narrator stayed in his room as a child—because he was ill. After the transition, the narrator discusses why he still stays in his room—because he has access to the world. The transition needs to show how those ideas are linked. Choice (A) provides a logical transition as written.

9. B

Difficulty: Easy

Category: Writing & Language / Effective Language Use

Strategic Advice: When two words or phrases in the sentence have the same meaning, the sentence is redundant and contains a concision error.

Getting to the Answer: In this sentence, "succinct" and "to the point" have the same meaning, so the correct answer will eliminate one. Choice (B) is correct.

10. C

Difficulty: Hard

Category: Writing & Language / Organization

Strategic Advice: To reorder a sentence within a paragraph, identify the information in the sentence and locate what sentence that information should logically precede or follow.

Getting to the Answer: As written, sentence 5 summarizes the freedom people experience when connected by the Internet. However, sentence 6 makes a claim about that freedom, and sentence 7 provides examples of that freedom. The summary in sentence 5 should logically follow both the claim and the examples. Choice (C) is correct.

11. B

Difficulty: Easy

Category: Writing & Language / Shifts in Construction

Strategic Advice: In addition to checking that underlined verbs agree with their subjects, also check to ensure that the verb tense remains consistent and logical. Unless the context in the passage tells you that the time frame has changed, the tense should not change.

Getting to the Answer: As written, this verb is in the past perfect tense. However, the context of the passage indicates that the action described by the verb continued to occur up until the present moment. Choice (B) correctly uses the present perfect tense.

12. D

Difficulty: Hard

Category: Writing & Language / Sentence Formation

Strategic Advice: Whenever you see a compound, series, or list, check to make sure that all of the items are in parallel form.

Getting to the Answer: The underlined phrase is part of a compound formed by the conjunction "and." Reread the sentence and identify the other part of the compound. In this sentence, "half two minds exchanging sophisticated ideas" forms the first part of the compound. The second part must be parallel. Choice (D) is correct.

13. A

Difficulty: Medium

Category: Writing & Language / Organization

Strategic Advice: Introductory transitions must logically connect the information and ideas in the sentences before and after the transition.

Getting to the Answer: In the sentence before the underlined transition, the author describes small talk as boring. In the following sentence, he compares a conversation without small talk to flying. The sentence suggests that small talk can be dispensed with only occasionally. This sentence is correct as written, or (A).

14. D

Difficulty: Medium

Category: Writing & Language / Organization

Strategic Advice: Paragraphs in a well-written passage will flow from the general to the specific. To put paragraphs in the most logical order, begin with the paragraph that introduces the central idea in broad terms.

Getting to the Answer: As written, paragraph 1 contains a very specific discussion of a particular form of speech. Paragraph 2 introduces the idea of conversation in general terms and outlines the narrator's thoughts about it. Only (D) arranges the paragraphs from the general to the specific.

EXTRA PRACTICE

1. B

Difficulty: Easy

Category: Writing & Language / Shifts in Construction

Strategic Advice: Identify the verb tense in the rest of the sentence to find the correct answer.

Getting to the Answer: The sentence switches verb tense mid-sentence as it is currently written. The other verb in the sentence, "was," indicates that the events happened in the past. The tense of the underlined verb should match and also be in a correct past tense. Choice (B) is correct because it correctly uses the past tense of "produce."

2. B

Difficulty: Medium

Category: Writing & Language / Organization

Strategic Advice: Look for the relationship between this sentence and the previous one. Doing so will help you choose the appropriate transition word. Read the word into the sentence to ensure that it makes sense.

Getting to the Answer: Choice (B) shows the relationship between the two sentences by giving an example of what kind of art the Post-Impressionists were creating.

3. D

Difficulty: Medium

Category: Writing & Language / Effective Language Use

Strategic Advice: Read the complete passage to learn more about the work of Impressionists. Then, substitute each word into the sentence to see which choice best fits into the context of the sentence.

Getting to the Answer: The passage states that Impressionists tried to paint exactly what they saw

in nature. Only (D) has the correct connotation and fits within the context of the sentence.

4. B

Difficulty: Medium

Category: Writing & Language / Sentence Formation

Strategic Advice: The verbs in a sentence have to be parallel.

Getting to the Answer: The correct answer is in the same form as the first verb in the sentence, "looking." That means that the -ing verb or gerund "attempting" in (B) is correct.

5. A

Difficulty: Easy

Category: Writing & Language / Effective Language Use

Strategic Advice: Check each word for its connotations and pick the answer choice that fits the context of the sentence. Substitute each answer choice for the underlined word to determine which works best.

Getting to the Answer: This sentence describes how Post-Impressionists focused on self-discovery in art by letting their personal experiences and emotions guide their interpretation of their subjects. Therefore, each artist had his or her own distinct, or "unique," vision. The underlined portion is correct as written, and the answer is therefore (A).

6. C

Difficulty: Hard

Category: Writing & Language / Development

Strategic Advice: Read the entire paragraph and determine the central idea. Look for a match to your prediction.

Getting to the Answer: The paragraph discusses different ways artists in the Post-Impressionism era painted. Choice (C) reflects this summary.

7. B

Difficulty: Hard

Category: Writing & Language / Effective Language Use

Strategic Advice: Watch out for answer choices that contain incorrect transition words.

Getting to the Answer: Choice (B) joins the sentences concisely and correctly by changing the verb tense of the first sentence to make it a dependent clause.

8. A

Difficulty: Easy

Category: Writing & Language / Usage

Strategic Advice: Read the sentence prior to the pronoun to determine whom the pronoun is referencing. Pronouns should not be ambiguous and must match the verb in number.

Getting to the Answer: The pronoun "they" refers to Paul Gauguin and Vincent van Gogh, so the pronoun needs to be plural and in the third person. Choice (A) is correct.

9. D

Difficulty: Hard

Category: Writing & Language / Development

Strategic Advice: Read the entire paragraph to identify the central idea. Find the answer choice that provides evidence about this idea. Remember to compare the scope of the evidence with the scope of the central idea.

Getting to the Answer: The paragraph concerns the Post-Impressionist period and what kinds of methods Post-Impressionists used to create their art. Choice (D) addresses the central idea by providing additional information about these methods.

10. B

Difficulty: Medium

Category: Writing & Language / Usage

Strategic Advice: First, determine whether the current sentence is correct as written. Then, evaluate the answer choices. Pay careful attention to which form of they're/their/there should be used in the sentence.

Getting to the Answer: "They're" is a contraction meaning "they are," which does not make sense in the context of the sentence. What is needed here is a possessive plural pronoun to match the antecedent "artists." Choice (B) is correct.

11. D

Difficulty: Medium

Category: Writing & Language / Organization

Strategic Advice: Try inserting this sentence into all of the possible places to figure out where it makes the most sense. See if the sentence is a logical extension of another sentence.

Getting to the Answer: Choice (D) is the most logical position for this sentence because it is a comment based on the quotation in sentence 5.

12. C

Difficulty: Medium

Category: Writing & Language / Effective Language Use

Strategic Advice: Think about the overall meaning of the sentence. Select the answer choice that makes the most sense in context. Watch out for choices like D that are similar in meaning but do not make sense in context.

Getting to the Answer: "Depletion" is the reduction of a resource, so (C) is correct.

13. D
Difficulty: Hard

Category: Writing & Language / Effective Language Use

Strategic Advice: Watch out for answer choices that are grammatically correct but do not focus on the most important element of the sentence, such as C.

Getting to the Answer: The most important element of the sentence is that biofuel is an alternative fuel source. Choice (D) is correct because this sentence places the emphasis on "alternative is biofuel."

14. A
Difficulty: Medium

Category: Writing & Language / Development

Strategic Advice: Look for the answer choice that clearly states the main topic of the paragraph and introduces the central idea supported by all of the details presented. Eliminate answer choices that contain details that would not effectively serve as a topic sentence.

Getting to the Answer: Topic sentences or introductory sentences of body paragraphs should generally introduce that paragraph's topic. While other answer choices address details disclosed in the paragraph, (A) is the most general and also uses the transition "until recently" to tie this paragraph to the one that precedes it.

15. A
Difficulty: Medium

Category: Writing & Language / Usage

Strategic Advice: Determine what the pronoun "it" refers to in this sentence. Keep in mind that the pronoun "its" is possessive and "it's" is a contraction of "it is."

Getting to the Answer: "It" refers to ethanol and is possessive. The possessive form of "it" is "its," so the sentence is correct as written. Choice (A) is correct.

16. B
Difficulty: Medium

Category: Writing & Language / Effective Language Use

Strategic Advice: Be careful of answer choices that are close in meaning to "horrible" but do not fit the established tone.

Getting to the Answer: Replace "horrible" with each of the answer choices. In this context, "dire," which means severe or urgent, best fits the tone and style of the sentence. Choice (B) is correct.

17. C
Difficulty: Medium

Category: Writing & Language / Quantitative

Strategic Advice: Look at the most recent data in the graph. Pay attention to the relationship between the two lines: the solid line represents the percentage of corn production used for ethanol, and the dotted line reflects the price of corn.

Getting to the Answer: In the most recent years displayed in the graph, the price of corn and the percentage of corn production used for ethanol have both increased. Choice (C) is correct.

18. A
Difficulty: Hard

Category: Writing & Language / Development

Strategic Advice: Determine the central idea of the paragraph. Eliminate answer choices that do not relate to it.

Getting to the Answer: In this paragraph, the author explains that ethanol is limited as a commercial fuel. Choice (A) describes one way in which ethanol use is limited and is therefore correct.

19. D

Difficulty: Easy

Category: Writing & Language / Organization

Strategic Advice: Read this paragraph in the context of the entire passage to determine its proper placement.

Getting to the Answer: This paragraph makes general statements about the central idea of the passage and draws a conclusion. Choice (D) is correct because paragraph 4 is an appropriate concluding paragraph.

20. B

Difficulty: Easy

Category: Writing & Language / Shifts in Construction

Strategic Advice: Read the first few sentences of the paragraph and pay attention to the verb tenses used in the following sentences.

Getting to the Answer: As written, the underlined portion is in the past perfect tense. The following sentence, however, uses the present perfect form of the verb "to develop." The underlined portion should also be in the present perfect form; therefore, (B) is correct.

21. C

Difficulty: Medium

Category: Writing & Language / Sentence Formation

Strategic Advice: Check to see if this sentence contains two independent clauses that create a run-on sentence without proper punctuation.

Getting to the Answer: This sentence contains two complete thoughts with two independent main clauses and should therefore be separated into two sentences with a period. Choice (C) is correct.

22. B

Difficulty: Medium

Category: Writing & Language / Organization

Strategic Advice: Read the previous sentence in conjunction with this one. Think about the relationship between the ideas in the two sentences.

Getting to the Answer: There is a cause-and-effect relationship between the ideas in the previous sentence and this sentence, but the underlined portion contains a concluding transition. "Therefore" is a cause-and-effect transition, so (B) is correct.

23. C

Difficulty: Medium

Category: Writing & Language / Effective Language Use

Strategic Advice: Use context clues to establish how the target word is used in the sentence. Then, imagine that the sentence has a blank in place of that word. Test each choice in its place, selecting the answer choice that makes sense within the context of the sentence.

Getting to the Answer: The opening sentences of the passage describe the bones as an unexpected find. "Tier" is a noun that means "a series of arranged rows" and is inappropriate here. Choice (C), "cache," is a noun meaning "hiding place," so it is correct.

24. C

Difficulty: Medium

Category: Writing & Language / Sentence Formation

Strategic Advice: Read the sentences carefully to determine the relationship between the two sentence parts. Think about grammatically correct ways to join clauses.

Getting to the Answer: "And" is a conjunction used between coordinating ideas. "Much larger than bison of that time" is a subordinate adverb clause expressing condition. "Although" is the only subordinating conjunction that expresses the relationship of the two ideas correctly. Choice (C) is correct.

25. D
Difficulty: Hard

Category: Writing & Language / Development

Strategic Advice: Identify the common idea that the sentences in the paragraph are supporting. Be aware of answer choices that provide a detail about a topic mentioned but not about the central idea of the entire paragraph.

Getting to the Answer: All of the sentences in this paragraph refer to the findings of the investigation at the site, not to the difficulties or methods of completing the investigation; (D) is correct.

26. A
Difficulty: Medium

Category: Writing & Language / Effective Language Use

Strategic Advice: Analyze the sentence and compare it to the answer choices presented. Consider whether all of the words in each choice are necessary to express the central idea.

Getting to the Answer: The repetition of phrases with similar meanings such as "materials found" and "artifacts" is unnecessary. Choice (A) correctly conveys the meaning using the fewest words.

27. D
Difficulty: Hard

Category: Writing & Language / Organization

Strategic Advice: Establish how the content of sentence 4 is related to the entire paragraph.

Getting to the Answer: The topic sentence identifies the scientific disciplines in the following order: "chemistry, geology, and biology." Sentence 4 needs to be placed before sentence 3 to achieve the established order; (D) is correct.

28. A
Difficulty: Easy

Category: Writing & Language / Punctuation

Strategic Advice: Determine if the two parts of the sentence contain both subjects and verbs; decide whether either part can stand independently as its own sentence.

Getting to the Answer: Removing the colon after "discovered" creates a run-on sentence. "Biology comes" and "archaeologists can" are the subject-verb combinations that make each part of the sentence independent. Choice (A) is correct.

29. D
Difficulty: Easy

Category: Writing & Language / Effective Language Use

Strategic Advice: Examine the sentence in relationship to other sentences in the paragraph. Think about the scientific nature of the content and determine which choice sounds the most specific to science.

Getting to the Answer: The noun "parts" is a general term meaning a portion. Choice (D), "subfield," is more exact when describing types of archaeology and is therefore correct.

30. B
Difficulty: Easy

Category: Writing & Language / Sentence Formation

Strategic Advice: A sentence is an idea that expresses a complete thought and contains a subject and a verb. Examine the sentence to find the subject and verb.

Getting to the Answer: Once the subject and verb are located, it is clear that the two clauses beginning with "which" cannot stand independently. Only (B) is a complete sentence and, therefore, is correct.

31. C

Difficulty: Hard

Category: Writing & Language / Development

Strategic Advice: Closely examine the topic sentence and the supporting details; identify the central idea of the paragraph. Read the paragraph with each answer choice added and consider which adds the most relevant information.

Getting to the Answer: Choice (C) is the only answer choice that adds supporting information about the central idea—the types of archaeology.

32. D

Difficulty: Medium

Category: Writing & Language / Sentence Formation

Strategic Advice: Identify the tense of the verbs used in the sentence. Parallel ideas must be expressed in the same grammatical form.

Getting to the Answer: The verbs describing the actions of the scientists are past tense. Correlative constructions require the past tense verb "dug" to be paired with the same form: "preserved" and "interpreted." Choice (D) is correct.

33. B

Difficulty: Medium

Category: Writing & Language / Usage

Strategic Advice: Ask how the word is used in the sentence; try substituting each answer choice in its place. Use the other words in the sentence to provide context clues.

Getting to the Answer: "Innate" is an adjective meaning existing in someone from birth. "Inert" means to have no ability to react. Because the final paragraph depicts archaeologists as translators of material items into something lifelike, (B) is correct.

CHAPTER 28

PREPARE

1. A

Difficulty: Medium

Category: Writing & Language / Development

Strategic Advice: Carefully consider sentences that seem to be making a claim that is central to the passage. Select the answer choice that matches the evidence that the author provides in the rest of the passage.

Getting to the Answer: After the first paragraph, the author explains how Dr. Marshall's findings fundamentally changed how the medical community understands ulcers. The underlined segment is correct as written because it accurately depicts Marshall as a disrupting force in the field. Choice (A) is correct.

2. B

Difficulty: Hard

Category: Writing & Language / Development

Strategic Advice: Sentences containing supporting details need to contribute to the author's central idea. Consider the context of the underlined section and select the answer choice that best advances the development of the author's argument.

Getting to the Answer: Choice (B) is correct. It develops the author's narrative by elaborating on how Dr. Marshall was outside of the mainstream of his field early in his career.

3. B

Difficulty: Hard

Category: Writing & Language / Development

Strategic Advice: Supporting details should confirm the central idea and not contradict specifics that are mentioned elsewhere. Look for the answer choice that assists the reader's understanding of the passage and is also in agreement with previously mentioned points.

Getting to the Answer: Choice (B) is correct because it links the current paragraph to the following paragraph, which mentions Dr. Marshall's experiments with an important type of bacteria. The other answer choices are either off-topic or conflict with details found elsewhere in the passage.

4. D

Difficulty: Easy

Category: Writing & Language / Development

Strategic Advice: The last sentence in a passage often serves to recap what the author has said up to that point, acting as a summarization of the central idea. It should not conflict with the rest of the passage or go off-topic.

Getting to the Answer: Choice (D) is correct because it accurately summarizes the accomplishments of Dr. Marshall as described in the passage.

PRACTICE

5. D

Difficulty: Medium

Category: Writing & Language / Development

Strategic Advice: Scrutinize details of densely factual passages to make sure they are on-topic and do not conflict with other details or the central idea.

Getting to the Answer: This passage is concerned with the details of human skin and explaining the properties and purposes of skin. Choice (D) abides by the author's narrative for the passage and is therefore correct.

6. A

Difficulty: Medium

Category: Writing & Language / Development

Strategic Advice: Pick the answer choice that is in line with the author's central idea and tone.

Getting to the Answer: In this passage, the author explains how the skin is essential to life by listing its various properties and processes for keeping the body in healthy operation. The underlined section is in line with the author's overall effort. Choice (A) is correct.

7. C

Difficulty: Medium

Category: Writing & Language / Development

Strategic Advice: Make sure details in the underlined section are relevant to the topic. Even if a detail matches the tone of the passage (in this case, strictly fact-based), it might not be relevant to the central idea.

Getting to the Answer: Most of the answer choices for this question sound legitimate and even factually correct. However, only (C) keeps the focus on the human skin and its characteristics, so it is correct. Remember, the focus of the paragraph is on the defensive functions of the skin, *not* on how those functions work at a cellular level. You also know that immediate medical attention is too extreme for any instance of skin breaking (small cuts, etc.).

8. A

Difficulty: Medium

Category: Writing & Language / Development

Strategic Advice: Concluding sentences often reassert or summarize the author's central idea; therefore, they cannot fundamentally conflict with the author's assertions.

Getting to the Answer: In this passage, the author has made clear that the skin is a very important organ that protects the body from a variety of illnesses and disorders, as well as from physical harm. Choice (A) is correct, as it ties preceding points and details together into a coherent conclusion for the author's argument.

PERFORM

9. A

Difficulty: Medium

Category: Writing & Language / Development

Strategic Advice: Scrutinize the answer choices for how they relate to the author's central ideas as well as how they potentially conflict with details that come later in the passage.

Getting to the Answer: Choice (A) is correct because—without going off-topic or conflicting with later details—it elaborates on the idea that Polk followed in Jackson's footsteps.

10. C

Difficulty: Easy

Category: Writing & Language / Development

Strategic Advice: Pay close attention to long lists of evidence to make sure that each component is in line with the central idea and context of the sentence.

Getting to the Answer: Choice (C) is correct because it is the only answer choice that both stays focused on matters of policy (as the first part of the sentence mentions) and supports the thesis that Polk and Jackson were in agreement on most points of public policy.

11. D

Difficulty: Easy

Category: Writing & Language / Development

Strategic Advice: The first sentence of a paragraph sets the paragraph's tone and purpose. Pay attention to what the other sentences of the paragraph are describing and pick the answer choice that is the best introduction for those details.

Getting to the Answer: This paragraph is concerned with explaining the chronology of Polk's early life. Choice (D) is correct because it states the place and date of Polk's birth, making it a logical introduction to the following sentences.

12. D

Difficulty: Medium

Category: Writing & Language / Development

Strategic Advice: Supporting details fit the context of the paragraph and do not contradict details found elsewhere in the passage. Select the answer choice that satisfies these guidelines.

Getting to the Answer: This paragraph is narrowly concerned with Polk's origins and early political career. Choice (D) fits the context and does not contradict later details.

13. C

Difficulty: Medium

Category: Writing & Language / Development

Strategic Advice: A paragraph's final sentence ideally guides the paragraph's central idea to a conclusion and remains linked to the central idea of the passage.

Getting to the Answer: Choice (C) is correct because it is the most effective conclusion for a paragraph tasked with explaining Polk's early political career. Choice (C) also makes a clear connection to the following paragraph, helping the narrative flow.

14. B

Difficulty: Medium

Category: Writing & Language / Development

Strategic Advice: Remember that supporting evidence needs to focus on and contribute to the central idea.

Getting to the Answer: The author's intent is to introduce the two main candidates in the 1844 election, leading to the following sentence that discusses their opinions of expansionism. Choice (B) is correct because it stays focused on the paragraph's topic and contributes to the argument that Polk recognized popular support for expansionism that other candidates overlooked or ignored.

15. A

Difficulty: Medium

Category: Writing & Language / Development

Strategic Advice: Examine details and parenthetical asides for relevance to the central idea. The goal is to make sure that no contradictions are being introduced into the narrative.

Getting to the Answer: No change is necessary because the underlined section touches on two central themes of the passage: Polk's support for expansionist policies and his Jacksonian view of America. Choice (A) is correct.

16. B

Difficulty: Hard

Category: Writing & Language / Development

Strategic Advice: Pay close attention to a paragraph's first sentence. It should set the stage for details to follow and also be in line with the passage's central idea.

Getting to the Answer: As alluded to in the first paragraph and explained clearly in the final paragraph, Polk did much to expand the borders of the United States. He even supported war with Mexico to gain territory. Choice (B) is correct.

EXTRA PRACTICE

1. B
Difficulty: Medium

Category: Writing & Language / Development

Strategic Advice: Identify the main idea of the paragraph. Eliminate options that do not support the main idea.

Getting to the Answer: Although sentence 3 is related to the main topic of the paragraph, coral reefs, the information in this sentence does nothing to support the main idea. Choice (B) is correct.

2. B
Difficulty: Medium

Category: Writing & Language / Organization

Strategic Advice: Read the preceding sentence along with this one and look for a relationship between the ideas in the sentences.

Getting to the Answer: The first sentence describes the importance of coral reefs, and this sentence explains how they are in danger of disappearing. "Unfortunately" is the best transition to use here, and (B) is the correct answer.

3. A
Difficulty: Medium

Category: Writing & Language / Quantitative

Strategic Advice: Evaluate the data presented in the infographic that accompanies the passage. Read each answer choice and eliminate those not supported by the data in the graph.

Getting to the Answer: Choice (A) is correct. As the pie chart shows and the caption confirms, about sixty percent of living reefs are in danger.

4. B
Difficulty: Medium

Category: Writing & Language / Effective Language Use

Strategic Advice: The two sentences in the passage contain redundant language. Look for the answer choice that retains the meaning of the two original sentences but is less wordy and redundant.

Getting to the Answer: Choice (B) is the correct answer because it contains the same information as the original sentences but in a more concise manner. While C is similar, it uses passive voice, which you should avoid using on the SAT.

5. D
Difficulty: Medium

Category: Writing & Language / Effective Language Use

Strategic Advice: Look for the answer that creates the clearest idea within the sentence.

Getting to the Answer: The resources referred to in the sentence are clean water and sunlight—things the reef needs to survive. These resources are vital to the coral reefs, so (D) is the correct answer.

6. B
Difficulty: Easy

Category: Writing & Language / Development

Strategic Advice: The correct answer will briefly describe the main idea of the paragraph and will be supported by the details in the paragraph. Be careful of answer choices like C that summarize a detail provided in the paragraph rather than the central idea.

Getting to the Answer: Choice (B) best describes the main idea of the paragraph. All of the details presented in the paragraph are related to how people engaging in activities near coral reefs often cause damage.

7. B

Difficulty: Easy

Category: Writing & Language / Usage

Strategic Advice: Check the verb tense in the sentences that follow this one. Be sure that the verb tense is consistent.

Getting to the Answer: To agree with the sentences in the rest of the paragraph, the verb in this sentence should be written in present tense. Because the noun is singular, (B) is the correct answer.

8. D

Difficulty: Medium

Category: Writing & Language / Organization

Strategic Advice: Read the paragraph with the sentence moved to the places suggested by the answer choices. Look for relationships between the ideas in the surrounding sentences.

Getting to the Answer: This sentence is a continuation of the idea introduced in sentence 3 (crabs might be damaging the coral) and belongs before sentence 4. Choice (D) is the correct answer.

9. C

Difficulty: Medium

Category: Writing & Language / Effective Language Use

Strategic Advice: Look for the answer that creates the clearest idea within the sentence.

Getting to the Answer: The word "obstruct" most clearly illustrates how the particles that settle on the coral keep sunlight from reaching the coral. Choice (C) is correct.

10. B

Difficulty: Easy

Category: Writing & Language / Effective Language Use

Strategic Advice: Avoid answers that are grammatically correct but wordy or redundant.

Getting to the Answer: The correct answer is the most concise choice. "Would suggest" fits grammatically and is the most concise choice, so (B) is the correct answer.

11. A

Difficulty: Medium

Category: Writing & Language / Development

Strategic Advice: Avoid answers that are related to the main topic but do not add relevant details to the paragraph.

Getting to the Answer: The paragraph explains how crabs and coral reefs help each other. Choice (A) is the best addition to this paragraph to support the central idea.

12. A

Difficulty: Medium

Category: Writing & Language / Development

Strategic Advice: Reread the paragraph to determine which answer choice best introduces the main point.

Getting to the Answer: The correct choice, (A), is the only one that accurately explains how the career is now popular and helpful but had to develop over time after a shift in health care needs.

13. D

Difficulty: Easy

Category: Writing & Language / Development

Strategic Advice: Reread the sentence and determine which answer choice creates the most focused sentence.

Getting to the Answer: The additional comments about the school's quality and programs are unnecessary. Choice (D) creates the most focused sentence.

14. B

Difficulty: Medium

Category: Writing & Language / Effective Language Use

Strategic Advice: Look for nearby context clues and use what you know of each answer choice's definition to determine which word most accurately reflects the intention of the sentence.

Getting to the Answer: The intention of the sentence is to state that students should acquire new hands-on medical knowledge through work experience. The word with the definition that best describes this acquisition is "accrue," (B).

15. B

Difficulty: Easy

Category: Writing & Language / Effective Language Use

Strategic Advice: Read the entire sentence for context clues and determine which answer choice creates a logical sentence without wordiness or redundancies.

Getting to the Answer: Because it eliminates wordiness and because the word "programs" is used later in the same sentence, (B) is correct.

16. D

Difficulty: Medium

Category: Writing & Language / Effective Language Use

Strategic Advice: Find context clues and determine which answer choice creates a logical sentence without wordiness or redundancies.

Getting to the Answer: Because there is still an exam to pass before these individuals become PAs, and because the repetition of the words "graduates" and "graduation" is redundant, (D) is the correct answer.

17. D

Difficulty: Medium

Category: Writing & Language / Organization

Strategic Advice: Review the answer choices to determine which creates a paragraph with the best logical progression of ideas.

Getting to the Answer: The paragraph discusses the steps a student must take in order to become a PA and does not discuss maintaining one's license until the end, as it is something someone does only after becoming a PA. Choice (D) is correct.

18. C

Difficulty: Medium

Category: Writing & Language / Effective Language Use

Strategic Advice: Use context clues to determine which answer choice best fits the context of the sentence and paragraph while conveying the author's intended meaning.

Getting to the Answer: The sentence suggests that doctors work alone while PAs work under supervision. The word with the definition that best describes a doctor's unsupervised work is "autonomously," (C).

19. A
Difficulty: Medium

Category: Writing & Language / Organization

Strategic Advice: Decide which answer choice offers the best transition for an accurate flow of ideas.

Getting to the Answer: Choice (A) offers the best transition in order to summarize why the previous information is important and to show the positive effects PAs have on the health care team.

20. C
Difficulty: Hard

Category: Writing & Language / Shifts in Construction

Strategic Advice: Evaluate whether the subject or object of the sentence is referred to by the pronoun and then determine which answer choice creates a logical and gramatically sound sentence.

Getting to the Answer: It is the PA who works under a physician, and because the pronoun refers to the object of the sentence, physicians, the appropriate pronoun to use in this situation is "whom." Therefore, (C) is correct.

21. B
Difficulty: Medium

Category: Writing & Language / Effective Language Use

Strategic Advice: Reread the paragraph and decide which answer choice maintains the style and tone of the author's voice.

Getting to the Answer: The author has not yet referenced him or herself, the reader, or any third party for an opinion in this passage. This makes the consistent tone found in (B) correct.

22. D
Difficulty: Medium

Category: Writing & Language / Development

Strategic Advice: Review the paragraph to determine which claim made by the author is lacking details or supporting evidence that would strengthen the author's case.

Getting to the Answer: The second sentence in the paragraph is the only one in which the author makes a claim based on projections, but the author fails to use specific figures. Adding these figures would strengthen this claim, thus (D) is correct.

CHAPTER 29

PREPARE

1. B
Difficulty: Medium

Category: Writing & Language / Effective Language Use

Strategic Advice: To answer a Precision question, reread the sentence containing the underlined word and determine what meaning the author wants to convey.

Getting to the Answer: In this sentence, the author contrasts imaginative readers who are able to enjoy ancient mythology with ordinary readers who are consumed by their everyday worries. "Prosaic" means ordinary. Choice (B) is correct.

2. D
Difficulty: Easy

Category: Writing & Language / Effective Language Use

Strategic Advice: Using two words with essentially the same meaning in the same sentence is redundant and creates a concision error.

Getting to the Answer: Because "understand" and "comprehend" have the same meaning, the correct answer will eliminate one of those words. Choice (D) is the only answer choice that does so and is therefore correct.

3. A
Difficulty: Medium

Category: Writing & Language / Effective Language Use

Strategic Advice: When answering a Style and Tone question, you will sometimes need to read the entire passage or paragraph before selecting the correct answer.

Getting to the Answer: This underlined portion is correct as written. The purpose of this paragraph is to suggest that the modern story mirrors modern life. In sentence 2, the author describes the modern story as having "complexity and ambivalence." By repeating the same phrase to describe the modern reader's life, the author has matched the style and tone to the purpose of the paragraph. Choice (A) is correct.

4. C
Difficulty: Hard

Category: Writing & Language / Effective Language Use

Strategic Advice: Remember that syntax errors do not necessarily indicate that a sentence is grammatically incorrect.

Getting to the Answer: The question stem asks you which of the answer choices most effectively combines the two sentences. Choice (C) does this by turning the second sentence into a modifying phrase that provides information about the action in the independent clause.

PRACTICE

5. D
Difficulty: Hard

Category: Writing & Language / Effective Language Use

Strategic Advice: Make sure the order in which words and phrases are written makes sense logically.

Getting to the Answer: As written, this sentence is hard to follow. The author is trying to emphasize the information that men also served as nurses during the Civil War. Choice (D) is correct because it is the only answer choice with grammatically and logically correct syntax.

6. B

Difficulty: Medium

Category: Writing & Language / Effective Language Use

Strategic Advice: Even if an underlined word or phrase sounds correct, analyze its meaning—both literal and figurative—to ensure it is appropriate in context.

Getting to the Answer: While it is easy to interpret a meaning from the underlined phrase "major victories," that meaning does not convey the author's intention. The phrase "major victories" suggests that of all the accomplishments of this organization, excluding men was one of the most important. Reread the sentences before and after the underlined phrase to understand that what the author means to convey is the idea that this exclusion occurred early in the history of the nurses' organization. Choice (B) corrects this error by explaining that this exclusion was one of the early victories within a series of accomplishments.

7. C

Difficulty: Easy

Category: Writing & Language / Effective Language Use

Strategic Advice: Avoid the temptation to use more words than necessary. The SAT requires concision; avoid wordiness and redundancy.

Getting to the Answer: As written, the underlined segment is redundant: "denied admission to" and "excluded from" have the same meaning. Look for the most succinct way to convey the author's intended meaning. Choice (C) is correct.

8. B

Difficulty: Medium

Category: Writing & Language / Effective Language Use

Strategic Advice: Style and Tone errors are nuanced—pay attention to the details in the sentences surrounding the underlined word or phrase.

Getting to the Answer: As written, the underlined portion does not match the style and tone of the passage because it includes the author's opinion while the rest of the passage offers no judgment on any of the situations discussed. Choice (B) correctly maintains the objective tone of the passage by omitting any subjective viewpoints.

PERFORM

9. B

Difficulty: Medium

Category: Writing & Language / Effective Language Use

Strategic Advice: Questions about the author's word choice require you to determine the author's intended meaning within the context of the sentence.

Getting to the Answer: Read the sentence to understand the context in which the underlined word, "imagine," is used. The author uses "imagine" to describe how certain groups portray the risks associated with genetically modified organisms. Because the author views these groups as the opposition, the word needs to convey a sense of resistance to the truth. As written, the sentence conveys too benign of a meaning. Choice (B) is correct.

10. D

Difficulty: Easy

Category: Writing & Language / Effective Language Use

Strategic Advice: A sentence is redundant when two words that mean the same thing are used to express one idea.

Getting to the Answer: "Interfere" and "tamper" have the same meaning and are used to express a single idea about intentionally changing nature. The correct answer will eliminate one of those words. Choice (D) is correct.

11. B

Difficulty: Medium

Category: Writing & Language / Effective Language Use

Strategic Advice: Do not automatically select the shortest answer choice when presented with a Concision question. The correct answer choice must fully convey the author's intended meaning.

Getting to the Answer: As written, the underlined segment is the shortest answer choice, but it is difficult to determine exactly which group of people "we" refers to. Choice (B) is correct because it specifies the range of people included in "we" most concisely.

12. B

Difficulty: Hard

Category: Writing & Language / Effective Language Use

Strategic Advice: Syntax questions often require you to recognize that grammatically correct sentence structure alone may not produce the most effective writing.

Getting to the Answer: Although the sentences are grammatically correct as written, the question stem asks which of the answer choices most effectively combines the two sentences. Because the second sentence provides additional information about the "certain bird species" mentioned in the first sentence, use the relative pronoun "that" to indicate which species could be affected by the decline in the insect population. Choice (B) is correct.

13. D

Difficulty: Medium

Category: Writing & Language / Effective Language Use

Strategic Advice: Auxiliary verbs, like the underlined "will," add functional or grammatical meaning like expressing tense, voice, or emphasis to the clause in which they appear. When an auxiliary verb is underlined, make sure it fits the context of the paragraph or passage.

Getting to the Answer: Throughout the paragraph, the author uses the auxiliary verb "could" to indicate that the possibility exists to complete the described actions—"could lead" and "could have." Nothing in the paragraph suggests that the author has shifted from conjecture (indicated by "could") to either certainty ("will" and "would") or necessity ("must"). Choice (D) is correct.

14. A

Difficulty: Medium

Category: Writing & Language / Effective Language Use

Strategic Advice: When an entire sentence is underlined, check for a syntax error.

Getting to the Answer: This sentence is correct as written. The author arranges the parts of the sentence in the most logical order by introducing the topic ("actual impact"), describing what is being impacted, and drawing a conclusion about the topic. Choice (A) is correct.

15. A

Difficulty: Medium

Category: Writing & Language / Effective Language Use

Strategic Advice: To answer Word Choice questions, reread the sentence containing the underlined word or phrase to determine the author's intended meaning.

Getting to the Answer: Determine that the underlined phrase "essential fallacy" provides information about the basis for the argument discussed in this sentence. Rephrase the sentence as: the argument is based on a false idea. Choice (A) is correct.

16. D

Difficulty: Medium

Category: Writing & Language / Effective Language Use

Strategic Advice: When answering a Style and Tone question, you will sometimes need to read the entire passage or paragraph before selecting the correct answer.

Getting to the Answer: In the first three paragraphs, the author focuses on the negative aspects of genetically modified organisms. In the fourth paragraph, he dismisses the counter argument raised by advocates for genetically modified organisms. The tone in the final paragraph becomes strident and accusatory. The final sentence must match this tone in order to effectively conclude the paragraph and the passage. Choice (D) is correct because it suggests that the stakes for the planet are enormous and our misplaced trust would have dire consequences.

EXTRA PRACTICE

1. B

Difficulty: Medium

Category: Writing & Language / Punctuation

Strategic Advice: Read the sentence to determine how the list within it should be formatted. If it is more of an aside than a direct part of the sentence's main structure, the list should be set off by punctuation.

Getting to the Answer: As the sentence is written, its many commas are confusing. Because there is a list in the sentence, the commas within that list should remain. However, the list of poetic forms is not directly related to the rest of the sentence, so this should be clarified with punctuation. Dashes are the best way to mark this as a separate thought. Choice (B) correctly adds dashes to both the beginning and end of the list.

2. A

Difficulty: Easy

Category: Writing & Language / Effective Language Use

Strategic Advice: Determine what the sentence is saying about the history of the haiku. Is "complex" the most accurate way to describe it?

Getting to the Answer: The passage describes the many forms and many centuries that comprise the history of haiku. Choice (A), "complex," perfectly describes the long, rich, and detailed history of the poetic form.

3. A

Difficulty: Hard

Category: Writing & Language / Development

Strategic Advice: Determine which answer choice makes the most sense as an introduction to this paragraph. Consider what the purpose of the paragraph is and locate a sentence among the answer choices that encapsulates that idea.

Getting to the Answer: The purpose of this paragraph, based on its other sentences, is to explain the history of haiku and how its structure has changed over time. Choice (A) is the only answer choice related to these ideas. While the other answer choices may briefly mention the structure of haiku or its history, they all focus on other aspects of haiku—its entertainment value, the difficulty of understanding its rules, or the challenge of writing it.

4. B

Difficulty: Easy

Category: Writing & Language / Development

Strategic Advice: Determine the purpose of this sentence within the passage.

Getting to the Answer: While it is interesting for the audience to know that "hokku" eventually became "haiku," the sentence's placement in the passage is not optimal. The next sentence returns the discussion to the hokku form. In addition, readers encounter another explanation of the name "haiku" later, in paragraph 5. Choice (B) is correct because the sentence should be omitted from paragraph 2.

5. C

Difficulty: Medium

Category: Writing & Language / Organization

Strategic Advice: Consider the information presented by the rest of the paragraph to determine what "alternating turns" refers to.

Getting to the Answer: Sentence 7 describes the specifics of different word games introduced in sentence 5, so it makes sense that it would follow sentence 5. Choice (C) is correct.

6. C

Difficulty: Easy

Category: Writing & Language / Organization

Strategic Advice: Make sure that this sentence clearly and precisely transitions from the topic of the previous paragraph to the topic of this paragraph.

Getting to the Answer: As currently written, the first sentence does not make a clear connection to the preceding paragraph. By making the discussion of time more precise, the beginning of this paragraph flows better from the previous paragraph. The reader understands more clearly how the details in each paragraph connect. Choice (C) is correct.

7. D

Difficulty: Medium

Category: Writing & Language / Effective Language Use

Strategic Advice: Determine the purpose of sharing this information with readers. The tone of the sentence should be suited to its purpose.

Getting to the Answer: The paragraph is a straightforward piece of informative writing. The original sentence and C are both too casual for the rest of the passage, while B is too formal and wordy. Choice (D) correctly communicates the information of this sentence with the right level of formality.

8. D

Difficulty: Hard

Category: Writing & Language / Development

Strategic Advice: Find the answer choice that clearly supports the topic sentence of the paragraph while elegantly tying into the next sentence.

Getting to the Answer: The topic sentence of this paragraph emphasizes the themes in Basho's work and how haiku became associated with nature and the seasons. Choice (D) provides examples of possible subjects of Basho haikus and is therefore correct.

9. C

Difficulty: Hard

Category: Writing & Language / Effective Language Use

Strategic Advice: Consider what the sentence is communicating and if any words can be eliminated to say the same thing more concisely.

Getting to the Answer: The sentence uses too many words to communicate its point. By combining ideas and eliminating wordiness, the sentence can flow more smoothly. Choice (C) is correct because it maintains the sentence's meaning and uses fewer words to do so.

10. B

Difficulty: Medium

Category: Writing & Language / Effective Language Use

Strategic Advice: Consider the precise relationship between Shiki and the other poets mentioned. The correct answer choice will describe his effect on them.

Getting to the Answer: It seems clear that Shiki's work was an influence on cummings and Pound. While "helped" and "aided" both generally suggest that his effect on them was positive, "inspired" is more accurate. Shiki had left his mark, and the other poets learned from him. Choice (B) is correct.

11. D

Difficulty: Medium

Category: Writing & Language / Effective Language Use

Strategic Advice: Read the sentence and determine whether its thoughts are joined logically. The correct conjunction will make clear the relationship between the thoughts.

Getting to the Answer: The two parts of the sentence are directly related; the writers are "taken with the brevity of the form" because of what it provides them. Neither the sentence as it is written nor choices B or C express this relationship. Choice (D) correctly combines the sentence while maintaining the relationship between the two clauses.

12. A

Difficulty: Hard

Category: Writing & Language / Effective Language Use

Strategic Advice: Read the complete sentence. The correct answer will flow smoothly from the preceding sentence and communicate the different phrases of the sentence in a logical order based on their importance.

Getting to the Answer: Choice (A) is correct, as the existing sentence arranges the phrases in the most logical order. The sentence begins, "During his time there," smoothly transitioning from the previous sentence and providing non-essential context for the rest of the sentence. The main point is that Tesla invented the alternating current system. This is the first time the alternating current system has been named, so it should be written out fully, and the nonessential information, "what we know in our homes as AC power," should come last, set off by the comma.

13. D
Difficulty: Easy

Category: Writing & Language / Development

Strategic Advice: Identify the sentence that contributes the least relevant information to the focus, or purpose, of the paragraph and the passage as a whole.

Getting to the Answer: The paragraph introduces Tesla and his professional activities and accomplishments. The passage as whole goes on to explore Tesla's scientific legacy. Sentence 5 provides accurate, but irrelevant, information regarding Tesla's personal interests and habits; therefore, the correct answer is (D).

14. A
Difficulty: Medium

Category: Writing & Language / Effective Language Use

Strategic Advice: Choose the most contextually appropriate word.

Getting to the Answer: Choice (A) is correct because "implemented" most accurately conveys the idea that Westinghouse first carried out the use of alternating current, which had already been developed, during the exposition.

15. D
Difficulty: Easy

Category: Writing & Language / Quantitative

Strategic Advice: The correct answer will reflect the correct data contained in the timeline.

Getting to the Answer: The timeline states that Tesla and Westinghouse displayed the AC system at the Columbian Exposition in 1893, so (D) is correct.

16. B
Difficulty: Medium

Category: Writing & Language / Development

Strategic Advice: Identify the subject of the paragraph and consider what the author wants to convey about it. That is the central idea. Then, select the answer choice that correctly conveys the central idea of the paragraph as supported by the details in the preceding sentences.

Getting to the Answer: The paragraph discusses the importance of Tesla's development of alternating current and its impact on daily life. In particular, it distinguishes the legacy of Tesla relative to the contributions of Edison. For this reason, (B) is correct because it is the only answer choice that emphasizes that Tesla's AC system was crucial (not just incidental) to the success of Edison's bulbs as fixtures in everyday life. "However, bulbs alone do not light our homes" makes clear that Edison's invention would not have done so well without Tesla's.

17. B
Difficulty: Medium

Category: Writing & Language / Organization

Strategic Advice: The correct answer will provide a clear, smooth transition of ideas that connects the content of the previous and current paragraphs. It will also place sentences in logical sequence.

Getting to the Answer: The previous paragraph discusses the development of Tesla's AC technology, while the current paragraph discusses Tesla's other inventions. Choice (B) is correct because it links Tesla's development of alternating current with his other innovations. Moving sentence 4 to the beginning of the paragraph also provides a logical sequence of ideas.

18. C

Difficulty: Medium

Category: Writing & Language / Quantitative

Strategic Advice: Read the information next to 1883 in the timeline and find the answer choice that matches that content. The correct answer will correspond to the same event in the passage and timeline.

Getting to the Answer: According to the timeline, in 1883, Tesla used alternating current to power a motor. This date corresponds to the information in sentence 3 of paragraph 3, making (C) correct.

19. D

Difficulty: Easy

Category: Writing & Language / Effective Language Use

Strategic Advice: The correct answer will demonstrate economy of word choice and retain active voice while preserving the meaning of the sentence.

Getting to the Answer: The sentence communicates that Tesla's inventions contributed to the development of future technologies. Choice (D) is correct because it uses minimal verbiage to express that Tesla's inventions led to later inventions.

20. B

Difficulty: Medium

Category: Writing & Language / Development

Strategic Advice: Consider other information in the passage. The correct answer will identify and remove the least essential supporting information to streamline the rhetoric. The least essential information will not alter the meaning of the sentence and will most likely be irrelevant or redundant.

Getting to the Answer: The sentence communicates Tesla's impact on wireless communications. Choice (B) is correct because it provides examples that, while somewhat relevant, are nonessential.

21. B

Difficulty: Hard

Category: Writing & Language / Sentence Formation

Strategic Advice: The correct answer will align the modifier with its subject without disrupting the syntax of the remainder of the sentence.

Getting to the Answer: The sentence begins "Edison may have invented the lightbulb" and proceeds to contrast Edison's achievement with Tesla's. The second part of the sentence is a dependent clause connected with "but" and should lead off with its subject "Tesla," followed by the modifier, "seeing no fame or fortune," and then proceeding with the rest of the sentence. Choice (B) does so and is therefore correct.

22. D

Difficulty: Medium

Category: Writing & Language / Effective Language Use

Strategic Advice: Choose the most contextually appropriate word.

Getting to the Answer: Choice (D) is correct because "pioneer" most correctly conveys the idea that Tesla was among the first people to make advances toward the use of electricity—and the lightbulb—in daily life.

CHAPTER 30

PREPARE

1. B
Difficulty: Medium

Category: Writing & Language / Sentence Formation

Strategic Advice: Longer, complex sentences often have parallel structures that need to be consistent. In other words, it is important that verbs are conjugated the same way if they are in the same tense and tied to the same subject.

Getting to the Answer: In this sentence, "task" is the subject and it has several verbs that follow it. The underlined section is incorrect because it is inconsistent with previous conjugations ("to protect and defend"). Choice (B) is correct.

2. C
Difficulty: Easy

Category: Writing & Language / Shifts in Construction

Strategic Advice: It is important to make sure that the underlined section uses verb tenses that not only match the sentence's context but also make logical sense. Be wary of abrupt changes in verb tense that conflict with the verb tense in the of rest of the passage.

Getting to the Answer: The underlined section has a present-tense conjugation that conflicts with conjugations in the previous sentences as well as the passage's logic. The rest of the paragraph consists of straightforward past-tense verbs that recount where SMOM has resided since its founding. Choice (C) is correct because it retains the verb tense found in this section of the passage.

3. B
Difficulty: Easy

Category: Writing & Language / Sentence Formation

Strategic Advice: When the underlined section includes the joining of two sentences, make sure that each sentence is grammatically correct. If one of the sentences is a fragment, the two sentences will need to be appropriately combined.

Getting to the Answer: The second sentence of the underlined section is a sentence fragment—it does not have a subject. Joining the two sentences together using a comma is the best answer choice, as commas can unite dependent clauses with independent clauses. Choice (B) is correct.

PRACTICE

4. A
Difficulty: Medium

Category: Writing & Language / Sentence Formation

Strategic Advice: Words such as *while, when*, and *because* are subordinating conjunctions—they work to join independent clauses with dependent clauses. Make sure that the subordinating conjunction is working in the context of the sentence and helping to make the author's intent clear.

Getting to the Answer: Here, the author is presenting a contrast between the aspects of the Sun that are easily identifiable (light, heat) and other phenomena that are less obvious. At the same time, the author admits that all of these aspects of the Sun are always happening simultaneously. The current construction of "Yet, while" most clearly conveys the author's meaning of contrast. Choice (A) is correct.

5. D

Difficulty: Hard

Category: Writing & Language / Shifts in Construction

Strategic Advice: Pronouns need to agree with the noun or noun phrase to which they refer. The noun is often in the same sentence but can sometimes be found in preceding sentences.

Getting to the Answer: The noun phrase to which the pronoun refers is found at the end of the previous sentence: "the Sun's most volatile surface activity." Since "activity" is singular, the pronoun must agree with a singular noun. "They" is plural and is thus incorrect. Choice (D) is correct because it matches the singular noun.

6. B

Difficulty: Medium

Category: Writing & Language / Sentence Formation

Strategic Advice: Pay close attention to modifier placement. If modifiers are misplaced or incorrectly used, they can change the author's meaning or harm the sentence's clarity.

Getting to the Answer: As the sentence is currently written, the modifier "powerful" is misplaced. The author's intent is to explain the power of the magnetic fields to prevent heat from reaching the Sun's surface. Choice (B) is correct because "powerful" is placed before "magnetic fields," thereby correctly modifying the noun.

PERFORM

7. C

Difficulty: Medium

Category: Writing & Language / Shifts in Construction

Strategic Advice: Active voice construction is almost always better than passive voice

construction, as it has the subject of the sentence performing the action. This makes a sentence simpler and clearer.

Getting to the Answer: Choice (C) is correct because it is an active voice construction and it is also not interrupted by parentheticals set off by commas.

8. B

Difficulty: Easy

Category: Writing & Language / Sentence Formation

Strategic Advice: When the passage presents a long, complex sentence, be sure that it is not a run-on that would be better presented as two or more separate sentences.

Getting to the Answer: The underlined section is a juncture within a very long sentence; this is made obvious by the comma and the transitional phrase "in fact." Before this juncture, the sentence discusses the accessibility of Eisenstein's work, and after, it addresses his lasting effect on film. These two ideas are more clearly presented in two separate sentences instead of the current run-on. Choice (B) is correct.

9. A

Difficulty: Easy

Category: Writing & Language / Sentence Formation

Strategic Advice: If the underlined section is a coordinating conjunction—a word or phrase that joins two equally important phrases or clauses—pay attention to the appropriateness of the word choice. Keep clarity of the sentence and passage in mind.

Getting to the Answer: No change is necessary because "and" clearly demonstrates that Eisenstein was pushed out of one pursuit and into another. The other answer choices would confuse the reader and harm the author's clarity. Choice (A) is correct.

10. B

Difficulty: Medium

Category: Writing & Language / Sentence Formation

Strategic Advice: Within complex sentences that contain parallel structure, make sure that verb conjugation, tense, and voice of the sentence are consistent.

Getting to the Answer: The underlined section is incorrect because it modifies a past-tense structure that was established earlier in the sentence with the phrase "He quickly found." The current construction also negatively affects the author's clarity and intent. Choice (B) is correct because it is consistent with the past-tense structure already established.

11. D

Difficulty: Medium

Category: Writing & Language / Shifts in Construction

Strategic Advice: Be aware of improper pronoun use, and keep in mind that not using a pronoun at all can also be incorrect. If the underlined section is a noun, consider whether a pronoun would be better suited for the quality of the narrative.

Getting to the Answer: Eisenstein's name is already mentioned in one other part of the sentence, so in this instance it is unnecessary to use it. A possessive pronoun is a better option as it improves the quality of the sentence by not unnecessarily repeating Eisenstein's name. Choice (D) is correct.

12. D

Difficulty: Medium

Category: Writing & Language / Sentence Formation

Strategic Advice: The correct use of modifiers includes vocabulary: making sure the word being used as a modifier has the appropriate definition for the context.

Getting to the Answer: Choice (D) is correct because "cumulative" is the correct word for the author's meaning. A montage is inherently cumulative: its meaning grows with the progression of each component shown.

13. C

Difficulty: Hard

Category: Writing & Language / Sentence Formation

Strategic Advice: Sentence fragments—stand-alone sentences that are missing either a subject or a predicate—should always be avoided because they are grammatically incorrect. Pay close attention to sentences that begin with "And," as they often can be combined with their preceding sentences.

Getting to the Answer: The sentence that begins with "And" is a sentence fragment because it has no subject. The best way to join this sentence with the previous sentence is by simply removing the period and making "And" lowercase. No other punctuation is needed. Choice (C) is correct.

14. A

Difficulty: Medium

Category: Writing & Language / Sentence Formation

Strategic Advice: Modifiers, while not always grammatically necessary, may be required for the author to make a point or emphasize a detail. Scrutinize their use to determine which answer choice preserves the author's intent in the sentence and context.

Getting to the Answer: Choice (A) is correct because its use of the modifying phrases "enormously famous 1925 hit" and "1927 celebration of the October Revolution" is correct. Their use is also rhetorically effective, as it's clear to which film each is referring, giving each movie context for the reader.

EXTRA PRACTICE

1. B

Difficulty: Medium

Category: Writing & Language / Development

Strategic Advice: Identify the common words in all the sentences of the opening paragraph.

Getting to the Answer: All the sentences in this paragraph refer to art as a form of communication throughout history, not to the devices required for digital communication; (B) is correct.

2. A

Difficulty: Easy

Category: Writing & Language / Effective Language Use

Strategic Advice: Determine how the word "prominent" is used in the sentence.

Getting to the Answer: The opening sentences of the passage describe art as a method of communication and the meeting place as an arena. Choice (A), "prominent," is an adjective meaning "noticeable," so it is the correct choice.

3. D

Difficulty: Easy

Category: Writing & Language / Punctuation

Strategic Advice: Determine whether the list of items is a series needing commas or semicolons.

Getting to the Answer: As the sentence is written, its many semicolons are unnecessary. No part of the sentence can stand independently. Because there is a list in the sentence, the commas within that list should remain.

4. C

Difficulty: Medium

Category: Writing & Language / Effective Language Use

Strategic Advice: Eliminate the redundant words from the sentence.

Getting to the Answer: Words with similar meanings, such as "create" and "craft," are unnecessary. Choice (C) correctly conveys the meaning of the sentence using the fewest words.

5. B

Difficulty: Medium

Category: Writing & Language / Effective Language Use

Strategic Advice: Examine the sentence in relationship to the rest of the paragraph.

Getting to the Answer: The students are learning from the interactive settings, not teaching them. Choice (B), "hone," is the correct verb to describe how to sharpen or improve expertise.

6. D

Difficulty: Hard

Category: Writing & Language / Organization

Strategic Advice: Identify how the content of sentence 6 is related to the entire paragraph.

Getting to the Answer: The compilation of the portfolio happens as a result of the projects discussed in sentence 4 but before the graduates begin their job searches; (D) is correct.

7. A

Difficulty: Easy

Category: Writing & Language / Punctuation

Strategic Advice: Determine if the two parts of the sentence can stand independently.

Getting to the Answer: The gerund phrase "taking on projects for external clients" cannot stand on its own because it lacks a subject. Choice (A) is correct.

8. C
Difficulty: Hard

Category: Writing & Language / Development

Strategic Advice: Identify the central idea of the paragraph in the topic sentence and the details presented in the support.

Getting to the Answer: The central idea is "graphic design features a variety of professional options." Only (C) supports the topic sentence by identifying these types of options. All other choices discuss additional education or salary.

9. B
Difficulty: Easy

Category: Writing & Language / Organization

Strategic Advice: Determine the relationship between the two sentence parts.

Getting to the Answer: The two sentence parts present opposing ideas; (B), the subordinating conjunction "although," is correct.

10. C
Difficulty: Medium

Category: Writing & Language / Sentence Formation

Strategic Advice: Identify the two verbs describing how graphic designers feel about their careers.

Getting to the Answer: Parallel ideas must be expressed in the same grammatical form. Correlative constructions require the transitive verb "satisfying" to be paired with the same form: "invigorating." Choice (C) is correct.

11. A
Difficulty: Hard

Category: Writing & Language / Development

Strategic Advice: Determine the main idea of the paragraph by closely examining the topic sentence.

Getting to the Answer: Choice (A) is the only option that adds relevant information to the rewards experienced by graphic designers in spite of the job competition.

12. A
Difficulty: Easy

Category: Writing & Language / Punctuation

Strategic Advice: Examine each answer choice and determine which presents the list in a grammatically correct manner with proper punctuation.

Getting to the Answer: The list is presented correctly as is, beginning with a colon and featuring the three items separated with commas with no additional information about the topic presented after the listed items. Choice (A) is correct.

13. C
Difficulty: Medium

Category: Writing & Language / Effective Language Use

Strategic Advice: Reread the sentence and select the answer choice that creates the most concise sentence. Minimize wordiness and awkward word combinations to ensure clarity.

Getting to the Answer: Choice (C) is correct as it creates the most concise sentence by removing unnecessary and awkward word choices while retaining the meaning of the sentence.

14. B

Difficulty: Hard

Category: Writing & Language / Shifts in Construction

Strategic Advice: Pay careful attention to any use of the passive voice. To avoid the passive voice, identify the subject and the object and make sure the subject comes before the verb.

Getting to the Answer: The sentence is passive as written, since the object ("educated guesses") should be preceded by the subject's actions. The verb "make" should come first and should be in the present tense. Choice (B) shows the correct construction of the sentence and eliminates the passive voice.

15. B

Difficulty: Medium

Category: Writing & Language / Organization

Strategic Advice: Study the surrounding sentences for context clues to determine which of the answer choices creates a logical flow of ideas.

Getting to the Answer: The preceding sentence discusses early humans using hands and feet to create music, and the following sentence discusses humans using tools to create music. The progression of ideas is a comparison of shared intentions and traits, so "Similarly," or (B), is correct.

16. C

Difficulty: Medium

Category: Writing & Language / Effective Language Use

Strategic Advice: Read the two underlined sentences and determine which answer choice best creates a logical and grammatically correct sentence. A grammatically correct sentence must contain a complete idea, utilizing both a subject and a predicate.

Getting to the Answer: Choice (C) is correct because it creates a logical, grammatically correct sentence with a subject and predicate.

17. D

Difficulty: Medium

Category: Writing & Language / Organization

Strategic Advice: Assess the central idea of both paragraphs and determine which answer choice creates an effective and logical transition from the previous idea while summarizing the next.

Getting to the Answer: The passage states music has affected all global cultures, and the noted paragraph explores two more examples showing how music is a social bonding tool. The correct answer, (D), is the only answer that creates a cohesive, logical transition while not limiting the number of cultures affected by music.

18. C

Difficulty: Hard

Category: Writing & Language / Development

Strategic Advice: Reread the sentence and select the answer choice that clearly conveys the author's full meaning. Sometimes adding a detail or two can improve a sentence and strengthen an author's claims.

Getting to the Answer: The author claims that directions for escape were embedded in well-known lyrics, implying that some people listening to the music may not have discovered the lyrics' true meaning. Choice (C) is correct as it makes this statement clear and direct for the reader and strengthens the author's claim in a concise manner.

19. A

Difficulty: Medium

Category: Writing & Language / Effective Language Use

Strategic Advice: Review the rest of the sentence. Look for context clues that can help you determine which answer choice makes the most sense based on the information provided.

Getting to the Answer: The sentence states that as of 1910, headphones created a shift in how we listen to music, implying that headphones are a relatively new invention. Since "advent" is the only word meaning the headphones first appeared at a specific point in time, (A) is correct.

20. D

Difficulty: Easy

Category: Writing & Language / Organization

Strategic Advice: Read the entire paragraph for sense. Then test the placement given in each answer choice to determine which one creates a paragraph with a logical progression of ideas.

Getting to the Answer: Choice (D) is correct because this sentence creates a transition into the subject discussed in the next paragraph.

21. D

Difficulty: Easy

Category: Writing & Language / Punctuation

Strategic Advice: The placement or lack of apostrophes can alter a noun's possessive meaning. Read the entire sentence to understand the author's intention. Which answer choice uses the correct punctuation to convey this idea?

Getting to the Answer: The nouns "Psychologists and sociologists" are not in possession of anything in this circumstance. Choice (D) correctly reflects this.

22. A

Difficulty: Medium

Category: Writing & Language / Development

Strategic Advice: Review the paragraph to assess areas in which the author may have left out facts or may have provided only partial information. Then determine which answer choice will have the greatest benefit to the reader.

Getting to the Answer: The author specifically mentions "recent studies" but does not cite any figures. Doing so will strengthen the importance of these studies, thus (A) is correct.

CHAPTER 31

PREPARE

1. C
Difficulty: Medium

Category: Writing & Language / Usage

Strategic Advice: Phrases that include the words *most* or *more*, or include adjectives that end in *-er* or *-est*, are points of comparison. Make sure the construction of the comparison is grammatically correct as well as appropriate for the sentence's context.

Getting to the Answer: If the sentence were explicitly comparing two directors, the current construction would be appropriate. When comparing three or more people, the superlative "most important" is correct. If an author does not specify the number of people or things in a group, assume that it is more than two and use the superlative. Choice (C) is correct because it uses the correct superlative construction.

2. B
Difficulty: Hard

Category: Writing & Language / Usage

Strategic Advice: Whenever an idea or topic is referred to by synonymous nouns in different parts of the same sentence, make sure that those nouns are in agreement.

Getting to the Answer: The underlined section is a synonym for a previously mentioned plural noun ("films"). While "work" can refer to a body of productions much like the singular form of "film" can, the author's intention is to use the plural form of the noun. Choice (B) is correct because it is in agreement with "films."

3. C
Difficulty: Medium

Category: Writing & Language / Usage

Strategic Advice: If the underlined section is a pronoun, make sure that it does not create ambiguity or confusion for the reader. If the pronoun's antecedent is unclear, consider replacing it with a noun.

Getting to the Answer: The use of "him" in this location can confuse the reader: Is the author referring to Kurosawa, one of the samurai, or someone else? Given that the author is describing the conception of the lead characters from the film *Seven Samurai*, we can be certain that the underlined section is referring to the characters' creator, Kurosawa. Choice (C) is correct.

4. A
Difficulty: Easy

Category: Writing & Language / Usage

Strategic Advice: An idiom is a combination of words that must be used together to convey either a figurative or literal meaning. Make sure that idioms used in the passage are appropriate for the context and are in agreement with the author's central ideas.

Getting to the Answer: The author is making the point that critics of Kurosawa made two contentions simultaneously—they charged he was both unoriginal and too Westernized. The current construction of "neither...nor" is both grammatically correct and appropriate for the context. Choice (A) is correct.

PRACTICE

5. B

Difficulty: Medium

Category: Writing & Language / Usage

Strategic Advice: Make sure that comparisons use the correct construction that is aligned with the central idea and context of the passage.

Getting to the Answer: The author is making a comparison involving all North American animals—definitely a group larger than two. A superlative construction is appropriate, but it also needs to align with the thesis that the opossum is a very unusual animal. Choice (B) is correct because it is grammatically correct and fits the author's central idea.

6. D

Difficulty: Medium

Category: Writing & Language / Usage

Strategic Advice: When a pronoun is the subject of a sentence, make sure that its antecedent is clear. If it is not clear to which noun the pronoun is referring, then replace the pronoun.

Getting to the Answer: The current construction of the sentence creates an ambiguity: does "It" refer to the opossum or the kangaroo? Since the passage describes the characteristics of the opossum, this sentence should be about that animal as well. Choice (D) is correct because it makes the sentence's subject clear to the reader.

7. C

Difficulty: Medium

Category: Writing & Language / Usage

Strategic Advice: Make sure that the proper prepositions are being used in the passage.

Getting to the Answer: The preposition "in" is incorrect given the context. The author is describing "limitations *on* the amount of food... that can be stored..." Choice (C) is correct. If idioms are tricky, think of an analogous situation. A computer's limited warranty has limitations *on* the kinds of things you can do with it. It doesn't have limitations *in* those things.

8. C

Difficulty: Easy

Category: Writing & Language / Usage

Strategic Advice: Review a pronoun's antecedent to make sure there is agreement throughout the sentence or section.

Getting to the Answer: Early in this sentence, the author establishes the singular possessive form ("the opossum's") as the antecedent of the pronoun in the underlined section. Also, except for an earlier section that discusses "the female opossum," the author uses the non-gendered pronoun "it" when referring to the animal. Choice (C) is correct because it is singular, possessive, and non-gendered.

PERFORM

9. A

Difficulty: Medium

Category: Writing & Language / Usage

Strategic Advice: Read the sentence in its entirety to make sure there is no subject-verb disagreement.

Getting to the Answer: The verb in the underlined section, "were," appears after the parenthetical remark set aside by dashes. The current version of the subject, "blimps," is in agreement with the verb. No change is necessary; (A) is correct.

10. B

Difficulty: Medium

Category: Writing & Language / Usage

Strategic Advice: Make sure that comparisons are in the appropriate format—comparative when comparing two things, superlative when comparing three or more things.

Getting to the Answer: In the previous sentence, the author states that the *Hindenburg* was "one of a kind." The ship was unique out of all airships, making superlative descriptions appropriate. Given the superlative construction and the author's focus on the ship's dimensions, (B) is correct because the reader can infer that the *Hindenburg* was the "largest" airship of its time.

11. C

Difficulty: Medium

Category: Writing & Language / Usage

Strategic Advice: Complex sentences can often benefit from the use of pronouns, reducing wordiness and repetition. That said, make sure that the use of a pronoun will not introduce ambiguity into the sentence.

Getting to the Answer: In a complicated sentence including multiple nouns, it is often better to avoid pronouns to preserve the clarity of the author's claims. Choice (C) is correct.

12. B

Difficulty: Hard

Category: Writing & Language / Usage

Strategic Advice: Check to see if the underlined section is part of an idiomatic expression, such as *either…or.*

Getting to the Answer: The sentence contains the first half of the idiomatic combination *not only…but also.* The use of "and" in this context is incorrect. Choice (B), "but also," is correct.

13. B

Difficulty: Easy

Category: Writing & Language / Usage

Strategic Advice: Pay attention to commonly confused words, such as *except* and *accept*, to make sure that careless mistakes do not go unaddressed in a passage.

Getting to the Answer: "It's" is a contraction of "it is" and is incorrect in this context. The sentence requires the singular possessive pronoun, "its." Choice (B) is correct.

14. C

Difficulty: Medium

Category: Writing & Language / Usage

Strategic Advice: Make sure the underlined section is using the appropriate prepositions.

Getting to the Answer: If the verb "rest" refers to a direct object, the preposition "on" is required. Choice (C) is correct because it correctly constructs the idiom.

15. D

Difficulty: Easy

Category: Writing & Language / Usage

Strategic Advice: Examine the use of nouns that are used as synonyms within the same sentence. They should agree in number, and their shared meaning should either be easily understood or previously explained by the author.

Getting to the Answer: At this point in the passage, the author has already established that "balloon" is a synonym for "blimp" and "airship." The underlined section is therefore the correct term, but it disagrees in number with the rest of the sentence in which the associated noun ("airship") is singular. Choice (D) is correct because it is in numerical agreement with the previous noun.

16. B

Difficulty: Easy

Category: Writing & Language / Usage

Strategic Advice: Examine the sentence's use of pronouns for agreement with antecedents.

Getting to the Answer: The sentence's use of "their" as a possessive pronoun conflicts with the antecedent "the airship," which is singular. Choice (B) is correct because it is a singular possessive pronoun in agreement with its antecedent.

EXTRA PRACTICE

1. B

Difficulty: Medium

Category: Writing & Language / Sentence Formation

Strategic Advice: Compare the two parts of the sentence. Is the second part a subordinate or coordinate clause?

Getting to the Answer: "Since" is a conjunction used between subordinating ideas. These two clauses are coordinating and require a coordinating conjunction meaning "in addition to." Choice (B) is correct.

2. D

Difficulty: Medium

Category: Writing & Language / Effective Language Use

Strategic Advice: Analyze how the underlined word is used in the sentence. Test each answer choice to see if it improves the overall clarity of the text.

Getting to the Answer: The opening sentences of the passage are about how the cold weather makes starting cars difficult. When used as a verb, "credit" means to have faith in something.

Choice (D), "blame," means to hold responsible, and is correct.

3. D

Difficulty: Hard

Category: Writing & Language / Organization

Strategic Advice: Review how the content of sentence 3 is related to the entire paragraph. Recall that transitions help the reader understand logical relationships between ideas. What words in sentence 3 signal a transition?

Getting to the Answer: Sentence 4 explains what happens when the number of electrons increases. Because sentence 3 further develops the explanation of what happens when the number of electrons decreases, the transition "likewise" is a clue that it should follow sentence 4. Choice (D) is correct.

4. A

Difficulty: Hard

Category: Writing & Language / Development

Strategic Advice: Identify the key details in the paragraph. Then, summarize them to find the central idea.

Getting to the Answer: All of the sentences in this paragraph describe how a battery is constructed and works. Choice (A) is correct.

5. D

Difficulty: Easy

Category: Writing & Language / Punctuation

Strategic Advice: Determine if the items listed need to be treated as a series.

Getting to the Answer: Since there are only two items, no commas are needed. Choice (D) is correct.

6. C
Difficulty: Easy

Category: Writing & Language / Usage

Strategic Advice: Determine the tense and the number of the subject. Then, predict the verb form that matches.

Getting to the Answer: Since "lead oxide" is singular and the paragraph is written in present tense, (C) is correct.

7. C
Difficulty: Medium

Category: Writing & Language / Effective Language Use

Strategic Advice: Establish how the underlined word is used in the sentence; consider the connotations and denotations of the answer choices. Remember that the correct term should reflect the scientific subject matter.

Getting to the Answer: "Boundary" is a term meaning a limitation. "Circuit," a noun, is the scientific term that means circumference or course. Choice (C) is correct.

8. B
Difficulty: Hard

Category: Writing & Language / Development

Strategic Advice: Closely examine the topic sentence and the supporting details; identify the central idea of the paragraph.

Getting to the Answer: Choice (B) is the only option that adds supporting information about how a current flows through a battery charger.

9. D
Difficulty: Medium

Category: Writing & Language / Effective Language Use

Strategic Advice: Look at how the word is used in the sentence; analyze its grammatical function. Use context clues to determine which choice is correct.

Getting to the Answer: "Practicality" is an adverb meaning in a practical manner; "probability" is a noun meaning likelihood. Choice (D) is correct.

10. A
Difficulty: Medium

Category: Writing & Language / Usage

Strategic Advice: Test all of the answer choices. Recall that contractions represent two words combined as one.

Getting to the Answer: The contraction "it's" is short for *it is* and is inappropriate here. Choice (A) is correct.

11. A
Difficulty: Hard

Category: Writing & Language / Quantitative

Strategic Advice: Study the graph carefully and consider how its data points connect to the content of the passage.

Getting to the Answer: The overall graph trend suggests that battery performance peaks at moderate temperatures, suffers slightly at higher temperatures, and declines greatly at lower ones. The lowest point of the *x*-axis indicates a temperature of approximately 30°F. At this temperature, for example, a battery-operated car can travel a distance of approximately 20 miles as shown on the *y*-axis, as opposed to peak performance of more than 40 miles. Since cold temperatures adversely affect the battery performance of an electric car, choice (A) is correct.

12. B

Difficulty: Hard

Category: Writing & Language / Effective Language Use

Strategic Advice: Consider the specific action being described by this word. Which answer choice is the most precise?

Getting to the Answer: The paragraph states that President Roosevelt asks Congress to declare war, an action that has a relationship to "The United States' entrance into World War II." This action leads directly to war. Choice (B), "signaled," conveys the most direct relationship between these two ideas and it is therefore correct.

13. B

Difficulty: Medium

Category: Writing & Language / Organization

Strategic Advice: Define the relationship between these two clauses, as well as between this and the previous sentence. A semicolon links two complete but separate independent clauses within a sentence.

Getting to the Answer: The sentence states two things: "Japan had not capitulated," and "it had strengthened its expansionist aims." The relationship is one of opposites. Both (B) and C link the two parts of the sentence in the correct way. Only (B), however, maintains the correct relationship with the previous sentence.

14. C

Difficulty: Medium

Category: Writing & Language / Shifts in Construction

Strategic Advice: Recall that the passive voice is used to describe a state of being. It requires an auxiliary verb and a past participle.

Getting to the Answer: The conflict in Japan is being described in the passive voice. To be grammatically correct, the verb form should be that of an auxiliary verb ("was") and a past participle ("understood"). Choice (C) is correct.

15. D

Difficulty: Hard

Category: Writing & Language / Development

Strategic Advice: Before reading the answer choices, think of a sentence that would make sentence 2 more credible if inserted here.

Getting to the Answer: Sentence 2 states that "American intelligence officials" had a theory about Japan's behavior. Therefore, the correct sentence will strengthen this idea. Choice (D) explains that as a consequence of America's wrong ideas about Japan, it had not bothered to defend Pearl Harbor well. This explanation supports the assertion made in sentence 2.

16. B

Difficulty: Medium

Category: Writing & Language / Punctuation

Strategic Advice: How can the relationship between Japan's plan and the phrase "destroy the Pacific Fleet" be clarified?

Getting to the Answer: The plan is to "destroy the Pacific Fleet." The two ideas are equivalent. The best way to convey this direct relationship is by introducing the phrase with a colon. Choice (B) is correct.

17. B

Difficulty: Medium

Category: Writing & Language / Effective Language Use

Strategic Advice: Identify the overall purpose and tone of the paragraph. The correct answer will convey the information needed to make the sentence effective without being excessively informal.

Getting to the Answer: In this sentence, Japan both plans and practices for months. These two ideas can be combined without changing the paragraph's informative tone. Choice (B) communicates the ideas of the sentence in the most elegant and neutral way, and it is therefore correct.

18. D
Difficulty: Medium

Category: Writing & Language / Effective Language Use

Strategic Advice: Consider whether the underlined text has any repetitive information. The correct answer will avoid excessive or redundant information.

Getting to the Answer: "8:00 AM" and "8:00 in the morning" convey the same idea. Contained within both "AM" and "in the morning" is the idea of time, so "o'clock" is unnecessary if one of these expressions is used. Choice (D) successfully communicates the time of day without being redundant.

19. A
Difficulty: Medium

Category: Writing & Language / Sentence Formation

Strategic Advice: Recall that a descriptive phrase that adds information without forming the main part of the sentence should use a participle, not a regular verb, in order to avoid creating a run-on sentence.

Getting to the Answer: Although the sentence should communicate that the bombs weighed

"over a ton and a half," the main verb in this sentence is "destroyed." Therefore, the phrase should include the present participle "weighing." Choice (A), the sentence as currently written, is the correct answer.

20. C
Difficulty: Hard

Category: Writing & Language / Effective Language Use

Strategic Advice: Read around the underlined word to find clues to its meaning. Then, pick the answer that offers the clearest and most concise meaning.

Getting to the Answer: In this context, military equipment is typically described using the expression "sustained damage." While the other choices may make sense grammatically, (C) provides a clear and concise term that makes sense in context.

21. A
Difficulty: Hard

Category: Writing & Language / Effective Language Use

Strategic Advice: Describe the purpose of this paragraph in your own words before looking at the answer choices.

Getting to the Answer: The rest of the paragraph describes how Japan's attack had not meant to provoke war but resulted in the United States entering the war. Choice (A) sets up the next sentence, in which Roosevelt makes clear that the United States is willing to go to war with Japan.

22. A
Difficulty: Easy

Category: Writing & Language / Quantitative

Strategic Advice: Be careful not to bring in outside knowledge. The correct answer choice will be explicitly supported by information in the timeline.

Getting to the Answer: The timeline presents a group of historical events, only one of which is reflected in the answer choices. Other choices may or may not be true, but only the sentence as currently written draws its facts from the timeline. Choice (A) is correct.

CHAPTER 32

PREPARE

1. D
Difficulty: Hard

Category: Writing & Language / Punctuation

Strategic Advice: When a period is underlined, make sure it correctly separates two complete sentences.

Getting to the Answer: Because the first clause is dependent, a period between the clauses creates a fragment. You can eliminate B and C because both choices are used to join independent clauses. By separating the clauses with a comma, the two clauses are properly connected, which makes (D) correct.

2. B
Difficulty: Medium

Category: Writing & Language / Punctuation

Strategic Advice: A semicolon is used to connect two independent clauses that express different ideas of equal weight.

Getting to the Answer: The clause after the semicolon is not an independent clause and must be correctly incorporated into the main sentence. The idea the sentence is expressing is Mallory's emphatic answer to the "non-climbers." A colon correctly combines the two clauses, indicating the emphasis the author places on Mallory's answer. Choice (B) is correct.

3. B
Difficulty: Easy

Category: Writing & Language / Punctuation

Strategic Advice: Make sure you don't confuse possessive determiners, contractions, and adverbs.

Getting to the Answer: "It's" is a contraction for "it is" and does not make sense in this sentence. "The" is an article and does not convey the sense of possession needed. The "it's" in the passage should be a possessive pronoun, which is "its." Choice (B) is correct.

4. A
Difficulty: Easy

Category: Writing & Language / Punctuation

Strategic Advice: Three or more items in a series must be separated using commas.

Getting to the Answer: This series contains three items and is correct as written. Separate each item with a comma and use the conjunction "and" with the comma to separate the final item from the rest of the series. Choice (A) is correct.

5. B
Difficulty: Hard

Category: Writing & Language / Punctuation

Strategic Advice: Make sure that phrases set off by commas are nonrestrictive.

Getting to the Answer: As written, the sentence incorrectly suggests that after receiving proper training, scientists make claims about chimpanzees. From the context of the sentence, it is clear that the chimpanzees receive the training. Read the sentence without the phrase "the scientists claim." Now, the sentence focuses on the chimpanzees and still makes logical sense without the information about the scientists. Choice (B) correctly sets off the phrase with commas, indicating that it is nonessential.

6. B
Difficulty: Medium

Category: Writing & Language / Punctuation

Strategic Advice: If the error is unclear, the underlined punctuation may be unnecessary.

Getting to the Answer: The comma with the conjunction "and" improperly separates the sentence into clauses and creates a fragment. Determine how the underlined infinitive verb "to communicate" relates to the other verbs in the sentence. In this sentence, "to communicate" forms a compound predicate with the verb phrase "are able to understand," with "chimpanzees" as the subject. The comma is unnecessary. Choice (B) correctly eliminates the punctuation.

PRACTICE

7. D
Difficulty: Easy

Category: Writing & Language / Punctuation

Strategic Advice: Use commas to separate three or more items forming a series or list.

Getting to the Answer: This series contains four items. Separate each item with a comma and use a comma with the conjunction "and" to separate the final item from the rest of the series. Choice (D) is correct.

8. C
Difficulty: Hard

Category: Writing & Language / Punctuation

Strategic Advice: When a period is underlined, make sure it's being used correctly.

Getting to the Answer: The period correctly separates two sentences but breaks up the flow of the ideas. The second sentence contributes useful information regarding the results of using the "12-note scale." Make the second sentence a modifying phrase, and connect it to the sentence with a comma. Choice (C) is correct.

9. B
Difficulty: Medium

Category: Writing & Language / Punctuation

Strategic Advice: When you see a phrase set off by commas, always read the sentence without the phrase to determine if the phrase is nonessential.

Getting to the Answer: Although the sentence is still grammatically correct without the information that is set off by the commas, an essential part of the meaning is lost. The author is stating that it is the group setting that distinguishes the improvisation found in jazz from the improvisation found in other types of music. Choice (B) properly removes the commas that set off the phrase.

10. A
Difficulty: Easy

Category: Writing & Language / Punctuation

Strategic Advice: When an underlined section features an apostrophe after a noun, check the noun's number.

Getting to the Answer: This sentence is correct as written. Although there are many styles of music, the noun "music" is a collective noun and singular. Choice (A) correctly uses the singular possessive.

PERFORM

11. B
Difficulty: Medium

Category: Writing & Language / Punctuation

Strategic Advice: When a comma is underlined, check to see if the parts of the sentence before and after the comma need to be separated.

Getting to the Answer: In this sentence, the comma separates the subordinate conjunction "although" from the clause it introduces and breaks the link between the dependent clause and the main clause. Choice (B) correctly eliminates the unnecessary punctuation.

12. C

Difficulty: Hard

Category: Writing & Language / Punctuation

Strategic Advice: Make sure period use is warranted—determine whether the sentences should really be separate.

Getting to the Answer: Although the second sentence is an independent clause and could stand on its own, the information in the second sentence belongs in the previous sentence. Choice (C) correctly uses a colon to indicate a break in thought to provide additional explanatory information.

13. D

Difficulty: Hard

Category: Writing & Language / Punctuation

Strategic Advice: A period separates independent clauses into sentences and indicates a strong break in thought. Make sure the context of the sentences requires them to be separated.

Getting to the Answer: Since both clauses form complete sentences, look at the information they share. Each sentence has Mauritius as its subject and a verb phrase providing information about the island. Combine the two sentences by creating a compound predicate joined by the conjunction "and." Choice (D) is correct.

14. A

Difficulty: Medium

Category: Writing & Language / Punctuation

Strategic Advice: Although a parenthetical or nonrestrictive phrase may appear in the beginning, middle, or end of a sentence, punctuation will always separate it from the rest of the sentence. Read the sentence without the parenthetical information to determine if the sentence still makes sense.

Getting to the Answer: This sentence is correct as written. Because the sentence makes logical sense without the phrase beginning with "making the dodo," the comma is necessary to correctly set off the phrase. Choice D may be tempting, but without the comma, the phrase incorrectly modifies "predators," suggesting that the predators themselves, not the dodo's failure to recognize the danger those predators posed, made the dodo easier to catch. Choice (A) is correct.

15. D

Difficulty: Easy

Category: Writing & Language / Punctuation

Strategic Advice: Separate three or more items in a series or list with commas. Separate the last two items with a comma and the conjunction "and."

Getting to the Answer: This series contains six distinct items. Separate each item with a comma and use the conjunction "and" with a comma to separate the final item from the rest of the series. Choice (D) is correct.

16. B

Difficulty: Easy

Category: Writing & Language / Punctuation

Strategic Advice: Watch out for easily confused words: keep straight your possessive determiners, contractions, and adverbs.

Getting to the Answer: "Who's" is a contraction for "who is" or "who has," which makes no sense in the context of the underlined portion. Choice (B) correctly uses "whose," the possessive form of the relative pronoun "who."

17. C

Difficulty: Medium

Category: Writing & Language / Punctuation

Strategic Advice: If a dash is used to introduce a break in thought, a second dash must be used to end the parenthetical phrase unless a period ends both the phrase and the sentence.

Getting to the Answer: Determine if the information after the dash is parenthetical or non-restrictive by reading the sentence without that information. Although the phrase provides a description of how the "colonial powers" treated Mauritius, the sentence makes logical sense without it. The phrase is therefore parenthetical and must be properly set off. Only (C) correctly sets off the phrase with both an opening and closing dash.

18. A

Difficulty: Medium

Category: Writing & Language / Punctuation

Strategic Advice: Avoid using unnecessary punctuation. Reread the sentence to determine how its parts are related.

Getting to the Answer: This sentence is correct as written because no punctuation is required. The phrase "through its advantageous geographic location and large labor force" completes the thought in the sentence by providing information on how Mauritius "balances" and "flourishes." Choice (A) is correct.

EXTRA PRACTICE

1. B

Difficulty: Medium

Category: Writing & Language / Usage

Strategic Advice: Consider the function of the underlined word in the sentence.

Getting to the Answer: The underlined word should be a plural possessive pronoun that refers to "coaches and trainers." Choice (B) is correct.

2. B

Difficulty: Medium

Category: Writing & Language / Effective Language Use

Strategic Advice: Think about the overall meaning of the sentence. Consider which answer choice most closely matches the author's intended meaning.

Getting to the Answer: The author explains that some people connect, or equate, the burning feeling experienced while exercising with burning calories. "Equate" is the most precise word to convey this meaning. Choice (B) is correct.

3. B

Difficulty: Medium

Category: Writing & Language / Organization

Strategic Advice: Two complete thoughts make up this sentence. Consider the relationship between the thoughts expressed on either side of the semicolon.

Getting to the Answer: The author presents contrasting ideas in this sentence. The relationship between these ideas is best expressed by inserting the transition word "instead" to indicate the contrast between the thoughts. Choice (B) is correct.

4. A

Difficulty: Hard

Category: Writing & Language / Development

Strategic Advice: The correct answer will include an idea that ties all of the information in the paragraph together. Try to put the central idea into your own words.

Getting to the Answer: This paragraph is primarily about how muscles use glucose to get the energy they need to move. Choice (A) is correct because it most effectively states the central idea.

5. C

Difficulty: Medium

Category: Writing & Language / Usage

Strategic Advice: Identify the noun in the clause. Determine whether the noun is singular or plural and what verb tense is used elsewhere in the sentence.

Getting to the Answer: The noun in this clause, "cells," is plural, and the rest of the sentence is written in present tense. Choice (C) is correct because it features the plural present tense form of the verb "to continue."

6. B

Difficulty: Medium

Category: Writing & Language / Punctuation

Strategic Advice: Determine the function of the phrase "found in vinegar" within the sentence. Remember that nonrestrictive elements must be set off from the rest of the sentence with commas before and after.

Getting to the Answer: The phrase "found in vinegar" modifies "acetic acid" and is not essential to the understanding of the sentence. Choice (B) is correct.

7. D

Difficulty: Medium

Category: Writing & Language / Effective Language Use

Strategic Advice: Reread the sentence with each of the answer choices in place of the underlined word. All of the answer choices are similar in meaning, so think about the connotation of

each one in relation to the overall meaning of the sentence.

Getting to the Answer: In this sentence, the connotation of "irritates" most precisely communicates the meaning of what the author is trying to convey to the reader: bothers. While "annoys" is similar to this meaning, it is mostly used when referring to people, not inanimate or biological objects like lactic acid. Choice (D) is correct.

8. C

Difficulty: Medium

Category: Writing & Language / Development

Strategic Advice: Identify the central idea of paragraph 4. Think about which sentences are essential to the understanding of the rest of the paragraph. The correct answer could be taken out without changing the meaning or the reader's understanding of the central idea.

Getting to the Answer: Although (C) is related to the central idea, the details in this sentence provide the least amount of support because they provide an example of a situation in which lactic acid builds up more quickly. The central idea of the paragraph, however, is the buildup and conversion of lactic acid during exercise. Choice (C) is correct.

9. C

Difficulty: Medium

Category: Writing & Language / Punctuation

Strategic Advice: Determine whether two complete thoughts are expressed in this sentence. Two complete sentences, each with a subject and predicate, become a run-on without proper punctuation.

Getting to the Answer: As written, this is a run-on sentence. Placing a semicolon between the two complete thoughts makes the sentence grammatically correct. Choice (C) is correct.

10. B

Difficulty: Easy

Category: Writing & Language / Usage

Strategic Advice: Read the entire sentence. Make sure that related pronouns agree in number and person.

Getting to the Answer: In this sentence, the author is referring to all human beings and uses "we" to do so. The underlined pronoun "you" does not match the use of the third person plural pronoun. Choice (B) is correct.

11. C

Difficulty: Hard

Category: Writing & Language / Quantitative

Strategic Advice: The correct answer will both reflect the information presented in the graph and be an appropriate conclusion for the passage. Avoid answers like B that do not strengthen the central idea of the passage.

Getting to the Answer: Choice (C) is correct because it contains details presented in the graph that are relevant to the central idea of the passage and provides an appropriate conclusion to the passage.

12. B

Difficulty: Medium

Category: Writing & Language / Quantitative

Strategic Advice: The table gives specific information about various bridges. Interpret the information to choose the correct answer choice.

Getting to the Answer: Choice (B) accurately reflects the information in the table since the Tower Bridge was not built until 1894.

13. B

Difficulty: Medium

Category: Writing & Language / Effective Language Use

Strategic Advice: Watch out for answer choices that may have incorrect transition words or be incorrect in usage or in punctuation.

Getting to the Answer: Choice (B) joins the sentences concisely and correctly by using the conjunction "and" to connect the two complete ideas.

14. D

Difficulty: Medium

Category: Writing & Language / Organization

Strategic Advice: Study the relationship between the two parts of the sentence to determine which transition word would work logically. Substitute each transition word in the sentence to see which fits best.

Getting to the Answer: Only "however" (a contrast transition) in (D) creates a correct and logical relationship between the two parts of the sentence because it discusses the difficulties that were encountered in building the bridge.

15. B

Difficulty: Easy

Category: Writing & Language / Effective Language Use

Strategic Advice: The context of the sentence suggests which word would have the correct connotation. Substitute each word choice in the sentence to see how it fits with the context.

Getting to the Answer: Only (B) correctly fits the context of the sentence, which suggests that the bridge was something that people very much wanted; "longed" embodies this notion.

16. C

Difficulty: Easy

Category: Writing & Language / Effective Language Use

Strategic Advice: Watch out for answer choices like A, which are extremely wordy. It is better to be as direct and simple as possible.

Getting to the Answer: Additional adjectives do not add more meaning to this content. Choice (C) is the most concise and effective way of stating the information in the passage and is therefore correct.

17. D

Difficulty: Easy

Category: Writing & Language / Usage

Strategic Advice: Reread the sentence to see what the antecedent is for the underlined pronoun and determine if the two agree.

Getting to the Answer: The antecedent in this sentence is "Roebling," which calls for a singular masculine possessive pronoun. Choice (D) is correct.

18. D

Difficulty: Medium

Category: Writing & Language / Effective Language Use

Strategic Advice: Consider the connotations of each word. Substitute each word choice back into the sentence to see how it fits with the context.

Getting to the Answer: Choice (D) fits with the context of the sentence, which suggests that such accidents do not happen often. While "special" in A and "exceptional" in B can indicate uniqueness, they are too positive. Choice (D) is correct.

19. C

Difficulty: Medium

Category: Writing & Language / Sentence Formation

Strategic Advice: Look at the other verb in the sentence to see if the verbs are parallel in structure.

Getting to the Answer: Choice (C) is the correct form of the verb that is parallel to "succumbed," which appears earlier in the sentence.

20. D

Difficulty: Hard

Category: Writing & Language / Development

Strategic Advice: To find the central idea of a paragraph, identify important details and summarize them. Then, find the choice that is the closest to your summary. Do not choose a detail rather than a central idea.

Getting to the Answer: The paragraph primarily discusses the hardships faced by workers building the bridge. Choice (D) most accurately summarizes the central idea of the paragraph.

21. B

Difficulty: Medium

Category: Writing & Language / Sentence Formation

Strategic Advice: Two complete thoughts should be two separate sentences. Be careful of inappropriate transition words.

Getting to the Answer: Choice (B) divides the two thoughts into two complete sentences by adding a period and capitalizing the first word of the second sentence and is therefore correct.

22. C

Difficulty: Hard

Category: Writing & Language / Development

Strategic Advice: To find the correct answer, look for the sentence that does not exclude any necessary details from the underlined portion.

Getting to the Answer: Choice (C) correctly maintains the author's inclusion of various details about when the bridge was completed and the significance of Emily's ride.

CHAPTER 33

EXTRA PRACTICE

Adapted from "Freedom or Death," a speech delivered by Emmeline Pankhurst on November 13, 1913, in Hartford, Connecticut

Mrs. Hepburn, ladies and gentlemen:

    Tonight I am not here to advocate woman suffrage. American suffragists can do that very well for themselves. I am here as a soldier who has temporarily left the field of battle in order to explain what civil war is like when civil war is waged by women. I am here as a person who, according to the law courts of my country, it has been decided, is of no value to the community at all: and I am adjudged because of my life to be a dangerous person.

purpose

war metaphor

    Now, first of all I want to make you understand the inevitableness of revolution and civil war, even on the part of women, when you reach a certain stage in the development of a community's life. It is quite easy for you to understand the desirability of revolution if I were a man. If an Irish revolutionary had addressed this meeting, and many have addressed meetings all over the United States during the last twenty or thirty years, it would not be necessary for that revolutionary to explain the need of revolution beyond saying that the people of his country were denied—and by people, meaning men—were denied the right of self-government. That would explain the whole situation. If I were a man and I said to you, "I come from a country which professes to have representative institutions and yet denies me, a taxpayer, an inhabitant of the country, representative rights," you would at once understand that that human being, being a man, was justified in the adoption of revolutionary methods to get representative institutions. But since I am a woman it is necessary in the twentieth century to explain why women have adopted revolutionary methods in order to win the rights of citizenship.

hypothetical

*must do
this bc
woman*

    You see, in spite of a good deal that we hear about revolutionary methods not being necessary for American women, we women, in trying to make our case clear, always have to make as part of our argument, and urge upon men in our audience the fact—a very simple fact—that women are human beings. I want to put a few political arguments before you—not arguments for the suffrage, because I said when I opened, I didn't mean to do that—but arguments for the adoption of militant methods in order to win political rights.

*kinds of
arguments
for ev.*

    Suppose the men of Hartford had a grievance, and they laid that grievance before their legislature, and the legislature obstinately refused to listen

more hypothet.

to them, or to remove their grievance, what would be the proper and the constitutional and the practical way of getting their grievance removed? Well, it is perfectly obvious at the next general election, when the legislature is elected, the men of Hartford would turn out that legislature and elect a new one: entirely change the personnel of an obstinate legislature.

But let the men of Hartford imagine that they were not in the position of being voters at all, that they were governed without their consent being obtained, that the legislature turned an absolutely deaf ear to their demands, what would the men of Hartford do then? They couldn't vote the legislature out. They would have to make a choice of two evils: they would either have to submit indefinitely to an unjust state of affairs, or they would have to rise up and adopt some of the antiquated means by which men in the past got their grievances remedied. We know what happened when your forefathers decided that they must have representation for taxation, many, many years ago. When they felt they couldn't wait any longer, when they laid all the arguments before an obstinate British government that they could think of, and when their arguments were absolutely disregarded, when every other means had failed, they began by the tea party at Boston, and they went on until they had won the independence of the United States of America. That is what happened in the old days.

It is perfectly evident to any logical mind that when you have got the vote, you can get out of any legislature whatever you want, or if you cannot get it, you can send them about their business and choose other people who will be more attentive to your demands, But it is clear to the meanest intelligence that if you have not got the vote, you must either submit to laws just or unjust, administration just or unjust, or the time inevitably comes when you will revolt against that injustice and use violent means to put an end to it.

effects of
men not
having rights

ex. of Am.
Rev.

war = inevitable

Sample Student Response #1

Emmeline Pankhurst is a militant suffragist, but she has not come to Hartford, Connecticut, to speak about suffrage. No, she makes that clear with the first line of her speech. Pankhurst does not want to explain why woman suffrage is just and necessary; she has come to explain why *the way* that she and her fellow suffragists fight for suffrage is just and necessary. To Pankhurst, the battle for woman suffrage is a civil war, and she is a soldier in that war ready to justify not her cause but her methods, not her ideas but her strategies, not her goals but her tactics. Pankhurst claims that the government, by denying women the vote to begin with, has left them with only protest and revolt as a means to win political change. She positions her speech as a defense of her methods, but as such, it also affirms her cause.

From the start, Pankhurst excites interest by claiming that the fight for woman suffrage is not merely a difference of opinion but a battle. She is not a reformer, an activist, or an ideologue. She is a soldier! She couches her argument in terms that demand the attention and the empathy of men and woman alike. After all, the United States is rooted in a history of revolution and civil war. Pankhurst draws a comparison with Irish revolutionaries as well. Anyone familiar with global events in of the late 19th and early 20th century would know that Irish revolutionaries were actively appealing to sympathies abroad, especially among Americans. In drawing this comparison, Pankhurst not only equates woman suffrage with political revolutions but also equates women with men, the underlying principle of the woman suffrage movement. She claims that if she were a male revolutionary, no one would doubt the right of her methods; it is only because she is a female revolutionary that there is any question. Furthermore, she makes clear that the battle itself is for "the rights of citizenship." By this rhetoric, she makes clear that suffrage is something to which women are entitled as citizens. This means that to deny woman suffrage is to deny them as citizens. She goes on to argue that the issue in question is not only suffrage but also women's status as human beings. To deny women suffrage is not just to deny them citizenship but to deny them humanity. Pankhurst appeals to her audience's higher emotions and sense of right, and weaves justification of her desired reform into her defense of the means to win that reform.

Pankhurst shifts back to defense of militant protest tactics, and reminds the audience that she is not there to discuss suffrage. In this way, she placates members of the audience who might question suffrage while again assuming the merit of suffrage. The end is just. She has only to justify her means. Pankhurst brings home the comparison to the *men* of Hartford. They are citizens with rights under their government. If they objected to the governance of their leaders, what would they do? Why, they would "turn out that legislature and elect a new one," of course! That's how political matters are resolved in democratic society. But what if they could not? Pankhurst argues that the men of Hartford, if denied their political rights as citizens, would do what their forebears had done. Here, she makes another emotional appeal by focusing on the heart of America. When denied their rights, the American revolutionaries used militant forms of protest, as demonstrated in the Boston Tea Party. When that failed, they took up arms and declared their independence. As Pankhurst explains, the political revolutionaries of the past had to choose between "two evils": submitting to "an unjust state of affairs" or rising up and using "antiquated means by which men in the past got their grievances remedied." Pankhurst appeals to the morality of her audience by making clear that she considers violent methods unpleasant. The implication is that she and the suffragists have been denied the preferred nonviolent solutions by being denied the vote. Again, Pankhurst skillfully weaves an argument for suffrage into her defense of the tactics to win suffrage.

Pankhurst concludes by reaffirming her underlying assumption—that suffrage is just and necessary. "It is perfectly evident to any logical mind," she says, suggesting that reason itself is on the side of the suffragists. She explains that when you have the vote, you don't need to use other protest methods—violent or otherwise; however, when you cannot take part in government in a legitimate way, then you must either submit or revolt. Pankhurst ties together the stated purpose of her speech with the underlying purpose. Submission is not an option. Their cause is just; therefore, their means, the only means open to the suffragists, is just. Throughout her speech, Pankhurst defends suffragists' militant activism, but in so doing, she justifies the cause of that activism. After all, if women had the vote, they would not need to revolt. To win revolutionary change, suffragists must adopt revolutions means. Pankhurst's argument feeds on itself, and the act of assumption becomes an act of persuasion.

Reading—4: The writer thoroughly understands the source text as evidenced by her use of paraphrases of Pankhurst's speech as well as direct quotations. She accurately summarizes Pankhurst's central idea (*Pankhurst does not want to explain why woman suffrage is just and necessary; she has come to explain why* the way *that she and her fellow suffragists fight for suffrage is just and necessary*) in the introduction and also cites many details and examples that support Pankhurst's purpose, explaining how these details interrelate with Pankhurst's central argument. This response demonstrates thorough comprehension of the source text.

Analysis—2: This response offers limited analysis of the source text and therefore partial understanding of the analytical task. In the second body paragraph, the writer lists different features of Pankhurst's speech (such as historical examples and appealing to the *audience's higher emotions and sense of right*), but does not expand on how these features contribute to or advance Pankhurst's central argument. Rather than an analysis of how Pankhurst persuades her audience that violent and nonviolent protest tactics are necessary to gain political rights for women, this response is more a summary of Pankhurst's speech.

Writing—3: The writer demonstrates effective use and control of standard written English in this mostly cohesive response. She includes her own central claim in the introduction (*To Pankhurst, the battle for woman suffrage is a civil war, and she is a soldier in that war ready to justify not her cause but her methods, not her ideas but her strategies, not her goals but her tactics*) and uses a variety of sentence structures. The two body paragraphs could be better organized—each seems like a hodgepodge of separate points rather than a cohesive, in-depth exploration of one feature of Pankhurst's argument, detracting from a coherent progression of ideas. While the overall style and tone is objective, the writer does deviate from formal writing at times: *Anyone familiar with global events in of the late 19th and early 20th century would know that Irish revolutionaries were actively appealing to sympathies abroad, especially among Americans.* Overall, the writing in this response is proficient.

Sample Student Response #2

Emmeline Pankhurst does appear in Hartford, Connecticut, to speak about suffrage. From the start of her speech, she makes clear that she does not want to explain why woman suffrage is necessary. Rather, she means to explain why the way that she and her fellow suffragists fight for suffrage is necessary. Pankhurst looks at the battle for woman suffrage as a civil war. She calls herself a soldier sent to explain her tactics in the war, not the importance of her side in the war. In her speech, Pankhurst explains that she and the suffragists must use violent means to win change because it is the only means open to them. She asserts that they cannot win reform any other way precisely because suffrage is denied to them. In this way, she uses her defense of her methods to actually justify the underlying cause—suffrage for women.

Pankhurst grabs her audience's attention by calling woman suffrage not just a political debate but a civil war. In the same way, she makes herself more than a reformer or an activist; she declares herself a soldier. In this way, she gets men and woman to listen to what she has to say. Her references to revolution and civil war also call up America's own history, rooted in political revolt. In addition to this comparison, she compares the struggle of suffragists with that of Irish revolutionaries. Not only is the woman suffrage movement a political revolution, she seems to say, but also women (revolutionary and otherwise) are equal with men. If she were a man, she says no one would doubt her right to revolt, but because she's a woman, she and her fellow suffragists have to explain themselves.

Pankhurst also claims that the struggle for suffrage is really a fight for "the rights of citizenship." She implies that by denying women the right to vote, the government is denying them citizenships. In using this rhetoric, she makes the idea that suffrage is something to which women are entitled as citizens clear. This means that to deny woman suffrage is to deny them as citizens. She goes on to say "that women are human beings," making the debate over suffrage also a denial of women's humanity. By doing this, Pankhurst tries to appeal to her audience's emotions and sympathies. She begins by talking about the way she works for political change, but by calling attention to the battle and to women as citizens and humans, she really makes the case for suffrage itself.

Finally, Pankhurst ties it all together in her final paragraph. She even suggests that reason itself is on her side by stating that it's "perfectly evident to any logical mind" and "clear to the meanest intelligence" that if you can vote, you can change government peacefully, while if you can't vote, you have to resort to other means. For this reason, using even violent means of protest and revolt to win suffrage is just. Pankhurst concludes by claiming that her tactics are needed precisely because women can't vote. This argument rests on the assumption that woman suffrage itself is right and necessary, and in a circular kind of way, ends up defending suffrage as well as the tactics to win suffrage.

Reading—2: This writer demonstrates some comprehension of the source text. He shortly relates an overview of Pankhurst's central purpose (*she does not want to explain why woman suffrage is necessary*). However, the writer does not go beyond what can be interpreted from Pankhurst's speech and misunderstands some important details. There is very little textual evidence used in the response.

Analysis—2: This writer demonstrates a partial understanding of the analytical task, offering a limited analysis of the source text. He is able to identify pieces of evidence Pankhurst uses, but is ineffective in explaining their importance in regard to the central argument. Also, the lack of direct quotations or paraphrases from the text leaves much of the writer's analysis unsubstantiated. There is also a lack of focus on the features of the text most relevant to furthering Pankhurst's central argument.

Writing—2: This response has little cohesion and demonstrates limited skill in the use and control of standard written English. Rather than using the introduction and conclusion as touchstones of the response, the writer merely uses the four paragraphs (including the two body paragraphs) to describe Pankhurst's argument as it unfolds. There is limited progression of ideas within paragraphs but this progression is absent from the overall response. The sentence structures utilized are repetitive and the style and tone are nowhere near as formal and objective as they should be. While there are some careless grammatical and spelling errors, they do not detract from the author's intended meaning.

CHAPTER 34

PRACTICE

Introductory Paragraph:

To demonstrate that you understand the source text, **paraphrase the author's central idea or claim:** Politically Correct English (PCE) is dangerous because using "politically correct" language doesn't get rid of elitism or unfairness.

List the three features you will analyze in your essay.

1. Diction

2. Appeal to authority

3. Juxtaposition

Body Paragraph #1: Diction

Where does the author use this feature? Throughout the essay; the author uses both colloquial and academic diction.

What example(s) of this feature can you cite from the source text (direct quotations or paraphrases)? "Insensitive and elitist and offensive and unfair" in the first paragraph; "taken very seriously *indeed*" in the second paragraph; "sort of funny in a dark way, maybe," in the third paragraph.

How does this example interrelate with the author's central claim? The author is using informal and formal language side-by-side to reinforce the fact that language itself, whether politically correct or not, is not indicative of societal attitudes.

How does this feature affect the author's audience? By alternating between formal and informal diction, the author keeps the audience on its toes.

Does achieving this effect help build the author's argument? Why or why not? Yes, because doing so proves that language is language—it doesn't matter what kind is used because the point still gets across.

What is the function of this feature and example in the overall text? The author's varied use of diction helps him subtly convey his central argument by using both politically correct and incorrect diction to make a point about language itself.

PERFORM

In his essay on the use of language, David Foster Wallace asserts that it is dangerous to promote strict use of Politically Correct English (PCE) because the use of PCE alone does not automatically make someone politically correct. Wallace effectively conveys the argument that PCE does not reverse instances of elitism or unfairness by using contrasting diction, appeals to authority, and juxtaposition.

Throughout the essay, Wallace uses both informal, colloquial diction and professional, academic diction. The seamless overlap of these two extremes not only forces Wallace's audience to pay attention but also reinforces the central argument that language itself, whether politically correct or not, is not indicative of societal attitudes or beliefs. In the first paragraph, Wallace writes that the "political realities of American life are themselves racially insensitive and elitist and offensive and unfair." The four adjectives Wallace uses to describe American political realities are progressively informal: "insensitive" could be considered PCE, while "unfair" evokes a child's temper tantrum. The use of four words that are similar in meaning but vary in sophistication to describe one concept strengthens Wallace's assertion that a point can be conveyed regardless of the type of language employed. The italicized word "indeed" in the second paragraph ("taken very seriously indeed") serves to emphasize that "prescriptive PCE is…silly." By highlighting the word "indeed" through italicization, Wallace underscores that the word itself does not enhance the statement in which it appears, but is merely a construction to enhance political correctness. By using both politically correct and incorrect diction, Wallace subtly enhances his central argument about how politically correct language is "sort of funny in a dark way, maybe."

EXTRA PRACTICE

Adapted from Vice President Spiro Agnew's 1969 speech "Television News Coverage."

Tonight I want to discuss the importance of the television news medium to the American people. No nation depends more on the intelligent judgment of its citizens. No medium has a more profound influence over public opinion. So, nowhere should there be more conscientious responsibility exercised than by the news media.

SA: TV should be responsible

Monday night a week ago, President Nixon delivered the <u>most important address</u> of his Administration, one of the <u>most important of our decade</u>. His subject was Vietnam. My hope, as his at that time, was to rally the American people to see the conflict through to a lasting and just peace in the Pacific. For 32 minutes, he reasoned with a nation that has suffered <u>almost a third of a million casualties in the longest war</u> in its history.

dramatic lang. emphasizes importance

When the President completed his address—an address, incidentally, that <u>he spent weeks</u> in the preparation of—his words and policies were subjected to <u>instant analysis and querulous criticism</u>. The audience of 70 million Americans was inherited by a small band of network commentators and self-appointed analysts, the majority of whom expressed in one way or another their hostility to what he had to say.

imagery = band of commentators

It was obvious that their minds were made up in advance. Those who recall the fumbling and groping that followed President Johnson's dramatic disclosure of his intention not to seek another term have seen these men in a genuine state of nonpreparedness. This was not it.

contrast w/ Johnson

One commentator twice contradicted the President's statement "about the exchange of correspondence with Ho Chi Minh.[1] Another challenged the President's abilities as a politician. A third asserted that the President was following a Pentagon line. Others, by the expressions on their faces, the tone of their questions, and the sarcasm of their responses, made clear their sharp disapproval.

supporting data = examples of bias

To guarantee in advance that the President's plea for national unity would be challenged, one network <u>trotted out</u> Averell Harriman for the occasion. All in all, Mr. Harriman offered a broad range of gratuitous advice challenging and contradicting the policies outlined by the President of the United States. Where the President had issued a call for unity, Mr. Harriman was encouraging the country not to listen to him.

AH = evidence of agenda

Now every American has a right to disagree with the President of the United States and to express publicly that disagreement. But the President of the United States has a right to <u>communicate directly</u> with the people who elected him, and the people of this country have the right to make up their own minds.

call to arms

When Winston Churchill rallied public opinion to stay the course against Hitler's Germany, he didn't have to contend with a gaggle of commentators raising doubts about whether he was reading public opinion right, or whether Britain had the stamina to see the war through. When President Kennedy rallied the nation in the Cuban missile crisis, his address to the people was not chewed over by a roundtable of critics who disparaged the course of action he'd asked America to follow.

At least 40 million Americans every night, it's estimated, watch the network news. Seven million of them view ABC, the remainder being divided between NBC and CBS. According to Harris polls and other studies, for millions of Americans the networks are the sole source of national and world news.

Now how is this network news determined? A small group of anchormen, commentators, and executive producers settle upon the 20 minutes or so of film and commentary that's to reach the public. This selection is made from the 90 to 180 minutes that may be available. Their powers of choice are broad.

They decide what 40 to 50 million Americans will learn of the day's events in the nation and in the world. These men can create national issues overnight. They can make or break by their coverage and commentary a moratorium on the war. They can elevate men from obscurity to national prominence within a week. They can reward some politicians with national exposure and ignore others.

The views of the majority of this fraternity do *not*—and I repeat, not—represent the views of America. Not only did the country receive the President's speech more warmly than the networks, but so also did the Congress of the United States.

Yesterday, the President was notified that 300 individual Congressmen and 50 Senators of both parties had endorsed his efforts for peace. As with other American institutions, perhaps it is time that the networks were made more responsive to the views of the nation and more responsible to the people they serve.

media left them alone

parallel examples: WC rallying public vs Hitler; JFK rallying U.S. in crisis.

statistics supporting strength of argument

contrast: small # elites vs millions

repetition of "they" & "they can" → emphasizes media power

central idea = media should reflect how "the nation" feels but not distort or persuade them

[1] Ho Chi Minh—president of North Vietnam, the enemy of the U.S. in the Vietnam War

Sample Student Response #1

While many people today get their news from different online sources, in the 1960s, a majority of Americans got their news from newspapers and television networks. Television in particular was a popular source of news, and presidents like Richard Nixon sometimes used it to communicate policy decisions to the American people. After Nixon gave a televised address about Vietnam, some network news correspondents disagreed with the president's position. Vice President Agnew disagreed with the network's criticism of the president's address. His argument? Network news coverage unduly influenced and did not accurately reflect popular opinion of the president's position on Vietnam.

After giving his implicit support for the president's address, Agnew begins his critique of the networks by explaining their outsize influence relative to the number of Americans who watch the news. He notes that at least 40 million people watch the news, yet what they see on the programs is decided by a relatively small number of people like producers and commentators. Then he explains this outsize influence by writing that they can "create national issues overnight," they can "elevate men from obscurity," and even "reward some politicians with national exposure." This is true today as it was then, but how does Agnew feel about this influence? The reader can see Agnew's opinion in the language he uses. For example, he describes news analysts as "self-appointed," which diminishes the reliability of their opinion in the reader's eyes.

Agnew does not restrict his criticism of network coverage to undue influence. He also argues that the opinion expressed on the networks did not accurately reflect that of Americans as a whole. His evidence for this idea can be seen in the last paragraph where he explains that over 300 congressmen and 50 senators "endorsed his efforts for peace." This implies that the will of Congress is also that of the American people. He also explicitly attacks Averell Harriman by contrasting Harriman's position with the president's, noting that other leaders such as Churchill and Kennedy were not criticized by media pundits. Agnew does this to equate the popular choices these leaders made during World War II and the Cuban Missile Crisis with Nixon's choices about Vietnam. The implication is that Churchill and Kennedy were correct, so Nixon must be too.

Throughout his speech, Agnew portrays the news networks as a minority of people with undue influence who are presenting an outsize opinion of Nixon's speech that does not "represent the views of America." In the end, the reader is left questioning the veracity and reliability of media coverage, something that many Americans continue to do today in the age of the Internet.

Reading—4: The writer demonstrates thorough understanding of the source text as evidenced by his use of direct quotations and paraphrases. He succinctly and accurately relays Agnew's central idea at the end of the introductory paragraph (*Network news coverage unduly influenced and did not accurately reflect popular opinion of the president's position on Vietnam*). The writer also references and cites many important details of Agnew's speech, making sure to interrelate them to the central idea. For example, at the end of the third paragraph, he states, *Agnew does this to equate the popular choices these leaders made during World War II and the Cuban Missile Crisis with Nixon's choices about Vietnam. The implication is that Churchill and Kennedy were correct, so Nixon must be too.* This response demonstrates thorough comprehension of the source text.

Analysis—3: This response offers effective analysis of the source text and demonstrates an understanding of the analytical task. The third paragraph is stronger than the second paragraph in that the writer cites evidence Agnew uses to support a claim and proceeds to explain why this evidence serves to advance Agnew's central argument. However, the second body paragraph is merely a summary of Agnew's speech.

Writing—3: The writer demonstrates effective use and control of standard written English in this mostly cohesive response. The introduction is not as focused as it should be; the writer focuses more on providing background information to Agnew's speech than presenting his own central claim. The manner in which the writer introduces his interpretation of Agnew's central idea (*His argument?*) is a bit too casual for an SAT Essay. Overall, the writing in this response is proficient. While the response is well written and conforms to standard written English, the fact that the writer does not provide his own central claim lowers his Writing score.

Sample Student Response #2

Today people get their news from different places like the Internet and television. But back in the 1960s, it was mainly from newspapers and television. Lots of people watched television news and presidents like Richard Nixon would explain their decisions on television to the American people. Nixon gave a speech about Vietnam and people on network news disagreed with what he said. In response, Vice President Agnew gave his own speech to support President Nixon. Agnew thought that the opinion of many in the network news was wrong because it was different than the opinion of a majority of Americans.

In his speech, we can see Agnew thinks they have too much power to influence opinion. He supports that idea with statements like the networks can "create national issues overnight" and "elevate men from obscurity." He doesn't think a small number of people should be able to do that.

We can also see that Agnew thinks a majority of Americans disagree with the opinion shown on networks. He says that a majority of Congress thinks that Nixon is right about Vietnam, so he probably thinks a lot of Americans must support Nixon's ideas about Vietnam too. He says that people supported Churchill and Kennedy, so they should support Nixon now. This is a good comparison, because he makes the readers think Nixon is a good leader like Kennedy and Churchill.

In conclusion, Agnew supports Nixon and doesn't approve of how the news networks are talking about him. He thinks the president knows what he's talking about when it comes to Vietnam. But now that we have the Internet, people have a choice about where to get their news.

Reading—2: This writer demonstrates some comprehension of the source text. She understands the surface function and central idea of Agnew's speech, but does not delve into important details; rather, she sticks to sweeping generalizations. Furthermore, the last sentence of the essay (*But now that we have the Internet, people have a choice about where to get their news*) veers from not only the central idea of Agnew's speech but also goes beyond the scope of the SAT Essay task.

Analysis—2: This writer demonstrates a partial understanding of the analytical task, offering a limited analysis of the source text. She summarizes Agnew's position and uses the third paragraph to partly discuss a comparison Agnew makes, but instead of accurately explaining how this comparison helps his argument, she qualifies it as "good." (*This is a good comparison, because he makes the readers think Nixon is a good leader like Kennedy and Churchill*)

Writing—2: This response has little cohesion and demonstrates limited skill in the use and control of standard written English. The writer never asserts her own central claim but merely describes the circumstances surrounding Agnew's speech. The lack of varied sentence structure and overuse of the third person plural ("we") also contribute to this low Writing score. Overall, the language used is far too casual for an SAT Essay response.

CHAPTER 35

Reading

the following passage discusses the interactions between sickle cell disease and malaria and their implications.

Sickle cell disease affects millions of people throughout the world, and it affects about 1 in 500 African Americans. It is the most common inherited
Line blood disorder in America. The disease causes severe
5 illness and shortens a person's life span if not treated. However, it is much more common than other disorders because it also has a surprising helpful side effect.

Sickle cell disease is caused by a small mutation in
10 a gene that carries the instructions to make hemo- globin, the protein in red blood cells that helps carry oxygen. Hemoglobin, like all proteins, is made from amino acids strung together like a chain in a certain sequence. The gene's instructions indicate which
15 amino acids to include and their sequence in the hemoglobin chain. The mutation in the gene changes the instructions and substitutes a different amino acid at one point in the sequence, thereby changing the properties of the hemoglobin protein. The hemo-
20 globin then tends to stick together and form long, thin structures. The structures grow long enough to push the red blood cell out of shape, forming a curved sickle-like shape that gives the disease its name.

25 The sickle-shaped red blood cells wear out faster than normal red blood cells, so a person with the disease often has a low red blood cell count. With fewer red blood cells, that person does not get enough oxygen in the blood, causing weakness and exhaus-
30 tion. The cells also tend to get stuck in the smaller blood vessels, causing pain and tissue damage.

We each receive two copies of the hemoglobin gene, one from each parent. A person with sickle cell disease receives the sickle cell gene from both
35 parents and consequently produces no normal hemoglobin. A person who receives only one sickle cell gene will produce both normal and abnormal

hemoglobin. This person will not have sickle cell disease but will carry the gene for it. Red blood cells
40 in people who carry the gene do not normally form the sickle shape. Carriers turn out to have an unusual advantage over people who have two normal copies of the gene: they are better able to survive malaria.

Malaria is a disease caused by a parasite that
45 invades red blood cells. It can be deadly, especially in young children. People who survive malaria infections gain a certain amount of immunity against future infections. After a few infections, their immune system is able to recognize and
50 destroy the parasites. When a parasite invades a red blood cell of a carrier, the cell forms the sickle shape. Since the sickle-shaped cells wear out rapidly, the parasite is destroyed with the cell soon after invading. The immune system removes the
55 worn out cells and recognizes the parasite, so it starts to attack the parasite even before it invades the red blood cells. The carrier is then more likely to survive the infection and also gains resistance to future infections.

60 It is therefore not surprising that the gene for sickle cell anemia is found mainly in people whose ancestors come from parts of the world in which malaria is common. People living in these areas have an increased chance of survival if they are carriers
65 of the sickle cell gene and so are more likely to live long enough to pass the gene on to their children. Therefore, although people with two copies of the gene were likely to die of the disease before they could pass it on, the gene still became common
70 because of the benefit to the carriers. Because modern medicine has treatments for both malaria and sickle cell disease, neither disease is as dangerous as it once was. Scientists hope to wipe out malaria in the future. The gene for sickle cell disease, however,
75 being a part of the human gene pool, will persist.

Sickle cell —causes disease, but has positive side effect

Cause: mutation in hem. gene

Hem sticks together, deforms cells

Cells wear out faster

Genes come from both parents

One copy = carrier, have advantage

Resistant to malaria

Sickle cell assoc. w/ malaria

Carriers likely to survive, though victims likely to die

Malaria gone; SC remains

Malaria Parasites in Blood of Children Living in a High-Malaria Area

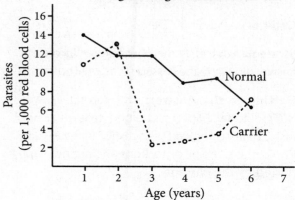

Adapted from Lucio Luzzatto, "Sickle Cell Anemia and Malaria."

1. C
Difficulty: Medium

Category: Reading / Global

Strategic Advice: Think about the central idea of the passage. Ask what the author's main point is. Eliminate answer choices that contain incorrect or incomplete information, such as B or D. The correct answer will reflect the overall message of the passage.

Getting to the Answer: The passage is mostly about how sickle cell disease and malaria interact, or (C).

2. D
Difficulty: Hard

Category: Reading / Inference

Strategic Advice: Use your Passage Map to look for specific clues that could support each of the answer possibilities. Determine which answer choice can be inferred from the information in the passage.

Getting to the Answer: Choice (D) is the only answer choice that is supported by the passage.

3. A
Difficulty: Medium

Category: Reading / Command of Evidence

Strategic Advice: Review your answer to the previous question. Then, determine which quotation directly supports that answer.

Getting to the Answer: Choice (A) is correct. It supports the inference that sickle cell disease is a major threat for African Americans.

4. B
Difficulty: Easy

Category: Reading / Vocab-in-Context

Strategic Advice: Read the sentence again and substitute all of the answer choices for the word "mutation." Determine which word makes the most sense and is the best substitution.

Getting to the Answer: Choice (B) is correct. The meaning of "mutation" is explained through context, specifically through the use of the words "changes" (line 16) and "changing" (line 18).

5. A
Difficulty: Hard

Category: Reading / Inference

Strategic Advice: Avoid answer choices that go too far or are not supported by direct evidence in the passage, such as C and D.

Getting to the Answer: The passage states that carriers of sickle cell disease have only one gene, but the presence of this one gene helps protect them from malaria. People with two genes have sickle cell disease, and they do not have extra protection from malaria. When considered together, these details lead to the inference that having one sickle cell gene is better than having two of the genes. Choice (A) is correct.

6. D

Difficulty: Medium

Category: Reading / Command of Evidence

Strategic Advice: Review your answer to the previous question. Check to see which answer choice relates to your answer and directly supports it with details.

Getting to the Answer: Choice (D) supports the inference that it is better to be a carrier of the sickle cell than to have the disease itself. This is the case for people who have one sickle cell gene.

7. D

Difficulty: Medium

Category: Reading / Synthesis

Strategic Advice: Study the graphic and summarize what information is being presented. Review the part of the passage where the benefits of being a sickle cell carrier are discussed. Determine where these ideas connect.

Getting to the Answer: Based on the information in the text and the graphic, (D) is the correct answer. The graph shows that children who are carriers of sickle cell disease have fewer parasites in their blood, which suggests protection against malaria.

8. C

Difficulty: Medium

Category: Reading / Vocab-in-Context

Strategic Advice: Substitute each answer choice for the word "pool" in the sentence. While all the words are synonyms of "pool," only one has the connotation that fits into the sentence.

Getting to the Answer: After trying each word in its place, it is clear that the meaning of "pool" is "group." The phrase "human gene pool" refers to the overall group of available human genes. Choice (C) is correct.

9. D

Difficulty: Easy

Category: Reading / Detail

Strategic Advice: Remember, you can locate the answer directly in the passage in a Detail question.

Getting to the Answer: The correct answer is (D). "Sickle-shaped red blood cells wear out faster than normal red blood cells" (lines 25–26). Choices A–C are all distortions and are not supported by the passage.

10. B

Difficulty: Medium

Category: Reading / Rhetoric

Strategic Advice: Make sure to read the text closely and decide why the author used this word. What effect was the author attempting to achieve? The correct answer will describe the author's purpose.

Getting to the Answer: The author is hoping to interest the reader by introducing this topic in an unexpected manner—one would not expect a terrible condition to have a helpful side effect. This matches (B).

11. A

Difficulty: Medium

Category: Reading / Rhetoric

Strategic Advice: Focus on *why* rather than *what* to figure out the author's purpose.

Getting to the Answer: Your Passage Map can help here. Paragraph after paragraph, the author seems to have a clear purpose: to instruct the reader about the connection between sickle cell disease and malaria, or (A). While the structure of red blood cells is mentioned, it is only detailed briefly in a portion of paragraph 2, making choice B incorrect. Diagnosis and treatment are not the focus either, eliminating answer choices C and D, as well.

Math

1. D

Difficulty: Medium

Category: Heart of Algebra / Linear Equations

Strategic Advice: You could start by cross-multiplying, but there are so many terms and parentheses that you are likely to forget to distribute a factor. Instead, simplify the numerators first. Don't forget to distribute the negative to both terms inside the parentheses on the right-hand side of the equation.

Getting to the Answer: Simplify the numerators, cross-multiply, and then solve for n using inverse operations. Don't try to do steps in your head – writing each step down will keep you organized.

$$\frac{3(n-2)+5}{4} = \frac{11-(7-n)}{6}$$
$$\frac{3n-6+5}{4} = \frac{11-7+n}{6}$$
$$\frac{3n-1}{4} = \frac{4+n}{6}$$
$$6(3n-1) = 4(4+n)$$
$$18n-6 = 16+4n$$
$$14n = 22$$
$$n = \frac{22}{14} = \frac{11}{7}$$

Choice (D) is correct.

2. C

Difficulty: Hard

Category: Heart of Algebra / Linear Equations

Strategic Advice: Pay careful attention to the units. They will lead you to the correct answer.

Getting to the Answer: Here, the units change from seconds to minutes. The light blinks once every 3.5 *seconds*, which is equivalent to

$$\frac{1\,\text{blink}}{3.5\,\text{seconds}} \times \frac{60\,\text{seconds}}{1\,\text{min}} = \frac{60\,\text{blinks}}{3.5\,\text{min}}$$ Over the

course of m minutes, the light will blink m times that amount, or $\frac{60m}{3.5}$ times, so the correct equation is $f(m) = \frac{60m}{3.5}$. Therefore, (C) is correct.

3. B

Difficulty: Easy

Category: Heart of Algebra / Linear Equations

Strategic Advice: Whenever a question gives you information about a total number of items and a total cost of those items, you should write one equation that represents the total *number* (here, the number of meals) and a second equation that represents the total *cost* (here, the school's total bill).

Getting to the Answer: The number of people who ordered veggie burgers plus the number who ordered roast beef sandwiches equals the total number of people, 56, so one equation is $v + r = 56$. This means you can eliminate A and D. Next, write the cost equation: cost per veggie burger (4.5) times number ordered (v) plus cost per roast beef sandwich (6.25) times number ordered (r) equals the total bill ($308). The cost equation is $4.5v + 6.5r = 308$. These two equations form the system in (B).

4. C

Difficulty: Hard

Category: Problem Solving and Data Analysis / Rates, Ratios, Proportions, and Percentages

Strategic Advice: This is a question where you will need to work backward. Normally, when there is a sale, you take the original price and multiply it by the discount to find the amount the shopper paid. But here, you know how much she paid and one discount amount, but not the other, so to work backward, you'll need to divide.

Getting to the Answer: Divide the amount Margo paid, $41.85, by 0.9 (because the discount for using her store credit card was 10%, or 0.1). This will tell you how much she would have paid if she hadn't used her store credit card: $\dfrac{\$41.85}{0.9} = \$46.50$. To find the amount of the sale discount, divide this by the original price: $\dfrac{\$46.50}{\$62.00} = 0.75$, which means she paid 75% of the price. In other words, the discount was 25%, making (C) the correct choice.

You could also try each answer choice, one at a time, but this will use up valuable time on Test Day.

5. A

Difficulty: Hard

Category: Passport to Advanced Math / Functions & Function Notation

Strategic Advice: The notation $(f \cdot g)(x)$ indicates a composition of two functions that can also be written as $f(g(x))$ and is read "f of g of x." It means that the output when x is substituted into $g(x)$ becomes the input for $f(x)$.

Getting to the Answer: Substitute 6 for x in $g(x)$, simplify, and then substitute the result into $f(x)$:

$$g(6) = \frac{6}{4} - 1 = \frac{3}{2} - 1 = \frac{3}{2} - \frac{2}{2} = \frac{1}{2}$$

$$f\left(\frac{1}{2}\right) = \left(\frac{1}{2}\right)^2 + \frac{5}{2} = \frac{1}{4} + \frac{5}{2} = \frac{1}{4} + \frac{10}{4} = \frac{11}{4}$$

Therefore, $(f \cdot g)(6)\ \dfrac{11}{4} = 2.75$, making (A) the correct choice.

6. C

Difficulty: Medium

Category: Passport to Advanced Math / Quadratics

Strategic Advice: Before resorting to the quadratic formula, try a couple different (and likely faster) factoring methods. All four choices contain i, so you should expect to see a negative number under a radical at some point.

Getting to the Answer: Although there are no factors of 7 that add up to 4, you can easily complete the square to find the roots of this equation. Start by subtracting 7 from both sides. Next, divide b (4) by 2, square the result, and add this final number to both sides. Once here, you'll have a perfect square trinomial, which you can factor and simplify further to find the roots:

$$x^2 + 4x + 7 = 0$$
$$x^2 + 4x = -7$$
$$\frac{b}{2} = \frac{4}{2} = 2 \to 2^2 = 4$$
$$x^2 + 4x + 4 = -7 + 4$$
$$(x + 2)^2 = -3$$
$$x + 2 = \pm\sqrt{-3}$$
$$x + 2 = \pm\sqrt{-1} \times \sqrt{3}$$
$$x = -2 \pm i\sqrt{-3}$$

Choice (C) is the correct answer.

7. C

Difficulty: Easy

Category: Passport to Advanced Math / Exponents

Strategic Advice: The question only asks how many values of x result in the expression being undefined; don't waste valuable time trying to simplify the expression as a whole.

Getting to the Answer: A rational expression is undefined for all values of x that result in a 0 denominator (regardless of whether or not you can cancel any common factors between the numerator and denominator). Set each factor in the denominator equal to 0 and solve for x:

$$x + 1 = 0$$
$$x = -1$$
$$x^2 - 9 = 0$$
$$x^2 = 9$$
$$x = -3, 3$$

There are three distinct values (-3, 0, and 3) that result in a 0 denominator, so (C) is correct.

8. B

Difficulty: Hard

Category: Passport to Advanced Math / Exponents

Strategic Advice: The area of a triangle is given by the formula $A = \frac{1}{2}bh$. When you know the area and either of the dimensions, multiply both sides of the formula by 2 (to get rid of the fraction), and then divide by the known dimension to find the other one.

Getting to the Answer: First, plug in what you know into the area formula: $3x^2 - 5x - 12 = \frac{1}{2}(3x + 4)h$. Multiply both sides by 2, and then solve for h using polynomial long division.

$$
\begin{array}{r}
2x - 6 \\
3x + 4 \overline{\smash{)}\, 6x^2 - 10x - 24} \\
\underline{-(6x^2 + 8x)} \\
-18x - 24 \\
\underline{-(-18x - 24)} \\
0
\end{array}
$$

The correct answer is (B). Note that you could have stopped as soon as you determined the first term in the quotient ($2x$), as (B) is the only answer choice that contains $2x$.

9. C

Difficulty: Easy

Category: Problem Solving and Data Analysis / Statistics and Probability

Strategic Advice: Being able to read information from a two-way table will earn you points on Test Day. Circling relevant information can help you stay organized.

Getting to the Answer: The question only asks about laptops and tablets, so ignore the column for smartphones. The technician sent 16 laptops and 12 tablets (a total of 28) off for repair out of the $72 + 58 = 130$ laptops and tablets that were brought in for service. This represents $\frac{28}{130} = \frac{14}{65}$ of the laptops and tablets, making (C) the correct answer.

10. D

Difficulty: Hard

Category: Additional Topics in Math / Geometry

Strategic Advice: A thorough understanding of the most commonly tested triangles on the SAT, the 30-60-90 and 45-45-90 special right triangles, will allow you to cruise through any questions that use them.

Getting to the Answer: Recall that the sides of a 30-60-90 triangle are in the ratio $x : x\sqrt{3} : 2x$. Because $\overline{QR} = 4$ and ΔQRT is a 30-60-90 triangle, you can conclude that $\overline{QT} = 4\sqrt{3}$. The question tells you that T is the midpoint of $\overline{QS}$, so $\overline{QS} = 2(4\sqrt{3}) = 8\sqrt{3}$. The question asks for the length of $\overline{RS}$, the hypotenuse of ΔQRS, so use the Pythagorean theorem to find it:

$$a^2 + b^2 = c^2$$
$$4^2 + (8\sqrt{3})^2 = c^2$$
$$16 + 192 = c^2$$
$$208 = c^2$$
$$\sqrt{208} = c$$
$$\sqrt{16 \times 13} = c$$
$$4\sqrt{13} = c$$

Choice (D) is correct.

Writing & Language

1. D
Difficulty: Medium

Category: Writing & Language / Development

Strategic Advice: After reading the entire passage, review the sentences presented here and determine which answer choice best captures the overarching idea of the passage rather than focusing on details or incorrect information.

Getting to the Answer: Unlike the other answer choices that focus on incorrect details, (D) is correct as it accurately sums up the central idea of the entire passage.

2. A
Difficulty: Easy

Category: Writing & Language / Usage

Strategic Advice: Review each answer choice against the subject of the sentence to determine which verb creates a grammatically correct agreement.

Getting to the Answer: Choice (A) is correct, as it is the only singular verb. The subject of the sentence, "the artist," is singular, and thus the verb must also be singular. All other answer choices agree with a plural subject.

3. D
Difficulty: Easy

Category: Writing & Language / Punctuation

Strategic Advice: Read the sentence with each answer choice taking the place of the underlined word and assess which is the correct possessive version of the noun in order to create a grammatically-correct and logical sentence.

Getting to the Answer: Because the "first mural" belongs to one world, the possessive version of the singular world in (D) is correct.

4. C
Difficulty: Medium

Category: Writing & Language / Effective Language Use

Strategic Advice: Reread the sentence for context clues to understand its intention. Then, determine which answer choice creates a logical sentence that matches that intention.

Getting to the Answer: "Depicted," or represented in an artistic manner, is the only word that correctly fits the intention of the sentence. Choice (C) is correct.

5. D
Difficulty: Medium

Category: Writing & Language / Effective Language Use

Strategic Advice: Read the paragraph to understand the purpose of the sentence and its context for sense; then replace the underlined portion of the sentence with the answer choice that creates a logical and grammatically correct sentence without redundancies.

Getting to the Answer: Choice (D) is correct because it eliminates the redundant word "ancient" (as it is used many times throughout the paragraph and "classical" also refers to a similar time period) while remaining grammatically and logically correct.

6. B
Difficulty: Medium

Category: Writing & Language / Sentence Formation

Strategic Advice: Modifiers must be placed precisely in order to make logical sense and create a grammatically correct sentence. Review the sentence to understand its meaning and then examine how the various placements of the modifier "nearly" affect the meaning of the sentence. Select the answer choice that creates a logical sentence.

Getting to the Answer: Choice (B) is correct as it places the modifier in a location that means many of the buildings contained murals.

7. B

Difficulty: Medium

Category: Writing & Language / Punctuation

Strategic Advice: Review the punctuation used in each answer choice to assess how each affects the meaning and structure of the entire sentence.

Getting to the Answer: Because the text after the word "town" is not a list or an independent clause and does not contain nonessential words or information, it does not need any within-sentence punctuation. Choice (B) is correct.

8. C

Difficulty: Medium

Category: Writing & Language / Effective Language Use

Strategic Advice: Imagine that there is a blank in the sentence instead of the word in question. Read the sentence with each word in the answer choices to assess how the definitions affect the sentence's meaning.

Getting to the Answer: "Deteriorate" is the only answer choice that directly relates to a problematic physical decomposition of the paint's properties; therefore, (C) is correct.

9. D

Difficulty: Hard

Category: Writing & Language / Organization

Strategic Advice: Read the paragraph to make sense of the content and carefully determine how the information should flow in order to create a logical argument.

Getting to the Answer: Sentence 4 discusses how egg is used instead of beeswax to create tempera paint. This should follow immediately after the sentences that discuss using beeswax to create encaustic paint (sentences 1 and 2); therefore, (D) is correct.

10. B

Difficulty: Medium

Category: Writing & Language / Shifts in Construction

Strategic Advice: Review the sentence to determine the established tense; then, determine which answer choice follows this tense and creates a grammatically correct sentence.

Getting to the Answer: Choice (B) is correct, as the sentence is written in the past tense, established by the phrase "were once used" earlier in the sentence.

11. D

Difficulty: Medium

Category: Writing & Language / Development

Strategic Advice: Reread the final paragraph to understand the central idea. Then, assess which details are supported by examples and which are not. Finally, determine which additional details noted in the answer choices will have the greatest benefit to the reader.

Getting to the Answer: The paragraph offers an example of murals being used to spread political and social messages, but no specific example is offered to support the claim that murals helped educate the illiterate. Therefore, (D) is correct.